20 Common Ele

Elements	Ato	
Aluminum (Al)	13	26.98
Barium (Ba)	56	137.33
Calcium (Ca)	20	40.08
Carbon (C)	6	12.01
Chlorine (Cl)	17	35.45
Copper (Cu)	27	63.55
Fluorine (F)	9	19.00
Helium (He)	2	4.00
Hydrogen (H)	1	1.01
Iron (Fe)	26	55.85
Magnesium (Mg)	12	24.31
Mercury (Hg)	80	200.59
Nitrogen (N)	7	14.01
Oxygen (O)	8	16.00
Phosphorus (P)	15	30.97
Potassium (K)	19	39.10
Silicon (Si)	14	28.09
Sodium (Na)	11	22.99
Sulfur (S)	16	32.07
Uranium (U)	92	238.03

Chemical Engineering Compact Encyclopedia

Mosen Asadi, PhD

MOE Book Publishing
Laguna Woods, California

Asadi, Mosen
Chemical Engineering Compact Encyclopedia

Illustration of figures, cover-and-inside design, copy editing, page layout, and publication by Mosen Asadi

Notice: The Author has compiled information believed to be reliable and complete. However, because technology continually evolves, the author shall *not* be responsible for any errors or damages from using this information.

ISBN: 978-0-578-26380-9

1) Chemical Engineering 2) Chemical Engineering Encyclopedia 3) Encyclopedia of Chemical Engineering 4) Chemical Industry

Printed in China

CONTENTS*

[* List of topics of sections is provided at the beginning of each section.]

PREFACE

ChemEng, in addition to central sciences (math, chemistry, and physics), is heavily rooted in its

- **Basics** (like atom, energy, energy balance, enthalpy, entropy, and much more).
- **Process Units** (like filtration, evaporation, crystallization, distillation, drying, and more).
- **Process Supplements** (like ChemEng process control, process economics, process safety, and more).

All three listed subjects are covered in this book. Around 900 topics are covered. Their content varies, from a few lines up to around 35 pages, depending on the context.

In authoring this book, I tried to follow the next two rules: 1) Keeping its **count pages** as least as possible by *not* using empty sentences. 2) Using exact **technical words** (because the 130-plus-year-old ChemEng field lacks standard terminology) and *not* using **multiple words** for the same concept.

[Please send a note to chemicaleng13@gmail.com to let me know of any error.]

Appreciation: I worked hard for 13 years to write this encyclopedia in the simplest possible writing style to help English-speaking and English-as-a-second-language students, academics, and practitioners involved internationally with the field of ChemEng (*life starts when we begin to help others*). I could *not* be promoted to such a scientific position to write this if I were *not* fortunate enough to meet some opportunities in my life. I, therefore, thank the Mighty Creator (study BIG BANG THEORY) for creating in me the next four desires:

- Eagerly studying ChemEng at a university in the beautiful city of Prague on a state-based scholarship.
- Proudly spending after-study life in the USA, a land of possibility with good libraries and coffee shops.
- Devotedly serving a branch of the chemical process industry to learn practical, research, and writing skills.
- Tirelessly writing, illustrating, and editing this to publish a valuable package reference source of ChemEng.

Dedication: This book is dedicated to my daughter (Miriam), my son-in-law (Darryl), and my grandchildren (Caleb, 11, and Lexi, 7), whose pictures are behind me. And to those scientists whose books are on my desk.

Study Readers' Guides

READER'S GUIDES

Cross References: Cross-references are shown in **orange** to draw your attention to key topics. The word, for example, pump on any page of the book tells you that a topic of PUMPS exists in the book's P Section, which gives sufficient information about the pumps and their types.

Related Topics: Related topics are discussed together. For example, energy and 32 types of it are discussed under ENERGY AND ITS FORMS. Similarly, all laws of motion are discussed under the topic of NEWTON'S LAWS OF MOTION. And the theories of special and general relativity are discussed under EINSTEIN'S THEORIES OF RELATIVITY. This treatment method saves time (because you do *not* have to go back and forth through the book to study the individual-related topics.)

Unit Systems: A quantity's SI unit (metric system) is used, followed by its equal US unit. In this way, calculations are done in SI units, and the final results are converted into US units at the end.

Technical Symbols: E_I is used instead of U to indicate internal energy, where E is for energy (as used in all scientific reference books) and subscript I is for internal. Likewise, E_H is used instead of A (from the German *Arbeit* for *work*) for Helmholtz free energy, where subscript H is for Helmholtz. The symbol S_S (one S for shear and one for stress) is used instead of the Greek letter τ (tau) to denote shear stress. D is used instead of p (Greek letter Wynne) to denote density, as used in most of today's reference books. The symbol d is used for diameter, as used in most new reference books.

Heat-Related Symbols: The symbol Q is used to symbolize the heat, and the **subscript** Q is used to symbolize a **heat-related quantity**. Say, heat energy is shown by E_Q (not Q) and heat transfer coefficient by U_Q (not U). This typical symbolization differentiates between heat-related and non-heat-related quantities, specifically between **heat** (Q) and **heat energy** (E_Q). I also tried to use relevant symbols. For example, heat flux (E_Q/A, where A is for the area) is denoted by E_q (not q) and heat flux rate (the time rate of E_q) by $\dot{E}_q$ (not $\dot{q}$).

Abbreviation Rules: Abbreviations are indicated by **capital letters** or starting with a capital letter, followed by a lower-case letter (or letters). Thus, the British thermal unit is shortened to BTU (*not* btu), pound per square inch to PSI (*not* psi) − Rotation per minute to RPM (*not* rpm) − Parts per million to PPM (*not* ppm). Also, the word liter is shortened to L (*not* l), pound to Lb (*not* lb), and Gallon to Ga (*not* ga). Bar (for pressure unit), *not* bar − Newton (for force unit), *not* newton.

English Technical Words Instead of Latin Words: English technical words are used for easier memorization, followed by equal Latin ones in parenthesis. Say, heat-releasing reaction (exothermic reaction).

Self-Defined Words Instead of Non-Self-Defined Words: For example, the word attached part is used instead of **fitting part** (simply **fitting**), the word detached part is used instead of **accessory**, and the phrase attached and detached parts are used instead of **auxiliaries**.

English Phrases Instead of Latin Phrases: Instead of, e.g. (*exempli gratia*), the English phrase "for example," for instance," or "say" is used. Instead of, i.e. (*id est*), the phrase "that is" is used. And instead of et al. (*et alii*), the word "cowriters" or "coauthors" is used.

Color Codes: In drawing figures, I used the color-coding of the chemical process industry, so air is shown in **blue**, steam in **aluminum**, solids in **brown**, liquids in **pink**, gases in **yellow**, and water in **green**.

Before starting to study this book, I (the author) would like you (the reader) to **review** (study quickly) the three frequently-used words of this book: 1) Chemical system (simply **system**; a small or large region, enclosed by a real or imaginary boundary), 2) Chemical process (simply **process**; a processing action that takes place in a system for certain purposes), and 3) Chemical process station (simply **station**; a part of a chemical process plant that performs a specific job). [It is also helpful to quickly review the list of the topics of all sections of this book (from A-Section to Z-Section) to become familiar with its topics.]

Author, May 2022, Laguna Woods, California, the US of America

INTRODUCTION

This encyclopedia can get to the hands of some readers unfamiliar with ChemEng (chemical engineering), particularly those young students who want to choose it as their subject study at a university. Thus, this two-page introductory guide is prepared to answer the following six (6) important questions:

- What is the definition of ChemEng?
- What is the historical age of ChemEng?
- What are the subject studies of ChemEng?
- What are the differences between ChemEng and chemistry?
- Can a chemist fill the gaps between ChemEng and chemistry?
- What are the job opportunities for new chemical engineers in the job market?

It is, yet, recommended that the young individuals, who intend to study ChemEng at a university, talk to an experienced chemical engineer to get more advice before making a final decision.

[Note: Terms (special words or phrases) written in orange refer to the same topics discussed in this book.]

Definition of Chemical Engineering

ChemEng is a certain type of engineering consisting of chemistry and MeEng (mechanical engineering). It mainly studies the chemical process plants' design, operation, and process control. [ChemEng often ranks the most or one of the three (3) most difficult engineering courses (along with aerospace engineering).]

Historical Age of Chemical Engineering

In 1887, the Massachusetts Institute of Technology (MIT) in the US of America and the University of Manchester in Britain opened a ChemEng course. Taking the listed year as its start, ChemEng was 133 years old in 2020. [The MIT was established in 1861 and opened its chemistry department in 1865 and MeEng in 1872.]

Subject Studies of Chemical Engineering

ChemEng studies **central sciences** (mathematics, chemistry, and physics) and **ChemEng process technology** (process units, devices, and instruments used in chemical process plants). Students, who enter a ChemEng department to obtain a bachelor (BS) degree, start studying lots of central sciences (probably more than other engineering courses). Then they study physical chemistry, thermodynamics, and a few more subjects. Further, for a few semesters, they study the next advanced topics.

- **Basics of ChemEng:** This part, which builds a foundation for the following two parts, covers definitions, basics, theories, mass-and-energy balances, and general equations and calculations of ChemEng.
- **Process Units of ChemEng:** This part, which is based on part one, covers processing techniques of ChemEng, like crystallization, distillation, evaporation, filtration, heat transfer, solid transfer, and more.
- **Process Supplements of ChemEng:** This part, which completes the first two parts, covers process control, process economics, process safety, and process design of ChemEng.

[This book covers all of the above-three-listed subjects, except the **process design of ChemEng**.]

Differences between Chemical Engineering and Chemistry

The main difference between these courses is that the ChemEng is in the engineering group taught in an engineering faculty. And chemistry is in the science group taught in a science faculty. Other differences are:

- ChemEng studies advanced math, chemistry, and physics, while chemistry studies advanced chemistry and the basics of math and physics.

- ChemEng covers the subjects at a process-plant (large) scale, while chemistry covers the subjects at a lab (small) scale. Say, ChemEng studies the distillation process in an oil refinery to process 50 000 m^3 crude oil/day, while chemistry deals with this process in a lab at, say, 1 000 mL/day (see Figures 1 and 2).
- ChemEng teaches process units, process control, and process economics, chemistry does *not*.

Can a Chemist Fill the Gaps between ChemEng and Chemistry

Yes. If you are a chemist and interested in becoming a chemical engineer by self-study and self-training, start studying this book as your all-inclusive reference source, improve your mathematical knowledge, and observe the operations of those process units of ChemEng that are available to you at an industrial scale.

Job Opportunities for New Chemical Engineers

After finishing a training course, a graduated chemical engineer can supervise the operation of a section of a chemical process plant–Can supervise the environmental activities of a plant–Can design a process for making a new product–Can be engaged in research projects–Can be involved in technical sales–and much more. Knowing that the chemical process industry is the world's largest industry consisting of many smaller industries, each with many sub-industries (Figure 3), producing about one million different products, a chemical engineer can access many attractive and well-paid jobs. [Often, ChemEng ranks one of the three best-paid engineering professions.]

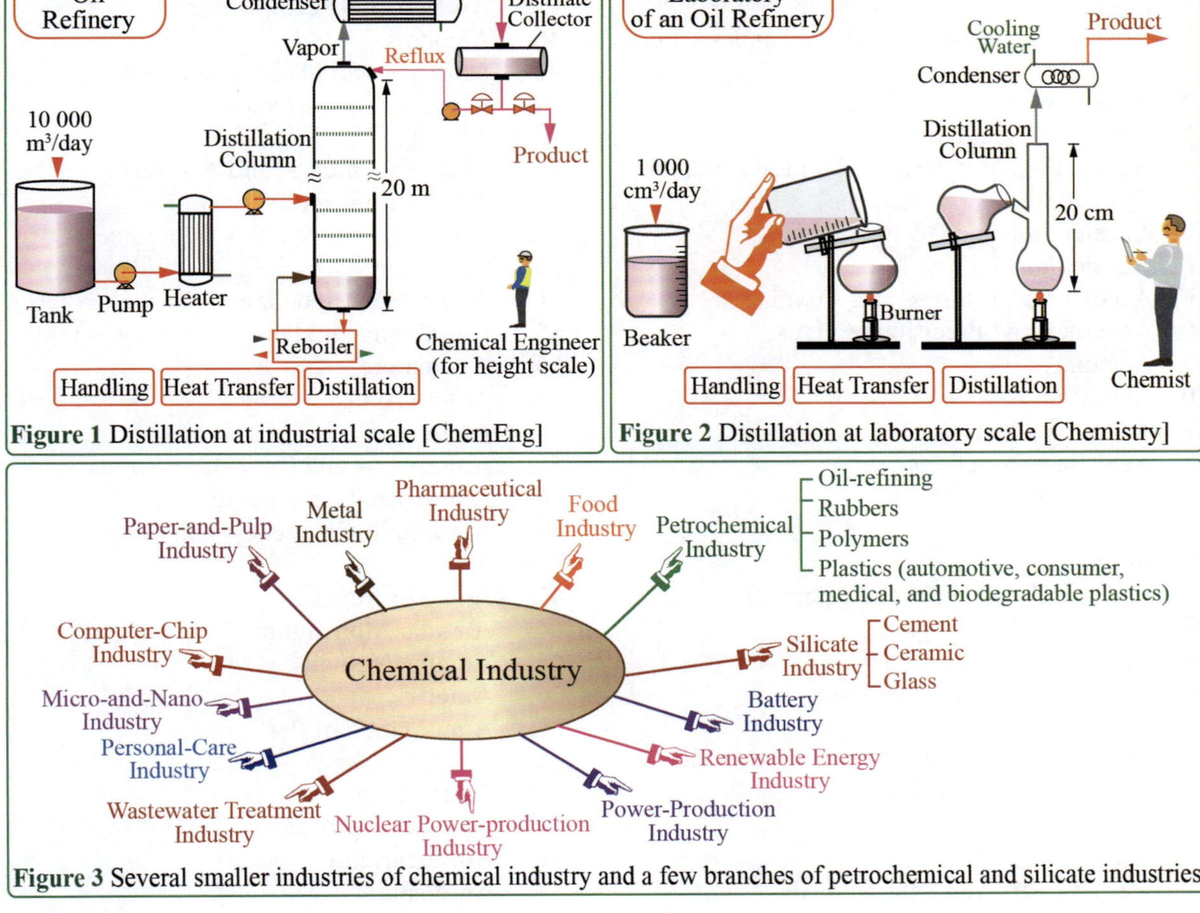

Figure 1 Distillation at industrial scale [ChemEng]

Figure 2 Distillation at laboratory scale [Chemistry]

Figure 3 Several smaller industries of chemical industry and a few branches of petrochemical and silicate industries

A Section

LIST OF TOPICS

1. Absolute Entropy
2. Absolute Humidity
3. Absolute Pressure
4. Absolute Quantity
5. Absolute Temperature
6. Absolute Vacuum
7. Absolute Vacuum Pressure
8. Absolute Value
9. Absolute Viscosity
10. Absolute Zero Temperature
11. Absolute, Atmospheric, Gauge, and Vacuum Pressures
12. Absorbance
13. Absorption and Adsorption
14. Accelerating and Nonaccelerating Reference Systems
15. Acceleration and Accelerometers
16. Accelerators
17. Accessories, Fittings, and Auxiliaries
18. Accuracy and Precision of Data
19. Acetone
20. Acid Rain
21. Acid-Base Indicators
22. Acid-Base Reactions
23. Acids, Bases, and Salts
24. Actinides
25. Activation Energy
26. Activity Coefficients and Equations
27. Adenosine Triphosphate
28. Adhesion and Cohesion
29. Adhesive and Cohesive Forces
30. Adhesive Bonds
31. Adiabatic, Isentropic, Isobaric, Isometric, and Isothermic Conditions
32. Aerosols
33. AIChE
34. Air, Dry Air, And Saturated Air.
35. Air Adiabatic Saturation Temperature
36. Air Density
37. Air Draft
38. Air Dry Bulb and Wet Bulb Temperatures
39. Air Jet Ejectors
40. Air Pollutants
41. Air Psychrometric Diagram
42. Air Pumps
43. Air Saturation Temperature
44. Air Specific Enthalpy
45. Air Wet Bulb Temperature
46. Alcohols
47. Aldehydes and Formaldehyde
48. Alkaline Earth Metals
49. Alkalinity
50. Alkanes, Alkenes, and Alkynes
51. Alkyl Group and Alkylation
52. Alloyants, Alloys, and Alloy Steels
53. Alpha Rays
54. Alpha, Beta, and Gamma Particles
55. Alternating and Direct Electric Currents
56. Alternators
57. Amino Acids
58. Ammonia
59. Amorphous and Crystalline Solids
60. Ampere and Ampere Second
61. Amplitude, Frequency, and Period
62. AMU
63. Angle of Repose
64. Angular Momentum
65. Angular Velocity
66. Anions
67. Annihilation of Particles
68. Anomers
69. Antielectron
70. Antifoaming Agents
71. Antilogarithm
72. Antimatters
73. Antineutrino

A-1
ABSOLUTE ENTROPY

Absolute entropy (S_{Abs}) is the entropy (S, disorder) of a system at absolute temperature (T_{Abs} = 0 K = – 273°C = – 460°F). According to the Thermodynamic Second Law, a pure system, such as a crystal, have minimum S (entropy) and E (energy) at T_{Abs} and, therefore, it is in the state of the lowest energy (known as the ground energy state). At T_{Abs}, a system's S is zero.

[As a close-related subject, study ENTROPY AND ENTROPY CHANGE.]

A-2
ABSOLUTE HUMIDITY

Discussed under the topic of HUMIDITY AND ITS WAYS OF MEASUREMENT.

A-3
ABSOLUTE PRESSURE

Study ABSOLUTE, ATMOSPHERIC, GAUGE, AND VACUUM PRESSURES.

A-4
ABSOLUTE QUANTITY

Absolute quantity is an independent physical quantity (simply **quantity**) of another quantity. For instance, absolute time is the time that is independent of an observer, as Newton assumed in his 1687's Law of Gravitation. In his 1905's principle of gravity spacetime, however, Einstein disapproved of Newton's idea and said that space and time are dependent on each other, so *none* of them can be **absolute**.

When the word **absolute** is used as a **qualifying** (determining) **word** in front of a quantity, it has several meanings, including the following:

- The **highest** or **lowest** limit. Absolute humidity, for example, is the highest reachable moisture in the air, and absolute temperature (T_{Abs}) is the lowest reachable temperature (T).
- The **highest** purity. Absolute alcohol, for example, is alcohol with the highest purity that can be produced.
- The **highest** quality that a device can have. A dew hygrometer is an **absolute hygrometer** because other hygrometers are calibrated against it.
- The **minimum** starting point. An absolute scale is a measuring system that begins at a minimum point and continues in one direction.
- An **unrecoverable** energy loss. When saying that the efficiency of an electric generator is **absolute**, it means that the generator's losses are unrecoverable.
- A **quantity** determined at zero pressure (P). Say, absolute pressure is a pressure (P) measured at vacuum pressure (zero P).
- A **quantity** determined at T_{Abs} (= 0K = – 273°C = – 460°F), where K is for the Kelvin scale. For example, absolute entropy is the entropy determined at T_{Abs}.
- A **quantity** per unit time–Say, **absolute thermal resistance** is the thermal resistance per time.
- A **quantity** independent of the **sign convention**–Say, the absolute value of both + 5 and – 5 is 5.

A-5
ABSOLUTE TEMPERATURE

Absolute temperature (T_{Abs}, also called **absolute zero temperature** or simply **absolute zero**) is the lowest temperature (T) to which a system can be cooled. T_{Abs} = 0K = – 273°C = – 460°F, where K is for Kelvin scale. [As seen, the degree sign (°) is *not* used with the Kelvin scale.] At T_{Abs}, molecules have minimal kinetic energy (E_K), moving slowly. As a result, the system's energy (E) and entropy (S) reach the lowest.

The Thermodynamic Third Law defines T_{Abs} by saying that the T_{Abs} can only be approached but *cannot* be reached. [Physicists used to think that it is impossible to achieve the T_{Abs} experimentally. But in 2003, American physicists at MIT (Massachusetts Institute of Technology) lowered the T of a piece of sodium (Na) to close to zero K. In 2013, a group of German physicists even broke this record by cooling a gas to below T_{Abs}.]

A-6
ABSOLUTE VACUUM

Study ABSOLUTE, ATMOSPHERIC, GAUGE, AND VACUUM PRESSURES.

A-7
ABSOLUTE VACUUM PRESSURE

Study ABSOLUTE, ATMOSPHERIC, GAUGE, AND VACUUM PRESSURES.

A-8
ABSOLUTE VALUE

Absolute value is a quantity without considering its sign. For example, the absolute value of both + 8 and – 8 is 8, showing as [8], where [] is the absolute sign. If the heat energy (E_Q) is in its absolute form, that is [E_Q], its value can be **positive** or **negative**. The E_Q value is **positive** if applied ON a system by its surroundings, so the E_Q of the system becomes greater. Instead, the E_Q value is **negative** if applied BY a system to its surroundings, so the system's E_Q becomes smaller.

A-9
ABSOLUTE VISCOSITY

Another name for VISCOSITY.

A-10
ABSOLUTE ZERO TEMPERATURE

Study ABSOLUTE TEMPERATURE.

A-11
ABSOLUTE, ATMOSPHERIC, GAUGE, AND VACUUM PRESSURES

Absolute pressure (P_{Abs}), atmospheric pressure (P_{Atm}), gauge pressure (P_G), and vacuum pressure (P_{Vac}) are different ways of expressing a fluid's pressure (P). Before defining each of these pressures, it is helpful to discuss the following four (4) general points:

- The P_{Abs} (an elevation-independent P) and P_G (an elevation-dependent P) are the two common ways of expressing a fluid P. [In this book, the P is given in P_{Abs}, unless mentioned otherwise.]
- Pressure measuring instruments are primarily calibrated in relation to P_{Abs}.
- In some reference books, P_{Abs} is shown by adding the letters (Abs) at the end of a unit, say, 850 mm Hg (Abs). [This way of designation is *not* used in this book. We, instead, say P_{Abs} = 850 mm Hg.]
- In some reference books, the letter "A" is used at the end of PSI (pounds per square inch, Lb/In^2) to designate **absolute**, and the letter "G" is used to designate **gauge**, so PSIA or PSIG. If, say, P_{Atm} = 14.7 PSIA and P_G = 30 PSIG, P_{Abs} will be 14.7 PSIA + 30 PSIG = 44.7 PSIG.
- Gauge pressure (P_G, the P relative to P_{Atm}) differs from pressure gauge (an instrument for measuring P_G).

Absolute Pressure

Absolute pressure (P_{Abs}) is a zero-referenced against a perfect vacuum, so it is *not* related to **elevation** (because it is related to P_{Vac}, an elevation-independent P)

For pressures greater than P_{Atm}, the P_{Abs} is the sum of the P_{Atm} and P_G (see Figure 1).

$$P_{Abs} = P_{Atm} + P_G \tag{1}$$

For pressures smaller than P_{Atm}, the P_{Abs} is the difference between P_{Atm} and P_{Vac} (see Figure 1).

$$P_{Abs} = P_{Atm} - P_{Vac} \tag{2}$$

In the US units, the two listed relations (equations) are written as:

$$\text{PSIA} = 14.7 + \text{PSIG} \tag{3}$$

$$\text{PSIA} = 14.7 - P_{Vac} \tag{4}$$

For the determination of a fluid P_{Abs} in a container (like a tank), one of the following ways is used:

- An open-end manometer (like the one shown in Figure 2) is used to read P_G, a barometer is used to read local P_{Atm}, and these two values are added together to get the P_{Abs}. If, for example, the local P_{Atm} is 101 kPa and a pressure source's P_G reading (by using a vacuum gauge) is 83 kPa, the P_{Abs}, according to Equation 1, is 101 – 83 = 18 KPa (= 2.6 Lb/In^2). If, similarly, a local P_{Atm} is 101 kPa and P_G reading is 345 kPa, the P_{Abs}, according to Equation 2, is 101 + 345 = 446 KPa (= 64.6 Lb/In^2).
- A closed-end manometer (shown in Figure 3) can directly read the P_{Abs}. [This method is easier and more accurate (because the measurement is direct and independent of elevation).]

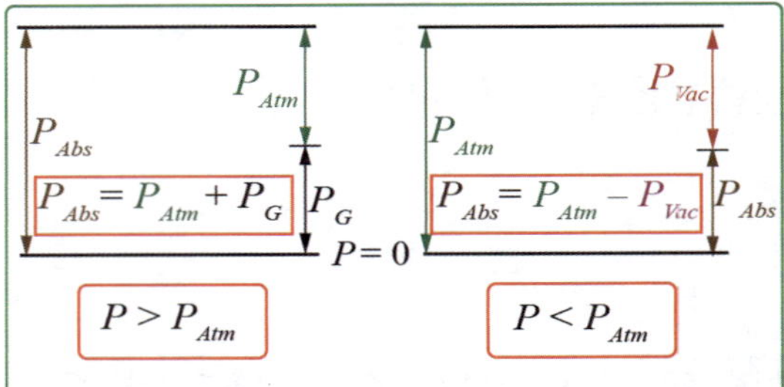

Figure 1 Absolute pressure (P_{Abs}) for pressures greater and smaller than P_{Atm}

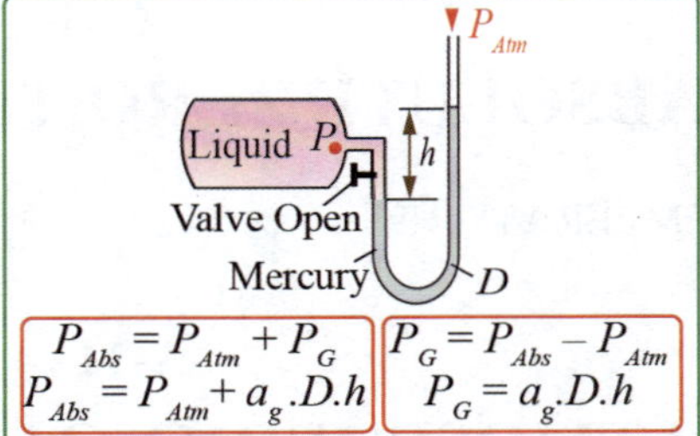

Figure 2 Measuring P_{Abs} and P_G with an open-end manometer

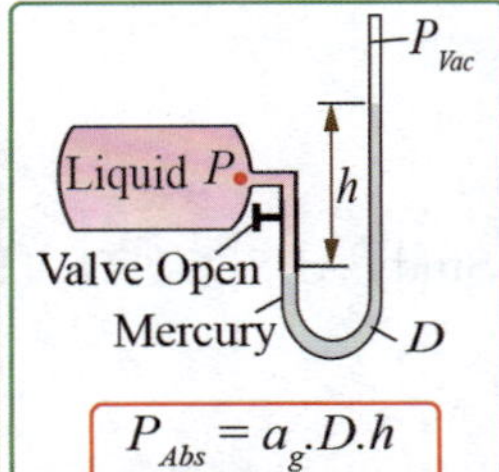

Figure 3 Measuring P_{Abs} with a closed-end manometer

An Example of Absolute Pressure

Given: A tank containing CO_2 gas with the gauge pressure (P_G) of 340 kPa (= 49 PSI), where the atmospheric pressure (P_{Atm}) in the tank is 740 mm Hg (= 28 In Hg, for inch mercury).

Wanted: Absolute pressure (P_{Abs}) in the tank (in kPa and PSI)

$$P_{Atm} = 740 \text{ mmHg} \times \frac{101 \text{ kPa}}{760 \text{ mmHg}} = 98 \text{ kPa } (=14.2 \text{ PSI})$$

$$P_{Abs} = P_{Atm} + P_G = 98 + 340 = 438 \text{ kPa } (= 63.4 \text{ PSI})$$

Consider a liquid at location A (shown with a red dot in Figure 3) in the Earth's gravitational field with the gravitational acceleration a_g. The liquid P (given in P_{Abs}) equates to the pressure difference (ΔP) in the tube of a closed-end manometer with a liquid of density D. So P_{Abs} at that point is the function of a_g, D, and h.

$$P_{Abs} = \Delta P = a_g.D.h \tag{5}$$

If a_g is in m/s², D is in kg/m³, and h is in m, P becomes in kg/m.s² = N/m² = 1 Pa, where N is for Newton (the force unit) and Pa is for Pascal (the pressure unit). The term $a_g.D$ is the liquid's specific weight.

Equation 5 is valid if the manometer liquid's D is much greater than the liquid under measurement's D. If the densities are numerically close to each other, Equation 5 becomes

$$P_{Abs} = \Delta P = a_g.D_1.h_1 - a_g.D.h \quad (6)$$

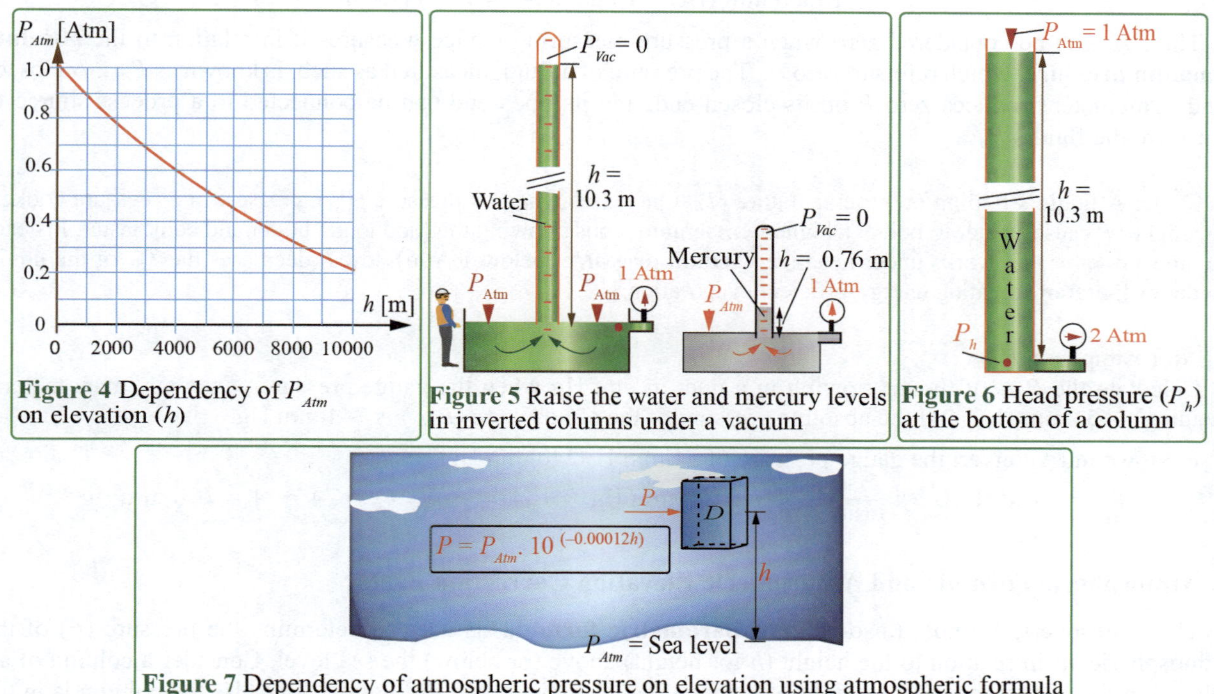

Figure 4 Dependency of P_{Atm} on elevation (h)

Figure 5 Raise the water and mercury levels in inverted columns under a vacuum

Figure 6 Head pressure (P_h) at the bottom of a column

Figure 7 Dependency of atmospheric pressure on elevation using atmospheric formula

Atmospheric Pressure

The term **atmospheric pressure** (P_{Atm}, also called **barometric pressure**) is used in two ways:

- As a way of measuring the unit of a system's P (pressure).
- As a way of expressing the P of atmospheric air (simply air).

We can say the following about P_{Atm} as a measuring unit:

- The P_{Atm} is the P of air that can raise mercury's height (h) in a column under a vacuum by 760 mm at 0°C.
- The P_{Atm} is dependent on elevation (the *greater* the h, the *lower* is P_{Atm}), as shown in Figure 4.

The P_{Atm} can also be visualized by applying it to a column of water or mercury (see Figure 5). The P_{Atm}, given in m Hg (meter mercury), thus, can be converted to m H_2O by using the D ratio of the Hg and H_2O.

$$\frac{D_{Hg}}{D_{H_2O}} = \frac{13600}{1000} = 13.6 \quad (7)$$

According to this expression, P_{Atm} at sea level (where P_{Atm} = 1 Atm) can be converted to m H_2O.

$$P_{Atm} = 0.76 \text{ m Hg} \times 13.6 = 10.3 \text{ m } H_2O$$

If the top surface of a liquid in a column is at P_{Atm}, the liquid's P at the bottom of the tank is *greater* than P_{Atm}. For example, a diver 10.3 m underwater feels 2 Atm pressure; that is, 1 Atm from P_{Atm} and 1 Atm from water's weight, as shown in Figure 6.

The equalities of P_{Atm} are:

$$1\text{Atm} = 1\text{ Bar} = 101\text{ kPa} = 760\text{ mm Hg} = 29.9\text{ In Hg} = 760\text{ Torr} = 10.3\text{ m } H_2O$$
$$= 10300\text{ mm } H_2O = 1\text{ kg/cm}^2 = 14.7\text{ PSI (Lb/In}^2\text{)}$$

The P_{Atm} can be considered zero when a pressure-measuring device measures it in relation to the **absolute vacuum pressure**, which refers to zero P. The pressure of a fluid, measured as such, is known as P_{Abs}. A closed-end manometer produces zero P on its closed-end, and its open-end can be connected to a process source to measure the fluid's P_{Abs}.

[Note: A liquid's boiling point temperature (T_{BP}) increases when its pressure (P) increases. In a pressure cooker, the higher P causes water to boil at a higher temperature, thus allowing the food to get hotter and cook faster. Instead, in an evaporator that works under negative **vacuum pressure** (below 1 Atm), low P decreases the T_{BP} of the liquid under evaporation, creating energy-efficient evaporation.]

An Example on P_{Atm}

Calculate the P_{Atm} of the air flowing in a duct in mm Hg when the gauge pressure of the air (manometer's reading) is 54 mm H_2O and the absolute pressure of the atmosphere (P_{Abs}) is 744 mm Hg.

First, we must convert the gauge pressure of 54 mm H_2O to mm Hg.

$$P_G = 54\text{mmH}_2\text{O} \times \left(\frac{760\text{mmHg}}{10300\text{mmH}_2\text{O}}\right) = 4\text{ mm Hg} \qquad P_{Atm} = P_{Abs} - P_G = 744 - 4 = 740\text{ mm Hg}$$

Atmospheric Formula and Atmospheric Elevation Correction Factor

The atmospheric formula (also called a **barometric formula**) is used to determine the pressure (P) of the atmospheric air in relation to the height (h for height) above (or below) the sea level. Consider a column of air placed in the atmosphere at the height of h above sea level, as shown in Figure 7. Because the column is in the gravitational field of Earth (near the Earth's surface), the P applied to the column by the air equates to the product of a_g (gravitational acceleration), D (density) of the air, and h.

$$P = -a_g.D.h \tag{8}$$

[The minus sign is because the P decreases as the h increases.] Considering the atmospheric air as an ideal gas and atmospheric pressure (the P at the sea level) as the reference pressure, and after some substitutions, the atmospheric (barometric) formula becomes

$$P = P_{Atm}.\text{E}^{\left(\frac{M_n.a_g}{R.T}\right)h} \tag{9}$$

Here, E is the sign for exponent, M_n is the air's molar mass, R is the gas constant, and T is the air's temperature. Using $M_n = 0.029$ kg/mole, $a_g = 9.81$ m/s^2, $R = 8.314$ (N.m)/(mole.K), and $T = 273$ K, the product of the constants inside the parentheses will be 0.00012 m^{-1}. Using h in m and $P_{Atm} = 101.3$ kPa, gives

$$P = 101.3\text{E}^{-0.00012h}\text{ [kPa]} \tag{10}$$

If P_{Atm} is given in mm mercury (Hg) and h in m, the atmospheric formula becomes

$$P = 760\text{E}^{-0.00012h}\text{ [mm Hg]} \tag{11}$$

And if P_{Atm} is given in inch (In) mercury and h in Ft, the atmospheric formula is written as

$$P = 29.9\text{E}^{-0.00039h}\text{ [In Hg]} \tag{12}$$

Using Equation 11, the P_{Atm} of a city that is 150 m above the sea level is $760\times10^{-0.00012\times150} = 760\times10^{-0.018} = 760\times0.96 = 730$ mm Hg. Likewise, the air pressure in a mine of 500 m deep and T of 40°C (= 313 K) is

$$P = 760.\mathrm{E}^{\left(\frac{M_n.a_g}{R.T}\right)h} = 760.E^{\left(\frac{-0.029\times9.81}{8.314\times313}\right)h} = 760.E^{-0.000109\times-500} = 760\times1.13 = 862 \text{ mm Hg}$$

[Note 1: The atmospheric formula gives slightly greater results than the real values (measured by a **barometer**). Say, the P_{Atm} at 150 m above the sea level using the formula is 730 mm Hg, while measured by a barometer is 746.]
[Note 2: The $\mathrm{E}^{-0.00012h}$ is known as the **atmospheric elevation correction factor**.]

Gauge Pressure

Gauge pressure (P_G) is a zero-referenced pressure measured against P_{Atm}, so it depends on **elevation** (because it is related to P_{Atm}). To get a fluid P_G, say, in a tank under P_{Atm}, do one of the following:

- Use a pressure gauge (like a Bourdon gauge) to read the P_G directly.
- Use a closed-end manometer to read the P_{Abs} and deduct the P_{Atm} (obtained from a barometer).

$$P_G = P_{Abs} - P_{Atm} \tag{13}$$

This equation tells us the following:

- A pressure gauge shows a zero P if the measuring fluid is open to the atmosphere.
- The P-value (in P_G) can be positive or negative. If, say, P_{Abs} = 70 kPa and P_{Atm} = 101 kPa, the P_G is

$$P_G = P_{Abs} - P_{Atm} = 70 - 101 = -31 \text{ kPa}$$

The P_G of – 31 means 70 kPa below P_{Atm} (as 101 – 31 = 70 kPa).

Vacuum Pressure

The word vacuum pressure (P_{Vac}), depending on the context, refers to the following:

- A system's pressure (P) with zero P (or no P). In this way, it is also called **absolute vacuum pressure**. When saying a fluid is at P_{Vac}, it is at zero P. [An approximate vacuum can be created by pumping the air out of a tank.]
- A system's P at **below zero** (at negative P or below P_{Atm}). When saying a condenser operates at negative P (or negative P_{Vac}), it means that its P is below P_{Atm} (= 1 Atm = 101 kPa = 14.7 PSI). For example, the P of 0.2 Atm (= 20 kPa) is negative (below 1 Atm).

[The term absolute vacuum pressure is also used to refer to a P with a value of zero or under zero, expressed in P_{Abs}. As said earlier, the pressures given in this book are in P_{Abs} unless mentioned otherwise.]

A-12
ABSORBANCE

Study LIGHT ABSORBANCE, INTENSITY, AND TRANSMITTANCE.

A-13
ABSORPTION AND ADSORPTION

Both absorption and adsorption are physical phenomena during which a physical change (but *not* chemical change) occurs. As you will see from their definitions, both are almost the same actions, but absorption is a **bulk process** during which one state is absorbed by the other state's (the absorbent's) whole volume. Instead, adsorption is a **surface process** during which one state is absorbed by only the other state's surface.

Absorption

During absorption, particles (atoms, molecules, or ions) of one state are absorbed by the **bulk** (under-the-surface) of another state. For example, absorption occurs when the molecules of a liquid are absorbed by the molecules of a solid or a gas. Or when the molecules of water (a liquid state) are absorbed (soaked) by a sponge (a solid state). Absorption also occurs in ion-exclusion chromatography. In this process, the molecules of a solution's nonionic compounds are absorbed by the resin pores, while its ionic compounds are *not*. So, the ionics move faster through the resin bed, and the nonionics stay behind, resulting in their separation.

Adsorption

During adsorption, A state's particles stick (adhere) to another state's **surface**, so a thin film of the adsorbate on the adsorbent's surface occurs. For example, the blood protein molecules stick to a bandage surface.

A-14

ACCELERATING AND NONACCELERATING REFERENCE SYSTEMS

Before these two technical words are defined, it is helpful to study the following comments about them:

- This book uses the non-confusing words of **accelerating reference system** instead of the **noninertial reference frame** and **nonaccelerating reference system** instead of the **inertial reference frame**.
- For massive systems (systems with mass, M), physics usually uses a reference system to express its relative speed (U). The reference system is *not* required for massless systems (like photons or other electromagnetic radiations). They move at the speed of light constant (c), which is the same if measured by an accelerating or a nonaccelerating observer.

Accelerating Reference Systems

An accelerating (noninertial) reference system is a moving reference system that is experiencing acceleration (a) and is under a force (F), such as the gravitational force (F_g, the force of gravity), which affects all systems in the Universe, but its effects are *not* the same, everywhere. Simply speaking, an accelerating system moves at different speeds under some F_g. A car moving at different speeds is an accelerating system. Similarly, an astronaut moves in a space shuttle in an accelerating reference system if the shuttle moves at different (non-constant) speeds. But the same astronaut is in a nonaccelerating reference system if the shuttle moves at a constant speed (when its engine is turned off). A feed, rotating in the basket of a centrifuge, is also in an accelerating system (because the basket rotates at different speeds in different operating cycles). In the basket, however, the F_g is negligible (because it is overcome by the centrifugal force, F_C).

Nonaccelerating Reference Systems

A nonaccelerating (inertial) reference system is *not* experiencing acceleration (a), and the net F acting on it is negligible (insignificant). So, a nonaccelerating system can be a non-moving system (at-rest system) or a moving system at a constant speed. The Earth, rotating around the Sun, is the most common example of a nonaccelerating system. The Sun is also a nonaccelerating system. Considering these examples, we realize that *no* place in the Universe is at full rest. If, for example, you are sitting in a train that is moving at a constant speed of 60 km/h (= 38 Mi/h), you are in one nonaccelerating system, which is under a small amount of F_g. You would feel the same as if you were in another train traveling at a constant speed of 120 km/h. When, similarly, an astronaut is in an aircraft that is constantly moving, the astronaut is in another nonaccelerating system but still under a small F_g. [Because the effect of F_g is relatively greater on an accelerating system, it should be accounted for in calculations. This statement does *not* apply to a nonaccelerating system, as the effect of the F_g is relatively negligible.]

A-15

ACCELERATION AND ACCELEROMETERS

Acceleration

Acceleration (a) is the time rate of the change of a system's velocity (V) or speed (U). Thus, acceleration measures how quickly a system's V (or U) changes. For example, a falling system accelerates (speedups) with *no* air resistance.

The concept of acceleration is familiar to us from cars. We say car A has better acceleration than car B because it accelerates from 0 to100 km/h (= 62 Mi/h) in 8 seconds and car B in 12 seconds. This means that car A can obtain speed in a shorter time. Consider a car that starts from zero speed and moves forward in a straight line at increasing speeds (accelerating). If it turns, a new acceleration occurs toward the new direction. The first acceleration, which a passenger in the car experiences as a force pushing him back into his seat, is a **linear acceleration**. And the second acceleration, which is a **nonlinear acceleration**, pushes the passenger to one side or the other side of its seat.

Numerically, acceleration can be defined as a system's change of V (velocity) or U (speed) per t (time).

$$a = \frac{V}{t} = \frac{U}{t} \tag{1}$$

When the motion is **linear** (constant), it means that the system moves at average velocity (whether the system starts from zero or has an initial velocity), the ordinary form of acceleration is used (see Figure 1).

$$a = \frac{\Delta V}{\Delta t} = \frac{V_2 - V_1}{t_2 - t_1} \tag{2}$$

The average acceleration (a_{Avg}) equates to the velocity difference (ΔV) per time difference (Δt)

$$a_{Avg} = \frac{\Delta V}{\Delta t} = \frac{V_2 - V_1}{t_2 - t_1} \tag{3}$$

From Equation 2, we can calculate the final velocity (V) of an accelerating system.

$$V = V_1 + a(t_2 - t_1) \tag{4}$$

When the motion is **nonlinear**, in other words, when the system moves faster and sometimes slower than average velocity, the differential form of acceleration is used (see Figure 2).

$$a = \frac{dV}{dt} \tag{5}$$

In Physics, the time rate of change of position is the velocity (V), and the time rate of change of velocity is acceleration (a).

$$V = \frac{dR}{dt} \tag{6}$$

$$a = \frac{dV}{dt} = \frac{d^2R}{d^2t} \tag{7}$$

The SI unit of acceleration is m/s^2 (read meter per second squared), and its US unit is Ft/s^2, where 1 m/s^2 = 3.281Ft/s^2.

Figure 3 compares the accelerations of three cars when car A is twice as powerful as car B, but it is powerful as car C. The masses of cars A and B are the same, but car C is twice massive as the other two. Referring to this information, we can say the following:

- The acceleration of A is double that of B because the force acting on A is double that of B, and both cars are equally massive (the *more* powerful the car's engine, the *greater* its acceleration).

- The acceleration of A is double that of C because A is half massive as C, and the forces acting on both cars are the same (the *lighter* the car, the *greater* is its acceleration for the same engine).

Force (F) is the driving force of a motion, and acceleration is the effect (or change) of that motion. Thus, when a system moves, it accelerates if its velocity (or speed) increases, decreases, or changes its direction. When talking about an at-rest system (motionless system), the system accelerates if a force acts on it, so it starts to move. A nonaccelerating system (inertial system) has zero a, or when it is moving, the **net force** on it is zero, so it is *not* accelerating. [**Net force** ($\sum F$) is the sum of all forces acting on a system.]

[Note: The word **coordinate acceleration** is also used in engineering to refer to the acceleration in a fixed **coordinate system**, a geometric system that uses a coordinate to determine that system's position.]

An Example on Acceleration

Given: A bike rider starts from rest ($t_1 = 0$) and reaches a final speed (U) of 12 m/s in 24 s

Wanted: Bike's acceleration after 6 s if its initial acceleration remains constant

At $U_1 = 0$ m/s, $U_2 = 12$ m/s, $t_1 = 0$, and $t_2 = 24$ s, the acceleration is

$$a = \frac{U_2 - U_1}{t_2 - t_1} = \frac{12-0}{24-0} = 0.5\ \text{m/s}^2$$

At $U_1 = 12$ m/s and $t_2 = 6$, $U_2 = U_1 + a.t = 12 + 0.5 \times 6 = 15$ m/s

$$a = \frac{U_2 - U_1}{t_2 - t_1} = \frac{15-12}{6-0} = 0.5\ \text{m/s}^2$$

Accelerometers

An accelerometer is an instrument used to measure a system's acceleration (a) in relation to a nonaccelerating reference system. For example, an accelerometer at rest on the surface of the Earth (a nonaccelerating reference system) measures acceleration in relation to the gravitational acceleration ($a_g = 9.81\ \text{m/s}^2 = 32.2\ \text{Ft/s}^2$ at or near the Earth's surface). Instead, an accelerometer in a free-fall motion measures acceleration in relation to zero acceleration, instead of 9.81 m/s^2, as free-fall systems do *not* accelerate.

Accelerometers have many applications, including in the space industry, for properly measuring a space shuttle or a missile orientation.

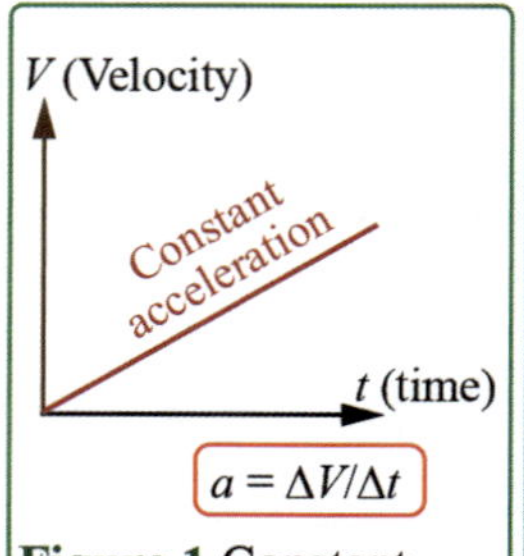

Figure 1 Constant acceleration as a result of linear motion

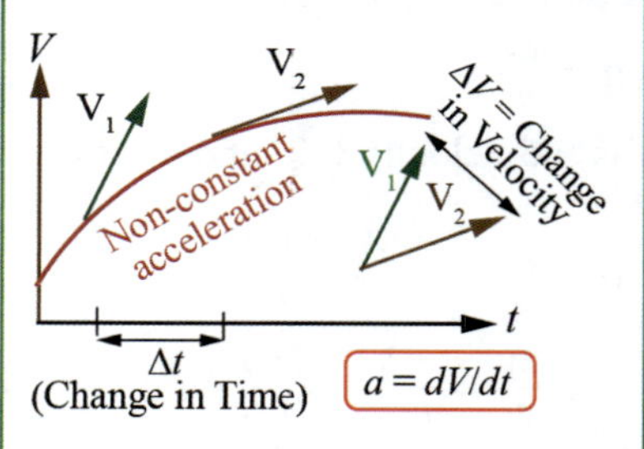

Figure 2 Non-constant acceleration as a result of non-linear motion

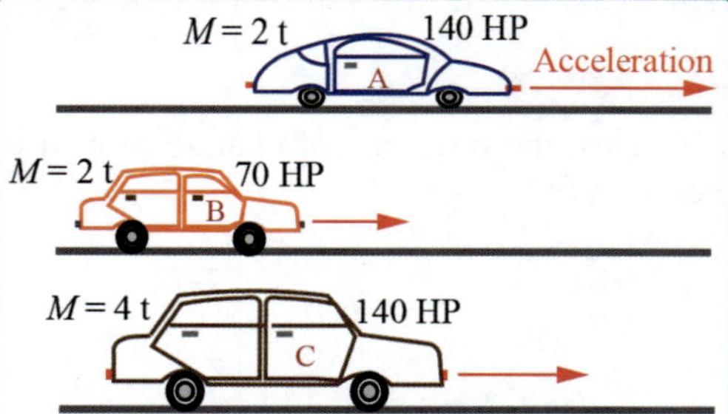

Figure 3 Comparison of acceleration of 3 cars with different M (mass) and HP (horsepower)

A-16
ACCELERATORS

Study PARTICLE ACCELERATORS.

A-17
ACCESSORY, FITTING, AND AUXILIARY PARTS

Study ATTACHED AND DETACHED PARTS.

A-18
ACCURACY AND PRECISION OF DATA

Accuracy and precision of data (values), in **statistics**, are the way of expressing the measured values of a test (experiment) for better evaluation of the data to achieve an exact result. All measurements have a degree of **uncertainty**, which depends on two factors−the limitations of the measuring instrument and the skill of the person who measures the measurement.

Accuracy

Accuracy is how **close** the **result** (test) **values**, gained by repeated measurements under unchanged conditions, are to the **actual value**, as shown in Figure 1. It, in short, indicates how close a measurement is to its actual value. [If a test is performed in a chemistry lab on an hourly basis, the **actual** (accepted) **value** is the average of all values obtained from that test in a day.]

Precision

Precision is how **close** the individual result values are to each other (see Figure 1) from test to test. In short, it indicates the reproducibility (repeatability) of a measurement.

By knowing the definitions of accuracy and precision, the word **being accurate** is *not* the same as **being precise**, although they are usually used equally. A test can be accurate (result values are close to the actual value), precise (result values are close to each other), or a combination of the two. These cases can be viewed using the right side of Figure 1.

After a test is done and the results are presented, we want to know how reliable (accurate and precise) the results are. The reliability of a test's values mainly depends on the following factors:

- Accuracy of the analyst, who performs the test,
- Accuracy of the procedure, which is used to perform the test,
- Accuracy of the instruments, which is used to perform the test, and
- Precision (repeatability) of all result values (reported values) obtained from the test.

Error: Error (E), in statistics, is defined as the experimental uncertainty. It places a numerical value on any uncertainty of a test. In practice, almost every performed test has one (or more) **error** (uncertainty), so to reach a correct result, we must be able to find the error (or errors) and try to eliminate it.

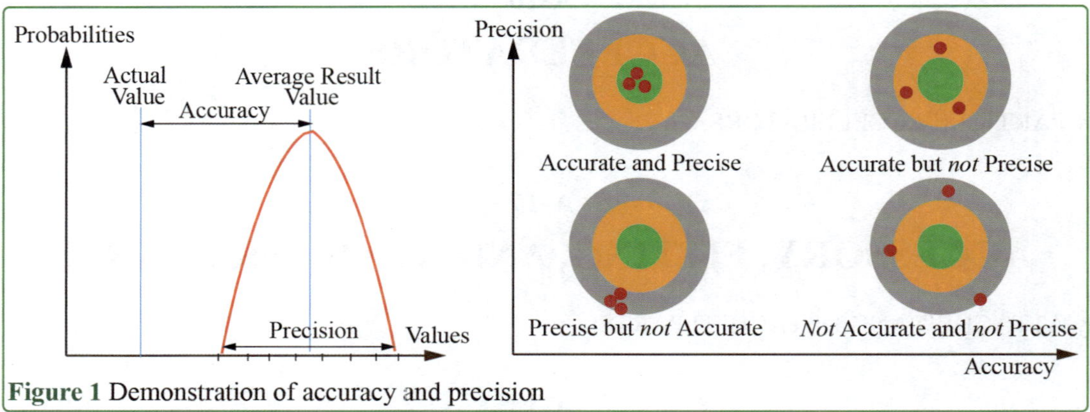

Figure 1 Demonstration of accuracy and precision

The two main errors are discussed next.

- **Systematic Errors:** These errors, which occur systematically (repeatedly on an ongoing basis), are caused by incorrect usage of an instrument, incorrect calibration of the instrument, incorrect averaging result values of a test, or all the above. A systematic error affects the measured values in the same direction, making them lower or higher than the actual value. Eliminating a systematic error is important for improving the **accuracy** of a test result (because such error *cannot* be improved by repetition).
- **Random Errors:** These errors, which occur randomly (occasionally), are caused by unpredictable changes in the measurements. For example, operating a ceiling fan in a lab can change the air-current direction toward an analytical balance to cause a random error. Minimizing random errors is important for improving the **precision** of a test result.

Remember the following about the errors:

- Although eliminating systematic errors improve accuracy, but do *not* change precision.
- Although systematic errors can be eliminated, random errors can only be minimized.

Percent error can be determined using the actual (accepted) value (AV) and result (test) value (RV).

$$E = \frac{\text{AV}-\text{RV}}{\text{AV}} \times 100 \tag{1}$$

If, for example, the density (D) of water at 4°C was measured in a lab to be 1.03 g/mL and the actual (accepted) value at that temperature is 1.00, the error would be.

$$E = \frac{1.00 - 1.03}{1.00} \times 100 = \pm 3\%$$

The value ±3 is the **error limit**, which indicates the test's high and low range values. In statistics, the error limit represents the uncertainty of a test, meaning that we can report the D as 1.03 ± 0.03 g/mL. The **confidence range** of this example is 100 – 3 = 97%.

[When a measurement is done, it includes all the certain digits plus one uncertain digit. These certain digits plus one uncertain digit are referred to as significant numbers (defined under ROUNDING NUMBERS).]

A-19

ACETONE

Acetone (CH_3COCH_3 with the chemical name of **propanone**) is the simplest ketone with a functional group of C=O (carbonyl group), linked to two hydrocarbon groups (CH_3). Some properties of acetone are given below.

- It is colorless, explosive, and volatile,
- It is a good solvent and is miscible with water in different proportions,
- It has many applications, including being used as a raw material for manufacturing plastics.

Some other properties of acetone are outlined next.

- Molar mass (M_n) = 58 g/mole,
- Density (D) = 791 kg/m^3 at 20°C,
- Enthalpy of formation (H_F) = 4310 kJ/kg,
- Molar enthalpy of formation ($H_{n.F}$) = 250 kJ/mole,
- Freezing point temperature (T_{FP}) = – 95°C (= –139°F),
- Melting point temperature (T_{MP}) = – 95°C (= –139°F),
- Boiling point temperature (T_{BP}) = 56°C (= 133°F),
- Vapor pressure (P_V) = 25 kPa at 20°C,
- Viscosity (η) = 3×10^{-4} Pa.s, and
- Refractive index = 1.359.

A-20

ACID RAIN

Acid rain is a word used in the environmental field to refer to atmospheric acidic precipitations (rain, fog, and snow) with a low PH (between 5 and 7, depending on the location of the rainwater source). The low PH is an indication of the acidity of rainwater. In addition to causing corrosion in metals, paints, and other exposed materials, acid rain causes land erosion and the formation of underground caves. Furthermore, it lowers the PH of lakes and oceans, harming fish and other aquatic animals. It also damages vegetation.

Acid rain forms when air pollutants react with water in the atmospheric air. For instance, CO_2 (carbon dioxide) reacts with the air's moisture to form carbonic acid (H_2CO_3). The CO_2 in the air can bring the PH of rainwater to about 5.5. [Since the Industrial Revolution (starting around the 1760s), the CO_2 content in the air has increased from about 300 to 420 PPM.]

SO_2 (sulfur dioxide) reacts with water to form sulfurous acid (H_2SO_3). [About 20 million tons of SO_2 is released into the atmosphere each year by combusting sulfur-containing coal and oil.] NOX (nitrogen dioxide, NO_2, and nitrogen oxide, NO) produced by coal-burning steam boilers also contribute to acid rain.

$$3NO_2 + H_2O \rightarrow 2\ HNO_3 + NO$$

$$2NO + H_2O \rightarrow 2HNO_3$$

A-21

ACID-BASE INDICATORS

An acid-base indicator (simply **titration indicator**, **color indicator**, or **indicator**) is used in the titrimetric analysis (simply **titration**) to change the color of a solution sample at a certain PH, called **endpoint**. Methyl orange (with color change at the PH of 3 to 4.4), methyl red (with color change at a PH of 5), bromthymol blue (with color change at PH of 7), and phenolphthalein (the PH of 8.3 to 10) are common indicators.

During titration, the PH changes sharply when it gets close to the endpoint. In solutions with a PH above 5, methyl red is yellow. In solutions with a PH below 5, it is **red**. And in solutions with a PH of 5, it is **orange** (as only a portion of it has been changed from yellow to **red**). In solutions with a PH below 9, phenolphthalein is colorless; and in solutions with a PH of 9 or above, it is pink.

Based on what has been said so far, the following are choices for choosing the right indicator:

- If a strong acid and a strong base are titrated, any indicator works (as the endpoint would be at PH 7).
- If a strong acid and a weak base are titrated, methyl orange works (as the endpoint is between 3 and 4.4).
- If a weak acid and a strong base are used, phenolphthalein works (as the endpoint is between 8.3 and 10).

A-22

ACID-BASE REACTIONS

An acid-base reaction is a chemical reaction (simply **reaction**) between an acid and a base to neutralize them. The product of an acid-base reaction is a solution containing a salt and water.

$$\text{Acid} + \text{Base} \rightarrow \text{Salt} + \text{Water}$$

$$\text{Molecular:} \quad HCl + NaOH \rightarrow NaCl + H_2O$$

$$\text{Ionic:} \ H^+ + Cl^- + Na^+ + OH^- \rightarrow Na^+ + Cl^- + H_2O$$

$$\text{Net ionic:} \quad H^+ + OH^- \rightarrow H_2O$$

Over the years, some notable chemists offered different acid-base theories and scientifically defined acid, base, and acid-base reactions. The most advanced theory is the Lewis theory, given in the 1920s. According to Lewis's theory, an acid is a chemical compound that can receive an electron pair, and a base is the one that can donate an electron pair. Therefore, an acid-base reaction is the exchange of electron pairs between an acid and a base.

A-23

ACIDS, BASES, AND SALTS

Based on Lewis's definition, an acid accepts an electron pair in an acid-base reaction, and a base donates its electron pair. These properties can be seen, say, in the reaction of hydrochloric acid (HCl), which accepts the electron pair of the NH_3, with ammonia (NH_3, a base), which donates it.

$$HCl + NH_3 \rightarrow NH_4Cl$$

Next, acids and bases are defined generally, and some of their properties are discussed.

Acids

An acid is a compound that ionizes in a solvent, such as water (H_2O), to release positive hydrogen ions (H^+). A few acids ionize almost completely, while others ionize partially. According to the ionizability (ionization ability) of their molecules in water, acids are classified into two classes:

- **Strong Acids:** A strong acid completely ionizes in a solvent. Nitric acid (HNO_3), for example, is completely ionized in water into hydrogen ions (H^+) and nitrate ions (NO_3^-).
- **Weak Acids:** A weak acid partially ionizes when dissolved in a solvent. Acetic acid (HCH_3COO, also called **vinegar acid**) and boric acid (H_3BO_3) are **weak acids**, as they are only partly ionized. Weak acids ionize slightly (less than 5%) and hardly give H^+.

The ionization of an acid (HA) to H^+ (hydrogen ion), rather H_3O^+ (hydronium ion), is generally shown as

$$HA + H_2O \leftrightarrow (H_3O)^+ + A^-$$

When, for example, HCl (hydrochloric acid) is mixed with H_2O, it releases a hydrogen ion (H^+) to a water molecule, forming a hydronium ion (H_3O^+) and a chloride ion (Cl^-). $HCl + H_2O \rightarrow H_3O^+ + Cl^-$. [Here, HCl behaves as acid, and H_2O behaves as a base (as it accepts an H^+ from HCl).]

The following are some other general properties of acids:

- **Commonalities:** All acids have several common properties. They have a sour taste and change the color of an acid-base indicator. For example, acids turn litmus paper red.
- **Conductivity:** Acids conduct electric current (I, electricity) because they form ions in water. This property can determine acids' strength (the *stronger* an acid, the *stronger* it conducts I). [An acid's strength can also be determined by its **dissociation constant**, K_A (the *stronger* an acid, the *greater* is its K_A). The K_A can be measured by titrimetric analysis.]
- **Reactivity:** Acids react with bases to form salts and water, known as **neutralization**. For example, HCl reacts with NaOH (sodium hydroxide) to produce sodium chloride ($HCl + NaOH \rightarrow NaCl + H_2O$). Most acids also react with metals to form hydrogen gas (H_2). Some acids react with carbonate to release carbon dioxide (CO_2). An example follows: $2\ HCl + CaCO_3 \rightarrow CaCl_2 + H_2CO_3$ and $H_2CO_3 \rightarrow CO_2 + H_2O$

Bases

A base (alkali) is a compound that ionizes in water to release hydroxyl ions (OH^-). Bases are classed into strong and weak, depending on the ability of their molecules to ionize in water. Sodium hydroxide (NaOH) is completely ionized in water to sodium ions (Na^+) and OH^- ions, so it is a strong base. Instead, calcium hydroxide [$Ca(OH)_2$] is a weak base, as it is only partially ionized. **Weak bases** produce OH^- ions slightly when reacting with water. When, say, ammonia (NH_3, a base) is mixed with water, it accepts an H^+ from a water molecule, resulting in the formation of an ammonium ion (NH_4^+) and a hydroxide ion (OH^-).

$$NH_3 + H_2O \rightarrow NH_4^+ + OH^-$$

In this reaction, NH_3 behaves as a base and H_2O as an acid (since it donates an H^+ to NH_3). Instead, H_2O behaves as a base when it reacts with HCl (since it accepts an H^+ from HCl). These examples tell us that the acid-base concept is a matter of **behavior** because a compound, like water, behaves, in one reaction, as a base but, in another reaction, as an acid. This is like our behavior (we are who we are, but our behavior changes depending on whom we are dealing with).

The following are some other general properties of bases:

- **Commonalities:** All bases have a bitter taste and change the color of an indicator; for example, they turn red litmus paper **blue** (the opposite of acids). Their solutions feel slippery like soapy water.
- **Conductivity:** Bases also conduct electric current (I, electricity) because they, too, form ions in water.
- The OH of bases is always written at the end of their formula, say, NaOH (sodium hydroxide).

Salts

Salts are compounds produced from a reaction between an **acid** and a **base**. Sodium chloride (NaCl), calcium chloride ($CaCl_2$), calcium sulfate ($CaSO_4$), and aluminum chloride ($AlCl_3$) are examples of salts. NaCl, for instance, is produced by the reaction of HCl with NaOH.

$$HCl + NaOH \rightarrow NaCl + H_2O$$

Salts are far less corrosive than the acids and bases from which they are produced. Both HCl and NaOH are highly corrosive, but NaCl is, by far, less damaging than either HCl or NaOH.

Some other properties of salts are outlined next.

- They are ionic compounds (they can be decomposed to ions),
- They can be inorganic compounds or organic compounds (contain carbon), and
- They consist of cations and anions, so salts are electrically neutral (with *no* electric charge).

In addition, salts are hydrolyzable, according to which they are divided into three classes:

- **Basic Salts:** A basic salt hydrolyzes in water (H_2O) to form hydroxide ions $(OH)^-$.
- **Acid Salts:** An acid salt hydrolyzes in water to form hydronium ions $(H_3O)^+$.
- **Neutral Salts:** A neutral salt is *neither* basic salt *nor* acid salt.

A-24
ACTINIDES

Actinides (also called **actinoids**) are 15 chemical elements. They start from actinium (Ac) through lawrencium (Lr), with the atomic number (N_Z, number of protons) of 89 through 103, written above of each actinide in Figure 1. The atomic mass (M_A) of each actinide is written below it.

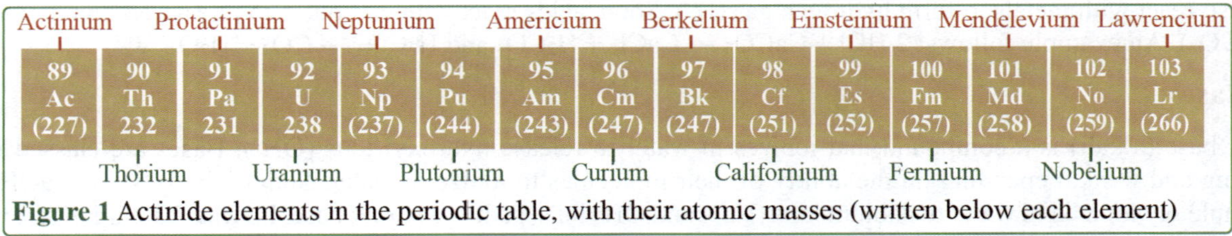

Figure 1 Actinide elements in the periodic table, with their atomic masses (written below each element)

Study the following generalities about actinides:

- They are called actinides because they fall after the element actinium (Ac).
- They are shown as an additional row below the main body of the periodic table of elements.
- Actinides and lanthanides have similar chemical and physical properties called **rare earth metals.**
- Uranium (U) and plutonium (Pu) are the most important actinides (they are used in the nuclear industry).

Next, some properties of actinides are outlined.

- The actinides heavier than uranium (U) are *not* found in nature but are produced by the nuclear decay process or synthetically in the laboratory.
- Neptunium (Np) and plutonium (Pu) are produced using the decay process. And elements after Pu are produced in the laboratory.
- The atomic bomb dropped on Nagasaki, Japan, in 1945, which was named Fat Man, had a Pu charge. The actinides used in the nuclear industry (like U) are first going under the uranium enrichment process.

A-25

ACTIVATION ENERGY

Discussed under the topic of ENERGY AND ITS FORMS.

A-26

ACTIVITY COEFFICIENTS AND EQUATIONS

Activity Coefficients

An activity coefficient (γ, Gamma) is a correction factor (a constant value), which is temperature-and-pressure dependent and is used in calculations (mainly in distillation) to adjust a liquid's molecular non-ideality in a mixture. For example, in the non-ideal binary mixture of ethanol and water, the molecules of water (a polar liquid) are strongly repulsed by those of ethanol (a non-polar liquid), requiring an γ greater than unity (as ethanol molecules tend to leave the liquid phase).

Activity coefficients are specific to a particular mixture, meaning that the γ used for the ethanol-water mixture is different from that used for the methanol-water mixture or ethanol-methanol-water mixture.

For a *non*-ideal binary mixture at vapor-liquid equilibrium (VLE), component A (lighter component, ethanol in the previous example) can be written using its molar fraction in the vapor phase (Y_A), that in the liquid phase (X_A), the vapor pressure of pure A above its liquid phase ($P_{V.A}$), and activity coefficient of A in the mixture (γ_A).

$$Y_A = X_A.P_{V.A}.\gamma_A \tag{1}$$

When dealing with an ideal VLE mixture, the component's activity coefficient is omitted, so

$$Y_A = X_A.P_{V.A} \tag{2}$$

And when dealing with a diluted ideal VLE mixture (a diluted ideal solution follows Raoult's Law of Vapor Pressure), the term $P_{V.A}$ can be eliminated from the previous equation.

$$Y_A = X_A \tag{3}$$

The last three equations are often used in distillation calculations. If, say, the non-ideal mixture of ethanol (component A) and water (component B) is under distillation at 1 Atm pressure, $Y_A = 0.56$, $X_A = 0.35$, the P_V of ethanol at 78.3°C (the ethanol's boiling point temperature) is 0.76 Atm, the P_V of water at 78.3°C is 0.35, so the γ for ethanol (A) and water (B) is

$$Y_A = X_A.P_{V.A}.\gamma_A \qquad 0.56 = (0.35)(0.76)(\gamma_A) \qquad \gamma_A = 2.1$$

$$Y_B = X_B.P_{V.B}.\gamma_B \qquad (1-0.56) = (1-0.35)(0.35)(\gamma_B) \qquad \gamma_B = 1.9$$

Activity Equations

An activity equation can simply determine the activity coefficient of a component. Usually, one (or more) activity coefficients are used in an activity equation or activity model. Activity equations and models are of a few kinds. In this book, the Antoine equation and Margules model are used.

Antoine Equation and Coefficients: Antoine equation (also called the **vapor pressure equation**) with its three (3) activity coefficients (A, B, and C) can calculate a pure liquid's vapor pressure (P_V) at a given T (temperature) when a vapor liquid equilibrium (VLE) occurs between its liquid and vapor.

$$P_V = 10^{\left(A-\frac{B}{C+T}\right)} \qquad \text{or} \qquad \log(P_V) = A - \frac{B}{C+T} \tag{4}$$

Its simplified form (when $C = 0$) is

$$\log(P_V) = A - \frac{B}{T} \tag{5}$$

The P_V unit is mostly in mm Hg absolute, and the T unit is °C. Antoine coefficients vary from liquid to liquid. The next table gives the coefficients of the Antoine equation for ethanol, methanol, and water.

[Note: Some Internet sites, such as Wikipedia.org, provide the Antoine coefficients for several pure liquids. Table 8 in the book's table section gives the water and ethanol vapor pressure (P_V) at various temperatures.]

Antoine Coefficients

	A	*B*	*C*
Ethanol	8.1122	1592.864	226.184
Methanol	8.0810	1582.271	239.726
Water	8.0713	1730.630	233.426

For example, the Antoine equation and coefficients can be used to determine the P_V of ethanol (when it is in equilibrium with its vapor phase) at 78.3°C (the ethanol's T_{BP}).

$$P_V = 10^{(8.1122 - \frac{1592.864}{226.184+78.3})} = 757 \text{ mm Hg} = 1 \text{ Atm} = 101 \text{ kPa}$$

At lower temperatures, the P_V reduces. For example, at 20°C, the ethanol's P_V reduces to

$$P_V = 10^{(8.1122 - \frac{1592.864}{226.184+20})} = 44 \text{ mm Hg} = 0.06 \text{ Atm} = 6 \text{ kPa}$$

Margules Equation and Coefficients: Margules activity coefficient (γ or γ_M) is used in calculations to adjust the non-ideality of an azeotropic liquid (azeotrope). Azeotrope between the molecules of a binary (two-component) mixture occurs because of strong dissimilarities between the components' molecules. A mixture of 96.5% by volume (= 95.5% by weight) of ethanol (C_2H_5OH) and 3.5% water (H_2O) is an example of an azeotropic liquid mixture. When this mixture goes under distillation, around the azeotropic point, the ethanol's molar fractions (X, a unitless quantity) in the vapor phase and liquid phase have almost the same concentrations. Thus, further separation of ethanol molecules from water molecules becomes impossible. To correct the ethanol's non-ideality behavior in calculations, an γ is needed. [In addition to the concentration, γ (activity coefficient) depends on the mixture's P (pressure) and T (temperature).] [Each mixture has its γ value, meaning that the γ used for the ethanol-water mixture is different from that used for the methanol-water mixture.]

In using γ_M (Margules activity coefficient), the following two cases may occur:

- **Repulsive Effect:** A repulsive effect (positive deviation from ideality) between molecules in the liquid phase of a binary mixture occurs because the molecules are dissimilar (unlike). Thus, they exert **repulsive forces** on each other. Say, the molecules of ethanol (a non-polar organic compound) and water (a polar inorganic compound) in their mixture create a repulsive effect (repulsion), which has γ greater than one (see Figure 1). For this reason, the molecules exert greater P on each other than if pure ethanol or pure water were present.
- **Attractive Effect:** An attractive effect (negative deviation from ideality) between molecules in the liquid phase of a binary mixture occurs because the molecules are similar, so they exert **attractive forces** on each other. For example, in the mixture of nitric acid and water, the molecules create an attractive effect with γ smaller than one but greater than zero (Figure 2). So, the molecules exert lower P on each other than if pure acid or pure water were present.

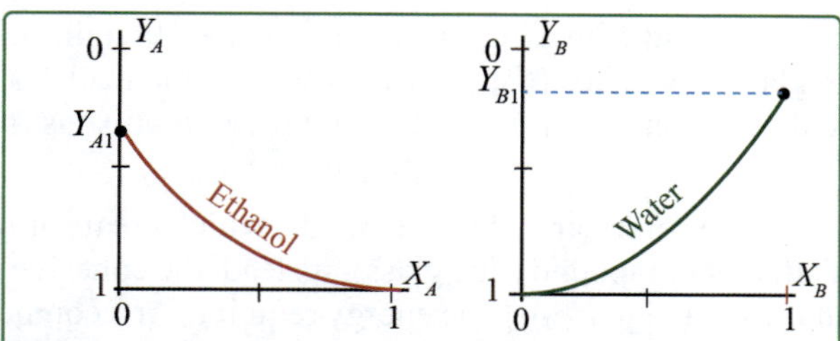

Figure 1 Dependency of concentration of a non-ideal binary mixture's liquid phase on its activity coefficient (γ) when **repulsion** occurs between its molecules

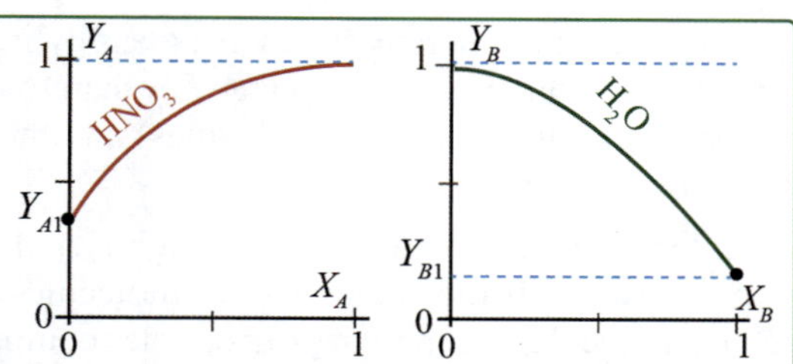

Figure 2 Dependency of concentration of a non-ideal binary mixture's liquid phase on its γ when **attraction** occurs between its molecules

A-27

ADENOSINE TRIPHOSPHATE

Adenosine triphosphate (ATP) is the main energy-carrying molecule in a human's cells. It is used as an energy source for our metabolism (the metabolic process). Because our body converts ATP back into its original chemical form, it continuously circulates in the body. An average human body contains 250 g (= 0.55 Lb) of ATP.

A-28

ADHESION AND COHESION

Adhesion and **cohesion** are identical sticking abilities, except that **adhesion** is the stickiness (scientifically **adherence**) of the molecules of **two** different compounds. In contrast, **cohesion** is the stickiness of the molecules of a **single** compound to each other.

As an example, the surface molecules of water have stronger adhesion than cohesion. Thus, when it is in a laboratory glass cylinder, its molecules stick (adhere) to the inside of the cylinder's wall and move up along the wall to form a **concave** meniscus (an inward curving at a liquid's surface), as shown in Figure 1 under ADHESIVE AND COHESIVE FORCES.

Instead, the mercury's surface molecules have stronger cohesion than adhesion. So, when mercury (Hg) is in the same glass cylinder, its molecules stick to each other and move down along the wall to form a **convex meniscus** (an outward curving at a liquid's surface in a narrow container), as shown in the same figure.

The adhesion and cohesion SI unit is g/m^2. The adhesion of crude oils ranges from 1 to 100 g/m^2, depending on their types (light, medium, and heavy). An extra-heavy crude oil adhesion is about 1 600 g/m^2.

A-29

ADHESIVE AND COHESIVE FORCES

Adhesive Force (F_A): The F_A is an attractive force between dissimilar molecules with a high adhesion (sticking of dissimilar molecules). **Cohesive Force (F_{Co}):** The F_{Co} is a force that occurs between similar molecules with a high cohesion (sticking of similar molecules to one another). The cohesion forces are relatively strong and participate in capillary action and surface tension.

Consider water in a glass cylinder as a liquid with a high $F_{A.}$ Because the water molecules are attracted to the glass molecules with stronger F_A than to its molecules (adhesion), its surface molecules stick to the glass molecules and move up along the wall to form a **concave** meniscus (see Figure 1).

Similarly, consider mercury (Hg) in a glass cylinder as a liquid with a high F_{Co}. Because the Hg molecules are attracted to each other with a stronger F_{Co} than to the glass molecules (cohesion), its surface molecules stick to each other (but *not* to the glass molecules) and move down along the wall to form a **convex meniscus** (see the right side of the same figure).

For water (a polar compound with a high F_A), the adhesive forces are adhesive bonds, which create attraction (sticking) between its molecules and the molecules of another compound (like glass). Instead, the cohesive forces attract the molecules for mercury (a nonpolar compound with a high F_{Co}). [The energy required for a compound's adhesion or cohesion comes from that compound's chemical bonds.]

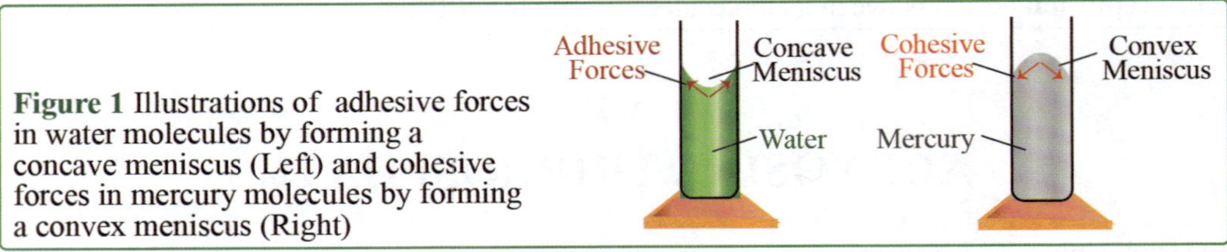

Figure 1 Illustrations of adhesive forces in water molecules by forming a concave meniscus (Left) and cohesive forces in mercury molecules by forming a convex meniscus (Right)

A-30

ADHESIVE BONDS

Discussed under CHEMICAL BONDS.

A-31

ADIABATIC, ISENTROPIC, ISOBARIC, ISOMETRIC, AND ISOTHERMIC CONDITIONS

A flowing fluid (liquid or gas) in a thermodynamic system (heat-involving system) flows under one of the following conditions with unique names:

- Adiabatic condition (constant-heat, $\Delta E_Q = 0$, condition)
- Isentropic condition (constant-entropy, $\Delta S = 0$, condition)
- Isobaric condition (constant-pressure, $\Delta P = 0$, condition)
- Isometric condition (constant-volume, $\Delta V = 0$, condition)
- Isothermic condition (constant-temperature, $\Delta T = 0$, condition)

Figure 1 demonstrates a pressure-volume (*P-V*) diagram of a fluid that flows under isothermic, adiabatic, and isometric (isochoric) conditions. Figure 2 shows an entropy-temperature (*S-T*) diagram of a fluid that flows under isentropic conditions. And Figure 3 shows a *P-V* diagram of a fluid that flows under an isobaric condition.

Adiabatic Condition

An adiabatic condition occurs when a closed thermodynamic system's E_Q (heat energy or simply **heat**) remains constant ($\Delta E_Q = 0$), but its *P* (pressure), *T* (temperature), or both can change. Here ΔE_Q means E_Q in one condition minus E_Q in another condition. When such a change occurs in a system, it is called an **adiabatic system**.

In an adiabatic (thermally-insulated) system, almost *no* heat transfer occurs between the system and its surroundings. When, however, work (W) is done on the system, its E_Q changes. Figure 4 shows an adiabatic (constant-E_Q) condition for a liquid flowing in an insulated-wall pipe. [It is better to say that the E_Q remains **almost** constant instead of constant (because *no* closed system is completely closed to the transfer of E_Q).]

Isentropic Condition

An isentropic condition in a system occurs when its S (entropy) remains constant ($\Delta S = 0$), but its V and T can change, where ΔS is the entropy change.

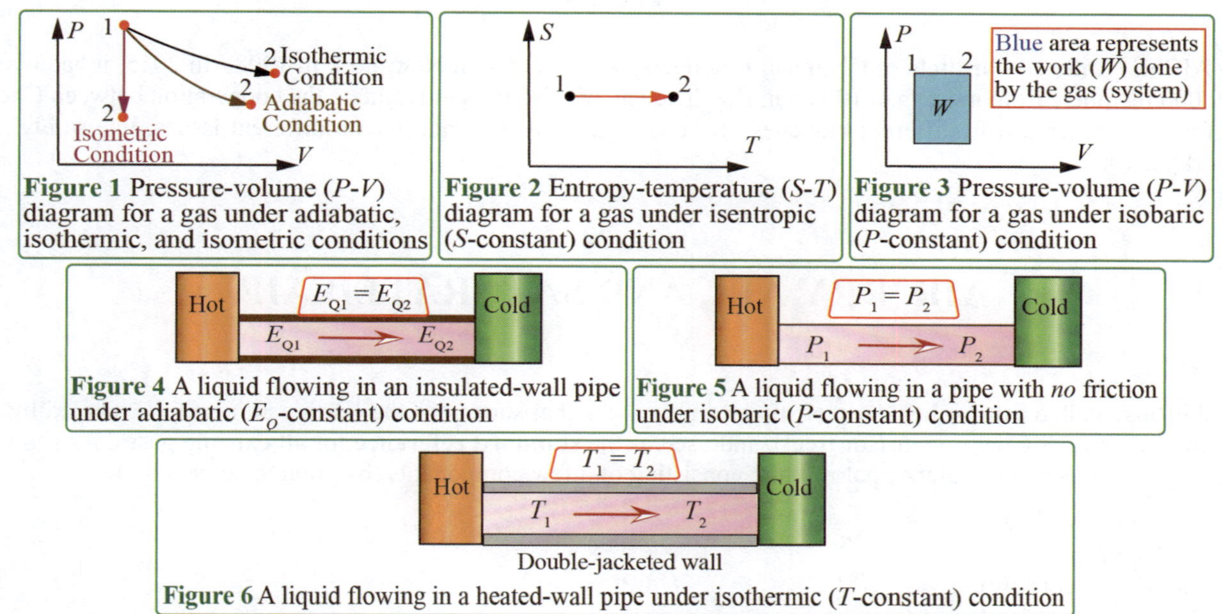

Figure 1 Pressure-volume (P-V) diagram for a gas under adiabatic, isothermic, and isometric conditions

Figure 2 Entropy-temperature (S-T) diagram for a gas under isentropic (S-constant) condition

Figure 3 Pressure-volume (P-V) diagram for a gas under isobaric (P-constant) condition

Figure 4 A liquid flowing in an insulated-wall pipe under adiabatic (E_Q-constant) condition

Figure 5 A liquid flowing in a pipe with *no* friction under isobaric (P-constant) condition

Figure 6 A liquid flowing in a heated-wall pipe under isothermic (T-constant) condition

Isobaric Condition

An isobaric condition occurs in a thermodynamic system when its P (pressure) remains constant ($\Delta P = 0$). A fluid flow in a pipe is under the isobaric (constant-P) condition when *no* friction (f) exists in the pipe. If E_Q (heat energy) enters an isobaric system, the system performs some work (W), as shown in Figure 3. By rule, the W is shown with a positive sign (because the system does it). Figure 5 shows a liquid that flows in a frictionless pipe under isobaric conditions.

Isometric Condition

An isometric (isochoric) condition in a closed thermodynamic system occurs when the system's V (volume) remains constant, so $\Delta V = 0$.

Isothermic Condition

An isothermic (isothermal) condition occurs when the T (temperature) of a closed thermodynamic system remains constant ($\Delta T = 0$), but its P (pressure), V (volume), or both can change. For example, an isothermic (constant-T) condition occurs for a liquid flowing in a double-jacketed-heated-wall pipe (Figure 6).

[Study Carnot cycle, a good example for **isothermic** and **adiabatic** conditions on an ideal gas in an ideal heat engine.]

A-32
AEROSOLS

Another name for PARTICULATE MATTERS.

A-33
AIChE

AIChE (American Institute of Chemical Engineers) was founded in New York in 1908. In 2015, it had over 50 000 members from more than 100 countries. The AIChE also tries to facilitate the cooperation between ChemEng departments with different branches of the chemical process industry on different issues, like safety in workplaces.

A-34
AIR, DRY AIR, AND SATURATED AIR

Air

Air (also called **atmospheric air** or **moist air**) is a gas that surrounds the Earth's atmosphere, inhaled by a human at about 8 g per minute (for free!), and used as the **standard reference** for all existing gases. As shown in Figure 1, it is an air-water-vapor mixture consisting of a few components (by volume percentage):

- 78% nitrogen (N_2),
- 21% oxygen (O_2),
- 1 to 4% water (H_2O),
- 1% argon (Ar), a noble gas,
- 0.04% (4 PPM) carbon dioxide (CO_2),
- Traces of other gases (such as NO and NO_2).

[N_2 is the solvent of the air (because its quantity is the greatest), so O_2 is dissolved in the air. For this reason, the air's combustion reactions do *not* occur explosively.]

The atmospheric (humid) air has several special properties, including the following:

- Its specific heat capacity (C_Q) is 1.005 kJ/(kg.°C) = 29 kJ/(kg.mole.°C),
- Its molecular mass (M_M) is 29 g and its M_n is 29 g/mole,
- Its density (D) at 1 Atm is 1.2 kg/m^3 = 0.07 Lb/Ft^3,
- Its thermal conductivity (K_{Th}) is 0.03 W/(h.m.°C),
- Its specific gas constant (R_{Sp}) is 0.287 kJ/(kg.°C),
- Its gas constant (R) is 287 (Pa.m^3)/(kg.°C),
- Its viscosity (η) is about 10^{-5} Pa.s, and
- Its relative humidity (W_R) is zero.

The following are two more properties of the air: 1) It becomes lighter as it warms and, thus, moves above the colder air. 2) It is clear, but it becomes smoggy (see SMOG) when it contains suspended water droplets (tiny drops). The air's density (D_{Air}) can be calculated by a practical equation that uses the air's specific humidity (W_{Sp}), air's T, and air's P.

$$D_{Air} = \frac{1+W_{Sp}}{0.622+W_{Sp}} \times \frac{P}{461.5T} \quad (1)$$

Study the following two (2) points about the density (D) of the air:

- The density (D) of the **atmospheric air** at 0°C is 1.01 kg/m^3 (= 0.06 Lb/Ft^3), which is lower than the D of the **dry air** (1.2 kg/m^3 = 0.07 Lb/Ft^3). This tells us that water is lighter than air because water (with M_M of 18 g) is lighter than either nitrogen (N_2, with M_M of 28 g) or oxygen (O_2, with M_M of 32 g).
- The D of air, like the P (pressure) of air, decreases with increasing altitude. It also changes with P_{Atm} (atmospheric pressure), T (temperature), and W (humidity).

Dry Air

The term **dry air** is used in scientific calculations to refer to a theoretical air assumed to be of zero moisture (although air always contains some water) and consisting of only 78% nitrogen (N_2) and 21% oxygen (O_2), as shown in Figure 2, although air consists of more components. Thus, the phrase "**on the dry-air basis**" refers to "**no-moist air**," usually used in calculations.

The dry air's molar mass (M_n) can be calculated as 0.78×28 + 0.21×32 = 29 g/ mole, where 28 is the M_n of N_2, and 32 is that of O_2. So, 100 moles of dry air have 78 moles of N_2 and 21 moles of O_2, giving a molar ratio of N_2 to O_2 of 78/21 = 3.7. Similarly, air to N_2 is 100/78 = 1.9, and air to O_2 is 100/21 = 4.8.

Specific enthalpy (H_{Sp}) of the **dry air** (shown as H_{SpDA}) is given in kJ/kg and calculated using its heat capacity ($C_{Q.D.A}$), its temperature ($T_{D.A}$), and a reference temperature (T_R, usually 0°C).

$$H_{SpDA} = C_{QDA}(T_{DA} - T_R) \tag{2}$$

At 1 Atm, T< 66°C, and an average value of 1.005 kJ/(kg dry air × °C) for $C_{Q.D.A}$ (dry-air's specific heat capacity), 1.88 for C_Q of water vapor, and W_{Sp} (the moist-air's specific humidity) from an air psychrometric diagram, C_{QMA} (moist-air specific heat capacity) can be calculated as

$$C_{QMA} = 1.005 + 1.88W_{Sp} \tag{3}$$

According to this equation, the C_Q of moist air with 0.02 kg water vapor/1 kg dry air is

$$C_{QMA} = 1.005 + 1.88 \times 0.02 = 1.04 \text{ kJ/(kg dry air} \times {}^{\circ}\text{C)}$$

Specific enthalpy of a moist air (shown as $H_{SpM.A}$), which is expressed in kJ/kg dry air, can be given as

$$H_{SpM.A} = C_{QM.A}(T_A - T_R) + W_{Sp}.H_E \tag{4}$$

In this equation, H_E is the water enthalpy of evaporation, equating to 2257 kJ/kg at 100°C (the boiling point temperature of water at 1 Atm). [The specific enthalpy of moist air can be determined from an **air psychrometric diagram** when the air's temperature (T) and relative humidity (W_R) are known.]

Specific volume (V_{Sp}) of the dry air (symbol $V_{SpD.A}$ and given in m^3/kg or Ft^3/Lb) is calculated using the dry-air's specific gas constant ($R_{SpD.A}$, given in m), the air's temperature (T_A), and the air's pressure (P_A).

$$V_{SpDA} = \frac{R_{Sp.DA}.T_A}{P_A} \tag{5}$$

The V_{Sp} of 1 kg of dry air plus the amount of the water vapor in the air is called the **specific volume of moist air**.

$$V_{SpD.A} = (22.4 + 0.082T_A)\left(\frac{1}{29} + \frac{W_{Sp}}{18}\right) \quad \text{m}^3\text{/kg dry air} \tag{6}$$

If, for example, the T of air is 80°C and its W_{Sp} is 0.02 kg water/kg dry air, the air's V_{Sp} is

$$V_{Sp} = (22.4 + 0.082 \times 80)\left(\frac{1}{29} + \frac{0.02}{18}\right) = 1.03 \text{ m}^3\text{/kg dry air}$$

[Note: As related topics, also study AIR DRY BULB AND WET BULB TEMPERATURES.]

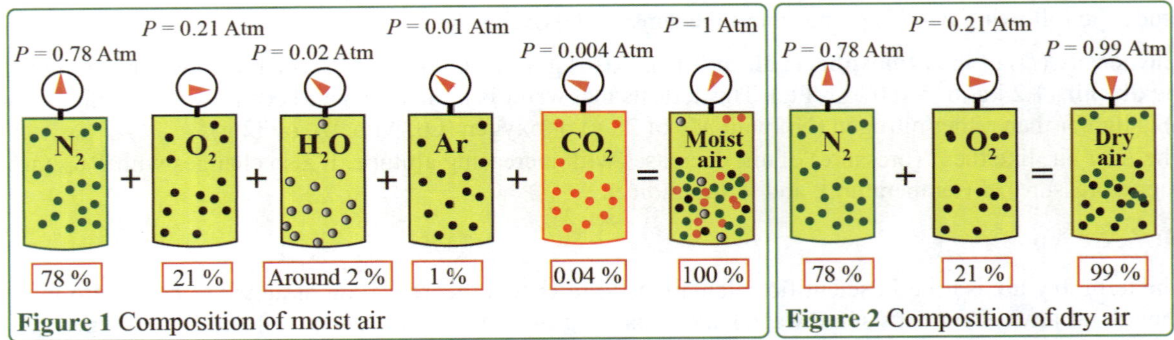

Figure 1 Composition of moist air

Figure 2 Composition of dry air

Saturated Air

Saturated air is the air that has the maximum (highest) amount of moisture content (the water vapor content) at a certain temperature (*T*). Thus, saturated air is maximally humid (moist) with vapor at a certain *T*. [Air always (and to some amount) is saturated with water.]

Saturated air and air's absolute humidity at a certain *T* equally refer to the highest (maximum) amount of moisture in the air that has reached the limit at that *T*.

A-35

AIR ADIABATIC SATURATION TEMPERATURE

Air adiabatic saturation temperature ($T_{A.Sat}$, simply called **air saturation temperature**) is the temperature (*T*) at which the air is saturated (maximally moist) when it is adiabatically cooled (*no* heat transfer occurs during an adiabatic process). At $T_{A.Sat}$, the air's humidity (air's moisture content) increases as some water evaporates to vapor and, therefore, part of the air's sensible heat converts to latent heat.

$T_{A.Sat}$, leaving a cooling device (like a cooling tower) or leaving a dryer after a reduction in its *T* in the dryer can be calculated as

$$T_{A.Sat} = T_{A1} - \frac{H_{E.A}(W_{Sp.A2} - W_{Sp.A1})}{1.005 + 1.88W_{Sp1}} \quad (1)$$

In this equation, T_{A1} is the air's *T* at the cooling device (or dryer), $H_{E.A}$ is the air's enthalpy of evaporation to the device (in kJ/kg), $W_{Sp.A2}$ is the air's specific humidity from the device (in kg water/kg dry air), and $W_{Sp.A1}$ is the air's specific humidity to the device (same unit). The value 1.005 is the dry-air's C_Q (specific heat capacity), and 1.88 is the C_Q of water vapor.

A-36
AIR DENSITY

Air density (D_{Air}) is the mass (M) per unit volume (V) of atmospheric air at a certain temperature (T) and pressure (P). Air density, like air pressure, decreases with increasing elevation (altitude). At atmospheric pressure (see-level pressure) and 15ºC, air density is 1.2 kg/m^3 (= 0.075 Lb/Ft^3). The **dry air**'s D is given using the Ideal Gas Law equation, which uses the air's P, T, and R (gas constant).

$$D = \frac{P}{R.T} \tag{1}$$

This equation can also be given using R_{Sp} (specific gas constant).

$$D = \frac{P}{R_{Sp}.T} \tag{2}$$

The **moist air**'s D can be calculated by using the air's specific humidity (W_{Sp}), T, and P.

$$D = \frac{1+W_{Sp}}{0.622+W_{Sp}} \times \frac{P}{461.5T} \tag{3}$$

A-37
AIR DRAFT

Air draft (simply **draft**) is the flow of atmospheric air from the higher-pressure point to the lower-pressure point. The draft, for example, in furnace operation occurs because of

- The pressure difference (ΔP) between the inside and outside of the furnace's stack (the *greater* is the ΔP, the *stronger* is the draft),
- The temperature difference (ΔT) between the inside and outside of the furnace's stack (the *greater* is the ΔT, the *stronger* is the draft),
- The stack's height of a natural-draft furnace (the *taller* the stack's height, the *stronger* is the draft).

The ΔT creates a density difference (ΔD) between the air at higher and lower-pressure points. This also helps the draft (the *greater* is the ΔD, the *stronger* is the draft). Thus, as the air warms up in a region, its T increases, and its D decreases. So, an air draft forms. When a draft caused by one (or more) of the above factors occurs in a chimney, it is called the chimney effect.

Conducting the right air draft is important in the furnace operation because

- Enough air is required in the furnace for the combustion of fuel, and
- Enough removing the flue gas from the furnace's stack is essential.

A-38

AIR DRY BULB AND WET BULB TEMPERATURES

Air Dry-Bulb Temperature

The air dry-bulb temperature (T_D, simply **dry-bulb temperature**) is a term used to theoretically express the temperature (T) of dry air (moisture-free air). [Scientists use the words **dry-bulb temperature** with some hesitation because air always (and to some extent) is saturated with water. We breathe wet air (but *not* dry air) unless a chemical or physical process dries it. The words **air actual temperature** (simply **air temperature**) and **air dry-bulb temperature** have the same meaning.]

Air Wet-Bulb Temperature

The air wet-bulb temperature (T_W, simply **wet-bulb temperature**) is the T of moist air when it is in contact with a liquid (mostly water) and becomes more saturated, called the saturated air. A wet-bulb thermometer, whose bulb is covered with a **wet cloth** (wick), can determine the T_W, as shown in Figure 1. When the wet cloth is exposed to moist unsaturated air, some water evaporates (because the vapor pressure of the wet cloth is higher than that of the air), so some water vapor (simply vapor) is formed. [The T_W is usually measured by an ordinary (uncovered) thermometer, the way the dry-air's T is measured. Therefore, the **air's wet-bulb temperature** is meant when using the word **air's temperature**.]

To realize the difference between T_D and T_W, consider an airstream with some humidity. The T of the airstream can be measured using two thermometers (see Figure 1). The first is an ordinary thermometer, which shows T_D (dry-bulb T or ordinary T). The second thermometer's bulb is covered with a wet cloth, so known as the **wet-bulb thermometer**. The air around the wet thermometer is saturated air. Evaporation of a small portion of water in wet cloth causes some water vapor to be formed. Part of the vapor condenses, which cools the remaining water in cloth, so T_W (measured by the wet-bulb thermometer) is lower than T_D (measured by an ordinary thermometer). T_D (the higher T) is the **air's dry-bulb temperature**, and T_W (the lower T) is the **wet-bulb temperature**.

Consider the evaporation process, during which the wet-bulb T of the wet cloth decreases (as evaporation gets some latent heat from the wet cloth). As the T of the wet cloth drops to below the air's dry-bulb T, the sensible heat starts to move from the air to the cloth, causing an increase in the cloth's T. Equilibrium occurs when the heat flow from the air to the cloth becomes equal to the heat of evaporation, required to evaporate the moisture from the cloth. This steady T in the air, indicated by a wet-bulb thermometer, is known as the air's wet-bulb T.

Knowing the following two (2) brief points is important:

- For **moist air** (a gas-vapor mixture), T_D (dry-bulb T) and T_W (wet-bulb T) are almost the same. However, in other gas-vapor mixtures, the difference between T_D and T_W can be large.
- Although an ordinary (uncovered) thermometer usually measures the air's temperature, scientists use the word **wet-bulb temperature** because air always (and to some amount) is saturated with water. Similarly, the word **air's temperature** means the air's wet-bulb temperature.

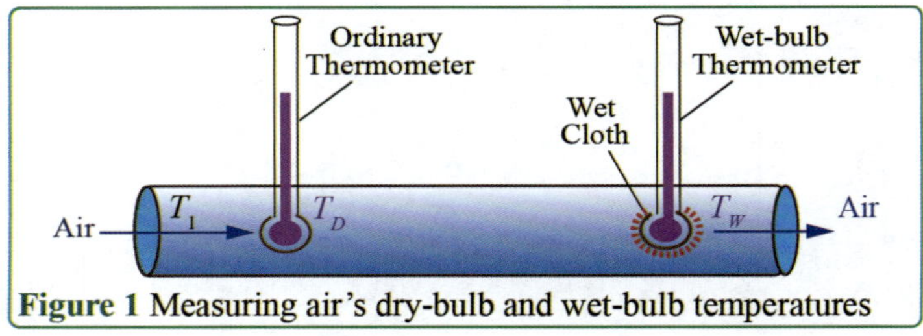

Figure 1 Measuring air's dry-bulb and wet-bulb temperatures

A-39

AIR JET EJECTORS

Discussed under JET EJECTORS.

A-40

AIR POLLUTANTS

As one of three types of pollutants, it is defined under POLLUTANTS.

A-41

AIR PSYCHROMETRIC DIAGRAM

An air psychrometric diagram (simply **psychrometric diagram**, **humidity diagram**, or **enthalpy diagram**), which is used in psychrometry, can determine some useful properties of air-vapor mixtures at constant pressure (P) when the air dry-bulb temperature (T_D) and air wet-bulb temperature (T_W) are known. Applying T_D and T_W on a humidity diagram allows us to determine the air's relative humidity (W_R), air's specific humidity (W_{Sp}), air's specific volume (V_{Sp}), air's specific enthalpy (H_{Sp}), and air's dew point temperature (T_{DP}). Some of these quantities, for example, are used in the energy balance calculations of a dryer.

Figure 1 shows a **humidity** (psychrometric) **diagram**. The main coordinates of the diagram are the air's T_D (actual T), drawn on the X-axis, and the air's specific humidity (W_{Sp}, in g water vapor per kg dry air), drawn on the Y-axis. Each of the ten (10) curves, shown in the diagram in **red** color, represents a humid-air's moisture content (in $\%W_R$) as a function of the air's T. The curve marked 100% is called the **saturation curve**, which gives W_R of saturated air as a function of the air's T. The sloping lines (shown in **blue**), running downward and to the right of the saturation curve, are called **air saturation lines**, where each line represents an air wet-bulb temperature (T_W, in °C).

As the first (1) example, we want to determine the specific humidity (W_{Sp}) of a saturated humid-air sample with 50% W_R at 22°C on the humidity diagram. Going up from $T = 22$°C until we reach the 50% W_R curve. From this point, we go right until we reach the Y-axis (the specific-humidity axis). This point gives us the sample's moisture content of 9 g of water vapor per kg of dry air (= 0.09 Lb of water vapor/Lb of dry air). The lines used in this example are shown in **green**.

As the second example, we want to determine an air sample's W_R (relative humidity) with a T_D of 20°C and T_W of 15°C. We go up on the 20°C line until reaching the 15°C line. This point intersects the 60% W_R curve.

As the third example, we want to determine an air sample's H_{Sp} (specific enthalpy) with a T_D of 32°C and W_R of 60%. We go up on the T_D of 32°C until our line intersects with the 60% W_R line. Then we go left on the adiabatic line to read H_{SP} of 80 kJ/kg dry air. The lines used in this example are shown in **brown**.

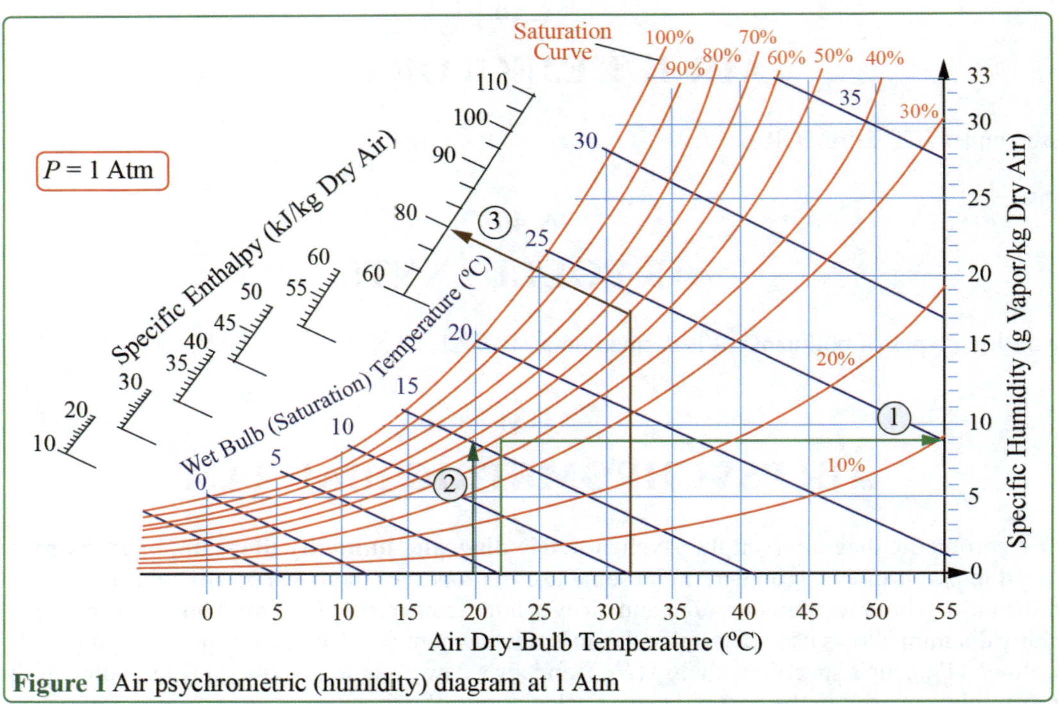

Figure 1 Air psychrometric (humidity) diagram at 1 Atm

A-42

AIR PUMPS

Discussed under COMPRESSORS.

A-43

AIR SATURATION TEMPERATURE

Simplified name for AIR ADIABATIC SATURATION TEMPERATURE.

A-44

AIR SPECIFIC ENTHALPY

Air specific enthalpy (H_{SpA}, simply **air enthalpy**) is the amount of heat energy (E_Q) in atmospheric air at constant pressure ($\Delta P = 0$). It is usually used in the energy balance (enthalpy balance) calculations of the drying process in a dryer.

The H_{SpA} is usually expressed on dry air. The SI unit of $H_{Sp.A}$ is kJ/kg dry air (like specific enthalpy), and its US unit is BTU/Lb, where 1 kJ/kg = 0.43 BTU/Lb.

A practical equation relates the H_{SpA} to the air's temperature (T) and air's specific humidity (W_{Sp}).

$$H_{SpA} = (996\,000 + 95T)T + (2\,490\,000 + 1970T)W_{Sp} \quad (1)$$

A-45

AIR WET BULB TEMPERATURE

Study AIR DRY BULB AND WET BULB TEMPERATURES.

A-46

ALCOHOLS

Alcohols are organic compounds with a general formula of R–OH, where R is for the alkyl group and OH is for the functional group bonded by a covalent bond. Say, an CH_3 (methyl group) covalently bonded to an OH (hydroxyl group) forms the methyl alcohol (CH_3OH, commonly methanol). Ethyl alcohol ($CH_3–CH_2–OH$, commonly ethanol), 1-propanol (propyl alcohol), and 2-propanol (isopropyl alcohol) are also alcohols. [1-propanol and 2-propanol are stereoisomers (see Figure 2 under ISOMERS.]

Alcohols have many applications. The simplest family member, methyl alcohol (methanol), is used as a fuel and solvent. Ethanol is blended with gasoline to be used as a fuel. Isopropyl alcohol ($CH_3CH–OH–CH_3$), at its 70% concentration, is used as rubbing alcohol and sterilizer in medicine. Ethylene glycol ($HO–CH_2–CH_2–OH$), with a freezing point temperature (T_{FP}) of −12ºC (= 10.4ºF), is used as antifreeze.

Some general properties of alcohols are given next.

- They are polar compounds (with a positive electric charge) and soluble in polar solvents.
- They can form hydrogen bonds between an oxygen atom and a hydrogen atom in separate molecules.
- They have high boiling point temperatures (T_{BP}). The T_{BP} of methanol is 64.7°C (= 148.5°F), that of ethanol is 78.4°C (= 173.1°F), and the T_{BP} of propanol is 97°C (= 207°F).

A-47

ALDEHYDES AND FORMALDEHYDE

Aldehydes

Aldehydes are organic compounds with a general chemical formula of R–CHO. The R group can be any alkyl chain (like $CH_3–CH_2$). Aldehydes' functional group (CHO) consists of a carbonyl group (C=O, a carbon double-bonded to oxygen) bonded to hydrogen (H). Methanal (generally formaldehyde) and ethanal ($CH_3–CH_2–CH_2–H–CHO$) are aldehydes.

Formaldehyde

Formaldehyde is the common name for methanal (shown as CH_2O or H−CHO), the simplest aldehyde (R−CHO). It is a colorless, hazardous, carcinogenic gas with a strong smell. Pure formaldehyde polymerizes into paraformaldehyde [$HO(CH_2O)_nH$], so it is stored as an aqueous solution (water-based solution). Industrially, formaldehyde is highly used (with about 10 Mt production worldwide). Among others, it is used in ion-exchange resin production.

Some other properties of formaldehyde are outlined as follows:

- Its boiling point temperature (T_{BP}) is −19ºC (= −2ºF),
- Its flashing point temperature is 64ºC (= 147ºF),
- Its vapor pressure (P_V) is below 1 Atm,
- Its density (D) is 815 kg/m^3 at 20ºC,
- Its molar mass (M_n) is 30g/ mole,
- Its solubility in water is 400 g/L.

The 40% aqueous formaldehyde solution is called **formalin**, used as a **biocide** (antimicrobial chemical for killing microbes). [The application of formaldehyde and formalin has been discontinued in most countries because of the following reasons:

- They are harmful to our health,
- They affect our natural environment, and
- They create safety risks during handling and application.]

A-48
ALKALINE EARTH METALS

Alkaline earth metals are six chemical elements in group 2 of the periodic table. Beryllium (Be), magnesium (Mg), calcium (Ca), strontium (Sr), barium (Ba), and radium (Rd) are alkaline earth metals. They are all silver-colored and soft with relatively low densities, boiling point temperature, and melting point temperature. Radium (Ra) and thorium (Th) occur in the nuclear decay of uranium (U), and the rest of the alkaline earth metals occur in nature.

Alkaline earth metals react with oxygen (O_2) to form oxides, like CaO (calcium oxide, commonly lime). They react with halogens (group 17, containing F, Cl, Br, I, and At) to form ionic halides, such as $CaCl_2$.

[The term **alkali metals** is used in chemistry to refer to lithium (Li), sodium (Na), potassium (K), rubidium (Rb), cesium (Cs), and francium (Fr).]

A-49
ALKALINITY

Alkalinity is the total amount of the soluble (non-filterable) carbonate $(CO_3)^{2-}$, bicarbonate $(HCO)^{3-}$, phosphate $(PO_4)^{3-}$, and hydroxide $(OH)^-$ of calcium (Ca), magnesium (Mg), sodium (Na), and potassium (K) in a sample. It may also be defined as the amount of acid that the sample under the test can get until it reaches a designated PH (8.2 in the case of total alkalinity). [In most industrial operations, carbonates and bicarbonates are the most-present components of alkalinity.]

The alkalinity of a solution sample is measured in a laboratory by titrimetric analysis. It is usually expressed in mg per L or mEq per L of the sample, where L is for liter, and mEq is for milliequivalent.

A-50

ALKANES, ALKENES, AND ALKYNES

Alkanes

Alkanes are organic compounds whose names end with the suffix *ane* and have a general chemical formula of C_nH_{2n+2}, where "n" is the number of carbon atoms. Having only C (carbon atom) and H (hydrogen atom) in their formula (composition) put them in the hydrocarbon group. Based on this definition, the number of hydrogen atoms in alkanes is twice the number of carbon atoms plus the two (2) end carbon atoms. Methane (CH_4), Ethane (C_2H_6), and propane (C_3H_8) are examples of alkanes. Methane (CH_4), the simplest alkane, has four hydrogen atoms (1×2+2=4), and the second family member of the alkanes has 6 hydrogen atoms (2×2+2=6) with the formula of C_2H_6. [The first few family members of alkanes (C_1 to C_{10}) are gases or liquids at room temperature and used as fuels. The higher members are solids.]

The alkanes are found in petroleum and natural gas. They are usually produced by fractional distillation of petroleum.

Alkenes

Alkenes are organic compounds whose names end with the suffix *ene* and have the general formula of C_nH_{2n}, where "n" is the number of carbon atoms being 2 or more. Ethane (C_2H_4, with the common name of ethylene), propene (C_3H_6, with the common name of **propylene**), and pentene (C_5H_{10}) are alkenes.

Alkenes have one chemical bond, and some have two or more double bonds. They have chemical polarity, are colorless, and their lower family members are in gaseous or liquid form at room temperature.

Alkynes

Alkynes are organic compounds whose names end with *yne* and have the general formula of C_nH_{2n-2}, where "n" is the number of carbon atoms being 2 or more. Ethyne (C_2H_2) and propyne (C_3H_4) are alkynes.

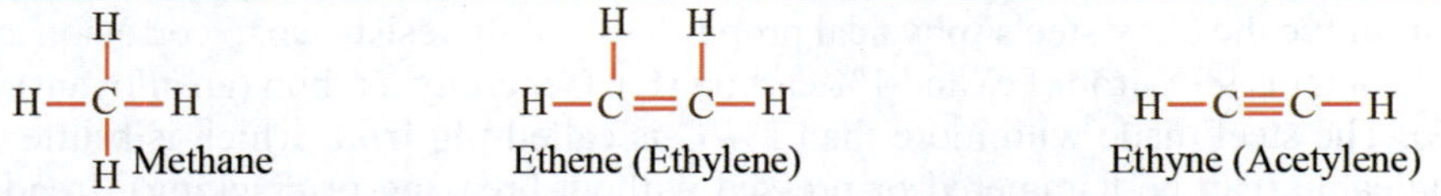

Figure 1 Methane is the simplest alkane, ethene is the simplest alkene, and ethyne is the simplest alkyne

A-51

ALKYL GROUP AND ALKYLATION

Alkyl Group: An alkyl group is a section of a molecule with the general formula of $R{=}C_nH_{2n+1}$. The letter R means many possible alkyl groups, and the subscript "*n*" indicates the number of linked carbons (C). For example, in a methane molecule (CH_4), R = CH_3 (methyl group) and $n = 1$.

Alkylation: Alkylation is the substitution of an alkyl group from one molecule. For example, the alkylation of an ammonia molecule (NH_3) substitutes an alkyl group for its hydrogen atoms (H).

Alkylation is an important process. In the oil-refining industry, the alkylation of isobutane [$HC(CH_3)_3$] is performed using an alkene to upgrade petroleum. In medicine, alkylation of DNA is used in chemotherapy (type of cancer treatment) to damage the DNA of cancer cells.

A-52

ALLOYANTS, ALLOYS, AND ALLOY STEELS

Alloyants: An alloyant is a substance, like iron (Fe), alloyed (mixing by melting) with another substance, like carbon (C), to improve the physical properties of an **alloy**, such as its strength and hardness. Alloy steel contains 99% Fe and 1% C as alloyants. Chromium (Cr), nickel (Ni), and manganese (Mn) are the main metallic alloyants, and carbon (C) is the main nonmetallic alloyant. The metallic alloyants are added to prevent corrosion, and C is used to increase the hardness. Copper (Cu), aluminum (Al), cobalt (Co), molybdenum (Mo), titanium (Ti), vanadium (V), zinc (Zn), and zirconium (Zr) are also alloyants that are used in a smaller amount. Stainless steel (a ferrous alloy) contains about 10% Cr and 0.1 C, both alloyed to Fe (about 90%).

Alloys: An alloy is formed from **alloying** (mixing by melting) a metal with one (or more) alloyant. Alloy steel, copper brass, and bronze are common alloys.

The following are the four (4) special properties of alloys:

- The physical properties of alloys change with cooling and heating.
- The molecular structure of an alloy determines many of its physical properties.
- The strength of an alloy is usually greater than each of its mixing components (alloyants).
- The melting point temperature of an alloy is lower than that of each of its mixing components.

Alloys can be in the form of crystal or amorphous compounds (without-form compounds), so they can be divided into **crystalline alloys** and **amorphous alloys**. If a liquid alloy is cooled rapidly, an amorphous alloy is formed.

Alloy Steel: Alloy steel (simply **steel**) is corrosive resistant steel produced from alloying two (or more) alloyants. Copper brass (mix of copper, Cu, and zinc, Zn), chrome steel (mix of Fe with 1, 5, or 20% Cr), and aluminum bronze steel (with 95% Cu and 5% Al) are other examples of alloy steel. Most metals are easily alloyed when they are melted. The content of the alloyants in alloy steel can be 1 to nearly 50% (by mass).

The alloyants can improve the alloy steels' physical properties (mainly resistance to corrosion and strength). The simplest alloy steel contains 99% iron (Fe) and 1% carbon (C). Generally, carbon (an alloyant) is used in a small amount (up to 2%). The steel made with more than 2% C is called **pig iron**, which is brittle (hard but easy to break) and *not* malleable (can be hammered or pressed without breaking or cracking). In addition to carbon, other alloyants, such as copper, aluminum, chromium, cobalt, molybdenum, nickel, titanium, vanadium, and zirconium, are used to produce different kinds of steel. Alloy steels are malleable and ductile (can be formed into a thin or thick wire).

Study the following useful information:

- Stainless steel is corrosive-resistant alloy steel consisting of Fe, Cr (chromium), and Ni (nickel) used as alloyants. Usually, it contains a minimum of 10% Cr.
- Carbon steel (also called mild steel) is steel with 0.05 to 2% by mass carbon and some other alloyants, like chromium (Cr), cobalt (Co), or molybdenum (Mo).

A-53

ALPHA RAYS

Another name for alpha particles (study ALPHA, BETA, AND GAMMA PARTICLES).

A-54

ALPHA, BETA, AND GAMMA PARTICLES

Alpha particles (α particles, α rays, or α radiation), beta particles (β particles, β rays, or β radiation), and gamma particles (γ particles, γ rays, or γ radiation) are produced when the nucleus of a nuclide goes under the decay process. During the decay process, the nucleus loses some of its mass (called **missing mass**) to release energy in the form of alpha, beta, and gamma particles. Alpha particles are the first particles that are released.

In 1903, Rutherford discovered alpha and beta particles and separated them experimentally by passing the radiation from a radioactive sample through an electric field (E-field). The method he used is shown in Figure 1. [As seen in the same figure, alpha rays reflect (deflect or turn) toward the negative electrode and beta rays toward the positive electrode. This experiment indicates that the α particles are electro-positively charged, and β particles are electro-negatively charged.]

Figure 2 demonstrates the **penetrability** of α, β, and γ particles. Alpha particles have the weakest **penetrability** of the three. A sheet of paper can stop alpha particles, so they are dangerous if we inhale a substance that emits α particles, eat food containing those particles, or when they contact a wound. A thin aluminum plate stops beta particles but partly penetrates the human body. And gamma particles partly stop and partly penetrate a thick lead plate, but completely penetrate the human body, so they are strong hazards.

Some other properties of α, β, and γ particles are outlined next.

- They are in the group of electromagnetic waves (EM waves or EM radiations).
- Alpha decay (a decay that emits alpha particles) occurs when helium (a nuclide consisting of two protons and two neutrons) decays.
- Beta decay occurs when a neutron changes to a proton or vice versa and emits (releases) beta particles. When the beta decay of an electron occurs in an atom, a neutron in the nucleus of that atom is changed to a proton. On the other hand, when the beta decay of positron occurs, a proton is changed to a neutron. In both cases, the nuclide under the decay process is changed to another nuclide.
- Gamma decay occurs when potassium-40 (a nuclide with a long halflife) deteriorates.

[Note 1: In an experiment, Rutherford directed electro-positively-charged alpha particles at a thin gold foil. Because many particles passed through the foil and only a few were reflected, he concluded that each gold atom is mostly empty space with a massively dense center. He called the point the nucleus and published a paper about it in 1909.]
[Note 2: Beta and gamma particles are radioactive elements (simply **radionuclides**), and their emissions remain for 5 to 50 years.]

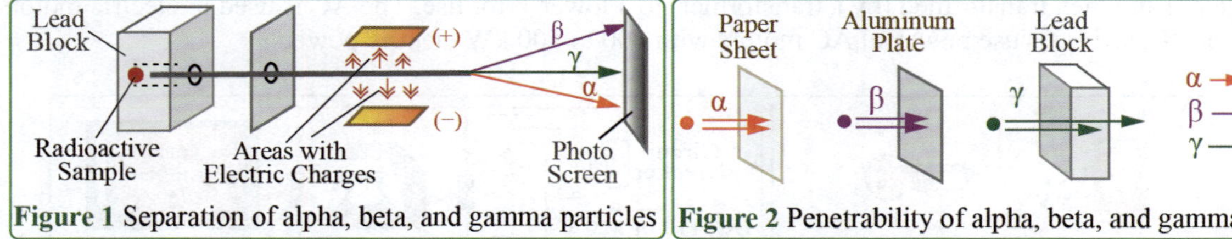

Figure 1 Separation of alpha, beta, and gamma particles

Figure 2 Penetrability of alpha, beta, and gamma particles

A-55

ALTERNATING AND DIRECT ELECTRIC CURRENTS

Alternating electric current (also called **alternating current electricity** or simply **alternating current**, AC) and direct electric current (also called **direct current electricity** or simply **direct current**, DC) are the two types of electric current (simply **current** or **electricity**), the flow of electric charges (q, simply **charges**) in an electric conductor. The AC and DC electricity is induced (produced) based on Faraday's Induction Law, invented by Faraday in the early1830s. AC and DC have different applications. Power plants and car batteries produce AC, while flashlight batteries produce DC (see Figure 1). The DC electricity in a flashlight battery flows from the battery's positive electrode (anode) toward its negative electrode (cathode).

Most electric devices use DC, such as TVs, computers, and house appliances (see Figure 2). [In chemical process plants, both are used. Most heavy equipment (like pumps, compressors, and centrifuges) use strong AC electricity, while process-control instruments use DC electricity.]

Alternating Current

AC electricity is an electric current whose electric voltage (V or V_E) alternates (reverses) as the opposite poles of the rotating magnet pass over it, as shown in Figure 3. For example, in 120 kV alternating current, the current alternates its direction 120 times per second. This is called the 60-cycle AC, which has 60 cycles per second, equal to 60 Hz (Hertz). [AC power has 60 Hz in some countries and 50 Hz in others.]

Based on what has been said here, the current-time graph of AC is sinusoidal (periodical), as shown in Figure 3. Figure 4 shows the production of AC by a simple electric generator (actually an alternator because it produces AC) when a wire coil (a wire loop with many turns) is rotating inside a cylindrical magnet. Typically, a generator is wired with three coils, evenly spaced around the axis so that when one coil is vertical, one of the others is at 120° to the vertical, and the other is at 240°.

In transferring AC, the amount of electric power (P_E, simply **power**) transmitted is the product of the I (electric current) multiplied by the V (electric voltage).

$$P_E = I.V \quad (1)$$

The **electric-power loss** ($P_{E.L}$) in a wire (because of heat energy transfer) is a product of the square of the wire's I and R (electric resistance).

$$P_{E.L} = I^2.R \quad (2)$$

Electric power (simply **power** or **electricity**) produced by power plants and delivered to residences, businesses, and industries, is in AC. The AC allows the power to be transmitted efficiently through power lines at high voltage (V) and then transformed (by a transformer) to a lower V for use. The AC is used in electric motors and generators. Centrifuges use powerful AC motors with 100 to 500 kW electric powers.

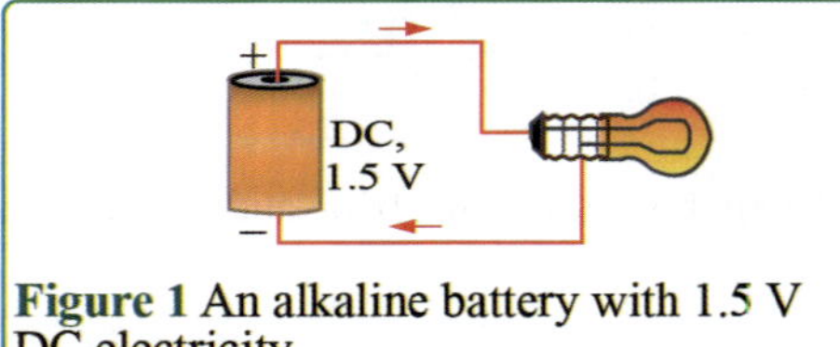

Figure 1 An alkaline battery with 1.5 V DC electricity

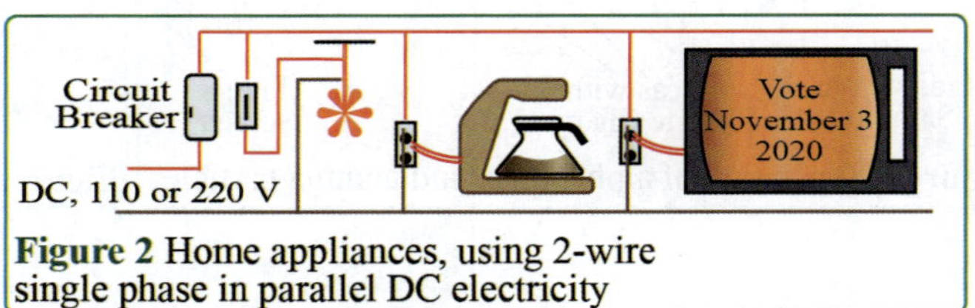

Figure 2 Home appliances, using 2-wire single phase in parallel DC electricity

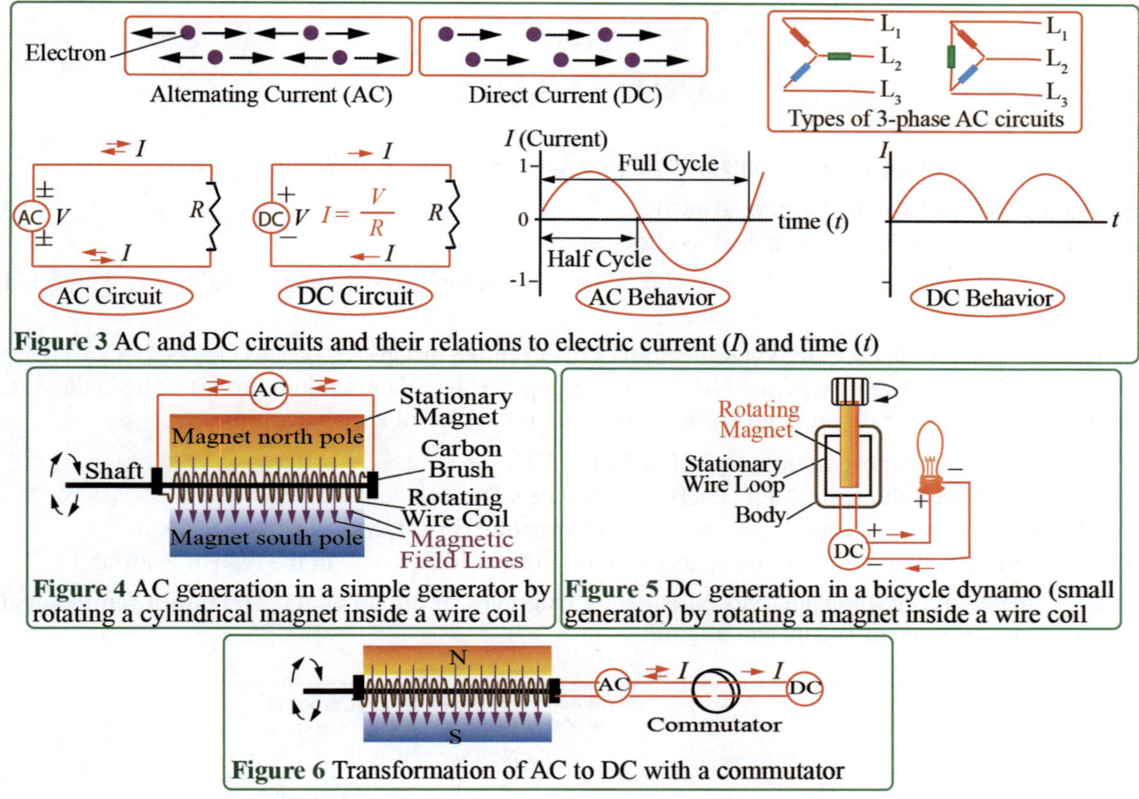

Figure 3 AC and DC circuits and their relations to electric current (I) and time (t)

Figure 4 AC generation in a simple generator by rotating a cylindrical magnet inside a wire coil

Figure 5 DC generation in a bicycle dynamo (small generator) by rotating a magnet inside a wire coil

Figure 6 Transformation of AC to DC with a commutator

Direct Current

A direct current (DC) is a current that flows in one direction, so the DC's positive and negative terminals do *not* alternate over time (see Figure 3). Defined so, the current-time graph of a DC is direct, as shown in the same figure. Figure 5 shows the formation of DC by a bicycle dynamo when a magnet is rotating inside a stationary wire loop.

The DC electricity in a flashlight battery flows from the battery's positive electrode (anode) toward its negative electrode (cathode).

An electric transformer or an electric commutator can transfer AC into DC (see Figure 6).

A-56
ALTERNATORS

Study ELECTRIC GENERATORS.

A-57

AMINO ACIDS

An amino acid is a compound that contains two functional groups in its molecular structure:

- Amino group (NH_2, also called **amine group**),
- Carboxyl group (COOH, also called **carboxylic group**).

Each group is connected to a carbon (C) atom. The asymmetric carbon (interior carbon) is connected to a variable group (shown by symbol R in Figure 1).

Usually, hydrogen (H) on the carboxyl group moves to the amino group (NH_2). This changes COOH (carboxyl group) to COO^- (carboxylate group) and NH_2 (amino group) to NH_3^+ (ammonium group). The changes tell us that amino acids are in their **dissociated state**. Some other properties of amino acids are:

- Most amino acids decompose in the range of 185 to 315°C,
- Most amino acids are soluble in water (H_2O) and alkaline solutions,
- Molecules of all amino acids are in one stereoisomer structure (in L-form), and
- Amino acids make proteins. [20 amino acids that form proteins differ only in the type of R group.]

Glutamine, melatonin, tryptophan, and tyrosine are examples of amino acids. **Melatonin** (amino acid and antioxidant) can treat sleep disorders and migraine.

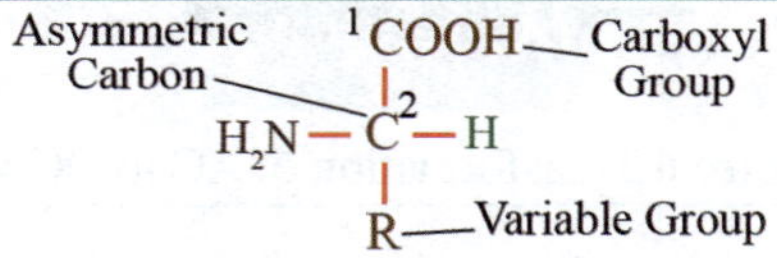

Asymmetric Carbon
^{1}COOH — Carboxyl Group
$H_2N-\overset{2}{C}-H$
R — Variable Group

Figure 1 Molecular structure of a typical amino acid

A-58

AMMONIA

Ammonia (NH_3) is an alkaline (base), noncondensing, corrosive, hazardous, and colorless gas with a special odor. It can be odorless by reacting with sodium bicarbonate ($NaHCO_3$) or acetic acid (HCH_3COO). It is easily liquefied because of hydrogen bonds between its molecules (see Figure 1).

As the only common weak alkaline gas that does *not* contain an OH^- (hydroxyl) functional group, when NH_3 reacts with H_2O (water), it takes an H^+ ion from the water molecule and produces an OH^- ion.

$$NH_3 + H_2O \rightarrow NH_4^+ + OH^-$$

Ammonia can be produced by nitrogen (N_2) and hydrogen (H_2) reactions.

$$N_2 + 3\ H_2 \longrightarrow 2\ NH_3$$

Because ammonia is noncondensing, it is usually vented out from the evaporators during the evaporation of an ammonia-containing solution. The venting process decreases the solution's PH (because the solution becomes less alkaline, so the solution's PH decreases).

Some other properties of pure ammonia are step-outlined next.

- Its density (D) is 0.88 kg/m^3 (it is lighter than atmospheric air with a density of 1.2 kg/m^3),
- Its molecular mass (M_M) is 17 g, and its molar mass (M_n) is 17 g/mole,
- Its specific heat capacity (C_Q) is 4.7 kJ/kg.°C (= 1.1 BTU/Lb.°F),
- Its boiling point temperature (T_{BP}) is – 33°C (= – 28°F), and
- Its solubility in water is high (33% by weight at 25°C).

Study the following brief-but-important points about ammonia:

- Liquid ammonia is stored below atmospheric pressure or at low temperature (T) because of its low T_{BP}.
- Ammonium hydroxide (NH_3OH, called **household ammonia**) is a 30% (by weight) of NH_3 in water.
- Ammonia's world production is about 180 million tons per year.

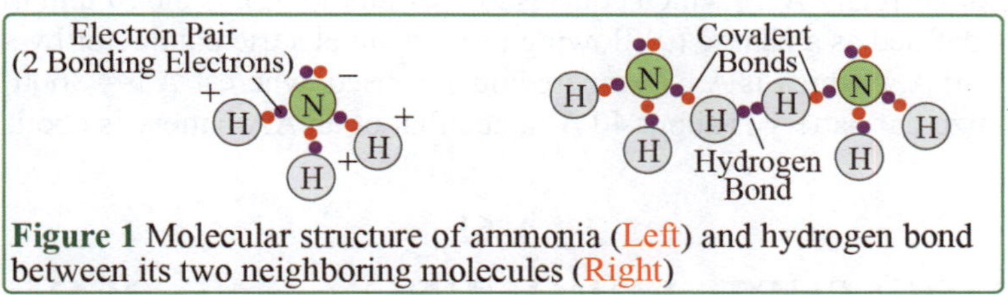

Figure 1 Molecular structure of ammonia (Left) and hydrogen bond between its two neighboring molecules (Right)

A-59

AMORPHOUS AND CRYSTALLINE SOLIDS

Amorphous Solids

An amorphous solid (a noncrystalline solid or a shapeless solid) consists of an unorganized and disorderly-repeating molecular structure (see Figure 1). Amorphous solids are also defined as solids with *no* molecular structure. Glasses (a family of silicates) are common examples of amorphous solids with unorganized and disorderly-repeating molecules. The molecules of powdered sugar are also amorphous.

Crystalline Solids

A crystalline solid has an organized and orderly-repeating molecular structure, called the **crystal lattice structure** (simply the **crystal structure**), as seen on the right side of Figure 1. Unlike amorphous powdered sugar with unorganized molecules, the molecules of table-crystalline sugar are crystalline with organized and orderly-repeating molecules. Table salt (sodium chloride, NaCl) and diamond are crystalline solids.

Polycrystalline Solids: A polycrystalline solid consists of many tiny crystals (crystallites or grains) with irregular shapes and orientations. Some metals and semimetals have polycrystalline molecular structures.

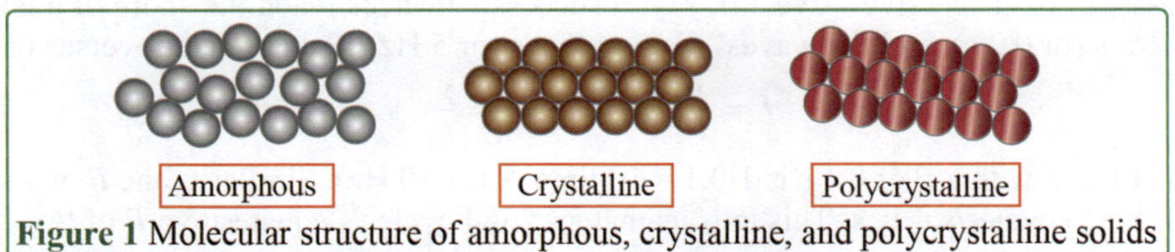

Figure 1 Molecular structure of amorphous, crystalline, and polycrystalline solids

A-60

AMPERE AND AMPERE SECOND

Ampere

Ampere (A, named after French physicist Andre Ampere, 1775–1836) is the SI unit of the electric current (I, simply **current**). It is defined as a current (I) that produces a force of 2×10^{-7} N/m between two one-meter wires placed 1 m apart, where N is for Newton (the SI unit of force), and m is for the meter.

Ampere Second

Ampere second (As or correctly A.s), which equates to 1 Coulomb (C), is the SI unit of the electric charge (q, simply **charge**). A.s is defined as a charge (q) flowing through an electric conductor by a current of 1 A for 1 s. Usually, the larger unit of A.s, which is A.h (Ampere hour), is used, where 1 A.h = 3600 A.s = 3600 C. Say, the capacity of a medium-size-car battery is about 40 A.h, and that of an AA battery is about 2 A.h.

A-61

AMPLITUDE, FREQUENCY, AND PERIOD

Amplitude: Amplitude (A) is the change of a periodic (repeating) quantity in a single period. In relation to the wave, A is half the height of a wave from its peak (the high part between two waves) or trough (the low part between two waves), as shown in Figure 1. In relation to the light, A indicates its intensity (the light luminous or brightness as seen by an observer) to determine how many photons hit a particular system at a time. In relation to the sound, A indicates a sound's intensity (the loudness of sound as heard by a listener).

[Amplitude has different units, depending on the usage. In relation to waves, the amplitude is a displacement, so it is expressed in the unit of length.]

Frequency: Frequency (f) is a rate quantity that expresses the number of times that a periodic system (like a wave or rotating basket of a centrifuge) repeats itself in a unit of time (t); say, in 1 s (second). Numerically, frequency is the number of cycles that pass by a given point per unit of time, as shown in Figure 2. If, say, 5 successive waves reach the edge of a lake in 1 s, the f of the waves is 5 waves/s or 5 Hertz (Hz, the SI unit of f). Similarly, if the centrifuge basket makes 1200 rotations per minute, the basket's f is 1200 RPM.

Frequency (f) and wavelength (λ) are related (the *longer* the λ of a wave, the *smaller* is its f), so in the subjects of light and other electromagnetic waves, f and λ are usually considered as two sides of the same coin by specifying one instead of the other. Because the waves of light travel through a vacuum at a constant speed, known as the speed of light constant (c), its f and λ are related as $f = c/\lambda$.

Period: Period (P) is the **time interval** to make one complete cycle. A wave's period is the time interval between the passages of successive waves. If, say, 5 successive waves reach the shore of a lake in 1 s, the P of these waves is 1/5 s (or 0.2 s), and the waves' f is 5 waves/s (or 5 Hz). P and f are reverses of each other.

$$f = \frac{1}{P} \quad \text{or} \quad P = \frac{1}{f} \tag{1}$$

Thus, the f of a wave with a P of 0.1 s is 1/0.1 = 10 times/s (or 10 Hz). Similarly, the P of a spring vibrating at f of 4 Hz is ¼ Hz = ¼ cycles/s = ¼ s. This tells us that an f of 4 cycles/s equates to a P of ¼ s.

The relation between a wave's U (speed), λ (wavelength), and its P (period) is

$$U = \frac{\lambda}{P} \tag{2}$$

Because it is easier to measure a wave's f (frequency) than its P, and because, numerically, the f and P are the reverse (reciprocal) of each other, we can write the previous equation as

$$U = \lambda . f \tag{4}$$

[Note: The symbol f shows both frequency and friction. This must *not* create confusion because these words are rarely used in one equation. P shows period and pressure, but *no* confusion can occur for the same reason.]

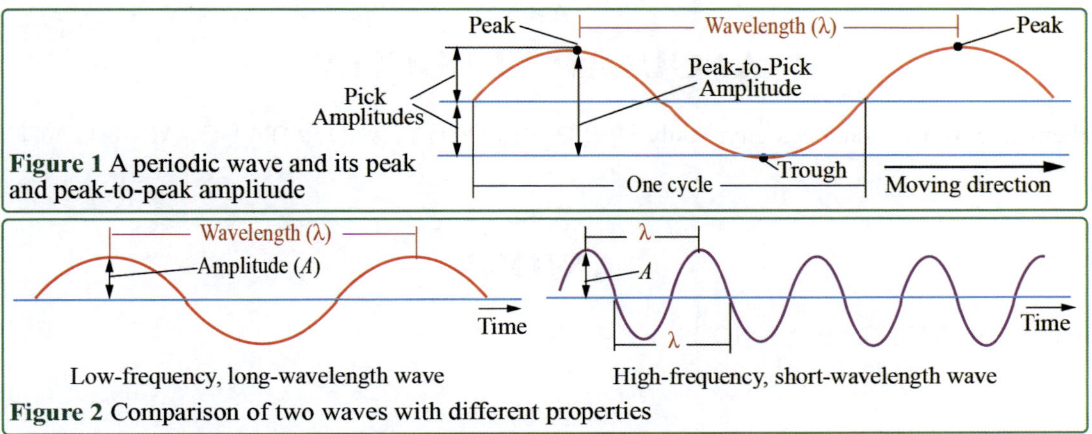

Figure 1 A periodic wave and its peak and peak-to-peak amplitude

Figure 2 Comparison of two waves with different properties

A-62
AMU

Abbreviated form of ATOMIC MASS UNIT.

A-63
ANGLE OF REPOSE

The angle of repose (the repose angle) is the steepest angle relative to the horizontal surface, to which a bulk material can be piled (loaded) without falling (sliding). At this angle, the material on the slope is on the edge of sliding. Figure 1 shows bulk sugar crystals conically piled on a surface and their angle of repose (the internal angle between the surface of the pile and the horizontal surface).

The repose angle can range from 0 to 90°. For example, the angle of dry sugar is between 30 and 35° and for wet sugar is 55° (depending on sugar coarseness). The angle of repose of dry sand is 35°, and that of wet sand is 45°. [The angle of repose has some industrial applications. For example, the repose angle is used in the design of silos, as the pressure applied on the silo walls by the stored material is different at different angles and depths.]

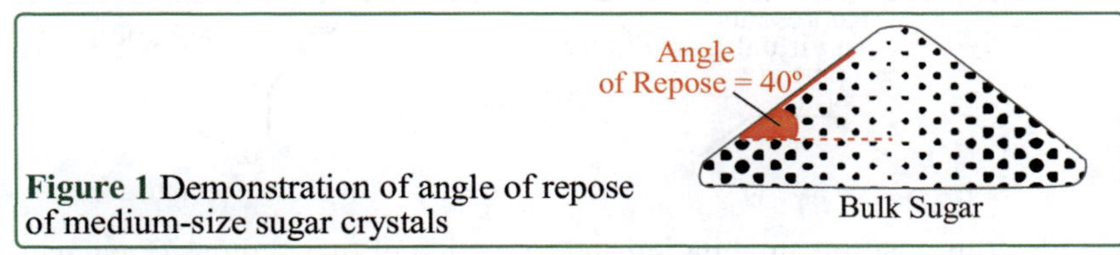

Figure 1 Demonstration of angle of repose of medium-size sugar crystals

A-64
ANGULAR MOMENTUM

Another name for ROTATIONAL MOMENTUM.

A-65
ANGULAR VELOCITY

Another name for rotational velocity. Study SPEED, VELOCITY, AND ROTATIONAL VELOCITY.

A-66
ANIONS

Study IONS, CATIONS, AND ANIONS.

A-67
ANNIHILATION OF PARTICLES

Annihilation of an atomic particle is its colliding (contacting) with its antiparticle (a particle with an opposite electric charge of its particle) to form a quantum particle (a particle with *no* sub-particle) and some energy (*E*). As shown in Figure 1, annihilation (destruction) occurs with formation, like the colliding of a hydrogen atom (an atomic particle) with antihydrogen (the antiparticle of hydrogen) and the formation of a photon. In this process (Figure 2), the *M* (mass) of hydrogen and antihydrogen convert into *E* in the form of E_{Ph} (photon energy), based on Einstein's equation ($E = M.c^2$). Similarly, two photons are formed when an electron collides antielectron (positron). The easiest way to think about the electron-positron annihilation is through the Feynman diagram, introduced in 1948 by Richard Feynman (1918–1988, an American physicist). This diagram (Figure 3) shows that an electron is absorbed, and two photons are released. [Electron-positron annihilation is performed in a particle accelerator.]

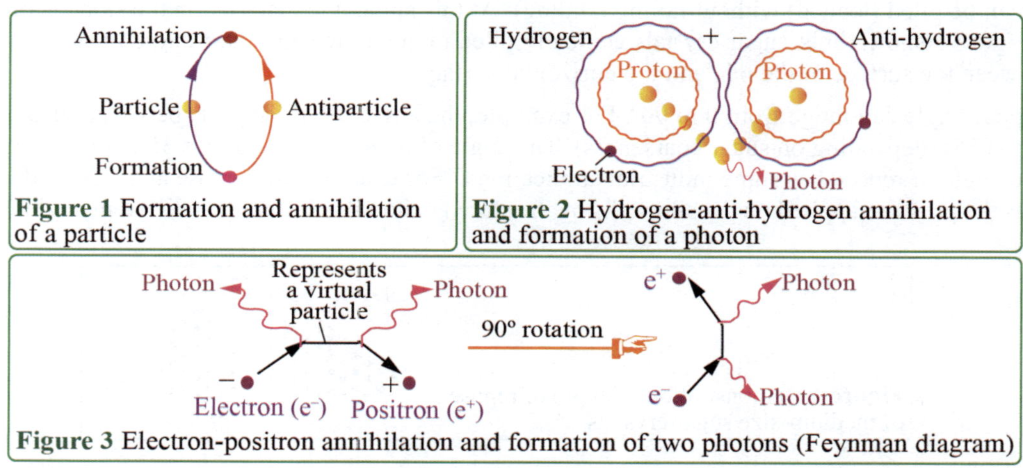

Figure 1 Formation and annihilation of a particle

Figure 2 Hydrogen-anti-hydrogen annihilation and formation of a photon

Figure 3 Electron-positron annihilation and formation of two photons (Feynman diagram)

A-68

ANOMERS

Anomers are two cyclic isomers that differ only in their molecular structures. For example, α-glucose and *β*-glucose are anomers, as shown in Figure 1. Carbon-1 (C-1) in glucose is an **anomeric carbon**. Glycosidic bonding (oxygen bonding, −O−) exists in the glucose molecular structure because of the anomeric carbon effect.

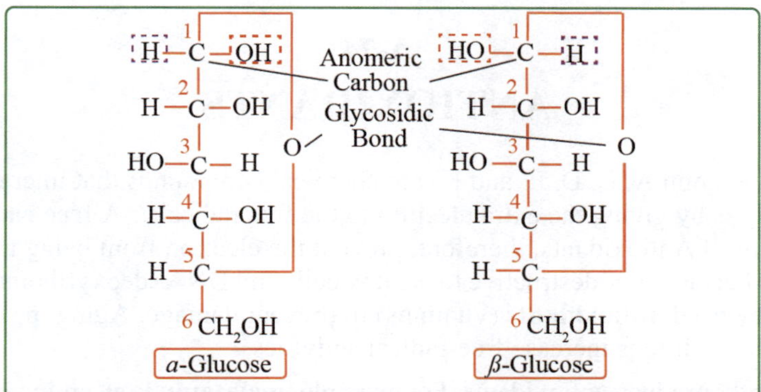

Figure 1 Demonstration of anomeric carbon and glycosidic bond in *a*-glucose and *β*-glucose in straight (Fischer) method

A-69

ANTIELECTRON

Another name for POSITRON.

A-70

ANTIFOAMING AGENTS

Discussed under the topic of FOAM AND ANTIFOAMING AGENTS.

A-71

ANTILOGARITHM

Study LOGARITHM AND ANTILOGARITHM.

A-72

ANTIMATTERS

Another name for ANTIPARTICLE.

A-73
ANTINEUTRINO

Antineutrino is the antiparticle of neutrino. An antineutrino exists for each neutrino (a Fermion with energy that obeys Fermi-Dirac statistics). Antineutrino has almost *no* mass, electric charge, and an opposite spin to a neutrino. In a nuclear chain reaction, an antineutrino is produced by beta minus decay (β^- decay)

A-74
ANTIOXIDANTS

Antioxidants (mainly vitamin A, C, D, E, and K) are chemical compounds that interact with free radicals and block the oxidation process by giving the extra electron to the free radicals. [A **free radical** is a highly reactive atom that lacks an electron.] Antioxidants, therefore, prevent the electron from being taken from a healthy cell. As a result, free radicals become non-destructive to healthy cells and DNA (deoxyribonucleic acid). Free radicals act like **oxidants,** so they need **antioxidants** (vitamins) to prevent damage. Aging, pollution, tobacco, radioactivity, and some medical conditions increase free-radical activities.

Our body *cannot* directly produce antioxidants. For example, **melatonin** is an amino acid and antioxidant with a free radical scavenger made in our brain from the amino acid **tryptophan**. When our eyes do *not* get enough light, melatonin is produced in the eye's pineal gland, causing tiredness. [Generally, most antioxidants can be produced in our body by consuming fruits and some vegetables.

A-75
ANTIPARTICLES

An antiparticle (also called **antimatter**) exactly matches the properties of its originated particle, but its electric charge (q) has an opposite value. For example, an electron and antielectron (called a positron) have the same properties, but the electron is an electro-negatively-charged particle, while the positron is electro-positively charged. Physicists think that most particles have antiparticles. So far, however, an antiparticle has *not* been predicted for photon, so it's an antiparticle.

As shown in Figure 1, annihilation produces two photons when an electron is in contact with its antiparticle (a positron). This statement tells us that all the mass (M) of electron and positron convert into energy (E) in the form of photon energy (E_{Ph}) by Einstein's equation ($E = M.c^2$). [The energy production is huge; just 10 mg of positrons can produce the energy of 428 t of TNT.]

The important point is that there is *no* antiparticle in the Universe now. For their creation, antiparticles need highly energetic gamma particles, which are rare because the special condition for their creation (extreme temperature) existed only during the first few seconds after the Big Bang. Also, antiparticles are unstable, so they quickly go through the decay process. So, the Universe contains plenty of particles and almost *no* antiparticles.

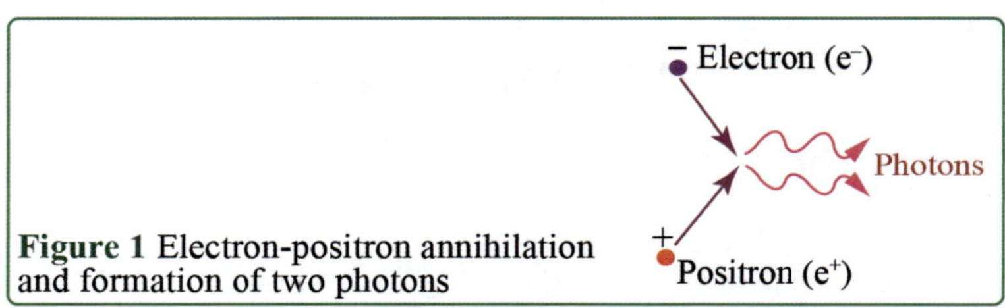

Figure 1 Electron-positron annihilation and formation of two photons

A-76

ANTOINE EQUATIONS AND COEFFICIENTS

Discussed under the topic of ACTIVITY EQUATIONS AND COEFFICIENTS.

A-77

APPROACH COOLING TEMPERATURE

Defined under EVAPORATIVE COOLING DEVICES.

A-78

AQUEOUS SOLUTIONS

An aqueous solution is a solution in which water is the solvent. For example, 25 g of NaCl is mixed with water to form 100 mL of 25% aqueous solution of NaCl.

The ability of a substance to dissolve in water depends on whether the substance can overcome the strong attractive forces that exist between the water molecules. If the substance *cannot* dissolve in water, the molecules of the substance form a precipitate. [Aqueous solutions are shown as **aq**, such as 25% NaCl (aq).]

A-79

ARCHIMEDES PRINCIPLE

Archimedes' principle is a physical chemistry concept named after Archimedes (287 BC – 212 BC, Greek scientist). This principle can be expressed in either of the following ways:

- When a system is partially or fully placed in a liquid, it experiences a weight reduction, equating to its weight (w, gravitational force exerted on a system by a mass).
- When a system is partially or fully placed in a liquid, it receives an upward buoyant force (F_B) that equates to the weight of the liquid that the system displaces.

Consider a system placed in water. If the weight of the water displaced is more than the system's weight, the system floats. Otherwise, the system sinks. And if the weights are equal, the system remains in place without floating or sinking. In equation form, Archimedes' principle for F_B can be given as

$$F_B = w = M.a_g = D.V.a_g \tag{1}$$

Here, w is the weight of the displaced liquid, M is the mass of the displaced liquid, D is the liquid's density, V is the displaced liquid's volume, and a_g is the buoyant-system's gravitational acceleration (= 9.81 m/s^2).

Knowing that the term $D.a_g$ is called specific weight (w_{Sp}), the F_B equation can be written as

$$F_B = D.V.a_g = w_{Sp}.V \tag{2}$$

Based on this equation, the F_B on a system that displaces 0.1 m^3 of water (with D of 1000 kg/m^3) is

$$F_B = D.V.a_g = 1000 \times 0.1 \times 9.81 = 981 \text{ (kg/m}^3\text{)(m}^3\text{)(m/s}^2\text{)} = \text{kg.m/s}^2 = \text{N or } 221 \text{ Lb}_F$$

As Figure 1 shows, the downward force on the system is its weight (w), and the upward force on the system is F_B (an upward force exerted on a system by a fluid). Thus, the net force on the system is the difference between F_B and w. If the net force is positive (when $F_B > w$), the system floats; if negative (when $F_B < w$), the system sinks; and if zero ($F_B = w$), the system stays in place without floating or sinking.

Based on Archimedes' principle, we can measure an irregular solid's volume (V), as shown in Figure 2. It is also used in the process control engineering in level measurement by a displacer gauge.

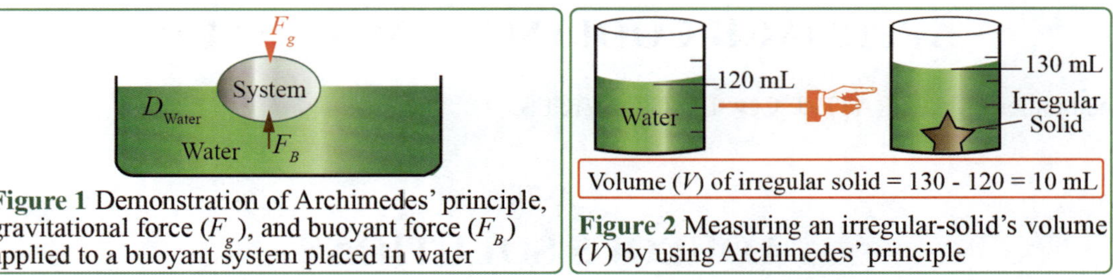

Figure 1 Demonstration of Archimedes' principle, gravitational force (F_g), and buoyant force (F_B) applied to a buoyant system placed in water

Figure 2 Measuring an irregular-solid's volume (V) by using Archimedes' principle

A-80

AREA

Area (A) is a vector quantity (a quantity with value and direction) representing a two-dimensional surface. The area of, say, a square is length square (L^2), and that of a rectangle is the length (L) multiplied by the width (W), that is $L.W$. Similarly, the area of a circle with a diameter d is $\pi.d^2/4$.

The SI unit of area is m^2, and its US unit is Ft^2, where m is for the meter, and Ft is for the foot.

A-81

ASH

Ash is incombustible soluble and insoluble salts of organic and inorganic compounds. Typical coal, for example, can have 4 to 12% ash, and coke has 12% ash. The flue gas carries the coal ash (fly ash) from a furnace during combustion. The ash particles are so small that ash is grouped in the class of particulate matter (simply **particulates**). In chemical process plants, flue gas (an air pollutant) is usually processed in a gas scrubber to remove its ash particles as much as possible, to prevent its harmful environmental effect.

Knowing the following brief points about ash is helpful:

- The ash determined by the conductometric method is called **conductivity ash.**
- The word **ash** without any **qualifying** (determining) **word** in front of it means **conductivity ash.**

A-82

ASYMMETRIC CARBON

An asymmetric carbon (also called **interior carbon**, **alpha carbon**, or **chiral carbon**) is an intermolecular carbon atom that is attached to four (4) different types of atoms or groups of atoms (Figure 1). For example, as shown in Figure 2, carbon 2 (or C-2) of an amino acid molecule is asymmetric. The C-2 is connected to a hydrogen (H) atom, an amino group (NH_2), a carboxylic group (COOH), and a variable group (shown by symbol R in the figure). Figure 3 shows the molecular structure of glucose, in which C–2 through C–5 are asymmetric.

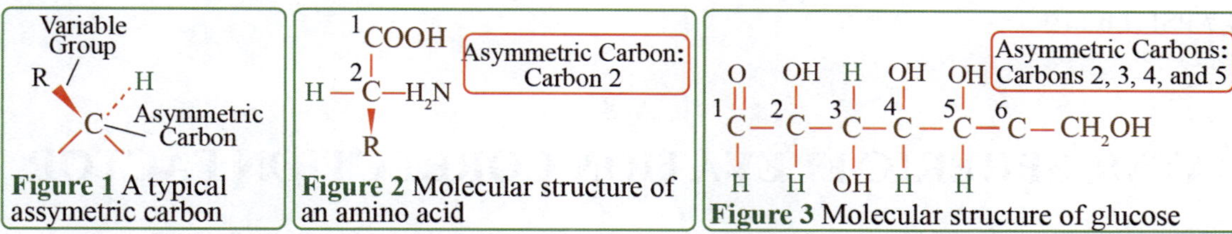

Figure 1 A typical assymetric carbon

Figure 2 Molecular structure of an amino acid

Figure 3 Molecular structure of glucose

A-83

AT REST SYSTEMS

In Physics, an at-rest system (a system at rest) is a motionless system with zero acceleration (a). [Remember that *no* place in the Universe is at rest (because the Earth, the Sun, and the Galaxies are also accelerating). However, in Physics, the Earth is considered a nonaccelerating reference system (inertial reference system), although it accelerates as it rotates around its axis and the Sun.]

The following are important to know about at-rest systems:

- Suppose the position of a system is *not* changing in relation to a given reference system (a frame of reference or simply reference). In that case, the system is **at rest** (motionless or stationary). When, for example, one grabs a book (like this) from the ground and raises it to 1 m (= 3 Ft), the book is raised from its **rest** position in relation to the ground (here, the reference system).
- The mass of an at-rest system is known as rest mass, and its energy is known as rest mass energy (E_M). All forms of energy act as E_M when they are at rest. [Because of mass-energy equivalency, some physicists use the word **rest mass** to refer to **rest mass energy**.]
- Because all motions seem relative and all at-constant-speed motions behave the same, we can say that one system is at rest and the others are moving.

A-84

ATMOSPHERE

The term atmosphere in science and engineering is used as

- **Earth's Atmosphere:** It is a layer of gases surrounding the Earth. Each planet has its atmosphere that is kept in place by that planet's gravitational force. The atmosphere contains air, which consists of molecular nitrogen (N_2), molecular oxygen (O_2), water (H_2O), argon (Ar), a small amount of carbon dioxide (CO_2), and traces of other gases.
- **Pressure's Unit:** Usually, its abbreviation, Atm, is used as a pressure unit, where 1 Atm = 1 bar = 101 kPa = 14.7 PSI (Lb/In^2).

A-85

ATMOSPHERIC ELEVATION CORRECTION FACTOR

Discussed under ABSOLUTE, ATMOSPHERIC, GAUGE, AND VACUUM PRESSURES.

A-86

ATMOSPHERIC FORMULA

Discussed under ABSOLUTE, ATMOSPHERIC, GAUGE, AND VACUUM PRESSURES.

A-87

ATMOSPHERIC PRESSURE

Discussed under ABSOLUTE, ATMOSPHERIC, GAUGE, AND VACUUM PRESSURES.

A-88
ATOM

An **atom** is a too-tiny (1 million atoms is only 0.01 mm in length) and a too-organized system with *no* definite outer boundary. An atom consists of its components (protons, neutrons, and electrons), subcomponents (quarks, the components of protons and neutrons), and electron shells (Figure 1). A **molecule** consists of two or more atoms joined together by chemical bonds. An atom is, thus, the elementary particle of an element, and a molecule is that of a compound. Say, a molecule of carbon (C, an element) consists of one kind of atom, while a molecule of water (H_2O, a compound) consists of two kinds of atoms (H and O).

Atoms (typically 0.1 nm in diameter) and molecules (typically 0.2 nm) are so small that 6.02×10^{23} atoms exist in 12 g of C, and 6.02×10^{23} molecules are in 18 g of H_2O, where 6.02×10^{23} is Avogadro's number.

The idea that the atom is a tiny particle goes back about 2500 years to the Greek philosopher Democritus. Still, it took several years until the physicists discovered some of its key unknown properties (Figure 1).

- 1687: Newton recognized the atom as an extremely tiny elementary particle (theoretic discovery of **atom**).
- 1897: Thomson J. J. proved the existence of one (or more) electron in an atom (discovery of **electron**).
- 1909: Rutherford discovered a small dense point in the atom's center (the discovery of **nucleus**).
- 1919: Rutherford proved the existence of protons in an atom's nucleus (discovery of **proton**).
- 1932: Chadwick J. proved the existence of neutrons in the nucleus (discovery of **neutron**).
- 1932: Dirac P. proved the antiparticle (antimatter) of the electron (discovery of **positron**).
- 1964: Two physicists proposed the existence of quarks in nucleon (discovery of **quark**).

[Note 1: Our today's knowledge of the atomic structure is based on a few atomic models, suggested by different distinguished physicists, mainly Bohr, whose model is discussed under ATOMIC MODELS.] [Note 2: Despite the development of the electronic microscope in the 1980s, it is still impossible to clearly see the inside of an atom, so we must imagine the behavior of subatomic particles when studying the atomic concepts.]

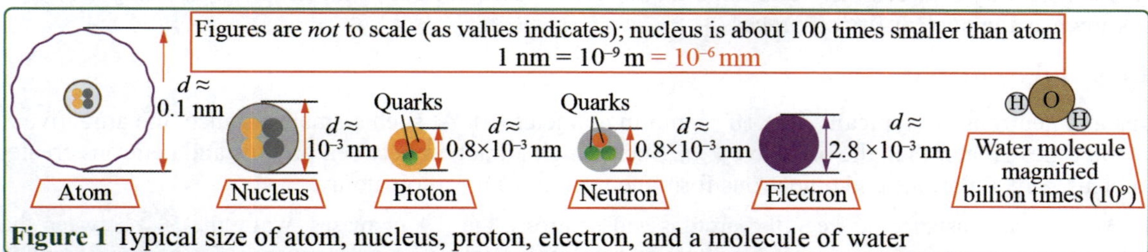

Figure 1 Typical size of atom, nucleus, proton, electron, and a molecule of water

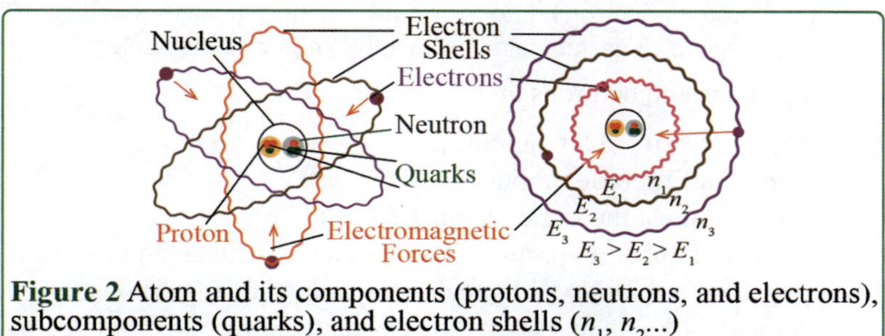

Figure 2 Atom and its components (protons, neutrons, and electrons), subcomponents (quarks), and electron shells (n_1, n_2...)

The following are some important characteristics of an atom:

- **Atomic Size and Mass:** It is hard to estimate atom size (because it has *no* outer boundary). However, the size of atoms is typically 10^{-7} mm in diameter. In solids, atomic size and atomic spacing are almost the same (see Figure 1). Atoms are so light that many trillions of them exist in each breath. The lightest atom is hydrogen (H), with a mass of 1.67×10^{-24} g. An oxygen atom (O) is 16 times heavier (26.7×10^{-24} g).
- **Atomic Charge:** Atoms are electrically **neutral** because an element's atom has the same number of protons (the electro-positively-charged particles) and electrons (electro-negatively-charged particles).
- **Atomic Decomposability:** Atoms *cannot* be decomposed by a chemical reaction but can be so by a nuclear reaction. Thus, the nucleus of an atom is *not* involved in a reaction and its electrons are the only ones participating in a reaction. This means that a reaction *cannot* create, destroy, or alter the nucleus. An atom's nucleus is involved in nuclear reactions. For example, the nucleus of a heavy nuclide (like uranium-235) in a nuclear fission process splits (fissions) to release a great amount of nuclear energy (E_N).
- **Atomic Attractivity and Repulsivity:** Atoms are attracted by attractive energy (E_A) when they are at a certain distance apart and repelled by repulsive energy (E_R) when compressed into one another. [An atom's sum of E_A and E_R equates to its E_P (potential energy).]

NUCLEUS

The atomic nucleus in an atom's center consists of protons (symbol p^+) and neutrons (n^0), together known as the **nucleon**. A few general properties of the nucleus are outlined next.

- Nucleus is dense because it carries almost the entire mass of an atom.
- Nucleus positive charges attract an equal number of electro-negatively-charged electrons.
- A typical nucleus is 10^{-12} mm in diameter (d), which is 10^5 times smaller than its atom. This tells us that a large space exists between the nucleus and **electron shells** (shells or orbits), used for orbiting the electrons around the nucleus. [Nuclei are in different sizes, depending on how many protons and neutrons they have.]
- In the nucleus, the repulsive FEM (electromagnetic force), created by positive charges of protons, keeps the protons and neutrons away to prevent their collision. And the attractive FSN (strong nuclear force), which is stronger than FEM, attracts them. In addition, FEM and FSN keep the quarks together in a proton and a neutron. [The instability between FEM and FSN in a nucleus causes nuclear chain reactions, splitting the nucleus, known as the nuclear fission process.]

Protons and Neutrons

Protons and neutrons are typically 0.8×10^{-12} mm in diameter (d). At such a small distance, the attractive F_{SN} is about 100 times greater than the repulsive F_{EM}. Such a high attraction between protons and neutrons creates a stable nucleus. Say, 6 protons and 6 neutrons form the nucleus of a carbon atom.

[Note: At a *greater* distance between the protons and neutrons, the F_{SN} increases; while the F_{EM} between them decreases at a *smaller* distance, so an unstable situation between attractive F_{SN} and repulsive F_{EM} occurs, creating an unstable nucleus. The optimum protons-neutrons ratio is also important to nucleus stability. If too many (or too few) neutrons are present, the nucleus becomes unstable and decayable, known as the nuclear decay process.]

Some other properties of protons and neutrons are:

- Proton's electric charge (q) is 1.6×10^{-19} C (Coulomb).
- Proton has an extremely large half lifetime (about 1.3×10^{34} years).
- Proton and neutron masses are almost the same (about 1.67×10^{-24} g).
- Protons and neutrons are made of quantum particles (with *no* sub-particles), quarks.
- Proton is made of two up quarks (*u*-quarks) and one down quark (*d*-quark), shown as *uud*.
- Neutron is made of two *d*-quarks (down quarks) and one *u*-quark, simply symbolized by *ddu*.
- A free proton can decay into a positron (an electron's antiparticle with a + charge) and a **neutral pion**.
- A free neutron can decay into a proton, an electron, and an antineutrino with a mean lifetime of 15 min.

ELECTRON

Electron (e^-) is a quantum particle with a negative electric charge. An atom's electron (electrons) constantly turns around the nucleus and its axis in **electron shells** (simply **shells** or **orbits**) or **subshells**, as shown in Figure 2. The neighboring atoms of an element do *not* collide (hit) each other simply because each atom's electrons repel the neighboring atoms' electrons. [Instead of the **electron shell** used by Bohr in his atomic model, the term **electron cloud** was used by Heisenberg and Schrodinger in their quantum atomic model to emphasize that it is hard to know exactly where an electron is located at the moment. So, they used the word **probability** (about 90%) of an electron in a shell.]

Electrons have dual properties, called electron's wave-particle duality. An electron acts like a wave when it turns around the nucleus and like a particle when it releases (or absorbs) a photon. [In 1926, Schrodinger proved that an electron's wave property could be calculated by a quantum wavefunction, which corresponds to the wavelength of the electron's wave. The wavefunction can determine an electron's energy (E) and, thus, its probable location in a shell (because an electron, moving in a certain shell, has a known amount of E.]

Next are some other properties of the electron:

- **Electron Size:** Electron has a tiny size (2.8×10^{-12} mm) that spectroscopy can detect.
- **Electron Mass:** It has a tiny mass of 9.11×10^{-28} g (almost massless). [Electron's mass equates to about 1% of the nucleus and is about 1000 times lighter than the lightest atom.]
- **Electron Structure:** It has *no* internal structure (because it does *not* contain sub-particles), so it is a **quantum** (non-composite) **particle** (a particle with *no* sub-particle).
- **Electron Behavior:** Electron behaves like a wave at this moment and like a particle at another.
- **Electron is a Fermion:** It, therefore, obeys the Fermi-Dirac statics (discussed under FERMIONS).
- **Electron Location:** An electron's situation in the electron shells is unique to each chemical element.
- **Electron Spins:** It rotates around its nucleus and its axis. Its rotation around the nucleus is called the **orbital rotation**, and that around its axis in clockwise (CW) or counterclockwise (CCW) is known as the **quantum spin** (simply spin), indicated by the quantum spin number (with the value of +½ and –½). [The electron spin direction determines its magnetic orientation (north-and-south magnetic poles).]
- **Electron Strength:** The valance (outer) electrons are the most weakly-bound electrons. This is why an atom's valence electrons are the only ones that participate in that atom's bonding process.

- **Electron Strength:** The valance (outer) electrons are the most weakly-bound electrons. This is why an atom's valence electrons are the only ones that participate in that atom's bonding process.
- **Electron Superposition:** Electron is in quantum superposition states, meaning its spin is in the more-than-one state; in other words, it can be in two different rotational states simultaneously.
- **Electron Speed:** It turns fast (at about 2 000 km/s) around its nucleus, caused by F_{EM} created by positive charges of a proton. Its F_{EM} creates an electromagnetic field around it.
- **Electron Charge:** It carries a negative electric charge (q) of 1.62×10^{-19} C, opposite to that of a proton with $q = 1.6\times10^{-19}$ C, so attraction energy between an electron and a proton has a tiny negative value. Here C is for Coulomb, the SI unit for electric charge.
- **Electron Energy:** Its energy (refers to its potential energy) is **quantized**, meaning that a given atom's electron (or electrons) in a shell has a different amount of energy than the same electron (or electrons) as it moves to another shell, as Bohr proved in 1913. This relates to an electron's distance from its nucleus (the *further* is an electron from its nucleus, the *more* energy it has). [Later, in 1926, Schrodinger proved that the energy of an electron corresponds to the wavelength of that electron's wave.]
- **Electron Decay:** An electron can decay into a proton and an antineutrino (the antiparticle of neutrino), so its decay is **beta minus decay** (see NUCLEAR DECAY PROCESS).

- **Electron Relocation:** It jumps from shell to shell (by releasing or absorbing energy). If an electron moves from one shell to another, it produces spectral lines different from other elements. Thus, spectral lines can be used to identify an element. Electron gets farther from its nucleus (goes up in shells) when it gains energy, acting at a higher energy-level shell. Instead, it gets closer to its nucleus when it loses energy, acting at a lower energy-level shell.

You should also be aware of the following three important points about electrons:

- **Electron Shells:** Electrons are in **electron shells** (simply **shells** or **orbits**). Each shell holds a maximum number of electrons (2 in the first shell, 8 in the second, 18 in the third, and likes). Valence (outer) electrons are the electrons in the **valence** (outer) **shell,** the farthest shell from the nucleus.
- **Electron Role in a Reaction:** The valence electrons are the only ones that participate in chemical reactions to create chemical bonds between the participating atoms. When a valence electron gets some energy to act in a reaction, it is called a **free** (liberated) **electron**, called **electron liberation**. The liberated electron can then act as a covalent bond or ionic bond in a reaction.
- **Electron Functionality:** When an electron jumps down from a higher energy-level shell to a lower energy-level shell, some energy, which equates to the difference in potential energy (E_P) between the two shells, is released. Similarly, electrons can move up to higher-energy shells. This process, called electron pumping, is used in some devices, such as a **laser** (Light Amplification by Stimulated Emission of Radiation). [Laser has many uses, including in medical surgery, where it produces a strong beam of light to focus on a tight spot and allow a high quantity of energy (E) on that spot.]

Quantization of Electron and Photon: Quantum leap is the jumping action of an electron from one shell to another. When electron leaps (jumps) from a higher-energy shell to a lower energy shell (see Figure 3), the **excess energy** is released in the form of a photon with a known amount of E_{Ph} (photon energy) and f (frequency). The action of releasing E by an electron is known as the **quantization of an electron to a photon.** A photon is a **quantized form of electron** (simply **photon originates from electron**).

When, oppositely, an electron leaps from a lower-energy shell to a higher-energy shell (see Figure 4), the difference in energies is absorbed by a photon to become an electron, with certain E and f. Absorbing E by a photon is called the **quantization of a photon to an electron**. For this reason, the released electrons are known as the **photoelectrons,** and the electron-releasing process from an atom is called the photoelectric effect.

More important points about the release (or absorption) of electrons are outlined next.

- The photon frequency (f) released (or absorbed) by an atom is proportional to the energy difference (ΔE) between the shells (the *greater* the ΔE between two shells, the *greater* is the photon f released from the shell. As shown on the right side of Figure 3, the energies and frequencies for transitions A and B equate to those of transition C.
- Because the energy between shells is discrete (different), the f of photon released (or absorbed) is also discrete. [The amount of released (or absorbed) photon energy (E_{Ph}) is determined from Planck's equation ($E_{Ph} = h.f$, where f is for frequency and h is Planck constant.]

Electron's Quantum Numbers

The electron's quantum numbers (simply **quantum numbers**) are four (4). The first three (3) are related to the electron's spin (turn) in a shell around its **nucleus**. And the fourth number is related to its spin around its **axis**. [Note that the nucleus also spins around its axis. This property is used in laboratory techniques, such as nuclear magnetic resonance and magnetic resonance imaging.]

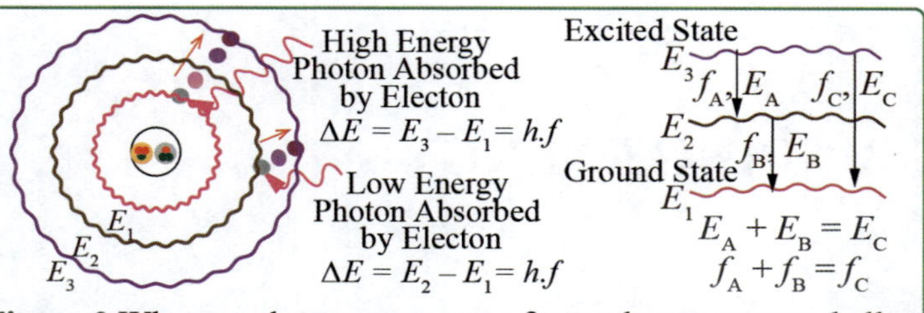

Figure 3 When an electron moves up from a lower-energy shell to a higher-energy shell, the difference in its energies is absorbed by a photon to become an electron with a known amount of E and f

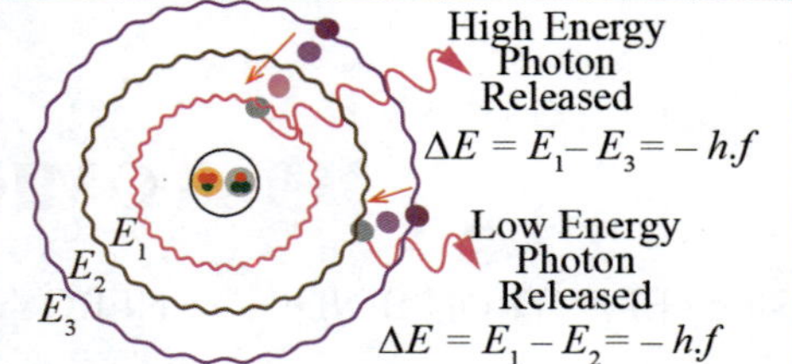

Figure 4 When an electron moves down from a higher shell to a lower shell, the difference in its energies is released in the form of a photon

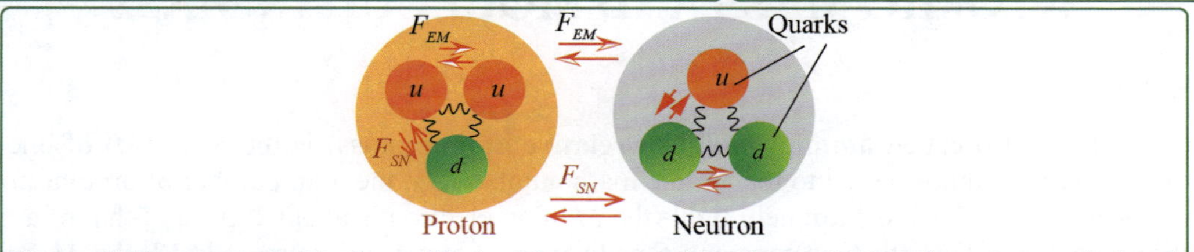

Figure 5 Electromagnetic force (F_{EM}) and strong nuclear force (F_{SN}) actions at atomic level

The four (4) electron quantum numbers are discussed next.

- **Principal Quantum Number** (n, also called **main quantum number** or simply a **quantum number**)**:** This number determines the electron shell (energy-level shell, simply **shell**) of an electron (the *greater* the n, the *farther* the electron is from the nucleus and the *more* energy it has), as shown in Figure 1 through 3. The n values are 1, 2, 3, 4, and so on. The n_1 shell (also written as $n = 1$) is the shell closest to the nucleus, and the electron (or electrons) located in that shell has the lowest energy (E). This exists because a system has lower potential energy (E_P) when closer to a reference point than farther from it. The n_2 shell or $n = 2$ (the second shell) is the next closest to the nucleus. And finally, the electron (or electrons) located at the farthest shell from the nucleus, known as valence electrons, have the highest E_P. [The value of n also determines a shell's size (the radius of shells *increases* as n *increases*).]
- **Angular Quantum Number** (l, also called the **orbital quantum number**, simply **orbital number**)**:** This number determines the rotational momentum (L) of an electron around its nucleus. The values of l are: $(n - 1)$, $(n - 2)$, $(n - 3)$, and so on. This means that the values of l are whole numbers and range from 0 to $n - 1$. In the first shell (n_1), thus, the value of l is 0 (because $1 - 1 = 0$). In the second shell (n_2 or $n = 2$ shell), the values of l can be 1 or 0 (because $2 - 1 = 1$ and $2 - 2 = 0$). As a result, two subshells of slightly different E_P are created there. Similarly, in the third shell, the l can be 2, 1, or 0 (because $3 - 1 = 2$, $3 - 2 = 1$, and $3 - 3 = 0$). As a result, 3 **subshells** are created.
- **Magnetic Quantum Number** (m)**:** This number is related to the orientation of the subshells. The m numbers range from –1 to 0 to +1. The value of the m depends on the value of l (angular quantum number). If, say, $l = 0$, then the only allowed value for the m is 0. And if $l = 2$, then the m may have the values of – 2, – 1, 0, +1, and +2.
- **Spin Quantum Number** (a spin number or **spin**)**:** This number gives the electron spin direction around its axis, CW or CCW. The electrons in one shell *cannot* have the same **spin numbers**. Thus, in one **electron shell**, the spin orientation of two electrons is always the opposite of each other; one has an **up** (north) orientation (shown as + ½), and the other one has a **down** (south) orientation (shown as – ½). [This rule also applies to electron pairs and **electron subshells**. Thus, each electron pair (or subshell) can have only two electrons, one with a spin of + ½ and another with – ½. Thus, the values of their spin numbers are + ½ and – ½.]

A-89

ATOMIC BINDING ENERGY

Study ELECTRON BINDING ENERGY.

A-90

ATOMIC MASS AND MOLECULAR MASS

Atomic Mass

Atomic mass (M_A, also called **atomic weight** or **relative atomic mass**) is the mass (M) of one atom of a chemical element. M_A is almost equal to the atomic mass number (N_A, the total number of protons and neutrons in an atom) because electrons are extremely light (the M of an electron is about 1/2000 of that of a proton). By this definition, the M_A of C (with 6 protons and 6 neutrons, as shown in Figure 1) is 12, the M_A of H (with 1 proton, as shown in Figure 2) is 1, and that of Mg (with 12 protons and 12 neutrons) is 24.

Molecular Mass

Molecular mass (M_M, also called **molecular weight**, M_W) is the M of one molecule of a chemical compound. Relating it to M_A, the M_M is the sum of the atomic masses of all atoms in a molecule.

Study the following must-to-know points about M_A (atomic mass) and M_M (molecular mass):

- Because the M of an atom is so tiny, the elements' M_A and compounds' M_M are expressed in AMU (atomic mass units), defined as 1/12 of the M of carbon 12 atom, with an exact mass of 12 AMU. By this definition, the M_A of hydrogen (H) is 1.008 AMU (or 1.66×10^{-24} g), where the value 1.66×10^{-24} is the conversion factor of AMU to gram (g). Similarly, the M_M of diatomic hydrogen molecule (H_2) is 2.016 AMU, and the M_A (or M_M) of magnesium (Mg) is 24 AMU. This means that Mg is two times heavier than C, so we obtain the same number of atoms of C and Mg when weighing the double amount of C.
- It is correct to increase the AMU value to g and say that the M_A of H is 1 g (or just 1 with *no* unit), the M_M of H_2 is 2g (or just 2), and the M_A (or M_M) of Mg is 24 g (or 24). This is because M_A becomes a ratio when it is divided by AMU. Because M_A is a ratio, it is **dimensionless**, so also called **relative atomic mass**.
- The M_A of isotopes of an element is given based on the weighted average (average giving points to priorities) of the atomic masses of all the isotopes of that element. M_A of; say, hydrogen (H) is given as the weighted average of its isotopes (deuterium, protium, and tritium). Similarly, carbon exists in nature as two isotopes: 98.9% in the form of C-12 (carbon-12) with an M_A of 12.0000 g and 1.1% in the form of C-13 with an M_A of 13.0034 g. So, the M_A of carbon is $12.0000 \times 0.989 + 13.0034 \times 0.011 = 11.868 + 0.143 = 12.01$ g
- Some authors use the term **molecular mass** (M_M) but mean molar mass (M_n). They say, for example, the M_M of water is 18 g/mole. In this way, $M_M = M_n = 18$ g/mole.

Next are the relations between the M_M (molecular mass), the M_n (molar mass), the mole (n), and the Avogadro's number ($N_{Avo} = 6.02\times10^{23}$) for water ($H_2O$).

M_M of H_2O (18 g) = M_n of H_2O (18 g/mole) = 1 mole of H_2O (18 g) = 6.02×10^{23} molecules of H_2O (18 g)

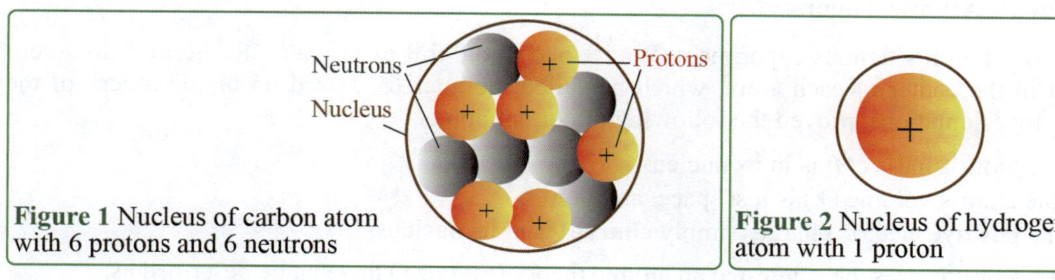

Figure 1 Nucleus of carbon atom with 6 protons and 6 neutrons

Figure 2 Nucleus of hydrogen atom with 1 proton

A-91

ATOMIC MASS NUMBER

Study ATOMIC NUMBER AND ATOMIC MASS NUMBER.

A-92

ATOMIC MASS UNIT

As a unit of mass (M), the atomic mass unit (AMU, symbol Da for Dalton or u) is used to express an element's atomic mass (M_A) or a compound's molecular mass (M_M). AMU is defined as 1/12 of the M of carbon 12 atom (C-12, read carbon 12), which has an exact mass of 12 AMU (12 g or just 12 with *no* unit), where 1 AMU = $1.822\ 539\ 066 \times 10^{-24}$ g.

For example, the M_A of hydrogen (H) is 1.008 AMU (1 g or just 1), and the M_M of diatomic hydrogen molecule (H_2) is 2.016 AMU (2 g or just 2). Similarly, the M_A and M_M of magnesium (Mg) is 24 AMU (24 g or just 24). This means that Mg is two times heavier (more massive) than carbon (C), so we obtain the same number of atoms when weighing twice as much Mg as C.

A-93

ATOMIC MODELS AND ATOMIC THEORIES

Atomic Models

An atomic model is a pictorial representation of an atomic theory. In the first quarter of the 20th century, four (4) important atomic models were offered in relation to four atomic theories by Rutherford (1911), Bohr (1913), Heisenberg (1925), and Schrodinger (1926). Because the last two models are similar, they are called the **quantum atomic model**, which is usually discussed in Physics under the same topic.

Remember the following:

- Each model is based on the previous one (or ones), so it is more advanced than its preceding one.
- All models are experimented on the hydrogen atom (with 1 electron), as shown in Figure 1.

Atomic Theories

An atomic theory is the detailed written version of an atomic model. Next, the three (3) important atomic theories are discussed.

Rutherford's Atomic Theory

In 1911, based on his famous experiment, Rutherford's gold foil experiment, Rutherford discovered a small dense point in the center of each atom, which he called the nucleus. Based on his discovery of the nucleus, Rutherford, by calculations, proved the following important points:

- Most of the atom's mass (*M*) is in its nucleus,
- Most of the atom's volume (*V*) is just space, and
- The atom's positive electric charge (simply **charge**) is in its nucleus.

Based on his discoveries, he suggested an atomic theory (Figure 1) that can be described as

- Electro-negatively-charged electrons surround the electro-positively-charged nucleus.
- Electrons spin around the nucleus at a relatively large distance from it as Earth orbiting the Sun.

Although Rutherford's atomic theory was an important start for knowing the atom's construction, his theory did *not* have convincing answers to some key questions, including the following:

- If an electron orbits the nucleus as a planet orbits the Sun, what is the reason for an electron *not* to gradually lose its energy (*E*) and crash into its nucleus as a planet crashes into another planet as it loses *E*?
- What occurs to an electron when a change of *E* occurs in its atom?
- Do all electrons of an atom have the same amount of *E*?

Bohr's Atomic Theory

In 1913, Bohr (Denmark) published his atomic theory in three articles, in which he considerably improved the 1911's Rutherford's atomic theory. Bohr's experiments on the hydrogen (H) atom (see the next Note and Figures 1 and 2) could answer the above-listed questions in the following ways:

- Although electrons spin the nucleus as planets orbit the Sun, an atom's electron stays in a certain **electron shell** (simply **shell**), and unlike planets, its *E* remains the same as it spins in the same shell.
- As a change of *E* occurs in an atom, its electron (or electrons) moves to another shell (an electron moves up to a higher-energy shell if its atom absorbs *E* and moves down to a lower shell if its atom loses *E*).
- Once an electron gets to the lowest energy shell (the ground-level shell or n_1), it *cannot* move further toward the nucleus, so there is *no* risk of crashing an electron into the nucleus.

While using spectroscopy on the hydrogen atom, Bohr observed that light is released from an electron in a series of colored lines, called the atomic spectral lines (Figure 3). He used this action to indicate an electron's jump (leap) from one shell to another. This brought him to the idea that when a hydrogen atom loses some *E* (say, by cooling), its electron moves down from a higher-energy shell (E_2) to a lower-energy shell (E_1). The difference between these two energies is released in the form of the photon energy (E_{Ph}) of a photon. Instead, the atom absorbs some *E* in the form of E_{Ph} when its electron moves up to a higher-energy shell. Bohr then used the wavelength (λ) of the released-or-absorbed photon to measure the *E* of an electron in a certain shell. And because the electron located in a shell has a different *E* than the same electron in the other shell, he could determine in which shell the electron is acting.

[Note: As the simplest element, a hydrogen atom has one electron, normally located on the n_1 shell, but can move to another shell. For example, it can move to the n_2 shell if it absorbs some energy. Symbol *n* is called the quantum number, a unitless number with a value of 1, 2, 3, and like. The lowest energy-level shell has a quantum number of $n = 1$. When an electron is in the $n = 1$ shell (n_1 shell), it is said to be in the ground energy state, and when that electron moves to a shell with *n* greater than 1 (say, to the n_2), the electron is in the excited energy state.]

Bohr used the word electron quantization to mean that the amount of an electron's energy on a certain shell is **quantized**, to mean that:

- An electron has a **fixed** amount of *E* when it is on a certain shell.
- An electron can be in one shell but *not* in between shells.

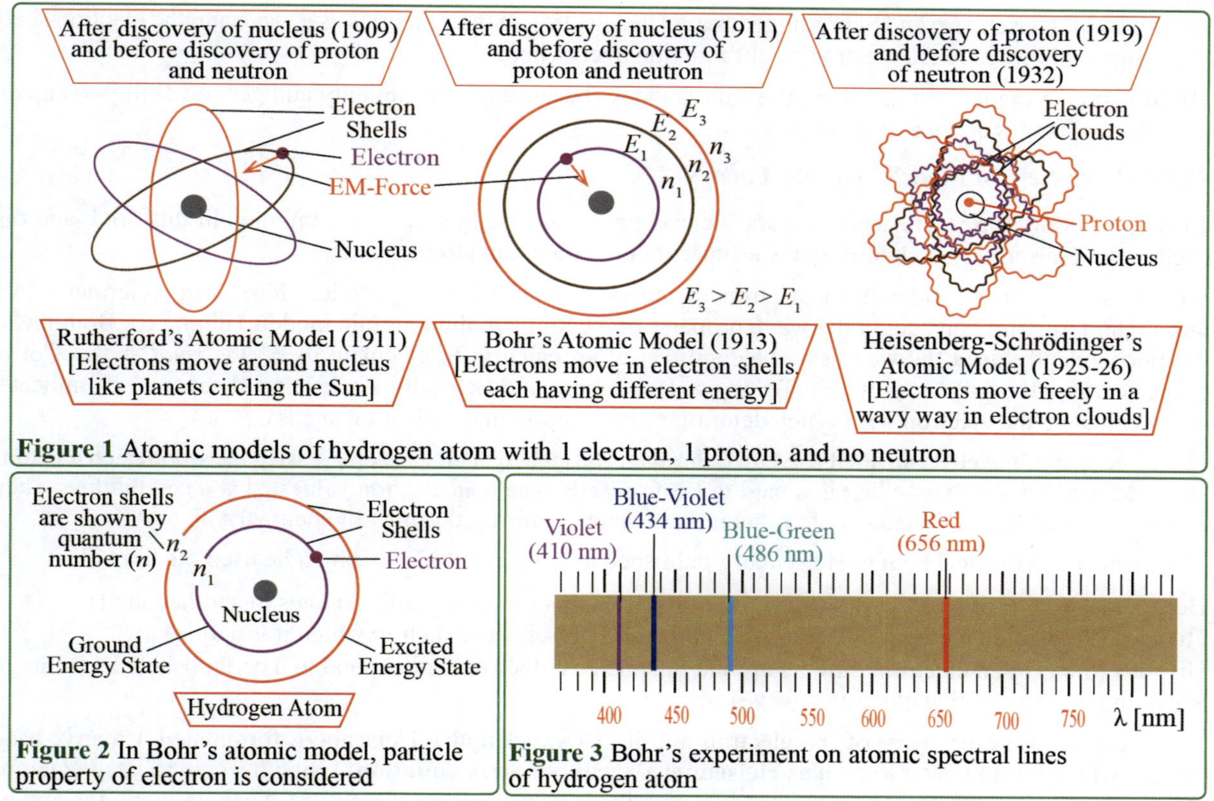

Figure 1 Atomic models of hydrogen atom with 1 electron, 1 proton, and no neutron

Figure 2 In Bohr's atomic model, particle property of electron is considered

Figure 3 Bohr's experiment on atomic spectral lines of hydrogen atom

Based on what has been mentioned so far about Bohr's theory, one can say that when an electron's E becomes greater (by absorption of some E), it jumps to a higher-energy-level shell. And when its E becomes lower, it jumps to a lower-energy-level shell. Consider an electron located in the n_1 shell (the closest to the nucleus with the lowest E). An atom's electron must absorb E in the form of the photon energy (E_{Ph}) of a photon to jump up from the n_1 shell to the n_2 shell, as we must spend E when climbing from one step of a ladder to the next step. Instead, an atom's electron releases E in the form of the E_{Ph} of a photon to jump down from the n_2 shell to the n_1 shell. Figure 4 shows the E released (in the amount of − 984 kJ) when the electrons of 1 mole of H atom move down from the n_2 shell to the n_1 shell, and the E absorbed (in the amount of + 984 kJ) when it moves up from the n_1 shell to the n_2 shell. [Example 1 under BOHR'S EQUATION proves the amount of released energy (E).]

Bohr's then concluded that

- Electrons can go from shell to shell but *cannot* freely move between two shells (when one is on a ladder, he can stay on any step but *cannot* stay between two steps).
- The E an electron releases when it jumps down to a lower-energy shell or absorbs when it jumps up to a higher-energy shell corresponds to the E_{Ph} of a photon. A decrease in E level from a higher-energy shell (say, n_2 or $n = 2$ shell) to a lower-energy shell (n_1), which equates to the difference in E between the two shells ($E_2 - E_1$), results in **release** (emission) of E in the form of E_{Ph} of a photon (see Figure 4). And an increase in E level from, say, $n = 1$ shell to $n = 2$ shell results in **absorption** of E in the form of E_{PH}.

Although Bohr considered the concept of quantization, his atomic theory, according to Heisenberg's atomic theory (1925) and Schrodinger's atomic theory (1926), had two weaknesses:

- It emphasizes the electron's particle property but not its wave property.
- It applies to single-electron atoms, like a hydrogen (H) atom.

Unlike Bohr, Heisenberg and Schrodinger treated the electron in their theories as a wave and the electron shells as a **cloudy region** where the electron might function everywhere.

[Bohr's atomic theory still has some usefulness today (because of its simplicity and general ability to explain energy-level changes at the atomic level.]

Heisenberg-Schrodinger's Atomic Theory

Because of similarities, Heisenberg's and Schrodinger's atomic theories are combined in this book and discussed under **Heisenberg-Schrodinger's atomic theory** (quantum atomic theory).

Unlike Bohr, who considered an electron in the electron shell as a particle, Heisenberg (Germany) and Schrodinger (Austria) considered the wave property of electrons in their atomic models (Figure 5). Both physicists independently used the wave's wavelength (λ) of an electron to calculate its E (the *smaller* the λ of an electron's wave, the *greater* is its E). To do so, Heisenberg and Schrodinger developed separate complicated math to calculate the electron's E (which determines its location in the electron shells).

[Note: Instead of the **electron shell** used by Bohr, both Heisenberg and Schrodinger used the word **electron cloud** (electron density) to emphasize that it is hard to know exactly where an electron is located at a certain time. They, therefore, replaced Bohr's certainty with quantum uncertainty (with a probability of about 90%).]

Heisenberg's Atomic Theory: Heisenberg published an article in 1925 in which he used the next ideas.

- Bohr's idea (the E of an electron located on a shell remains the same until it moves to another shell),
- His idea (the λ of an electron indicates its E and that represents the shell in which it is acting),
- His idea (the E of an electron, moving around the nucleus, does *not* correspond to a certain shell, as Bohr stated, but to the λ of that electron's wave).

Based on the wave property of the electron and its λ (wavelength), Heisenberg formulated a matrix-based equation, which became later known as **Heisenberg's wave-matrix equation**. Using his complicated equation, one can determine an electron's E (energy) in a certain electron shell (see Figure 5). Then knowing the amount of an electron's E can determine its location in a shell, with some degree of probability (around 90%). [In math, a **matrix** is a rectangular group of values (numbers) with which a mathematical function can be solved. Heisenberg used the matrix property to determine the probable position of a set of electrons in quantum theories.]

While experimenting on his equation, Heisenberg realized that it is impossible to simultaneously measure two properties of an electron (or any other quantum elementary particle, like a photon) with perfect accuracy. We, he said, *cannot* measure, say, both E and V (velocity) of an electron with accuracy. The inaccuracy exists because the measurement of one quantity changes the other quantity's real value (the *more* precise an electron is measured, the *less* precisely its other property can be measured). He solved this problem by offering a principle known later as Heisenberg's uncertainty principle.

Schrodinger Atomic Theory: Shortly after Heisenberg published his atomic theory, Schrodinger published an article in 1926, in which he used the following ideas:

- Bohr's idea (the E of an electron located on a shell remains the same until it moves to another shell),
- Heisenberg's idea (the λ of an electron is the indication of its location in the electron cloud), and
- Heisenberg's idea (the E of an electron moving around the nucleus corresponds to the λ of its wave).

Schrodinger used the electron's λ (wavelength) to make its location in a shell measurable mathematically. He considered the λ of an electron's wave as its quantum wavefunction (simply **wavefunction**), shown by the Greek letter Ψ (psi). Then he developed a differential equation, known later as **Schrodinger's wavefunction equation**, to determine an electron's E, which determines the electron's location in electron shells (simply **shells**), with some uncertainty (around 90%).

Solving wavefunction square (ψ^2) and using two real variables of x (position) and t (time) for a hydrogen atom gives the probability of the location of the hydrogen's electron in a certain electron cloud (Figure 5).

$$\psi^2(x,t)$$

The ψ^2 of an electron is a positive real number that gives the electron cloud in which it is located (the *greater* the ψ^2, the *more* likely the electron is in that electron shell), with some degree of certainty (around 90%). Thus, wave-matrix (Heisenberg) and wavefunction (Schrodinger) equations involve some probability.

In his atomic theory, Schrodinger also proved that

- The uncertainty of the location of an electron is the range of possible locations of that electron in the electron cloud found by the wavefunction.
- A quantum system's measurement (observation) affects that system immediately, reducing the number of probabilities to only one. This property is called the **collapse of the wavefunction**.

Heisenberg's wave equation is harder to be used than Schrodinger's wavefunction equation. [in 1930, Dirac (1902–1995, British physicist) combined these equations into a single equation (**Dirac wave equation**).]

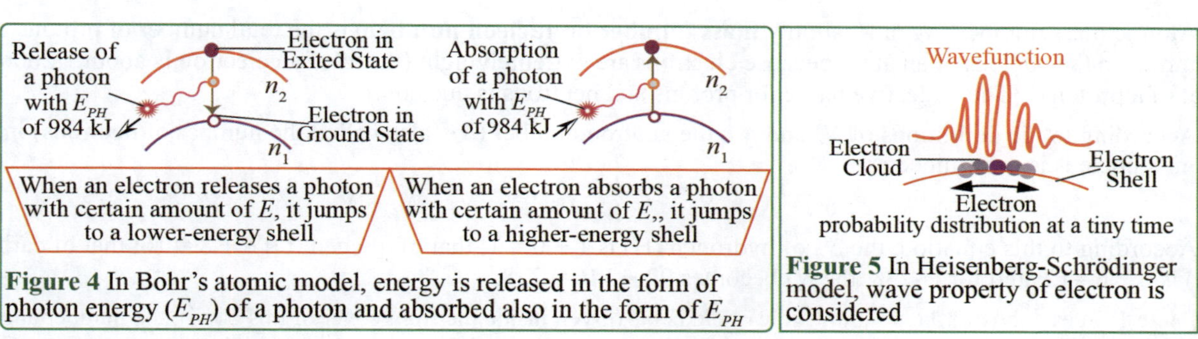

Figure 4 In Bohr's atomic model, energy is released in the form of photon energy (E_{PH}) of a photon and absorbed also in the form of E_{PH}

Figure 5 In Heisenberg-Schrödinger model, wave property of electron is considered

A-94

ATOMIC NUMBER AND ATOMIC MASS NUMBER

Atomic Number

The atomic number (N_Z or Z; also known as the **proton number**) is the number of protons in the nucleus of an atom. Because the number of protons and electrons of each atom is the same, N_Z also indicates the number of electrons in an atom. Because, for example, hydrogen (H) has 1 proton and 1 electron, its N_Z equates to 1. N_Z of oxygen (O) is 8, that of carbon (C) is 6, and that of uranium-238 (U-238) is 92.

[In each box of the periodic table of elements (inside the book's front cover), the number above an element's symbol is the N_Z. Hydrogen (H, with 1 proton) has an N_Z of 1; helium (He, with 2 protons per atom) has an N_Z of 2; and so on. The number below each element's symbol is the atomic mass number (N_A). Carbon (C) has N_Z of 6 and N_A of 12.]

Atomic Mass Number

Atomic mass number (N_A or A, simply **mass number** or **nucleon number**) is the total number of protons and neutrons in the nucleus of an atom because electrons are extremely light (the M of an electron is about 1/2000 of that of a proton). [The collective name for protons and neutrons is nucleon.]

According to the definitions of N_Z and N_A, the neutron number (N_N, also called the number of neutrons) in an atom's nucleus is determined as

$$N_N = N_A - N_Z \qquad \text{or} \qquad N_A = N_Z + N_N$$

According to this equation, the N_A of hydrogen (H) is 1 + 0 = 1; that of oxygen (O) 8 + 8 = 16; that of carbon (C) is 6 + 6 =12; and for U-238, the N_A becomes 92 + 146 = 238.

[Note 1: In each box of the periodic table of elements (given inside the front cover of this book), the number above each element's chemical symbol is the atomic number (N_Z, number of protons), and the number below the symbol is the atomic mass (M_A, previously **atomic weight**). Consider $^{6}_{12}C$. Number 6 above C indicates carbon's N_Z, and number 12 below C indicates its M_A. Also, note that some periodic tables show the symbol of an element just with one of these numbers. For example, ^{6}C or $_{12}C$. Furthermore, some write the M_A in front of the element; for example, C-12 (carbon-12) or U-238 (uranium-238).]

[Note 2: An atom's N_A (atomic mass number) approximates its M_A (atomic mass) because the mass of an atom's electrons is negligible. The M_A of O is 15.999, but it is approximated to 16, which is its N_A (mass number).]

A-95

ATOMIC PARTICLES

Discussed under the topic of PARTICLE AND ITS TYPES.

A-96

ATOMIC SPECTRAL LINES

The atomic spectral lines (simply **spectral lines**) of an element are several colored-narrow beams (bands or lines) that are specific to that element and can be seen on dark background in spectrometry (also called spectroscopy). Spectral lines are formed by jumping an element's electron from a high-energy shell (electron shell) to a low-energy shell.

When an electron jumps (leaps) from a higher shell to a lower shell, a photon of light is released, causing the electron to be cooled. The process of jumping an electron from a higher-energy shell to a lower one through the release of a photon is called emission. Notably, each element's emission is specific to that element, so the spectral lines of an element are different from those of other elements.

Consider hydrogen (H) under spectrometry. The emitted (reflected) light can be observed as four (4) colored lines (see Figure 1). These lines (counting from the right) are called **hydrogen spectral lines**. Spectral lines are visible because they have a wavelength (λ) greater than 400 nm (where nm = 10^{-9} m).

The question here is, "why H has 4 spectral lines?" This question has two (2) answers. 1) There are also lines 5 and 6 in the ultraviolet range of the spectrum (since they have λ less than 400 nm). 2) Although H has one electron, it contains several electron shells (apparently 6). Because the difference in energy between the two shells of the H atom converts to a photon with a certain λ, each spectral line can tell us the electron's location at a time. When, for example, the hydrogen electron moves down from, say, its second shell (n_2) to its first shell (n_1), it releases a photon with a certain λ and E_{Ph} (photon energy). Similarly, when the electron moves down from n_3 to n_1, it releases a photon with shorter λ and greater E_{Ph}. [Because the distance between the shells gets greater as they get farther from the nucleus, the energy difference between the shells (and between the electrons) increases. And vice versa (as shells get closer together).]

Bohr used the spectral lines of a hydrogen atom to determine its electron's E in different shells by measuring that electron's λ.

$$\lambda = \frac{1}{R\left(\frac{1}{4}-\frac{1}{n^2}\right)} \quad (1)$$

In this equation, R is **Rydberg's constant** (for hydrogen $R = 1.1 \times 10^7$ m^{-1}), and n is a quantum number (a unitless number, like n_1, n_2), so λ becomes in m.

It is important to know about the following two brief points:

- Every element has a unique set of spectral lines, identifying that element.
- Because the atoms of each element absorb or release electromagnetic waves (EM waves) over a certain wavelength range, the spectral lines of a given element are specific to that element, as shown in Figure 1.

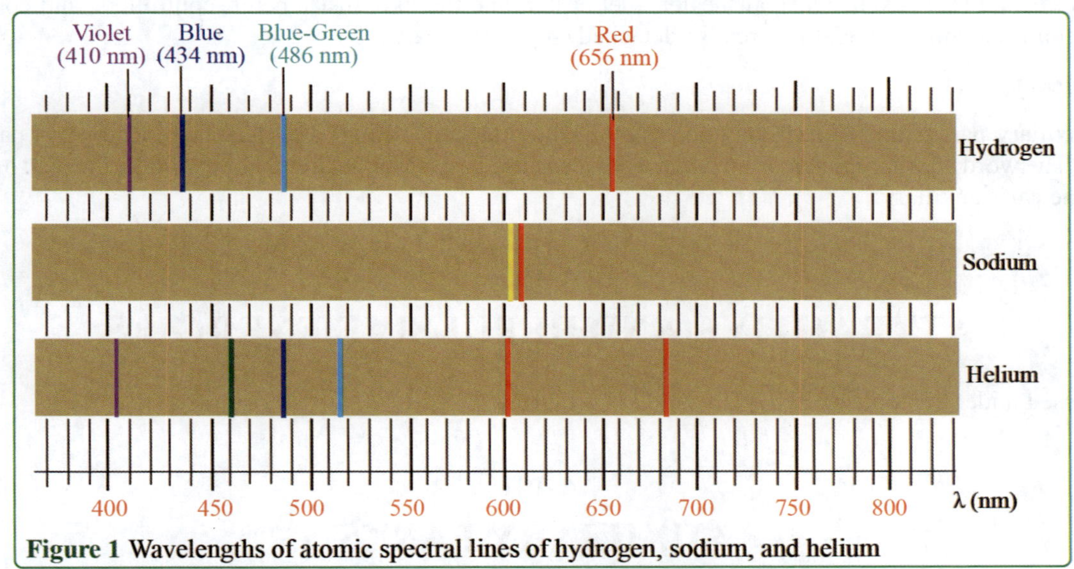

Figure 1 Wavelengths of atomic spectral lines of hydrogen, sodium, and helium

A-97

ATOMIC THEORIES

Study ATOMIC MODELS AND ATOMIC THEORIES.

A-98

ATOMIC WEIGHT

See RELATIVE ATOMIC MASS.

A-99

ATTACHED, DETACHED, AND AUXILIARY PARTS

Attached Parts

An attached part (also called **fitting parts** or simply **fittings**) is a part that is attached to a device (equipment or auxiliary). For example, the main **attached** (fitting) **parts** of a steam boiler (simply **boiler**) are the furnace, burner, fuel pump (in oil-fired boilers) or bunker (in coal-fired boilers), feedwater valves, safety valves, blow-down valves, steam valves, steam-stop valves, pressure gauges, vacuum gauges, and more. Similarly, the main attached parts of a pump are the shaft, impeller (wheel), bearings, and seals. And valves, elbows, and tees are the attached parts of a pipe. [Instruments and controllers can be considered attached or detached parts of a boiler.]

Detached Parts

A detached part (also called an **accessory part** or simply an **accessory**) is a part that is *not* attached to a device. For example, the main **detached** (accessory) **parts** of a steam boiler are the condensate tank, feedwater pump, feedwater heater (heat exchanger), air heater, fuel heater, and the like. Instruments, controllers, and computers used to control a boiler's operation are also detached (separated) parts.

Auxiliary Parts

An auxiliary part (simply **auxiliary**) consists of both attached (fitting) and detached (accessory) parts of a device. [The word auxiliary is also used when a device is used as additional help. For example, the jack of a car's tires is the car's auxiliary.]

A-100

ATTRACTIVE AND REPULSIVE ENERGIES

Discussed under the topic of ENERGY AND ITS FORMS.

A-101

AUXILIARY PARTS

Study ATTACHED AND DETACHED PARTS.

A-102

AVERAGES OF DATA

An average of data expresses a test's values (data or entries). For better accuracy and precision, a test's average value is expressed in one of the following ways: mean, median, and weighted average.

Mean

The mean (the ordinary average) of a value (data) set, which is shown as $\bar{x}$ (read x bar), is calculated by adding the values and dividing the result ($\sum x$) by the number of values (n).

$$\bar{x} = \frac{\Sigma x}{n} \tag{1}$$

Here, $\sum$ (sigma) is the symbol for summation, and x is for each value.

Median

The median (midpoint average) is the value in the middle of the results, so 50% (one-half) of the values are above the median, and 50% are below the median. For example, in a city, the median price of the homes is where half the homes are sold for more than the median and half for less.

To find the median, follow the next steps:

- List the values in the order from highest to lowest or vice versa.
- If the number of values is odd, the median is the middle value. If the number of values is even, the median is the average of the two middle values.

Weighted Average

Weighted average (also called **weighted mean**) is an average that gives the priorities to the important points. It is usually used when the values of a data set have different weights (greatness), so some values have a **greater effect** (weight) on the average than others. The weighted average for the weight of each value (x) can be calculated as

$$\bar{x}_w = \frac{\Sigma(x{,}w)}{\Sigma w} \tag{2}$$

To find the weighted average, follow the next steps:

- List the values (x) in one column,
- List the weights (w) in another column,
- Find the sum (total) of the weights (Σw),
- Multiply each value (x) by its weight (w) and find their sum ($\Sigma x.w$), and
- Divide the sum determined in step 4 ($\Sigma x.w$) by the sum determined in step 3 (Σw).

Consider carbon (C) that exists in nature as two isotopes: 98.9% in the form of C-12 (carbon-12) with atomic mass (M_A) of 12.0000 g and 1.1% in the form of C-13 with M_A of 13.0034 g. To find the real average M_A of carbon, the mean (ordinary) average [(12.0000 + 13.0034)/2 = 12.50)] is *not* an accurate result (because it does *not* consider that 98.9% of carbon has M_M of 12.00). We, thus, must use a weighted average.

x	w	$x.w$
12.0000	0.989	11.868
13.0034	0.011	0.143
	$\sum w = 1.00$	$\sum x.w = 12.01$

$$\bar{x}_w = \frac{\sum x.w}{\sum w} = \frac{12.01}{1.00} = 12.01$$

[The mean, median, and weighted are all averages, but each works better in particular situations. Here are helpful guidelines for selecting the average of choice:

- Use **mean** when the data do *not* contain extreme values,
- Use **median** when the data contain extreme values (out-of-line values), and
- Use **weighted** when data contain a value (or values) that weighs more than other values.]

A-103

AVOGADRO'S GAS LAW

Discussed under the topic of GAS LAWS.

A-104

AVOGADRO'S NUMBER

Avogadro's number ($N_{Avo} = 6.022 \times 10^{23}$; also called **Avogadro's constant**) is the number of atomic particles (atoms, molecules, or ions) in a mole. As a proportionality constant that relates a substance's mass (M) to its molar mass (M_n), N_{Avo} tells us that equal volumes of gases under the same conditions of temperature (T) and pressure (P) contain an equal number of particles. [It is better to use the word **Avogadro's constant** because **Avogadro's number** was initially defined as the number of atoms in one mole of atomic hydrogen. When this number was confirmed in the early 20th century, it was named after Avogadro.]

Because mole is defined as the mass (M) of a substance that contains as many particles as are in 12 g carbon-12 (C-12) and because 6.02×10^{23} particles are in 12 g C-12, the N_{Avo} is the base for expressing the M of any substance. For example, 6.02×10^{23} atoms are in 12 g of carbon (C, with an atomic mass of 12 g/mole), 6.02×10^{23} molecules in 18 g of water (H_2O, with M_n of 18 g/mole), and 6.022×10^{23} molecules in 342 g of sugar ($C_{12}H_{22}O_{11}$, with M_n of 342 g/mole). N_{Avo}, thus, is a constant number with the unit of 1/mole.

As a numerical example, let us express the relations between the number of molecules (expressed by N_{Avo}), M_M (molecular mass), M_n (molar mass), and mole for water (H_2O).

6.022×10^{23} Molecules of water (= 18 g) = M_M of water (= 18 g) = M_n of water (= 18 g) = Mole of water (= 18 g)

A-105
AZEOTROPIC DISTILLATION

Discussed under the topic of DISTILLATION PROCESS.

A-106
AZEOTROPIC LIQUID MIXTURE

An azeotropic liquid mixture (simply **azeotrope**) is a mixture that its components' molecules get to an azeotropic (non-ideal) behavior at a certain concentration (*C*). For example, an azeotropic behavior occurs between the molecules of a binary (two-component) mixture because of strong forces between the components' molecules at a certain concentration (called **azeotropic point**). For example, the ethanol-water behaves idealistically when its ethanol's *C* is below 96.5% by volume (= 95.5% by mass = 0.91 molar fraction). Once the mixture reaches its azeotropic point, it becomes an azeotropic mixture and starts to behave non-ideally; scientifically, *not* obey Raoult's Law of Vapor Pressure (simply **Raoult's Law**). Considering this law, an azeotropic binary mixture, which consists of a lower-boiling component (LBC, the component with lower T_{BP}, boiling point temperature) and a higher-boiling component (HBC, the component with higher T_{BP}), can fall under one of the following groups:

- **Positive Azeotropes:** A positive azeotropic mixture indicates a **positive deviation** from Raoult's Law. In this case, LBC sticks to LBC and HBC to HBC. As a result, the molecules of both components readily escape from the liquid phase (stuck-together phase) to the vapor phase (because of strong **repulsive forces** that exist between the molecules). Thus, a positive azeotropic mixture boils *below* the T_{BP} of its pure LBC. For example, the ethanol-water mixture indicates a positive deviation from Raoult's Law when it reaches its azeotropic point, equal to 96.5% by volume (= 95.5% by mass = 0.91 molar fraction) ethanol (EOH). At P_{Atm} (atmospheric pressure), ethanol boils at 78.4°C, water boils at 100°C, but their azeotropic mixture boils at 78.2°C (*lower* than the ethanol's T_{BP}). The strong **repulsive forces** between the molecules of a positive azeotropic mixture's components cause the mixture to boil at temperatures *below* the T_{BP} of its pure LBC (lower boiling component). The mixture's components (EOH and H_2O) are *not* miscible in an azeotropic situation, so they *cannot* be separated during an ordinary (fractionating) distillation. Thus, the minimum boing *T* for an EOH-water solution of such *C* is 78.2°C. If therefore, a higher *C* of EOH is required, an azeotropic distillation or extractive distillation is performed. [When a positive azeotrope is tested at constant pressure (*P*), it is called a **temperature-minimum positive azeotrope**, as shown on the left side of Figure 1 for the EOH-water mixture. When tested at constant *T* (temperature), it is called a **pressure-maximum positive azeotrope**, as shown on the right side of the same figure, where the symbol P_V is for vapor pressure.]
- **Negative Azeotropes:** A negative azeotropic mixture **deviates** negatively from Raoult's Law, so the LBC sticks to the HBC more strongly than LBC does to LBC and HBC does to HBC. As a result, the molecules of both components do *not* readily escape to the liquid phase (because of strong **repulsive forces** that exist between the molecules). Thus, a negative azeotropic mixture boils *above* the T_{BP} of its pure HBC. For example, an HCl-water solution consisting of 20.2% (by mass) HCL (hydrochloric acid) and 79.8% H_2O indicates a negative deviation. At P_{Atm}, HCl boils at −84°C and water boils at 100°C, but their azeotropic mixture boils at 110°C (*higher* than the water's T_{BP}). Figure 2 shows the **temperature-minimum negative azeotrope** at constant P_{Atm} and **pressure-maximum negative azeotrope** at constant *T* for the HCl-water mixture.

Based on miscibility, azeotropes are grouped into two (2) classes:

- **Homogeneous Azeotropes:** A homogeneous azeotrope consists of components that are miscible with each other in all proportions. For example, the EOH-water mixture is a homogeneous azeotrope because a certain amount of EOH (ethanol) can be mixed with water.
- **Heterogeneous Azeotropes:** A heterogeneous azeotrope consists of immiscible components. For example, the chloroform-water mixture is a heterogeneous azeotrope. If the same amount of chloroform ($CHCl_3$, with water solubility of 0.8 g/100 mL at 20°C) and water are shaken together and let the mixture stand, the mixture separates into two layers. The top layer mostly consists of H_2O with a small amount of $CHCl_3$ dissolved in it, and the bottom layer is mostly $CHCl_3$ with a small amount of H_2O. Their mix boils at 53.3°C, lower than either the T_{BP} of $CHCl_3$ (61.2°C) or H_2O (100°C). The vapor, formed during boiling, consists of 97% $CHCl_3$ and 3% H_2O regardless of initial C before boiling (evaporation). And if the vapor is condensed, the condensate will again contain two layers, each with the same composition as before boiling.

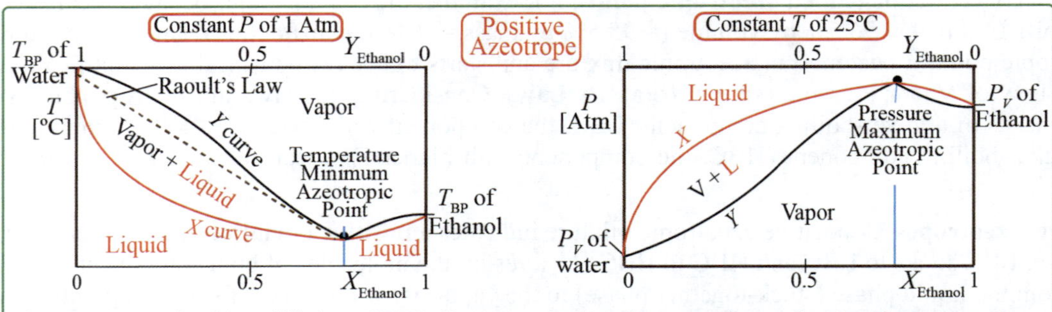

Figure 1 Vapor-liquid equilibrium (VLE) diagrams of ethanol-water mixture for showing mixture's temperature minimum azeotropic point (left) and pressure maximum azeotropic point (right)

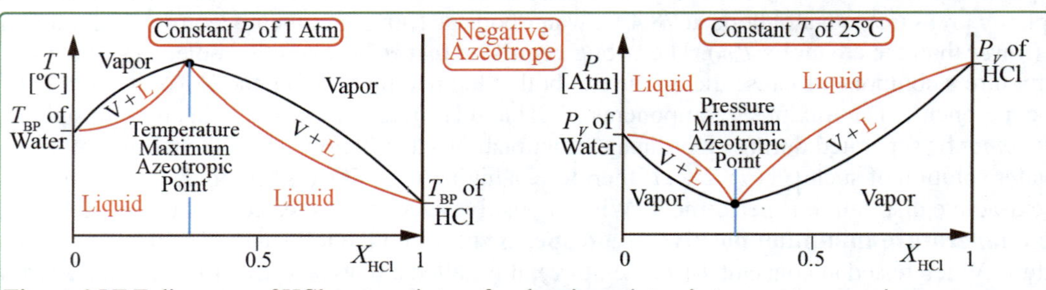

Figure 2 VLE diagrams of HCl-water mixture for showing mixture's temperature maximum azeotropic point (left) and pressure minimum azeotropic point (right)

B Section

LIST OF TOPICS

1. Bar
2. Barometers
3. Barometric Condensers
4. Barometric Formula
5. Barometric Height and Barometric Leg
6. Barometric Pressure and Barometric Formula
7. Bases
8. Batch and Continuous Chemical Processes
9. Batteries
10. Becquerel
11. Belts and Belt Conveyors
12. Bernoulli Equation
13. Bernoulli Principle
14. Beta Particles
15. Big Bang Theory
16. Binding Energy
17. Biochemical and Chemical Oxygen Demands
18. Biodiesel
19. Bioethanol
20. Biofuels
21. Biogas
22. Biological Half Lifetime
23. Biomasses
24. Blackbody and Blackbody Radiation
25. Blackholes
26. Blowers
27. BOD
28. Body (in Physics)
29. Bohr
30. Bohr's Atomic Model
31. Bohr's Atomic Theory
32. Bohr's Equation
33. Boilers
34. Boiling Depression and Boiling Elevation Temperatures
35. Boiling Elevation Temperature
36. Boiling Point Diagrams
37. Boiling Point Temperature
38. Boiling Process
39. Boltzmann's Constant and Stefan-Boltzmann's Constant
40. Bond Energy
41. Bosons, Fermions, and Hadrons
42. Boundary Layer and Stream Layers in Fluid Flow
43. Bourdon Gauge
44. Boyle's Gas Law
45. Brasses
46. Brix
47. Broglie
48. Broglie's Theory of Duality of Matter
49. Bromine, Chlorine, Florine, and Iodine
50. Brownian Motion of Particles
51. BTU
52. Bubble Point and Dew Point Calculations
53. Bubble Point and Dew Point Pressures
54. Bubble Point and Dew Point Temperatures
55. Buffering Effect
56. Buffers
57. Bulk Density
58. Bulk Material Handling Process
59. Buoyant Force
60. Bypass
61. Byproduct

B-1
BAR

Bar (from Latin *baros*, weight) is one of the units of measurement of pressure (P). It is defined as exactly 100 kPa, where Pa is for Pascal (the main unit of P in the SI units).

B-2
BAROMETERS

A barometer is a simple instrument that uses the height (h) of a column of mercury (Hg) to measure the atmospheric pressure (P_{Atm}) of air or other gases in mm of Hg (mercury), where 1 mm Hg = 1 Torr. In its old form, shown in Figure 1, a mercury barometer uses a vacuum at the top of a glass tube, placed in a Hg dish. Because of P_{Atm}, the Hg pushes the tube up until the P (pressure) at the bottom of the tube (because of the weight of Hg) is balanced by P_{Atm}. The weight of the column of Hg equates to the weight of the air outside the tube (the P_{Atm}). For this reason, P_{Atm} is often measured in mm Hg (or In Hg), corresponding to h of the mercury column, where "In" is for inch.

Under sea-level conditions, atmospheric air exerts pressure to raise the mercury in the tube to the height (h) of 760 mm (= 0.76 m = 29.9 In). If the dish were filled with water, h would be 10.3 m (= 34 Ft) because the density (D) of Hg is 13.6 times greater than that of water (13.6/0.76 = 10.3), as shown in Figure 2.

Figure 3 shows a typical aneroid barometer, which measures P_{Atm} with *no* use of a liquid. Instead, it uses a small, flexible metal box called an aneroid capsule (cell) made from an alloy of copper and beryllium. A small change in P_{Atm} causes the capsule under the vacuum to expand or contract. The expansion (or contraction) drives a small lever that displays the P_{Atm} on the face of the barometer.

MEMS (micro electro mechanical system) barometers are extremely small instruments for measuring P_{Atm}. Because of their extremely small size (0.001 to 0.1 mm), these manometers can be used in cellphones and wrest clocks.

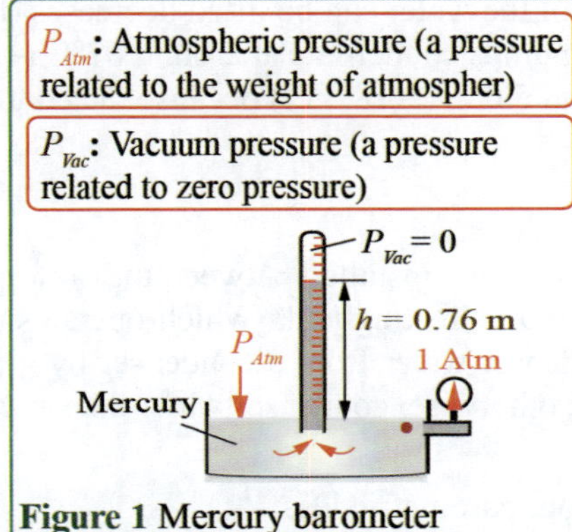

Figure 1 Mercury barometer

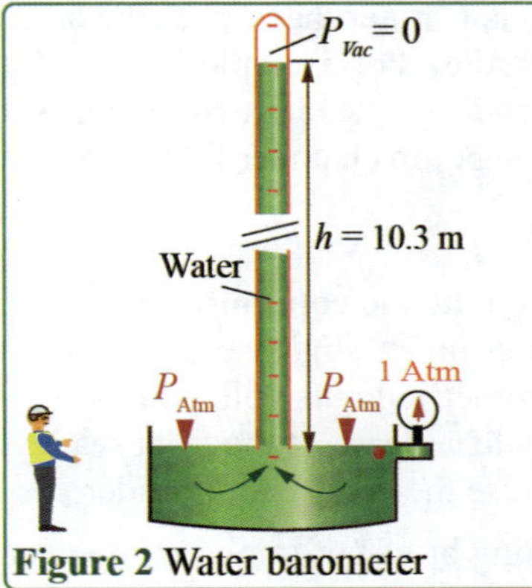

Figure 2 Water barometer

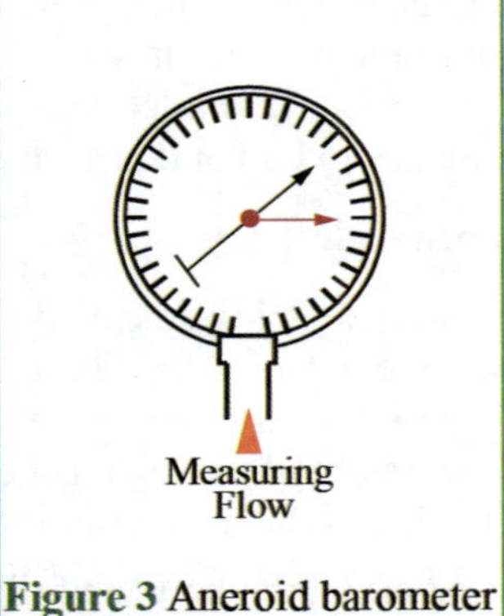

Figure 3 Aneroid barometer

B-3

BAROMETRIC CONDENSERS

Discussed under the topic of CONDENSERS.

B-4

BAROMETRIC FORMULA

Study ATMOSPHERIC PRESSURE AND ATMOSPHERIC FORMULA.

B-5

BAROMETRIC HEIGHT AND BAROMETRIC LEG

Barometric Height

Barometric height (h_B, where subscript *B* is for **barometric**) is the height (*h*) of 10.3 m (= 34 Ft) of water in a column at 20ºC (= 68ºF) and at atmospheric pressure (P_{Atm} = 1 Atm = 14.7 PSI). One Atm pressure (the sea-level pressure) can lift water in a column under vacuum pressure (P_{Vac}) of zero to h_B of 10.3 m at 20°C, as shown in Figure 1. That is why the **barometric leg** of barometric condensers, which operate under slight negative P_{Vac}, must equate to h_B (= 10.3 m = 10300 mm = 34 Ft = 408 In), at least. Otherwise, water does *not* flow down the leg. As the result of h_B, condenser water from the condenser flows down through the condenser's leg by gravity as fast as it is condensed, without breaking the condenser's P_{Vac}.

The following two important points must be made about barometric height (h_B):

- The h_B of a liquid can be estimated by comparing its density (*D*) with the water's density (1000 kg/m^3 at 4ºC). As shown in Figure 2, the barometric height of mercury (Hg, a liquid 13.6 times denser than water) is 0.76 m (= 29.9 In) because 10.3/13.6 = 0.76.
- When the water's temperature (*T*) is warmer than 20°C, the height of the water can be lifted decreases (because of the increase in vapor pressure). For example, a pump that pumps condensate at around 67°C (= 153°F) to a steam boiler *cannot* produce a head pressure greater than 5.6 m (= 18.4 Ft) because the condensate begins to boil at that *T,* and the pump chamber fills with vapor.

Barometric Leg

A barometric leg (also called a **barometric column**) is a long vertical pipe installed between the bottom of a barometric condenser (which operates under slight negative P_{Vac}) and a collecting tank (which operates under P_{Atm}). The main function of the barometric leg is collecting the condenser water from a condenser by gravity. Thus, the height of the leg must equate, at least, to the h_B at sea level; otherwise, condenser water does *not* flow down the leg of the condenser (because the condenser is under P_{Vac}).

It is important to know the following brief-but-important points about barometric legs:

- A barometric leg must be designed according to the local h_B. The height decreases by 1 m for every 1000 m increase in elevation from sea level.
- The distance between the lower edge of the condenser's flange to the condenser-water level in the seal (collecting) tank should be at least 10 m, as shown in Figure 3. [The legs are usually designed 1 m longer than the local barometric height to allow for unstable conditions.]

Because of the leg's height, a barometric leg can remove condenser water from a condenser without breaking its P_{Vac}. The condenser-water level in the leg corresponds to the difference between the P_{Atm} in the seal tank and P_{Vac} in the condenser. As a result, water flows down the leg by gravity as fast as it condenses without breaking its P_{Vac}.

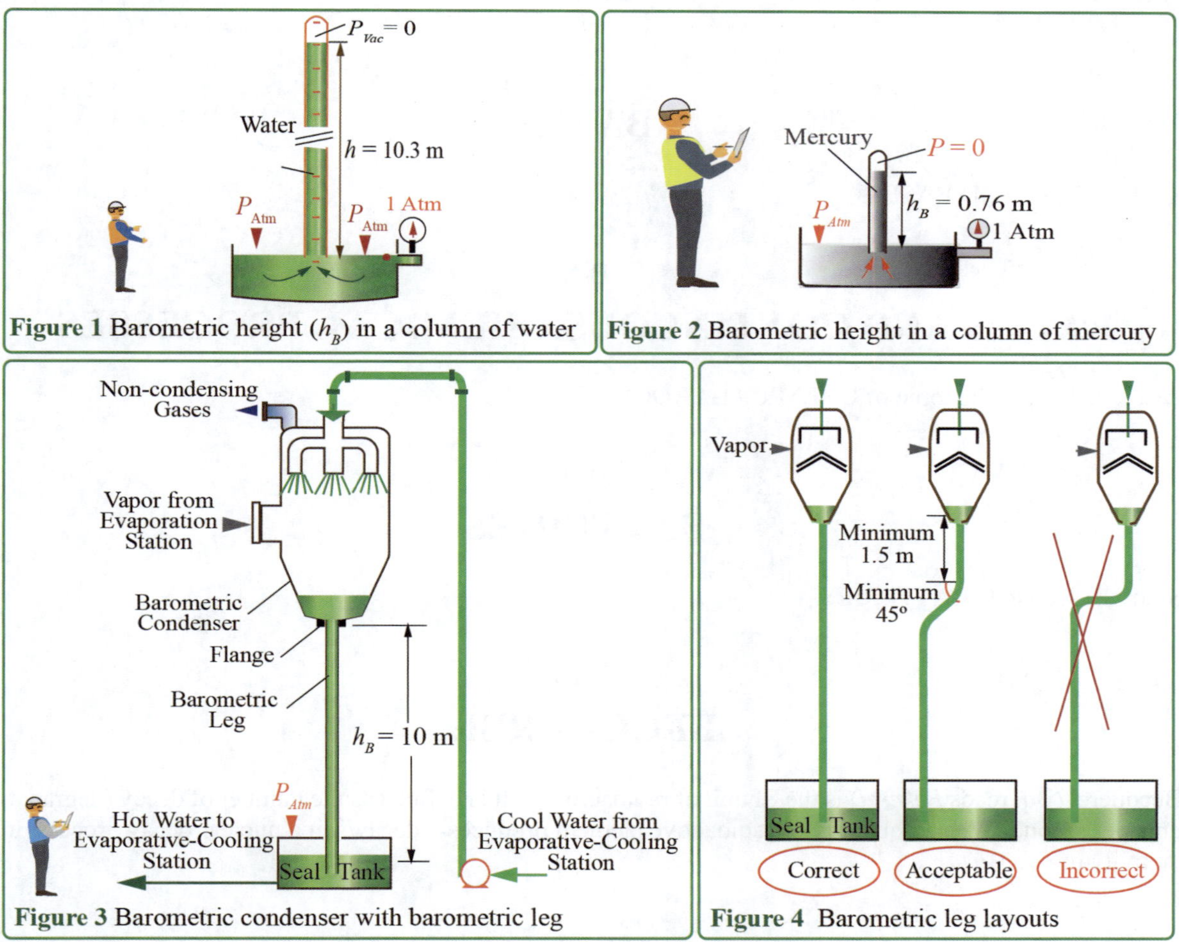

Figure 1 Barometric height (h_B) in a column of water

Figure 2 Barometric height in a column of mercury

Figure 3 Barometric condenser with barometric leg

Figure 4 Barometric leg layouts

The difference in elevation between the condenser and seal tank must be such that the water's liquid head (h) in the leg exceeds the pressure difference (ΔP) between the condenser and seal tank.

In receiving the condenser water from a condenser, remembering the next three points are important:

- The leg must be submerged enough into the seal tank *not* to pull air.
- The seal tank must have enough capacity to prevent the water level drop to a point lower than about 0.5 m (= 20 In) above the leg to *not* break the condenser's P_{Vac}. At the start of the operation, the seal tank is filled to the height mentioned above. Under normal operating conditions, the condenser-water level in the leg automatically adjusts itself because of a negative P_{Vac} that exists in the condenser.
- The connection of the leg to the seal tank must be straight. However, a connection with a 45° angle is a good layout, but *not* more than that, as shown in Figure 4.

B-6

BAROMETRIC PRESSURE AND BAROMETRIC FORMULA

Study ATMOSPHERIC PRESSURE AND ATMOSPHERIC FORMULA.

B-7

BASES

Study ACIDS AND BASES.

B-8

BATCH AND CONTINUOUS CHEMICAL PROCESSES

Discussed under the topic of CHEMICAL PROCESSES.

B-9

BATTERIES

Study ELECTRIC BATTERIES.

B-10

BECQUEREL

Becquerel (Bq; reads *Bekerel*) is the SI unit of radioactivity. It is defined as the number of decay (degradation) events per second. When a quantity of radioactive element produces 1 decay/s in a nuclear decay process, it has an activity of one Bq.

B-11

BELTS

A belt (referred to as a **mechanical belt**) is an endless loop made of flexible material (often rubber) and used in the following ways:

- As an attached part of a belt conveyor (a carrier of loose solid material), as shown in Figure 1.
- As a connector for connecting two shafts, one of which is driven by a drive (Figure 2).

In both ways, the kinetic energy (E_K) of a drive (such as an electric motor) is converted to mechanical energy (E_M) to move the belt.

Belts are divided into many types, including flat belts (Figure 3), V-belts, round belts, and more. A V-belt (Figure 4) is usually used to transfer electric power (simply **power**). V-belts have many applications, including in the cars' engines.

V-belts provide long service without slippage and alignment problems. As shown in the figure, the cross-section of such a belt has a V shape that tracks in the groove of the pulley, preventing the belt from slippage.

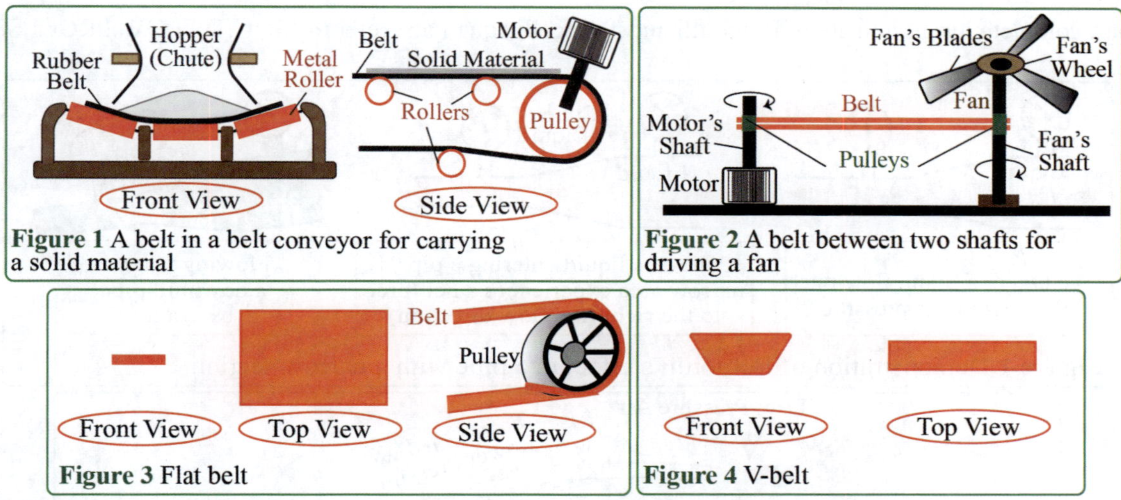

Figure 1 A belt in a belt conveyor for carrying a solid material

Figure 2 A belt between two shafts for driving a fan

Figure 3 Flat belt

Figure 4 V-belt

B-12

BERNOULLI'S EFFECT AND BERNOULLI'S EQUATION

Bernoulli's Effect

Bernoulli's effect (also called **Bernoulli's principle** or **pressure-drop effect**) is a principle in Physics created by Daniel Bernoulli (1700–1782, Swiss physicist) in the 1730s. It can be defined in the next ways:

- In a fluid flow process, a fluid's pressure *decreases* as its velocity *increases* and vice versa (see Figure 1).
- In a steady fluid flow, the sum of all forms of energy (E) is the same at all points in that flow.
- In a steady fluid flow, the net resultant of all energies applied to a flow is zero.

Bernoulli's Equation

Bernoulli's equation (also called **mechanical-energy equation**) and Torricelli equation are usually used in ChemEng in their different forms to mainly calculate the energy (E) used when a liquid is flowing in a pipe by a pump and pressure drop (generally pressure difference, ΔP) during the flow of that liquid. Both equations also calculate the shaft work (W_S) in pumps, compressors, fans, and likes.

The energies that a pump uses to elevate a liquid from location 1 to 2 are the following:

- **Pressure Energy:** This is the E used to overcome the liquid's change in density (ΔD).
- **Kinetic Energy** (E_K)**:** This is the E used to overcome the liquid's change in velocity (ΔV).
- **Potential Energy** (E_P)**:** This is the E used to overcome the liquid's change in elevation (Δh).
- **Frictional Energy** (E_f)**:** This is the E used to overcome the frictions in pipes, pumps, and liquid.
- **Shaft Work** (W_S)**:** This is the E in the form of W (work), used on a pump's shaft.

Using all five terms gives us the complete form of the Bernoulli equation.

$$\frac{P_1-P_2}{D}+\frac{V_1^2-V_2^2}{2}+a_g(h_1-h_2)+E_f-W_S=0 \qquad (1)$$

In this equation, P_1, P_2, V_1, and V_2 can be recognized from Figure 1. D is the flowing liquid's density, and a_g is the flowing liquid's gravitational acceleration. All the energy terms used in this equation are in the unit of specific energy (J/kg), which is the energy (in J) per unit mass (in kg) of the fluid to be pumped.

[For a complete discussion about Bernoulli and Torricelli equations, refer to LIQUID FLOW PROCESS.]

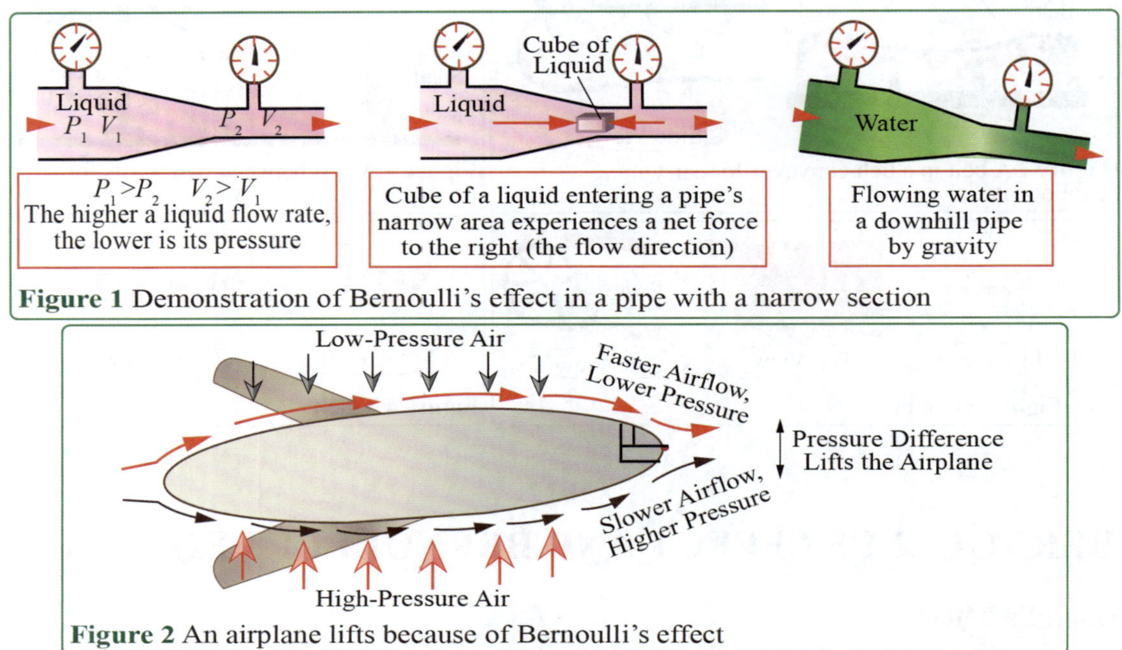

Figure 1 Demonstration of Bernoulli's effect in a pipe with a narrow section

Figure 2 An airplane lifts because of Bernoulli's effect

B-13
BERNOULLI'S EQUATION

Discussed under BERNOULLI'S EFFECT AND BERNOULLI'S EQUATION.

B-14
BETA PARTICLES

Study ALPHA AND BETA PARTICLES.

B-15

BIG BANG THEORY

The Big Bang (BB) theory was suggested in the 1930s by a few cosmologists, cosmophysicists who study the origin and evolution of the **cosmos** (Universe) from its start (when space and time started) until now. [At the first, physicists, including **Fred Hoyle** (1915–2001), did *not* like it, but after some improvements, it became a respective theory. This theory suggests that a big and fast explosion occurred about 13.8 billion years ago (BYA) in a teeny system called the **Big Bang singularity** (BB singularity, a single-dense point with a huge amount of heat energy) that expanded fast (3×10^8 m/s) in all directions like a balloon to create the Universe (Figure 1).]

Universe Age: In the 1930s, **Edwin P. Hubble** predicted the age of the Universe using a constant, now **Hubble's expansion constant**, a unit of length equal to 3 million **lightyears** (LY), where 1 LY (the distance light travels in 1 year) is 9.5×10^{12} km. He proved that two planets, 3 million LY apart, distance from each other 70 km/s. By his calculations and extrapolation back to the BB singularity, the age of the Universe is estimated to be 13.8 BY (billion years), and the Earth (measured in radioactive rocks) is 4 BY old.

Universe Temperature: Hawking predicted that the Universe's temperature (T) right after the Big Bang was about ten thousand million °C, almost the same as inside an atomic bomb explosion. It then dropped to one thousand million °C about 100 seconds after the Big Bang. At such high temperatures, everything was in the form of plasma, in which hardly anything could have survived. The T dropped later to a few thousand °C, allowing the formation of atoms and some elements (like hydrogen and helium). Then gravitational force, stars, and galaxies slowly (in billion years) originated.

Universe Size: The size of the Universe is estimated to be infinite, so the word **observable Universe** is used in Physics to mean a spherical space with a diameter of about 8.65×10^{23} km (= 91×10^{12} LY) and mass of 10^{50} t (tons). [Comparing these data with the Earth's diameter of only 2024 km = 2.1×10^{-10} LY and mass of 6×10^{21} t, we can realize how small is the Earth and how huge is the observable Universe.] [Some models estimate that the observable Universe could be 7 trillion LY apart, while still constantly expanding.]

Universe Evolution: A cosmological model converts the entire time of the Universe into a single day. The start of the time ($t = 0$) is when Big Bang started at 12:00 AM, and the end of the time is the next day at 12:00 AM. Then, the model roughly divides the Universal evolution into six (6) periods:

- **Period 1** (origin of the Universe)**:** About 13.8 BYA, at 12:00 AM.
- **Period 2** (origin of the Galaxies)**:** About 13 BYA, around 1:54 AM.
- **Period 3** (origin of the Solar System)**:** About 4.5 BYA, around 5:00 PM.
- **Period 4** (origin of natural life on Earth)**:** About 4 BYA, around 7:00 PM.
- **Period 5** (origin of plants and animals)**:** About 0.5 BYA, around 11:03 PM.
- **Period 6** (origin of human ancestors)**:** About 14 MYA, about 11: 58:15 PM.

As the timeline of the Big Bang shows in Figure 2, the age of the human ancestors (about 14 BY), compared to the age of the natural life (about 4 BY), is tiny. It took many years for one branch of mammals to gradually evolve into brainy creatures named **human-chimp ancestors**. The evolution of our ancestors continued until about 4 MYA when they split into human-like individuals and chimps. The evolution has continued until the present-type smart-and-talkative humans (Homo Sapiens) evolved around 300 000 years ago (YA) in East Africa. Then around 200 000 YA, early humans started to migrate to Asia and later to Europe.

Today, all physical theories, including Einstein's general relativity, the Big Bang, and Hawking's birth of the Universe, reject the religion-based idea that the Universe has existed the way it is now (known as the **steady-state universal theory**). Physicists, instead, say: 1) The Universe, from its start, has been going through numerous changes, and 2) The life of all living creatures has been evolving (because of changes in genes).

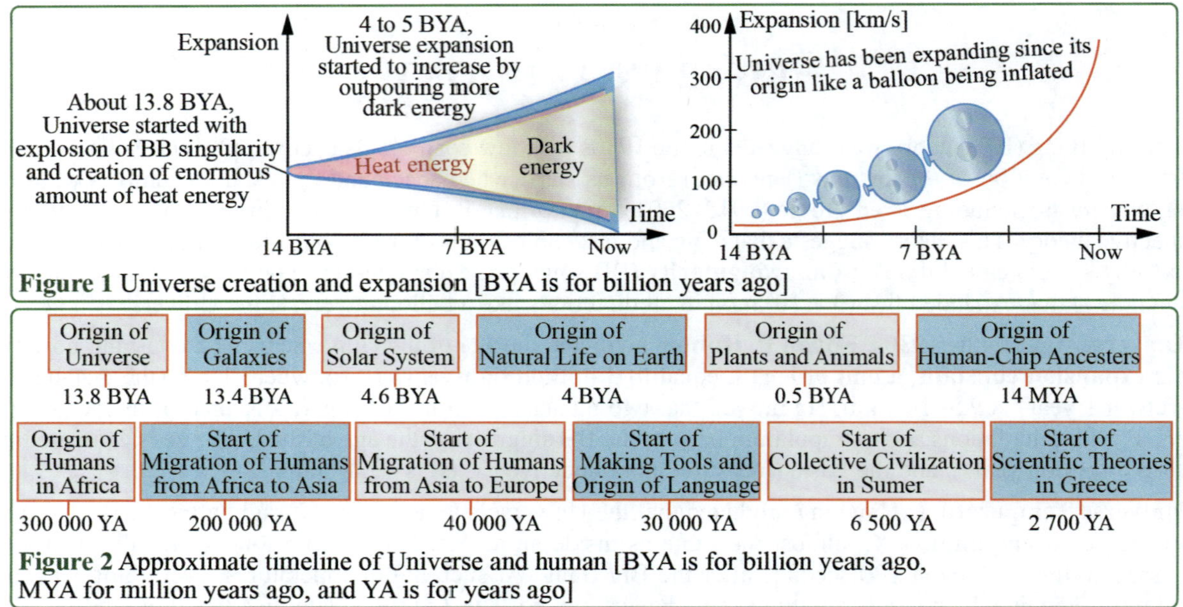

Figure 1 Universe creation and expansion [BYA is for billion years ago]

Figure 2 Approximate timeline of Universe and human [BYA is for billion years ago, MYA for million years ago, and YA is for years ago]

Thus far, humans have discovered many unknowns, including the foundation of classical physics (in 1687 by Newton), the Industrial Revolution (in the1760s by Europeans), electric power production (in the late 1880s by Edison and Tesla, based on Faraday and Maxwell discoveries), theories of relativity (in the early 1900s by Einstein), quantum physics (in the 1920s by several European physicists), first-landed humans on the Moon (in 1969 by US astronauts), internet networking (in the 1980s by US scientists), GPS (Global Positioning Systems) in the 1990s by US scientists, and many more. Despite these discoveries and finding answers to many hard questions, the following three (3) questions remained unanswered in the humans' minds:

- **Was the Big Bang a Supernatural Event?** This question has one answer. The **theists** (the believers in God), **atheists** (the non-believers in God), **agnostics** (the ones who *neither* believe *nor* disbelieve in God), and **cosmophysicists** (mostly agnostics) all say, "yes, the Big Bang was a supernatural event."
- **Who was the Creator of that Supernatural Event?** This question has four answers. Theists say "God." Atheists say "chance." Agnostics say, "we don't know." And cosmophysicists say, "regardless of our belief or disbelief in God, we can continue discovering unknowns of the Universe."
- **Does God Exist?** This is the hardest question that has come to the human mind, as *no* scientist (of any kind) could (or will be able to) find a verifiable answer to that because God's existence (or nonexistence) *cannot* be proved experimentally in a lab or mathematically on paper. This, thus, leaves us to refer to our deep conscience to find an answer to this hard question. Some, including this author, think that the Mighty Creator created the BB singularity, caused its rapid explosion and expansion, and managed all-natural evolutions that have been orderly happening in the Universe since the Big Bang time. For those who may ask, "where was the singularity before the Big Bang when there was *no* space to locate it?" – The answer is that the singularity was massless and timeless, so *no* space-and-time (spacetime) was needed to locate it.

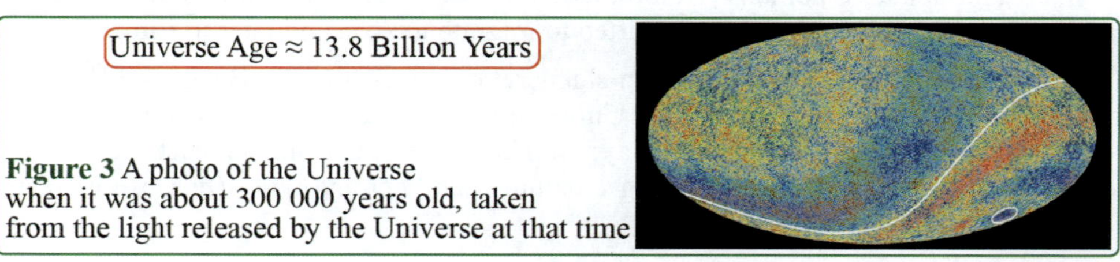

Figure 3 A photo of the Universe when it was about 300 000 years old, taken from the light released by the Universe at that time

B-16

BINDING ENERGY

This topic is discussed under ELECTRON BINDING ENERGY and NUCLEAR BINDING ENERGY.

B-17

BIOCHEMICAL AND CHEMICAL OXYGEN DEMAND

Biochemical Oxygen Demand

Biochemical oxygen demand (BOD) is a slow (five-day) biochemical test to estimate the amount of organic compounds in a sample. It determines the amount of oxygen used by microorganisms (the *higher* is the oxygen demand and, consequently, the *higher* is the BOD). BOD test is run at a certain temperature (*T*) over five days to allow microbes to oxidize the organic compounds biochemically.

Chemical Oxygen Demand

Chemical oxygen demand (COD) is a quick (two-hour) chemical test for the same purpose. Both BOD and COD tests are expressed in mg/L (= PPM). [On the same sample, the result of a COD test is about twice the BOD test. Although the test results correlate well, the COD test is preferred (because it is a quick test).] The COD test determines the amount of organic compounds in a wastewater sample.

The sample's BOD is determined by comparing the amount of **dissolved oxygen** (DO) left at the end of the five-day test with the amount at the beginning. The difference between these two values is the amount of oxygen consumed. The determination is made by diluting a measured quantity of the sample with a measured quantity of dilution water. The dilution water is deionized water (DI water) saturated with oxygen, to which an inorganic **nutrient buffer** (a nutrient for the growth of bacteria) is added.

In the COD test, an extra measured quantity of potassium dichromate ($K_2Cr_2O_7$) and concentrated sulfuric acid (H_2SO_4) is added to the sample, and the mixture is heated (at 150°C) in a closed-cap vial to oxidize the organic compounds. Part of the dichromate is consumed in the oxidation, and the COD is determined spectrophotometrically by measuring the increase in the **green** color intensity of the chromium (Cr^{+3}). The intensity of the **green** color is proportional to the concentration of organic compounds in the sample.

B-18

BIODIESEL

Discussed under the topic of ETHANOL, BIOETHANOL, AND BIODIESEL.

B-19

BIOETHANOL

Discussed under ETHANOL, BIOETHANOL, AND BIODIESEL

B-20

BIOFUELS

Biofuels are carbon-based compounds produced from biomasses. Bioethanol (C_2H_5OH), biodiesel, and syngas (a synthetic gas) are the main biofuels. Compared with fossil fuels, biofuels produce less carbon dioxide (CO_2), making them environmentally safer. [CO_2 acts as a greenhouse gas.]

B-21

BIOGAS

Biogas is a gas mixture consisting of methane (CH_4, 60 to 80%), carbon dioxide (CO_2), water vapor, and a small amount of hydrogen sulfide (H_2S). It is produced in an anaerobic wastewater system from the breakdown of organic compounds by anaerobic bacteria without oxygen. [Existing H_2S with a strong odor of rotten egg in biogas is the main problem when wastewater is treated anaerobically (because the public's tolerance for odor is low).]

[Safety Note: Biogas is explosive (when mixed with air), corrosive, and toxic. When designing an anaerobic system, these properties must be considered. Warning signs for hazards are required in the area around a biogas source. Operators working in and around biogas systems must be trained to respond to leaks, what actions they should take, and who they should contact.]

B-22

BIOLOGICAL HALF LIFETIME

Discussed under the topic of HALF LIFETIME.

B-23

BIOMASSES

Biomass is a plant resource used to produce bioethanol (renewable energy) and biodiesel. It can be used directly to produce heat energy (E_Q) or indirectly after converting it to different biofuels. The main biomasses used for bioethanol production are sugarcane, corn, sugarbeet, potato, rice, barley, and wheat.

In general, wood is also biomass that can be directly burned to produce E_Q. In particular, **cellulosic biomasses** (cellulose-containing biomasses), like cane bagasse and beet pulp, are fermentable biomasses. In addition, some low-maintenance, fast-growing crops, like straws and grasslands (steppes), are grown solely for their high lignocellulose and energy contents. These low-cost crops are the most used biomasses in this group. [**Lignocellulose** is the plants' dry substance, mainly consisting of **carbohydrate polymers** (cellulose and hemicellulose) and **lignin** (an organic polymer in the plants' tissues).]

B-24

BLACKBODIES AND BLACKBODY RADIATION

Blackbodies

A blackbody is a body (system) that *cannot* release electromagnetic radiation (EM radiation or EM waves, like light). It is called a **blackbody** because it does *not* glow at low temperatures. Instead, a **white body** can release EM radiation. Say, graphite (a crystalline form of carbon) is a blackbody (because it releases only 3% of the EM radiation).

Because *no* EM radiation is released from a blackbody, its released energy depends only on its temperature (T) and *not* on its chemical composition. In 1900, Planck formulized the photon energy (E_{Ph}), released from the surface of a blackbody in relation to its T (temperature) and released light's λ (wavelength), known later as Planck's equation ($E = h.f$), where h is Planck's constant and f is the frequency of the released (emitted) radiation. To calculate blackbody's E, Planck assumed that the light (the light energy) is quantized (broken down into tiny packets; see QUANTIZATION), meaning it travels in tiny-separate packets, known as **quanta** (plural of quantum). This is known as Planck's quantum theory.

Many systems glow when they are heated. Electric-stove iron and barbecue coal glow red at high temperatures. However, iron and coal (blackbodies) appear black at room temperature (≈ 25ºC). This tells us that a blackbody releases E (energy) in the form of E_{Ph} (photon energy).

Figure 1 shows a model for demonstrating a blackbody's structure. The model is a **cavity** (hollow space) with a black surface and a small hole. The incoming EM radiation goes through the hole into the cavity. After some time, the radiation's T becomes the same as the cavity's wall, reaching thermal equilibrium. Because the hole allows some radiation to escape, the released radiation from the cavity can approximate blackbody radiation, expressed by Planck's equation, as said a moment ago.

Figure 2 shows the relation between wavelength (λ) and intensity (I) of radiations of a blackbody at different temperatures. Referring to this figure, we can say the following two (2) brief points:

- A blackbody's λ decreases with increasing its T, so its I (which indicates E_{Ph}) increases with increasing T (the total area under the curve increases).
- A blackbody releases E_{Ph} at every λ (because the first curve in the figure touches the x-axis at infinite λ).

Next, the other important properties of blackbody are outlined.

- A blackbody does *not* release visible light when cold, so it appears black.
- A blackbody releases light when it gets hot (above 800ºC), glowing. A blackbody's releasing property increases with increasing its T. Blackbody radiation (energy), thus, temperature-related radiation.
- A blackbody is an ideal reference with a perfect radiation-absorbing property, so its surface T can be measured by measuring the wavelengths (λ) released from its surface, as shown in Figure 2.

Blackbody Radiation

Blackbody radiation (energy) is released by a perfect absorber of electromagnetic radiation (EM radiation). Bodies glow at higher frequencies as they are heated. This is more evident for dark bodies (systems), such as iron and coal (which efficiently absorb and release heat energy). Glowing coal releases most of its light in the high-frequency **red** and **orange**, but barely any **blue**, as shown in Figure 2.

[Today, physicists think that even blackholes emit blackbody radiation in the form of so-known as the **Hawking radiation** (blackhole radiation), after Hawking (1942 –2018).]

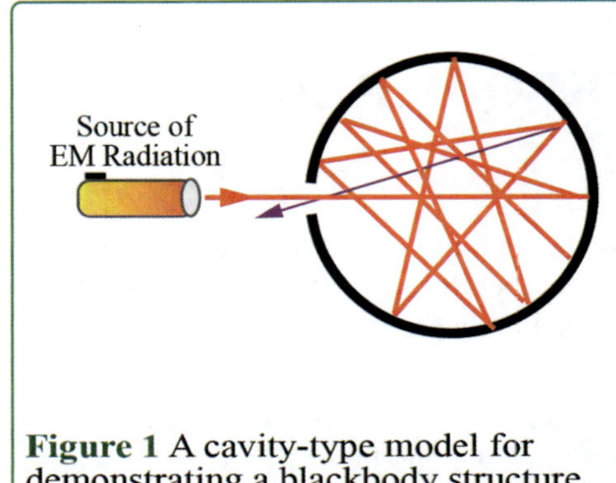

Figure 1 A cavity-type model for demonstrating a blackbody structure

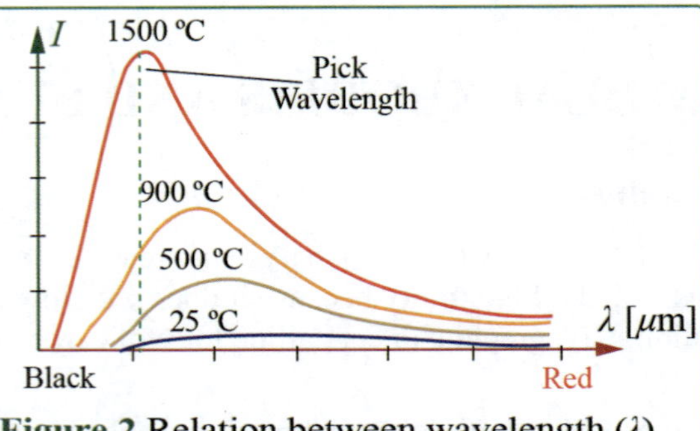

Figure 2 Relation between wavelength (λ) and intensity (I) of a blackbody radiation at different temperatures

B-25

BLACKHOLES

A blackhole (often written **black hole**) is a dense system in space with a **singularity** in the middle and an **event horizon** surrounding the singularity's surface. It is the residue of a super (giant) star when its energy (E) is almost finished, so it collapses (falls) into its gravity well and shrinks gradually by a huge gravitational force (F_g) to a much smaller volume, known as a blackhole singularity (see Figure 1 and 2). Therefore, a blackhole can be viewed as a dead-dark-compacted system in space with extreme density (D) so that light *cannot* be reflected (returned) from it, causing it to be **non-observable**. But, its horizon is **observable** (because it is *not* compact as the blackhole). [Blackholes are small because they are very compact (a blackhole with its horizon as massive as the Sun would be less than 6 km.)]

[The concept of **blackhole** was first predicted in 1915 by Karl Schwarzschild (1873–1916, a German physicist), and then was developed by some cosmophysicists, including Penrose and Hawking, known as the Penrose-Hawking blackhole singularity theory (developed in the 1970s).]

The Physics Laws *cannot* easily govern blackholes. For example, when a system gets to a blackhole's event horizon, it starts to move very fast, and when it gets to its singularity, it *cannot* get out. Some other properties of blackholes are the following:

- They can curve spacetime around themselves, as shown in Figure 3.
- Their lifetime is extremely long. Based on the **blackhole evaporation theory**: Blackholes that lose more mass (M) than they gain are expected to disappear over a long period (more than 10 billion years).
- Their rotating velocity is extremely high (up to 150 km/s), so they have high rotational momentum (L).
- They release **blackhole radiation** (Hawking radiation) from their event horizon's area with different wavelengths, depending on their temperature. [**Hawking radiation** is a type of EM radiation made by **gravitational vacuum polarization** in the event horizon, where moving radiation is *not* a problem.]

Hawking also predicted that

- Much of the mass (M) of stars is in the form of blackholes.
- Blackholes occupy around one-fourth (1/4) of the entire Universe.
- Blackholes are *not* completely free of energy (E), so they release a bit of Hawking radiation. [Because of releasing E, blackholes gradually shrink and ultimately die over a long time (in around 10 billion years).]
- The F_g of a blackhole is the same as a conventional system of the same M (often conversely described).

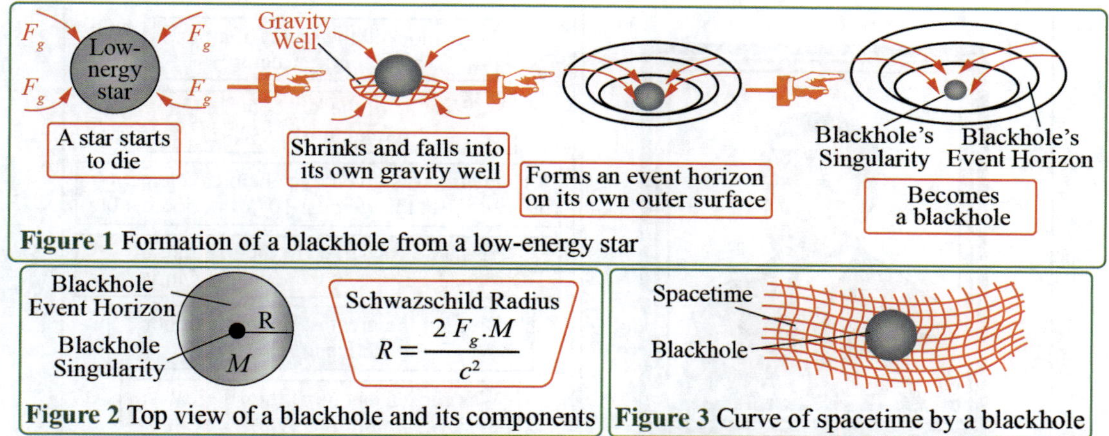

Figure 1 Formation of a blackhole from a low-energy star

Figure 2 Top view of a blackhole and its components

Figure 3 Curve of spacetime by a blackhole

B-26
BLOWERS

Discussed under the topic of COMPRESSORS, FANS, AND BLOWERS.

B-27
BOD

Abbreviated form of BIOCHEMICAL OXYGEN DEMAND.

B-28
BODY (in Physics)

The term **body** is used in physics and engineering to refer to a system with a certain mass and shape that can move in a three-dimensional (3-D) direction. A boundary can enclose a body. [Instead of the word **body**, the word **system** is often used in this book.]

B-29
BOHR

Niels Bohr (1885–1962) was a Danish physical chemist who received the Nobel Prize in Physics in 1922 for his atomic theory [see Bohr's atomic theory]. In 1920, Bohr founded the Institute of Theoretical Physics at the University of Copenhagen, now known as the Niels Bohr Institute. [Interesting to know that he barely missed selection as a goalkeeper in Denmark's national football team in 1908.]

As a person, he was a likable, shy, and softly-spoken man. As a physicist, he was one of the two best experimentalists on atomic subjects to reach first-hand results (the other one was Rutherford). For example, he conducted several experiments on the light's duality properties after Einstein's 1905 paper about this subject (see Einstein's theory of light duality). He discovered that electrons, like light, have wave-particle duality properties.

Bohr [Illustrated specifically for this book]

Unlocked the secret of atom and atomic structure

Was one of the key contributors of quantum physics

His name was given to a chemical element (bohrium, Bh, the element 107 of periodic table)

His name was given to the Institute of Theoretical Physics in Copenhagen University

Brought the greatest scientific honor to Denmark

Was chosen as one of the 10 greatest physicists of all time by *Physics World*

Some of Bohr's memorable achievements

Bohr concluded the following:

- We can only experience the wavelike property or particlelike property of an electron at any given time, but never both at the same time. This means that each property must be tested in a separate experiment.
- We must accept that experiments *cannot* necessarily give consistent results. We, however, must hold all the possibilities in mind at once.

Combining the listed two ideas is known as Bohr's theory of complementarity.

He could express his scientific views excellently with other physicists (study Copenhagen Interpretation). In one of his communications, he said, "When talking about atom, language can be used only as in poetry."

[Planck, Einstein, Rutherford, Bohr, Heisenberg, Schrodinger, and Broglie can be named as the seven (7) top quantum physicists. And Newton, Faraday, and Maxwell as the three (3) top classical physicists. The ten (10) pioneers contributed to Physics more than all physicists.]

B-30

BOHR'S ATOMIC MODEL

Discussed under the topic of ATOMIC MODELS AND ATOMIC THEORIES.

B-31

BOHR'S ATOMIC THEORY

Discussed under the topic of ATOMIC MODELS AND ATOMIC THEORIES.

B-32

BOHR'S EQUATION

Bohr drove an equation and published it in 1913 to determine an electron's energy (refers to potential energy) located on each electron shell. Bohr's equation for the energy of an atom's *n*th shell is given as

$$E_n = -\frac{R.h.c}{n^2} \quad (1)$$

In this equation, R is the Rydberg's constant (for hydrogen $R = 1.097 \times 10^7\ m^{-1}$), h is Planck's constant (= 6.625×10^{-34} J.s), c is the speed of light constant (= 3×10^8 m/s), and n is the quantum number, so E_n becomes in J (Joule). The product of $R.h.c = -2.179 \times 10^{-21}$ kJ/atom. To calculate Rhc in kJ/mole, we must multiply $R.h.c$ by the Avogadro's number ($N_{Avo} = 6.022 \times 10^{23}$), so $R.h.c$ becomes −1312 kJ/mole. Study the next Note and Example.

[As seen from Equation 1, the energy of an electron has a **negative** value. This is because the attraction energy between an electron (with an electric charge of 1.6×10^{-19} C, where C is for coulomb) and a proton (with an electric charge of 1.6×10^{-19} C) has a negative value. And this value becomes more negative as they get closer to each other (when an electron gets closer to its nucleus, it gets closer to the protons of that atom). As an electron climbs from the $n = 1$ shell to the $n = 2$ shell, it is less strongly attracted to the nucleus, and its energy is less negative. This tells us that an atom must absorb energy until its electron (or electrons) can move from the $n = 1$ shell to the $n = 2$ shell.]

An Example on Bohr's Equation

Wanted: The E_n of electron in the hydrogen (H) atom, when it is in the $n = 2$ shell, where $R.h.c = -2.179 \times 10^{-21}$ kJ/atom.

$$E_2 = -\frac{R.h.c}{n^2} = -\frac{R.h.c}{2^2} = \frac{-R.h.c}{4} = \frac{-2.179\times10^{-21}}{4} = -5.448 \times 10^{-22}\ \text{kJ/atom}$$

And E_2 in kJ/mole will be

$$E_2 = -5.448 \times 10^{-22} \times 6.022 \times 10^{23} = -328\ \text{kJ/mole}$$

We could also find E_2 by dividing E_1 by 4, because $E_2 = E_1/n^2 = E_1/2^2 = -1312/4 = -328$.

B-33

BOHR'S THEORY OF COMPLEMENTARITY

This subject is briefly discussed under the topic of BOHR.

B-34

BOILERS

Study STEAM BOILERS.

B-35

BOILING DEPRESSION AND BOILING ELEVATION TEMPERATURES

Boiling Depression Temperature

The boiling depression temperature (T_{BD}, also called **boiling point depression**) of a liquid is the decrease in its boiling point temperature (T_{BP}) below that of water, which has a T_{BP} of 100°C at 1 Atm (the atmospheric pressure, P_{Atm}). In another context, the T_{BD} of a liquid is the difference between the T_{BP} of that liquid and water, both at the same P (pressure). For example, water boils at 86°C in an evaporator, operating at negative vacuum pressure (P_{Vac}) of 0.6 Atm. If a solution at the same P boils at 80°C, its T_{BD} is 86°C – 80°C = 6°C.

Besides P, the T_{BD} of a solution is a function of concentration, C (*T_{BD} increases as C increases*), so T_{BD} is a colligative property (a concentration-dependent property).

Boiling Elevation Temperature

The boiling elevation temperature (T_{BE}, also called **boiling point elevation**) of a liquid is the increase in its boiling point temperature (T_{BP}) above that of water, which has a T_{BP} of 100°C at 1 Atm (the atmospheric pressure, P_{Atm}). If, therefore, water is evaporated instead of a solution in an evaporator, we have no T_{BE} (boiling elevation temperature). Because the T_{BE} of a liquid is usually given in relation to P (pressure), the T_{BE} can also be defined as the difference between the T_{BP} of that liquid and water, both at the same P. If, for example, we add some sugar to water and the sugar solution boils at 102°C at the same P, the T_{BE} of the solution would be 102°C – 100°C = 2°C.

Besides P, a solution's T_{BE} is a function of concentration, C (*T_{BE} increases as C increases*), so T_{BE} is a colligative property. A practical equation calculates T_{BE} when a solution's dissolved solids (DS) value is known.

$$T_{BE} = \frac{2DS}{100-DS} \tag{1}$$

According to this equation, a 50% sugar solution has a T_{BE} of 2°C, so its T_{BP} increases to 102°C (see Figure 1). Adding solute (here sugar) to a solvent (here water) increases the solution's T_{BP}.

A simple equation also calculates the T_{BE} of an ideal solution (a solution with up to 15% DS content) when the solution's molality (m, moles/one kg of solution) is known.

$$T_{BE} = K_{BE}.m \tag{2}$$

In this equation, K_{BE} is the boiling depression constant (in °C.kg/mole of solute). For example, K_{BE} for water and ideal solutions is 0.5°C.kg/mole. Molality (m) is given as

$$m = \frac{M_S}{M_{Mol}.kg_{Sol}} \tag{3}$$

In this equation, M_S is the mass of the solute (in g), M_n is the solute's molar mass (g/mole), and kg_{Sol} is the solution's quantity (kg).

An Example on T_{BE}

Given: A sugar solution with DS of 10% by mass and the K_{BE} for 10% sugar solution of 0.5°C.kg/mole. The molar mass (M_n) of sugar is 342 g/mole.

Wanted: T_{BE} (boiling elevation temperature) of sugar solution at P_{Atm}

The 10% sugar solution contains 10 g of sugar in 100 g of solution, so $M_S = 10$ g, and the amount of solution is 100 mL (or 0.1 kg). The molality equation calculates the molality (m) of the solution.

$$m = \frac{M_S}{M_n \times kg_{Sol}} = \frac{10}{342 \times 0.1} = 0.3 \text{ mole/kg } (= 0.3 \text{ m})$$

$$T_{BE} = K_{BE}.m = 0.5 \times 0.3 = 0.15\ ^{\circ}\text{C}$$

Because the T_{BP} of water at 1 Atm is 100°C, the T_{BP} of this solution is

$$T_{BP} = 100 + 0.15 = 100.15\ ^{\circ}\text{C}$$

If we had used $T_{BE} = 2\ DS/100 - DS$, the T_{BE} would be 0.2.

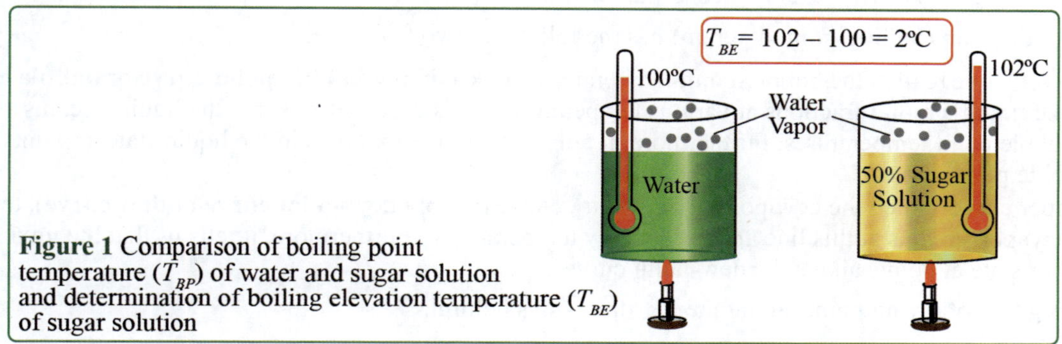

Figure 1 Comparison of boiling point temperature (T_{BP}) of water and sugar solution and determination of boiling elevation temperature (T_{BE}) of sugar solution

B-36

BOILING ELEVATION TEMPERATURE

Discussed under BOILING DEPRESSION AND BOILING ELEVATION TEMPERATURES.

B-37

BOILING POINT DIAGRAMS

A boiling-point diagram (T_{BP} diagram, also called ***XY* diagram**) shows a phase diagram and boiling point temperature (T_{BP}) and concentration (usually in molar fraction, X) for one mole (n) of a binary (two-component) mixture at constant pressure (P) and various temperatures (T). T_{BP} diagrams at constant P have many applications, including the distillation process.

As we change a binary mixture's T, each component's molar fraction (X) in the mixture's liquid phase and vapor phase changes. If, thus, holding the P constant (usually at 1 Atm), we can compare molar fractions of both components at various T. The molar fraction of component A in the liquid (L) phase (shown by $X_{n.A}$) is related to that of component B in the L phase (shown by $X_{n.B}$) as

$$X_{n.A} + X_{n.B} = 1 \qquad (1)$$

Similar equations can be written for molar fractions of A and B in the vapor (V) phase.

$$Y_{n.A} + Y_{n.B} = 1 \qquad (2)$$

If plotting the results of these two equations in a single diagram, we get a **boiling point diagram** of that binary mixture.

For making a T_{BP} diagram at constant *P*, the molar fractions of each component in the liquid phase ($X_{n.A}$ and $X_{n.B}$) are plotted on the *X*-axis, and temperatures are plotted on the *Y*-axis. When the points are connected for different temperatures, a graph like in Figure 1 is produced. Any given *X* (molar fraction in the liquid phase) and *Y* (molar fraction in the vapor phase) can be represented by two points. The points are shown by connecting a horizontal line, called the isotherm (constant-temperature) line. [**Isotherm** is a line, or a curve, of pressure (*P*) in relation to volume (*V*) of a fluid when the fluid's *T* is constant ($\Delta T = 0$).]

As a real example, consider an ethanol-water mixture, whose boiling-point diagram is shown in Figure 2. The molar fraction of ethanol (with T_{BP} of 78.4°C) in the liquid (*L*) phase is related to the molar fraction of water (with T_{BP} of 100°C) in the *L* phase, based on Equation 1. Similarly, the ethanol's molar fraction in the vapor (*V*) phase, according to Equation 2, is related to that of water.

Any T_{BP} diagram (boiling-point diagram) has the following two (2) curves:

- The lower curve, called the bubble-point temperature **curve** (simply **bubble-point curve** or **bubble curve**), gives the liquid's molar fractions at various temperatures. This curve tells us that the liquid streams are at their bubble point temperatures. Furthermore, it tells us that the mixture is in the liquid state at points below the bubble point curve.
- The upper curve, called the dew point temperature **curve** (simply **dew-point curve** or **dew curve**), tells us that the vapor streams at this line are at their dew temperatures. Furthermore, it tells us that the mixture is in the vapor state at points above the dew-point curve.

Knowing the following points about the T_{BP} diagram is helpful:

- Both liquid and vapor phases exist between the dew curve and bubble curve. At a certain *T*, liquid with a certain *X* is in equilibrium with vapor with a certain *Y*.
- The dew and bubble curves joint where the mixture becomes one pure component. That is $X_{n.1} = 0$ and $X_{n.2} = 1$ or $X_{n.1} = 1$ and $X_{n.2} = 0$. And *T* at each point corresponds to the T_{BP} of that pure component.
- The mixture boils at *T* given by the bubble curve.

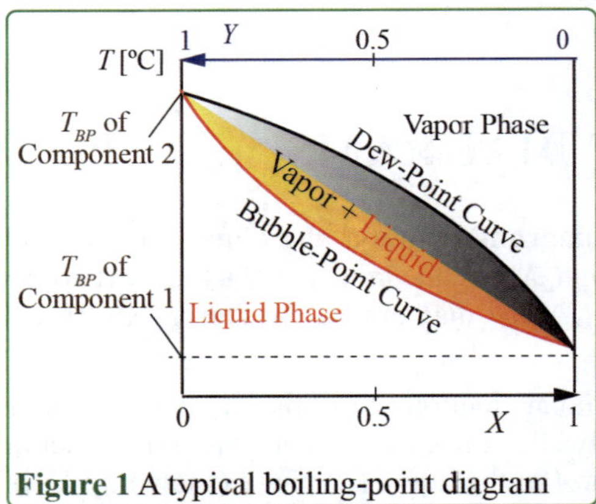

Figure 1 A typical boiling-point diagram

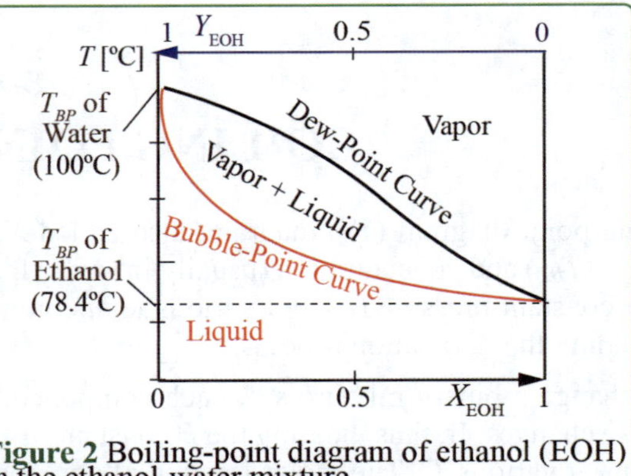

Figure 2 Boiling-point diagram of ethanol (EOH) in the ethanol-water mixture

B-38

BOILING POINT TEMPERATURE

The boiling point temperature (T_{BP}, simply **boiling point** or **boiling temperature**) of a liquid is the temperature (T) at which boiling starts at the pressure (P) surrounding that liquid. Usually, T_{BP} is determined at atmospheric pressure (P_{Atm} = 1 Atm = 14.7 PSI, the pressure at sea level) because T_{BP} varies greatly with P, as shown in Figure 1 for water. A liquid starts to boil when it is heated to the T that the vapor pressure (P_V, ↑), surrounding the liquid, applied to it, is equal (or greater) than the P_{Atm} (↓). [Arrows indicate the direction of the pressures.] Therefore, the T_{BP} is usually defined as the T, at which liquid boils at P_{Atm} (*at P_{Atm}, different liquids boil at different temperatures*). Differences in the strength of molecular attractions explain why different liquids have different T_{BP} at the same P_{Atm}.

The word **normal boiling-point temperature** (T_{NBP}) is also used to refer to the T_{BP} of a liquid at P_{Atm}, so the T_{BP} of a liquid at P_{Atm} equates to its T_{NBP}, as shown in Figure 1 for water. [This is why in textbooks, the word **boiling point temperature** is used to mean **normal boiling point temperature**.]

The T_{BP} of a liquid depends on the following:

- **Pressure** (P)**:** The *greater* the liquid P, the *greater* is its T_{BP}. A liquid at high P has a higher T_{BP} than at P_{Atm}. At P_{Atm}, water boils at 100ºC (= 212ºF), but when its P is increased to, say, 40 Atm (= 588 PSI) in a steam boiler, water boils at 250ºC (= 482ºF), and the steam T is also at 250ºC. This phenomenon is called boiling point elevation (T_{BPE}). Instead, a liquid under negative vacuum pressure (P_{Vac}) has a lower T_{BP} than when that liquid is at P_{Atm}. Consider an evaporator that operates under P_{Vac}. The low P in the evaporator decreases the T_{BP} of the evaporating liquid, resulting in an energy-efficiency operation. Water, for instance, boils at 86°C in an evaporator, which operates at 0.6 Atm (= 60 kPa = 9 PSI). The decrease of a liquid's T_{BP} below that of water is called boiling depression temperature (T_{BD}).

  Molecular Mass (M_M)**:** With some exceptions, the *greater* the liquid M_M, the *greater* is its T_{BP}. At P_{Atm}, acetone (with M_M of 58 g) boils at 56.6 °C (= 134°F), methanol (with M_M of 32 g) at 64.7°C (= 148°F), ethanol (with M_M of 46 g) at 78.3°C (= 173°F), and water at 100ºC (= 212ºF). [Note that liquids with similar M_M to water are usually in the gaseous phase at room temperature (around 25ºC or 77 ºF). If this applied to water, *no* liquid water would exist on Earth. Also, note that once one of these liquids reaches its T_{BP}, it will remain at that T until the boiling process is complete and all of the liquid is boiled.]
- **Altitude:** The *lower* the altitude, the *higher* is the T_{BP} (since P_{Atm} varies with altitude), as seen in Figure 2.

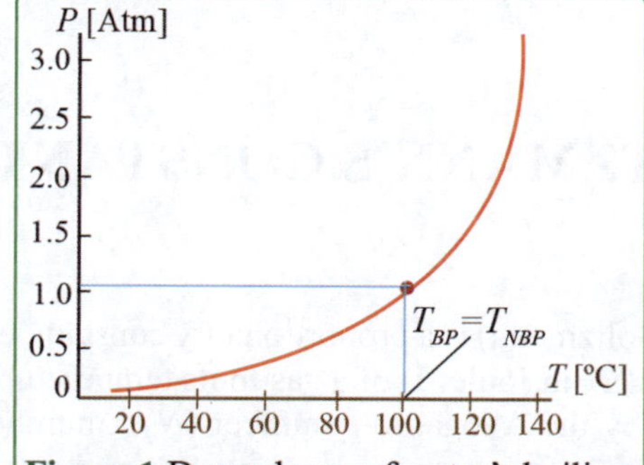

Figure 1 Dependency of water's boiling point temperature (T_{BP}) on pressure (P)

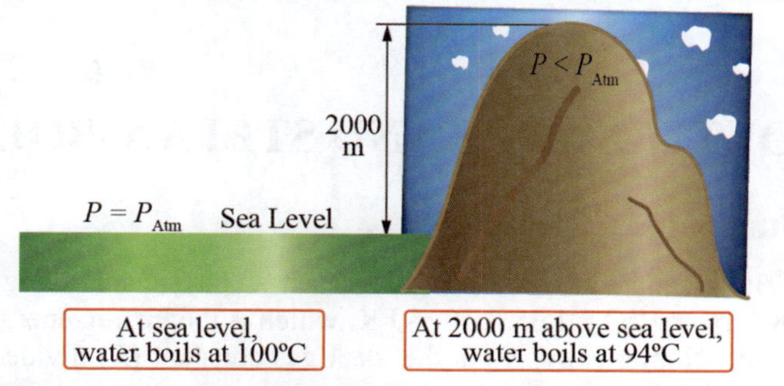

Figure 2 Boiling point temperature (T_{BP}) of water at two different altitudes (the *lower* the altitude, the *higher* is the T_{BP})

B-39

BOILING PROCESS

As one of the process units of ChemEng, boiling is a phase-change process (latent heat process) by which a liquid changes into a vapor when its temperature (T) reaches its boiling point temperature (T_{BP}). The boiling process is the **rapid form** of the evaporation process with the following differences:

- The boiling of a liquid occurs only when the liquid reaches its T_{BP}. Instead, evaporation can occur without reaching a liquid's T_{BP} (water evaporates without reaching its T_{BP}). [Scientists, however, use the word **evaporation** even when the liquid reaches its T_{BP}.]
- Boiling occurs at a liquid-solid interface when a liquid is heated in a container to its T_{BP}. Instead, evaporation can occur without contacting a liquid-solid interface. [Industrially, both boiling and evaporation are performed at a solid-liquid interface in a vessel.]
- Boiling is an all-over process because molecules anywhere (on the surface and under the surface) in the liquid move to the vapor phase. Instead, evaporation is a surface process (only molecules near the vapor-liquid surface move to the vapor phase).

The heat energy (E_Q) is added to a liquid during boiling to increase the liquid's T to reach its T_{BP}. A liquid starts to boil when the vapor pressure ($P_V\uparrow$) applied to its molecules is equal to or greater than the atmospheric pressure ($P_{Atm}\downarrow$). [Arrows indicate the approximate direction of forces.] Therefore, T_{BP} is defined as the T, at which a solution boils at P_{Atm} (1 Atm = 14.7 PSI, the pressure at sea level). When the molecules leave the liquid phase during boiling and evaporation, they take their E_Q, so the released vapor has some E_Q.

Liquids boil under vacuum pressure (P_{Vac}) at temperatures below their T_{BP}. For example, water (with T_{BP} of 100°C at 1 Atm) boils at 86°C in an evaporator, which operates at P_{Vac} of 0.6 Atm (= 60 kPa = 9 PSI).

In boiling, the heat transfer process mainly occurs by **convection** between a liquid and a solid so that the general convection equation can be used. The heat transfer rate ($\dot{E}_Q$), heat transfer area (A, the area through which convection occurs), and the driving force of the heat transfer ($\Delta T = T_H - T_S$) are related through a proportionality constant called the heat transfer coefficient (U_Q).

$$\dot{E}_Q = U_Q.A(T_H - T_S) \qquad (1)$$

If, for example, the heating medium's U_Q is 10 kW/h.m².°C, A is 2 m², T_H (heating medium's T) of a boiling device is 108°C, and T_S (tubes-surface's T) is 38°C; then $\dot{E}_Q$ from heating medium to the tubes is

$$\dot{E}_Q = 9 \times 2(108 - 38) = 1260 \text{ kW/h}$$

B-40

BOLTZMANN'S AND STEFAN-BOLTZMANN'S CONSTANTS

Boltzmann's Constant

The Boltzmann's constant (K_B, after Austrian physicist Ludwig Boltzmann) is a proportionality constant, equal to 1.38×10^{-23} J/°C = 1.38×10^{-23} J/K, which is the kinetic energy (E_K in Joule, J) of a gas to its temperature (T, in Kelvin). Numerically, K_B is the ideal gas constant (R) divided by the Avogadro's number (N_{Avo}, number of atomic particles in one mole).

$$K_B = \frac{R}{N_{Avo}} \qquad (1)$$

Applying K_B in the ideal gas equation ($P.V = n.R.T$) gives another expression for the Ideal Gas Law.

$$P.V = N_{Avo}.K_B.T \qquad (2)$$

Stefan-Boltzmann's Constant

Stefan-Boltzmann's constant (K_{SB} or Greek letter sigma, Ő; after Slovenian physicist Josef Stefan and Austrian physicist Ludwig Boltzmann) is a proportionality constant, equal to 5.67×10^{-8} W/m^2.K^4 = 5.67×10^{-8} W/m^2.°C^4, where W is for Watt and m is for the meter.

K_{SB} has some applications, including in Stefan-Boltzmann's Law (total intensity radiated over all wavelengths increases as the T increases) and in heat transfer by radiation from a system's surface to its outside.

B-41

BOND ENERGY

Another name for ELECTRON BINDING ENERGY.

B-42

BOSONS, FERMIONS, AND HADRONS

Bosons (the name comes from Satyendra Bose, 1894−1974, Indian physicist), **Fermions** (the name comes from Enrico Fermi,1901−1954, Italian physicist), and **hadrons** are particles that some of them are elementary particles and some are composite particles. They contain energy and carry electromagnetic force (EM force). The classification of Bosons, Fermions, and hadrons is shown in Figure 1. These particles and their member-family particles account for most of the total known particles (around 60).

Before discussing these particles, it is important to define the **Bose-Einstein** (B-E) **statistics** and **Fermi-Dirac** (F-D) **statistics**.

- **Bose-Einstein** (B-E) **Statistics:** In B-E statistics, the interaction of any two particles of an atom leaves the resultant atom **symmetrically**. This means that the system's quantum wavefunction before the interaction is the same as after. This tells us that more than one particle can occupy a single position in B-E statistics.
- In F-D statistics, the interaction of any two particles of an atom leaves the atom in a **non-symmetric state**. This means that the system's wavefunction before the interaction is the same as after interaction but with a **minus sign**. This tells us that more than one particle *cannot* occupy a position in F-D statistics.

Bosons

Bosons are bosonic force-carrying particles that obey B-E statistics. In other words, bosons are particles that mediate force. Thus, the photon is the boson for electromagnetic force (F_{EM}). Bosons have a spin of 0, 1, or 2. The 7 currently known **Bosonic particles** are:

- **Gluons:** Gluons are the force-carrying particles of the strong nuclear force (F_{SN}).
- **Photons:** Photons are the force-carrying particles of electromagnetic force (F_{EM}).
- **W-Bosons and Z-Bosons:** They are the force-carrying particles of the weak nuclear force (F_{WN}). [W- and Z-Bosons were predicted in the 1960s and observed in 1983 at CERN.]
- **Gravitons:** Gravitons are the force-carrying particles of gravitational force, the weakest of the four fundamental forces. [The existence of graviton has *not* been observed yet (because of its insufficient energy.]

- **Higgs Bosons:** Higgs Bosons are massive (the mass of a Higgs particle is 126 times greater than a proton). They have a zero spin and are produced by **quantum excitation** (moving a particle, like an electron, from the ground state) of the Higgs field. [Higgs Boson was suspected to exist in the 1960s and proved to exist in 2012 by the particle accelerator of CERN.]
- **Gauge Bosons:** Gauge Bosons can carry any of the fundamental forces of nature, commonly called **gauge forces**. All known gauge Bosons have a spin of 1.

Fermions

Fermions are charged particles that obey F-D statistics and spin a half-integer (½). Some fermions are elementary particles, such as electrons, quarks, and neutrinos. And some are composite particles, like protons and neutrons.

Hadrons

A hadron is a subatomic, composite particle made of two (or more) quarks, kept together by the F_{SN} (strong nuclear force) in a similar way as molecules are kept together by the F_{EM} (electromagnetic force).

As Figure 1 shows, hadrons are classed into **baryons** (made of 3 quarks) and **mesons** (1 quark and 1 antiquark). Proton and neutron are baryons. A **pion** (any of 3 subatomic particles) is a meson.

Scientists discovered that hadrons might consist of short-lived subparticles, and many hadrons can decay into other hadrons.

A few important properties of **mesons** are outlined next.

- They are unstable (their lifespan is about a few hundredths of a microsecond).
- Their diameter is roughly one Fermi (about 2/3 the size of a proton or neutron).
- Their effect is like a photon, the force-carrier of electromagnetic force (EM force).

The difference between the **hadron** and **lepton** is whether one interacts through the F_{SN}. Hadrons can interact with all four fundamental forces of nature. Leptons, instead, can participate in the electromagnetic, weak, and gravitational forces but *not* in the strong force.

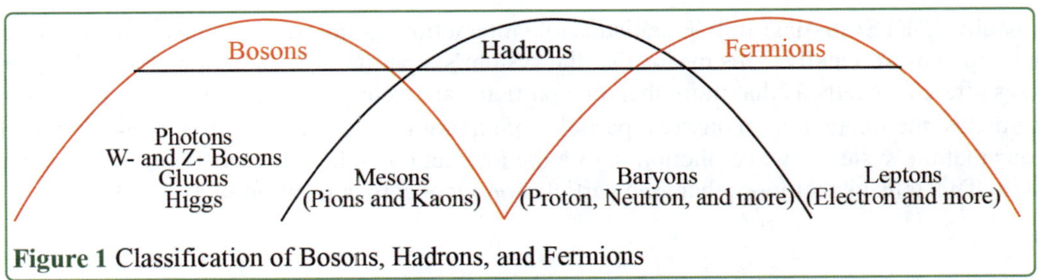

Figure 1 Classification of Bosons, Hadrons, and Fermions

B-43
BOUNDARY AND STREAM LAYERS IN FLUID FLOW

Boundary layers and stream layers (in some textbooks called **streamlines**) are frequently used in liquid flow processes. Consider a flowing liquid in a pipe and visualize this flow as many imaginary layers, which slide smoothly over each other (like playing cards) while flowing in a certain direction. The thin layers flowing next to the pipe's wall are **boundary layers**, and those in the middle (at the **center** of the flow) are **stream layers** (see Figure 1).

Before studying the rest of this topic, it is helpful to study the next Note.

[Note: In this book, the word **stream layer** is used instead of **streamline** (usually used in other textbooks) to indicate 1) A liquid flows like layers (but *not* like lines), 2) To match the word with **boundary layers** (usually used in all textbooks). This treatment eliminates the reader's confusion because both are the layers of a liquid, one flowing in the middle of a pipe (I call it **stream layers**) and the other moving along the wall (everybody calls it **boundary layers**).]

The main differences between boundary layers and stream layers in the flow of a liquid in a pipe are:

- The boundary layers move slower because the molecules next to the pipe's wall *stick* to the wall's surface, making them move at low (if *not* at zero) velocity (V, rather **average velocity** $\bar{V}$) in this area. Further away from the wall, the molecules move slowly but *not* as slowly as the molecules next to the wall. And further away from the wall toward the center of the flow, the molecules move at their maximum velocity.
- The flow at the boundary layers is turbulent, while the flow at the stream layers is laminar.

In Figure 1, each arrow shows the approximate magnitude of that area's velocity. As seen, the lengths of arrows are *not* the same. The arrows indicating the stream layers in the middle of the flow are shown longer and ahead of the arrows of the boundary layers to indicate that a steady flow (fully-developed or uniform flow) with maximum velocity is at the center of the flow where the stream layers are. The stream-layer arrows show a **steady profile** (distribution) that stays the same as long as the next two conditions are met:

- **No Object Exists in the way of the Flow.** As an object, assume a flat plate is placed parallel to flow in a pipe (see Figure 2). The plate causes the flow to be interrupted, and more boundary layers are formed next to the plate's edges. Soon after leaving the plate, the velocities of the boundary layers gradually increase until they become the same as the velocities of stream layers. Then, boundary layers behave like stream layers, and flow becomes fully developed again. Let us now see the behavior of layers when the plate is standing at 45° against the direction of flow (see Figure 3). When the liquid molecules reach the face of the plate, their momentum (mass × velocity) prevents them from making a sharp turn around the plate, thus starting to move unsteady and *not* occupy the entire pipe's cross-section. Because of the sharp change in the velocity profile, a backwater zone, called eddy current (vortex), occurs in the back of the plate. After a while, the molecules move more evenly, and the layers occupy the entire pipe's cross-section. At this time, the flow behaves again as a fully-developed flow.
- **No Sudden Change Occurs in the Flow:** As a sudden change, consider a flowing liquid that enters a pipe, as shown in Figure 4. The layers next to the inside-wall surface behave like boundary layers (with low velocity). First, boundary layers occupy only part of the pipe's cross-section. As the liquid moves farther down the pipe, these layers thicken until they reach their maximum thickness when they reach the center of the pipe. Because boundary layers are affected by friction (f, resistance to motion), which exists close to the wall surface, the velocity of the layers at the wall is small (though *not* zero). But by the time they get to the center of the pipe, their movement increases gradually until they reach a velocity equal to the velocity of the stream layers. From this point on, the whole flow (boundary and stream layers) moves further in an organized and uniform manner, scientifically known as a **fully-developed flow**.

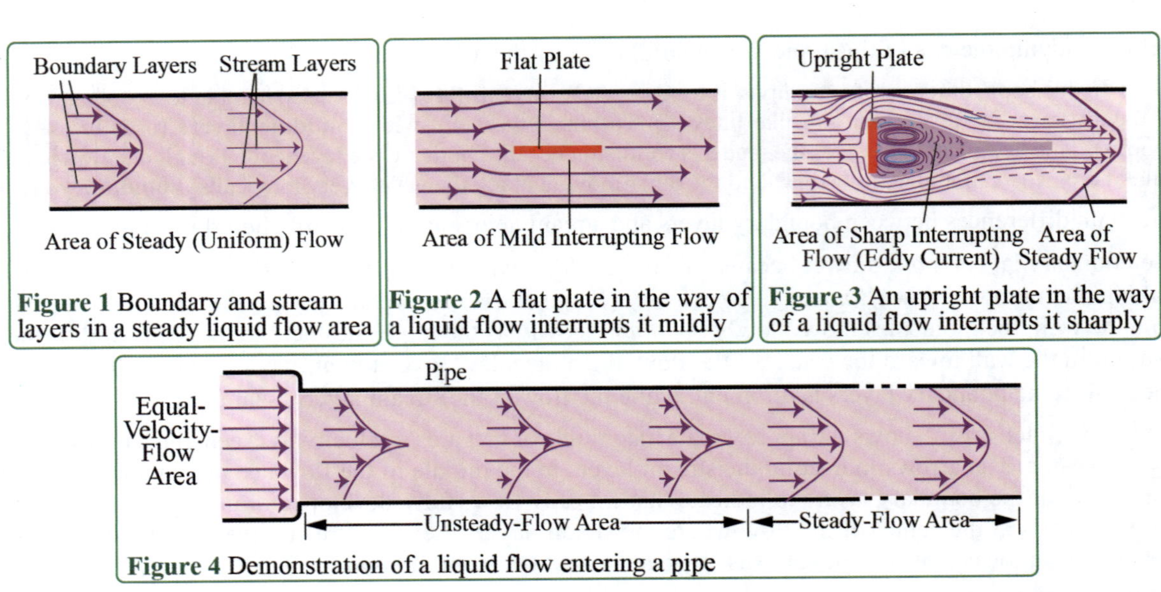

Figure 1 Boundary and stream layers in a steady liquid flow area

Figure 2 A flat plate in the way of a liquid flow interrupts it mildly

Figure 3 An upright plate in the way of a liquid flow interrupts it sharply

Figure 4 Demonstration of a liquid flow entering a pipe

B-44
BOURDON GAUGE

Discussed under PROCESS CONTROL OF CHEMICAL ENGINEERING.

B-45
BOYLE'S GAS LAW

Discussed under GAS LAWS.

B-46
BRASS

See COPPER BRASS.

B-47
BRIX

The term Brix (study Notes 1 and 2) refers to the percentage (by mass) of non-filterable solids of a solution measured by a refractometer. In refractometric tests, samples are filtered to remove suspended solid particles (filterable solids) before being tested by a refractometer.]

[Note 1: The term **Brix**, which comes from the inventor of the hydrometer scale, Adolf Brix (1798–1870, a German scientist), is *not* recommended because it is *not* self-defined. Scientists, instead, use the term refractometric dissolved solids to pass their points to the readers.]

[Note 2: Although the terms Brix, soluble solid, dissolved solid, and dry substance are used equally to indicate the same meaning but are different. **Brix**, **soluble solids**, and **dissolved solids** are correct terms when referring to a solution's nonfilterable solids. The **dry substance** is a correct term when referring to a solution's nonfilterable solids and filterable solids. The word **refractometric dissolved substance** is correct when referring to nonfilterable solids of a solution measured by a refractometer. This is because, in a refractometric test, the sample is usually filtered to remove suspended solid particles (filterable solids); before being tested by the refractometer.]

B-48

BROGLIE

Louis Broglie (more correctly, Lois Victor Pierre Reymond de Broglie, 1892–1987) was a French physicist who discovered the wavelike behavior of particles, known later as Broglie's theory of duality of matter. In this theory, which was his PhD thesis and brought him the Nobel Prize in Physics in 1929, Broglie said that all particles, particularly electrons, can act as particles and waves, but never both at the same time. In this sense, he proved that an electron has a wavelength (λ), later called **Broglie's wavelength**, which its value depends on that electron's mass (M) and velocity (V) in the form of $\lambda = h/(M.V)$, where h is Planck constant. This relationship is known as **Broglie's equation**.

As the person, Broglie was an honored man with the following personality:

- He was an **aristocrat** (a person of the highest rank in his society) who carried the French title of **duke**.
- He was interested in humanities (the study of human culture) but became a physicist.
- He never got married in his life.

[Planck, Einstein, Rutherford, Bohr, Heisenberg, Schrodinger, and Broglie can be named as the seven (7) top quantum physicists. And Newton, Faraday, and Maxwell as the three (3) top classical physicists. The ten (10) pioneers contributed to Physics more than all physicists.]

Broglie receives the Nobel Prize in physics in 1929 [Illustrated specifically for this book]

He was one of the key contributors of quantum physics for his discovery of wave-particle duality of matters

1928

He was elected the member of the French Academy of Sciences

1944

He and Heisenberg played a leading role in establishment of the European Organization for Nuclear Research, known by its French abbreviation CERN, in Switzerland

1954

Some of Broglie's scientific and memorable achievements

B-49

BROGLIE'S THEORY OF DUALITY OF MATTER

Broglie, in 1927, discovered that an atomic particle (atom, molecule, or ion), subatomic particle (electron, proton, and neutron), and quantum particle (a particle with *no* subparticle like the photon) could have wave-particle properties. His theory (his PhD thesis) was later called **Broglie's theory of duality of matter**.

Before Broglie's discovery, physicists thought matter consisted of particles with *no* wavelike property. As for this statement, it is helpful to know the following:

- Planck, Einstein, and Bohr previously proved the photon's wave-particle duality in their theories. Broglie further proved that atomic particles and particles of all matters have wavelike and particlelike properties.
- The electrons' wave property can be easily detected (because of their large wavelengths and extreme tiny mass, M), so it is better to describe an electron with its wave property.
- A molecule's wave property *cannot* be easily detected (because of its extremely short wavelength), so it is better to describe it with its particle property.

Broglie mostly tested his theory on the electron (an electronegative particle) to develop **Broglie's equation** to calculate its wavelength (λ), known as **Broglie's wavelength.**

$$\lambda = \frac{h}{M.V} \qquad (1)$$

Here, h is Planck's constant (= 6.625×10^{-34} J.s), M is the particle's rest mass, V is the particle's velocity, and $M.V$ is the particle's momentum (p).

Broglie's equation tells us the following:

- A particle's λ is inversely proportional to its M (the *larger* the M, the *smaller* is the λ of a wave).
- A particle's λ is inversely proportional to its p (the *larger* the p, the *smaller* is the λ of a wave).
- Every particle has some energy (E) because of mass-energy equivalency. And the amount of a particle's E depends on that particle's λ (the *smaller* a particle's λ, the *greater* is its E).
- When an electron moves around the nucleus, it has wave property, and when it emits (releases) energy as a photon, it has particle property.

Broglie's theory about electrons can be outlined as

- Electrons have wave property when they turn around the nucleus and particle property when releasing E in the form of the photon energy of a photon.
- The faster an electron rotates, the more its behavior is like a wave of energy.
- The slower an electron rotates, the more its behavior is like a particle of matter,

[Note: The concept of duality of matter depends on the properties of the matter under study. For example, an electron behaves like a **wave** when it is orbiting the nucleus and like a **particle** when it releases (or absorbs) a photon with a certain amount of energy. Similarly, the behavior of a photon can be visualized as a **wave** when it is moving and as a **particle** when it shines on the surface of a metal, causing the metal to release an electron, a phenomenon known as the photoelectric effect.]

B-50

BROMINE, CHLORINE, FLUORINE, AND IODINE

As halogens, these elements are discussed under the topic of HALOGENS.

B-51

BROWNIAN MOTION OF PARTICLES

Brownian motion is the random (irregular) motion of suspended solid particles in a liquid or the air. Under a microscope, particles suspended in a liquid appear to shake randomly because of the frequent colliding of their atoms with the liquid's atoms. In the air, colliding occurs between invisible atoms with visible particles.

First, this motion was observed by Robert Brown (1773–1858, Scottish botanist), from where the name Brownian comes. In 1905, Einstein used this idea in one of his papers, Motion of Suspended Particles, to say that Brownian motion can be explained as colliding atoms and molecules in a liquid with suspended particles, causing them to vibrate back and forth. In his paper, Einstein also calculated how far, on average, the Brownian particles can move in a certain time. For a particle 1 μm (= 10^{-6} m) long, he predicted this distance is about 6 μm/min.

Three years later, a French scientist could prove solid particles' Brownian motion by using an advanced microscope and more accurate calculations. In 2002, Brownian motion was observed more clearly under an electronic scanning microscope.

B-52

BTU

BTU (British thermal unit) is the heat energy (E_Q) unit in the US units. One BTU is the amount of E_Q that can increase the temperature (T) of 1 Lb of water by 1°F. 1 BTU ≈ 1 kJ, where J is for Joule.

B-53

BUBBLE POINT AND DEW POINT CALCULATIONS

Bubble-point (BP) and dew-point (DP) calculations are the steps used to calculate the concentration (composition) of vapor in a vapor-liquid mixture when the mixture's vapor phase is in equilibrium with its liquid phase. This mixture is in phase equilibrium or vapor-liquid equilibrium (VLE). [BP and DP calculations are useful in VLE calculations, particularly in the distillation process.]

Vapor-liquid mixtures involving bubble point (saturated liquid) or dew point (vapor phase) calculations are

- In the phase equilibrium condition, two phases in a mixture are in contact with each other for enough time until the transfer of molecules between the phases stops. And the mixture reaches an equilibrium (stable) condition.
- In the equimolal (equal-molarity) condition, when 1 mole of a liquid evaporates, 1 mole of its vapor condenses if the mixture's components have a similar molar enthalpy of evaporation.

Bubble-Point Calculation

The bubble-point (BP) calculations are steps that calculate the composition of **vapor** in a vapor-liquid mixture if the composition of the **liquid** is known and the mixture is in phase equilibrium at constant pressure (P) and temperature (T). [The word **temperature** refers to a liquid's bubble point temperature, defined as the T, at which the first bubble of a liquid's vapor begins to form.]

The BP calculations can fall under one of the following cases:

- **Bubble-Point Pressure Calculations:** The bubble-point pressure calculations (BPP calculations) are used to calculate the composition of a mixture's **vapor** and P if its liquid's composition is known and the mixture is in phase equilibrium at constant T. The diagram for 1 mole of a binary mixture is called the *PXY* diagram (*P*-versus-*XY* diagram), discussed under VAPOR LIQUID EQUILIBRIUM DIAGRAMS.
- **Bubble-Point Temperature Calculations:** The bubble-point temperature calculations (BPT calculations) are used to calculate the composition of a mixture's **vapor** and T if its liquid's composition is known and the mixture is in phase equilibrium at constant P. The diagram for 1 mole of a binary mixture is called the *TXY* diagram (*T*-versus-*XY* diagram), which is discussed under the same topic.

[Note: ChemEng mostly deals with calculations in which the liquid's composition (bubble point) and the system's P are known than the vapor's composition (dew point) and P.]

The next basic equation is used in BPP calculations of an ideal binary mixture when its vapor phase is in equilibrium with its liquid phase.

$$Y_A = P_A . X_A \tag{1}$$

In this equation, Y_A is the molar fraction (a unitless quantity) of component A in the vapor phase, X_A is in the liquid phase, and P_A is the partial pressure of A.

Note that if the liquid phase of the system acts as a non-ideal solution (mostly it is the case), we have to apply the activity coefficient (K_{Act}) of component A to Equation 1.

$$Y_A = P_A . X_A (K_{Act})_A \tag{2}$$

Dew-Point Calculation

The dew-point (DP) calculations determine the composition of a **liquid** in a vapor-liquid mixture if the **vapor** composition is known and the mixture is in phase equilibrium at a certain P and T (temperature). [The word **temperature** used here refers to a vapor's dew point temperature, defined as the T, at which a vapor begins to condense into its liquid.]

DP calculations can fall under one of the following cases:

- **Dew-Point Pressure Calculations:** The dew-point pressure calculations (DPP calculations) are used to calculate the composition of a mixture's liquid and P if the vapor composition is known and the mixture is in phase equilibrium at a certain T.
- **Dew-Point Temperature Calculations:** The dew-point temperature calculations (DPT calculations) are used to calculate the composition of a mixture's liquid and T if the vapor composition is known and the mixture is in phase equilibrium at a certain P.

[Note: For detailed bubble-point and dew-point calculations, refer to Chapter 7 of *Chemical Process Analysis*, authored by W.L Luyben and L.A. Wenzel.]

B-54

BUBBLE POINT AND DEW POINT PRESSURES

Bubble Point Pressure

The bubble-point pressure (correctly **liquid bubble-point pressure** and simply **bubble pressure**) of a liquid in a vapor-liquid mixture consisting of two components is the pressure (P) at which the first bubble of **vapor** begins to form when heating that liquid. This occurs slightly below that liquid's boiling point temperature.

Dew Point Pressure

The dew-point pressure (correctly **vapor bubble-point pressure** and simply **dew pressure**) of vapor in a vapor-liquid mixture consisting of two components is the P at which the first droplet (dew) of liquid begins to form when cooling it. This occurs slightly above that vapor's condensation point temperature (T_{CP}).

B-55

BUBBLE POINT AND DEW POINT TEMPERATURES

Bubble-point temperature and dew point temperature are useful data, particularly in the distillation's vapor liquid equilibrium (VLE) calculations. Usually, both are measured at P_{Atm} (atmospheric pressure). Figure 1 shows the boiling point diagram, and bubble point and dew point curves of a typical binary mixture with components A and B at P_{Atm}. In the figure, point A represents pure A, and B represents pure B. The **red** line represents the **liquid bubble-point curve** (X curve)**,** and the **silver** line represents the **vapor dew-point curve** (Y curve).

Bubble Point Temperature

The bubble-point temperature (correctly **liquid bubble-point temperature** and simply **bubble temperature** or **bubble point**) of a liquid in a vapor-liquid mixture consisting of two components is the temperature (T) at which the first bubble of vapor begins to form when heating that liquid. This occurs slightly below that liquid's boiling point temperature (T_{BP}).

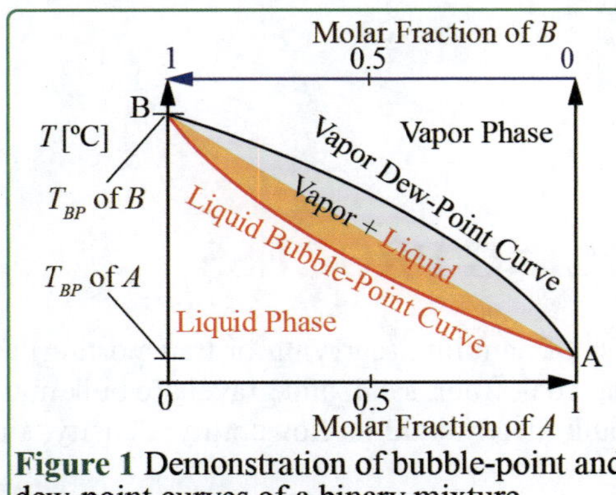

Figure 1 Demonstration of bubble-point and dew-point curves of a binary mixture

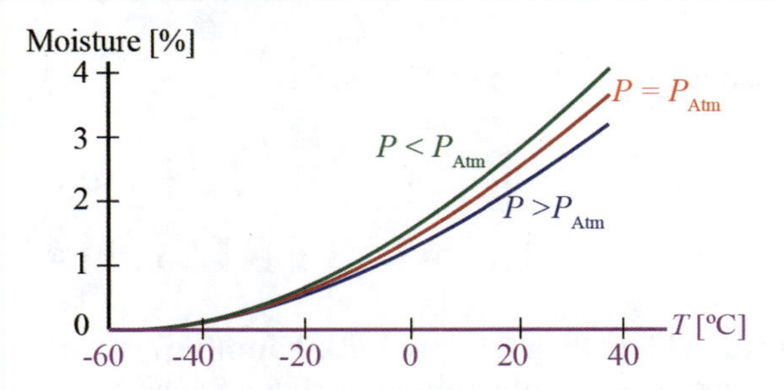

Figure 2 Relation between amount of vapor in air and air's temperature at P_{Atm} (**red** curve), at P lower than P_{Atm} (**green**), and at P higher than P_{Atm} (**blue**)

Dew Point Temperature

The dew-point temperature (correctly **liquid dew-point temperature** and simply **dew temperature** or **dew point**) of vapor in a vapor-liquid mixture consisting of two components is the T at which the first droplet (dew) of liquid begins to form when cooling that vapor. This occurs slightly above that vapor's condensation point temperature (T_{CP}).

As for the air, dew temperature is the *T*, at which water vapor in the air begins to condense into liquid water. In this way, it is called the **air's dew temperature** (air's dew point). In the early morning, we can see dew when *T* drops and water condenses on a solid surface. The air's dew *T* depends on the air's absolute humidity (W_{Abs}), so the *greater* the W_{Abs}, the *less* is the difference between the air's dew *T* and the actual air's *T*. Figure 2 shows the maximum humidity that air can contain at different pressures and temperatures.

Dew temperatures can be obtained from a steam table. If, for example, the partial pressure of water vapor is 2 kPa, then dew *T* can be directly obtained as the corresponding saturation temperature, 18ºC. This statement helps us to give a new definition of dew temperature. When an air-vapor mixture is cooled at constant *P*, the mixture becomes saturated. Further cooling results in condensation of the mixture

B-56

BUFFERING EFFECT

The buffering effect (also called buffering capacity) improves the stability of a solution under a certain condition by adding base or acid. If, for example, a certain low-PH solution goes under the evaporation process at a high temperature (*T*), its stability reduces notably. Thus, a base, like [$Ca(OH)_2$], can bring its PH up, making the juice thermostable (resistant to heating without alteration) during the evaporation process by establishing an equilibrium (stability) between the solution and its dissociated ions.

B-57

BUFFERS

A buffer is a solution that contains a weak acid and its salt or a weak base and its salt. A buffered solution can keep its PH almost constant when a small amount of acid or base is added or when the solution goes under evaporation. [In biochemistry, the word **nutrient buffer** refer to nutrient for bacteria growth.]

B-58

BULK DENSITY

Discussed under the topic of DENSITY.

B-59

BULK MATERIAL HANDLING PROCESS

Bulk material handling (simply **bulk handling**) is the process of handling (carrying or transporting) the dry solid bulk materials (simply **bulk materials**). Sugar, salt, cement, coal, flour, sand, and gravel are bulk materials. In bulk-handling operations, the most important properties of bulk material are its flowability, density, angle of repose, and moisture content.

Bulk-handling devices (equipment) are of different types: belt conveyors, screw conveyors, bucket conveyors, pneumatic conveyors, and drag-chain conveyors (elevators). In the first three, the transport of bulk material is performed by converting the kinetic energy (E_K) of an electric motor (simply **motor**) to mechanical energy (E_M) to move the carrying part on which bulk material is transported. In pneumatic transport conveyors, the transport of bulk material is performed by the pressured air. [Road truckers (truck dumpers), railcars (railcar dumpers), front-end loaders, and even ship loaders are also bulk-handling machines.]

Belt Conveyors: A typical belt conveyor (Figure 1) consists of a wide endless belt, two (or more) metal **pulleys** that move the belt, several rubber **rollers** that support the belt, and a motor to drive the belt. If a motor powers a conveyor's pulley, it is called a **powered belt conveyor**. And if it is unpowered, it is called an **idler belt conveyor**. The powered conveyors are usually run on a variable speed motor to move the belt at 1 to 2 m/s.

A pulley, which has a round shape, can have one (or more) groove that functions as a track for the belt and prevents slippage. The number of metal pulleys and rubber rollers in a conveyor is different (depending on the length of the belt used). The belt conveyors are designed to roll over both the pulleys and rollers.

Belt conveyors have a lot of applications in today's chemical plants because of their smooth and simple operation and little noise. The general properties of belt conveyors include the following:

- Their belts can be up to 240 m (= 800 Ft) in length and 60 to 240 cm (= 24 to 96 In) wide, with up to 500 t/h capacity. [Large belt conveyors have more drive motors.]
- They can handle up to 45° incline (depending on the carried-feed type) and horizontal and vertical curves through changes in elevation or direction. [The carrying feed's cross-section is the function of the surcharge angle, which is related to the angle of repose.]

Screw Conveyors: A typical screw conveyor (Figure 2) consists of a central shaft, a U-shaped shell (channel or trough), and a helical screw blade (ribbon), which is attached to the shaft of a motor. The shell is usually filled below the shaft with the bulk materials because filling causes the carrying material to be damaged by grounding between the screw and the shell.

Bucket Conveyors: A typical bucket conveyor (elevator), shown in Figure 3, consists of several buckets (scoops), a rubber belt (a metal chain in older models) to carry the buckets, and a motor to drive the belt (or chain). In addition, it has a feed chute for loading the buckets, a hopper for unloading the buckets, and a casing for protecting the handling material. The buckets are made of steel or plastic, depending on the use. The feed chute is sized to prevent the overloading of the buckets. A deflector is installed on each bucket to prevent the material from turning over. [Upright bucket elevators or inclined bucket conveyors have a control instrument (such as a zero-speed detector) to prevent them from running backward in motor failure or shaft breakage.]

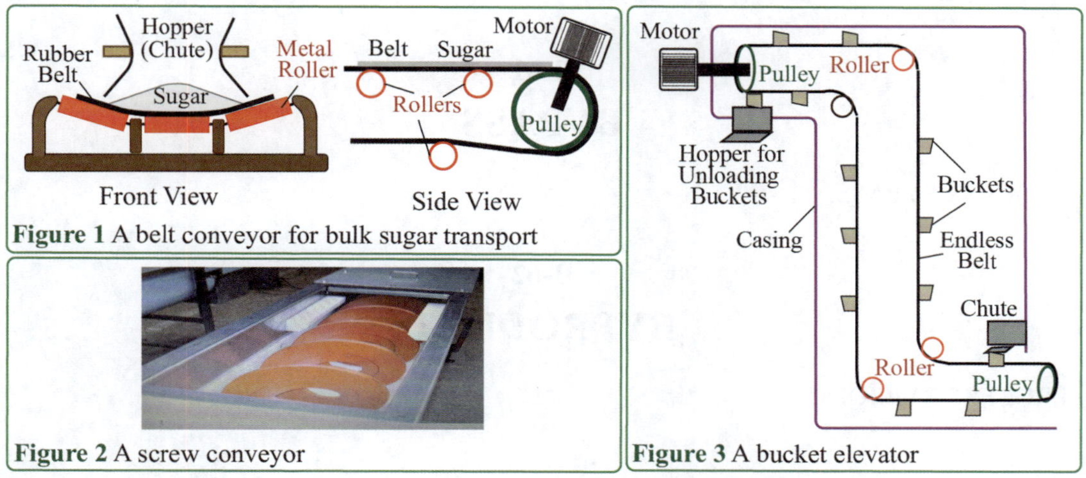

Figure 1 A belt conveyor for bulk sugar transport

Figure 2 A screw conveyor

Figure 3 A bucket elevator

Pneumatic Transport: In a pneumatic system, the pressured air sucks bulk material through a duck. The pressure and velocity of the used air are two important criteria for transporting material. The air's pressure is adjusted to be greater than the handling material needs (typically 3 times).

B-60

BUOYANT FORCE

Buoyant force (F_B, also called **buoyancy force** or simply **buoyancy**) is an upward force (F) exerted on a system by a fluid (liquid or gas). Based on Archimedes' principle, the F_B acting on a fluid is related to the displaced fluid's weight (w), fluid's density (D), displaced fluid's volume (V), and the displaced fluid's gravitational acceleration ($a_g = 9.81$ m/s^2).

$$F_B = w = D.V.a_g \tag{1}$$

Knowing that the term $a_g.D$ is called specific weight (w_{Sp}), the F_B equation can be written as

$$F_B = D.V.a_g = w_{Sp}.V \tag{2}$$

Based on this equation, F_B on a system that displaces 0.1 m^3 of water (with D of 1000 kg/m^3) will be

$$F_B = D.V.a_g = 1000 \times 0.1 \times 9.81 = 981\ (\text{kg/m}^3)(\text{m}^3)(\text{m/s}^2) = \text{kg.m/s}^2 = \text{N or } 221\ \text{Lb}_\text{F}$$

Some of the properties of F_B (Buoyant force) are outlined next.

- The F_B acts against the gravitational force (F_g), which acts downward as the result of a system's weight (w). Thus, when a freefalling system is in the air, a F_B is applied to the system by the air.
- The F_B exists in a fluid in a tank because P in the fluid changes with depth (*P on the bottom of the tank is greater than on its top.*) The pressure difference (ΔP) results in an upward net force known as F_B. When, thus, a system is placed in a liquid, the difference in P results in F_B.
- The F_B, according to Archimedes' principle, equates to the weight (F_g exerted on a system by a mass) of the fluid that is replaced by the system placed in a liquid.

If a system is either less dense than the liquid or has an appropriate shape (as in a boat), the F_B keeps the system floating on the liquid's surface.

B-61

BYPASS

Study PROCESS BYPASS.

B-62

BYPRODUCT

Study PROCESS BYPRODUCT.

C Section

LIST OF TOPICS

1. Cake, Mud, Sludge, and Slurry
2. Calorie, Calorimetry, and Calorimeter
3. Capacitance and Capacitors
4. Capillary Action
5. Carbohydrates
6. Carbon, Carbon Dioxide, and Carbon Monoxide
7. Carbon Sequestration
8. Carbonyl and Carboxyl Groups
9. Carboxylic Acids
10. Carnot Cycle
11. Catalysts
12. Cations
13. Caustic Soda
14. Cavitation
15. Celsius, Kelvin, and Fahrenheit Scales
16. Cement and Concrete
17. Central Processing Unit
18. Centrifugal Acceleration and Centripetal Acceleration
19. Centrifugal Force and Centripetal Force
20. Centrifugal Process
21. Centrifugal Pumps
22. Centrifuges
23. Centripetal Acceleration
24. Centripetal Force
25. Ceramics
26. CERN
27. Chain Reactions
28. Charge and Charge Number
29. Charles's Gas Law
30. Chelates and Chelation
31. Chemical Affinity
32. Chemical and Physical Changes
33. Chemical and Physical Properties
34. Chemical Bonds
35. Chemical Components
36. Chemical Composition
37. Chemical Compounds
38. Chemical Elements
39. Chemical Energy
40. Chemical Engineering
41. Chemical Engineering Process Units
42. Chemical Equation
43. Chemical Equilibrium
44. Chemical Formulas
45. Chemical Oxygen Demand
46. Chemical Polarity
47. Chemical Potential
48. Chemical Potential Energy
49. Chemical Potential Gradient
50. Chemical Processes
51. Chemical Process Design
52. Chemical Process Economy
53. Chemical Process Industry
54. Chemical Process Plant
55. Chemical Process Station
56. Chemical Reaction Order
57. Chemical Reaction Rate and Reaction Rate Constant
58. Chemical Reactions
59. Chemical Reactors
60. Chemical Reagents
61. Chemical Substances
62. Chemical Symbols
63. Chemical Systems
64. Chimney Effect
65. Chlorofluorocarbons
66. Chromatographic Process
67. Circulation, Recirculation, and Recycling
68. Clapeyron Equation
69. Clarification Process and Clarifiers
70. Classical Physics
71. Closed System
72. Coagulants
73. Coal
74. COD
75. CODATA

76. Coefficient of Friction
77. Coefficient of Variation
78. Coefficient of Viscosity
79. Coefficients, Constants, and Proportionality Coefficients, and Proportionality Constants
80. Cohesion
81. Cohesive Energy
82. Cohesive Force
83. Coke
84. Colliders
85. Colligative Properties
86. Collision Theory
87. Colloids
88. Color and Colorimetry
89. Color Charge
90. Colorants
91. Coloring Substances
92. Combined Gas Law
93. Combustion Engines
94. Combustion Reactions and Combustion Air Requirement
95. Components
96. Composite Particles
97. Composition
98. Compounds
99. Compressed Natural Gas
100. Compressibility Factor
101. Compressible and Incompressible Flows
102. Compressible and Incompressible Fluids
103. Compressors, Fans, and Blowers
104. Computer and Quantum Computer
105. Concentration, Concentration Difference, and Concentration Gradient
106. Concrete
107. Condensate and Condensate Trap
108. Condensation Film
109. Condensation Height
110. Condensation Point Temperature
111. Condensation Process
112. Condensed Substances
113. Condensed Systems
114. Condenser Water, Condensate, and Condensate Trap
115. Condensers
116. Conductive Diffusion
117. Conductive Diffusion Coefficient
118. Conductive Heat Transfer Coefficient
119. Conductive Heat Transfer Process
120. Conductivity
121. Conductometers
122. Conductors
123. Conformation
124. Conservation Laws
125. Conservation of Angular Momentum
126. Conservation of Energy
127. Conservation of Linear Momentum
128. Conservation of Mass
129. Conservation of Rotational Momentum
130. Conserved Quantities
131. Constant
132. Continuity Equation
133. Continuous Processes
134. Convective and Conductive Diffusion Coefficients
135. Convective and Conductive Heat Transfer Coefficients
136. Convective Heat Transfer Process
137. Convective Mass Diffusion
138. Convective Mass Transfer Coefficient
139. Cooling Approach Temperature
140. Cooling Effect Temperature
141. Cooling Load
142. Cooling Ponds
143. Cooling Process
144. Cooling Tower Characteristic
145. Cooling Towers
146. Copenhagen Interpretation of Quantum Theories
147. Copper Brass
148. Corrosion and Rusting
149. Coulomb and Coulomb's Law
150. Covalent Bonds
151. Covalent Compounds
152. CPU
153. Critical and Excess Masses
154. Critical Mass
155. Critical Moisture Content
156. Critical Point
157. Critical Pressure
158. Critical Temperature and Critical Pressure
159. Crosslinking Process
160. Crude Oil and Fuel Oil
161. Cryogenic Gases
162. Cryogenic Process
163. Cryogenic Temperature
164. Crystal Deformity

165. Crystal Occlusion
166. Crystal Size Distribution
167. Crystalable Solute
168. Crystalline Density
169. Crystalline Solids
170. Crystallinity
171. Crystallization Coefficients
172. Crystallization Law
173. Crystallization Process and Crystallizers
174. Crystallization Rate
175. Crystallization Water
176. Crystallizers
177. Crystals
178. Curie Temperature
179. Current
180. Current Density
181. Curvature of Spacetime
182. Cyclones

C-1

CAKE, MUD, SLUDGE, AND SLURRY

The terms **cake**, **mud**, **sludge**, and **slurry** are often used in the filtration and sedimentation processes. All three contain suspended solid particles (simply **suspended solids** or **suspended particles**) and dissolved solid particles (simply **dissolved solids** or **dissolved particles**) with different concentrations. The order of concentration of these compounds (from the thickest to the thinnest) is cake, mud, sludge, and slurry.

Cake: Cake (filter cake) is a fine thick mixture containing fine suspended-and-dissolved solids retained on a filter's filter medium or a filtering centrifuge's screen.

Mud: Mud is a watery mixture thinner than cake, so it has higher moisture than cake but less than sludge and slurry. Mud becomes slurry by further addition of a liquid (usually water).

Sludge: Sludge is slightly thinner than mud, containing fine suspended-and-dissolved solids. Sludge looks like a suspension solution (simply **suspension**). [The word **sludge** is often used in wastewater treatment operations, such as the product of an anaerobic reactor (Anamet).]

Slurry: Slurry is thinner than sludge. A lime slurry (used in wastewater operations for neutralization) and coal slurry are two examples of slurries. Slurry becomes cake by filtration in a membrane filterpress (see FILTERS) or thickening in a sedimenting centrifuge (see CENTRIFUGES).

Next, three (3) generalities about cake, mud, sludge, and slurry are outlined.

- The cake is *not* flowable (so it is *not* pumpable), but it is transportable. The mud, sludge, and slurry are flowable (pumpable) but *not* transportable.
- A **cake** is diluted by adding a liquid to become a **pumpable slurry**.
- **Mud**, **sludge**, or **slurry** can be thickened in a filter or centrifuge to become a **cake** (transportable).

[Note: It is generally cheaper to transport liquids than solids, so solids can be suspended in a liquid to form a slurry, transported by a pump (usually a centrifugal or piston pump) in a pipe.]

C-2

CALORIE, CALORIMETRY, AND CALORIMETER

Calorie

A calorie (cal) is the US unit of heat energy (E_Q), equal to 4.184 J (joule), so 1 cal is 4.184 times larger than 1 J. It is usually used to express E_Q in the following two ways:

- Gram calorie (small calorie, shown as **cal**) is the amount of E_Q needed to raise the temperature (T) of 1 g of water by 1°C (from 15 to 16°C).
- Kilo calorie (large calorie, shown as **Cal**) is the E_Q needed to raise the T of 1 kg of water by 1°C.

$$1 \text{ cal} = 4.186 \text{ J} \qquad \text{or} \qquad 1 \text{ kcal} = 1\text{Cal} = 1000 \text{ cal} = 4.186 \text{ kJ}$$

[Note: Commonly, the terms **Calorie** and energy are used equally. We say, for example, the energy content of 1 g sugar is 4 Calories (Cal or Kcal) = 4 000 calories (cal). So, when 1 g of sugar decomposes, its energy heats 4 g of the body's water by 1°C.]

Calorimetry

Calorimetry is a laboratory technique that uses a calorimeter to measure the E_Q (heat energy) transferred (released or absorbed) during a chemical reaction (simply **reaction**) under constant pressure (P) condition or constant volume (V) condition.

Calorimeters

Calorimeters are of two kinds: **constant-pressure calorimeters** and **constant-volume calorimeters**.

Constant-Pressure Calorimeter: This is usually used to measure the enthalpy change (ΔH) during a reaction. Its simple one consists of an insulated container with a lid and a thermometer. A solution sample's known mass (M) with known specific heat capacity (C_Q, simply **heat capacity**) is placed in the calorimeter to measure the ΔH, a. Because the container prevents heat transfer between the sample and its surroundings, a reaction in the sample changes its temperature (T), which can be read from a thermometer. The following two cases can occur:

- If T is increased, it indicates that the reaction is a heat-releasing (exothermic) reaction.
- If T is decreased, it indicates that the reaction is a heat-absorbing (endothermic) reaction).

Because the reaction in the calorimeter occurs at constant P and *no* heat transfer between the calorimeter and its outsides is assumed, the measured E_Q equates to the sample's enthalpy change ($\Delta H = E_Q$), which can be calculated from the sample's M (mass), C_Q (heat capacity), and ΔT (temperature difference).

$$\Delta H = M.C_Q.\Delta T = M.C_Q(T_2 - T_1) \quad (1)$$

Considering the calorimeter as the system and assuming no heat transfer between the system and its surroundings, the system's enthalpy balance (heat balance) balance can be given as

$$H_R + H_S = 0 \quad (2)$$

In this equation, subscripts R is for reaction and S is for sample (or solution).

An Example on Constant-Pressure Calorimeter

Calculate the enthalpy change per mole of HCL when 200 mL of 0.4 M HCL is mixed with 200 mL of 0.4 M of NaOH in a calorimeter, where M is for molarity. Because of the reaction, the T of the formed solution increases from 25 to 28°C. The heat capacity (C_Q) of the formed solution is 4.2 J/g.°C, and its D is 1.0 g/mL

$$M = 200 + 200 = 400 \text{ g}$$

$$\Delta T = T_2 - T_1 = 28 - 25 = 3°\text{C}$$

$$\Delta H = M.C_Q.\Delta T = 400 \times 4.2 \times 3 = 5040 = 5 \times 10^3 \text{ kJ}$$

Because the solution's T is increased during a reaction in a system, the reaction is heat-releasing, so a minus sign must be added to the front of the result value. The minus sign can be proved by using Equation 2, which consists of two enthalpy changes occurring in the system, one is related to the reaction (H_R), and the other is related to the solution (H_S), so

$$\Delta H = H_R + 5 \times 10^3 = 0 \qquad H_R = -5 \times 10^3 \text{ kJ}$$

The minus sign proves that the reaction is a heat-releasing (exothermic) reaction.

To calculate the ΔH per mole of HCl, we use the amount of HCl (200 g) and its molar mass (35.5 g/mole).

$$\Delta H = -5 \times 10^3 \times \frac{35.5}{200} = -888 \text{ kJ/mole}$$

Constant-Volume Calorimeter: This is usually used to measure the caloric value of food (like sugar) and the enthalpy of combustion of a fuel (like ethanol). Its simple one consists of a cylindrical container, about a beverage can, with thick steel walls and ends.

To perform a test, the container around the calorimeter is filled with a certain amount of water. The sample is placed in the calorimeter, filled with oxygen (O_2), and an electric spark is used to combust the sample with oxygen. The system's enthalpy (heat) balance can be expressed as

$$H_R + H_C + H_W = 0 \quad (3)$$

Here, subscripts R is for reaction, C is for calorimeter, and W is for water. Study the next Example.

An Example on Constant-Volume Calorimeter

Calculate the enthalpy (heat) change per gram of sugar (sucrose, $C_{12}H_{22}O_{11}$) and the molar enthalpy of sugar, where the molar mass of sugar is 342.3 g/mole. A constant-volume calorimeter with a heat capacity (C_Q) of 834 J/°C is used for the test. The container around the calorimeter contains 1500 g of water (with a specific heat capacity, C_Q, of 4.2 J/g.°C and density of 1.0 g/mL). Because of the combustion reaction, the water's T increases from 25 to 27.3°C.

In the calorimeter, sugar is oxidized to carbon dioxide gas (CO_2) and water (H_2O) in the following way:

$$C_{12}H_{22}O_{11}\ (s) + 12\ O_2\ (g) \rightarrow 12\ CO_2\ (g) + 11H_2O\ (l)$$

We can balance the system by combining Equations 3 and 1.

$$H_R + H_C + H_W = 0 \qquad \Delta H = M.C_Q(T_2 - T_1)$$

$$H_R + C_{Q.C}(T_2 - T_1) + M_W.C_{Q.W}(T_2 - T_1) = 0$$

$$H_R + 834(27.3 - 25) + 1500\times 4.2(27.3 - 25) = 0 \qquad H_R = -\ 16400\ J = 16.4\ kJ/g$$

At 342.3 g/mole, the sugar's molar enthalpy is −16.4 × 342.3 = −5614 kJ/mole.

C-3
CAPACITANCE AND CAPACITORS

Study ELECTRIC CAPACITANCE AND ELECTRIC CAPACITORS.

C-4
CAPILLARY ACTION

Capillary action is the rise of polar liquid in a narrow tube (called capillary tube), caused by the interaction of adhesive forces (F_A) with cohesive forces (F_C). Consider a laboratory glass (a polar compound) cylinder. The molecules of water (a polar compound with high adhesion) pull themselves up through the cylinder because the F_A acting on water molecules is stronger than F_C acting on them. In other words, capillary action (an upward force) is stronger than the gravitational force (F_g, a downward force). For example, in a tree, capillary action overcomes the F_g, causing water molecules to pull up through the capillary tubes of the tree's branches.

Similarly, in a laboratory glass cylinder containing a liquid, the adhesive forces in the liquid interact with the glass molecules, causing a curve at the liquid surface. The curving **phenomenon** (an observable event) is known as the meniscus. A meniscus occurs because of the strong adhesive forces between water and glass molecules. Figure 1 shows the formation of a concave meniscus in water when a glass tube with a small diameter is placed in water. This process can be divided into two steps: 1) Adhesive forces form a relatively sharp meniscus. 2) Cohesive forces start to minimize the surface area of the meniscus.

[Note that the diameter of a capillary tube plays an important role in the rise of a liquid in that tube (the *smaller* the diameter of a capillary tube, the *higher* a liquid rises in it), as shown in Figure 2.]

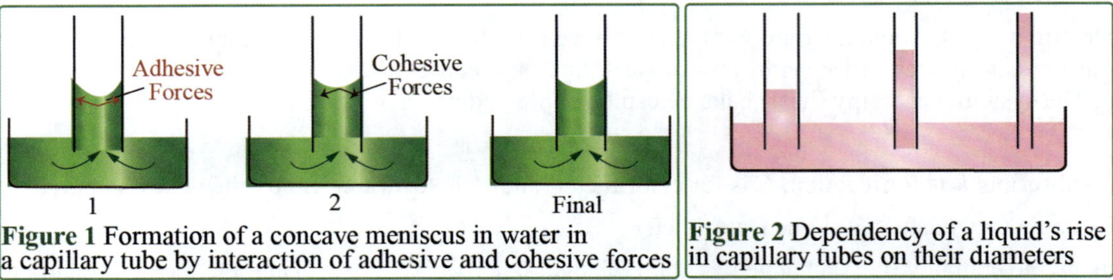

Figure 1 Formation of a concave meniscus in water in a capillary tube by interaction of adhesive and cohesive forces

Figure 2 Dependency of a liquid's rise in capillary tubes on their diameters

C-5

CARBOHYDRATES

Carbohydrates are a class of chemical compounds containing sugars, starches, and dietary fibers. Carbohydrates are composed of carbon (C), hydrogen (H), and oxygen (O). In the body, all carbohydrates eventually convert to **glucose** ($C_6H_{12}O_6$) to release energy (in dietary science calories). About half of the released energy is used to maintain our body's activities. The remainder is used to maintain the body's temperature (T). In addition, part of glucose is converted to **glycogen** (a polysaccharide) and stored in the liver and muscles to be used later. When the body needs energy (calorie), glycogen is broken down into glucose to maintain blood glucose levels.

Sugars (scientifically **saccharides**) are in the group of carbohydrates. Sucrose (read *soo'kros*; the chemical name for sugar), glucose (*gloo'kos*), and fructose (*froo'ktos*) are the most known saccharides.

C-6

CARBON, CARBON DIOXIDE, AND CARBON MONOXIDE

Carbon

Carbon (C) is a chemical element in group 14 and period 2 of the periodic table of elements. Its atomic mass number (N_A or A; the total number of protons and neutrons of an atom) is 12, and its atomic number (N_Z or Z; the total number of protons) is 6, so it has 6 neutrons (that is 12 – 6 = 6). Its atomic mass (M_A, the mass of one atom of an element) is 12, and its molar mass (M_{Mol}) is 12 g/mole. Carbon is only stable if all its 4 chemical bonds are used. For example, in a methane (CH_4) molecule, 4 covalent bonds connect a carbon atom to each hydrogen atom.

The most important types of carbon are the following two:

- **Graphite** is a crystalline carbon with carbon atoms arranged in a hexagonal form (see CRYSTAL). It exists in nature under standard conditions. Under high pressure and temperature, graphite converts to diamond. It is used to produce pencils, lubricants, and thermal conductors. Graphite is a good electric conductor.
- **Graphene** is another crystalline form of carbon, discovered in 2004 at the University of Manchester and won the 2010 Noble Prize in Physics for both of its discoverers. Graphene consists of carbon atoms arranged in a single thick layer with a hexagonal shape. Although it is light, it is the strongest known material (100 times stronger than steel). Graphene can be used in a transistor to switch electric current on and off. It can also be used in other fields, such as flexible touchscreens and nanotubes (nano-sized tubes).

- **Diamond** is a dense crystalline form of carbon arranged in a cubic form. It has high metastability (but *not* as high as graphene). Because of its high molecular rigidity, a diamond can be contaminated by very few impurities (such as element boron) at a low level (about one PPM, part per million). Diamond, unlike graphite, is a poor electric conductor.

Carbon has the following three isotopes with different N_A:

- Carbon-12 with 6 protons and 6 neutrons and, therefore, an N_A of 12,
- Carbon-13 with 6 protons and 7 neutrons and, hence, an N_A of 13,
- Carbon-14 with 6 protons and 8 neutrons and, thus, an N_A of 14.

Carbon-12 (or C-12), by far, is the most common isotope of carbon. C-12 is *not* a radioactive element (simply **radionuclide** or **nuclide**), as its nucleus is stable. Carbon-13 (C-13), also a non-radionuclide, makes about 1.1% of all-natural carbon. C-14, a less common isotope of carbon, is a radionuclide (because its nucleus is stable) with a halflife of 5730 years.

When C-14 (a radionuclide) decays (undergoes nuclear decay process), it changes to nitrogen (N-14; with 7 protons and 7 neutrons), a non-radionuclide, and emits beta rays (C-14 is a beta-ray emitter). [Fortunately, the amount of C-14 in the atmosphere is in trace amount. Because all three isotopes of carbon react with oxygen (O_2) to form carbon dioxide (CO_2) and plants absorb CO_2, all plants contain a tiny bit of radioactive C-14. And because all animals eat either plants or plant-eating animals, all living beings on the Earth contain a trace of C-14. Because carbon halflife is 5730 years, half of the C-14 atoms now present in a plant or animal that dies today will decay in the next 5730 years.]

Listed next are some other properties of carbon (C-12):

- Its electronegativity (E_{Neg}) is 2.5, making it a strongly electronegative element,
- Its enthalpy of combustion ($H_{C,}$) is 53 000 kJ/kg (22 790 BTU/Lb),
- Its molar enthalpy of formation ($H_{n.F}$) is zero.

Carbon Dioxide Gas

Carbon dioxide (CO_2) is a colorless gas with an acidic odor. CO_2 is composed of a carbon atom (C) covalently double bonded to two oxygen atoms (O=C=O). Some general properties of CO_2 are outlined next.

- Its molar mass (M_n) is 44 g/mole.
- Its content in the atmospheric air is low (0.04% by volume or 400 PPM) and is regulated by the photosynthetic process and greenhouse effect.
- Since the Industrial Revolution, the air CO_2 content has increased from about 300 to about 420 PPM in early 2020, leading to global warming.
- The major damage of the increase in CO_2 content in the air is that it reacts with water to form carbonic acid (H_2CO_3), a component of acid rain. This increases the PH of oceans, harming aquatic animals.

Listed next are some other properties of carbon dioxide (CO_2):

- Its conversion to carbon monoxide (CO) is difficult and slow.
- Its critical point occurs at approximately 31°C (= 87.8°F) and 73 Atm (= 1073 PSI).
- Its density (D) is 1.56 kg/m^3, about 60% greater than humid air (with D of about 1 kg/m^3).
- It sublimates by the direct change from its solid state to its gas state or condenses by the direct change from its gas state to its solid state.

[Note: CO_2 is *not* an air pollutant, but it absorbs infrared radiation released by the Earth. CO_2 and water vapor (two major greenhouse gasses) act like glass in a greenhouse. The term **greenhouse** is used because a glass greenhouse traps the heat energy (E_Q) of the Sun inside to keep the plants warm, the way the greenhouse gases act in the atmosphere, causing global warming. Allowing the Sun's rays to enter the atmosphere but preventing the infrared radiation from leaving the Earth is called the greenhouse effect.]

Carbon Monoxide Gas

Carbon monoxide (CO) is a colorless, odorless, tasteless gas with high **toxicity**. CO is composed of a carbon atom (C) covalently triple bonded to one oxygen atom (C≡O). Its molar mass (M_n) is 28 g/mole.

CO is formed in a furnace with insufficient oxygen to react with a fossil-based fuel to produce CO_2. The generated CO moves with the furnace flue gas to the atmosphere if it is *not* removed from the flue gas by a chemical way, such as contacting it with an adsorbent to oxidize CO to CO_2.

CO damages to the environment include the following:

- CO is one of the major air pollutants and is highly toxic. If breathed, it binds tightly with hemoglobin, preventing oxygen transport from the lungs to the rest of the body. In chemical process plants, CO forms in a furnace by burning a fossil-based fuel and moving its flue gas to the atmosphere.
- CO is an ozone-depleting compound, destructing the **ozone layer** (part of the atmosphere with ozone, O_3).

[The main source of carbon monoxide (CO) in chemical plants is coal-burning boilers. Using an adequate amount of airflow (at low excess air requirement, EAR) in the furnace combustion chamber decreases the CO content of the flue gas (advantage). Instead, it increases the NO content (disadvantage). In a pulp dryer, the amount of released CO is a function of the dryer combustion temperature (*T*). At 600ºC, the CO released from the dryer is relatively low, and as the *T* increases, the CO increases nonlinearly, reaching more than 400 PPM at over 900ºC. This occurs because higher inlet *T* burns the pulp, increasing CO production.]

C-7

CARBON SEQUESTRATION

Carbon sequestration (removal) is the process of removing CO_2 (carbon dioxide) from the atmospheric air to reduce the environmental pollution's negative effect and reverse (mitigate) global warming and climate change. We know that CO_2 is naturally removed (captured) from the atmospheric air by natural biological and chemical activities, so these activities can be artificially accelerated biologically (such as converting crops into the non-crop fast-growing plants) and industrially (like the carbon-capture-and-storage process).

Biologically, the atmospheric CO_2 can be reduced in many ways, such as **forestry** (planting trees on cropland to capture CO_2 from the atmosphere and grow biomass), **vegetation** (converting land into woodland, grassland, and steppes cause the reduction of soil's CO_2 by a notable amount), **carbon farming** (applying atmospheric CO_2 into the crop's soil, crop's roots, and crop's leaves), and more.

Industrially, carbon dioxide is mainly reduced by absorption into a liquid or solid.

In the process of absorption into a solid, CO_2 can be removed from a stream by reacting it with a metal oxide, like CaO (calcium oxide) or MgO (magnesium oxide), to form a stable carbonate precipitate (↓). Ca and Mg are found in nature abundantly in the form of silicates.

$$Ca_2SiO_4 + 2\ CO_2 \rightarrow CaCO_3\downarrow + SiO_2$$

$$Mg_2SiO_4 + 2\ CO_2 \rightarrow MgCO_3\downarrow + SiO_2$$

These reactions are heat-releasing (exothermic) reactions, so they occur naturally.

C-8

CARBONYL AND CARBOXYL GROUPS

A carbonyl group (a functional group) contains an aldehyde group (H–C=O) or a ketone group (–C=O). A carboxyl group is a functional group containing a –COOH group.

C-9
CARBOXYLIC ACIDS

A carboxylic acid is an acid that contains a carbonyl group (C=O) and a hydroxyl group (O–H) attached to a variable group (shown by symbol R), as shown in Figure 1. Acetic acid (HCH_3COO), which gives vinegar the sour test, and methanoic acid (H–COOH, also known as **formic acid**), which occurs in ants, are examples of carboxylic acids.

Carbonyl Group
Variable Group R
Hydroxyl Group
Acetic Acid (CH_3COOH)

Figure 1 General molecular structure of carboxilic acids (left) and acetic acid (right)

C-10
CARNOT CYCLE

The Carnot cycle, which was first developed by Sadi Carnot (1796–1832, a French mechanical engineer) in 1824, describes the stages that an ideal gas in a thermodynamic (heat-involving) engine (like a heat engine) performs some useful work (W) under ideal operating conditions. He proved that a thermodynamic system can only perform work when a temperature difference (ΔT) exists. And the performed work equates to the multiplying product of ΔT and the E_Q (heat energy) absorbed.

$$W = \Delta T . E_Q \tag{1}$$

In a Carnot cycle, heat energy (E_Q) is released isothermally by a hot reservoir and absorbed by a cold reservoir (see Figure 1).

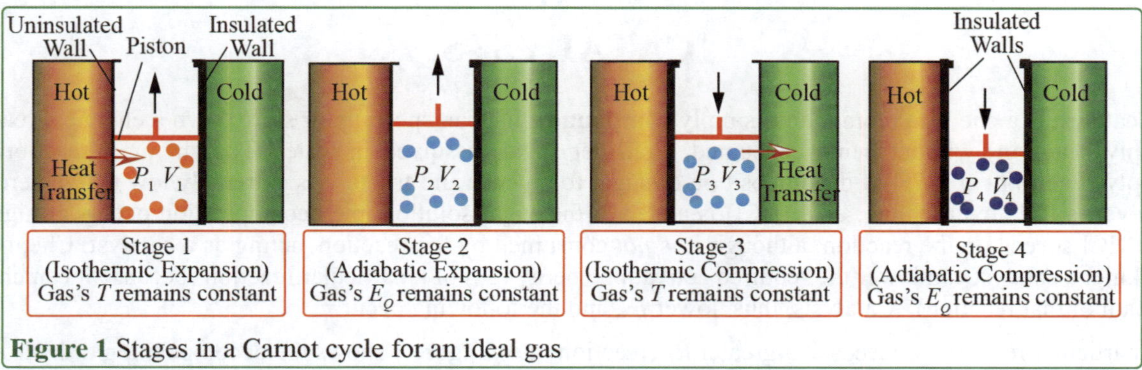

Figure 1 Stages in a Carnot cycle for an ideal gas

Considering an ideal gas (the system) in a cylinder, the gas goes through the next four (4) stages:

- **Isothermic Expansion (Stage 1):** In this stage, the gas (which is in heat transfer with the hot reservoir at T_H through an uninsulated wall) expands by reduction of pressure (P) in the cylinder. As the result of expansion, the gas pushes the cylinder's piston up, doing some W (work) on its outsides (surroundings). This expansion is isothermic because the gas's temperature (T) in the cylinder remains constant at T_H, as it is in heat transfer with the hot reservoir, but *not* with the cold reservoir, which is at T_L.

- **Adiabatic Expansion** (Stage 2)**:** In this stage, the gas (which is still in heat transfer with the hot reservoir) expands further in the cylinder by reducing P, so the gas pushes the piston further up, doing work on its outsides. This expansion is adiabatic because the gas's E_Q remains constant, as an insulated wall between the cylinder and the cold reservoir prevents the heat transfer between them.
- **Isothermic Compression** (Stage 3)**:** In this stage, the gas (which is in heat transfer with the cold reservoir at T_C) cools and, so, is compressed. As a result, outsides push the piston down, doing work on the system. The compression is isothermic because E_Q can be transferred from the cylinder into the cold reservoir through an uninsulated wall, so the gas's T remains constant in this stage (like the first stage).
- **Adiabatic Compression** (Stage 4)**:** In this stage, the gas (which is *not* in heat transfer with either of the reservoirs) is further compressed. This compression is adiabatic because the gas's E_Q remains constant (as the cylinder's both sides are insulated in this stage).

As seen in Figure 1, in the first-and-second stages of the Carnot cycle, the gas (the system) is expanding, and in the third and fourth stages, it is compressing. But the expansion and compression each go through two changes; isothermic and adiabatic. In the isothermic (T-constant) stage, a heat transfer (the transfer of E_Q) with surroundings occurs, while in the adiabatic (E_Q-constant) stage, *no* heat transfer with surroundings occurs.

After these experiments, Carnot calculated useful W (work) in a heat engine by using T_H (the highest T in the hot reservoir), T_C (the lowest T in the cold reservoir), and the E_Q transferred between the reservoirs, based on Equation 1.

$$W = \frac{\frac{T_H}{T_C}}{T_H} \times E_Q = \left(1 - \frac{T_C}{T_H}\right) E_Q \tag{2}$$

Then, he calculated the efficiency of a simple heat engine (E_H) as

$$E_H = \left(1 - \frac{T_C}{T_H}\right) \tag{3}$$

Although Carnot wanted to convert the highest possible E_Q into useful W in a heat engine, it was somehow far from 100% efficient (because of some losses of E_Q during the cycle).

C-11

CATALYSTS

A catalyst is a chemical compound (simply **compound)** that can speed up or slow down a chemical reaction (simply **reaction**) without being consumed. Consider sugar dissolved in water. The chemical reaction rate (simply **reaction rate,** R_R) of decomposition of sugar to glucose and fructose is extremely low (if *not* zero). If, however, a little hydrochloric acid (HCl) is added to the sugar solution, the decomposition occurs at high R_R. Here HCl speeds up the reaction, although it is *not* consumed by the reaction, acting as a catalyst. Chemically speaking, a catalyst can lower the required activation energy (E_a) of a particular reaction (because it can change the path of that reaction). Catalysts, thus, lower E_a, and the following occur:

- A particular reaction proceeds at a greater R_R (reaction rate). Figure 1 shows the decomposition of hydrogen peroxide (H_2O_2) and its required E_a with a catalyst (in this case, MnO_2) and without the catalyst. Note that without the catalyst, the decomposition process goes very slowly.
- A particular reaction proceeds at a lower temperature and pressure than required.

As a result of these advantages, catalysts can considerably reduce the production costs of a typical chemical process plant.

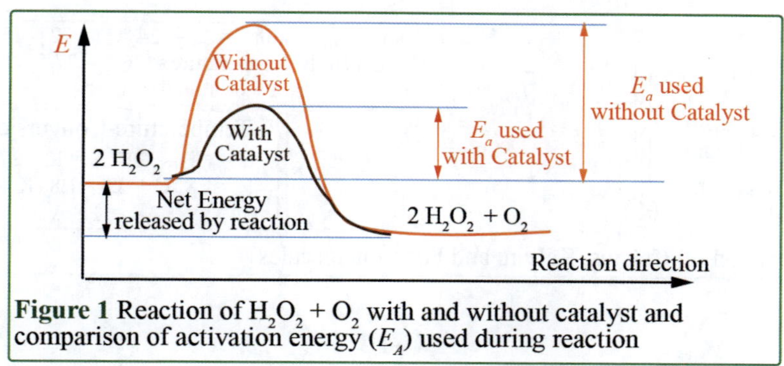

Figure 1 Reaction of $H_2O_2 + O_2$ with and without catalyst and comparison of activation energy (E_A) used during reaction

C-12

CATIONS

Study IONS, CATIONS, AND ANIONS.

C-13

CAUSTIC SODA

Caustic soda is a common industrial name for sodium hydroxide (NaOH), so it is discussed under SODIUM CARBONATE, SODIUM CHLORIDE, AND SODIUM HYDROXIDE.

C-14

CAVITATION

Simplified name for PUMP CAVITATION.

C-15

CELSIUS, KELVIN, AND FAHRENHEIT SCALES

Celsius scale (symbol °C) and Kelvin scale (symbol K, with *no* degree sign, °) are two ways of expressing the temperature (T) of a system in the SI units, and the Fahrenheit scale (°F) is used in the US units.

Celsius Scale (T_C): The T_C is based on 0°C for the freezing point temperature (T_{FP}) of pure water and 100°C for the water's boiling point temperature (T_{BP}), both at 1 Atm (atmospheric pressure, P_{Atm}).

Kelvin Scale (T_K): The T_K, which is used for expressing T of thermodynamic (heat-involving) systems, is based on absolute temperature (T_{Abs}, where $T_{Abs} = 0\ T_K = -273\ T_C$. Thus, the Kelvin scale uses T_{Abs} as its zero T and 373.15 as the water T_{BP}. The relation between T_K and T_C is $T_K = T_C + 273.15$

Fahrenheit Scale (T_F): The T_F is based on 32°F for the T_{FP} of pure water and 212°F for the water's T_{BP}, both at 1 Atm. Figure 1 compares the three scales and their conversion factors.

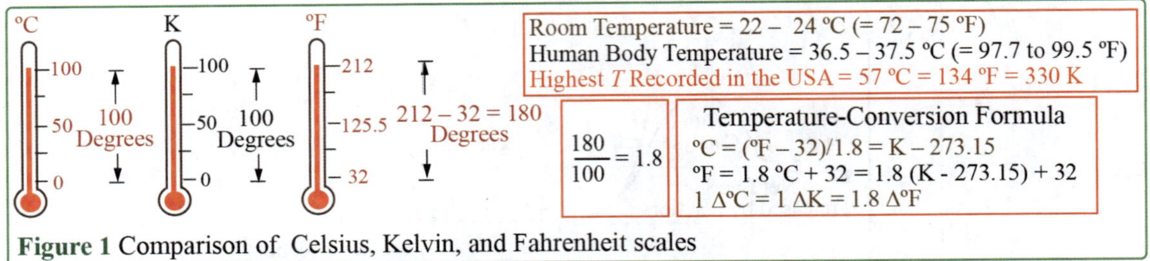

Figure 1 Comparison of Celsius, Kelvin, and Fahrenheit scales

C-16

CEMENT AND CONCRETE

Cement

Cement (also called **Portland cement**) is a silicate used as constructing material. [The word **cement** can be used in its generic sense to refer to any kind of adhesive. Our purpose in this book is the cement used as a constructing material.]

Cement mainly consists of silicon oxide (SiO_2), calcium (Ca), and aluminum (Al). It is produced by mixing limestone ($CaCO_3$), gypsum ($CaSO_4$), kaolin (Al_2O_3), and sand (SiO_2). The mixture (simply **mix**) is heated in a kiln at 1 450°C to form a melt, called the **clinker**, which is then cooled and ground to produce cement powder. During the heating process and at about 1 100°C, the decomposition of limestone occurs.

$$CaCO_3 \rightarrow CaO + CO_2$$

The main components of cement are tricalcium silicate ($3CaO\text{-}SiO_2$), dicalcium silicate ($2CaO\text{-}SiO_2$), tricalcium aluminate ($3CaO\text{-}Al_2O_3$), and tetra calcium aluminoferrite ($4CaO\text{-}Al_2O_3\text{-}Fe_2O_3$).

When cement reacts with water, it forms a **mortar** (a thick fluid) that can bind with other materials, such as bricks and stones.

Cement products are grouped into three types. Type 1 is used for general purposes, Type 3 is used for where the cement must set rapidly, and Type 3 has a low heat of hydration and is used for, say, dam (because the hydration reactions are extremely heat-releasing reactions). Cement is mainly used in the production of concrete.

Concrete

Concrete consists of cement, aggregates (sand, gravel, and crushed stone), slags (various metal oxides, such as MgO and FeO), and water. In some cases, an additive is added to a cement's ingredients to improve the concrete's physical properties, like the stiffness (hardness). Aggregates, which take about 60 to 70% of the concrete's volume, are fine (at the size of sand) or coarse (at the size of gravel). The aggregate size and quantity are selected to control a newly-produced concrete's thickness, workability, and future strength properties. The water-to-cement ratio at the time of making concrete and the reinforcement used also affect these elements.

When the concrete's ingredients are mixed, cement reacts with water to form a mortar (a thick fluid) that binds the concrete's ingredients together. The mortar is easily pourable and moldable into a desired shape. Gradually the mix goes through a series of hydration reactions to become stiff and then hard, known as the concrete. The concrete becomes hard after days.

Concrete is mainly used in foundation construction, roads, bridges, and dams. Its global usage is twice steel, plastic, wood, and aluminum. [The ready-mix concrete industry, the largest branch of the concrete industry, will exceed $600 billion in revenue by 2025.]

C-17

CENTRAL PROCESSING UNIT

A central processing unit (CPU) is a computer processor (such as a resistor, transistor, or capacitor) that carries the instructive data of a program for controlling a process, such as handling an input/output (I/O) operation. The main component of a CPU is an arithmetic logic unit (ALU), which is a digital electronic circuit that performs arithmetic and bitwise operations on integer binary numbers.

C-18

CENTRIFUGAL ACCELERATION AND CENTRIPETAL ACCELERATION

Centrifugal Acceleration

Centrifugal acceleration (a_C, also called **rotational acceleration** or **angular acceleration**) is the acceleration (a) of a rotating system that acts **away** from the system's circular path with radius R when the system rotates at a rotational velocity of ω (omega) around an axis or a central point.

$$a_C = R.\omega^2 \tag{1}$$

In words, this equation tells us that,

- The *greater* the radius R, the *greater* is the a_C.
- If car A drives at twice the speed of car B through the same curve, car A comparatively experiences 4 times a_C (because $2^2 = 4$), so it is more at the risk of flipping over.
- When driving a car, it is more difficult to make a sharp turn (a turn with a small curving radius) than a moderate turn (because a_C acts away from the rotating system's center, as shown in Figure 1).

The relation between V (the velocity of a moving system on a straight path, given in m/min or Ft/min) and ω (the rotational velocity of a system moving on a curved path, given in several rotations/min or RPM) is

$$V = R.\omega \qquad \text{or} \qquad \omega = \frac{V}{R} \tag{2}$$

Thus, a_C acting on a rotating system (such as the basket of a centrifuge) can also be given as

$$a_c = R.\omega^2 = R\left(\frac{V}{R}\right)^2 = \frac{V^2}{R} \tag{3}$$

Centrifugal acceleration is usually expressed in m/s^2 or Ft/s^2.

Centripetal Acceleration

Centripetal acceleration (a_{CP}) is the acceleration (a) of a rotating system that acts **toward** the system's circular path with radius R when the system rotates at a rotational velocity of ω around an axis or a central point.

As a numerical example, we can calculate the a_{CP} of a moving ball with a mass (M) of 0.3 kg while moving 1 m every second circularly with a radius (R) of 0.8 m. The circumference of the moving circle is

$$2\pi.R = 2\times3.14\times0.8 = 5 \text{ m}$$

With a circumference of 5 m, the velocity (V) of the ball is 5 m/s, so its acceleration (a) will be

$$a = \frac{V^2}{R} = \frac{5^2}{0.8} = 31 \text{ m/s}^2$$

We can use this result and the equation for Newton's Second Law of Motion ($F = M.a$), which also applies to the rotational motions, to calculate the ball's a_{CP}.

$$a_{CP} = M.a = 0.3 \times 31 = 9.3 \text{ kg.m/s}^2 = 9.3 \text{ N}$$

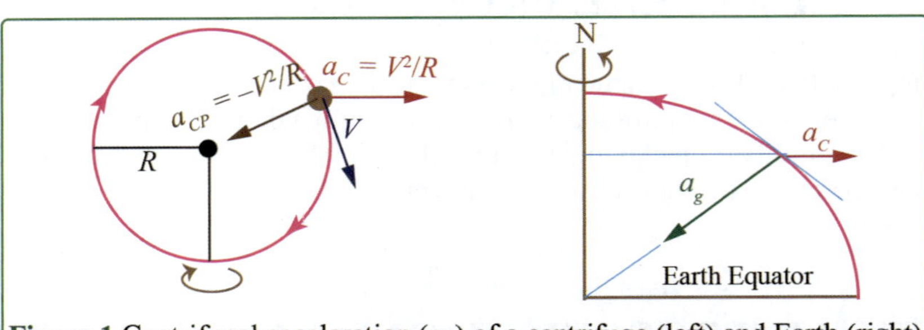

Figure 1 Centrifugal acceleration (a_C) of a centrifuge (left) and Earth (right)

C-19

CENTRIFUGAL FORCE AND CENTRIPETAL FORCE

Centrifugal force (F_C, also called **C force**) and centripetal force (F_{CP}) are related to a rotating system, acting in different directions; F_C acts **away** from the center of a rotating system, and F_{CP} **toward** the axis of rotation. In short, F_C is a disoriented force, and F_{CP} is an oriented force. These forces are discussed next in more detail.

Centrifugal Force

Centrifugal force (F_C, also called C-force) is a center-away force (F) that acts **parallel** to the axis of a rotating system and tries to pull the system **away** from its circular path when the system rotates around an axis or a central point. The two (2) important properties of F_C are outlined next.

- It is only present when a system is rotating, and
- It is the opposite of the centripetal force (F_{CP}).

Outlined next are the two (2) important differences between F_C and F_{CP}:

- F_C acts away from the center of rotation, away from the curvature of the path, while F_{CP} acts toward the center of rotation, toward the curvature of the path.
- F_C keeps the rotation out of its circular path and creates an out-of-balance rotation, while F_{CP} tries to keep the rotation on its circular path to prevent it from out-of-balance rotation.

As a simple example, tie one end of a string to your finger and another end to a small object with mass M (see Figure 1) and rotate the string by your finger. The F_C is the force that acts parallel on the string away from the center of rotation. And the force, which your finger applies **perpendicularly** (vertically at 90° angle) on the string toward the center of rotation to keep the string on its circular path and prevent it from out-of-balance rotation, is F_{CP}.

Consider the basket of a vertical-shaft centrifuge, which rotates horizontally like a household clothing washer. F_C, which acts horizontally away from the basket's shaft (the center of rotation), forces the feed farther away from the shaft toward the wall of the basket and, from there, forces the liquid through the basket's screen. Figure 2 shows the direction of F_C and F_{CP} in the rotating basket of a centrifuge. In this figure, ω (omega) is the rotational velocity of the basket ($\omega = \alpha/t$, where a is the **rotational angle** in radian and t is time)

In the centrifugal process, the F_C is more important than F_{CP} because it forces the feed toward the basket's wall. Similarly, in a centrifugal pump (see PUMPS), the F_C pushes the liquid out when the pump's shaft rotates at a high-but-uniform rotation (revolution). So, F_C is the only factor that causes the reduction in the liquid-removal time, compared with a non-centrifugal process (a process just under gravitational force, F_g).

Under the topic of CENTRIFUGAL PROCESS, the equations for F_C and F_{CP} were derived as

$$F_C = M.a_C = M\frac{V^2}{R} = M\frac{2V^2}{d} \quad (1)$$

$$F_{CP} = -M.a_C = -M\frac{V^2}{R} = -M\frac{2V^2}{d} \quad (2)$$

M is the mass of the rotating system (in kg), a_C is the centrifugal acceleration (in m/s^2), V is the centrifuge basket's rotational velocity (in m/s), and R is the basket's radius (in m; $R = d/2$, where d is for diameter), so F_C becomes in kg.m/s^2 = N (Newton). F_{CP} is also expressed in N. [Equation 2 got a minus sign because F_{CP} acts backward, toward the center of the rotating system.]

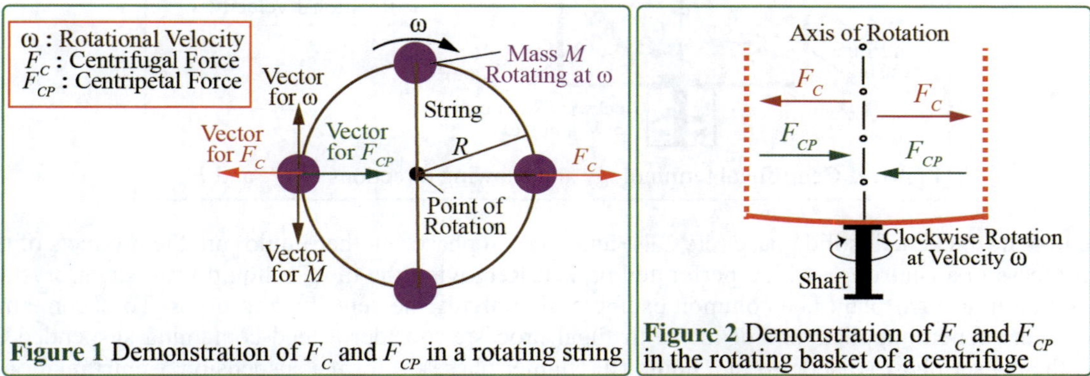

Figure 1 Demonstration of F_C and F_{CP} in a rotating string

Figure 2 Demonstration of F_C and F_{CP} in the rotating basket of a centrifuge

Centripetal Force

Centripetal force (F_{CP}) is a center-oriented force that acts **perpendicularly** (vertically at a 90° angle) toward the axis of a rotating system and tries to make it follow a circular path when the system rotates around an axis or a central point. The three (3) important properties of F_{CP} are outlined next.

- It is only present when a system is rotating,
- It is the opposite of the centrifugal force (F_C), and
- It continually changes the direction of the rotating system, but *not* its velocity.

C-20
CENTRIFUGAL PROCESS

BASICS

As a process unit of ChemEng, centrifugation is a separation process performed in a centrifuge to separate suspended solid particles (simply **solid particles** or **suspended particles**) from a suspension solution (simply **suspension**). The cause (driving force) of the centrifugation is the centrifugal force (F_C), which is created by the rotation of a centrifuge's basket (Figure 1). The F_C has the next two properties: 1) It is much stronger than gravitational force (F_g). 2) It acts horizontally sideward, while F_g acts vertically downward.

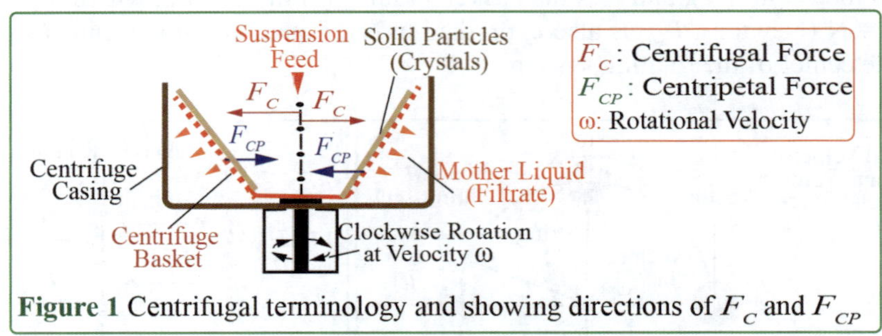

Figure 1 Centrifugal terminology and showing directions of F_C and F_{CP}

A concentrated (thickened) solid phase (crystals) and a liquid phase (mother liquid) are the products of the centrifugal process in a centrifuge with a perforated basket. Removing the mother liquid from sugar crystals after crystallization in a sugar plant is a common example of applying the centrifugal process. To become more familiar with the general applications of the centrifugal process, consider a feed containing suspended crystals (usually, the denser phase) dispersed in a liquid (the lighter phase) to form a suspension. Centrifugation can be done on this suspension to perform the following:

- Remove mother liquid from crystals to increase the purity of the crystals, so-called **purification**,
- Classify different-size crystals into two fractions, so-called **classification**,
- Settle crystals in the form of sediment, so known as sedimentation,
- Reduce water content to produce a cake, so-called **thickening**.

The listed cases have a wide range of applications. Centrifugation separates two immiscible liquids based on their density differences (ΔD) in an oil plant. In a wastewater treatment plant, it is used to decrease the water content in sludge to produce filter cake (which is suitable for transport). **Gas centrifuges** (discussed under CENTRIFUGES) are used in uranium enrichment in the nuclear industry,

In some centrifuges, the **basket** (bowl) is mounted on a vertical **shaft**, driven by a vertically-mounted drive motor (simply motor or drive) from the top. Hence, the basket rotates horizontally (Figure 2). The design is the same in centrifuges, but the shaft is driven from the bottom (Figure 3).

As a result of the basket's high rotation around the centrifuge's **shaft** (the axis of rotation), the following two forces are formed in the basket (see Figure 4):

- Centrifugal Force (F_C)**:** The F_C acts horizontally away from the basket's shaft (the center of rotation) and toward the basket's wall. The F_C, which is much greater than F_g, acts as a force (F) to push the feed's particles farther away from the shaft, toward the basket's wall. [Thus, the level of the particles at the basket's wall is higher than at the shaft.] The quantity of F_C depends on the basket's rotational velocity (ω), so the *greater* the ω, the *greater* is the F_C. The F_C makes the centrifugation a highly-efficient separation process compared with a non-centrifugal process (under only F_g, known as **gravitational sedimentation** or simply sedimentation).

- Centripetal Force (F_{CP}): In centrifugation, F_{CP} acts vertically toward the basket's shaft.

Listed next are two important differences between F_C and F_{CP}:

- The F_C acts away from the center of rotation (away from the curvature of the path) toward the basket's wall. Instead, the F_{CP} acts toward the center of rotation (toward the curvature of the path).
- The F_C keeps the rotation out of its circular path and creates an out-of-balance rotation. Instead, the F_{CP} tries to keep the rotation on its circular path and prevent out-of-balance rotation.

In centrifugation, however, F_C is much more important than F_{CP} because it is the F_C that forces a liquid to move toward the basket's wall and out of its screen's holes.

Based on the type of centrifuge that is used in a particular operation, the centrifugal process can be classified into three major classes: 1) Centrifugal filtration process, 2) Centrifugal sedimentation process, and 3) Gas centrifugal process.

Centrifugal Filtration Process

A centrifuge used for filtration has a basket whose wall is perforated (slotted), and a filtering medium (made of canvas or metal woven cloth) covers the wall. [These are known as **filtering centrifuges** (filtration centrifuges) or commonly **centrifuges**.]

Consider a suspension feed, which contains a solid phase (usually, the denser phase) dispersed in a liquid phase (usually, the lighter phase), placed in the basket of a filtering centrifuge, as shown in Figure 4. As a result of the basket's rotation along its vertical axis (the shaft) at high-and-uniform rotation, an F_C is developed, which forces the solid particles toward the wall of the basket and builds, so-called a filter cake (later – just cake) of solids on the filtering medium of the basket. The F_C also forces the liquid (the filtrate) through the cake, the filtering medium, and the holes of the basket's wall. Unlike sedimentation, centrifugal separation does *not* require a difference in density (D) between the two phases. If there is a density difference, centrifugal sedimentation is preferred because it usually operates faster, producing greater efficiency than centrifugal filtration.

Centrifugal Sedimentation Process

Centrifuges used for sedimentation (also called **settling**, **decantation**, or **clarification**) have an **imperforated** (non-perforated) basket, so known as **sedimenting** (decanting) **centrifuges**. Consider the same feed as in the previous case, but it is placed in the basket of a sedimenting centrifuge. The F_C causes the solid particles to move away from the basket's shaft to build a denser layer (in the form of a ring) on the basket wall. Unlike in a filtering centrifuge, the liquid moves on the opposite side toward the shaft and builds a liquid layer next to the denser layer, as shown in Figure 5.

A centrifugal sedimenting centrifuge can separate a mixture of solid-liquid, liquid-liquid, solid-liquid-solid, liquid-liquid-solid, or two immiscible liquids. In most cases, centrifugal sedimentation is performed to settle fine solid particles dispersed in a liquid. Such a process is called sedimentation (clarification) when the clarity of the liquid phase is of prime concern. And the term **classification** is used when dispersed particles are different in densities and sizes, so separation of the particles into two fractions is required. And the term **thickening** is used when a solid-settling process is performed to form a concentrated stream.

As shown in Figure 6, when a mixture of two **immiscible liquids** with different densities is in a sedimenting centrifuge, and the centrifuge's basket is at rest (non-rotating), the heavy liquid forms a layer on the bottom of the basket under a layer of light liquid. Figure 7 shows the same centrifuge, but its basket is now rotating. As a result of F_C, two (2) layers are formed. The heavy liquid forms a layer next to the inside wall of the basket, and the light liquid forms a layer next to the heavy liquid toward the shaft.

Gas Centrifugal Process

The gas centrifugation is performed in special centrifuges (called **gas centrifuges**), with different characteristics than ordinary centrifuges. A typical gas centrifuge is shown in Figure 8 under CENTRIFUGES.

While filtering and sedimenting centrifuges operate at normal speeds of 1000 to 2000 R/min (depending on their duties), gas centrifuges act at high speeds (around 80 000 R/min). The most important application of the gas centrifugal process is the uranium enrichment process to separate uranium-235 from uranium-238.

In the centrifugal station of a uranium enrichment plant, the gaseous uranium hexafluoride (UF_6) is passed through a series of gas centrifuges called the **cascade**. The F_C in each centrifuge pushes the heavier uranium 238 (U-238, the unwanted component) closer to the wall of the centrifuge's rotor (the basket) than the lighter uranium 235 (U-235, the wanted component). As a result, the gas closer to the wall becomes depleted (reduced) in U-235, whereas the gas near the center of rotation becomes slightly enriched in U-235. Then the stream that is slightly enriched in U-235 is directed into the next stage of the cascade, while the slightly depleted (reduced) stream is recycled back into the previous stage of the cascade. This process is repeated many times in the cascade until the desired level of enrichment is achieved. [In general, detailed information is unavailable about the gas centrifugal process and gas centrifuges (because of the secrecy of their usage in the nuclear industry.)]

Centrifugal sedimentation is primarily chosen over the centrifugal filtration when the solid particles are fine and when,

- A higher density of the solid phase over the liquid phase is a requirement,
- The high cake purity through cake washing is *not* a requirement,
- The minimal residual cake moisture is *not* a requirement.

[Note 1: Centrifugal sedimentation is mostly used to separate solid particles dispersed in a liquid. If solid particles are too small to be settled easily, a coagulant is added to the feed.]

[Note 2: In a cake bed, solidosity + porosity = 1, where **solidosity** is the volume fraction of the cake's solids and **porosity** is the volume fraction of the cake's empty spaces.]

Besides sufficient F_C, the next listed factors are important in having a high **centrifugal separation rate** (C_R, discussed later) in a filtering centrifuge or a high **centrifugal settling rate** in a sedimenting centrifuge.

- Low liquid phase viscosity (η),
- High basket's rotational velocity (ω),
- Large density difference (ΔD) between two phases,
- Sufficient solid fraction (*not* more and *not* less than enough), and
- Large solid particles with high porosity produce a transportable cake.

Centrifuge solid yield (also called **centrifuge efficiency**), the percentage ratio of the mass of the solid particles leaving and entering the centrifuge in the feed, is a good indication on both operational and mechanical sides of a centrifugal process. For a given centrifuge, the centrifuge efficiency is usually evaluated by

- The developed F_C (the *greater* the F_C, the *more* efficient is the centrifugal process),
- The thickness of the cake layer (the *thicker* the layer, the *more* efficient is the centrifugal process),
- The amount of cake's moisture (the *lower* the cake's moisture content, the *more* efficient is the process). [The cake's moisture content depends on the cycle time for a batch centrifuge and solid content for a continuous centrifuge, both being discussed under CENTRIFUGES.]

Design-wise, the inside diameter (d) of a centrifuge basket determines its operating speed (the *larger* the d, the *slower* it can be operated) and, consequently, the lower its efficiency. For example, a centrifuge with a basket of 1 m in diameter can be operated at 2 200 rotations per minute (R/min or RPM) without any vibration. But a 1.4 m basket can be operated as such only up to 1 800 RPM with no vibration.

The F_C depends on the next factors.

- Radius (R) of the centrifuge's basket,
- Speed of rotation (RPM) of the basket, and
- Density (D) of the particles under the centrifugal process.

If R and RPM are fixed, the controlling factor is the D of the particles (the *heavier* the particles, the *greater* is the F_C acting on them). Suppose two liquids are in a centrifuge's basket when one is twice as dense. The F_C per unit volume will be twice as great for the heavier liquid as the lighter liquid, so the heavy liquid passes the lighter liquid and moves toward the basket wall (as seen in Figure 5).

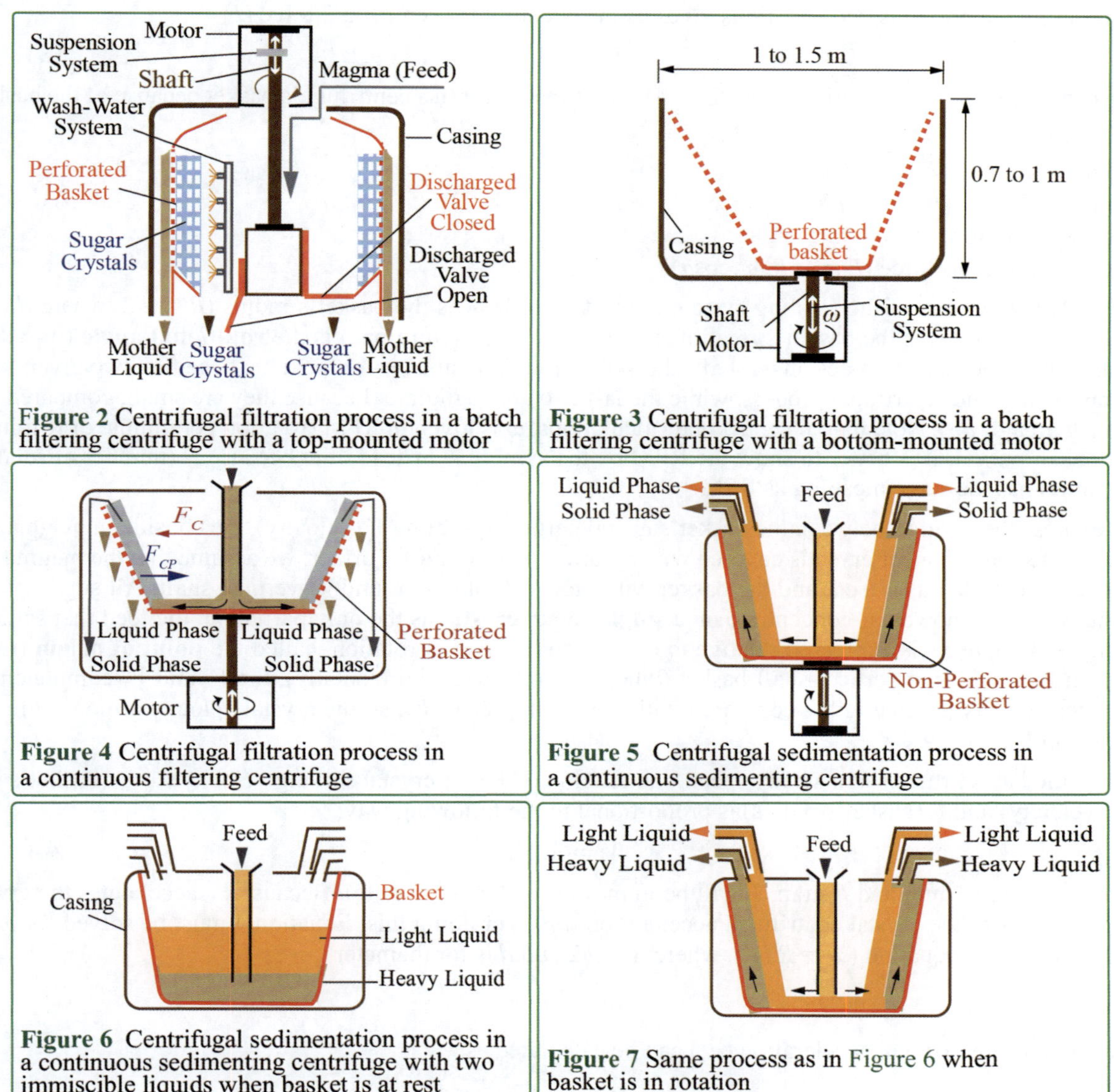

Figure 2 Centrifugal filtration process in a batch filtering centrifuge with a top-mounted motor

Figure 3 Centrifugal filtration process in a batch filtering centrifuge with a bottom-mounted motor

Figure 4 Centrifugal filtration process in a continuous filtering centrifuge

Figure 5 Centrifugal sedimentation process in a continuous sedimenting centrifuge

Figure 6 Centrifugal sedimentation process in a continuous sedimenting centrifuge with two immiscible liquids when basket is at rest

Figure 7 Same process as in Figure 6 when basket is in rotation

Centrifugal Equations

We start this subtopic with the mathematical result of Newton's Second Law (the force law), which says a force (F) acting on a system equates to that system's mass (M) multiplied by its acceleration (a),

$$F = M.a \tag{1}$$

We know that the centrifugal acceleration (a_C) equates to the acceleration (a) of a rotating system that acts **away** from the system's circular path with radius R when the system rotates at a rotational velocity of ω (omega) around an axis or a central point.

$$a_C = R.\omega^2 \tag{2}$$

Combining the previous two equations gives us the equation for centrifugal force (F_C).

$$F_C = M.R.\omega^2 \tag{3}$$

We can now apply this equation to the four (4) forces that occur in a centrifuge's basket because of the basket's rotation (see Figure 8).

- Centrifugal force ($F_C = M.R.\omega^2$),
- Centripetal force ($F_{CP} = -M.R.\omega^2$),
- Displacement force ($F_D = M.R.\omega^2.\sin\alpha$),
- Ordinary (normal) force ($F = M.R.\omega^2.\cos\alpha$).

Here, M is the mass of the rotating system (basket + feed), R is the basket's radius ($R = d/2$, where d is for diameter), ω (omega) is the basket's rotational velocity ($\omega = \alpha/t$), α (alpha) is the **rotational angle** (in radian), through which the basket rotates on its shaft (the axis of rotation), and t is for the time. [The first two given forces are important in the centrifugal process, while the last two are negligible (because they are small, compared with the much greater F_C). Note that in centrifugal calculations, ω is given in RPM (rotation per minute or R/min). In equations, however, it is better to show the RPM by the symbol N instead of ω because N (number of rotations per minute) has the same meaning as RPM.]

To express the relation between the basket's ω and particles' settling V (velocity), we consider a magma consisting of suspended sugar crystals covered with syrup (mother liquid). Further, we assume that the magma is in the centrifuge basket as a feed, and the basket with radius R rotates around its vertical shaft. All sugar crystals are under F_C. We, however, concentrate on a **single sugar crystal** as the only particle in the feed that settles at velocity V. Usually, v is expressed relative to a point on the axis of rotation, called the **point of origin** (O), as shown in Figure 9. In a vertical-shaft basket (whose basket rotates horizontally), the V_Z and V_Y components of the vector velocity are negligible compared with the much greater V_X, so the crystal velocity at point P mainly depends on V_X.

When the basket rotates at a steady speed, the relation of V (the crystal settling velocity) to ω (basket's rotational velocity) and R (basket's radius) is proportional in the following way:

$$V = R.\omega \tag{4}$$

If ω is given in 1/min and R in m, V will be in m/min (meter per minute). Because F_C accelerates the crystal, we must calculate the crystal centrifugal acceleration (a_C). For doing this, Equation 4 must be solved for ω and substituted into a_C equation ($a_C = R.\omega^2$), where $R = d/2$ and d is for diameter.

$$\omega = \frac{V}{R} \tag{5}$$

The basket's centrifugal acceleration (a_C) can be calculated as

$$a_C = R.\omega^2 = R\left(\frac{V}{R}\right)^2 = \frac{V^2}{R} = \frac{2V^2}{d} \tag{6}$$

In general, to accelerate a system with mass M that settles at velocity V, a centrifugal force (F_C) must be applied. Then, the F_C can be defined by its relation to M (mass) and a_C.

$$F_C = M.a_C = M\frac{V^2}{R} = M\frac{2V^2}{d} \tag{7}$$

Similarly, **centripetal force** (F_{CP}) at radius R is defined as

$$F_{CP} = -M.a_C = -M\frac{V^2}{R} = -M\frac{2V^2}{d} \tag{8}$$

In Equations 7 and 8, M is the mass of the rotating feed (in kg), a_C is the centrifugal acceleration (in m/s^2), V is the settling velocity (in m/s), and R is the rotational radius (in m), so F_C becomes in kg.m/s^2 = N (for Newton), which is the unit of force.

Equation 7 tells us that doubling the M of a rotating feed increases the F_C by 2, but doubling the basket's V (or RPM) increases the F_C by 4.

F_C tries to force the system farther away from the axis of rotation. For example, in a sugar factory centrifuge's high-rotating basket, the mother liquid from crystals is removed because of F_C (the F_C forces the liquid to move toward the basket's wall and out of the basket's screen). So, F_C is the only factor causing the decrease in the syrup-removal time compared with a non-centrifugal process (centrifugation just under F_g), where F_g is the gravitational force. Thus, it is important to know a centrifuge's separation ability when comparing it. The **centrifugal separation factor** (G_F) and **centrifugal separation rate** (C_R) express a centrifuge separation ability. These are discussed next.

Centrifugal Separation Factor

The centrifugal separation factor (G_F, also called **G-factor**, or simply G) compares the separation ability of a centrifugal operation with a non-centrifugal operation (a separation process under only F_g). G_F compares a centrifugal operation (a separation process under F_C) with a non-centrifugal operation (a separation process under F_g). For example, G_F of 500 F_g tells us that F_G is 500 times greater than F_g. [G-factor can be as low as $100F_g$ (for slow-speed-large-diameter basket filtering centrifuges) or as high as $1200F_g$ (for high-speed-smaller-diameter filtering centrifuges). In a high-speed sedimenting centrifuge, G_F can reach up to 10 000F_g. And in a **gas centrifuge**, it can get as high as 500 000F_g, because these centrifuges operate at an extremely high speed (around 80 000 RPM.)]

Generally, G_F (G-factor) is important because

- It can develop an F_C that exceeds the F_g by G_F.
- It can indicate the separating power of a centrifuge for a unit of mass (M) of a feed that moves at a certain rotation per unit of time (t).

G_F is a unitless quantity that numerically expresses the ratio of a centrifuge's F_C to F_g (where $F_g = M.a_g$, where a_g is gravitational acceleration).

$$G_F = \frac{F_C}{F_g} = \frac{F_C}{M.a_g} \tag{9}$$

To calculate G_F, we must substitute Equation 7 into 9.

$$G_F = \frac{F_C}{F_g} = \frac{M(\frac{2V^2}{d_B})}{M.a_g} = \frac{2V^2}{a_g.d_B} \tag{10}$$

As seen from this equation, G_F mainly depends on the following:

- Rotational velocity, V (the *greater* the V, the *greater* is the G_F).
- Basket's diameter, d_B (the *greater* the d_B, the *lower* is the G_F), so a large-diameter centrifuge has a lower G_F at the same v. In addition, the *greater* the d_B of a centrifuge, the *slower* it can be operated, and consequently, its efficiency reduces.

The basket diameter is important, and, therefore, **gas centrifuges** (discussed under CENTRIFUGES), which operate at extremely high speed, are made with a smaller diameter for the next two main reasons.

- To achieve a high G_F,
- To prevent vibration and breakage of attached parts (fittings).

The dependability of G_F on N (rotation per minute) is shown in Figure 10 for a centrifuge with a 1 m basket diameter (d_B).

The rotating basket (with diameter d_B), which has a circumference of $\pi.d_B$, can create a rotational velocity of V in the rotating feed when it constantly (uniformly) rotates N times in 60 seconds.

$$V = 2\pi.R_B\frac{N}{60} = \frac{\pi.d_B.N}{60} \quad (11)$$

[The symbol V was used for feed's rotational velocity, and N for basket's rotational velocity instead of ω because it is given in RPM.]

Now, we can substitute V into Equation 10 to calculate G_F (centrifuge separation factor).

$$G_F = \frac{2\left(\frac{\pi.d_B.N}{60}\right)^2}{a_g.d_B} = \frac{\pi^2.d_B.N^2}{1800a_g} \quad (12)$$

The gravitational acceleration (a_g = 9.81 m/s^2) numerically almost equates to $\pi^2 = (3.13)^2 = 9.86$, so π^2 and a_g are crossed out of the previous equation, so G_F becomes

$$G_F = \frac{d_B.N^2}{1800} = 5.6 \times 10^{-4}d_B.N^2 \quad (13)$$

In the case of a **batch centrifuge**, the thickness of the cake (d_C) is usually incorporated into Equation 10 to achieve a more accurate result, as the cake's thickness is usually much greater than in a continuous one.

$$G_F = 5.6 \times 10^{-4}(d_B - d_C)N^2 \quad (14)$$

The term $d_B - d_C$ is called the **effective separation diameter**.

With d in inch (In), the constant in the last two equations is 1.4×10^{-5}, so the US unit of G_F can be given as

$$G_F = 1.4 \times 10^{-5}d_B.N^2 \quad (15)$$

As seen from the listed equations, G_F mainly depends on the following:

- Speed of rotation (N; the *greater* the N, the *greater* is the G_F).
- Basket's diameter (d_B; the *greater* the d_B, the greater is the G_F). This, however, has a limit because the *larger* the d_B, the *slower* it can be operated, and, consequently, its efficiency *decreases*. This is why gas centrifuges (special centrifuges that operate at an extremely high speed of around 80 000 R/min) are smaller in diameter to prevent vibration and breakage of attached parts (fittings).

Example 1 on Centrifugal Process

Given: A batch centrifuge with the following related values:

Rotating-feed's mass (M)	1000 kg (= 1 t)
Centrifuge-basket's diameter (d_B)	1.27 m (= 50 In)
Number of rotation/min (N)	1100

Wanted: 1) Centrifugal force, 2) Centrifuge separation factor (G_F), and 3) Centrifuge separation time (t_S)

Assumption: A non-centrifugal operation takes 50 hours (3 000 minutes) to do the same job

Because the basket has a circumference of C = πd = 3.14×1.27 = 4 m, it gives the feed particles a velocity (V) of 4 m/s. And the V of this magnitude creates a centrifugal acceleration (a_C) of

$$a_C = \frac{2V^2}{d_B} = \frac{2\times4^2}{1.27} = 25 \text{ m/s}^2$$

$$F_C = M.a_C = 1000 \times 25 = 25 \times 10^3 \text{ kg.m/s}^2 = \text{N (Newton, the force unit)}$$

$$G_F = 5.6 \times 10^{-4} \times d_B.N^2 = 5.6 \times 10^{-4} \times 1.27 \times 1100^2 = 860$$

This means that the feed is under a centrifugal force of 860 times greater than the gravitational force (F_g), so the separation time is 860 times shorter than a non-centrifugal operation. A G_F of this magnitude shortens the separation time (*from a few hours to a few minutes*). Since we assumed that the non-centrifugal operation takes 3 000 min, the centrifuge separation time (centrifuge cycle time, t_C) should be 860 times shorter. So, the t_S of this centrifuge is 3000/860 = 3.5 minutes.

Centrifugal Separation Rate

Centrifugal separation rate (C_R) expresses the velocity of the mother liquid (the less-denser phase) through the basket's feed bed. The modified Stokes' Law equation calculates the C_R. This equation uses the basket's rotational speed (N), the basket's diameter (d_B), the particle's average diameter (d), the denser phase's density (D_1), the mother liquid's density (D_2), and the mother liquid's viscosity (η).

$$C_R = \frac{N^2.d_B.d^2(D_1 - D_2)}{3280\eta} \qquad (16)$$

Using N in 1/s, d_B and d in m, D in kg/m^3, and η in kg/m.s will give C_R in m/s. Consider a sugar magma (sugar crystals covered with syrup) in the centrifuge basket to remove the mother liquid from the crystals. C_R mainly depends on the d_B, the d (the average diameter of crystals), and the η.

Example 2 on Centrifugal Process

Given: A continuous centrifuge for processing solid particles suspended in water

Centrifugal separation rate (C_R)	2 m/s
Water viscosity (η)	6×10^{-4} Pa.s (= 6×10^{-4} kg/m.s)
Centrifugal-basket's diameter (d)	1 m
Solid particles diameter (d_S)	80 µm (=80×10^{-6} m)
Solid density (D_1)	1065 kg/m^3
Water density (D_2)	995 kg/m^3

Wanted: Rotational speed (N) in R/min (rotation per minute)

$$C_R = \frac{N^2.d_B.d_S^2(D_1 - D_2)}{3280\eta} \qquad N^2 = \frac{3280C_R.\mu}{d_B.d_S^2(D_1 - D_2)} = \frac{3280\times2\times6\times10^{-4}}{1\times80\times10^{-6}(1065-995)} = 703 \text{ R/s}^2$$

$$N = 26.5 \text{ R/s} \qquad N = 26.5 \times 60 = 1590 \text{ R/min}$$

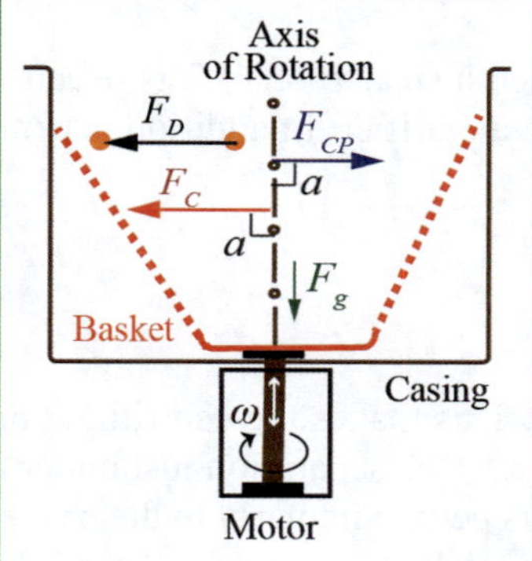

Figure 8 Forces acting in the basket of a centrifuge at a steady-speed rotation

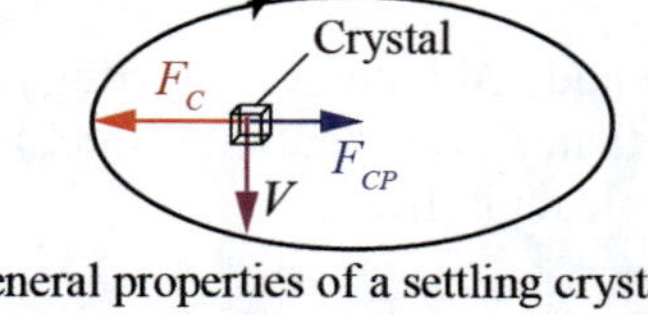

General properties of a settling crystal

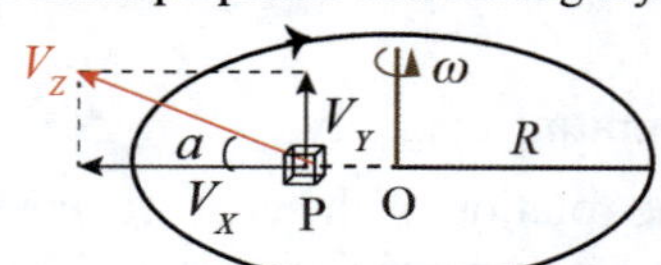

Settling property of a crystal at point P in relation to point O (origin)

Figure 9 General and settling properties of a settling suspended particle (in our example, a settling sugar crystal)

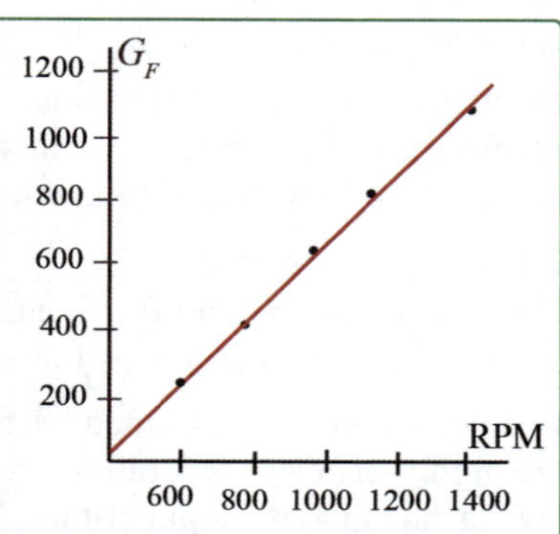

Figure 10 Relation between centrifugal separation factor (G_F) and rotation per minute (RPM) for a centrifuge with 1 m basket

C-21
CENTRIFUGAL PUMPS

Discussed under PUMPS.

C-22

CENTRIFUGES

An industrial centrifuge is a heavy device (equipment) that applies a centrifugal force (F_C) to perform the centrifugal process. In its typical design, a centrifuge consists of attached parts (such as basket, electric drive motor, feed, and discharge valves) and detached parts (such as feed tank, instruments, controllers, and computers for process control). Before going into details, study the next Notes.

[Note 1: The term **centrifuge** is accepted in most scientific literature as the name for the equipment. Some, instead, use the word **centrifugal** (away-from-the-center) for the equipment. This is incorrect because the word **centrifugal** is used as a **qualifying** (determining) **word**, such as centrifugal process, centrifugal force, or centrifugal duty. This book uses the word **centrifuge** (*not* centrifugal).]

[Note 2: The first centrifuge was invented in the early 17th century to separate cream from milk. Later, the sugar industry, which uses several centrifuges in a sugar factory, has greatly contributed to the design and operation of batch and continuous filtering centrifuges.]

[Note 3: A centrifuge used for **centrifugal filtration** (discussed under CENTRIFUGAL PROCESS) is commonly called the **centrifuge**. Thus, if the type of a centrifuge is *not* mentioned, a **filtering centrifuge** is meant.]

[Note 4: **Supporting structure** and **foundation** of centrifuges must be strong and correctly designed because they are heavy equipment and subjected to strong vibration. In top-suspended centrifuges, the motor, which is located above the basket, is supported by a heavy-metal horizontal bar, connected to a strong supporting frame at each end. In designing the supporting frame, enough headroom between the ground and the frame should be applied to ease the access to a centrifuge's attached parts (fittings).]

Centrifuges, in a broad range, are divided into three (3) types:

- Filtering centrifuges (simply **centrifuges**),
- Sedimenting centrifuges, and
- Gas centrifuges.

In some chemical process plants, filtering and sedimenting centrifuges are used instead of clarifiers because a centrifuge uses F_C, which is much stronger than F_g (gravitational force) used in a clarifier. In addition, a centrifuge has the following advantages over a typical clarifier:

- Centrifuge saves time,
- Centrifuge has greater effectiveness, and
- Centrifuge is smaller in size for a given operating capacity.

In a centrifuge, F_C is formed because of the rotation of the centrifuge basket. This makes the centrifugation a more highly-efficient separation process than a non-centrifugal separation process (the separation just under F_g, known as the **gravity separation**). In a centrifuge, the quantity of F_C, which acts perpendicularly to the basket's shaft, depends on two factors:

- Basket's rotational velocity, ω (the *greater* the ω, the *greater* is the F_C), and
- Basket's radius, R (the *smaller* the R, the *greater* is the F_C).

[Note: The basket's rotational velocity, usually expressed in RPM (R/min or rotation per minute), is important in designing a centrifuge. While ordinary filtering and sedimenting centrifuges operate at 1000 to 2000 rotations per minute (R/min or RPM), **gas centrifuges**, which are used in the uranium enrichment process to separate uranium-235 from uranium-238, operate at a high RPM (around 80 000 RPM).]

Centrifugal Separation Factor and Separation Rate

The **centrifugal separation factor** (G_F, G-factor, or G) and **centrifugal separation rate** (C_R) are used in the following ways:

- The G_F is used to find how strong a centrifuge can create F_C; in other words, it expresses the ratio of a centrifuge's F_C to F_g. [As a ratio, the G_F is a unitless quantity.]
- The C_R is used to evaluate the separation ability of a centrifuge. In other words, it expresses a rate at which the separation of two phases of different densities occurs in a centrifuge. [As a rate, the C_R is given in m/s.]

[The G_F and C_R are discussed in more detail under CENTRIFUGAL PROCESS.]

FILTERING CENTRIFUGES

Filtering centrifuges are used in the **centrifugal filtration process** (discussed under CENTRIFUGAL PROCESS). [Note: Both batch and continuous filtering centrifuges use some type of filter media (such as a metal screen), which covers the perforated wall of the basket, hence known as the **filtering centrifuges**, **centrifugal filters**, or simply **centrifuges**).]

Because of the filtering system, batch filtering centrifuges are loaded so that the liquid does *not* build up in the basket during the loading (feeding) step. Otherwise, the solid particles settle, causing high vibration. This is *not* of concern for continuous centrifuges because the **centrifuge separation rate** (C_R) exceeds the feed rate.

Filtering centrifuges are of two main kinds:

- Batch filtering centrifuges (simply **batch centrifuges**), and
- Continuous filtering centrifuges (simply **continuous centrifuges**).

When, in general, a high-quality product is required, **batch centrifuges** are often preferred because they have the following advantages over the continuous types:

- Higher recovery,
- Lower moist product,
- Higher-purity product,
- Better washing capability,
- Less cross-contamination,
- Less solid-lumps formation,
- Higher operating flexibility,
- Fewer fines loss to the filtrate,
- Higher operating cleanability, and
- Higher operating and maintaining inspectability.

Despite these advantages, continuous centrifuges are the preferred choice, in many industries, over the batch types when the feed properties and processing conditions allow. This is because continuous centrifuges offer the following advantages over the batch types:

- Lower labor cost,
- Lower capital cost,
- Lower maintenance cost,
- Higher operating capacity,
- Lighter weight, requiring lighter supporting structure,
- Higher F_C (500 to 2000) than batch centrifuges (200 to 500),
- Lower solid retention time because of operating at faster rotation,
- Higher efficiency (short cycle and *no* delay for loading and unloading), and
- Better coordination of centrifugal station with the station before and after.

Despite these advantages, continuous centrifuges *cannot* produce high-quality products in some cases. For example, sugar factories do *not* use continuous types for the highest-purity magma to produce refined-crystallized sugar (the table sugar with 99.95% purity). Continuous centrifuges break the sugar crystals during feeding (because of the high-speed rotation of the basket), so high-moisture crystals and crystal lumps are produced.

However, the sugar industry uses continuous types to centrifuge between-the-product magmas (called high-raw magma and low-raw magma), which are then remelted in a high-purity juice to produce liquor. The liquor is then crystallized to produce white magma centrifuged in a batch centrifuge.

Batch Filtering Centrifuges

Batch filtering centrifuges (simply **batch centrifuges**, also called **batch centrifugal filters**) come in different designs, drive motors (simply motors or **drives**), and capacities. In most centrifuges, the **basket** (bowl) is mounted on a vertical **shaft**, driven by a motor, so the basket rotates horizontally. In some special cases, such as when the coarse crystals must be separated, the basket is mounted on a horizontal shaft, rotating vertically. The basket, shown in Figure 1, is mounted on a vertical shaft driven by a top-mounted motor. And the basket, shown in Figure 2, is also mounted on a vertical shaft, but a bottom-mounted motor runs it. In both designs thus, the basket rotates horizontally. A batch centrifuge supported from the top and unloaded from the bottom is called a **top-suspended bottom-unloaded centrifuge**.

The loading capacity of the older batch centrifuges is up to 1000 kg/load (cycle) or less, while modern types can operate with loads up to 2500 kg/cycle, depending on the operating uses.

The total operating time per charge (cycle time) depends on the centrifugal duty. Some feeds need a shorter cycle time (2 to 3 minutes) and some longer (3 to 5 minutes). Cycle time also depends on the control system of the centrifuge (the *better* a centrifuge is controlled, the *better* is its efficiency and, therefore, the *shorter* is its cycle time.)

Vertical-shaft centrifuges have a much wider demand in chemical process plants than horizontal-shaft centrifuges. This is because vertical-shaft centrifuges allow crystals to deposit evenly on the basket's wall. Next, **vertical-shaft centrifuges** are described.

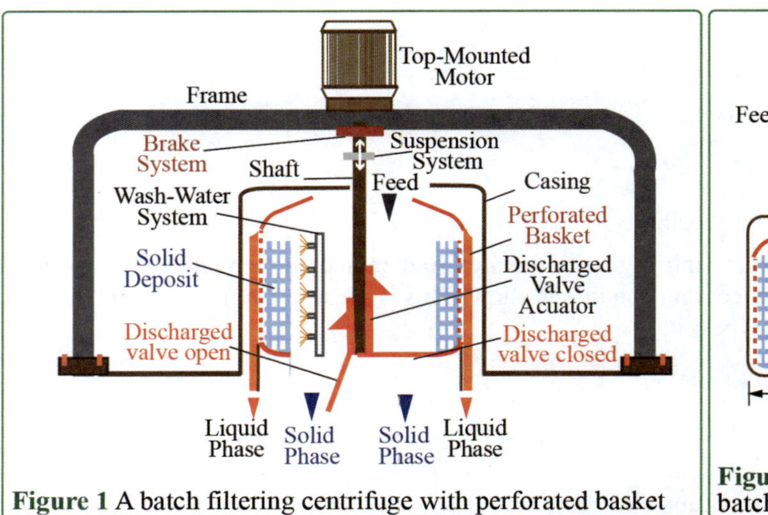

Figure 1 A batch filtering centrifuge with perforated basket

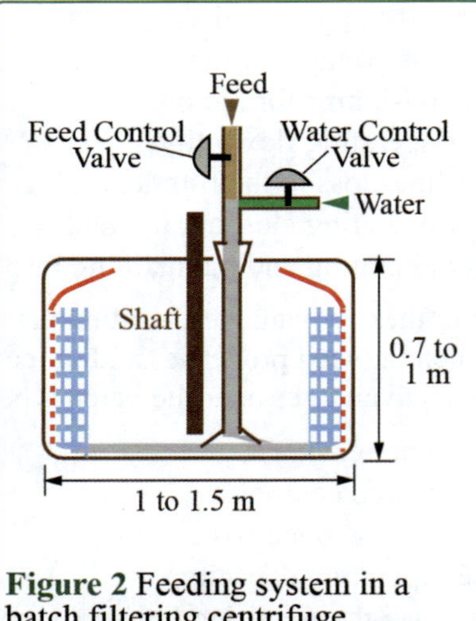

Figure 2 Feeding system in a batch filtering centrifuge

Basket: The size and strength of the material used to build a basket are important for centrifugal duty at its highest capacity and lowest vibration. A batch centrifuge contains a vertical basket (bowl), usually made of stainless steel in its typical design. The basket is 1 to 1.5 m (= 40 to 60 In) in diameter and 0.7 to 1 m (= 28 to 39 In) in height. The height of a basket is smaller than its diameter (with a ratio of about 0.7) to prevent out-of-balance rotation. The rotational velocity of a typical centrifuge is up to 2000 RPM.

The basket is perforated with a typical hole diameter of 5 mm. The holes occupy about 10 to 20% of the basket's total area.

The diameter size of the basket is one of the factors that influence the centrifuge operating speed and vibration (the *larger* the diameter, the *more* vibration). For example, a centrifuge with a 1 m basket can be operated up to 2200 rotation (*R*)/min without a considerable vibration, while a 1.4 m basket can conveniently operate up to only 1800 *R*/min. The centrifuge-separation factor (G_F or G-factor), explained under CENTRIFUGAL PROCESS, follows the speed rule (the *larger* the basket's diameter, the *slower* it can be operated and, therefore, the *smaller* is its G_F.) The baskets have rubber pads to absorb the basket's shaking to reduce the vibration at high rotations. [Modern batch centrifuges are equipped with sensors to detect vibration and stop the motor when an unusual out-of-balance situation occurs.]

Basket Screen: The perforated wall of a basket is covered with two screens, a **baking screen** (installed on top of the basket wall) and a **filtering screen** (installed on top of the baking screen). Both screens are usually made of stainless steel or copper brass. The baking screen is in the form of woven wire with larger holes (typically 4 mm). And the filtering screen has different thickness and size hole, depending on the particle size to be centrifuged. For example, the sugar industry uses filtering screens about 0.5 mm thick with rectangle holes of 0.4×4 mm or round holes of 0.5 mm. With given specifications, a typical screen has about 20% open area. A centrifuge with a 1 m basket has a 1 m^2 filtering area.

A screen lifetime ranges from 100 000 to 150 000 cycles, but ammonia (NH_3) in the washing water can notably decrease the lifetime of the screens (because NH_3 damages the metals). **Duplex stainless-steel** screens are chrome-plated on the working side, so they have a long lifetime (because of high corrosion resistance).

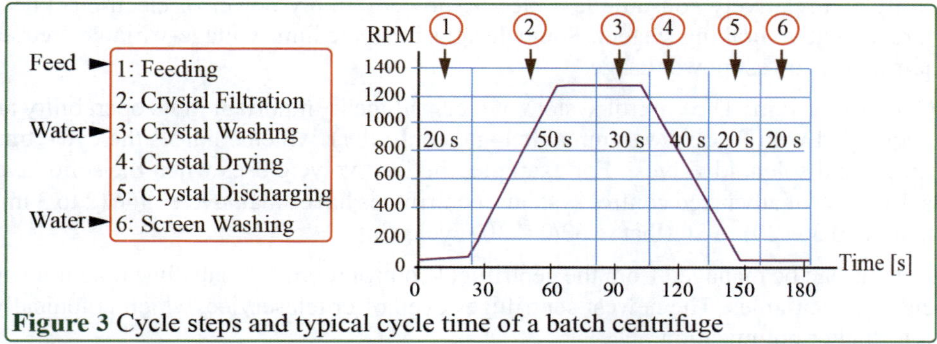

Figure 3 Cycle steps and typical cycle time of a batch centrifuge

Basket Suspension System: The central shaft attached to the motor's head by coupling is connected to the thrust and bearings and the bottom of the basket. Because the basket is suspended, carries the weight of the shaft and feed, and operates at high speeds, its suspended system must

- Have strong thrust and bearings.
- Be designed carefully to prevent vibration.

Basket Balance: Vibrations mainly occur because of unbalanced loads and are sometimes unavoidable, so the centrifuge's support structure (frame) must be strong enough to resist vibration and support its weight. The basket has rubber pads to absorb vibration at high rotations (around 2000 *R*/min). [Modern centrifuges are equipped with a **balance sensor** to detect extreme vibration and stop the motor.]

Basket Washing System: Usually, 3 to 5 spray nozzles are installed on a vertical pipe to wash the solid-deposit layer. As shown in Figure 1, the sprays are installed to spread the wash liquid evenly across the height of the inside of the solid-deposit layer. Washing can remove almost all the mother liquid from the solid particles with minimum wash liquid use if the particle layer has uniform pores. The sugar industry, for example, uses hot water (usually condensate without ammonia) as a wash liquid to remove the thin layer of the mother liquid from the surface of the sugar crystals.

Basket Feeding System: Figure 2 shows a batch centrifuge feeding system. A valve loads a preset amount of feed close to the shaft at the bottom of the basket. [The loading system of a batch centrifuge usually has a second valve to prevent feed from dripping into the basket after the loading step.] After discharge from the valve, the feed goes toward a feed plate attached to the shaft and rotates with it. The sloping feed plate directs the feed into the center of the basket, from where it flows evenly toward the basket's wall to form a uniform solid layer.

The feeding capacity of older centrifuges is 1000 to 1200 kg per cycle. New models can centrifuge 1750 to 2200 kg of feed.

Basket Discharge System: The deposit is discharged from the bottom of the basket through the discharging valve (or door). The valve fits tight to prevent air from being drawn into the basket in the closed position. An adjustable **discharging blade (plow)** installed inside the basket removes the remaining deposit from the basket. The blade moves inward and downward during discharge to move the solids layer from the basket wall. After discharge, the blade returns to its original position. The blade is actuated by a direct or an indirect drive. Blades have some tips, which wear, so need replacing. Some centrifuges have a blade pivot outside the basket to stop it if it meets an obstruction.

Centrifuge Motor: Suspended centrifuges generally require powerful drive motors (simply **drives** or motors) as they must rotate the basket, shaft, and a large load of feed in each cycle. Generally, batch types require stronger motors than continuous ones because the batch centrifuges must accelerate and decelerate extensively in each operating cycle. Depending on their loading capacity, batch centrifuges use variable-frequency DC (direct current) motors from 100 to 500 kW/h.

Some suppliers use **variable-frequency AC** (alternating current) motors for larger centrifuges. Such motors can operate flexibly and relatively consume less electric power (simply power or electricity) because they are equipped with a regenerative braking system. Some designs have medium-voltage-variable-frequency (MVVF) AC motors, requiring the lowest power usage.

Centrifuge Control System: The control system of a centrifuge is important in its operability and efficiency. Centrifuges are equipped with PLC (programmable logic controller), which controls the cycle time in different stages, basket speed, and solenoid valves. For example, the feed valve closes when the solid layer reaches the preset thickness. Because of advanced control systems, centrifuges have small cycle time (2 to 3 minutes), which equates to 20 (that is 60/3 = 20) to 30 (that is 60/2 = 30) cycles/h.

The control systems can be managed from the centrifugal control room. A centrifuge operator can preset cycle washing time and other variables. The newest centrifuges even offer teleservice, which graphically displays the operational data for better optimization.

Operating Cycle: The operating cycle of a typical batch centrifuge consists of six steps, as shown in Figure 3. The steps are outlined next.

- **Charging** (feeding)**:** The basket receives the preset amount of feed while rotating slowly (usually 150 to 300 RPM, rotation per minute).
- **Solid Filtration:** Feeding stops and speed increases constantly to reach its full level and then continues at a constant rotation for a preset time. [Achieving the maximum speed in the shortest time possible is important for a batch centrifuge.] Setting the spin time at this stage is usually determined by experience based on operating conditions and requirements. High F_C pushes the feed toward the basket's wall, discharging the liquid through the basket screen. The solid particles are too large to pass through the basket, so they build up a solid layer of typically 150 to 200 mm (6 to 8 In). Although most of the liquid is removed from the solids, the solids retained on the screen contain a thin layer of liquid, which needs to be washed and centrifuged a bit more.
- **Solid Washing** (deliquoring)**:** Washing starts as the deposited solids on the screen become like a packed bed because the spaces between the solid particles are still filled with the liquid. Thus, the solids layer is sprayed for a few seconds, typically with hot water once or twice. Washing removes the thin layer of the liquid from the surface of the solid particles.
- **Solid Drying:** Drying starts as the liquid level reaches below the solid surface. As a result of drying, more liquid passes the basket to achieve the preset solid with the desired moisture content.

- **Solid Discharging:** A mechanical brake slows the rotation, and a plow discharges the deposited solids.
- **Screen Washing:** The screen is washed to prepare the screen for the next cycle.

Continuous Filtering Centrifuges

In a continuous filtering centrifuge (simply **continuous centrifuge**), feed flow rate, filtrate flow rate, and solid flow rate from the centrifuge are constant because the basket receives the feed at a constant rate and rotates at a constant RPM. A right RPM (rotation per minute) of the basket provides the next results:

- It makes the solids slide over the basket wall at an appropriate velocity,
- It develops a uniform distribution of the solids over the basket wall,
- It reduces the operating time of the solids for dewatering.

Continuous centrifuges are broadly divided into the following two classes:

- Continuous centrifuges with vertical shaft and horizontal basket (Figure 4 and Figure 5)
- Continuous centrifuges with horizontal shaft and vertical basket (as seen in Figure 6)

The first-type centrifuges are much more popular in the chemical process industry than the second ones, so a typical continuous centrifuge with a vertical shaft and a horizontal basket is discussed next.

Supporting Structure: Although continuous centrifuges are usually lighter than the batch types and are subject to less unbalanced vibration (because of rotation at constant speed), they also need a strong and stiff supporting structure. The drive motor, located below the basket, is connected to the foundation.

Basket: The basket of a continuous centrifuge has a conical shape with an angle of about 25º (Figure 4) or a cylindrical shape (Figure 5). Mostly**,** baskets have a conical shape, with the top diameter (the large side) of 0.8 to 1.6 m, depending on the loading capacity. Many holes with a diameter of about 10 mm are in the basket's wall for quick drainage of the separated liquid. The total area of the holes is 10 to 20% of the basket area. The design and material of the basket are of the utmost importance because of the high-speed rotation and centrifugal force involved in the operation of continuous centrifuges, so baskets are made of strong stainless steel.

The feed is entered continuously into the middle of the rotating basket through a feed pipe, and water is sprayed continuously over the feed to the feed pipe.

Basket Suspension System: The basket is suspended on an anti-vibration system. This design creates a suspension mechanism that helps the basket rotate uniformly even when unusual vibrations occur at high speed.

The central shaft, which is attached to the motor's head by a coupling, is connected to the thrust and bearings and the bottom of the basket. Because the basket is suspended, carries the weight of the shaft and feed, and because it operates at high speeds, its suspended system must

- Have strong thrust and bearings.
- Be designed carefully to prevent vibration.

[The **centrifugal force** (F_C) is higher in continuous centrifuges than in the batch types, as the continuous types are usually operated at a higher speed. The high speed creates high F_C, which can reach up to 3 000 F_g at the top of the centrifuge.]

Screen Design: The screens used for continuous centrifuges are relatively thinner than those for batch ones. The following three types of screens are used: 1) Sheet-metal screens, 2) Metal-coated screens, and 3) Wedge-wire screens.

For example, metal-coated and wedge-wire coated screens are used in the sugar industry. Metal-coated screens are made by deposition of nickel (Ni) with a coating of hard chrome (Cr) on both sides. The opening size of the screens used in the sugar industry is in the range of 50 μm (= 0.05 mm) to 100 μm (= 0.1 mm). Different industries use screens with different opening sizes, depending on the size of the processed solids. The weight of the screen can be used as a quick judgment for checking its use for a particular operating feed.

The wedge-wire screens are relatively much stronger and less damageable. The slots of these screens are parallel to the axis of rotation. Wedge-wired screens have a higher open area than woven-wire ones.

Because of fine construction, screens can easily be damaged by foreign materials and even solid lumps. Thus, they must be visually inspected periodically for damage and wear. If the chrome layer is gone, the underlying nickel wears quickly. [Small holes can be repaired using a low-temperature silver solder, performed on the back of the screen.]

Feeding-and-Washing Design: The feed flow is controlled by the position of the feed valve. A feed funnel is located at the top center of the basket for receiving a constant amount of feed. Washing liquid (usually hot water) is also sprayed at the feed funnel. Some suppliers offer a special design distributor which effectively mixes the feed and washing liquid. Constant rotation and feeding create an equal centrifugal force (F_C), causing the feed's uniform distribution and minimizing solid particle breakage. The centrifugal force of continuous centrifuges is as high as 3000 at the top of the basket, relatively higher than those in batch centrifuges.

The area between the feed and the top surface of the basket is usually enclosed to prevent air from being sucked into the basket. The rotating basket at high-speed acts like a large pump sucking a large amount of air into the basket. This can hurt the operating temperature and efficiency of the centrifuge.

The liquid enters the grooves from the basket and moves out. Different sealing covers are used at the top of the basket to prevent mixing the separated solids and liquid.

Unloading: While in the basket, the feed gains speed and moves up toward the large end of the basket. A deposit (cake) layer moves up by a **reciprocating pusher**. Each stroke of the pusher moves the deposit toward the top of the basket, from where it falls continuously into a collector chute. The liquid flows through the basket screen and is discharged from the bottom.

Drive Motor: The basket of a continuous filtering centrifuge is driven from the bottom by a motor whose size depends on the basket size and centrifugal duty. The motors used in continuous centrifuges are relatively smaller than the batch ones because their baskets rotate continuously. The speed depends on the processing material and the basket size; however, it can reach 2200 R/min. Nowadays, suppliers use standard motors in 30 to 130 kW electric power, depending on the basket size and load weight.

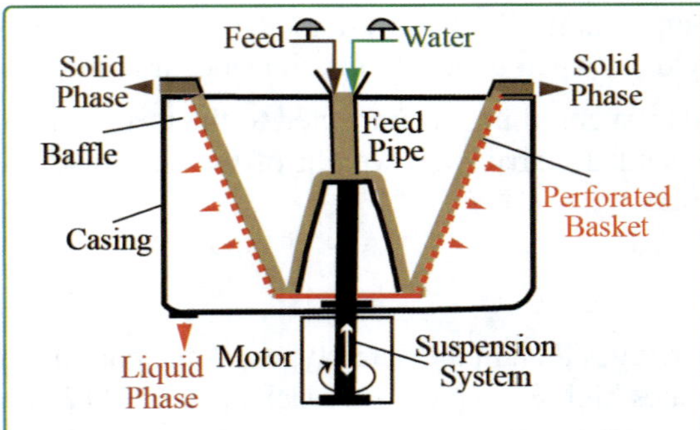

Figure 4 Continuous filtering centrifuge with conical basket and vertical shaft

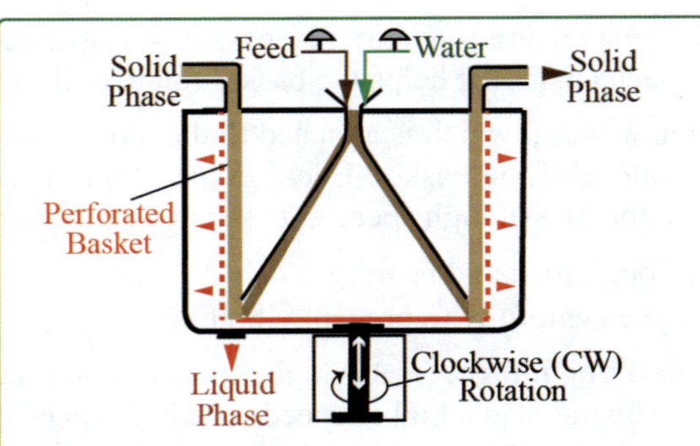

Figure 5 Continuous filtering centrifuge with cylindrical basket and vertical shaft

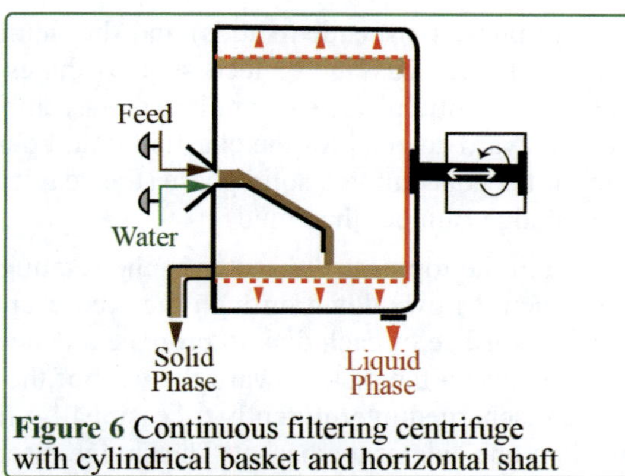

Figure 6 Continuous filtering centrifuge with cylindrical basket and horizontal shaft

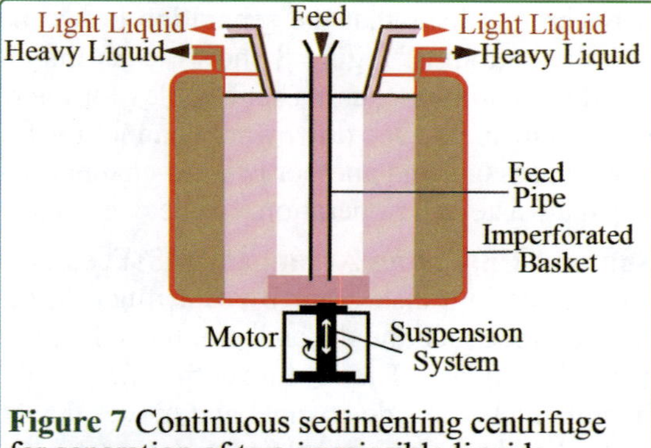

Figure 7 Continuous sedimenting centrifuge for separation of two immiscible liquids

SEDIMENTING CENTRIFUGES

Sedimenting (decanting) centrifuges are mostly used in the sedimentation process to separate suspended particles dispersed in a liquid using a centrifugal force (F_C), which is produced by high-speed rotation of the centrifuge's basket. Most sedimenting centrifuges operate like continuous centrifuges unless designed specifically for batch operation. So, when talking about a sedimenting centrifuge, its continuous type is meant.

In a sedimenting centrifuge, the separation can be in the form of

- **Thickening:** In a thickening centrifuge, suspended particles in a sludge settle to produce filter cake (transportable). The thickening process is used, for example, in wastewater treatment systems.
- **Clarification:** In a clarification centrifuge, suspended particles are separated from the liquid phase because the clarity of the liquid phase is the main concern.
- **Classification:** In a classification centrifuge, the particles are separated into two different-size fractions. Classification is done because the user is interested in the size of classified particles. [The cumulative mass fraction measures the size distribution of the particles (see CRYSTAL SIZE DISTRIBUTION).]
- **Dewatering:** In a dewatering centrifuge, suspended particles settle to form a deposit with a high solid concentration. It is, for example, used to dewater coarse coal and rubber crumb.

Figure 7 shows the separation of two immiscible liquids in the basket of a sedimenting centrifuge. The feed enters from the top in a funnel. In the basket, two layers are formed. One is the **high-density** (heavy) **liquid**, which flows upward along the wall to leave the basket. The other layer is the **low-density** (light) **liquid**, which flows toward the center of the basket and then upward to leave the basket.

Sedimenting centrifuges (centrifugal filters) come in different designs, such as disk sedimenting centrifuges, three-phase decanter centrifuges, disk-nozzle centrifuges, and self-cleaning disk centrifuges. Here, a typical disk sedimenting centrifuge, one of the most common sedimenting centrifuges, is discussed.

Sedimenting Disk Centrifuges

Sedimenting disk centrifuges (centrifugal disk filters) have different applications, such as dewatering the underflow of a clarifier to produce a transportable cake in wastewater treatment operations. Figure 8 illustrates a typical basket of a disk centrifuge with a top-feeding and top-unloading design. A typical self-cleaning disk centrifuge description follows.

Basket and Disks: The basket of a disk sedimenting centrifuge is mounted on a vertical shaft, driven by an electric motor with a belt drive. The basket's wall is imperforated (with *no* holes) and has a truncated cone shape with an angle of 40 to 55° with horizontal to improve the feed movement. The diameter of the basket's top (the larger side) ranges from 0.5 to 2.5 m (= 20 to 100 In), depending on the feeding capacity. In the basket, 50 to 100 disks are installed with a narrow space of 0.3 to 3.3 mm (= 0.011 to 0.12 In) between the disks. [In Figure 8, the number of disks is much reduced to show the feed movement's direction.]

It is between the disks that the separation between the solid phase (suspended solids) and the liquid phase occurs. As the bottom of Figure 8 shows, each disk has a hole for the passage of feed, a set of holes for the passage of the liquid phase, and a set of holes for the passage of the solid phase. When disks are assembled, the holes create 3 channels. One downward channel for feed, one upward channel for the clarified liquid phase (the lighter phase) passage, and another upward channel passage for the concentrated solid phase (the heavier phase) passage. [In a wastewater operation, the heavier phase is the sludge (thinner than mud).]

Loading-and-Unloading Arrangement: Feed is loaded from the top near the center of the rotating basket and is accelerated in a distributor by centrifugal force (F_C). Then it flows down through the feed channel and enters the areas between the disks. Here, the solids settle on the surface of each disk to produce a concentrated solid phase (the sludge). The F_C forces the sludge to move in between the disks toward the wall of the basket, from where it enters the side channel and moves upward to be discharged intermittently (occasionally) from the top of the basket through two outlets (ports), each positioned on one side of the basket. The sludge discharge is controlled by a **hydraulic valve**, which opens to discharge the sludge at preset intervals. The clarified liquid released from the disks enters the middle channel, from where it is discharged from the top through two ports.

Some disk centrifuges are made to discharge the sludge manually (called **manual-cleaning** or **solid-retaining** disk centrifuges). They are used when the feed has low-solid content (less than 0.5% on volume) to separate a two-liquid-phase feed.

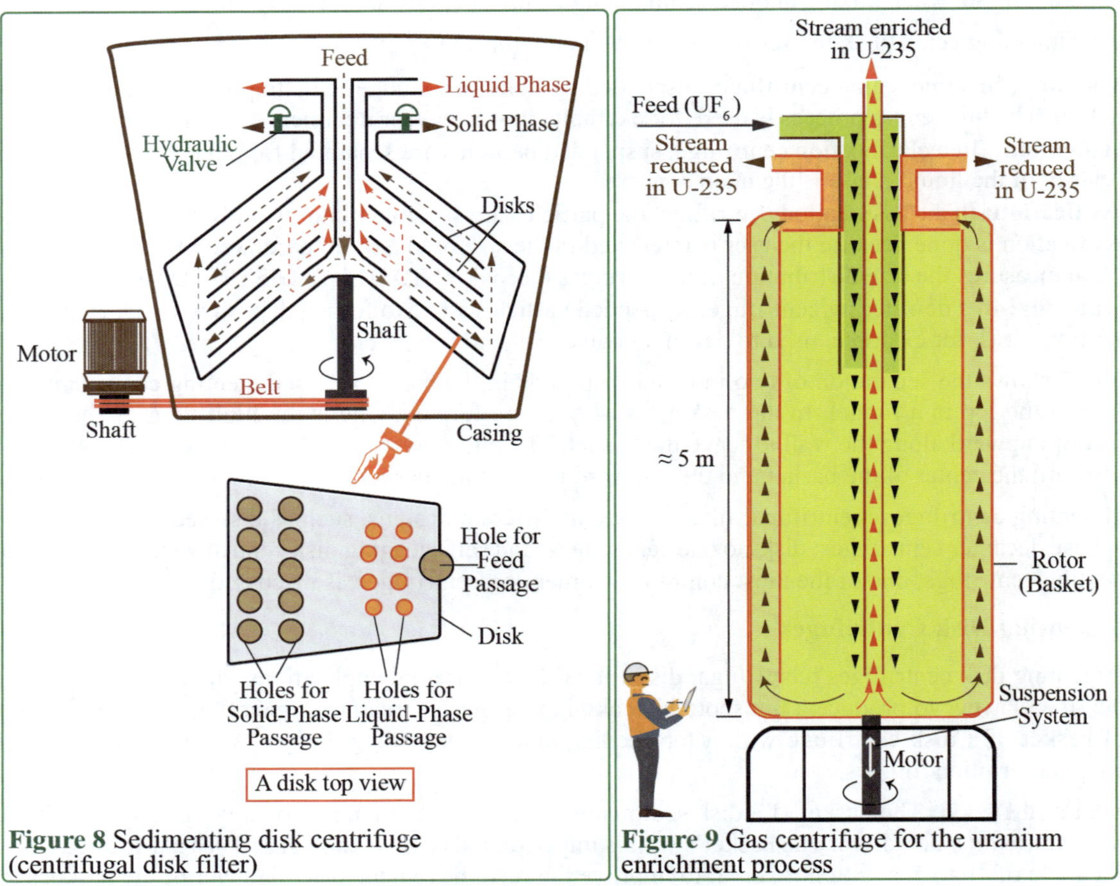

Figure 8 Sedimenting disk centrifuge (centrifugal disk filter)

Figure 9 Gas centrifuge for the uranium enrichment process

GAS CENTRIFUGES

Gas centrifuges are highly-complicated centrifuges, mostly used in the nuclear industry for the uranium enrichment process. In this process, natural uranium is converted into a gaseous-soluble form of **uranium hexafluoride** (UF_6). The UF_6 is then processed in a set of gas centrifuges (known as a **cascade**), which operate in connection.

[The number of gas centrifuges used in an enrichment process is too many (in several hundred) if the process intends to produce uranium 235 (simply U-235) with high purity (80% or more) from uranium 238 (simply U-238) to use in a nuclear weapon. Thus, a complicated-and-secret enrichment process is involved.]

Typically, a gas centrifuge, shown in Figure 9, is about 5 m (= 16 Ft) in height and about 20 cm (= 8 In) in diameter. Its unique design allows feed to flow continuously in and out of each centrifuge.

Gas centrifuges must spin at extremely high speed (around 80 000 rotations per minute, R/min) to separate the feed's components, with a slight difference in densities, from each other. For comparison, ordinary centrifuges used in usual chemical process plants operate up to 2 000 R/min, and household washing machines operate at around 1 000 R/min. As said under CENTRIFUGAL PROCESS,

In the gas-centrifugal process, the following occurs in a cascade:

- The centrifuge's rotor (the basket of a gas centrifuge), which rotates at high speed, causes the heavier gas molecules (the U-238) to move toward the wall of the rotor, while the slightly lighter gas molecules (the U-235), which is the **wanted component**, move toward the center of the rotor.
- The slightly enriched stream in U-235 is directed into the cascade's next stage, while the slightly depleted stream, which is reduced in U-235 content, is recycled back into the cascade's previous stage.
- The process is repeated many times in the cascade until the desired level of U-235's enrichment is achieved.

Provided below are two important points about gas centrifuges.

- Because of their usage in the nuclear industry, detailed info on gas centrifuges is unavailable.
- In the 1950s, Gernot Zippe (1917–2008, an Austrian-German mechanical engineer) designed the first gas centrifuge for the enrichment of U-235, based on a slight difference in density between U-235 and U-238.

CENTRIFUGE CAPACITY

The capacity of a centrifuge is usually expressed in two ways:

- Loading capacity (the amount of feed that a centrifuge can process),
- Output capacity (the amount of product that a centrifuge can produce).

These data are important for a centrifuge's designing calculations and day-to-day operation. It is, however, difficult to generally determine the loading capacity of a centrifuge exactly because it very much depends on the quality of the processing feed. Centrifuge manufacturers prefer to offer the **nominal loading capacity** (C_{NL}). On the other hand, the centrifuge users prefer to use the **practical loading capacity** (C_{PL}) for processing a specific feed. The C_{NL} is lower than C_{PL}, particularly in larger centrifuges, because **nominal solids layer thickness** (typically 200 mm) *cannot* be easily achieved. So, it is recommended to fill the basket to about 90% of its C_{NL}.

The nominal loading capacity (C_{NL}) of a batch-filtering centrifuge per cycle is given as

$$C_{NL} = [\pi(d_B - d_C)d_C.h_B]\frac{D}{DS} \quad (1)$$

Using d_B (basket's diameter) in m, d_C (deposit-ring's diameter) in m, h_B (basket's height) in m, D (deposit's density) in kg/m^3, DS (feed's dry-solid content) in %, will result C_{NL} in kg/cycle. Study the next example.

Example 1

Given: A batch centrifuge with the following data:

Basket's height (h_B)	1.1 m (= 43 In)
Basket's diameter (d_B)	1.5 m (= 60 In)
Deposit-ring diameter (d_C)	0.14 m (= 6 In)
Deposit density (D)	1020 kg/m^3
Feed dry solid content (DS)	53%

Wanted: 1) Centrifuge nominal loading capacity (C_{NL}), 2) The amount of centrifuged feed at 15 cycles/h, 3) If the centrifuge meets its nominal capacity of 1346 kg or *not*, and 4) Utilization rate,

$$C_{NL} = [3.14(1.5 - 0.14)0.14 \times 1.1]\frac{1020}{0.53} = 1266 \text{ kg/cycle}$$

The amount of centrifuged solid at 15 cycles/h is

$$1266 \times 15 = 18\,990 \quad \text{kg/h or } 456 \text{ t/day}$$

Nominal capacity (1346 kg) *cannot* be met unless the thickness of the solid layer (d_2) is increased to150 mm (0.15 m).

$$[3.14(1.6 - 0.15)0.15 \times 1.1]\frac{1020}{0.53} = 1346$$

This equates to a utilization rate of (1266/1346)×100 = 94%

The C_N (nominal output capacity) of a **continuous filtering centrifuge** is given in relation to its ability to produce filtrate (the centrifuge's liquid output). The capacity of such a centrifuge is nearly proportional to the filtrate's volumetric flow rate ($\dot{V} = V/t$, where V is for volume and t is for time).

$$C_N \approx \dot{V} \approx \frac{D_L.N^2(R_B^2 - R_L^2)}{2\eta\left(\frac{R_{FC}}{A_{CA}}\times\frac{M_K}{A_{CL}}+\frac{R_{FM}}{A_F}\right)} \tag{2}$$

Using D_L (filtrate's density) in kg/m^3, N (basket's rotational velocity) in 1/s, R_B (basket's inside radius) in m, R_L (liquid ring's radius) in m, η (filtrate's viscosity) in kg/m.s, R_{FC} (filter-cake resistance) in m/kg, A_{CA} (cake's arithmetic mean surface area) in m^2, A_{CL} (cake's logarithmic mean surface area) in m^2, A_F (filter-medium surface area, which equates to the inside area of the basket) in m^2, M_K (cake's mass) in kg, and R_{FM} (filter medium resistance) in 1/m will result in C_N in m^3/s. [R_{FM} is of 10^{-10} to 10^{-11}.]

The nominal output capacity (C_N) of a **continuous sedimenting centrifuge** is given in relation to its ability to produce filter cake (simply **cake**), so C_N is nearly proportional to the cake's $\dot{V}$.

$$C_N \approx \dot{V} \approx \frac{2\pi.N^2.R_B^2.h_B.V_P}{a_g} \tag{3}$$

When N (basket's rotational velocity) is given in 1/s, R_B (basket's radius) in m, h_B (basket's height) in m, V_P (particles settling velocity) in m/s, and a_g (gravitational acceleration = 9.81 m/s^2), the capacity of the centrifuge becomes in m^3/s.

In designing a batch centrifugal station, the number of centrifuges required is calculated from the nominal capacity of the centrifuge and the feed volume to be centrifuged. Usually, an extra centrifuge is considered for periodic maintenance.

CENTRIFUGE POWER USAGE

Centrifuges consume a high amount of electric power (P_E, expressed in W/h or Wh). However, modern centrifuges' use of electric power (simply power) has been improved considerably. For example, the modern batch centrifuges use a regenerative braking system, which recovers P_E as the basket's rotational velocity slows. This system reduces the net power usage of a centrifuge greatly.

Continuous centrifuges consume more power than batch ones (because they must produce higher F_C). In addition, the power used to accelerate a continuous centrifuge is *not* recovered by a regenerative brake mechanism.

The typical power usage of a medium-size continuous centrifuge is about 5 to 10 kW/h per ton of feed processed. The power usage of a batch centrifuge depends on the cycle time. At 20 cycles/h, a typical-medium-size batch centrifuge requires 1 to 2 kW/h (1 kW/h = 3.6 MJ/h) power per t feed. At 15 cycle/h, the required power of such a centrifuge increases from 1.3 to 2.3 kW/h. And at 10 cycles/h, the required power is 1.5 to 2.5 kW/h.

The electric power (P_E) required to operate a continuous centrifuge can be calculated as

$$P_E = \frac{1}{2}\left(\frac{\pi}{600}\right) M.d_B^2.N^2 \tag{4}$$

When M (mass of processing feed) is given in kg, d_B (basket's diameter) in m, N (basket's rotational velocity) in 1/s, then P_E becomes in kg.m^2/s^2 = J.

Suppose we show all quantities in Equation 4, except N^2, by the constant K, so for a given centrifuge, $P_E = K.N^2$. This means that, for example, at 1500 R/min (rotation per minute), we need to apply 2.25 times more power than 1000 R/min because $(1500/1000)^2 = 2.25$.

OPERATING PROBLEMS IN RUNNING A CENTRIFUGE

Several problems can happen in the operation of a centrifuge. The problems and causes discussed here are written particularly for batch filtering centrifuges. However, some can also be applied for filtering and sedimenting centrifuges (which mostly operate continuously).

Low Solid Recovery: Centrifugal solid recovery (also called **centrifuge yield** or **centrifuge efficiency**) is the percentage ratio of the mass of the solid particles leaving a centrifuge and entering it into the feed. It helps evaluate the efficiency on both operational and mechanical sides.

Typically, a filtering centrifuge may leave about 2 to 10% of the mass of the deposited cake as mother liquid on the particles' surface in a very thin layer. The deposit is washed during centrifugation to remove this liquid from solid particles. Other possible operational causes of the low solid yield are:

- High air-content feed,
- High solid-content feed,
- High foam-content feed,
- Wrong wash-water usage,
- Fine-solid particles increase the void fraction (ε_F), so particles become more packed and, consequently, prevent easy liquid passage, and
- High charge related to operational norms (loading a centrifuge more than 90% of its nominal capacity).

On the mechanical side, centrifuges must have enough **capacity** to handle the loads easily. Some chemical-process plants increase the number of centrifuge cycles to cover the centrifuge's low capacity or increase the amount of wash water. Both are *not* appropriate approaches because they sacrifice performance. Other possible mechanical causes of the low solid yield of a batch filtering centrifuge are the following:

- Low charge because of technical norms (like the use of a small feed valve or motor),
- Wrong screen setup (its polished surface must be toward the inside of the basket),
- Use of wrong distance between spray nozzles and the deposit-layer surface,
- Inappropriate inspection of the screen and basket for possible damage,
- Use of inappropriate nozzles for washing deposit layer,
- Use of damaged screen (particularly with holes),
- Wrong time set up for different steps.

Basket Vibration: When the basket vibrates, the rotation axis swings (oscillates), causing the basket to sound unusually loud, like an unbalanced clothes washer at home. If this situation is *not* corrected, the centrifuge can be damaged. Modern centrifuges have some sensors to detect high vibration and stop the motor. Most notably, the **load** a centrifuge carries must be balanced in its basket to run smoothly at its operating speed. Other usual causes for vibration of a centrifuge's basket are the following:

- Bent spindle,
- Clogged screen holes,
- Slippage of the screen,
- Solids stuck on the basket wall,
- Wrong load amount (too high or too low),
- Charging at high speed (above 300 rotations/min),
- Processing a feed with low suspended-solid-particles content,
- Using a high amount of solder (more than 5 g) to repair the screen's holes.

[Note: Vibration and basket's diameter (d) are inversely related (the smaller the d, the greater is the vibration) because the diameter of a centrifuge is directly proportional to its operating capacity (the greater the capacity, the larger is its d, so the smaller is its acceleration and, consequently, its vibration). That is why newer centrifuges with larger baskets relatively vibrate less.]

Unusual Screen Damage: Outlined next are some possible causes of unusual screen damage.

- Basket vibration,
- Wrong screen installation,
- High-speed rotation during unloading,
- Bumping the blade to the screen while unloading,
- Not enough gap between blade (plow) tip and screen,
- Existence of foreign materials or lumpy particles in the feed.

Centrifuged Deposit is too Wet: In a batch filtering centrifuge, wet cake discharged ideally should *not* have high moisture content. The amount of moisture depends on the feed under the process. For example, centrifuged sugar crystals should *not* have above 0.3% moisture. Centrifuged sugar with high moisture (above 0.6%) creates problems during transportation to the drying process station (because it gets hard). During drying, sugar moisture is reduced to about 0.03%.

The following are the reasons for cake (deposit) with high moisture content:

- **Short Drying Step:** If the drying time during the spin step is short, enough liquid does *not* pass through the basket to achieve the desired low moisture content.
- **Fine Solid Particles:** At the same centrifuge-separation factor (C_F) and liquid viscosity, extra-fine particles impede the separation of the liquid from the feed, causing high moisture content in the centrifuged product.
- **Too Viscous Feed:** It is difficult to release the liquid from the solid particles when the feed is too viscous.
- **Too Concentrated Feed:** When feed has too high dry substance (*DS*), it slows down the separation of the liquid from the solids, which also causes high moisture content of the cake.

C-23
CENTRIPETAL ACCELERATION

Study CENTRIFUGAL ACCELERATION AND CENTRIPETAL ACCELERATION.

C-24
CENTRIPETAL FORCE

Study CENTRIFUGAL FORCE AND CENTRIPETAL FORCE.

C-25
CERAMICS

As a silicate, ceramic is an amorphous (noncrystalline) composed mainly of silicon dioxide (SiO_2, simply **silica**). The ceramic components are bonded by ionic bonding and covalent bonding (strong chemical bonds). Because of strong bonds in their atoms, a ceramic's molecules do *not* exchange bonds easily, causing the following good properties:

- They are low in electric conductivity (K_E),
- They are low in reactivity (even at high temperatures),
- They are high in resistivity against corrosion and oxidation, and
- They are hard and brittle. Therefore, they can be used in many applications.

Because of these properties, ceramics have many applications, including in the linings of an industrial furnace, sanitary equipment, packing material for distillation columns, refractory bricks, and more.

Ceramics are in a wider class, called the silicates (mainly glass, ceramic, and cement), and are made by heating a mixture of silicates and other minerals and subsequent cooling of the **melt** (a molten state).

C-26
CERN

CERN is the French abbreviation for the European Organization for Nuclear Research, founded in 1954 in Switzerland with the help of some European countries. This large research facility has the most powerful particle accelerator, the Large Hadron Collider (LHC), a 27 km (= 17 Mi). The collider is a long tunnel located on the Swiss-French border. LHC can accelerate particles close to the speed of light constant in opposite directions before colliding them for complicated research purposes. The CERN's 8 000 magnets control the beam of particles. [After World War II, Broglie and Heisenberg played a leading role in establishing CERN.]

C-27
CHAIN REACTIONS

Defined under CHEMICAL REACTIONS.

C-28

CHARGE AND CHARGE NUMBER

Charge

The word **charge** is often used in Physics as a simplified form of the electric charge in studying some subjects, such as electromagnetism. It is also used to refer to the color charge in quantum chromodynamics.

Charge Number

A charge number (N_C, also called **valence number**) is a unitless quantity that expresses the following:

- Electric charges (q) of ions (cations or anions) in a chemical reaction,
- Replaceable hydrogen ions (H^+) in an acid or hydroxide ions (OH^-) in a base, and
- Chemical bonds that a given ion can make with other ions to form a chemical substance during a reaction.

As for the first case, consider NaCl (salt), which is formed by reacting 1 sodium cation (Na^+, with N_C of 1) with 1 chlorine anion (Cl^-, with N_C of –1), as $Na^+ + Cl^- \rightarrow NaCl$. Similarly, 1 calcium ion (Ca^{+2}, with N_C of 2) reacts with 2 chloride ions (Cl^-) to form neutrally-charged calcium chloride, as $Ca^{2+} + 2\ Cl^- \rightarrow CaCl_2$.

As for the second case, the N_C of **acids** equates to the number of hydrogen ions (H^{+1}) they can release. For example, the N_C of hydrochloric acid (HCl) is 1 because 1 mole of it releases 1 mole of H^+. The N_C of sulfuric acid (H_2SO_4) is 2 (because 1 mole releases 2 moles of H^+). The N_C of **bases** equates to the amount of hydroxyl ion (OH^-) released. The N_C of, for instance, sodium hydroxide (NaOH) is 1 (because 1 mole of NaOH can release 1 mole of OH^-). And that of calcium hydroxide, $Ca(OH)_2$, is 2 (because 1 mole can release 2 moles of OH^-). Ammonia (NH_3, an alkaline gas) releases 1 OH^- when it reacts with water ($NH_3 + H_2O \rightarrow NH_4 + OH$), so its N_C = 1.

As for the third case, in the NaCl example, Na^+ needs a chemical bond to connect to Cl^- because their ions' N_C is 1. Similarly, in the $CaCl_2$ example, Ca^{+2} needs 2 bonds (of the same type) to connect to 2 chloride ions (Cl^-) because the N_C of Ca^{+2} is 2.

[Charge number (N_C) is often used in calculations of equivalent mass (M_{Eq}).]

C-29

CHARLES'S GAS LAW

Discussed under GAS LAWS.

C-29

CHARLES'S GAS LAW

Discussed under GAS LAWS.

C-30
CHELATES AND CHELATION

Chelates

A chelate (*ki-leite*) is a chemical compound that can form two (or more) separate covalent bonds with different ions (mostly metal ions). An example of chelate is ethylenediaminetetraacetic acid dihydrate (EDTA.2H_2O, simply EDTA), which can make bonds with cations, mainly calcium cation (Ca^{2+}), magnesium cation (Mg^{2+}), and iron cation (Fe^{2+}) in a solution sample. Because of the chelate property, EDTA is used in the laboratories to determine a sample's hardness (the total soluble salts of Ca and Mg). EDTA is used in some chemical process plants to clean hardness from evaporators' tubes and boilers' feedwater to absorb Ca^{2+} and Mg^{2+} (the main hardness components).

Chelation

Chelation (*ki-lei-shen*) uses a chelate (like EDTA) to form covalent bonds with a metal ion, mainly Ca^{2+}, Mg^{2+}, and Fe^{2+}.

C-31
CHEMICAL AFFINITY

As another name for **attractive energy**, it is defined under ENERGY AND ITS FORMS.

C-32
CHEMICAL AND PHYSICAL CHANGES

Chemical Changes

A chemical change occurs when a chemical substance's chemical composition and chemical properties change to form a new substance (or substances). For example, a chemical change in water occurs when an electric current goes through its molecules to cause a chemical reaction. During the reaction, the energy (E) of the current causes the water molecules to decompose into atoms that then create chemical bonds to form hydrogen molecules (H_2) and oxygen molecules (O_2), which are different from water molecules (H_2O).

$$2\,H_2O \rightarrow 2\,H_2 + O_2$$

[A chemical change occurring in a reaction is usually shown by an arrow (→), like the listed reaction.]

Physical Changes

A physical change occurs when a substance's physical properties change, but its composition and chemical properties remain the same. For example, a physical change in water occurs when heated from 30ºC to 50ºC. And a chemical change in water occurs when a new substance (or substances) is formed, as said a moment ago.

[Physical changes usually occur in connection with a phase change, which is a physical change. Evaporation of water (a liquid) into vapor (a gas) or melting ice (a solid) to liquid water is, thus, physical changes (because the water in both liquid form and solid form has the same composition of H_2O).]

C-33

CHEMICAL AND PHYSICAL PROPERTIES

Chemical Properties: A chemical property is the property of a substance related to that substance's composition. Thus, when a substance goes under a reaction, that substance's composition also changes. A substance's chemical properties are the chemical identities of that substance. When, for example, atmospheric oxygen reacts with iron (Fe), corrosion occurs, causing the composition of Fe to be changed to FeO.

Physical Properties: A physical property is a property that can be observed, sensed, and measured directly. The physical properties of a chemical system (simply **system**) are changed during a physical change. When a solution's temperature (T, a physical property) changes, some of its other physical properties also change.

For example, area, boiling point temperature, color, density, elasticity, length, intensity, mass, mass flow rate, momentum, plasticity, permeability, permittivity, resistance, solubility, and time are physical properties.

C-34

CHEMICAL BONDS

Chemical bonds (simply **bonds**) bind (connect) the particles (atoms, molecules, or ions) together in a chemical reaction to form a compound (or compounds). In a compound, bonds can be viewed as **binding forces** (more correctly, electromagnetic forces) between the atoms of a compound. For example, two (2) hydrogen atoms (H) bind to each other to form a hydrogen molecule (H_2). **Bonding** (intermolecular connection) occurs by bond energy (E_B), **released** when a bond is **formed** and **absorbed** when a bond is **broken**. Thus, forming new bond releases energy (E), and breaking the bond takes E.

The way the bonds hold a compound's atoms together determines the **strength** of that compound. Based on the strength, bonds are divided into two major groups:

- **Strong** (Primary) **Bonds:** Covalent, ionic, and metallic bonds are strong bonds.
- **Weak** (Secondary) **Bonds:** Hydrogen bonds, dipole-dipole bonds, and van der Waals are weak bonds.

As for the bonding process, the following general statements can be said:

- An atom's valance (outer) electrons are the only ones that participate in that atom's bonding process (because they are the most weakly-bound electrons). Taking one (or more) electron occurs on the weakest electron from the valance shell of an atom.
- A molecule's total valence electrons (outer electrons) is 8; that is, $2(1\ e^-) + 6\ e^- = 8\ e^-$ (or 4 electron pairs).

Covalent Bonds

As the strongest bonds, the covalent bonds are formed between two (or more) atoms by sharing or transferring (giving or taking) those atoms' valence electrons.

The covalent bonds usually join nonmetals to nonmetals. Most nonmetal molecules are bonded together by a single electron pair (two valence electrons that act as a chemical bond), double electron pair, or triple electron pair (see Figure 1). One electron pair is shared between the atoms in a **single covalent bond**. The bond between two hydrogen atoms in a hydrogen molecule (H_2) is a single bond, shown as H–H (simply H_2).

[Single covalent bonds are the weakest of the three covalent bonds.] Two electron pairs are shared between the atoms in a **double covalent bond**. The bonds between two oxygen atoms in an oxygen molecule are double covalent bonds, so an oxygen molecule is shown as O=O (simply O_2). [Double bonds are stronger than single bonds.] In a **triple covalent bond**, three pairs of electrons are shared. The bond between C and N in cyanide (CN) is a triple bond, so shown as C≡N (simply CN), as shown in Figure 1. [Triple covalent bonds are the strongest of all three.]

The bonds between carbon (C) and nitrogen (N) atoms in a cyanide molecule (CN), between oxygen and each of the 2 hydrogen atoms in a water molecule (H_2O), and between C and each of the 4 hydrogen atoms in a methane molecule (CH_4) are also covalent, as shown in Figure 1.

Knowing the following about covalent bonding is helpful:

- The compounds that are bonded covalently (electronically) are known as covalent compounds. Water (H_2O), methane (CH_4), and ethylene (C_2H_4) are examples of covalent compounds.
- The strength of covalent bonds varies depending on how many electron pairs are shared between the atoms (the *greater* the number of shared electron pairs, the *stronger* is the bond).

Because in covalent bonding, atoms interact with one another electronically, two situations are possible:

- **Oxidation:** This is the loss of an electron (or electrons) by an element (or a compound) in an oxidation-reduction reaction. The element (or compound) that loses the electron (e^-) is oxidized.
- **Reduction:** This is the gain of an electron (or electrons) by an element (or a compound). The element (or compound) that receives the electron is reduced.

Glycosidic Bond: Glycosidic bond (also called **oxygen bond**) is one type of covalent bond that consists of oxygen linkage (–O–) to connect a monosaccharide unit (molecule) to another unit, which may be (or may *not* be) another monosaccharide. For example, starch consists of many glucose (monosaccharide) units connected by alpha 1:4 glycosidic bonds (see Figure 1 under STARCH).

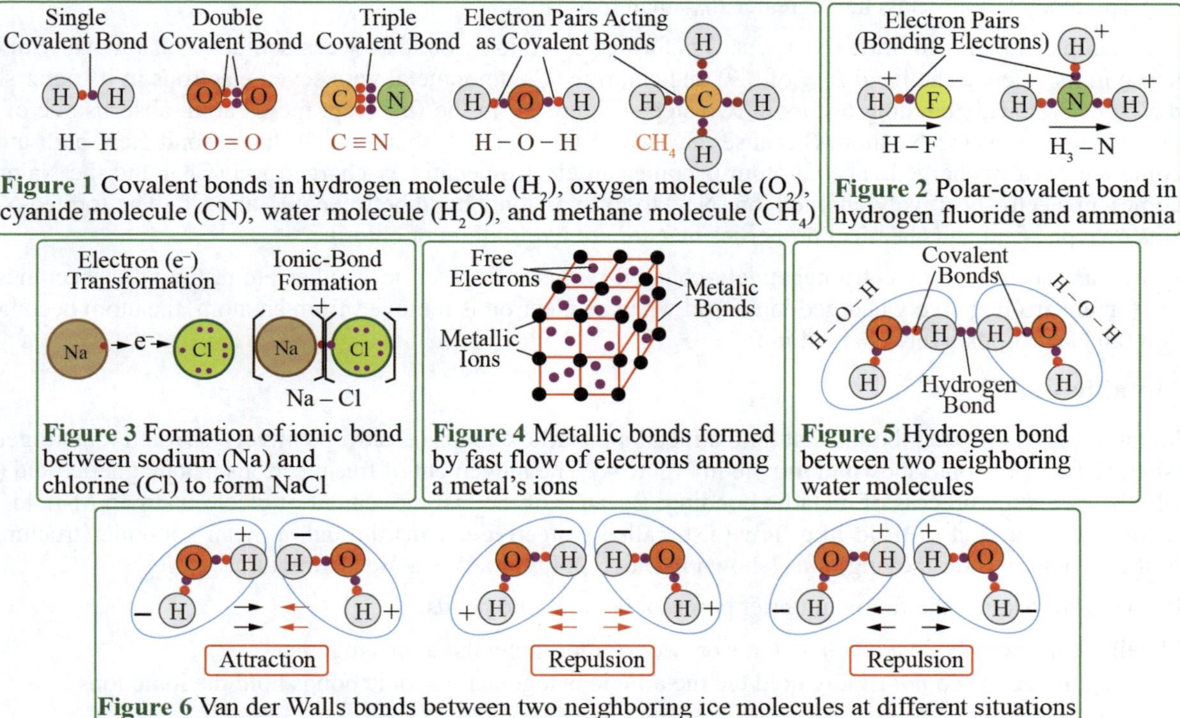

Figure 1 Covalent bonds in hydrogen molecule (H_2), oxygen molecule (O_2), cyanide molecule (CN), water molecule (H_2O), and methane molecule (CH_4)

Figure 2 Polar-covalent bond in hydrogen fluoride and ammonia

Figure 3 Formation of ionic bond between sodium (Na) and chlorine (Cl) to form NaCl

Figure 4 Metallic bonds formed by fast flow of electrons among a metal's ions

Figure 5 Hydrogen bond between two neighboring water molecules

Figure 6 Van der Walls bonds between two neighboring ice molecules at different situations

Polar-Covalent Bonds

The polar-covalent bonds (simply **polar bonds**; also called **dipole-dipole bonds**) form between atoms of two elements with different electronegativity (E_{Neg}), resulting in sharing electrons unevenly between the two atoms. In general, the *greater* is an atom's E_{Neg}, the *greater* is its ability to pull electrons toward itself when it makes a bond with another atom.

Consider the formation of a polar covalent bond between a hydrogen atom (H, a nonpolar atom with E_{Neg} of 2.2) and a fluorine atom (F, a polar atom with E_{Neg} of 4) to form hydrogen fluoride (HF, a polar compound). Because of greater E_{Neg}, the F atom pulls the shared electron pairs toward itself than the H atom (see the left side of Figure 2). Thus, the electron pairs are closer to the F atom. For this reason, the F side of the bond is slightly **negative**, and the H side is slightly **positive**. This difference in electric charges is known as the **dipole** (read *die pole*) and is shown by an arrow pointing to the negative side of the bond ($\overrightarrow{H-F}$). [A delta notation (δ^+ and δ^-) is usually used to indicate bond polarity).

In a molecule of ammonia (NH_3, a polar covalent compound), the nitrogen (N) atom has a little more polarity than the hydrogen (H) atom has (because the E_{Neg} of the N atom is greater than E_{Neg} of H), so the N atom pulls the shared electron pairs toward itself, as shown on the right side of Figure 2.

When the E_{Neg} of two elements differs, a polar covalent bond may form between them, as in H + F → HF. When, instead, the E_{Neg} of the elements are the same, *no* polar covalent bond is formed between them (as in H + H → H_2), so they are bonded by another type of bond and, therefore, called a **nonpolar bond**.

Ionic Bonds

As weak bonds, the ionic bonds are formed by losing or gaining electrons between atoms of two elements, resulting in electrically-charged ions, known as the **ionic bond**. An ionic bond between two atoms occurs when the shared electrons are transferred from the less electropositive atom to the more electronegative atom. For this reason, ionic bonding occurs between a nonmetal and a metal because they are different in electronegativity (E_{Neg}). [In general, nonmetals have greater E_{Neg} than metals.]

For example, sodium chloride (Na Cl, salt) is formed by an ionic bond between sodium (Na, a metal with one electron in its valence shell and E_{Neg} of 0.9) and chlorine (Cl, a nonmetal with seven electrons in its outer shell and E_{Neg} of 3.2). This bonding occurs in two steps (Figure 3). In the first step, the Cl atom absorbs one of the valence electrons of the Na atom (because the E_{Neg} of Cl is greater than Na). In the second step, both atoms become electrically charged. The Cl atom becomes an electro-negatively-charged ion (Cl^-), and the Na atom becomes an electro-positively-charged ion (Na^+) to form an ionic bond between Na^+ and Cl^-. The formed NaCl has its own physical and chemical properties that are *not* like sodium or chlorine.

[When an electron (an electro-negatively-charged particle) is given to another atom, the atom becomes an anion (an electro-negatively charged ion). And when an electron is removed from an atom, the atom becomes a cation (an electro-positively charged ion).]

Metallic Bonds

Metallic bonds are weak bonds that hold a metal's metallic cations (electro-positively-charged ions) together by sharing free electrons (shown in **purple** in Figure 4). The movement of free electrons in a magnetic field (M-field) also helps the process of metallic bonding. Because of the fast movement of electrons in an M-field, the electrons create a kind of **fluid-like flow** (also called **collective ocean**) through a metal's atomic structure to hold the stationary (non-moving) ions (shown in **black** in Figure 4) in a metal structure.

It is helpful to know the following brief points about metallic bonds:

- Metallic bonds can bond a metal's atoms or two (or more) metals' atoms together.
- The metallic bonds do *not* rigidly hold the metallic ions together, as ionic bonds hold the ionic ions.

Hydrogen Bonds

As the second weakest bonds, the hydrogen bonds are formed by an electron pair between the neighboring molecules of the same compound or between the molecules of different compounds. The bonds between neighboring water molecules (H_2O – H_2O) are typical hydrogen bonds (see Figure 5). When a hydrogen atom (H) of a water molecule forms a hydrogen bond with the hydrogen atom of the neighboring water molecule by a pair of electrons, the two neighboring water molecules behave as charged molecules because of an electric dipole formed between the O and H atoms in an OH bond. Thus, one molecule becomes a **bond donor** and the other one a **bond acceptor**.

The bonds between nitrogen (N), oxygen (O), or fluorine (F) with an electronegative atom are also hydrogen bonds. And so the bond between CH_3 and OH in the molecule of methanol (CH_3OH).

Van der Waals Bonds

As the weakest of all bonds, the Van der Waals bonds (named after the developer, Johannes Van der Waals, a Dutch physicist, 1837–1923) are formed by slight non-uniform (imbalance) in the electric charge distribution in molecules. If, say, an electrically neutral molecule has a more negative charge on one end than the other, the molecule would attract other similar molecules. Thus, the Van der Waals forces can be attractive or repulsive. As a result, the electrically-charged molecule might be unevenly distributed, making one part of a molecule slightly positive and the other slightly negative. Van der Waals bonds exist in ice and dry ice (the solid form of carbon dioxide). Figure 6 shows van der Waals between two neighboring ice molecules at different situations.

C-35
CHEMICAL COMPONENTS

Study CHEMICAL ELEMENTS, COMPOUNDS, ND COMPONENTS.

C-36
CHEMICAL COMPOSITION

The chemical composition of a chemical compound indicates the number of its chemical elements in one of its molecules. For example, one molecule of salt (sodium chloride, NaCl) composes of one sodium (Na) atom and one chlorine (Cl) atom. In mass percentage, a salt molecule composes of 39.3% Na atoms (23/58.5 = 39.3%) and 60.7% of Cl atoms (35.5/58.5 = 60.7%), where 23 is the molecular mass (M_M) of Na and 35.5 is the M_M of Cl. Similarly, one molecule of sugar (sucrose, $C_{12}H_{22}O_{11}$) composes of 12 carbon (C) atoms, 22 hydrogen (H) atoms, and 11 oxygen (O) atoms. In percentage, a sugar molecule composes of 42% C atoms [(12×12)/342 = 42%], 6.5% H atoms [(22×1)/342 = 6.5%], and 51.5% O atoms [(11×16)/342 = 51.5%], where 12 is the M_M of C, 1 is the M_M of H, and 16 is that of O.

The chemical composition of a mixture is the individual substances constituting that mixture, so it quantifies that mixture's concentration. [Because the concentration is expressed in different ways (in mass fraction, molar fraction, volume fraction, molarity, molality, and normality), more ways describe a mixture's composition.]

C-37
CHEMICAL COMPOUNDS

Study CHEMICAL ELEMENTS, COMPOUNDS, ND COMPONENTS.

CHEMICAL ELEMENTS, COMPOUNDS, AND COMPONENTS

Chemical Elements

A chemical element (simply **element**) consists of only one type of atoms, so it is pure. For example, pure hydrogen (H) composes of only hydrogen atoms. Pure iron (Fe) is an element, too.

Elements have some other properties that can be summarized as

- Atoms of two (or more) elements combine in a definite mass ratio to form one (or more) chemical compound. For example, 2 g of hydrogen (H; with molecular mass, M_M, of 1) react with 16 g of oxygen (O; with M_M of 16) to produce 18 g of water (H_2O; with M_M of 18). So, the **mass ratio** of H to O is 2 to 16 (or 1 to 8). And the **proportion ratio** between them is 1 to 2. [Many other compounds contain H and O, but only H_2O has a mass ratio of 1 to 8 and a proportion ratio of 1 to 2.]
- All atoms of an element have the same atomic mass (M_A), and atoms of different elements have different atomic masses.
- An element *cannot* be chemically decomposed into atoms (see CHEMICAL REACTION).

The following are other useful information about elements:

- Chemistry knows 118 elements, 94 of these exist in nature; the others are produced artificially in the lab. The balance of protons and neutrons in heavier elements can make them unstable, meaning that they can go through a process known as radioactive decay.
- All elements are named by IUPAC (International Union of Pure and Applied Chemistry) and listed in an organized table known as the periodic table of elements (simply **periodic table**).

Chemical Compounds

A chemical compound (simply **compound**) consists of two (or more) chemical elements. Elements in a compound have a certain proportion ratio. In more detail, a compound's molecules are composed of atoms from more than one element held together by chemical bonds. Some compounds, like sugar ($C_{12}H_{22}O_{11}$), consist of molecules, while others, such as salt (NaCl), consist of ions. Some other properties of a compound are:

- It has a chemical formula.
- It has a constant chemical composition and constant chemical and physical properties.
- It *cannot* be decomposed to its elements by a physical change but by a chemical change.

It is also helpful to know the following before finishing this subtopic:

- In chemistry, the terms compound and substance are usually used equally.
- Organic compounds and inorganic compounds are two types of chemical compounds.
- Antoine Lavoisier (1743–1794) was the first who presented the notion of element and compound.

Chemical Components

A chemical component (simply **component**) is a constituent of a chemical compound. [In modern chemistry, the term **components** is usually used instead of **species**.] The **number of components** (C_N) in a reactive-fluid system can be calculated by using the system's number of constituents (C_{N1}), the number of reactions that occur in the system (R_N), and the system's number of constraints (C_{N2}).

$$C_N = C_{N1} - R_N - C_{N2} \tag{1}$$

Consider the solution mixture of ethanol and water. This system (mixture) has two (2) constituents (C_2H_5OH and H_2O), *no* reaction, and *no* constraint (limitation), so the system's C_N is $2 - 0 - 0 = 2$.

As another example, consider the reaction of $CaCO_3 \rightleftharpoons CaO + CO_2$. This system has three constituents; two solids ($CaCO_3$ and CaO), one gas (CO_2), one reaction, and *no* constraint, so its C_N will be $3 - 1 - 0 = 2$.

Furthermore, consider water in the liquid state. This system has 3 independent constituents, water (H_2O), hydronium cations (H_3O^+), and hydroxyl anions (OH^-). In the system, one reaction occurs, as given below.

$$2\,H_2O \rightleftharpoons (H_3O)^+ + (OH)^-$$

Thus, the C_N of this system with one constraint (because of the reaction's reversibility) is $3 - 1 - 1 = 1$.

Being aware of the following brief points about C_N (the number of components) is helpful:

- When two phases of the same compound exist in a system with different concentrations, the system contains two components. For example, two components are in a supersaturated sugar solution (because sugar concentration in the solid phase is different from the liquid phase.

[The C_N has some applications in fluid systems, including determining the number of degrees of freedom in a system used in the phase rule (Gibbs phase rule).]

C-39

CHEMICAL ENERGY

Simplified name for CHEMICAL POTENTIAL ENERGY.

C-40

CHEMICAL ENGINEERING

Discussed in the book's INTRODUCTION.

C-41

CHEMICAL ENGINEERING PROCESS UNITS

Study PROCESS UNITS OF CHEMICAL ENGINEERING.

C-42

CHEMICAL EQUATION

A chemical equation is the symbolic representation of a chemical reaction using chemical symbols and chemical formulas. The reactant (or reactants) in a chemical equation is given on the left-hand side and the product (or products) on the right-hand side, as shown below.

$$2\,HCl + 2\,Na \rightarrow 2\,NaCl + H_2$$

According to IUPAC nomenclature rules, this equation is read as "hydrochloric acid plus sodium yields sodium chloride and hydrogen gas" or simply "2 HCl plus 2 Na yield 2 NaCl and 1 H_2." [The coefficients in this equation are the absolute values (with *no* sign).]

C-43

CHEMICAL EQUILIBRIUM

Discussed under the topic of EQUILIBRIUM.

C-44

CHEMICAL FORMULAS

A chemical formula (also called **molecular formula** or simply **formula**) concisely expresses the symbol and number of a compound's atoms. For example, the chemical formula of sugar (sucrose) is $C_{12}H_{22}O_{11}$. This formula tells us that a sugar molecule consists of 12 atoms of carbon (C), 22 atoms of hydrogen (H), and 11 atoms of oxygen (O), with a molecular mass (M_M) of 342 g. And according to the Law of Definite Composition, the sugar's components (C with M_M of 12 g, H with M_M of 1 g, and O with M_M of 16 g) are always in a fixed mass ratio. Expressing the ratio in mass percentage, a sugar molecule consists of 42% C atoms [(12×12)/342 = 42], 6.5% H atoms [(22×1)/342 = 6.5], and 51.5% O atoms [(11×16)100/342 = 51.5].

The use of dotes, parentheses, brackets, dashes, plus signs (+), minus signs (–), subscripts, and superscripts may be required for writing a compound's formula. For instance, the aluminum sulfate's formula is written with parenthesis as $Al_2(SO_4)_3$, and the formula of calcium sulfate dihydrate ($CaSO_4.2H_2O$, a hydrate) is written with a centered dot that separates the two parts of the formula.

C-45

CHEMICAL OXYGEN DEMAND

Study BIOCHEMICAL AND CHEMICAL OXYGEN DEMANDS.

C-46

CHEMICAL POLARITY

Chemical polarity (simply **polarity**) is a property of a molecule related to the existence of an electric dipole (also called **electric dipole moment**, simply **dipole moment** or **dipole**) in that molecule. A molecule with a dipole (read *die pole*) has unequal electric charges on each side. Consider a water molecule (a polar molecule). Here, hydrogen (H) atoms are slightly positive, and the oxygen atom (O) is slightly negative (because the electronegativity of O is greater than H). In a water molecule, thus, two electron pairs act as covalent bonds between two H atoms and one O atom. The more electronegative oxygen atom pulls the electron pairs toward itself, so a negative dipole and a positive dipole are formed, as shown in Figure 1. The dipole then acts as a hydrogen bond between two neighboring water molecules.

Similarly, a sugar molecule ($C_{12}H_{22}O_{11}$) contains seven O–H covalent bonds. The H atoms are slightly positive, and the O atoms are slightly negative, forming seven (7) dipoles, which create hydrogen bonds between the neighboring sugar molecules. [The bond between the sugar molecule's two rings is a glycosidic bond (oxygen bond), as shown on the right-hand side of the same figure.]

[Note: As a related subject, study POLAR AND NONPOLAR COMPOUNDS.]

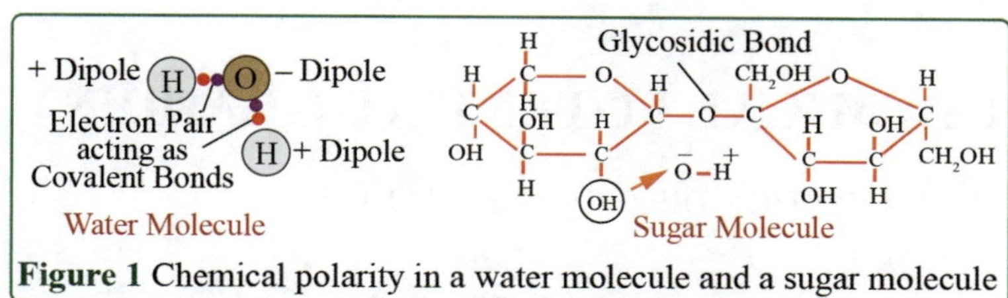

Figure 1 Chemical polarity in a water molecule and a sugar molecule

C-47

CHEMICAL POTENTIAL

The chemical potential (μ, mu) of a chemical component (simply **component**) is its potential (ability) when it goes through a concentration change (generally concentration difference, ΔC). Thus, a component's μ in a fluid (liquid or gas) is the difference in C (concentration) between two points in that fluid or between two fluids. Knowing the following two (2) points is important:

- Because the μ acts like the ΔC, the words **chemical potential** and **concentration difference** are used equally, and both are expressed in units of concentration (like molar concentration).
- The Greek letters used for chemical potential and viscosity are different. For chemical potential, the letter μ (mu) is used, while for viscosity, η (eta) is used. Note also that μ is also used to abbreviate **millimeters**.

An μ (chemical potential) can occur in a system by the following:

- Concentration change,
- Phase change (state change), and
- Chemical reaction (simply **reaction**).

A component's molecules are likely to move (scientifically **diffuse**) from an area with a higher μ to the area with a lower μ. This is also true for C (concentration) as molecules diffuse from an area with a higher C to an area with a lower C. Similarly, at a certain temperature (T), molecules have a higher μ in an area with a higher C and a lower μ in an area with a lower C.

Let us now consider an example *not* based on C but on a phase change. The water molecules have a lower μ than the molecules of an ice cube (the water's solid phase). When, therefore, an ice cube is added to a glass of water, some of the water molecules convert from solid to liquid (because of lower μ in the molecules of water phase), so the ice cube shrinks (melting occurs). If we start now to cool down the water-ice mixture to below 0°C, the water molecules convert from liquid to solid (because of higher μ in the molecules of the ice phase), so the ice cube grows (crystallization occurs).

Knowing the following points about the μ (chemical potential) is also helpful:

- Although μ plays a key role in some cases, it exhibits undesirable properties that discourage its use. Fugacity (f), for example, can be used in a system at phase equilibrium instead of μ to make the calculations easier.
- Chemical potential is an extensive quantity, which depends on the components' quantity in a sample.

C-48

CHEMICAL POTENTIAL ENERGY

Discussed under the topic of ENERGY AND ITS FORMS.

C-49

CHEMICAL POTENTIAL GRADIENT

Another name for CONCENTRATION DIFFERENCE GRADIENT.

C-50

CHEMICAL PROCESSES

A chemical process (simply **process**) is a chemical, physical, or both action that occurs in a chemical system (simply **system**). Knowing the following brief points about the process is useful:

- The word **process** is used in ChemEng reference books (like this book) to make studying a subject easier.
- A process can occur in an extremely small system, like an electron in an atom, or as large as generating electric power in a power plant (or even acting gravitational force in the entire Universe).

When a process occurs in a system, the system goes through one, two, three, four, or all the next changes:

- Chemical change,
- Physical change,
- Phase change,
- Mass change,
- Enthalpy change.

The processes used in ChemEng are called process units of ChemEng (unit operations of ChemEng), which are discussed in this book alphabetically.

Chemical processes are divided into two groups: batch and continuous processes.

Batch Processes

A batch process is an interruptible operating process used in a chemical process plant to process a certain amount of raw material. A batch process is usually used to meet one (or more) of the next situations:

- The production is seasonal,
- A small-volume production is required, and
- The process must be performed under restricted operating conditions.

A batch process has the next main characteristics.

- It may proceed in a non-steady manner,
- It is a closed system (mass *cannot* enter or leave the system), and
- Its controlling parameters do *not* change greatly with time (t) because it proceeds quickly.

Continuous Processes

A continuous process is a nonstop operating method used in chemical plants to process a large quantity of raw material (or raw materials) when a nonstop production is needed.

A continuous process has the next main properties.

- It may (or may *not*) proceed in a steady-state manner,
- It is an open system (both mass and energy can enter or leave the system), and
- Its controlling parameters change with time considerably, although it is a non-interrupted operation.

Comparison of Batch and Continuous Processes

For the same processing inputs, the advantages of a batch process over a continuous process are:

- Production of better quality and uniform products, and
- Less dependency on control systems (automation).

Instead, a continuous process has some advantages over a batch process:

- Less man work,
- Less supervision,
- Less operating costs,
- Less energy consumption,
- Less floor space requirement.

In a typical batch process, like the reaction of A and B in a reactor, the feeds (A and B) are added to the reactor, and after a certain time when the reaction is complete, the process is stopped, and the product (C) is removed from the reactor. The same steps are then repeated for the feeds' next batch. A batch process, thus, is:

- A closed system (energy can enter or leave the system, but mass *cannot*) because *no* mass enters or leaves the system during the process.
- A non-steady-state process because the variables (like temperature) may change.

[In the mass balancing of a **batch process**, the amount of mass (M) is considered, while in a continuous process, $\dot{M}$ (mass flow rates) or $\dot{V}$ (volumetric flow rate) is used.]

In a typical continuous process, like A + B = C + D in a reactor, the feeds (A and B) continuously enter the process, and the products (C and D) leave the process, meaning that while the reaction is proceeding, the materials move through the reactor.

In a batch process, a reactor's **volumetric capacity** (V_C) is the product of A (reactor's cross-sectional area), V (the flow's velocity), and t (time), where $A = \pi R^2 = \pi d^2/4$.

$$V_C = A.V.t \tag{1}$$

When A is in m^2, V is in m/h, and t is in h (hour), the V_C becomes in m^3.

In a continuous process, the reactor's V_C (volumetric capacity or volumetric flow rate) equates to the reactor's A (area) multiplied by its V (velocity).

$$V_C = A.V \tag{2}$$

For example, the V_C of a continuous reactor can be 50 m^3/h. [As seen from these equations, the V_C of a reactor is *not* dependent on its height (h), regardless it operates continuously or discontinuously.]

Reversible and Irreversible Processes

A process is **reversible** when it can return to its original condition by the same path. For example, melting ice at 0°C is a reversible process, as adding heat energy (E_Q) to the mixture of water and ice converts ice to water. And removing E_Q from the mixture returns the mixture to its original condition. [Spontaneous (unforced) processes are *not* reversible (because they occur in one direction).]

Instead, a process is **irreversible** when it *cannot* return to its original condition by the same path. A gas expansion into a vacuum is irreversible, as some work must be done to return it to its original condition.

C-51

CHEMICAL PROCESS DESIGN

This topic is *not* covered in this book.

C-52

CHEMICAL PROCESS ECONOMY

Study PROCESS ECONOMICS OF CHEMICAL ENGINEERING.

C-53

CHEMICAL PROCESS INDUSTRY

The chemical process industry (simply **chemical industry**) applies the principles of ChemEng to produce around one million different products. By rough estimation, two out of three industrial facilities are chemical process plants (simply **chemical plants**). The chemical industry, by far, is the world's largest industry, which divides into smaller industries, each consisting of several branches. In a short definition, any industry that processes a chemical compound (or more compounds) to produce a product is included in this classification. Figure 3 under INTRODUCTION gives several smaller industries of the main chemical process industry.

It is helpful to know the following brief information about the chemical process industry:

- The world's three largest chemical-producing companies are BASF (Germany), Dow Chemical (USA), and Sinopec (China). In 2018, the BSAF's sales were over 74 billion dollars, that of Dow was 70 billion dollars, and the sales of Sinopec were 69.2 billion dollars.
- As the largest sub-industry of the chemical industry, the food industry had \$3.2 trillion in annual sales globally in 2011 (about one-third of it was in the US of America). The pharmaceutical sub-industry had \$1 trillion (about one-third of it was in the US of America).

C-54

CHEMICAL PROCESS PLANT

As the elementary unit of the chemical process industry (simply **chemical industry**), a chemical process plant (simply **chemical plant**) is a facility that processes raw material (materials) into products and byproducts. An oil refinery for processing crude oil, a plant for biofuel production from biomass, and many other chemical productions and processing facilities are examples of chemical plants. Such a facility processes raw materials on thousands of tons a day.

A chemical plant usually consists of several process stations (simply **stations**), like filtration, evaporation, and crystallization stations. Each station consists of one or more process units of ChemEng. And each process unit (unit operation) has related attached parts (fittings) and detached parts (accessories).

C-55

CHEMICAL PROCESS STATION

A chemical process station (simply **process station** or **station**) is a term frequently used in this book to indicate a section of a chemical process plant (simply **chemical plant**) assigned to do a particular duty (job). The reason that the term station is, comparatively, more appropriate is that today's chemical plants usually have a high operating capacity, so for; say, an evaporation process, they need to use more than one evaporator (some use up to 12 evaporators), so we are talking about a set of evaporators that operate in connection with each other and with other devices. In this way, the term **evaporating station** refers to a large section of a chemical plant that consists of attached parts (like evaporator bodies, valves, and pipes), detached parts (like heat exchangers and condensers), and instruments (like controllers). Notably, each station usually employs one or more process units of ChemEng (unit operations of ChemEng). Evaporating station, for example, consists of three process units: heating, evaporation, and condensation processes.

[Note: The term **in-process product** or simply **in-product** is used in this book to indicate the product of an individual station in a chemical plant, as opposed to the final product of that plant. For example, the concentrated liquid stream from the evaporation station is an in-product because it must be processed further to produce the main product.]

C-56

CHEMICAL REACTION ORDER

Chemical reaction order (simply **reaction order**) is the exponent to which the concentration (C) of a reactant or product of a chemical reaction (simply **reaction**) is raised. In other definition, the reaction order of a reactant is the exponent of its C in a **reaction-rate equation** (defined in a moment). Consider the following typical reaction with stoichiometric coefficients of a, b, c, and d:

$$a.A + b.B \rightarrow c.C + d.D \qquad (1)$$

The chemical reaction rate (simply **reaction rate**, R_R) for this reaction's reactants (A and B) is

$$R_R = K_R(C_A)^a(C_B)^b \qquad (2)$$

In this equation, called the **reaction-rate equation**, a is the reaction order for A, and b is that for B. K_R is a proportionality constant, called **reaction rate constant** (simply **rate constant**), C_A is the concentration of component A, and C_B is that of B. For a reaction that is described by Equation 2, the reaction is "a^{th}" order in relation to component A, "b^{th}" order in relation to component B, and "$a + b$" order in relation to the overall reaction. For example, for a reaction with $a = 1$ and $b = 2$, the reaction is **first-order** in relation to A, **second-order** in relation to B, and **third-order** overall. As a real example, consider the reaction for the decomposition of N_2O_5.

$$2\ N_2O_5 \rightarrow 4\ NO_2 + O_2$$

The rate equation for this reaction is

$$R_R = K_R(C)_{N_2O_5} = K_R[N_2O_5] \qquad (3)$$

The reaction is first order in relation to N_2O_5 (because N_2O_5 carries an exponent of 1). If the concentration (C) of N_2O_5 decreases by half, the rate is half as fast. If, similarly, C of N_2O_5 is doubled, the rate of reaction doubles. Thus, a first-order reaction has a constant (fixed) rate of concentration change.

Similarly, we can consider the reaction of NO and Cl_2 ($2\ NO + Cl_2 \rightarrow 2\ NOCl$) with the rate equation of

$$R_R = K_R(C_{NO})^2(C_{Cl_2}) = K_R[NO]^2[Cl_2] \qquad (4)$$

This reaction is **second-order** in NO, **first-order** in Cl_2, and **third-order** overall. [For some reactions, the reaction orders do *not* equate to the stoichiometric coefficients.]

C-57

CHEMICAL REACTION RATE AND REACTION RATE CONSTANT

Chemical Reaction Rate

The chemical reaction rate (R_R, simply **reaction rate**) is a quantity that shows how fast a chemical reaction occurs. It shows how fast the reactants' concentration (C) decreases and that of products increases with time (t). A reaction's R_R can be determined by measuring the product's appearance rate or the reactant's disappearance rate. The R_R is expressed, among others, in mole/t. A substance's C under a reaction in a solution can be determined, among others, by measuring the light absorbance (a C-related quantity) passing the solution.

Some reactions are extremely fast (like the combustion reaction of a fuel), some are slow (like the drying of concrete), and some are extremely slow (like the rusting of iron (Fe) caused by its reaction with atmospheric oxygen (O_2). In this way, the *faster* a reaction, the *greater* is its R_R, so the reaction of a fuel with O_2 has a lot greater R_R than Fe with O_2.

The reaction's R_R can be determined by the change in the reactant's concentration (ΔC) divided by the change in time (Δt).

$$R_R = -\frac{\Delta C}{\Delta t} \quad (1)$$

[The minus sign used here is because the C of the **reactant** *decreases* with time. The R_R, however, is always expressed as a positive quantity. Instead, when the product's R_R is calculated, the equation will have a positive sign (because the C of the **product** *increases* with time).]

Consider the decomposition of sugar (sucrose, $C_{12}H_{22}O_{11}$) to ethanol (C_2H_5OH) with the help of brewer yeasts, which act as an enzymatic catalyst in the production of ethanol from sugarcane juice or molasses in Brazil and some other countries. A graph of the sugar concentration (C) in the fermentation process in relation to time is given in Figure 1. For example, the rate of change of sugar in 8 h of fermentation (see the same figure) will be

$$R_R = -\frac{\Delta C}{\Delta t} = -\frac{\Delta C_2 - \Delta C_1}{8} = -\frac{0.5 - 15.1}{8} = 22 \text{ g/L}$$

The four (4) main factors that control the R_R of a reaction are the following:

- **Concentration of Reactants:** The concentration of the reactant (or reactants) is directly proportional to the R_R (the *more* concentrated the reactants, the *faster* the reaction occurs). This occurs because as the C increases, *more* molecules of the reactants are in each volume to contact each other.
- **Types of Chemical Bonds of Reactants:** The chemical bonds of the reactant (or reactants) affect the R_R because some bonds break faster than others in reactions.
- **Temperature of Reaction:** The temperature (T) of a reaction also goes proportionally with the R_R (the *higher* the T of a reaction, the *faster* the reaction occurs). This statement is true because the molecules' average kinetic energy (E_K) increases as the T increases. [Typically, a temperature increase of 10ºC above room temperature causes the R_R to double (or triple).]
- **Use of Catalyst:** The use of catalyst in a reaction also follows R_R proportionally (the *more* a catalyst is used, the *faster* a reaction occurs). Consider sugar (sucrose, $C_{12}H_{22}O_{11}$) dissolved in water (H_2O). The rate of decomposition of sugar to glucose and fructose is almost zero. But as a little hydrochloric acid (HCl) is added to the solution, the decomposition occurs at a high rate without being consumed.

R_R can also be discussed in the context of collision theory, which studies

- Collision energy (scientifically activation energy, E_a),
- Collision frequency (f_C, also called **collision rate**),
- Collision orientation (O_{XYZ}).

R_R can then be expressed as the product of the three (3) listed collision factors.

$$R_R = E_a.f_C.O_{XYZ} \tag{2}$$

Reaction Rate Constant

The reaction rate constant (K_R) is a proportionality constant that relates a reaction's R_R (reaction rate) to a reactant's concentration (C) in that reaction.

$$R_R = K_R.C \tag{3}$$

This equation, called the **reaction-rate equation**, can be written for both **irreversible reaction** (the products do *not* react to reform the reactants) and **reversible reaction** (the products react to reform the reactants). Consider the general expression for an irreversible reaction.

$$A + B \rightarrow C + D \tag{4}$$

R_R for the reactants (A and B) and K_R of this reaction are given as

$$R_R = K_R.C_A.C_B \tag{5}$$

$$K_R = \frac{C_A.C_B}{C_C.C_D} \tag{6}$$

Some symbolize the concentrations as [] and write this equation as

$$K_R = \frac{[A][B]}{[C][D]} \tag{7}$$

For a reversible reaction, K_R will be

$$K_R = \frac{C_C.C_D}{C_A.C_B} \tag{8}$$

Thus, knowing K_R and the concentrations of the reaction's three components (A, B, and C), the C of the unknown component (D) can be determined.

Further, Equation 8 tells us that

- Equilibrium occurs when the forward reaction rate equates to the backward (reverse) reaction rate, so the reactants reach steady-state values.
- All other concentrations will be changed to maintain the same K_R if one concentration is changed. There is, therefore, different K_R at different temperatures.

In the case that stoichiometric coefficients a, b, c, and d exist, Equation 3 is shown as

$$a.A + b.B \rightarrow c.C + d.D \tag{9}$$

Then R_R for the reactants (A and B), shown as R_{R1}, and that for the products, shown as R_{R2}, are given as

$$R_{R1} = K_{R1}(C_A)^a(C_B)^b \tag{10}$$

$$R_{R2} = K_{R2}(C_A)^a(C_B)^b \tag{11}$$

When the reaction is in equilibrium, R_{R1} equates to R_{R2}, so we can equate these two equations to give

$$\frac{K_{R1}}{K_{R2}} = K_R = \frac{(C_A)^a(C_B)^b}{(C_A)^a(C_B)^b} \tag{12}$$

Some write this equation as

$$K_R = \frac{[A]^a[B]^b}{[C]^c[D]^d} \tag{13}$$

R_R has the unit of mole/(volume.time), such as mole/L.s, where the term volume often refers to a reactor's volume (V), in which the reactants are processed. C_A and C_B are in mole/volume; say, mole/L, known as the molarity. And K_R has the unit of inverse time (in second). [As a practical example, study the next Example.]

Note that for gases (gas phases), C_A and C_B are often expressed as their partial pressures, shown as P_A and P_B, so Equation 10 becomes

$$R_R = K_C . P_A^a . P_B^b \tag{14}$$

An Example on K_R

Given: In the reaction of H_2 (g) + Cl_2 (g) ↔ 2 HCl (g), where g stands for gaseous form, the concentration of H_2 is 0.2, that of Cl_2 is 0.3, and that of HCl is 1.8, all in mole/L.

Wanted: The reaction rate constant (K_R) at a certain temperature

This reaction has two reactants and one product. Equation 6 or 7 can calculate the K_R.

$$K_R = \frac{C_{\text{HCL}}^2}{C_{\text{H2}} . C_{\text{Cl2}}} = \frac{[\text{HCl}]^2}{[\text{H}_2][\text{Cl}_2]} = \frac{[1.8]^2}{[0.2][0.3]} = 54$$

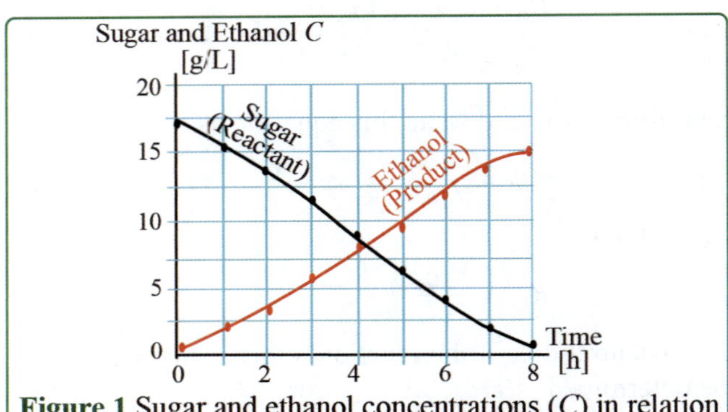

Figure 1 Sugar and ethanol concentrations (C) in relation to time during fermentation of sugar to ethanol

C-58

CHEMICAL REACTIONS

A chemical reaction (simply **reaction**) occurs when its reactant's (or reactants') molecules,

- Contact (collide) to create collisions (contacts) between the molecules. [Because the concept of collision and its affecting factors in chemical reactions are important, they are usually discussed under a separate-and-broad topic, named collision theory.]
- Have access to a certain amount of energy (E), known as activation energy (E_a).

Consider a chemical substance (elements or compounds) that participates as the reactant in a reaction. As soon as the substance's molecules get the required E_a, the molecules collide (contact) and break the chemical bonds, so atoms can be exchanged or rearranged to cause a reaction.

The following points are important to remember:

- When a reaction starts, it proceeds at a certain rate, known as the chemical reaction rate (R_R).
- In a chemical laboratory, a reaction can occur on a small scale in a beaker, while in a chemical process plant, a reaction occurs on a large scale in a chemical reactor (simply **reactor**).

During a reaction, the following are true:

- Atoms are rearranged to form new substances (elements or compounds),

- The principle of conservation of mass remains the same (*no* atoms are lost),
- The nucleus of the participating atoms remains in its original form and shape,
- The electrons of the atoms, however, participate in the chemical reaction process,
- One or more chemical changes and physical changes start taking place immediately.

From what has been said here, one can say that a **chemical reaction** *cannot* change the nucleus of the participating atoms, while a nuclear reaction can. This is the main difference between these reactions.

We consider a single chemical reaction, generally written as A + B → C + D. In this reaction, A and B are **reactants**, and C and D are the **products**. The arrow sign symbolizes a chemical change, meaning that the reactants A and B are changed (converted) into products C and D.

The ratios in which substances combine or form, known as the **reaction coefficients** (usually shown as a, b, c, and d), are written in front of the reactants and products, where coefficient 1 is omitted.

$$a.A + b.B \rightarrow c.C + d.D$$

The reaction coefficients are negative for reactants and positive for products. [Note that more reactants and products can participate in a reaction than those listed here.]

We should be aware that the reactants for the desired reaction can often undergo an undesired reaction (also called a **side reaction**), so we often deal with two (2) reactions.

$$A + B \rightarrow C + D$$

$$A + B \rightarrow E + F$$

We must maximize the desired reaction and minimize the undesired reaction. This can be achieved by selecting the right conditions (like temperature, pressure, and concentration) and chemical reactor (simply **reactor**) to maximize the ratio of desired-to-undesired reactions and produce a product with the highest possible efficiency.

Based on the reversibility, reactions are divided into two groups:

- **Reversible Reactions.** In a reversible reaction, the products react to reform the reactants. In other words, the conversion of reactants to products and that of reactants to products occur simultaneously. When a reversible reaction becomes at equilibrium stability, it can be expressed as a.A + b.B ↔ c.C + d.D.
- **Irreversible Reactions:** In an irreversible reaction, only the reactants react, and products do *not* react to reform the reactants.

Because one mole of all substances always contains 6.02×10^{23} particles (where 6.02×10^{23} is Avogadro's number), the mole concentration (simply **mole**) is used for reactions. Say, 1 mole of carbon atoms (12 g of C, containing 6.02×10^{2} atoms of C) reacts with 1 mole of oxygen (32 g of O_2, containing 6.02×10^{2} molecules of O_2) to produce 1 mole of carbon dioxide (44 g of CO_2, containing 6.02×10^{2} molecules of CO_2). $1\ C + 1\ O_2 \rightarrow 1\ CO_2$. This reaction tells us

- The total number of atoms on each side of the equation is always the same, meaning that the number of C and O on both sides is balanced.
- There are the same number of particles in 12 g C, 32 g O_2, and 44 g CO_2.
- An oxygen molecule (O_2) is 2.67 times as massive as a C atom (because 32/12 = 2.67), and a CO_2 molecule is 3.67 times more massive than a C atom (as 44/12 = 3.67).

The listed reaction, thus, in its complete form, will be

$$1\ \text{kg C} + 2.67\ \text{kg } O_2 \rightarrow 3.67\ \text{kg } CO_2$$

Another point that either of these reactions tells us is that the reaction, from one side, is a combustion reaction, during which the carbon (C) in fuel burns in atmospheric oxygen (O_2), and from another side, is a heat-releasing reaction, during which some energy (E) in the form of heat energy (E_Q, simply heat, Q) is released. When, in this case, 1 kg of C reacts with 2.67 kg O_2, 53 000 kJ of E_Q is released (shown usually with a **negative** sign). The reaction, thus, in its real complete form, can be written as

$$1 \text{ kg C} + 2.67 \text{ kg } O_2 \rightarrow 3.67 \text{ kg } CO_2 - 53\ 000 \text{ kJ of } E_Q$$

As for the energy (E) and mass (M), during a reaction,

- Some E, which is formed by breaking the reactants' chemical bonds, is transferred.
- The transfer of E of a reaction is equivalent to the appearance or disappearance of a tiny amount of M because E and M are equivalent, based on Einstein's equation ($E = M.c^2$).

Let us consider here a question, "can a reaction occur by itself?" This question has two answers:

- Yes. When the reaction *decreases* the E_Q, it goes from a higher-E situation to a lower-E situation, so it can occur by itself. Such a reaction, thus, releases some E_Q to its outside.
- No. If the reaction *increases* the E_Q, it goes from a lower-E situation to a higher one, so it *cannot* occur. Such a reaction, thus, occurs if some E_Q is supplied to it from outside.

Using these concepts, we are now able to differentiate between the next two reactions:

- Heat Releasing Reaction**:** This is a **negative** (exothermic) **reaction** because it releases E_Q.
- Heat Absorbing Reaction**:** This is a **positive** (endothermic) **reaction** because it absorbs E_Q.

Several other reactions are alphabetically listed next.

- **Chain Reaction:** A reaction during which the product of the reaction causes more subsequent reactions, so a chain reaction is a self-generating series of reactions.
- **Combustion Reaction:** A reaction during which combustible components of a fuel react with oxygen from the air to produce carbon dioxide (CO_2), water (H_2O), and E_Q. [This subject is more discussed under the topic of COMBUSTION REACTIONS.]
- **Corrosive Reaction:** A reaction during which a compound (usually a metal) reacts with oxygen (O_2) and water (H_2O) in the air (the air's moisture content or humidity) to produce rust. [This subject is more discussed under the topic of CORROSIVE REACTIONS.]
- **Decomposition Reaction:** A reaction during which a compound decomposes into simpler compounds. For example, when we dissolve salt (NaCl, an ionic compound) in water (a nonionic compound), it deionizes (decomposes) to positive sodium ion (Na+) and negative chlorine ion (Cl–).
- **Dehydration Reaction** (also known as a condensation reaction)**:** A reaction during which one molecule of water is formed.
- **Electrochemical Reaction:** A reaction during which the reactants react with the help of the electric current. [This subject is more discussed under the topic of ELECTROCHEMICAL REACTIONS.]
- **Halflife Reaction:** A reaction during which the concentration (C) of an oxidation-reduction reaction is decreased to half its initial value.
- **Hydration Reaction:** A reaction during which a substance combines with water (H_2O); in other words, it requires one molecule of water to occur.
- **Hydrogenation Reaction:** A reaction during which one molecular hydrogen (H_2) reacts with a substance, usually with a catalyst.
- **Ionization Reaction:** A reaction in which an ionic compound ionizes when it is dissolved in a solvent. For example, NaCl in water ionizes to Na^+ and Cl^-.
- **Order Reaction:** In a **first-order reaction**, the reaction rate (R_R) is proportional (shown by a proportionality constant k) to the concentration (C) of the reactant; $R_R = k.C$. In other words, C in the reaction-rate equation is raised to the power of one when the reaction occurs. Similarly, in a **second-order reaction**, the R_R is proportional to C of the reactant squared; $R = k.C^2$. Thus, C in the reaction-rate equation is squared (raised to the power of 2) when the reaction occurs, as discussed under CHEMICAL REACTION ORDER.

- **Neutralization Reaction:** A reaction between an acid and a base to produce a salt. Hydrogen chloride, for example, reacts with calcium hydroxide to form calcium chloride: $2\ HCl + Ca(OH)_2 \rightarrow CaCl_2\downarrow + 2\ H_2O$. The salt's positive ion (Ca^{2+}) comes from the base, and its negative ion (Cl^-) comes from the acid.
- **Oxidation-Reduction Reactions** (also called **reduction-oxidation reactions** or simply **redox):** These are two-part reactions in which an electron (or electrons) is transferred from one reactant to another reactant. The particle that releases the electron (e^-) is **oxidized**, and the particle that receives the electron is **reduced**. [More discussion under the topic of OXIDATION REDUCTION REACTIONS.]
- **Nuclear Reaction:** Discussed under the topic of NUCLEAR REACTIONS.

C-59

CHEMICAL REACTORS

A chemical reactor (simply **reactor**) is an enclosed vessel where a chemical reaction (or more reactions) occurs. In designing a reactor, we should be aware that the desired reaction's reactants can often undergo an undesired reaction (also called **side reaction**), as discussed more under CHEMICAL REACTIONS. A reactor, thus, should be designed to maximize the ratio of desired-to-undesired reactions to produce a product with the highest possible efficiency. Reactors come in different designs for different applications.

The reactors are of two types: 1) Continuously stirred reactors (CS reactors) and 2) Plug reactors. A typical CS reactor consists of a tank where the reactants are completely stirred to keep the reaction uniform.

C-60

CHEMICAL REAGENTS

A chemical reagent (simply **reagent**) is a chemical compound or a mixture of more compounds used in a laboratory in performing quantitative analysis. In preparing a reagent, one or more chemical substances are used. The general steps in preparing a reagent are outlined next:

- Find out the molecular mass of the chemicals,
- Calculate the amount of chemicals needed,
- Measure the right amount of chemicals,
- Dissolve them in deionized (DI) water,
- Adjust it to the exact volume, and
- Standardize it if instructed.

C-61

CHEMICAL SUBSTANCES

A chemical substance (simply **substance**) is a chemical element (simply **element**, such as carbon, C) or a chemical compound (simply **compound**, such as water, H_2O). Thus, a substance has a definite and constant chemical composition. [In chemistry, the terms **substance** and **compound** are often used equally.]

Substances can be in solid, liquid, gas, or plasma. For example, water, water vapor, and ice are three (3) different forms of the same substance, water.

C-62

CHEMICAL SYMBOLS

A chemical symbol is a one-letter or two-letter abbreviation for each chemical element (simply **element**). For example, K is the chemical symbol for potassium, and Mg is for magnesium. [Elements are presented in the periodic table of elements given inside the front cover of this book.]

C-63

CHEMICAL SYSTEMS

A chemical system (simply **system**) is a certain area (region) enclosed with a **boundary**. Although systems' sizes do *not* usually define them, Physics recognizes the macro and micro-size systems. When talking about a system in this book, we do *not* pay attention to its size and mass because the system of interest can be as small as an atom or as big as a chemical process plant. A tiny massless particle, a human, or the entire Universe can be a system when assumed to be limited to an **imaginary boundary**, through which *no* energy (E) or mass (M) enters or leaves. This is why physics considers the sum of all energies and masses in the Universe constant (the concept of the Thermodynamic First Law).

As illustrated in Figure 1, a **boundary** is an enclosing surface that separates a system from its **surrounding environment** (everything **outside** the boundary of a system). A system (small or large) can, thus, be enclosed by one of the following boundaries:

- **Real boundary** (such a system is called a **physical system** or simply a **system**).
- **Imaginary boundary** (such a system is called an **imaginary system**).
- Real and imaginary boundaries.

The word **system** is often used in this book to generalize a subject and make it easier to study, so it is helpful to remember its four (4) main characteristics:

- Its size and its massiveness do not define it,
- It can exist in all three phases (solid, liquid, or gas),
- It is a place for occurring one (or more) chemical process (simply **process**), and
- It can be described by one (or more) variables, such as temperature, pressure, volume, and like.

Classification of Systems

The most important system for us (chemical engineers) is a thermodynamic (heat-involving) system. Based on the transferability of E (energy) and M (mass), systems are grouped into three classes: 1) Open systems (an open system is open to both E and M), 2) Closed systems (a closed system is close to M but open to E), and 3) Isolated systems (an isolated system is close to both M and E).

Based on the transferability of E_Q (heat energy, simply heat), systems are divided into:

- Adiabatic Systems: No heat transfer between the system and its outsides (surroundings) occurs.
- Isothermic Systems: No temperature change (ΔT) between the system and its outsides occur, so T = constant and $\Delta T = 0$.

Based on **stability**, systems are divided into:

- Stable system
- Unstable system

According to the unchanged variable, stable systems are grouped into 1) Mass stability, 2) Pressure stability, 3) Thermal stability, and 4) Phase stability. [All of these systems are defined under STABLE SYSTEMS.]

Based on homogeneity, systems are divided into:

- Homogeneous system (when the system has uniform properties),
- Heterogeneous system (when the system has more than one phase, like ice in water).

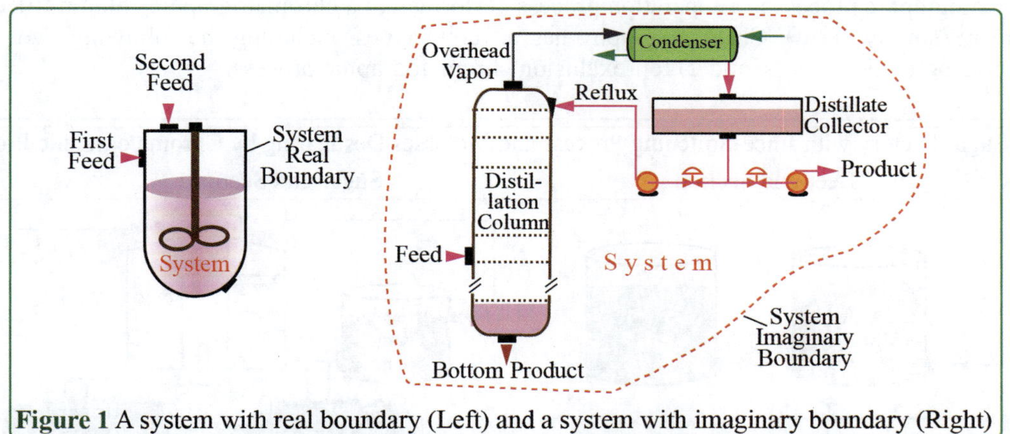

Figure 1 A system with real boundary (Left) and a system with imaginary boundary (Right)

C-64

CHIMNEY EFFECT

The chimney effect is a **process** (referred to as a chemical process) that occurs in the stack (chimney) of a furnace. The chimney effect occurs because of the following reasons:

- The temperature difference between the warm air inside of the stack and cool air outside the stack,
- The pressure difference between the inside and outside of the stack's air, and
- The density difference between the inside and outside of the stack's air.

As air warms, it becomes lighter (less dense), moving upward, while colder air is heavier and moves below the warmer air. This happens in the stack of a natural-draft furnace. An air draft occurs as the result of the chimney effect. In the furnace operation, an air draft is needed to

- Supply air to the combustion chamber of the furnace for the combustion of fuel, and
- Move the **stack gas** (the flue gas) out of the furnace's stack.

C-65

CHLOROFLUOROCARBONS

A chlorofluorocarbon (CFC) is a chemical compound with a low boiling point temperature (T_{BP}) that destructs the **ozone layer** (part of the atmosphere containing ozone, O_3). This is the reason that chlorofluorocarbons are known as ozone-depleting compounds. The ozone layer filters harmful rays from sunlight preventing damage to our skin. $CFCl_3$, which was used as a refrigerant, is an example of a CFC compound. [CFC compounds are *not* used anymore because of their ozone-depleting effect.]

C-66

CHROMATOGRAPHIC PROCESSES

The chromatographic process is a separation process performed in a chromatographic column filled with ion-exchange resin (simply **resin**). Chromatography has different types, including the following two: 1) Ion-exchange chromatographic process, and 2) Ion-exclusion chromatographic process.

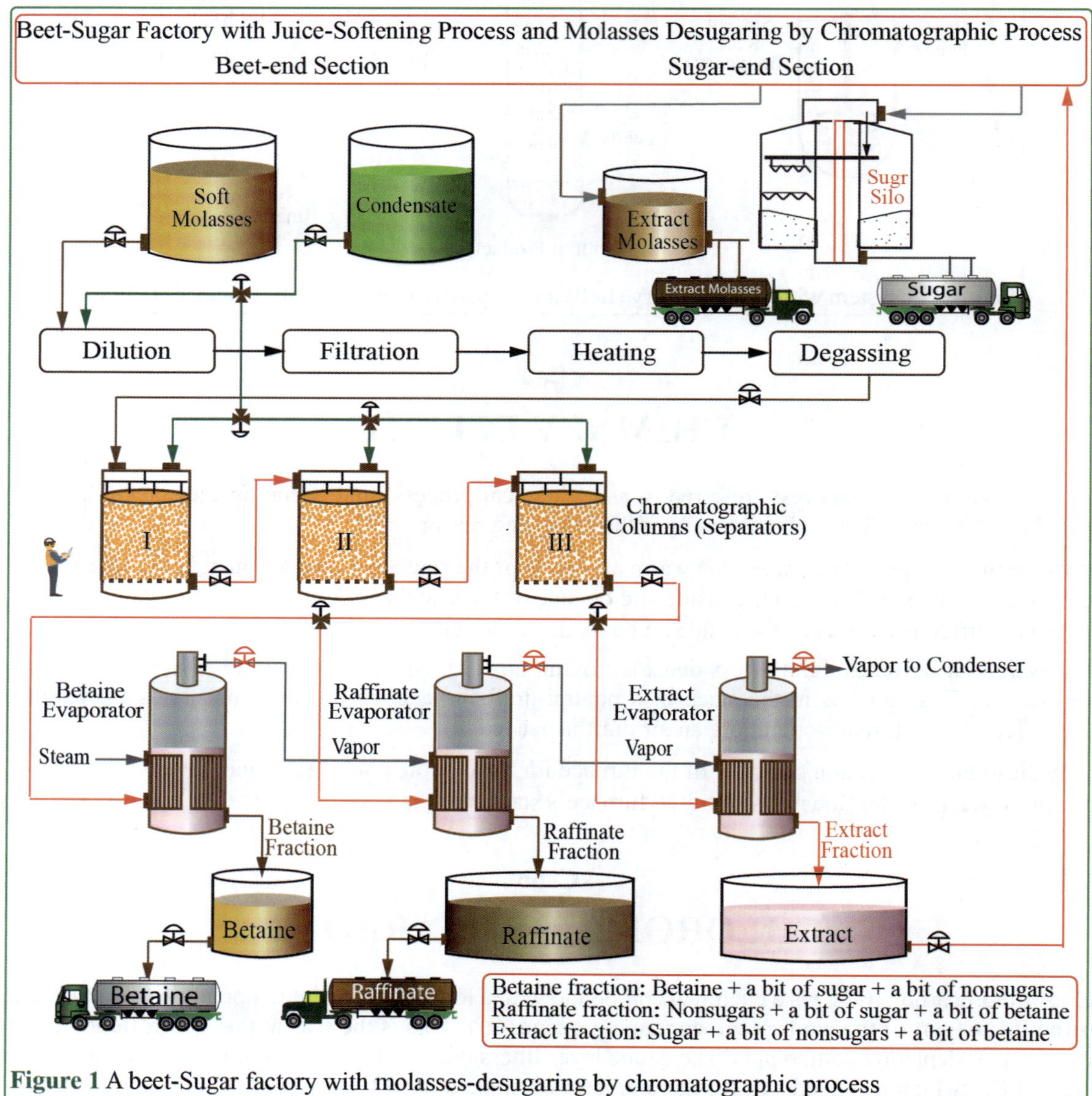

Figure 1 A beet-Sugar factory with molasses-desugaring by chromatographic process

Ion-Exchange Chromatographic Process: Ion-exchange chromatography is the process of exchanging some of a solution's ions with the **exchanging ions** of the resin functional group. This process is used, for example, in the water-softening process.

Ion-Exclusion Chromatographic Process: Ion-exclusion chromatography is the process of separating a solution's components by using resin, based on the following:

- **Chemical Affinity:** Different chemical affinities (absorption capability) of the resin particles create exclusivity (rejection) for ionic compounds and inclusivity (adsorption) for nonionic compounds.
- **Molecular Size:** Different molecular sizes (represented by molecular masses) of the components in the solution cause some of the solution's components to penetrate the pores of the particles and some *not*.

Ion-exclusion chromatography is used in many branches of the chemical process industry. The beet-sugar industry uses molasses desugaring by chromatographic (MDC) process to separate sugar (sucrose, $C_{12}H_{22}O_{11}$) in molasses from **nonsugars** (all dissolved solids except sugar). The MDC process is briefly discussed here (for detailed information, refer to this author's other book, *Beet-Sugar Technology Handbook*).

Figure 1 shows the MDC process. The chromatographic column is filled with styrene-divinylbenzene-based resin with an average particle size of about 0.3 mm. The soft-diluted molasses (with about 60% dissolved solids, *DS*) is fed to the column, followed by elution water (with molasses to water ratio of 1 to 6). As the solution feed is pumped to a column, the nonionic components (like sugar) do *not* ionize in the solution and create an opposite charge to the resin particles, so they become absorbed by the resin particles, moving through the resin bed more slowly. Instead, the ionic compounds are excluded (rejected) from the resin, moving through the column quickly. Water now reaches the resin, penetrates its pores, dissolves the nonionic components, and removes the nonionics from the pores. Thus, nonionics appear later in the **effluent** (output solution from the separator).

This explanation tells us that a series of **exclusion-inclusion** (rejection-absorption) actions between the resin and the components in the molasses occur, causing sugar molecules to stay behind. As in a race, a competition between ionics and nonionics occurs. The winners are **ionics** (nonsugar molecules), which appear in the effluent first, and the losers are **nonionics** (sugar molecules), which appear later (after eluting the resin with water).

C-67

CIRCULATION, RECIRCULATION, AND RECYCLING

The words **circulation**, **recirculation**, and **recycling** are often used in ChemEng, but some do *not* pay attention to their differences and use them equally. Although the terms circulation and recirculation can be used almost equally, the term recycling has a completely different definition. These terms are discussed here based on their chemical and environmental engineering applications.

Circulation

Circulation is the process of circulating the **entire content** of a container in that container for some beneficial operating purposes, including the next:

- Increasing the settling rate of a suspension,
- Increasing the reaction rate of a chemical reaction,
- Increasing the heat transfer rate of a heat transfer process,
- Decreasing the amount of foam in a mixer, a tank, and the like,
- Decreasing the retention time of a batch process in a chemical reactor,
- Increasing the operating capacity of a continuous process in a container, and
- Improving the mixing of a fluid, solution, mixture, or suspension in a mixer (see Figure 1).

Recirculation

Recirculation is the continuous return of a **portion** of a container's content to another container or from the bottom of a container to its top for beneficial operating purposes.

Figure 2 shows a continuous recirculation between two tanks to improve a chemical reaction. The recirculation rate between tank A (reservoir) and tank B (receiver) is in the ratio of 7 to 1 (that is 7 times the original feed or 700%), meaning that for every ton of liquid feed entering tank A, 7 t of liquid is pumped from B to A.

Figure 3 shows a recirculation in a tank for heating a liquid by a heat exchanger and keeping the liquid's temperature (*T*) unchanged in the tank. [This example tells us that recirculation can also be performed between a tank and a device (equipment).]

Recycling

Recycling is the process of reusing waste materials for some good reasons, including the following:

- Reducing environmental pollutants,
- Using lesser raw materials, and
- Saving in energy cost.

In environmental science, the word **recycling** means the cycle of a substance in nature. For example, the **nitrogen cycle** is the recycling process of nitrogen (N) in the environment.

Many waste products of chemical plants are recycled for reuse. For example, **gypsum** ($CaSO_4.2H_2O$), the waste product of the fertilizer plants, is recycled to be used in plaster and drywall industries. Similarly, **lime residue** ($CaCO_3$ + some minerals), produced in a beet-sugar factory, is recycled as a soil enhancer and PH reducer on the farms or as compost.

Today, many household products, such as paper, plastic, glass, metal, rubber, and polyethylene, are recycled to be reused as raw materials to produce new products, which come to the market again. **Biodegradable wastes**, such as garden waste, are also recyclable for composting purposes.

[Note: Nuclear waste can NOT be recycled, as they are hazardous and single-use material. Because of security concerns, Yucca Mountain in Nevada was selected for nuclear waste disposal in the US of America. In this country, the Office of Health, Safety, and Security of the Department of Energy can be contacted.]

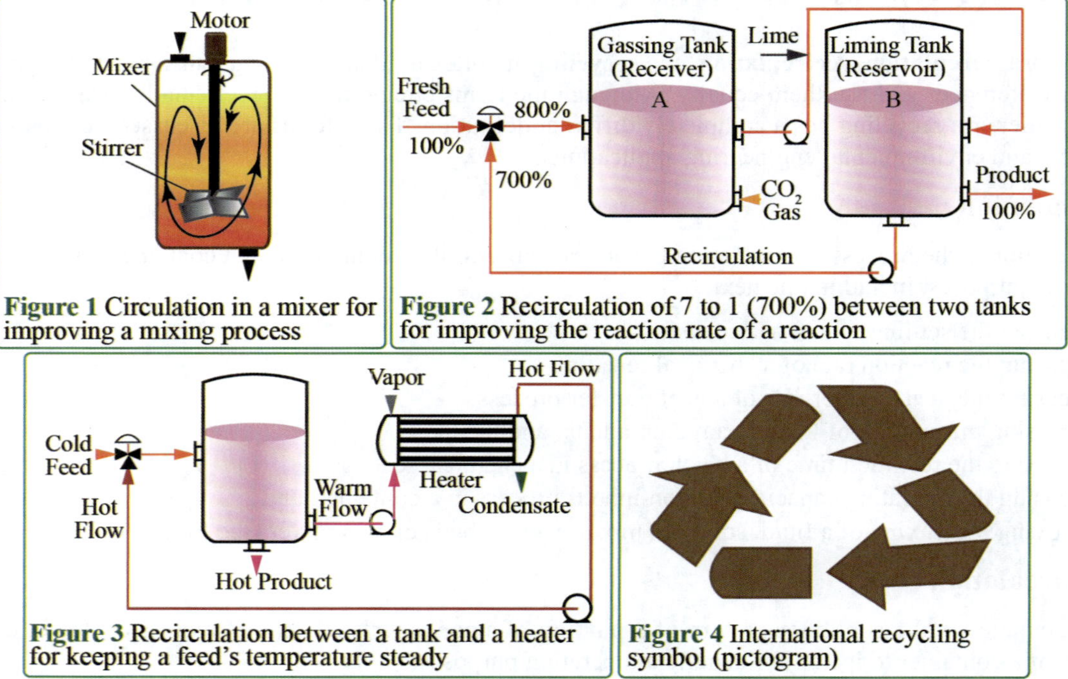

Figure 1 Circulation in a mixer for improving a mixing process

Figure 2 Recirculation of 7 to 1 (700%) between two tanks for improving the reaction rate of a reaction

Figure 3 Recirculation between a tank and a heater for keeping a feed's temperature steady

Figure 4 International recycling symbol (pictogram)

C-68

CLAPEYRON EQUATION

The Clapeyron equation (also called the **Clausius-Clapeyron equation**) characterizes a phase change between two phases containing the same chemical component (simply **component**). On a phase diagram (pressure-temperature diagram), the Clapeyron equation gives the slope (the rise-to-run ratio) of the coexistence line (the line that separates the phases). It gives the necessary relation for the pressure difference (ΔP) and temperature difference (ΔT) occurring during a phase change in a process (like evaporation or distillation).

C-69

CLARIFICATION PROCESS AND CLARIFIERS

CLARIFICATION PROCESS

This is another name for sedimentation, so study SEDIMENTATION PROCESS.

CLARIFIERS

A clarifier (also called **decanter** or **thickener**) is a device used to perform the sedimentation (settling) process by separating settleable suspended solid particles (simply **suspended particles**) from a suspension solution (simply **suspension**). The gravitational force (F_g) is the driving force of sedimentation.

Based on their useability, clarifiers can be divided into two main groups: 1) Wastewater clarifiers and 2) Process clarifiers.

Wastewater Clarifiers

A wastewater clarifier (sludge clarifier) is used in chemical process plants to separate the suspended and solid particles existing in wastewater from a suspension, which is the input of a wastewater clarifier. And the clarifier's outputs are **clarified liquid**, **thickened suspension**, and **scum** (foamy particles that float on the surface of a wastewater suspension). The thickened suspension consists of densely settled solids (sludge) accumulated in the clarifier's bottom. [Sludge is thinner than mud.]

In its typical design, a wastewater clarifier (Figure 1) consists of a large cylindrical tank (usually with more than 4000 m^3 volume) with a narrow cone bottom. It is 50 to 100 m (= 150 to 300 Ft) in diameter and 2 to 4 m (= 6 to 12 Ft) deep. It contains a rake connected to a central shaft, driven by an adjustable electric motor. The rake, which turns slow (at around 12 rotations per hour), has several arms.

The feed enters the bottom center of the clarifier and moves upward through the feeding pipe. The heavier particles sink downward and gradually make a sludge layer in the bottom, and the clear water stays on the top, from where it spills over the edge of the tank into a **trough** (channel). The rakes gently move the sludge layer at the bottom to the clarifier's center, which is discharged by gravity. Usually, the sludge is pumped by a pump to a mud-settling pond or goes through a thickening centrifuge to produce cake (transportable).

In a clarifier, gravitational force (F_g), which acts downward toward the bottom of the clarifier, is the driving force of the sedimentation of the suspended particles. The density difference between solids and water also helps in the sedimentation of the denser particles. Clarifiers are large enough to slow the flow of the suspension so that the impurities settle faster than the upward fluid flow. By introducing the feed water at the bottom of the clarifier, the settling sludge helps catch the suspended particles from the feed water. Clarified water (overflow) is constantly removed from the top of the clarifier and sludge (underflow) from its bottom.

Clarifier operation depends on the nature and amounts of suspended particles and dissolved solids, pH, temperature, and required throughput of the feed wastewater.

Settling the particles in a clarifier depends on their size and interaction with other particles. Particles' Brownian motion causes them to collide (bump), stick together, become bigger, and settle fast. If these processes are happening too slowly, the particles do *not* settle properly.

You should also be aware of the following problems when operating a clarifier:

- If the clarity of the overflow is *not* sufficient, increasing the volume of underflow relative to the overflow can solve this problem.
- If a clarifier operates under its design capacity, the sludge buildup in its bottom can be high. Increasing the underflow removes the settled sludge and restores the clarifier to its design capacity.

The average **retention time** (t_R) of feed in a clarifier is 2 to 3 hours, depending on the particle size. A clarifier's t_R, can be calculated by using its tank volume (V) and influent rate (actually, volumetric flow rate, $\dot{V}$). For example, the t_C of a clarifier that its tank's V is 100 m^3 and receives a flow of 50 m^3/h is

$$t_R = \frac{V}{\dot{V}} = \frac{100}{50} = 2\ \text{h}$$

The $\dot{V}$ (also called **volumetric capacity** or simply **capacity**) of a clarifier can be calculated from its cross-sectional area ($A = \pi R^2 = \pi d^2/4$) and particles' settling velocity (V, also called **settling rate**, R_S).

$$\dot{V} = A.V \tag{1}$$

The $\dot{V}$ of a **batch** centrifugal clarifier is calculated similarly, except the sedimentation time (t) is included in the previous equation.

$$\dot{V} = A.V.t \tag{2}$$

This equation shows that a clarifier's processing capacity depends on its settling area, *not* its height. Therefore, a higher capacity per unit of floor area can be obtained by using a **multiple-compartment clarifier**, where the compartments have a lower depth than a single-compartment clarifier.

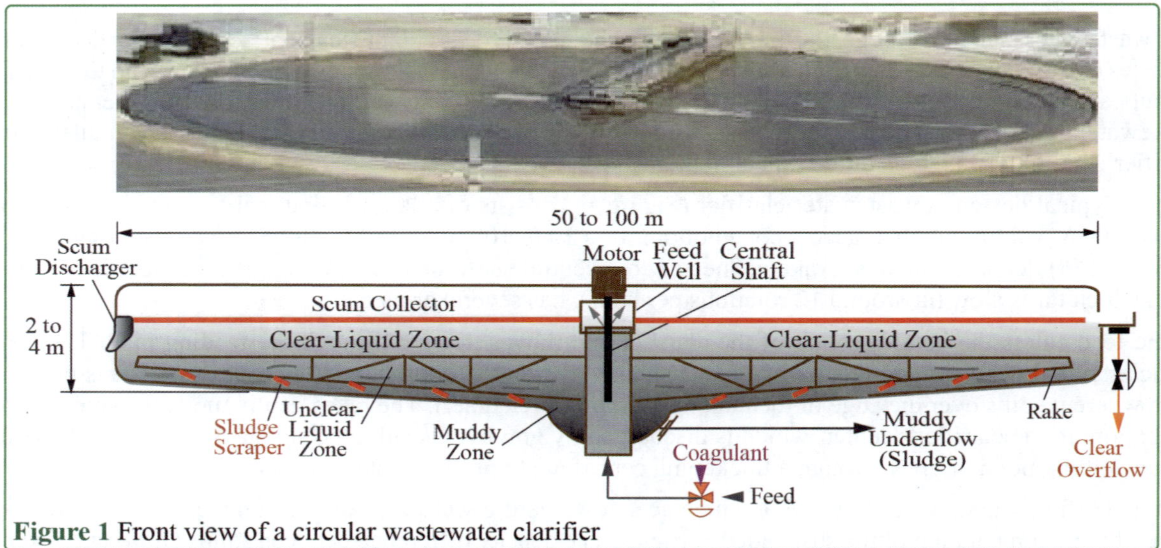

Figure 1 Front view of a circular wastewater clarifier

Sedimenting Centrifuges: A sedimenting centrifuge (also called a **centrifugal clarifier**) operates using the centrifugal force (F_C), which acts toward the centrifuge wall.

The following are the advantages of centrifugal clarifiers (sedimenting centrifuges) over gravity (G) clarifiers:

- The centrifugal clarifiers can settle solid particles much faster than the G clarifiers (F_g is weaker than F_C).

- The centrifugal clarifiers are more effective in separating fine solid particles than G clarifiers.
- The centrifugal clarifiers are smaller for a given capacity than G clarifiers.

For these advantages, centrifugal clarifiers, to a large extent, have replaced gravity (G) clarifiers in many chemical process plants.

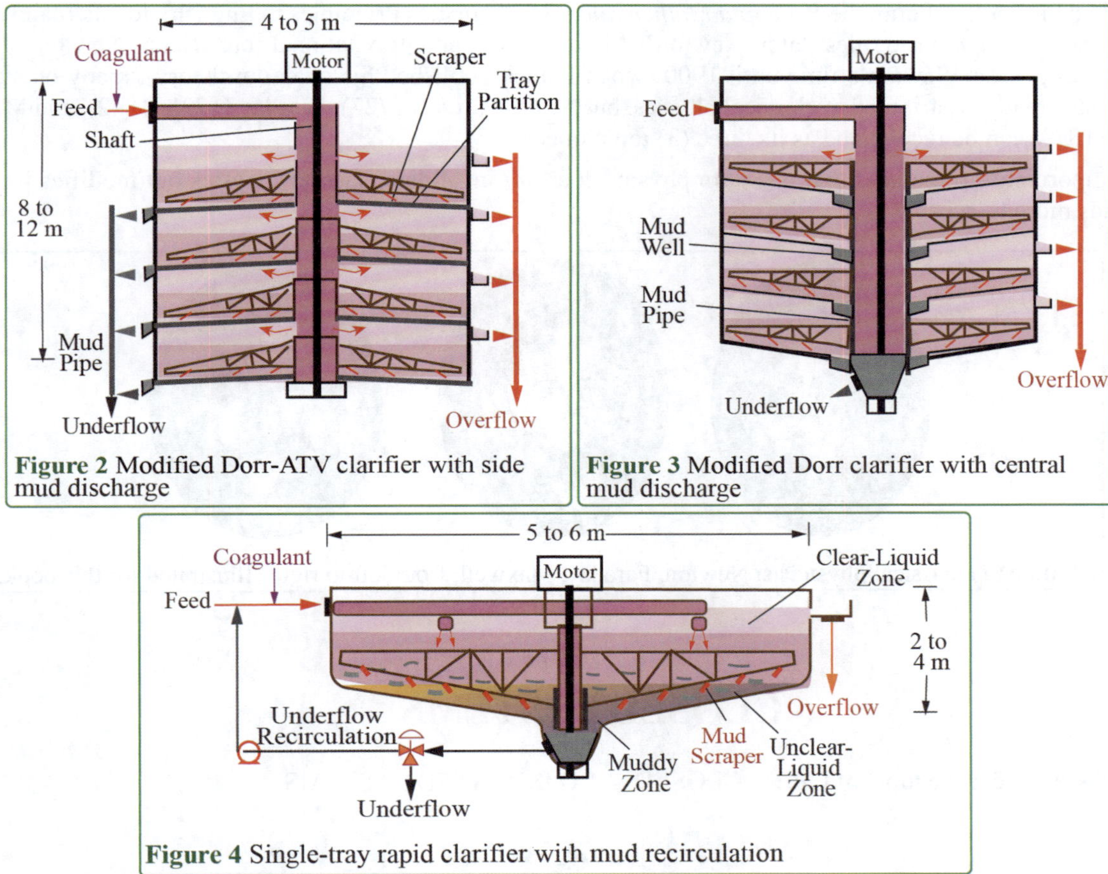

Figure 2 Modified Dorr-ATV clarifier with side mud discharge

Figure 3 Modified Dorr clarifier with central mud discharge

Figure 4 Single-tray rapid clarifier with mud recirculation

Process Clarifiers

A process clarifier, which is smaller than a wastewater clarifier and is covered, is used as a pre-filtration to separate the coarse suspended particles from a process stream. For example, most sugar factories use a modified Dorr clarifier to settle the suspended particles of the precipitated calcium carbonate ($CaCO_3$) from the processed juice by sedimentation in a four-compartment (four-tray) clarifier (Figure 2), which might be considered as four (4) separate clarifiers, stacked on top of each other. The feed is split equally to each compartment on the top of the clarifier through a centrally-located feed pipe.

Figure 2 shows a modified Dorr-ATV clarifier, and Figure 3 shows another modified design of the Dorr types. These two are almost similar in design and operation, but the mud from each compartment (tray) is discharged separately in the Dorr-ATV clarifier. In contrast, in the clarifier shown in Figure 3, the mud from each tray goes to a central pipe, and the whole mud from all trays is discharged from a deep cone at the bottom. Figure 4 shows the front view of a continuous rapid clarifier used in many chemical process plants. This clarifier has a single tray and provides vigorous sludge circulation. A single-tray clarifier's cost is lower (for the same capacity) than a multi-tray clarifier and simpler to operate.

C-70

CLASSICAL PHYSICS

Classical physics (also called Newtonian physics) is the pre-1900 physics that started in 1687 when Newton published his book in Latin, the *Principia Mathematica* (Mathematics Principles in English), to talk mainly about motion and its three basic rules (later, Newton's Motion Laws) and gravitational force (later, Newton's Law of Gravitation). From Newton's time until 1900 (when Planck published his quantum theory), many outstanding physicists greatly contributed to classical physics, but Newton (1642–1727), Faraday (1791–1842), and Maxwell (1831–1879) can be recognized as its three (3) top pioneers.

[It is important to remember that quantum physics does *not* invalidate classical physics but modifies its basics and adds more to it.]

All time top classical physicists, Newton, Faraday, Maxwell, from left to right [Illustrated for this book.]

C-71

CLOSED SYSTEMS

Discussed under the topic of OPEN, CLOSED, AND ISOLATED SYSTEMS.

C-72

COAGULANTS

A coagulant (also called **flocculent** or **settling aid**) is a polymeric compound used in the sedimentation process to coagulate (get together) fine suspended solid particles (simply **suspended particles**) to increase their sedimentation (settling) rate. For example, adding a proper coagulant to the feed of a clarifier makes suspended particles larger and heavier to settle faster.

One of the most important functions of the coagulants is that they can coagulate (solidify) the colloids by positioning themselves between the colloidal particles. This occurs because a coagulant's particles have positive electric charges, absorbing the electro-negatively charged colloidal particles. The formed neutrally-charged particles are larger, heavier, and *no* longer sticky, so they can settle faster during sedimentation and *not* plug the pores of a filter during filtration. This process is called **coagulation** (synonym for **flocculation**).

Coagulants are divided into the following two (2) main groups:

- **Polymeric Coagulants:** Polyacrylamide, polyethylene oxide, and polyamine polymers are examples of this group. Polymeric coagulants are polyelectrolytes because they have characteristics of both **polymers** (long-chained molecules) and **electrolytes** (charged particles).

- **Nonpolymeric Inorganic Coagulants:** Calcium oxide (CaO) and aluminum oxide (Al_2O_3) are in this group.

The choice of proper coagulant is established experimentally, however. Most chemical plants use polymeric coagulants, which are water-soluble, have long chains, and have a high molecular mass (M_M). In this way, the *greater* the M_M, the *longer* is the chain length, and the *greater* the coagulant's coagulability.

[The terms **coagulant** and **flocculant** are usually used equally, although coagulants have a smaller molecular chain and larger net charge than flocculants. In this book, the word **coagulant** is used.]

C-73

COAL

Coal is a fossil fuel formed in layers by heat (Q) and pressure (P) on the plants buried underground, with an approximate chemical formula of $C_{135}H_{96}O_9NS$. Coal is harvested through mining. It mainly consists of hydrocarbons (have carbon and hydrogen). It also contains sulfur (S), nitrogen (N), and 4 to 12% ash (a noncombustible compound).

The largest source of SO_2 in the atmospheric air is produced from coal combustion. Thus, coal with low sulfur is in demand because of its low sulfuric acid (H_2SO_4) formation during combustion. Sulfuric acid attacks boiler metals. The sulfur in coal also creates SO_2 air pollution, contributing to acid rain (atmospheric precipitation such as rain, fog, and snow, with a PH less than 5.5). It contains high ash (4 to 20%), which also causes air pollution if it is *not* filtered.

Oil, coal, and natural gas are the main world's energy resources, even as renewable energy has rapidly increased. In chemical process plants, coal is used in combustion reactions to produce steam. Then, the steam is used in a steam turbine to produce electricity. Coal has many other uses, including in refining metals.

A few important properties of typical medium-size coal are outlined next.

- It is still the world's largest source of energy (E) for generating electricity,
- Its enthalpy of combustion is about 26 000 kJ/kg (= 11 160 BTU/Lb),
- Its bulk density (D_B) is about 750 kg/m^3 (= 47 Lb/Ft^3).

Coals are classed according to their **grade** (size), **heat value** (heat energy or enthalpy), and ash content. **Anthracite**, **bituminous**, and **lignite** are the three (3) main kinds of coal. [The order given here indicates the coal with the highest **heat value** to the lowest.] **Pulverized coal**, produced in a **coal pulverizer** (coal mill), creates a higher efficiency in the coal-fired furnaces than solid coal. Pulverized coal is highly explosive, so special considerations must be made in its handling. In addition, it needs a larger furnace to complete combustion. Coal can also be used in other ways, including the following:

- **Coal Liquefaction:** This method produces coal slurry, which improves the coal's heat value and reduces air pollution.
- **Coal Gasification:** This method is used to produce syngas (synthetic natural gas, SNG), which is a mixture of hydrogen (H_2) and carbon monoxide (CO). The syngas can then be converted into synthetic gasoline.

C-74

COD

Abbreviated form of CHEMICAL OXYGEN DEMAND.

C-75

CODATA

CODATA (Committee on Data for Science and Technology) was established in 1969 in Paris as one branch of the **International Council for Science** (an international non-governmental organization established in 1931 in Paris). The main function of CODATA is to provide up-to-date values of the fundamental physical constants, like the speed of light constant (c), Planck's constant (h), and gravitational constant (K_G). In 2019, CODATA published the new definitions for SI units. Besides others, the value of h was changed by a bit.

C-76

COEFFICIENT OF FRICTION

Study FRICTION FACTOR, FRICTION FORCE, AND FRICTION COEFFICIENT.

C-77

COEFFICIENT OF VARIATION

The coefficient of variation (C_V, also called **variation coefficient**) describes the precision of a set of measurements (the *lower* the C_V value, the *more* precise and uniform are the measurements). A low C_V value characterizes a better **uniformity** (distribution). In the crystallization process, the C_V expresses the size uniformity of the crystals (the *lower* the C_V value, the *more* uniformed the crystals are), so the minimum possible value of variation is desired. A high C_V value, on the contrary, is an indication of a wide and poor distribution size. For example, a C_V of less than 35% is required for sugar crystals in the sugar industry. The C_V requirements are different in different industries. [Lower C_V can be achieved with a larger mean aperture (M_A).]

The sugar industry determines the crystal size distribution by testing a given amount of sugar sample (typically 100 g) on a screen test. [For choosing the right size, the screens (usually 5 to 7 screens) are chosen so that the total weight of the top two screens would contain 10 to 20% of the sample, and the total two bottom screens, 70 to 80% of the sample. The top and bottom screens are chosen so that the sugar remaining on each does *not* exceed 1% of the sample.]

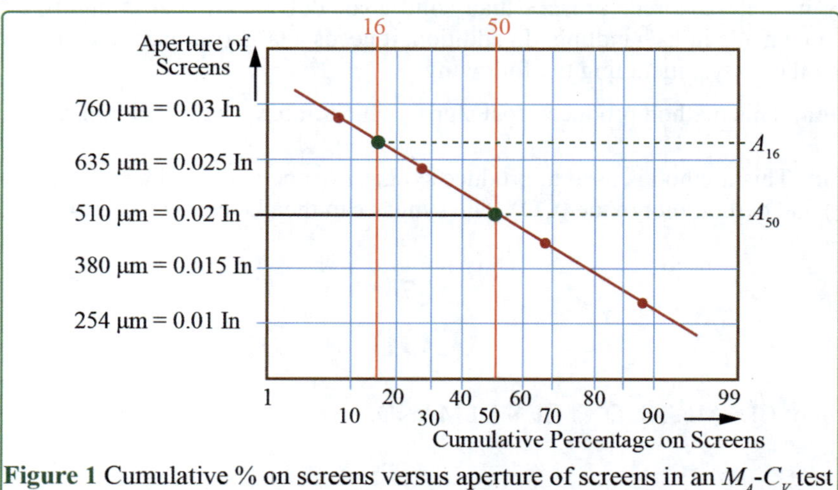

Figure 1 Cumulative % on screens versus aperture of screens in an M_A-C_V test

C-78

COEFFICIENT OF VISCOSITY

Another name for VISCOSITY.

C-79

COEFFICIENTS, CONSTANTS, PROPORTIONALITY COEFFICIENTS AND CONSTANTS

The words **coefficient**, **constant**, **proportionality coefficient**, and **proportionality constant** are often used in Mathematics, science, and engineering. Although some writers do *not* pay attention to the differences between them and use them equally, each has its definition and application, as discussed next.

In **math**, these words are defined in the following ways:

- **Coefficient:** A coefficient is a unitless, non-fixed quantity dependent on a **variable** (an unknown quantity), changing in time. A coefficient is usually written before a variable to multiply that variable. In equation $2X + 3Y$, numbers 2 and 3 are coefficients since each depends on a variable (X or Y).
- **Constant:** A constant is a fixed quantity independent of a variable, so it does *not* change in time. In equation $2X + 3Y + 4$, number 4 is a constant (because it is independent from a variable). However, some mistakenly consider 2, 3, and 4 constant numbers. [Note: The constants used in math are *not* measurable (but calculable) and do *not* have **dimension** (unit), so-called dimensionless (unitless).]
- **Proportionality Coefficient:** This is *not* used in mathematics.
- **Proportionality Constant** (K_P)**:** The K_P relates two variables. If the **ratio** of two variables (X and Y) equates to K_P, they are **directly proportional** through K_P. Instead, if the **product** of two variables equates to K_P, then the two variables are **inversely proportional** through K_P.

In **Physics** and **ChemEng**, coefficients and constants are used as discussed next

Proportionality Coefficients without Dimension

A proportionality coefficient (C_P, simply **coefficient**) is used to express the relation between two quantities. Consider the **spring's deformation coefficient** (K, a unitless number), used in Hook's Law ($F = K.L$, where F is force and L is length) as a C_P. If, say, F is doubled, L will also double. If, for example, an F of 2 N (where N is for Newton, the force unit) is applied on a spring, it stretches 1 cm, and if F is 4 N, the spring stretches 2 cm. We can then express this test as

$$2 = 1 \times 2$$

$$4 = 2 \times 2$$

$$F = 2L$$

Thus, the value 2 in this example plays as the spring's C_P. Similarly, if an F of 6 is applied to a spring, it stretches 2 cm, and if F is 12 N, the spring stretches 4 cm. We can then express this test as

$$6 = 3 \times 2$$

$$12 = 3 \times 4$$

$$F = 3L$$

Here, the value 3 is the spring's C_P. These examples tell us that a coefficient is *not* a fixed quantity.

Proportionality Coefficients with Dimension

Examples of proportionality coefficients with dimension (unit) are convective and conductive heat transfer coefficients. The convective heat transfer coefficient (U_Q), with an SI unit of kJ/(m^2.ºC), relates the convective (direct) heat transfer to the driving force of the transfer, the temperature difference (ΔT). And conductive heat transfer coefficient (K_T), with the unit of W/(h.°C), relates the conductive heat transfer to the driving force of the transfer (ΔT). [Dimentional coefficients are often used in ChemEng to relate a flux (F_X, such as mass flux, heat flux, or momentum flux), to its corresponding driving force (F_D) by the general equation of $F_X = K_P.F_D$. For example, the amount of heat transfer is the proportionality between the heat flux and the F_D of heat transfer (temperature gradient).]

Physical Constants

A physical constant (simply **constant**) is a fixed (does *not* change in time) and dimensional quantity that relates two (or more) quantities. The speed of light constant (c), Planck's constant (h), and gravitational constant (K_G) are three important physical constants. The unit of c is length per time, that of h is energy multiplied by time (usually J.s), and the unit of K_G is N.m^2/ kg^2. [Speed of light constant (c = 299 792 792) is the largest, and Planck's constant (h = 6.626 070 × 10^{-34} J.s) is one of the smallest constants used in Physics.] Thus, the main difference between coefficient and constant is that a coefficient is *not* a fixed quantity, while a constant is.

Proportionality Constants

A proportionality constant (K_P) is used similarly as a constant. For example, the gas constant (R), which relates the pressure (P), volume (V), quantity (in mole, n), and temperature (T) of a gas as $P.V = n.R.T$, is a proportionality constant with a unit (dimension). Thus, if the values of variables in this equation are known, we can calculate the R (which equates to 0.0821 Atm.L/K.mole).

C-80
COHESION

Study ADHESION AND COHESION.

C-81
COHESIVE ENERGY

Another name for SURFACE ENERGY.

C-82
COHESIVE FORCE

Study ADHESIVE AND COHESIVE FORCES.

C-83
COKE

Coke is burned coal at about 1000ºC in the absence of air. As a fuel, it is used industrially in many processes, including the following:

- In metallurgical furnaces to produce iron,
- In a limekiln to decompose $CaCO_3$ for producing CaO and CO_2,
- In a chemical reactor to produce syngas (a synthetic gas consisting of H_2, CO, and CO_2).

A typical coke consists of minimum 80% carbon (C), about 12% ash, 5% oxygen (O), 1% nitrogen (N), 0.5% sulfur (S), and 6% water (H_2O). The following are some other properties of a typical coke:

- Its bulk density (D_B) is 400 kg/m^3 (= 25 Lb/Ft^3),
- Its combustion temperature is around 700ºC (= 1290 ºF),
- Its enthalpy of combustion is about 28 000 kJ/kg (= 12 173 BTU/Lb).

C-84
COLLIDERS

Study PARTICLE ACCELERATORS.

C-85
COLLIGATIVE PROPERTIES

The colligative property of a solution depends on its concentration (*C*) but *not* its chemical properties (identities). In more detail, this property depends on a solute's molarity (*M*, molar concentration). Boiling depression temperature, boiling elevation temperature, osmotic pressure, and vapor pressure are colligative properties.

For example, when saying that the osmotic pressure (P_O) is a colligative property, we mean that the P_O depends on the solute's molarity of the solution in which P_O occurred. The P_O that occurs during the osmosis process on the salty seawater depends on the molarity of the salt (NaCl, the solute) on each side of the membrane. This means that the same amount of P_O would occur in the solution for given molarity if other types of solute were used instead of salt. [Solute is a substance being dissolved in a solvent.]

C-86
COLLISION THEORY

The collision theory (also called a **molecular collision**) talks about how and how fast a chemical reaction (simply **reaction**) occurs when the molecules of its reactant (or reactants) collide (contact) with each other repeatedly. The collision theory can be discussed in the context of the following three (3) factors:

- **Activation Energy** (E_a), also called **collision energy**): A reaction does *not* occur unless the involving molecules get enough energy (*E*) in the form of E_a (the *E* necessary to cause a reaction to occur) to collide (contact) other reacting molecules sufficiently. This means that the collision between the reactants must provide enough E_a before chemical bonds of the reactants' molecules are broken and bonds of the product's (or products') molecules are formed. Then, the reactants' (or reactants') molecules change to the products' molecules. The E_a required for forward and backward (reverse) reactions can be better understood as we consider the reaction of $A + B \rightarrow C + D$, and Figures 1 and 2. This reaction does *not* occur unless at least one collision between A and B occurs at the **reactive site**. If A and B have large molecules (like protein or polymer), then the likelihood of their collisions at the reactive site is much smaller, comparatively. Then its chemical reaction rate (R_R, simply **reaction rate**) is much slower than a simple case. [The R_R depends on the concentration (C) of A, B, C, and D.] Every reaction can be described as having a forward direction and a backward direction. As shown in Figure 1, the forward reaction is more favorable, as E_a required for it is less than that for the backward reaction. And E_A of the products is lower than that of the reactants.

- **Collision Frequency** (f_C)**:** This is the number of collisions per unit of time. The f_C is affected by the reactants' C and T (temperature), as the *more* concentrated and *hotter* the reactants, the *more* frequently their molecules collide. This is because 1) more molecules exist in each volume, and 2) high T increases the molecules' kinetic energy. At constant T, the R_R doubles as C doubles. For some, the R_R almost doubles when T increases by 10°C. The f_C is also affected by whether the reaction occurs in a gas or a liquid phase. [When it occurs in a gas, pressure (P) is also an affecting factor.]
- **Collision Orientation** (O_{XYZ})**:** This is the molecular direction and velocity at which the molecules move at the time of the collision. For a reaction to properly occur, the colliding molecules must have a certain orientation (as in billiard balls). For example, carbon and oxygen molecules react easier to form carbon dioxide (CO_2) when they collide parallelly. [In some cases, a temporary product, known as an **activated compound**, forms during a reaction for a short period, and then its molecules are rearranged to form the main product. Figure 2 shows the formation of a compound during the reaction of $A + B \rightarrow C + D$.]

Considering what has been said, the R_R (reaction rate) is the multiplicating product of the three listed factors.

$$R_R = E_a \times f_C \times O_{XYZ} \tag{1}$$

Catalysts can reduce some reactions' required E_A (activation energy), so:

- A catalyst can force a reaction to proceed at a higher R_R than without a catalyst (see Figure 3).
- A catalyst can force a reaction to proceed at a lower T and P than would otherwise be required.

Irreversible and Reversible Reactions: If a forward reaction's R_R is greater than its backward reaction, it is **irreversible** (A + B → C + D). And if a backward reaction's R_R is considerably greater than its forward reaction, it is **reversible** (A + B ← C + D).

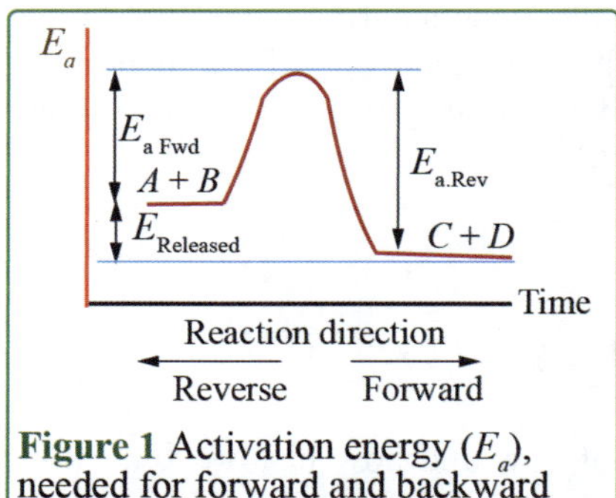

Figure 1 Activation energy (E_a), needed for forward and backward directions in reaction A + B ↔ C + D

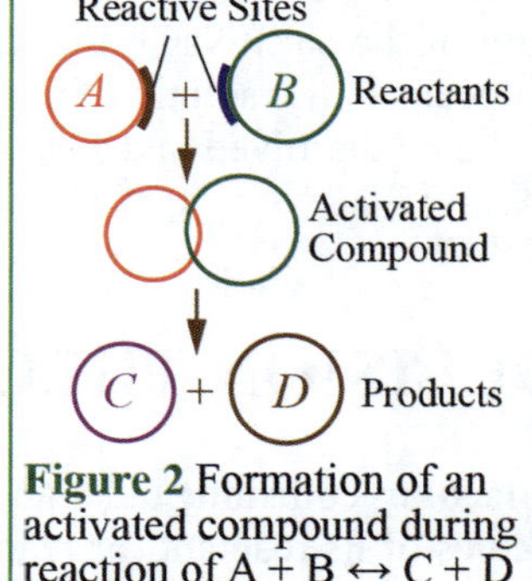

Figure 2 Formation of an activated compound during reaction of A + B ↔ C + D

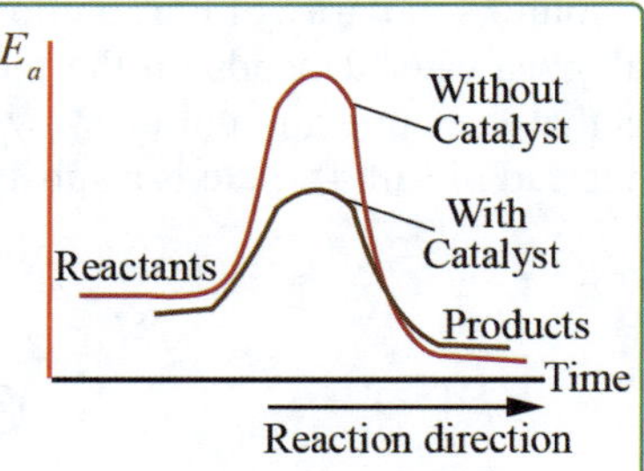

Figure 3 Effect of a catalyst on the required E_a during the forward reaction of A + B → C + D

C-87

COLLOIDS

Colloids are in a large group of dispersions, so it is discussed under DISPERSIONS.

C-88
COLOR AND COLORIMETRY

Color and colorimetry (spectrophotometry) are used in many branches of the chemical process industry.

Color

Color comes to our eyes when a system is observed. We observe a system's color when the reflected (returned) light from that system is more intense to our eyes in some colors than the others. Because color originates from light and light can be different in intensity, the wavelength (λ) of the reflected light can represent the color of a system under observation. Our eyes can only recognize the light within a certain wave range, called the **visible light range** (with λ of about 400 to 700 nm). This means that the shortest λ of light that we can recognize is 400 nm and the longest one is 700 nm. For example, the sky seems **blue** because the air's molecules are more effective in scattering (spreading) **blue** light to our eyes than the other colors. Sun is yellow because as the sunlight moves, more and more of its color spectra (particularly blue) are absorbed by the air's molecules, leaving the scattered light yellowish.

The color of a system depends on

- The properties of the observing eye,
- The way the eye sends the message to the brain,
- The way the brain interprets the receiving message,
- The surface properties of the system under observation,
- The reflection (bouncing-back) properties of the system under observation,
- The color of the system's background. Say, the color of a red apple remains red in our brain at midday when the sunlight is white, and it looks to us orange at sunset when the sunlight is orange.
- The λ (wavelength) of the reflected light (we observe color when the λ of the reflected light is stronger than the wavelengths of other reflected lights). An apple appears red because its surface molecules absorb all colors from the light, except red, which is reflected in our eyes. Similarly, the sky is **blue** because the air molecules absorb all colors from the light except **blue** (see Figure 1).

A visible light's spectrum (ray) consists of seven (7) primary colors, each corresponding to a certain wavelength (λ). These colors are **red** (with λ between 700 and 635 nm), **orange** (with λ between 635 and 590 nm), yellow (with λ between 590 and 560 nm), **green** (with λ between 560 and 520 nm), **cyan** (with λ between 520 and 490 nm), **blue** (with λ between 490 and 450 nm), and **violet** (with λ from 450 to 400 nm).

Colorimetry

Colorimetry (spectrophotometry) is an analytical technique that uses a **colorimeter** (spectrophotometer) to measure the color of a solution sample by measuring how much the sample absorbs the light when it passes through the sample. The light absorption (absorbency) is expressed by absorbance (A), which is the measure of the intensity (I) of a light's ray (spectrum) absorbed or reflected (bounced back) when the ray passes through a colored (light-absorbing) solution (see Figure 1).

In a spectrophotometer, a light's narrow beam (band) with a certain wavelength (λ) passes the sample, the light's absorbance (A) or transmittance (T) is measured, and its A or T value is converted numerically to indicate the color of the sample.

In a spectrophotometer, a light's narrow beam (band) with a certain wavelength (λ) passes the sample, the light's absorbance (A) or transmittance (T) is measured, and its A or T value is converted numerically to indicate the color of the sample.

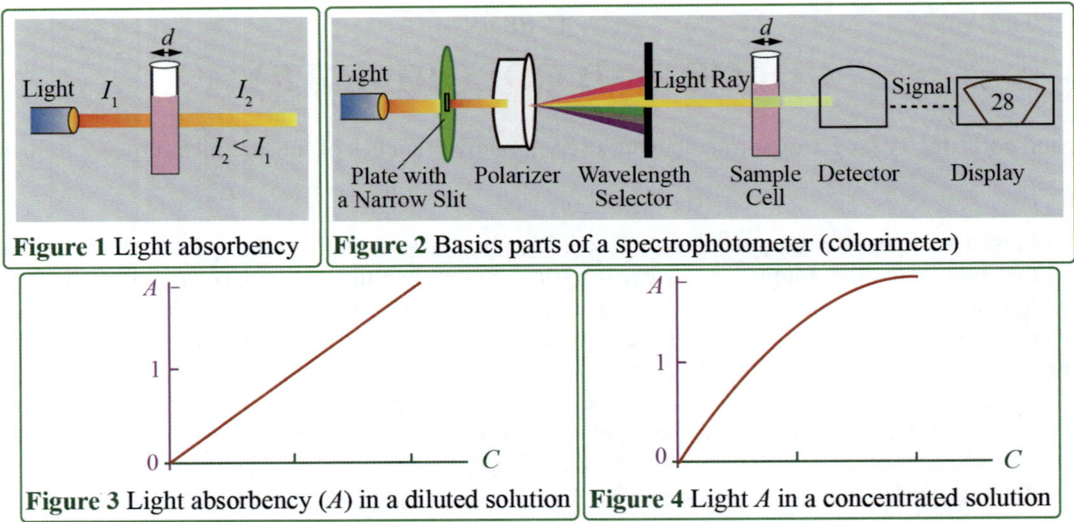

Figure 1 Light absorbency

Figure 2 Basics parts of a spectrophotometer (colorimeter)

Figure 3 Light absorbency (*A*) in a diluted solution

Figure 4 Light *A* in a concentrated solution

A simple typical spectrophotometer mainly consists of the following parts (see Figure 2):

- A light source for providing a thin beam of light,
- A plate with a narrow slit for making a light's thin beam (light's ray),
- A polarizer for polarizing (breaking) the light's ray to its components,
- A wavelength selector for selecting the wavelength at which the test is measured,
- A sample cell with a known outside diameter (in a round cell) or width (in a square cell),
- A detector (photocell) for measuring the amount of the absorbed light by the solution sample and generating an electric current proportional to it, and
- A display for indicating the received signals in transmittance (*T*) or absorbance (*A*) in numerical values.

[Note: Spectrophotometers usually operate at a wide range of wavelengths (350 to 880 nm, where nm = 10^{-9} m or 1 m = 10^9 nm). The violet range (with wavelength below 350 nm) is used in advanced models. A wide range of wavelengths is required because different substances absorb best at different wavelengths. For example, sugar solutions have the maximum absorbance at 420 nm.]

Spectrophotometry mainly depends on the following:

- **Light's Wavelength:** Each substance absorbs (or releases) the light over a certain range of wavelengths.
- **Beer-Lambert Law:** The amount of light transmitted through a medium gets weaker **exponentially**.

In a spectrophotometer, light first passes through a narrow slit to create a light with a narrow beam (band). Then it passes through a prism to create a light ray (beam). As a light ray with a certain wavelength (λ) passes through a sample, part of its intensity (*I*) is absorbed by the sample (the *darker* the sample, the *more* of the light's ray is absorbed by it). When the sample is colored, the leaving *I* after passing the sample (I_2) is less than the entering *I* (I_1, the light intensity of the reference). According to the **Beer-Lambert Law**, the light's *A* is directly proportional to the sample's concentration (*C*) and the sample's **thickness** (shown as *d* in Figure 1). This statement applies to the light's *T* (transmittance), too.

$$T = \frac{I_2}{I_1} \qquad \text{or} \qquad \%T = \frac{I_2}{I_1} \times 100 \qquad (1)$$

The spectrophotometer's detector is calibrated before measuring the sample's *T*. The calibration is performed by assigning distilled water a value of 100 *T* (because the absorbance of pure water is 0) and 0 for *T* by blocking the detector so that *no* light can enter. The spectrophotometer then compares a sample's intensity of the transmitted light (unabsorbed light) to the transmitted light of a **reference** (distilled water).

The inverse (reciprocal) log of T is absorbance (A), which measures the portion of the light absorbed by the sample:

$$A = \text{Log}\frac{1}{\%T} \tag{2}$$

The light's absorbance (A) changes **linearly** when the light passes through a **diluted solution** (see Figure 3). In a **concentrated solution**, it changes non-linearly (Figure 4). We can use the linear dependency of A (absorbance) with C (concentration) in diluted solutions to measure a sample's A and, consequently, color. The **Beer-Lambert equation** calculates a sample's **absorptivity coefficient** (A_A), which measures the sample's **color** (the *greater* a sample's A_A, the *darker* is the sample's color).

$$A_A = c = \frac{A}{d.C} \tag{3}$$

A is absorbance (unitless), d is the sample cell's thickness (the path length of cuvette or the distance the light passes through the sample, in cm), and C is the sample's concentration (in g/L). Using these units, A_A (or c, the color) becomes L/g.cm. [If we use the same concentrated sample, cuvette size, and wavelength for all our measurements, Equation 12.9 shows a linear (positive) relationship between c (color) and A.]

When expressing the path length in mm (millimeter), we must multiply the previous equation by 10, so the color becomes L/g.mm.

$$A_A = c = 10\frac{A}{d.C} \tag{4}$$

Example 1 on Spectrophotometry

Given: The concentration of a compound in a solution is 6 g/L, the diameter (d) of the sample cell is 2.54 cm, and the amount of light transmitted through the solution is 50%.

Wanted: Sample's absorbance (A) and absorbtivity (A_A, or color)

$$A = -\text{LogT} = -\text{Log}\frac{I_2}{I_2} = -\text{Log}\frac{50}{100} = 0.3 \qquad A_A = \frac{A}{d.C} = \frac{0.3}{2.54\times 6} = 0.02$$

The sample's C (concentration) when using its DS (dissolved substance) content and D (density) is given as

$$C = \frac{DS.D}{100} \tag{5}$$

Substituting C into Equation 4 gives

$$A_A = 1000\frac{A}{d.DS.D} \tag{6}$$

In the sugar industry, the value of A_A (measured at 420 nm) multiplied by 1000 is reported as ICUMSA-420 color (IU-420). Therefore, the color equation becomes

$$A_A = 10^6\frac{A}{d.DS.D} \tag{7}$$

Because A is the inverse log of T, this equation becomes,

$$A = \text{Log}\frac{1}{\%T} = -\text{Log}\%T = -(\text{Log}T - \text{Log}100) = -\text{Log}T + 2 = 2 - \text{Log}T \tag{8}$$

Using $A = 2 - \log T$ in this equation, we obtain

$$A_A = 10^6\frac{2-\text{Log}T}{d.DS.D} \tag{9}$$

Example 2 on Spectrophotometry: Calculate the color of a sugar solution sample if its DS is 50.2%, its T (transmittance) is 90.4%, its D (density) is 1.23, and the sample cell's d (diameter) is 25.4 mm (= 1 In).

$$A_A = 10^6\frac{2-\text{Log}T}{d.DS.D} = 10^6\frac{2-\text{Log}90.4}{25.4\times 50.2\times 1.23} = 28$$

C-89

COLOR CHARGE

Color charge is a quantum particle (a particle with *no* subparticle) that acts as the source of strong nuclear force (F_{SN}) in atoms. Color charges exist in some quantum particles, like quarks (the particles of protons and neutrons), photons (the particles of light), and gluons (the particles of F_{SN}). In this way, the F_{SN} keeps quarks of different color charges in a proton together.

[The term **color** in color charge has *nothing* to do with color (the visual property of the human eye). The name was used since its introduction in the late 1960s because the charge responsible for F_{SN} between particles can be viewed as the three primary colors to which the human vision is sensitive: **red**, **green**, and **blue**.]

Particles with color charge, like proton and neutron, have corresponding antiparticles and feel the F_{SN}, while particles without the color charge, such as an electron, do *not* feel that. Quantum chromodynamics (QC) takes its name from this property of color charge. According to QC, a quark's color charges (red, green, and blue) combine to appear colorless, while in an antiquark, three anti-colors of anti-red, anti-green, and antiblue combine to be colorless. Gluons, instead, can take two colors and two anti-colors.

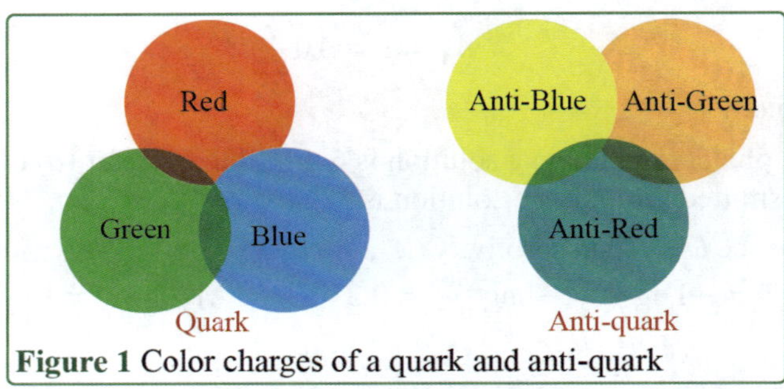

Figure 1 Color charges of a quark and anti-quark

C-90

COLORANTS

Another name for COLORING SUBSTANCES.

C-91

COLORING SUBSTANCES

Coloring substances (also called **colorants**) have complex polymeric structures composed of many organic compounds. The following are some general properties of colorants:

- They cause darkness in products, particularly in food products,
- Some of them, like colloids, are *not* dissolvable but rather suspended,
- They are **electro-negatively charged**, so their molecules can be absorbed by electro-positively-charged molecules, such as the molecules of active carbon, or by the particles of anionic ion-exchange resin.

[Note: The chemistry of colorants and color formation is too complex to indicate with simple chemical equations, so this topic does *not* concern with color chemistry.]

In a chemical plant that produces a product (or products), particulate to the amount of colorant content and color appearance, reducing colorants in the **in-process products** is important because they negatively affect its value. [The term **in-process** (intermediate) **product** or simply **in-product** is used in this book to denote an individual station's product in a chemical plant. For example, centrifuged magma from the centrifugal station is an in-product because it must be processed further to produce the plant's main product.]

Colorants are *not* necessarily present in the raw material of a food plant, but they are formed during operation steps. As an example, the juice inside the cells of sugarbeet (the raw material of a beet-sugar plant) is colorless or off-white, but processed beet juice is brown or dark brown, mainly because of the following:

- Exposure to high temperature (T),
- Interaction of organic compounds that form colorants.

The importance of colorants in a particular product, thus, makes color measurement an important subject in the laboratories of those chemical plants. Such a laboratory is usually equipped with one (or more) instruments to test a sample for colorant content. [Because of conciseability reasons, it is impossible to discuss all techniques that can measure a sample's color here. This book, however, discusses one of them, spectrometry.]

C-92

COMBINED GAS LAW

Discussed under the topic of GAS LAWS.

C-93

COMBUSTION ENGINES

Study EXTERNAL COMBUSTION ENGINES.

C-94

COMBUSTION REACTIONS AND COMBUSTION AIR REQUIREMENT

Combustion Reaction

A combustion reaction (simply **combustion**) is a rapid chemical reaction (simply **reaction**) that occurs between the combustible components of a fuel and oxygen (O_2) in the air to create heat energy (E_Q). Based on this definition, combustion reactions are heat-releasing reactions (exothermic reactions), known as **negative reactions** (release E_Q). The simplest example of combustion is the burning of a match. Industrially, combustion reactions occur in many devices, such as a furnace, an internal combustion engine (like a car's engine), and a limekiln. In a limekiln, a combustion reaction occurs between coke (or natural gas) and air to decompose limestone (mainly $CaCO_3$) to produce quicklime (CaO) and carbon dioxide (CO_2).

$$100 \text{ kg } CaCO_3 \rightarrow 56 \text{ kg } CaO + 44 \text{ kg } CO_2 - E_Q$$

This equation tells us the following:

- The reaction is a heat-releasing (exothermic) reaction, usually shown with a **negative** sign.
- During the decomposition of limestone in the kiln, the limestone loses approximately 44% of its mass, which is taken from the kiln as CO_2 gas.

Before fuel can react with oxygen, it must be heated to the ignition temperature (T_{Ig}). As fuel molecules start to react with oxygen molecules in the air, the fuel's carbon-hydrogen bonds break, and C (carbon) and H (hydrogen) molecules combine with O (oxygen) molecules to produce CO_2, H_2O, and some E_Q.

$$C + O_2 \rightarrow CO_2 - E_Q$$

$$2\ H_2 + O_2 \rightarrow 2\ H_2O - E_Q$$

These equations tell us that carbon and oxygen are the most important components of the combustion reaction, so their mixing ratio must be in a certain range, as discussed next.

Combustion Air Requirement

The combustion air requirement (CAR) is the air required to combust a fuel's mass unit, usually expressed in kg/kg (or Lb/Lb). CAR is calculated based on fuel analyses on a dry basis. [In calculations, the word dry air (or **on a dry basis**) gives a solid definition of theoretical air.]

Without sufficient air, combustion reaction is incomplete because,

- It produces carbon monoxide (CO), which is toxic (hazardous).
- It increases fuel usage, which is costly.

Now, we can define the following three terms, which are usually used in CAR calculations:

- **Theoretical Air Requirement** (TAR)**:** TAR is the amount of dry air (*not* oxygen) required for a combustion reaction. It is determined stoichiometry (theoretically) based on a reaction's reactants and products.
- **Practical Air Requirement** (PAR)**:** PAR is the amount of dry air (*not* oxygen) required for a complete combustion reaction. It is determined practically, based on the day-to-day practice. PAR is greater than TAR because excess air above TAR is needed to complete fuel combustion. Incomplete combustion produces carbon monoxide (CO), which is a hazard! And we know that all carbon (C) in the fuel does *not* oxidize to carbon dioxide (CO_2) and all the hydrogen (H_2), either.
- **Excess Air Factor** (EAF): EAF is the ratio of PAR (the practical or actual amount of air) to TAR (the theoretical amount of air) for fuel combustion, so it tells us about the amount of excess air (which is free!).

$$EAF = \frac{PAR}{TAR} \tag{1}$$

Often, an EAF of 1.3 to 1.5 (which equates to 30 to 50% excess air) is used. Here are three numerical examples. (1) For combustion of each cubic meter (m^3) of C in a fuel, theoretically, 2 kg of oxygen ($C + O_2 \rightarrow CO_2$) is needed, so the TAR value is 2 kg of O_2 per m^3 of C. Using an EAF of 1.4, the PAR value will be $2 \times 1.4 = 2.8$ kg oxygen per m^3 of C. (2) For combustion of each m^3 of natural gas, 10.2 m^3 dry air (discussed under the topic of AIR) are needed. Using an EAF of 1.4, the PAR value will be $10.2 \times 1.4 = 14.3$ m^3 of dry air per m^3 of natural gas. (3) To burn 1 kg of fuel oil, 13.4 kg of dry air is needed, so the TAR is 13.4 and PAR will be $13.4 \times 1.4 =$ 18.8 kg of dry air per kg of fuel oil.

C-95

COMPONENTS

Simplified name for CHEMICAL COMPONENTS.

C-96

COMPOSITE PARTICLES

It is defined under ELEMENTARY PARTICLES.

C-97
COMPOSITION

Study CHEMICAL COMPOSITION.

C-98
COMPOUNDS

Study CHEMICAL COMPOUNDS.

C-99
COMPRESSED NATURAL GAS

Compressed natural gas (CNG) is natural gas stored at high pressure. CNG requires more volume than compressed natural gas (CNG), and its specific energy (the energy per unit mass) is 2.4 times smaller than CNG and 0.6 times smaller than diesel fuel.

C-100
COMPRESSIBILITY FACTOR

Study IDEAL GAS COMPRESSIBILITY FACTOR.

C-101
COMPRESSIBLE AND INCOMPRESSIBLE FLOWS

In ChemEng, all **liquid flows** are generally known as incompressible, except a few used in hydraulics.

Compressible Flow

A compressible flow is a high-speed gas flow in which a gas's density (D) changes considerably. In ChemEng, almost all **gases** are considered compressible fluids, as their density can vary by more than 5% when flowing in a pipe.

Incompressible Flow

An incompressible flow is a liquid flow with the following properties:

- Its density (D) does *not* appreciably change (D = constant), and
- Applying pressure (P) *cannot* compress its volume (V) greatly.

Compressible and incompressible flows are similar in many ways. However, two important differences between them are the following:

- Unlike in liquid (incompressible) flow, some considerable changes occur to the properties of the gas (mainly to its density and volume) when it flows from its **reservoir** (the starting point; say, a tank) to a **media** (the endpoint; say, a pipe), or conversely from media to the reservoir. So, the variations of these factors must be considered in calculations.

- Unlike liquid flow, the Reynolds number (N_R) is *not* used in a gas-flow classification. Instead, another dimensionless parameter, known as the Mach number (N_M), is used to classify the gas flows into the **sonic flow** (with N_M of nearly 1), **subsonic flow** (with N_M of less than 1), and **supersonic flow** (N_M of greater than 1).

C-102
COMPRESSIBLE AND INCOMPRESSIBLE FLUIDS

Gases are compressible fluids because

- Pressure (*P*) can compress their volume considerably,
- The density (*D*) of them changes considerably when their *P* or *T* (temperature) changes,
- Intermolecular forces (F_{Int}) between gases' particles are minimal, so they move freely, are far apart, and, therefore, are compressible.

Liquids are incompressible fluids because

- Pressure (*P*) *cannot* compress a liquid's volume (*V*) considerably,
- A liquid's *D* does *not* change considerably when its *P* or *T* changes, and
- Intermolecular forces (F_{Int}) between particles of a liquid are high, so the particles *cannot* move freely, are *not* far apart, and, therefore, are incompressible.

C-103
COMPRESSORS, FANS, AND BLOWERS

Compressors, blowers, and fans are blowing devices for moving air (a gas). They are almost similar in operation, but different in performance, particularly in the discharge pressure (*P*) of the moving gas, as outlined next.

- Compressors can create the highest discharge *P* in the range of 10^4 to 8.3×10^4 kPa (= 1450 to 12000 PSI),
- Fans can generate the lowest discharge *P* in the range of 0.5 to 25 kPa (= 0.07 to 3.6 PSI), and
- Blowers can generate discharge *P* in the range of 3.5 to 55 kPa (= 0.5 to 8 PSI).

Because these devices have the same functionality, they are almost similar in operation but different in efficiency. [The **American Society of Mechanical Engineers** (ASME) uses a **compression ratio** (CR, the ratio of discharge-to-suction pressure of a blowing device) to rate compressors, fans, and blowers. Based on this rating, the CR for compressors is more than 1.2. For the fans is up to 1.1. And the CR for blowers is from 1.1 to 1.2.]

The disadvantage of the compressors over fans is the sealing of their attached parts (fans are better sealed). This makes the fans operate at higher temperatures than compressors (which are limited to 150°C = 300°F).

Another marker is the **compression ratio** (the ratio of discharge-to-suction pressure of a blowing device), up to 1.1 for the fans, up to 1.2 for the blowers, and more than 1.2 for the compressors.

Compressors

A compressor (also called the **gas compressor** or **gas pump**, and **air compressor** when it moves air) is installed in a piping system to move a gas through a pipe from one point to another at a certain *P* and constant flow rate. High *P* in the flowing gas is formed in the same way as in a liquid under pumping by a pump.

Like pumps, compressors use one of the following two effects to move a gas:

- **Ram Effect:** A compressor that operates based on the ram effect rams (pushes) the gas into its **suction-end** with constant volume (*V*) by its high-speed impeller (ring + blades). Then it discharges the gas from its **discharge end**. A compressor that operates based on this principle is called a **centrifugal compressor**.

- **Trapping Effect:** A compressor that operates based on the trapping effect holds (traps) the gas into its suction-end by its impeller, squeezes it into a smaller *V* until a desired *P* is reached, and discharges it. A compressor that operates based on this principle is called a **positive displacement compressor**.

Compressors use electric energy or steam as a source of energy to perform shaft work (W_S) on a gas to perform the following:

- Compressing (decreasing volume) of the gas,
- Overcoming the frictions that resist the flow of the gas,
- Increasing *P*, E_{Me} (mechanical energy), and *V* (velocity) of the gas.

In a compressor, the kinetic energy (E_K) and potential energy (E_P) do *not* change considerably, and *no* considerable frictions occur, so the Bernoulli equation will be simplified to the following form:

$$dW_S = \frac{dP}{D} \tag{1}$$

Integration of this equation between the suction pressure (P_S) and the discharge pressure (P_D) gives the compressor's shaft work (W_S) applied on a gas with a density of *D*.

$$W_S = \int_{P_S}^{P_D} \frac{dP}{D} \tag{2}$$

Types of Compressors

Compressors are classified into **centrifugal** and **positive-displacement** (PD) **compressors**.

Centrifugal Compressors: A typical centrifugal compressor (Figure 1) operates on the same principle as a centrifugal pump (discussed under PUMPS), meaning that a gas is moved by a centrifugal force (F_C), which is formed by turning its impeller's blades (vanes). Because of F_C, the gas velocity at the inlet (V_1) increases to V_2 at the outlet, and the decrease in volume increases the pressure of the gas to P_2. In a centrifugal compressor, the gas flows radially (horizontally) along with the compressor's casing.

Today's centrifugal compressors are **multistage** with two (or more) sets of blades on a single shaft to discharge a gas at a higher *P*. The shaft is driven by either an electric motor or a gas engine. In a typical multi-stage centrifugal compressor, the discharge gas from the first set of blades provides suction for the second set; the discharge from the second provides suction for the third set. And so on. Multistage centrifugal compressors have a suction capacity of up to 500 000 m^3/h and can discharge a gas with about 70 MPa (= 10 150 PSI) at the discharge side.

Figure 2 shows an **axial** (axial-flow) **compressor**, which operates like a centrifugal compressor. But the gas flows axially (vertically) parallel to the axis of rotation, while in a centrifugal pump, the gas flows radially (horizontally) along with the compressor's casing. An axial compressor has an airfoil (aerodynamic) body, in which a shaft rotates a set of blades. The rotating blades cause the velocity of the gas to increase considerably as the gas leaves the compressor.

Positive-Displacement Compressors: In a positive-displacement (PD) compressor, gas moves by trapping (holding) a fixed amount of it and displacing it by applying a force (*F*) into the compressor's discharge section. PD pumps come in many types, including reciprocating and lobe-type compressors.

Reciprocating (piston) **compressors** are in the class of PD compressors. A reciprocating compressor uses a piston driven by a shaft to increase the *P* of the inflow gas. In such a compressor, the intake gas enters the suction section, from where it flows into the compressor's cylinder. The gas gets compressed by the piston in a **reciprocating motion** (the piston enters and leaves the cylinder to move the gas out of the cylinder at a high *P*), as shown in Figure 3.

Lobe-type compressors are one kind of piston compressors, with two or three **lobes** (rotors), which are installed in the compressor's housing. Figure 4 shows a double-lobe compressor, and Figure 5 shows a tri-lobe compressor. Note that the compressor's rotors (lobes) do *not* touch each other.

Compressor Operating Curve

A compressor operating curve (compressor performing curve) indicates the relationship between the pressure (P) a compressor can develop and the compressor's **capacity** (flow rate). As shown in Figure 6, the head pressure (P_h, pressure expressed in unit length) of a compressor decreases as its capacity increases. Instead, as the compressor's capacity decreases, its head increases until it reaches a maximum point (called **surge point**), at which the flow of the gas is at its minimum. A **surge point** is when a maximum head and minimum flow occurs in compressor operation.

The operating point gets closer to the surge point if the demand for gas decreases. If this situation gets to its limit, the compressor loses the ability to increase the discharge P, so the following occurs:

- Flow-reversal situation (the return of gas from high-P side to low-P side),
- A large audible sound can be heard from the compressor,
- Excessive vibration of the compressor.

[A compressor's surge limit mainly depends on the compressor's RPM, gas P, gas T, and gas composition. A surge mainly occurs at low demand when the compressor's impeller runs at low RPM (lower than 50% of design speed). Although the surge-limit situation is a cyclic process (can be returned to normal when the demand is increased), it can greatly damage a compressor's operability if it continues for a long time.]

Fans

A fan increases the P of air (or another gas) to move it through a device (like the furnace of a forced-draft boiler). Fans are also used for cooling and ventilation of buildings. Fans are also used for cooling and ventilation of buildings. These three devices are rated based on

Fan selection mainly depends on the volumetric flow rate ($\dot{V}$) of the air to be moved and the air quality. Fans are rated at a standard air (a dry-clean air with a density of 1.2 kg/m^3 = 0.075 Lb/Ft^3 at 1 Atm).

Fans are divided into three main types: 1) Centrifugal fans, 2) Axial fans, and 3) Airfoil fans.

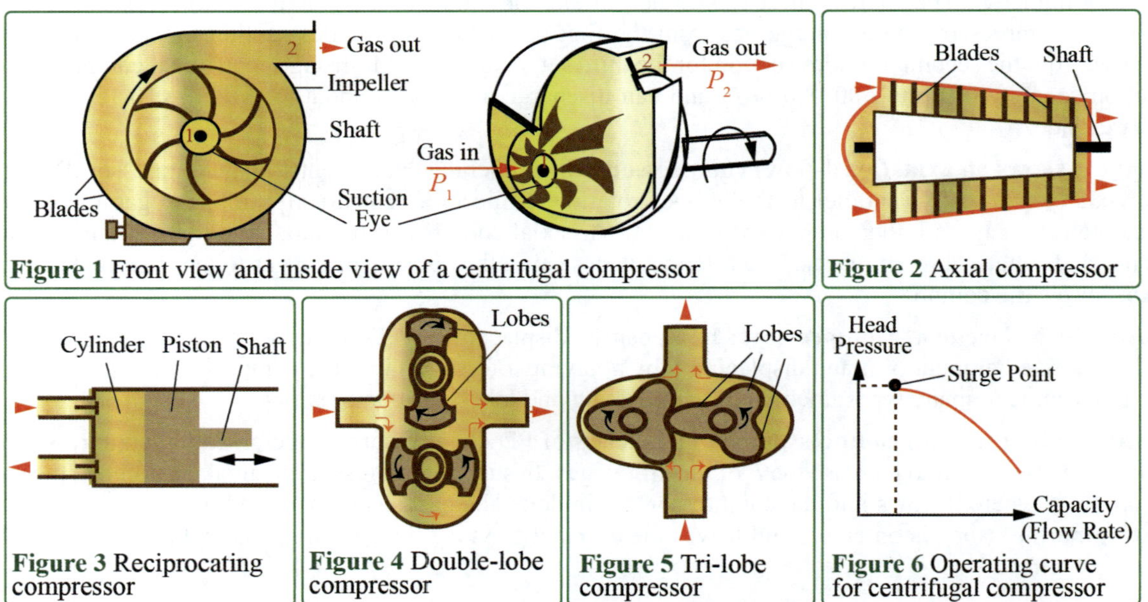

Figure 1 Front view and inside view of a centrifugal compressor

Figure 2 Axial compressor

Figure 3 Reciprocating compressor

Figure 4 Double-lobe compressor

Figure 5 Tri-lobe compressor

Figure 6 Operating curve for centrifugal compressor

Centrifugal Fans: As shown in Figure 7, a typical centrifugal fan consists of an impeller (ring + blades) connected from one side to the fan's shaft and from the other side to several blades. An electric motor connected to the fan's shaft by a bearing system (or a belt) is used as a drive. The air enters from the side of the fan, turns typically by 90° by the fan's impeller, accelerates by a centrifugal force (F_C) when moving over the fan's blades, and exits the fan while making another turn. Changing airflow direction twice, once when the air enters the fan and once when the air leaves it, increases air discharge *P* considerably.

A centrifugal fan can move 1700 to 2000 m^3/h (1000 to 1180 Ft^3/min) of air at discharge *P* of 5 to 25 kPa (0.7 to 3.6 PSI). Theoretically, when a fan operates at half speed, its air suction ability reduces by 50%, while its HP (horsepower) is reduced only by $1/8^{th}$ of full speed.

Centrifugal fans come with **radial-straight blades**, **forward-curved blades**, and **backward-curved blades**. Figure 8 shows a centrifugal fan with forward-curved blades, and Figure 9 shows the same fan with backward-curved blades. A centrifugal fan creates an airflow with constant $\dot{V}$ (volumetric flow rate) and *U* (speed).

Centrifugal fans have the next advantages over axial fans: 1) They are cheaper than axial fans, 2) They are simpler in construction than axial fans, and 3) They operate quietly over a wide range of conditions.

These advantages make them one of the most widely used fans for moving low to medium volume airflows. The efficiency of centrifugal fans is 55 to 65%, where the remaining energy converts to heat energy.

Axial Fans: As shown in Figure 10, an axial fan creates axial airflow by moving its blades in a vertical (top-to-bottom) manner, so the produced airflow is parallel with the shaft (which is installed horizontally). The air-flow, in other words, is axially in and axially out, so airflow moves through the fan with *no* change in direction. A typical industrial axial fan has 5 to 9 blades and can discharge airflow with a pressure of 0.5 to 0.75 kPa (= 0.07 to 1 PSI), depending on its size and electric drive. The propeller, tube-axial-blade, and vane-axial-blade are the main types of axial fans. Vane-axial-blade fans, for example, are used for forcing air into the furnace of the forced-draft furnaces.

Airfoil Fans: As shown in Figure 11, an airfoil fan has aerodynamic-shaped blades to decrease the airflow resistance, resulting in high efficiency.

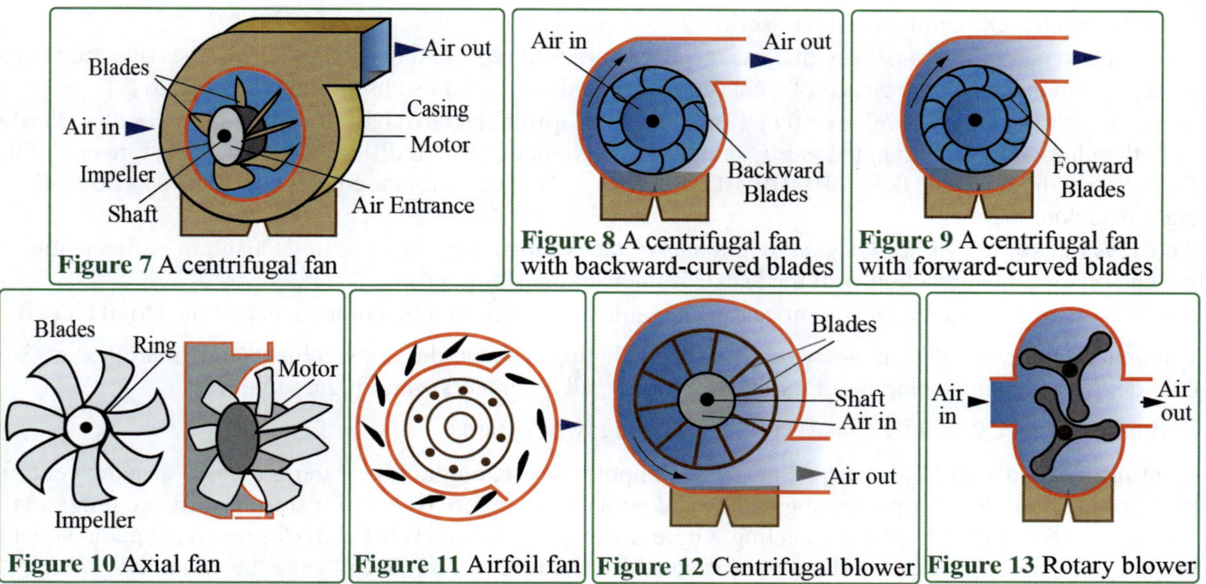

Figure 7 A centrifugal fan

Figure 8 A centrifugal fan with backward-curved blades

Figure 9 A centrifugal fan with forward-curved blades

Figure 10 Axial fan

Figure 11 Airfoil fan

Figure 12 Centrifugal blower

Figure 13 Rotary blower

Blowers: A blower moves air (or other gases) in a device, like moving air in a dryer. Centrifugal, backward-curved-blade, and radial-blade are three of many types of blowers. Figure 12 shows a centrifugal blower, in which air enters at the center of a spinning impeller and spreads between the impeller's blades (vanes).

C-104

COMPUTER AND QUANTUM COMPUTER

A computer is a digital device that can process information in the form of **binary numbers** (**binary digits**, or simply **bits**), where a **byte** (a computer's basic unit of information) is equivalent to 8 **bits** (binary digits). The next table indicates the units used in the computer field.

Unit	Size
Byte (B)	8 bits
Kilobyte (kB)	1000 bytes
Megabyte (MB)	10^6 (million) bytes
Gigabyte (GB)	10^9 (billion) bytes
Terabyte (TB)	10^{12} (trillion) bytes

The five (5) main differences between a **classical computer** (CC) and a **quantum computer** (QC) are:

- An CC (classical computer) is much slower than a QC (quantum computer), as a CC can process a **bit** (0 or 1) at a time, while a QC uses many bits (called **quantum bits** or **qubits**) to perform the same process at a time. In addition, increasing the qubits of a QC increases its storing capacity exponentially. For example, 4 qubits can store $2^4 = 16$ numbers, 8 qubits can store $2^8 = 256$ numbers, 16 qubits can store $2^{16} = 65536$ numbers, and *n* qubits can store 2^n numbers. As a result, a QC can have a huge processing capacity. [The computer capacity is measured in FLOPS (floating-point operations per second) to express how many single operations (say, deducting 2 from 6) it can perform a second. The term FLOPS gets a G (for Giga = 10^9) to be read as GFLOPS (simply G). Today, when writing this book, an average desktop CC can produce 7 G (= 7×10^9 FLOPS), which is too small compared to a QC expected to produce about 10^9 G (= $10^9 + 10^9 = 10^{18}$ FLOPS). Such a QC can forecast the world's two-week weather.]
- An CC uses many tiny transistors that use electric charges to represent data, while a QC uses quantum cryptography. [In an CC, the presence of a charge corresponds to 1, and its absence corresponds to 0.]
- In an CC, a **bit** can have a value of 0 or 1, while a QC's **qubit** can have both 0 and 1 values simultaneously, as both values are kept entangled (see Quantum Entanglement). Stated differently, a CC can store one of the following eight numbers: 000, 001, 010, 011, 100, 101, 110, and 111, at a time, while a QC can store all eight listed numbers.
- An CC is **hackable**, while a QC is *not*, as a hacker faces superposed states (study Quantum Superposition), which collapse by interacting with the hacker's interruption (for good).
- An CC uses larger components to process data, while a QC uses smaller components (at the atomic level).

Computers come in different shapes and sizes, including laptops, desktops, tablets, and smartphones. Some digital devices contain a computer. Despite this variety, all computers work in the same way.

A simple typical CC mainly consists of the following two (2) parts:

- **Computer Hardware:** This part includes the computer's case, monitor, keyboard, mouse, speaker, central processing unit (CPU, for processing data), random-access memory (RAM, for storing software programs and data), electric circuits (for connecting wirelessly to the internet), WIFI chip (for receiving audio signals), graphic card, and sound card. [**Hardware** is so-called because it is **hard** to change the variables.]
- **Computer Software:** This part mainly consists of the instructive programs that the hardware can perform. [**Software** is so-called because it is **easy** to change the variables.]

Built-in storage, like hard disks, can have a capacity of 250 GB to 1 TB. While removable storage with less capacity, like USB **flash drives**, is used for transferring information from one computer to another. [About 3 billion laptop-and-desktop computers are used globally.]

C-105

CONCENTRATION, CONCENTRATION DIFFERENCE, AND CONCENTRATION GRADIENT

Concentration

A solution's concentration (*C*) is the amount of solute (dissolved solids) in that solution (the solvent). Thus, a solution's *C* indicates how much solute is dissolved in a certain amount of solution. It is usually expressed as a salute's *M* (mass) per the solution's unit mass or per the solution's unit *V* (volume).

- **Mass Percent Concentration:** The percent by mass (% *M/M*, also called **percent mass fraction** or simply **mass fraction**) is the solute's mass (M_S) divided by the total solution's mass (M_{Sol}) times 100 or (M_S /M_{Sol})×100. It can be alternatively expressed as [(g solute/(g solute + g solvent)]×100. A solution with 80% by mass (by weight) dissolved solids (*DS*) contains 80 g of *DS* in 100 g of solution. [The same concept as **mass percent concentration** is a mass fraction (X_M) with a denominator of 100. For example, a solution containing 60% by *M* of ethanol and 40% of water means that its ethanol's X_M is 0.6 and water's X_M is 0.4.]
- **Mass-Volume Percent Concentration:** The prevent mass/volume (% *M*/*V*) is the *M* of solute divided by the total *V* of solution times 100. For example, a 20% *M/V* calcium chloride ($CaCl_2$) solution contains 20 g of $CaCl_2$ per 100 mL of solution, or 20 g of $CaCl_2$ is mixed with water to form 100 mL of $CaCl_2$ solution.
- **Volume Percent Concentration:** The percent by volume (% *V*) is volume parts per hundred volumes. A 20% by *V* of ammonium hydroxide (NH_4OH) solution contains 20 mL of NH_4OH per 100 mL of solution. [Note: Percent by volume is *not* the same as mixing 20 mL of NH_4OH with 80 mL of water (because the total volume will *not* be exactly 100 mL when mixed).]

Remember the following important points about concentration:

- Concentration, in chemistry, is also expressed by molarity (*M*), normality (*N*), molality (*m*), mass fraction (X_M), volume fraction (X_V), and molar fraction (X_n).
- Concentration is expressed by parts per when a solute in a solution sample is too low. Parts per million (PPM) and parts per billion (PPB) are two (2) types of parts per.
- The concentration of an acid (or base) does *not* express its strength because the word strength of an acid in chemistry refers to the amount of ionization (breaking).

Concentration Difference

Concentration difference (ΔC, also called **chemical potential**) is the difference in *C* between two points in a fluid (liquid or gas) or between two fluids. The ΔC is given in units of concentration. [Concentration difference (shown by the symbol $\Delta C = C_2 - C_1$) does *not* mean the **concentration gradient**, as defined next.]

Concentration Gradient

Concentration gradient ($\Delta C/L$, also called **potential chemical gradient**) is the concentration difference (ΔC) between two points in a fluid (or between two fluids) per unit length (*L*) or per differential (final-minus-initial) length, shown as *dL* or *dx*. [When using *dx*, we mean that *C* (concentration) changes only along the *x*-axis direction, so it is only a function of *x*. $\Delta C/L$, in other words, describes how fast and in which direction *C* of a solution changes around a given point. Assume that a solution's *C* does *not* change with time. At each point in the solution, $\Delta C/L$ shows the direction of the mass transfer by diffusion at its greatest. And the quantity (magnitude) of $\Delta C/L$ determines how fast the mass (*M*) diffuses in that direction. $\Delta C/L$ is the driving force for the mass transfer by diffusion. Also, note that a **gradient** is a change in the value of a quantity (like concentration) per change in *L*.]

The SI unit of concentration gradient is mole/m or kmole/m, where m is for meter and k is for a kilo. The concentration gradient's US unit is mole/Ft or kmole/Ft, where Ft is for feet.

C-106

CONCRETE

Study CEMENT AND CONCRETE.

C-107

CONDENSATE AND CONDENSATE TRAP

Study CONDENSER WATER, CONDENSATE, AND CONDENSATE TRAP.

C-108

CONDENSATION FILM

Condensation film is a thin layer of condensate that covers the surface of the tubes (or plates) of a heat exchanger when the vapor contacts the tubes (which are colder than vapor), and condensation of the liquid occurs. Condensate film creates a considerable resistance to heat transfer.

C-109

CONDENSATION HEIGHT

Condensation height (h_C) is the height between the points where vapor enters the bottom of a barometric condenser and the cooling-water distribution level at the top of the condenser, as shown in Figure 1 under CONDENSATION PROCESS.

C-110

CONDENSATION POINT TEMPERATURE

The condensation point temperature (T_{CP}, simply **condensation point**) of a gas is the temperature (T) at which it changes to liquid at the pressure (P) around that gas. Usually, T_{CP} is defined at atmospheric pressure (P_{Atm} = 1 Atm = 14.7 PSI, the pressure at sea level). At 1 Atm, water vapor condenses at 0°C to water.

At a given P (pressure), *different* gases have *different* T_{CP} because each gas's molecular attraction is different. If heat energy (E_Q) is gradually and uniformly released from a gas, its T stays at the T_{CP} until complete condensation.

C-111
CONDENSATION PROCESS

BASICS

As a process unit of ChemEng, condensation is a heat transfer process performed in a condenser to condense a vapor to a liquid by cooling the vapor. Condensation mainly occurs because of the following:

- Temperature (T)**:** A vapor starts to condense when its T reaches its condensation temperature.
- Pressure (P)**:** A vapor starts to condense when its vapor pressure ($P_V\uparrow$) is equal to or lower than the atmospheric pressure ($P_{Atm}\downarrow$). [Arrows indicate the rough direction of P.] Water vapor (vapor phase of water), for example, starts to condense to liquid water when the P_V applied to its molecules is equal to or lower than the P_{Atm} (= 1 Atm ≈ 100 kPa ≈ 14.7 PSI). For this reason, the condensers are operated under negative vacuum pressure (P_{Vac}) to easier condense a gas.

Condensation is a supporting process unit (unit operation) of ChemEng because it helps the main process units, such as distillation and evaporation. In association with distillation, the non-contact condensers (discussed under CONDENSERS) are used, for example, in oil refineries to condense the following fractions: gasoline, kerosene, diesel fuel, motor oil, asphalt, tar, petrochemicals, **liquid petroleum gas** (LPG), and more. In association with evaporation, it is used in many chemical process plants (simply **chemical plants**), for example, a chemical plant with a multiple-effect-evaporating station (discussed under EVAPORATION PROCESS). In this station, the vapor from the last effect is usually condensed in a direct-contact condenser (called the barometric condenser). Condensation is also used in power plants for treating a process stream, consisting of condensing gas and some noncondensing gases (like air, ammonia, and carbon dioxide).

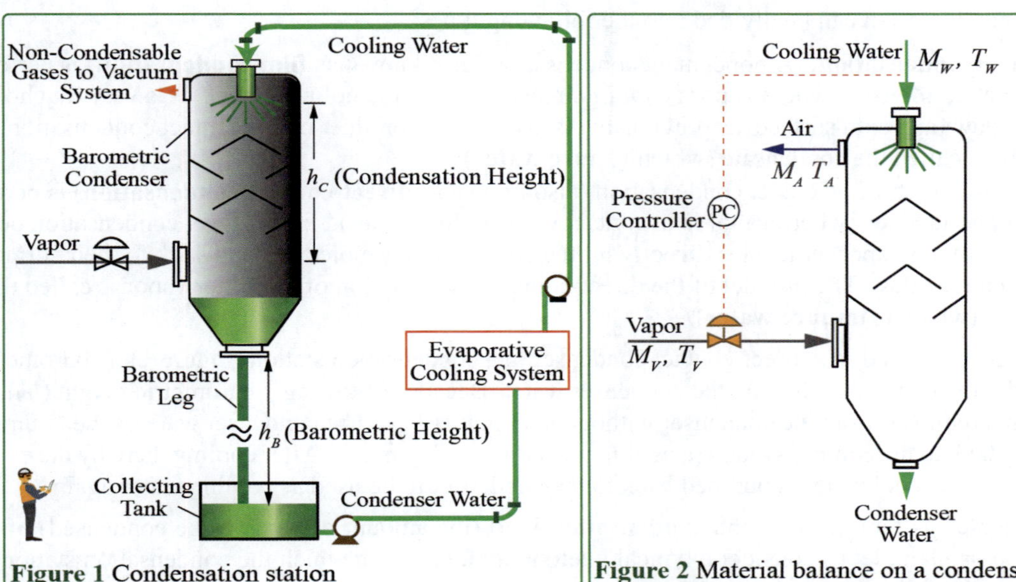

Figure 1 Condensation station

Figure 2 Material balance on a condenser

In condensation, both of the following heat transfer processes are involved:

- Temperature change (a sensible heat process), because T of vapor reduces during the process,
- Phase-change (a latent heat process) because a major portion of vapor changes to a liquid.

Thus, part of the enthalpy change ($\Delta H = E_Q$, heat energy) that occurs during condensation is a temperature change enthalpy (called sensible enthalpy or non-phase-change enthalpy), and part is phase change enthalpy (called latent enthalpy), known as the enthalpy of condensation.

Condensing water vapor (the gas phase of water) on a cold surface to form **dew** (a small drop of water) on a cool night is a typical example of condensation. Dew forms as water vapor molecules meet a cold surface because they cool down to their T_C. In the beginning, condensation occurs as a thin liquid layer called the **condensate film**, but as condensation continues, the thickness of the film increases until dew forms. To better understand the process of condensation and the factors affecting it, consider a gas under condensation in a condenser. Next are the important factors that contribute to the condensation of this gas:

- Kinetic Energy (E_K)**:** On average, the molecules of a gas, compared to a liquid, have a greater E_K, so they are *not* attracted to adjacent molecules by intermolecular forces (F_I). As the gas is cooled, its molecules start to move slower. When T of the gas reaches its T_C, the molecules move at their slowest, so the F_{Int} can get the molecules closer to each other, forming a liquid.
- Density (D)**:** As a gas is cooled, the D of some of its molecules becomes greater than others. Because the high-density molecules move slower than the low-density ones, they do *not* have enough E_K to overcome F_{Int}, so they *canno*t stay in the gaseous form and condense to liquid form.
- Pressure (P)**:** As a gas is cooled, its P starts decreasing, and when it starts to condense, its vapor pressure (P_V) becomes equal (or lower) than the atmospheric pressure (P_{Atm}). The T_C (condensation temperature) is defined at P_{Atm} (= 1 Atm = 14.7 PSI).

Industrial condensation is performed on two vapors: 1) **Pure Vapor:** A pure vapor consists of only a **condensing** (a condensable) **gas**, like water vapor. 2) **Mixed Vapor:** A mixed vapor of two gasses consists of condensing and noncondensing gases. [A **mixed vapor of more gases** consists of condensing and two (or more) noncondensing gases. Industrially, this is the most dominant case.]

Industrial condensation can be divided into the following types:

- **Noncontact Condensation:** A noncontact condensation (also known as **film condensation**) is performed in a **noncontact condenser** (where vapor is *not* in direct contact with cooling water). It is very much like the creation of dew on a cold surface, as previously discussed. The product of noncontact condensation of the water vapor is called the condensate (which is **pure water**).
- **Contact Condensation:** Contact condensation (also known as **direct-contact condensation**) is performed in a **contact condenser** (where vapor is in contact with cooling water). In this type, condensation occurs because slow-moving vapor molecules **directly** hit the cooling water molecules and stick to their surface to form liquid molecules. The product of the direct-contact condensation of the water vapor is called the condenser water (which is **impure water**).

The vapor is condensed in a direct-contact condenser in a condensation station (Figure 1). A barometric leg is installed under the condenser to draw the condenser water. Because of the leg's barometric height (h_B), the condenser water is removed from the condenser without breaking its P_{Vac}. The condenser water is then pumped from the collecting tank to the cooling system (a cooling tower or cooling pond). After cooling there by the evaporative cooling process, the cool water is pumped back to the condenser to be used as cooling water again.

To make ourselves familiar with the **condensation load** (the amount of vapor to be condensed) of a typical chemical process plant, let us consider a typical **beet-sugar factory**, in which the condensation station receives the vapor from the following stations:

- **Evaporation Station:** A typical last effect of a multiple-effect evaporating station in such a plant operates at a slightly negative vacuum pressure (typically about 20 kPa = 0.2 Atm = 3 PSI). This P corresponds to the saturated vapor of 60°C. This vapor enters a barometric condenser to be condensed. The amount of the last-effect vapor depends on the daily capacity of the factory and its heat (thermal) efficiency. Usually, a typical beet factory produces around 16 t vapor in its last effect for each 100-t beet processed.

- **Crystallization Station:** Each crystallizer has a barometric condenser that receives a vapor at about 12 kPa (= 0.12 Atm = 1.8 PSI) P_{Vac}, corresponding to the saturated vapor of 50°C (lower than the last effect of the evaporating station). A typical three-stage crystallization station in a beet-sugar plant produces around 14 t vapor for each 100-t beet processed.
- **Filtration Station:** Vacuum filters in the filtration station operate at around 30 kPa (= 0.3 Atm = 4.4 PSI) pressure, corresponding to the saturated vapor of about 70°C. The condensing load of vapor coming from the filtration station is low compared with the other two stations.

The vapors from all the three listed stations are condensed by direct-contact condensers, which operate in a typical sugar plant under a slight P_{Vac} of about 14 kPa (= 0.14 Atm = 2 PSI).

The amount of cooling water entering a condenser to the amount of vapor entering that condenser is called the **water-to-vapor ratio**. [We will talk more about this ratio later, but for familiarity, remember that the typical practical range for this ratio is between 4-to-1 and 5-to-1.]

FACTORS AFFECTING CONTACT CONDENSATION

Consider a condensation station with a barometric contact condenser (discussed under CONDENSERS). Assume the vapor entering the condenser consists of a condensing gas (water vapor) and three noncondensing gases (air, ammonia, and CO_2). In addition to the type of condenser used to cool such vapor, the main factors affecting the **condensation rate** (R_{Con}) are the following two:

- **Temperature Difference** (ΔT): The ΔT between the cooling water entering the condenser and condenser water affects the R_{Con} (the greater the ΔT, the greater the R_{Con}).
- **Amount of Noncondensing Gases:** The amount of these gases in a condensing gas significantly reduces the R_{Con} (the *greater* the amount of noncondensing gases, the *smaller* is the R_{Con}). R_{Con} is reduced because noncondensing gases diffuse (penetrate) into the condensing gas, reducing the T_C of the vapor under condensation. Thus the R_{Con} is reduced, particularly in the condenser's last part (because of the accumulation of noncondensing gases in that area). The mass diffusion of these gases into the vapor phase also reduces the partial pressure of the condensing gas.

As for the effect of noncondensing gases on the R_{Con}, consider air (the major noncondensing gas) with the mass flow rate of $\dot{M}$, entering a condenser. The major sources of this air are the following:

- **Air Coming with Vapor:** This air is dissolved in the feed and released during evaporation. It is roughly estimated that the $\dot{M}$ of air from this source is around 60 kg/h.
- **Air Coming with Cooling Water:** This air is released from the cooling water in the condenser, which operates under negative vacuum pressure (P_{Vac}). It is roughly estimated that the $\dot{M}$ of air is around 40 kg/h.
- **Air Coming from Condenser's Leaks:** Because condensers operate under P_{Vac}, any leak sucks air into the condenser (the condenser can be tested for air leak by a vacuum test.) It is roughly estimated that the amount of air from this source is negligibly low (if *not* zero).

Considering the approximate numbers given here, the rough estimate of the total mass flow rate ($\dot{M}$) of air from the above three sources in that typical plant is 100 kg/h. According to the example given under the topic of VOLUMETRIC FLOW RATE, the volumetric flow rate of this air is 698 m^3/h. This is a large amount of air that must be constantly removed from the top of the condenser to prevent its accumulation. Otherwise, the condensation rate is reduced considerably.

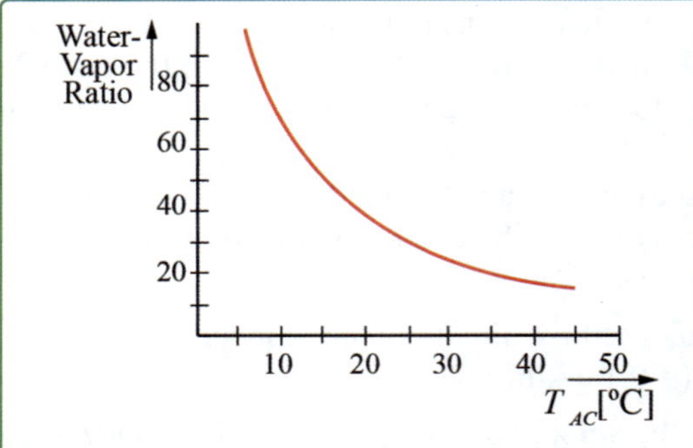

Figure 3 Dependency of water-to-vapor ratio on approach cooling temperature (T_{AC}) across a counterflow condenser

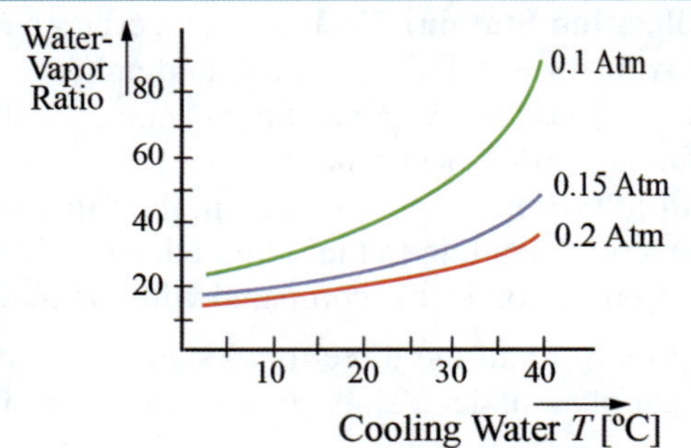

Figure 4 Dependency of water-to-vapor ratio on cooling water temperature and on condenser's pressure, assuming T_{AC} of 3°C

The following factors also affect the **condensation rate** (R_C) of a barometric condenser:

- Condensation Height (h_C): The h_C is the distance between the points where vapor enters the bottom of a condenser and the water-distribution level at its top. An h_C of 4 to 5 m (= 13 to 17 Ft) for condensers without the baffles is recommended. An h_C of 3 to 4 m is usually used for condensers with two to four baffles. However, some reference books suggest that the h_C must be chosen according to the vessel's diameter, where the optimum h_C is 3 to 4 times the vessel's diameter.
- Temperature Difference (ΔT): The ΔT affects the following three (3) variables: 1) Water-to-vapor ratio (the *greater* the ΔT, the *smaller* is the ratio and, consequently, the *less* cooling water is required). 2) Amount of pressure (P_{Vac}) in the condenser. 3) And capacity of the vacuum pump.

MASS BALANCING OF CONDENSATION

Because condensation is a phase-change process, it involves heat transfer and mass transfer. Thus, it is governed by the heat-transfer and mass-transfer rules and equations (like heating and evaporation).

Water-to-Vapor Ratio in Barometric Condensers

Figure 2 shows a contact-barometric-counterflow condenser for a condenser mass balance. It is helpful to know that the **condensation rate** (R_{Con}, condensation load per unit time) of a typical sugar plant that processes 6000 t sugarbeet/day is about 1 800 t/day (= 75 t/h or 75 000 kg/h). Knowing the condensation rate, we can calculate the heat energy rate ($\dot{E}_Q$), released during condensation by the basic heat transfer equation.

$$\dot{E}_Q = \dot{M}.C_Q(T_1 - T_2) \qquad (1)$$

In this equation, $\dot{M}$ is the vapor's mass flow rate (75 000 kg/h), C_Q is the water's specific heat capacity (C_Q = 4.186 kJ/kg.°C), T_1 is the temperature of the vapor going to the condenser (T_1, typically 60°C), and T_2 is the condenser water's temperature (T_2, typically 35°C).

$$\dot{E}_Q = \dot{M}.C_Q(T_1 - T_2) = 75000 \times 4.186(60 - 35) = 785 \times 10^4 \text{ kJ/h}$$

In such a condenser, the ratio of water consumption (M_W) to vapor condensed (M_V) can be calculated as

$$\frac{M_W}{M_V} = \frac{H_V - H_{W2}}{H_{W2} - H_{W1}} \qquad (2)$$

The H_V is the vapor's enthalpy, H_{W1} is the water's enthalpy entering the condenser, and H_{W2} is leaving the condenser, so knowing these variables and the amount of vapor entering a condenser (M_V) determines the M_W.

To estimate the rate of vapor ($\dot{M}_V$) entering a condenser, we consider a typical chemical process plant with an evaporation rate of about 30 kg/h per m^2 heating surface area. [Knowing the $\dot{M}_V$ is important in calculations to design a condenser.] Knowing $\dot{M}_V$, we can write the mass balance of the condenser, shown in Figure 2.

$$\dot{M}_W . C_Q . T_1 + \dot{M}_V . H_V = (\dot{M}_W + \dot{M}_V)\lambda_Q . T_2 \quad (3)$$

In this equation, $\dot{M}_W$ is the rate of the cooling water entering the condenser, $\dot{M}_V$ is the rate of vapor entering the condenser to be condensed, C_Q is the heat capacity of water, H_V is the enthalpy of vapor entering the condenser, T_1 is the temperature of vapor entering the condenser, and T_2 is the temperature of condenser water leaving the condenser. Equation 2 can be written as

$$\dot{M}_W . T_1 = (\dot{M}_W + \dot{M}_V)T_2 - \frac{\dot{M}_V . H_V}{\lambda_Q} \quad (4)$$

$$\dot{M}_W . T_1 - \dot{M}_W . T_2 = \dot{M}_V . T_2 - \frac{\dot{M}_V . H_V}{\lambda_Q} \quad (5)$$

$$\dot{M}_W = \frac{\dot{M}_V (H_V - T_2)}{\lambda_Q (T_1 - T_2)} \quad (6)$$

Thus, the ratio of water to vapor can be written as

$$\frac{\dot{M}_W}{\dot{M}_V} = \frac{H_V - T_2}{\lambda_Q (T_1 - T_2)} \quad (7)$$

This ratio is important (because it determines the amount of water required to condense a given amount of vapor in a condenser). The required water amount mainly depends on the following:

- Approach Cooling Temperature (**T_{AC}**)**:** This is the difference between the cooling water's T leaving the condenser and the cooling water's T entering the condenser. Thus, the *higher* the T_{AC}, the *less* cooling water is required to condense a certain amount of vapor (see Figure 3).
- **Vacuum Pressure (**P_{Vac}**) in the Condenser:** This is the P under which the condenser operates. Assuming a typical amount of T_{AC} of 3°C, the *higher* is the P_{Vac}; the *less* cooling water is required to condense a certain amount of vapor (as shown in Figure 4). In other words, colder water creates higher P_{Vac} at certain T_{AC}.

At condensers' typical operating P_{Vac} of 10 to 20 kPa (0.1 to 0.2 Atm or 1.5 to 3 PSI), Equation 6 can be written for practical purposes in the following way:

$$\frac{\dot{M}_W}{\dot{M}_V} = \frac{570}{(T_1 - T_2)} \quad (8)$$

As a numerical example, assume that the temperature of the vapor going to a condenser (T_1) is 60°C and that of condenser-water (T_2) is 35°C); the water-to-vapor ratio will be

$$\frac{\dot{M}_W}{\dot{M}_V} = \frac{570}{(T_1 - T_2)} = \frac{570}{60 - 35} = 23$$

The denominator of the right side of Equation 7 gets smaller as T_2 (the T of condenser water leaving the condenser) increases, so the water-to-vapor ratio increases.

C-112

CONDENSED SUBSTANCES

A condensed substance is a chemical substance (simply **substance**) in its liquid or solid form. Usually, when the term **condensed substance** is used, a liquid substance or a solid substance is meant at room temperature (around 25°C or 77 °F). Liquids and solids are called condensed substances because,

- Their molecules do *not* move freely,
- Their volumes are *not* compressible (pressure *cannot* compress them), and
- Their densities in the liquid phase and solid phase are approximately the same.

C-113

CONDENSED SYSTEMS

A condensed system is a system that contains a liquid or a solid. Usually, when the term **condensed system** is used, a liquid system or a solid system is meant at room temperature (around 25ºC or 77 ºF). Similarly, when the term condensed substance is used, a liquid or solid substance is meant at room temperature. The term liquid phase or solid phase is also used to refer to a condensed system.

C-114

CONDENSER WATER, CONDENSATE, AND CONDENSATE TRAP

Condenser water and **condensate** are *not* the same, as discussed next.

Condenser Water

Condenser water is impure water formed in a contact condenser. Condenser water collected in a barometric condenser's **seal tank** is also called **seal water**. The seal water is pumped to the cooling tower or cooling pond to be cooled and pumped back to the condensation station to be used again as the cooling water.

Condensate

Condensate is pure water with *no* or minimum dissolved solids (*DS*) produced in a noncontact condenser of the condensation process. In chemical process plants, condensate is formed from water vapor or steam that has partly lost its heat energy (E_Q) value and condensed to water (H_2O) in a noncontact condenser.

One of the most important properties of condensate is its amount of scale-causing salts (SC salts), which is usually measured with a conductometer. A conductometer measures the specific conductance ($K_{E.Sp}$) of a solution sample in µS/cm, where S (Siemens) is the SI unit of electric conductance (K_E). A high-quality condensate has a low $K_{E.Sp}$ in the range of 0 to 4 µS/cm, corresponding to 0 to 2 PPM of SC salts.

The two main properties of a high-quality condensate are 1) Alkaline PH (typically 8.5) and 2) Low oxygen content (maximum 0.02 PPM).

[Note: All condensates produced in a chemical plant *cannot* be used in the steam boilers. This is because of **scale-causing salts** in an impure condensate that deposits on the boiler's tubes. In a chemical plant with **multiple-effect evaporation** (discussed under EVAPORATION PROCESS), the boiler's feedwater is supplied mainly (up to 85%) from the highest quality condensate produced from the steam's condensation entering the first-effect evaporator. The balance is covered by the condensate produced in the second-effect evaporator. If, however, more high-quality condensate is needed, **soft makeup water** (the city or well water, processed by water softening process) is added to the condensate (boiler feedwater).

Condensate Trap

A condensate trap is installed in a piping system to separate the condensate from the air and other gases. A condensate trap operates based on the differential density between the condensate and the gas mixture. In designing a condensate trap, attention must be paid to its vent location. Figure 1 shows the correct and wrong ways of connecting a vent to a condensate trap.

Instead, a steam trap separates the condensate from the steam or vapor in a piping system.

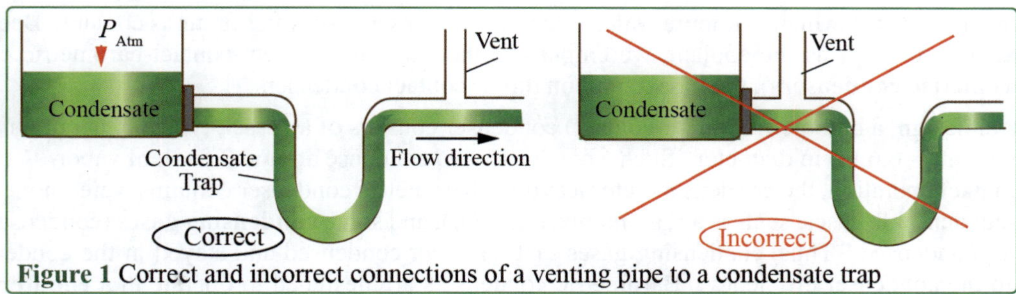

Figure 1 Correct and incorrect connections of a venting pipe to a condensate trap

C-115
CONDENSERS

As used in a system involving heat transfer, a condenser is a heat exchanger by which the condensation process is performed. Condensers change a vapor to a liquid by lowering the temperature (T) of the vapor. Most condensers used in chemical process plants operate under slight negative vacuum pressure (P_{Vac}), typically 10 to 20 kPa (0.1 to 0.2 Atm). P_{Vac} is used in a condenser for the following reasons:

- To move vapor and air in the condenser's vessel,
- To remove condenser water from the condenser's barometric leg.

Condensers that serve a condensation station are usually designed to have a vacuum pump for creating P_{Vac}. Usually, a combination of the following helps to produce a P_{Vac}:

- Condensation of the vapor and velocity of the vapor and cooling water entering the condenser.
- Using a piston or liquid-ring vacuum pump (discussed under VACUUM PUMPS).

In chemical plants with a multiple-effect-evaporating station (discussed under EVAPORATION PROCESS), the vapor from the last-effect evaporator is usually condensed into liquid in a contact condenser (discussed later). Condensers are also associated with the distillation process because the vapor from a distillation column must be condensed into liquid in a noncontact condenser.

Condensers are generally classed into two types:

- Contact condensers (also called the **spray condensers**),
- Noncontact condensers (also called **surface condensers**).

Before getting to the detail of each type, let us compare these condensers. The advantages of the contact condensers over the noncontact ones are the following:

- **Construction Cost:** They are less expensive.
- **Maintenance Cost:** They require less maintenance.
- **Approach Cooling Temperature:** They achieve a close approach cooling temperature (T_{AC}). This is particularly important for a factory in a warm area (because the average cooling water T is high).

The advantages of the noncontact condensers over contact condensers are the following:

- **Condensation Efficiency:** They create a higher condensation effect (6 to 18 times).
- **Produced Condensate:** They produce less condensate (10 to 20 times).
- **Cooling Medium:** They require less cooling water.

CONTACT CONDENSERS

The vapor directly contacts the coolant (cooling medium) in a contact condenser, so the vapor condenses while mixing with the coolant. When steam or vapor is the feed of a contact condenser, the product of the condenser is called condenser water, which is impure water. Contact condensers use water or air as coolant. Because most chemical plants use water as the coolant, we emphasize the water-used-direct-contact-barometric condensers (further **barometric condensers**), the most common direct-contact condensers.

In a general design, a barometric (direct-contact) condenser consists of a vessel, typically about 4 m (= 13 Ft) in height and 2 m (= 6.6 Ft) in diameter. Such a condenser can condense around 0.5 t/ h of vapor. As a result of the direct-contact operation, the condenser water leaving a barometric condenser contains water, noncondensing gases (non-condensable gases, such as air, ammonia, and CO_2), and some **condensing gases** (condensable gases) that have *not* condensed. Thus, condensing gases that have *not* condensed and stayed in the condenser water contribute to the condenser efficiency. Barometric condensers are designed to operate in a **counter** (counter-current) or **cocurrent** ways. Most chemical plants prefer counter condensers over the cocurrent ones because of the following two (2) main reasons:

- Counter condensers require less cooling water,
- Counter condensers give higher **cooling efficiency**. If water is used as the cooling medium, a 2 to 4°C approach cooling temperature (T_{AC}) can be easily achieved. In the case of using air as the cooling medium, T_{AC} of 4 to 8°C is possible.

Counter-current barometric condensers are direct condensers that operate under a small negative vacuum pressure (P_{Vac}), created by condensation of the vapor entering the condenser. Because of P_{Vac},

- Removing the condenser water from a barometric condenser requires a barometric leg.
- The removal of noncondensing gases requires a vacuum pump or jet ejector.

A barometric leg is installed under the condensing vessel of the condenser. The barometric condensers come in different types, including the following three (3):

- Barometric condensers with a single tray,
- Barometric condensers with multiple trays,
- Barometric condensers with spray jets.

Barometric condensers with a single tray (left drawing in Figure 1) usually have a vessel of around 4 m (= 13 Ft) in height and 1.5 to 2 m in diameter. [Note: The condenser height refers to the distance between the vapor-entering level at the bottom of the vessel and the water-distribution level at the top. This height is shown with h_C and is called condensation height. An h_C of 1.5 to 2 m for a condenser vessel 4 m tall is recommended.]

Cooling water (which enters from the top at a velocity of 2 to 3 m/s) flows downward through a **spray-type distributor** to be mixed uniformly with the vapor, which comes to the condenser at a typical velocity of 20 to 30 m/s. Such velocity creates a typical P_{Vac} of 12 kPa (0.12 Atm = 1.8 PSI) in the condenser. A tray, called the **rain tray**, is mounted below the water's distributor to create a uniform distribution of water over the entire circumference of the condenser. The tray also allows noncondensing gases to flow up and be pumped out of the condenser by a vacuum pump.

Vapor, which enters the bottom at a velocity of around 40 m/s, flows upward opposite the cooling water's direction. Such a velocity creates about 20 kPa (= 0.2 Atm = 9.9 Lb/In^2) P_{Vac} in the condenser.

Barometric condensers with multiple trays (middle drawing in Figure 1) have a similar design and operate like condensers with a single tray. But the cooling water is mixed with the vapor through a few disc-type trays. Well-designed multiple-tray condensers provide good condensation efficiency, and the temperature of the non-condensing gases leaving the condenser is close to the temperature of the cooling water.

Barometric condensers with spray jets (right drawing in Figure 1) spray the cooling water with high P through multiple high-velocity jets. Because of high pressure, the non-condensing gases flow down with the stream of the condenser water. These condensers need a high amount of cooling water, so they are *not* popular.

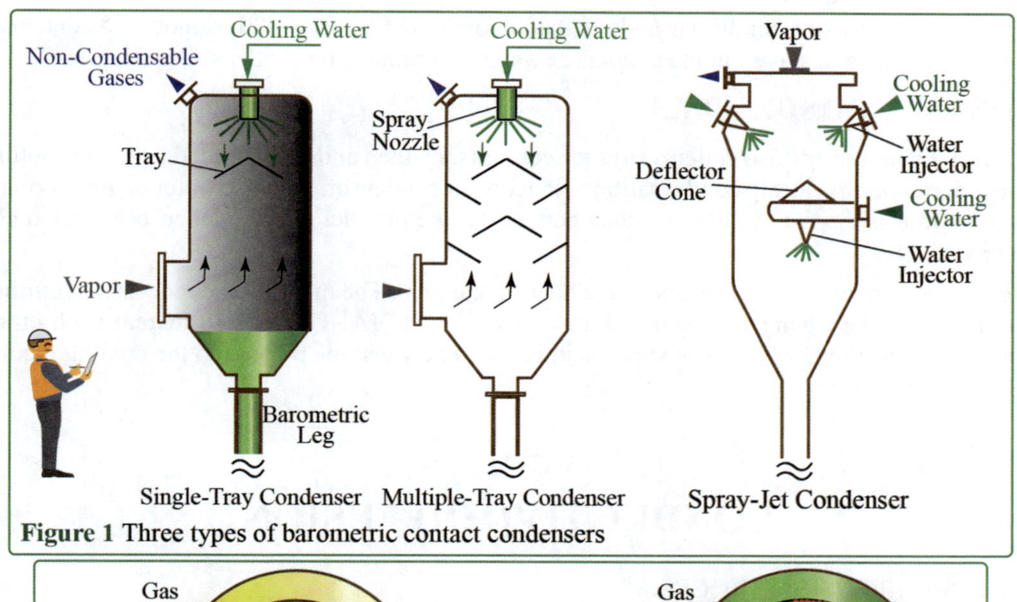

Figure 1 Three types of barometric contact condensers

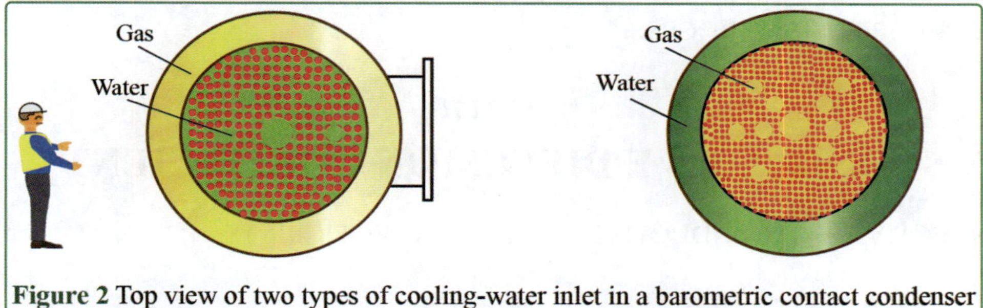

Figure 2 Top view of two types of cooling-water inlet in a barometric contact condenser

Efficiency of a Contact Condenser

A **condenser's efficiency** is defined as the amount of condensable gases it can condense in unit time (t); in other words, the ratio of the amount of condensable gases in the condenser water to that in the vapor entering the condenser. The operating efficiency of a barometric condenser is a function of the following factors:

- **Water-to-Vapor Ratio:** This is the ratio between cooling water and the vapor entering a condenser. A ratio around 30 is optimum. This value, however, depends on the condenser's design and the cooling water T (the *cooler* the cooling water, the *lesser* the cooling water is needed).
- **Temperature of Cooling Water** ($T_{C.W}$): The $T_{C.W}$ also depends on the plant's geographical location. In areas with a moderate climate, a $T_{C.W}$ of around 20°C is recommended.
- **Condensation Height** (h_C): For good condensation efficiency, an h_C of 1.5 to 2 m for a condenser vessel 4 m tall at a vapor rate of 2 t/h is recommended.
- **Vapor Velocity** (V_V)**:** The practical v_V is 20 to 30 m/s. Such vapor velocity can create a negative vacuum pressure (P_{Vac}) of about 0.12 Atm (12 kPa = 1.8 PSI) in the condenser.
- **Noncondensing-Gas Removal:** Because noncondensing gases do *not* condense, they must be removed (from the top of the condenser) to prevent their accumulation. An insufficient removal decreases the condensation temperature and, consequently, the efficiency of the condenser.
- **Design of Cooling-Water Inlet to the Condenser:** The way the cooling water enters a condenser is an important factor in the condenser's efficiency. The cooling water enters from the top center or around the sides (see Figure 2). Both designs in a condenser with multiple trays create a uniform distribution of water over the entire circumference of the condenser and ensure proper cooling of noncondensing gases and their flow through a center tray up and out of the condenser.

Considering the above-listed conditions and good non-condensable removal, the amount of condensable gases that have *not* condensed and stayed in the condenser water determines the condenser's efficiency.

NONCONTACT CONDENSERS

In a **noncontact condenser** (also called a **surface condenser**), the vapor is separated from the cooling medium (coolant), so it does *not* mix during condensation. Noncontact condensers also use water or air as coolant. When steam or water vapor is the feed of a noncontact condenser, the product of the condenser is called condensate, which is pure water.

The design of the noncontact condensers is like heat exchangers. The most-used condensers are **tube** (tubular) and **shell-and-tube** heat exchangers (discussed under HEAT EXCHANGER). A **tube heat exchanger** consists of a pipe located inside another pipe. The vapor is introduced between the pipes, and the cooling medium moves inside the smaller pipe.

C-116

CONDUCTIVE DIFFUSION

Discussed under DIFFUSION PROCESS.

C-117

CONDUCTIVE DIFFUSION COEFFICIENT

Study CONVECTIVE AND CONDUCTIVE DIFFUSION COEFFICIENTS.

C-118

CONDUCTIVE HEAT TRANSFER COEFFICIENT

Study CONVECTIVE AND CONDUCTIVE HEAT TRANSFER COEFFICIENTS.

C-119

CONDUCTIVE HEAT TRANSFER PROCESS

Discussed under the topic of HEAT TRANSFER PROCESS.

C-120

CONDUCTIVITY

Study ELECTRIC CONDUCTANCE and THERMAL CONDUCTANCE.

C-121

CONDUCTOMETERS

A conductometer (conductivity meter) is an instrument that measures a solution sample's ash (soluble inorganic compounds) based on conductometry. Conductometry is based on the electric conductance (K_E, conductivity) of a sample when an electric current (I, simply **current**) passes through the sample (the *higher* the K_E, the *higher* is the sample's ash content). [The ash determined by conductivity is called **conductivity ash**.]

Solutions carry current at different speeds, depending on their ionization ability. Ionic compounds (electrolytes), like salt (NaCl), produce a lot of ions in a solution, forming a **conducting solution** that carries current easily. Instead, nonionic compounds (nonelectrolytes), like sugar (sucrose, $C_{12}H_{22}O_{11}$), do *not* ionize, forming a **nonconducting solution**. Thus, measuring a solution's K_E can confirm the presence of ionic compounds in it.

Conductometers are usually calibrated to measure the K_E of a solution sample in specific conductance (K_{Sp}), which is expressed in S/m instead of S (Siemens, the unit for K_E). the K_{Sp} depends on R_E (electric resistance), A (the cross-sectional area of the conductometer's electrodes), and d (the distance between electrodes).

$$K_{Sp} = \frac{1}{R_E} = K_C \frac{A}{d} \qquad (1)$$

K_C (the cell constant, in 1/m) is determined by measuring the R_E of a standard solution of known K_{Sp} and using a sample cell of 1 cm long and 1 cm^2 of surface area.

C-122

CONDUCTORS

Study ELECTRIC CONDUCTORS, SEMICONDUCTORS, AND INSULATORS. Also, study THERMAL CONDUCTORS AND THERMAL INSULATORS.

C-123

CONFORMATION

Conformation, in chemistry, refers to an organic (carbon-based) molecule that can twist and turn along its carbon-carbon single bond, resulting in different spatial (3-dimensional) orientations of that molecule.

C-124

CONSERVATION LAWS

The theories of conservation, which became laws later, talk about the most important conserved quantities: energy (E), mass (M), momentum (p), and rotational momentum (L). Before defining these four (4) conserved quantities, it is helpful to pay attention to the following points:

- Mole is also a conserved quantity because the masses entering and leaving a system can be given in moles instead of mass units.
- Matter, unlike mass, is *not* a conserved quantity.

Energy Conservation Law

The Energy Conservation Law states that energy (or any type of it) *cannot* be created or destroyed in an isolated system (M and E *cannot* enter and leave an isolated system) but can only be converted from one form into another (or be transferred between systems). Another expression of this law says that the total energy (E) of an isolated system remains constant (the same) over time (t). This law can be expressed as $\Delta E = 0$ for the total amount of energy (E) in the Universe if we consider it an isolated system.

As shown in Figure 1, any decrease in the potential energy (E_P) indicates an increase in the kinetic energy (E_K) and vice versa when friction forces can be ignored.

As we said under CHEMICAL AND PHYSICAL CHANGES, when a chemical change occurs, an energy transformation also occurs. This statement can be demonstrated in water electrolysis to hydrogen and oxygen gasses. As shown on the top of Figure 2, when water is electrolyzed, energy is absorbed from the electric current, so the chemical potential energy (E_{CP}) of the products (H_2 and O_2) is greater than that of the reactant (H_2O). And when H_2 is burned in O_2, some E is released, so the E_{CP} of the product (H_2O) is lower than that of the reactants (H_2 and O_2). These examples tell us that E *cannot* be created or destroyed but can only be converted from one form into another.

Mass Conservation Law

The Mass Conservation Law says that mass (M) *cannot* be created or destroyed in a system; it can only be changed into a different substance. In another expression, this law says that the M of an isolated system remains constant with time. Considering the Universe as a closed-isolated system, M can *neither* be created *nor* destroyed in the Universe, but it can be rearranged.

Based on this law, during a chemical reaction in a closed system (M *cannot* enter or leave the system), the total M of the reactants must equate to the total M of the products. This is also true during a nuclear reaction or radioactive decay. The decomposition of H_2O to H_2 and O_2 demonstrates this law. For example, 100 g of H_2O decomposes into 11.2 g of H_2 and 88.8 g of O_2'

$$H_2O \rightarrow H_2 + O_2$$

$$100\text{ g} \rightarrow 11.2\text{ g} + 88.8\text{ g}$$

$$100\text{ g reactant} \rightarrow 100\text{ g products}$$

[Einstein formulated the mass-energy conservation law ($E = M.c^2$), which states that M and E are interchangeable under special conditions. The conditions have been created in a nuclear reactor and a particle accelerator, and this relationship was verified.]

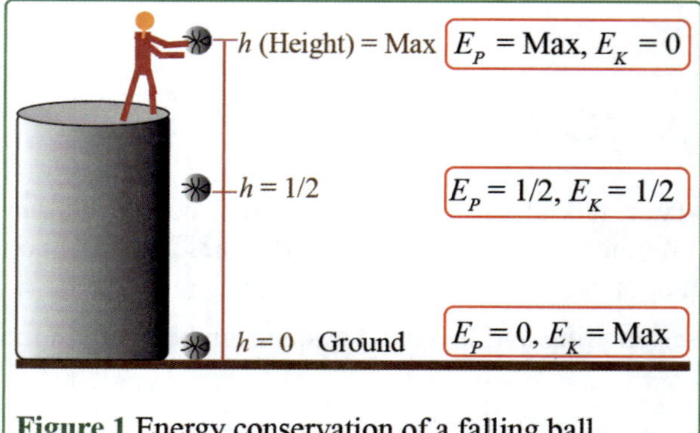

Figure 1 Energy conservation of a falling ball

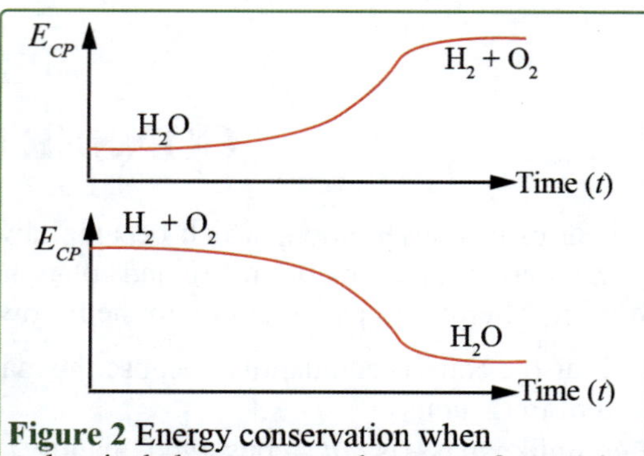

Figure 2 Energy conservation when a chemical change occurs because of a reaction

Linear Momentum Conservation Law

The Linear-Momentum Conservation Law states that an isolated system's linear momentum (p, simply **momentum**) remains constant with time in both quantity and direction if *no* external force (F) affects the system. Based on this principle, if a momentum (mass × velocity) is given to one part of an isolated moving system in one direction, then some other part (or parts) of the system must simultaneously be given the same momentum in the opposite direction to remain constant in its motion.

$$\Delta p_1 = -\Delta p_2 \tag{1}$$

[In quantum physics, conservation of momentum is applied to massless particles. If thus, a stationary particle (with zero momentum) splits into two moving particles, those sub-particles must have equal and opposite momentum.]

Rotational Momentum Conservation Law

The Rotational-Momentum Conservation Law says that an isolated system's rotational momentum (L, also called **angular momentum**) remains constant with time in both quantity and direction if *no* external torque (a twisting effect of a force applied to a rotating system) acts on the system.

C-125
CONSERVATION OF ANGULAR MOMENTUM

Another name for CONSERVATION OF ROTATIONAL MOMENTUM.

C-126
CONSERVATION OF ENERGY

Discussed under the topic of CONSERVATION LAWS.

C-127
CONSERVATION OF LINEAR MOMENTUM

Discussed under the topic of CONSERVATION LAWS.

C-128
CONSERVATION OF MASS

Discussed under CONSERVATION LAWS.

C-129
CONSERVATION OF ROTATIONAL MOMENTUM

Discussed under CONSERVATION LAWS.

C-130

CONSERVED QUANTITY

The most important conserved quantities are energy (E), mass (M), linear momentum (p), and rotational momentum (L). The conserved quantities are discussed under the topic of LAWS OF CONSERVATION. [In chemistry, mole is considered a conserved quantity because the masses entering and leaving a system can be given in moles instead of mass units (like kg).]

C-131

CONSTANT

Study COEFFICIENT, CONSTANT, AND PROPORTIONALITY CONSTANT.

C-132

CONTINUITY EQUATION

The continuity equation (also called **mass equation**) is used in ChemEng to express the steadiness of a fluid flowing in a pipe with a different cross-sectional area (A). In other words, this equation tells us that the mass flow rate ($\dot{M}$) of a fluid remains constant in two sections of a pipe with different A when the flow is *steady*.

$$\dot{M}_1 = \dot{M}_2 \tag{1}$$

Continuity, however, occurs at different velocities (V). We know from the topic of LIQUID FLOW PROCESS that a liquid $\dot{M}$ (in kg/time) in a pipe is the product of that liquid's density (D in kg/m^3) multiplied by its volumetric flow rate ($\dot{V}$, in m^3/s). Also, we know from there that a liquid's $\dot{V}$ is the product of the liquid's **average velocity** ($\bar{V}$, in m/s) multiply by A (in m^2), where $A = \pi R^2 = \pi d^2/4$ and d is the pipe's inside diameter. With constant D through the pipe, the following are obtained:

$$\dot{M} = D.\dot{V} \qquad \dot{V} = \bar{V}.A \tag{2}$$

Combining these equations gives,

$$\dot{M}_1 = D.\dot{V}_1 = D.\bar{V}_1.A_1 \qquad \dot{M}_2 = D.\dot{V}_2 = D.\bar{V}_2.A_2 \tag{3}$$

According to Equations 2 and 3 (continuity equations), $\dot{V}$ (volumetric flow rate) and $\dot{M}$ (mass flow rate) in a pipe with different A remain constant when the flow in the pipe is steady.

Figure 1 shows a steady liquid (incompressible) flow with constant D in a pipe with two unequal cross-sectional areas (where $A_1 < A_2$). Assume in time dt (where d is for differential and t is for time), the liquid in space X_1X_2 in the smaller-diameter section reaches space X_3X_4 in the larger-diameter section. Let the small distance between X_1 and X_2 be equal to dX_1 and between X_3 and X_4 equal to dX_2. Similarly, the differential cross-sectional area at distance X_1X_2 is dA_1 and at X_3X_4 is dA_2. According to the Law of Mass Conservation (mass *cannot* be created or destroyed in a process), the mass (M) contained in the X_1X_2 section must equate to the mass in the X_3X_4 section, and because distance X_1X_2 = dX_1 and X_3X_4 = dX_2, the following is a valid expression:

$$D_1.dX_1.A_1 = D_2.dX_2.A_2 \tag{4}$$

Dividing both sides of this equation by the time step t, we obtain

$$D_1\frac{dX_1}{t}A_1 = D_2\frac{dX_2}{t}A_2 \tag{5}$$

The term dX_1/t is the liquid's velocity in the initial section, and dX_2/t is that in the final section, so

$$D_1.V_1.A_1 = D_2.\bar{V}_2.A_2 \quad (6)$$

This equation, called the **continuity equation**, tells us that the mass flow rate ($\dot{M} = D.\bar{V}.A = D.\dot{V}$) remains constant in two sections of a pipe with different A when the flow is incompressible (with constant D) and steady (with constant $\dot{M}$).

In a horizontal pipe shown in Figure 2 and based on mass conservation, the $\dot{M}$ in location 1 equates to the $\dot{M}$ in location 2, that is $\dot{M}_1 = \dot{M}_2$ or $D_1.\bar{V}_1.A_1 = D_2.\overline{V}_2.A_2$. The continuity equation also tells us that the average velocity must also be the same at 2 as at 1, that is $\bar{V}_2 = \bar{V}_1$ when the flow is incompressible and steady.

The arguments made for the horizontal pipe here also apply to the downward pipe (Figure 3). Thus, *no* matter whether the flow is uphill or downhill, the average velocity of a liquid in a steady flow through a constant-diameter pipe is the same everywhere along the length of the pipe.

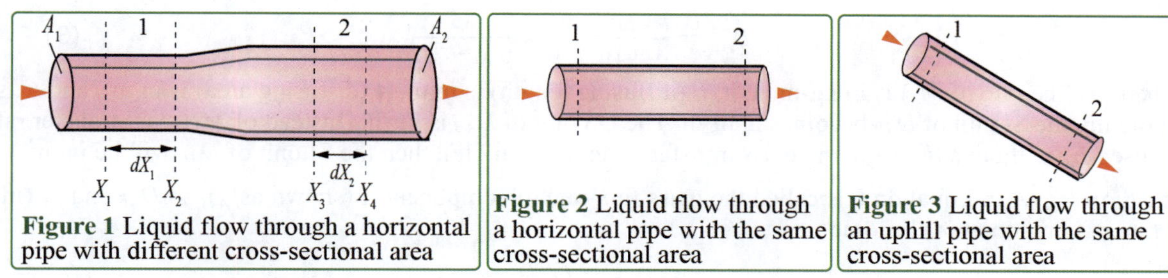

Figure 1 Liquid flow through a horizontal pipe with different cross-sectional area

Figure 2 Liquid flow through a horizontal pipe with the same cross-sectional area

Figure 3 Liquid flow through an uphill pipe with the same cross-sectional area

C-133

CONTINUOUS PROCESSES

Discussed under the topic of CHEMICAL PROCESSES.

C-134

CONVECTIVE AND CONDUCTIVE DIFFUSION COEFFICIENTS

Convective and conductive diffusion coefficients are used as proportionality coefficients in a diffusion process.

Convective Diffusion Coefficient

The convective diffusion coefficient (also called **convective mass transfer coefficient**) of the diffusing component A, shown as K_A, indicates how fast A molecules diffuse directly through *non*-diffusing B molecules by convective diffusion (direct diffusion). Numerically, K_A is given as

$$K_A = \frac{\dot{M}_A}{A.\Delta C} = \frac{\dot{M}_A}{A(C_{A1} - C_{A2})} \quad (1)$$

When $\dot{M}_A$ (mass diffusion rate) is given in kgmole/h, A (area) in m^2, and C (concentration) in kgmole/m^3, the SI unit of K_A becomes in m^3/(m^2.h) = m/h (length per unit time or velocity). For example, the air's KA is about 0.1 m/s, so it diffuses (moves) in a dryer at 0.1 m/s. The K_A can also be expressed based on $\dot{J}_A$ (mass flux rate of A), which is defined as $\dot{M}_A$ per unit area (A) and concentration (C).

$$K_A = \frac{\frac{\dot{M}_A}{A}}{\Delta C} = \frac{\dot{J}_A}{\Delta C} \quad (2)$$

Conductive Diffusion Coefficient

The conductive diffusion coefficient (also called **diffusion coefficient**, **mass diffusion coefficient**, **momentum diffusion**, or **momentum diffusivity**) of diffusing component *A*, shown as D_{AB}, indicates how fast *A* molecules diffuse through the unit area of a phase boundary. In simple words, the D_{AB} indicates the **diffusivity** of *A* through the phase boundary by conductive diffusion. [Symbol D_{AB} indicates that component *A* diffuses through *B* (the non-diffusing component). If, as an alternative, *B* were the diffusing component, the symbol D_{BA} would have been used instead of D_{AB}.]

The D_{AB} of component *A* can be calculated from the component's $\dot{M}_A$ (the mass diffusion rate of *A* diffused in unit time), ΔL (the difference in diffusing length), *A* (the area of phase boundary through which the diffusion occurs), C_{A1} (the concentration of diffusant *A* in location 1 at the start of the process), C_{A2} (the *C* in location 2 at the end of process), and ΔC_A (the concentration difference of component *A* between location 1 and 2).

$$D_{AB} = \frac{\dot{M}_A . \Delta L}{A . \Delta C_A} = \frac{\dot{M}_A}{A} \times \frac{\Delta L}{(C_{A1} - C_{A2})} \quad (3)$$

When $\dot{M}_A$ (the rate of M_A) is in kg-mole/h, *L* (diffusing length) is in m, *A* (diffusing area) is in m^2, and *C* is in kg-mole/m^3, the SI unit of D_{AB} becomes in m^2/h. The US unit of D_{AB} is Ft^2/h. [Instead of $\dot{M}_A$ (mass transfer rate), if we use M_A (without a *dot* sign, the mass transfer given in kg-mole), then the SI unit of D_{AB} will be in m^2.]

The term $\dot{M}_A/A$ in Equation 6 is called the mass flux rate of component *A* (shown as $\dot{J}_A$), so D_{AB} and $\dot{J}_A$ (mass flux rate of component *A*) become

$$D_{AB} = \dot{J} \frac{\Delta L}{\Delta C_A} \quad (4)$$

$$\dot{J}_A = \frac{D_{AB}}{\frac{\Delta L}{\Delta C_A}} = D_{AB} \frac{\Delta C_A}{\Delta L} \quad (5)$$

This equation relates $\dot{J}_A$ to the $\Delta C_A/\Delta L$ (concentration gradient, the diffusion driving) through D_{AB}. Usually, a **minus sign** is used on the right side of this equation to indicate that a force equal to the negative driving force must be used to diffuse the molecules from the higher-concentrated side to the lower-concentrated side (in the + *X*-axis direction). Instead, the **plus sign** means that the molecules diffuse in the – *X*-axis (lower to higher *C*).

Einstein, in 1906 formulated D_{AB} and proved that in an ideal solution (with low concentration and so behaves like a pure solution) with temperature *T* and viscosity η, D_{AB} of diffusant *A* equates to

$$D_{AB} = K_A \frac{T}{\eta} \quad (6)$$

This equation, which is known as Einstein's diffusion equation, can also be written as

$$K_A = D_{AB} \frac{\eta}{T} \quad (7)$$

Together, Einstein's diffusion equation and Fick's diffusion equation is the **Einstein-Fick diffusion equation**.

$$\dot{M}_A = D_{AB} . A \frac{C}{L} = (K_A \frac{T}{\eta})(A \frac{C}{L}) \quad (8)$$

A few data are tabulated for diffusion coefficient (D_{AB}), so it is necessary to use available estimated data for different phases in calculations. The next table lists the practical values of D_{AB} in cm^2/s for different phases.

D_{AB}	[cm^3/s]
Gas-to-gas diffusion	0.1 to 0.7
Liquid-to-liquid diffusion	0.2×10^{-5} to 2×10^{-5}
Liquid-to solid diffusion	1.0×10^{-6} to 1.5×10^{-6}
Solid-to-solid diffusion	2.5×10^{-11} to 1.3×10^{-26}
Gas-to-solid diffusion	0.65×10^{-4} to 8.50×10^{-7}

C-135

CONVECTIVE AND CONDUCTIVE HEAT TRANSFER COEFFICIENTS

Convective and conductive heat transfer coefficients are two proportionality coefficients used to express how a material conducts (flows) the heat energy (E_Q, simply heat and scientifically enthalpy) in a heat transfer process. As discussed next, each has its scientific definition and application in ChemEng.

Convective Heat Transfer Coefficient

Convective heat transfer coefficient (U_Q or h; simply **heat transfer coefficient**) is used to express how a material conducts the E_Q in a convective heat transfer process. As a proportionality coefficient, the U_Q relates the convective (direct) heat transfer to the transfer's driving force, the temperature difference ($\Delta T = T_H - T_S$), through a solid wall. Here, T is for temperature, subscript H is for heating medium, and subscript S is for solid surface. For example, in an evaporator, the ΔT is the difference in T between steam (or vapor) and the liquid feed. In a heat exchanger, ΔT is the difference in T between hot and cold fluid streams.

A material's U_Q can be calculated as the amount of E_Q transferred through the 1 m^2 heat transfer area (A) to create a ΔT of 1°C.

$$U_Q = \frac{E_Q}{A.\Delta T} \quad (1)$$

This equation tells us that the U_Q is directly proportional to E_Q and disproportional to ΔT between two streams (the *greater* the ΔT between the streams, the *lower* is the U_Q). [This equation is usually used with the ΔT_{Avg} rather than the logarithmic mean temperature difference (LMTD or ΔT_{LM}). The LMTD, however, is *not* used (because ΔT is a rough estimation between the heating medium and the liquid under heat transfer).]

The SI unit of U_Q is kJ/(m^2.°C), and its US unit is BTU/(Ft^2.°F). [Often, the E_Q is given as heat transfer rate ($\dot{E}_Q = E_Q/t$), which is the amount of E_Q through 1 m^2 of a stream to create a ΔT of 1°C in 1 s. In this case, the U_Q becomes in kJ/(s.m^2.°C), equating to kW/(h.m^2.°C), where W is for Watt, h is for an hour, °C is for the degrees centigrade, s is for the second, and J is four Joule. Thus, 1 kJ/(s.m^2.°C) = 1 kW/(h.m^2.°C) = 176 BTU/(h.Ft^2.°F). For example, U_Q of water is 1 kJ/(h.m^2.°C) = 1 kW/(h.m^2.°C) = 176 BTU/(h.Ft^2.°F).]

Conductive Heat Transfer Coefficient

Conductive heat transfer coefficient (K_T or K_Q, also called **thermal conductance** or **thermal conductivity**) expresses how a material conducts E_Q in a conductive heat-transfer process (Figure 1). As a proportionality coefficient, it relates the conductive heat transfer to the transfer's driving force (the ΔT). Thus, a thermal conductor has a high K_T and a low R_T (thermal resistance), while a thermal insulator has a low K_T and a high R_T. A material's K_T is the reciprocal (inverse) of its R_T (or vice versa).

A material's K_T can be calculated from the temperature change (ΔT) when an E_Q flows through it.

$$E_Q = K_T.\Delta T \quad \text{or} \quad K_T = \frac{E_Q}{\Delta T} \quad (2)$$

If E_Q is in W/h and T is in °C, the SI unit of K_T becomes in W/(h.°C), which equates to J/(s.°C).

Specific Thermal Conductivity: The specific thermal conductance ($K_{T.Sp}$, also called **specific thermal conductance**) is the K_T (conductive heat transfer coefficient) per unit A (area) of a material. The $K_{T.Sp}$ is expressed using Fourier's heat conduction equation and the heat transfer rate ($\dot{E}_Q = E_Q/t$, where t is for time).

$$\dot{E}_Q = K_{T.Sp}.A\frac{\Delta T}{L} \quad \text{or} \quad K_T = \frac{\dot{E}_Q}{A} \times \frac{L}{\Delta T} \quad (3)$$

In this equation, A is the conductor's area, L is the conductor's length, and $\Delta T/L$ is the temperature gradient (the **driving force** of heat transfer). If $\dot{E}_Q$ is in W/h, A is in m^2, L is in m, and ΔT is in °C, $K_{T.Sp}$ becomes in W/(h.m.°C). [Note that 1 W/h = 1 J/s, so W/(h.m.°C) = J/m.°C.] The $K_{T.Sp}$ of dry air is 0.03, that of water is 0.6, that of stainless steel is 40, and that of copper is 400, all in W/(h.m.°C).

[Note 1: For simplicity reasons, sometimes the term **specific thermal conductance** ($K_{T.Sp}$, also called **specific thermal conductivity**) is abbreviated to just **thermal conductance** (K_T). In such cases, the given quantity unit can determine the purpose of the technical writer, as the $K_{T.Sp}$ is expressed in W/(h.m.°C), while K_T is given in W/(h.°C).]

[Note 2: Generally, solids have greater $K_{T.Sp}$ than liquids and gases.]

[Note 3: The $K_{T.Sp}$ values for some solids, liquids, and gases are provided in Table 7 in the Table Section of this book.]

[Note 4: The heat-transfer areas (A_Q) are constructed from tubes or plates in many types of heat-transfer devices (equipment). The calculations may then be based on either a tube's inside (or outside) area or diameter when using a tube. Thus, the choice must be given because the results of calculations will *not* be the same for both choices.]

Overall Heat Transfer Coefficient

As the reverse of the overall heat resistance, the overall heat transfer coefficient (U_{QO}, where subscript O is for overall) is the sum of heat transfer coefficients (U_Q) that exist in a heat transfer process. Usually, U_{QO} is used to calculate a combined convective-and-conductive heat transfer process, in which different heat resistances exist. In a heat exchanger, for example, heat transfers in three steps: 1) Heat transfer from fluid 1 (hot fluid) to the solid wall, 2) Heat transfer in the wall, and 3) Heat transfer from the wall to fluid 2 (cold fluid). Then the U_{QO} is the total of all resistances.

$$\frac{1}{U_{QO}} = \frac{1}{U_{Q1}} + \frac{1}{U_{Q2}} + \frac{1}{U_{Q3}} + \frac{L}{K_{Th}} \tag{4}$$

In this equation, the U_{Q1} is the U_Q of fluid 1, U_{Q2} is the U_Q of fluid 2, U_{Q3} is the U_Q of the solid wall between the two fluids, the L is the wall's thickness, and the K_{Th} is the wall's thermal conductivity.

In a heat transfer process occurring in a heat exchanger, the heat resistance depends on,

- The ΔT between hot and cold streams (the *greater* the ΔT; the *lower* is the resistance), and
- The liquid feed's DS (the *greater* the DS, the *higher* is the resistance), where DS is for dissolved solids.

Thus, the *greater* the ΔT and the *lower* the DS, the *lower* is the U_Q, and the *easier* is the heat-transfer process. In addition to the listed factors, the U_Q depends on the equipment tubes' **cleanliness** (the *cleaner* the tubes, the *greater* is the U_Q, and the *easier* is the heat transfer).

Some practical equations exist that calculate U_Q, including the following two:

$$U_Q = \frac{503T}{DS} \tag{5}$$

$$U_Q = 7T\left(\frac{V}{1.8}\right)^{0.8} \tag{6}$$

In these equations, T is the temperature (in °C) of vapor (or steam), DS is the dissolved solid (in %) of the liquid feed under the heat transfer process, and V is the velocity (in m/s) of the liquid feed under heat transfer. [For simplifying the calculation, a liquid feed's velocity is considered 1 to 2 m/s.]

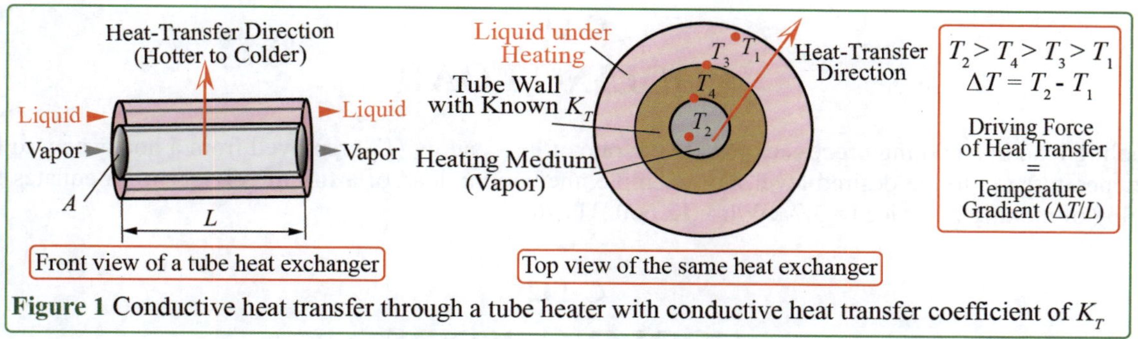

Figure 1 Conductive heat transfer through a tube heater with conductive heat transfer coefficient of K_T

C-136
CONVECTIVE HEAT TRANSFER PROCESS

Discussed under the topic of HEAT TRANSFER PROCESS.

C-137
CONVECTIVE MASS DIFFUSION

Discussed under the topic of DIFFUSION PROCESS.

C-138
CONVECTIVE MASS TRANSFER COEFFICIENT

Another name for convective diffusion coefficient. It is discussed under the topic of CONVECTIVE AND CONDUCTIVE DIFFUSION COEFFICIENTS.

C-139
COOLING APPROACH TEMPERATURE

Defined under EVAPORATIVE COOLING DEVICES.

C-140
COOLING EFFECT TEMPERATURE

Defined under EVAPORATIVE COOLING PROCESS and EVAPORATIVE COOLING DEVICES.

C-141
COOLING LOAD

Cooling load in a cooling process expresses the rate of heat energy (E_Q) removed from a hot system to lower its temperature (T) to the desired level. For example, the cooling load of a **ton of refrigeration** equates to the enthalpy of melting of 1 t ice (= 3.7 kW/h = 12 660 BTU/h).

C-142
COOLING PONDS

Discussed under EVAPORATIVE COOLING DEVICES.

C-143
COOLING PROCESS

This topic is *not* covered in this book.

C-144
COOLING TOWER CHARACTERISTIC

Cooling-tower characteristic (CTC) is a term mainly used in the evaporative cooling process to mean the ratio of a device's cooling effect temperature (T_E) to its driving force (F_D). For example, a cooling tower CTC is

$$CTC = \frac{T_E}{F_D} = \frac{T_{W1}-T_{W2}}{H_W-H_A} \quad (1)$$

Here, $T_{W1}$is the warm inlet water's temperature (T) to the cooling tower, T_{W2} is the cool outlet water's T from the cooling tower, H_W is the inlet water's enthalpy, and H_A is the inlet air (the cooling medium) enthalpy.

You should also be aware of the following points about cooling tower characteristics (CTC):

- The CTC is dependent on the operating conditions and independent of the cooling tower's dimensions.
- The CTC can be effectively reduced by increasing the air quantity to the cooling tower and air-water contact area using suitable packing.
- The CTC for a given cooling approach temperature (T_A) can be determined from a graph (given in Perry and coauthors 2007, pages 12-18) or by Equation 1.

C-145
COOLING TOWERS

Discussed under EVAPORATIVE COOLING DEVICES.

C-146

COPENHAGEN INTERPRETATION OF QUANTUM THEORIES

Copenhagen interpretation of quantum theories (simply **Copenhagen interpretation**) is a term used by Bohr in the 1920s to mean the combination of his atomic theory (Bohr's atomic theory) with that of Heisenberg (Heisenberg's wavematrix theory) and Schrodinger (Schrodinger's wavefunction theory) on electron's dual behavior. [The word **Copenhagen** refers to the Copenhagen University (where Bohr taught Physics), and **interpretation** was used to emphasize discussions about quantum theories.]

Three quantum physicists in debate, known as Copenhagen Interpretation of Quantum Physics, in a restaurant. This author taught of a non-happening party to illustrate their portraits for this book.

As for the electron's dual (wave-particle) property, these physicists thought that the electron is neither one nor the other but a combination of both. A particular situation (wave or particle) appears when an experimenter selects which aspects must be measured. Light behaves like a photon (light particle) when an experimenter observes (experiments) it. However, the act of observation generates uncertainty so that once one property is measured precisely, the other becomes affected, resulting in probability, as Heisenberg proved.

Consider two quantumly entangled electrons (study Quantum Entanglement of Particles). According to the Copenhagen idea, when a physicist measures the spin direction of one of the electrons, he instantly knows the spin direction of the other one (it must spin in the opposite direction to obey the quantum rules), *no* matter how far apart the electrons are. But, according to Einstein's idea, two electrons, which are apart from each other, *cannot* pass an instant signal (because *nothing* can travel faster than the speed of light). This is why Einstein called quantum entanglement "a **spooky** (strange) action at a distance" because of lacking theoretical support.

C-147

COPPER BRASS

A copper brass (simply **brass**) is an alloy steel that consists of about 70% copper (Cu) and 30% zinc (Zn). The proportions of these two elements can be varied to produce a range of alloy steels with varying properties. Copper brass is used in pipes used in heat exchangers, evaporators, and crystallizers. It is also used to produce valves, casings, and electric products. The combination of **malleability** (ability to form a thin metal sheet by hammering it), acoustic, and gold-like shininess properties of brass have made it the metal of choice in producing some musical instruments, such as saxophone.

Aluminum (Al) makes copper brass stronger and resistant to corrosion. The thermal conductivity (K_T) of brass is high (110 W/h.m.°C), while that of stainless steel is low (40 W/h.m.°C). Its thermal expansion is about 15 µm/m.°C, higher than stainless steel.

C-148

CORROSION AND RUSTING

Corrosion and rusting have the same definition, but the word **corrosion** indicates the gradual deterioration of any chemical substance (simply **substance**). The word **rusting** is used for only **corrosion** of iron (Fe). Both processes happen in the presence of oxygen (O_2) and water (H_2O) in the air by the oxidation-reduction reaction, which is a two-step reaction. [The words **corrosion** and **rusting** (and sometimes even **oxidation**) are used equally because of their similar definitions.]

Corrosion

Corrosion is the gradual deterioration of a corrosive substance by an oxidation-reduction reaction. Many metals, alloys, and steels corrode. For example, about one-fifth of the steel used annually in the US chemical process industry corrodes, causing considerable damage. The corroding process occurs differently. Aluminum corrodes but forms a coating cover on its surface (called a **passivation layer**) that protects its bulk from further rusting.

Corrosion can also occur in polymers (plastics, rubbers, and more) and silicates. Plastics, for example, corrode from exposure to sunlight. Because of the availability of oxygen (a strong oxidizing agent) and moisture at the Earth's surface, corrosion can affect locally on a small spot or start across a wide area to make a thin film on the surface and diffuse further to corrode deeper.

Some other important points about corrosion are outlined next.

- Salts are generally far less corrosive than acids and bases from which they are formed.
- The corrosion effect is independent of the strength of the acid or base. A dilute solution of a strong acid or a strong base may have little corrosivity simply because only a few hydronium ions (H^+) or hydroxide ions (OH^-) are available in such solutions. [A concentrated solution of a weak acid (like acetic acid, HCH_3COO) may be just as corrosive as or even more corrosive than a dilute solution of a strong acid, like hydrochloric acid (HCl).]
- The corrosion effect increases with salt (NaCl) in water.
- The most corrosive elements are Ni, Co, Fe, Cr, Zn, Al, Mg, and Na, given from the highest to the lowest. And the least corrosive elements are Au, Pt, Cu, and Pb, given from the lowest.

Rusting

Rusting is the process of deterioration of iron (Fe) to iron oxide trihydrate [($Fe_2O_3.3H_2O$)], which is the main component of **rust** (a brown-reddish substance). Rusting of Fe occurs in the next oxidizing-reducing ways:

- **Oxidation:** Fe (the reducing agent) releases one electron to be oxidized to iron cation (Fe^{2+}).
- **Reduction:** O_2 (the oxidizing agent) absorbs the released electron to be reduced and reacts with H_2O to form a hydroxide anion (OH^-).

Then the Fe cation (Fe^{2+}) and OH anion (OH^-) combine to produce an iron hydroxide molecule [$Fe(OH)_2$], which reacts with OH^- to produce a rust molecule ($Fe_2O_3 .3H_2O$).

$$2\ Fe \rightarrow 2\ Fe^{2+} + 4\ e^- \quad \text{Oxidation reaction}$$

$$O_2 + 4\ e^- + 2\ H_2O \rightarrow 4\ OH^- \ \text{Reduction reaction}$$

$$2\ Fe^{2+} + 4\ OH^- \rightarrow 2\ Fe(OH)_2$$

$$2\ Fe(OH)_2 + 2\ OH^- \rightarrow Fe_2O_3.3H_2O$$

The listed reactions can be combined into one reaction.

$$4\ Fe + 3\ O_2 + 3\ H_2O \rightarrow 2\ Fe_2O_3\ .3\ H_2O$$

The formation of rust proceeds from the surface of the iron to its bulk, to the point that finally, the entire iron converts to rust over time. This tells us that the surface rust does *not* protect the underlying iron. Iron rusts faster in the presence of salty water, such as seawater.

Control of Corrosive and Rusting Activity

For controlling corrosive activity, the following two methods are usually used:

- Painting.
- Metallic Coating: In metallic coating (called **galvanization** or **passivation**), a metal is coated by a **thin protective layer** (passive thin layer) of a noble metal (such as cobalt, chromium, nickel, and zinc). The zinc (Zn) oxidizes to zinc oxide (ZnO), preventing further oxidation. Similarly, the aluminum (Al) oxidizes to aluminum oxide (Al_2O_3), which is insoluble in water, forming a thin coat that protects the aluminum from further oxidation. [The thin layer of Al_2O_3 rust is transparent, so light passes through it. This is the reason that aluminum maintains its metallic shine.]

C-149

COULOMB AND COULOMB'S LAW

Coulomb

Coulomb (C), which is named after French physicist Charles Coulomb (1736–1806), is the SI unit of the electric charge (q, simply **charge**). It is defined as the charge (q) that flows through an electric conductor by an electric current (I, simply **current**) of 1 A (Ampere) in one second (s). Thus, 1 C = 1 A × 1 s or A.s (Ampere second, often written wrongly as As). Since 2019, C has been defined as the number of charges carried by a proton, equating to $1/(1.602\ 176\ 634 \times 10^{-19})$ charges. Based on this definition, one electron has the same charges but opposite signs, so the amount of an electron's charges is – 1 C.

Instead of A.s (Ampere second), its **practical unit,** Ampere hour (A.h, often written in reference books as Ah and read Ampere hour), is used, where 1 A.h = 3600 A.s = 3600 C. For example, the capacity of a medium-size-car battery is about 40 A.h, and that of an AA battery is about 2 A.h.

Coulomb's Law

Coulomb's Law is a principle in Physics published in 1784 by Coulomb. It states that a proportionality constant (the Coulomb's constant, $K_C = 8.99 \times 10^9\ N.m^2/C^2$) can relate the attractive force (F_{At}) between two charged particles to those particles' charges (q_1 and q_2) and the distance (L for length) between the charges.

$$F_{At} = K_C \frac{q_1.q_2}{L^2} \quad (1)$$

In this equation, F_{At} is in N (Newton), q is in C (Coulomb), and L is in m (meter), so K_C becomes in N.m^2/C^2.

[The F_{At} between the charges works if the charges have opposite signs, so q_1 and q_2 are signed quantities.] [As seen, Coulomb's Law is formulized like Newton's Law of Gravitation.]

C-150

COVALENT BONDS

Discussed under CHEMICAL BONDS.

C-151

COVALENT COMPOUNDS

A covalent (electrolyte) compound is a compound whose molecules are joined by covalent bonds (strong chemical bonds). Water (H_2O), methane (CH_4), ethane (C_2H_4, commonly ethylene), and sucrose ($C_{12}H_{22}O_{11}$, commonly sugar) are examples of covalent compounds.

Covalent compounds are of two types:

- **Polar Covalent Compounds:** When the electronegativity (E_{Neg}) of two elements differs, a polar covalent bond forms between them, resulting in a polar covalent compound, as in $H + F \rightarrow HF$.
- **Nonpolar Covalent Compounds:** When the E_{Neg} of the elements is the same, *no* polar covalent bond is formed between them, resulting in a nonpolar covalent compound, as in $H + H \rightarrow H_2$. Thus, the atoms of a nonpolar covalent compound are bonded by a **nonpolar covalent bond** (or bonds).

C-152

CPU

Abbreviated term for Central Processing Unit.

N-153

CRITICAL AND EXCESS NUCLEAR MASSES

Critical nuclear mass (simply **critical mass**) and excess nuclear mass (simply **excess mass**) of a nuclide (a radioactive element) are important in nuclear chain reactions, particularly in a nuclear fission process performed in a nuclear reactor of a nuclear power plant or in fueling a nuclear weapon. In both fission and fueling a nuclear bomb, two or more **critical masses** are brought together to make an excess mass (a mass above the critical mass) to assure that the fission in a reactor or explosion in a bomb will occur.

Critical Nuclear Mass

The critical excess mass (M_{CN}) of a nuclide is its minimum mass (M) needed to sustain a nuclear chain reaction. The use of critical mass is *not* enough to assure that a nuclear fission process in a nuclear reactor or explosion in a nuclear bomb will occur. Thus, the use of an excess mass is required.

Excess Nuclear Mass

The excess nuclear mass (M_{EN}) of a nuclide is a mass greater than its M_{CN} (critical nuclear mass). An excess mass (M_{EN}) assures that a nuclear fission process in a nuclear reactor or explosion in a nuclear bomb will occur. It is calculated based on the difference between a nuclide's atomic mass (M_A) and its atomic mass number (N_A, the sum of protons and neutrons). Because the M_A of elements and M_M (molecular mass) of compounds are usually given in AMU (atomic mass unit), a nuclide's M_{EN} (excess mass) can be defined as its AMU minus its N_A, where AMU is defined as 1/12 of the M of an atom of carbon-12 (C-12, read **carbon 12**), with 6 protons and 6 neutrons and a mass of exactly 12 AMU. Thus, one proton (or one neutron) has a mass of 1 AMU. A **free proton** (a proton outside the nucleus) has a mass of 1.00728 AMU, and a **free neutron** has a mass of 1.00867 AMU. The combined mass of 6 free protons and 6 free neutrons is [(6×1.00728) + (6×1.00867) = 12.09570], which is a bit greater (by 0.09570 AMU) than the mass of one C-12 nucleus (12.000 AMU). This tiny excess mass equates to about 0.1% of the original mass of the participating reactants. According to Einstein's equation ($E = M.c^2$), the M_{EN} (usually shown with a **negative** sign) is then converted in a nuclear reactor to nuclear energy (E_N). Therefore, based on the mass-energy equality, we can say that a nuclide's excess mass represents that nuclide's E_N (nuclear energy) relative to the E_N of C-12.

Considering a nuclide's M_{EN} (excess mass) and E_N (nuclear energy) and what has been discussed so far, two cases may occur:

- If the nuclide's M_{EN} is **negative**, its E_N is *greater* than the E_N of C-12,
- If the nuclide's M_{EN} is **positive**, its E_N is *smaller* than the E_N of C-12.

Assume a nuclear fission reaction occurs on ONE atom of uranium-235 (U-235). The split (fission) of U-235 starts when a neutron ($^1_0$N) hits (collides) the nucleus of U-235 to convert it to U-236, which then splits into the smaller nuclei of barium-141 (Ba-141, with 56 protons and 85 neutrons) and krypton-92 (Kr-92, with 36 protons and 56 neutrons). Then the reaction releases 3 neutrons and a tiny amount of E_N.

$$^{235}_{92}\text{U} + ^{1}_{0}\text{N} \rightarrow ^{236}_{92}\text{U} \rightarrow ^{141}_{56}\text{Ba} + ^{92}_{36}\text{Kr} + 3(^{1}_{0}\text{N}) + E_N$$

The M_A (atomic mass) of U-235 is 235.043 930 AMU, and its N_A (atomic mass number) is 235 (it has 92 protons and 143 neutrons), making a M_{EN} (excess mass) of + 0.043 930 AMU. The **plus sign** here tells us that one atom of U-235 has slightly more M than its nucleus. The M_{EN} of the neutron is + 0.008 665, making the total M_{EN} of the reactants 0.043 930 + 0.008 665 = + 0.052 595 AMU. While the total M_{EN} of the products equates to the M_{EN} of Ba-141, that of Kr-92, and that of 3 neutrons, so – 0.085 588 – 0.073 843 + 3 × 0.008 665 = – 0.133 436 AMU. Comparing the M_{EN} of the reactants with that of the products tells us that the M_{EN} of the **reactants** is *greater* than that of the **products** so that the fission CAN occur.

The E_N yielded from splitting ONE atom of U-235 can be calculated by using the conversion factor of 1 AMU = 931.494 MeV/c^2 (where M is for mega, eV is for electron volts, and c is for speed of light constant) multiplied by the difference between the reactants' M_{EN} and the products' M_{EN} [0.052 595 – (– 0.133 436) = 0.186 031)]. Thus, the E_N will be 931.494 × 0.186 031 = 139.9 MeV (= 2.2×10^{-8} kJ). [This tells us that the conversion of a tiny amount of M_{EN} of 1 atom of U-235 creates a small amount of E_N, but when many (in trillions) of atoms of U-235 split (fission) in a nuclear reactor, the produced E_N is huge (in tons of MeV).]

C-154
CRITICAL MASS

This is the short name for Nuclear Critical Mass.

C-155
CRITICAL MOISTURE CONTENT

Study MOISTURE AND ITS TYPES.

C-156
CRITICAL POINT

A critical point (C-point) is usually used in a phase diagram to indicate the point at which critical temperature (T_C) and critical pressure (P_C) occur. A substance that exists under these conditions is called a **supercritical fluid**. The C-point occurs at high temperatures and pressures. For example, the C-point in water occurs at T_C of 374ºC and P_C of 218 Atm, as shown in Figure 2 under PHASE DIAGRAM. At C-point, therefore:

- No phase boundary exists between liquid and vapor phases.
- Liquid and vapor phases are at equilibrium (stable) conditions.
- The liquid phase and gaseous phase become indistinguishable.

C-157
CRITICAL PRESSURE

Study CRITICAL TEMPERATURE AND CRITICAL PRESSURE.

C-158
CRITICAL TEMPERATURE AND CRITICAL PRESSURE

Critical Temperature

The critical temperature (T_C, also called **critical point temperature**) of a pure chemical substance is the temperature (T), at which all three (3) phases (solid, liquid, and gas) of that substance approach each other, resulting in only one phase. T_C can also be defined as the highest T, at which a liquid can boil when heated or gas can condense when cooled. At temperatures higher than T_C, *no* distinction is recognized between the liquid and vapor phases.

In water, T_C occurs at 374ºC (= 705ºF = 647 K), which is the highest T, at which liquid water boils when heated or water vapor condenses when cooled. In carbon dioxide gas (CO_2), T_C occurs at about 31°C.

Critical Pressure

The critical pressure (P_C, also called **critical point pressure**) of a pure substance is the pressure (P), at which the liquid phase and vapor phase of that substance approach each other, resulting in only one phase. No distinction can be made between the liquid and vapor phases at pressures higher than P_C. In water, P_C occurs at around 218 Atm (= 218×10^2 kPa = 3200 PSIA), which is the highest P, at which liquid water boils when heated or water vapor condenses when cooled. In CO_2, P_C occurs at about 73 Atm.

A substance's T_C and P_C are usually studied in a phase diagram, in which the substance's critical point (C-point) represents that substance's T_C and P_C. At C-point, *no* distinction exists between liquid and gas phases.

C-159

CROSSLINKING PROCESS

Crosslinking (also called polymerization) is the process of bonding, particularly covalent bonds (strong bonds), between the monomers (units or chains) of a polymer. The bonds that link the monomers together are called **crosslinks**. For example, rubber crosslinking (called **vulcanization of rubber**) is done by the addition of heat and sulfur (S), where sulfur creates crosslinks (bonds) between the rubber's chains at high temperatures. The vulcanization process increases the strength of rubber.

In general, the presence of crosslinks provides a few benefits to the properties of some compounds, such as

- It increases the strength between the rubber's chains (monomers).
- It increases a polymer's strength, resilience, and elasticity. [Polymers that have more than 200% elastic elongation (three times the original length) and can be returned to their original length are called elastomers.]
- It protects an ion exchange resin (a polymer) against high operating temperatures and PH ranges.

C-160

CRUDE OIL AND FUEL OIL

Crude Oil

Crude oil (simply known as **oil** or **petroleum**) is a naturally-occurring, unrefined, and complex mixture of hydrocarbons formed over millions of years when the remains of sea creatures are trapped in sediments and converted by heat and pressure to carbon-based compounds. In addition to carbon, crude oil contains nitrogen, sulfur, and a trace amount of metals (such as iron).

Oil, coal, and natural gas are still the main world's energy resources, although renewable energy has rapidly increased. In an oil refinery, the components of crude oil are separated from each other by the distillation process, producing gasoline, diesel fuel, kerosene, fuel oil, and natural gas.

The density (D) of crude oil ranges from 770 to 990 kg/m^3, depending on its types (light, medium, and heavy crude oils). And because the seawater's D is about 1003 kg/m^3, even the heaviest crude oil floats on seawater. When, however, the light components of oil evaporate, its D increases, so it sinks to the bottom.

Light, medium, and heavy crude oils and bitumen are the types of crude oil, from the lightest to the heaviest. The light crude oil's D is 770 kg/m^3, and bitumen is 998 kg/m^3.

The flashing point temperature (T_{FP}) of the light crude oil is -30°C, of the medium crude is -10°C, of the heavy crude is -3°C, and that of bitumen is greater than 100°C.

Viscosity (η) of light crude is 1 Pa.s, medium crude is 9, heavy crude is 820, and bitumen is too high (about 260 000 Pa.s).

Fuel Oil

Fuel oil (simply **oil**) is a fraction obtained from crude oil (petroleum) by the distillation process in the oil refineries. Fuel oil has lower volatility than gasoline (mainly octane, C_8H_{18}, a hydrocarbon). It is mainly used for its heat energy (E_Q, heat content) in homes, different industries, ships, and some special cars. In chemical-process plants, fuel oil is mainly burned in the furnace of steam boilers to produce steam.

A few important properties of typical fuel oil are listed next.

- Its bulk density (D_B) ranges from 890 to 990 kg/m^3 (= 55.5 to 62 Lb/Ft^3).
- Its enthalpy of combustion (H_C) is about 43 000 kJ/kg (= 18 450 BTU/Lb).

- Its flashing point temperature (T_{FP}) ranges from 44 to 60°C (= 111 to 140°F).

On a broad scale, fuel oils are classed based on the refining standards into

- **Distillate Fuel Oil** (DFO, also called **light fuel oil):** It is further subclassed into four groups: 1) Number (#) 1 oil, 2) Number 2 oil, 3) Number 3 oil, and 4) Number 4 oil. Number 1, 2, and 3 are diesel fuel oils used in diesel cars.
- **Residual Fuel Oil** (RFO, also called **heavy fuel oil** or **furnace fuel oil**): It is further subclassed into two groups: 1) Number 5, and 2) Number 6 oil.

Number 1 fuel oil has the highest combustibility and viscosity (η), and number 6 is the lowest. Thus, the *highest* the number of a fuel oil, the *more* it needs to be preheated before being used in a furnace. Say, number 6 needs preheating to 100 to 125°C (= 212 to 257°F), while # 5 needs 75 to 105°C (= 167 to 221°F).

C-161
CRYOGENIC GASES

A cryogenic gas can reach a low temperature (T). Hydrogen, oxygen, nitrogen, helium, argon, neon, and natural gas (predominantly methane, CH_4) are cryogenic gases. Cryogenic gases are used in the cryogenic process (liquefying a cryogenic gas by applying a very low T of about –150°C). For example, natural gas is used to produce liquefied natural gas (LNG), which is used as a cryogenic fuel in vehicles, satellites, rockets, and more.

C-162
CRYOGENIC PROCESS

As one of the process units of ChemEng, cryogenic is the process of liquefying a cryogenic gas (like oxygen) by reaching its cryogenic temperature (T_{Cry}, a very low temperature of about –150°C or –238°F). The process starts with compressing a cryogenic gas in a high-pressure compressor (P). The compressed gas is then cooled around T_{Cry} in a special refrigerator close to atmospheric pressure (P_{Atm}). As a result of condensation in the refrigerator, liquefied gas is produced. Sometimes, the cryogenic process involves the removal of certain components, such as water and heavy hydrocarbons, from the processing gas. During compression, the processing gas's heat energy (E_Q, the enthalpy, H) is decreased, and then during condensation at T_{Cry}, E_Q starts to increase.

The cryogenic process is used in some areas, including producing high-quality liquefied fuels (with high purity of 99.5%), known as **cryogenic fuels**. These fuels are produced from liquefied gases, such as liquid oxygen (with high purity of 99.5%), liquid hydrogen, and liquefied natural gas (LNG).

Cryogenic fuels must be stored at T_{Cry}. They are used in engines that operate in space (like satellites and rockets) because they can combust without oxygen. LNG occupies about 1600 times less volume than natural gas and requires less than **compressed natural gas** (CNG), making it easier to store and transport. The LNG's specific energy (the energy per unit mass) is 2.4 times greater than CNG and 0.6 times greater than diesel fuel. These properties make the LNG a cost-efficient fuel to transport over long distances where pipelines do *not* exist. LNG is usually carried in cryogenic road tankers and sea carriers. LNG can be used in natural gas vehicles, satellites, rockets, and more.

Today, the cryogenic industry is big and advanced. The nuclear, space, food, and transportation industries need cryogenic products. Liquid hydrogen and liquid helium (He) productions have been increased during the last four decades by a factor of 10. The food industry uses a large amount of liquid nitrogen (N_2) for food freezing and preservation. The medical industry uses cryogenic surgery to cure some diseases like Parkinson. MRI (magnetic resonance imaging) uses cryogenic superconducting magnets.

[Note: Cryogenics is a branch of ChemEng, which studies the properties and behavior of cryogenic gases (the gases that can reach a low temperature, such as oxygen, hydrogen, and nitrogen) and uses them in the cryogenic process. Sometimes, **cryogenics** is wrongly used to refer to **cryogenic gases**.]

C-163

CRYOGENIC TEMPERATURE

The cryogenic temperature (T_{Cry}) is an extremely low temperature of approximately –150°C (= –238°F = 123 K). Some cryogenic processes are performed at T_{Cry}. At the T_{Cry}, helium (He) becomes a superfluid, so its atoms lose their colliding ability and become motionless (with zero viscosity).

C-164

CRYSTAL DEFORMITY

Discussed under CRYSTALLIZATION PROCESS.

C-165

CRYSTAL OCCLUSION

A crystal occlusion is a small pocket on the face of a crystal that occurs during the crystallization process. Although the pockets in a sugar crystal are *not* large enough to be seen by an ordinary microscope, they can be observed under electronic scanning microscopes that significantly build up an image.

C-166

CRYSTAL SIZE DISTRIBUTION

Study PARTICLE SIZE DISTRIBUTION.

C-167

CRYSTALABLE SOLUTE

A crystalable solute (solute of interest) is a solute whose molecules have the highest ability to crystallize in a solution (mother liquid crystallization). A solute of interest indicates more changes in solubility with the solution's concentration (C) and temperature (T) than its other solutes (called non-crystalable solutes or impurities). Thus, some molecules of the crystalable solute solidify to initiate the crystal growth, while non-crystalable solutes stay in the mother liquid with *no* change (*no* crystallization).

In the diffusion process, the molecules of a crystalable solute have a much better ability to diffuse (move). Instead, the molecules of non-crystalable solute (or solutes) do *not* have a high diffusing ability. Thus, the crystalable (diffusing) solute molecules diffuse through the non-crystalable (non-diffusing) solute.

C-168
CRYSTALLINE DENSITY

See PARTICLE DENSITY.

C-169
CRYSTALLINE SOLIDS

Study AMORPHOUS AND CRYSTALLINE SOLIDS.

C-170
CRYSTALLINITY

Crystallinity (crystallization ability) is a new term used in crystallography to describe how a given crystalable solute crystallizes in a solution under certain conditions. Sugar (sucrose, $C_{12}H_{22}O_{11}$), with monoclinic-shaped crystals, has a complicated crystallinity (study CRYSTAL).

C-171
CRYSTALLIZATION COEFFICIENTS

Crystallization coefficients are three (3) dimensionless quantities used in the crystallization process to numerically express the state of solubility, saturation, and supersaturation of a **crystalable solute** in a solution, where **crystalable solute** (the solute-of-interest) is the solute with the highest crystallization ability (because its solubility changes more than the other solutes present in that solution). [Generally, the word coefficient is used in Physics as a dimensionless ratio that compares the change of a variable related to another variable.]

The three (3) coefficients used in the crystallization process are the following:

- **Solubility Coefficient** (K_S)**:** It indicates the state of solubility of a crystalable solute in a pure solution when that solution is under crystallization at a certain temperature (T). K_S has the same definition as **solubility**.
- **Saturation Coefficient** (K_{Sat})**:** It indicates the state of solubility of a crystalable solute in an impure solution when that solution is under crystallization at saturation and a certain T. In other words, K_{Sat} compares the solubility of the crystalable solute in an impure sample solution with that solute in a pure solution. Thus, it tells us the effect of impurities on the solubility of the solute in an impure sample solution.
- **Supersaturation Coefficient** (K_{Sup})**:** It indicates the state of solubility of a crystalable solute in a supersaturated solution (pure or impure) when that solution is under crystallization. In other words, K_{Sup} compares the solubility of the crystalable solute in a saturated solution with that solute in an unsaturated solution.

To formulize these coefficients, we define them in the solute-to-solvent (S_1-to-S_2) ratio, where solute can be sugar and solvent can be water.

- K_S is the S_1-to-S_2 ratio in a pure saturated solution (Sat) at a given T.
- K_{Sat} is the S_1-to-S_2 ratio in an **impure sample solution** ($I.S$) to that ratio in a **pure solutio**n (P), both at saturation and the same T.
- K_{Sup} is the S_1-to-S_2 ratio in an **impure sample solution** ($I.S$) to that ratio in an **impure solution** (I), both at the same T and purity.

$$K_S = \left[\frac{S_1}{S_2}\right]_{Sat} = \left[\frac{\%S}{100-\%S}\right] \quad (1)$$

$$K_{Sat} = \frac{\left[\frac{S_1}{S_2}\right]_{I.S}}{\left[\frac{S_1}{S_2}\right]_P} \quad (2)$$

$$K_{Sup} = \frac{\left[\frac{S_1}{S_2}\right]_{I.S}}{\left[\frac{S_1}{S_2}\right]_I} \quad (3)$$

[Comparing the last two equations tells us that the difference between K_{Sat} and K_{Sup} is in their denominators.]

When, for example, a sugar solution at 20ºC is saturated, its $K_S = K_{Sat} = 2$. This means that the maximum sugar solubility at 20ºC is 2 g, so its sugar-to-water (solute-to-solvent) ratio is 2-to-1. This solution consists of 2 parts sugar and 1 part of water (or 2 g sugar and 1 g water), with 66.7% (by mass) sugar.

Based on what has been explained, K_{Sup} can indicate if a solution (pure or impure) is unsaturated ($K_{Sup} < 1$), saturated ($K_{Sup} = 1$), or supersaturated ($K_{Sup} > 1$).

[Note: In an unsaturated solution or saturated solution, the crystalable solute does *not* start to crystallize until the solution becomes supersaturated (because, as said earlier, supersaturation is the cause of the crystallization process) by evaporating it (removing the solution's water) or by cooling it (changing the solution's solubility).]

Example

Given: An impure-sugar solution with dissolved solids (*DS*) content of 80% and purity (*P*) of 94% is under crystallization at a supersaturation situation at 76ºC.

Wanted: 1) K_S of the solution, considering that sugar solubility in a pure solution at 76ºC and saturation is 3.5, meaning that $(S_1/S_2)_P = 3.5$, 2) K_{Sup} of the solution, considering that sugar solubility in a saturated impure solution with a purity of 94% at 76ºC is 3.4, meaning that $(S_1/S_2)_I = 3.4$, 3) If the solution has the right supersaturity for seeding

The solution's sugar content (S_1) can be calculated from the purity (*P*) equation.

$$S_1 = \frac{DS \times P}{100} = \frac{80 \times 94}{100} = 75.2\%$$

$$\left(\frac{S_1}{S_2}\right)_{I.S} = \frac{S_1}{100-DS} = \frac{75.2}{100-80} = 3.8 \qquad K_{Sat} = \frac{\left[\frac{S_1}{S_2}\right]_{I.S}}{\left[\frac{S_1}{S_2}\right]_P} = \frac{3.8}{3.5} = 1.1$$

Impurities have increased the sugar solubility by 1.1 to 1 (or 9%).

$$K_{Sup} = \frac{\left[\frac{S_1}{S_2}\right]_{I.S}}{\left[\frac{S_1}{S_2}\right]_I} = \frac{3.8}{3.4} = 1.1$$

This is a good supersaturity for seeding because experience shows that an impure sugar solution with a purity (*P*) of around 94% can be seeded at K_{Sup} of 1.1 to 1.2 to create satisfactory crystallization efficiency.

C-172

CRYSTALLIZATION LAW

Crystallization Law (also called **Δ*L* Law** or ***dL* Law**, where *d* is for differential and *L* is for the length of the crystal in its tinniest time quantity of *dt*) is an expression that generalizes the **growth rate** (R_G, discussed under CRYSTALLIZATION PROCESS) of the crystals of a given substance that grow under ideal conditions.

In crystallization, an ideal condition has the following properties:

- All crystals in the mother liquid (the solution around crystals) grow in a uniform supersaturation coefficient range and at the same temperature (*T*), and
- All crystals grow from birth at a rate governed by supersaturation.

Under such ideal conditions, all crystals grow **invariantly** (uniformly) to maintain their geometric uniformity. So, a tiny change in a crystal's length (*dL*, where *d* is for differential) can be expressed with R_G and *dt* (tiny change in time) as

$$dL = R_G.dt \qquad (1)$$

[Such ideal conditions are hard to create in practice; however, the utmost attempt must be made to create nearly-ideal conditions to produce uniform crystals.]

A crystal size can also be calculated by its length (*L*, in m), volume (*V*, in m^3), and total surface area (*A,* in m^2) as

$$L = \frac{6V}{A} \qquad (2)$$

In practice, *L* is equal to the crystal size distribution (CSD, the average size of the produced crystals and their uniformity) determined by **screening tests** and some calculations.

C-173
CRYSTALLIZATION PROCESS AND CRYSTALLIZERS

1. CRYSTALLIZATION PROCESS

As an important process unit of ChemEng, crystallization (the reverse of the melting process) is a heat-absorbing process (endothermic process) performed in a crystallizer to crystallize the molecules of a crystalable solute (solute-of-interest) to produce crystals. The cause (driving force) of crystallization is the changes in the crystalable-solute's solubility; or, in more detail, the solubility difference between when a solution is in undersaturated and saturated situations, both at the same temperature (T). Let us first study Figure 1 and the upcoming Note.

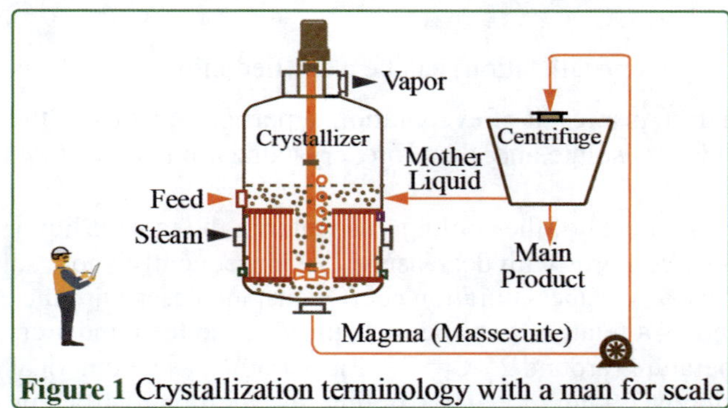

Figure 1 Crystallization terminology with a man for scale

[Note: The word **crystalable solute** (solute of interest) is consistently used here for the solute whose molecules have the highest ability to crystallize in the solution under crystallization. The word **solution feed** (simply **feed**) refers to what is fed to the crystallizer. And the word **mother liquid** (mother liquor) is used when the feed is nucleated. Thus, feed does *not* have nucleated (seeded) particles or crystals, while the mother liquid contains one or both. The word magma is used when the process gets toward the end, and the mother liquid becomes too dense. Thus, magma is the product of the crystallization station.]

When a solution is under evaporative crystallization, it changes from unsaturated to saturated and then supersaturated because a portion of the mother liquid (the solution around crystals) gradually evaporates into vapor. Some scientists, however, go deeper into the subject and consider the chemical potential energy of the crystalable solute as the cause of crystallization when the mother liquid goes through concentration changes and, thus, through solubility changes to become supersaturated. So, supersaturation is related to the solubility, and solubility is related to the concentration difference (ΔC, also called **chemical potential**) between the solute's concentration in the supersaturated solution, in which a crystal is growing (C_1), and the saturated solution around the crystal (C_2). So, $\Delta C = C_1 - C_2$. Crystallization, thus, does *not* initiate if supersaturation is *not* properly maintained. For this reason, supersaturation, whose quantity is numerically expressed by the supersaturation coefficient (K_{Sup}), is practically considered the driving force of crystallization. Instead, the viscosity (η) of the mother liquid is the crystallization's **opposing force**.

As a heat-absorbing process, crystallization involves the next two heat transfer processes:

- **Temperature-Change Process:** This process occurs because the T of the solution under crystallization increases to reach its boiling point temperature (T_{BP}).
- **Phase-Change Process:** This process occurs because some crystalable solute molecules go from the liquid phase to the solid phase.

Thus, part of the enthalpy change (ΔH) that occurs during crystallization is a temperature-change enthalpy (sensible enthalpy or sensible heat), and part is phase-change enthalpy (latent enthalpy or latent heat).

The following are also key points in crystallization:

- Both crystallization and diffusion (a contributor to crystallization) are mass transfer processes. Diffusion contributes to crystallization by moving (scientifically **diffusing**) the crystalable solute molecules through the phase boundary between the liquid and solid phase to initiate crystal growth.
- Crystallization differs from the evaporation process because, in crystallization, the concentration process follows by the formation of crystals, which will grow gradually in the saturated mother liquid to the desired size. In evaporation, instead, the goal is to concentrate a solution.

[Note 1: Many natural phenomena, such as water crystallization (the ice formation), occur by a combination of crystallization and diffusion, so some of their rules and equations will be discussed here.] [Note 2: Crystallization can be performed on a solution (like salty seawater to salt crystals) or a vapor. However, **solution crystallization** (simply **crystallization**) is predominant and is the subject of this topic. Also, note that the term crystallization used here does *not* refer to melt crystallization.]

Solution crystallization (simply crystallization) can be classified into

- **Evaporative crystallization:** As a result of evaporation, a portion of water in the solution feed evaporates, so the remaining water holds less solute and, therefore, crystallization occurs (solubility *decreases* with *decreasing* water content).
- **Cooling crystallization:** As a result of the cooling, the water in the mother liquor holds less solute, so crystallization occurs (solubility *decreases* with decreasing T). Consequently, more solute molecules position themselves on the crystals as K_{Sup} (supersaturation coefficient) increases with the cooling of mother liquor. [The word **cooling** used here is a relative word because the T of the feed under crystallization can be much higher than the room temperature (around 25ºC = 77 ºF).] At 60ºC, as a numerical example, the sugar solubility in a pure sugar solution is 2.9 g/g of water. Cooling this solution to 40ºC, its solubility decreases to 2.3 g/g of water. The difference in sugar (2.9 – 2.3 = 0.6 g) is then used in crystallization.

Let us now briefly overview the steps involved in the evaporative crystallization.

- **Evaporation:** It boils the feed to increase its DS (dissolved solids) content.
- **Seeding:** It adds fine solute particles to the feed at the right DS content and K_{Sup}.
- **Mass Diffusion:** It relocates the solute molecules from the mother liquor to the seed particles.
- **Crystal Growth:** It positions the diffused solute's molecules on the seed particles in a layer-by-layer fashion until particles become large crystals.

Because of the highly purified product produced from relatively impure solutions, **crystallization efficiency** is high because crystallization leaves impurities in the mother liquid, providing a high-impurity-elimination effect of up to 98%. Under correct operating conditions, the impurities are excluded from crystallization (because their solute's solubility changes much less compared to the crystalable solute). For these reasons, crystallization has wide applications in the chemical process industry.

Magma (mother liquor + crystals) is the product of the crystallization station, which then goes to the **centrifugal station** (or **filtration station**) to remove the remaining liquid from crystals. The wet-centrifuged crystals then go to the **drying station** to produce dry crystals with high purity. Sugar crystals, for example, after going through the centrifugal process and drying process, have a purity of above 99.9%, making sugar one of the purest food products. [The purity (P) of the crystals, among other factors, depends on the purity of the feed (the *greater* the purity of the feed, the *greater* is the purity of the crystals).]

1.1 NUCLEATION

Nucleation is the preparing process, during which the formation of the **nuclei** (the plural of **nucleus**) occurs by adding tiny solid particles of the crystalable solute to the solution feed. Each new solid nucleus grows when the solution becomes supersaturated and instead dissolves when the solution becomes saturated or unsaturated (undersaturated).

The nucleation process is of two types:

- **Nucleation without the Seeding:** A self-nucleation (seedless nucleation) occurs by evaporation or cooling when the supersaturation coefficient (K_{Sup}) reaches a certain range (called **metastable zone**). In self-nucleation, some solute molecules solidify at the right K_{Sup} to prepare a solid foundation for crystallization.
- **Nucleation with the Seeding:** A seeded nucleation occurs by adding fine particles of the crystalable solute to the feed at the right K_{Sup} to prepare a solid foundation for the process. For example, seeding is done in the sugar crystallization process by dispersing a slurry of fine sugar particles (5 to 10 microns in size) to the feed. The sugar seed particles (the crystalable solute) grow until they become the desired-size crystals.

1.2 SUPERSATURITY AND VISCOSITY, OPPOSING FORCES

In crystallization, two forces act against each other: supersaturity (supersaturation action) as the driving force and viscosity (η) as the opposing force. And the crystallization rate (R_C) is closely related to these variables (supersaturation and viscosity). Crystallization does *not* happen if the mother liquid is *not* in a supersaturity situation (the *higher* the supersaturity, the *higher* is the R_C). And it does *not* proceed at the right rate if the η of the mother liquor is too high (the *higher* the η, the *lower* is the R_C). Other factors, such as temperature (T) and stirring, also play important roles. But once they are established and kept under control, their effects on optimization of the crystallization process become less important. Thus, most of the discussion on this topic is about establishing the correct supersaturity and viscosity in the mother liquid.

The process of supersaturation in a solution containing crystalable solute molecules can be achieved by:

- **Evaporation:** For a solute whose solubility is independent of the solution's temperature (T), as with salt (NaCl) and potassium chloride (KCl), supersaturation can be achieved by evaporating the solution feed.
- **Cooling:** For a solute whose solubility increases with increasing T, as with potassium nitrate (KNO_3) and sodium sulfite (Na_2SO_3), cooling can achieve supersaturation.
- **Evaporation, Cooling, or Seeding:** These options are used for a solute whose solubility increases extremely with increasing T, as with sugar ($C_{12}H_{22}O_{11}$) and sodium nitrate ($NaNO_3$). Sugar can be satisfactorily crystallized by evaporation with *no* cooling, cooling without evaporation, by the combination of both, or by **seeding** (adding fine particles of crystalable solute to mildly supersaturated solution). At 100ºC, 477 g of sugar dissolves in 100 g of water, but this ratio is only 200 to 100 at 20ºC. So, cooling the solution by 80ºC causes 277g more sugar to crystallize. [In sugar crystallization, a rapid supersaturation can be formed by seeding when sugar solution (pure or impure) is saturated.]

As Figure 2 shows, R_C (crystallization rate) increases notably with increasing the solution's K_{Sup} (supersaturation coefficient). At a low K_{Sup}, the R_C is low, if *not* zero, but as the solution becomes more supersaturated, the R_C gets greater exponentially. Considering this statement, we can say that a crystal in a solution with a K_{Sup} of 1.4 grows two times faster than a solution with a K_{Sup} of 1.2 compared with a saturated solution with a K_{Sup} of 1. The reason follows.

$$R_C = \frac{(K_{Sup})_1 - 1}{(K_{Sup})_2 - 1} = \frac{1.4 - 1}{1.2 - 1} = \frac{0.4}{0.2} = 2$$

At the same K_{Sup}, the main variables that affect R_C (crystallization rate) are:

- T (temperature): Increasing T increases the R_C because it decreases η (the opposing force of crystallization),
- DS (dissolved solid): Increasing DS decreases R_C (because it increases viscosity, η).

Coordinating Model: To better prepare the readers for the crystal-growth subject, a pure sugar solution is used as a coordinating model and study the solubility changes of sugar (the crystalable solute) as the solution's T (temperature). This can be discussed with the help of a sugar **solubility graph**, which represents the relation between the solute's solubility coefficient (K_S, the solute-to-solvent ratio, S_1/S_2) and solution's T (see Figure 3). In the graph, we see three lines ($K_{Sup} = 1$, $K_{Sup} = 1.2$, and $K_{Sup} = 1.5$), where K_{Sup} is for supersaturation coefficient. The lines divide the graph into the following four (4) zones:

- **Unsaturated Zone** ($K_{Sup} < 1$)**:** This is a **non-nucleation** zone in which *no* nucleation and, consequently, *no* growth activity occurs.
- **Low Supersaturated Zone** ($K_{Sup} = 1$ to 1.2)**:** This is a mild nucleation zone in which nucleation occurs safely by further evaporation, and some growth activity occurs at a low rate.
- **Optimum Supersaturated Zone** ($K_{Sup} = 1.2$ to 1.5)**:** This zone, also called the **growing zone** or **metastable zone**, is a safe-growing zone in which nucleation continues by further evaporation and crystals grow safely at an ideal rate. [We, thus, must keep K_{Sup} of the solution in this range (later, I will discuss how to do so).]
- **Extreme Supersaturated Zone** ($K_{Sup} > 1.5$)**:** This is an **unsafe-growth** zone in which crystals grow extremely, so the risk of **defected** (false) **crystal formation** exists.

Consider the saturated line ($K_{Sup} = 1$) in Figure 3. At point A, the system is in a stable (equilibrium) condition, so *no* exchange of the molecules between two phases (liquid and solid) occurs. Or, if the exchange occurs slowly, the rates of the crystal-occurring process and crystal-dissolving process are the same. From point A, a supersaturated condition can be obtained by evaporation (case 1), seeding (case 2, in which K_{Sup} rapidly increases), or by cooling (case 3). The combination of cases 1 and 2 is called the **evaporative crystallization with seed nucleation**, which is practiced in the sugar plants, and we will briefly discuss it next.

As evaporation proceeds, the number of free water molecules gradually reduces until the solution reaches a low K_{Sup} of about 1.1. At this point, the solution is seeded with finely powdered sugar to form mother liquor (solution + seed particles). Seeding causes a rapid increase in K_{Sup} of mother liquor. From now on, the conditions are kept so that the liquor stays in the **optimum-supersaturated zone** (growing zone) with K_{Sup} of 1.2 to 1.4. During this time, some sugar molecules move toward seed particles and position themselves on their surface to create the first layers on each sugar seed particle. The thickness of each layer is about 1 nm = 10^{-6} cm, which a strong microscope can see.

At the early stage of crystallization (after nucleation), the molecular diffusion is relatively faster (because nucleated crystals are far apart). As K_{Sup} increases during the later crystallization stage, the molecular movement slowly decreases (because the crystals are relatively closer), causing a slower crystallization rate (R_C). The slow molecular movement continues to some extent, but it stops after a while. The mother liquid becomes **saturated** (non-growing condition) after the crystals absorb the excess sugar molecules in the mother liquid. Hence, the system is again in a stable (equilibrium) condition, causing the stop of the molecular movement.

As evaporation continues, the concentration of the mother liquid increases, so K_{Sup} increases to high points, again, and the system becomes stressed (exhausted) and, consequently, the mother liquid becomes **supersaturated** (growing condition). To release the stress, the molecules start to move by diffusion again toward the existing crystals and position themselves on the faces, so more new layers build, making the crystal a bit larger. Going through **saturation** and **supersaturation** and vice versa, repeatedly continue until the desired-size crystals are produced. At the end of crystallization, the mother liquid and the crystals are in contact long enough to reach equilibrium, so the mother liquid and the liquid around the crystals are saturated and at the same C (concentration) and T (temperature).

After studying the upcoming Notes, pause because, in the rest of the discussion, we will go one step deeper and discuss the crystal growth in more detail and provide its equations.

[Note 1: During the growing period, holding supersaturation coefficient (K_{Sup}) in an optimum range ($K_{Sup} = 1.2$ to 1.5) is the most important factor in doing the right job in crystallization. When the K_{Sup} passes the optimum range and enters the unsafe (liable) zone, the risk of forming false crystals occurs (an unwanted situation). In industrial practices, K_{Sup} is maintained in the safe supersaturated zone by periodically feeding the crystallizer while evaporation continues. During the early stage of the growing period, the feeding process is done at a higher rate (because crystals are far apart, allowing a greater crystallization rate, R_C). The feeding is then reduced during the later stage, as the crystals are relatively closer to each other, so they grow at a slower rate.]

[Note 2: The T of the liquid phase (the mother liquid) and solid phase (the crystals) are nearly the same, so in the crystallization discussions and calculations, the mother liquid's T is considered the T of the system.]

[Note 3: When a solute solubility increases appreciably with T, the solution's K_{Sup} can be expressed as temperature difference (ΔT) instead of concentration difference (ΔC). The ΔT is related to K_{Sup} and, therefore, it is used in process control of crystallization (discussed later).]

[Note 4: In theory, what applies to the **crystal-growth process** approximately applies to the **diffusion process**. This statement has an exception. Almost all solutes diffuse from one liquid phase to another liquid phase during the diffusion process. But in crystallization, just the crystalable solute's molecules diffuse from the liquid phase to the solid phase (the crystal). Remember that the diffusion direction in both cases is perpendicular to the phase boundary between two phases, as shown in Figure 4.]

1.3 CRYSTAL GROWTH

Crystal growth is a buildup process that occurs on each crystal layer-by-layer (like the **ring of an onion**) until the crystal grows to the desired size. [The crystal growth process occurs at the molecular (non-visible) level, so we must use our imaginary senses to study this subtopic.]

The growth process can be measured by the crystallization rate (R_C, also called **growth rate**). R_C is directly proportional to the mother liquid's supersaturation (whose quantity is expressed by supersaturation coefficient, K_{Sup}), which is the crystallization driving force, and indirectly proportional to the mother liquid's viscosity (η), which is the opposing force of crystallization.

$$R_C = \frac{K_{Sup}}{\eta} \quad (1)$$

Theoretically, this equation is an easy way to control the crystal growth. But practically, *no* instrument (as of writing this book) exists to directly measure a solution's K_{Sup}. And we know, by now, that the solution K_{Sup} should be kept at a correct-and-uniform range during the entire process, particularly during the **nucleation** and **growth** periods. This makes the control of crystallization difficult. [Later, under Control of Crystallization Station, we talk about how the K_{Sup} can be controlled indirectly.]

We mentioned earlier that evaporative crystallization (simply **crystallization**) consists of four steps: 1) Evaporation (boils the syrup to increase its dissolved solids content), 2) Seeding (adds fine sugar seed particles to the liquor at the right DS content and K_{Sup}), 3) Mass diffusion (relocates sugar molecules from the mother liquor to the seed particles), and 4) Crystal growth (positions the diffused sugar molecules on the seed particles in a layer-by-layer fashion until particles become large crystals).

Unlike the first two steps, the last two (mass diffusion and crystal growth) are, theoretically, complicated subjects. As a practical example, we add powdered sugar to warm water to make a supersaturated sugar solution and application of crystal growth.

The processing cycle of growing a nucleated particle to a small crystal and the processing cycle of a small crystal to become a crystal of the desired size is the same. In each cycle, which consists of two sections, the crystalable solute molecules (sugar molecules in our example) diffuse (move) from the bulk of the supersaturated mother liquid to the crystals' faces to fill their empty spaces and complete a layer (base unit of a crystal).

The growing cycle of a crystal in a supersaturated solution proceeds in two (2) sections (see Figure 4):

- **Diffusing Section:** During this section, which occurs in the bulk of the mother liquid, the crystalable solute's molecules diffuse through a phase boundary to make the distance L and sit on the existing crystal. [The **cause** (driving force) of the first section is the **difference in solute concentration** between the mother liquid (C_B, where subscript B is for **bulk**), which is in a supersaturated situation, and the thin layer of the liquid around the crystal (C_L, where subscript L is for **layer**), which is in a saturated situation, so $C_B - C_L$ is the cause of the diffusing section.]
- **Reacting Section:** During this section, which occurs at the surface of the existing crystal, the new molecules seated on the surface of the crystal start to make a chemical reaction with the existing molecules to create chemical bonds with them. [The **cause** of the reacting section is *not* concentration difference (because *no* ΔC exists on the surface of the crystals) but heat energy (E_Q), which is released during the third-step diffusion (discussed in a minute). E_Q acts as E_a (activation energy) to remove molecules from the liquid phase and

place them on the surface (face) of the solid phase (the crystal). While on the surface, E_Q acts as E_S (surface energy) to create a new crystal surface by creating hydrogen bonds between the dislocated-solute molecules and the existing crystal molecules.] [Note that at a given M (mass), finer crystals have larger surface area than the coarser ones. Thus, the amount of E_S per unit M of the finer crystals is comparatively greater. [More talk about the reacting section later.]

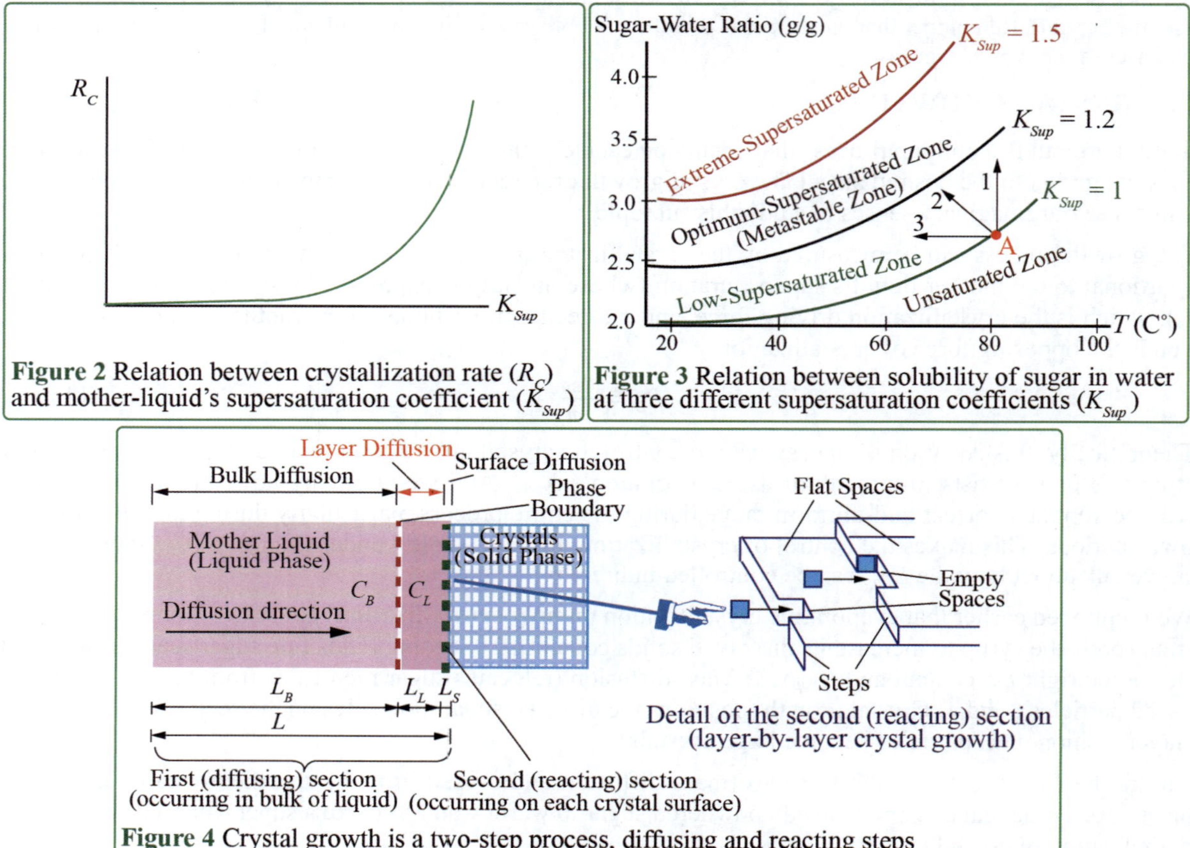

Figure 2 Relation between crystallization rate (R_C) and mother-liquid's supersaturation coefficient (K_{Sup})

Figure 3 Relation between solubility of sugar in water at three different supersaturation coefficients (K_{Sup})

Figure 4 Crystal growth is a two-step process, diffusing and reacting steps

1.3.1 Individual Steps of Diffusing and Reacting Sections

Now that you have been introduced to the crystal-growth theory and its equations, we can be more specific and focus on individual steps that occur during the **first** (diffusing) **section** and the **second** (reacting) **section** of the crystal growth.

As shown in Figure 4, the diffusing section occurs in three steps, as outlined next.

- **First-Step Diffusion** (bulk diffusion)**:** In the first diffusing step, the crystalable solute's molecules diffuse by convective diffusion from the bulk of the solution to make the distance L_B (where subscript B is for **bulk**) and position themselves on the boundary between the mother liquid and the solution around the crystals.
- **Second-Step Diffusion** (layer diffusion)**:** In the second diffusing step, the solute's molecules diffuse through the liquid-liquid phase boundary by conductive diffusion to make the distance L_L (where subscript L is for **layer**). [**Phase boundary** is an extremely-thin diffusional layer with a few nm thicknesses between two phases, where 1 nm = 10^{-6} mm.]
- **Third-step diffusion** (surface diffusion)**:** In the third step, the solute's molecules diffuse, again, by convection to make the distance L_S (subscript S is for **surface**) and sit on the surface of the crystals.

To study the **second** (reacting) **section** of crystal growth, we consider a **cluster** (group) consisting of a sugar molecule surrounded by several water molecules, known as a water cluster, rather sugar-water cluster. Such a cluster can be viewed as the **growth unit** of the crystal-growth process. Further, we assume many of these clusters are in a supersaturated sugar solution (mother liquid). After going through the individual diffusing steps, each cluster positions itself on a nucleated sugar particle. This process continues until a nucleated particle grows to become a desired-size crystal. Thus, the formation of a crystal occurs in the next order:

Water cluster → Nucleated particle → Crystal

The following three (3) conditions can exist for a **water cluster** (a growth unit):

- **Normal Condition:** If the crystallization condition is normal and the mother liquid is optimally supersaturated, the movement (diffusion) of the water cluster continues normally. So, it places itself on a nucleated particle. This process continues until the empty spaces on all faces of the particle become completely flat, so a **normal** (invariant) **crystal** with the desired size is formed over a certain time.
- **Abnormal Condition:** If the condition is abnormal and the mother liquid is *not* sufficiently supersaturated, the water cluster dissolves in the liquid, so the nucleated particle does *not* grow to a crystal.
- **In-between Condition:** If the crystallization condition is normal and abnormal, the cluster *cannot* fill a space, so the crystal would *not* maintain its normal crystallographic shape and becomes spherical without any face. Consequently, an **abnormal crystal** (known as a **variant** or **deformed crystal**) is formed. [Sometimes, the condition is normal, but the purity of the mother liquid is too low (that is, impurities are too high), so in addition to the crystalable solute (sugar), some non-crystallable solutes may crystallize (so **impure-deformed crystals** are produced).]

We now assume a normal condition and outline the three (3) individual steps that a water cluster goes through during the reacting (second) section to become a desired-size crystal.

- Movement of a water cluster toward a crystal's space,
- Positioning of the cluster into a space of each face of a crystal, and
- Releasing E_Q by the cluster acts as the cause of the reaction with existing crystal molecules.

As the result of what has been discussed so far, we can summarize the subject of crystal growth as follow:

- It is a layer-by-layer process (similar to an **onion ring**), occurring in an identical and orderly manner.
- It occurs in 2 sections (each involving 3 steps), where the first section takes much longer than the second.
- Its first section's cause is concentration difference, and that of the second section is surface energy.
- Its first section is a mass-diffusion process, and its second section is a chemical reaction process.
- Its first section is an energy-absorbing process, and the second one is an energy-releasing process.

1.3.2 Crystal Growth Equations

Crystallization rate (C_R, also called **growth rate**) can be expressed as the amount of the crystalable-solute's mass (M) per unit time (t) of the first (diffusing) section because the time of the second (reacting) section is negligible compared to that of the first. It is important to know the following about the R_C:

- It is usually measured in g.m^2/min.
- It increases considerably with increasing K_{Sup} of the solution, as shown in Figure 2. At low K_{Sup}, it is low, if *not* zero, but it becomes more supersaturated and exponentially greater. A crystal in a solution with K_{Sup} = 1.4 grows two times faster than a solution with K_{Sup} = 1.2 (compared with a saturated solution with K_{Sup} = 1).

We can simplify the formulation of the R_C equations by using the following close-to-reality assumptions:

- The distance (L for length) that the molecules must diffuse in the **first-step diffusion** (a convective diffusion), shown as L_B (where B is for **bulk**), is nearly sufficient to be taken as the overall distance for all three steps of the first (diffusing) section. This is because L_B (the bulk diffusing length) and t_B (the bulk diffusing time) are much larger in the first step than those in the second and third steps, as shown in Figure 4.

- The diffusion coefficient (D_{AB}) of the **second-step diffusion** (a conductive diffusion) is nearly sufficient to be considered the overall diffusion coefficient for all three steps. [Symbol D_{AB} indicates that A diffuses through B, where B is the non-diffusing solute. If B were the diffusing solute, the symbol D_{BA} would have been used instead of D_{AB}.]

Based on these assumptions, the first section's crystallization rate (R_{C1}, mass diffusion per unit time in the diffusing section, in kg/s) can be given by using D_{AB} (diffusion coefficient, in m²/s), L_B (the bulk diffusing length, in m), A (the phase boundary's area, in m²), C_B (solute's concentration in the bulk-diffusing area, kg/m³), and C_L (solute's concentration in the layer-diffusing area, kg/m³), where subscript L is for **layer**.

$$R_{C1} = \dot{M} = \frac{dM}{dt} = D_{AB}.A\frac{\Delta C}{L_B} = \frac{D_{AB}}{L_B}A(C_B - C_L) \quad (2)$$

The second section's crystallization rate (R_{C2}, mass diffusion per unit time in the reacting section) can be given by using K_R (**reaction rate constant**), C_L, C_S (solute's concentration in the surface-diffusing area), and order of reaction (reaction order, an exponent shown by symbol R).

$$R_{C2} = \dot{M} = \frac{dM}{dt} = K_R.\Delta C^R = K_R(C_L - C_S)^R \quad (3)$$

At a stable (equilibrium) condition, both sections of the crystal growth proceed at the **same rate**. Considering this statement and knowing that the order of reaction on the surface of the crystal is equal to one (because the reaction is of **first-order**), Equation 2 becomes equal to Equation 3.

$$\frac{D_{AB}}{L_B}A(C_B - C_L) = K_R(C_L - C_S)^R \quad (4)$$

We can also eliminate difficult-to-measure concentrations of C_L and C_S from this equation because C_B can be considered the main cause (driving force) of both sections of the crystal growth, so

$$\frac{D_{AB}}{L_B}A.C_B = K_R \quad (5)$$

The term D_{AB}/L_B is a coefficient, shown by the symbol K_d, so

$$A.C_B = \frac{K_d}{K_R} \quad (6)$$

The term K_d/K_R is called the crystallization coefficient (K_C), so the overall crystallization rate (R_C) would be

$$R_C = K_C.A.C_B \quad (7)$$

This equation represents both growth sections. In detail, the crystalable solute molecules diffuse at a rate of R_C from the mother liquid with a viscosity of η to the crystal with a surface area of A, position themselves on the crystal structure, and react with the existing crystal.

Because K_C directly depends on the solution's T (temperature) and indirectly on the η (viscosity), Equation 7 can also be written as

$$R_C = K_C\frac{T}{\eta}A.C_B \quad (8)$$

The R_C of a **normal** (invariant) **crystal** can also be given as the $\dot{M}_A$ (the mass crystallization rate of the crystalable solute). The $\dot{M}_A$ is the amount of the diffusing solute A diffused in unit time through the non-crystalable solute B (a non-diffusing solute).

$$R_C = \dot{M}_A = \frac{2D_{AB}A}{D_n} \quad (9)$$

In this equation, D_{AB} is the diffusion coefficient of the crystalable solute A when diffusing through the non-crystalable solute B. The C_A is the concentration of A, and D_n is the molar density of the crystalable crystal.

1.3.3 Crystal Growth Law

The crystal-growth law (the ΔL law of crystal growth) generalizes the crystallization rate (R_C) of **all crystals** when they are assumed to be spherical with radius R and surface area of $4\pi.R^2$ and grow under ideal conditions to form normal crystals. The ΔL, which is the characteristic length of a crystal in its tinniest differential time quantity of dt, indicates the size of the crystal when it grows in a solution under ideal conditions, meaning that 1) The solution is under a uniform supersaturation range. 2) The solution is at an appropriate temperature (T). 3) *No* new nucleation occurs in the solution. Based on the listed statements, ΔL Law can be formulized as

$$\Delta L = R_C, dt \tag{10}$$

[Theoretically, the average size of crystals can be calculated by their average length (L, in mm), volume (V, in mm^3), and their total surface area (A, in mm^2).

$$L = \frac{6V}{A} \tag{11}$$

The **screening test** (see CRYSTAL SIZE DISTRIBUTION) determines the crystals' average size.]

1.4 CRYSTAL DEFORMITY

Crystal deformity (crystal defect) is the deformation of crystals from their ordinary geometric shape. It occurs during crystal growth when the mother liquid, in which the crystals grow, is under non-ideal conditions.

[Note: It is almost impossible (and uncommon) that all the crystals of a crystalable solute (the solute of interest), produced industrially, to be **normal** (invariant) in shape. When, however, the defects are too high, they negatively affect the quality of the product. Usually, an impure solution under crystallization makes more deformed crystals than a pure solution.]

As an example, Figure 5A shows the top faces of a sugar crystal grown undeformed under **normal conditions** in a pure sugar solution. Deformity in the sugar crystals (or other crystals) can be from two sources:

- **Outside Sources:** Crystallization under high supersaturation, improper seed use, or improper stirring may cause deformities in the crystals.
- **Inside Sources:** Certain impurities in the feed, similar solubility properties, can create deformities. For example, in the beet-juice or cane-juice crystallization, raffinose and invert sugar are the main impurities that cause the deformity of the sugar crystals. These impurities accumulate in the middle of the crystal, so the crystalable-solute molecules crystallize around them, causing crystal deformation.

The crystal defect may differ depending on the crystalable solute under process. With, for example, sugar crystals, the defect can take the following shapes:

- **Elongation:** This occurs when crystals grow more on the sides, making the crystals a needlelike shape, which can be seen by the naked eye when the crystals are large. Elongation in sugar crystals occurs to the width-to-height ratio of up to 4 to 1, while this ratio in a normal sugar crystal is 1.6 to 1. Figure 5B shows the top faces of an elongated sugar crystal grown in a sugar solution containing unsuitable impurities, like raffinose, in the class of sugars (saccharides). The raffinose molecules get to the layers of sugar crystals during crystallization, causing elongation in sugar crystals.
- **Twining:** This occurs when two crystals grow together, so a larger crystal is formed. Figure 5C shows the top faces of a twin sugar crystal grown under abnormal conditions.
- **Conglomeration:** This occurs when more crystals grow together, so a conglomerated crystal is formed. The conglomeration of crystals is seen when **rock candy** is produced. [Later, under the subsection of Operating Problems of Crystallization Station, you will learn the causes of the crystal deformities.]

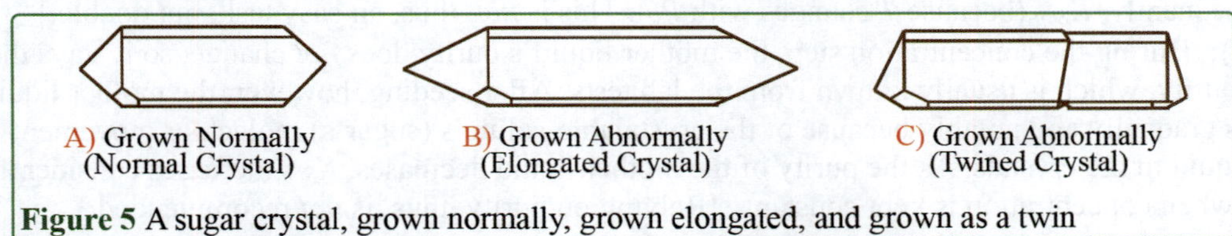

Figure 5 A sugar crystal, grown normally, grown elongated, and grown as a twin

1.5 CONTROL OF CRYSTALLIZATION STATION

Crystallization is a delicate process, so it needs to be controlled by a skilled operator and automated process control. When the crystallization station is only controlled by an operator (with *no* control system), the quality of the product depends on the operator's skill. Critical points, such as seeding time, control of dissolved solids content, and most importantly, supersaturation of the solution under crystallization, are estimated by:

- **Observations:** These are unreliable (*no* two operators control the crystallization similarly).
- **Laboratory Tests:** These *cannot* give sufficient-and-fast information, so create after-the-fact results.

A control system, instead, does *not* create the listed disadvantages so that it can provide some benefits:

- It creates immediate results,
- It simplifies the operation of the crystallizers,
- It helps in producing the right-size high-quality crystals,
- It saves steam consumption of the crystallization station, and
- It can control some additional variables, such as feed and vapor supply, the temperature of the condensate, vacuum pressure in the crystallizers, stirrers' speed, and more.

As for the control of a crystallizer, the mother liquid's supersaturation (its quantity is shown by supersaturation coefficient, K_{Sup}) must be controlled. During concentrating, seeding, and early growing, the mother liquid should be kept at a different but correct K_{Sup}. Then during the later growth stage until the end of the process, the mother liquid's K_{Sup} and magma's crystal content should be controlled closely. [Notably, *no* instrument is available that can directly control K_{Sup}, the most important factor in controlling the crystallization's operation.] Thus, crystallization scientists have tried to measure other variables by different techniques and relate them to K_{Sup} by calculations. It must be said here that although the calculations are done by **computer**, relating variables to K_{Sup} affects the accuracy of the measurements. In addition, the **data tables** on K_{Sup} are *not* suitable for a computer control system. However, the crystallization station should be controlled automatically, as explained next. [To simplify the topic, we apply process control on a crystallization station as is in a sugar factory (as the most suitable way for our purpose).]

When an impure sugar solution is under crystallization, the four (4) main interrelated variables affecting K_{Sup} are the dissolved solid (DS = Brix) concentration of the mother liquid (DS_{ML}), its purity (P_{ML}), temperature (T_{ML}), and its saturation coefficient (K_{Sat}), where subscript ML used here stands for mother liquid. Thus, K_{Sup} can be expressed as a function of these independent variables as

$$K_{Sup} = f(DS_{ML} T_{ML} P_{ML} K_{IP}) \tag{15}$$

Each of these variables relates to K_{Sup} in the following different ways:

- Dissolved Solids (DS)**:** Mother liquid's DS is related to K_{Sup} directly (the *larger* the DS, the *greater* is the K_{Sup}). As the feed is ready to be seeded, the mother liquid's DS increases notably, so it helps estimate K_{Sup}.
- Temperature (T)**:** Temperature is the best way to control the mother liquid's K_{Sup} because a direct relation between the T and K_{Sup} exists (increasing T *increases* the K_{Sup}). As a rough idea, when a higher-purity sugar solution is under crystallization, a 4ºC change in the crystallizer temperature changes K_{Sup} by about 0.4 units. When a low-purity solution is processed, 4 to 8ºC change, depending on the purity, creates the same change in K_{Sup}. [The crystallizer should be kept under constant vacuum pressure (P_V) to control the mother liquid's T and, consequently, K_{Sup} (because T changes with P_V). This is *not*, thus, an easy task, but doable.]
- Purity (P)**:** During the concentration step, the mother liquid's purity does *not* change, so it stays the same as the feed purity, which is usually known from the lab tests. After seeding, however, the mother liquid's purity decreases gradually and notably because of the crystalable-solute's (sugar's) molecular movement from the mother liquid to the crystals. As the purity of the mother liquid decreases, K_{Sup} increases considerably, particularly when concentration is kept constant. [Relying on purity, thus, is *not* recommended.]

- Saturation Coefficient (K_{Sat}): Since K_{Sat} indicates the effect of impurities on the crystalable solute's solubility in an impure solution, the mother liquids with different K_{Sat} can hold different amounts of the crystalable solute, resulting in different K_{Sup}. [K_{Sat} measurement, thus, is a problematic task.]

As a result of these explanations, the mother liquid's *DS* (shown as DS_{ML}) is the only variable that can be used to estimate K_{Sup}. We also know that the direct measurement of *DS* (particularly when the mother liquid contains crystals; at this point, it is called magma) is a challenge, too. Thus, we should find an easy-measurable variable related to the *DS* and K_{Sup}. Or relate another easy-measurable variable directly to K_{Sup}. For doing so, the following methods have been used in the chemical industry to control a crystallization station:

- Refractometric method,
- Conductometric method,
- Microwave method,
- Temperature-controlled method,
- Boiling-elevation-temperature method, and
- Dielectric-constant method.

Next, the first two methods are discussed.

1.5.1 Refractometric Method

Refractometry is based on the refractive index (R_I) of a beam (ray) of light when it enters a different medium. The refractometric control method uses the direct relation between the *DS* concentration and the R_I of the solution under crystallization at a constant temperature (*T*). This way, R_I can indirectly represent the *DS* concentration of the sample. Special refractometers are available for online measurement of *DS* in the crystallizers, tanks, and pipes. Unlike lab refractometers, an online refractometer is *not* affected by crystals in the solution (because they are equipped with an energy source). Usually, cesium-137 (Cs-137), which gives gamma rays for a long period (its half lifetime is 32 years, meaning in 32 years, Cs-137 loses 50% of its content), is used as the source of energy. Because the Cs-137 is a radioactive element, it is placed in a double-wall, waterproof, stainless steel box, mounted at the crystallizer's bottom. The source sends constant energy to the **detector** (installed outside the crystallizer). The frequency (*f*) reaching the detector is inversely related to the solution's concentration (*C*). The *C* values enable the control of the mother liquid's supersaturation. These refractometers are also equipped with automatic temperature compensation (ATC) for variations in the standard temperature (20ºC).

1.5.2 Conductometric Method

The **conductometric method** (conductivity method) is based on the electric resistance of an electric current passing through a solution. Conductivity (refers to electric conductivity, K_E) is related to the activity of the molecules, which is related to the *DS* concentration of the solution under the test.

In a solution with high purity (*P*), the K_E of the solution is *not* linear to its *DS* concentration (because of the low ash content in a high-purity solution). But it is linear to its *T* (K_E *increases* with *increasing T*). The conductometric method, thus, can be used successfully in low-purity solutions (below 90% purity), in which the ash content is high, as K_E increases with increasing impurities (decreasing purity).

Suspended solids and precipitated sediments do *not* affect K_E. Although the conductivity method requires keeping several variables constant (say, feed *DS*, *T*, and vapor pressure), it correlates closely with the K_{Sup} of the solution (the K_E of the solution *decreases* with *increasing the* K_{Sup} and with *increasing* its crystal content). [The **radio-frequency-conductivity probes** (transducers) can measure K_E using radio frequency, providing greater sensitivity, and reducing signal drift.]

1.6 OPERATING PROBLEMS OF CRYSTALLIZATION STATION

Several problems can occur in the crystallization station, such as low crystallization rate (R_C) and improper crystal size distribution (CSD). We start this subsection by talking about problems related to R_C and CSD and their causes. Then, we will outline other problems that usually may occur in the crystallization station. [To exemplify our discussion, we use sugar crystallization as performed in a typical beet-sugar plant.]

Low Crystallization Rate

In the sugar crystallization, for example, the normal time for the first-stage crystallization is 2 to 3 hours, 4 to 8 hours for the second stage, and 8 to 12 hours for the third stage. [The time differences are because of the differences in the purity of the feed used in different stages.] Possible causes of low R_C are the following:

- **Insufficient Steam:** Using insufficient steam or using low-pressure steam cause a slow process (low R_C).
- **Insufficient Discharge of Condensate:** When the crystallization process proceeds slowly, part of the steam chest (the heating section of a crystallizer) is filled with condensate, causing less steam to the chest, and lowering R_C. In such a situation, the amount of discharged condensate must be carefully controlled.
- **Insufficient Stirring:** Insufficient stirring causes crystals to stay at the bottom of a crystallizer, so there is little crystal surface exposed to the supersaturated solution present in the higher area.

Other causes of the slow crystallization process are the following:

- Insufficient removal of noncondensing gases
- Excessive scale on heating tubes
- Insufficient heating surface
- Low feed concentration

Improper Crystal Size Distribution

The existence of the fine crystals in excessive amounts is a disadvantage because, in the centrifugal (or filtration) station, fine crystals easily pass the centrifuge screen (or filtering medium) and become part of the mother liquid, which must be recrystallized (disadvantage). In one of the techniques used to reduce the number of fine crystals, an external circulation-and-heating system is installed outside the main crystallizer body to recirculate heated magma (mother liquor + crystals) to the crystallizer.

Produced Crystals are Twined or Conglomerated

Twined crystals (growing two crystals together) and **conglomerated crystals** (growing more crystals together) are produced when magma's T is *not* carefully regulated during the process. In these situations, the steam and feed intakes must be regulated to maintain the T constant and the supersaturation coefficient (K_{Sup}) in the safe zone. Improper seed use and stirring system are the other reasons.

Produced Crystals are Elongated or Rounded Corner

Crystals elongated along one or two faces are produced when some impurities are in the feed. Crystals with rounded corners and edges are produced when the crystals break into fragments by hitting an inappropriate stirrer used in a crystallizer.

2. CRYSTALLIZERS

A crystallizer is a device (equipment) used for performing the crystallization process. In its typical design, a crystallizer consists of a closed-round vessel that, in its lower section, crystallization of the solution feed occurs. And in its upper section, the vapor, produced by evaporation of the feed, moves to be discharged. The lower (heat-transfer) section receives steam or vapor, so a heat transfer process from the heating medium to the solution through the walls of the heating tubes occurs. As a result of the heat transfer, some vapor is produced that goes to the vapor section. In a crystallizer, however, the heating medium is *not* in direct contact with the solution because the heat energy (E_Q) is transferred through the walls of the heating tubes, which are in the lower (heat-transfer) section of the crystallizer.

Because many products are marketed today in the crystalline form and crystallization of different products requires special operating conditions, many types of crystallizers are on the market. From an operability viewpoint, crystallizers fall into one of the following types:

- Batch crystallizers, and
- Continuous crystallizers.

For a given processing input, the advantages of a continuous crystallizer over a batch one are:

- Less man work,
- Less supervision,
- Less operating cost,
- Higher energy efficiency,
- Less floor space requirement.

On the other hand, a batch crystallizer has the following advantages over a continuous one:

- Fewer problems with the high-purity feed,
- Less dependency on control and automation systems,
- More uniform crystals (smaller coefficient of variation, *CV*).

One of the general norms (criteria) for choosing a crystallizer, *no* matter what type, is how its mixer uniformly mixes the magma to create a homogeneous mixture. So, a good crystallizer has the next properties.

- It keeps crystals in contact with its mother liquid in all parts of the crystallizer body,
- It keeps crystals in suspension and movement in the crystallizer body,
- It prevents crystals from settling to the bottom of the crystallizer,
- It prevents crystals from accumulating in hidden locations,
- It equalizes concentration in the crystallizer body,
- It equalizes temperature in the crystallizer.

In addition, a good crystallizer is the one that

- Operates in a way that the supersaturation exists in the entire magma,
- Operates in a way that the Crystallization Law of crystal growth applies to the crystals.

As for the capacity to produce the crystals with the desired size and quality, crystallizers are mainly chosen based on the following:

- The required retention time, and
- The rate of the material under crystallization.

In one type of general classification, crystallizers are classified into three (3) classes:

- **Crystallizers with Internal Circulation:** In a crystallizer with internal circulation, a mixer mixes the entire magma in the entire body of the crystallizer.
- **Crystallizers with External Circulation:** In a crystallizer with external circulation (like a draft-tube-baffle crystallizer), a portion of the magma is continuously pumped out and back again to the crystallizer's body.
- **Crystallizers with Internal and External Circulation:** Such a crystallizer has both internal and external mixers, so known as the mixed-suspension, mixed-product-removal (MSMPR) crystallizers, and the process is called MSMPR crystallization.

In all types of circulating crystallizers, the speed and direction of rotation of the mixer's stirrer are usually chosen to achieve a good mixing because crystals tend to settle to the bottom of the crystallizer, where there may be a little or *no* chance of crystal growth. In addition, the magma leaving a crystallizer with a good mixing system is uniform so that the mother liquid can get to the state of saturation and supersaturation (the cause of crystal growth) easily. [The choice of a good mixing system in a crystallizer is particularly evident when a magma with high viscosity is under crystallization.]

Based on a broad classification, the following are the most important types of crystallizers: 1) Evaporative crystallizers, 2) Cooling crystallizers, and 3) Evaporative-cooling crystallizers.

[Because almost all crystallizers operate at negative vacuum pressure (P_{Vac}), except cooling crystallizers, the word **evaporative crystallizer** refers to the **vacuum-evaporative crystallizer**.]

2.1 EVAPORATIVE CRYSTALLIZERS

The evaporative (vacuum-evaporative) crystallizers can be further subclassified into

- Batch-Vacuum-Evaporative (BVE) Crystallizers
- Continuous-Vacuum-Evaporative (CVE) Crystallizers

Figure 6 shows a typical **BVE crystallizer**, which generally looks like a Robert evaporator. Such crystallizer consists of a closed cylindrical tank and some auxiliaries (attached and detached parts). The diameter of a BE crystallizer is typically 5 to 6 m, and its height is 5 to 7 m. A barometric condenser produces P_{Vac} to be used in the crystallizer. [P_{Vac} is maintained by a vacuum pump placed between the crystallizer and the condenser.] The tank of the crystallizer, which is also called the **crystallizer's body**, consists of two sections:

- **Steam Section** (steam chest)**:** The space for receiving steam or vapor.
- **Vapor Section:** The space above the feed for releasing vapor.

In the center of the heating section of a BE crystallizer, a wide **circulating pipe** (also called **draft pipe** or **downtake pipe**) 1.5 to 2 m in diameter (30 to 50% of the crystallizer diameter) is installed to circulate the magma (also called **massecuite**) Two perforated plates (called **tube plates**) are at a distance equal to the length of the **heating tubes**. One of the tube plates is welded horizontally to the outside diameter of the circulating pipe, and the other is welded to the inside diameter of the pipe. The tube plates have the same number of round holes as the number of **heating tubes** (1000 to 1500). The heating tubes are vertically rolled into the holes of the tube plates. For rolling, holes of the tube plates have a clearance of 0.25 mm, compared with the tubes' outside diameter. The inside diameter of the tubes is 100 to 120 mm (= 4 to 4.7 In) with a thickness of 1.5 mm. The heating tubes are wider than in the Robert evaporators to ease the magma circulation. Figure 7 shows the direction of steam, condensate, and noncondensing gases of a BVE (batch-vacuum-evaporative) crystallizer. And Figure 8 shows the cross-section of the heating tubes of the same crystallizer.

The bottom plate of the tube plates is placed above the base of the crystallizer to allow for the circulation of the magma. In addition to that, the circulating pipe and a stirrer improve the magma's circulation. The propeller of the stirrer is driven by a shaft connected to an electric motor. In general, propellers are driven from the top or bottom. Like the one shown in Figure 6, the top-driven stirrers have a suspended shaft. Size-wise, the stirrer diameter is close to the inside diameter of the circulating pipe.

In one design of BE crystallizers, like the one used in the sugar plants, the ratio of the heating surface area to the volume of the crystallizer is 4 to 6. These crystallizers are made with a capacity of 40 to 100 t feed. A crystallizer, say, 5 m (= 15 Ft) high and 4.5 m (= 13.5 Ft) in diameter, has a volume of 80 m^3 (= 2820 Ft^3). [The height of the feed is *not* held more than 2 m (= 6 Ft) above the upper plate of the **steam section** (the heating section of the crystallizer) to eliminate the carrying boiling material out of the crystallizer.] Deducting the volume of the space above the feed, which is used to release vapor and eliminate entrainment, from the total volume makes the useful volume of the crystallizer about 50 m^3 (= 1770 Ft^3). This is approximately 60% of the total volume of the crystallizer. Assume processing magma with a density of 1.5 t/m^3. This makes the crystallizer's useful capacity of about 75 t.

The discharge outlet at the bottom of the crystallizer has a hydraulic valve. At the top of the crystallizer, an entrainment separator removes water droplets from the vapor. Condensate is removed from the bottom by two ports. The vapor formed rises to the top and enters the condenser through a valve. If the magma creates NC gases (such as air, ammonia, and carbon dioxide gas), they are discharged from the bottom of the crystallizer.

The following are usually installed on the body of a crystallizer for different purposes:

- A simple refractometer to measure the concentration of the solution,
- A few sight glasses for observing the crystallization process,
- A special microscope to magnify the crystals, and
- A sampling valve for taking samples.

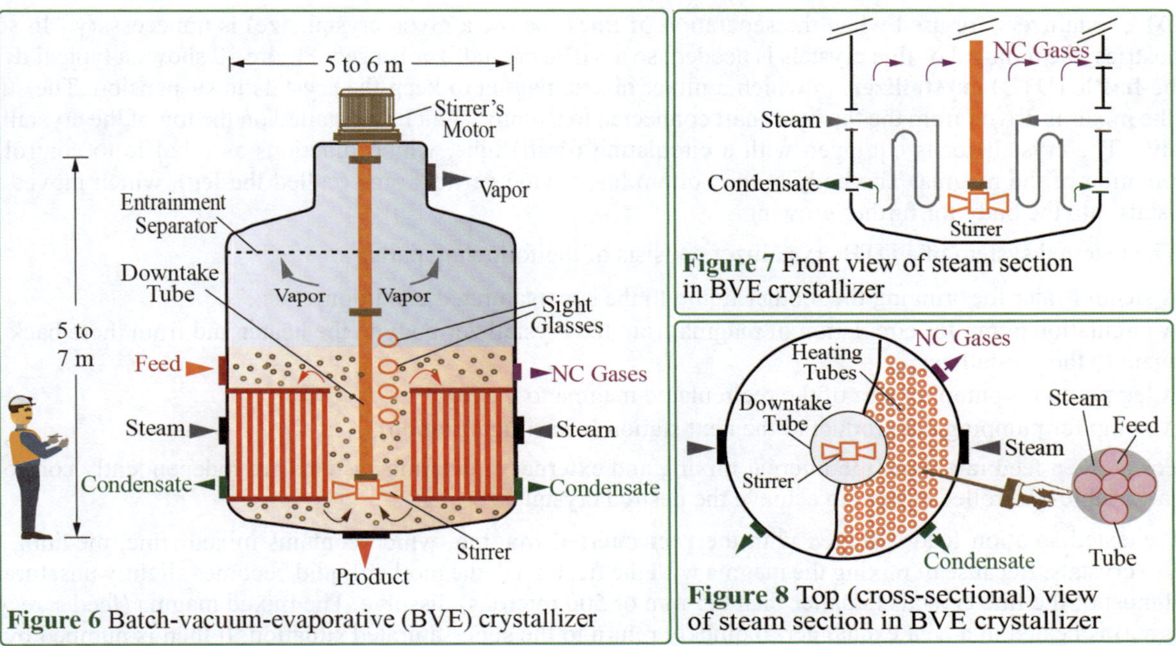

Figure 6 Batch-vacuum-evaporative (BVE) crystallizer

Figure 7 Front view of steam section in BVE crystallizer

Figure 8 Top (cross-sectional) view of steam section in BVE crystallizer

A thermometer is also installed above the heating section and another one at a full-crystallizer level to show the temperature of the boiling material and released vapor, respectively. A pressure gauge is also installed to indicate the vacuum pressure (P_{Vac}) of the upper part of the crystallizer. Steam injectors are also installed inside the crystallizer to clean after each strike.

The magma moves inside the heating tubes (with *no* direct contact with the steam) below and above the tube plates, flows downward in the circulating pipe to the bottom section, and moves upward in the tubes.

Steam is introduced into the steam section between the heating tubes. The heat from the steam passes through the tubes to the magma, evaporating water in quantity equal to the mass of the vapor produced and the steam condensed. The temperature difference between the steam and the magma causes evaporation.

In BE crystallizers, like the ones used in the sugar plants for the first-stage crystallization, solution feed enters the middle of the circulating pipe. At the end of the strike, the product magma is discharged from the bottom of the crystallizer. After being separated from the mother liquid (mother liquor) in a batch centrifuge, the crystals are dried and sold as the final product (the table sugar).

In summary, each strike of a batch operation systematically involves the following steps: 1) Crystallizer preparation, 2) Feed evaporation, 3) Seeding, 4) Crystal growing, 5) Charging more feed, 6) Concentrating mother liquid, 7) Discharging, and 8) Cleaning the crystallizer for the next strike.

Continuous-evaporative (CE) **crystallizers** are today's most-used crystallizers. They can be generally divided into the following major types: 1) Continuous-Evaporative-Single (CES) Crystallizers, and 2) Continuous-Evaporative-Chamber (CEC) Crystallizers.

Continuous-evaporative-single (CES) crystallizers are of the following types: 1) Draft-Tube (DT) Crystallizers, and 2) Draft-Tube-Baffle (DTB) Crystallizers.

Figure 9 shows a typical **draft-tube** (DT) **crystallizer** that operates in continuous mode. These crystallizers are used in the production of many organic and inorganic crystals, such as potassium chloride (KCl) and ammonium sulfate [$(NH_3)_2SO_4$]. Such substances can grow on the walls of the crystallizer and need long operating cycles. In such cases, the baffle is unnecessary, and the internal circulator is sized to have the minimum nucleation influence on the crystallization.

DT crystallizers are used when the separation of fines (below a given crystal size) is unnecessary. In some industries, the removal of fine crystals is needed, so a baffle crystallizer is used. Figure 10 shows a typical **draft-tube-baffle** (DTB) **crystallizer**, in which a mixer mixes magma to keep the crystals in suspension. The stirrer of the mixer is driven from the top by a shaft connected to a motor, which is installed on the top of the crystallizer body. The crystallizer is equipped with a circulating (draft) tube, which functions as a baffle to control the circulation of the magma. The body at the bottom has a wide vertical pipe (called the **leg**), which moves fine crystals into the body for further growing.

The external system of a DTB crystallizer consists of the following parts:

- A steam heater for bringing the mother liquid to the supersaturated condition;
- A circulation pump for circulation of magma from the crystallizer body to the heater and from there back again to the crystallizer;
- A leg pump for pumping part of the recirculated magma to the leg;
- A pump for pumping the product to the next station (centrifugal station).

For a given feed rate, both the internal mixing and external circulation systems are independently controlled by a variable-controlled system to achieve the desired crystal size.

Preheated solution feed is mixed with the **recirculated magma**, which contains mixed (fine, medium, and large) crystals. Because of mixing the magma with the fresh feed, the mother liquid becomes slightly unsaturated, and most of the fine crystals (smaller than 0.5 mm or 500 microns) dissolve. The mixed magma (feed + recycle magma) is heated in a heat exchanger to quickly return to the supersaturated situation. It then is pumped by the circulation pump to the crystallizer body at the top of the leg. And part of the mixed magma is pumped by the leg pump to the bottom of the leg. The leg acts as a crystal classifier because there is *no* stirrer in the leg, the larger crystals settle, and the fine ones move upward in the flowing stream of the mother liquid toward the top and enter the crystallizer body. All fine crystals pass the baffle, enter the recirculated line, and mix with the fresh feed. The whole described process continues until the magma product, pumped out of the crystallizer near the bottom of the leg, contains larger-desired-size crystals. The crystallizer product is then sent to the centrifugal (or filtration) station to separate the mother liquid. In some designs of DTB crystallizers, the leg has a baffle for better classification of the crystals.

Figure 11 shows an **evaporative-single** (ES) **crystallizer** that operates in continuous mode. In its simple design, the ES crystallizer body and its barometric condenser look like a batch-evaporative (BE) crystallizer, as discussed earlier.

In its vertical design, an **evaporative chamber** (EC) **crystallizer** (Figure 12) is used in the sugar industry to make sugar crystals. This crystallizer operates in continuous mode and has four separated chambers (compartments) installed on top of each other. Each chamber is a batch crystallizer with attached parts (valves, heating tubes, mixer, and more) and detached parts (supply pump and drive motor). The mixer of each chamber, which keeps the crystals in suspension and prevents them from settling, is driven from the top of the chamber by a shaft connected to a motor. The feed and external seed magma enter the top chamber and move by gravity to the chamber below. Finally, the product magma leaves from the bottom of the last chamber.

The EC continuous crystallizers are energy efficient because they use low-pressure steam. The separation of chambers allows any chamber to be bypassed for cleaning. During cleaning, the content of the dirty chamber is emptied into the chamber below, and a procedure like that for cleaning an evaporator (described under EVAPORATORS) is followed.

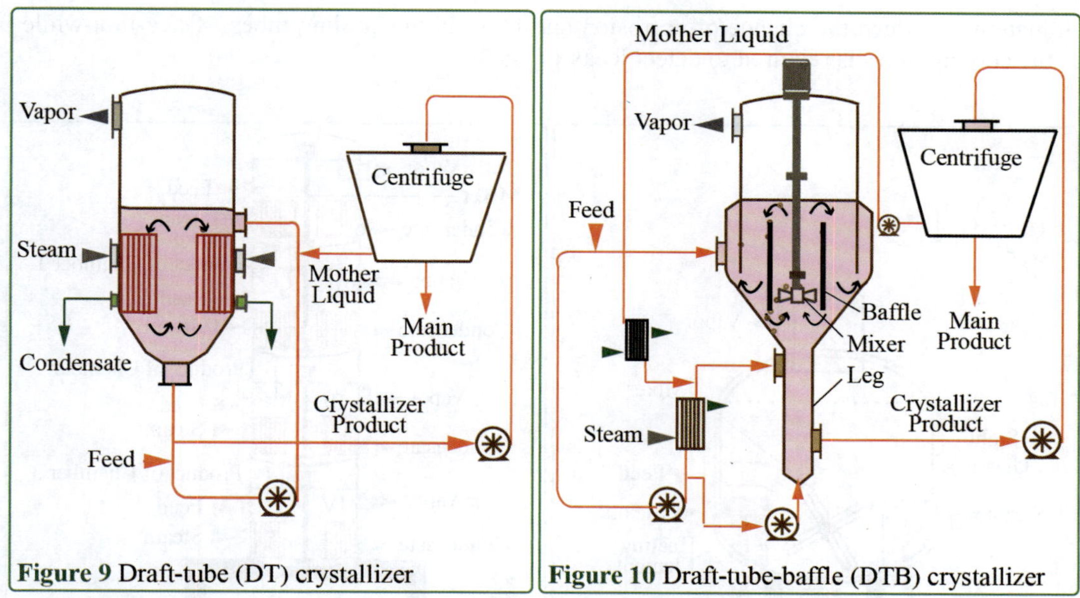

Figure 9 Draft-tube (DT) crystallizer

Figure 10 Draft-tube-baffle (DTB) crystallizer

2.2 COOLING CRYSTALLIZERS

Cooling crystallizers are used to complete the crystallization job by treating the hot magma dropped from an evaporative crystallizer. By gradually cooling the magma (crystals + mother liquid), supersaturation increases, and crystals grow larger. Like evaporative crystallizers, they are of two types; batch and continuous.

In a **batch-cooling** (BC) **crystallizer**, the hot magma stays in the crystallizer for some time (typically from 12 to 24 hours) under constant mixing until it gradually cools and crystallization is complete. Then it is pumped to the centrifugal (or filtration) station to separate the mother liquid from the crystals. The empty crystallizer is then refilled with a new batch of hot magma.

In a **continuous-cooling** (CC) **crystallizer**, the full capacity of the equipment is always used. Compared to batch type, a CC crystallizer is more controllable and less expensive to operate. CC crystallizers are of two types: Horizontal and vertical.

The hot magma enters the first tank in a **horizontal-continuous-cooling crystallizer**, usually consisting of a few U-shaped horizontal tanks (20 to 80 m^3 capacity) connected by chutes. A mixer, rotating about 1 R/min, gradually moves the magma to the succeeding tank. Consequently, the magma cools gradually on its way until it leaves the last compartment, from where it enters the distributor. The mixer in each tank helps the heat transfer and prevents crystals from settling. In some designs, the flow is divided into two parallel paths to improve the cooling effect. Cooling water that runs through cooling tubes moves counter (opposite) to the magma flow. Cooling water enters at the coldest end of the crystallizer and leaves the warmer end.

Some horizontal cooling crystallizers *cannot* handle viscous (stiff) magma because of limitations in the drive mechanism of their stirring elements. So, the magma's *DS* (dissolved solids) entering these crystallizers *cannot* be as high as required for optimum performance.

A **vertical-continuous-cooling crystallizer** (see Figure 13) requires less floor space for installation than a horizontal one. In a vertical cooling crystallizer, the magma is held at the lower-temperature end for a longer time in the cycle, so it cools faster. Typically, a vertical cooling crystallizer is 3 to 5 m in diameter with different heights to have a capacity of 100 to 300 m^3. This crystallizer contains two cooling elements. One is installed in the top half of the unit, and the other is in the bottom half. Cooling elements get the cooling water in series, with the top element receiving the coldest cooling water. [Water used for cooling crystallizers must be clean and free of contamination to reduce the chance of corrosion and leaks in the cooling tubes. Once-in-a-while pressure testing of the cooling tubes is required to detect leaks.]

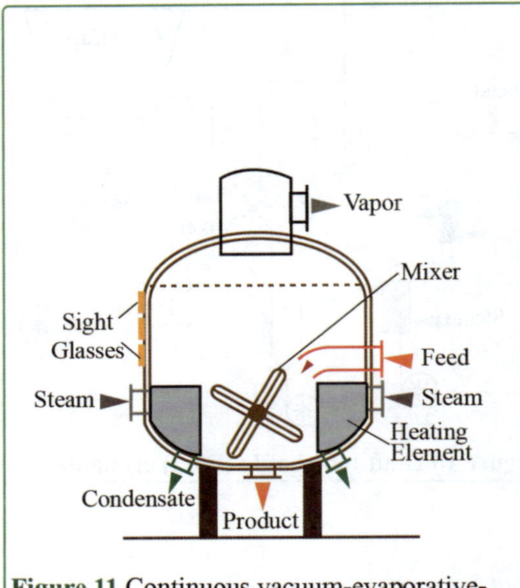

Figure 11 Continuous vacuum-evaporative-single (VES) crystallizer

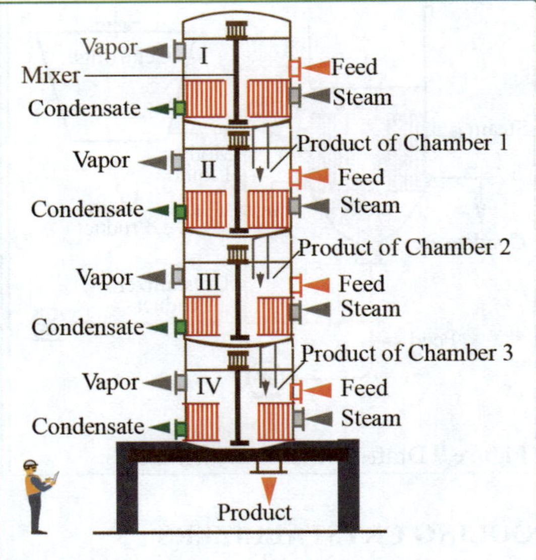

Figure 12 Continuous vacuum-evaporative-chamber (VEC) crystallizer

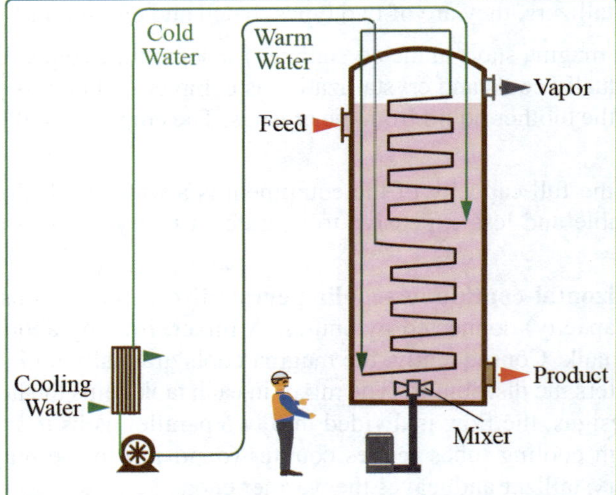

Figure 13 Cooling design in a vertical-continuous-cooling crystallizer

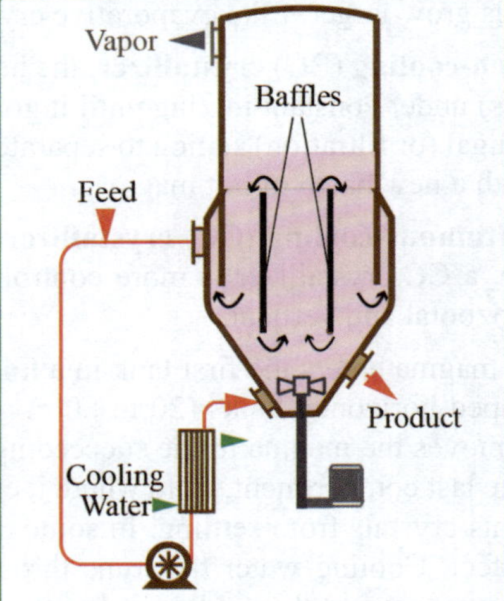

Figure 14 Draft-tube continuous cooling crystallizer with two baffles

A **draft-tube** (DT) **cooling crystallizer** with a baffle is shown in Figure 14. A draft-tube crystallizer is installed vertically and operates continuously. It has an internal circulation (with the help of a mixer) and external circulation (with the help of a pump) to move the magma throughout the crystallizer body. The mixer is driven from the bottom of the crystallizer by a shaft connected to a motor. In the external circulation, a portion of the hot magma is pumped to a heat exchanger to be partially cooled to increase supersaturation quickly. The magma is then recycled back to the crystallizer's evaporating body. Here, the magma moves upward at a low velocity so that large crystals can settle and return to the main circulation. At the same time, the fines are eventually destroyed by increasing or decreasing temperature, creating additional supersaturation.

Some cooling crystallizers have two counter-rotating mixers, which better suspend the crystals in the mother liquid (also called **mother liquor**).

2.3 OPERATING PROBLEMS IN RUNNING A CRYSTALLIZER

Most crystallizers operate under negative vacuum pressure (P_{Vac}). One of the main problems that can occur during the operation of a crystallizer is when the P_{Vac} in the crystallizer is insufficient. The P_{Vac}, usually maintained by the condensers, must be enough in each crystallizer. Low P_{Vac} in a crystallizer mainly occurs because of a leak. Leaks mainly occur because of corrosion. A suspect crystallizer must be checked for leak by a vacuum test. The test result should *not* be more than 10 kPa (about 70 mm Hg) in 60 minutes. This value is about 10 kPa in 30 minutes in older crystallizers.

Other causes of low P_{Vac} in a crystallizer are the following: 1) The vacuum pump does *not* work properly, 2) The cooling water in the condenser is *not* enough, 3) The cooling water temperature in the condenser is high, and 4) Leak in fittings (the attached parts) of the crystallizer or condenser.

C-174
CRYSTALLIZATION RATE

Crystallization rate (R_C, also called crystal growth rate, R_G) is the mass (M) of a solute crystallized on a crystal surface unit area in unit time. R_C is usually expressed in g.m^2/min. [Refer to the subtopic of Crystal Growth under CRYSTALLIZATION PROCESS for more information.]

C-175
CRYSTALLIZATION WATER

Crystallization water (also called **hydration water**) is the water (H_2O) present in a **crystalline compound** (crystal) in definite proportions. Some crystals contain one, two, or more molecules of H_2O per molecule of crystal. In the crystals of calcium sulfate dihydrate ($CaSO_4.2H_2O$, known as **gypsum**), for example, calcium sulfate holds two molecules of water. Crystals of $CaSO_4.2H_2O$ convert to $CaSO_4.H_2O$ (called the plaster of Paris) if heated to 128°C (262°F). And they become completely anhydrous if heated much higher than 128°. These types of chemical compounds are known as hydrates. The chemical formula of hydrates is written with a **centered dot** (•) to separate the compound from water.

C-176
CRYSTALLIZERS

Study CRYSTALLIZATION PROCESS AND CRYSTALLIZERS.

C-177
CRYSTALS

A crystal (crystalline solid) is a three-dimensional solid composed of atoms (or molecules) arranged in an organized and orderly-repeating pattern, known as the **crystal lattice structure** (simply the **crystal structure**).

The following are two special terms used in crystallography:

- **Crystal Habit:** This word indicates how a given crystal is formed.
- **Unit Cell:** This is the smallest pattern of atoms (or molecules) that can be repeated to form a crystal. The three (3) common unit cells are simple, faced, and body-centered units. As shown in Figure 1, a **simple unit** has atoms at the corner of the cell, a **faced-centered unit** has extra atoms in the center of the unit's surface, and a **body-centered unit** has an extra atom in its center.

A typical crystal has the following general properties:

- It has some flat surfaces, known as the crystal faces (simply **faces**).
- Each of its faces makes a definite angle, called the **facial angle**, with its neighboring faces,
- Its interatomic (or intermolecular) distances are constant and are specific to that substance's crystal.
- It grows in a supersaturated solution in a layer-by-layer way, like stacking many identical bricks on top and next to each other to build a cubic wall.
- All crystals of the same substance grow to have the same facial angles. All faces, however, may *not* have the same external appearance because different faces can grow at different rates, depending on the conditions under which the crystals grow.

Based on the shape of the faces and facial angles (angles between faces), crystals are classified into seven crystalline systems: cubic, rhombic, rhombohedral, tetragonal, hexagonal, monoclinic, and triclinic. [Note: A given substance may crystallize in one, two, or more types, depending on the crystallization conditions.]

Coordinating Model: To easier describe the generalities of the crystal types, it is better to choose a coordinating model for a cubic crystal (with six faces), as shown in Figure 2, and assume that it was grown under ideal conditions, so it maintained its geometric similarity during growth. This model can then be used to easily describe the structure of all types of crystals and their general properties.

Three vectors can define the model: A (the horizontal vector), B (the vertical vector), and C (back vector). Vectors represent the **faces** of the crystalline model in 3-dimensional directions (X, Y, and Z), as is usual in Physics. Vector A represents the length of the crystal along the X-axes from the origin to the edge of the crystal. Vector B and C are defined similarly along the axes Y and Z, respectively. And finally, there are three (3) **facial angles** (shown by α, β, and γ), which are the angles between the vectors (between the crystal faces). Angle α is between vectors A and B, angle β is between A and C, and angle γ is between B and C.

Figure 3 shows a salt crystal, with chlorine anions (Cl^-) at four corners and sodium cations (Na^+) at alternating corners of the cube. In general, a cubic crystal can be described as $A = B = C$, and $\alpha = \beta = \gamma = 90^o$.

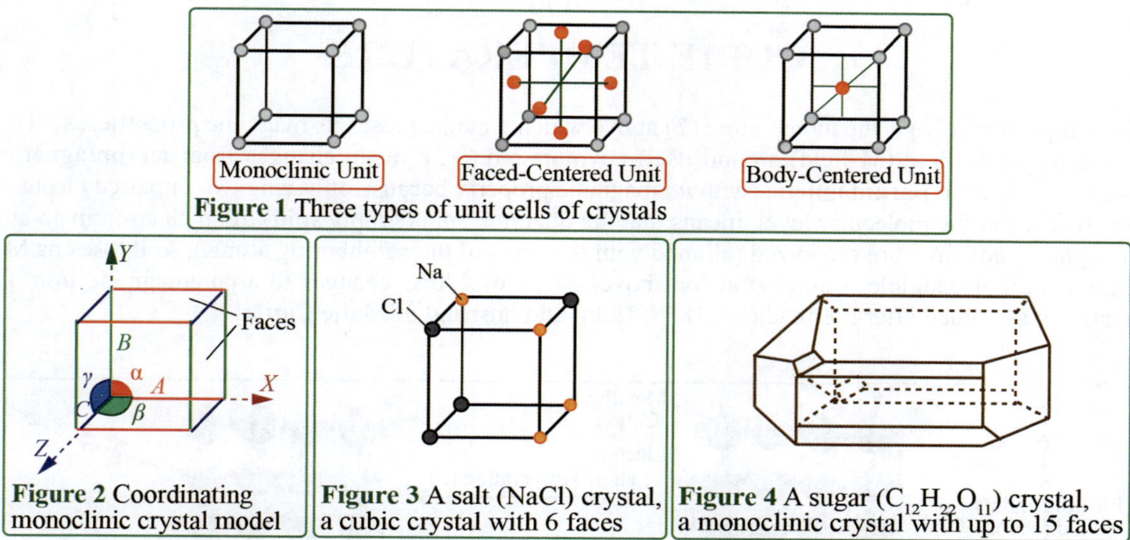

Figure 1 Three types of unit cells of crystals

Figure 2 Coordinating monoclinic crystal model

Figure 3 A salt (NaCl) crystal, a cubic crystal with 6 faces

Figure 4 A sugar ($C_{12}H_{22}O_{11}$) crystal, a monoclinic crystal with up to 15 faces

Figure 4 shows a sugar crystal grown under ideal conditions. Sugar has a monoclinic crystal with up to 15 faces. A monoclinic crystal can be described as $A \# B \# C$, $\alpha = \beta = 90°$, and $\gamma \neq 90°$. Thus, a sugar crystal has unequal lengths ($A \neq B \neq C$) with one symmetrical vector (vector A), so it makes a 90° angle with the other two vectors (B and C), so $\alpha = \beta = 90°$. And γ is equal to 103° 30'.

Based on our coordinating model, the seven crystal types can be described in the following ways:

- Cubic: $A = B = C$, and $\alpha = \beta = \gamma = 90°$
- Rhombic: $A \# B \# C$, and $\alpha = \beta = \gamma = 90°$
- Rhombohedral: $A = B = C$, and $\alpha = \beta = \gamma \# 90°$ (but < 120°)
- Tetragonal: $A = C \# B$, and $\alpha = \beta = \gamma = 90°$
- Hexagonal: $A = C, B \# C$, $\alpha = \gamma = 90°$, and $\beta = 120°$
- Monoclinic: $A \# B \# C$, $\alpha = \beta = 90°$, and $\gamma \neq 90°$
- Triclinic: $A \# B \# C$, and $\alpha = \beta = \gamma \# 90°$

As can be seen, each type is characterized based on the following: 1) Relative length of axes; for example, for cubic type $A = B = C$. 2) Interfacial angles; for example, for cubic type $\alpha = \beta = \gamma = 90°$. 3) The width-to-height ratio of each face; for example, this ratio in a sugar crystal is about 1.6 to 1, and it can get up to 4 to 1 in an elongated sugar crystal, which is unusually wide.

Based on the dominant type of chemical bond to hold the crystal together, crystals (crystalline solids) can be divided into four (4) classes:

- **Covalent Crystals:** In covalent crystals, covalent bonding can form between the atoms of the same element (such as the carbon atoms of the diamond) or between atoms of different elements (like silicon atoms and oxygen atoms). Covalent bonds join nonmetals to nonmetals.
- **Ionic Crystals:** In ionic crystals, which join a metal to a nonmetal, ionic bonding forms when electrons are given by atoms of one element and gained by atoms of another element. Say, sodium and chlorine combine to form ionically bonded sodium chloride (NaCl), as shown in Figure 2 under CHEMICAL BONDS.
- **Molecular Crystals:** In molecular crystals, bonds are between molecules and atoms. Ice has such bonds.
- **Metallic Crystals:** Metallic bonding forms between valence electrons and the metal atoms in metallic crystals. It is the sharing of many electrons between many positive ions, where the electrons act as a glue to give the metal a solid structure (see Figure 4 under CHEMICAL BONDS).

C-178

CURIE TEMPERATURE

Curie temperature (T_C) is the temperature (T) above which a magnet loses its magnetic properties, so it *cannot* produce a magnetic field (M-field) around itself anymore. At T_C, a metal changes from **ferromagnetic** (can produce an M-field) to **paramagnetic** (with *no* magnetic property because of having two unpaired electrons per molecule). This, at the molecular level, means that the quantum spin (simply **spin**) of an electron in an atom of a paramagnet is *not* anymore organized (aligned with the spins of the neighboring atoms), so it loses its M-field (see Figure 1). For example, iron (Fe) at (or above) its T_C of 770°C changes to a paramagnetic iron. [Curie temperature was named after Pierre Curie (1858–1906) and husband of Marie Curie.]

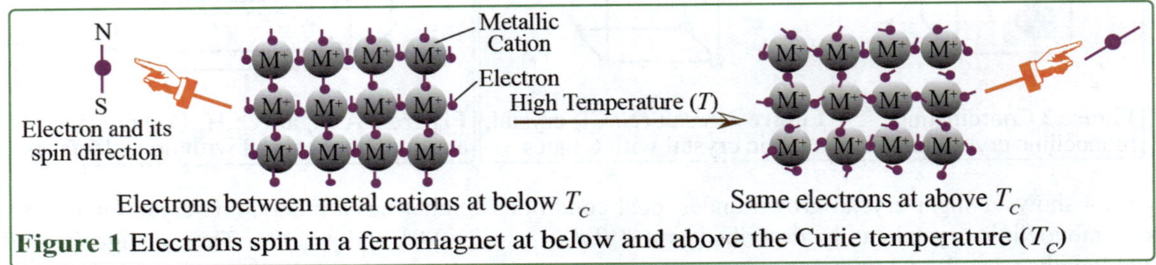

Figure 1 Electrons spin in a ferromagnet at below and above the Curie temperature (T_C)

C-179

CURRENT

Simplified name for ELECTRIC CURRENT.

C-180

CURRENT DENSITY

Simplified name for ELECTRIC CURRENT DENSITY.

C-181

CURVATURE OF SPACETIME

Discussed under EINSTEIN'S THEORIES OF RELATIVITY.

C-182

CYCLONES

Simplified name for **gas cyclones**. They are discussed under PARTICULATE REMOVING DEVICES.

D Section

LIST OF TOPICS

1. Dalton's Law of Partial Pressure
2. Darcy-Weisbach Equation and Friction Factor
3. Dark Energy and Dark Matter
4. Decantation Process and Decanters
5. Decay Process
6. Decomposition Reactions
7. Definite Composition and Multiple Composition Laws
8. Defoamers
9. Deformation of Material
10. Degrees of Freedom
11. Dehydration Reactions
12. Deionized Water
13. Density and its Forms
14. Derivation and Integration
15. Desiccation Process
16. Detached Parts
17. Detergents
18. Deuterium
19. Devices
20. Dew Point Calculations
21. Dew Point Pressure
22. Dew Point Temperature
23. Dialysis Process
24. Diesel Fuel
25. Differentiation
26. Diffusion Coefficient
27. Diffusion Pressure Deficit
28. Diffusion Process
29. Diffusivity Coefficient
30. Diffusivity Flux
31. Diffusivity Flux Rate
32. Dimension and Dimensional Analysis
33. Direct Current
34. Discharge Head
35. Dispersions
36. Dissolved Solid Substances
37. Dissolved Substances
38. Distance and Displacement
39. Distillate Reflux
40. Distillation Columns
41. Distillation Process
42. Distilled Water
43. Distribution Coefficient
44. DNA and RNA
45. Donnan Membrane Effect
46. Draft
47. Drag Coefficient
48. Drag Force
49. Drams
50. Dry Air
51. Dry Bulb Temperature
52. Dry Bulb Thermometer
53. Dry Steam
54. Dry Substances
55. Dryers
56. Drying Process
57. Ductility
58. Dust
59. Dynamic Viscosity
60. Dynamics

D-1

DALTON'S LAW OF PARTIAL PRESSURE

Study PARTIAL PRESSURE AND DALTON'S LAW OF PARTIAL PRESSURE.

D-2

DARCY-WEISBACH EQUATION AND FRICTION FACTOR

Darcy-Weisbach Equation: The Darcy-Weisbach equation (also called **Darcy-Weisbach head-loss equation**) is used in piping-system subjects to calculate a flowing liquid's head loss (h_L) in a pipe related to the friction (f) that exists in that pipe.

$$h_L = \frac{f_D.L.V^2}{d.a_g} \quad (1)$$

When L (the pipe's length) is in m (meter), V (the liquid's average velocity or half of its maximum velocity) is in m/s, d (the pipe's diameter) is in m, and a_g (gravitational acceleration of the flowing liquid) is in m/s^2, the h_L becomes in m. The term f_D (a unitless quantity) in the equation is the **Darcy-Weisbach friction factor**

Darcy-Weisbach Friction Factor (simply **Darcy friction factor**)**:** The Darcy friction factor (f_D, a unitless quantity) signifies resistance caused by the wall of a pipe when a viscous liquid flows through it. The f_D depends on a flow's Reynold number and the pipe's roughness. [The Fanning friction factor (f_f) and Darcy-Weisbach friction factor (f_D) are two important friction factors. The f_D is 4 times the f_F.]

D-3

DARK ENERGY

Discussed under the topic of ENERGY AND ITS FORMS.

D-4

DARK MATTER AND BARYONIC MATTER

Dark Matter: Dark matter is a hypothetical (unseen) form of matter that, according to cosmophysicists, accounts for about 85% of the matter in the Universe and about 27% of the Universe's energy density. [It is called **dark matter** because it does *not* interact with the electromagnetic field (EM-field), which means it does *not* absorb, release, or reflect light or other electromagnetic radiations (EM-radiations) and is, therefore, difficult to detect (identify).]

The main evidence for dark matter is calculations that physicists conducted to prove that many galaxies would decompose (or would *not* have formed) if they would *not* contain a large amount of dark matter. [The latest cosmological model says that the total mass-energy of the Universe contains 27% dark matter, 5% baryonic (ordinary) matter, and 68% dark energy.]

Baryonic Matter: Baryonic matter (also called ordinary matter) is the ordinary matter that is composed mainly of baryons and is experienced in everyday life. Cosmophysicists' calculations indicate that 5% of the universal matter is in the form of baryonic matter.

D-5

DECANTATION PROCESS AND DECANTERS

The decantation process is another name for SEDIMENTATION PROCESS. And decanters is another name for CLARIFIERS.

D-6

DECAY PROCESS

Study NUCLEAR DECAY PROCESS.

D-7

DEFINITE COMPOSITION AND MULTIPLE COMPOSITION LAWS

Study LAWS OF DEFINITE COMPOSITION AND MULTIPLE COMPOSITION.

D-8

DECOMPOSITION REACTIONS

Defined under CHEMICAL REACTIONS.

D-9

DEFOAMERS

Study FOAM AND DEFOAMERS.

D-10

DEFORMATION OF MATERIAL

In Physics, the deformation of a material is the change that happens in its shape as its atoms or molecules become stretched and rearranged. The extent of deformation in a material is proportional to the force (F) applied to that material (Hooke's Law). The two important types of deformation are:

- **Elastic Deformation** (elastic strain)**:** This is a material's temporary alteration, returning to its original shape once F is removed. A spring, for example, bounces back after being stretched.
- **Plastic Deformation:** This is a material's permanent alteration, so it does *not* return to its original shape.

[Material engineers use the words **elastic deformation** and **elastic strain** equally. They consider strain the measure of deformation in a material's length (L). When a strain (deformation) occurs in a material, they say that the material is under **stress** (load), so stress is the cause of strain.]

D-11

DEGREES OF FREEDOM

Discussed under PHASE RULE.

D-12

DEHYDRATION REACTIONS

Defined under CHEMICAL REACTIONS.

D-13

DEIONIZED WATER

Deionized water (DI water or soft water) is pure water prepared by one of the following three techniques:

- Distillation process,
- Reverse osmosis process, or
- Ion exchange resin chromatographic process.

[The distillation process produces the distilled water, and both the reverse osmosis process and ion exchange process produce the **deionized** (DI) **water**.]

Water quality is determined by its scale-causing salts (**limesalt hardness** or simply **hardness**) content. To specify the amount of hardness in water, its electric conductance (K_E, the ability to carry electric current) is measured. The city water and well water usually have high K_E (because they contain a considerable amount of Ca and Mg salts), so they are characterized as hard water. Boiling hard water precipitates calcium carbonate (CO_3Ca) and magnesium carbonate (CO_3Ca), which are *not* desired. Thus, hard water *cannot* be used in a steam boiler as feedwater or in a laboratory as reagent water unless treated by one of the above-listed techniques.

D-14

DENSITY AND ITS FORMS

Density

As a physical quantity, the density (*D*, its complete name is **volumetric mass density**) of a chemical compound (simply **compound**) is its mass (*M*) per its volume (*V*) at a specified temperature (*T*) and pressure (*P*).

$$D = \frac{M}{V} \tag{1}$$

M may be in kilograms (kg) or pounds (Lb), and *V* may be in cubic meters (m^3) or cubic feet (Ft^3). Thus, the SI unit of density is kg/m^3, and its US unit is Lb/Ft^3. For example, the density of water at 4°C is 1000 kg/m^3 (= 62.4 Lb/Ft^3), and that of mercury (Hg) is 13600 kg/m^3 (= 868.6 Lb/Ft^3). We say that mercury is denser (has greater density) than water.

We think of *D* as the **lightness** or **heaviness** of the same-size systems so that it can compare the masses of two compounds with the same *V*. For example, *D* of iron (Fe) is greater than aluminum (Al) because the *M* of 1 m^3 of Fe is more than 1 m^3 of Al, as shown in Figure 1.

Two important properties of density are outlined next.

- It is usually given at STP (standard temperature and pressure), and
- Materials with a more compact molecular structure have a higher density.

In general, a substance in its solid form is denser than in its liquid form. [Water (H_2O) is an exception. Solid water (the ice) is much less dense than water, so ice cubes always stay at the top of a glass of water. The D of warmer water is less than colder water. This behavior continues until it reaches 4°C. At below 4°C, water becomes less dense as it freezes (see Figure 2).] Figure 3 shows the dependency of the air's D on its T.

The D of a liquid sample can be determined by **pycnometer** as

- Determine the M (mass) of the empty pycnometer (M_1) at 20°C,
- Fill it to the top of the capillary with the sample,
- Determine the M of the filled pycnometer (M_2),
- Obtain the M of the sample by subtraction $M_2 - M_1$,
- Rinse pycnometer with deionized (DI) water, fill it again, and weigh it (M_3),
- The M of the water (which equates to its V) is equal to $M_3 - M_1$, and
- Divide the M of the sample ($M_2 - M_1$) by the V of water ($M_3 - M_1$) to determine the liquid D.

Density has different forms, bulk density, particle density, molar density, gas density, and specific density.

Bulk Density

Bulk density (D_B) is the density (D) of a bulk solid (a solid of many particles). D_B is given as the M of a bulk solid divided by the particles' total V, where the total V equates to the V of the particles and the empty spaces (void fraction) between them. Knowing the following points is important:

- D_B is an approximate density (because different-sized particles create different void spaces.)
- Because the D_B considers the empty spaces between the particles and different-sized particles occupy different empty spaces, we can say that the larger the particles, the larger the empty spaces and, consequently, the smaller the D_B of the material. Similarly, the finer the particles, the larger the D_B of the material.

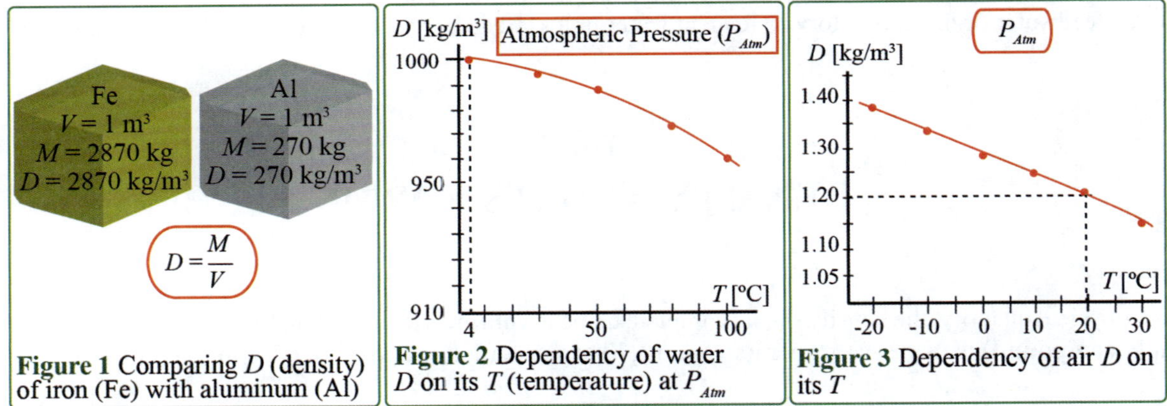

Figure 1 Comparing D (density) of iron (Fe) with aluminum (Al)

Figure 2 Dependency of water D on its T (temperature) at P_{Atm}

Figure 3 Dependency of air D on its T

Particle Density

Particle density (D_P) is the density of one particle of a solid material. The D_P does *not* consider empty spaces between the particles, so its value for a given solid is correct and greater than D_B. [Instead of particle density, **crystalline density** is used when the solid substance is in the crystalline form, like a sugar crystal.

Void fraction ($\mathcal{E}_F$, also called porosity) is related to D_B and D_P in the following way:

$$D_B = D_P(1 - \mathcal{E}_F) \qquad (2)$$

$$\mathcal{E}_F = 1 - \frac{D_B}{D_P} \quad (3)$$

As example, the D_B of fine-size sugar crystals is about 880 kg/m^3 (= 55 Lb/Ft^3), that of medium-size sugar crystals is 860 kg/m^3 (= 54 Lb/Ft^3), and that of coarse sugar is 840 kg/m^3 (= 52 Lb/Ft^3). The D_P of a sugar crystal is 1588 kg/m^3 (= 99.2 Lb/Ft^3).

Using the D_B of medium-size sugar and the D_P of sugar in Equation 3, the $\mathcal{E}_F$ becomes 0.46. Thus, empty spaces occupy 46% of the medium-size bulk sugar. The $\mathcal{E}_F$ is highest with a bed of uniformly sized particles. [In the filtration process and centrifugal process, high $\mathcal{E}_F$ (void spaces or porosity) between molecules of bulk material are advantageous. Instead, in the **packing process** and **storing process**, a low $\mathcal{E}_F$ is advantageous (because the material occupies less packing area).]

Molar Density

The molar density (D_n) of a substance is the mass (M) of one mole (n) of that substance divided by its volume (V). D_n is given in mole/m^3 (mole per cubic meter). For example, the D_n of sugar crystal (with a molar mass of 342 g/mole) is 0.342 mole/m^3. The D_n is expressed as

$$D_n = \frac{n}{V} \quad (4)$$

The D_n of a substance can also be expressed as its D (density) divided by its M_n (molar mass).

$$D_n = \frac{D}{M_n} \quad (5)$$

To find the D_n of an ideal gas, we can substitute the term $D_n.V$ from Equation 4 for n in the ideal-gas equation ($P.V = n.R.T$).

$$P.V = D_n.V.R.T \quad (6)$$

$$D_n = \frac{P}{R.T} \quad (7)$$

In this equation, the P is for the pressure (in Atm) of the gas, T is for its temperature (in K), and R is the gas constant (0.0821 Atm.L/mole.K), giving D_n of the gas in mole/L.

Gas Density

The density of a gas is the product of its molar density (D_n) multiplied by its molar mass (M_n).

$$D = D_n.M_n \quad (8)$$

To find the D of an ideal gas, we can combine this equation with Equation 7.

$$D = \frac{P}{R.T} M_n = \frac{P.M_n}{R.T} \quad (9)$$

This equation (the **modified-ideal-gas law**, see GAS LAWS) calculates the D of an ideal gas. It could also be used for a liquid if its D is assumed to be constant.

[Note 1: Because the density of gases is small, it is usually expressed in g/L. For example, the density of hydrogen is 0.09 g/L.] [Note 2: The density of gases is more affected by temperature (T) and pressure (P) than the D of liquids and solids, as shown in Figures 2 and 3.] [Note 3: Warm air is less dense than cold air. This is why hot air in a balloon takes its passengers up to the sky.]

Example 1 on Gas Density

Calculate the volume (V) occupied by CO_2 gas (with a molar mass of 44 g/mole) at 20ºC and 1 Atm, and its density (D)

We can find the V of the gas from the ideal gas equation ($PV = n.R.T$) and use that to calculate the gas D.

$$V = \frac{n.R.T}{P} = \frac{1\times0.0821(20+273)}{1} = 24\text{ L} \qquad D = \frac{P.M_n}{R.T} = \frac{1\times44}{0.0821\times293} = 1.8\text{ g/L}$$

The V of 1 mole CO_2 increased from 22.4 to 24 L when its P was kept constant at standard (1 Atm), but its T was increased from zero (standard T) to 20ºC. [Note that this increase in V from 22.4 to 24 L applies to any gas under the same conditions.]

Example 2 on Gas Density

Calculate the molar density (D_n) of methane (CH_4, with a molar mass, M_n, of 16 g/mole(at STP and its D.

The D_n and D of the methane at standard temperature (T = 0ºC = 273K) and pressure (1 Atm) are

$$D_n = \frac{P}{R.T} = \frac{1}{0.08205 \times 273} = 0.0446 \text{ mole/L} \qquad D = D_n . M_n = 0.0446 \times 16 = 0.714 \text{ g/L}$$

Note that we can also calculate the density of a gas by using the molar volume (the volume of one mole) at STP, which is 22.4 L for any gas, as a conversion factor.

$$D = 16 \times \frac{1}{22.4} = 0.714 \text{ (g/}\cancel{\text{mole}}\text{)(}\cancel{\text{mole}}\text{/L)} = \text{g/L}$$

The density of methane is lower than that of dry air. Dry air density at STP is 1.2 g/L.

Specific Density

Specific density (D_{Sp}, also called **specific gravity**) is the density (D) of a **liquid** or a **solid** to the density of **water** at 4°C temperature. [D of water at 4°C is 1000 kg/m^3 (= 62.4 Lb/Ft^3).]

Standard references are different for different phases, as outlined next.

- For solids and liquids, water is the standard reference. For example, D of mercury (Hg) is 13600 kg/m3 (= 868.6 Lb/Ft3), so the SI unit of D_{Sp} of mercury becomes 13600/1000 = 13.6, which equates to 868.6/62.4 = 13.9 in US units. Water D_{Sp} in both units equates to one.
- For gases, air (refers to dry air, whose D is 1.2 kg/m3 = 0.075 Lb/Ft3) is the reference substance.

The specific density (D_{Sp}) of a gas is its density (D) divided by the hydrogen density (0.09 g/L), used as standard, at the same temperature (T). In another context, it is the molar mass (M_n) of a gas divided by the M_n of hydrogen (H_2). Hydrogen's M_n is 2 g/mole, so its D_{Sp} is 2/2 = 1. Similarly, the M_n of water vapor (H_2O) is 18 g/mole, so its D_{Sp} is 18/2 = 9. The M_n of oxygen (O_2) is 32 g/mole, so its D_{Sp} is 32/2 = 16. And the air's M_n is 29 g/mole, so its D_{Sp} is 29/2 = 14.5. Specific density (D_{Sp}) is a dimensionless quantity (unitless) expressing the ratio of two values with identical units.

Knowing the following about D_{Sp} is also helpful:

- Sometimes, the **specific density** (D_{Sp}) of a gas is given in relation to air. The air's M_n is 29 g/mole, so its D_{Sp} is one. Similarly, the M_n of oxygen (O_2) is 32 g/mole, so its D_{Sp}, in relation to air, is 32/29 = 1.1.
- The D_{Sp} is a **unitless** quantity (as it is the ratio of two densities), so a substance's D_{Sp} numerically equates to its D.

Relative Density

Relative density (D_{Rel}; formerly called **specific gravity**) is the ratio of a substance's density (D) to the density of a reference substance at the same temperature (T). Water at 4°C is the reference substance of liquids and solids. Thus, for liquids and solids, the D_{Rel} and D_{Sp} are the same. And dry air is the reference substance for gases.

[The D_{Rel} is a **unitless** quantity (without unit) because it is the ratio of two numbers having identical units. So, the D_{Rel} of a substance numerically equates to its density.]

D-15

DERIVATION AND INTEGRATION

Derivation and integration are mathematical procedures used in **calculus** for solving some functions (equations), such as linear, quadratic, curve, trigonometric, logarithmic, and many more functions. Before getting to the details of derivation and integration (together **calculus**), it is helpful to be aware of the following generalities about them:

- **Calculus** calculates a variable quantity at a **changing rate**, while **algebra** calculates a variable quantity at an **unchanging rate** (it either does *not* change or changes at a **constant rate**).
- In **calculus**, a **tiny** (infinitesimal) **change** of variable x is shown by dx (reads derivative of x or d form of x). In **algebra**, a **normal change** (small or large, but *not* tiny) of variable x is often shown by Δx (reads delta x or Δ form of x). A normal change in algebra is also called **final-minus-initial change**.
- The word **tiny** or **infinitesimal**, used in integral and differential subjects, refers to when a variable quantity is minimized to approach zero (shown by $\rightarrow 0$) but *not* equal to zero. [Although a derivative value is tiny (extremely small), it can represent a large action. For example, dL (differential length) can represent a large distance over which a rocket travels in the sky to hit a target.]
- Solve a derivative function; it must be integrated.
- Integration is the reverse of derivation.

DERIVATION

Derivation (differentiation) is the process of finding the **derivative** (origin) of a function when the function **changes** by a **tiny** (infinitesimal) amount. The derivation of a function is the slope (S, steepness, the rise-to-run ratio) of that function, anywhere the function is well behaved. A function is well behaved in an area where an appropriate slope exists at every point of that area. For example, an appropriate slope exists at any point on a **linear function** (like $y = 2x$) or a point on a **curved function** (like $y = x^2$). Thus, the words **derivation** and **slope** are used in calculus equally.

Slope (S) is the ratio of the derivative of the rise (dy) to the derivative of the run (dx) of a linear line (straight line or simply **line**) or a curved line (simply **curve**).

$$S = \frac{dy}{dx}$$

The letter d used here is the symbol for derivation, and dy/dx (reads *dee y dee x*) is the derivative (the slope) of y (the dependent variable) to x (the independent variable). Because the slope is a ratio and derivation is a slope, a differential (derivative) equation expresses a function's **rate** of change when the function changes by a tiny amount. Thus, a derivation indicates the **rate** of change of a quantity. The rate of change of position is speed. And the rate of change in speed is acceleration. This, however, is *not* a complete definition of derivation because its proper definition, as you will study later, must include the word limit ($\lim \rightarrow 0$).

In **algebra**, to find the slope of a curve at a point, we need two points on that curve. This can be seen in Figure 1, which shows the value table and graph (chart) for the curve $y = x^2$. To find the slope at point P on this curve, you must follow the next general steps:

- Draw a straight line to connect point P to the X-axis,
- Pick another point (Q) on the curve and draw a straight line to connect the point Q to the X-axis,
- Show the first point on the X-axis by x and the second point by $x + L$, so the difference between these two points equates to L.
- Show the y value for x as $f(x)$ and the y value for $x + L$ as $f(x + L)$.
- Use the x and y values in the slope (S) equation to find the slope at point P.

$$S = \frac{y_2 - y_1}{x_2 - x_1} = \frac{f(x+L) - f(x)}{x + L - x} = \frac{f(x+L) - f(x)}{L}$$

This equation, which gives the difference in the y_2 and y_1 over L, is the slope for the line PQ, called the **normal line** (see Figure 1), at the point P. This, however, is a rough estimate for the slope for the curve $y = x^2$ at point P (because the line PQ is a straight line). The exact determination of the slope is possible with the use of calculus, as discussed next.

In **calculus**, to find the exact slope of a curve at a point, we must proceed differentially by narrowing L to a very close-to-zero value (the *closer* the L value gets to zero, the *more* accurate is the slope at the desired point). To do so, we must make L infinitely smaller by taking the limit as L approaches zero. In the **limit**, when L approaches zero, the **normal line** becomes a **tangent line** (a line that barely touches a curve at a point and has the same slope as the curve at that point). A tangent line is shown in Figure 2. The limit of a normal line's slope is the tangent line's slope. Thus, we can find the tangent line's slope (which has the same slope as our curve at point P) by using the next version of the previous equation.

$$S = y' = \frac{dy}{dx} = \lim_{L \to 0} \frac{f(x+L) - f(x)}{L}$$

In this equation (the **derivative equation**), the symbols *y*' and *dy*/*dx* are equally used for *S*, and the symbol $L \to 0$ refers to when a quantity is minimized to approach zero but *not* equal to zero. This applies to the word **infinitesimal** (tiny), which is often used in derivation to refer to a tiny amount of a quantity, but *not* zero. It is usually shown as $\to 0$. [The slope of a **curved line** (simply **curve**) changes if we choose different points on that curve, so the curved-line slope is a variable quantity.]

To see how the **derivative equation** works, we use it to find the derivation of the curve $y = 3x^2 + 2$.

$$y' = \lim_{L \to 0} \frac{3(x+L)^2 + 2 - (3x^2 + 2)}{L} = \lim_{L \to 0} \frac{3(x^2 + L^2 + 2xL) + 2 - 3x^2 - 2}{L}$$

$$y' = \lim_{L \to 0} \frac{6Lx + 3L^2}{L} = \lim_{L \to 0} \frac{L(6x + 3L)}{L} = \lim_{L \to 0} (6x + 3L)$$

At $L = 0$, the answer is $y' = 6x$.

The derivative operations could be shorter if we used the derivation rules. For example, we can solve $y = 3x^2 + 2$ by derivation **power rule** ($x^n = n.x^{n-1}$) and find the answer as $3 \times 2x^{2-1} = 6x$, faster.

Basic Derivation Rules

Constant Rule:

$$y = c \quad \to \quad y' = 0$$
$$y = 2 \quad \to \quad y' = 0$$

Power Rule:

$$y = cx^n \quad \to \quad y' = c.n.x^{n-1}$$

Examples:

$$y = 2x \quad \to \quad y' = 2 \times 1 \times x^{1-1} = 2x^0 = 2$$
$$y = 2x^3 + 3x^2 - 4x + 5 \qquad y' = 2 \times 3x^{3-1} + 3 \times 2x^{2-1} - 4 + 0 = 6x^2 + 6x - 4$$

Sum Rule:

$$y = gx + hx \quad \to \quad y' = g'x + h'x$$
$$y = gx - hx \quad \to \quad y' = g'x - h'x$$

Examples:

$$y = 2x^3 - 3x^2 + 4x \rightarrow \quad y' = 6x^2 - 6x + 4$$

$$y = \sin x - \cos x \quad \rightarrow \quad y' = \cos x - (-\sin x) = \cos x + \sin x$$

Product Rule:

$$y = gx.hx \quad \rightarrow \quad y' = gx.h'x + hx.g'x$$

In words, the product rule is "first × *d* (second) + second × *d* (first)," where *d* is for derivative.

Example:

$$y = (x^2 + 2)(x^3 + x) \rightarrow y' = (x^2 + 2)(3x^2 + 1) + (x^3 + x)(2x) = 5x^4 + 9x^2 + 2$$

Quotient Rule:

$$y = \frac{gx}{hx} \quad \rightarrow \quad y' = \frac{hx.g'x - gx.h'x}{[h(x)]^2}$$

You may better remember the shortcut for differentiating a quotient (fraction).

$$y = \frac{gx}{hx} \quad \rightarrow \quad y' = \frac{\text{LowdHi} - \text{HighdLo}}{\text{Low.Low}}$$

In this equation, *d* is for derivative, *Hi* is for high, and *Lo* is for low. Study the next two examples.

$$y = \frac{x^2+1}{3x-2} \quad \rightarrow \quad y' = \frac{(3x-2)(2x)-(x^2+1)(3)}{(3x-2)^2} = \frac{3x^2-4x-3}{(3x-2)^2}$$

$$y = \frac{x}{\sin x} \quad \rightarrow \quad y' = \frac{(\sin x)(1)-x(\cos x)}{(\sin x)^2} = \frac{\sin x - x(\cos x)}{\sin^2 x}$$

Chain Rule:

[Derivative of OUTSIDE, leaving inside alone][Derivative of INSIDE]

$$y = g[hx] \quad \rightarrow \quad y' = [gx][h'x]$$

Examples:

$$y = (x^2 + x)^4 \quad \rightarrow \quad y' = [4(x^2 + x)^3][2x + 1] = (4x^2 + 4x)^3(2x + 1)$$

$$y = \sin(x^2 - 3x) \quad \rightarrow \quad y' = [\cos(x^2 - 3x)][(2x - 3)]$$

$$y = (1 + \cos 2x)^3 \quad \rightarrow \quad y' = 3(1 + \cos 2x)[(-\sin 2x)(2)] = -6(1 + \cos 2x)(\sin 2x)$$

Exponential Rule:

$$y = e^x \quad \rightarrow \quad y' = e^x dx$$

$$y = e^{x^2-2} \quad \rightarrow \quad y' = e^{x^2-2}(2xdx)$$

Logarithmic Rule:

$$y = \ln x \quad \rightarrow \quad y' = \frac{1}{x} dx$$

Trigonometric Rules:

$$y = \sin (x) \rightarrow \; y' = \cos (x)$$

$$y = \cos (x) \rightarrow \; y' = \sin (x)$$

$$y = \tan (x) \rightarrow \; y' = 1/\cos^2 (x)$$

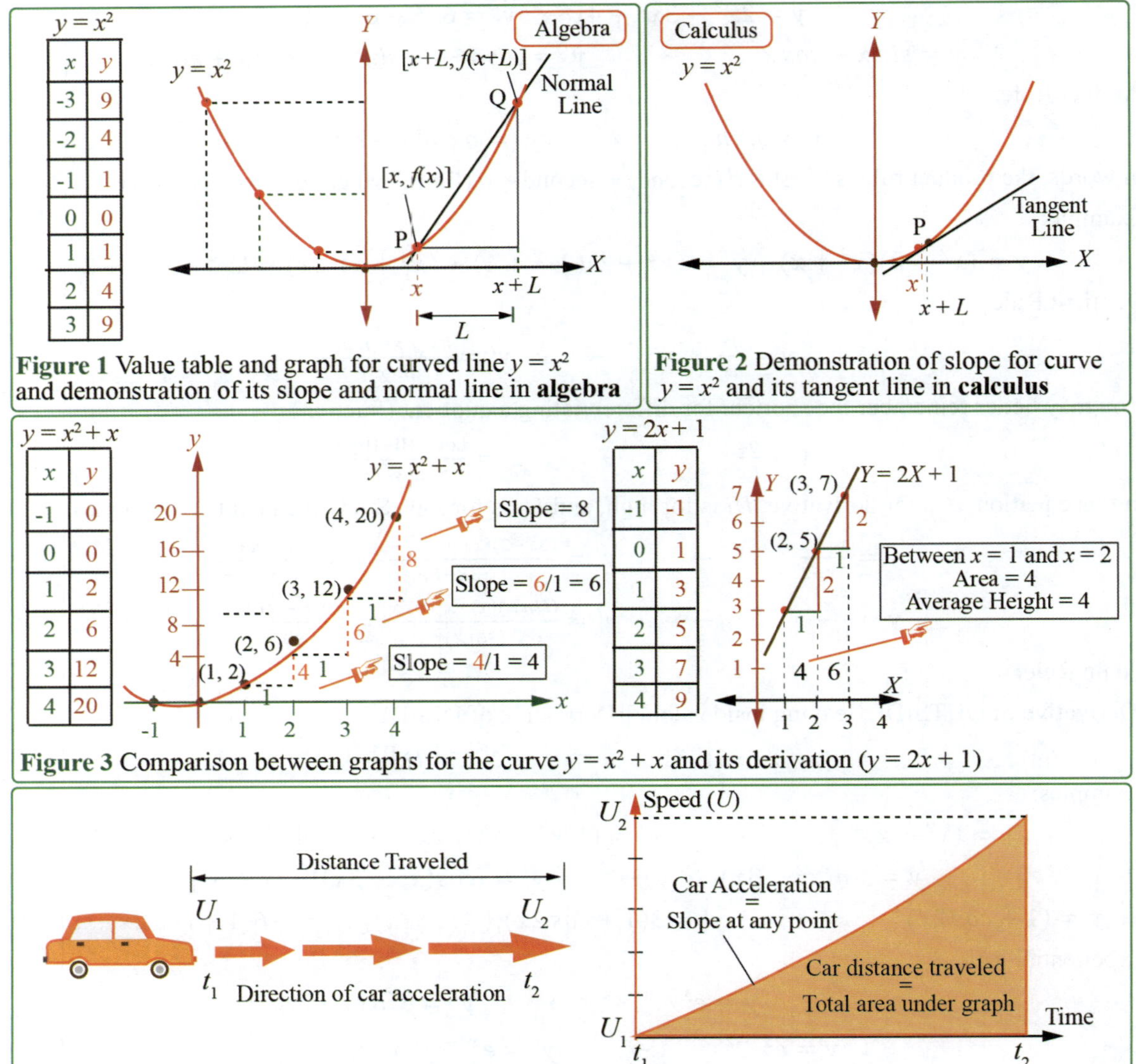

x	y
-3	9
-2	4
-1	1
0	0
1	1
2	4
3	9

Figure 1 Value table and graph for curved line $y = x^2$ and demonstration of its slope and normal line in **algebra**

Figure 2 Demonstration of slope for curve $y = x^2$ and its tangent line in **calculus**

x	y
-1	0
0	0
1	2
2	6
3	12
4	20

x	y
-1	-1
0	1
1	3
2	5
3	7
4	9

Figure 3 Comparison between graphs for the curve $y = x^2 + x$ and its derivation ($y = 2x + 1$)

Figure 4 An accelerating car, its acceleration, and distance traveled (shaded orange)

Implicit Derivation

Consider the implicit derivation of $x^3 + x^2y^2 - xy^3$. It is impossible to solve for x in relation to y or y in relation to x unless we use the implicit derivation. For finding the slope (y' or dy/dx) of this function, we treat x^2y^2 and xy^3 as products and use the product rule.

$$3x^2dx + x^2d(y^2) + y^2d(x^2) - xd(y^3) - y^3dx = 0$$

$$3x^2dx + x^2(2ydy) + y^2(2xdx) - x(3y^2dy) - y^3dx = 0$$

$$x^2(2ydy) - x(3y^2dy) = -3x^2dx - y^2(2xdx) + y^3dx$$

$$(2x^2y - 3xy^2)dy = -(3x^2 + y^22xy^2 - y^3)dx$$

We have to solve for dy/dx to find the slope function.

$$\frac{dy}{dx} = -\frac{3x^2 + y^2 2xy^2 - y^3}{2x^2y - 3xy^2}$$

We can find the value of the slope at, say, $x = 1$ and $y = 2$ as

$$\frac{dy}{dx} = -\frac{3 \times 1^2 + 2^2 \times 2 \times 1 \times 2^2 - 2^3}{2 \times 1^2 \times 2 - 3 \times 1 \times 2^2} = -\frac{27}{8} = -3.4$$

This means the graph of $x^3 + x^2y^2 - xy^3$ goes through the point (1, 2) and has a slope of –3.4 at this point.

Integration-Derivation Relation

We start this subtopic by studying the function $x^2 + x$ and its derivative, $2x + 1$, shown in Figure 3. Considering *f* (function) and *F* (anti-derivative of *f*), we can say the following:

- **Integration and Derivation are closely Related:** On graph *f*, the number of **rises** (which are 4, 6, and 8) equates to the areas on graph *F* (which are also 4, 6, and 8).
- **Integration is the Reverse of Derivation:** This is because the total **rises** on *f* between (1, 2) and (4, 20), which is 4 + 8 = 12, equates to the **area** under *F* between 1 and 4 (which is also 4 + 8 = 12). This tells us that the *S* (slope) of *f* gives the heights of *F*.

Applications of Derivation

In general use, derivation has many applications, such as calculating a curve's slope or a function's slope and determining a **tiny change** in a quantity. For example, the tiny distance (called **differential distance**, *dL*) of a moving system from one point to another in a tiny time of *dt* can be solved differentially. In ChemEng, derivation can be used when the rate of a physical quantity must be determined.

Calculating the Rate of a Quantity: Consider a car that moves from point 1 to 2 on a straight line at an almost constant (unchanged) rate of speed (*U*) to make a distance *L* per unit time (*t*), as shown in Figure 4. The car's average speed can be calculated as $U = L/t$, where *L* is for length (distance). The same figure shows the *U* (speed) of the car in relation to *t* (time) when it is accelerating (it is *not* moving at a constant rate, but sometimes faster or slower than average speed), which is often the case. We use the equation for a differential form of speed. The distance (*L* for length) the car is moving from point 1 is a function of *t* or $L = f(t)$. The car's rate of change of *L* relative to *t*, which is the definition of speed (*U*), is

$$dU = \frac{L_2 - L_1}{t_2 - t_1} = \frac{dL}{dt}$$

Likewise, the car's rate of change of *U* relative to *t*, which is the definition of acceleration (*a*), is

$$a = \frac{dU}{dt} = \frac{\frac{dL}{dt}}{dt} = \frac{dL}{dt^2}$$

This equation tells us that if a function gives the **distance** of a quantity in relation to time, the first derivation of that quantity gives its **speed**, and the second derivation gives its **acceleration**. So, we choose a little bit of distance (*dL*) to calculate speed and acceleration **differentially** (infinitesimally).

Assume that the *L* of a moving system at $t = 2$ s (seconds) is represented by the function $f(L) = 2t^2$, and we want to find *u* (speed) and *a* (acceleration) at time $t = 2$ s. Because the derivation of $2t^2$ is $2 \times 2t = 4t$, the *dL* at time $t = 2$ is $2t^2 = 2 \times 2^2 = 8$ m (meter). Derivation of *t* is 1, so at $t = 2$, the *dt* is $1 \times 2 = 2$, so the speed is

$$U = \frac{dL}{dt} = \frac{8}{2} = 4 \text{ m/s}$$

Because the derivation of $4t$ is 4, the *dL* at time $t = 2$ is $4t = 4 \times 2 = 8$ m. And derivative of t^2 is $2t$, so at $t = 2$, the *dt* will be $2 \times 2 = 4$. Then acceleration is

$$a = \frac{dL}{dt^2} = \frac{8}{4} = 2 \text{ m/s}^2$$

INTEGRATION

Integration (integral) is used in calculus to solve a derivative (differential) function. It can calculate a quantity when that quantity **changes** by a **tiny** (infinitesimal) amount in a tiny time (t). We can understand it better by considering it as the area under a curve.

Basic Integration Rules

Constant Rule:

$$\int k dx = kx + C$$

Example:

$$\int 2 = 2x + C$$

Because the derivative of a constant is zero, x^2 can have many anti-derivatives, such as $x^3/3 + 1$, $x^3/3 - 1$, $x^3/3 + 2$, and many more. The constants 1, − 1, + 2, and many more are known as the **constant of integration**. Say, the integral of acceleration (a) gives velocity (V) plus a constant.

Power Rule:

$$\int x^a dx = \frac{x^{a+1}}{a+1} + C$$

Examples:

$$\int x^2 dx = \frac{x^{2+1}}{2+1} = \frac{x^3}{3} + C$$

$$\int -4x^2 + 3x - 1 = \frac{-4x^3}{3} + \frac{3x^2}{2} - x + C$$

Chain Rule:

$$\int (ax+b)^n dx = \frac{(ax+b)^{n+1}}{a(n+1)} + C \qquad \text{for } n \neq -1$$

Division Rule:

$$\int \frac{1}{x} dx = ln\, x + C$$

$$\int \frac{1}{2x} dx = ln\, 2x + C \qquad \int \frac{c}{ax+b} dx = \frac{c}{a} ln(ax+b) + C$$

Exponential Rule:

$$\int e^{ax} dx = \frac{1}{a} e^{ax} + C$$

Definite Integral: A definite integral (simply **integral**) of variable x is usually given as

$$\int_a^b f(x)dx$$

The sign ∫ is the symbol for **integral**, values a and b are the **domains** (ordinances) of the integral, $f(x)$ is the function of x, d is the symbol for derivation (differential), and x is the variable of integral.

The integral $f(x)$ over an interval $[a, b]$ is given as

$$\int_a^b f(x)dx = F(b) - F(a)$$

The sign F (some use f') in this equation is for the anti-derivative of function f. This equation, called the **second fundamental theorem of calculus**, works as a general principle to calculate integrals. As a numerical example, consider the next simple integral.

$$\int_0^1 x^2 dx$$

For solving this integral, it is sufficient to find an anti-derivative whose derivative equates to $x^3/3$ because the derivative of $x^3/3$ is $(3x^{3-1})/3 = x^2$. [The easiest way is to look at the integration rules given earlier. According to the integration power rule, we have $\int x^a dx = (x^{a+1})/(a+1) = x^{2+1}/(2+1) = x^3/3$.]

$$\int_0^1 x^2 dx = \left[\frac{x^3}{3}(1)\right] - \left[\frac{x^3}{3}(0)\right] = \frac{1^3}{3} - \frac{0^3}{3} = \frac{1}{3} - 0 = \frac{1}{3}$$

Similarly, the integral of length (L) expresses position.

$$\int_1^2 dL = L_2 - L_1$$

This integrates L between points 1 and 2. Using, say, the interval between time $t = 0$ (which reflects L_1) and $t = 5$ minutes (which reflects L_2) and knowing that the integral of dL is L, we can integrate our equation.

$$\int_0^5 dL = L_2 - L_1 = 5 - 0 = 5$$

Applications of Integration

The most basic applications of integration in ChemEng are the following three (3):

- Calculation of a quantity,
- Calculation of area (A) under a curve, and
- Calculation of the volume (V) of a non-geometric shape.

Calculation of a Quantity: As a numerical example, let us look at the integration of the work equation ($W = F.L$) over a length of L within a specified (infinite) small change in L (shown as dL) from initial point 1 to final point 2 by a force (F). The integration of $W = F.L$ over dL from 1 to 2 gives the W in its integral form.

$$W = \int_1^2 F.dL = F(L_2 - L_1)$$

This equation tells us that the force moves a system by a tiny length of dL, where L is the variable of integral and dL means that we are integrating over L within a specified change in L from point 1 to 2.

Here, we consider the compression of a gas (a system) at constant temperature (T), which changes its volume (V) and pressure (P). Figure 5A shows a cylinder containing the gas with an initial pressure of P_1 and an initial volume of V_1. The V of the gas can be compressed by weight with mass M, placed on the piston, as shown in Figure 5B. When the two stops on the cylinder sides are released, the piston moves down by the mass M_1. This compresses the gas from the initial state of P_1 to the final state of P_2.

Figure 6A shows the gas's pressure-volume ($P-V$) graph when compressed in one step by applying mass M_1 on the piston. The work (W) done is shown by the shaded area in the same figure. [W done on the gas is positive (because $V_2 < V_1$) and can be calculated by $W = M.a_g.h$, where M is mass, a_g is the gravitational acceleration ($a_g = 9.8$ m/s^2 = 32.2 Ft/s^2), and h is the height through which the M is dropped. This is known as the gravitational work.]

Figure 6B shows the $P-V$ diagram of the gas when work is done in two steps by using M_2, which is half large as M_1, to compress the gas to volume $(V_1 + V_2)/2$. Figure 6C shows the compression when the work is done in five steps using a smaller mass. As seen from the same figure, the gaps are getting smaller, and thus, the estimate for W becomes more exact. Finally, Figure 6D shows the compression when W is done in infinite steps using M_n

(a tiny mass). In the infinite case, which is the most exact of all cases, W can be calculated by integrating the flow work equation ($W_F = P.V$) on an interval of V_1 and V_2.

$$W_F = \int W_F = \int_{V1}^{V2} P.dV = P(V_2 - V_1)$$

This equation tells us that the tiny mass compresses the gas by an infinitesimal (tiny) volume of dV for each infinitesimal step. [The P used here is *not* the P of the gas, but the external P, applied by the piston, determined by $P = M.a_g/A$, where A is the cross-sectional area of the cylinder.] For example, for $V_1 = 0$ and $V_2 = 4$, the result of the integral will be

$$W_F = P(V_2 - V_1) = P(4 - 0) = 4P$$

We use $P = F/A$ for the pressure, whose integration over an area of A in a specified small change in A (shown as dA) from initial state 1 to final state 2 will give P in its integral form.

$$P = \frac{F}{\int_1^2 dA} = \frac{F}{A_2 - A_1}$$

Calculation of Area under a Curve: The exact area (A) under the curve $f(x)dx$ on an interval (such as a and b) can be determined as

$$A = \int_a^b f(x)dx = \lim_{n\to\infty} \sum_{i=1}^{n} f(x_i).\left(\frac{b-a}{n}\right)$$

Consider function $f(x) = y = x^2 + 1$ between 0 and 3. In Figure 7A, a rough area is estimated by drawing three (3) rectangles under the curve and then determining the sum of their areas between 0 and 3. Each rectangle has a width of 1, and the height of the function gives the rectangle height. In this way, rectangle 1 has a height of $f(0) = 0^2 + 1 = 1$, so its area is $1 \times 1 = 1$, rectangle 2 has $f(1) = 1^2 + 1 = 2$, so its area is $2 \times 1 = 2$. And rectangle 3 has a height of $f(2) = 2^2 + 1 = 5$, so its area is $5 \times 1 = 5$. Adding these three areas gives a sum of $1 + 2 + 5 = 8$. As seen from the same figure, this is a rough estimate of the area under the curve, which is *not* acceptable to a scientist (because of the three big gaps between the rectangles).

But, as Figure 7B shows, if drawing six (6) smaller rectangles, we will see that the gaps are getting smaller and, thus, our estimate from the area becomes more exact. This happens because of an increase in the number of rectangles and a decrease in gaps between them (the *more* the rectangles, the *more* exact is the result).

To calculate the area of each rectangle separately, the next general rule (the **left-rectangle rule**) is used.

$$A_n = \frac{b-a}{n}[f(x_0) + f(x_1) + f(x_2) + \cdots + f(x_{n-1})]$$

In this equation, A_n is the area under the curve for the nth rectangle, a and b are the integral's **intervals** (domains), n is the number of functions (here rectangles), $(b - a)/n$ is the width of each rectangle, and the values of $f(x_0)$ …. $f(x_{n-1})$ are the heights of the rectangles. The width of each rectangle $(b - a)/n$ equates to the length of the total distance from 0 to 3. We use this rule for six rectangles (see Figure 7B).

$$A_6 = \frac{3-0}{6}[f(0) + f(0.5) + f(1) + f(1.5) + f(2) + f(2.5)]$$
$$= 0.5[1 + 1.25 + 2 + 3.25 + 5 + 7.25] = 9.9$$

This result is still *not* satisfactory unless we increase the number of rectangles to reach **infinitely** thin rectangles, as shown in Figure 7C. For example, for $n = 100$, the area calculated by this rule is close to 12, which is quite satisfactory for us (chemical engineers) because the area is divided into an infinite number of tiny thin rectangles to make the gaps negligibly small.

Now, we calculate the area under the curve $y = x^2 + x$, between $x = 1$ and $x = 3$. The integral of this function in relation to x will be

$$\int_1^3 (x^2 + x)dx$$

We can use the integral rules to solve this curve for $x = 1$ and $x = 3$ as

$$\left[\frac{x^3}{3} + \frac{x^2}{2}\right]_1^3 = \left[\frac{3^3}{3} + \frac{3^2}{2}\right] - \left[\frac{1^3}{3} + \frac{1^2}{2}\right] = [9 + 4.5][0.3 + 0.5] = 13.5 + 0.8 = 14.3$$

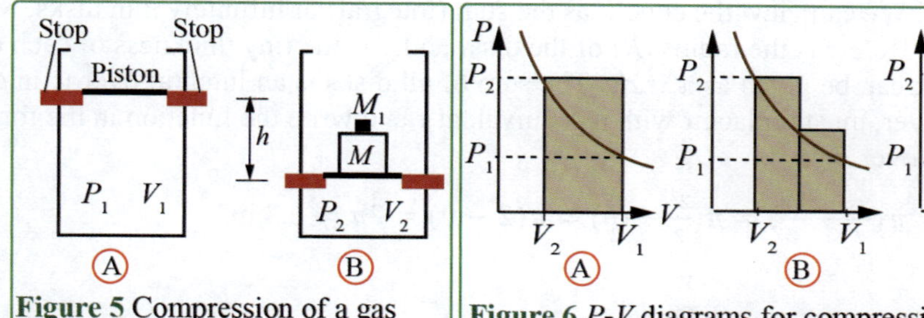

Figure 5 Compression of a gas from P_1V_1 to P_2V_2

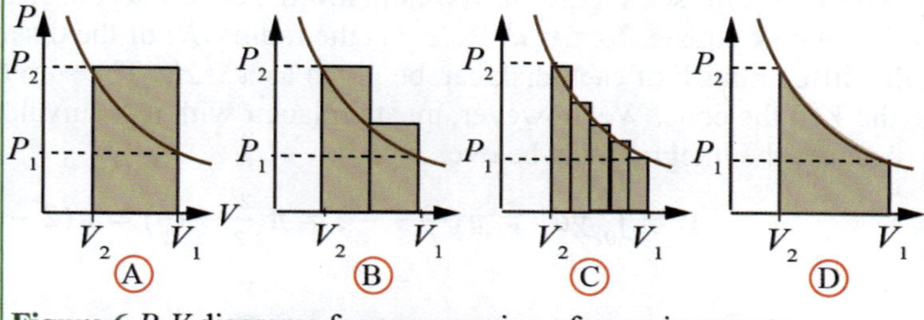

Figure 6 *P-V* diagrams for compression of a gas in one step, two steps, five steps, and in infinite number of steps

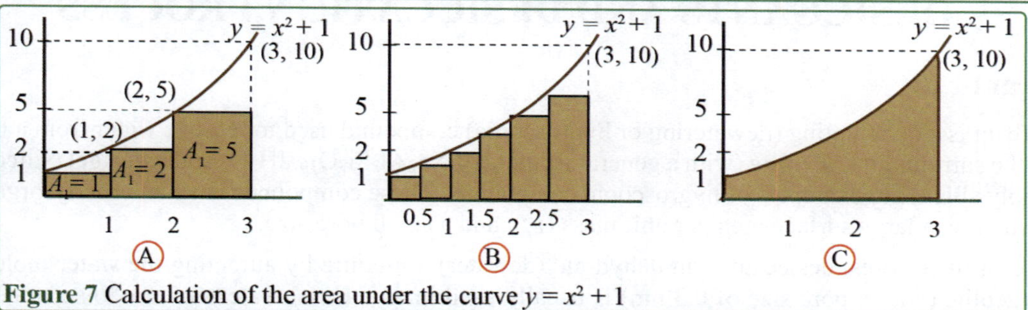

Figure 7 Calculation of the area under the curve $y = x^2 + 1$

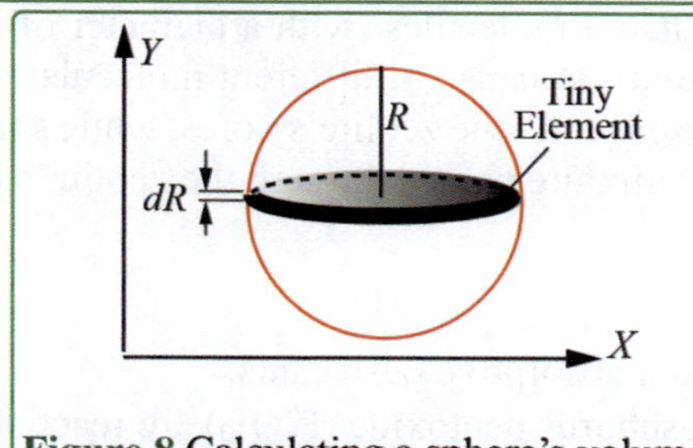

Figure 8 Calculating a sphere's volume

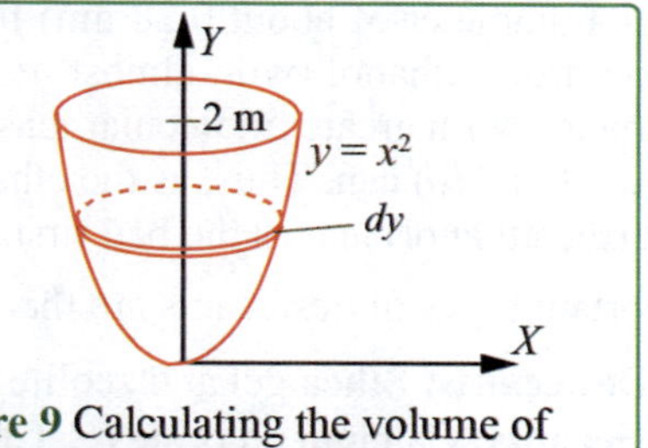

Figure 9 Calculating the volume of a cone generated by rotating $y = x^2$

Calculation of Volume: We consider a sphere to calculate a geometric volume (V). The sphere's differential (tiny) element, shown in Figure 8, is cylindrical with a radius R and a tiny thickness of the dR. The cylindrical element's differential volume (dV) equals its A (surface area) multiplied by dR, so $dV = A.dR$. We can view this by minimizing A and R equally to reach zero. The V of that element becomes minimized, also. The A of a cylinder equates to $A = \pi.R^2$, so the V of the cylindrical element will be

$$dV = \pi.R^2.dR$$

The sum of the elements from 0 to R is a hemisphere, and twice the hemisphere will give a sphere, so the V of the spherical element will be $dV = 2\pi.R^2.dR$. As said earlier, to solve a derivative equation, it must be integrated, so we integrate this equation in relation to R, according to integral rules.

$$V = 2\pi \int_0^R R^2.dR = 2\pi \left[R^2.R - \frac{R^3}{3}\right]_0^R = 2\pi \left[\left(R^3 - \frac{R^3}{3}\right) - \left(0 - \frac{0^3}{3}\right)\right] = 2\pi \left(\frac{2R^3}{3}\right) = \frac{4}{3}\pi.R^3$$

If we want to calculate the sphere's *V* from the bottom (*A*) to a certain level (*B*), we have to use the domains of the integral (*A* and *B*).

$$V = \int_A^B dV$$

As another example, we can calculate the *V* (volume) of a **cone**, generated by rotating $y = x^2$ around the *Y*-axis from $y = 0$ to $y = 2$ m (see Figure 9). We can view the cone *V* as the sum (integral) of infinitely thin disks, where the *V* of each disk equates to $\pi.x^2.d$. Here *x* is the radius (*R*) of the disk, and *d* is the tiny thickness of each disk. Thus, the differential *V* of each disk can be given as $\pi.x^2.dy$. The sum of all disks is an integral over *y*; in other words, the *V* of the cone. We, however, must replace *x* with its equivalent *y* and write the function in the form of $\pi y^2 dy$ (because the integral must be over *dy*).

$$V = \int_0^2 ydy = \pi(\frac{y_2^2}{2} - \frac{y_1^2}{2}) = \pi(\frac{2^2}{2} - \frac{0^2}{2}) = \pi(2 - 0) = 2\pi = 6.3 \text{ m}^3$$

D-16

DESICCANTS AND DESICCATION PROCESS

Desiccants

A desiccant is a dehydrating (dewatering or hygroscopic) compound used to remove water from a moist compound or the surrounding. **Zeolite** (with a general formula of $Na_2Al_2Si_3O_{10}.2H_2O$) and **silica gel** (silicon dioxide, SiO_2, simply **silica**) are examples of hygroscopic compounds. These compounds have an orderly-organized molecular structure, a large surface area per unit mass (*M*), and a small pore size.

Because of their pores, desiccants can dehydrate (dewater) a mixture by attracting the water molecules. For example, zeolite (with a pore size of 0.3 nm) is usually used in an ethanol-water mixture to separate the water molecules (with a diameter of about 0.28 nm) from the ethanol molecules (with a diameter of about 0.44 nm) and produce anhydrous ethanol (with almost *no* H_2O content). Because of different molecular sizes, the larger molecules of ethanol (with greater molecular mass, M_M) *cannot* enter the zeolite's pores, while smaller molecules of water (with smaller M_M) can. Thus, as the ethanol-water mixture passes through the zeolite's bed, the greater M_M component (the ethanol) leaves the bed first.

The two important types of desiccants are the following:

- **Absorptive Desiccants:** Silica gel and zeolite are common absorptive desiccants.
- **Reactive Desiccants:** Calcium chloride ($CaCl_2$) and phosphorus pentoxide (P_4O_{10}) are reactive desiccants that react with H_2O to form hydrates. For example, P_4O_{10} reacts with water to form phosphoric acid as $P_4O_{10} + 6\ H_2O \rightarrow 4\ H_3PO_4$. A crystallized form of P_4O_{10} is used in desiccators.

Desiccation Process

As the opposite of **humidification**, desiccation is the partial removal of water from a moist compound or the surrounding by a desiccant. [Desiccation is also called the molecular-sieve process because of using a desiccant that its molecular structure is organized like a sieve. The desiccation process is performed in a small desiccator in a lab. When performed on a large column in a chemical process plant, it is called the **molecular-sieve process**. For example, the molecular-sieve process uses zeolite on a hydrous ethanol mixture (with about 5% water content) to produce anhydrous ethanol (below 0.3% water content).]

D-17

DETACHED PARTS

Study ATTACHED AND DETACHED PARTS.

D-18

DETERGENTS AND SOAPS

Detergents and soaps are surfactants (surface-active substances) that reduce the surface tension of water. Both have cleansing properties and kill microorganisms by denaturing their proteins. The molecular structure of detergents and soaps is similar in that both contain a polar head attached to a nonpolar tail. The polar head typically consists of either a sulfate group (SO_4^-) or a sulfonate group (SO_3^-). Their nonpolar heads attract the nonpolar molecules of grime (dirt plus grease) to form a conglomeration, then washed with water.

Detergents

A detergent is a sulfated surfactant, like **alkylbenzene sulfonate** or **sodium lauryl sulfate** (SLS). SLS is also the main ingredient of most toothpaste and dishwashing liquids. SLS is **biodegradable** (microorganisms can break its molecules once released into the environment). Detergents act like soaps but are more soluble in hard water (because a detergent's sulfonate group is less polar than soap's carboxylate group).

Soaps

Soap is a fatty acid salt (a carboxylic acid salt with a long aliphatic chain). During cleaning, soap dissolves fat particles, washed with water. Soaps are grouped based on the type of alkali used in their production. Sodium soaps, produced from sodium hydroxide, are firm solids, while potassium soaps, produced from potassium hydroxide, are softer or often liquid.

D-19

DEUTERIUM

Defined under HYDROGEN.

D-20

DEVICES

A device (also called **equipment**), in general, is a tool for a particular purpose. In ChemEng, large devices used in chemical process plants perform a particular process to achieve a particular technical goal. Usually, a device has several attached and detached parts. A pump, a compressor, a thermometer, a filter, an evaporator, an electric generator, a dryer, and a distillation column are examples of devices. Engines (like a car's engine), machines (like a heat pump and steam turbine), motors (like the motor of a centrifuge), and instruments (like thermometers, manometers, and flowmeters) are devices, also.

D-21

DEW POINT CALCULATIONS

Study BUBBLE POINT, DEW POINT, AND ISOTHERMIC FLASHING CALCULATIONS.

B.22

DEW POINT PRESSURE

Defined under the topic of BUBBLE POINT AND DEW POINT PRESSURES.

D-23

DEW POINT TEMPERATURE

Defined under the topic of BUBBLE POINT AND DEW POINT TEMPERATURES.

D-24

DIALYSIS PROCESS

As one type of membrane separation process, dialysis is a diffusion process in which a solution diffuses through a semipermeable membrane that is **permeable** (diffusible) to the solution's smaller molecules and **impermeable** (non-diffusible) to its larger molecules. The driving force (the cause) of dialysis is the concentration difference (ΔC) between the two sides of the membrane. Thus, its driving force (the ΔC) is greater when the following two points are met: 1) The decrease in the osmotic pressure (P_O) on the feed-side (side 1), and 2) The decrease in the concentration of the product side (side 2); in other words, the increase in the system's Gibbs-Donnan effect (the effect of unequal molecular distribution on each side of a membrane).

A **dialysate** is usually added to side 1 (the feed-side) to improve these conditions. This causes the dialysate's molecules to diffuse through the membrane to side 2 (the product-side), increasing the permeability of the small molecules to side 2. If, for example, the blood of a patient with kidney disease is under dialysis, adding a salt (NaCl) solution (a dialysate) to side 1 causes the blood's small (wanted) molecules to diffuse to side 2 easily. Instead, the blood's large (unwanted) molecules (mainly the proteins) are absorbed by the salt molecules and remain in side 1. Then, the clean blood with wanted molecules from side 2 returns to the patient's body, and the used salt solution with unwanted molecules from side 1 goes to the used salt container (see Figure 1).

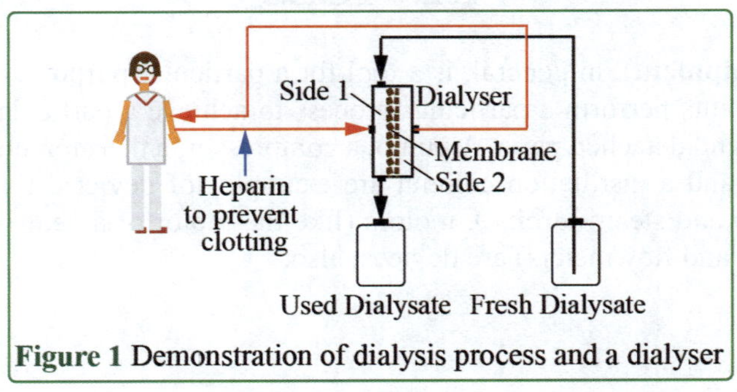

Figure 1 Demonstration of dialysis process and a dialyser

Technically, the dialysis process is a three-step diffusion process, so we can use an equation like the one given under the MEMBRANE SEPARATION PROCESS to solve a dialysis process. There, we said that when a diffusing system is in a steady-state, the mass-transfer (mass-diffusivity) rate of all three steps is equal, so we show all three of them by the same symbol of $\dot{M}_A$ (the rate of M_A), which is the amount of mass transfer of A in unit time or **diffusion rate of A**.

$$\dot{M}_A = \frac{C_{A1} - C_{A2}}{\frac{1}{K_{A1}.A} + \frac{\Delta X_M}{D_{AB}.A.\varepsilon_p} + \frac{1}{K_{A2}.A}} = \frac{\Sigma F_D}{\Sigma R} \tag{2}$$

In this equation, C_{A1} is the concentration of A on side 1, and C_{A2} is that on side 2, K_{A1} is the convective diffusion coefficient of A on side 1, and K_{A2} is on side 2. And A is the total membrane's diffusing area, X_M is the membrane thickness, D_{AB} is the diffusion coefficient of A through the membrane, and ε_p is the **membrane porosity** (where subscript p is for **porosity**). The nominator of Equation 2 is the overall **driving force** of the dialysis process (F_D), and its denominator is the process's overall resistance (the sum of the resistances for individual steps). To better clarify the dialysis process, study the next Example.

An Example on Dialysis Process

In a dialyzer for reducing urea from the blood of a patient with kidney disease, urea passes through a membrane to the dialysate side (side 2) to be absorbed by a salt solution (dialysate). The next values are given:

X_M (membrane's thickness)	20 µm = 20×10^{-6} m
A (membrane area)	1 m^2
ε_p (membrane porosity)	50%
C_{A1} (concentration of urea on blood side or side 1)	2×10^{-2} mole/L
C_{A2} (concentration of urea on dialysate side or side 2)	1.5×10^{-2} mole/L
D_{AB} (diffusion coefficient of urea through the membrane)	6×10^{-8} m^2/min
K_{A1} (convective diffusion coefficient of urea on blood side)	4.8×10^{-2} m/min
K_{A2} (convective diffusion coefficient of urea on dialysate side)	3×10^{-2} m/min

Calculate: $\dot{M}_A$ (mass-transfer rate of urea or urea molecular absorption to the salt)

$$\dot{M}_A = \frac{C_{A1} - C_{A2}}{\frac{1}{K_{A1}.A} + \frac{\Delta X_M}{D_{AB}.A.\varepsilon_p} + \frac{1}{K_{A2}.A}} = \frac{2\times10^{-2} - 1.5\times10^{-2}}{\frac{1}{4.8\times10^{-2}\times1} + \frac{20\times10^{-6}}{6\times10^{-8}\times1\times0.5} + \frac{1}{3\times10^{-2}\times1}}$$

$$\dot{M}_A = \frac{0.005\ \text{mole/L}}{20.8\frac{\text{min}}{m^3} + 666.7\times\frac{\text{min}}{m^3} + 33.3\frac{\text{min}}{m^3}} \times 1000\frac{L}{m^3} = \frac{5}{720.8} = 0.007\ \text{mole/min}$$

D-25

DIESEL FUEL

Diesel fuel is a fuel used in diesel engines. It is produced from crude oil in oil refineries by the distillation process. Today, biodiesels are also produced in a considerable amount. [Environmentalists recommend the use of ultra-low-sulfur diesel (ULSD) fuel.]

D-26

DIFFERENTIATION

Study DERIVATION.

D-27

DIFFUSION COEFFICIENT

Study CONDUCTIVE AND CONVECTIVE DIFFUSION COEFFICIENTS.

D-28

DIFFUSION PRESSURE DEFICIT

The diffusion pressure deficit (DPD) is the difference in pressure (P) between the pure water and a given solution under the diffusion process. Assume that a red beet is sliced and placed in a cup of warm water. The water molecules enter each beet's cell through its wall by osmosis, producing juicy water. As a result of osmosis, a P, known as the P_O (osmotic pressure), develops in the produced juice. In this example, the DPD is the difference between the P of water entering the cells and the juice's P_O.

In general, the following can be said about DPD (diffusion pressure deficit):

- It is directly proportional to the concentration of the solution under the diffusion process,
- It *decreases* with a dilution of the solution under diffusion and *increases* with the solution's concentration.

D-29

DIFFUSION PROCESS

BASICS

As a process unit of ChemEng, diffusion (molecular diffusion or mass diffusion) is a mass transfer process during which the molecules of a diffusing component (or components) move (diffuse) in a phase (or from one phase to another phase through a phase boundary). Diffusion always occurs from an area of high concentration (C) to the areas of lower C. [A **phase boundary** (interface) is a very thin layer between two phases with a thickness of a few nm (1 nanometer = 10^{-9} m = 10^{-6} mm) to a few µm (1 micrometer = 10^{-6} m or 10^{-3} mm).]

Molecular diffusion occurring in various directions at different velocities proceeds because of changes in equilibrium caused by the concentration difference (ΔC, also called **chemical potential**) of a **diffusing component** (diffusant) between one part and another part of a fluid (liquid or gas) or between two fluids. Instead of ΔC, scientists prefer to use $\Delta C/L$ (concentration gradient) as the driving force of diffusion to include the diffusing length (L). In addition, $\Delta P/L$ (pressure gradient), $\Delta T/L$ (temperature gradient), or heat flux (E_Q/A) can cause (or contribute) to the diffusion process, where E_Q is heat energy and A is heat transfer area.

[Note 1: Although both diffusion fluid flow processes are **mass transfer processes** but are *not* the same. When mass diffuses at a **molecular level** by $\Delta C/L$, it is called the **diffusion process**, but when mass diffusion occurs in **bulk** (under-the-surface) by $\Delta P/L$, it is called the **fluid flow process**, where P is for pressure.]

[Note 2: The diffusion process participates in several process units, including crystallization, distillation, evaporation, evaporative cooling, drying, gas absorption, leaching, liquid extraction, membrane separation, and a few more processes *not* discussed in this book.]

[Note 3: Although **diffusion** and **extraction** processes have some similarities, some differences exist between them that are outlined under EXTRACTION PROCESS.]

The diffusion process has some similarities with the heat transfer process because:

- Both heat and mass transfers occur by **convection**, **conduction**, or both.
- Both have a similar driving force. Diffusion occurs by $\Delta C/L$ when one part of a phase is at a higher C than the other part. Or one phase is at a higher C than the other phase, and heat transfer occurs by $\Delta T/L$ when one part of a system is at a higher T than the other.

For these reasons, some equations related to these processes are similar.

The following are the three main types of diffusion:

- **Convective Diffusion** (diffusion by convection)**:** In convection, the molecules diffuse convectively (collectively) from one part to the other part of a fluid. Thus, convective diffusion is a direct mass-transfer process that occurs in the bulk of a fluid.
- **Conductive Diffusion** (diffusion by conduction, simply **diffusion**)**:** In conduction, the molecules diffuse conductively (individually) from a system's higher concentrated side to a lower concentrated side through a phase boundary. Thus, conductive diffusion is an indirect mass-transfer process in a certain location.
- **Combined Diffusion** (multi-step diffusion or diffusion by convection-and-conduction)**:** In combined diffusion, the molecules diffuse by both convection and conduction.

Before discussing the types of diffusion in more detail, it is helpful to outline the main differences between **convective diffusion** and **conductive diffusion**.

- In convection, the molecules diffuse much *faster* than in conduction,
- In convection, diffusion occurs by molecular bulk flow, while conduction is flowless.
- In convection, the molecules diffuse collectively, while in conduction, they move individually.
- In convection, the molecules diffuse in a *certain* direction (usually *parallel* to the diffusion direction), while in conduction, they diffuse in *different* directions.

It is also helpful to mention that chemical reactions can occur by convection, conduction, or both. When, say, two liquids are in a chemical reactor, they diffuse by convection across *no* boundary and then react with each other. And when a liquid and a gas are in a reactor, they diffuse by conduction through a liquid-gas boundary (the surface of the liquid and gas) and then react. In both cases, molecular diffusion occurs in opposite directions at different rates. [Equations related to **reaction-diffusion** are *not* covered in this book.]

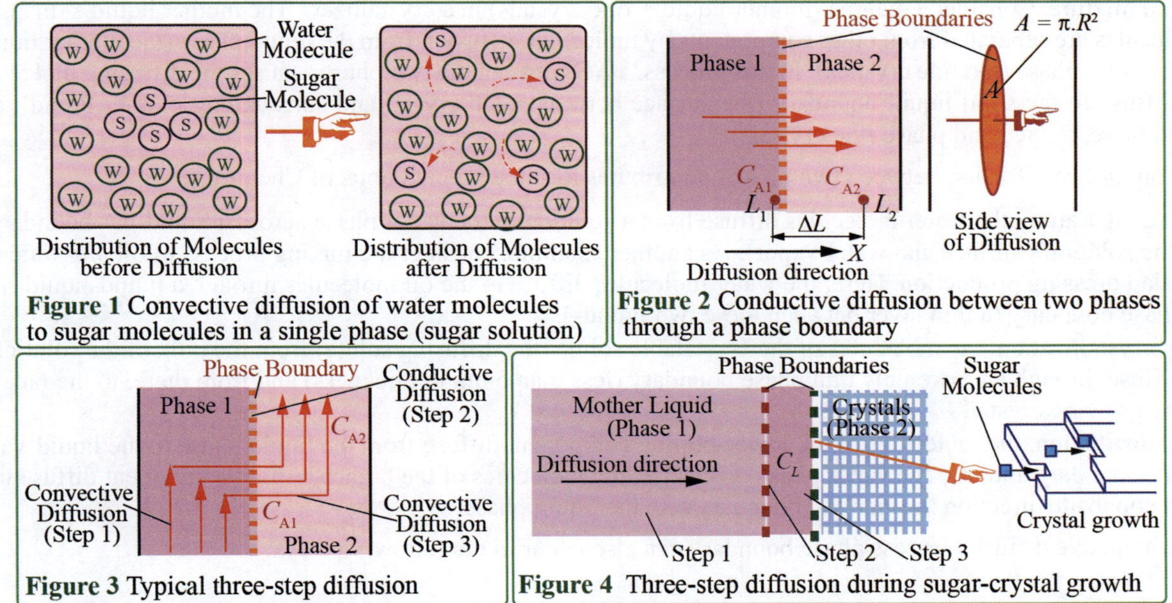

Figure 1 Convective diffusion of water molecules to sugar molecules in a single phase (sugar solution)

Figure 2 Conductive diffusion between two phases through a phase boundary

Figure 3 Typical three-step diffusion

Figure 4 Three-step diffusion during sugar-crystal growth

CONVECTIVE DIFFUSION

In a convective diffusion (also called **mass diffusion by convection**), a fluid's diffusant molecules diffuse from one part to another part of that fluid parallel to the diffusion direction. The main *goal* of convective diffusion is the mixing of a fluid. Consider adding a few sugar crystals to a glass of water and stirring it to make the water molecules (see Figure 1). The diffusion of water (W) molecules through S (sugar) molecules creates a new distribution of W molecules in S molecules.

When diffusant A diffuses by convection through the non-diffusing component B in a direction parallel to the diffusion direction, the amount of component A diffused in unit time (diffusion transfer rate of A), shown usually by the symbol $\dot{M}_A$ (the rate of M_A), can be given by using the convective diffusion coefficient of A (K_A, also called the **mass transfer coefficient** of component A).

$$\dot{M}_A = \frac{M}{t} = K_A.A(C_{A1} - C_{A2}) \quad (1)$$

In this equation, A is the cross-sectional area through which the diffusion occurs, and subscript A is for the diffusing component (diffusant). The C_{A1} is the concentration of component A in the bulk of fluid in location 1 at the start of diffusion, C_{A2} is that in location 2 when the diffusion is finished, and the term $C_{A1} - C_{A2} = \Delta C$ is the driving force of the diffusion. If K_A is given in m/h, area (A) in m^2, and concentration (C) in kgmole/m^3, the SI unit of $\dot{M}_A$ becomes kgmole/h. The US unit of $\dot{M}_A$ is Lbmole/h.

[When, similarly, B is the diffusing component, and its molecules move by diffusion through A molecules from location 1 to location 2, we must use the coefficient for component B (the K_B) to calculate the diffusion of B molecules into A molecules.]

CONDUCTIVE DIFFUSION

In a conductive diffusion process (simply **diffusion process**), a fluid's diffusant molecules diffuse from one phase to another phase through a phase boundary between two fluid phases (Figure 2). [Conductive diffusion can also occur in a single phase with *no* phase boundary. Because conductive diffusion through phase boundary has more applications in ChemEng, our discussion here will be about it only.]

The main *goal* of conductive diffusion is to separate one (or more) components from other components in a liquid mixture. Consider a magma (mother liquid + fine crystals) in a crystallizer. The mother liquid's diffusing molecules are separated from other components by molecular diffusion from the liquid phase (the mother liquid) to the solid phase (the fine crystals). In this process, a ΔC between the two phases causes the diffusing molecules to diffuse to the solid-liquid boundary (the surface between each crystal and surrounding mother liquid), and from there, to the solid phase (the crystals).

Conductive diffusion between two phases contributes to some process units of ChemEng:

- In evaporation, the water molecules diffuse from a solution to the vapor phase across a liquid-gas boundary (the solution's surface and water vapor). As another example, consider the mixing process of oil and water in salad dressing production. Here, the water molecules diffuse to the oil molecules through a liquid-liquid phase boundary (a thin layer between these two liquids).
- In crystallization, the molecules of the crystalable solute (the diffusing solute) from the bulk of the solution diffuse through an extremely thin phase boundary (less than 5 nm in thickness) and from there, to the face of the growing crystal.
- In distillation, the molecules of the lower-boiling component diffuse from the liquid phase to the liquid-vapor boundary and into the vapor phase. Likewise, the molecules of the higher-boiling component diffuse in the opposite direction through the boundary into the liquid phase.

Conductive diffusion across phase boundary can also occur in the following ways:

- **Heat Diffusion:** In diffusion caused by E_Q (heat energy), the liquid feed must be first heated to become ready for diffusion. Brewing tea in a teapot is a simple example of heat diffusion (**infusion** in the tea drinkers' language). During infusion, E_Q from the hot water changes the nature of the cell's protoplasm, causing it to be permeable. As a result of infusion, the tea's soluble components (like flavors, caffeine, antioxidants, and colorants) diffuse (infuse) from the tealeaf's cells to the water. The diffusion of components decreases because the tealeaf will *no* longer contain such components. Here, the main cause of diffusion is ΔC (concentration difference), and the minor cause is ΔP (pressure difference) between inside and outside the protoplasm. Industrially, a similar diffusion occurs on sliced sugarbeet in a beet diffuser.
- **Membrane Diffusion:** In diffusion with the help of a membrane (a membrane separation process), the diffusing component's molecules pass through the membrane, from the side with a lower solute concentration (C) to the side with a higher solute C, as shown in Figure 1 under OSMOSIS PROCESS.

To run equations on a **conductive diffusion**, we assume that,

- A diffusant diffuses through a *non*-diffusing component (component B) across a phase boundary.
- The diffusant proceeds steadily in the X-axis direction perpendicular to the boundary between the two phases.

Keeping these in mind and paying attention to Figure 2, the mass transfer rate of the diffusant (component A), shown as $\dot{M}_A$ (the rate of M_A) can be expressed by a general equation between flux (F_X, the amount of a quantity per unit area), a proportionality coefficient (C_P), and the driving force (F_D) of the process.

$$F_X = C_P . F_D \tag{2}$$

The C_P can be represented by the diffusion coefficient (D_{AB}) of component A in a mixture with components A and B. [Symbol D_{AB} is used to indicate that A diffuses through B (the non-diffusing component). If instead, B was the diffusing component, the symbol D_{BA} would have been used instead of D_{AB}.] D_{AB} can relate $\dot{M}_A$ (**mass diffusion rate** of diffusant A or amount of diffusant A diffused in unit time) to $\Delta C_A/\Delta L$ (where L is the diffusion distance) when molecules of component A move from location 1 to location 2 (see Figure 2). Considering these statements and knowing that $\Delta C_A = C_{A1} - C_{A2}$ (where C_{A1} is the concentration of A at phase boundary and C_{A2} is that at some distance from the boundary) leads us to

$$\dot{M}_A = \frac{M_A}{t} = D_{AB}\frac{\Delta C_A}{\Delta L} = D_{AB}\frac{C_{A1}-C_{A2}}{L_1-L_2} \tag{3}$$

Because diffusion occurs across an area of A, this equation must be multiplied by A. Further, it is better to replace ΔL (the difference in diffusing length) with ΔX (because we assumed that the diffusion proceeds in the X-axis direction or horizontal-axis direction). Thus,

$$\dot{M}_A = D_{AB}.A\frac{\Delta C_A}{\Delta X} \tag{4}$$

This equation gives the diffusion transfer rate of diffusant A ($\dot{M}_A$, the amount of A diffused in unit time) in relation to the diffusion driving force, F_D (the $\Delta C_A/\Delta X$), which tends to produce diffusion, and the opposing diffusion force (a resistance, $R = 1/D_{AB}.A$), which tends to oppose (resist) that diffusion.

Sometimes, Equation 4 is given in its differential (d) form to indicate the diffusion applied on a small infinitesimal thickness (dX), through which the diffusion occurs.

$$\dot{M}_A = D_{AB}.A\frac{dC_A}{dX} \tag{5}$$

Either Equation 3 or 4 is known as Fick's diffusion equation, which states that $\dot{M}_A$ (the transfer rate of diffusant A) across area A is proportional to the concentration gradient ($\Delta C_A/\Delta L$ or dC_A/dX) through D_{AB}.

In Fick's equation, D_{AB} is usually given in m^2/h, so if area (A) is in m^2, C (concentration) is in kgmole/m^3, and length (L or X) is in m, the SI unit of $\dot{M}_A$ becomes in kgmole/h. Its US unit is Lbmole/h, where Lb is for pound.

[Usually, a **minus sign** is used on the right side of Fick's equation (Equation 3, 4, or 5) to indicate that the molecules diffuse in the X-axis direction (from the higher concentrated side to the lower-concentrated side).

Instead, the **plus sign** means that the molecules diffuse in the $-X$-axis direction (lower to higher concentration). The diffusion direction is determined by the shear force (F_S) that must be applied to the liquid to flow.]

Let us write Equation 4 in the following form:

$$\frac{\dot{M}_A}{A} = D_{AB}\frac{\Delta C_A}{\Delta L} \tag{6}$$

The term $\dot{M}_A/A$ is called mass flux rate ($\dot{J}$), so

$$\dot{J}_A = \frac{\dot{M}_A}{A} = D_{AB}\frac{C_{A1}-C_{A2}}{\Delta L} \tag{7}$$

This equation relates $\dot{J}_A$ to $\Delta C_A/\Delta L$ (concentration gradient, the driving force of diffusion) through D_{AB}. [The driving force can also be expressed in molar fraction (X, a unitless quantity) as $X_{A1} - X_{A2}$.]

For example, in diffusion between a liquid phase and vapor phase, the diffusion transfer coefficient of component A in the liquid phase (K_X) and that in the vapor phase (K_Y) is given as

$$K_X = \frac{\dot{J}_A}{X_{A1}-X_{A2}} \tag{8}$$

$$K_Y = \frac{\dot{J}_A}{Y_{A1}-Y_{A2}} \tag{9}$$

In these equations, $\dot{J}_A$ is the mass flux rate, X_{A1} is the molar fraction of component A in the liquid phase at the phase boundary, X_{A2} is that at a distance from the boundary, Y_{A1} is the molar fraction of component A in the vapor phase at the boundary, and Y_{A2} is that at a distance from the boundary. That is to say, the units for K_X and K_Y are the same as $\dot{J}_A$ (because molar fractions are unitless numbers).

THREE-STEP DIFFUSION

Figure 3 shows a typical three-step diffusion, in which a liquid's molecules go through the following three diffusing steps to complete the diffusion-transfer process:

- **First-Step Diffusion:** In this step, the molecules diffuse by **convection**, collectively from side 1 (input side) toward the boundary between two phases.
- **Second-Step Diffusion:** In this step, the liquid's molecules diffuse by **conduction**, individually through the phase boundary.
- **Third-Step Diffusion:** This step is like step 1, so the molecules diffuse, again, by **convection** from the boundary toward side 2 (output side).

The easiest way to express the main difference between the two listed diffusions is to look at the flow. If, as said earlier, a flow exists, diffusion occurs convectively, and if there is *no* flow, diffusion occurs conductively. Earlier, we derived the diffusion equations in relation to concentration difference (ΔC) for convective and conductive diffusions. We can, thus, use Equation 1 twice, each with a different diffusion coefficient, and Equation 4 once, and add them together to obtain the equation for the entire 3-step diffusion process.

$$\dot{M}_A = K_{A1}.A(C_{A1} - C_{A2}) + D_{AB}.A\frac{\Delta C_A}{\Delta X} + K_{A2}.A(C_{A1} - C_{A2}) \tag{10}$$

The term C_A equates to $C_{A1} - C_{A2}$, so after solving the equation for$\dot{M}_A$, we obtain

$$\dot{M}_A = \frac{C_{A1}-C_{A2}}{\frac{1}{K_{A1}.A}+\frac{\Delta X}{D_{AB}.A}+\frac{1}{K_{A2}.A}} \tag{11}$$

The nominator of this equation ($C_{A1} - C_{A2}$) is the overall **driving force** of the diffusion process (F_D), and its denominator is the overall resistance that occurs in all diffusing steps (R_O).

$$\dot{M}_A = \frac{C_{A1}-C_{A2}}{\frac{1}{K_{A1}.A}+\frac{\Delta X}{D_{AB}.A}+\frac{1}{K_{A2}.A}} = \frac{\Sigma F_D}{\Sigma R_O} \tag{12}$$

Figure 4 shows a three-step diffusion during the crystal growth of sugar. As explained in the subtopic of Crystal Growth under the topic of CRYSTALLIZATION PROCESS, in the first step, the sugar molecules diffuse by convection from the bulk of the mother liquid to make a certain distance and position themselves on the boundary between the mother liquid and the solution around the crystals. In the second step, the sugar molecules diffuse through the liquid-liquid boundary by conduction to reach the crystals. In the third step, the molecules diffuse, again, by convection to make a certain distance and sit on the surface of the crystals.

[Note 1: If the diffusion goes through a real membrane, the membrane's diffusing area for step 2 must be given based on the **membrane porosity** (ε_p), as discussed under MEMBRANE SEPARATION PROCESS.] [Note 2: To become more familiar with the diffusion process, study the upcoming Example and Examples given under MEMBRANE SEPARATION PROCESS and DIALYSIS PROCESS.]

An Example on Diffusion Process

Given: In a diffuser used in a beet-sugar factory, sugar (sucrose) molecules diffuse through the beet-cell wall (protoplasm) to the warm diffusion water. The following values are given:

ΔX (the cell protoplasm's thickness)	2 µm = 2×10^{-6} m
A (total protoplasm diffusing area)	1 m^2
C_{A1} (concentration of sugar inside the cells)	0.5 mole/L
C_{A2} (concentration of sugar outside the cells)	0.005 mole/L
D_{AB} (diffusion coefficient of sugar across protoplasm at 70°C)	4×10^{-6} m^2/h
K_{A1} (convective diffusion coefficient of sugar inside the cells)	3.8 m/h
K_{A2} (convective diffusion coefficient of sugar outside the cells)	2.8 m/h

Wanted: $\dot{M}_A$ (mass-transfer rate of sugar to the diffusion water) per unit area (1 m^2) of protoplasm

$$\dot{M}_A = \frac{C_{A1} - C_{A2}}{\frac{1}{K_{A1}.A} + \frac{\Delta X}{D_{AB}A} + \frac{1}{K_{A2}.A}} = \frac{0.5 - 0.005}{\frac{1}{3.8 \times 1} + \frac{2 \times 10^{-6}}{4 \times 10^{-6} \times 1} + \frac{1}{2.8 \times 1}}$$

$$\dot{M}_A = \frac{0.495[\frac{mol}{L}]}{0.26[\frac{h}{m^3}]+1[\frac{h}{m^3}]+0.36\frac{h}{m^3}} \times 1000[\frac{L}{m^3}] = \frac{495}{1.62} = 307 \text{ mole/h}$$

Considering the sucrose molar mass of 342 g/mole, the mass transfer rate of sugar in kg/h will be

$$307\left[\frac{\text{mole}}{\text{h}}\right] \times 342\left[\frac{\text{g}}{\text{mole}}\right] = 104994 \text{ g/h or } 105 \text{ kg/h}$$

D-30

DIFFUSIVITY COEFFICIENT

Another name for DIFFUSION COEFFICIENT.

D-31

DIFFUSIVITY FLUX AND DIFFUSIVITY FLUX RATE

Another name for MASS FLUX AND MASS FLUX RATE.

D-32

DIMENSION AND DIMENSIONAL ANALYSIS

Dimension

Dimension is a fundamental measurable quantity for describing a system or an event. Length (L), width (d), height (h), and time (t) are the four (4) main dimensions. [The time has been used as the fourth dimension since 1905 when Einstein, in his principle of gravity spacetime, suggested the word spacetime to mean a combination of 3-dimensional space (length, width, and height) and one-dimensional time.]

In math, dimension is the minimum number of coordinates (X, Y, and Z) needed to specify a **point** (a system with *no* dimension). As shown in Figure 1, a line has one dimension (because only one coordinate is required to specify a point). A surface area, such as a **plane** (a flat 2-dimensional surface), is two-dimensional (2-D) because two coordinates are needed to specify a point. Likewise, three coordinates (X, Y, and Z) are required to locate a point on a cube, so it is 3 dimensional (3-D). As shown in the same figure, two points can be connected to create a line, two parallel lines can be connected to form a square, and three parallel lines (or two parallel squares) can form a cube.

We, humans, are a four-dimensional (4-D or 3 + 1) system; as we move through space (with three dimensions) and through time (with one dimension), so experiencing four dimensions all the time.

One valid concept says that extra small dimensions exist (in addition to 4-D) but are so small that points representing each line can curl into a circle, as shown in Figure 2. These small dimensions might be difficult to see, but they can hide a lot of systems that show themselves in arguably surprising ways when studied from the 4-D dimensions that we are used to seeing.

Dimensional Analysis

A dimensional analysis expresses relations among physical quantities by identifying their dimensions. Mass (M), time (t), length (L, the distance), and electric charge (q) are basic physical quantities. All other physical quantities can be expressed in relation to these quantities. For example, velocity (V) is L/t. Similarly, electric current (I, simply **current**) is q/t.

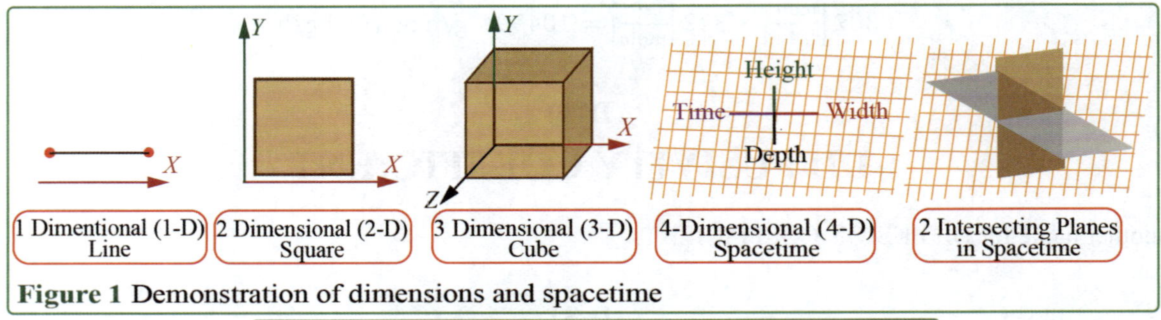

Figure 1 Demonstration of dimensions and spacetime

Figure 2 Points representing a line can curl into a circle

D-33
DIRECT CURRENT

Study ALTERNATING AND DIRECT ELECTRIC CURRENTS.

D-34
DISCHARGE HEAD

Study PUMP LIQUID HEADS.

D-35
DISPERSIONS

A dispersion (also called **dispersion solution**) is a one-phase liquid (like a solution) or a two-phase liquid mixture (like a colloid or emulsion). Dispersions are roughly divided into four classes: 1) Solutions, 2) Colloids, 3) Emulsions, and 4) Suspensions.

Solutions

A solution is a one-phase dispersion consisting of a chemical substance (or more) dissolved in a liquid. A substance dissolved in a liquid to form a solution is called the solute, and the liquid is called the solvent. Solutions are homogeneous because their solute molecules are evenly distributed in the solvent molecules. Sugar, for example, dissolved in water (a liquid), makes a solution. Similarly, ethanol (a liquid) in water makes a solution.

Study the following about the solutions:

- A solution's solute (or solutes) is in a lower proportion than the solvent.
- A solution's solute (or solutes) and solvent are combined chemically, so *none* of them retain their identity after mixing to form the solution.
- The main difference between **liquid** and **solution** is that a liquid is made of a single solute, so it is pure, but a solution is made from one (or more) solutes. In other words, when a solute (or more) is dissolved in a liquid (solvent), it becomes a solution.

Colloids

A colloid (comes from the Greek for **glue**) is a two-phase dispersion (mixture) in which the particles of one phase (called the **dispersed phase**) are dispersed (disorderly distributed) in the other phase. The dispersed phase of a colloid can be an insoluble solid, liquid, or gas dispersed in a liquid or solution. Pectin, dextran, and colorants are colloids. Smoke (fine solids dispersed in the air) are colloids.

The following are the two major operating problems caused by colloids:

- **Sedimentation Problems:** Because colloids are dispersions, their particles are un-settleable under normal conditions, causing problems during sedimentation. Usually, a coagulant is used to make the colloids' particles settleable, neutral, and destabilized. This process is known as **colloid** (colloidal) **coagulation** because the coagulant coagulates (gets them together to become larger) the particles. [The colloid particles are electro-negatively charged, so the positively-charged coagulant's particles can neutralize them.]
- **Filtration Problems:** Because colloids' particles are large (10 to 1000 nm, about 5 to 5000 times larger than a typical solution's molecules), they cause filtration problems.

[A colloid's molecules can be distinguished from a solution's molecules by shining a light through them. If it is a colloid, the light beam is visible as it reflects (because of large molecules), and if it is a solution, the light beam is invisible (because of small solute molecules). This is known as the **Tyndall effect**.]

Emulsions

An emulsion (also called **emulsion solution**) is a two-phase dispersion (simply **dispersions**); one phase (the dispersed phase) is dispersed in the other phase (called the **continuous phase**). An emulsion can consist of two or more immiscible liquids (like oil-in-water or water-in-oil). **Milk**, which consists of milk fat (lipid) dispersed in water, is an oil-in-water emulsion. **Butter**, which consists of water dispersed in butterfat, is a water-in-oil emulsion. Hand and face creams are water-in-oil emulsions. Municipal sludge (a dispersion) is an industrial emulsion.

[Incorrectly, some use the term **emulsion** and colloid equally. In emulsions, both phases are liquids, while in colloids, the dispersed phase can be solid, liquid, or gas.]

Emulsifiers: An emulsifier is a compound that stabilizes an emulsion by increasing its stability in a particular mixing medium. Egg yolk and mustard are examples of food emulsifiers. And surfactants (like detergents) are examples of industrial emulsifiers.

An emulsifier usually consists of a water-soluble (hydrophilic) component and a water-insoluble (hydrophobic) component. An emulsifier that is more soluble in water and less in oil forms an oil-in-water emulsion. An emulsifier that is more soluble in oil and less in water forms a water-in-oil emulsion.

Sometimes, one phase of the emulsion can act as an emulsifier to produce a new emulsion in which the droplets (tiny drops) of one phase join and disperse in the other phase. Joining the droplets can be prevented by using a surfactant to lower the surface tension between the two liquid phases.

Suspensions

A suspension (also called **suspension solution**) is a two-phase solution mixture in which one phase is disorderly dispersed in the other phase. The dispersed phase is usually suspended particles, while the continuous phase can be liquid or gas. By this definition, a suspension is a liquid-solid or gas-solid mixture. A magma consisting of sugar crystals and mother liquid is a thick suspension. The presence of protein in a salt solution makes a suspension. Similarly, fine suspended particles in a gas form a **suspension gas**, generally called particulate matter, which is a gas-solid mix. [The word **suspension** is often used in wastewater treatment operations to refer to a two-phase solution mix containing suspended and dissolved solid particles.]

Both colloids and suspensions are a two-phase mixture, but the following differences exist between their particles (consisting of many molecules):

- The colloids' particles are un-settleable, but suspensions' particles are.
- The colloids' particles can be solid, liquid, or gas, but suspensions' particles are solid.
- The colloids' particles (10 to 1000 nm) are smaller than the suspensions' particles (larger than 1000 nm).

D-36
DISSOLVED SOLID SUBSTANCES

See DISSOLVED SOLIDS.

D-37

DISSOLVED SOLIDS

A dissolved solid (*DS*) consists of soluble (non-filterable) molecules in a solution. By operational definition, the dissolved solids of a solution are those solids that can pass through a filter with a fine sieve size of 2 μm or smaller. When a solution sample is filtered in the lab to remove the suspended solids (filterable solids), the dissolved solids stay in the sample. A solution's dissolved solids are expressed in mass percentage.

A solution's concentration (*C*) can be calculated by knowing its *DS* and density (*D*).

$$C = \frac{DS.D}{100} \tag{1}$$

[Note: Although the terms **dissolved solid**, soluble solid, dry substance, and Brix are used equally to indicate the same meaning but are different. **Dissolved solid** and **soluble solid** are correct terms when referring to a solution's non-filterable solids. The **dry substance** is a correct term when referring to a solution's filterable solids (suspended solids) and nonfilterable solids. Brix (also called refractometric dissolved substance or simply **dissolved substance**) is a correct term for a solution's nonfilterable solids measured by a refractometer because the samples are filtered to remove suspended solids before being tested by a refractometer.]

D-38

DISTANCE AND DISPLACEMENT

As vector quantities, **distance** and **displacement** are different (see Figure 1). Assume that your workplace is 2 km (= 1.25 Mi) away from your home. If you go to work taking a different road and your car's odometer shows 3 km after setting it to zero, your distance traveled is 3 km, but your displacement is 2 km. Also, note that distance traveled up (or right) is a **positive displacement** but going down (or left) is **negative**. Next, these quantities are defined. Both distance and displacement are expressed as the same units, m (meter) in SI units and Ft (foot) in US units.

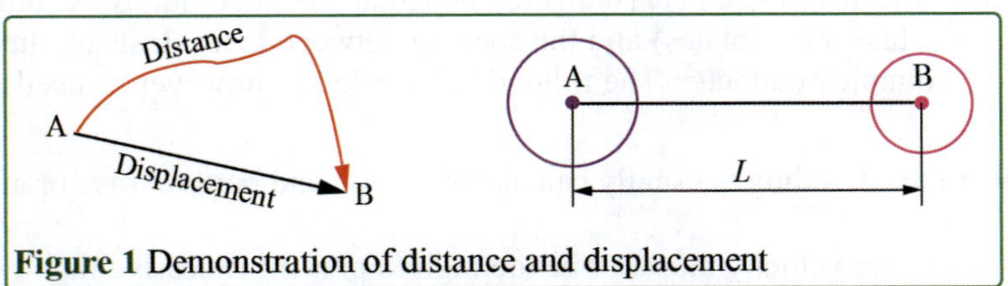

Figure 1 Demonstration of distance and displacement

Distance (*L* for length; refers to **displacement distance**) is a length (*not* necessarily the shortest) in space, as shown in Figure 1. [The words **distance** and **length** are usually used equally, and both are shown by the symbol *L*. **Length** (*L*) also shows the width of a system. We say, for example, the distance from point A to B is 1 km (= 0.6 Mi), and the width (length) of a wall is larger than its height.]

Distance is a positive quantity, but going down (or left) is a negative distance. In the case of two systems, distance is the length between their centers, as shown on the right side of Figure 1. The distance P_1P_2 between points P_1 and P_2, with coordinates (X_1, Y_1) and (X_2, Y_2), is expressed by the distance equation:

$$\overline{P_1P_2} = \sqrt{(X_1 + X_2) + (Y_1 + Y_2)} \tag{1}$$

Displacement (*S*) is the shortest distance from an initial to the final point of a system undergoing motion along a straight line in space (see Figure 1). Thus, displacement quantifies a motion's distance and direction.

D-39

DISTILLATE REFLUX

Distillate reflux (simply **reflux**) is the partial return (recirculation) of the distillate (product of the distillation process) to the upper section of a distillation column. The downflowing reflux in the column causes some cooling and, consequently, condensation of upflowing vapor, so more mass transfer occurs between the liquid and vapor. Reflux improves notably the separation efficiency (S_E) of the components with lower boiling point temperature (T_{BP}), known as the **lower-boiling component** (LBC or component *A*), from the components with higher T_{BP}, called **higher-boiling component** (HBC or component *B*).

The following are related quantities to the distillate reflux:

- **Reflux Flow Rate** (R_R): R_R (simply reflux rate) is the amount of reflux per unit time (in m^3/s or m^3/h).
- **Reflux Ratio** (R_X)**:** R_X is the rate ratio of the top product to the bottom product of a distillation column, where $R_X = R_R/D$ and D is the amount of distillate. As a ratio, the R_X is a unitless quantity.

A relation exists between T_P (the number of theoretical trays), R_X (reflux rate), and S_E (separation efficiency) of a distillation column. In this way, the *greater* is the R_X for a given N_T, the *greater* is the S_E. Alternatively, the *greater* the R_X to achieve the desired S_E, the *fewer* N_T is required. The right R_X and N_T, thus, are important factors for achieving the desired S_E in distillation. [The subject of the **number of theoretical trays** (plates) is discussed in the subtopic of Theory of Distillation Trays under DISTILLATION PROCESS.]

D-40

DISTILLATION COLUMNS

A distillation column (tower) is the most important part of a distillation system, and, thus, its design for a particular distillation process is important. In its typical design (Figure 1), an industrial column is a closed-round-vertical vessel, usually built from carbon steel or stainless steel. Columns come in different sizes, from 6 to 30 m (20 to 100 Ft) tall and 1 to 6 m (3 to 20 Ft) in diameter, depending on their duties. A column height is calculated based on the number of actual trays (plates) and the spacing between them. Instead, the number of trays is *not* needed for estimating a column's diameter. The following knowledge, however, is needed to estimate the diameter of a column:

- **Vapor-and-Liquid Load:** Loading is usually calculated for top and bottom trays or above and below the feed trays.
- **Vapor Velocity:** The vapor velocity must *not* be too high to prevent excessive liquid droplet entrainment, known as **priming**, which reduces column efficiency. The priming occurs when the vapor velocity through the column is excessively high, so too much foam is formed so that the vapor rises to the next tray above the foamy tray.

A column's diameter can be estimated by using the vapor's maximum mass flow rate ($\dot{M}_{Max}$, in kg/s), the vapor's density (D, in kg/m^3), and maximum vapor's velocity (V_{Max}, in m/s).

$$d = \sqrt{\frac{4\dot{M}_{Max}}{\pi . D_V . V_{Max}}} \tag{1}$$

In designing a column, some factors must be taken into consideration. Reflux rate is one of those factors. A reflux rate of about 20% increase over minimum reflux flow is usually used.

Some industries use **single-feed columns**, while some use **multiple-feed columns**. A column, therefore, can have two (or more) sections, each with different liquid and vapor flow rates. In a single-feed column, the feed is introduced in the middle of the column to improve the separation efficiency (S_E). In a single feed with reflux, the column theoretically divides into two sections: the **upper section** (the **rectifying section**) is above the feed plate, and the **lower section** (the **stripping section**) is below the feed plate, as shown in Figure 1. In the rectifying (upper) section, the vapor becomes enriched with a **lower-boiling component** (LBC) as it is brought into contact with the reflux. In the stripping (lower) section, the liquid stream gradually loses LBC until it becomes minimized in its content.

The contact between the vapor phase and liquid phase is the most important duty of a distillation column. This is achieved by the internal design of the column, based on which the columns are divided into two (2) large groups: **plate columns** and **packed columns**.

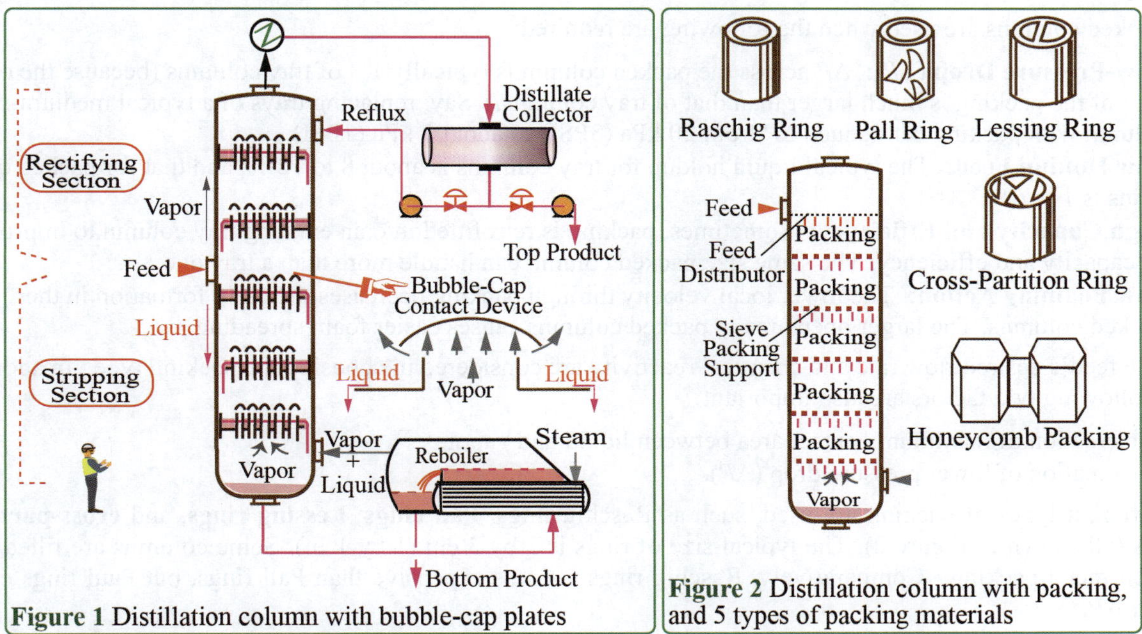

Figure 1 Distillation column with bubble-cap plates

Figure 2 Distillation column with packing, and 5 types of packing materials

Plate Columns

A typical plate column has several plates (trays) stacked one above the other so that the liquid feed moves downward from plate to plate to cover the surface of each plate, and the vapor moves upward to contact the feed at each plate. Plates are usually bolted to the shell of a column, typically 66 cm (= 2 Ft) from each other. **Bubble-cap plates** and **valve plates** are the oldest and most-effective vapor-liquid contact plates used in a distillation station, and **sieve** (perforated) **plates** are the newest and the most cost-effective ones. In a bubble-cap plate, as shown in Figure 1, vapor moves upward through the plate's hole, goes through the cap riser, and moves down toward the surface of the plate. Because there is a space between the riser and cap, the vapor bubbles through the liquid on the plate. A valve tray has a flapper that can move up and down as the vapor's flow rate changes.

Packed Columns

Figure 2 shows a typical packed column and five types of packing materials. Such a column consists of a packing support plate, packing, and feed distributor. Packed columns need an effective feed distributor to efficiently contact vapor and liquid streams.

The three (3) main disadvantages of packed columns over plate columns are the following:

- **Capacity:** Usually, packed columns are smaller in height and diameter than plate columns. This, relatively, decreases the capacity of packed columns. For this reason, packed columns are used for distillation when the separation of components in the feed is relatively easy. A packed column should be designed for 20 to 40% more capacity to achieve the same result.

- **Separation Efficiency:** Packed columns provide lower S_E than plate columns. They are relatively less efficient in liquid distribution (because the liquid tends to move toward the wall, causing less liquid-vapor contact). For this reason, packed columns are designed to allow maximum liquid and vapor distributions by considering enough free cross-sectional available area.
- **Cleaning:** Packed columns require more cleaning than plate columns.

Packed columns, however, have the following two main advantages compared with plate columns:

- **Pressure Drop:** Packed columns create lower pressure drop (ΔP).
- **Capital Cost:** Packed columns need lower capital costs.

Packed columns are used when the following are required:

- **Low-Pressure Drop** (ΔP)**:** ΔP across the packed column is typically 1/3 of tray columns (because the open area of the packing is much larger than that of tray columns.) Say, replacing trays of a typical medium-size column with packing can reduce ΔP from 20 kPa (3PSI) to about 7 kPa (1PSI).
- **Low Holdup Feed:** The typical liquid holdup for tray columns is about 8 to 12 %, and that for packed columns is 1 to 6%.
- **High Capacity and Efficiency:** Sometimes, packing is retrofitted into an existing tray column to improve its capacity and efficiency. The same size packed column can handle more than a tray one.
- **Low Foaming Action:** The lower local velocity through packing decreases the foam formation in the packed columns. The larger open area in packed columns causes easier foam spreading.

The feed's desired flow rate and chemical reactivity are considered in choosing the packing type. In addition, the following two factors are also important:

- The creation of maximum contact area between liquid and vapor,
- The creation of lower pressure drop (ΔP).

Different types of packing are used, such as Raschig rings, **Pall rings**, **Lessing rings**, and **cross-partition rings** (all shown in Figure 2). The typical size of rings is 3 by 3 cm (1 by 1 In). Some columns are filled with woven-metal packing. Comparatively, Raschig rings are less expensive than Pall rings, but Paul rings create lower ΔP.

Structured metal packing, **structured ceramic packing**, and **structured polymer packing**, which create low ΔP and high efficiency, are also used to pack the columns.

Metal structured packing consists of a corrugated (textured) thin pad and perforated metal sheets. Texturing promotes easy wetting of the packing's surface. The metal sheets, made from corrosion-resistant material, are thin (about 0.2 mm) and layered vertically to fit into a column with a certain diameter. The bottom of Figure 2 shows a honeycomb packing made from propylene.

Ceramic structured packing, made of ceramics, provides low ΔP, high efficiency, more effective contact between liquid and gas, and acidic-medium applications.

D-41
DISTILLATION PROCESS

BASICS

As an important process unit of ChemEng, distillation is an efficient separation process performed in a distillation column (tower) to separate one preferentially, two, or more components of a liquid mixture based on the components' different boiling point temperatures (T_{BP}) and relative volatilities (α, alpha). Industrially, it is used when a large amount of a liquid feed must be distilled.

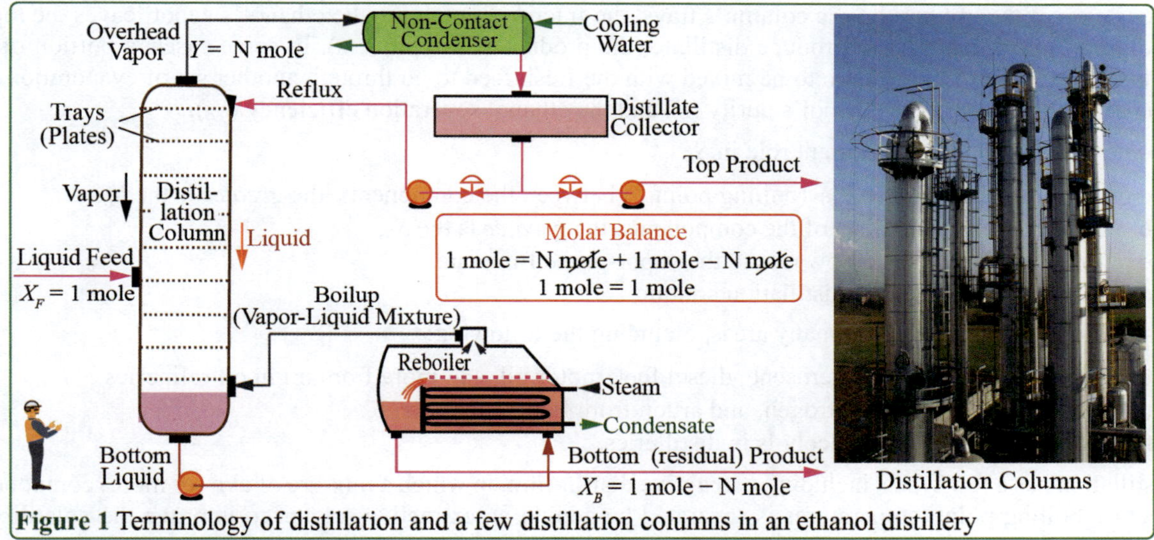

Figure 1 Terminology of distillation and a few distillation columns in an ethanol distillery

As a heat-absorbing process (endothermic process), distillation involves two heat transfer processes:

- Temperature-change (sensible heat) process, because T (temperature) of the feed increases to T_{BP},
- Phase-change (latent heat) process since some components go from L (liquid) phase to V (vapor) phase.

In addition to the heat transfer process, a few other process units participate in distillation, including mass transfer, mass diffusion, evaporation, and condensation.

Distillation is based on different T_{BP} and volatility of a solution mixture's components. After evaporation of the mixture's lower-boiling components (LBC), the vapors released from the distillation column are separately condensed to produce nearly pure liquid fractions. And the higher-boiling components (HBC) accumulate in the bottom product. [Note: When a binary (two-component) solution is under distillation, component A is called the **lower-boiling component** (LBC, simply **light component** or **component** $\boldsymbol{A}$), which has lower T_{BP} and higher volatility. And component B is called the **higher-boiling component** (HBC, simply **heavy component** or **component** $\boldsymbol{B}$), with higher T_{BP} and lower volatility. Also, note that the terms **light** and **heavy**, used in distillation, refer to **volatility,** *not* density (D), as is used in the extraction process.]

Inside the column, the heat energy (E_Q) causes part of the feed to evaporate, and the **trays** (plates) or **packing** containing phase-contact devices create a countercurrent contact between the L (liquid) phase, which moves downward, and V (vapor) phase, which moves upward. As a result, the light component's molecules diffuse from the L phase to the liquid-vapor boundary and into the V phase. Likewise, the heavy component's molecules diffuse in the opposite direction through the boundary and into the L phase. These processes continue until a liquid-vapor equilibrium (VLE) occurs between the phases.

The VLE does *not* remain forever and changes from a VLE to a non-VLE situation (and vice versa), creating a **separation** (fractionation) between the components with different volatilities. Thus, the V phase (leaving the top of the column) has much more of the light (volatile) component than the L phase (leaving the bottom of the column). The top vapor is condensed to produce the **distillate**. Part of the distillate is often returned into the column as distillate reflux (simply **reflux**).

Distillation must go through sufficient equilibrium stages related to a column's number of trays (N_P) to provide a high separation efficiency (S_E) between the components. Consider the distillation of a binary solution, like ethanol-water solution. When this mixture is partially evaporated in the distillation column, the light component (the ethanol), which has higher relative volatility and vapor pressure (P_V), concentrates in the V (vapor) phase, resulting in a difference in composition between the L (liquid) and V phases. After successive evaporation and condensation of the mixture on the column's trays, the fraction containing the ethanol's vapor leaves the top of the column to be condensed to produce distillate (the product of the process). In some cases, a portion of the distillate is returned to the column to be mixed with the fresh feed to go through another set of evaporation and condensation to increase the ethanol's purity (P) and the ethanol separation efficiency (S_E).

The next factors play an important role in S_E:

- The *greater* the difference in T_{BP} (boiling point T) between the components, the *greater* is the S_E.
- The *greater* is the α (volatility) of the components, the *greater* is the S_E.
- The ratio of the liquid-phase flow rate to the vapor-phase flow rate.
- The number of trays (N_T) in a distillation column.

Distillation applications are in many areas, including the following:

- In the production of gasoline, kerosene, diesel fuel, motor oil, and more from oil in oil refineries,
- In the production of oxygen, nitrogen, and argon from liquefied air, and
- In the production of different alcohols in distilleries.

Distillation has a few types, including **extractive distillation**, in which a mixture of two (or more) components with close boiling-point temperatures is separated by adding an extractive solvent to improve the volatility of azeotropic liquid mixtures.

As an energy-absorbing process, distillation is an energy-intensive process, increasing the operating cost of a distillation station. As to energy balance, heat energy (E_Q, simply heat and scientifically enthalpy) enters the reboiler at the bottom and leaves the condenser at the top.

[A chemical engineer needs to be familiar with the basics of distillation and its mass-balance and number-of-trays calculations, so-called equilibrium-stage calculations. Giving such information is the main goal of the rest of this topic. However, the design of a large distillation system requires good familiarity with computerized simulation programs (simply **simulators**), which is beyond the scope of this topic.]

BATCH DISTILLATION

Batch distillation is used when small or periodic (on-and-off) production is needed. As discussed next, it is divided into batch distillation without distillate reflux (simply reflux) and batch distillation with reflux.

Batch Distillation without Reflux

Figure 2 shows a simple batch distillation system with *no* reflux but a short column, a reboiler (for evaporating the bottom liquid), a non-contact condenser (for condensing overhead vapor), and connecting pipes. The solution feed enters the column, where the feed's LBC gets to its T_{BP} to produce vapor. The evaporation rate is maintained to keep the reboiler in a steady condition. In the reboiler, steam, which is used as a source of heat energy (E_Q), flows inside the tubes, and feed flows outside (the shell-side) the tubes. The vapor-liquid mixture (**boilup**), generated in the reboiler, leaves the top of the reboiler and enters the bottom of the distillation column. The residual liquid (**bottom product**) leaves the bottom of the reboiler. [The overhead product (**distillate**) contains much more of the light component than the bottom product.]

Some common problems can occur in a simple-equipped batch distillation system. These problems are related to one or other of the following causes:

- Presence of two components with very close T_{BP},
- Presence of one or more components in relatively small quantities, and
- Formation of an azeotropic liquid mixture even if the components' T_{BP} are sufficiently apart.

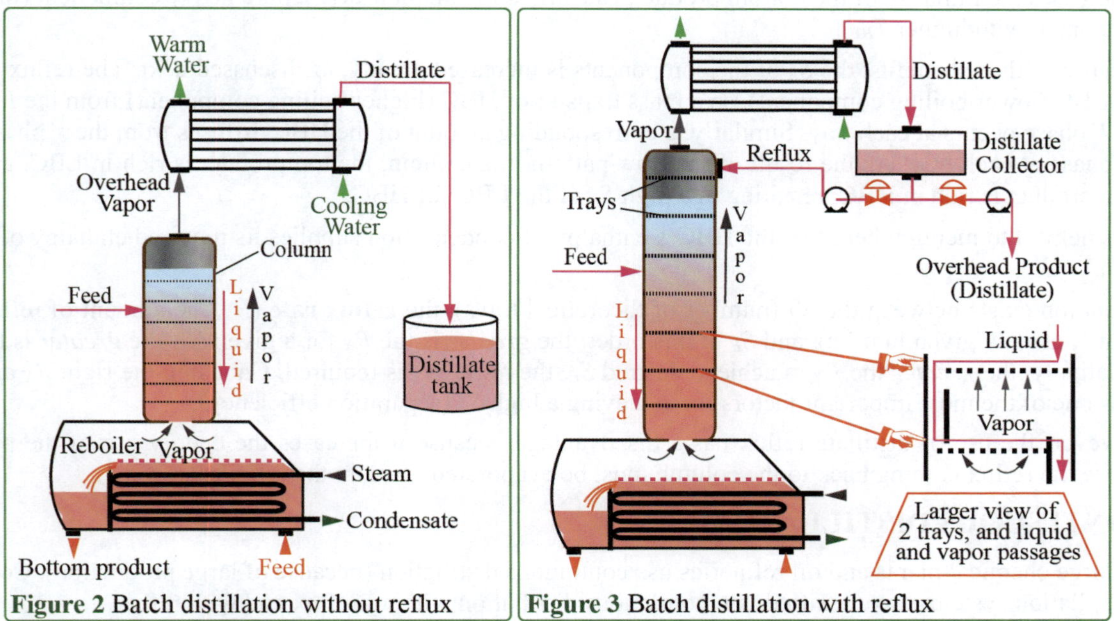

Figure 2 Batch distillation without reflux

Figure 3 Batch distillation with reflux

Batch Distillation with Distillate Reflux

As Figure 3 shows, a batch-distillation system with a column, a reboiler, a non-contact condenser, a reflux pump, a distillate pump, and a distillate holding tank (called the **distillate collector**) for receiving the distillate (overhead) product. Depending on the feed, a continuous column can operate at atmospheric pressure (P_{Atm}), above P_{Atm}, or vacuum pressure (P_{Vac}).

In the system shown in the same figure, several trays (plates) with phase-contact devices are in the column to ease a close contact between the vapor and liquid phases to improve the separation of the components. The trays are often of **sieve** (perforated) **type** with openings to allow easy countercurrent passage of the vapor and liquid through the phase-contact devices and, therefore, through each other.

The vapor from the reboiler enters the column, flows up through the trays, and leaves the column at the top. The vapor goes to a condenser to be partially or totally condensed, and the condensate (the distillate) from the condenser goes to the distillate collector.

At the top of the column, a distillate reflux process is performed. A portion of the distillate from the distillate collector returns to the column. And the rest of the distillate goes to the distillate receiver as the product of the process, called the **distillate** (overhead) **product**. [Comparatively, a distillation system with reflux produces higher separation efficiency (S_E) than a simple batch system when both process the same feed.]

On its way down in the column, the distillate reflux contacts the upflowing vapor from the reboiler. For close contact with the surface of each tray, reflux provides some cooling and condensation of a portion of the vapor, so more mass transfer occurs between the L (liquid) phase and V (vapor) phase on all the trays. After some time, the vapor-and-liquid phases on each tray approach composition, thermal, and pressure equilibria.

At the column bottom (the hottest section), the liquid stream is partially evaporated in the reboiler and pumps back to the column as a **boilup**. The rest of the bottom liquid is pumped out as the **bottom product**.

The use of distillate reflux achieves the following two benefits:

- It increases the purity of the overhead product, causing it to contain nearly a pure light component (the component with lower T_{BP}).
- It increases the impurity of the bottom product, causing it to contain nearly a pure heavy component (the component with higher T_{BP}).

Because of these benefits, the S_E of the components is increased greatly, as discussed next. The reflux is rich in the LBC (lower boiling component), so a mass transfer of HBC (higher boiling component) from the L phase to the V phase occurs at each tray. Similarly, a corresponding amount of the HBC diffuses from the V phase into the L phase at each tray. As the result of the flow pattern in a column, the top product is rich in LBC, and the bottom product is rich in HBC, resulting in a high S_E of the LBC for HBC.

[It is helpful to mention here that the HBC's enthalpy of condensation supplies its required enthalpy of evaporation.]

A relation exists between the N_T (number of theoretical trays), the **reflux rate** (R_X, the amount of reflux per unit time, usually given in m^3/s), and S_E in this order; the *greater* is the R_X for a given N_T, the *greater* is the S_E. Alternatively, the *greater* the R_X to achieve desired S_E, the *fewer* N_T is required. Choosing the right R_X and N_T, thus, is one of the most important factors for achieving a high S_E (separation efficiency).

However, the use of distillate reflux has a disadvantage because it increases the energy use of the process (because the reflux coming back to the column must be evaporated again in the reboiler).

CONTINUOUS DISTILLATION

All large chemical plants and oil refineries use continuous distillation (because of large production). Continuous distillation systems are classified into continuous distillation without reflux and with reflux.

Continuous Distillation without Reflux

Figure 4 illustrates a continuous distillation without distillate reflux, known as the **flashing distillation**. Such a distillation system separates the components with a wider range of T_{BP} and volatility. Instead, distillation with reflux is usually used to separate the components with closer T_{BP} and volatility. The liquid feed is preheated near its T_{BP} (bubble point temperature) in a heat exchanger with the bottom product or steam. Some continuous operations use a **reboiler** (usually **cattle type**) installed horizontally next to the column. A reboiler has a heating section with several **heating tubes** (see the same figure). Steam, which is used as a source of heat energy (E_Q, simply heat and scientifically enthalpy) to evaporate the feed partially, flows inside the tubes, and feed flows outside (the shell-side) of the tubes.

The feed near T_{BP} enters the feed tray and moves downward toward the bottom of the column through the trays' holes. The vapor coming from the reboiler moves upward through the tray's holes. On its way down, the liquid covers the surface of each tray to be in contact with the vapor. Because the vapor passes through the liquid at each tray, it is enriched in the LBC (lower-boiling component) as it moves up in the column. After leaving the top of the column, vapor (mainly consisting of LBC) goes to a condenser and from there to the accumulator, in which a certain level of liquid is maintained.

The liquid level at the column's bottom (the hottest section) is controlled so that when the desired level has been reached, some liquid leaves the column to be pumped to the reboiler for the reheating process.

Maintaining the right pressure (P) in a distillation column is important. The P in the bottom area of the column must be maintained higher than in the top for the vapor to flow upward.

Figure 5 shows a continuous **fractional distillation**, with a column with a single feed point and *no* reflux to separate components in crude oil in an oil refinery. The oil is first heated in a reboiler to 400°C, and the mixture of hot liquid and vapor then goes to the column's bottom section (the hot section). Natural gas leaves the top of the column as the **top product**. The components with greater T_{BP} (boiling point temperature) than natural gas, like ethanol and gasoline, condense and leave the column's upper section (the less-hot section) as liquids. The components with greater T_{BP} condense and leave the column's middle section as liquids. And the one with the highest T_{BP} leaves the column's lower part (the hot section) as the **bottom product**.

Figure 6 shows three different liquid-and-vapor flow patterns in a distillation column. The left side of this figure shows a **bubble-cap tray**, in which the vapor goes through the cap riser, and after hitting the cap, it moves down toward the tray's surface and finally bubbles through the liquid on the tray. A space exists between the riser and cap to allow the passage of the vapor.

Continuous Distillation with Reflux

Figure 7 shows the basics of a continuous distillation system with sieve-type trays and **distillate reflux** (simply **reflux**). And Figure 8 illustrates a continuous column with bubble trays, bubble-cap phase contact, and reflux. In both systems, feed enters the column at one point, so-known as the **single-feed column**. The feed point divides a column into a **rectifying** (upper) **section** and a **stripping** (lower) **section**.

A portion of the condensate (**distillate reflux**) is pumped back to the column's top tray to provide an overhead stream. The reflux flows down through each tray while contacting the upflowing vapor. The vapor from the top of the column is then condensed in a non-contact condenser (see CONDENSERS). The liquid from the condenser goes to the distillate accumulator. Some of the liquid from the distillate accumulator is removed as the distillate product, and some go back as reflux to the column. The column produces another product (rather a byproduct), called the **bottom product**.

In the reboiler, the liquid circulates naturally by its decrease in density (D). It enters the bottom of the reboiler, in which the liquid partially evaporates, causing its D to be decreased. The decrease in D causes the vapor-liquid mixture (called **boilup**) to rise to the top of the reboiler. From there, it enters the column's lower (stripping) section.

Consider a binary mixture of ethanol (LBC with T_{BP} of 78°C) and water (HBC with T_{BP} of 100°C). In the column with certain T and P, most molecules of the LBC (higher-boiling component) relocate to the vapor (V) phase, and most of the HBC (higher-boiling component) stay in the liquid (L) phase. Then, the vapor enriched in LBC is condensed in a condenser to produce a nearly pure solution of LBC, called **distillate product**, whose first portion has the greatest concentration of LBC. As the process proceeds, the liquid mixture reaches its T_{BP}, so some components get into the distillate, but the LBC (the ethanol) has a larger portion. Purer ethanol liquid, thus, can be obtained by condensing the first portion of the vapor.

As the process continues, the released vapor (mainly LBC) becomes in equilibrium with the residual liquid (mainly HBC). But the concentration of the components in each phase (liquid and vapor) is *not* the same. If we take two sets of samples during distillation, vapor-phase samples show a *greater* concentration of the LBC than the liquid-phase samples. This occurs because the LBC has lower T_{BP}. The separation efficiency (S_E), thus, depends on the T_{BP} (the *greater* the difference in T_{BP}, the *greater* is the S_E). The S_E also depends on the volatility (α) of the components in the same way (the *greater* is the α, the *greater* is the S_E).

The design of a distillation column to accomplish a specified separation involves the next two main steps: 1) Mass balance of components, and 2) Determination of the number of trays.

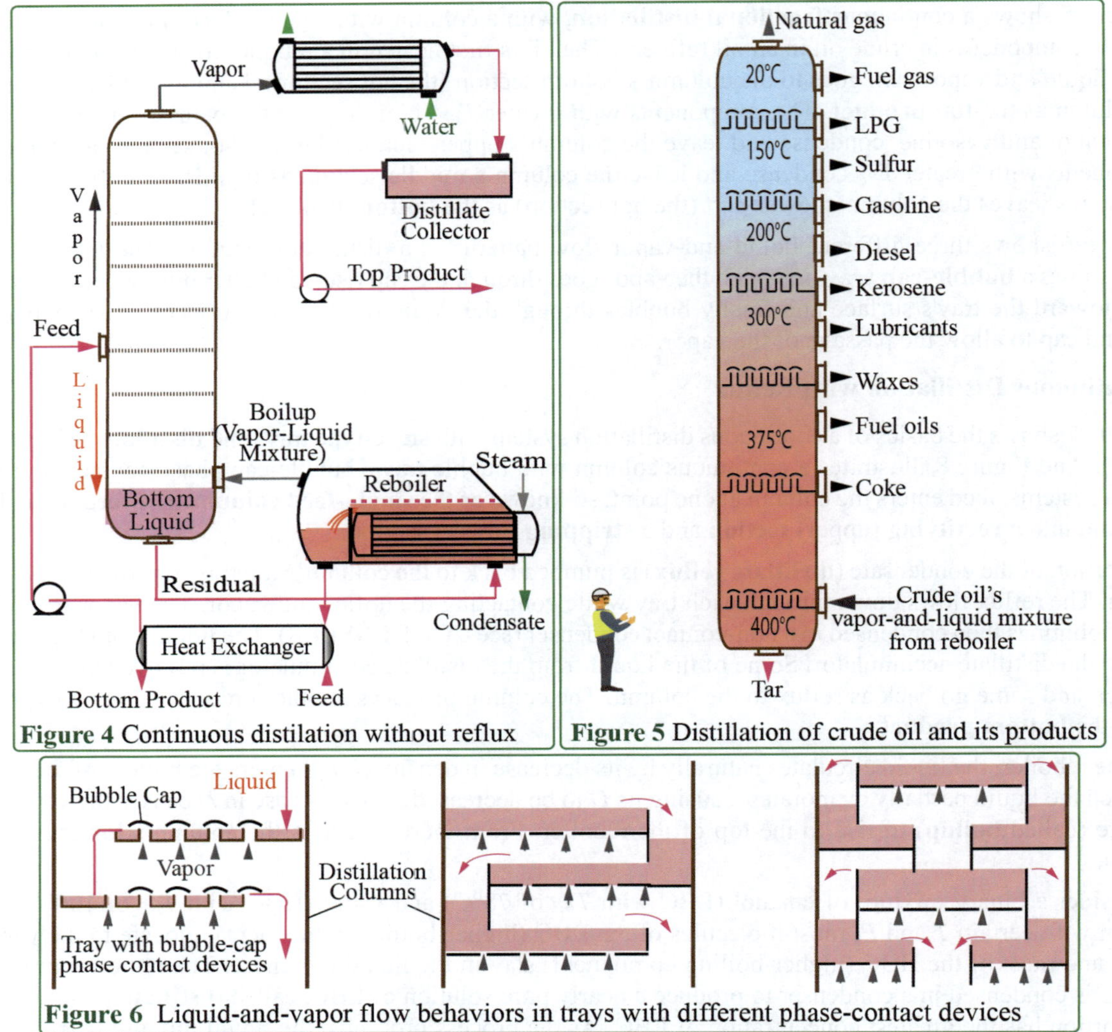

Figure 4 Continuous distilation without reflux

Figure 5 Distillation of crude oil and its products

Figure 6 Liquid-and-vapor flow behaviors in trays with different phase-contact devices

AZEOTROPIC DISTILLATION

Azeotropic distillation is a special type of distillation that is used to distill an azeotropic liquid mixture (simply **azeotrope**), a mixture that one (or more) of its components' molecules behaves non-ideally (azeotropically) at a certain concentration (*C*). For example, an azeotropic behavior occurs during distillation of the ethanol-water mixture when the mixture reaches a *C* of 96.5% by volume (= 95.5% by mass) ethanol and 3.5% water. The azeotropic situation occurs because of strong forces between the molecules at that *C*. Once that *C* has been reached during distillation, the liquid and vapor fractions have almost the same composition ($X_A \approx Y_{n\text{-}A}$), where $X_{n\text{-}A}$ (simply shown as X_A) is the molar fraction of component *A* (ethanol) in the liquid phase and $Y_{n\text{-}A}$ (simply shown as Y_A) is in the vapor phase.

[When **repulsive forces** cause the azeotropic behavior, the mixture is called the **minimum boiling** (positive) **azeotropic mixture**. Instead, when **attractive forces** are the cause, the mixture is called the **maximum boiling** (negative) **azeotropic mixture**. In such situations, the ethanol and water are *not* miscible, so their molecules *cannot* be separated from each other anymore by ordinary distillation.]

An **azeotropic distillation column** and a **decanter** produce anhydrous ethanol (Figure 9). In the azeotropic column, a third component, known as the **separating agent** (also called an **entraining agent** or simply **entrainer**), is added to the mixture to break (interrupt) the azeotrope. Different entrainers, like **cyclohexane** (C_6H_{12}), **pentane** (C_5H_{12}), and **hexane** (C_6H_{14}), are used. Cyclohexane is usually used in the azeotropic distillation of ethanol-water mixture (with about 95% ethanol content) to produce anhydrous ethanol (with about 99.7% ethanol content).

Adding cyclohexane to the anhydrous ethanol (ethanol-water mixture to the azeotropic (dehydration) column forms a low-boiling ternary heterogeneous mixture of ethanol-water-cyclohexane with a T_{BP} of about 63ºC, which is less than that of ethanol (78.4ºC) and cyclohexane (80.8ºC). In addition, the ternary mixture, which consists of two immiscible liquid phases, changes the components' relative volatility. As a result, the separation efficiency (S_E) of the ethanol and water during the azeotropic distillation increases. [As shown in the same figure, the added cyclohexane (a separating agent) is recovered in a decanting column and is returned to the azeotropic column.]

In the azeotropic distillation, the ternary mixture (ethanol + water + cyclohexane) from the azeotropic column is sedimented in the decanting column to form a mixture containing two layers. The upper portion (recovered cyclohexane) returns to the azeotropic column. And the bottom portion mainly consists of water. The top product of the azeotropic column is an anhydrous ethanol solution with 99.3 to 99.7% ethanol.

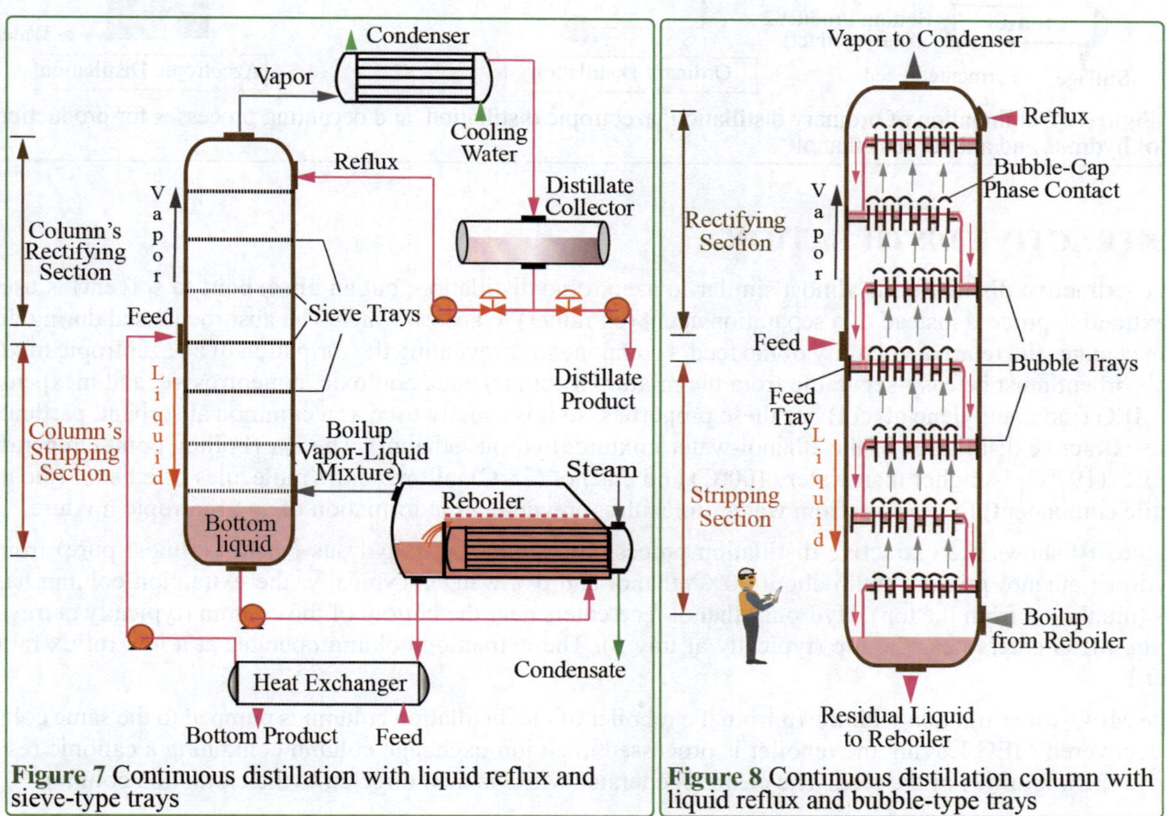

Figure 7 Continuous distillation with liquid reflux and sieve-type trays

Figure 8 Continuous distillation column with liquid reflux and bubble-type trays

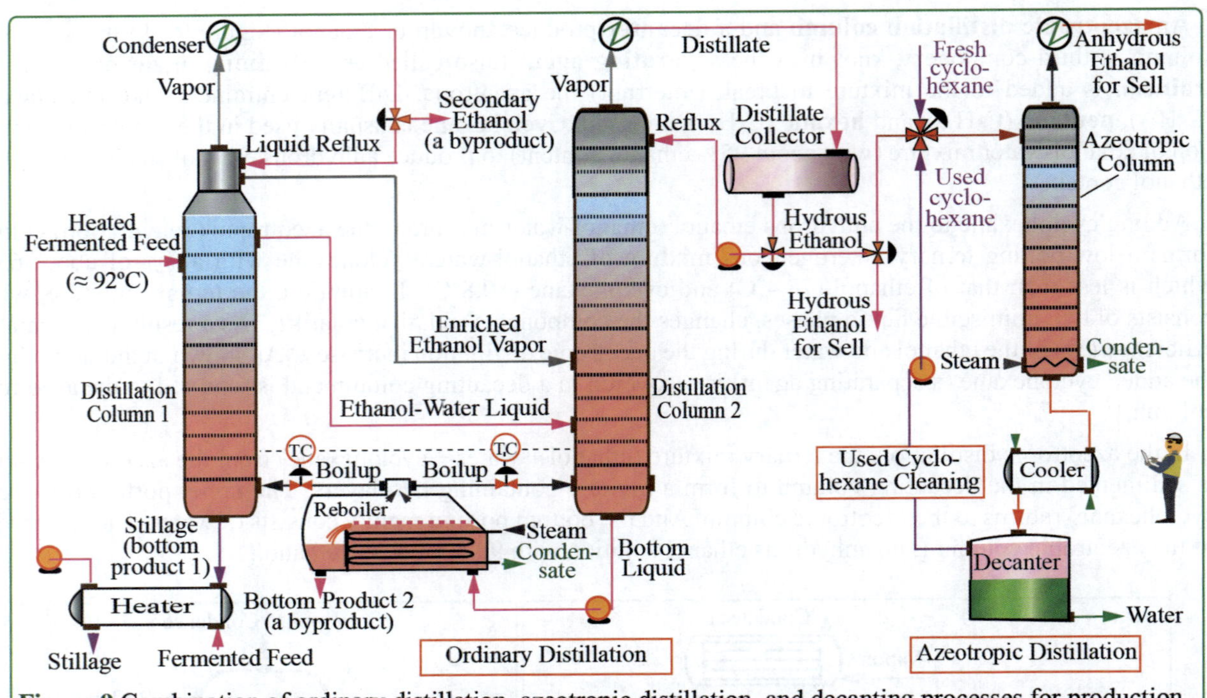

Figure 9 Combination of ordinary distillation, azeotropic distillation, and decanting processes for production of hydrous and anhydrous ethanol

EXTRACTIVE DISTILLATION

The extractive distillation is almost similar to azeotropic distillation, but an **absorbent** (a solvent) is used in the extractive process instead of a separation agent (entrainer) to absorb water. The absorbent used during distillation changes the relative volatility of the feed's components, preventing the formation of an azeotropic mixture. An absorbent must be easy-separable from the mixture's components, nontoxic, noncorrosive, and inexpensive. The MEG (mono ethylene glycol) has these properties, so it is usually used as a common absorbent, particularly in the extractive distillation of the ethanol-water mixture (hydrous ethanol). The T_{BP} (boiling point temperature) of MEG (197ºC) is higher than water (100ºC) and ethanol (78ºC), allowing the molecules of ethanol (the more volatile component) to separate from water molecules, preventing the formation of an azeotropic mixture.

Figure 10 shows the extractive distillation process for producing anhydrous ethanol (almost pure) from an anhydrous ethanol mixture (with about 90% ethanol and 5% water). Typically, the extraction column has 40 trays (numbered from the top). Hydrous ethanol feed enters near the bottom of the column (typically at tray 35), and the MEG enters near the top (typically at tray 5). The extraction column operates at a low reflux ratio of about 1.

The MEG-water fraction withdrawn from the reboiler of the distillation column is pumped to the same column. The recovered MEG leaving the reboiler is processed in an ion-exchange column containing a cationic resin to remove the impurities of the feed. The clean regenerated MEG is then directed to the extraction column.

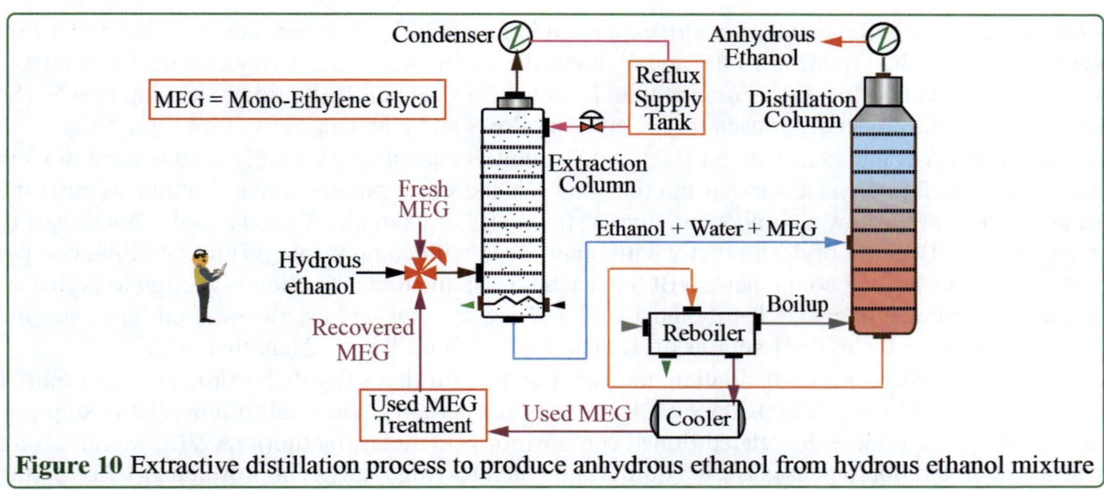

Figure 10 Extractive distillation process to produce anhydrous ethanol from hydrous ethanol mixture

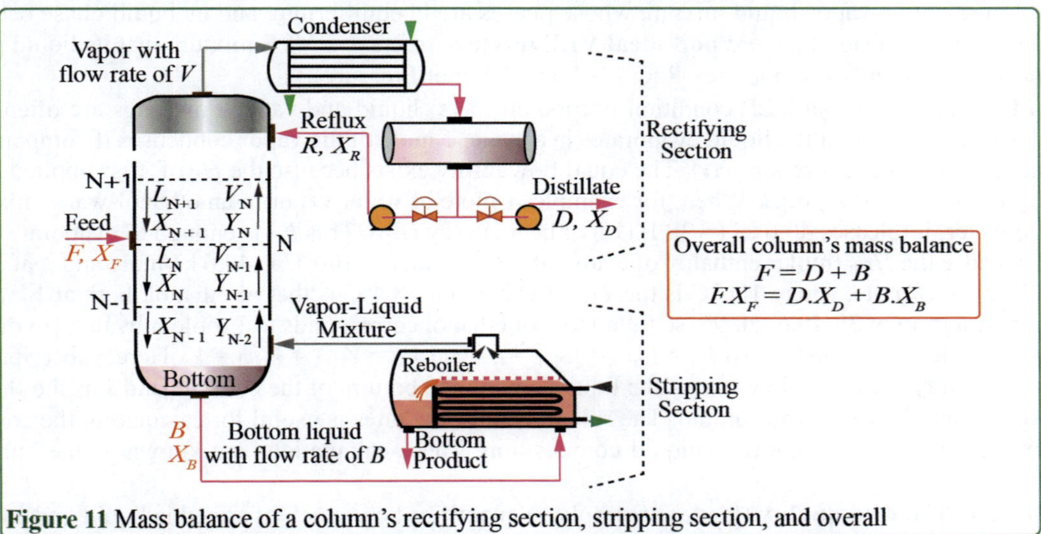

Figure 11 Mass balance of a column's rectifying section, stripping section, and overall

MASS BALANCE OF DISTILLATION

The mass balance of the components entering and leaving a distillation column can determine the **operating lines**, the **number of trays** (N_T), **reflux rates** (R_R), and more. [For conciseability reasons, this subtopic focuses only on the mass balancing of binary distillation systems. Readers interested in multicomponent balancing can refer to Chapter 22 of *Unit Operations of Chemical Engineering*, 7th Edition.]

The design of a distillation column to achieve a specified separation involves the next two main steps: 1) Mass balance of components, and 2) Determination of the number of trays.

These subjects will be discussed for a distillation column with stripping and rectifying sections, reflux, and reboiler. Before starting, it is important to know the following introductory points:

- **Tray Numbering:** The trays of a one-section (rectifying or fractionating) column with a single feed point and *no* reflux are usually numbered serially from the top-down or bottom-up. The trays of a two-section column (with rectifying and stripping sections) are mostly numbered around the feed tray (shown with N). The tray above is N + 1, and below it is N – 1 (Figure 11). [In calculations, the feed tray is considered in the **stripping** (lower) **section**.]

- **Flow Rates:** A stream's flow rate is usually expressed in kmole/h (kg mole per hour), called molar flow rate. The symbol L shows the liquid flow rate, and V shows the vapor flow rate. A tray's number is used as a subscript to show a stream's flow rate. For example, L_N is the flow rate of the liquid (L) leaving tray N. [So, 4 flows exist for a binary system for each tray, 2 entering flows and 2 leaving flows (see Figure 11).]
- **Molar Fractions:** A component's molar fraction (X, a unitless quantity) is usually used instead of its mass fraction, so X is the liquid phase's molar fraction, and Y is the vapor phase's molar fraction. A tray's number is used as a subscript to show a component's molar fraction. For example, X_N is the molar fraction of the liquid leaving tray N. Because of dealing only with binary feed with components A (lower-boiling component, LBC) and B (higher-boiling component, HBC) in each phase; one molar fraction is enough to define a stream's concentrations, like $X_A = 1 - Y_A$ and $Y_A = 1 - X_A$. [Subscripts are usually omitted for binary mixtures, so if X and Y are the molar fractions of A, then $X = 1 - Y$ and $Y = 1 - X$ are that of B.]
- **Vapor-Liquid Equilibrium:** In distillation, the vapor and liquid flows finally become in equilibrium, called the vapor-liquid equilibrium (VLE). Once VLE happens at a certain P, the equilibrium relationship can be used as a model to determine the related flows' compositions (in molar fraction). [A VLE mixture is a mixture whose vapor and liquid phases are in equilibrium when leaving a tray. The word ideal VLE mixture is also used to refer to a vapor-liquid mixture whose phases are in equilibrium, and its liquid phase behaves as an ideal solution. Instead, the word **non-ideal VLE mixture** refers to a VLE mixture that its liquid phase that behaves **non-ideally** (do *not* obey Raoult's Law of Vapor Pressure).]
- **Equal Flow Rates:** Once a VLE condition occurs, all trays' liquid and vapor flow rates are often constant. Thus, at VLE, as 1 mole of the liquid evaporates in a stage, 1 mole of the vapor condenses if components have a similar enthalpy of evaporation (H_E). The equal flowability exists because the H_E of A is supplied by the H_C (enthalpy of condensation) of B. When, for example, 1 mole of water vapor in an ethanol-water mixture condenses to water, it releases 40.6 kJ (= 39 BTU) of heat energy (E_Q). This E_Q is enough to evaporate 1 mole of ethanol because the $H_{E.n}$ (molar enthalpy of evaporation) of water at 100°C is 40.6 kJ/mole and that of ethanol at 78.4°C is 39 kJ/mole, where 100°C is the T_{BP} of water and 78.4°C is that of ethanol, both at 1 Atm. These values create a ratio of 39/40.6 = 0.96, so 0.96 mole of ethanol corresponds to 1 mole of water. [In distillation, the flow rates are often constant, so $L_N = L_{N+1} = L_{N-1} = L$. And $V_N = V_{N+1} = V_{N-1} = V$. Here, subscripts indicate the number of trays, L is the flow rate of the liquid leaving the bottom of the column, and V is the flow rate of the vapor leaving the top of the column. The rule of equal flow rates is useful for calculating the composition of a mixture's vapor if we know its liquid composition. These calculations are known as the bubble point calculations.]
- **Feed Quality:** The **feed quality** (feed-q or simply q) quantifies how much of a feed is liquid and vapor.
- **One-Component Calculations:** In calculations of a binary mixture, only one component is balanced, usually the lighter component (lighter-boiling component, LBC, or component A).

Relative Volatility

The relative volatility (α) measures the difficulty of separating two components of a binary mixture from each other. The relative volatility of the components A and B (shown as α_{AB}) is related to the separation efficiency (S_E) of the components (the *greater* is the α_{AB}, the *easier* is the separation of the components from each other and, thus, the *greater* is the S_E of the components). Thus, α_{AB} should be high in distillation to give a high S_E, like the separation of methanol from water with a large α_{AB} of around 2.5 (as α_{AB} gets closer to one, S_E approaches a low value). When a binary VLE mixture with components A and B is under distillation and compositions are expressed in molar fractions (X and Y), the relative volatility of A (light component) to B (heavy component), shown as α_{AB}, is

$$\alpha_{AB} = \frac{\frac{Y_A}{Y_B}}{\frac{X_A}{X_B}} = \frac{Y_A.X_B}{X_A.Y_B} \quad (1)$$

The term Y_A/X_A (the molar fraction of A in the vapor phase to A in the liquid phase) in this equation is called the distribution coefficient (K-value) of component A when the two phases are at equilibrium.

$$K_A = \frac{Y_A}{X_A} = \frac{Y}{X} \tag{2}$$

Because X and Y are the molar fractions of A, then $(1 - X)$ and $(1 - Y)$ are the molar fractions of B, so subscripts are usually *not* used in Equation 1.

$$\alpha = \frac{Y(1-X)}{X(1-Y)} \tag{3}$$

Solving for Y gives a frequently-used separation equation that indicates the nonlinearity relationship of X to Y through α:

$$Y = \frac{\alpha.X}{1+(\alpha-1)X} \tag{4}$$

The α is T dependent, but P independent. In most distillation systems, α is constant under normal operating T and P, so the simple form of the volatility equation can be used to calculate Y (the light component's molar fraction in the vapor phase) if we know X (the light component's molar fraction in the liquid phase).

$$Y = \frac{X}{1+X} \tag{5}$$

According to this equation (simple volatility equation), Y is a non-straight (non-linear) function of X.

[When an **ideal VLE mixture** is under distillation, α equates to the vapor pressure (P_V) of component A (the light component), so the P_V of A is usually used in calculations instead of α.]

Mass Balance of a Two-Section Column With Reflux and Reboiler

For mass balancing a typical distillation system, we use the next usual simplifying assumptions:

- A binary mixture with components A (in our case, ethanol) and B (water) is under distillation
- A good phase equilibrium exists between the vapor and liquid streams leaving each tray.
- The feed enters the column as a saturated liquid at its bubble point temperature.

Because feed enters the column as a saturated liquid, the feed quality (q) will be

$$q = \frac{L_S - L_R}{F} \tag{6}$$

L_S is the liquid flow rate in the column's stripping section, L_R is the liquid flow rate in the rectifying section, and F is the feed's flow rate, all in mole/time or kmole/time. As this equation tells us, q is the fraction of the liquid feed, so it determines the thermal condition of the feed to the column.

When the feed enters the stripping (lower) section, the liquid flow rate in the stripping section (L_S) is

$$L_S = L_R + F \tag{7}$$

And the vapor flow rate in the stripping section (V_S) will be

$$V_S = V_R + F \tag{8}$$

For the column's flow-rate balance, the total flow of feed (F), distillate (D), and bottom product (B) are used.

$$F = D + B \quad \text{or} \quad B = F - D \tag{9}$$

Similarly, the total component balance of F, D, and B is used for the column's component balance.

$$F.X_F = D.X_D + B.X_B \tag{10}$$

X_F is the molar fraction of LBC (lower boiling component) in the **feed**, X_D is that in the **distillate**, and X_B is in the **bottom** product. Equations 9 ($B = F - D$) and 10 can solve the D.

$$D = \frac{F(X_F - X_B)}{X_D - X_B} \tag{11}$$

Eliminating D gives

$$B = \frac{F(X_D - X_F)}{X_D - X_B} \tag{12}$$

Or

$$\frac{B}{F} = \frac{X_D - X_F}{X_D - X_B}$$

Reflux Rate, Reflux Ratio, and Minimum Reflux Ratio: As for the distillate reflux flow, the following three (3) quantities are used:

- **Reflux Flow Rate** (R_R)**:** The R_R is the reflux flow rate per unit time (usually in m^3/s or m^3/h).
- **Reflux Ratio** (R)**:** The R is the ratio (a unitless quantity) of R_R (the amount of the reflux returned to the column from the overhead condenser) to D (the amount of distillate removed from the column) or R_R/D.
- **Minimum Reflux Ratio** (R_M)**:** The R_M is the minimum amount of liquid reflux (L) needed to be returned to a column to produce a certain amount of distillate (D) with desired concentration, or $R_M = L/D$.

The next equation is usually used to determine the R_M (the minimum L-to-D ratio) of a binary mixture when the feed enters a column at its bubble point T:

$$R_M = \frac{1}{\alpha - 1}\left(\frac{X_D}{X_F} - \frac{\alpha(1 - X_D)}{(1 - X_F)}\right) \tag{13}$$

And when the feed enters a column at its dew point T, the next equation is used:

$$R_M = \frac{1}{\alpha - 1}\left(\frac{\alpha . X_D}{\alpha . X_F} - \frac{\alpha(1 - X_D)}{(1 - X_F)}\right) \tag{14}$$

In these equations, α is the relative volatility of the light component (A) to the heavy component (B), X_D is the distillate's molar fraction of A, and X_F is the feed's molar fraction of A.

Another relationship exists between R_R, N_T (a column's number of trays), and S_E (a column's separation efficiency) that indicates "the *greater* is the R_R for a given N_T, the *greater* is the S_E. Alternatively, the *greater* is the R_R to achieve the desired S_E, the *fewer* N_T is required." [Thus, choosing the right R_R and N_T is the most important factor for achieving the desired S_E in a distillation column with a certain number of trays (N_T).]

Because reflux is a saturated liquid at its bubble point T, the liquid flow rate in the column's rectifying (upper) section (L_R) will be

$$L_R = R_R = R_X . D \tag{15}$$

Once L_R has been calculated, L_S (the liquid flow rate in the column's stripping section) can be calculated from Equation 6 (feed-quality equation).

Knowing L_R, the V_R (the vapor flow rate in the column's top section above the feed tray) can be calculated.

$$V_R = L_R + D \quad \text{or} \quad V_R = R_R + D \tag{16}$$

A similar equation can calculate the liquid flow rate in the column's bottom section.

$$L_S = V_S + B \tag{17}$$

Because we assumed the feed enters the column as saturated liquid, the q (feed quality) equates to 1, so the stripping section's liquid flow rate (L_S) will be

$$L_S = L_R + q . F \tag{18}$$

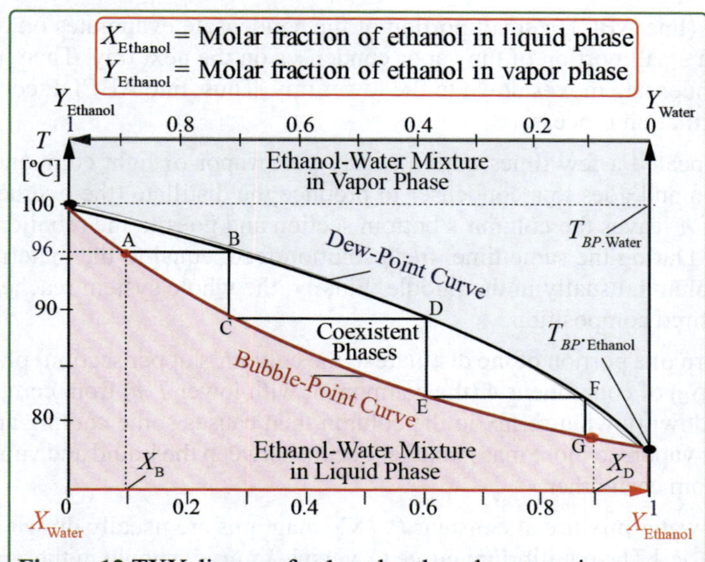

Figure 12 TXY diagram for 1 mole ethanol-water mixture at constant pressure (*P*) of 1 Atm

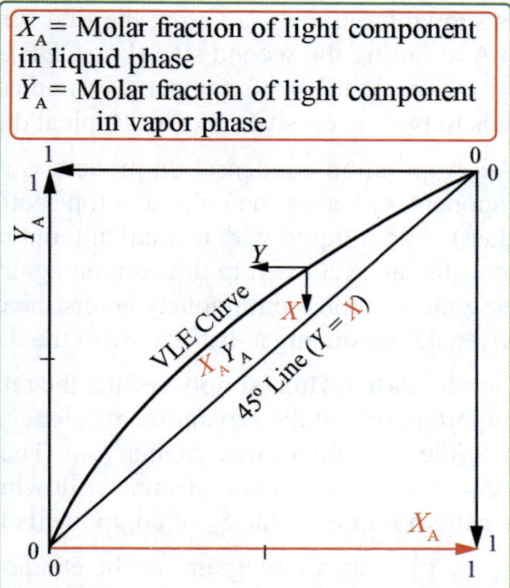

Figure 13 XY diagram for 1 mole ethanol-water mixture at constant *P*

THEORY OF DISTILLATION TRAYS

The **trays** (plates) are installed inside a distillation column to transfer the mass between the liquid and vapor phases. The mass transfer between the phases continues in a countercurrent way on each tray until a VLE (liquid-vapor equilibrium) is established between the phases. Maximum mass transfer between the phases occurs in a column at a certain pressure (*P*), so when the vapor and liquid phases leave the column, the composition (concentration) of each component in each phase is different. Thus, a **separation** (fractionation) between the components with different T_{BP} (boiling point temperature) occurs. Distillation must go through sufficient VLE steps, equal to a column's number of trays (N_T), to provide satisfactory separation efficiency (S_E) between the components.

Figure 12 shows the boiling point diagram of the ethanol-water mixture (a binary mixture) at a constant *P* of 1 Atm. Such a phase diagram is also called TXY diagram as it shows a component's liquid and vapor phases in relation to their *T* at constant *P*. In the diagram, two temperature-related quantities are recognized:

- **Bubble Point Temperature:** At points below the bubble point temperature curve (simply **bubble-point curve**), the mixture is in the liquid state, so this curve indicates the liquid compositions. [The **bubble point temperature** of a liquid is the *T* slightly below its boiling point temperature (T_{BP}).]
- **Dew Point Temperature:** At points above the dew point temperature curve (simply **dew-point curve**), the mixture is in the vapor state, so this curve indicates the vapor compositions. [A vapor's **dew point temperature** is the *T* slightly above its condensation temperature (T_C).]

And between bubble and dew curves, both phases (liquid and vapor) exist, known as the **coexistent phases**. In the coexistent area, the relative amounts of the two phases can be drawn by the Mc-Thiele method (discussed later). In this case and as shown in the same figure, the mixture boils at the *T* given by the lower curve (red), so a liquid of 0.1 molar fraction ethanol (LBC) and 0.9 molar fraction water (HBC) boils at about 96ºC under P_{Atm}. And the vapor of this liquid, which is richer in water and has the composition B, can be condensed by lowering the *T* along the line BC. If evaporating a small portion of the condensate, the produced vapor contains the composition D. During distillation, the evaporation-condensation processes of the ethanol-water mixture are repeated more times to produce vapor with a high amount of ethanol. These steps are repeated to produce a product distillate with the highest ethanol concentration. [If a distillation column operates with a reboiler, the number of theoretical trays is reduced by one (because the reboiler acts like one tray.]

As shown in Figure 12, during the first step (line ABC), a small portion of the condensate evaporates on one tray. And during the second step (line CDE), a small portion of the vapor condenses on the next tray. Then, the vapor moves up to the next upper tray, and condensate moves down to the lower tray. Thus, line ABCDE corresponds to two successive trays in a typical distillation process.

The evaporation-condensation process is repeated a few times until a nearly-pure vapor of light component (component A) leaves the column's top section and goes to a condenser to produce the distillate (the overhead product). And a liquid with a small amount of A leaves the column's bottom section and goes to the reboiler to be reheated and returned to the column again. During the same time, fresh solution feed, equal to the materials leaving the column, continuously enters the column, usually in the middle. Finally, the whole system reaches a steady state, producing a distillate with the desired composition.

The **distillate reflux** (simply **reflux**, the return of a portion of the distillate to the column's upper section) plays an important role in the separation efficiency (S_E) of component A (the component with lower T_{BP}) from component B (the component with higher T_{BP}). The downflowing reflux in the column then causes some cooling and, consequently, condensation of some upflowing vapor, so more mass transfer occurs between the liquid and vapor. This pattern improves the S_E of components from each other.

Figure 13 is an XY diagram for the ethanol-water mixture at constant P. [XY diagrams are usually drawn for constant P because most applications are isobaric.] The equilibrium curve (Y versus X curve) shown in the same figure relates the concentrations of the liquid and vapor phases in equilibrium with each other, known as the **vapor-liquid equilibrium** (VLE). The VLE curve and 45º line (on which $X = Y$) pass the (0,0) corners of the diagram, but each with a different slope.

DETERMINATION OF NUMBER OF TRAYS

To provide a sufficient vapor-liquid contact and separation efficiency (S_E) of the components, we must carefully determine a distillation column's **number of trays** (N_T, also called the **number of theoretical trays**). The number of **actual trays** (N_{Act}) is often more than the **theoretical trays** (N_T) because the establishment of VLE in each tray is *not* complete. A relationship between N_{Act}, N_T, and E_T (tray efficiency) exists.

$$N_{Act} = \frac{N_T}{E_T} \tag{19}$$

Based on the duties of a distillation column, one of the following methods is usually used to model a distillation system and determine the N_T:

- Calculation Method
- McCabe-Thiele graphical Method
- McCabe-Thiele Computer Program Method
- Computerized Simulation Program (Simulator) Method

[The last method uses computerized simulation programs for more complicated cases, like when a column is fed at two (or even more) points. This method is *not* covered in ordinary textbooks like this one.]

Determination of Number of Trays Using Calculation Method

This subtopic provides the equations for determining the N_T (number of trays) of a column with stripping and rectifying sections for a binary (two-component) system, like an ethanol-water solution. Only one (usually the light component) balance is sufficient for a binary system.

Stripping Section Equations: As shown in Figure 11, the component balance for the N tray in the stripping (lower) section can be written as

$$L_S.X_{N+1} = V_S.Y_N + B.X_B \tag{20}$$

The component balance for tray 1 (or X_1) in the bottom of the stripping section (the **reboiler section**) is

$$L_S.X_1 = V_S.Y_B + B.X_B \tag{21}$$

The component balance for X_2 will be

$$L_S.X_2 = V_S.Y_1 + B.X_B \tag{22}$$

For obtaining the total number of trays in the stripping section, we continue the tray-to-tray calculations until a liquid composition near the liquid feed composition (X_F) is obtained.

Rectifying Section Equations: As shown in Figure 11, the component balance for the N (feed) tray in the rectifying (upper) section will be

$$L_R.X_{N+1} + F.X_F = V_R.Y_N + B.X_B \tag{23}$$

To obtain the total number of trays in the rectifying section, we continue the tray-to-tray calculations until a liquid composition equal to or greater than the desired distillate composition (X_D) is obtained.

The next Example makes the subjects of calculating a distillation column's liquid flow rates, vapor flow rates, and the number of trays clearer.

Example 1 on Distillation

Determine the number of trays using the calculation method in a two-section column when 100 kg-mole/h of a saturated binary solution enters the column as a feed with an LBC composition (X_F) of 0.50 kg-mole/h. The distillate's composition (X_D) is 0.96 and the bottom product's composition (X_B) is 0.03 kg-mole/h.

Assumptions: A reflux ratio of $R_X =$ 2.5 and constant relative volatility of $\alpha = 2$ are assumed to obtain the column's VLE. A saturated feed solution with 50% vapor and distillate reflux are also assumed.

Equations 11 and 9 can calculate the distillate's flow rate (D) and the bottom's flow rate (B).

$$D = \frac{F(X_F - X_B)}{X_D - X_B} = \frac{100(0.5-0.03)}{0.96-0.03} = 50.5 \text{ kg-mole/h}$$

$$B = F - D = 100 - 50.5 = 49.5 \text{ kg-mole/h}$$

The rectifying section's liquid flow rate (L_R) will be

$$L_R = R_R = R_X.D = 2.5 \times 50.5 = 126.3$$

Because the feed enters the column as saturated liquid, the q (feed quality) equates to 1, so the stripping section's liquid flow rate (L_S) can be calculated as

$$L_S = L_R + q.F = 126.3 + (1)(100) = 226.3$$

V_R (the rectifying section's vapor flow rate) and V_S (the stripping section's vapor flow rate) are:

$$V_R = L_R + D = 126.3 + 50.5 = 176.8 \text{ kg-mole/h} \qquad V_S = L_S - B = 226.3 - 49.5 = 176.8 \text{ kg-mole/h}$$

V_R and V_S are equal because the feed is saturated liquid. Under this situation, the feed changes the liquid flow rates in the stripping and rectifying sections but does *not* change the vapor flow rates between them.

For the component balance of the bottom tray (the reboiler is taken as tray 1), we use the next equation to calculate vapor composition (Y_B).

$$Y_B = \frac{\alpha.X_B}{1+(\alpha-1)X_B} = \frac{(2)(0.03)}{1+(2-1)(0.03)} = 0.058 \text{ kg-mole/h}$$

We use the next equation for the component balance of the stripping section's trays.

$$L_S.X_1 = V_S.Y_N + B.X_B$$

$$X_1 = \frac{(V_S.Y_B)+(B.X_B)}{L_S} = \frac{(176.8)(0.058)+(49.5)(0.03)}{226.3} = 0.052 \text{ kg-mole/h}$$

For tray 1:

$$Y_1 = \frac{\alpha.X_1}{1+(\alpha-1)X_1} = \frac{(2)(0.052)}{1+(2-1)(0.052)} = 0.099 \text{ kg-mole/h}$$

$$X_2 = \frac{(V_S.Y_1)+(B.X_B)}{L_S} = \frac{(176.8)(0.099)+(49.5)(0.03)}{226.3} = 0.084 \text{ kg-mole/h}$$

For tray 2:

$$Y_2 = \frac{\alpha.X_2}{1+(\alpha-1)X_1} = \frac{(2)(0.084)}{1+(2-1)(0.084)} = 0.155 \text{ kg-mole/h}$$

$$X_3 = \frac{(V_S.Y_2)+(B.X_B)}{L_S} = \frac{(176.8)(0.155)+(49.5)(0.03)}{226.3} = 0.128 \text{ kg-mole/h}$$

We must continue with these calculations until a value of X_{N+1} greater than the feed composition ($X_F = 0.50$) is achieved.

Tray #	X_N	Y_N
0	0.030	0.058
1	0.052	0.099
2	0.084	0.155
3	0.128	0.227
4	0.184	0.311
5	0.250	0.400
6	0.319	0.484
7	0.385	0.653
8	0.516	0.981

The value X_8 in this table is greater than the feed composition ($X_F = 0.5$), so the required trays in the stripping section are 7.

For the component balance of the rectifying section's top tray, we use Equation 23 to calculate the X values from tray 8 until the vapor composition is greater than the distillate composition ($X_D = 0.96$).

$$L_R.X_{N+1} + F.X_F = V_R.Y_N + B.X_B$$

$$X_8 = \frac{V_R.Y_7 + B.X_B - F.X_F}{L_R} = \frac{176.8 \times 0.653 + 49.5 \times 0.03 - 100 \times 0.5}{126.3} = \frac{66.935}{126.3} = 0.530$$

Tray 8:

$$Y_8 = \frac{\alpha.X_8}{1+(\alpha-1)X_8} = \frac{(2)(0.53)}{1+(2-1)(0.53)} = 0.693$$

$$X_9 = \frac{176.8 \times 0.693 + 49.5 \times 0.03 - 100 \times 0.5}{126.3} = \frac{74.001}{126.3} = 0.586$$

We must continue with these calculations until a vapor composition greater than the distillate composition of $X_D = 0.96$ is achieved.

Tray #	X_N	Y_N
8	0.530	0.693
9	0.586	0.739
10	0.650	0.788
11	0.719	0.837
12	0.788	0.881
13	0.849	0.918
14	0.901	0.948
15	0.943	0.971
16	0.975	0.987

The value X_{16} in this table is greater than the desired distillate composition ($X_D = 0.96$), so 15 trays are required to achieve this distillation duty.

Determination of Number of Trays Using McCabe-Thiele Method on a Graph Paper

For applying the **McCabe-Thiele method** (simply the Mc-Thiele method) on a graph paper, you first need to become familiar with the operating lines.

Operating Lines

Usually, four (4) operating lines are used in MC-Thiele graphical method:

- Reference operating line,
- Feed quality operating line,
- Section operating line, and
- Vapor-liquid equilibrium (VLE) operating line

Reference Line

A reference line (also called **45° line**) is a straight (linear or $X = Y$) line that connects the 0-0 corners of a phase diagram, with the intercept of 0 and slope (S) of 1.

The reference (45°) line has the following properties:

- It is used to draw all other **operating lines**, and
- Both X_B (the bottom's molar fraction of light component) and X_D (the distillate's molar fraction of light component) are on the 45° line.

Feed Quality Line

A feed-quality line (simply **feed line** or **q-line**) is a straight line that starts from X_F (the feed's liquid molar fraction of LBC) on a 45° (reference) line and connects to the intersection of the SO (stripping-operating) line and RO (rectifying-operating) line with the slope of $-q/(1-q)$.

A feed line (q-line) has the following properties:

- It is used to draw the SO and RO lines of a two-section column with stripping and rectifying sections.
- It expresses the feed's thermal (heat) condition when it enters a column. Saturated-liquid feed at bubble-point T, $q = 1$, saturated vapor at dew-point T, $q = 0$, and liquid-vapor mixture, $q = 0.5$ (see Figure 14-D).

The q-line's slope [$S = -q/(1-q)$] intersects the 45° line at X_F. The intersection of the q-line and the SO line is important because it is at that point that the column changes from the stripping action to the rectifying action. The **feed quality** (feed-q or simply q) determines the fraction of the feed that is liquid by the feed's thermal properties. Generally, Equation 6 determines q.

$$q = \frac{L_S - L_R}{F}$$

A feed entering a distillation column can be in one of the following states:

- Saturated liquid at its bubble point T, as shown in Figure 14-A (see the next Note).
- Saturated vapor at its boiling point temperature or dew point temperature (Figure 14-B).
- Mixture of liquid (L) and vapor (V). This case can be studied by referring to Figure 14-C.

Most columns operate like the first case when the feed enters as a liquid at its bubble point T (in other words, near its boiling point T). We consider this case to write the q-line equation.

$$Y = -\frac{q}{1-q}X + \frac{X_F}{1-q} \tag{24}$$

In the q-line's equation, Y is the LBC's flow rate in the vapor phase, X is the flow rate in the liquid phase, the q is for q-value, and X_F is the composition of the liquid feed. As the equation indicates, the q-line is a straight line with a slope of $-q/(1-q)$ that intersects the 45° line at X_F, so all lines' intersections fall on the q-line.

Drawing the *q*-Line: For drawing a *q*-line, start at X_F at 45° line and draw a line with slope $-q/(1-q)$. The *q*-line slopes for the listed three (3) cases can be studied in Figure 14-D.

[Note: In distillation, often, the word **bubble point temperature** is used to indicate the temperature (T) of a liquid stream, which is at or slightly below its **boiling point temperature** (T_{BP}). Similarly, **dew point temperature** indicates the T of a stream at or slightly above its condensation temperature.]

Section Operating Lines

A section operating line represents the liquid-to-vapor (L-to-V) flow rate ratio of a one-section (stripping) column or each section of a two-section column. Thus, a two-section column with **stripping** (lower) and **rectifying** (upper) sections has two section operating lines, **stripping operating** (SO) **line** and **rectifying operating** (RO) **line**.

A section line generally has the following characteristics:

- It can be generally shown as $Y = aX + b$, where a is the line's slope, and b is its intercept (a point where the line crosses the Y-axis). X is the light component's flow rate in liquid, and Y is in the vapor phase.
- It is straight if the L/V of a column with one feed point is constant (Figure 15A).
- Its slope (S) in a one-section column is the column's L/V (Figure 15D). In a two-section column, each section's S is the L/V in that section (Figure 15E), where the L/V in each section is different from the other.

The SO-line slope equation for the light component for the feed plate (N plate) of a one-section column is

$$Y_{N+1} = \frac{L}{V}X_N + \frac{BX_B}{V} \tag{25}$$

The SO-line is a straight line that starts at the intersection of the 45° line and X_B (bottom concentration). The SO-line slope equation for the light component for the N tray of a two-section column is

$$Y_{N+1} = \frac{L_S}{V_S}X_N + \frac{B.X_B}{V_S} \tag{26}$$

The RO-line is a straight line that starts at the intersection of the 45° line and X_D (distillate concentration). The RO-line slope equation for the light component for the N tray of a two-section column is

$$Y_{N+1} = \frac{L_R}{V_R}X_N + \frac{D.X_D}{V_R} \tag{27}$$

When saturated liquid reflux reenters a column at its bubble point temperature, the $L_R = R_R$, and $V_R = R_R + D$. The R_R is the **reflux flow rate**. Using these terms in the previous equation yields the RO-line slope equation for tray N of a column with reflux.

$$Y_{N+1} = \frac{R_R}{R_R+D}X_N + \frac{D.X_D}{R_R+D} \tag{28}$$

Dividing the right-hand side of this equation's numerators and denominators by D, we get the RO-line slope equation of the column's rectifying section.

$$Y_{N+1} = \frac{R_R}{R_R+1}X_N + \frac{X_D}{R_R+1} \tag{29}$$

Thus, the RO-line slope (S) given in Equations 27 and 29 are equal.

$$S = \frac{L_R}{V_R} = \frac{R_R}{R_R+1} \tag{30}$$

Rearranging to solve for R_R gives

$$R_R = \frac{S}{1-S} \tag{31}$$

Drawing Section Operating Lines

We want to see how to draw operating lines for a one-section (stripping) column and each section of a two-section column.

Drawing SO Line: Follow the next steps to draw a SO (stripping-operating) line.

- Calculate the SO line's slope (L_S/V_S), where L_S is the liquid's flow rate and V_S is the vapor's flow rate, both in the **stripping** section. Assume that that the $L_S = 0.9$ and $V_S = 0.6$, then the SO line's slope (S) is 0.9/0.6 = 1.5. [The SO line's slope is always **greater** than unity (one).]
- Start at X_B (the LBC's molar fraction in the bottom product) on a 45° line and draw an upward straight line with slope L_S/V_S until it connects to the q-line (as shown in Figures 15A, B, and C).

Drawing RO Line: For drawing a RO (rectifying-operating) line, follow the next steps:

- Calculate the RO line's slope (L_R/V_R), where L_R is the liquid's flow rate and V_R is the vapor's flow rate, both in the **rectifying** section. Assume that the $L_R = 0.6$ and $V_R = 0.8$, then the RO line's S is 0.6/0.8 = 0.75. [The RO line's slope is always **less** than unity.]
- Start at X_D (the light component's molar fraction of the distillate product) on a 45° line and draw a downward straight line with slope L_R/V_R until it connects to the q-line (as shown in Figures 15D and E).

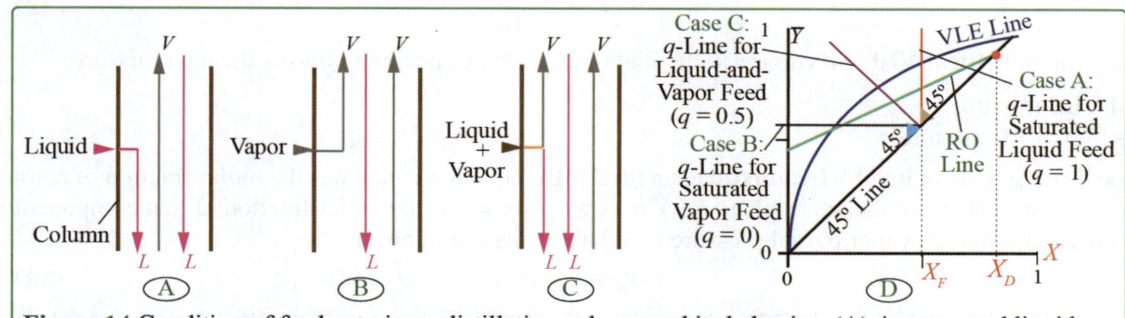

Figure 14 Condition of feed entering a distillation column and its behavior: (A) As saturated liquid, (B) As saturated vapor, (C) As mixture of liquid and vapor, (D) q-lines for all three cases

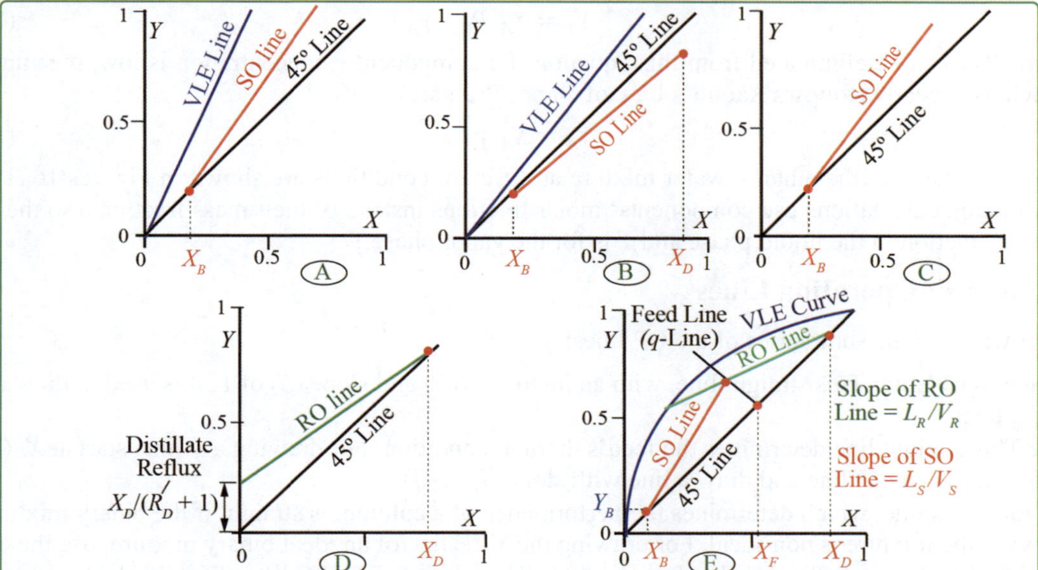

Figure 15 Operating lines: (A) For a one-section column when K-value of VLE line is constant, (B) For a one-section column when K-value of VLE line is not constant, (C) For stripping section of a two-section column, (D) For rectifying section of a two-section column, (E) For stripping and rectifying sections of a two-section column when feed enters the column as mixture of liquid and vapor

Vapor-Liquid Equilibrium Line

A vapor-liquid equilibrium line (VLE line) has the following properties:

- It determines the performance of a distillation column by representing the LBC (component A) concentrations at different temperatures and constant P in an XY diagram (X-versus-Y diagram) when the VLE is established (when vapor and liquid flows are in equilibrium with each other) in the column.
- The VLE line of an ideal mixture is straight, representing the components' partial pressure (PP) of that mixture. A non-ideal mixture (in most cases) requires activity coefficients (temperature-and-pressure dependents correction factors) to cover the mixture's non-ideality.

Drawing VLE Line: The VLE line of a mixture starts from the (0, 0) point of an *XY* diagram and connects to the compositions of that mixture's vapor and liquid flows. The VLE line of an ideal mixture is straight (see Figures 15A and B). Instead, the VLE line of a non-ideal mixture is curved (see Figures 15E and F). For drawing a binary mixture's VLE curve, the components' relative volatility (α) is used.

$$Y = \frac{\alpha X}{1+(\alpha-1)X} \tag{32}$$

Ideal and Non-Ideal VLE Mixtures: In distillation, we always deal with one of the next mixtures:

- Ideal VLE mixture
- Non-ideal VLE mixture

When dealing with an **ideal VLE mixture**, an ideal VLE equation calculates the molar fraction of component *A* (the light component) in the vapor phase (Y_A) in a tray if we know the molar fraction of that component in the liquid phase (X_A) and its vapor partial pressure ($P_{P.A}$) above its liquid phase.

$$Y_A = X_A . P_{P.A} \tag{33}$$

When dealing with a **non-ideal VLE mixture** (mostly is the case), a non-ideal-VLE equation can be written if a component's correction factor, called activity coefficient (γ_A), is applied to the previous equation.

$$Y_A = X_A . P_{P.A} . \gamma_A \tag{34}$$

The term $P_{P.A}$ can be eliminated from this equation if a component's concentration is low, meaning that the mixture behaves ideally (follows Raoult's Law of Vapor Pressure).

$$Y_A = X_A . \gamma_A \tag{35}$$

The VLE diagrams of the ethanol-water mixture at different conditions are shown in Figures 16, 17, and 18. [Most distillation calculations use components' molar fractions instead of their mass fractions, so the letter *X* is for the molar fraction in the liquid phase and *Y* is for the vapor phase.]

Summaries of Operating Lines

The following are the summaries of the OP lines:

- **reference (45°) Line:** This straight line, with an intercept of 0 and slope (*S*) of 1. It is used to draw all other operating lines.
- ***q*-Line:** This straight line determines the feed's thermal condition. For drawing a *q*-line, start at X_F (feed's molar fraction) at a 45° line and draw a line with slope $-q/(1-q)$.
- **VLE Line:** This line, which determines the performance of a column, is straight if the binary mixture is ideal and curvy if the mixture is non-ideal. For drawing the VLE line of an ideal binary mixture, use the components' partial pressure (P_P), as used in Equation 34. For drawing the VLE line of a non-ideal mixture, use the component's P_P and γ (activity coefficient), as used in Equation 34 or 35.
- ROP Line: This straight line represents a liquid-to-vapor (*L*-to-*V*) flow rate ratio of a column's rectifying section. For drawing the ROP, start at X_D on 45° line and draw a downward straight line with slope L_R/V_R until it connects to the *q*-line.

- **SOP Line:** This straight line represents the L-to-V flow rate ratio of a one-section (stripping) column or the stripping section of a two-section column. For drawing the SOP, start at X_B on a 45° line and draw an upward straight line with slope L_S/V_S until it connects to the q-line.

Now that you have become familiar with the operating lines, we can discuss how to determine the N_T (number of trays) using the Mc-Thiele method.

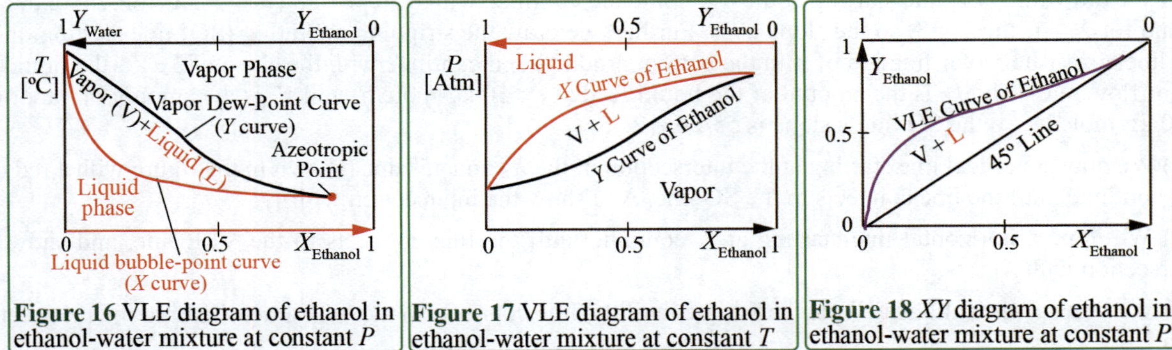

Figure 16 VLE diagram of ethanol in ethanol-water mixture at constant P

Figure 17 VLE diagram of ethanol in ethanol-water mixture at constant T

Figure 18 XY diagram of ethanol in ethanol-water mixture at constant P

Mc-Thiele Method for a One-Section Column

The McCabe-Thiele method (simply the Mc-Thiele method) is a graphical step-by-step procedure to determine a column's number of trays (N_T). Figure 19 shows the application of the Mc-Thiele method for 1 mole of a binary mixture in a one-section (stripping) column.

For determining the N_T using the Mc-Thiele method, follow the next steps:

1. Draw the 45° line on an XY diagram.
2. Mark X_B (the light component's molar fraction in the bottom product) and X_D (the light component's molar fraction in the distillate product) on the X-axis.
3. Draw the VLE line and SO line on the diagram.
4. Draw a vertical line at the intersection of the X_B and 45° line (shown in the same figure with a red dot) and continue until the line connects to the SO line. And show the intersection with 1. [For drawing the step lines, use the area between the 45° and SO lines.]
5. Draw a horizontal line starting at point 1, continue until the line connects to the VLE line, and show the intersection with X_1.
6. Draw a vertical line starting at X_1, continue until the line connects to the VLE line, and show the intersection with 2.
7. Continue with stepping up until reaching or passing the X_D on the 45° line. [The step-by-step procedure can be started either at the bottom of the SO line or at the top of that line. Here we start at the bottom of the SO line.]
8. Count the number of steps needed to go from X_B to X_D. The number of steps equals the number of theoretical stages built to achieve a desired separation at the specified L/V ratio.

Example 2 on Distillation

Determine the number of trays using Mc-Thiele's graphical method in a one-section column when the liquid feed flow rate to the column is 55 kg-mole/h, with an LBC composition of 2.5-mole percent and HBC of 97.5 mole %. The bottom of the column contains a heating coil to produce vapor from the feed. The liquid and vapor rates can be assumed to be the same on all trays. The distillation goal is a purity of 0.3-mole percent of component

A in the bottom product (so, $X_B = 0.3\%$ molar fraction) when the vapor (V) flow rate is 20 kg-mole/h. The K-value for component A in the column is assumed to be 3 or $Y_A = 3\ X_B$.

1) We draw the 45° line starting at the 0-0 point and connecting a straight line to the 0-0 point of the other corner of an XY diagram (see Figure 19).

2) We locate points $X_B = 0.03\%$ and $X_F = 2.5\%$ on the X-axis and 45° line.

3) We draw the VLE line starting at the 0-0 point and continue with a slope of 3 (in $Y = 3X$, for $X = 0$, the $Y = 0$; and for $X = 1$, the $Y = 3$, so the slope is 3). Further, we draw the stripping operating (SO) line starting on the 45° line at X_B (the molar fraction of A in the bottom product) and continue with the slope of L_S/V_S (the liquid-to-vapor flow rate). The L_S is the amount of the liquid feed ($L_S = 50$ kg-mole/h) and V_S is the amount of vapor ($V_S = 20$ kg-mole/h), so the SO line's slope is 55/20 = 2.75.

4) We draw a vertical line starting at the intersection of the X_B and 45° line (shown in the figure with a red dot) and continue until the line connects to the SO line. And show the intersection with 1.

5) We draw a horizontal line starting at 1, continue until the line connects to the VLE line, and show the intersection with X_1.

6) We draw a vertical line at X_1 and continue until the line connects to the VLE line, showing the intersection with 2.

7) We continue with stepping up until reaching the X_D on the 45° line.

8) As the same figure shows, a total of 6 trays is needed to achieve this separation.

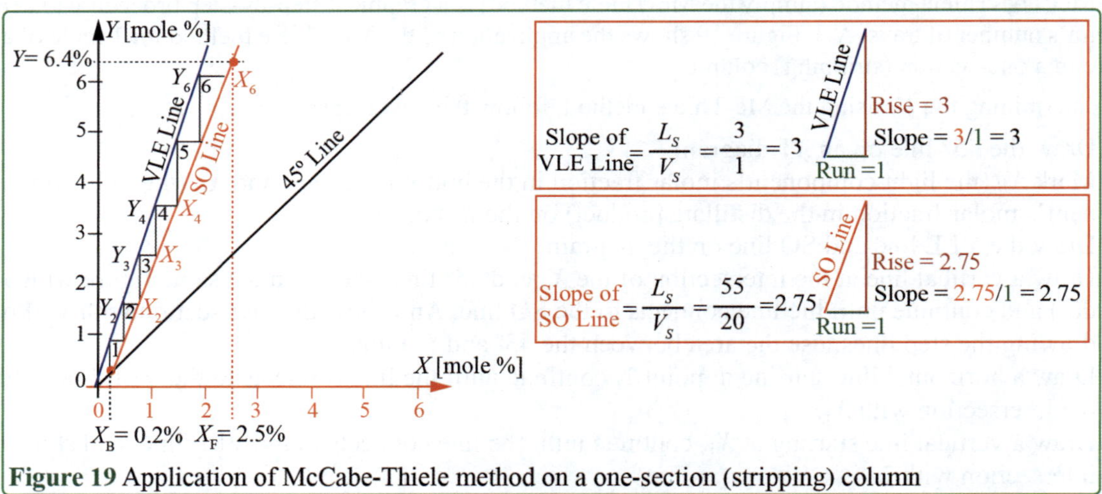

Figure 19 Application of McCabe-Thiele method on a one-section (stripping) column

Mc-Thiele Method for a Two-Section Column

For a step-by-step procedure of the Mc-Thiele method to graphically determine the number of trays (N_T) in a two-section column, follow the next steps:

1. Draw a 45° ($X = Y$) line and the VLE curve on an XY diagram.
2. Locate X_F, X_B, and X_D on the X-axis and 45° line.
3. Calculate the q-line's slope $[-q/(1-q)]$ and draw the q-line from the X_F point on the 45° line.
4. Calculate the D from the equation $D = F(X_F - X_B)/(X_D - X_B)$ and B from the equation $B = F - D$.
5. Calculate the R_R (the reflux flow rate) from equation $R_R = R_X.D$, where R_X is the reflux ratio.
6. Calculate the L_S (the LBC's liquid flow rate in the stripping section) from the equation $L_S = L_R + q.F$, where $L_R = R_R$ if the reflux is saturated liquid (most cases). Thus, $L_S = R_R + q.F$
7. Calculate the V_R (the LBC's vapor flow rate in the rectifying section) from $V_R = L_R + D$.

8. Calculate the V_S (the LBC's vapor flow rate in the stripping section) from $V_S = L_S - B$.
9. Calculate the RO-line's slope as $S_{RO} = L_R / V_R$ and the SO-line's slope as $S_{SO} = L_S / V_S$.
10. Draw the RO line from the point X_D on the 45° line with a slope of L_R / V_R.
11. Draw the SO line from the point X_B on the 45° line to the q-line and RO line intersection. [Note: At this point, you better check to ensure that the slope of the SO line equates to L_S / V_S. If it is *not*, some mistakes have been done in calculations or graph. Recheck your calculations.]
12. Draw a vertical line starting at the intersection of X_B, SO line, and 45° line (shown in Figure 22 with a red dot) and continue until the line connects to the SO line. And show the intersection (the point of connection) with 1. [For drawing the step lines, we use the area between the 45° and SO lines.] [When a step crosses the SO and RO lines (which occurs on the q-line, this tray is the optimum feed tray).]
13. Continue with stepping up in the rectifying area until reaching or passing the X_D on the SO line. This tray is the top tray in the column's rectifying section.

The upcoming Example makes the subject clearer.

Example 3 on Distillation

Determine the number of trays using Mc-Thiele's graphical method in a two-section column when 100 kg-mole/h of ethanol-water solution enters the column as the feed with ethanol composition (X_F) of 0.40 kg-mole/h. The distillate's ethanol composition (X_D) should be 0.90, and the bottom product's ethanol composition (X_B) should be 0.02 kg-mole/h. The feed entering the column is saturated liquid at its bubble point T. The column operates at 1 Atm pressure (the *XY* diagram for the ethanol-water mixture at P_{Atm} is given in Figure 20). Equimolal flows in the column are assumed. The tray efficiencies are assumed to be the same on all trays and in the partial reboiler. A reflux ratio of $R = 2.5$ (2.5 moles to 1 mole of product).

1) We draw the 45° line on the equilibrium (*XY*) diagram for 1 mole of the mixture feed.

2) We locate the points $X_F = 0.40$, $X_B = 0.02$, and $X_D = 0.90$ on the X-axis and 45° line (see Figure 20).

3) The q-line is at a 45° angle with the 45° line at point X_F, so $q = 1$ (as feed is saturated liquid at its bubble point T).

4) The D (distillate flow rate) and B (bottom flow rate) are calculated as

$$D = \frac{F(X_F - X_B)}{X_D - X_B} = \frac{100(0.4 - 0.02)}{0.90 - 0.02} = 43.2 \text{ kg-mole/h}$$

$$B = F - D = 100 - 43.2 = 56.8 \text{ kg-mole/h}$$

5) The R_R (reflux flow rate) is the R (reflux ratio) times D, so $R_R = R \times D = 2.5 \times 43.2 = 108$ kg-mole/h. Because the reflux is saturated liquid, $L_R = R_R = 108$ kg-mole/h.

6) $L_S = L_R + q.F = R_R + q.F = 108 + (1 \times 100) = 208$ kg-mole/h.

7) $V_R = L_R + D = 108 + 43.2 = 151.2$ kg-mole/h.

8) $V_S = L_S - B = 208 - 65.8 = 142.2$ kg-mole/h.

9) The RO-line's slope (S_{RO}) $= L_R / V_R = 108/151.2 = 0.71$, and $S_{SO} = L_S / V_S = 208/142.2 = 1.46$.

10) The RO line is drawn from the point X_D on the 45° line with a slope of L_R / V_R, which is 0.71.

11) The SO line is drawn from the point X_B on the 45° line to the intersection of the q-line and the RO line. The SO's slope is checked to ensure that it is 1.46.

12) A vertical line was drawn at the intersection of X_B, SO line, and 45° line (shown in the figure with a red dot) and continued until the line connects to the SO line. The graph starts to form the steps up. The first step is the reboiler. The next step is tray 1, and so on.

13) The steps in the rectifying area are done when reaching (or passing) the X_D on the 45° line. This is the top tray in the column's rectifying section, so the column must have 11 trays (the first one is for the partial reboiler).

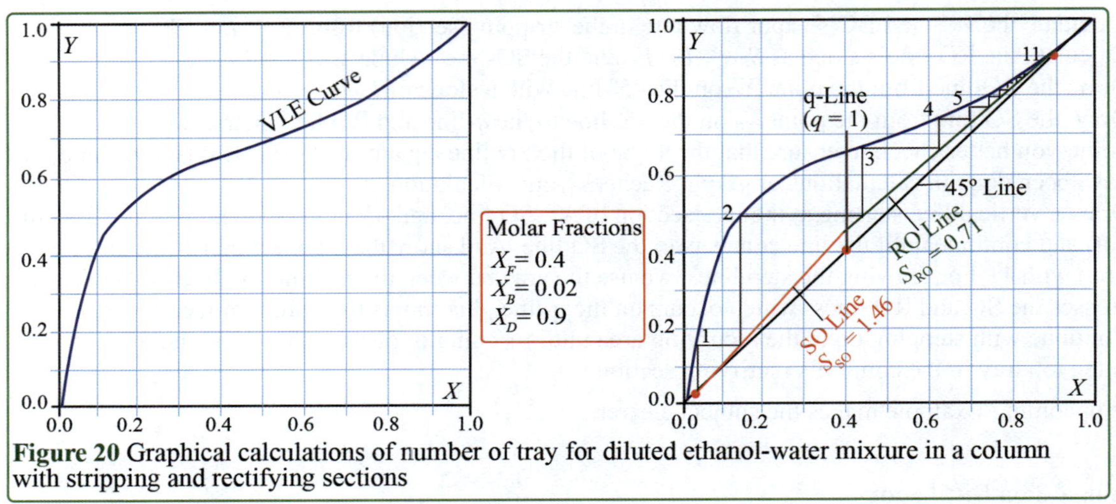

Figure 20 Graphical calculations of number of tray for diluted ethanol-water mixture in a column with stripping and rectifying sections

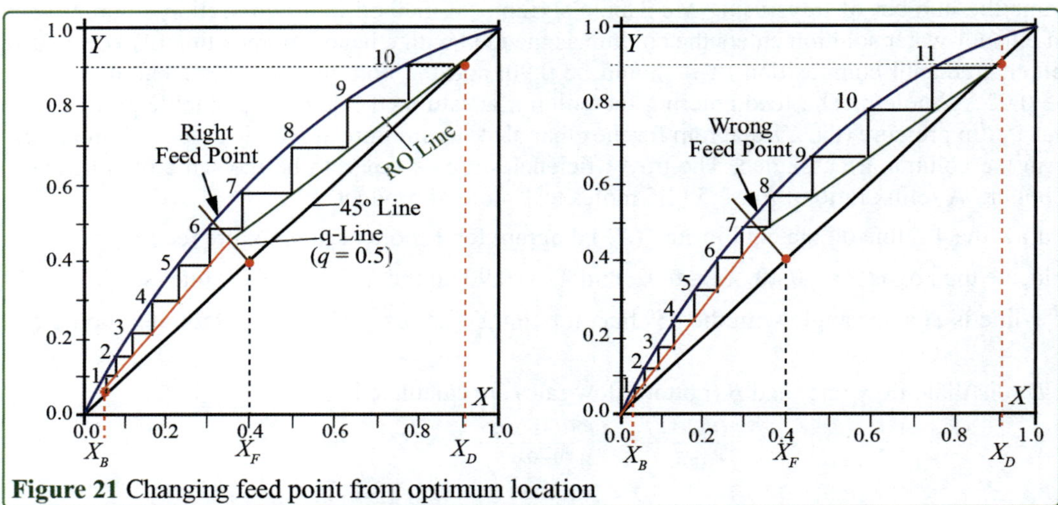

Figure 21 Changing feed point from optimum location

Determination of Feed Tray Location

As discussed earlier, mostly a feed entering a column can be in the following three (3) states:

- Saturated liquid at its bubble point T with $q = 1$ (see Figure 14A).
- Saturated vapor at its dew point T with $q = 0$ (see Figure 14B).
- Mixture of liquid and vapor, with $q = 0.5$ (see Figure 14C).

In the first case (the A case), when the feed enters as a saturated liquid at its bubble point T (in most cases), the L_S (the liquid's flow rate in the stripping section) can be calculated if we know F (the feed's flow rate) and L_R (the liquid's flow rate in the rectifying section), both usually in mole/time or kmole/time.

$$L_S = F + L_R \tag{36}$$

In the second case (the B case), when the feed enters as vapor, V_R (the vapor's flow rate in the rectifying section) can be calculated if we know F and V_S (the vapor's flow rate in the stripping section).

$$V_R = F + V_S \tag{37}$$

In the third case (the C case), when the feed enters as a mix of liquid and vapor, q (the **feed's liquid fraction**), the fraction of the feed that is liquid (the liquid's number of moles in the feed per feed's total number of moles), must be calculated.

$$q = \frac{L_S - L_R}{F} \tag{38}$$

When the feed is saturated liquid at its bubble-point temperature (case A), $q = 1$; when it is saturated vapor at its dew-point T (case B), $q = 0$; and when it is a mix of liquid and vapor (case C), which means it is between its bubble-point temperature and dew-point temperature, $q = 1/2$. [The q-line (feed line) slopes for these three cases can be recognized in Figure 14D.]

If the **feed tray** (the tray to which the feed enters) is positioned at the wrong point, a more unnecessary number of trays will be required, causing a decrease in the process efficiency.

The number of ideal trays can be found by the step-by-step (Mc-Thiele) method when operating lines have been drawn. With this in mind, we try to use the usual step-by-step method to find the right point for the feed tray and to find the smaller possible number of trays for a typical distillation process. As seen from the left side of Figure 21, the number of trays for the column is 10. As we move the feed point from tray 7 to 8, as seen from the right side of the same figure, the stripping operating (SO) line and rectifying operating (RO) line change location, increasing the required number of trays to 11. Thus, the optimum location for feed is on tray 7. Feeding above or below the optimum tray causes the following:

- It *increases* the number of trays, causing the lower quality of both the top and bottom products,
- It *decreases* the efficiency of the distillation process.

[Note 1: Usually, the liquid on the feed tray does *not* have the same composition as the feed except by chance, even the location of the feed tray is optimum.] [Note 2: In large columns, feed enters the column on two (or more) trays, above and below the theoretical optimum feed tray.]

Determination of Number of Trays Using McCabe-Thiele Method on a Computer

The **Microsoft Excel program** can solve the McCabe-Thiele method (simply the Mc-Thiele method). Excel is usually used when a distillation process must handle complicated distillation duties, such as when

- The OP (operating) and VLE (vapor-liquid-equilibrium) lines of the system are curvy,
- The feed deviates from ideal-solution properties, like when an azeotropic liquid is under distillation.

We discuss creating the VLE (vapor-liquid equilibrium) data and related operational parameters in Excel, which can help draw the VLE lines for complicated duties. [The method used here is like in *Rules of Thumb for Chemical Engineers*, 5th Edition, authored by Stephen Hall.]

Vapor-Pressure Equation: The vapor-pressure equation (also called the Antoine equation), which relates the vapor pressure (P_V) of a pure liquid mixture to that mixture's temperature (T) at 1 Atm (= 760 mm Hg), is

$$P_V = 10^{\left(A - \frac{B}{C+T}\right)} \tag{39}$$

A, *B*, and *C* are Antoine coefficients. [Note: The Antoine coefficients for some liquids can be obtained from a few internet sites, such as **ddbst.com/calculation.html**. The Antoine coefficients for ethanol, methanol, and water are given under the topic of Activity Equations and Coefficients.]

Excel Method on an Ideal VLE Mixture: To apply the Excel method to a **binary ideal VLE mixture**, we study a methanol-water mixture (with 40% methanol), which behaves ideally under distillation at P of 1 Atm. We assume that the feed enters the column as a saturated liquid at its bubble point T, so $q = 0.5$.

The Excel worksheet (spreadsheet) for VLE data for this example can be created as

- Open a worksheet in Excel and enter Antoine coefficients (*A*, *B*, and *C*) for methanol (CH_3OH, simply MOH) and water (H_2O) on the top left side of the worksheet (see Figure 22).

- Column A is for the molar fractions of MOH (component A) in the liquid phase (X_A), so type 0.0, 0.1….1.0 down the column on cells A10 until A20.
- Column B is for the molar fractions of MOH in the vapor phase (Y_A). It relates the Y_A to the MOH's vapor pressure (P_V, column C). Column B is calculated based on the ideal VLE equation ($Y_A = X_A.P_{V.A}$), so type A10*(D10/760) in cell B10 and copy it down.
- Column C is for the bubble-point T (in °C) of each liquid's concentration. It needs an **iterative calculation**, meaning that by changing the bubble-point T in column C, the vapor P and, therefore, the partial P of the liquid change. The goal is the sum of the partial pressures in each set to be 760 mm Hg in column H. This can be done by using Excel's **Goal-Seek function**. First, enter (F10+G10) in cell H10 and copy it down the column. Next, use the Goal-Seek function to find the T in column C10, which gives 760 in column H10. From the **Data** tab, select the "What-if-Analysis" button. Then select **Goal Seek** from the drop-down menu. Enter H10 in the "Set cell" text box, 760 in the "To value" box, and C10 in the "By Changing" box, and click OK. Excel finds the T that gives 760 in column H10. [**Repeat** these steps for C11 through C20.]
- Column D is for the vapor pressure (P_V) of MOH. It is calculated using the Antoine equation (Equation 38), so type 10^($A$4–$B$4/($C$4+$C10)) in D10 and copy it down the column.
- Column E is for the P_V of water. It is also calculated using the Antoine equation, so type 10^($A$5–$B$5/($C$5+$C10)) in E10 and copy it down the column.
- Column F is for the partial pressure (P_P) of MOH. The P_P of a component equates to its molar fraction multiplied by its P_V, so type A10*D10 in F10 and copy it down the column.
- Column G (the water P_P) is calculated by typing (1–A10)*E10 in G10 and copying it down.
- Column H, which is for the column total P, is calculated by entering F10 + G10 in H10 and copying down.

After constructing the VLE data, we draw a chart (graph) in Excel (see Figure 22). [In this situation, a scatter (*XY*) chart that compares pairs of values is the best way to graph the data.] For drawing a scatter chart, select (highlight) the molar fraction columns (A10 through B10) on the VLE data. Choose Scatter from "Insert menu," Then, continue as follow:

- Choose the option of "Smooth lines without markers,"
- Format both the X-axis and Y-axis from 0.1 to 1.0 when the chart appears,

Then try to resize the chart to become square by performing the following:

- Click **Insert** on the Excel toolbar and choose **Scatter** and then **Scatter with smooth lines**,
- Format X-axis after the chart appears by clicking from 0.1 to 1.0 and determining major units at 0.1 and minor units at 0.05,
- Resize the chart to square by clicking its top-right corner and dragging it to the left.

For determining the N_T, we use the Mc-Thiele method to determine the N_T graphically.

Excel Method on a Non-Ideal VLE Mixture: To apply the Excel method to a **binary non-ideal VLE mixture**, we study the ethanol-water mixture with 40% ethanol under distillation at P of 1 Atm. [At high ethanol concentrations (above 15%), the ethanol-water mixture behaves non-ideally (as it is an azeotropic liquid mixture).]

The steps involved in making an Excel worksheet for VLE data for this example are like the previous example. But, because dealing with a non-ideal mixture, we must use the activity coefficient (γ) to calculate the molar fraction of a solution's component in the vapor phase. The Excel worksheet for constructing the diagram of this mixture under distillation is shown in Figure 23.

[Note: The equations for determining the **adjusting parameters** for **activity coefficients** are beyond the scope of most ChemEng books and this one. The parameters used here were taken from *Rules of Thumb for Chemical Engineers*, which obtained the data from DETHERM, a site that provides data for many pure components and mixtures.]

Methanol (CHOH)–Water (H_2O) at 1 Atm

	A	B	C	D	E	F	G	H
2	Antoine Coefficients					Molar Fractions		
3	*A*	*B*	*C*			Feed	Bottom	Distillate
4	8.0810	1582.271	239.728	Methanol		0.40	0.02	0.95
5	8.0713	1730.630	233.426	Water		0.60	0.98	0.05
6								
7	Molar Fractions		Bubble	P_V		Partial pressure (P_P)		
8	Methanol		Temp.	[mm Hg]		[mm Hg]		
9	*X*	*Y*	[°C]	Methanol	Water	Methanol	Water	Total
10	0.00	0.00	100.0	2651.5	760.0	0.0	760.0	760
11	0.10	0.28	93.7	2165.5	603.8	216.5	543.5	760
12	0.20	0.48	88.5	1818.9	495.3	363.8	396.2	760
13	0.30	0.62	84.0	1561.7	416.4	468.5	291.5	760
14	0.40	0.72	80.2	1364.4	357.1	545.7	214.3	760
15	0.50	0.80	76.8	1208.9	311.1	604.4	155.6	760
16	0.60	0.86	73.8	1083.6	274.7	650.1	109.9	760
17	0.70	0.90	71.2	980.6	245.2	686.5	73.5	760
18	0.80	0.94	68.8	894.8	220.8	715.8	44.2	760
19	0.90	0.91	66.6	822.2	200.5	739.9	20.1	760
20	0.10	1.00	64.5	760.0	183.3	760.0	0.0	760

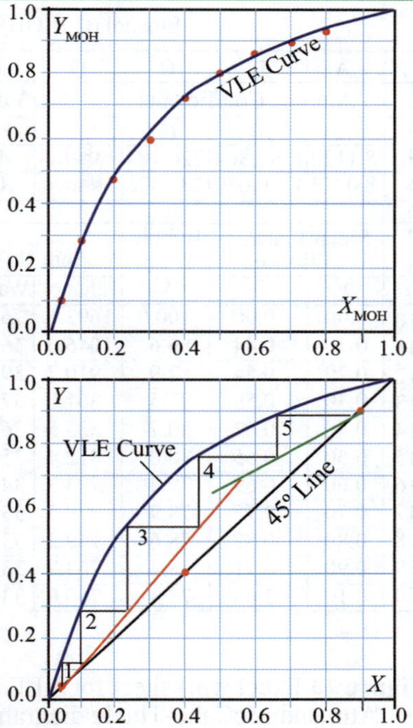

Figure 22 Excel worksheet for VLE data of methanol-water-mixture at 1 Atm and McCabe-Thiele diagram for calculating number of trays

The formulas used in the Excel columns for this example are like the previous worksheet given in Figure 22, except for the following:

- Column F, which is for the adjusted activity coefficient of ethanol, is calculated by entering EXP(($F$4+2*($F$5-$F$4)*A10)*(1-A10)^2) in F10 and copying it down the column.
- Column G, which is for the adjusted activity coefficient of water, is calculated by entering EXP(($F$5+2*($F$4-$F$5)*(1-A10))*A10^2) in G10 and copying it down the column.
- Column H (partial *P* of ethanol) is calculated by entering A10*D10*F10 in H10 and copying it similarly.
- Column I (the partial *P* of water) is calculated by entering (1–A10)*E10*G10 in I10 and copying it down.
- Column J, which is for the column total *P*, is calculated by entering H10 + I10 in J10 and copying down.

The drawing of the chart for this example is the same as we have done for the previous example. The first step of finding the N_T is adding operating lines to the graph and continuing as the previous example.

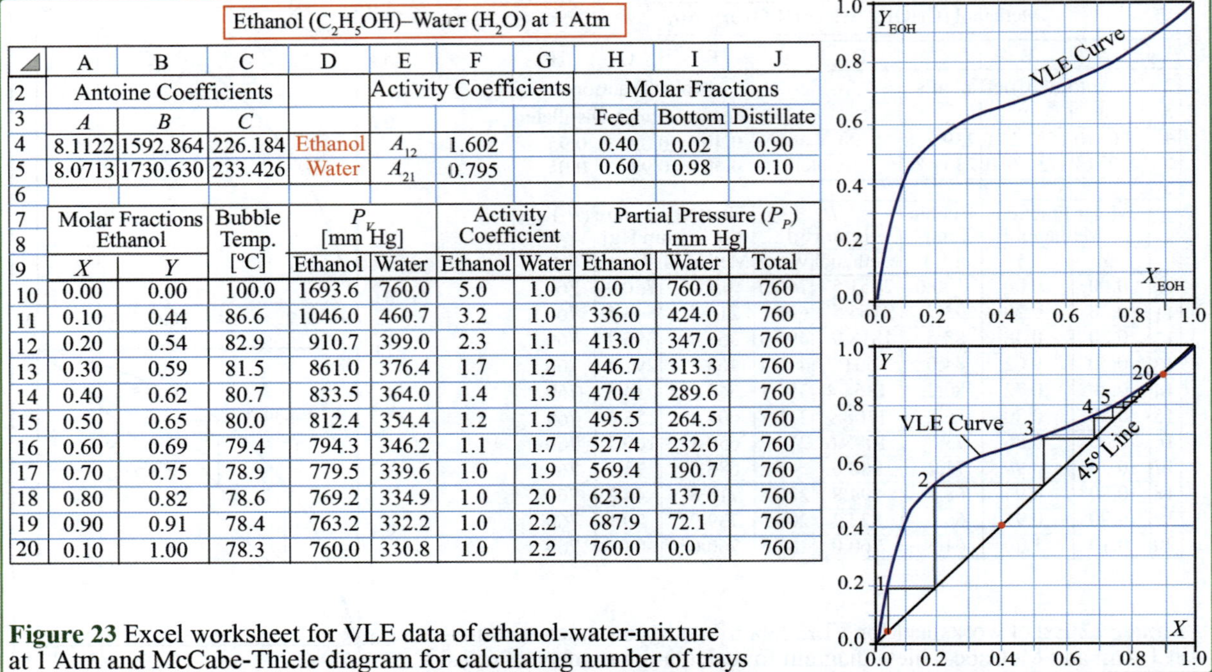

Ethanol (C_2H_5OH)–Water (H_2O) at 1 Atm

	A	B	C	D	E	F	G	H	I	J
2	Antoine Coefficients				Activity Coefficients			Molar Fractions		
3	*A*	*B*	*C*					Feed	Bottom	Distillate
4	8.1122	1592.864	226.184	Ethanol	A_{12}	1.602		0.40	0.02	0.90
5	8.0713	1730.630	233.426	Water	A_{21}	0.795		0.60	0.98	0.10
6										
7–8	Molar Fractions Ethanol		Bubble Temp. [°C]	P_V [mm Hg]		Activity Coefficient		Partial Pressure (P_P) [mm Hg]		
9	*X*	*Y*		Ethanol	Water	Ethanol	Water	Ethanol	Water	Total
10	0.00	0.00	100.0	1693.6	760.0	5.0	1.0	0.0	760.0	760
11	0.10	0.44	86.6	1046.0	460.7	3.2	1.0	336.0	424.0	760
12	0.20	0.54	82.9	910.7	399.0	2.3	1.1	413.0	347.0	760
13	0.30	0.59	81.5	861.0	376.4	1.7	1.2	446.7	313.3	760
14	0.40	0.62	80.7	833.5	364.0	1.4	1.3	470.4	289.6	760
15	0.50	0.65	80.0	812.4	354.4	1.2	1.5	495.5	264.5	760
16	0.60	0.69	79.4	794.3	346.2	1.1	1.7	527.4	232.6	760
17	0.70	0.75	78.9	779.5	339.6	1.0	1.9	569.4	190.7	760
18	0.80	0.82	78.6	769.2	334.9	1.0	2.0	623.0	137.0	760
19	0.90	0.91	78.4	763.2	332.2	1.0	2.2	687.9	72.1	760
20	0.10	1.00	78.3	760.0	330.8	1.0	2.2	760.0	0.0	760

Figure 23 Excel worksheet for VLE data of ethanol-water-mixture at 1 Atm and McCabe-Thiele diagram for calculating number of trays

Tray Efficiency of Distillation Columns

Theoretical trays of a distillation column often *cannot* achieve sufficient separation between the vapor and liquid phases, so two types of efficiencies are usually used to determine the difference between the **number of theoretical trays** (N_{TT}) and the number of **actual trays** (N_{AT}), overall efficiency and Murphree vapor-phase efficiency (simply **Murphree efficiency**).

Overall Efficiency (E_O): The E_O determines the performance of **all trays**. It is the ratio of the N_{TT} needed to achieve the desired separation to the N_{AT} performing the same separation ($E_O = N_{TT}/N_{AT}$). If, for example, the N_{TT} is 6 and it was found in practice that the N_{AT} should be 10 to achieve the desired separation, the E_O is 60%. Typical numbers for E_O are between 50 and 70%. An easy separation with large relative volatility, like methanol from water (with a high α_{AB} of about 2.5), has a low E_O (about 50% in the methanol-water mixture). Instead, a difficult separation with a low α_{AB} has a high E_O.

Murphree Efficiency (E_M): The E_M determines the performance of a **single tray**. It is the ratio of the actual change in vapor concentration (*C*) leaving a tray to the theoretical change in *C*. Based on this definition and considering the left-hand side of Figure 23; the E_M can be written for the N (feed) tray as the change in vapor composition (concentration) between the N tray and the next tray below (tray N – 1) divided by the change in vapor composition between the vapor leaving the N tray if it would be at equilibrium with the liquid leaving the tray N – 1 and the vapor leaving the tray N – 1.

$$E_M = \frac{Y_N - Y_{N-1}}{Y_N^* - Y_{N-1}} \tag{40}$$

Y_N is the composition of actual vapor leaving the N tray, Y_{N-1} is the composition of actual vapor entering the N tray from tray N – 1 below, and Y^*_N is the composition of vapor that is in equilibrium with the liquid going down from the tray N to tray N + 1. [For determination of the E_M, liquid samples are taken from different plates for testing, and the vapor compositions are determined from an Mc-Thiele diagram.]

The right-hand side of Figure 23 is a portion of an Mc-Thiele diagram with the N-tray's E_M of about 0.7 (point B on line ABC), which is a fraction of the vertical ABC line between the OP (operating) line and the VLE (vapor-liquid-equilibrium) line. If the E_M were 100%, the AB line must go up to point C. In other words, because $E_M = 0.7$, the AB line is 70% of the ABC line.

When the E_M is known, it can be used in the Mc-Thiele diagram to determine the N_{AC} (number of actual trays) from N_{TT} (number of theoretical trays). The diagram for the N_{TT} found in the previous two examples can be compared with the N_{AC}. Figure 25 shows the entire Mc-Thiele diagram for the methanol-water mixture with Murphree tray efficiency (E_M) of 0.7, and Figure 26 shows the diagram for the ethanol-water mixture.

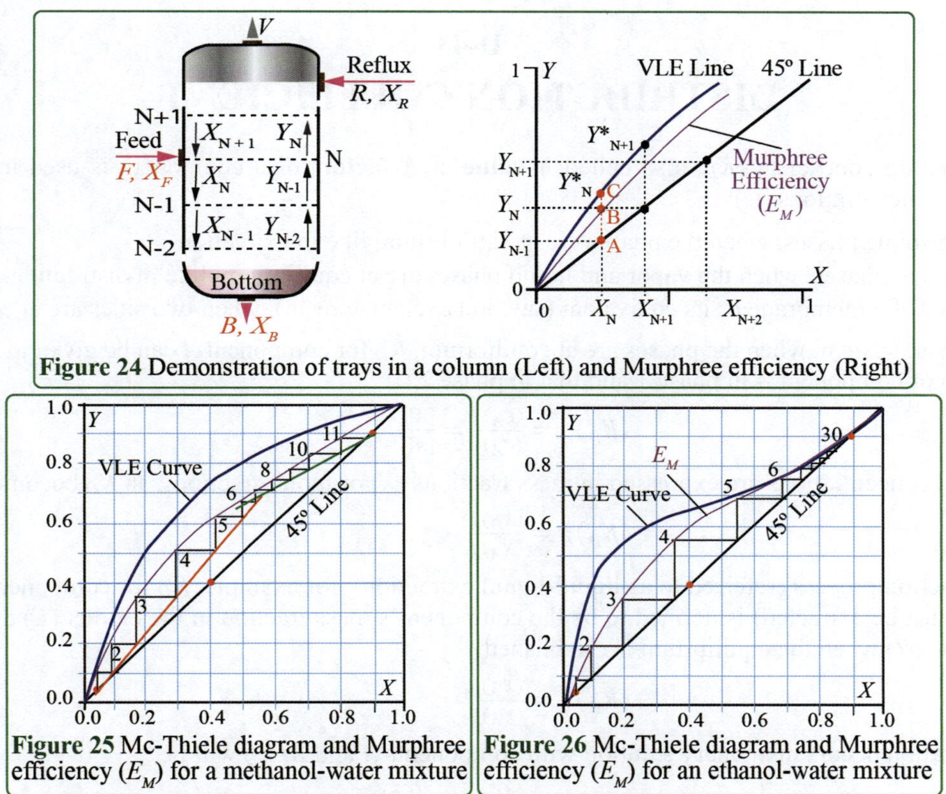

Figure 24 Demonstration of trays in a column (Left) and Murphree efficiency (Right)

Figure 25 Mc-Thiele diagram and Murphree efficiency (E_M) for a methanol-water mixture

Figure 26 Mc-Thiele diagram and Murphree efficiency (E_M) for an ethanol-water mixture

D-42

DISTILLED WATER

Distilled water is purified water produced by the distillation of hard water and then condensed in a condenser. Quality distilled water has a specific conductance of 0 to 4 μS/cm, corresponding to 0 to 2 PPM of scale causing salts (calcium and magnesium soluble salts, such as $CaCO_3$, $CaSO_4$, and $MgSO_4$).

D-43

DISTRIBUTION COEFFICIENT

The distribution coefficient (K_D, also called ***K*-value** or ***K*-factor**) of a component is used to compare the component's concentrations (C):

- In two immiscible phases, when the phases are at equilibrium, like in extraction,
- In two miscible phases, when the vapor and liquid phases are at equilibrium, like in distillation.
- On two sides of a membrane or its equivalent (say, ion exchange resin), when two sides are at equilibrium.

In a two-phase system, when the phases are at equilibrium, K_D for component A can be given in relation to the concentration of component A in phase 1 and that in phase 2.

$$(K_D)_A = \frac{(C_A)_1}{(C_A)_2} = \frac{[A]_1}{[A]_2} \tag{1}$$

Sometimes, concentrations are expressed in mass fractions (X) or molar fractions, so K_D becomes

$$(K_D)_A = \frac{(X_A)_1}{(X_A)_2} \tag{2}$$

In the extraction process (referred to as liquid-liquid extraction), for example, K_D for component A (the component that must be extracted) is defined to be the component's mass fraction in the extract (E) divided by that in the raffinate (R) when the equilibrium is established.

$$(K_D)_A = \frac{(X_A)_E}{(X_A)_R} \tag{3}$$

If the separation occurs in a binary solution with components A and B, K_D will be

$$(K_D)_{AB} = \frac{(C_A)_1}{(C_A)_2} = \frac{(C_B)_2}{(C_B)_1} \tag{4}$$

K_D can numerically determine the S_E (separation efficiency) of a component from another component (the *greater* the K_D, the *greater* is the S_E and, therefore, the *easier* is the separation of the components from each other). In practice, K_D is usually used to express S_E of a separation process (like ion-exclusion chromatographic process) by comparing the K_D of two (or more) components when passing through a bed of ion-exchange resin (simply **resin**) or its equivalent (like a semipermeable membrane). The separation of components occurs because of the Gibbs Donnan effect, which can be simply explained by considering a binary (two-component) solution containing the following:

- Anionic component (like salt with K_D of 0.2 cm^2/h; later – component A),
- Nonionic component (like sugar with K_D of 0.04 cm^2/h; later – component B).

If such a solution slowly passes through a chromatographic column filled with resin, A stays at a much higher concentration in the liquid phase than in the resin phase (pores inside the resin). This occurs because A-molecules (the salt molecules) have greater K_D, making them non-diffusible through the resin's pores. Instead, B-molecules (the sugar molecules) have lower K_D, making it diffusible into the resin's pores. This results in an unequal concentration (C) distribution in the liquid phase and solid phase (resin).

The inequality in C occurs because the A molecules have a smaller chemical affinity for resin (smaller **chemical diffusivity** through resin), moving faster through the resin bed. Instead, the B molecules have a greater chemical affinity (greater diffusivity through the resin), so they stay in a higher concentration in the resin phase than in the liquid phase. As a result, molecules of B move slower through the resin. For this example, the S_E of each component depends on the component's K_D (the *greater* the component's K_D, the greater is its S_E). Because of the difference in S_E, a separation between A (the non-diffusible component with greater K_D) and B (the diffusible component with smaller K_D) occurs. K_D for A and B can be written in relation to the resin phase (shown with subscript R) and solution phase (shown with subscript S) as

$$(K_D)_A = \frac{(C_A)_R}{(C_A)_S} \qquad (K_D)_B = \frac{(C_B)_R}{(C_B)_S} \tag{5}$$

Or

$$(K_D)_{AB} = \frac{\frac{(C_A)_R}{(C_A)_S}}{\frac{(C_B)_R}{(C_B)_S}} = \frac{(C_A)_R(C_B)_S}{(C_A)_S(C_B)_R} \tag{6}$$

The K_D is usually called K-factor when used in the distillation process to compare the volatility of two components, known as relative volatility (α), the molar fraction of A to B, shown as $(K_D)_{AB}$ or a_{AB}.

$$a_{AB} = \frac{\alpha_A}{\alpha_B} = \frac{\frac{Y_A}{X_A}}{\frac{Y_B}{X_B}} = \frac{Y_A . X_B}{X_A . Y_B} \tag{7}$$

Here, X_A is the mass fraction of component A in the liquid phase, and Y_A is that in the vapor phase. X_B and Y_B are defined similarly.

D-44
DNA AND RNA

DNA is the simplified form of deoxyribonucleic acid (DNA), and RNA is for ribonucleic acid (RNA). Both are biological polymers, but instead of amino acids as the repeating units, they have a chain of nucleotides. Each nucleotide consists of three basic structural units: a base, a pentose sugar, and a phosphate group. The sugar in RNA is called ribose, reduced in DNA by losing oxygen to form deoxyribose.

DNA and RNA are nucleic acids, probably the largest macromolecules known. They are essential for all known forms of life to encode, transmit, and express genetic information.

D-45
DONNAN MEMBRANE EFFECT

Study GIBBS-DONNAN EFFECT.

D-46
DRAFT

See AIR DRAFT.

D-47

DRAG COEFFICIENT

The drag coefficient (K_D) is a unitless number used to quantify the drag (resistance) of a system in a free-fall motion. It depends on the shape of the free-fall system (the *more* aerodynamic the shape of a system, the *smaller* is its K_D) and the system's surface area (the *greater* a system's surface area, the *greater* is its K_D). For example, the K_D of a sphere is 0.47, and that of a half-sphere is 0.4.

In a liquid flow process, K_D depends on the liquid's drag force (F_D), the liquid's density (D), the liquid's velocity (V), and the surface area through which the liquid flows (A_R).

$$K_D = \frac{2F_D}{D.V^2.A} \quad (1)$$

Remember that the surface area refers to a reference surface area, depending on what type of K_D is under measurement. If, for example, we measure a car's K_D, the reference area is *not* the cross-sectional area of a sphere (which equates to $4\pi.R^2$), but just $\pi.R^2$, where R is for radius.

D-48

DRAG FORCE

Drag force (F_D, sometimes called air **resistance force** or **fluid resistance force**) is a resistance force that acts against a moving system (like a moving car or a flowing liquid in a pipe). For example, the F_D can act against gravitational force (F_g) in a free-fall motion (see Figure 1). Similarly, it can act against the downward settling of particles in a sedimentation process. Unlike other resistance forces, the F_D depends on a moving system's velocity (V). For example, in a liquid flow in a pipe, the F_D depends on the liquid's D (density), the liquid's V, and the pipe's d (diameter).

$$F_D = D.V^2.d \quad (1)$$

In a free-fall system, the F_D depends on the system's V, D, d, and K_D (drag coefficient).

$$F_D = \frac{1}{2}D.V^2.d.K_D \quad (2)$$

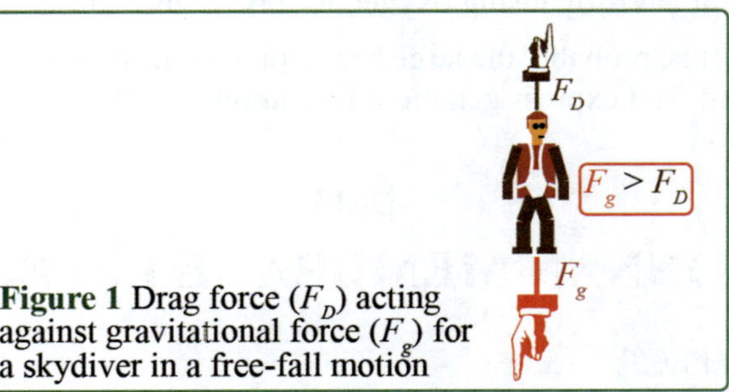

Figure 1 Drag force (F_D) acting against gravitational force (F_g) for a skydiver in a free-fall motion

In a free-fall system, when the air's F_D (drag force) is small, the F_g cancels the air's F_D, so the system falls at a constant gravitational acceleration ($a_g = 9.8$ m/s$^2 = 32.2$ Ft/s^2) and is independent of its mass (M). Thus, the V (velocity) of the system falling from rest ($V_0 = 0$), in relation to a_g and time t, will be

$$V = V_0 + a_g.t = a_g.t \quad (3)$$

And the free-fall system's V, in relation to a_g and h (height), will be

$$V = \sqrt{V_0^2 + 2a_g(h - h_0)} = \sqrt{2a_g.h} \quad (4)$$

D-49

DRUMS

Study TANKS, VESSELS, AND DRUMS.

D-50

DRY AIR

Discussed under the topic of AIR, DRY AIR, AND SATURATED AIR.

D-51

DRY BULB TEMPERATURE

See AIR DRY BULB TEMPERATURE.

D-52

DRY BULB THERMOMETER

Discussed under the top THERMOMETER.

D-53

DRY STEAM

Simplified name for SATURATED DRY STEAM.

D-54

DRY SUBSTANCES

A dry substance (*DS*) consists of soluble (non-filterable) and insoluble (filterable) molecules in a solution. If a solution sample is filtered to remove the suspended solids (filterable solids) before being tested, the sample's dry substances are left after evaporation. The dry substances are expressed in mass percentage (see PERCENTAGES).

[Note: Although the terms dry substance, soluble solid, dissolved solid, and Brix are used equally to indicate the same meaning but are different. A **dry substance** refers to a solution's nonfilterable and filterable solids. **Soluble solid** and **dissolved solid** are correct terms when referring to a solution's just nonfilterable solids. Brix is a correct term when referring to a solution's nonfilterable solids, measured by a refractometry (because in a refractometric test, the sample is filtered to remove filterable solids before being tested with a refractometer. Note that it is recommended to use refractometric dissolved solid (*RDS*) instead of Brix.]

D-55
DRYERS

A dryer is a device (equipment) in which a drying process is performed on a wet substance (like wet sugar crystals). Many different types of dryers are used by different branches of the chemical process industry. In a broad concept, the dryers can be divided into two main groups:

- The dryers are used for drying moist solid particles, crystals, and powder.
- The dryers that are used for drying slurry-type feed (which have high liquid content).

In general, too many designs of each type are on the market. Here we discuss a few of them.

Rotary-Drum Dryers

A typical rotary-drum dryer consists of a rotating horizontal drum 2 to 3 m (= 6 to 10 ft) in diameter and 15 to 20 m (= 45 to 60 Ft) long. The drum, supported on two sets of rollers and gears, rotates at a low speed by a motor, which drives one of the gears. As shown in Figure 1, the dryer is slightly inclined toward the discharge end. The wet feed particles enter the dryer's upper end (feed end), and the dry particles are discharged from the lower end (product-end). The particles in the dryer are moved by the incline of the drum and the lifting flights. The **flights** (lifters) are mounted to the drum and rotate with it. Flights are of different designs, from long-narrow individual plates to individual scoops. The speed of the motor and, to a lesser extent, the shape of the flights determine the residence time of the feed in the dryer.

The feed enters the dryer through a feed chute at the upper end. The air goes through a heat exchanger (to be heated), to a filter (to be filtered), and is forced to the dryer by a fan and exits the dryer from the upper end. As the drum rotates, the lifting flights lift the particles and shower them down through the current of air. The particles are lifted and fall several times during one drum rotation, causing better drying. At the lower end, the dry feed is discharged into a conveyor.

Rotary-Louver Dryers

Figure 2 shows a typical rotary-louver dryer-cooler (simply **roto-louver dryers**), consisting of two rotating drums (one in the other) and several angle-adjustable baffles and louvers. The diameter of the inner drum gradually increases toward the discharge end. At the drum's feed-end, heated air is forced by a fan into the dryer to pass through the feed's particles at about 0.5 m/s and leave the dryer at the end of the drum through a stationary outlet. And the dried-and-cooled particles leave the end of the dryer by a fan. The retention time of the feed in the dryer can be adjusted by changing the bed depth, achieved by adjusting the rotation speed of the drum. This can also be done by adjusting the baffles' angle at the discharge end.

Each louver is connected to the outer drum by a baffle, dividing the area between the inner and outer drums into several smaller sections. This pattern creates passages for the drying air to move through the louvers and the particles. In addition, it has the following benefits:

- It makes the particles move toward the discharge end, so *no* slope is needed for the drums.
- It makes the crystal bed like semi-fluidization, with minimum damage to the particles.

The main advantage of a rotary-louver dryer over a rotary-drum dryer is that it handles the particles more gently, so *no* damage to them occurs.

Fluidized Dryers-Coolers

Fluidized dryers-coolers (simply **fluidized-bed dryers** or **fluidized dryers**), which started to cool the bulk particles since the 1980s, have been gaining popularity to the extent that they are now used in many chemical plants for both drying and cooling the wet bulk particles. [The process is called fluidization because the particles in the dryer behave like a fluid that is constantly flowing through a gaseous medium.]

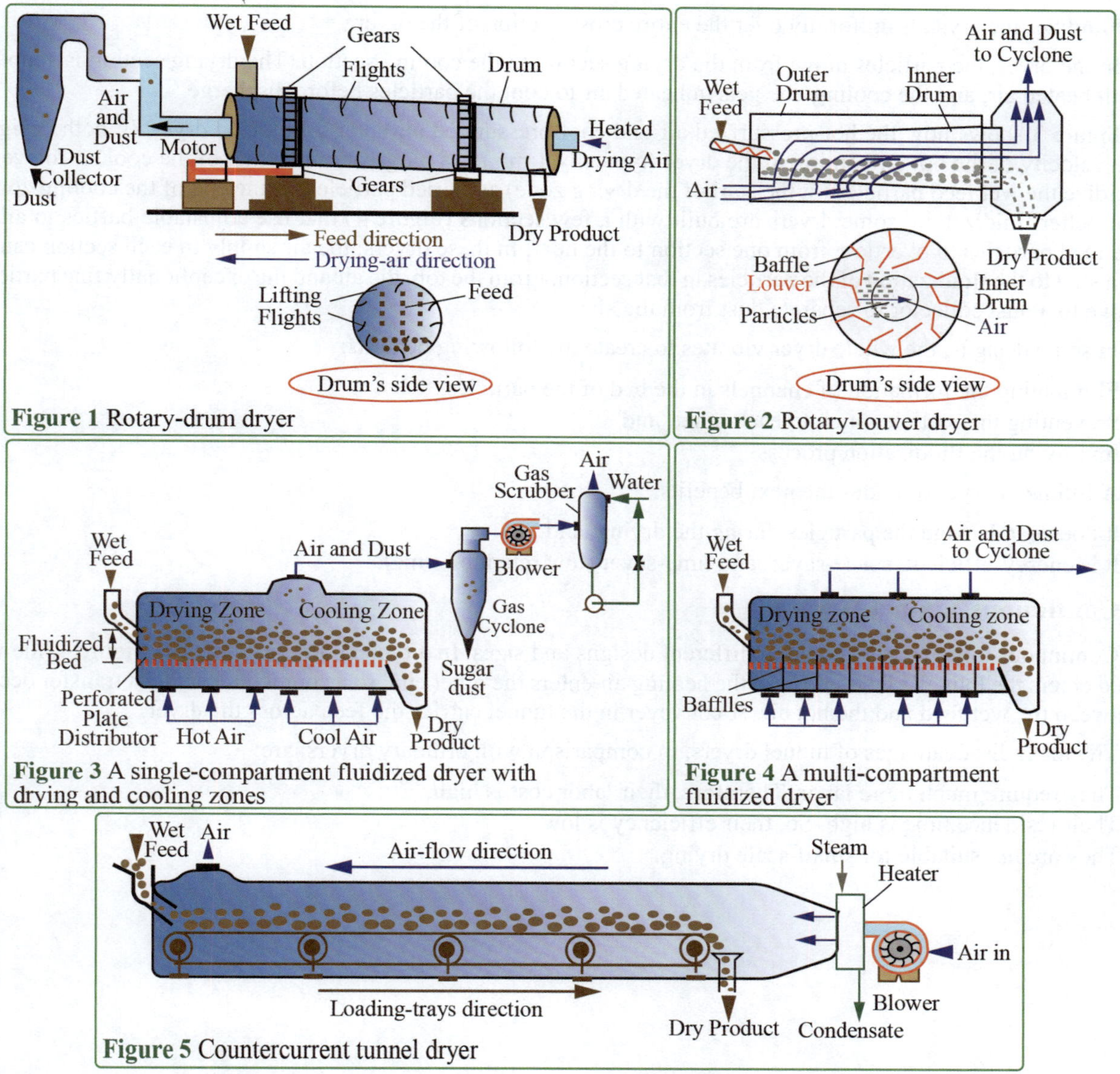

Figure 1 Rotary-drum dryer

Figure 2 Rotary-louver dryer

Figure 3 A single-compartment fluidized dryer with drying and cooling zones

Figure 4 A multi-compartment fluidized dryer

Figure 5 Countercurrent tunnel dryer

For the reason of full fluidization and close contact between individual particles and the drying medium (usually heated air), the following occurs:

- A high heat transfer between the particles makes them reach their equilibrium moisture content (W_E, the lowest moisture removal from a product) during a short retention time (typically 30 seconds).
- A high mixing of the particles in the dryer makes them have a uniform temperature.

A typical fluidized dryer for drying and cooling purposes has an inlet at the top to receive the wet feed particles and a perforated distributor plate at the bottom. Heated drying air enters the dryer below the distributor at a certain velocity (V), passes the distributor's holes, and enters the dryer.

A correct design distributor,

- Supports the bed of the particles,
- Provides sufficient pressure drop to distribute the air evenly, and

- Fluidizes the crystals uniformly over the entire cross-section of the dryer.

In the dryer, the particles move from the drying section to the cooling section. The drying section is supplied with heated air, and the cooling one gets unheated air to cool the particles before discharge.

Figure 3 shows how the hot-pressurized air and cool-pressurized air enter a fluidized dryer. In both designs, the velocity of the hot air coming to the dryer (typically 1 m/s) is a bit greater than that of the cool air to evenly fluidize the wet feed particles (at the start of the drying zone) and dried particles (at the end of the cooling zone). For better fluidization, some dryers are built with a few sections (Figure 4) that use adjustable baffles to allow the feed particles to overflow from one section to the next. In these dryers, the air supply to each section can be adjusted to the fluidization of the particles in that section. From the top, the air and the exceptionally fine particles move to a dust collector to separate dust from the air.

In some designs, the whole dryer vibrates to create the following benefits:

- Eliminating the formation of channels in the bed of the particles,
- Preventing the particles stick to each other, and
- Improving the fluidization process.

A fluidized dryer provides the next benefits:

- It does *not* damage the particles during the drying, and
- It is energy-efficient, space-saver, and time-saver (low retention time).

Continuous Tunnel Dryers

Continuous tunnel dryers come in different designs and sizes. In a typical design, shown in Figure 4, the wet feed enters the tunnel's feed-end, and the heating air enters the other end, so a countercurrent heat transfer occurs between the wet feed and the hot air. A conveyer in the tunnel carries the feed across the dryer.

The main disadvantages of tunnel dryers, in comparison with ordinary dryers, are:

- They require much more labor. Therefore, their labor cost is high.
- Their residence time is high. So, their efficiency is low.
- They are *not* suitable for small-scale drying.

D-56

DRYING PROCESS

BASICS

As a process unit of ChemEng, drying is a heat-absorbing process performed in a dryer to remove moisture (the trace amount of a liquid, usually water) from a moist-solid feed using hot air (Figure 1). Drying has a few types. Under this topic, you will learn the detail of drying by using warm air, known as **convective drying** (simply **drying**). The cause (driving force) is the concentration difference between the warm air (the heating medium) and the moist feed. The warm-and-pressurized air brings heat energy (E_Q, simply heat and scientifically enthalpy) to the dryer and forces the produced vapor out of the dryer. A drying station is usually the last (or one of the last) stations of a chemical process plant, so the drying product is ready for packing, storing, or shipping.

The moist feed under the drying process can have the following properties:

- It can be in different forms, such as crystals, particles, powders, flakes, or slabs,
- Its moisture can be on the surface, inside, or on the surface and inside of the solid,
- Its moisture content can be in the range of 0.2 to 8% when it enters the drying station, and
- Its moisture content, when it leaves the drying station, is reduced to an acceptable level (for example, 0.05% in table sugar crystal, 0.5% in table salt crystals, or 4% in dried coal).
- The drying process is a simultaneous heat transfer and mass transfer. In addition, evaporation and diffusion also participate in drying. During drying, moisture in each particle moves (scientifically diffuse) to its surface by diffusion and is removed from the particle surface by evaporation.

The rate of moisture removal from the particles mainly depends on the next factors:

- Drying time (t_D) of the moist feed in the dryer. [The t_D of a moist feed can be completely different from another moist feed so that it may range from a few seconds to a few hours.]
- The way the particles under drying are moving in the dryer.
- Drying air and feed temperatures.

Moisture in moist-solid particles exists in the following three (3) forms:

- **Surface** (free) **Moisture:** This moisture, which exists on the surface of the particles in a high amount, escapes fast from the particles during drying.
- **Interior** (bound) **Moisture:** This moisture exists near the surface of the particles, so it escapes slowly. It creates a problem in a dry product if it remains in the product after the drying and conditioning processes. This moisture removal occurs by the diffusion of water molecules from a product through its bulk.
- **Inherent** (permanent) **Moisture**: This moisture, which exists in the middle of the moist solid particles in a tiny amount, does *not* escape from the particles during drying. [However, it does *not* create any problem in packing, storing, or shipping a dry product.]

During the surface-moisture removal, T (temperature) is the main driving force of the drying process, while during the interior-moisture removal, T is *not*, by far, the main driving force as the concentration difference (ΔC) between one part and another part of the product is.

To become more familiar with drying, we consider the drying of sugar crystals with a typical moisture content of 0.5%. The water molecules are diffused from the sugar crystals using hot drying air in a sugar dryer. The air humidity gradually increases during drying. When the crystals enter a dryer, their **surface moisture** is removed first. Thus, the main part of E_Q (heat energy) entering the dryer with the drying air evaporates crystals' surface moisture. Almost all the remaining moisture left in the crystals is **interior moisture**, from which a small amount is removed during drying, but most of it is removed only over time when the crystals are out of the dryer. Thus, the complete removal of interior moisture to the desired level continues during the cooling of the warm sugar crystals. Cooling is usually performed in a cooler under sufficient air current with low relative humidity (W_R)

until the dry product reaches the equilibrium moisture content (W_E, the lowest practical moisture removal from a product), with around 0.03% moisture content for sugar crystals.

Figure 2 shows the drying temperature (T) of a moist-solid feed in relation to the drying time (t) in a typical dryer. The T of the feed particles increases fast from T_1 (initial T) to T_2, where T_2 equates to the boiling point temperature (T_{BP}) of the particles' surface moisture. Then, the particles' T remains almost the same until the final drying stage, during which their T increases rapidly to T_3.

Figure 3 shows the relation between the surface moisture content (W) and drying time (see the top of the figure) and between the drying rate (R_D) and drying time (see the bottom of the same figure) in a three-stage drying.

Particles of a moist feed entering a dryer go through a **drying rate curve**, like Figure 4, which shows the relation between R_D and surface-moisture reduction of solid particles. Such a moisture reduction goes through the following three rate stages:

- **Initial-Drying-Rate Stage:** During this short stage (AB in Figure 4), the R_D is too low, and drying occurs on the surface moisture. The feed under the drying and the water experience a slight T increase to create conditions for the next-drying stage.
- **Constant-Drying-Rate Stage:** During this stage (BC), the R_D is fast and constant, so a high surface-moisture reduction occurs. Under optimum operating conditions, the fast-drying stage continues for a certain period until the moisture content is reduced to the critical moisture content (W_C). [Most often, W_C is *not* identifiable (because it is an approximate value).]
- **Falling-Drying-Rate Stage:** During this stage (CD), the R_D becomes lower, so the rest of the surface moisture and a small portion of the interior moisture are removed. [During the falling stage, the solid particles are heated to their final T.]

As for the rapidity of the moisture reduction, drying can be performed in one of the next two ways:

- **Ideal Drying:** The feed's particles go through all the above-listed drying stages, so all the surface moisture and a small portion of the interior moisture are removed.
- **Rapid Drying:** The feed's particles only go through the constant drying stage, so the surface moisture is *not* sufficiently removed, and obviously, *no* interior moisture is removed.

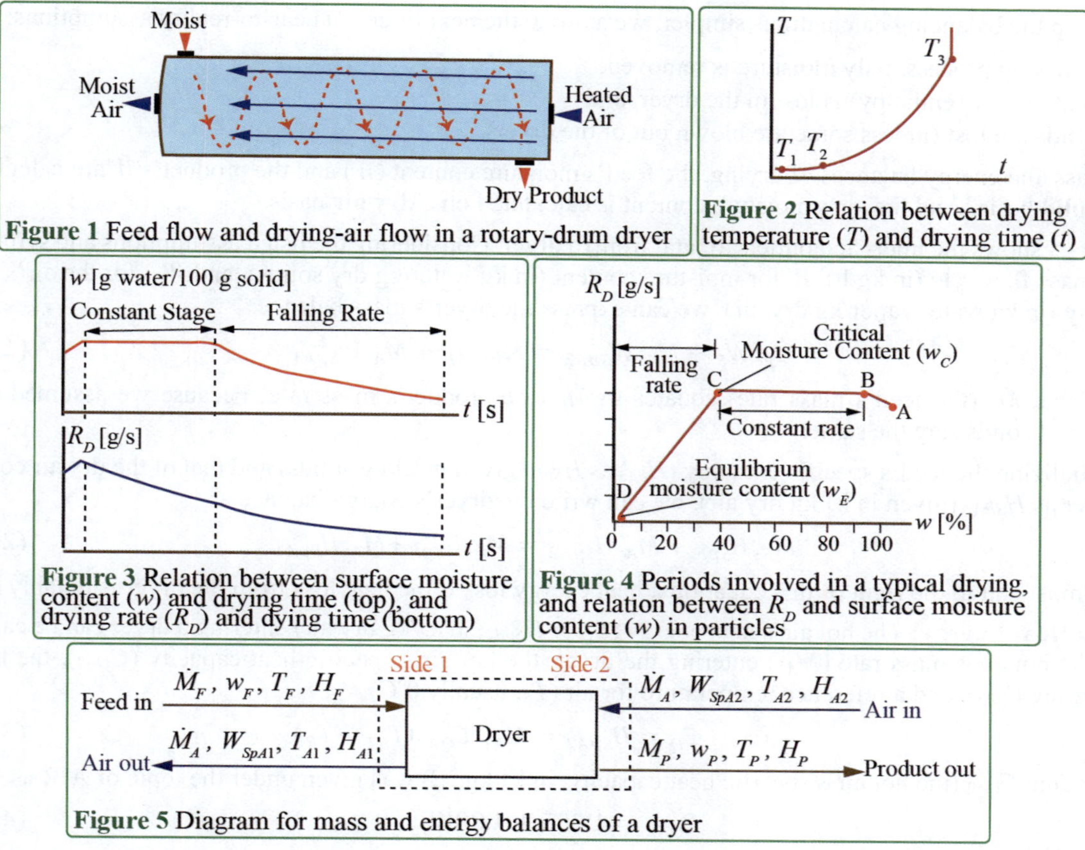

Figure 1 Feed flow and drying-air flow in a rotary-drum dryer

Figure 2 Relation between drying temperature (T) and drying time (t)

Figure 3 Relation between surface moisture content (w) and drying time (top), and drying rate (R_D) and dying time (bottom)

Figure 4 Periods involved in a typical drying, and relation between R_D and surface moisture content (w) in particles

Figure 5 Diagram for mass and energy balances of a dryer

You should also be aware of the following generalities about the drying process:

- The drying air's T is usually constant, but it may change as drying continues.
- The drying rate (R_D) depends on the feed's particle size (the *larger* the particles, the *smaller* the surface area, and, therefore, the *greater* is the R_D).
- Some chemical plants dry and cool the moist-and-hot feed in the same dryer. This method saves a great amount of E_Q (heat energy). This exists because the moist feed enters the dryer with a high enthalpy (H, heat value), high T, and low moisture content. For example, in sugar plants, the drying-and-cooling process on moist sugar crystals is performed in the same dryer, which has both drying and cooling zones. Moist sugar at typically below 1% moisture content and 60ºC enters the drying zone of the dryer. Here **conditioned drying air** (filtered air typically at about 25ºC and about 60% RH) is blown to the dryer's drying zone to sufficiently dry the moist sugar to the desired level of typically 0.05% moisture content and 35ºC.

MASS BALANCE AND ENERGY BALANCE OF A DRYER

During drying of a moist feed in a dryer, E_Q (heat energy) is transferred from the hot air to the feed surface. A dryer's efficiency is evaluated by conducting a mass and energy balance. An efficient dryer offers an optimum mass transfer and heat-energy transfer between the heating medium (mostly hot air) and the feed. A combination of these two produces a product that is optimally dried. We can calculate some useful operating data from the mass and energy balances, including the following:

- Hot air requirement (air flow rate, $\dot{M}_{Air}$),
- Heat energy (E_Q) requirement (actually, heat energy rate, $\dot{E}_Q$), and
- Moisture removal rate from a feed ($\dot{M}.w$, where $\dot{M}$ is for mass rate and w is moisture content).

To keep the balancing calculations simpler, we assume the next three (3) near-to-reality assumptions:

- In the drying process, only moisture is removed,
- No heat energy (enthalpy) is lost in the dryer, and
- No solids are lost (unless some are blown out of the dryer).

In mass and energy balances of drying, the feed's moisture content (W) and the product's W are calculated on a **dry solid** basis. And the air's moisture content is calculated on a **dry air** basis.

Figure 5 shows the inlets and outlets to (and from) a dryer. Considering the listed assumptions and symbolizing $\dot{M}$ for mass flow rate (in kg/h), W for moisture content (in kg water/kg dry solids), and W_{Sp} for the air's specific humidity (in kg water vapor/kg dry air), we can express the dryer's mass balance.

$$\dot{M}_F . W_F + \dot{M}_A . W_{SpA2} = \dot{M}_P . W_P + \dot{M}_A . W_{SpA1} \quad (1)$$

Note that $\dot{M}_F$ (the feed's mass rate) equates to $\dot{M}_P$ (the product's mass rate) because we assumed that the amounts of solids stay the same.

Symbolizing the feed's specific enthalpy (H_{Sp}) as H_{SpF} (given in kJ/kg solids) and that of the dry air coming to the dryer as H_{SPA2} (given in kJ/kg dry air), we can write the dryer's energy balance as

$$\dot{M}_F . H_{SpF} + \dot{M}_A . H_{SpA2} = \dot{M}_P . H_{SpP} + \dot{M}_A . H_{SpA1} \quad (2)$$

[We must add to the right of this equation a heat energy loss if the heat loss from the dryer is notably high.]

Air's Heat Energy: The hot air's heat energy (E_Q or H_{SpA2}, in kJ/kg dry air) entering a dryer can be calculated using the hot air's mass rate ($\dot{M}_{A1}$) entering the dryer, the hot air's specific heat capacity (C_{QA2}), the hot air's temperature (T_{A2}), and a reference temperature for air (T_R, usually 0ºC).

$$E_Q = H_{SpA2} = \dot{M}_{A1} . C_{QA2}(T_{A2} - T_R) \quad (3)$$

The value C_{QA2} (the hot air's specific heat capacity, in kJ/kg.ºC) was given under the topic of AIR as

$$C_{QA2} = 1.005 + 1.88 W_{Sp} \quad (4)$$

In this equation, 1.005 is the hot air's C_Q [in kJ/(kg dry air×ºC)], and 1.88 is the C_Q of water vapor (in kJ/kg.ºC). [The heat-energy content (enthalpy) of hot air is a relative term and requires the selection of a reference T and P (pressure), where in psychrometric calculations, the reference T is 0ºC and P is 1 Atm.]

Air's Temperature: The air adiabatic saturation temperature ($T_{Sat.A}$), which is the T of the wet air, leaving a dryer, can be calculated as

$$T_{Sat.A} = T_{A1} - \frac{H_{E.A1}(W_{Sp.A2} - W_{Sp.A1})}{1.005 + 1.88 W_{Sp.A1}} \quad (5)$$

The T_{A1} is the air's T at the entrance to the dryer, $H_{E.A.1}$ is the hot air's enthalpy of evaporation at the entrance (in kJ/kg, given in Table 1), $W_{Sp.A2}$ is the air's specific humidity at the exit from the dryer (in kg water/kg dry air), and $W_{Sp.A1}$ is the air's specific humidity at the entrance to the dryer. Study the next Example for familiarity with the practical data used in Equation 5.

Example 1 on Drying

Calculate the temperature of humid air leaving a dryer ($T_{Sat.A}$) operating under the following conditions:

Hot air's temperature to the dryer (T_{A1})	55°C
Hot air's wet-bulb temperature to the dryer (T_{WA})	30°C
Specific humidity of hot air to dryer ($W_{Sp.A1}$)	0.01 kg water/kg dry air
Specific humidity of humid air from the dryer ($W_{Sp.A2}$)	0.02 kg water/kg dry air

Table 1 gives us the value for $H_{E.A1}$ (hot air's enthalpy of evaporation at 55°C) as 2383 kJ/kg.

$$T_{Sat.A} = T_{A1} - \frac{H_{E.A1}(W_{Sp.A2} - W_{Sp.A1})}{1.005 + 1.88 W_{Sp.A1}} = 55 - \frac{2383(0.02 - 0.01)}{1.005 + 1.88 \times 0.01} = 47\ °C$$

Drying Time: The drying time (t_D), which refers to the time of constant drying step needed to sufficiently dry the product in a dryer at a reasonable rate, can be calculated as

$$t_D = \frac{H_L(W_P - W_C)}{U_Q.A_P(T_A - T_P)} \quad (6)$$

The H_L is the water's enthalpy of evaporation (in kJ/kg) at heated air wet-bulb temperature, W_P is the product's initial moisture content (in kg water/kg dry product), W_C is the product's critical moisture content (in kg water/kg dry product). The U_Q is the air's convective heat transfer coefficient [in W/(h.m^2.°C) or kJ/(m^2.°C], A_P is the product's surface area (in m^2), T_A is the heated air temperature to the dryer (in °C), and T_P is the product's T from the dryer (in °C).

The next equation can also calculate the t_D during the constant drying period.

$$t_D = \frac{0.62R.T\ (W_P - W_C)}{K_A.A_P.M_{n.W}.P_{Atm}(W_{Sp.P} - W_{Sp.A})} \quad (7)$$

The value 0.62 is the ratio of the molar mass of water (M_n = 18 g/mole) to that of air (M_n = 29 g/mole). R is the air's gas constant [= 287 (Pa.m^3)/(kg.°C)], T is the mean of heated air's and product's surface temperatures (in Kelvin, K), K_A is the air's convective diffusion coefficient (in m/s). $M_{n.W}$ is the water's molar mass (= 18 kg/kmole), the P_{Atm} is the air's atmospheric pressure (= 101.3 kPa), the $W_{Sp.P}$ is the product surface's specific humidity (in kg water/kg dry air), and the $W_{Sp.A}$ is the air's specific humidity (in kg water/kg dry air). [Note that the T in Equation 7 is the mean T of heated air and the product's T.]

Example 2 on Drying

Given: A rotary-drum dryer that works under P_{Atm} is used to dry wet sugar crystals (product). The dryer uses air that is heated from 35ºC and 60% W_R (relative humidity). Following data are available:

Product's initial moisture content (W_P)	0.5%
Product's critical moisture content (W_C)	0.3%.
Air's convective diffusion coefficient (K_A)	0.1 m/s.
Average surface area of crystals	0.3×0.3 = 0.09 mm^2 = 9×10^{-5} m^2
Product-surface's temperature (T_P)	33ºC
Air's gas constant (R)	8.314 m^3.kPa/(kgmole.K)
Water's molar mass (M_n)	18 kg/kgmole

Assumption: The rate of moisture removal from the surface of crystals during the constant drying step can be described by mass transfer from the crystals' surface to the heated air moving through the crystals.

Calculate: Drying time (t_D) during the constant drying step

We start with converting the values of W_P and W_C to a mass fraction.

$$W_P = 0.5/0.5 = 1 \text{ kg water/kg solid}$$

$$W_C = 0.3/0.7 = 0.4 \text{ kg water/kg solid}$$

We convert the air's T and product's T to Kelvin, make a mean of them, and use it as the T_A in Equation 7.

$$T_A = 35 + 33 = 68^{\circ}C = 341 \text{ K} \quad 341/2 = 170 \text{ K}$$

An air psychrometric diagram can determine the $W_{Sp.P}$ (the product's specific humidity) at saturation. To do so, we use the product's wet-bulb T of 33ºC to find the value of 0.03 kg water/kg dry air for $W_{Sp.P}$. Having values of heated air of 35ºC and 60% W_R; we can find the air's specific humidity ($W_{Sp.A}$) from the same graph as 0.02 kg water/kg dry air.

$$t_D = \frac{0.62R.T_A\ (W_P - W_C)}{K_A.A_P.M_{n.W}.P_{Atm}(W_{Sp.P} - W_{Sp.A})} = \frac{0.62\times8.314\times170(1-0.4)}{0.1\times9\times10^{-5}\times18\times101.3(0.03-0.02)} = 3090 \text{ s or } 51 \text{ min}$$

D-57
DUCTILITY

Discussed under the topic of ELASTICITY AND PLASTICITY OF MATERIAL.

D-58
DUST

Dust is a gas in the air with fine particles (smaller than 500 μm) and *no* considerable pressure (*P*). Dust particles are suspended solid particles from different sources, such as soil lifted by the wind. Dust particles (smaller than 500 μm) are smaller than particles of particulate matter (smaller than 10 μm). Both, however, are combustible under ordinary conditions and become explosive under specific conditions. The factors affecting the **explosion** (sudden fire) of dust in a dusty area are the following:

- **Particles Size:** The *smaller* the dust particles, the *higher* is the risk of explosion, and the *more* violent the explosion is.
- **Particles Concentration:** The *more* the particles in each volume, the *higher* is the risk of explosion. [The amount of dust in the air must *not* exceed the minimum explosion dust concentration (20 g/m^3).]
- **Air Temperature:** The *higher* the air *T* (temperature) and the *lower* the W_R (relative humidity), the *higher* is the risk of explosion.

To reduce **fugitive dust** (the particulates of traffic, wind, dirt, and other materials) outside of the processing buildings of a chemical process plant, the following are recommended:

- Not letting dusty materials accumulate onsite of the plant.
- Applying water or calcium chloride ($CaCl_2$) to gravel roads is a temporary solution for dust reduction. Paving problematic roads is a more permanent solution.

Under unsuitable conditions, **spontaneous combustion** (combustion that does *not* need an external ignition) occurs in extremely dusty areas. For example, several major sugar-dust explosions have occurred in the sugar silos, causing loss of life and extensive property damage. Investigations proved that almost all began with a small explosion and increased because **fire** follows the **pressure rise**, creating more explosions on its way. The following are a few safety precautions:

- **Good Cleaning:** The dusty areas must be cleaned regularly. Furthermore, dust should *not* accumulate on equipment, walls, and tanks.
- **Adequate Ventilation:** Adequate ventilation should be provided to control dust accumulation.
- **Electrical System:** All electrical devices installed in related devices should be explosion-proof and confirmed with the highest security codes.
- **Relative Humidity:** Air recirculation to a dusty area must contain at least 50% W_R and be filtered to remove dust. Constant addition of fresh air to the recirculation line is also required.
- **Welding and Grinding:** Welding, grinding, and drilling should be avoided in dusty areas. When these activities are necessary, the area should be cleaned first, and the facility's safety manager should supervise the entire process.
- **Ventilation:** Proper ventilation and airflow are required in dusty areas.
- **Dust-Removal Equipment:** Dust collectors (gas scrubbers) must be installed in dusty areas.

D-59

DYNAMIC VISCOSITY

Defined under the topic of VISCOSITY.

D-60

DYNAMICS

Dynamics is a branch of Physics that studies the systems' motion (a change in the position of a system in relation to time). Among others, dynamics also studies the effect of different forces and torques on the motion of a system.

E Section

LIST OF TOPICS

1. Eddy Current
2. Edison
3. EDTA
4. EFCE
5. Einstein
6. Einstein's Diffusion Equation
7. Einstein's Equation
8. Einstein's Gravitational Field Equation
9. Einstein's Principle of Gravity Spacetime
10. Einstein's Principle of Length Contraction
11. Einstein's Principle of Mass Energy Equality
12. Einstein's Principle of Mass Expansion
13. Einstein's Principle of Speed of Light
14. Einstein's Principle of Time Dilation
15. Einstein's Theories of Relativity
16. Einstein's Theory of General Relativity
17. Einstein's Theory of Light Duality
18. Einstein's Theory of Photoelectric Effect
19. Einstein's Theory of Special Relativity
20. Ejectors
21. Elastic Force, Elastic Modulus, and Elastic Strain
22. Elastic Potential Energy
23. Elasticity and Plasticity of Material
24. Elastics, Elastomers, and Plastics
25. Electric Batteries
26. Electric Capacitance and Electric Capacitors
27. Electric Charge
28. Electric Circuit
29. Electric Conductance and Electric Inductance
30. Electric Conductivity
31. Electric Conductors, Semiconductors, and Insulators
32. Electric Current and Electric Current Density
33. Electric Dipole
34. Electric Energy
35. Electric Field and Magnetic Field
36. Electric Force and Magnetic Force
37. Electric Generators and Electric Motors
38. Electric Insulators
39. Electric Potential
40. Electric Potential Energy
41. Electric Power
42. Electric Resistance
43. Electric Transformers
44. Electric Voltage
45. Electricity
46. Electrochemical Potential
47. Electrochemical Reactions
48. Electrolytes and Electrolysis
49. Electromagnetic Energy
50. Electromagnetic Field
51. Electromagnetic Force
52. Electromagnetic Induction
53. Electromagnetic Radiation
54. Electromagnetic Waves
55. Electromagnetism
56. Electron
57. Electron Affinity
58. Electron Binding Energy
59. Electron Pairs and Electron Lone Pairs
60. Electron Volt
61. Electronegativity
62. Electronic Microscope
63. Electrostatic Force
64. Electrostatic Precipitators
65. Elementary Particles and Elementary Quantum Particles
66. Emissivity
67. Emulsions
68. Endothermic Process
69. Endothermic Reactions
70. Energy Absorbing Reactions
71. Energy and its Forms
72. Energy Balance
73. Energy Conversion
74. Energy Density
75. Energy of Reaction

E-1

EDDY CURRENT

The eddy current (also called **vortex**) is an area in a fluid flow in which the fluid stream behaves like a turbulent flow (non-developed flow). When a flowing liquid in a pipe reaches an object (like a half-open valve), a stream that contains large eddy currents (**vortexes** or **vortices**) starts to form. Eddy current move in a non-fully-developed manner, as shown in Figure 1. Eddy currents can be observed in a cup of tea when mixing to dissolve the sugar crystals, in a cigarette's smoke rings, and an airplane's wingtip.

Figure 2 illustrates a liquid flow in a pipe in three different regions:

- **Unsteady Region:** This is a short distance of unsteady flow immediately at the entrance to the pipe, shown in Figure 2 with unequal arrows (for unequal velocity vectors).
- **Steady Region:** This is the area after the entrance region, shown in Figure 2 with uniform arrows.
- **Eddy Region:** The region where the liquid hits an object, shown with non-uniform arrows in Figure 2.

In a pipe, eddy currents reduce the velocity of the flow, causing a large pressure drop (generally known as pressure difference, ΔP) in the flow. In a heat exchanger, eddy currents affect the flow's temperature, causing the flowing fluid's molecules near the wall of the exchanger to move faster than the molecules in the middle of the pipe. This behavior increases the rate of heat energy (E_Q, simply heat and scientifically enthalpy).

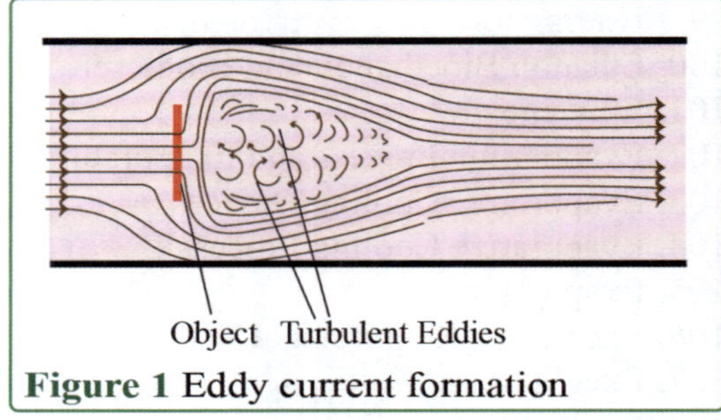

Figure 1 Eddy current formation

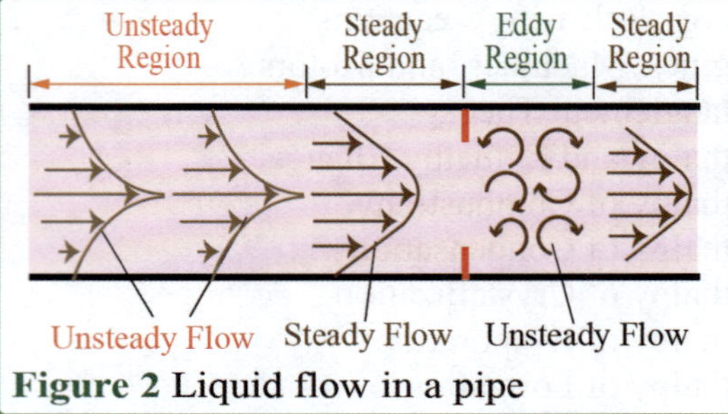

Figure 2 Liquid flow in a pipe

E-2

EDISON

Thomas Alva Edison (1847–1931) is one of the most creative inventors and developers. He is known as the man who electrified the entire world. He was born in Milan, Ohio, and raised in Port Huron, Michigan. At the age of 13, he started to sell newspapers and vegetables on the train from Port Huron to Detroit and spent most of his profit buying devices for electric experiments, his favored hobby for his entire life.

Edison achieved many industrial successes, including the following:

- He developed electricity production (also called **power production**) on an industrial scale. This invention had a huge impact on any industry and household worldwide.
- He had 1093 US patents, including an electric vote recorder (1867), microphone (1876), phonograph (1877, the early version of gramophone), electric lightbulb (1879), and rechargeable battery (the 1890s).
- He established the first research laboratory (in 1876) in Menlo Park, New Jersey, and the Edison Electric Light Company (in 1878) in New York, which later became today's General Electric Company (GE).
- He favored direct current (DC) electricity but finally accepted that alternating current (AC) electricity is a more cost-effective and practical electricity distribution.
- His first steam-generating power plant started in London in January 1882 to distribute 110 V direct-current electricity to street lamps and several homes near distance. Shortly after (in September of the same year), his New York power plant started distributing 110 V electricity to 59 customers in lower Manhattan.

Edison, photographed in 1922
[copied from Wikipedia]

E-3
EDTA

EDTA is abbreviated for ethylenediamine tetra-acetic acid, a polycarboxylic acid with the chemical formula of $[CH_2N(CH_2CO_2H)_2]_2$. EDTA is produced as salts, mainly as a sodium salt (called disodium EDTA or EDTA-2Na) and sometimes with 2 molecules of water (EDTA dihydrate or EDTA.$2H_2O$). EDTA-2Na is a water-soluble white powder used in both laboratory and operation as a chelate (a compound that can form two, or more, separate covalent bonds with different ions, mainly Ca, Mg, and Fe).

The following are a few uses of EDTA: 1) It is used in labs to determine a sample's hardness content by attaching it to its Ca and Mg cations. 2) It is used to clean an evaporator's tubes and boiler feedwater by combining with their Ca^{2+} and Mg^{2+}. 3) It can be used in some products, such as soda, beer, soap, and detergents, to get the trace metal ions together that would otherwise produce unwanted precipitates.

E-4
EFCE

EFCE (European Federation of Chemical Engineering) was founded in Paris, France, in 1953. As of 2015, EFCE has over 160 000 members from over 30 countries

E-5

EINSTEIN

As one of the two most talented physicists (Newton the second one), Albert Einstein (1879–1955) was a German-Swiss-American physicist. He was born in Germany, took Swiss nationality in 1901, became a US citizen in 1933, and died in the USA at 76. [Einstein was cremated, and his ashes were spread on the ground of the Institute for Advanced Study of Princeton University in New Jersey.]

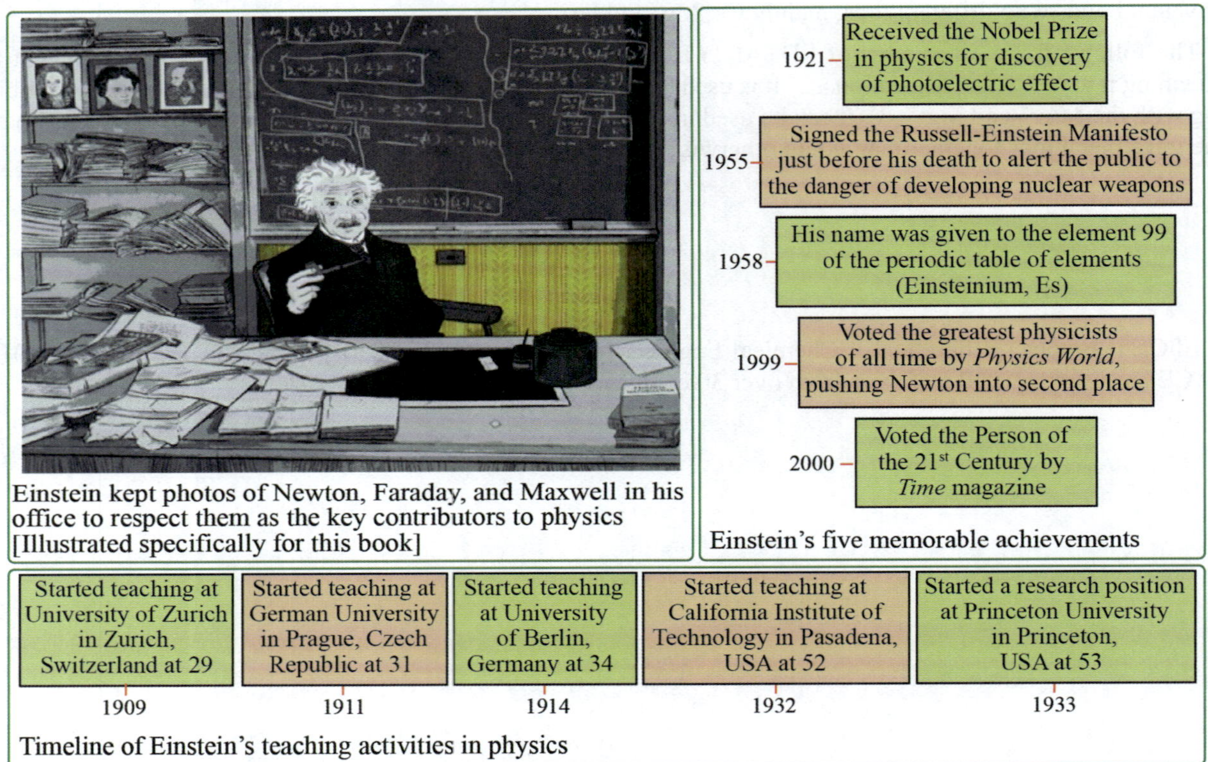

Einstein kept photos of Newton, Faraday, and Maxwell in his office to respect them as the key contributors to physics [Illustrated specifically for this book]

Einstein's five memorable achievements

Timeline of Einstein's teaching activities in physics

The following are some other Einstein's achievements:

- He worked on many theories, including the theory of unification of physics.
- His equality equation ($E = M.c^2$) became the most famous equation ever formulized.
- His idea about the constant speed of light directed him to space-and-time dependability.
- He is the only man whose deep understanding of Physics is greater than any man before him.

During his school years in Germany, Einstein was an average student but excellent in math and physics. During his late school years, Einstein kept asking himself, "what would we see if we would sit on a beam of light?" The answer he found later was the principle of speed of light. During his university years at Zurich Polytechnic in Switzerland, he was *not* satisfied with typical answers to some key physics concepts. In 1905, after his graduation at the age of 26, while he was a scientific nobody working in the Patent Office in Bern, Switzerland, Einstein published the following four (4) important scientific articles:

- **Transformation of Light** (June 1905)**:** In this paper, Einstein talked about the photoelectric effect and the relation between light and electricity. In this paper, he also contributed to Planck's quantum theory by saying that light releases its energy, known as the photon energy, in individual units (packets), each consisting of many particles (photons of light). [Later, in 1921, this paper won him the Noble Prize in Physics.]

- **Motion of Suspended Particles** (July 1905)**:** In this paper, Einstein discussed the movement of the suspended solid particles in a liquid, known later as the Brownian motion of particles.
- **Electrodynamics of Moving Bodies** (September 1905)**:** In this paper, Einstein discussed the theory of special relativity about the relative motion of systems moving at a constant speed. He proved that the speed of light is constant and independent of an observer's and the light source's speed, so *no* reference system is needed to define the speed of light constant (c). This discovery led him to conclude that space and time are closely dependent, and it makes more sense if they were combined into one quantity of spacetime.
- **Inertia of a Moving Body in Relation to its Mass** (November 1905)**:** In this paper, Einstein discussed the principle of mass-energy equality and his famous equality equation ($E = M.c^2$). [Time, however, does *not* run at the same speed at c.]

His papers of 1905 (Einstein's year of miracles) changed the idea of physicists about mass, energy, gravitational force (simply **gravity**), and space and time (together spacetime, as he named it). Between 1915 and 1919, he wrote four more articles about general relativity to remove the limitation of his 1905's special relativity. [In his life, Einstein wrote many scientific papers, but just one book (*The Meaning of Relativity*).]

It is also interesting to know the following about Einstein:

- Einstein's idea of spacetime and its relation to gravitational force was so strange at its time that he did *not* get the Noble Prize for it. But, he got a Noble Prize in Physics later in 1921 for the photoelectric effect.
- Physicists believe that Physics advanced far more in the 20th century than in any previous century, and Einstein created those advances far more than any other physicist.
- During the last two decades of his life, Einstein's main goal was to connect his principle of gravity and spacetime with some quantum theories to create the theory of unification of physics. Unfortunately, he could *not* complete this task until he died in 1955. [This theory remains unsolved.]
- After he died, medical scientists suggested that in Einstein's brain, areas involved with data processing were larger compared with a normal brain. Instead, those involved in language and speech were smaller.

The following four statements can familiarize you with Einstein's thoughts about life and Physics:

- Imagination is more important than knowledge, the first holds the entire world, but the second is limited.
- Education is *not* the learning of facts but the training of the mind to think better.
- Life is like riding a bicycle. To keep your balance, you must keep moving.
- If you *can't* explain it simply, you *don't* understand it well enough.

This topic can come to an end by saying the following:

- Most physicists think that Einstein's work was worthy of 4 Nobel Prizes; one for photoelectric effect (the one he got one for), special relativity, mass-energy equality, and general relativity. He just got one because his relativity theories seemed surprisingly premature to be understood, at the time, by the Nobel referees.
- Although Einstein did *not* agree with a few theories of quantum physics (like quantum entanglement), his theories of the duality of light and photoelectric effect established it with some other top physicists.
- Planck, Einstein, Rutherford, Bohr, Heisenberg, Schrodinger, and Broglie can be named as the seven (7) top quantum physicists. And Newton, Faraday, and Maxwell as the three (3) top classical physicists. The ten (10) pioneers contributed to Physics more than all physicists.

E-6

EINSTEIN'S DIFFUSION EQUATION

Einstein, in 1906, formulated the diffusion coefficient (D_{AB}) for use in the diffusion process occurring through a phase boundary or membrane. He proved that when an ideal solution (which has low concentration and, so, behaves like a pure solution) is under diffusion, the D_{AB} of diffusing component A (also called diffusant A) can be given in relation to non-diffusing component B, and the solution's temperature (T) and viscosity (η).

$$D_{AB} = K_A \frac{T}{\eta} \tag{1}$$

Symbol D_{AB} is used to indicate that A diffuses through B. D_{BA} would have been used instead of D_{AB} if B were the diffusing component.

Einstein's diffusion equation can be combined with Fick's diffusion equation to write the **Einstein-Fick diffusion equation**.

$$M_A = (K_A \frac{T}{\eta})(A \frac{C}{L}) \tag{2}$$

Here, M_A is the mass of diffusant A, T is the temperature of the solution under diffusion, η is the viscosity of the solution, A is the area through which the diffusion occurs, C is the concentration of diffusant A, and L is the diffusing length the diffusant diffuses.

The previous equation can be written in rate form to indicate the amount of A diffused in unit time.

$$\dot{M}_A = \frac{K_A}{t} \times \frac{T}{\eta}(A \frac{C}{L}) \tag{3}$$

In the previous equations, coefficient K_A (where subscript A is for diffusant A) is inversely proportional to T and directly proportional to D_{AB} and η. In addition, K_A is inversely proportional to the following:

- **Molar Mass:** The molar fraction (M_n) of the diffusant inversely affects the diffusion (the *larger* the M_n of diffusant A, the *smaller* is its K_A and D_{AB} and, consequently, the *slower* it diffuses). Consider a solution containing KCl, sugar (sucrose), and protein in a column containing ion exchange resin that operates at 70ºC. KCl molecules (with small M_n of 75 g/mole and large D_{AB} of 0.2 cm^2/h at 70ºC) diffuse the ion-exchange resin particles faster than sugar molecules (with M_n of 343 g/mole and small D_{AB} of 0.04 cm^2/h at 70ºC) and protein molecules (with a large M_n and a small D_{AB} of 1.3×10^{-3} cm^2/h at 70ºC).
- **Friction:** A friction (f), or frictions, on the way of diffusion inversely affects the diffusion. Consider a diffusant with spherical-shaped molecules under diffusion. If, therefore, friction exists on its way, the diffusion rate becomes affected less or more, depending on the solution's η (viscosity) and molecule's R (radius) in the following way:

$$f = 6\pi . R . \eta \tag{4}$$

E-7

EINSTEIN'S EQUATION

Einstein's equation is the simplified word for Einstein's mass-energy equality equation, discussed in the Principle of Mass-Energy Equality subtopic under EINSTEIN'S THEORIES OF RELATIVITY.

E-8

EINSTEIN'S GRAVITATIONAL FIELD EQUATION

Einstein's gravitational field equation (simply **Einstein's gravitational equation** or **Einstein's field equation**) is an equation used by Einstein in 2015 in his theory of general relativity to express gravitational force (F_g, simply **gravity**). In other words, it expresses how the rest mass energy (simply **mass energy**, E_M) curves the spacetime in a gravitational field (G-field). He used three (3) **tensors** to solve his equation. [A **tensor** (T), in math, is a quantity that consists of two (or more) components. Vector and scalar quantities are simple examples of tensors, as each has two components. Because tensors can simplify the solution of some mathematical equations, many have been used in physics, such as the Maxwell tensor, used by Maxwell to express the close relationship between electric charges and electric current.]

Einstein used the following equation to express the relationship between the three (3) tensors:

$$T_E + A.T_M = \frac{8\pi.K_G}{c^4}.T_{SEM} \qquad (1)$$

Here, T_E is **Einstein's tensor**, A is a constant expressing the energy density or vacuum energy of the spacetime, T_M is the **metric tensor**, K_G is the gravitational constant, c is the speed of light constant, and T_{SE} is known as the **stress-energy** tensor, which uses mass, energy, pressure, and shear components to express the G-field of the spacetime.

The T_E (Einstein's tensor) is defined as

$$T_E = T_R - \frac{1}{2}T_M.R \qquad (2)$$

T_R is the Ricci curvature tensor (a quantity the geometry of given metric tensor changes), and R is the scalar curvature. Substituting Equation 2 into 1 and showing the terms $8\pi.K_G/c^4$ as K_E (Einstein's gravitational constant = 2.077×10^{-43} in 1/N), Einstein's gravitational (EG) equation can be written in its final form.

$$T_R - \frac{1}{2}T_M.R + A.T_M = K_E.T_{SE} \qquad (3)$$

The unit of each term on the left side of this equation is $1/L^2$, where L is for length. The whole expression on the left represents the curvature of spacetime. The equation's right side represents the spacetime's E_M content. Thus, the EG equation can determine how a massive system can curve spacetime.

As for the EG equation, it is important to know the following points:

- The EG equation works fine for all cases, except for extreme F_g around a singularity (like the Big Bang singularity at its earliest moments or the blackhole singularity). For this reason, it is easier to study such a singularity without considering the effect of the F_g on it.
- The EG equation is an advanced substitute for Newton's gravitational equation (NG equation), which can calculate the F_g as an attractive force between any two systems with masses of M_1 and M_2, located in the distance L from each other. [Most gravity-related calculations are still solved using the NG equation, as it is simpler than the EG equation and gives enough accuracy for most ordinary systems.]

E-9

EINSTEIN'S PRINCIPLE OF GRAVITY SPACETIME

Discussed under the topic of EINSTEIN'S THEORIES OF RELATIVITY.

E-10

EINSTEIN'S PRINCIPLE OF LENGTH CONTRACTION

Discussed under the topic of EINSTEIN'S THEORIES OF RELATIVITY.

E-11

EINSTEIN'S PRINCIPLE OF MASS-ENERGY EQUALITY

Discussed under the topic of EINSTEIN'S THEORIES OF RELATIVITY.

E-12

EINSTEIN'S PRINCIPLE OF MASS EXPANSION

Discussed under the topic of EINSTEIN'S THEORIES OF RELATIVITY.

E-13

EINSTEIN'S PRINCIPLE OF SPEED OF LIGHT

Discussed under the topic of EINSTEIN'S THEORIES OF RELATIVITY.

E-14

EINSTEIN'S PRINCIPLE OF TIME DILATION

Discussed under the topic of EINSTEIN'S THEORIES OF RELATIVITY.

E-15

EINSTEIN'S THEORIES OF RELATIVITY

In one of his four (4) articles of 1905, called **Electrodynamics of Moving Bodies**, Einstein presented his **theory of relativity**, later called the **theory of special relativity** (TSR). However, he felt later that this theory was incomplete, as it only covered the nonaccelerating reference systems but *not* accelerating systems. He, therefore, worked on it theoretically and experimentally and published his findings between 1915 and 1919 in four (4) more articles under the name of the **theory of general relativity** (TGR), which considered both nonaccelerating (inertial) and accelerating (noninertial) reference systems.

In relativity theories, as their names suggest, Einstein proved that everything is **relative** (comparative), so it is impossible to correctly estimate a moving (relativistic) system's speed without relating it to a reference system. In simple words, these theories tell us what different observers see by comparison. Without seeing the ground (a nonaccelerating reference) from the window, we *cannot* estimate how fast our train moves.

Assume you are traveling on a train and fire a fire gun twice. To an observer next to you, they occur at the same location. Instead, to an observer on the ground, they occur at two separate locations (as the train moves between the two events). This example tells us that the time is relative, also. The rate at which a clock ticks on the moving train differs from the observer's wristwatch rate.

Assume that you are sitting in a train moving at a constant slow speed of 8 km/h (= 5 Mi/h) relative to an observer standing on the ground, so you and the observer are in a nonaccelerating (inertial) system. Further, assume that another train is moving next to your train at the same speed of 8 km/h. While looking at the other train, it may seem that you are *not* moving relative to another train (because *no* relative speed exists between two trains). In other words, you're stationary in relation to the other train. But you would feel a relative speed of 8 km/h between you and the observer standing on the ground. If you then start walking at 4 km/h in the same direction, it seems to the ground observer that you are moving at 12 km/h. This simple example tells us that speed (distance per time) is **relative** to a reference system.

Einstein chose the speed of light constant (c) as a reference system to prove its TSR (theory of special relativity) and remove the limitations of Newton's Law of Gravitation. And the purpose of the TGR (theory of general relativity) was to remove the limitation of the TSR by talking about both a **nonaccelerating** (inertial) **system** and an **accelerating** (noninertial) **system**, a system that experiences acceleration.

1. CONSEQUENCE PRINCIPLES OF SPECIAL RELATIVITY THEORY

In the TSR (theory of special relativity), Einstein discussed the following seven related principles (rules): 1) Principle of Equivalence Laws, 2) Principle of Gravity-Spacetime, 3) Principle of Speed of Light, 4) Principle of Mass-Energy Equality, 5) Principle of Time Dilation, 6) Principle of Length Contraction, and 7) Principle of Mass Expansion. These are discussed next.

1.1 Principle of Equivalence Laws of Physics of Special Relativity

The principle of equivalence laws of Physics introduces Einstein's idea that the laws of Physics work the **same** in different reference systems, regardless of an observer's speed. Einstein first proved this rule for all nonaccelerating systems in the TSR. But later in the TGR, he also proved that the equivalence-laws principle works on the accelerating systems. Consider the following two systems: 1) The Earth, a common nonaccelerating system in Physics (under constant gravitational acceleration of a_g). 2) A space shuttle that travels in the sky at constant acceleration, like a_g ($\approx 10\ m/s^2$ on the Earth's surface).

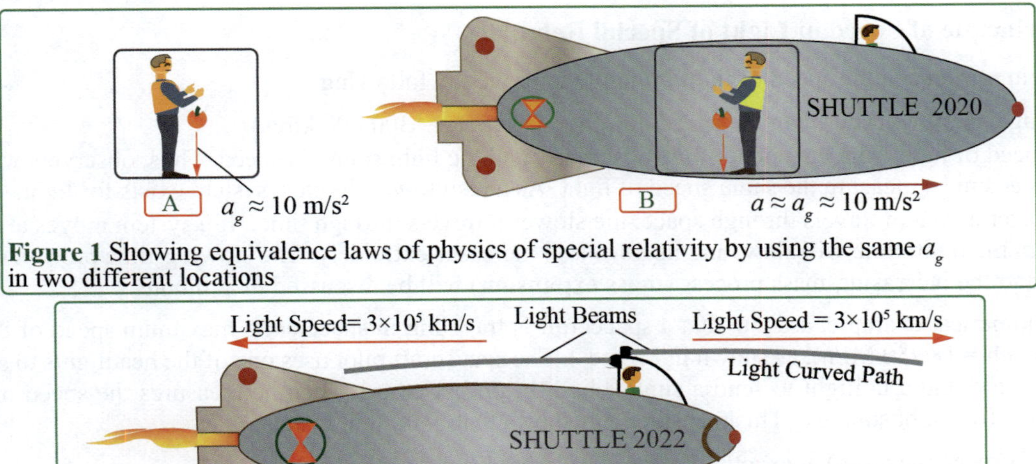

Figure 1 Showing equivalence laws of physics of special relativity by using the same a_g in two different locations

Figure 2 Showing speed-of-light constant of special relativity by using a space shuttle and its pilot as observer

Further, consider the A section of Figure 1 that shows a person in a box on the ground under constant acceleration of a_g, created by gravitational force (F_g, symbolically shown by a falling **apple**). And the B section of the same figure shows another person in a similar box in a shuttle in space under almost the same a_g (when the shuttle's engine is off). Under the assumption that both systems and persons in them (the observers) are massively the same, we can apply the equivalence principle to both systems and say the following:

- Persons (observers) in both systems would feel the same force, equivalent to F_g.
- Person in the shuttle does *not* feel that his time is passing more quickly.
- Persons and apples in both systems experience *no* acceleration ($a = 0$).
- Apples in both systems fall with the same velocity. [According to the principle of free-fall motion, if the person on the ground and the person in the shuttle release 2 apples with different masses, all 4 apples fall side-by-side (with the same velocity and with the same a).]

[Later, Einstein contributed more to the equivalence principle in his TGR, as discussed later.]

1.2 Principle of Gravity Spacetime of Special Relativity

Newton in his 1687's gravitation theory (Newton's Law of Gravitation), assumed that space is a non-absolute quantity, time is an absolute quantity, and both are independent of each other. If, according to this idea, a beam of light is sent from one point to another, different observers moving at different speeds would agree on the time that the light's beam traveled (because time is absolute). But would *not* agree on how far the beam traveled (because space is non-absolute). According to Newton's idea, different observers measure different speeds of light. This idea seemed wrong to Einstein, as he thought that time is relative, *not* absolute (because each observer has his measure of time). If, say, a system moving close to the speed of light constant (c), its clock ticks slower relative to a clock on the Earth. Thus, the following are true:

- Space and time are dependent on each other, so *none* of them can be absolute, and
- All observers measure the same speed for the light, regardless of their speed.

Einstein in his 1905's gravitation theory (Einstein's principle of gravity of special relativity), went further and proved that space and time are linked closely. Therefore, it makes more sense to combine them into one quantity, spacetime. Later, in general relativity, he proved that mass (M) causes curve (warp) in spacetime, so-called the curvature of spacetime.

1.3 Principle of Speed of Light of Special Relativity

Einstein introduced the speed of light principle to prove the following:

- Nothing can move faster than the speed of light constant (c = 300 000 km/s).
- The speed of light is independent of the observer's and the light source's speed. Thus, observers with different speeds must measure the same speed of light. As a result, *no* reference system exists for light.
- The faster a system travels through space, the slower it travels through time. If a system moves at a speed close to the light, time will slow, and its M (mass) increases extremely. The slowing-time process (**time dilation**) and the increasing-mass process (**mass expansion**) will be discussed in a minute.

As a numerical example, assume that a spacecraft is traveling in space at its maximum speed of 8.3 km/s (= 30 000 km/h = 18 750 Mi/h), as shown in Figure 2. The spacecraft pilot uses one of the headlights to send a light beam forward and a taillight to send a similar light beam backward. Then he measures the speed of light that leave these two light sources. This measurement shows that both light beams:

- Move in space (vacuum) at exactly the speed of light ($1\ c = 3\times10^5$ km/s),
- Move equally, regardless of the speed of the **observer** (the pilot), who travels much slower than c,
- Move equally, regardless of the speed of the **source** (spacecraft), unlike other quantum particles (particles with *no* subparticle) that are dependent on the speed of the motion's source.

1.4 Principle of Mass-Energy Equality of Special Relativity

Einstein published the equality equation (Einstein's equation) in his fourth article of 1905 to prove that mass (M) and energy (E) are equivalence (interchangeable) under special conditions. He formulized mass-energy relationship through speed of light constant (c = 300 000 km/s), a proportionality constant.

$$E = M.c^2 \quad (1)$$

In his equation, which became the most famous equation ever formulized, Einstein used c^2 (the square of c) because of the nature of energy. When a system (small or large) is moving, say, 2 times as fast as another system, it doesn't have 2 times the energy, but $2^2 = 4$ times. The Einstein equation tells us that a system with M exhibits an E, given by $M.c$. Conversely, a system with E exhibits an M, given by E/c.

Einstein derived his equation by considering a given. When a system emits light (releasing E) in opposite directions, its V (velocity) does *not* change (since the c does *not* change). And because the system's V remains constant, its M must change. Then he found that the M is reduced by an amount proportional to the E released (emitted), so the change in M is E divided by the square of c.

$$M = \frac{E}{c^2} \qquad \text{Or} \qquad E = M.c^2$$

Einstein's simple equation ($E = M.c^2$) is *not* complete for a moving particle with mass M, as the particle's momentum ($p = M.V$) must be considered. This brings the equation to the next general form.

$$E^2 = (M.c^2)^2 + (p.c)^2 = M^2.c^4 + p^2.c^2 \quad (2)$$

Thus, we are facing the following two cases:

- For a **massive-but-moveless** (at-rest) **system**, $V = 0$ and, therefore, p becomes zero too. Thus, the momentum section of the equation eliminates, leaving the term $E^2 = M^2.c^4$. Taking the square root of each side (because all quantities here are positive) gives $E = M.c^2$.
- For a **massless-but-moving system** (like a photon), $M = 0$, so the equation becomes $E = p.c$.

According to Einstein's equation, an extremely small amount of nuclear fuel in a nuclear reactor can be converted to a large amount of nuclear energy (because of the large value of c^2). Generally, we can say the following about the term c^2:

- The energy created from mass can move at c^2.
- The c^2 determines the energy existing in the nucleus of a radioactive element.
- When a system is at rest, it has some energy, equal to $M.c^2$, stored in its nuclear mass.

Consider the mass energy (E_M) released by nuclear fission of one atom of uranium-235 (U-235) in the reactor of a nuclear power plant. The E released from the nucleus of the U-235 atom during fission is about seven million times (7×10^6) greater than the E released from the explosion of one molecule of TNT. Now, we can calculate the E equivalent to 1 g of the U-235. We must square the value of c and multiply it by 1 g, so

$$E = (1/10^3 \text{ kg})(c) \approx (3\times10^8 \text{ m/s})^2 \approx 3\times10^{13} \text{ kg.m}^2/\text{s}^2 \approx 3\times10^{13} \text{ J} \approx 30\times10^9 \text{ kJ}$$

30×10^9 (= 30 billion) kJ of E_Q (heat energy), released from 1 g of the U-235, can produce electricity for about 2 500 average-size homes for a year. To have a sense of 30×10^9 kJ of E_Q, we can compare it with coke. When 1 g of coke burns, it approximately releases 30 kJ of E_Q (or 30 000 kJ/kg coke).

Based on Einstein's equation, adding 90 MJ (= 25 W/h) of any form of E to a system increases its M by 1 μg (microgram) without adding any M to that system, where W is for Watt. [Scientists measured the mass of a piece of coal and then measured the total mass of ash and smoke after the coal had been burned. The result showed that the M after the test is less than the M before. Calculations proved that the difference in mass (ΔM) multiplied by c^2 equals the missing M, which was released in the form of E while burning the coal.] [In $E = M.c^2$, the term $E = E_M$ (the mass energy) and $M = M_R$ (rest mass) when the system is non-moving.]

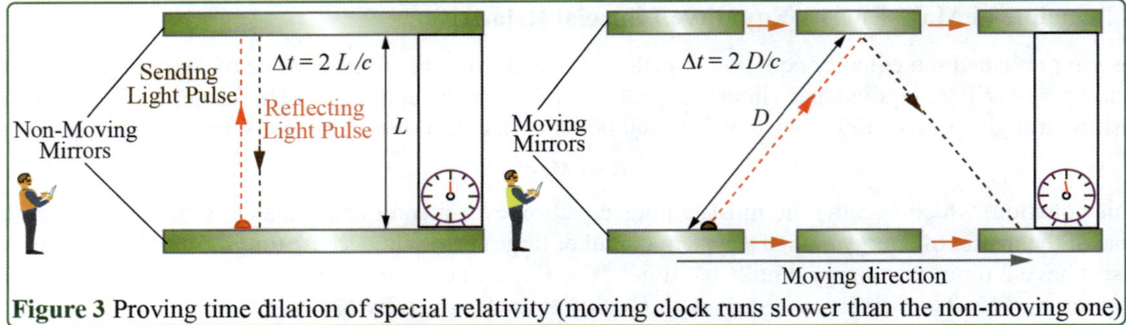

Figure 3 Proving time dilation of special relativity (moving clock runs slower than the non-moving one)

1.5 Principle of Time Dilation of Special Relativity

The time-dilation principle introduces Einstein's idea that time slows down in any reference system (the *faster* a system travels through space, the *slower* it travels through time). In other words, at high speeds, space contracts in the direction of moving. Our time experience depends on how fast we travel relative to a reference observer's time. Thus, the *faster* we travel, the *more* time slows down for us, or the *faster* we travel, the *slower* our clock runs. This statement tells us that time is relative to the speed of a moving system. Thus, *no* clock exists at the center of the Universe, to which all of us can set our watches reliably.

The time dilation of a relative motion is very small unless the system (or the clock) moves at a very high speed, close to the speed of light (c). For example, a clock moving at 0.5 c (relative to a stationary observer) ticks about 83% faster than if it were at rest (relative to the same observer). If a clock moves close to the c, time slows by less than one part in a billion. If, however, a clock moves at c, time stops for it completely. For a photon of light moving at c, the space shrinks to zero, so it does *not* experience time (so it can be everywhere, at the same time, in the Universe). [And if a system travels faster than light, it travels back in time, as the time-dilation principle suggests.]

Consider the GPS (Global Positioning Systems) satellites (starting their duties in 1995). If the atomic clocks located in these satellites were *not* tuned to Einstein's time-dilation math, they would lose about 47 microseconds each day compared with the clocks on the Earth. The reasons follow.

- GPS satellites orbiting at high speed, compared to a stationary (at-rest) system, and
- GPS satellites experience a weaker gravitational force (F_g) than a clock on the Earth.

Knowing that physicists express time-dilation effects at speeds close to the speed of light, let us study a hypothetical (imaginary) example. A spacecraft starts traveling at 0.99 c, relative to the Earth, directly toward a star that is 1 lightyear (LY = 5.8 trillion Mi) away from the Earth. We can then say:

- If the astronaut looks at the craft's clock, he sees it ticking at its normal rate (because *no* relative speed exists between the craft's clock and him; in other words, he is stationary in relation to the craft's clock).
- If the astronaut looks at Earth's clock (with a remote device), he sees, according to the time-dilation math, it is ticking 1/7 (that is 14%) times faster than the craft's clock (because a relative speed of 0.99 c exists between the craft's and the Earth's clocks).
- If the astronaut travels at the same speed of 0.99 c for 1 year to reach the star, he will find 7 years have passed when he returns to the Earth, so his twin brother looks to him as 7 years older. [But the astronaut did *not* feel his life passing more quickly during travel.]
- The astronaut reaches the star in just 1/7 year, measured by the craft's clock. This is because the distance between the Earth and the star is *no* longer 1 LY but 1/7 (or 0.14) LY. As viewed by an observer on the Earth, the clock on the Earth would have registered a total time of 1 year (*not* 1/7 years). This statement is true because the astronaut is traveling at 99% of c directly toward the star, so the distance (the length in space) is contracted by 1/7, according to Einstein's theory of length contraction.

- If the astronaut returns immediately after reaching the star to the Earth at the same speed of 99% of c, the total round-trip time, recorded by the craft's clock, for the astronaut would be 1/7 + 1/7 = 2/7 = 0.3 years. As viewed by an observer on the Earth, the clock on the Earth would have registered a total time of 2 years (*not* 0.3 years) for the astronaut's round-trip journey.

As said, the amount of time dilation increases with speed. Consider a simple clock and two mirrors, between which a light pulse bounces back and forth. Further, assume that the clock kicks once the light pulse reaches each mirror. In the at-rest clock (the left side of Figure 3), the light pulse travels a path with a length of $2L$, and the total time for the light beam to travel its path is

$$\Delta t_1 = \frac{2L}{c} \tag{3}$$

In the moving clock (the right side of the same figure), which moves at the speed of U relative to the at-rest clock, the light pulse takes a longer path. In this case, the total time for the light beam to pass its path is

$$\Delta t_2 = \frac{2D}{c} \tag{4}$$

Thus, a **relativistic adjustment factor** (symbol γ, gamma) must be used to indicate the ratio between U (the system's speed) and c (the light's speed).

$$\gamma = \frac{1}{\sqrt{1-\left(\frac{U}{c}\right)^2}} \tag{5}$$

According to this equation, the γ factor (ratio) for a system that travels at 90% c is 7.1, that for a system traveling at 99.99% of c is 70.7, and that for a system traveling at exactly c is infinite.

[Note: In 1971, American physicists proved the principle of time dilation by placing 4 identical atomic clocks in flights traveling twice around the world, 2 flying east and 2 flying west. Comparing the times with a similar clock on the Earth, they found that the moving clocks had a tiny delay, equal to a fraction of a second (microsecond). This experiment agreed with the time-dilation equation (Equation 3).]

1.6 Principle of Length Contraction of Special Relativity

This principle introduces Einstein's idea that the *faster* a system moves, its moving **length contraction** is *greater*. When, for example, a system quickly passes you (the observer), it seems to you shorter, compared to its actual length, by a factor that depends on its **speed** relative to yours. Thus, to correctly specify a fast-moving system's length, we need to know the speed of the reference.

Consider a measuring meter stick, exactly 1 m (= 100 cm) in length. Now imagine that the stick is moving at $0.5c$, relative to you (the observer) standing on the ground. While moving at that speed, space is contracted by 83%, so the stick seems 83 cm (0.83 of its at-rest length) to you. At a relative speed of $0.99c$, the space contracts by 14%, so the stick seems 14 cm (1/7 of its at-rest length) to you.

A system's contracted length (L) can be calculated from its at-rest length (L_0), its speed (U), and speed of light constant (c).

$$L = L_0\sqrt{\frac{1-U^2}{c^2}} \tag{6}$$

1.7 Principle of Mass Expansion of Special Relativity

On the principle of mass expansion, Einstein proved that the *faster* a massive system moves, the *greater* is its moving (relativistic) mass (M). When, for example, a system with a mass of 1 kg is moving at 0.5 c, relative to an observer, it has a moving mass of about 1.2 kg. When this system moves at 0.9 c, it has a mass of about 2.3 kg. And when it is moving at 0.99 c, it will have a mass of about 7 kg. The mass-energy equivalency is the M increase at high speeds (the E that a system has in relation to its motion will add to its M). Thus, a massive system can never reach the c because its M would have become infinite, regardless of its at-rest mass.

Einstein discovered that the mass increase depends on the following:

- **Length Contraction:** Mass increase is proportional to the *decreasing* length of a moving system (the *faster* a system moves, the *greater* is the decrease in its length.)
- **Time Dilation:** Mass increase is proportional to the *decreasing* rate of a moving clock (the *faster* a system moves through space, the *slower* it moves through time.) A fast-moving clock runs a tiny bit slower than the stationary one.

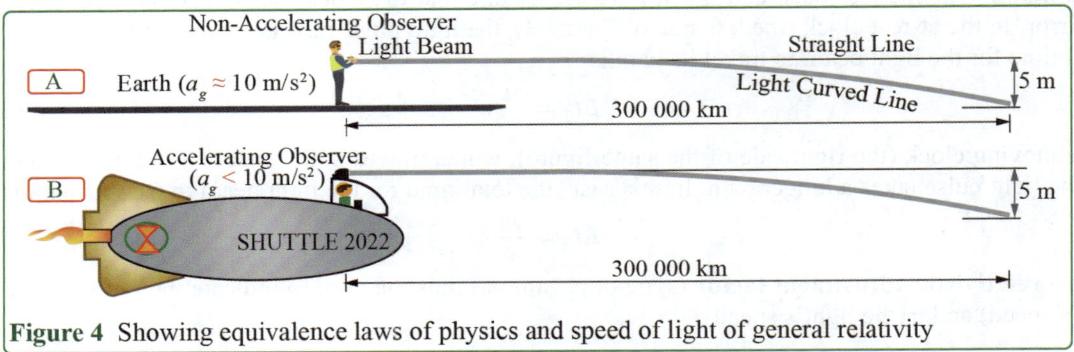

Figure 4 Showing equivalence laws of physics and speed of light of general relativity

2. CONSEQUENCES OF GENERAL RELATIVITY THEORY

In the TGR (theory of general relativity), Einstein completed his equivalence laws and the gravity-spacetime principle, as discussed below.

2.1 Principles of Equivalence Laws and Speed of Light of General Relativity

The A section of Figure 4 shows a man standing on the ground (nonaccelerating system) and having a flashlight in his hand to send a light beam forward. The B section of the same figure shows an astronaut piloting a spacecraft at high speed and some **acceleration**, so the system accelerates. The astronaut uses a headlight to send a light beam ahead. Then both observers (at-rest man on the ground and astronaut in the spacecraft) measure the speed of light. The tests show that both light beams in empty spaces move at exactly the speed of light ($1\ c = 3\times10^5$ km/s), regardless of the speed of the observers.

As shown in A and B cases, each light beam curve falls behind its path by 5 m (meter) in 1 s (second) after traveling 3×10^5 km. The similarities in the results of these experiments prove to us that: 1) All reference systems with 1 a_g are equivalent. 2) What is true for a non-accelerating system (the man on the ground under some F_g) is also true for an accelerating system (the pilot in the spacecraft under acceleration and negligible amount of F_g). This example tells us that F_g affects all systems in the Universe, but its amount is *not* the same everywhere. 3) Light beams behave in the same way, regardless of the speed of the observers (the man and the pilot).

2.2 Principle of Gravity-Spacetime of General Relativity

Earlier in special relativity, Einstein considered time as the fourth dimension and suggested that "space by itself and time by itself *cannot* make sense, called by him the spacetime. As a quantity, thus,

- Spacetime is *not* an absolute quantity, as space and time are dependent on each other.
- Spacetime can be curved (bent) by massive systems, known as the curvature of spacetime.

Einstein used a gravitational-field model to explain his **principle of gravity-spacetime** (principle of curvature of spacetime), as shown in Figure 5. Referring to this model, he said that F_g (gravitational force) is *not* an attracting force between two massive systems (systems with mass, M), as Newton said in around 1687, but the result of those systems curving space at a time. The *more* massive a system, the *greater* its F_g is, and the *more* it curves the spacetime. Thus, F_g can be viewed as a curved spacetime around a massive system. In other words, spacetime is **flat** in the absence of M and **curved** in the presence of M.

Later, physicists predicted that the F_g curves the spacetime by its particles (the gravitons). Spacetime is related to M (mass), and as M is related to E (energy), all forms of E, including the E_{Ph} (photon energy), can curve the spacetime and create F_g.

[Note 1: The principle of spacetime was so strange at its time that Einstein did *not* get the Noble Prize for it. In 1919, however, a British physicist could show the effect of F_g on spacetime during a solar eclipse by taking several photos, showing how the apparent position of stars shifted near the Sun.]

[Note 2: When a journalist told Arthur Eddington (1882–1944, a British physicist) that now there are only three people who understand how properly the spacetime principle works and asked him what he thinks about it. Eddington, after a long pause, said, "I am thinking who the third person would be."]

[Note 3: Although Einstein's principle of gravity spacetime has completed Newton's Law of Gravitation, most gravity-related calculations are still solved using Newton's gravity equation, as it gives sufficiently accurate results for most systems with ordinary mass and speed.]

[Note 4: Some physicists, including Einstein, have tried to formulize the F_g in the context of quantum physics (QP) to solve the theory of unification of physics. These attempts have *not* been successful yet.]

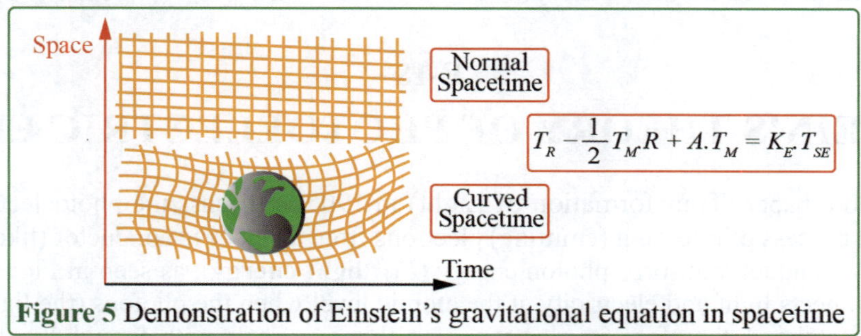

Figure 5 Demonstration of Einstein's gravitational equation in spacetime

E-16
EINSTEIN'S THEORY OF GENERAL RELATIVITY

Study EINSTEIN'S THEORIES OF RELATIVITY.

E-17
EINSTEIN'S THEORY OF LIGHT DUALITY

Einstein published an article (Transformation of Light) in 1905 to describe his theory of wave-particle light duality. In his paper, he says that the quantum particles of light (referred to as light energy) and other electromagnetic radiations (EM radiations or EM waves), known as photons, *cannot* be described as particles or waves but as a combination of both. This means that photons have dual (double) properties, known as **wave-particle duality**, based on which all kinds of EM radiations have the following main properties:

- They act like waves when moving and particles when releasing energy, but *not* both simultaneously.
- They spread all over to occupy a large area in space while moving.

Einstein said in his article that "we have two different pictures of the same reality; separately *none* of them fully explains the behavior of light, but together they do." By this statement, he wanted to prove that one aspect, which acts at lower energy, is wavelike. Instead, another aspect that acts at higher energy (when light releases energy) is particlelike. Thus, *no* dividing line exists between the light's two properties (because light behaves as a wave now and as a particle in a tiny fraction of time later, depending on the process and how fast it travels.

In his article, Einstein agrees with Planck's quantum theory, which says light is quantized while moving, meaning that a beam of light (light energy) is a discontinuous (quantized) stream of energy packets, called by Planck the **quanta** (the plural of quantum) of light. And by Einstein, the photons of light. We can, thus, say a photon is a quantum of light (the quantum particle of light or a packet of light.)

Einstein's theory of wave-particle duality was more investigated later by different physicists. In the late 1920s, Bohr offered a concept known as the Copenhagen interpretation of quantum theories (simply CIQT or **Copenhagen interpretation**), combining his atomic theory (Bohr's atomic theory) with Heisenberg and Schrodinger's theories about the dual property of electrons in an atom. The Copenhagen group came to the idea that the real electron is *neither* one *nor* the other but a mix of both. A particular situation (wave or particle) appears when an observer (experimenter) selects which aspects to measure. The act of measurement generates an uncertainty that Heisenberg discovered (Heisenberg's Uncertainty Principle). Once one property is measured precisely, the other becomes less precise (because the measurement of one property affects the other property's situation).

[Note: Although Einstein's duality theory was, and still is, a difficult subject to prove with certainty, many other theories have been proved based on it. For example, Broglie, in 1927, proved that the duality theory *not* only works on photons but also on electrons and matters (study Broglie's Theory of Duality of Matter.)]

E-18

EINSTEIN'S THEORY OF PHOTOELECTRIC EFFECT

Einstein published a paper (Transformation of Light) in 1905 to discuss the photoelectric effect (later, PE effect), which is the process of releasing (emitting) electrons from an electric conductor (like most metals). This effect occurs when a conductor absorbs photon energy (E_{Ph}, **light energy**), as seen in Figure 1. In the physics language, the PE connects light and electricity at the atomic level when the photons (the light's particles) shine on the surface of a metal and, therefore, its electrons start to move freely with enough kinetic energy (E_K). The released electrons are known as the free electrons (photoelectrons). And the process of releasing electrons (which is the formation of electric current in the metal) is called the PE effect. Photoelectric solar power panels generate electricity from the Sun based on the PE effect. [Einstein used the word photoelectric because **photo** represents light and **electric** represents electricity.]

For escaping an electron from a conductor and becoming a free electron (photoelectron), the electron must contain an E_K equal to (or greater than) W (work), which here represents the E_P (potential energy) of electrons at the metal's surface. Because the free electrons in the conductor have different E_K (because of their distance from the conductor's surface), ranging from nearly zero at its bottom to a high E_K at the surface ($E_{K.S}$), an electron must absorb energy between W and $W - E_{K.S}$ to be released from the conductor. Thus, the W that must be applied to release a free electron, which is called the **work function** (W_F or φ), will be

$$W_F = W - E_{K.S} \qquad (1)$$

And the minimum E_{Ph} required for a photon for an electron to become a photoelectron is then equal to

$$W_F = h.f \qquad (2)$$

In this equation, h is Planck's constant, and f is the photon frequency. When, therefore, a photon's f is *less* than the **critical frequency**, it *cannot* release an electron. In other words, when a photon's λ (wavelength) is *greater* than the **critical wavelength**, it *cannot* release an electron. Thus, the light wave's λ, but *not* its I (intensity), is a factor for an electron to become a photoelectron (the *shorter* the λ, the *easier* an electron to become a photoelectron). Thus, a photon of **red** light (with λ of 700 nm) does *not* have enough E_{Ph} to release an electron from its shell, while a photon of **violet** light (with λ of 400 nm) does, as shown in Figure 2. In addition, the shining light's **brightness** (illumination) is a factor for an electron to become a photoelectron (the *brighter* is the light, the *more* electrons are released because the *brighter* the light, the *more* photons are there to act in releasing electrons from the metal).

While performing experiments on the PE effect, Einstein discovered the following:

- As Planck discovered earlier, light behaves as streams of individual particles (the photons), which travel in the quantized stream (in the form of separate energy packets).
- The photons always have a quantized amount of energy (study QUANTUM AND QUANTIZATION).

[Historical Note: Planck's quantum theory in 1900 and Einstein's theory of PE effect in 1905 inspired younger physicists, mainly Bohr (1913), Heisenberg (1925), and Schrodinger (1926), to develop their atomic theories (study ATOMIC MODELS AND ATOMIC THEORIES). These theories then gradually laid the foundation of quantum physics in the 1920s.]

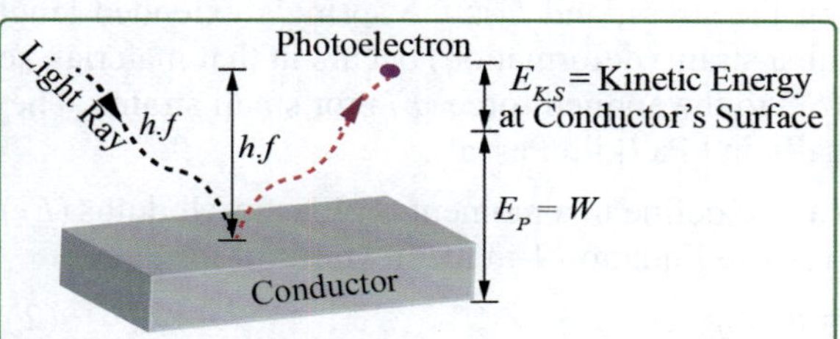

Figure 1 Showing the energy needed by a photon to remove an electron from a conductor

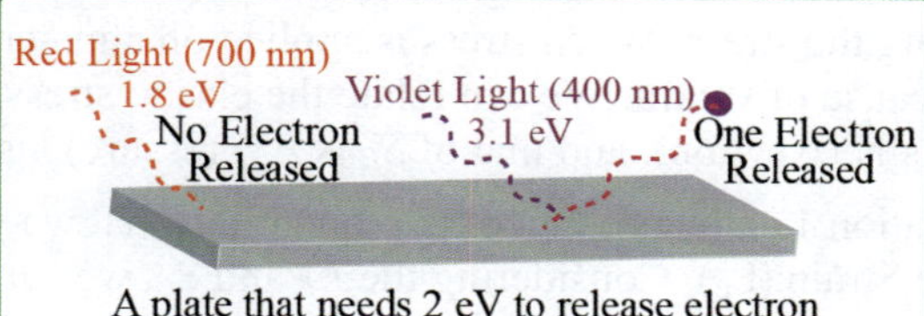

Figure 2 Photoelectric effect cannot occur with red light, but occurs with violet light

E-19
EINSTEIN'S THEORY OF SPECIAL RELATIVITY

Study EINSTEIN'S THEORIES OF RELATIVITY.

E-20
EJECTORS

Study JET EJECTORS.

E-21
ELASTIC FORCE, ELASTIC MODULUS, AND ELASTIC STRAIN

The words **elastic** (tensile) **force**, **elastic modulus**, and **elastic strain** are often used in material engineering without the qualifying word (elastic or tensile). These quantities are related to the deformation (strain) of elastics, while hardness and strength are related to the deformation of plastics. To better understand these quantities, we start this topic with two figures. Figure 1 shows the types of stress (load in the form of force) that can be applied to a material (system), and Figure 2 shows a **spring** that is often used in textbooks to represent an **elastic material** (a material that gets to its original shape if the load is removed).

In material engineering, three (3) different forces are usually used to test a material (Figure 1):

- **Elastic Force:** An elastic (tensile) force is a force that is applied on a material's surface in opposite directions at opposite places on opposite sides to **pull** the material.

- **Compressive Force:** A compressive force is a force that is applied on a material's surface in opposite directions at opposite places on opposite sides to **push** the material, as shown in Figure 2.
- **Shear Force:** A shear force is a force that is applied on a material's surface to **push** (or pull) the material.

Elastic Force

An elastic force (F_E, **tensile force**) is a load (stress) in the form of a force (F) applied to a material's unit area (A) to deform (strain) it. Referring to Figure 2, F_E applied on a spring (an elastic system) is formulized as

$$F_E = \left(\frac{S_E}{L_0}\right)\left(\frac{L-L_0}{L_0}\right) \quad (1)$$

Here, S_E is the **elastic stress**, which is the amount of stress (load) that must be overcome to pull the spring apart, L_0 is the spring's original length before applying the stress, and L is the spring's extended length after applying the stress. When stress is applied on a material, a strain (deformation) occurs in that material, so **stress** is the cause of **strain**. We can relate the elastic stress (S_E) to the applied force (F_E) for small strains. The SI unit of F_E is N (Newton), and that of S_E is P (pressure), usually in kPa (kilo Pascal).

Equation 1 is the product of two quantities that we want to define in a moment. 1) Elastic Modulus (E_E) and 2) Elastic Strain ($\mathcal{E}_E$). Considering the E_E and $\mathcal{E}_E$, we can rewrite Equation 1 in the next useful form.

$$F_E = E_E.\mathcal{E}_E \quad (2)$$

Elastic Modulus

Elastic modulus (E_E, **Young's modulus**, **tensile modulus**, **modulus of elasticity**, or simply **modulus**) is the elastic response to the applied elastic stress (S_E). Thus, the E_E can estimate how much a material extends under a stress (load). Using the spring example, the E_E can be defined by the first set of parentheses in Equation 1.

$$E_E = \frac{S_E}{L_0} \quad (3)$$

Based on this equation, the *greater* a material's modulus, the *more* stress is needed to create the same displacement. Thus, **soft materials** have a low modulus, and **stiff materials** have a high modulus. For example, a fluid deforms without stress, so its modulus is zero. Modulus is given in unit P per unit L, usually in kPa/m.

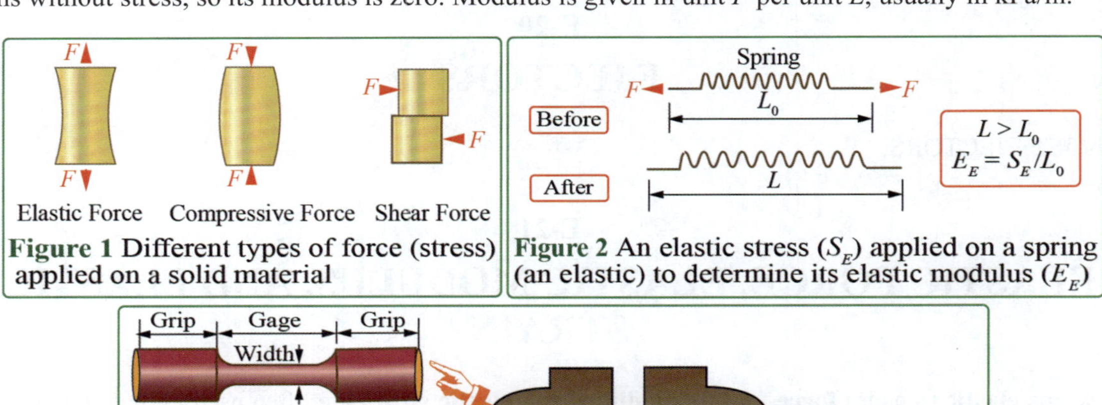

Figure 1 Different types of force (stress) applied on a solid material

Figure 2 An elastic stress (S_E) applied on a spring (an elastic) to determine its elastic modulus (E_E)

Figure 3 A typical tensile tester

Figure 3 illustrates a tensile (elastic) tester for measuring a material's modulus. A typical metal sample (specimen) consists of wider sections (called **grips**) used for gripping the sample by the tester's discs and the narrower section (called **gage**), which is for deformation and failure that occur in the sample under the test.

Elastic Strain

Elastic strain (ε_E) is the increase in length (ΔL) of an elastic material caused by a stress per its original length (L_0). Defined so, ε_E is the displacement (ΔL) relative to the original position (L_0), so-called **relative displacement**. Using the spring example, ε_E can be defined by the second set of parentheses in Equation 1.

$$\varepsilon_E = \frac{\Delta L}{L_0} = \frac{L - L_0}{L_0} \tag{4}$$

If, for example, L_0 of a sample is 1.002 m and L (final length after applying a load) is 1.004 m, then $\Delta L = 0.002$ and ε_L will be 0.002/1.002 = 0.002 m/m, so % strain (% **elongation**) becomes 0.002 × 100 = 0.2 %.

Strain is dimensionless but is often given in units of length/length, like m/m.

Knowing the following strain-related points is helpful:

- When a strain occurs in a material, it is said that it is under a stress, so **stress** is the cause of **strain.**
- At the atomic level, ε_E is pulling atoms of material apart if the material under stress is elastic.
- Material engineers use the words **strain of material** and deformation of material equally.

We briefly define the following terms to summarize this topic.

- **Elastic Force** (F_E)**:** The amount of force (F) applied on an elastic material.
- **Elastic Modulus** (E_E)**:** The amount of elastic response to the applied elastic stress (load).
- **Elastic Strain** (ε_E)**:** The increase in length of a material caused by a stress per its initial length.

E-22

ELASTIC POTENTIAL ENERGY

Defined in the subtopic of Potential Energy under ENERGY AND ITS FORMS.

E-23

ELASTICITY AND PLASTICITY OF MATERIAL

Elasticity and plasticity are important physical properties of materials used in material engineering.

Elasticity

Elasticity is the property of a material to go through a temporary (returnable) **deformation** (strain) when a load (stress) in the form of a force is applied to it. The elasticity of an elastic (tensile) material is its **elastic modulus** (also called **Young's modulus**, **modulus of elasticity**, or simply **modulus**), which is a quantity that measures a material's **stiffness**. In other words, the proportionality coefficient between the stress and strain is the modulus (the *greater* the modulus, the *stiffer* the material is). Conversely, like a fluid, a soft material deforms without stress to have zero modulus.

In practice, the **elastic deformation point** (simply **elastic point**) of an elastic material (simply **elastic**) is determined by a **stress-strain test** in a **strength tester** (Figure 1), and the resulting data from the test are usually summarized in a stress-strain diagram (Figure 2).

Consider an elastic wire under a load (stress) in a strength tester. The load applied to the wire in the tester is proportionally increased. At the start, the stress-strain line is linear (see Figure 2), so stress is proportional to strain (Hook's Law). Applying more load on the wire gets to its **elastic point** (point A), a temporary strain (as the wire gets to its original length if the load is removed). As the applied load increases, the wire gets to its **plastic point** (point B), a permanent deformation (the wire will *not* return to its original length if the stress is removed). With a further increase in stress, the wire reaches its **maximum strength point** (point C), close to its **breaking point** (point D).

At the atomic level, elasticity can pull atoms apart or push them toward each other through an applied force (F). A simple way to visualize elasticity between two atoms is to imagine that each atom is connected to one side of a metal spring, as shown in Figure 3. As a result of the spring movement, a reversible deformation of atoms occurs. This statement means that the atoms can return to their original positions, as the atomic deformation (strain) is an elastic (returnable) deformation.

Plasticity

Plasticity (flexibility) is the physical ability of a material to go through a permanent **deformation** (strain) when a stress (load) is applied on it. A stress-strain test can determine the plastic deformation point of a plastic material. Like elasticity, the resulting data from a plasticity strength test are usually summarized in a stress-strain diagram (Figure 2).

The two main differences between elastics and plastics are the following:

- Elastics, like rubbers, can return to their original shape after the applied load is removed, known as the **elastic response**. Plastics, instead, *cannot* return to their original shape after the applied load is removed, so-called the **plastic response**.
- Elastics undergo a final deformation, while plastics first undergo an elastic deformation and then through the final deformation, so elastics are *less* flexible than plastics.

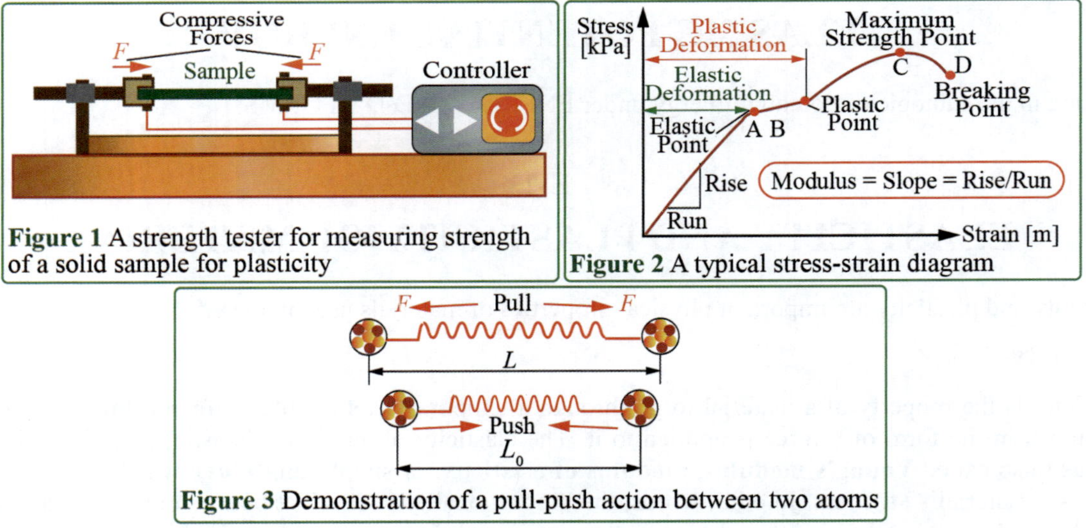

Figure 1 A strength tester for measuring strength of a solid sample for plasticity

Figure 2 A typical stress-strain diagram

Figure 3 Demonstration of a pull-push action between two atoms

E-24

ELASTICS, ELASTOMERS, AND PLASTICS

Elastics

The word elastic is often used to describe a certain type of **elastomers**.

Elastomers

An elastomer is a polymer with viscoelasticity (viscosity and elasticity), weak intermolecular forces, and low tensile modulus (simply **modulus**). In other definition, a polymer that has more than 200% elastic elongation (three times the original length) and can be returned to its original length is an elastomer.

Plastics

Plastics are chemical compounds (simply **compounds**) made from polymers (mostly made from petrochemicals, the byproducts of an oil refinery). [The words **plastic** and **polymer** are often used equally, although some polymers are *not* plastics. This is the reason that the word **polymer plastic** is used.]

Some of the long-chain hydrocarbons, which are *not* converted into fuels, are used as the monomers to be polymerized to produce plastics. Chemical reactions that form a plastic are called **polymerization reactions**. After polymerization, the liquid polymer is processed by **extrusion process** (a continuous process) to squeeze the liquid polymer into solid polymer sheets. Solidification can also be done by the **molding process** (a batch process), in which the liquid plastic is injected into a mold to get its final solid shape.

E-25

ELECTRIC BATTERIES

An electric battery (simply **battery**) is a device (equipment) that creates an electric voltage (V_E or V, simply **voltage**) in an electric circuit. A battery has two connections (called **electrodes**) with a voltage difference. The voltage difference creates an **electric circuit** between the electrodes. The direct current (DC) in a battery flows in the circuit from the positive electrode (anode) toward the negative electrode (cathode).

Today, batteries have many applications, including in mobile phones, combustion cars, electric cars, and even spacecraft.

Batteries store the chemical potential energy (E_{CP}, simply **chemical energy**) to produce immediate electric energy (E_E, simply **electricity**). The main difference between electricity produced by batteries and that produced on a large scale in power plants for households and industry is that the electricity supplied by batteries is much smaller (in the range of Volts, V) than that produced in power plants (in the range of MV). A typical voltage for a battery is 1.5 V (DC), and for a car, the battery is 12 V (AC, alternating current). High-voltage batteries power electric vehicles (Evs). Electricity for household usage in the USA is 110 to 220 kV (DC).

A typical flashlight battery has two conducting **electrodes**. One of them is usually made of carbon (an electric conductor). And one is a small storage for storing an electrolyte (the *larger* the amount of electrolyte used in a battery, the *longer* the battery will last).

The voltage produced by a battery depends on connecting to an electric resistance (simply **resistance**). Two (or more) batteries can be connected in two ways:

- **Batteries in Series:** As shown in Figure 1, the positive terminal of the first battery is wired to the negative terminal of the second. The series (row) arrangement increases the voltage (V) produced in the resistor, but the batteries' lifetime becomes half of the similar batteries.

- **Batteries in Parallel:** As shown in Figure 2, the positive terminal of the first battery is wired to the positive terminal of the second and the negative of the one to the negative of the other. The parallel arrangement does *not* increase the *V* produced in the resistor, but the batteries' lifetime remains the same.

The connection of a battery to two or more resistors (like lightbulbs) can be done in two (2) ways:

- **Lightbulbs in Series:** Two bulbs are connected to a battery by wiring it to the first bulb, to the second bulb, and back to the battery's other end, so the bulbs have the same current circuit (see Figure 3). The series connection creates equal light intensity (brightness) in bulbs, but the total amount of light given by both bulbs is less than if we had just one similar bulb. However, the battery's **lifetime** would be greater than a parallel connection. Because the light intensity of a bulb gives a rough estimate of the current through it (electric intensity *increases* with *increasing* current), the series circuit has a smaller current than a standard circuit. This statement tells us that the resistance created by two bulbs in a series is greater than that of a single bulb. And the same light intensity in each bulb tells us that the current through each bulb is the same. The wiring was in series in the older Christmas tree lights, so if one bulb defected, the rest of the bulbs would be affected (because the current in one bulb passes through the others). You will see in a moment that the parallel connection does *not* have this disadvantage
- **Lightbulbs in Parallel:** Two bulbs are connected to a battery by wiring one end of the battery to the other, so each bulb has its current circuit (Figure 4). In contrast to the series connection, the current in one bulb does *not* pass through the other in the parallel connection. We can disconnect one bulb and observe that the other is *not* affected to test a parallel connection. The battery's lifetime is the same. These tell us that the battery's voltage lowers as it supplies more current. The wiring is parallel in the newer Christmas tree lights, so if one bulb becomes defective, the other bulbs still give light.

Small batteries (flashlight-type and car batteries) are roughly divided into the following two classes:

- **Non-Rechargeable** (dry-cell) **Batteries:** These batteries are used in flashlights, clocks, watches, and more. A **carbon-zinc battery** (D battery) with a 1.5 V capacity (AAA) is a common non-rechargeable battery. Such a battery can supply 375 mA (milli Ampere) for about 400 minutes, yielding a total E_E (electric energy) of about 13 kJ (kilo Joules). **Alkaline batteries** are also in this class of batteries. They last about 60% more than D batteries, so they are more expensive, comparatively. **Silver** and **lithium** batteries provide more E_E in smaller volumes, costing more. These batteries are mostly used in wristwatches and cameras.
- **Rechargeable** (storage) **Batteries:** These batteries are used in smart cellphones, computers, traffic signals, and other consumer electronics. Most are lithium-ion (Li-ion) batteries recharged with an electric charger. For recharging, the positive terminals of the battery and charger are connected, and the negative terminals are connected. The charger forces the electric current (*I*, simply **current**) to run back through the battery. This type of setup reverses the chemical reactions and refreshes the battery. The E_E is then stored as E_{CP} for later use. Car batteries are rechargeable. A typical car battery has six (6) cells, each producing 2 V (Volts), totaling 12 V when operating together in **series** (the positive electrode of one cell is connected to the negative electrode of the next cell).

[The amount of electric current stored in large batteries is given in A/h (Ampere per hour), with the total power in kW/h (Watt per hour, Watt-hours, or Wh. For example, the capacity of a battery used in a medium-size car is about 40 A/h, and an AA battery has a capacity of about 2 A/h.]

Batteries used for Hybrid and Electric Vehicles: **Hybrid electric vehicles** (HEVs) and **battery electric vehicles** (BEVs) use high-voltage rechargeable batteries to produce high electric power. Most of them are lithium-ion (Li-ion) batteries, with high energy density per their weight. Lithium polymer batteries, nickel-cadmium, and nickel-metal-hydride batteries are also used in modern BEVs. Tesla uses lithium-ion batteries in their cars to achieve around 250 Mi (= 400 km) per charge.

[Electric vehicles are equipped with a regenerative braking technique that uses the vehicle's momentum ($p = M.V$, where M is mass and V is velocity) to recover energy that would be otherwise lost (dissipated), as heat energy (E_Q), in a conventional vehicle with a disc-braking system.]

The technique of battery production for vehicles has been advancing fast in the last 20 years. The following are a few general information available as of 2020 about batteries used in BEVs:

- Their lifetime range is 5 to 10 years.
- Most of their parts are safely recyclable.
- They can run up to 400 km (= 250 Mi) per charge.
- Their production cost has fallen considerably since 2010.
- Their weight is equal to about half of the vehicle's total weight.
- Their operating cost is notably lower than fuel for equivalent combustion vehicles.
- Their charging releases hydrogen, oxygen, and sulfur, which are harmless if properly vented.
- Their capacity ranges from about 20 kW/h to about 100 kW/h. For example, the batteries used in Nissan Leaf have 24 to 60 kW/h, and those used in Tesla Model S have 60 to 100 kW/h.

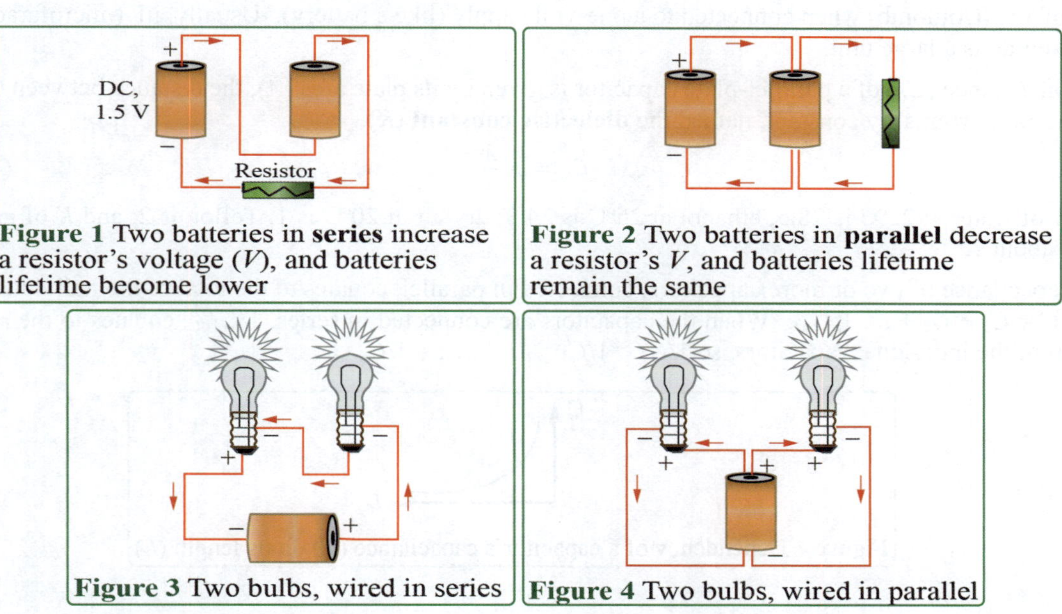

Figure 1 Two batteries in **series** increase a resistor's voltage (V), and batteries lifetime become lower

Figure 2 Two batteries in **parallel** decrease a resistor's V, and batteries lifetime remain the same

Figure 3 Two bulbs, wired in series

Figure 4 Two bulbs, wired in parallel

E-26

ELECTRIC CAPACITANCE AND ELECTRIC CAPACITORS

Electric Capacitance

Electric capacitance (C_E, simply capacitance) is the main property of a capacitor (an electric capacitor. It is defined to be the ratio of the change in a system's electric current (simply **current**) to that system's voltage (also called **electric potential**). It is easy to understand electric capacitance because it can be viewed as an equivalent of a storage tank for storing current.

The C_E of a simple plate electric capacitor can be determined by ε_0 (plate's vacuum permittivity), ε_{Rel} (plate's relative permittivity), A (plate's surface area), and L (plate's length).

$$C_E = \varepsilon_0 . \varepsilon_{Rel} . \frac{A}{L} \tag{1}$$

This equation can be simplified by assuming that the only term in the equation that can be changed is L so that the remaining terms can be shown by constant K.

$$C_E = \frac{K}{L} \qquad (2)$$

As Figure 1 shows, the relation between C_E and L is non-linear, so a small change in L creates a large C.

The SI unit of capacitance is **Farad** (F), named after Faraday (a British physicist).

Electric Capacitors

A capacitor has a **capacitance property** (it can be electrically charged). Thus, a capacitor can accept and store an electric charge, so when it is connected to a battery, the electrons flow between the capacitor and the negative and positive terminals of the battery. The flow of electrons continues until the voltage (also called **electric potential**) across the capacitor equals the applied voltage. Thus, voltage is the driving force that pushes the electric charges; in other words, the electric current (simply **current**) through a capacitor (a conductor).

The capacitance of capacitors is measured in **Farad** (F). A capacitor has the capacitance of 1 F if it stores a charge of 1 C (Coulomb) when connected to a one-volt supply (like a battery). Usually, μF (microfarad) is used because Farad is a large unit.

The capacitance (C_E) of a parallel-plate capacitor is given by its plate area (A), the distance between the plates (d), and a proportionality constant, named the **dielectric constant** (K).

$$C_E = K\frac{A}{d} \qquad (3)$$

The K of water at 25ºC is 78.5, ethanol at 25ºC is 24.3, dry air at 20ºC is 1, Teflon is 2, and K of granulated sugar is about 2.

The capacitance of two or more capacitors, connected in parallel, equates to the total of the individual capacitances ($C = C_1 + C_2 + ... + C_n$). When the capacitors are connected in series, $1/C_{Total}$ equates to the reciprocal (reverse) of the individual capacitors, so $1/C_T = 1/C_1 = 1/C_2 .... = 1/C_n$.

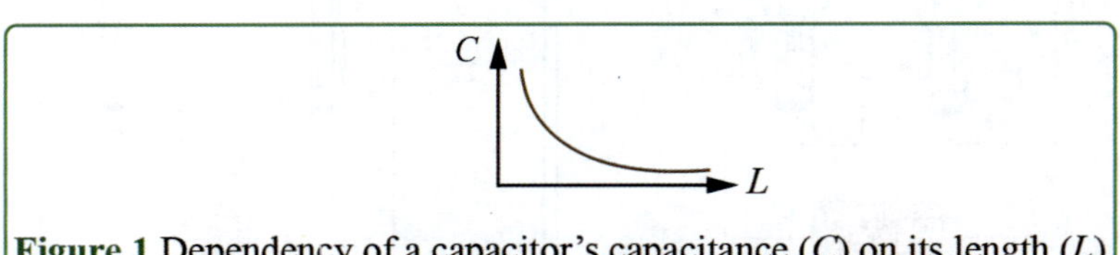

Figure 1 Dependency of a capacitor's capacitance (C) on its length (L)

E-27
ELECTRIC CHARGE

The electric charge (Q_E, simply **charge**) is the flow of electrons through an electric conductor (such as a metal wire). Because the flow of electrons through a conductor over a certain time (t) creates an electric current (I_E, simply **current**), Q_E can be expressed as the product of I_E and t.

$$Q_E = I_E . t \qquad (1)$$

Electric charges are the main source of electromagnetic force (F_{EM}). In an atom, F_{EM} is produced by positive electric charges of protons. In nature, F_{EM} can be produced by positive charges of thunderstorms.

The SI unit of Q_E (electric charge) is ampere per second (A/s, often written in reference books as As or A.s and read it ampere second), where A/s = 1 C (Coulomb; another unit for electric charges). The practical unit of Q_E is A/h (some write it Ah or A.h and read it ampere-hour), where 1 A/h = 3600 C.

Some particles (like a proton) are electro-positively charged, some (like an electron) are electro-negatively charged, and some (like neutron) are neutral. A neutral particle can become electrically charged by absorbing or losing electrons. Two (2) properties of electric charges are given next.

- They can create an electric field or magnetic field around themselves, and
- They can determine the strength of a system's electric force.

Knowing the following points about electric charges is helpful:

- They can flow through an electric conductor but *cannot* through an electric insulator.
- They can also be carried, besides conductors, by ions in an electrolyte (see the upcoming Note 1).
- Two electro-positively-charged systems, like two electro-negatively charged systems, experience a **repulsive force**. Instead, an electro-positively-charged system and an electro-negatively-charged system experience an **attractive force**. Thus, the force (F) direction between two differently-charged systems depends on the charges' signs (*like* charges *repel* and *unlike* charges *attract*.)
- They can be calculated by measuring a force (F) experienced by a particle in an electric field of known strength. The F exerted by an electric field on a particle carrying only one or more excess electrons is very small. This very small force can be compared with the gravitational force applied to a particle with a mass of 10^{-12} g (one million millionth grams).

E-28
ELECTRIC CIRCUIT

An electric circuit (simply **circuit**, also called **electric network** or electric loop) is a closed interconnection between one **electric component** (like an electric voltage, electric resistor, electric battery, electric switch, and more) and one (or more) **electric element** (like a current source, electric resistance, electric capacitance, and more). Figure 1 illustrates a circuit consisting of a source of electric voltage (V_E or V) with an electric current of I_E and an electric resistor with an electric resistance of R_E. This is a closed electric loop because it gives a return path for the current. This loop can be expressed based on Ohm's Law as $V_E = I_E \times R_E$.

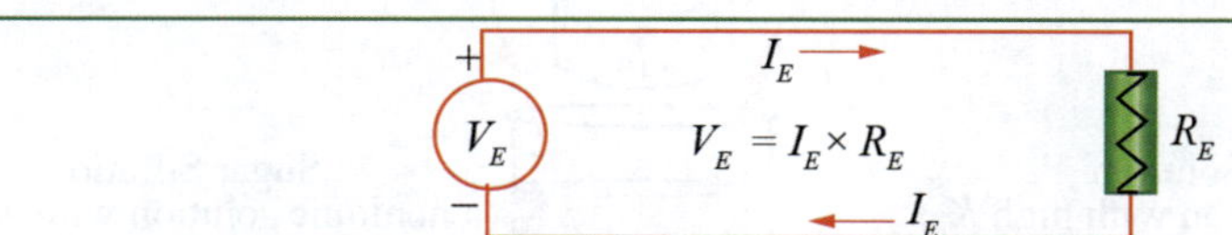

Figure 1 A simple electric circuit with an electric voltage of V_E and electric resistance of R_E

E-29
ELECTRIC CONDUCTANCE AND ELECTRIC INDUCTANCE

Electric Conductance

Electric conductance (K_E, also called **electric conductivity** or simply **conductivity**) expresses how a material conducts an electric current (I_E) that flows through it. So, an electric conductor (simply **conductor**) has a high K_E and a low R_E (electric resistance). Instead, an electric insulator (simply **insulator**) has a low K_E and a high R_E. A material's K_E is the reciprocal (inverse) of its R_E (or vice versa).

The fast-moving ability of free electrons in a metal structure is responsible for its K_E and thermal conductivity (K_Q).

A conductor's K_E can be calculated using Ohm's Law ($V_E = I_E.R_E$), which considers V_E (electric voltage) as the driving force of the I_E through a conductor and R_E as the opposing force of that current.

$$K_E = \frac{1}{R_E} = \frac{I}{V_E} \qquad (1)$$

The SI unit of K_E is S (Siemens), equating to $1/\Omega = A/V$, where Ω (omega) is for Ohm, A is for Ampere, and V is for Volt.

Ionic compounds (electrolytes), such as salt (NaCl), produce many ions in a solution to form a **conducting solution**, so the solution conducts K_E easily. Instead, nonionic compounds (nonelectrolytes), such as sucrose (sugar, $C_{12}H_{22}O_{11}$), do *not* ionize in solution, so they do *not* produce ions, forming a **nonconducting solution** (with zero conductivity), as shown in Figure 1. Thus, measuring the K_E of a solution can indicate if it is an ionic solution or a non-ionic solution.

Conductometers (lab instruments for measuring ash content of solution samples) are calibrated to measure the K_E of a sample in **specific electric conductance** ($K_{E.Sp}$). The $K_{E.Sp}$, expressed in S/m instead of S, depends on A (the cross-sectional area of the conductometer's electrodes) and d (distance between electrodes).

$$K_{E.Sp} = \frac{1}{R_E} = K_C \frac{A}{d} \quad (2)$$

K_C (the cell constant, in 1/m) is determined by measuring the R_E of a standard solution of known $K_{E.Sp}$ and using a sample cell of 1 cm long and 1 cm^2 of surface area.

[Note 1: For simplicity reasons, sometimes the term **specific electric conductance** ($K_{E.Sp}$, simply **specific conductance** or **specific conductivity**) is abbreviated to just **electric conductance** (K_E). In such cases, the given unit of the quantity can determine the purpose of the writer because the $K_{E.Sp}$ is expressed in S/m, but K_E in S.]

Electric Inductance

An electric inductance (also called **electric induction** or simply **inductance**) is a quantity that expresses how a material opposes an electric current that flows through it. According to Faraday's Induction Law, a magnetic field (M-field) charge in a conductor induces (produces) a V_E in that conductor, a process called electromagnetic induction. [Electric inductance (induction) and electromagnetic induction are different quantities.]

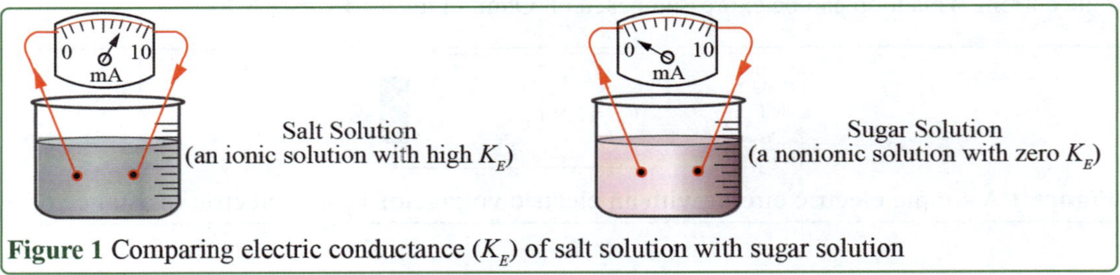

Figure 1 Comparing electric conductance (K_E) of salt solution with sugar solution

E-30

ELECTRIC CONDUCTIVITY

Another name for ELECTRIC CONDUCTANCE.

E-31

ELECTRIC CONDUCTORS, SEMICONDUCTORS, AND INSULATORS

Electric Conductors: An electric conductor (simply **electroconductor** or just **conductor**) is a chemical compound (simply **compound**) with atoms containing free electrons, so it can easily conduct an electric current (I_E, simply **current**). Thus, a conductor has a high electric conductance (K_E) and a low electric resistance (R_E). In other definition, a conductor has many electric charges that are free to move.

[The word **superconductor** is also used to refer to a highly conducting material with no R_E. For creating superconductivity in a compound, it must be cooled to very low temperatures (about – 260ºC), but in 1986, two physicists developed a ceramic that could superconduct at – 163ºC (= – 261ºF). Among other uses, superconductors are used in a particle accelerator to produce a large magnetic field.]

Electric Semiconductors: An electric semiconductor's K_E value is between a conductor and insulator. In other definition, a semiconductor has a small number of electric charges that are free to move, far less than a conductor. Silicon (a semiconductor) is used in modern electronics, such as computer processors, digital cameras, and light-sensitive photodetectors.

Most metals are good conductors. Electrolytes, plasma, and some polymers are nonmetal conductors. A perfect insulator does *not* exist, but some materials, like glass and some plastics, are insulators. Ceramics are semiconductors

Knowing the following brief points is helpful:

- Copper (Cu), which has the highest K_E, is a standard for all other conductors to be compared.
- If an electric current passes through a conductor, the movement of the electrons' electric charges creates a magnetic field. This phenomenon is the idea behind making an **electromagnet**.

Electric Insulators: An electric insulator (simply **electroinsulator** or just **insulator**) has a low K_E (electric conductance) and a high R_E (electric resistance). An insulator does *not* allow electric charges to move freely through it, so charges *cannot* move, causing **static electricity**.

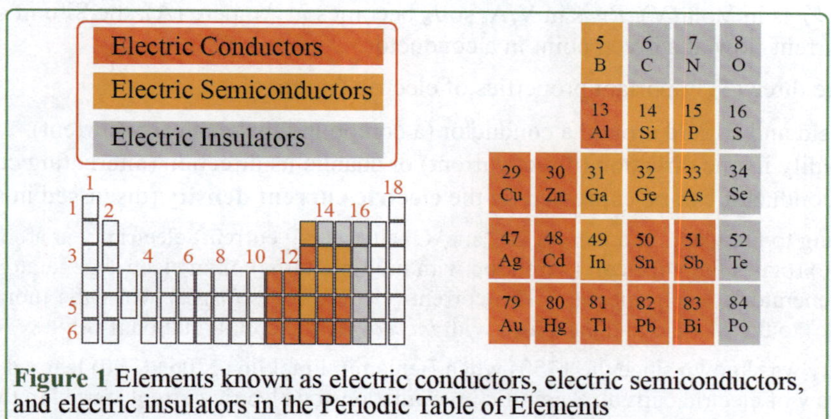

Figure 1 Elements known as electric conductors, electric semiconductors, and electric insulators in the Periodic Table of Elements

E-32

ELECTRIC CURRENT AND ELECTRIC CURRENT DENSITY

Electric Current

An electric current (I_E, simply **current**) is the flow of electricity (the flow of electric charges) in an electric conductor (simply **conductor**). Figure 1 shows a current's direction in a conductor, the electric field (E-field) that the current produces around itself, and the direction of the E-field lines. Current flows because of an electric voltage (V_E) between two points in a conductor.

As for the charge carriers of a current's electric charges, we can say the following:

- In metals (electric conductors), the charge carriers are electrons (electro-negatively-charged particles).
- In electrolytes (nonmetal conductors), negative AND positive charge carriers may be present.
- In semiconductors, negative OR positive charge carriers may be present.

It is helpful to study the following about the currents:

- In a conductor, the electro-negatively-charged electrons flow in the current's opposite direction (see Figures 1 and 2), and the electro-positively-charged atomic nuclei stay fixed.
- The electrons in a conductor move slowly, but the electric field (E-field), which flows through the electrons, moves very fast (at around 200 000 km/s, which is like the speed of sound constant). We see the light immediately when turning a lamp's switch on.

Because the flow of electrons (electronegatively-charged particles) through a conductor forms charges (q), current (I_E) can be defined as the flow of electric charges (Q_E) through a conductor per time (t).

$$I_E = \frac{Q_E}{t} \tag{1}$$

Current can also be defined by using Ohm's Law, which considers V_E as the driving force of the I_E through a conductor and R_E (electric resistance or simply **resistance**) as the opposing force of the I_E.

$$I_E = \frac{V_E}{R_E} \tag{2}$$

In this equation, V_E is in Volt (V), R_E is in V/A, so I_E becomes in Ampere (A), the SI unit of I_E. An ohmmeter can measure the current flow at a given point in a conductor.

The following are three (3) important properties of electric current (I_E):

- It produces M-field and E-field around a conductor (a compound that can carry current).
- It may move steadily in one direction (direct current) or change its direction (alternating current).
- Its strength in a conductor can be expressed by the **electric current density** (discussed in a moment).

[Note 1: According to Faraday's Induction Law, an AC (alternating current) electricity is produced when a device (like a steam turbine) rotates the **wire coil** (wire loop with multiple turns) of an electric generator in a magnetic field (produced by the generator's electromagnet). The current (electricity) is *largest* when the motion is perpendicular (vertical at 90° angle) to the M-field and *increases* with *increasing* the coil's rotational velocity.]

[Note 2: Electricity was known since the 1750s when Benjamin Franklin (1706−1790) learned from an experiment that lightning is a flow of electric current. Scientific investigations on electric current started in the 1830s by Faraday and Maxwell. And its practical applications started in the late years of 19th century when inventors like Edison and Tesla were able to put it into industrial production. In 1879, Edison showed his first lightbulb to the public and said, "*we will produce electricity so cheap that only the rich people will burn candles*."]

Electric Current Density

An electric current density (J, simply **current density**) is a quantity that expresses the strength of an electric current (I_E) per area (A) of a conductor, like a metal wire.

$$J = \frac{I_E}{A} \quad (1)$$

In this equation, I_E is in Ampere, and A is in m^2, so J becomes in A/m^2.

The direction of a current density is arbitrary. If the moving electric charges are negative (electrons), the direction of J is opposite to the current's direction. And if the charges are positive (protons), the direction of J is the same as the current's direction.

[Note: In ChemEng, the symbol J is used for both the molar flux rate and **current density**, but they are *not* usually used in the same equation so that *no* confusion can occur.]

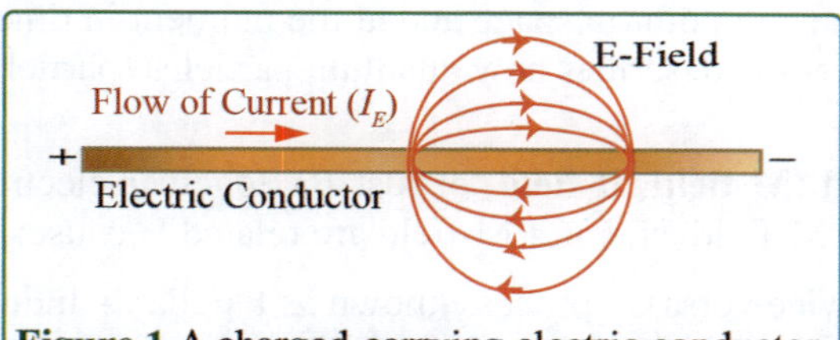

Figure 1 A charged-carrying electric conductor creates an E-field around itself

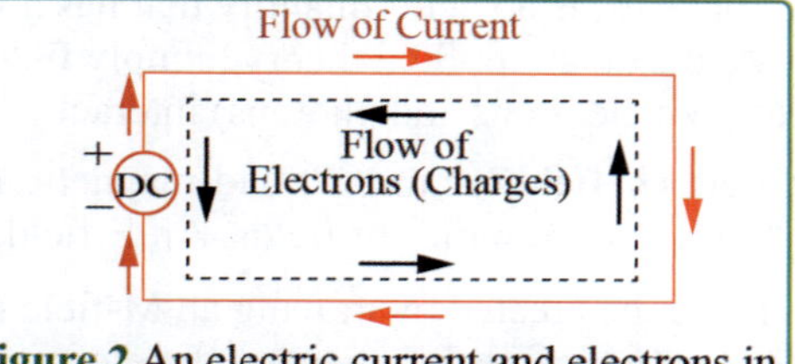

Figure 2 An electric current and electrons in an electric circuit move in opposite ways

E-33

ELECTRIC DIPOLE

Electric dipole (also called **electric dipole moment**, simply **dipole**) is the separation of positive and negative electric charges (Q_E) from each other in a molecule or a system. As for a molecule, it is related to its chemical polarity (simply **polarity**). A molecule with a dipole (read *die pole*) has unequal electric charges on every side. For example, in a water molecule (H_2O, a polar molecule), the hydrogen (H) atoms are slightly positive, and the oxygen atom (O) is slightly negative (because the electronegativity of O is greater than H). Thus, the two electron pairs that act as covalent bonds between two H atoms and one O atom are polarized. The polarization occurs because the more electronegative O atom pulls the electron pairs toward itself to become electronegative charged (with $-Q_E$). And the H atoms become electropositive charged (with $+Q_E$). As a result, negative and positive dipoles are formed (see Figure 1).

An electric field (M-field) around an electric conductor with electric charges also makes a dipolar system, as shown in Figure 2.

The SI unit for electric dipole is C.m (Coulomb-meter). Debye (D) is also used, where 1 D = 10^{-18} C-cm.

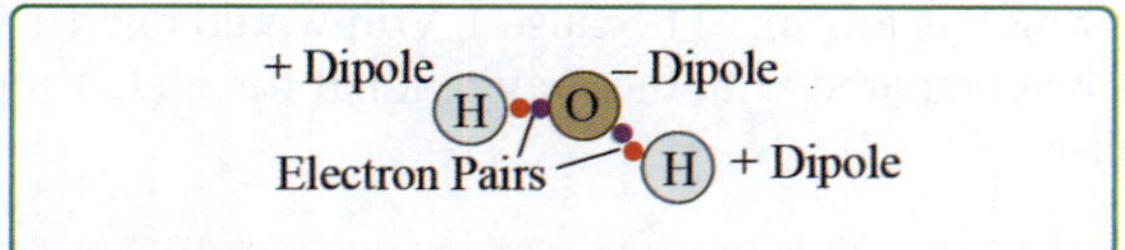

Figure 1 Formation of dipoles in a water molecule

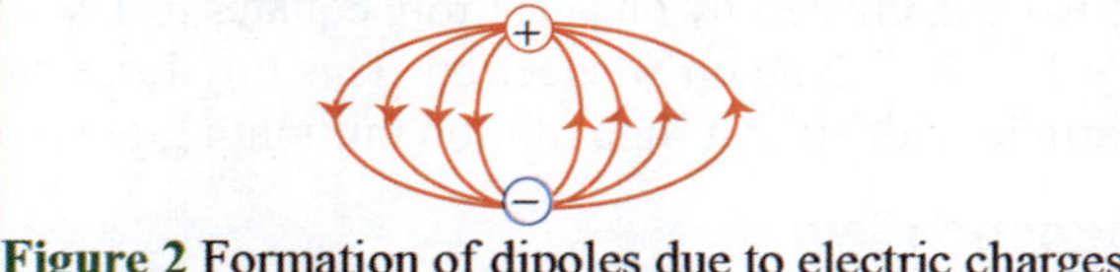

Figure 2 Formation of dipoles due to electric charges

E-34

ELECTRIC ENERGY

Discussed under the topic of ENERGY AND ITS FORMS.

E-35

ELECTRIC FIELD, MAGNETIC FIELD, AND ELECTROMAGNETIC FIELD

Field

A field, in classical physics, is a system in space that can change some physical properties of another system. A **field theory** describes how a field behaves and how a system interacts with a field when placed in it. A field, in quantum physics, is a vector quantity that has a value at a point in space and at the moment in time, together spacetime. And a quantum field theory (simply **field theory**) describes how quantum particles (particles with *no* subparticles, like electrons and photons) interact.

Electric field (**E-field**, or just ***E***) and magnetic field (**M-field**, **B-field**, or just ***B***), together electromagnetic field (EM field), are examples of fields. An E-field, an M-field, and an EM-field are related because:

- An E-field can be created by moving an M-field (or vice versa), a process known as Faraday's Induction Law, based on which electric generators, electric motors, and electric transformers operate.
- An EM-field has the properties of E-field (represented by the word electro in electromagnetic) and M-field (represented by magnetic in electromagnetic).

Electric Field

An E-field (E) is an invisible (imaginary) space around an electric system, which carries electric charges (Q_E) and, thus, electric current (I_E). Study the following main properties of an E-field:

- An E-field, like an M-field, is a vector quantity (a quantity with value and direction).
- E-field can be visualized as circular **field lines** traditionally directed from the positive to the negative charge of an electric conductor (see Figure 1).

An E-field (E) can be created by applying an electric voltage (V_E) across a distance (L, for length).

$$E = \frac{V_E}{L} \quad (1)$$

Because a charged particle in an E-field experiences a small force (F), the E can also be defined as F applied on a system that contains Q_E (electric charge).

$$E = \frac{F}{Q_E} \quad (2)$$

The previous two equations show us that the SI unit of E-fields is Volt per meter (V/m) or Newton (N) per Coulomb (C), where 1 V/m = 1 N/C. Newton is the unit of F and Coulomb is the unit of Q_E.

The E-field, created by one electron, equates to 1 V/m, which is too small because 1 V/m would exert a force of only 1.6×10^{-9} dyne on an electron. This tiny force can be compared with the gravitational force (F_g) applied to a particle with 10^{-12} g (one million millionth grams) mass.

Magnetic Field

An M-field (B) is a force field around a magnetic system (like a magnet) or a current-carrying conductor. According to Faraday's Induction Law, an electric current (simply current or electricity) can be generated by turning a **wire coil** (a wire loop with multiple turns) in an M-field (see Figure 2). An M-field can be visualized as **field lines** surrounding that field and can be experienced by a small **ferromagnet** (permanent magnet) and a **compass** (see Figure 3). This is possible because an M-field is **dipolar**, with a **north** (N) **magnetic pole** and a **south** (N) **magnetic pole**, where the field lines are directed from its N magnetic pole to the S pole.

An M-field can be created around an electro-wire coil (a coil connected to a power supply), as shown in Figure 4. An M-field system also exists around the Earth's space (Figure 5). [The Earth's M-field protects us from skin sicknesses by blocking ultraviolet radiation.]

Next, two other properties of E-fields are outlined.

- An M-field, like an E-field, is a vector quantity (a quantity with value and direction).
- An M-field's strength and direction can be expressed by its magnetic moment (M-moment).

The SI Unit of M-field is A/s but is also expressed as N/m.A, where A is for Ampere, s for second, N for Newton (the force unit), and m is for the meter. [The SI Unit of **magnetic flux density** (simply **magnetic flux**; M-field per surface area) is Tesla (T), where 1 T equates to 1 N.s/C.m (= Weber per m^2).]

Electromagnetic Field

EM-field ($\mathcal{E}$) is the non-direct-visible space around a system under the effect of the electromagnetic force (F_{EM}). The EM field can carry energy (E) and momentum (p = mass × velocity) from place to place. Thus, it has different values at different points of the space. In quantum physics, the EM field is a **massless** field with quantization ability (acting in tiny-separated quantities).

Remember the following important points about EM-fields:

- In nature, an EM-field can be formed by a thunderstorm's electric charges. The Earth's EM field causes a **compass** needle to orient in the North-South direction, which is used, say, by birds for their navigation.
- In industry, an EM-field can be formed by passing an electric current through a **wire coil** (a wire loop with multiple turns) because the movement of electrons (with negative charges) creates such a field around the coil. Thus, the strength of an EM-field depends on a current's strength (the *greater* the current, the *stronger* is the field). This is the idea behind making electricity by turning an **electromagnet**, as shown in Figure 2.

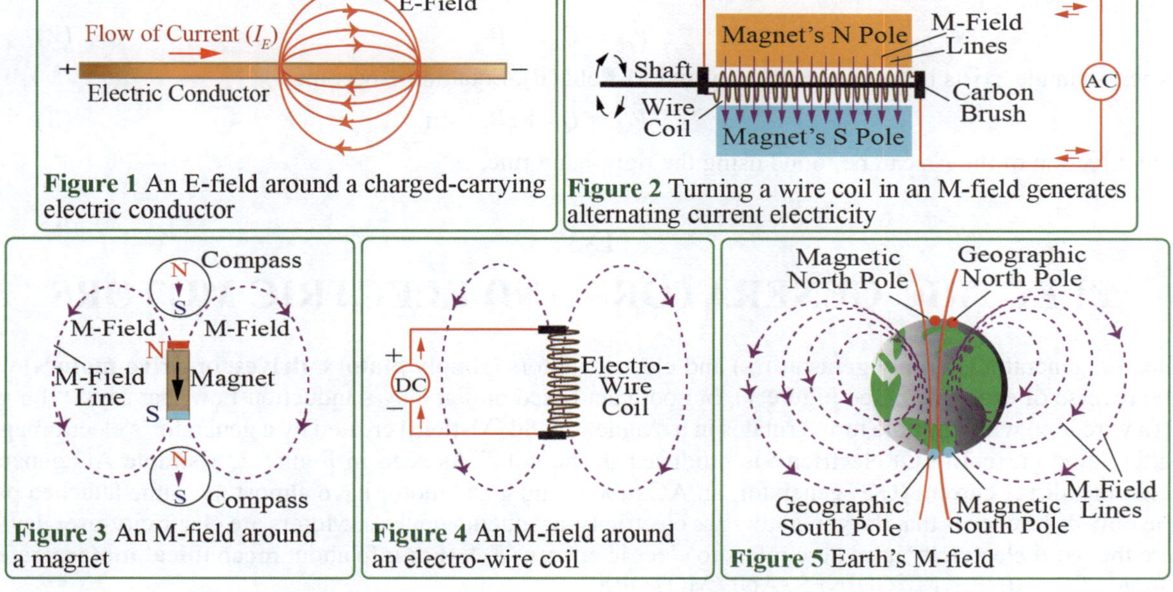

Figure 1 An E-field around a charged-carrying electric conductor

Figure 2 Turning a wire coil in an M-field generates alternating current electricity

Figure 3 An M-field around a magnet

Figure 4 An M-field around an electro-wire coil

Figure 5 Earth's M-field

E-36

ELECTRIC FORCE AND MAGNETIC FORCE

Electric Force

Electric force (F_E or E-force) is a force (F) created by positive charges of protons of an atom. As the result of F_E, the following events occur in an atom:

- Protons are kept away (repelled) from each other.
- A stable grouping of protons and neutrons in an atom's nucleus occurs (because of competition between F_E and nuclear force). Say, 6 protons and 6 neutrons group to form the nucleus of a carbon atom (C).

Magnetic Force

Magnetic force (F_M or M-force) is a force (F) carried by a magnetic field (simply M-field, B-field, or just B). An F_M results from the motion of electric charges (Q_E, simply **charges**) in an M-field, so an F_M can be viewed as an F whose act depends on an M-field. Study the following:

- Two (2) systems with charges moving in the same direction have an attractive force between them.
- Two systems with charges moving in opposite directions have a repulsive force between them.

Lorentz Force Law can describe the F_M of a charged particle. According to this law, a particle of charge Q_E moving with velocity V in the field of B and an electric field of E experiences a magnetic force of F_M.

$$F_M = q.V.B \tag{1}$$

In this equation, F_M is in Newton (N), q is in Coulomb (C), and V (the charge's velocity) is in m/s, so B (the charge of M-field) becomes in N.s/C.m, which equates to 1 Tesla (T).

We can write the previous equation in the vector form as

$$\vec{F}_M = Q_E.\vec{V}.\vec{B} \tag{2}$$

When an angle exists between the velocity and M-field (B), Equation 1 becomes

$$F_M = Q_E.V.B.sin\alpha \tag{3}$$

The direction of the F_M can be found using the right-hand rule.

E-37

ELECTRIC GENERATORS AND ELECTRIC MOTORS

Electric generators (simply **generators**) and electric motors (simply **motors**, **drives**, or **drive motors**) work in the reverse of each other (see Figure 1), but both act based on Faraday's Induction Law that says, "if a **wire coil** (a wire loop with multiple turns) rotates in a magnetic field (M-field) created by a generator's electromagnet, an alternating current (AC) electricity is produced in the coil." As seen in Figure 2, a simple AC generator (alternator), direct current (DC) generator, an AC motor, and a DC motor have almost the same attached parts, so the only difference is that the generators are electricity-producing devices. Motors are electricity-user devices, where the word **electricity** used here refers to electric energy (E_E). [For info about **mechanical motors**, refer to the topic of ENGINES, MACHINES, AND MOTORS.]

Electric Generators

An electric generator is a device that converts E_K (kinetic energy) of the turbine's shaft into E_E for generating AC electricity, the so-called AC generator (or **alternator**). In the steam and electricity production station of a chemical process plant, the E_Q (heat energy) in steam (produced in a steam boiler) is converted into E_K (kinetic energy) in a steam turbine to perform W_S (shaft work) on the generator's shaft, around which a coil is looped (together called the **rotor**). And turning the rotor turns the M-field, created by the electromagnet (called the **stator**), which causes the flow of electrons in the coil and, thus, the generation of AC electricity. Most generators, such as those used in power plants, produce AC electricity. As for this statement, you (chemical engineers) should be aware of the following terminologies:

- Generators that generate AC electricity are called **alternators**.
- Generators that generate DC through an attached electric transformer are **DC generators**.
- Generators that generate pulsing DC through an attached **electric commutator** are **dynamos**.

[It is important to mention that it is easier to get the electricity from the **stator** than from the **rotor**. This is why larger generators have a rotating electromagnet (a magnet connected to a source of electricity) mounted on the generator's shaft. Thus, the shaft and electromagnet act as the generator's **rotor**, and the stationary wire coil, in which the AC electricity is generated, acts as its **stator**.]

Under the heading of FARADAY'S INDUCTION LAW, we said that the amount of induced (produced) AC in a generator mainly depends on the change in its M-field (double the change, double the AC produced). Doubling the M-field can be achieved by adding a second wire coil into the stator, as shown in Figure 2.

In addition to the rotor and stator, a typical generator has an **electric governor** (see the same figure) that maintains the rotor's constant (synchronous) speed. [The most common rotating speed is 3 000 RPM for 50 Hz generators and 3 600 RPM for 60 Hz generators.] Furthermore, a generator has carbon-made **electric brushes** to supply the electricity to the stator. An **electric commutator** is a rotary electric switch that periodically reverses the generated current's supply of AC electricity. [As shown in Figure 2, in a DC generator, the parts are the same, but it has an attached commutator to convert the AC to DC.] A bicycle dynamo is the simplest DC generator, with a magnet turning (by one of the bicycle's wheels) inside a stationary (fixed) coil to supply the DC (Figure 3).

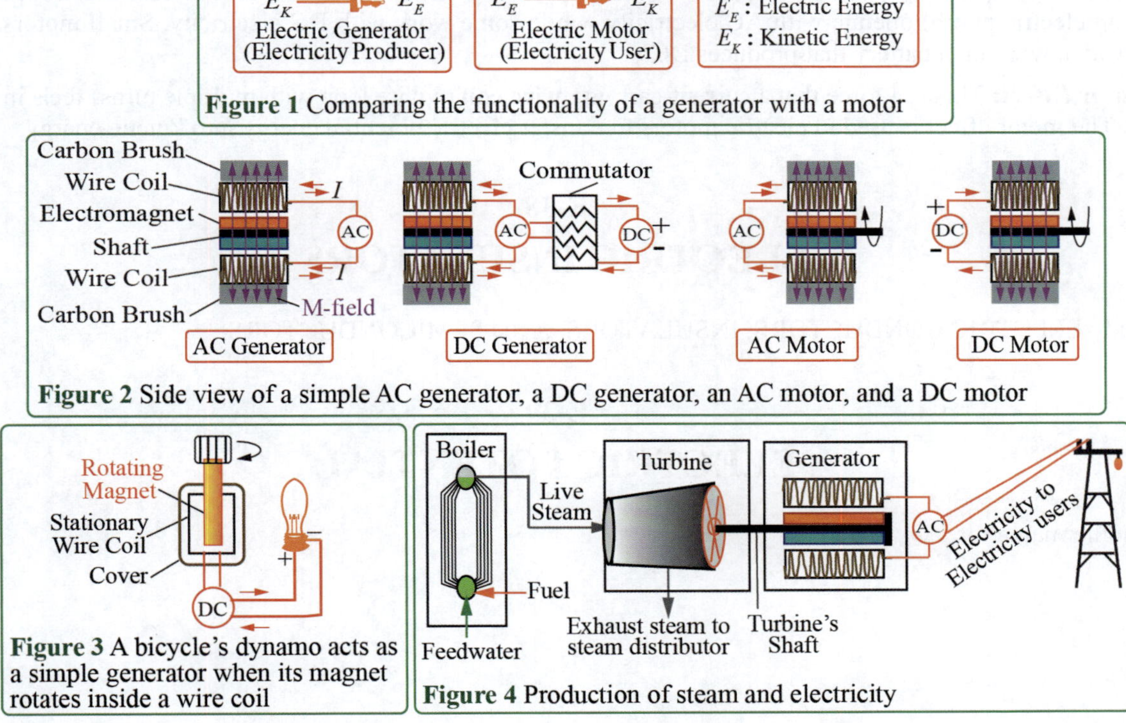

Figure 1 Comparing the functionality of a generator with a motor

Figure 2 Side view of a simple AC generator, a DC generator, an AC motor, and a DC motor

Figure 3 A bicycle's dynamo acts as a simple generator when its magnet rotates inside a wire coil

Figure 4 Production of steam and electricity

Consider a chemical process plant's steam and power production station (see Figure 4). The E_Q (heat energy) in steam (produced by a steam boiler) is converted in a turbine into E_K to perform W_S (shaft work) on the generator's shaft, around which a coil is looped, together called the **rotor**. And turning the rotor turns the M-field, created by the stator (electromagnet), which causes the flow of electrons in the coil and, thus, the generation of AC electricity.

Generator's Efficiency: A generator's efficiency (E_G), which is contrary to the E_G of a steam turbine, is an absolute quantity, meaning that the losses of generators are unrecoverable (irrecoverable).

The output electric voltage (V_E) of a generator depends mainly on the next factors:

- RPM of its rotor, which indicates the strength of its M-field, and
- Size and number of its electromagnets.

A small electric generator used in a power plant can produce about 2 MW/h (= 2 000 kW/h) of electric power (E_E, electricity), enough to cover about 330 homes. Generators are presently available up to 25 MW/h, but larger sizes are also built. [A medium-size chemical process plant (like a beet-sugar factory) uses one 25 MW/h generator, but it prefers to have two half-sized generators, should one unit need a repair.]

Electric Motors

An electric motor (simply **motor**) is a device that converts E_E (electric energy) into E_K (kinetic energy) for different purposes. As mentioned at the beginning of this topic, motors are almost identical to generators. The only difference between them is that the generators are electricity producers, and motors are electricity users. Usually, motors produce a rotating force on their rotor for different purposes. For example, consider a centrifuge motor, which converts E_E into E_K to perform a shaft work (W_S) for turning the basket of the centrifuge. As another example, a solar boiler in a solar power plant works as a motor to use Sun's solar energy (radiant energy) to convert water into steam. The E_K of steam then drives a turbine, which runs a generator to produce AC electricity. A typical solar power plant produces about 300 MW/h of electricity.

Turbines, pumps, compressors, fans, mixers, and tools like an electric drill are also motors. Most large motors (like an electric pump) operate with AC electricity, while some work with DC electricity. Small motors like a wristwatch work on a battery that produces DC.

Motor Effect: This is a force that a current-carrying **wire coil** (a wire loop with multiple turns) feels in an M-field. The motor effect is used in electric motors to transfer electric potential energy into kinetic energy.

E-38
ELECTRIC INSULATORS

Study ELECTRIC CONDUCTORS, INSULATORS, AND SEMICONDUCTORS.

E-39
ELECTRIC POTENTIAL

Another name for VOLTAGE.

E-40

ELECTRIC POTENTIAL ENERGY

Discussed under the subtopic of Potential Energy under ENERGY AND ITS FORMS.

E-41

ELECTRIC POWER

Electric power (P_E, simply **power** or **electricity**) is a system's ability to do a work (the *more* power a system has, the *more* work it can do each time, *t*). In Physics, P_E is defined as a time rate (quantity/*t*) at which work (*W*) is done. Because *W* (work) can be viewed as *E* (energy), the P_E can be taken as *W* per *t* (time) or as a system's E_E (electric energy) per *t*.

$$P_E = \frac{W}{t} = \frac{E_E}{t} \tag{1}$$

The SI unit of P_E is W/h (watt/ hour, often written Wh or W), which equals J/s (joule per second). A 100 W (= 0.1 kW) lightbulb uses 100 J of P_E each second. The **practical unit** of P_E is kW per hour (kW/h; often written kWh or kW), where 1 kW/h is the amount of energy equivalent to a power of 1 kW running for 1 h. 1 kW/h can be defined as the amount of power used by a 100 W lightbulb when is on for 10 h. Thus, 1 kW/h = 1 kJ/s and 0.7457 kW/h = 1HP, where HP (horsepower) is the US unit of P_E, where 1 HP = 550 Ft.Lb$_F$/s (simply Ft.Lb/s). All units of P_E refer to the rate of E_E produced in a power-producing device (like an electric generator) or used by a power-user device (like an electric motor).

Household lightbulbs are usually rated 60, 75, or 100 W/h. A house electric heater uses about 1500 W/h. A medium-size industrial electric generator can produce about 2 MW/h (= 2 000 kW/h) of P_E, and this amount of power is enough to cover about 660 medium-size homes. Hydrodynamic generators, which produce power from moving hot gases through a magnetic field with *no* rotors, can generate around 25 MW/h.

Paying attention to the following important points is recommended:

- Instead of W/h (watt per hour), which is a correct abbreviation, the words Wh, W.h, or just W are often used to express power use per certain time (in h). For familiarity with W/h, a typical US household uses electric power (simply power or electricity) at an average rate of about 1000 W/h. For a small community of 1000 households, this adds up to 1 million W/h (or 1 MW/h). A typical coal-fired power plant produces about 500 MW/h of electricity, a typical nuclear power plant produces about 1500 MW/h, and a hydroelectric dam can produce more than 10 000 MW/h of electricity.
- Electric power (P_E) and electric energy (E_E) are different. P_E is a **rate** (quantity/time), but E_E is a **quantity**.
- The US electric power consumption is high (about 10 kW/h or 36 MJ/h per person).

E-42

ELECTRIC RESISTANCE AND ELECTRIC RESISTORS

Electric Resistance

An electric resistance (R_E, also called **electric resistivity** or simply **resistivity**) is a quantity that expresses how an **electric component** (like a resistor, a capacitor, a switch, and more) resists the flow of an electric current (*I*, simply **current**). Defined so, an electric insulator (simply **insulator**) has a high R_E and a low K_E (electric conductance). In contrast, an electric conductor (simply **conductor**) has a low R_E and a high K_E. A material's K_E is the reciprocal (inverse) of its R_E (or vice versa).

While moving through a conductor, electric charges experience resistance to their movement, reducing a current progress through the conductor. A conductor's R_E can be determined by Ohm's Law ($V_E = I_R.R_E$) using V_E (electric voltage) as the driving force of the I_E (electric current) and R_E as the opposing force of the current.

$$R_E = \frac{1}{K_E} = \frac{V_E}{I_E} \quad (1)$$

The SI unit of R_E is Ω (omega, for Ohm), which is V/A, where V is for Volt (the SI unit of voltage), and A is for Ampere (the SI unit of current). An ohmmeter can measure the R_E of a circuit with I_E current.

Electric Resistors

An electric resistor (simply **resistor**) can reduce an electric current, divide electric voltage, adjust signal levels, and terminate an electric conductor. An electric resistor can be viewed as an equivalent of a friction force (a force that resists the motion of a system) in an electric circuit.

E-43

ELECTRIC TRANSFORMERS

An electric transformer (simply **transformer**) is a device (equipment) for decreasing or increasing the voltage (V) of an alternating current (AC) or for converting AC to DC (direct current). Transformers work based on Faraday's Induction Law (if a coil rotates in a magnetic field, an AC is produced in the loop). A simple typical transformer mainly consists of two **wire coils** (see Figure 1). An AC in the primary **wire coil** (a wire loop with multiple turns) creates a magnetic field (M-field), which causes the electric current (I) to flow through a second wire loop. By varying the number of coils in each loop, the electric voltage can be changed to the desired level. For example, a personal computer has a transformer in its power plug to decrease the voltage to 12 V.

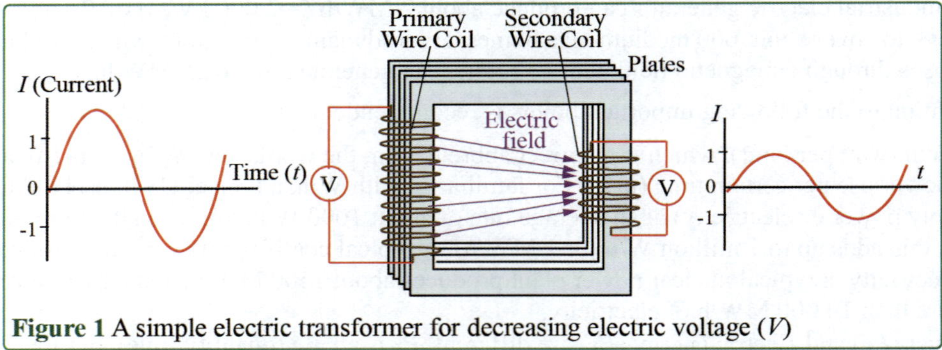

Figure 1 A simple electric transformer for decreasing electric voltage (V)

E-44

ELECTRIC VOLTAGE

Electric voltage (V_E or V, simply **voltage**; also called **electric potential**) is the difference in electric energy (E_E, the flow of electrons) between two points in an electric conductor (simply **conductor**, like a metal wire) per electric charges (Q_E) existing in that conductor.

$$V_E = \frac{E_E}{Q_E} \quad (1)$$

According to Ohm's Law, voltage is the driving force for flowing an electric current (I_E) through a conductor, whereas electric resistance (R_E) is the opposing force of the current. Thus,

$$I_E = \frac{V_E}{R_E} \quad (2)$$

A battery is an example of a device that creates a voltage in an electric circuit. A battery has two connections (called **electrodes**) with a voltage difference. In a battery, a direct current (DC) electricity flows from the positive electrode (anode) toward the negative electrode (cathode).

The voltage in a system (such as the voltage in a battery) can be measured by a voltmeter (potentiometer). A simple voltmeter has a coil of fine wire suspended in a strong magnetic field.

Volt (V) is the unit of voltage (*V*). A typical voltage for a flashlight AAA battery is 1.5 volts (DC). The voltage is 12 volts (AC) for a car battery, whereas AC is for alternating current. Electricity for household usage in the US of America is 110 to 220 kV (AC).

E-45
ELECTRICITY

Another name for ELECTRIC ENERGY.

E-46
ELECTROCHEMICAL POTENTIAL

The electrochemical potential ($\bar{\mu}$, usually abbreviated to ECP) of a chemical component is that component's chemical potential. Its SI unit is J/mole, where J is for Joule (the unit for energy), and the mole is the unit for concentration. The two important characteristics of the ECP are the following:

- Each component has an ECP at a certain point, representing how easy or difficult adding more of that component to that location.
- When a component is at equilibrium, its EPC remains constant.

A component's molecules may move from an area with higher ECP to an area with lower ECP. This occurs because of the electric potential energy of the molecules in the lower ECP area than in the higher ECP area. If, say, a glass of water has more dissolved sugar on one side than on the other side, each sugar molecule will randomly diffuse by convective diffusion (see DIFFUSION PROCESS) to the area with fewer sugar molecules. The diffusion (movement) of molecules continues until an equilibrium (called **diffusion equilibrium**) occurs among the molecules anywhere in the water. Scientists say that diffusion occurs because the sugar molecules have more chemical potential in the higher-concentration area than in the lower-concentration area. In simple words, a concentration difference of sugar molecules exists in those areas.

E-47
ELECTROCHEMICAL REACTIONS

An electrochemical reaction is a chemical reaction of reactants with the help of the electric current, as in electrolysis. Figure 1 shows two laboratory beakers with two metal electrodes, a zinc anode (Zn) and a copper cathode (Cu), connected by an electric circuit. The electrodes are immersed in two different aqueous solutions, 1 M $ZnSO_4$ and 1 M $CuSO_4$ (M is for molarity). In the solutions, an oxidation-reduction reaction occurs. At the anode, two electrons (e^-) are released, causing the oxidation reaction of zinc (Zn) to produce zinc cation (Zn^{2+}). At the cathode, the released electrons, which flow through the circuit, are gained, causing the reduction of the copper cation (Cu^{2+}) to copper (Cu).

$$Zn \rightarrow 2\ e^- + Zn^{2+} \quad \text{Oxidation}$$

$$Cu^{2+} + 2\ e^- \rightarrow Cu \quad \text{Reduction}$$

The overall reaction is the total of these two half-reactions.

$$Zn + Cu^{2+} \rightarrow Zn^{2+} + Cu$$

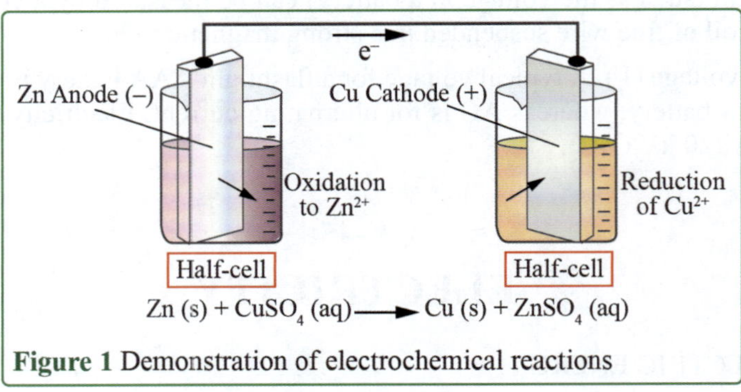

Figure 1 Demonstration of electrochemical reactions

E-48

ELECTROLYTES AND ELECTROLYSIS

Electrolytes

An electrolyte (also called **electrolytic compound**) is an ionic compound that ionizes to ions when dissolved in a solvent. For example, water-based sodium chloride (NaCl, called brine) is an electrolyte, so it reacts with water (H_2O, a solvent) to produce sodium hydroxide (NaOH) and chlorine ions (Cl_2), which are used often in the chemical process industry.

$$2\ NaCl + 2\ H_2O \rightarrow 2\ NaOH + H_2 + Cl_2$$

Most acids, bases, and salts are electrolytes. When saying a compound is an electrolyte, it does *not* mean that it carries an electric current (electron conductor). Acids, for example, are electrolytes that carry hydrogen ions but are *not* current carriers. Salts, instead, are both electrolytes and current carriers.

When, for example, salt (NaCl, an electrolyte) is dissolved in water, it ionizes to the sodium cation (Na^+) and anion chlorine (Cl^-) to produce an (electrolyte).

$$NaCl \rightarrow Na^+ + Cl^-$$

Some gases are electrolytes, too.

Electrolysis

Electrolysis is an electrolytic process that uses electric energy (E_E) to separate the elements of a substance, such as the ionization of an electrolyte or purifying metal from natural ore. The change (or changes) that occur during an electrolytic process is a chemical change.

A typical electrolyzer consists of an **electro-positively-charged anode** and an **electro-negatively-charged cathode**, both connected to a direct current (DC) electricity with different voltages, depending on the substance under the electrolytic process.

Figure 1 shows the electrolysis of water (an electrolyte), in which water goes through an oxidation-reduction reaction to produce hydrogen (H_2) and oxygen (O_2).

$$2\,H_2O \rightarrow 2\,H_2 + O_2$$

An oxidation-reduction reaction consists of two parts, and each is called a **half-reaction**. In the electrolysis of H_2O, the two half-reactions (together known as an oxidation-reduction reaction) proceed as

$2\,H_2O \rightarrow 4\,e^- + 4\,H^+ + O_2$ Oxidation (**release** of electron or **increase** in the oxidation state)

$4\,H^+ + 4\,e^- \rightarrow 2\,H_2$ Reduction (**gain** of electron or decrease in the oxidation state)

At the anode, as seen, four electrons (e^-) are released, causing the oxidation of the H_2O to hydrogen cation (H^+) and the formation of oxygen gas (O_2). At the cathode, the released electrons, which flow through the circuit connecting the two electrodes, are gained, causing the reduction of the hydrogen cation (H^+) to hydrogen gas (H_2).

Figure 2 shows the electrolysis of an aqueous solution of **sodium chloride** (NaCl, called **brine**) to produce sodium hydroxide (NaOH) and chlorine gas (Cl_2).

$$2\,NaCl + 2\,H_2O \rightarrow 2\,NaOH + H_2 + Cl_2$$

The oxidation-reduction reaction can be written as

$2\,NaCl \rightarrow 2\,e^- + 2\,Na^+ + Cl_2$ Oxidation

$2\,Na^+ + 2\,e^- + 2\,OH^- \rightarrow 2\,NaOH$ Reduction

The anode releases two electrons, causing the oxidation of the NaCl to produce sodium cation (Na^+) and chlorine gas (Cl_2). The cathode gains the electrons, causing the reduction of the sodium cation (Na^+). At the same time, H_2O molecules split to produce hydrogen cation (H^+) and hydroxide anion (OH^-), and OH^- reacts with Na^+ to form NaOH. [As seen in Figure 2, a **semipermeable membrane** separates the electrodes to allow the passage of ions, but *not* the bulk flow of the NaCl and NaOH from one side of the reactor.]

Aluminum, calcium, magnesium, potassium, and sodium are metallic electrolyzed ores to produce pure metals. Figure 3 shows the purification of aluminum (Al) by the **Hall-Heroult process**, in which aluminum ore (called **bauxite**, mainly aluminum oxide, Al_2O_3) is dissolved in molten **cryolite** (sodium hexafluoroaluminate, Na_3AlF_6) to decrease the bauxite's melting point temperature from 2072°C to about 950°C for easier electrolysis. A strong DC is passed through the molten to form $AlOF_3^{2-}$.

The anode releases 4 electrons by oxidation of the mixture to form aluminum hexafluoride ions [$(AlF_6)^{3-}$]. At the same time, the fluoride ions (F^-) of the cryolite react with the Al_2O_3 of the bauxite to form various aluminum fluoride ions, such as $AlOF_3^{2-}$, which are also oxidized to $(AlF_6)^{3-}$.

$2\,AlOF_3^{2-} + 6\,F^- + C \rightarrow 4e^- + 2\,(AlF_6)^{3-} + CO_2$ Oxidation

The cathode gains the electrons by reduction of the aluminum hexafluoride ion. At the same time, the Al^{3+} cation in the AlF_6^{3-} is reduced to elemental aluminum.

$AlF_6^{3-} + 3\,e^- \rightarrow 6\,F^- + Al$ Reduction

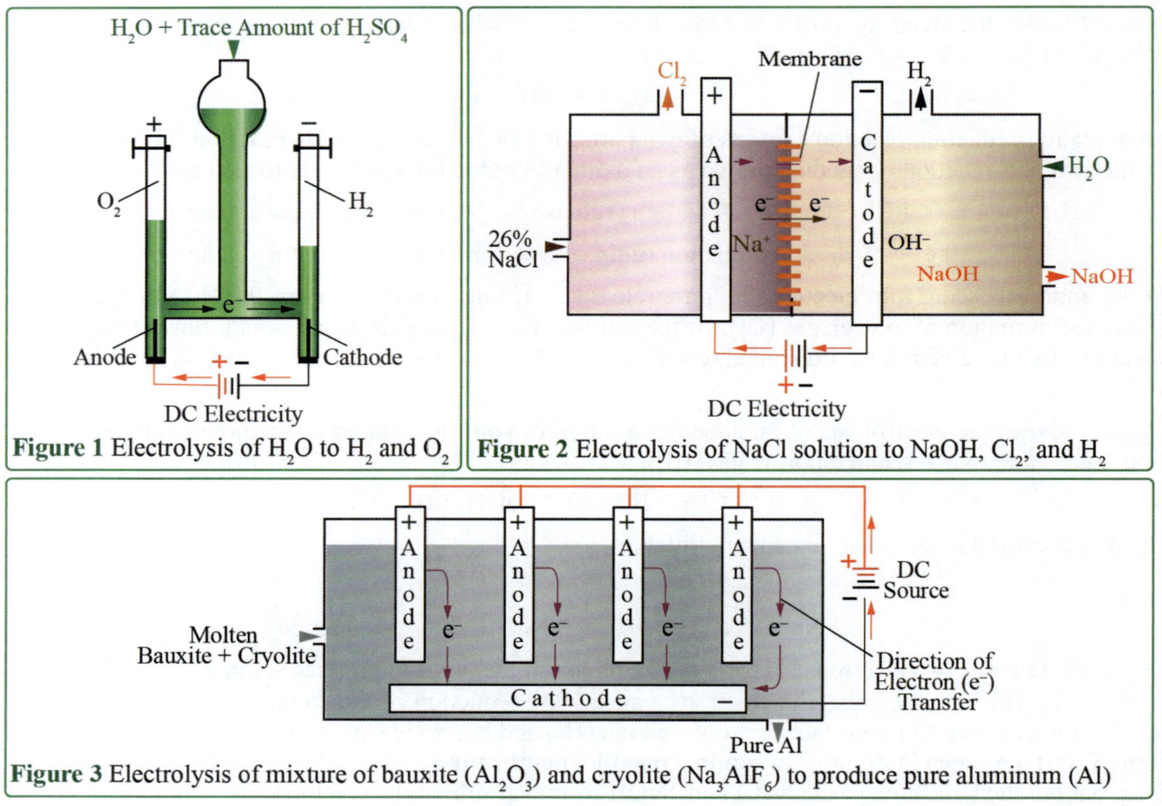

Figure 1 Electrolysis of H_2O to H_2 and O_2

Figure 2 Electrolysis of NaCl solution to NaOH, Cl_2, and H_2

Figure 3 Electrolysis of mixture of bauxite (Al_2O_3) and cryolite (Na_3AlF_6) to produce pure aluminum (Al)

E-49

ELECTROMAGNETIC ENERGY

Discussed under the topic of ENERGY AND ITS FORMS.

E-50

ELECTROMAGNETIC FIELD

Discussed under ELECTRIC FIELD, MAGNETIC FIELD, AND ELECTROMAGNETIC FIELD.

E-51

ELECTROMAGNETIC FORCE

Discussed under FUNDAMENTAL FORCES OF NATURE.

E-52
ELECTROMAGNETIC INDUCTION

Electromagnetic induction (simply **induction**) is a process of placing an electric conductor, like a **wire coil** (a wire loop with multiple turns), in a changing magnetic field (M-field) to produce (induce) an electric current in the conductor. This definition tells us that a close relation exists between magnetism and electricity, known as Faraday's Induction Law (if some magnetic field lines pass through a wire coil, alternating current electricity is produced in the coil). [Electromagnetic induction and electric inductance are *not* the same.]

E-53
ELECTROMAGNETIC RADIATIONS

Study ELECTROMAGNETIC WAVES.

E-54
ELECTROMAGNETIC WAVES

As invisible waves to the human eye, **electromagnetic waves** (EM waves or **EM radiations**) are carried by photons (the particles of the EM-waves). The EM-waves transfer energy (E), known as photon energy (E_{Ph}), through the oscillation of an electric field (E-field) and magnetic field (M-field). In this way, an EM wave is formed from oscillating E-field and M-field. And as shown in Figure 1, the wave direction and E-field and M-field oscillations are all perpendiculars.

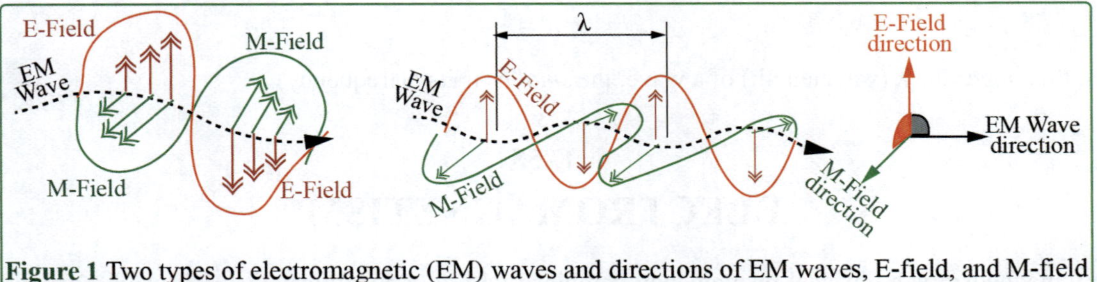

Figure 1 Two types of electromagnetic (EM) waves and directions of EM waves, E-field, and M-field

[Light, X-rays, alpha rays, gamma rays, infrared waves, microwaves, radio waves, and TV rays are in the class of EM waves.]

EM waves do *not* need a particle-containing medium to move through a vacuum. Each EM wave has a specific wavelength (λ), frequency (f), and photon energy (E_{Ph}). Some other characteristics of an EM wave are outlined next.

- It heats a surface that absorbs its waves.
- It exhibits the properties of both waves and particles.
- It can travel at the speed of light in space without a medium.
- It is the photon's movement (because an electron releases a photon).
- It has wave-particle property by moving like a wave and releasing energy as a particle (see the Note).
- It is more energetic if its λ is shorter (or its f is greater) because a much smaller distance exists between the peak of its waves, and vice versa (less energetic if its λ is longer).

[Note: In the subject of the photon's dual properties, known as the wave-particle duality, low-energy photons (like radio waves) behave like waves, while high-energy photons (like X-rays) behave more like particles, but never both at the same time.]

Next are some other properties of EM waves:

- They have different photon energy (E_{Ph}), the energy carried by the photons.
- They consist of packets, where each packet consists of several photons that carry the electromagnetic force.
- They have different intensities. The intensity of a particular EM wave indicates its energy (known as **photon energy**), which increases with decreasing wavelength. X-rays and γ-rays are more energetic than light.
- They have a different amount of radiation. **Sunburn** on a human face is an example of a mild radiation effect, although nearly the entire Sun's ultraviolet spectrum is absorbed by the Earth's atmosphere.

The following are the seven (7) most important types of EM waves (in the order of longest-to-shortest λ or lowest-to-highest *f*):

- Radio wave (with λ of 1 m to 100 km and *f* of 300 MHz to 3 kHz), where M is for Mega (10^6).
- Microwave (with λ of 1 mm to 1 m and *f* of 300 GHz to 300 MHz), where G is for Giga (10^9).
- Infrared wave (with λ of 750 nm to 1 mm and *f* of 400 THz to 300 GHz), where T is for Tera (10^{12}).
- Visible light wave (with λ of 400 to 700 nm and *f* of 770 THz to 400 THz).
- Ultraviolet wave (with λ of 10 to 400 nm and *f* of 30 PHz to 750 THz), where P is for Pita (10^{15}).
- X-ray (with λ of 0.01 to 10 nm and *f* of 30 EHz to 30 PHz), where E is for Eta (10^{18}).
- Gamma-ray (with λ < 0.02 nm and *f* of above 15 EHz).

The relation between a wave's *U* (speed), λ (wavelength), and its *f* (frequency) is

$$U = \lambda . f \quad \text{or} \quad \lambda = \frac{U}{f} \tag{1}$$

Because all EM waves always travel through a vacuum at the speed of light constant (*c*), their λ is related to their *f* as

$$\lambda = \frac{c}{f} \tag{2}$$

Thus, the *longer* the λ (wavelength) of a wave, the *smaller* is its *f* (frequency).

E-55

ELECTROMAGNETISM

Electromagnetism is a physical phenomenon combined with two quantities; electricity and magnetism. It is represented by an electromagnetic force (F_{EM} or EM force), which is carried by an electromagnetic field (EM field), a field composed of an electric field (E-field), and a magnetic field (M-field). EM force is responsible for electromagnetic waves (radiations), such as light waves (radiations).

E-56

ELECTRON

Defined under the topic of ATOM.

E-57

ELECTRON AFFINITY

Study ELECTRONEGATIVITY, ELECTRON AFFINITY, AND IONIZATION ENERGY, as these are related subjects.

E-58

ELECTRON BINDING ENERGY

Electron binding energy (E_{EB}, also called **atomic binding energy** or **bond energy**) is the energy (E) in an atom's electrons. It is used as bond energy in a chemical reaction (simply **reaction**).

The two main differences between E_{EB} and E_{NB} (nuclear binding energy, simply **nuclear energy**) are:

- E_{EB} participates in a chemical reaction, while E_{NB} participates in a nuclear reaction. In a chemical reaction, the electrons are the only ones that participate in the reaction. In contrast, in a nuclear reaction, both nucleus and electrons of an atom contribute to the reaction.
- E_{EB} is much smaller (on the order of million times) than the E_{NB} because protons and neutrons (together called the nucleon) are attached by the strong nuclear force (F_{SN}).

[The term **nuclear binding energy** (simply **nuclear energy**) is used in nuclear reactions, while in the chemical reactions, the word **electron binding energy** is used.]

In a chemical reaction, E_{EB} causes the following:

- Breaking chemical bonds between two atoms by taking some electrons from them, and
- Joining two atoms together by giving them electron (or electrons).

During a chemical reaction, E_{EB} converts to heat energy (E_Q, simply heat and scientifically enthalpy) to ease the process of breaking bonds or joining bonds. Therefore, each chemical bond has an E_Q, equating to its E_{EB}. For example, the H–C–H bond has 414 kJ (= 393 BTU) of E_Q per mole of CH_2. This means that 414 kJ of E_Q, which equates to 414 kJ of E_{EB}, is absorbed as 1 mole of CH_2 breaks apart, and the same amount of E_Q is released when two hydrogen atoms and one carbon atom are joined to form CH_2.

The E_Q of the H–H bond is 436 kJ/mole of H_2 (= 414 BTU/mole), that of the H–O bond is 464 kJ/mole of HO (= 441 BTU/mole), and that of 6 electrons in a carbon atom is 1.65×10^{-13} kJ (= 1030 electron volt).

[Note 1: Conventionally, a **positive** E_Q, which equates to E_{EB}, represents the amount of E **absorbed** as a bond breaks, and a **negative** E_Q represents the amount of E **released** as a bond form.]

[Note 2: Because the bonds that break in the reactant's molecules are *not* the same bonds that form in the product's molecules, the amount of E_Q absorbed when the reactant's molecules break is *not* the same as the amount of E_Q released as the product's molecules form.]

[Note 3: Some reactions, however, require adding some E_Q from outside to force the reactants to react with each other. Such a reaction is called a heat-absorbing reaction (endothermic reaction).]

E-59

ELECTRON PAIRS AND ELECTRON LONE PAIRS

Electron Pairs: An electron pair (also called **pair of electrons**) consists of two (2) valance electrons (the outer-shell electrons of an atom) that are paired and participate in the chemical bonding process between atoms, also known as the **bonding electron pair**, so atoms are bonded **electronically** (but *not* **chemically**).

The following dots express two important properties of electron pairs:

- The maximum valence electrons in one atom is 8; that is, 2(1 e^-) + 6 e^- = 8 e^- (or 4 electron pairs).
- The two electrons in an electron pair have opposite spins because they are in the same shell or subshell. The electrons in one shell (or subshell) *cannot* have the same **spin quantum numbers** (simply a spin number or **spin**). Thus, the spin numbers of electrons in an electron pair are + ½ and – ½.

Electron Lone Pairs: An electron lone pair also consists of two valence electrons paired but do *not* participate in the bonding process, known as the **non-bonding electron pair**. Electron pairs participate in the bonding process of many compounds, including water (H_2O), ammonia (NH_3), and hydrochloric acid (HCl). Figure 1 shows the electron pairs and electron lone pairs in a water molecule.

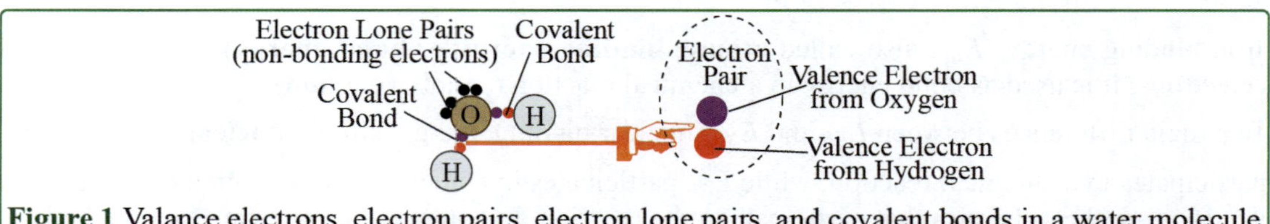

Figure 1 Valance electrons, electron pairs, electron lone pairs, and covalent bonds in a water molecule

E-60

ELECTRON VOLT

Electron Volt (eV) is one of the units of energy (*E*) commonly used to measure a particle's energy in nuclear reactions. It is defined as the *E* that an electron gets from an electric field of 1 V (volt), where 1 eV = 1.60×10^{-16} kJ and 1 MeV (mega electron volt) = 1.60×10^{-10} kJ. The nuclear mass excess (expressed in AMU) can be converted into nuclear energy using 1 AMU = 931.494 MeV/c^2, where *c* is the speed of light constant.

E-61

ELECTRONEGATIVITY, ELECTRON AFFINITY, AND IONIZATION ENERGY

Electronegativity (E_{Neg}), electron affinity (E_{Af}), and ionization energy (E_{Ion}) are electron-and-energy-related concepts. In the periodic table of elements, E_{Neg}, E_{Af}, and E_{Io} increase from left to right and bottom to top (see Figure 1). All three are expressed in one of the units of energy (*E*), usually in kJ/mole, where J is for Joule.

Electronegativity: An element's electronegativity (E_{Neg}) is the minimum amount of energy (*E*) used in a chemical bonding process to **absorb** a valence electron (outer electron) from its reacting partner. Each element needs a different amount of E_{Neg} to absorb an electron (the *greater* the E_{Neg} of an element, the *greater* is its attraction ability for electrons when bonded).

Fluorine (F, with E_{Neg} of 4) is the first most electronegative element, oxygen (O, with E_{Neg} of 3.2) is the second most electronegative element, and francium (Fr, with E_{Neg} of 0.8) is the least electronegative element. For example, consider hydrogen (H, with E_{Neg} of 2.2) and chlorine (Cl, with E_{Neg} of 3.2). Because Cl has greater E_{Neg}, it can absorb electrons than H when they react to form HCL (hydrogen chloride). E_{Neg} is, thus, a useful quantity to determine the **strength** of a chemical bond in a chemical reaction (because atoms are bonded electronically). [When two elements have the same E_{Neg}, *no* polar covalent bond is formed between them (as with H + H → H_2), so the bond is **nonpolar**. Instead, when two elements differ in E_{Neg}, a polar bond forms between them, as with H_2 + O → H_2O and H + Cl → HCl.]

Electron Affinity: An element's electron affinity (E_{Af}) is the minimum amount of energy (E) used in a bonding process to **release** a valence electron from its reacting partner. Each element needs a different amount of E_{Af} to release an electron (the *greater* the E_{Af} of an element, the *greater* is its releasing ability for electrons when bonded). When an electro-negatively-charged ion (X^-) **releases** an electron (e^-) to its reacting partner, it becomes a neutral atom (X^0).

$$X^- + E_{Af} \rightarrow X^0 + e^-$$

And when a neutral atom (X^0) **absorbs** an electro-negatively-charged electron (e^-) from its reacting partner, the neutral atom becomes an electro-negatively-charged ion (X^-, an anion).

$$X^0 + e^- \rightarrow X^- + E_{Af}$$

The last two paragraphs tell us that E_{Af} can have a **positive** or **negative** value, which can be both a positive E and a negative E.

Study the following two (2) important points about E_{Af} (electron affinity):

- E_{Af} is used when the element under the test is in the gaseous state ONLY, as in the case of ionization energy (E_{Ion}). This exists because the energy level changes by contacting the atoms in the liquid or solid state.
- E_{Af} of elements varies greatly across the periodic table. For example, the E_{Af} of sodium (Na) is 53, and that of chlorine (Cl) is 349, both in kJ/mole. By combining Na and Cl in equal amounts, therefore, Cl absorbs an electron from Na to form a sodium cation (Na^+) and a chlorine anion (Cl^-), which then produces an ionic bond between them to form salt (NaCl).

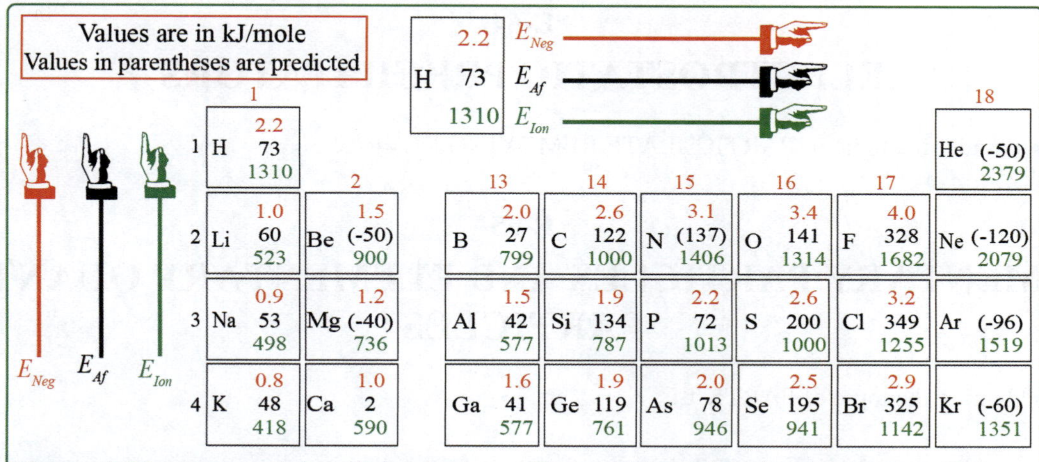

Figure 1 Electronegativity (E_{Neg}), electron affinity (E_{Af}), and ionization energy (E_{Ion}) of several elements and indication of their trends

Ionization Energy: The ionization energy (E_{Ion}, also called **ionization potential**) of an element is the minimum amount of E needed to remove a valence electron from that element's neutral atom (X^0) to form a positively-charge ion (X^+, a cation).

$$X^0 + E \rightarrow X^+ + e^-$$

Study the following four (4) important points about E_{Ion} (ionization energy):

- The E_{Ion} is used when the element under the test is in the gaseous state ONLY, as in the case of E_{Af}.
- The E_{Ion} is a positive E (since E is absorbed from outside when an electron is removed from an atom).

- Because the size of atoms decreases from left to right in the periodic table, the atoms are held more strongly, so it takes more E_{Ion} to remove an electron from their valence shells. For example, it takes about 4 times as much E_{Ion} to remove an electron from a lithium atom (Li, group 1) as a neon atom (Ne, group 18).
- The amount of E needed to remove the first electron is called the **first ionization energy**. When the first electron is gone, the removal of succeeding electrons becomes more difficult (because of the increase of attractive energy between electrons).

E-62

ELECTRONIC MICROSCOPES

Discussed under MICROSCOPES.

E-63

ELECTROSTATIC FORCE

The electrostatic force (F_{ES}) is the force (F) that exists between two systems because of their electric charges (q, simply **charges**). The F_{ES} can be **attractive** (when pulling charges of opposite sign together; that is, + − or − +) or **repulsive** (when pushing charges of the same sign; that is, + + or − −).

E-64

ELECTROSTATIC PRECIPITATORS

Discussed under the topic of PARTICULATE REMOVING DEVICES.

E-65

ELEMENTARY PARTICLES AND ELEMENTARY QUANTUM PARTICLES

Discussed under the topic of PARTICLE.

E-66

EMISSIVITY

The term **emissivity** (ε) is used in Physics to express the ability of a substance's surface to emit (radiate) thermal radiation, which is the photon energy generated by electromagnetic radiation (EM radiation or EM waves), to the environment around it (the surroundings). Mathematically, emissivity (ε, a unitless quantity) is the ratio of EM radiation emitted from a given surface to a black surface (which absorbs all EM radiation). In other words, emissivity is the property of a surface that describes how its radiation varies from the ideal of a blackbody (a warm body that releases and absorbs the maximum possible amount of EM radiation). Objects with low emissivity (lower than 1) emit EM radiation at a comparatively lower rate.

When EM radiations hit the surface of an object, they convert to heat energy (E_Q, simply heat and scientifically enthalpy), so the surface emits thermal radiation in the form of E_Q. Thus, emissivity is important in the heat transfer by radiation from a given surface to its surroundings.

$$\dot{E}_Q = \varepsilon . K_{SB} . A . T^4 \quad (1)$$

In this equation, which is called the Stefan-Boltzmann equation, $\dot{E}_Q$ is the rate of heat transfer by radiation, K_{SB} is Stefan-Boltzmann constant (= 5.67×10^{-8} W/m^2.K^4 = 5.67×10^{-8} W/m^2.°C^4), A is the cross-sectional area from which radiation emits (in m^2), and T is the surface's temperature (in Kelvin, K, or °C). [While a surface emits thermal radiation to the environment around it, the environment also emits E_Q back to that surface, and the net transfer is the difference between these two values.]

The fourth power of T in Equation 1 says the thermal radiation from a surface is *not* large at low temperatures, like room temperature (around 25ºC or 77 ºF). However, we can see the thermal radiation emitted from a hot object. Sun (with T of 5 400 K) looks white to us, while a planet with over 8000 K looks blue.

Emissivity occurs on Earth's surface by emitting the sunlight's thermal radiation to the atmosphere. The concept of emissivity is used in some industries. In the solar industry, it is used because the surface of solar collectors has low emissivity, so it emits very little E_Q. In the energy-efficient window industry, high emissivity causes a window to cool itself by emitting thermal radiation to the environment. Emissivity is also used in infrared sensors to measure a system's T using thermal radiation.

E-67
EMULSIONS

Emulsions are in a large group of dispersions, so it is discussed under DISPERSIONS.

E-68
ENDOTHERMIC PROCESS

Another name for HEAT ABSORBING PROCESS.

E-69
ENDOTHERMIC REACTIONS

Another name for HEAT ABSORBING REACTIONS.

E-70
ENERGY-ABSORBING REACTIONS

Study HEAT ABSORBING AND HEAT RELEASING REACTIONS.

E-71

ENERGY AND ITS FORMS

ENERGY

As the World's living force (F), energy (E, from the Latin *Energia*) is hard to be defined because:

- It has several forms (types), each having its definition and characteristics.
- It is *not* fully known to us (because we do *not* know what it is and how it works).

Energy and its forms are discussed under this topic in their fullest possible way as they are one of the most important subjects that a chemical engineer needs to know. [Before going through the detail of energy, it is helpful to mention that the general concept of energy is meant when discussing **energy** without mentioning its forms. Instead, particular energy, which has its definition and properties, is meant when a form of energy (like potential energy) is mentioned. This general rule is followed in this book, as well.]

Generally, energy (E) can be defined as the ability of a system that can perform the following:

- It can be estimated by a system's temperature, T (the *higher* a system's T, the *higher* is its E).
- It can be converted to heat energy (E_Q; simply heat and scientifically enthalpy, H).
- It can perform useful work (W), say, shaft work (W_S) or flow work (W_F).
- It can overcome a system's resistance and cause a system's motion.

In defining E, knowing the following three (3) points is helpful:

- Because W (work) is the product of a system's F (force) times L (length); that is, $W = F.L$, energy (E) is the ability of a system that can force (pull or push) another system.
- Because E is equivalent to M (mass) through c (speed of light constant) by Einstein's equation ($E = M.c^2$), M can be viewed as concentrated E.
- Because E is the ability of a system to do W and W is Gibbs free energy (E_{GF}), E can be viewed as E_{GF}.

Based on what has been said so far, E, E_Q, H, W, and E_{GF} are similar quantities, with the same SI unit of J (Joule) and US unit of BTU (British thermal unit), where 1 kJ $\approx$1 BTU. [In the nuclear industry, MeV (mega electron volt) is used as the energy unit (1 MeV = 1.60×10^{-10} kJ).] The derived unit of energy, W/h (also written as Wh or just W), is used for electric power consumption, where W is for Watt and h is for an hour.

Here are 25 more general properties of E.

- It is *not* a substance (element or compound),
- It is *not* the same as electric power (electricity),
- It is *not* a system's property, but that system's ability,
- It is *not* measurable, but it can be determined indirectly,
- It is always positive; therefore, it can curve the spacetime,
- It is generated in fossil fuels in the form of heat energy (E_Q),
- It is generated in the nucleus of an atom in the form of nuclear energy (E_N),
- It is quantized to tiny-separated quantities, called the **quanta** (the plural of quantum),
- It is moved as light energy (photon energy) by individual packets, each having many photons,
- It is related to work and force by $E = W = F.L$; therefore, it can move a system to some distance (L),
- Its form of heat energy (E_Q) can move from point A to point B by conduction, convection, or radiation,
- Its fast-moving ability can be expressed by a proportionality constant, named speed of light constant (c),
- Its flow as heat (simple word for heat energy, E_Q) has the same meaning as enthalpy change (ΔH),
- Its content in the nucleus of an atom is given by $M.c^2$, where M is mass and c is the speed of light,
- Its content in an inertial (nonaccelerating) system is equivalent to that system's inertial mass,
- Its flow as heat (Q) takes a one-way direction (from a higher-energy system to a lower one),

- Its quantity in a system or a region of space per unit volume is called energy density,
- Its *decrease* in a system is proportional to the *increase* in that system's entropy (S),
- Its main forms are heat energy (E_Q), kinetic energy (E_K), and potential energy (E_P),
- Its main sources are fossil fuels (oil, gas, and coal), biofuels, and nuclear fuels,
- Its crisis in 1973, 1979, 1990, and 2008 affected every household and industry,
- Its price changes unpredictably ($150 in mid-2008 and $30 six months later),
- Its effect on the economics of the chemical process industry is enormous,
- Its effect on today's international politics and environment is significant,
- Its world cost is about 10% of the world GDP (Gross Domestic Product).

As a physical quantity (simply **quantity**), energy is in the next classes:

- Conserved quantity (its quantity in a closed system stays unchanged),
- Extensive quantity (it depends on a system's size when it moves),
- Fixed quantity (it is independent of time, t, when travels),
- Scalar quantity (has quantity with *no* specific path), and
- State quantity (it is independent of a process path).

Energy is **conserved** (is *not* creatable, destroyable, or losable) but can be converted to mass (M), or vice versa, in a nuclear reaction, which is governed by Einstein's equation ($E = M.c^2$). Study the next Notes.

[Note 1: The statement "energy can *never* be created or destroyed" may create a question, "how was it made? The answer is that the Universe started with the **net** total E of zero, and it is still zero but differently distributed.] [Note 2: Because energy is *not* losable, the word **energy loss** is an incorrect expression when talking about heat energy (E_Q).] [Note 3: Energy is one of the most studied scientific subjects. Since Industrial Revolution, technology has gone through many important **scientific changes**. The development of renewable energy, which started after the first crisis in oil prices in1973, is one of the changes. **Renewable energy** is also discussed under this topic.]

FORMS OF ENERGY

Energy exists in different forms (types). Next, 31 forms of energy are discussed alphabetically.

1. ACTIVATION ENERGY

The activation energy (E_a, also called **collision energy**) is the amount of energy (E) necessary to cause a chemical reaction to occur. In another definition, E_A is the E that the reactants' molecules of a reaction must have to **become active**, **move fast**, and **start reacting**. [In chemistry, the words "**to become active, move fast, and start reacting**" are expressed in one word, **collide**.] Usually, the E_a is given to the reaction in the form of E_Q (heat energy) from an outside source. E_a functions in the following ways:

- It breaks the chemical bonds between the reactants' molecules,
- It increases the reactant molecules' kinetic energy (E_K) to **collide** with each other, and
- It increases the temperature (T) of the reacting medium to help the occurrence of the reaction.

Because E_a is used in the collision theory, chemical reaction, chemical reaction rate, and more, it is important to understand it deeply. We, thus, consider Figure 1 and analogically (equivalently) compare E_A with the E that a young man spends start cutting the grass of an uphill area with a lawnmower. Once he spends the needed E_K (as E_a) to cut uphill, the downhill E_P (potential energy) available to him helps him continue cutting the grass in the downhill area, which is at a lower level, so he has lower E_P in the downhill area.

As a real example, consider Figure 2, which shows the combustion reaction in a system (like a furnace) between carbon (C) in fuel and oxygen (O_2) in the air to produce carbon dioxide (CO_2). As a result, some E_Q is released (by definition, shown with a **negative** sign), so $C + O_2 \rightarrow CO_2 - E_Q$. This reaction, or any other, does *not* start by itself (fuel can be stored indefinitely with *no* reaction with O_2 in the air) unless it gets some energy (in this case, from **ignition**), known as E_a (activation energy). Once some E as E_a is spent to initiate the reaction of C and O_2, a certain amount of E_Q is released, so it is a heat-releasing reaction.

The released E_Q is notably greater than the E_a, as seen in the same figure. The amount of the released E_Q equates to the difference in the E_Q level of the reactants and that of the products. This means that the reactants are at a higher energy state than the products. [Note that the E_Q given to the reaction from outside to start acting is different than the E_Q released by a heat-releasing reaction.]

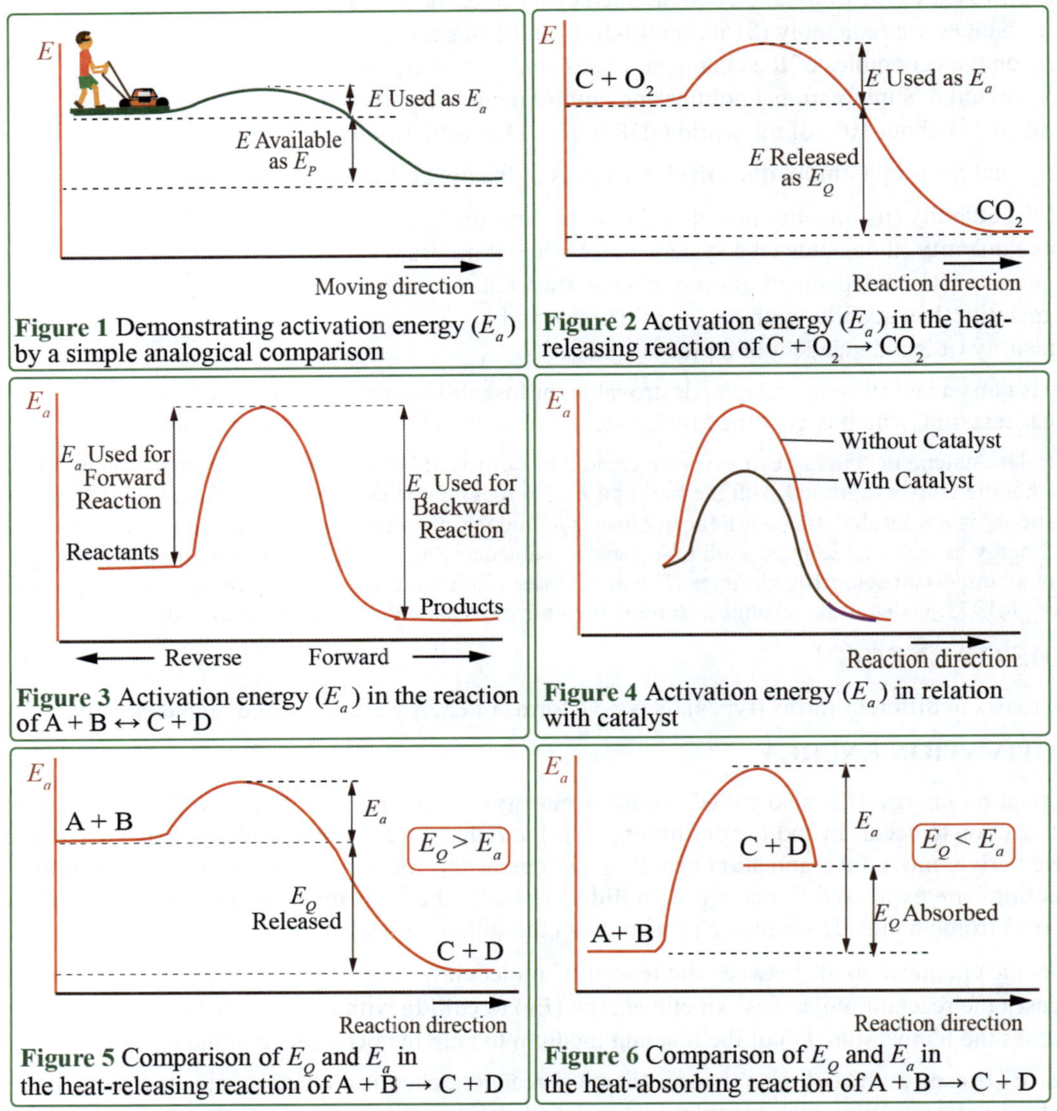

Figure 1 Demonstrating activation energy (E_a) by a simple analogical comparison

Figure 2 Activation energy (E_a) in the heat-releasing reaction of $C + O_2 \rightarrow CO_2$

Figure 3 Activation energy (E_a) in the reaction of A + B ↔ C + D

Figure 4 Activation energy (E_a) in relation with catalyst

Figure 5 Comparison of E_Q and E_a in the heat-releasing reaction of A + B → C + D

Figure 6 Comparison of E_Q and E_a in the heat-absorbing reaction of A + B → C + D

A reaction can have a **forward direction** or **backward** (reverse) **direction**. In the reaction of A + B = C + D, as shown in Figure 3, the forward reaction has more chance of occurring (because the E_a required for the forward reactions is less than that for the backward reactions).

Catalysts can help some reactions by lowering their required E_A, so a catalyst acts in the following ways:

- It helps the reaction to proceed at a greater rate than would otherwise be done, as shown in Figure 4,
- It helps a reaction proceed at a lower T and P (pressure) than would otherwise be required.

The activation energy (E_a) does *not* affect the overall **energy of reaction** (enthalpy of reaction, H_R), as H_R equates to $(E_{CP})_R - (E_{CP})_P$, but *not* $E_Q - E_a$. The E_{CP} is for chemical potential energy, subscript R is for the reactant, and subscript P is for the product.

Considering the reaction of A + B = C + D and Figures 5 and 6, we can compare the E_a needed to initiate an HR (heat releasing) reaction with that of an HA reaction (heat absorbing reaction) in the following ways:

- While both HR and HA reactions need E_a, an HR reaction needs less E_a than an HA reaction. An HR reaction gets part of its needed E_a from its own releasing E_Q to keep going, while the HA gets its entire energy need from an outside source.
- In an HR reaction, the reactants start at a higher energy state than the products, so the reaction proceeds from reactants to products. While in a HA reaction, the reactants start at a lower energy state than the products, so the reaction needs to get some energy to proceed.

2. ATTRACTIVE ENERGY

The attractive energy (E_A or U_A, also known as **chemical affinity**) is the energy (E) that holds the atoms (or molecules) of a chemical compound (simply **compound**) together, so the E_A between atoms is what causes them to approach each other. When two atoms join, the E_A is inversely proportional to the separation distance (L, the separation length, or bond length) between them. Thus, the *further* the atoms are from each other, the *weaker* is the E_A and, consequently, the *less* they attract each other.

$$E_A = -\frac{a}{L^m} \tag{1}$$

In this equation, a and m (known as the **attractive exponent**) are constants, where the constant m (which depends on the outer surface of the atom or molecule) has a value of 1 for atoms and 6 for molecules.

Atoms attract each other only to a certain distance. If the conditions are suitable, they form a compound. They will maintain a certain distance from each other by **repulsive energy** (E_R), **positive** energy, while **attractive energy** (E_A) is **negative** energy, both by convention.

The sum of E_A and E_R in an atom (or molecule) equates to that atom's (or molecule's) E_P (potential energy), as shown in Figure 7.

$$E_P = E_A + E_T = -\frac{a}{L^m} + \frac{b}{L^n} \tag{2}$$

Here, b and n are constants, where n is the **repulsive exponent**. The constant n (which depends on the outer surface of the atom or molecule) has a value of 1 for atoms and 6 for molecules.

The E_A also works between molecules. Say, in the ion-exclusion process, the molecules of nonionic compounds (like sugar) in the solution feed show much more attractive ability toward the resin (refers to ion-exchange resin) than the molecules of ionic compounds (say, most salts). As a result of attraction to the resin pores, the nonionic compounds move much slower through the resin bed than the ionic compounds.

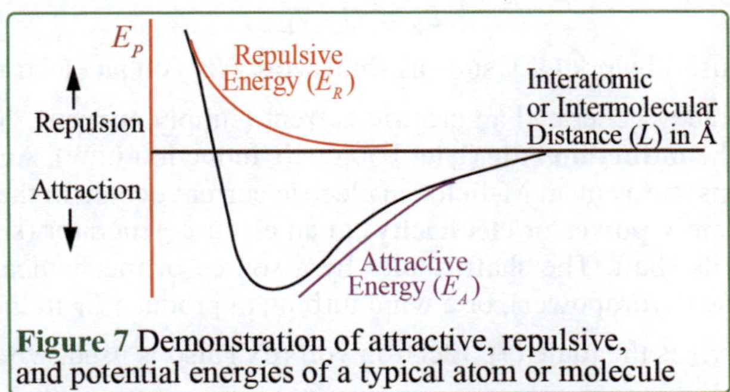

Figure 7 Demonstration of attractive, repulsive, and potential energies of a typical atom or molecule

3. BINDING ENERGY

The binding energy (E_B) is the minimum amount of energy (E) needed to remove a particle from a system of particles or to dissociate a system of particles into smaller individual systems of the particle during a chemical reaction. Each system typically has a lower E than its origin system, as a bound system is typically at a lower E level than its unbound components. The reason follows. According to Einstein's equation ($E = M.c^2$), a system's E_T *decreases* if its total mass (M) *decreases*.

[Comparing the definition of E_B with E_{EB} (electron binding energy), we can say that these energies are the same, but the term E_B is used when talking about the removal of a particle from a system of particles, but the term E_{EB} is used when talking about the removal of an electron from an atom's valance shell.]

4. CHEMICAL POTENTIAL ENERGY

The chemical potential energy (E_{CP}, simply **chemical energy**) is a potential energy (E_P) related to the composition of a system. It exists in the particles (atoms, molecules, or ions) of a compound when that compound goes through one or both of the following situations:

- One (or more) chemical reaction.
- One (or more) phase change.

When, for example, a fuel reacts with oxygen, it goes through both chemical reactions and phase changes to convert its E_{CP} to E_Q (heat energy). Before the reactions and phase change occur, the fuel molecules must overcome **activation energy** deficiency, equal to its Helmholtz free energy, to convert their E_{CP} to E_Q.

The energy that comes to our body in food to be converted to E_Q to perform activities is in the form of E_{CP}. Thus, we can say that every food contains the E_{CP}, given in J (Joule) in the SI system.

5. DARK ENERGY

Dark energy (E_D) is a form of E whose origin and properties are *not* yet well-known to us. Cosmophysicists (the physicists who specialized in **cosmology**, the study of the origin and evolution of the cosmos) think that the cosmos (Universe) was (and still is) filled with E_D to accelerate the expansion of the Universe.

On the amount of E_D, different physicists suggest different values. Some say that about 70% of the E in the Universe is in $E_{D,}$ and its amount remains **constant** in time, while the others consider it a non-constant E. Both groups, however, think that the E_D has a huge negative pressure (P).

6. ELECTRIC ENERGY

Electric energy (E_E, simply **electricity** or **power**) is one type of E that occurs in an electric conductor (simply **conductor**, like a metal wire) by flowing electrons (particles with electric charges). The flow of E_E in a conductor creates an electric current (I, simply **current**). A conductor that is carrying a current with electric charges of Q_E and electric voltage of V_E can carry E_E equal to

$$E_E = Q_E . V_E \quad (3)$$

The E_E can perform some useful work (W), such as shaft work (W_S) on an electric motor (like a pump).

In 1831 (see Figure 8), Faraday generated an electric current (simply **current**, I_E) from a changing magnetic field (M-field), discovering the **induction rule** (later Faraday's Induction Law). According to this law, if a **wire coil** (a wire with multiple turns) turns in an M-field, an electric current occurs in the coil. This is the idea behind generating electric power (simply **power** or **electricity**) in an electric generator (simply **generator**), which has a wire coil wrapped around its shaft. The shaft rotates by a source of mechanical energy (E_{Me}), like a steam turbine, a water-falling turbine (hydropower), or a wind turbine to produce E_E in the loop.

Like energy, the SI unit of E_E is the joule (J). Electron volt (eV) also is used, where 1 eV = 1.602×10^{-19} J.

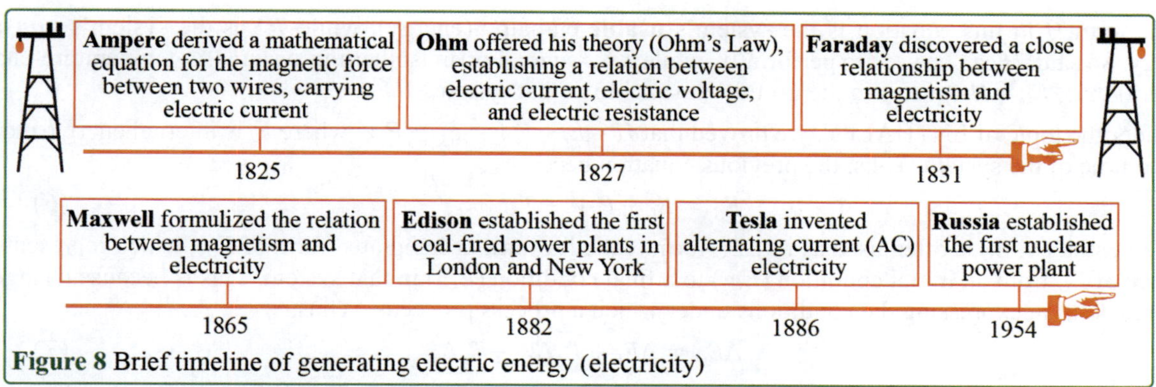

Figure 8 Brief timeline of generating electric energy (electricity)

7. ELECTRIC POTENTIAL ENERGY

The electric potential energy (E_{EP} or U_E) is a system's potential energy (E_P) that is related to the structure of a point that carries electric charges (q) in that system. The E_{EP} can create an electric current (I, simply **current**) in a wire coil, a wire with multiple turns (loops). The coil is mounted on a shaft, allowing it to turn.

8. ELECTROMAGNETIC ENERGY

The electromagnetic energy (E_{EM} or EM energy) is the E carried by electromagnetic waves (EM waves). We know that the photons are the energy carriers of the EM waves (EM radiations). Although photons are massless, causing the EM waves to carry *no* mass (M), they (the EM waves) carry E, named the EM energy. It is noteworthy that photons also carry momentum (mass × velocity) because they can apply pressure to a system.

Light rays (beams), gamma rays, X-rays, infrared rays, microwaves, and radio waves are some forms of EM energy.

9. ELECTRON BINDING ENERGY

The electron binding energy (E_{EB}) is the minimum energy (E) needed to remove an electron from its electron shell (simply **shell**) during a chemical reaction. For example, the E_{EB} for removing an electron from the valance shell of a chloride ion (Cl^-), with an electric charge of -1, is the amount of E needed to remove that electron from a neutral chlorine atom. In this example, the E_{EB} of the chlorine atom has the same quantity as the electron affinity of that atom. [Remember that electronegatively-charged electrons remain in their shell because of the electropositively-charged nucleus.]

10. GIBBS FREE ENERGY

The Gibbs free energy (E_G, simply **Gibbs energy**) is one form of energy (E) that was introduced by Willard Gibbs (1839 – 1903, an American physical chemist) in the 1870s. The E_G is defined to be the amount of free E of a heat-involving (thermodynamic) closed system that can perform **useful** (mechanical) work (W) at constant temperature ($\Delta T = 0$) and constant pressure ($\Delta P = 0$), the usual laboratory conditions to run a test.

[Note: In other reference books, the Gibbs free energy is usually shown by the letter G (for Gibbs). In this book, the Gibs free energy is denoted by the symbol E_G to incorporate E for energy and G for Gibbs.]

Comparing the definition of E_G and E_H (Helmholtz free energy), we can see that the main difference between them is that the E_G is related to the heat-involving closed systems. At the same time, E_H is related to the non-heat-involving systems. So said, E_G can be used for a physical process (like a heat transfer process or phase change process), while E_H can be used for a chemical process (like a chemical reaction).

The E_G (in kJ, kilo Joule) of a heat-involving closed system (like a tank with warm water) can be calculated by the system's enthalpy (H, in kJ), its temperature (T, in K, Kelvin), and entropy (S, in kJ/K).

$$E_G = H - T.S \quad (5)$$

The term H in this equation is the system's **usable** enthalpy (energy), while $T.S$ is the system's **unusable** energy. So said, H can be used to perform W, while $T.S$ *cannot*. For an isothermic system (*no*-temperature-change system) thus, $E_G = H$ equates to the useful W available in that system.

Under the topic of ENTHALPY, we proved that $H = E_I + P.V = E_Q + P.V$, where E_I is internal energy and V is the volume of the system. Thus, the previous equation becomes

$$E_G = E_I + P.V - T.S \quad (6)$$

Like enthalpy, E_G is often used as its ΔE_G form (called Δ form or integrated form of E_G), which represents the change of E_G from an initial condition (E_{G1}) to a final condition (E_{G2}) in that system. This is because changes in E_G are useful in expressing the conditions under which a process proceeds. Thus,

$$\Delta E_G = \Delta E_I + P.\Delta V - T.\Delta S \quad (7)$$

Applying derivation to this equation gives us the differential (final-minus-initial) form (*d* form) of E_G when V is changed by an infinitesimal (tiny) amount.

$$dE_G = dE_I + P.dV + V.dP - T.dS - S.dT \quad (8)$$

At constant T, the term $T.dS$ becomes zero, so this equation becomes,

$$dE_G = dE_I + P.dV - T.dS \quad (9)$$

This equation tells us that the E_G of liquid increases as its P increases. If, thus, we measure a system's E_G at two different pressures (P_1 and P_2, where $P_2 > P_1$) at constant T, the E_{G2} (E_G at P_2) is given as

$$E_{G2} = E_{G1} + \int_{P1}^{P2} VdP \quad (10)$$

The E_G of a gas is more dependent on P than that of a liquid. For an ideal gas, the E_G of the gas is given as

$$E_G = E_{G2} - E_{G1} = n.R.TLn\frac{P_2}{P_1} \quad (11)$$

In this equation, the n is the amount of the gas (given in mole), the R is the ideal gas constant, and the Ln is the sign of a natural logarithm.

11. GRAVITATIONAL POTENTIAL ENERGY

As one type of energy (E), the gravitational potential energy (E_{GP}, simply **gravitational energy**) of a system is related to the mass (M), potential energy (E_P), and gravitational acceleration (a_g) that are applied to that system. Because a system's E_P is related to its height (h), its E_{GP} can be formulized using its M, a_g, and h.

$$E_{GP} = M.a_g.h \quad (12)$$

As energy, E_{GP} can perform W (work), known as the W_G (gravitational work), on another system to elevate it to the h against a_g. For example, a system held above the floor has E_{GP} because it can work (W) on another system as it falls. Similarly, water stored behind a dam has a lot of E_{GP} to drive a generator.

In a pumping system, E_{GP} is the E used to overcome the change in height (called the **liquid head**).

Example 1 on E_{GP}

Given: A man raises a book (like this one) with a mass of 1.2 kg against a_g to a height (h) of 1.5 m above a desk. The surface of the desk is 0.7 m above the floor's surface.

Wanted: 1) E_{GP} of the book relative to the desk, 2) E_{GP} of the book relative to the floor

Using gravitational acceleration (a_g) of 9.81 m/s^2 and h = 1.5 m, E_{GP} of the book becomes

$$E_{GP} = M.a_g.h = 1.2 \times 9.81 \times 1.5 = 17.6 \text{ kg(m/s}^2\text{)m} = \text{kgm}^2/\text{s}^2 = 17.6 \text{ J}$$

In the second case, h = 1.5 + 0.7 = 2.2 m above the floor, so E_{GP} of the book is

$$E_{GP} = 1.2 \times 9.81 \times 2.2 = 25.9 \text{ J}$$

Example 2 on E_{GP}

Given: A solution is pumped at 110 kg/s from a tank to another tank located 20 m above the first tank

Wanted: Increase in potential energy rate relative to the first tank

$$\Delta\dot{E_P} = \dot{M}.a_g(h_2 - h_1) = 110 \times 9.81[(0 - (-20)] = 21560\ (kg/s)(m/s^2)(m) = kg.m^2/(s^2.s) = J/s$$

12. HEAT ENERGY

As the most important type of energy (E), the heat energy (E_Q; see Note below) is the E in transfer (transit), so a system can absorb or release it from another system in one of three ways: 1) By convection in liquids, 2) By conduction in solids, and 3) By radiation in space.

The E_Q between the two systems is the **heat content** (heat-energy value or enthalpy value) that moves the Q (heat) from the hotter system to the colder system because of the temperature difference (ΔT) between the systems. Thus, *no* heat transfer occurs ($\Delta E_Q = 0$) between two systems if their temperatures are the same.

[Note: **Heat energy** is shown in this book by the symbol E_Q and **heat** by Q, while in some other books, heat energy is usually shown by Q, and heat is *not* symbolized. Showing heat energy by E_Q and heat by Q is helpful because this symbolization indicates the minor differences between these two words. It is, however, also important to know that the term **heat energy** is traditionally called **heat** and scientifically enthalpy (H) or enthalpy change (ΔH), so $E_Q \approx Q \approx H \approx \Delta H$.]

The following are there (3) important properties of heat energy (E_Q):

- E_Q is easy to feel because of its association with temperature (T),
- E_Q can be viewed as sensible and latent forms of energy because it can change both a system's T (so-called sensible heat) and that system's phase (so-called latent heat), and
- E_Q is a path quantity, so a system's E_Q *cannot* be calculated unless its path (from initial to final) is known.

1 kg of a compound (like water or stainless steel) needs a different E_Q to increase its T by 1°C. The amount of E_Q needed to increase the T of 1 kg of a mass (M) by 1°C at constant atmospheric pressure (P_{Atm} = 1 Atm), without phase change, is called specific heat capacity (C_Q, simply **heat capacity**).

$$E_Q = M.C_Q.\Delta T = M.C_Q(T_2 - T_1) \quad (13)$$

This is known as the heat-energy equation, which can also be written in the rate form as

$$\dot{E}_Q = \dot{M}.C_Q.\Delta T = \dot{M}.C_Q(T_2 - T_1) \quad (14)$$

As a system's internal energy can be changed by a certain amount of E_Q or W (work), these quantities (E_Q and W) are equivalent. While both E_Q and W are energies, two differences exist between them:

- E_Q is caused by a ΔT, while W is caused by force (F), and
- E_Q is lower-quality energy, while W is higher-quality energy.

When a fuel (oil, coke, coal, or natural gas) goes under a combustion reaction in a steam boiler, its energy (in the form of **chemical potential energy**) converts to E_Q, which is absorbed by the water to produce steam. This happens because the chemical bonds of fuel molecules break to release energy. For example, some E_Q is released when in a boiler's furnace; carbon in natural gas reacts with oxygen in the air.

$$1\ kg\ C + 1\ kg\ O_2 \rightarrow CO_2 + 49\ 000\ kJ\ E_Q$$

This tells us that the enthalpy of combustion (H_C) of carbon (*not* natural gas) is 49 000 kJ/kg (= 21 066 BTU/Lb in US units). This also tells us that the reaction is heat-releasing (an exothermic reaction), a negative reaction (because it releases E_Q).

13. HELMHOLTZ FREE ENERGY

As one type of energy (E), the Helmholtz free energy (E_H, simply **Helmholtz energy**) was introduced by Hermann Helmholtz (1821–1894, a German physicist). The E_H is defined as the amount of free E of a non-heat-involving (non-thermodynamic) system that can perform **usefully** (mechanical or non-expansion) work (W) at constant temperature ($\Delta T = 0$) and constant pressure ($\Delta P = 0$), the usual lab condition to run a test.

[Note: The Helmholtz free energy is usually shown by the letter A (from the German *Arbeit* for work). In this book, the Helmholtz free energy is denoted by the symbol E_H to incorporate E for energy and H for Helmholtz.]

Comparing the definition of E_H and E_G (Gibbs free energy), one can see that the main difference between them is that the E_H concerns non-heat-involving systems, while E_G concerns heat-involving systems. So said, E_H can be used for a chemical process (like a chemical reaction), while E_G can be used for a physical process (like heat transfer process or phase change process).

Consider the simple chemical reaction of A + B → C + D in a chemical reactor (a closed system). The reaction's E_H (in kJ) can be determined by using its internal energy (E_I, in kilo Joule, kJ), its temperature (T, in Kelvin, K), and its entropy (S, in kJ/K).

$$E_H = E_I - T.S \tag{15}$$

The term E_I in this equation is the system's usable energy, while $T.S$ is its unusable energy (E). In other words, E_I is the amount of E that is used to perform the reaction, while $T.S$ does *not*.

Like enthalpy, ChemEng is *not* so much concerned with the E_H of a system as it is with the changes in E_H; that is, ΔE_H (called integrated form or Δ form), which is changes between two situations (final state, E_{H2}, and initial state, E_{H1}) in that system. This is because changes in E_H are useful in expressing the conditions under which a chemical reaction occurs. Thus,

$$\Delta E_H = -\Delta P.V - T.\Delta S \tag{16}$$

Taking differential in this equation gives us the differential (final-minus-initial) form (d form) of E_H when V is changed by an infinitesimal (tiny) amount.

$$dE_H = -P.dV - V.dP - T.dS - S.dT \tag{17}$$

At constant T and P, this equation becomes,

$$dE_H = -P.dV - T.dS \tag{18}$$

14. INTERACTION ENERGY

As one type of energy (E), the interaction energy (E_{IN}) is formed by **interaction** between two (or more) systems being under study. The E_{IN} can contribute to a system's **total energy** (defined under this topic). [The word **interaction** used here is the effect that two (or more) interacted systems have on one another.]

In the case of interaction of two systems, A and B, the E_{IN} can be calculated from the E of the interacted system [shown as E (A, B)], the E of A before being interacted [shown as $E(A)$], and the E of B before being interacted [shown as $E(B)$].

$$\Delta E_{IN} = E(A, B) - [E(A) + E(B)] \tag{19}$$

In the case of interaction of N systems, the interacted system's total E_{IN} can be calculated from the generalization of the previous equation.

$$\Delta E_{IN} = E(A_1, A_2, \ldots A_N) - \textstyle\sum_{i=1}^{N} E(A_i) \tag{20}$$

At the molecular level, the E_{IN} is formed by the interaction between the molecules of a compound, so it depends on their location (the *closer* the molecules to each other, the *greater* is the E_{IN} between them).

15. INTERNAL ENERGY

The internal energy (E_I or U in some other textbooks) is the sum of energies that can exist in a **thermodynamic** (heat-involving) **system**. [The kinetic energy (E_K) and potential energy (E_P) of a thermodynamic system are *not* included in this definition because both are the system's external properties related to the system's motion (E_K) and position (E_P). Therefore, the main difference between a system's E_I and E_M (mechanical energy) is that the E_I *cannot* account for changes in a system's E_K and E_P, while the E_M can.]

Instead, in a microscopic system (a system of particles), the E_I is the system's total of E_K and E_P, as the energy of a particle equates to the total of its subparticles energies, which are in the form of E_K and E_P. In addition, subparticles' motion (like rotational motion) in a particle is important in the quantity of that particle's E_I. Solids' molecules move at a much slower speed (U) than fluids' molecules, so their E_I is comparably small. If a solid or fluid is under the heating process, its E_I increases, and therefore, its particles move more rapidly. This increases the temperature (T) of the system (solid or fluid), so a system's T can be used as an estimate for its E_I (the *higher* a system's T, the *higher* is its E_I). Because the E_I of a microscopic system is comprised of E_P and E_K, we can say that such a system's E equates to its E_I.

In a closed thermodynamic system, the following statements can be made about E_I:

- Heat transferred at constant P equates, by definition, to ΔH (enthalpy change), while the heat transferred at constant V (volume) is ΔE_I (internal-energy change).
- If E_Q is added to a closed system from its outside and performs W (work) on its outsides, its E_I equates to the E_Q given to the system, minus the W performed on its outsides.

$$E_I = E_Q - W \tag{21}$$

If both E_Q and W are added to a closed system from the system's outsides, the system's E_I becomes

$$E_I = E_Q + W \tag{22}$$

And for an infinitesimal (tiny) change in the situation, the differential form (d form) is used.

$$dE_I = dE_Q \pm dW \tag{23}$$

These three equations define the Thermodynamic First Law. When an adiabatic process (a process with *no* heat transfer) occurs in a closed thermodynamic system (energy can enter or leave the system, but mass *cannot*), the system's E_I can be calculated from W done on that system to change it from one state to another.

$$\Delta E_I = W \tag{24}$$

The symbol Δ represents the quantity of E_I from an initial state (E_{I1}) to a final state (E_{I2}), so $\Delta E_I = E_{I2} - E_{I1}$. The previous equation tells us the following:

- The W (work) is done ON the system by its surroundings,
- The W and E_I are **positive** when W is done on the system by its surroundings, and
- The system's E_I (internal energy) increases when W is done on it by its surroundings.

The other form of the previous equation is

$$\Delta E_I = -W \tag{25}$$

This equation, instead, tells us that,

- The W is done BY the system on its surroundings,
- The W and E_I are **negative** when W is done by the system on its surroundings, and
- The system's E_I (internal energy) decreases when it does some W on its surroundings.

Usually, the internal energy is expressed in molar quantity to give the change (Δ) in molar internal energy (ΔE_I) in J/mole, where J is for Joule.

16. IONIZATION ENERGY

Study ELECTRONEGATIVITY, ELECTRON AFFINITY, AND IONIZATION ENERGY (as these topics are electron-energy-related subjects).

17. KINETIC ENERGY

As an important type of energy (*E*), the kinetic energy (E_K) of a moving system is the *E* related to that system's mass (*M*) and velocity (*V*).

$$E_K = \frac{1}{2}M.V^2 \quad (26)$$

If *M* is in kg, *V* in m/s, the E_K becomes in kg.m²/s² = J (Joule). [The factor ½ in the equation of E_K is used because a system moves at an **average velocity** (which is ½ of maximum velocity). This factor makes the E_K compatible with other forms of *E*.]

A moving ball, a speeding car, a liquid flowing in a pipe, and the steam entering a steam turbine all have E_K. The E_K of a rotating system, which has a moment of inertia of *I* and rotational velocity of *ω* (omega), is

$$E_K = \frac{1}{2}I.\omega^2 \quad (27)$$

E_Q also depends on the **observer** that measures it. If, say, a car passes you (the observer) at a high rate of speed, you measure a lot of E_K. But if you were in that car, you measured the car's E_K as zero (because the car is motionless relative to you).

At the atomic level, E_K is the *E* related to an atom's motion. Assume that one atom of iron (Fe) with a mass of 9.296×10^{-26} kg/56 nucleons (=1.66×10^{-27} kg/nucleon) moves at a velocity of 8×10^4 m/s. The E_K of that iron atom is extremely small.

$$E_K = \frac{1}{2}1.66 \times 10^{-27} \times (8 \times 10^4)^2 = 5.3 \times 10^{-18}\ \text{kg.m}^2/\text{s}^2 = \text{J}$$

If that atom of Fe would travel at the speed of light constant ($c = 3\times10^8$ m/s), its E_K would still be small.

$$E_K = \frac{1}{2}1.66 \times 10^{-27} \times (3 \times 10^8)^2 = 7.5 \times 10^{-11}\ \text{J}$$

Example 1 on E_K

Given: A 72-kg person runs at 4 m/s

Wanted: Person's E_K relative to the ground and person's E_K if he doubles the speed (*U*) to 8 m/s

$$E_{K1} = \frac{1}{2}M.U^2 = \frac{1}{2}\times 72 \times 4^2 = 576\ \text{kg.m}^2/\text{s}^2 = 576 \qquad E_{K2} = \frac{1}{2}\times 72 \times 8^2 = 2304\ \text{J}$$

In the first case, the person's E_K is 576 J, and in the second case is 2304 J. As you see, E_K became squared of the speed, so each doubling of speed creates a fourfold increase in E_K.

Example 2 on E_K

Given: A 200 mm pipe in which water flows at a volumetric flow rate ($\dot{V} = V/t$) of 220 m³/h

Wanted: Kinetic-energy rate (E_K/t) of the water flow, where density (*D*) of water is 1000 kg/m³

The cross-sectional area (*A*) of the pipe with a 200 mm (= 0.2 m) diameter is

$$A = \pi\frac{d^2}{4} = 3.14 \times \frac{0.2^2}{4} = 3.14 \times 10^{-2}\ \text{m}^2$$

The flow's linear velocity (*V*), mass (*M*), and kinetic-energy rate are

$$V = \frac{\dot{V}}{A} = \frac{220}{3.14\times10^{-2}} = 7006\ \text{m/h}\ (= 2\ \text{m/s}) \qquad M = V.D = 220 \times 1000 = 220000\ \text{kg}$$

$$\dot{E}_K = \frac{E_K}{t} = \frac{1}{2}\times\frac{M,V^2}{t} = \frac{220000\times2^2}{2\times3600} = 30\ \text{kg.m}^2/(\text{s}^2.\text{s}) = \text{J/s}$$

18. MASS ENERGY

Mass energy (E_M, also called **rest mass energy** or **matter energy**) is an at-rest system's energy. Einstein's equation ($E_M = M.c^2$) gives the E_M, where M is for mass and c is the speed-of-light constant). Knowing the following brief points about E_M (mass energy) is important:

- All forms of energy act as E_M when they are at rest. Because of this fact, the mass energy in Einstein's equation is generally shown by E, the symbol for energy, and rarely by E_M. So, $E = E_M$ when talking about an at rest (non-moving) system.
- E_M is distinct from other types of E because a tiny amount of excess nuclear mass (M_{EN}) has a large amount of E_M stored in it.
- E_M is *not* usually considered in ordinary calculations because it is *not* an easily **reachable** (accessible) E.
- Based on Einstein's equation, adding 90 MJ (= 25 W/h) of any form of E to a system increases its M by 1 μg (micrograms) without adding any M to that system.

19. MECHANICAL ENERGY

Mechanical energy (E_M) is the energy (E) related to a system's motion and position. Thus, a system's E_M is the sum of its kinetic energy (E_K, the energy related to a system's motion) and potential energy (E_P, the energy related to a system's elevation). Thus, the E_M can account for the changes in E_K and E_P of a system, while internal energy (E_I, a system's sum of energies, except E_K and E_P) *cannot*. However, a system's E_M can be converted into the E_I of that system, but it is *not* possible to recover all the E_I and get the same amount of E_M back.

20. NUCLEAR ENERGY

Nuclear energy (E_N, also called **nuclear binding energy**) is the energy (E) that exists in an atom's nucleus to hold the protons and neutrons together. In a nuclear reaction, the protons and neutrons (collectively called **nucleons**) are detached to release a large amount of E_N in the form of E_Q (heat energy).

The two (2) main differences between E_N and E_{EB} (electron binding energy) are outlined next.

- E_N participates in a nuclear reaction, while E_{EB} participates in a chemical reaction. Both the nucleus and electrons of an atom participate in a nuclear reaction. In a chemical reaction, the electrons are the only ones that participate in the reaction.
- E_N is much greater (on the order of million times) than the E_{EB}, as protons and neutrons are attached by the strong nuclear force (F_{SN}).

[The term **nuclear energy** is used in nuclear reactions, while in the chemical reactions, the term **electron binding energy** is used.]

An atom nucleon's mass (M) is greater than its nucleus. According to Einstein's equation ($E = M.c^2$), this extra mass, the excess nuclear mass (M_{EN}, simply **excess mass**), equals that atom's E_N. The tiny amount of an atom's M_{EN}, formed during a nuclear reaction, transforms into a large amount of E_N because the speed of light constant (c, speed of light in a vacuum) is too large. [An atom produces a tiny amount of E_N, but when an enormous number of atoms (in trillions) split, the produced E_N is huge. If 1 kg of U-235 splits, it produces 57.4×10^9 kJ of E_N, so its enthalpy of combustion (H_C) is 57.4×10^9 kJ/kg. This is about 2.1 million times more than the energy released from burning 1 kg of coal (with the H_C of about 27 000 kJ/kg).]

Some nuclei release E_N when they **split** in the nuclear fission process, while others release E_N when joining the nuclear fusion process.

The following are helpful to know about nuclear energy (E_N):

- The amount of E_N in the nuclei of different atoms is *not* the same. This explains why some nuclear reactions release energy while others absorb energy.
- The element with the highest E_N is nickel-62.

In its useful industrial application, E_N is released in the nuclear power plants, mainly by the nuclear fission process, which is the fission (split) of the nucleus of a radioactive element (nuclide). This energy generates E_Q, which can be used in a turbine to produce electricity. Presently, uranium-235 (U-235, an isotope of uranium) is the most common nuclide used as nuclear fuel in the reactors of nuclear power plants. U-235 can strongly absorb **thermal neutrons** (the neutrons that sustain a nuclear chain reaction) to release a huge amount of nuclear energy. [The nuclear energy released from each stage of nuclear fission in a nuclear power plant is about 200 MeV (million electronvolts), where 1 MeV = 1.61×10^{-13} joules (J).]

21. PARTICLE SELF-ENERGY

Particle self-energy (E_{PS}, where subscripts *P* is for particle and *S* is for self; simply called **self-energy**) is one form of energy (*E*) that exists in an elementary particle (a massive or massless particle) as a result of interactions with a system, in which it functions. The E_{PS} is related to a particle's changes in a system. For example, an electron moving in a particulate shell (system) has a different E_{PS} than if it jumps to another shell (another system). Because of the E_{PS}, an electron can repulse (keep away) itself from its atom's nucleus.

22. PHOTON ENERGY

Photon energy (E_{Ph}, also called **radiant energy**, **quantum energy**, **light energy**, or **solar energy**) is the energy (*E*) of a photon, the quantum particle (a particle with *no* subparticle) of light, and other electromagnetic radiations. [Photon energy is shown in this book by the symbol E_{Ph} to include the symbols for both energy (*E*) and photon (shown by subscript *Ph*). In most books, it is shown just by the symbol *E*.]

The photon energy depends on the frequency (*f*) of that photon's wave (the higher the *f* of the wave, the greater the E_{PH}), so Planck's equation can express it.

$$E_{Ph} = h.f \tag{28}$$

Because *f* and λ (wavelength) of a photon's wave are related by $\lambda.f = c$, Planck's equation can be written as

$$E_{Ph} = \frac{h.c}{\lambda} \tag{29}$$

In this equation, which is known as the Planck-Einstein equation, the *h* is given in J.s, the *c* (speed of light constant) in m/s, and λ in m, so E_{Ph} becomes in (J.s)(m/s)/m = J (Joule).

Photon energy (E_{Ph}) also relates to the color of the light. For example, blue light consists of higher-frequency photons, so photons have more energy than red ones.

For example, a solar boiler in a solar power plant uses the Sun's solar energy to convert water into steam. The steam drives a steam turbine (simply **turbine**), which drives an electric generator (simply **generator**) to produce electricity. [A typical solar power plant produces about 300 MW/h of electricity.]

23. POTENTIAL ENERGY

The potential energy (E_P or *U*) of a system is related to its height (*h*, **elevation**) and gravitational acceleration (a_g = 9.8 m/s^2 on Earth) applied to it.

$$E_P = a_g.h \tag{30}$$

For example, falling water (system) from a dam has some E_P because of its height from the ground (a reference system). The E_P required by a pump to overcome a change in height during pumping a liquid is the product of a_g multiplied by the pump's liquid head ($h_2 - h_1$, in m or Ft).

$$E_P = a_g(h_2 - h_1) \tag{31}$$

As its name indicates, E_P has the potential (ability) to do the following:

- To be converted into other forms of energy; for example, the E_P of the falling water from a dam can be converted to electric energy (E_E) in a turbine.
- To do work by bringing a system into motion.

In addition to height, E_P can be in many forms, like pressure and stress (load in the form of force). Instead, kinetic energy (E_K) can be only in the form of velocity. As shown in Figure 9, water stored in an elevated tank contains E_P as pressure energy (E_{Pr}), but it contains only E_K when it gets to a lower-level elevation.

The E_P exists in every chemical substance particle (atom, molecule, or ion). In solid particles, almost half of the energy is E_P, and the other half is E_K. In gas particles, almost all the energy is in E_K (because of much intense particle movement of gases).

At the atomic level, E_P is the sum of an atom's attractive energy (E_A) and repulsive energy (E_R). In addition, it causes the conversion of atoms to ions when it acts as ionization energy (E_{Ion}) in a reaction, so

$$E_P = E_A + E_R + E_{Ion} \tag{32}$$

Potential energy (E_P) is of several kinds, such as the following:

- **Chemical potential energy** (E_{CP}) is related to a system's composition.
- **Electric potential energy** (E_{EP}) equals $1/2C.V^2$, where C is capacitance and V is voltage.
- **Elastic potential energy** (E_{ELP}) equals $1/2K.L^2$, where K is deformation coefficient, and L is length.
- **Magnetic potential energy** (E_{MP}) equals $m.B$, where m is magnetic moment, and B is magnetic field.
- **Gravitational potential energy** (E_{GP}) is related to a system's mass, gravitational acceleration, and height.
- **Surface potential energy** (E_{SP}) is related to microscopic parameters, such as the length (L) of the chemical bonds in a chemical reaction.

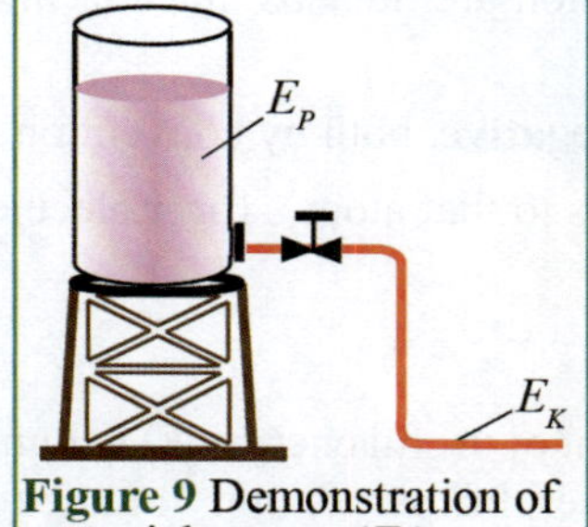

Figure 9 Demonstration of potential energy (E_p) and kinetic energy (E_K)

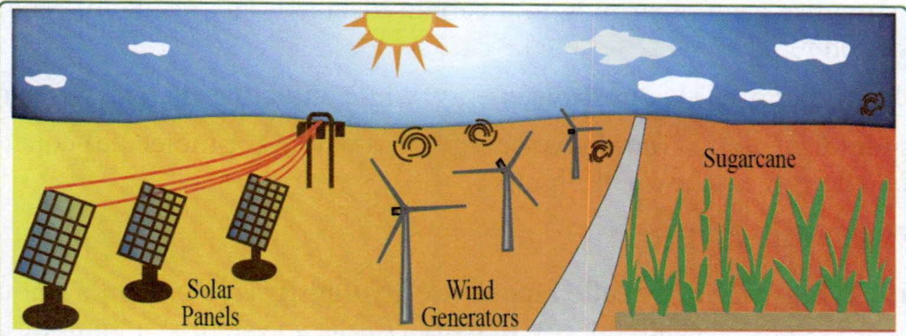

Figure 10 Three important resources of renewable energy; sunlight, wind, and biomasses

24. PRESSURE ENERGY

Pressure energy (E_{Pr}) is one kind of energy (E) that is related to the pressure (P) of a moving fluid (liquid or gas). It is mainly used in Bernoulli's equation to overcome the density change (ΔD) when a liquid moves from point 1 to 2. In a liquid flow process, E_{Pr} can be expressed as

$$E_{Pr} = \frac{\Delta P}{D} \tag{33}$$

If P is in N/m^2, D in kg/m^3, the E_{Pr} becomes in (N/m^2)/(kg/m^3) = (N.m)/kg = J/kg (the unit of specific energy).

25. RENEWABLE ENERGY

Renewable energy (E_{Re}) is the energy produced from some natural resources, such as solar (sunlight), wind, biomass, and geothermal (heat generated deep in the Earth). See Figure 10. [The word **nonrenewable energy** refers to oil, natural gas, coal, coke, or nuclear energy.] Knowing the next brief points about E_{Re} is important:

- Its resources exist in all countries, unlike fossil fuels that exist only in a limited number of countries.
- It is mainly used in industry as heat energy to produce heat and electricity or used in cars as fuel.
- It accounts for about 20% of the world's electricity production and is growing considerably.
- The world's largest geothermal power plant is in the US of America, with 750 MW/h.

- The world's largest solar power plant is in the USA, with a capacity of 350 MW/h.
- Denmark produces approximately half of its electricity need from wind energy.
- Brazil is one of the advanced countries in E_{Re} with the production of bioethanol from sugarcane.
- Since the first energy crisis in 1973, which has notably affected every household and industry, the study of renewable energy has been the world's hottest political subject.

[Note: Instead of the term renewable energy **resources**, some incorrectly use the word renewable energy **sources**. The word **resource** means a supply that can be used, like when saying, "a country's main resources are oil and coal." Instead, the word **source** means a place from where something comes, like saying, "Australia is one of the largest sources of iron globally," or saying corn and sugarcane are the largest sources of bioethanol.]

26. REPULSIVE ENERGY

The repulsive energy (E_R or U_R) is the energy (E) that keeps the atoms (or molecules) of a chemical compound (simply **compound**) apart. When two atoms join, the E_R is inversely proportional to the separation distance (L, the separation length or bond length) of those atoms (the *closer* the atoms, the *stronger* is E_R and, consequently, the *more* they repel each other).

$$E_R = \frac{b}{L^n} \quad (34)$$

Here, b and n (known as **repulsive exponents**) are constants. The constant n (which depends on the outer surface of an atom or molecule) has a value of 1 for atoms and 6 for molecules.

Atoms repulse each other only to a certain distance. The results of repulsion are nucleus–nucleus and electron–electron repulsions.

Repulsive energy (E_R) is **positive** energy, while attractive energy (E_A) is **negative**, both by convention.

The sum of E_R and E_A (attractive energy) in an atom (or molecule) equates to that atom's (or molecule's) E_P (potential energy), as shown in Figure 7.

27. SPECIFIC ENERGY

Specific energy (E_{SP}, also called **mass-energy density**) is a system's amount of useful energy (E) per unit mass (M) of that system. Instead, **energy density** (E_D) is a system's amount of useful E per its unit volume (V). For example, the E_{SP} of ethanol is about 27 000 kJ/ kg, and its E_D is about 21 000 kJ/L. [The term **useful energy** refers to accessible energy, so inaccessible energy, such as **rest mass energy**, is *not* included in this definition.]

In most cases, the specific energy, and in some cases, energy density, is used to express the energy of fuels and heat-related quantities, like specific enthalpy, Gibbs free energy, and Helmholtz free energy.

The SI unit of specific energy (E_{SP}) is kJ/kg, and its US unit is BTU/Lb, where 1 kJ/kg = 0.43 BTU/Lb. And that of energy density (E_D) is kJ/L and BTU/Ga. As said earlier, the E_{SP} of ethanol is about 27 000 kJ/ kg, and its E_D is about 21 000 kJ/L.

[Note: The terms **specific energy** and **specific enthalpy** (specific heat) are used equally to compare the strength of fuels. For example, the specific energy of LNG (liquefied natural gas) is 2.4 times greater than CNG (compressed natural gas) and 0.6 times greater than diesel fuel.]

28. SURFACE ENERGY

A surface energy (E_S or γ, gamma; also known as **cohesive energy**) in a condensed substance (a liquid or a solid) occurs because its surface molecules contain more energy (E) than its under-the-surface (bulk) molecules. Thus, the excess E in the surface molecules of a substance is its E_S.

A good way to view the E_S is to relate it to the needed work (W) to remove a liquid's molecules from its surface and build a new surface. Based on this analogy (a simple example to understand a concept), we can say that a liquid's surface molecules need less W to be removed than its bulk molecules (because the surface molecules have fewer nearest neighbors than those in bulk). So, some W is needed to move the liquid's molecules from the bulk to the surface. Thus, a new surface with an extra surface is formed. The W needed to form the new surface is proportional to the area (A) of the new surface by a proportionality constant named the E_S.

$$W = E_S.A \tag{35}$$

$$E_S = \frac{W}{A} \tag{36}$$

The E_S creates a new crystal surface during the crystal growth in crystallization. At a given M (mass), finer crystals have a larger surface area than the coarser ones, so the E_S per unit M of fine crystals is greater.

[Surface energy (E_S or γ) and surface tension (γ) are identical quantities, except that the E_S applies to liquids and solids, while γ (gamma) applies only to liquids. When, thus, talking about a liquid, its E_S and γ have the same meaning, the same value, and the same SI unit (or US unit). Both E_S and γ are expressed in J/m^2 (= N/m), where N (Newton) is the SI unit of force (F) and m^2 (square meter) is the SI unit of area. Both E_S and γ of water at 25°C are 0.07 J/m^2 (= 0.07 N/m). A sugar crystal (a solid) E_S is 0.22 J/m^2.]

29. TOTAL ENERGY

Total energy (E_T) is the sum of all forms of E that exist in a system, like a thermodynamic system, an atom, or a quantum particle (a particle with *no* subparticle). When, however, the amount of a system's internal energy (E_{Int}), kinetic energy (E_K), and potential energy (E_P) is far greater than the other energies, the sum of the E_{Int}, E_K, and E_P can be taken as the E_T of a closed system (energy can enter or leave the system, but mass *cannot*).

$$E_T = E_{Int} + E_K + E_P \tag{37}$$

Two ways exist to increase a thermodynamic system's E_T; to give the system some heat energy (E_Q) or do work (W) on it. Similarly, E_T decreases when the system releases some E_Q or does some W. This statement is the expression of the Thermodynamic First Law for a closed system.

$$E_T = E_Q + W \tag{38}$$

The sign of E_Q is + if heat enters a system and – if heat leaves the system. The sign rule applies to W in the same way. Thus, it is better to write the previous equation as

$$E_T = \pm E_Q \pm W \tag{39}$$

For a condensed substance (liquid or solid) in a closed system at constant P_{Atm}, the work term ($W = P.V$) can be ignored. Similarly, the E_K and E_P are unimportant here, so we arrive at the First Law's **practical form**.

$$E_T = E_{Int} = E_Q \tag{40}$$

This equation can be written in the differential form (*d* form) for very small changes of state,

$$dE_T = dE_{Int} = dE_Q \tag{41}$$

[A bound system is typically at a lower E level than its unbound components, as, according to Einstein's equation ($E = M.c^2$), a system's E_T decreases if its total mass (M) decreases.]

30. VACUUM ENERGY

Vacuum energy (E_V) is one form of E in space in the entire Universe. Some physicists think that E_V comes from electron pairs that exist in space but destroy in a short time, so they *cannot* be observed. However, the effects of E_V can be observed experimentally in a **spontaneous-emission process**. An electron undergoes an excited energy state to be changed to a state with lower energy and, thus, emits (releases) a photon with E_{PH}.

31. ZERO-POINT ENERGY

Zero-point energy (E_Z) is the lowest energy (E) that a quantum system contains. E_Z is also defined as the E of a quantum system in a ground energy state. Instead, an excited energy state is a state with E greater than E_Z. So defined, every quantum system contains E_Z. [A quantum system's E_Z constantly changes, as Heisenberg's uncertainty principle describes.]

E-72

ENERGY BALANCE

Energy balance, in ChemEng, is a series of calculations to determine the usage of heat energy (E_Q, simply heat and scientifically enthalpy) entering and leaving a device (like an evaporator), a station (like an evaporating station with more than one evaporator), or a chemical process plant (a facility with more stations). [The terms **energy balance**, **heat balance**, and **heat-energy balance** are often used equally.] For example, the energy-balance report of a boiler-house station shows how much fuel (oil, coal, or natural gas) is used each day to produce steam for running the plant's steam turbines, evaporation station, and heating station. Then, the amount of energy usage is expressed per unit of the raw material processed to develop a number that can be used as the base for comparing the plant's day-to-day E_Q usage. Usually, in a chemical plant, the energy used to produce steam is calculated per 100 t of the raw material processed by that plant. Typically, the number in a beet-sugar plant is about 10 MW/h per 100 t of sugarbeet processed.

Energy-balance calculations are based on the following:

- Conservation of energy (energy remains unchanged in a completely isothermic system),
- E_Q and ΔH (enthalpy change) equality ($E_Q = \Delta H$), as proved under ENTHALPY,
- Specific enthalpy (H_{Sp}, energy per unit mass; in kJ/kg or BTU/Lb).

Based on these points, the First Law's mathematical expression can express energy transfer from one system to the next as E_Q, which has the same meaning as ΔH when a process occurs at constant P ($\Delta P = 0$).

$$(E_Q)_{In} = (E_Q)_{Out} + (E_Q)_{Ac} \quad (1)$$

Ac subscript is for accumulation (see Note 1). The practical First-Law equation for an open system (see Note 2), which is at a **steady-state condition** [*no* accumulation, $(E_Q)_{Ac} = 0$], becomes

$$(E_Q)_{In} = (E_Q)_{Out} \quad (2)$$

[Note 1: Instead of the word **accumulation of energy**, some use the word **loss of energy**. This is incorrect because energy *cannot* be lost. But part of it *cannot* be utilized because it leaves the system (poor isolation), stays in the energy source, converts into less-useful forms of energy, or all the above. For example, when some reactions occur in a steam boiler between the components of fuel and oxygen, about 85% of the fuel's E_Q is absorbed by the boiler's water. The rest is released from the boiler's stack or stays in fuel (because of incomplete combustion).]

[Note 2: Most of the systems dealing with energy balance are **open systems** (more on this under OPEN SYSTEM.]

[Note 3: To realize how energy balancing is important in the process economics (profitability) of a chemical plant, consider that energy cost is usually the second **operating cost** (after the raw-material cost) in most chemical plants. The only way to judge whether the energy is used efficiently is by conducting an energy balance from a chemical plant, or even better, from its heat-user stations (process stations), like the evaporation station. That is why energy balance is one of the two most important calculations in ChemEng; the other one is mass balance.]

[Note 4: Today, energy balancing is performed by computer daily in almost all chemical plants because 1) It helps the profitability of such a facility, and 2) It is a useful tool for keeping track of the use of energy resources (oil, gas, and coal) and their environmental impact.]

[Note 5: Energy balancing of a process requires a particular procedure that fits that given process. This is why heat balancing is discussed separately for different processes in this book. For example, you can find heat balancing under condensation, evaporation, evaporative-cooling, heating, liquid flow processes, and more. Studying the energy-balance section of these topics can improve your skill in the energy balancing subjects.]

The two most important areas that need an in-depth energy balance to operate efficiently are the following:

- Energy balance on an existing heat-involved process unit (unit operation),
- Energy balance on a new heat-involved process unit at the time of designing.

To become here a little familiar with a real energy balancing, consider the limekiln of a chemical plant, in which limestone (calcium carbonate, $CaCO_3$) is decomposed by a fuel's heat energy (E_Q) to produce quicklime (CaO) and carbon dioxide gas (CO_2).

$$CaCO_3 \rightarrow CaO + CO_2 + 1812 \text{ kJ of } E_Q$$

This heat-absorbing reaction (endothermic) needs 1812 kJ of E_Q to decompose 1 kg of $CaCO_3$. This energy is most frequently supplied by coke or natural gas. If the plant uses coke, which has an enthalpy of combustion (H_C, or **heat value**) of about 28000 kJ/kg (or 12468 BTU/Lb), the amount of coke needed to decompose 100 kg of $CaCO_3$ will be

$$100 \times \frac{1812}{28000} = 6.5 \qquad [\text{kg}][(\cancel{\text{kJ/kg}})/\cancel{\text{kJ/kg}})] = 6.5 \text{ kg coke (or \% coke on } CaCO_3)$$

This value tells us that the theoretical mixing ratio of $CaCO_3$ to coke is 100 to 6.5. But in normal day-to-day operations, a plant uses an average of 8 to 10 kg coke per 100 kg of limestone. The difference between theoretical and practical values is the amount of heat energy (E_Q) unaccounted for during operation. If, in a day, the plant uses, say, 8.1 kg coke per 100 kg of limestone, the kiln's **heat efficiency** (E_H) will be

$$E_H = \frac{6.5}{8.1} \times 100 = 80\%$$

The remaining 20% is the E_Q loss, from which some remain in CO_2 gas and some escape to the atmosphere. This simple heat balance indicates how a chemical plant controls its limekiln station's heat-energy efficiency. Note that this balance could have been done directly from the amount of limestone and coke and by applying the coke's enthalpy of combustion (H_C); of course, if the plant had the scales for weighing limestone and coke.

Energy Balance on an Open System

We now balance an **open system**, through which E_Q flows in a liquid into and out of a tank at a **steady state** (at a constant mass), as shown in Figure 1. Assume that a mixer performs shaft work (W_S) on the system (the liquid in the tank), so W_S is positive. Putting E_Q, W_S, H (enthalpy), E_K (kinetic energy), and E_P (potential energy) into the practical Thermodynamic-First-Law equation [$(E_Q)_{\text{In}} = (E_Q)_{\text{Out}}$], the system can be balanced as

$$H_1 + E_{K1} + E_{P1} \pm E_Q = H_2 + E_{K2} + E_{P2} \pm W_S \qquad (3)$$

Using Δ sign to show differential (final-minus-initial) form and rearranging Equation 3, we get

$$\Delta(H + E_K + E_P) = \pm E_Q \pm W_S \qquad (4)$$

This equation gets a dot sign (•) to indicate **rate** (the time-based form of a quantity).

$$\Delta(\dot{H} + \dot{E}_K + \dot{E}_P) = \pm \dot{E}_Q \pm \dot{W}_S \qquad (5)$$

Equations 4 and 5 are generally used as a basic energy-balance equation in calculations of **open systems** at a **steady-state** (*no* accumulation or $\dot{M}_{In} = \dot{M}_{Out}$), where $\dot{M}$ is the mass flow rate (mass, M, per time, t). When using such an equation, however, knowing the following 9 points are important:

- In some cases, E_K, and in most cases E_P, are negligibly small so that they can be omitted,
- If heat flows from the system to its surroundings, then a – sign is used in front of E_Q,
- If heat flows from outside to the system, a + sign must be used in front of E_Q,
- When work is done on the surroundings, then a + sign is used in front of W_S,
- When work is done on the system, then a – symbol is used in front of W_S,
- When *no* moving parts exist in the system to perform work, then $W_S = 0$,
- If velocities of entering and leaving streams are the same, then $\Delta E_K = 0$,

- If temperatures of the system and its outsides are the same, then $E_Q = 0$,
- If entering and leaving streams are at the same height, then $\Delta E_P = 0$.

Convention-sign rules sometimes confuse heat balancing, so it is helpful to explain more about them, as outlined next.

- If heat is **added to a system,** E_Q is **positive** (+). When, for example, water absorbs fuel energy in a boiler, it produces steam. In this process, some heat is added to the boiler (the system), so E_Q is +. In other words, the system goes from a lower-enthalpy state to a higher-enthalpy state.
- If heat is **taken from a system**, E_Q is **negative** (−). When, for example, the steam condenses in an evaporator (the system), the condensate takes some E_Q from the evaporator (the system), so E_Q is −. Likewise, in a steam turbine, some E_Q of the steam is taken from the turbine (the system) to act as shaft work (W_S) to turn the shaft, so E_Q is −. [In both cases, in another context, the evaporator and turbine (the systems) go from a higher-enthalpy to a lower-enthalpy state.]
- If work is done **on the system** (by the surroundings), W_S is **positive**. When, for example, steam is pumped into an evaporator (the system), the pump's W_S is +.
- If work is done **on the outside** (by the system), W_S is **negative**. In the turbine example, because work is done on the shaft (the surroundings) by the turbine (the system), W_S is –.

In addition to these cases, the following two more situations may occur with the system:

- If more than one E_Q flow, a W_S, or both exists in the system, the individual values must be added algebraically, and then, the net values of E_Q and W_S are used in Equations 4 and 5.
- If a mass flow rate ($\dot{M}$) enters and leaves a system at a steady-state ($\dot{M}_{In} = \dot{M}_{Out}$), in another context, if the system is open, Equation 5 can be written in the rate form.

$$\dot{M}\Delta(\dot{H} + \dot{E}_K + \dot{E}_P) = \pm\dot{E}_Q \pm \dot{W}_S \quad (6)$$

The next very close-to-reality assumptions are often used to simplify the energy-balance calculations.

- Heat energy equates to enthalpy,
- Temperatures are given in the mean average,
- The effect of the liquid head (h) is mostly negligible,
- As a rule of thumb, 1 kg of steam or vapor can evaporate 1 kg of water,
- Total enthalpy (H, total heat-energy content) is the sum of sensible enthalpy and latent enthalpy, and
- Sensible enthalpy is the enthalpy of a liquid or condensate, latent enthalpy is the enthalpy of vapor, and the total enthalpy is the enthalpy of the steam.

Now, you are in a good position to start calculating some examples of heat balancing. As starting example, we consider a steam turbine as an open and steady-state system, as shown in Figure 2, to calculate its heat-energy balance. So, study the upcoming two Examples.

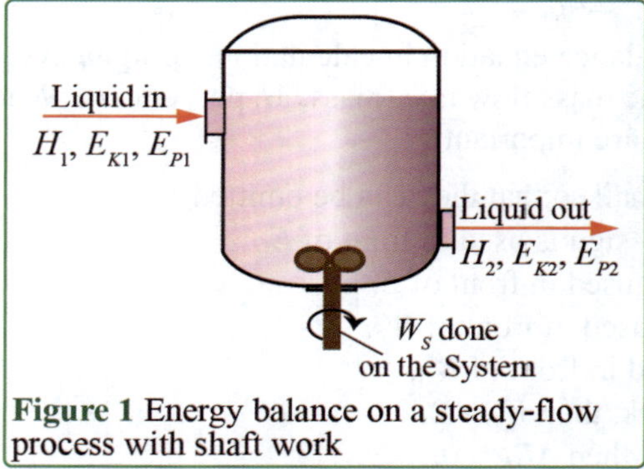

Figure 1 Energy balance on a steady-flow process with shaft work

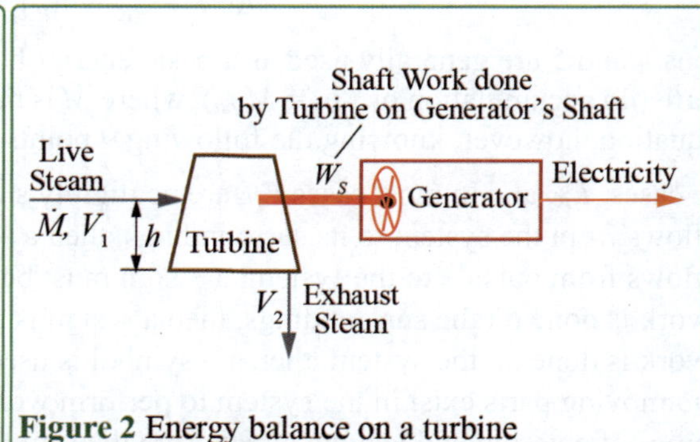

Figure 2 Energy balance on a turbine

Example 1 on Energy Balance

Given: In a turbine (see Figure 2), steam enters and leaves equally. The following values are known:

Steam's flow rate ($\dot{M}$)	2.5 kg/s
Steam's velocity in (V_2)	70 m/s
Steam's velocity out (V_1)	400 m/s
Steam's shaft work rate ($\dot{W}_S$)	1400 kJ/s = 1400 kW/h
Steam rate used by the turbine ($\dot{E}_Q$)	220 kJ/s = 220 kW/h
Steam level difference at inlet and outlet (Δh)	−4 m

Wanted: 1) Rate of enthalpy change of the steam in the turbine ($\Delta\dot{H}$), and 2) Turbine's steam's rate of specific enthalpy change ($\Delta\dot{H}_{Sp}$)

We want to determine the rate of the decrease in steam's heat value ($\dot{H}_1 - \dot{H}_2$) due to the turbine's shaft work (which runs a generator to produce electricity). Because the rates of W_S and E_Q are in kJ/s, we must calculate the rate of kinetic energy ($\dot{E}_K$) and potential energy ($\dot{E}_P$) in kJ/s, also.

The change in kinetic energy rate change ($\Delta\dot{E}_K$) from an initial state (E_{I1}) to a final state is

$$\Delta\dot{E}_K = \frac{\dot{M}}{2}(V_2^2 - V_1^2) = \frac{2.5}{2}(400^2 - 70^2) = 193875\ (\text{kg/s})(\text{m}^2/\text{s}^2)$$

$$= 193875(\text{kg.m}^2/\text{s}^2)/\text{s} = 193875\ \text{J/s} = 194\ \text{kJ/s}$$

Because steam leaves the turbine 4 m below where it was entered, the potential energy rate ($\Delta\dot{E}_P$) would be

$$\Delta\dot{E}_P = \dot{M}.F_g(h_2 - h_1) = 2.5 \times 9.8(0 - 4) = -98$$

$$(\text{kg/s})(\text{m/s}^2)(\text{m}) = -98\ (\text{kg.m}^2/\text{s}^2)/\text{s} = -98\ \text{J/s} = -0.1\ \text{kJ/s}$$

The change in potential energy is small (this is a typical result), so we can neglect it. Because heat is taken from the turbine (the system) to turn the turbine's shaft (the surroundings), E_Q and W_S are negative. $\Delta\dot{H}$ (the rate of enthalpy) is

$$\Delta\dot{H} = -E_Q - W_S - \Delta E_K - \Delta E_P = -220 - 1400 - 194 - 0 = -1814 \quad \text{kJ/s}$$

$$\Delta\dot{H}_{Sp} = \frac{\Delta\dot{H}}{\dot{M}} = \frac{-1814}{2.5} = -726\ (\text{kJ/s})/(\text{kg/s}) = -388\ \text{kJ/kg}$$

Example 2 on Energy Balance

Calculate the shaft work rate ($\dot{W}_S$) done by a turbine, to which steam enters and leaves equally.

Steam's flow rate to the turbine ($\dot{M}$)	2.5 kg/s
Steam's temperature (T_S)	360°C (= 680°F)
Steam's pressure (P_S)	1000 kPa (= 10 Atm = 145 PSIA)
Exhaust steam's pressure ($P_{E.S}$)	101 kPa

Assumptions: 1) Steam enters and leaves at the same level, so the change in E_P is zero, and 2) Kinetic energy is too small so that it can be neglected

$$\pm\dot{E}_Q \pm \dot{W}_S = \dot{M}\Delta(\dot{H} + \dot{E}_K + \dot{E}_P)$$

The E_Q can be dropped as *no* noticeable change in temperature exists between the system (the turbine) and its surroundings (the turbine's shaft). From Table 2 (Supersaturated Steam Table) in the Table Section of the book, the specific enthalpy of superheated steam at 360°C and 1000 kPa is 3178.9 kJ/kg. From Table 1 (Saturated Steam Table), the enthalpy of saturated steam at 101 kPa is 2676.1 kJ/kg. Thus, the $\dot{W}_S$ can be calculated as

$$\dot{W}_S = -\Delta\dot{H} = -\dot{M}(\dot{H}_{Out} - \dot{H}_{In}) = -2.5(3178.9 - 2676.1) = -1257 \quad (\text{kg/s})(\text{kJ/kg}) = -1257\ \text{kJ/s} = -1257\ \text{kW/h}$$

The work is negative because the turbine releases energy to the shaft (the surroundings).

E-73

ENERGY CONVERSION

Energy conversion is the ability of energy (E) to be changed to other forms of energy. Consider a typical power-and-steam-production station in a chemical-process plant as a large thermodynamic system. This station mainly consists of a steam boiler (assume that the factory is small, so it has only one boiler), a steam turbine, and some steam pumps. The following energy conversions occur in this chemical plant:

- The boiler uses a fuel's chemical potential energy (E_{CP}) to convert water to steam. This is the conversion of E_{CP} to E_Q (heat energy), so $E_{CP} \rightarrow E_Q$, where the arrow sign ($\rightarrow$) means conversion.
- Steam is pumped to the turbine, in which $E_Q \rightarrow E_K$ (kinetic energy).
- The E_K drives the turbine's generator to produce electric energy (E_E), so $E_K \rightarrow E_E$.
- The E_E runs auxiliary equipment (like pumps and compressors), meaning $E_E \rightarrow E_{Me}$ (mechanical energy).

After these energy conversions, the turbine's exhaust steam (the steam leaving the turbine) goes to the pressure adjuster and then to the evaporation station to evaporate some water from the liquid under evaporation. Here, the steam creates vapor that is used by the factory's vapor users (like heat exchangers). A portion of steam and vapor condenses during evaporation into condensate and returns to the boilerhouse as boiler feedwater. And part of the condensate is used by the condensate users.

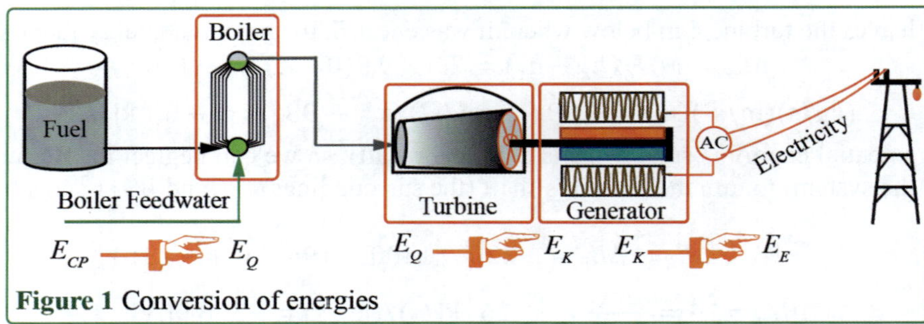

Figure 1 Conversion of energies

E-74

ENERGY DENSITY

The energy density (energy content) is the amount of useful energy (E) in a system per unit volume (V) of that system. Instead, specific energy (E_{Sp}) is the amount of useful E in a system per its unit mass (M). For example, the energy density of ethanol is about 21 000 kJ/L, and its specific energy is about 27 000 kJ/ kg. [The term **useful energy** used here refers to accessible (extractable) energy, so this definition does *not* include inaccessible energy, such as **rest mass energy**.]

In some cases, energy density, and in most cases, specific energy, are used to mainly express the energy in fuels and the heat-related quantities, like specific enthalpy, Gibbs free energy, and Helmholtz free energy.

The SI unit of energy density is kJ/m^3, and its US unit is BTU/Ft^3, where 1 kJ/m^3 = 0.027 BTU/Ft^3. And that of specific energy is kJ/kg and BTU/Lb, where 1 kJ/kg = 0.43 BTU/Lb.

[Note 1: The terms **specific energy** and **specific enthalpy** are often used equally to compare the strength of different fuels. For example, the specific energy (specific enthalpy) of LNG (liquefied natural gas) is 2.4 times greater than CNG (compressed natural gas) and 0.6 times greater than diesel fuel.] [Note 2: The term energy density is also used in cosmology to refer to the energy in a region of space per unit volume.]

E-75
ENERGY OF REACTION

Another name for ENTHALPY OF REACTION.

E-76
ENERGY RELEASING REACTIONS

Study HEAT ABSORBING AND HEAT RELEASING REACTIONS.

E-77
ENGINES, MACHINES, AND MOTORS

Engines, machines, and motors are **mechanical** devices (equipment) that convert energy (E) into mechanical energy (E_{Me}) to perform work (W). In this book, the word **motor** refers to the **mechanical motor**. **Electric motors** are discussed under ELECTRIC GENERATORS AND MOTORS.

The terms **engine**, **machine**, and **motor** are often used equally in general conversations. But, some minor differences exist between them, as explained next.

- Engines and machines are usually mechanical, while motors can be mechanical, electrical, or both.
- Engines are more complex than machines and motors because the number of processes occurring in an engine is greater than those in a machine or motor. For example, we say a car's engine or an airplane's engine. Heat pumps, instead, are machines (because they are less complex than a car's engine).

[An internal combustion engine is an engine in which combustion (the reaction of a fuel with air) occurs.]

E-78
ENTANGLEMENT THEORY

Study QUANTUM ENTANGLEMENT.

E-79

ENTHALPY AND ENTHALPY CHANGE

ENTHALPY

A system's (or a substance's) enthalpy (H) is the change of heat energy (E_Q, simply **heat**) at constant pressure ($\Delta P = 0$), where Δ is for **difference** and P is pressure. A system's enthalpy can also be defined as its ability to supply E_Q (heat energy) and perform W (work) at constant P, so it is the total of both.

$$H = E_Q + W \quad (1)$$

Because a system's enthalpy change (ΔH) equates to its E_Q, the ΔH (the difference between the initial enthalpy, H_1, and final enthalpy, H_2) of a heat-involving system can be used to determine the system's E_Q.

$$E_Q = \Delta H = H_2 - H_1 \quad (2)$$

Enthalpy (H) is expressed in J (Joule) or BTU (British thermal unit), where 1 kJ ≈1 BTU. It is also expressed in the following two ways:

- In kJ/kg and called specific enthalpy (H_{Sp}), but often shortened to just **enthalpy**.
- In kJ/mole and called molar enthalpy (H_n). This unit is mostly used in chemical reactions.

Specific enthalpy (H_{Sp}, also called **specific heat**) is H per unit M (mass).

$$H_{Sp} = \frac{H}{M} \quad (3)$$

Scientifically, a substance's H_{Sp} is the amount of E_Q needed to raise the T (temperature) of 1 kg of that substance by 1°C (without changing its phase). The SI unit of H_{Sp} is kJ/kg, and its US unit is BTU/Lb, where 1 kJ/kg = 0.43 BTU/Lb. For example, the enthalpy of combustion (H_C) of ethanol is 26 800 kJ/kg (= 11 524 BTU/Lb), and that of natural gas is about 49 000 kJ/kg (= 21 070 BTU/Lb).

Based on how enthalpy affects a substance's T or phase, it is classed into

- Temperature-change enthalpy (sensible enthalpy), and
- Phase-change enthalpy (latent enthalpy).

Sometimes, one of them or both can be involved. For example, the enthalpy of reaction (H_R or λ_R) can be sensible, latent, or both. [The reference T for H determination of many substances is 25°C and is the T, at which H is defined as zero.]

ENTHALPY CHANGE

The enthalpy change (ΔH) is the change in enthalpy (H) from an initial (1) state to a final (2) state in a heat transfer process.

$$\Delta H = H_{Net} = H_2 - H_1 \quad (4)$$

Because a system's ΔH equates to its E_Q (as will be proved in a moment), this equation can be written as

$$E_Q = \Delta H = H_{Net} = H_2 - H_1 \quad (5)$$

[Because it is *not* possible to measure a system's H directly, the enthalpy change (ΔH) is used in calculations. Under the following two conditions, ΔH equates to E_Q: 1) When the system under study is a closed system (E can enter or leave the system but mass *cannot*), and 2) When the system under study is under constant P.]

When a system is under these two conditions, its H can be calculated as

$$\Delta H = H_2 - H_1 = E_Q + W = E_Q + P.V \quad (6)$$

For a condensed substance (a liquid or solid) at constant P, the work term ($W = P.V$), known as the flow work (W_F), can be eliminated because ΔP or ΔV are zero or very close to zero. Elimination of W leads us to the practical form of the Thermodynamic First Law for enthalpy of a condensed substance at constant P.

$$\Delta H = E_Q \tag{7}$$

For example, the ΔH of a liquid in a mixer, which operates under constant P_{Atm} (atmospheric pressure), can be approximated by the E_Q released from the mixer during the mixing process. Similarly, when hot-wet sugar crystals enter a dryer (which works at P_{Atm}) to be dried, some E_Q is released from the wet crystals that dry the crystals. Thus, the ΔH of the sugar crystals can be used as its E_Q in the dryer's heat balance calculations.

The ΔH is the release or absorption of enthalpy between the product (or products) and reactant (or reactants) in a chemical reaction.

$$\Delta H = H_P - H_R \tag{8}$$

Thus, the following two cases can occur:

- **Negative** values of ΔH or E_Q indicate that energy is transferred from a reaction (system) to its surroundings, specifying that the reaction is a **heat-releasing** (exothermic) **reaction**.
- **Positive** values of ΔH or E_Q indicate that energy is transferred from the outsides to the reaction, specifying that the reaction is a **heat-absorbing** (endothermic) **reaction**.

The enthalpy change in a reaction can be measured in a calorimeter by measuring the enthalpy (heat) transferred (released or absorbed). As a numerical example, we can calculate the enthalpy change for the oxidation of one teaspoonful (5 g) of sugar (with a molecular mass of 342.3) with oxygen (O_2) in our body.

$$C_{12}H_{22}O_{11}\ (s) + 12\ O_2\ (g) \rightarrow 12\ CO_2\ (g) + 11\ H_2O\ (l)$$

We know that one mole of sugar (342.3 g) releases 5620 kJ (= 1342.6 kcal) of enthalpy (heat energy, E_Q) in a calorimeter. Because the reaction releases heat, the amount of ΔH involved is shown with a negative sign. Thus, we first convert the sugar sample (5 g) to mole and apply the negative sign.

$$5\text{g} = \frac{\text{1 mole sugar}}{\text{342.3 sugar}} = 1.5 \times 10^{-2}\ \text{mole sugar}$$

$$E_Q = 1.5 \times 10^{-2} \times -5620 = -84\ \text{kJ}$$

This tells us that a level teaspoon of sugar (5 g) supplies 84/4.184 = 20 Cal, where 4.184 is the conversion of kJ to kcal (or Cal). This equates to 84/5 = 16.8 kJ/g = 20/5 = 4 Cal/g = 4 000 cal/g sugar. According to the definition of a calorie, when 1 g of sugar in our body decomposes, its energy heats 4 g of water in our body by 1°C (which is *not* a large caloric content!).

The following summarizes the subjects of enthalpy, enthalpy change, and specific enthalpy:

- The enthalpy (H) of a system *cannot* be measured directly. Thus, the enthalpy change (ΔH) between two situations (initial state, H_1, and final state, H_2) is measured. If, for example, a system requires 1000 kJ of E_Q to move a heat (Q) from system A to system B, then the enthalpy in system B is 1000 kJ more than in system A. Assuming no E_Q loss, the ΔH = 1000 kJ. [This is why the term **enthalpy** always refers to the **enthalpy change** (ΔH, the differential form of enthalpy).]
- The term **heat** (Q) is often used traditionally instead of **enthalpy** (H), **enthalpy change** (ΔH), and **heat energy** (E_Q) to almost indicate the same meaning, so $Q \approx H \approx \Delta H \approx E_Q$. To be, however, very correct, scientists differentiate these words depending on the context. The term **heat** (Q) is used when talking about the flow of E_Q. **Enthalpy** (H) discusses the **heat value** (heat-energy value or enthalpy value) of a system, a substance, or a fuel. **Enthalpy change** (ΔH) discusses enthalpy in its differential (final-minus-initial) form. And **heat energy** (E_Q) is used when discussing a heat transfer between two systems. We say, for example, system A requires 1000 kJ of E_Q to move a heat (the flow of E_Q) to system B. [In the case that the term **heat** is generally used or these four (4) words are used equally, paying attention to the above-listed explanations, and

the context of the subject can clear a writer's exact purpose.] [Using ΔH in energy balance instead of E_Q simplifies the calculations, as ΔH values are determined for many substances (like steam and vapor). Table 1, given in the Table Section of this book, is an example of steam tables.]

- In almost all cases, the term **enthalpy** simply refers to **specific enthalpy** (H_{Sp}), enthalpy per mass (M) given in kJ/kg or BTU/Lb. In some cases, a substance enthalpy is expressed in kJ/mole or BTU/mole to refer to the molar value of the enthalpy.
- Enthalpies (rather specific enthalpies) given in steam tables are taken at the very-close-to-reality assumption that at 0ºC (standard temperature), the H_{Sp} of water is zero.
- **Enthalpy rate** ($\dot{H}$) is enthalpy per unit time (t, usually in second or hour), while **specific enthalpy rate** ($\dot{H}_{Sp}$) is enthalpy per unit mass (M) per unit time (t).
- Like energy, enthalpy (rather ΔH) is a state quantity, meaning that the amount of ΔH does *not* depend on how the process goes from one system to the next (from an initial state to the final state). For example, the amount of ΔH when 100 kg of a liquid is heated from, say, 30 to 60°C is independent of the steps taken from the initial to the final state; in other words, enthalpy (H) is a state quantity. This means that the amount of E_Q used is the same if we heat first the liquid from 30 to 40°C and then from 40°C to 60°C, or heat it with *no* delay to 60°C. This is also known as Hess's Law.

E-80

ENTHALPY OF COMBUSTION

Enthalpy of combustion (H_C or λ_C, also known as the **heat of combustion** or **heat content**) is the heat energy (E_Q, simply heat and scientifically enthalpy) released from the combustion of a mass unit (usually 1 kg or 1 Lb) of a fuel at atmospheric pressure (P_{Atm} = 1 Atm ≈ 100 kPa).

The SI unit of H_C is kJ/kg, and its US unit is BTU/Lb, where 1 kJ ≈ 1 BTU (British thermal unit) and 1 kJ/kg = 0.43 BTU/Lb. Because H_C is usually given per unit mass (M), it is also known as the **specific enthalpy of combustion** or specific energy. When, for example, 1 kg of coke burns, approximately 28 000 kJ of E_Q is released, so H_C of coke is 28 000 kJ/kg (= 12 040 BTU/Lb). The H_C of coal is about 27 000 kJ/kg (= 11 610 BTU/Lb), and that of ethanol is 26 100 kJ/kg. [Sometimes, however, H_C is expressed in kJ/mole or BTU/mole and called **molar enthalpy of combustion**.]

The enthalpy (H) released in a fuel combustion is a latent enthalpy (phase-change enthalpy). When, for example, 1 kg of natural gas, which is mainly methane (CH_4), reacts with molecular oxygen (O_2) in the air, 49 000 kJ of E_Q is released, according to the following reaction:

$$1 \text{ kg } CH_4 + 2 \text{ kg } O_2 \rightarrow 1 \text{ kg } CO_2 + 2 \text{ kg } H_2O - 49\,000 \text{ kJ } E_Q$$

This reaction tells us that the H_C of natural gas is 49 000 kJ/kg (= 21 070 BTU/Lb).

When, instead, 1 kg carbon (C) in natural gas reacts with molecular oxygen (O_2) in the air, 53 000 kJ (= 53 000 BTU) heat energy (E_Q) is released, based on the following equation:

$$1 \text{ kg C} + 2.67 \text{ kg } O_2 \rightarrow 3.67 \text{ kg } CO_2 - 53\,000 \text{ kJ } E_Q$$

Thus, the H_C of C in natural gas is 53 000 kJ/kg (= 22 790 BTU/Lb).

For practical purposes, the following equations can be used to calculate a fuel H_C:

$$H_C = 33878C + 144460\left(H - \frac{O}{8}\right) + 9436S \text{ kJ/kg} \quad (1)$$

$$H_C = 14540C + 62000\left(H - \frac{O}{8}\right) + 4050S \text{ BTU/Lb} \quad (2)$$

The C is for % carbon, H is % hydrogen, O is % oxygen, and S is % sulfur in the fuel.

[Note: The term **enthalpy of combustion** is often used instead of enthalpy of reaction (H_R) when discussing a fuel.]

E-81

ENTHALPY OF CONDENSATION

Enthalpy of condensation (H_{Con} or λ_{Con}, also known as the **heat of condensation**) is the heat energy (E_Q, simply heat and scientifically enthalpy) released when a mass unit (usually 1 kg or 1 Lb) of a gas condenses to a liquid. The change in the H_{Con} (the ΔH_{Con}) is usually measured at atmospheric pressure (P_{Atm} = 1 Atm ≈ 100 kPa) and condensation temperature (T_{Con}) of the gas under condensation.

Because of phase change during condensation of a gas, the enthalpy involved is a latent enthalpy (phase-change enthalpy). This is the reason that H_{Con} is given at the liquid's T_{Con}. When 1 kg water vapor at 0ºC and 1 Atm condenses to water, it releases 2 257 kJ of E_Q, where 0ºC is the T_{Con} of water at 1 Atm. The H_{Con} of water, thus, is 2 257 kJ/kg (= 970 BTU/Lb). Similarly, the H_{Con} of ethanol (C_2H_5OH) at 78.4°C is 855 kJ/kg (= 363 BTU/Lb), where 78.4°C is the T_{BP} (boiling point temperature) of ethanol at 1 Atm.

The SI unit of H_{Con} is kJ/kg, and its US unit is BTU/Lb, where 1 kJ ≈ 1 BTU (British thermal unit) and 1 kJ/kg = 0.43 BTU/Lb. Sometimes, it is given in older units like cal/g. Because H_{Con} is usually given per unit mass (M), it is also known as the **specific enthalpy of condensation**. Sometimes, however, H_{Con} is expressed in kJ/mole or BTU/mole and called **molar enthalpy of condensation** ($H_{C.n}$). The water's H_{Con} is 40.6 kJ/mole (= 39 BTU/mole).

[Note 1: Enthalpy of condensation and enthalpy of evaporation are numerically the same with the opposite signs. In another context, the T at which a substance condenses or evaporates is the same. For water, this condensing-evaporating T is 100°C, meaning that at the same T of 100°C, water vapor condenses to water, and water evaporates to vapor.] [Note 2: At homes, the H_C is used in cooling systems.]

E-82

ENTHALPY OF CRYSTALLIZATION

Study ENTHALPY OF FREEZING.

E-83

ENTHALPY OF EVAPORATION

Enthalpy of evaporation (H_E, λ_E, or λ_Q; also called the **heat of evaporation**, **latent heat of evaporation**, or **latent enthalpy of evaporation**) is the heat energy (E_Q, simply heat and scientifically enthalpy) needed to evaporate a mass unit (usually 1 kg or 1 Lb) of a liquid to vapor. The H_E of liquids is usually determined at atmospheric pressure (P_{Atm} = 1 Atm ≈ 100 kPa) and at their boiling point temperature (T_{BP}). [For the reason that H_E is usually expressed per unit mass (M), it is also called **specific enthalpy of evaporation**.]

Because of phase change during evaporation of a liquid, the enthalpy (H) involved is a latent enthalpy (phase-change enthalpy). This is the reason that H_E is given at the liquid's T_{BP}. One kg of water, at 100ºC and 1 Atm, needs 2 257 kJ (= 2 144 BTU) of E_Q when it evaporates to water vapor, where 100ºC is the T_{BP} of water at 1 Atm. Thus, the water H_E at 1 Atm and 100ºC is 2 257 kJ/kg.

The SI unit of H_E is kJ/kg, and its US unit is BTU/Lb, where 1 kJ ≈ 1 BTU (British thermal unit) and 1 kJ/kg = 0.43 BTU/Lb. Sometimes it is expressed in kJ/mole and called molar enthalpy of evaporation ($H_{n.E}$).

A liquid H_E can be calculated using its $H_{n.E}$ (molar enthalpy of evaporation) and M_n (molar mass).

$$H_E = \frac{H_{n.E}}{M_n} \times 1000 \quad (1)$$

For example, the H_E of ethanol (with $H_{n.E}$ = 39 kJ/mole and M_n = 46 g/mole) at 1 Atm and 78.4°C (the T_{BP} of ethanol) is

$$H_E = \frac{39}{46} \times 1000 = 848 \text{ kJ/kg} (= 367 \text{ BTU/Lb})$$

[Note 1: In steam tables, the difference between the vapor's enthalpy and liquid's enthalpy at a given T (temperature) or a given P (pressure) is the enthalpy of evaporation at that T or P.]

[Note 2: Enthalpy of evaporation (H_E) and enthalpy of condensation (H_C) are numerically the same with the opposite signs. In other words, the T, at which a substance evaporates or condenses, is the same. For water, this evaporating-condensing T is 100°C, meaning that at the T of 100°C, water evaporates to water vapor, and water vapor condenses to water.]

[Note 3: The H_E diminishes with increasing T and vanishes completely at critical temperature (T_C) because the liquid and vapor phases no longer exist above T_C, so only one phase exists.]

E-84

ENTHALPY OF FORMATION

Enthalpy of formation (H_F or λ_F, also called **heat of formation**) is the heat energy (E_Q, simply heat and scientifically enthalpy, H) that occurs during the formation of a mass unit (usually 1 kg or 1 Lb) of a chemical substance (simply **substance**) in a chemical reaction (simply **reaction**). The H_F of a substance is usually measured at standard conditions (25°C and 1 Atm), also called **standard enthalpy of formation**.

Because temperature and phase change during a substance formation, the enthalpy involved can be a sensible enthalpy (a temperature-change enthalpy), a latent enthalpy (phase-change enthalpy), or both.

The SI unit of H_F is kJ/kg, and its US unit is BTU/Lb, where 1 kJ ≈ 1 BTU (British thermal unit) and 1 kJ/kg = 0.43 BTU/Lb. Because H_F is usually expressed per unit mass (M), it is also called **specific enthalpy of formation**. Sometimes, however, H_F is expressed in kJ/mole or BTU/mole and called molar enthalpy of formation ($H_{n.F}$). Numerically, the H_F of ethanol (C_2H_5OH) is 6 022 kJ/kg. This is the ΔH that occurs during the formation of 1 kg of C_2H_5OH, consisting of 2 mole C, 3 mole H_2, and ½ mole O_2. Similarly, the H_F of sugar (sucrose, $C_{12}H_{22}O_{11}$) is 6 494 kJ/kg. And that of carbon dioxide is 8 955 kJ/kg.

E-85

ENTHALPY OF FREEZING

Enthalpy of freezing (H_{FZ} or λ_{FZ}, also called **heat of freezing**) is the heat energy (E_Q, simply heat and scientifically enthalpy) required during the freezing of a mass unit (usually 1 kg or 1 Lb) of a liquid to solid. The H_{FZ} is usually measured at atmospheric pressure (P_{Atm} = 1 Atm ≈ 100 kPa) and freezing point temperature (T_{FP}) of the liquid under freezing.

Because of phase change during the freezing of a liquid, the enthalpy (H) involved is a latent enthalpy (phase-change enthalpy). Therefore, H_{FZ} is given at the liquid's T_{FP}. Numerically, to freeze 1 kg of water to the ice at 0°C and 1 Atm, 333 kJ of E_Q (heat energy) is needed, so H_{FZ} of water is 333 kJ/kg. The H_{FZ} is numerically the same as the **enthalpy of crystallization** of water and enthalpy of melting (H_M) of ice.

The SI unit of H_{FZ} is kJ/kg, and its US unit is BTU/Lb, where 1 kJ ≈ 1 BTU (British thermal unit) and 1 kJ/kg = 0.43 BTU/Lb. Because H_{FZ} is usually given per unit mass (M), it is also known as the **specific enthalpy of freezing** (specific heat of freezing). Sometimes, however, H_{Fre} is expressed in kJ/mole or BTU/mole and called **molar enthalpy of freezing** ($H_{FZ.Mol}$).

[Enthalpy of freezing (H_{FZ}), enthalpy of melting (H_M), and **enthalpy of crystallization** are numerically the same with the opposite signs. In other words, the T (temperature) at which a substance freezes, crystallizes, or melts, is the same. For water, this freezing-crystallizing-melting T is 0°C, meaning that at 0°C, water freezes (crystallizes) to ice, and at the same T, ice melts to water.]

E-86

ENTHALPY OF MELTING

Enthalpy of melting (H_M or λ_M, also called **enthalpy of fusion**) is the heat energy (**E_Q,** simply heat and scientifically enthalpy) required during melting (fusion) of a mass unit (usually 1 kg or 1 Lb) of a solid to liquid. The change in H_M (the ΔH_M) is usually expressed at atmospheric pressure (P_{Atm} = 1 Atm ≈ 100 kPa) or standard conditions (25°C and 1 Atm). Because of phase change during melting, the enthalpy (H) involved is a latent enthalpy (phase-change enthalpy*)*.

The SI unit of H_M is kJ/kg, and its US unit is BTU/Lb, where 1 kJ ≈ 1 BTU (British thermal unit) and 1 kJ/kg = 0.43 BTU/Lb. Because H_M is usually given per unit mass (M), it is also called **specific enthalpy of melting**. Sometimes, however, H_M is expressed in kJ/mole or BTU/mole and called the **molar enthalpy of melting** ($H_{M.n}$). For example, the H_M of ice is 333 kJ/kg. This is numerically the same as the enthalpy of freezing (H_{FZ}) of water. We need 333 kJ heat energy (E_Q) to melt 1 kg of ice into water. Or when 1 kg of water freezes to ice, 333 kJ of E_Q is released. Therefore, to melt 1 kg ice from 0°C (= 273 K) to water at 20°C (= 293 K), we need 333 + (20 × 4.187) = 415 kJ. Water's specific heat capacity (C_Q) is 4.187 kJ/kg.°C (= 1 BTU/Lb.°F). This means that for each °C that 1 kg of water is heated, 4.187 kJ of E_Q is needed.

[Note: Enthalpy of melting (H_M), enthalpy of freezing (H_{FZ}), and enthalpy of crystallization are numerically the same with the opposite signs. In other words, the T, at which a substance melts or freezes (crystallizes), is the same. For water, this melting-freezing-crystallizing T is 0°C, meaning that at 0°C, ice melts to water at the same T, water freezes (crystallizes) to ice.]

E-87

ENTHALPY OF MIXING

Enthalpy of mixing (H_{Mix} or λ_{Mix}, also called **heat of mixing**) is the heat energy (**E_Q,** simply heat and scientifically enthalpy) that occurs during the mixing of a mass unit (usually 1 kg or 1 Lb) of a mixture. The change in H_{Mix} (the ΔH_{Mix}) is usually expressed at atmospheric pressure (P_{Atm} = 1 Atm ≈ 100 kPa) or standard conditions (25°C and 1 Atm). In the mixing process, almost the entire E_Q used by the stirrer is converted to heat energy (E_Q), known as the enthalpy of mixing.

Because *no* phase change, but temperature change, occurs during mixing, the enthalpy (H) involved is a sensible enthalpy, a non-phase-change-but-temperature-change enthalpy.

E-88

ENTHALPY OF REACTION

Enthalpy of reaction (H_R or λ_R, also called **heat of reaction** or **energy of reaction**) is the heat energy (E_Q, simply heat and scientifically enthalpy) that occurs (produced or consumed) when a mass unit (usually 1 kg or 1 Lb) of a reactant (reactants) is converted to product (products) during a chemical reaction. The H_R is usually expressed at standard conditions (25°C and 1 Atm), called the **standard enthalpy of reaction**.

H_R (the H involved in a reaction) can be a sensible enthalpy (a temperature-change enthalpy), a latent enthalpy (phase-change enthalpy), or both. The H_R, thus, determines whether a reaction is a heat-releasing reaction or a heat-absorbing reaction. When ΔH_R is **negative**, the reaction is a heat-releasing (exothermic) reaction, and when ΔH_R is **positive**, the reaction is a heat-absorbing (endothermic) reaction.

The SI unit of H_R is kJ/kg, and its US unit is BTU/Lb, where 1 kJ ≈ 1 BTU (British thermal unit) and 1 kJ/kg = 0.43 BTU/Lb. Because H_R is usually given per unit mass (M), it is also known as the **specific enthalpy of reaction** (specific heat of reaction). Sometimes, however, H_R is expressed in kJ/mole or BTU/mole and called molar enthalpy of reaction. [Note: The term enthalpy of combustion is usually used instead of **enthalpy of reaction** when talking about the combustion reaction of a fuel.]

E-89

ENTHALPY OF SUBLIMATION

Enthalpy of sublimation (H_S or λ_S, also known as the **heat of sublimation**) is the heat energy (E_Q, simply heat and scientifically enthalpy) required for changing a mass unit (usually 1 kg or 1 Lb) of a substance from the solid phase to the gaseous phase, without going through the liquid phase. The change in H_S (the ΔH_R) is usually expressed at atmospheric pressure (P_{Atm} = 1 Atm ≈ 100 kPa) or standard conditions (25°C and 1 Atm). H_S can be considered as the enthalpy of melting plus enthalpy of evaporation. Because of phase change during a substance sublimation, the enthalpy (H) involved is a latent enthalpy (phase-change enthalpy).

The SI unit of H_S is kJ/kg, and its US unit is BTU/Lb, where 1 kJ ≈ 1 BTU (British thermal unit). Because H_S is usually expressed per unit mass (M), it is also known as **specific enthalpy of sublimation**. Sometimes, however, H_S is expressed in kJ/mole or BTU/mole and called **molar enthalpy of sublimation**.

E-90

ENTHALPY-ENTROPY DIAGRAM

The enthalpy-entropy diagram (also called the ***H-S* diagram** or **Mollier diagram**) provides quick access to some properties of a thermodynamic process at high pressure (P) and temperature (T). The *H-S* diagram shown in Figure 1 is a helpful tool for steam properties, like determining the efficiency of a steam turbine (simply **turbine**). An *H-S* diagram's main coordinates are steam's enthalpy (refers to specific enthalpy, H_{Sp}, in kJ/kg), drawn on the Y-axis, and steam's entropy (refers to specific entropy, S_{Sp}, in kJ/kg.°C), drawn on the X-axis. It also indicates the lines of constant P (**red**) in absolute P of kPa, and constant T (**blue**) in °C.

For example, an *H-S* diagram can determine the enthalpies of the entering and exiting steams to and from a turbine. It can also determine a turbine's efficiency if the P and T of the entering and leaving steams to and from the turbine are known. A vertical line on the diagram from the initial condition (live steam) to the final condition (exhaust steam), shown in **green**, represents a turbine's efficiency. [An example of using an *H-S* diagram is shown below Figure 1.]

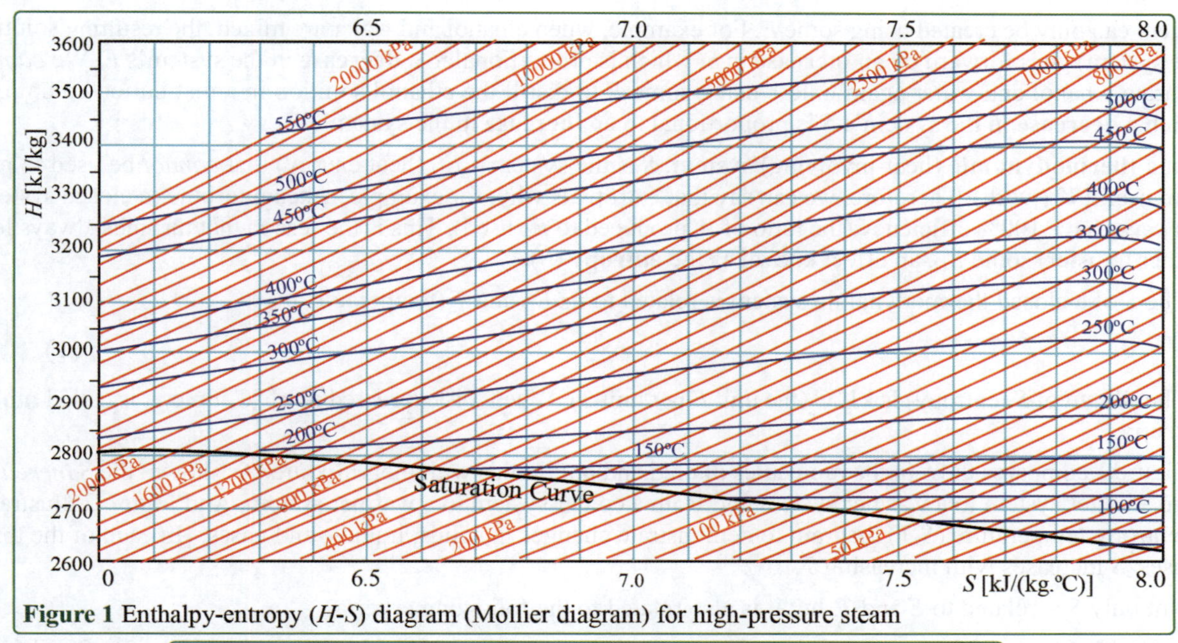

Figure 1 Enthalpy-entropy (*H-S*) diagram (Mollier diagram) for high-pressure steam

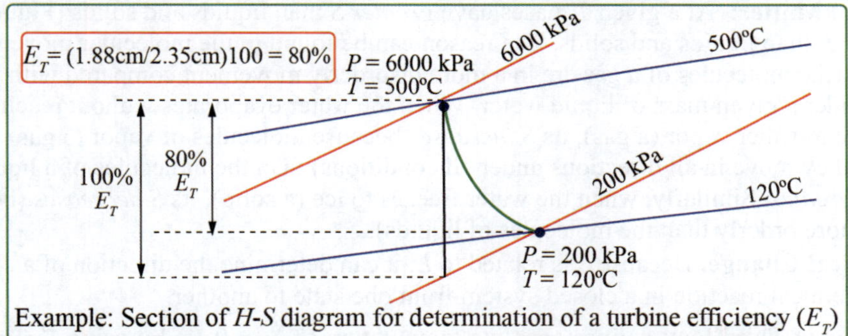

Example: Section of *H-S* diagram for determination of a turbine efficiency (E_T)

E-91

ENTRAINMENT AND ENTRAINMENT SEPARATORS

Discussed under the topic of LIQUID ENTRAINMENT.

E-92

ENTROPY AND ENTROPY CHANGE

Entropy

Entropy (S) is a system's disorderliness. A poor-ordered system with a low amount of E (energy) is high in S, and a perfectly-ordered system with a high E is low in S. Said so, disorderly systems have *high S*, but *less E*. And orderly systems have *less S*, but *more E*. As a common example, a broken cup of coffee on the floor is in a disordered state (with a high S), while a glass cup of coffee on the table is in a high order state (with a low S). The floor situation *cannot* be corrected unless spending some E to clean it and lower the S. A neatly ordered system can only be created using some E. For example, when ethanol and water are mixed, the resulting solution (the system) goes forward by an **increase** in S, which is proportional to a **decrease** in the system's E. We *cannot* separate ethanol and water again unless using some E to distill the ethanol solution in a distillation column, in which a **decrease** in the system's S is proportional to an **increase** in the system's E.

In a **thermodynamic** (heat-involving) **system**, S is the system's E_Q (heat energy) that *cannot* be used to perform useful W (work). Therefore, we can say that entropy is why, for example, a steam turbine (a closed system) can *never* have 100% efficiency (the ratio of W produced to E_Q used). This is the reason that turbines always lose (rather transfer) some E_Q, an effect known as the **entropy** (S).

The S of a closed thermodynamic system is related to its E_Q and T (temperature).

$$S = \frac{E_Q}{T} \quad (1)$$

The SI unit of S (entropy) is kJ/ºC (the unit E per unit T). When S is expressed in kJ/ºC.mole, it is called **molar entropy**.

Figure 1 compares the S in the molecules of cold and hot liquids with their mixture. As shown, the S *increases* from a hotter system to a warmer system and from a colder system to a warmer system. And Figure 2 illustrates an entropy-temperature (S-T) diagram to demonstrate changes in solids, liquids, and gases. [In each of the three phases, S increases with increasing T.]

Not only S is related to E and T, but it is also related to the following criteria:

- **System's State of Matter:** At a given T, gases have *greater* S than liquids and solids (Figure 2). Similarly, gases have *lower* E than liquids and solids. The reason can be found in the molecular movement disorder of these substances (the molecules of a gas are in a more disorderly movement compared with those of a liquid or a solid). Consider a given mass of liquid water. When the water evaporates without reaching its boiling point temperature to water vapor (a gas), its S *increases* because molecules of vapor (a gas) move in a more disorderly way (they move in all directions under all conditions) than the molecules of a liquid. This means that S is getting *greater*. Similarly, when the water freezes to ice (a solid), its S *decreases* (because molecules of solids move more orderly than the molecules of liquids).
- **System's Chemical Change:** Because S is related to E, it can determine the direction of a chemical change occurring in a chemical reaction in a closed system from one state to another.

The Thermodynamic Third Law defines absolute temperature (T_{Abs} = 0 K) by using S. The law says that a system's S only approaches a constant value when the system's T approaches T_{Abs}. At T_{Abs}, the S and E of a pure system (like crystal molecules) are zero, so the system is in the ground energy state.

[Note: Some physicists think that over time (in billions of years), the S (entropy) gradually *increases* hugely (because the molecules usually tend to become more disorderly). If this theory is correct, *not* enough E will remain in the Universe (a closed system) to sustain life, a process called the **heat death of the Universe**. The heat death can be prevented only by giving a huge amount of E to the Universe over time.]

Entropy Change

The entropy change (ΔS) of a system, in which a change (chemical or a physical) occurs, can be calculated by the E_Q added to the system in very small increments (additions) and the T, at which the change occurs.

$$\Delta S = \frac{E_Q}{T} \quad (2)$$

This equation expresses the Thermodynamic Second Law, which can be combined with the practical form of the Thermodynamic First Law ($\Delta H = E_Q$) to rewrite the entropy equation (Equation 1) in its useful form.

$$\Delta S = \frac{E_Q}{T} = \frac{\Delta H}{T} \quad (3)$$

In a chemical process or a chemical reaction, the ΔS is the sum of the entropies of the products minus the sum of the entropies of the reactants.

$$\Delta S = \sum S_{Pro} - \sum S_{Rea} \qquad (4)$$

[Entropy changes are calculated from values of standard entropies (Table. 15, at the end of the book).]

As a numerical example for a chemical process, we calculate the ΔS for evaporating 1 mole of liquid ethanol (with S of 160.7 J/°C.mole) to vapor ethanol (with S of 282.7 J/°C.mole).

$$C_2H_5OH\ (L) \rightarrow C_2H_5OH\ (G)$$

$$\Delta S = S\,[C_2H_5OH\ (L)] - S\,[C_2H_5OH\ (G)] = 282.7 - 160.7 = 122\ J/°C$$

Notice that the process went from a more ordered condition (liquid, L) to a less ordered condition (gas, G), resulting in a positive value for the ΔS.

As a numerical example for a chemical reaction, we calculate the ΔS for oxidation of 1 mole of ethanol vapor, using the S values from Table. 15.

$$C_2H_5OH\ (G) + 3\ O_2\ (G) \rightarrow 2\ CO_2\ (G) + 3\ H_2O\ (G)$$

$$\Delta S = 2\ S\,[CO_2\ (G)] + 3\ S\,[H_2O\ (G)] - \{S\,[C_2H_5OH\ (G)] + 3\ S\{O_2\ (G)]\}$$

$$\Delta S = 2 \times 213.7) + 3 \times 188.8 - [282.7 + 3 \times 205.1] = 96.1\ J/°C$$

The number of moles of gases increases for this reaction from 4 to 5, resulting in a positive value for ΔS.

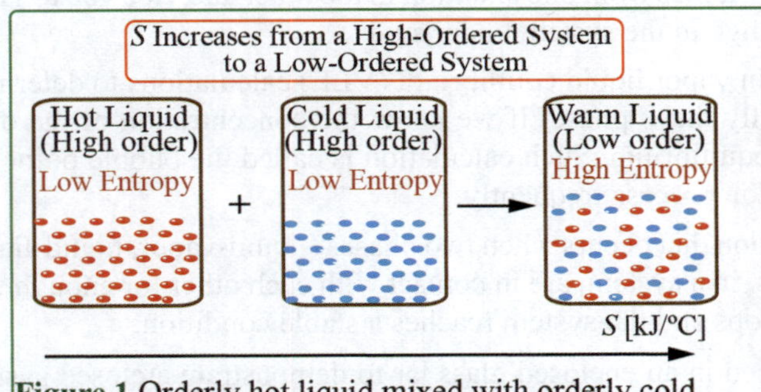

Figure 1 Orderly hot liquid mixed with orderly cold liquid forms disorderly warm liquid with high S (entropy)

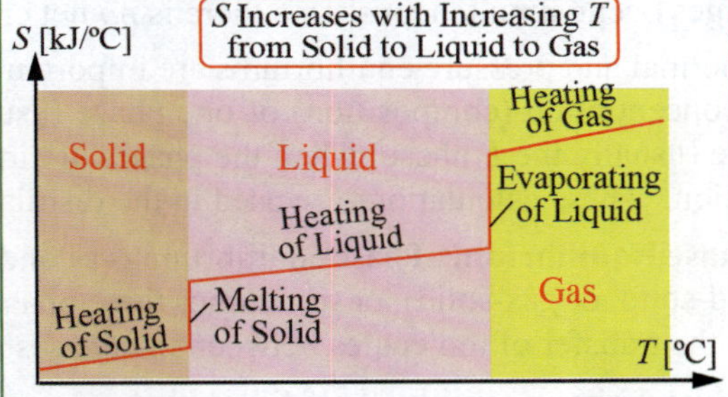

Figure 2 Entropy-temperature (S-T) diagram for phase changes in solids, liquids, and gases

E-93

ENZYMES

An enzyme is a large molecular catalyst used to accelerate (speed up) a chemical reaction. Most enzymes are proteins with specific structures and shapes. An enzyme can only act on one type of **substrate** (a compound on which an enzyme works). In our body, almost all reactions in the cells need enzymes to occur.

In enzyme chemistry, the name of enzymes often ends with ***ase*** and often describes the substrate on which the enzyme works. For example, the enzyme **sucrase** changes sucrose (sugar) in our body to fructose.

$$C_{12}H_{22}O_{11} + H_2O + \text{Enzyme} \rightarrow C_6H_{12}O_6 + C_6H_{12}O_6$$

Then in the liver, the fructose is converted to glucose. [Fructose and glucose are isomers (compounds with the same chemical formula but different structures).]

An enzyme can only work on one type of substrate. As shown in Figure 1, the following occurs: 1) the substrate enters the enzyme's active site, 2) the enzyme forms a complex with the substrate, 3) the enzyme changes the substrate to a product, and 4) the product leaves the enzyme's active site.

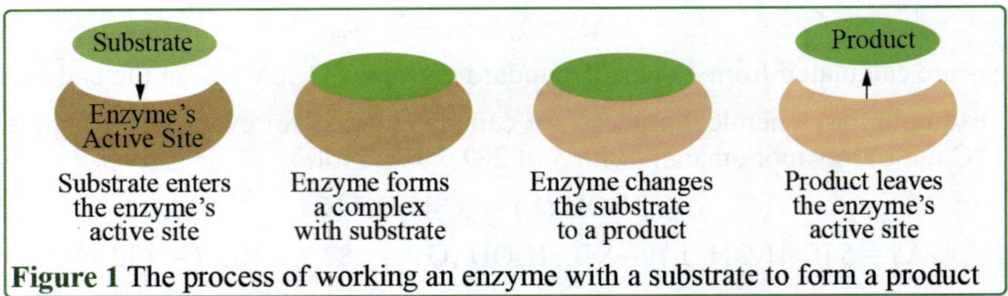

Figure 1 The process of working an enzyme with a substrate to form a product

E-94

EQUILIBRIUM

Equilibrium (stability) is the condition of stability in a system when *no* change in concentration (C), temperature (T), or pressure (P) occurs in that system. If a change occurs to a **stable system** (a system at equilibrium), the equilibrium shifts to the direction that partially relieves the change, but the system moves toward equilibrium again. It may seem to us that *nothing* is happening at equilibrium. Something is changing because the system *cannot* hold its equilibrium forever, so it constantly switches from one situation to the other and vice versa. These changes occur simultaneously, so there is *no* net change in the system under study.

Thermal and pressure equilibriums are important in vapor liquid equilibrium (VLE) calculations to determine the concentration (composition) of one phase (usually the V phase) if we know the concentration of the other phase (usually the L phase) when the phases are in equilibrium. Such calculation is called the bubble point calculation. These calculations are used in the distillation process frequently.

Phase Equilibrium: Phase equilibrium is a condition that occurs when two phases (liquid-vapor, liquid-liquid, liquid-solid, or gas-solid), or sometimes three phases, in a system, are in contact with each other for enough time until the transfer of molecules between the phases stops and the system reaches a stable condition.

Figure 1 shows a beaker half-full with water, placed in an enclosed glass jar to demonstrate a closed system. A small drop in the water level occurs at the start, indicating that some evaporation is happening, so the system is *not* at equilibrium. After some time, the water level becomes constant, indicating that the rate of evaporation and condensation equalize. This indicates that the system is at phase equilibrium, meaning that a phase equilibrium occurs between the vapor phase and the liquid phase of water, known as the VLE.

The phase equilibrium between chemical components occurs in some ChemEng process units. Consider a binary solution containing ethanol and water under distillation at certain T and P. Phase equilibrium usually occurs between the two phases of ethanol and water over a long period. When, finally, equilibrium occurs between them in the vapor and liquid phases, the C between phases stops changing at this T and P. If some changes occur slowly, it occurs at an equal rate.

As another example, consider a two-phase saturated solution containing sugar and water under crystallization at certain T and P. This system is at **liquid-solid equilibrium** (LSE) when the concentration of sugar (the component understudy) does *not* change greatly at this T and P.

Usually, a system, which is in phase equilibrium, is also in the following three (3) equilibriums:

- **Chemical Equilibrium:** $[(E_{CP})^L = (E_{CP})^V = (E_{CP})^S]$, where E_{CP} is for chemical potential energy.
- **Thermal** (heat) **Equilibrium:** $T^L = T^V = T^S$, where T is for temperature.
- **Pressure equilibrium:** $P^L = P^V = P^S$, where P is for pressure.

[In the first case, the phases' E_{CP} is the same, but *not* the components' concentration (C) in the phases. The C, in general, will *not* be the same in all phases, which are in equilibrium with each other.]

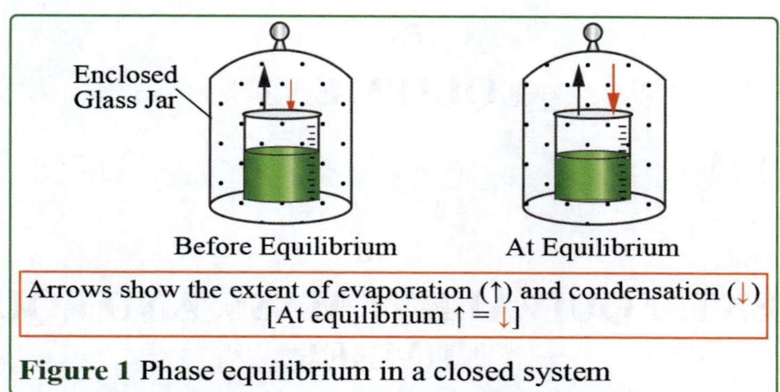

Figure 1 Phase equilibrium in a closed system

Chemical Equilibrium: Chemical equilibrium is a condition that occurs in a chemical reaction when its reactants and products are at a fixed concentration and have *no* tendency to change with time. At chemical equilibrium, the forward reaction proceeds at the same rate as the backward (reverse) reaction. [Note that the reaction rate of the forward and backward reactions are *not* zero but equal and slow. Therefore, chemical equilibrium is a dynamic condition, but *not* a static one, although the reaction seems to have stopped.]

Thermal Equilibrium: Thermal (heat) equilibrium is a condition that occurs between two (or three) phases when the phases are kept in contact enough until *no* net change of T occurs between them (because *no* further heat transfer occurs between them). If we keep a liquid phase in contact with a vapor phase with different temperatures, eventually, a situation is reached when both phases become at thermal equilibrium. When T of the vapor (V) phase and liquid (L) phase in a system is in equilibrium, the thermal equilibrium is expressed as

$$T^V = T^L \tag{1}$$

Pressure Equilibrium: Pressure equilibrium is a condition that occurs between two (or three) phases (or systems) when the phases are kept in direct contact enough until their pressures become equal. Similarly, an equation can be written for **pressure equilibrium** between V and L phases in a system.

$$P^V = P^L \tag{2}$$

E-95
EQUILIBRIUM MOISTURE CONTENT

Discussed under MOISTURE, CRITICAL MOISTURE, AND EQUILIBRIUM MOISTURE CONTENTS.

E-96
EQUILIBRIUM RELATIVE HUMIDITY

Equilibrium relative humidity (W_{ER}) is the lowest air humidity to hold a product without creating any problem during its packing, storing, and shipping. A relation between W_{ER} and water activity (A_W) exists.

$$A_W = \frac{W_{ER}}{100} \tag{1}$$

If, for example, the A_W of the sugar crystals is 0.6 at 25°C, the W_{ER} of its crystals is 60%. This means that at the air's relative humidity (W_R) of 60% and temperature (T) of 25°C, the sugar crystals reach their equilibrium moisture content (about 0.03%). Thus, the sugar crystals under these optimum conditions (W_{ER} of 60% and 25°C) *neither* absorb *nor* lose moisture unless they are exposed to high humidity or extreme T.

E-97

EQUIPMENT

Another name for DEVICE.

E-98

EQUIVALENT, EQUIVALENT MASS, AND EQUIVALENT NUMBER

Equivalent: Equivalent (Eq) is the amount of a chemical substance (simply **substance**) that corresponds to one mole of charge number (N_C, simply **charge**). For example, 1 mole of the sodium ion (Na^+) contains 1 mole of **positive** charge that equates to 1 Eq of Na^+. But 1 mole of the calcium ion (Ca^{2+}) contains 2 moles of positive charge, so 1 Eq of Ca^{2+} equates to ½ moles of Ca^{2+}. For the chlorine ion (Cl^-), 1 mole contains 1 mole of a **negative** charge, equating to 1 Eq of Cl^- ions. Thus, the Eq of Na is 1, Eq of Ca is 2, and Eq of Cl is 1. If then, 1 mole of Na^+, 1 mole of Ca^{2+}, and 1 mole of Cl^- dissolve in water, the produced solution contains 1 Eq of Na^+, 2 Eq of Ca^{2+}, and 1 Eq of Cl^- ions.

[Note: When the amount of a substance in a sample is too small, it is expressed in mEq (milliequivalent), where 1 Eq = 1000 mEq. For example, mEq expresses the limesalt hardness content in a water sample.]

Equivalent Mass: Equivalent mass (M_{Eq}, also called **equivalent weight**) is a substance's mass (M) of one equivalent (Eq). A substance's M_{Eq} is calculated from its M_M (molecular mass) or M_n (molar mass) and N_C (charge number).

$$M_{Eq} = \frac{M_M}{N_C} \tag{1}$$

The M_{Eq} has a unit of mass (in g equivalent or mg equivalent, simply g Eq or mg Eq) because N_C is unitless. When, in general, the N_C of a substance is ±1, its M_{Eq} is the same as its M_M, and if the N_C of a substance is ±2, its M_{Eq} equates to its M_M divided by 2.

Using Equation 1, the M_{Eq} of the Na (with M_M of 35.5 g and N_C of 1), Ca (with M_M of 40 g and N_C of 2), and Cl (with M_M of 35.5 g and N_C of 1) will be

$$M_{Eq-Na} = \frac{23}{1} = 23 \text{ g Eq} \qquad M_{Eq-Ca} = \frac{40}{2} = 20 \text{ g Eq} \qquad M_{Eq-Cl} = \frac{35.5}{1} = 35.5 \text{ g Eq}$$

The following are some other examples for M_{Eq}:

- M_{Eq} of sulfuric acid (H_2SO_4, with M_M of 98 g) is 98/2 = 49 g (or gEq or just Eq) because 1 mole of this acid can release 2 moles of hydrogen ion (H^+).
- M_{Eq} of calcium oxide (CaO, with M_M of 56 g) is 56/2 = 28 gEq because the N_C of both elements is 2 (Ca^{2+} is electro-positively charged, and O^{-2} has negative charges).
- M_{Eq} of calcium hydroxide [$Ca(OH)_2$, with M_M of 74 g] is 74/2 = 37 gEq because 1 mole of this base can release 2 hydroxyl ions $(OH)^-$.
- M_{Eq} of aluminum hydroxide [$Al(OH)_3$ with M_M of 78 g] is 78/3 = 26 gEq because 1 mole of this base can release 3 $(OH)^-$ ions.
- M_{Eq} of EDTA.2H_2O (ethylenediamine tetra-acetic acid dihydrate, with M_M of 372 g) is 372/2 = 186 g because EDTA can make two bonds to a metal ion (such as calcium).

Considering the M_{Eq} of H_2SO_4 and CaO, if we measure 48 g of H_2SO_4 and 28 g of CaO, both will have the same number of molecules because they are weighted based on their M_{Eq} ratio (because one molecule of H_2SO_4 reacts with one molecule of CaO to form one molecule of $CaSO_4$ and one molecule of H_2O.

Knowing the following two points are important:

- Sometimes, the term **number of equivalents** is used instead of **equivalent mass** (M_{Eq}) to refer to the quantity of M_{Eq} in a solution.
- When the amount of a substance in a sample is too small, it is expressed in mEq (milligram equivalent) instead of gEq (gram equivalent). For example, the content of limesalt hardness in water samples is given in mEq per 100 mL of the sample.

Equivalent Number: The **number of equivalents** (N_{Eq}) of a substance in a solution sample can be calculated from the M of the substance and its M_{Eq}.

$$N_{Eq} = \frac{M}{\frac{M_M}{N_C}} = \frac{M}{M_{Eq}} \qquad (2)$$

For example, we can calculate the N_{Eq} of 20 g CaO (with M_M of 56 g) in a solution sample as

$$N_{Eq} = \frac{M}{\frac{M_M}{N_C}} = \frac{20}{\frac{56}{2}} = \frac{20}{28} = 0.7 \text{ gEq} = 700 \text{ mEq}$$

Similarly, the N_{Eq} of CaO in a 3% (mass/volume) solution sample can be calculated as

$$N_{Eq} = \frac{M}{M_{Eq}} = \frac{3}{28} = 0.1 \text{ g Eq/100 mL} = 100 \text{ mEq/100 mL}$$

E-99

ESTERS

An ester is a chemical compound with a carbonyl group (C=O) linked to its two hydrocarbon groups (CH_3), as shown in Figure 1. Usually, esters are formed from the reaction of a carboxylic acid and an alcohol, so they are named based on their parents' alcohol and acid, with the ending of the suffix "ate." The right side of Figure 1 shows the molecular structure of ethyl ethanoate ($CH_3COOC_2H_5$, also called **ethyl acetate**), an ester formed from alcohol and acyl groups. Methyl propanoate ($C_2H_5COOCH_3$) is an ester, too. Tri-esters (with a molecular structure containing three ester groups) exist in nature as oils and fats (lipids).

$R_1—C(=O)—O—R_2$ $H_3C—C(=O)—O—CH_2—CH_3$

Figure 1 Molecular structure of ester, left, and ethyl ethanoate ($C_4H_8O_2$), right

E-100

ETHANOL, BIOETHANOL, AND BIODIESEL

ETHANOL AND BIOETHANOL

The words **ethanol** and **bioethanol** are used equally because both are the same chemical compounds, with the same chemical formula (C_2H_5OH) and chemical properties but different production resources. The word **ethanol** is particularly used when the production resource is crude oil and **bioethanol** (renewable energy) when the resource is biomass. Because most of the world's ethanol production is from biomass, for simplicity reasons, scientists usually use the word **ethanol** for both. We follow this trend in this book.

The chemical formula of ethanol (simply **EOH**) is C_2H_5OH. Its empirical formula is C_2H_6O, where the letter E in EOH is for **ethanol** and OH in EOH and C_2H_5OH is the functional group of alcohols. The ethanol's chemical name is ethyl alcohol, the same alcohol in edible alcoholic beverages. It is also shown as $CH_3–CH_2–OH$ (Figure 1) to indicate that the C of the methyl group ($CH_3–$) is attached to the C of the methylene group ($–CH_2–$), which is attached to a hydroxyl group (–OH).

Based on its formula, ethanol (C_2H_6O) consists of 2 moles of C (carbon), 3 moles of H_2 (hydrogen), and ½ mole of O_2 (oxygen). Percentage wise, an ethanol molecule (C_2H_6O) consists of 52.2% by mass carbon atoms [(2×12)/46 = 52.2%], 13% hydrogen atoms [(6×1)/46 = 13%], and 34.8% oxygen atoms [(1×16)/46 = 34.8%], where 12, 1, and 16 are the M_M (molecular mass) of C, H, and O, respectively.

Pure ethanol is highly flammable. If an ignition source is applied to ethanol, it will catch fire at its flashing point temperature (T_{FP}) of 14°C (= 57°F). Ethanol is a colorless, low-density, volatile, and highly flammable liquid. It is miscible in water and is potable (used in alcoholic beverages). Several other properties of pure ethanol are outlined next.

- It is alkaline (with a PH of 8 to 9),
- Its research octane number is 108,
- Its molar mass (M_{Mol}) is 46 g/mole,
- Its density (D) is 807 kg/m^3 at 20°C,
- Its enthalpy of freezing (E_{FZ}) is 109 kJ/kg,
- Its enthalpy of formation (H_F) is 6022 kJ/kg,
- Its enthalpy of evaporation (H_E) is 848 kJ/kg,
- Its enthalpy of condensation (H_{Con}) is 848 kJ/kg,
- Its enthalpy of combustion (H_C or λ_C) is 26100 kJ/kg,
- Its critical point temperature (T_C) is 243°C (= 469°F),
- Its critical point pressure (P_C) is 63 Atm (= 926 PSIA),
- Its entropy is 160.7 J/°C.mole in liquid form and 282.7 in vapor form,
- Its freezing point temperature (T_{FP}) is about –114°C (= –173°F),
- Its boiling point temperature (T_{BP}) is about 78.4°C (= 173°F),
- Its ignition temperature (T_{Ig}) is about 365°C (= 689°F),
- Its specific heat capacity (C_Q) is about 2.4 kJ/(kg°C),
- Its vapor pressure (P_V) is 6 kPa (at 20°C = 68°F),
- Its electric conductivity (K_E) is below 50 μS/m,
- Its viscosity (η) is 6×10^{-4} Pa.s (at 20°C), and
- Its refractive index is 1.361 (at 20°C=68°F).

[For calculating pure ethanol's vapor pressure (P_V), study ACTIVITY EQUATIONS, MODELES, AND CO-EFFICIENTS.]

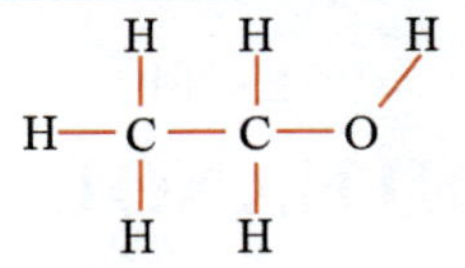

```
     H   H    H
     |   |   /
 H — C — C — O
     |   |
     H   H
```

Figure 1 Molecular structure of ethanol (C_2H_5OH)

Ethanol (or bioethanol) has many uses, mainly as a fuel and production of edible alcoholic beverages. As a fuel, ethanol (or bioethanol) reacts with oxygen to form carbon dioxide and water.

$$C_2H_5OH + 3\ O_2 \rightarrow 2\ CO_2 + 3H_2O + \text{Energy}$$

Specific heat capacity (C_Q, in kJ/kg.°C) of ethanol (C_2H_5OH) at different concentration

C_2H_5OH	5°C	20°C	40°C
5%	1.0	1.0	
10%	1.0	1.0	1.0
40%	0.8	0.8	0.9
70%	0.7	0.7	08
100%	0.5	0.5	0.6

In 2018, the world the three top ethanol producers were the United States (from corn, with the production of 60.8 Mm^3 = 16 063 MGa), Brazil (from sugarcane, with the production of 30 Mm^3 = 7 920 MGa), and EU (from different crops, with the production of 5.4 Mm^3 = 1 430 MGa).

In comparison with gasoline, knowing the following two (2) indicators is recommended:

- **Gasoline Equivalency:** The gasoline equivalency of ethanol is about 1.5, meaning that 1.5 units (L or Ga) of ethanol can replace 1 unit of gasoline.
- **Energy balance:** The energy balance of corn ethanol produced in the USA is about 1.3, meaning that 1 energy unit (say, kJ) of fuel is required to grow corn and process it to ethanol to produce 1.3 energy units from the ethanol. The energy balance for cane ethanol produced in Brazil is much higher (about 8 times).

As discussed next, ethanol and bioethanol originate differently, requiring different production methods.

Ethanol Production from Crude Oil

Ethanol can be produced from crude oil by fractional distillation in oil refineries. The crude oil is first heated in a reboiler to 400°C, and the mixture of hot liquid and vapor then goes to the bottom section of the distillation column, which is much warmer than the top section. Natural gas leaves the top of the column as the top product. The components with greater T_{BP} (boiling point temperature) than natural gas, like ethanol and gasoline, condense and leave the column's upper part (the less-hot section) as liquids. The components with greater T_{BP} condense and leave the column's middle section. And the one with the highest T_{BP} leaves the column's lower part (the hottest section) as the bottom product.

Ethanol Production from Biomass

Ethanol can be produced from biomass resources containing sugars, such as corn juice (mainly in the USA), sugarcane juice (mainly in Brazil), and sugarbeet juice (mainly in Europe) by fermentation in distilleries. The source's filtered juice (corn juice, cane juice, or beet juice) is mixed with **yeast** and allowed to ferment in a reactor for 4 to 12 h to produce a dilute solution with about 10% ethanol. After filtration, the impure ethanol solution goes to the distillation station to increase its purity to about 96% using its low boiling point temperature (T_{BP}). The vapor stream containing ethanol from the distillation column enters a non-contact condenser, from where the ethanol is collected as the **top product**. Components other than ethanol are collected in the residual, known as the **bottom product**. The ethanol-water mixture from the distillation column has about 5% water, so it is treated to reduce the water content by azeotropic distillation, extractive distillation, or molecular-sieve process. Anhydrous ethanol is the product of the process. [Instead of processing cane juice, some distilleries ferment the mixture of the juice and molasses to produce ethanol.]

Here the way of producing cane juice in a cane-sugar factory is explained. In the cane-to-ethanol-and-sugar process, the cane is washed, chopped, and shredded. Then, the shredded cane is squeezed by a set of mills to remove cane juice. The fiber residue, called the bagasse, is used as fuel in a special furnace to produce steam and electricity in the factory's steam-and-power production station. The cane juice goes to the purification station to produce a juice with higher purity in sugar (sucrose) content. The purified juice then goes to the filtration station to be filtered. At this point, the filtered juice, depending on what product, sugar or ethanol, is intended to be produced, is processed in one of the following ways:

- **Juice-to-Sugar Process:** The evaporation process concentrates the filtered juice to increase its *DS* (dissolved solids) content. The thick juice is crystallized to produce magma (mother liquid + crystals) in the crystallization station. The magma is processed in the centrifugal station (with several centrifuges) to separate the sugar crystals from the mother liquid (the liquid around the crystals). The wet sugar crystals are then dried in the drying station to produce market-quality sugar (the product). The mother liquid is recrystallized after being mixed with fresh thick juice (the product of the evaporating station). After another crystallization and centrifugation, molasses (the process's byproduct) is produced.
- **Juice-to-Ethanol Process:** This method was explained a moment ago.

Bioethanol is produced with different specifications. As an example, it is produced in Brazil with the following specifications:

- **Anhydrous Ethanol Blend:** This is pure ethanol with almost *no* water. This product is mixed with fossil-based gasoline at a 25% to 75% ratio, known as the E25 blend. This product is used in **flex-fuel vehicles** to increase gasoline's octane number and decrease fossil-based gasoline and air pollution.
- **Hydrous Ethanol:** This is pure ethanol with up to 15% water. This product is mainly used in special engines without mixing with any additives, known as E-100. [The production cost of hydrous bioethanol is less than anhydrous ethanol.]

[Note: Brazil is the most advanced country in producing cane-based bioethanol. In 2018, Brazil produced 30 Mm^3 (= 7 920 MGa) of ethanol from cane juice or cane molasses in about 400 modern factories. In that year, 55% of the cane crop was used to produce ethanol, 44% for sugar, and 1% for alcoholic beverages. In Brazil, about 40% of the gasoline usage and about 20% of the total energy usage comes from cane-based ethanol. And over 90% of the cars are **flex-fuel vehicles** that can use pure ethanol, ethanol blend, or fossil-based gasoline.]

BIODIESEL

As one fuel type used in diesel engines or heating oil, biodiesel is produced from biomasses, like sugarcane. It can also be produced from waste animal fats or vegetable oils by reacting with alcohol. Officially, biodiesel is a mono-alkyl ester that can be used alone or mixed with petrodiesel in any proportion. Pure biodiesel is called B100, and the 5% mixed with 95% petrodiesel is called B5. Today, biodiesels are produced in a considerable amount.

E-101

ETHYLENE

Ethylene (C_2H_4, with the chemical name of **ethene**) is a gaseous hydrocarbon, which can be viewed as two methylene groups ($-CH_2-$) connected covalently by a double bond ($CH_2=CH_2$). It is the simplest alkene. It is colorless with an aromatic odor. Its use in the chemical process industry is high (about 200 Mt in 2020).

Below are some properties of ethylene (C_2H_4):

- It is polymerized to produce polyethylene [$(C_2H_4)_n$], the world's most widely used plastic.
- It is oxidized to produce ethylene oxide (C_2H_4O), the main raw material in the production of surfactants.
- It can be alkylated with benzene () by an alkyl group from one molecule with another molecule) for the production of ethylbenzene ($C_6H_5C_2H_5$ or $C_6H_5CH_2CH_3$).

E-102
EVAPORATION PROCESS AND EVAPORATORS

1. EVAPORATION PROCESS

As an important process unit of ChemEng, evaporation (vaporization) is a heat transfer process performed in an **evaporator** to concentrate a solution by boiling it to its boiling point temperature (T_{BP}). During evaporation, some of the solution's volatile liquid (mostly water) is converted to vapor. The evaporation cause (driving force) is the temperature difference (ΔT) between the heating medium (industrially, steam) and the liquid under evaporation, $\Delta T = T_S - T_L$. Water can be partially evaporated from a water-containing solution by increasing T (temperature) to its T_{BP} of 100°C and forming water vapor. Evaporation, unlike boiling, can occur without reaching T_{BP} (water in a container evaporates without reaching its T_{BP}). But industrially, it is done by applying heat energy (E_Q, simply heat and scientifically enthalpy, H) of steam to increase the evaporation rate. Evaporation is used in many chemical process plants. [Figure 1 is about special terms used in evaporation.]

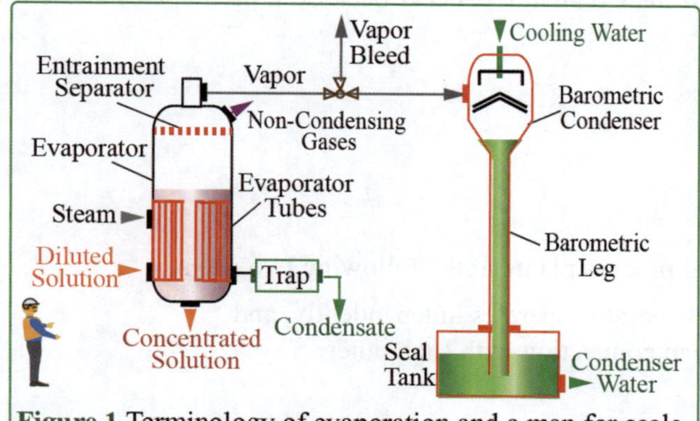

Figure 1 Terminology of evaporation and a man for scale

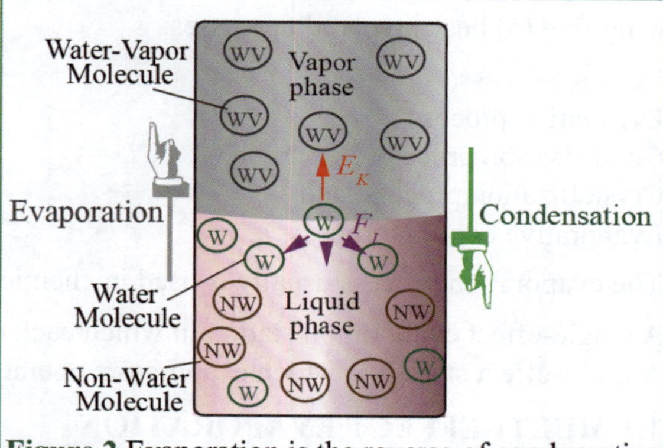

Figure 2 Evaporation is the reverse of condensation

As a heat-absorbing process, evaporation involves both of the following heat transfer processes:

- Temperature-change (sensible heat) process, because T of the liquid increases to reach its T_{BP}, and
- Phase-change (latent heat) process because part of the liquid changes to vapor.

Thus, part of the enthalpy change (ΔH) that occurs during evaporation is temperature change enthalpy (sensible enthalpy), and part is phase change enthalpy (latent enthalpy, also known as the enthalpy of evaporation), which changes a liquid at its T_{BP} to vapor.

[Note: The terms **heat energy** (E_Q) and enthalpy change (ΔH) have the same meaning when a process occurs at constant pressure (P). Traditionally, however, the term **heat** (Q) is often used instead of heat energy, enthalpy (H), or enthalpy change, so $Q \approx E_Q \approx H \approx \Delta H$.]

To understand evaporation at the molecular level, consider a water-based solution (aqueous solution) under evaporation in an evaporator. The important factors that affect the evaporation of the solution are:

- Kinetic Energy (E_K)**:** As the solution is heated, its molecules gain some E_K, so they move faster, and as the solution reaches its T_{BP}, the molecules move at their fastest. Thus, the molecules gain enough E_K to overcome intermolecular forces (F_I) and move to the solution's surface. They escape the surface to become vapor molecules (see Figure 2). [A solution's molecules, compared to a gas, generally have a low amount of E_K, so they are comparably more attracted to adjacent molecules by F_I. Also, note that the vapor molecules escaping the solution take their E_Q with them, so the released vapor contains a notable amount of **heat value** (heat-energy value or enthalpy value).]

- Density (D): As the solution is heated, the D of some of its molecules becomes smaller than others, so low-density molecules move to the solution's surface.
- Pressure (P): As the solution is heated, it starts to evaporate, and its vapor pressure (P_V) becomes equal (or greater) than the atmospheric pressure (P_{Atm}), so the liquid molecules can easier move to the vapor phase.

The general definition of evaporation includes the following two classes:

- Evaporation under atmospheric pressure (P_{Atm}), and
- Evaporation below P_{Atm} is called evaporation under P_{Vac} (vacuum pressure) or negative P_{Vac}.

Evaporation under P_{Vac} is used to decrease the T_{BP} of the solution under evaporation (at a *lower P*, a given solution boils at a *lower T*). Most discussions of this topic are about this kind of evaporation because, in most chemical plants, evaporation is performed under vacuum pressure, as it improves the following:

- Energy usage of the process by lowering the T_{BP} of the solution,
- Quality of the product (because most products are temperature sensitive), and
- Operating efficiency of the process by easing the feed's circulation in the evaporators.

In ChemEng, evaporation is considered the **central heat transfer process** because it participates in the following five (5) heat-involved processes:

- Boiling process,
- Distillation process,
- Condensation process,
- Crystallization process, and
- Evaporative cooling process.

The evaporation process usually is used in chemical process plants in the following two ways:

- A single-effect evaporation station in which each evaporator operates independently, and
- A multi-effect station in which evaporators operate in connection with each other.

1.1 MULTI-EFFECT EVAPORATION

A multiple-effect-evaporation station consists of several attached parts (mainly evaporators and mixers) and detached parts (mainly condensers, pumps, instruments, controllers, and computers). A typical station usually consists of 3 to 6 **effects** (for reasons, study STEAM ECONOMY). In larger chemical process plants, each effect consists of 1 to 3 evaporators, called **bodies**. For example, a four-effect evaporating station with 2 bodies in the first three effects (shown usually by symbols 1A, 1B, 2A, 2B, and 3A and 3B) and 1 body in the fourth effect contains 7 evaporators. [Under this topic, however, we consider that each effect has only 1 evaporator (body), so when talking about a 4-effect evaporating station, we mean the station has 4 evaporators that operate in connection with each other, as shown in Figure 3.]

In a multiple-effect evaporation station, the liquid feed's T_{BP} (boiling point temperature) in each effect is reduced using lower P_{Vac} (vacuum pressure). This considerably reduces the station's energy use (improves its steam economy), which is the main goal of multi-effect evaporation.

To become familiar with multi-effect evaporation, consider a **four-effect-evaporating station** in a small typical beet-sugar plant, which processes 100 t beet/h. [This is a scale-down consideration because typical medium-size beet factory processes about five times more. Also, note that such a factory has more evaporators (bodies) in each effect.] The evaporating station processes thin juice (the feed) to concentrate it (to increase its dissolved solids, *DS*, content) to produce the thick juice (the station's product).

- Steam with P of around 230 kPa (≈ 2.3 Atm ≈ 33 PSI), corresponding to the saturation temperature of 125°C (Table 1, given in Table Section of the book), enters effect 1.
- Vapor from effect 1 (at about 112°C) is used as the source of heat energy in effect 2. Vapor from effect 2 (at about 102°C) is used in effect 3. And so on.

- Feed is heated in a heat exchanger to around its T_{BP} before entering effect 1.
- Partially concentrated juice from effect 1 enters effect 2, and so on until it leaves effect 4 (the last effect) as the product with the desired *DS* content.

A multi-effect station gets E_Q from

- Steam coming from the boilerhouse,
- Vapor coming from individual effects, and
- Flashing heat energy coming from flashing evaporation.

The flashing evaporation occurs because the *T* of the feed entering an effect is higher than that effect. So, part of the feed flashes (cools fast because of lower *T*) into vapor, releasing some E_Q, known as **flashing heat**. The released heat, which can cause flashing evaporation, equates to the enthalpy change (ΔH) between *T* of the feed and *T* of the effect (to which the feed enters).

Because all effects operate under negative P_{Vac}, the T_{BP} of the feed to each effect decreases (*the lower the* P_{Vac}, *the lower is the* T_{BP}), so ΔT between the steam and the feed under evaporation increases. A decrease in the T_{BP} and increase in the ΔT improve the **heat transfer rate** ($\dot{E}_Q$) in each evaporator and, therefore, the station's steam economy (E_S) becomes greater.

The evaporating station sends out **vapor bleeds** (study VAPOR BLEEDING PROCESS), used by vapor users (such as heat exchangers). With three vapor bleeds, the mass balance of the process (according to the first up-coming Example) tells us that the station uses 33 t/h of steam to,

- Process 130 t/h feed with 15% *DS* to 30 t/h concentrated product with 65% *DS*,
- Evaporate 100 t/h water to produce 100 t/h vapor to be used by vapor users,
- Produce 75 t/h condensate for boilers and other condensate users, and
- Develop a steam economy (E_S) of 100/25 = 4 t water/t steam.

Let us assume here that all evaporators of a four-effect evaporation station are Robert type (explained under EVAPORATORS) and operate under a small P_{Vac}. We can talk now about the operation of this station, as

- Feed enters 1 (the first-effect evaporator). Partially concentrated product from 1 enters 2. After more concentration (*C*), the product leaving 2 enters 3. And so on. Finally, a product with the desired *C* leaves 4 (the last-effect evaporator).
- Steam enters 1. Heat energy (E_Q) from the steam goes through the wall of the tubes to the feed, evaporating part of its water in quantity equal to the mass of the vapor produced in 1. The vapor leaving 1 (at the same *T* as the boiling feed) is used as the heating medium in 2 to remove some of the feed's water. The vapor from 2 is used in 3. And so on. The vapor from 4 enters a barometric condenser (a direct-contact condenser) to be condensed. The condenser maintains the last-effect *P* at a small negative P_{Vac}.
- The steam entered to 1 becomes the condensate from 1. The vapor from 1 becomes the condensate from 2. And so on. Each effect works as a condenser for its previous effect.
- The main part of the product coming from 1 goes to 2 for further concentration, and part of it goes to the flashing tank 1 to be flashed to produce condensate and vapor. The flashing tank 1 separates the condensate from the vapor. The condensate 1 from flash tank 1 is pumped to the boiler-feedwater tank. The same process occurs in flashing tank 2. Condensate 2 is pumped to the boiler-feedwater tank, from there to the boilerhouse as the boilers' feedwater. The condensate 3 from flashing tank 3 is pumped to the condensate tank, and the vapor is pumped to the vapor line going to 2.
- The vapor coming from 4 enters the barometric condenser. There, it gets mixed with the condenser's cooling water to produce the condenser water, which leaves the condenser and goes to the **seal** (collection) **tank** through the condenser's barometric leg. The hot condenser water from the seal tank is pumped to an evaporative cooling device (pond, cooling tower, or wet surface air cooler) to be cooled. After cooling, the cool stream gets some **makeup water** and is used, again, as cooling water in the condenser.

In a multi-effect station, the P_{Vac} in each evaporator is maintained by a vacuum pump placed between each evaporator and its flashing tank. The vacuum in the last effect is maintained by the barometric condenser, which keeps the last effect at a slight P_{Vac} (around 70 kPa = 0.7 Atm = 10 PSI). Because the *T* of the feed entering an effect is higher than the *T* of the effect it enters, it cools down (flashes) to the *T* of the entering effect.

A **condensate flashing tank** (simply **flashing tank**) is installed under each effect evaporator for flashing evaporation and separation of condensate from vapor (see Figure 3). The flashing tank gets the condensate, makes flashing on it, and sends the flashing vapor to the previous effect's vapor line. And the rest of the condensate is pumped to the condensate users (see the Note below).

[Note 1: Because of high quality, the condensate from the first flashing tank is usually pumped to the boilerhouse to be used as feedwater for steam boilers. The lower-quality condensates from the other flashing tanks end up in the last flashing tank and are pumped to the condensate users.]

[Note 2: The flashing evaporation on condensate improves the E_S (steam economy) because the released vapor is used again.]

As a rule, each kg of flashing vapor from condensate from the Ith effect evaporates an additional (N – I) kg of water. Assume that condensate comes from the third effect at 100°C (= 212°F) and enters the third flashing tank, which is at 95°C (= 203°F), so the condensate cools down to 95°C. As a result of losing 5°C, an enthalpy of condensation (H_C), which equates to the difference in enthalpy (*H*) between these two temperatures, will be formed. Numerically, this can be explained as

Enthalpy of saturated liquid at 95°C	398 kJ/kg (from Table 1, given in Table Section)
Enthalpy of saturated liquid at100°C	419 kJ/kg (from Table 1)
Difference	21 kJ/kg

Here are the other advantages of a multi-effect station over a single-effect station:

- In multi-effect evaporation, the steam is used as many times as there are effects in the station. This treatment greatly improves steam efficiency (E_S, also called evaporation efficiency). [A limit, however, exists to the number of effects that work efficiently (more talk about it later.]
- In multi-effect evaporation, the vapor produced by each effect is *not* only used in the next effect, but the **vapor users** can also use it outside of the evaporating station (like in a heat exchanger). Sending vapor to a vapor user is called the vapor bleeding process. And shifting a vapor to a lower-grade vapor (a vapor with a lower heating ability) is called the vapor-shifting process. These two processes greatly save the vapor used in evaporation and improve the station's E_S. [In some modern chemical plants, the amount of heat required to be used by **vapor users** is up to half of the total steam usage. Assume that the vapor users use 40% of the total steam usage. This means that the steam use would be 40% higher if steam had been used instead of vapor. Figure 3 shows a 4-effect station that sends vapors 1, 2, and 3 to the vapor users.
- In multi-effect evaporation, the vapor leaving each evaporator is used in the next one, while in single effect, the vapor leaving an evaporator is discarded.
- In multi-effect evaporation, the amount of vapor going to the barometric condenser and, therefore, the amount of cooling water used by the condenser is comparably smaller.
- In multi-effect evaporation, the feed can be concentrated to the desired level of *DS* content. A single-effect evaporator *cannot* (in some cases) concentrate the feed to the desired level, particularly when the feed must be concentrated to a higher level (like in a typical sugar plant, the feed with about 15% *DS* must be concentrated to around 65% *DS*). This *cannot* be done in a single-effect station.
- In multi-effect evaporation, higher-pressure steam can be used than in a single-effect evaporator.

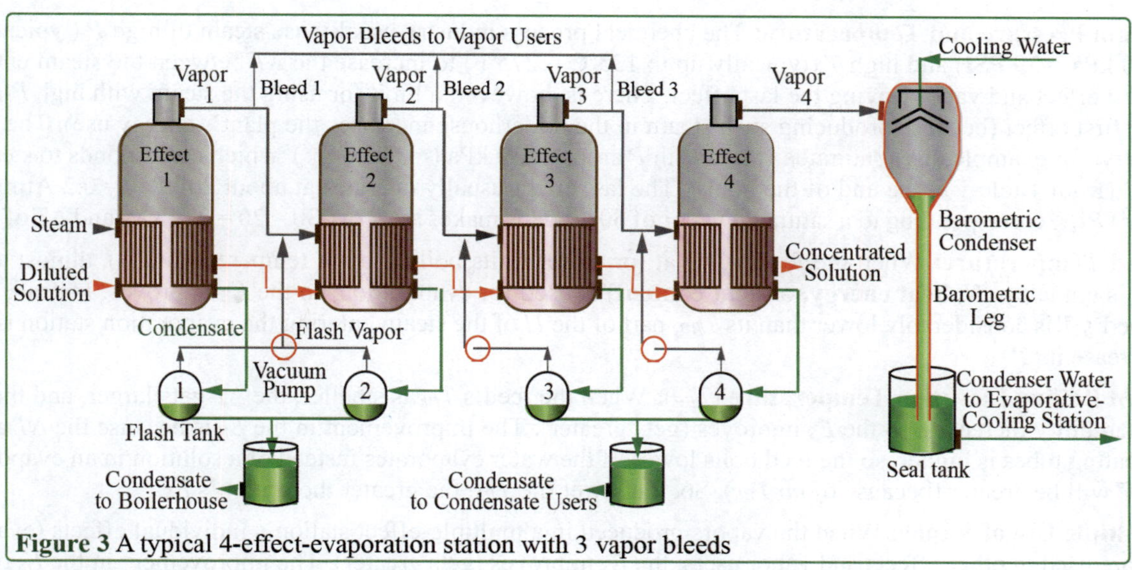

Figure 3 A typical 4-effect-evaporation station with 3 vapor bleeds

1.1.1 Steam Efficiency of Multiple-Effect Operation

The steam efficiency (E_S, also called **evaporation efficiency**) indicates the efficiency of an evaporation station (regardless of being a single-effect or multiple-effect station). Numerically, E_S is the mass of **water evaporated** (M_W) per mass of steam used (M_S) in an evaporator or an evaporating station.

$$E_S = \frac{M_W}{M_S} \tag{1}$$

Usually, the E_S is expressed as the tons of water evaporated per one ton of vapor used, so the *greater* the M_W, the more efficient is the evaporation process.

Major Factors: The five **major** factors affecting a multiple-effect evaporation station's E_S are: 1) Number of effects, 2) Steam pressure and temperature, 3) Feed temperature (T), 4) Feed boiling elevation temperature (T_{BE}), and 5) Multiple-use of vapor. These are discussed next.

Number of Effects (N_E): When the N_E is reasonably *greater* (discussed in a moment), the M_W (the amount of water evaporated) per a certain amount of steam becomes *greater* (advantage). In a multiple-effect evaporation station, M_W and N_E are practically related as

$$M_W = \frac{1.1}{N_E} \tag{2}$$

According to this equation, in a single-effect evaporator, the amount of M_W for 1 kg (or t) of steam used is 1.1 (that is, 1 kg of steam is used to evaporate 1.1 kg of water) and increases as the number of effects increases in a multi-effect station. Each effect, however, does *not* contribute to steam efficiency (E_S) equally, as we notice now. In a two-effect, the amount of M_W for 1 kg of steam used is (1.1)/2 = 0.6 kg. In a three-effect, the M_W is (1.1)/3 = 0.4 kg. In a four-effect, the M_W is 0.3 kg. And in a five-effect operation, the M_W is 0.2 kg for 1 kg of steam. This example proves the following two important facts:

- **Greater E_S:** The reasonably *greater* the E_S (steam efficiency), the *more* efficiently the station operates (because the station evaporates more water per t steam used).
- **N_E Limit:** The water evaporated (M_W) in a single-effect station compared to a two-effect is 1.1 – 0.6 = 0.5 t. However, when comparing a four-effect with a five-effect, the M_W is only 0.3 – 0.2 = 0.1 t. This tells us that a **limit** to N_E exists that works efficiently. That is why stations with four effects (and in some chemical plants, up to five effects) are the most common.

Steam Pressure and Temperature: The chemical process industry usually use steam of high P (typically up to 270 kPa = 39 PSI) and high T (typically up to 135°C = 275°F) to increase the ΔT between the steam entering the first effect and vapor leaving the last effect. There is, however, a limit for using the steam with high P-and-T in the first effect (because producing such steam in the boilerhouse increases the plant's energy use). The sugar industry, for example, uses saturated steam with P around 230 kPa (= 33 Lb/In^2), which corresponds to steam of 125°C (from Table 1 at the end of the book). The last effect usually operates at about 20 kPa (= 0.2 Atm = 2.9 Lb/In^2) P_{Vac}, corresponding to a saturated vapor of 60°C. This makes a ΔP of 230 – 20 = 210 kPa and ΔT of 65°C.

Feed Temperature: When the feed's T is at (or close) to its boiling point temperature (T_{BP}), almost all the steam's enthalpy (H, **heat energy,** or **heat content**) is used for evaporation, so the E_E improves. Instead, when the feed's T is considerably lower than its T_{BP}, part of the H of the steam entering the evaporation station is used to increase its T.

Feed Boiling Elevation Temperature (T_{BE}): When the feed's T_{BE} is smaller, the ΔT gets larger, and the heat transferability increases, so the E_S improves (gets greater). The improvement in the E_S is because the ΔT across the heating tubes is higher, so the feed boils lower. If the water evaporates instead of a solution in an evaporator, the ΔT will be greater (because of *no* T_{BE}). So, the lower the T_{BE}, the greater the station's E_S.

Multiple Use of Vapor: When the vapors produced in a multiple-effect station's individual effects (evaporators) are used in other effects and vapor users, the E_S improves (gets greater). The improvement in the E_S occurs because the enthalpy (heat) value (H) in most heat users is later returned to the evaporation station. For example, the heat used to increase the feed's T is returned to the evaporation station in the feed.

Minor Factors: The four (4) **minor** factors affecting a multiple-effect evaporation station's E_S (steam efficiency) are discussed next.

Liquid Head (h): The h (the feed level above the heating surface) negatively affects the E_S (the *greater* the h, the *less* steam-efficient is the station). The liquid head (h) in a tube evaporator (like Robert evaporator) should be kept at such a height that the top tube's sheet is covered. Such a feed level increases the heat-transfer rate (because the ΔT across the heating tubes becomes greater), so the liquid boils at a lower T, causing an improvement in the station's E_S. Instead, a high feed level decreases (worsens) the station's E_S.

Pressure Difference (ΔP): The ΔP between the first and last effect positively affects the E_S (the *greater* the difference in P, the *greater* is the available ΔT and, therefore, the *more* steam-efficient is the station).

Amount of Evaporated Water: The amount of vapor formed in the last effect influences the station's E_S because it ends up in the condensation station and is, therefore, wasted in the cooling water. [Vapor-bleeding process, vapor-shifting process, and increasing the sum of **vapor bleeds** to be used by the heat users are the best ways to decrease the amount of vapor from the last effect and, consequently, improve (increase) the E_S.]

Non-condensing Gases (NC gases): The NC gases (like air, ammonia, and carbon dioxide), produced in individual effects by evaporating the feed, negatively influence the E_S. These gases mix with the vapor and move with its flow to the next effect. Because NC gases do *not* condense, they decrease the condensation temperature (T_{Con}) of the condensing gases. As a result, the ΔT across the heating tubes is gradually reduced, causing the evaporation rate to be reduced, so the E_S decreases. [The NC gases are usually removed from each effect before their concentration becomes too great (typically, more than 10% of existing vapor). In some operations, the NC gases are discharged continuously at about 1% of the vapor entering each evaporator. This operation is achievable if 1) A positive vapor-flow path from inlet to vent outlet exists in the evaporator. 2) The vent's discharge points are enough and are located furthest from the vapor inlet. The NC gases are vented to the next effect's vapor line, the last-effect condenser, or to the atmosphere (if vapor pressure is above P_{Atm}).]

In addition to the listed factors, the steam pressure adjustment affects the evaporation station's E_S. The adjusting is called the **pressure reduction process** if the steam used in an evaporator is at a greater P than needed. And if the vapor is at a lower P than is needed, the adjusting is called the vapor recompression process.

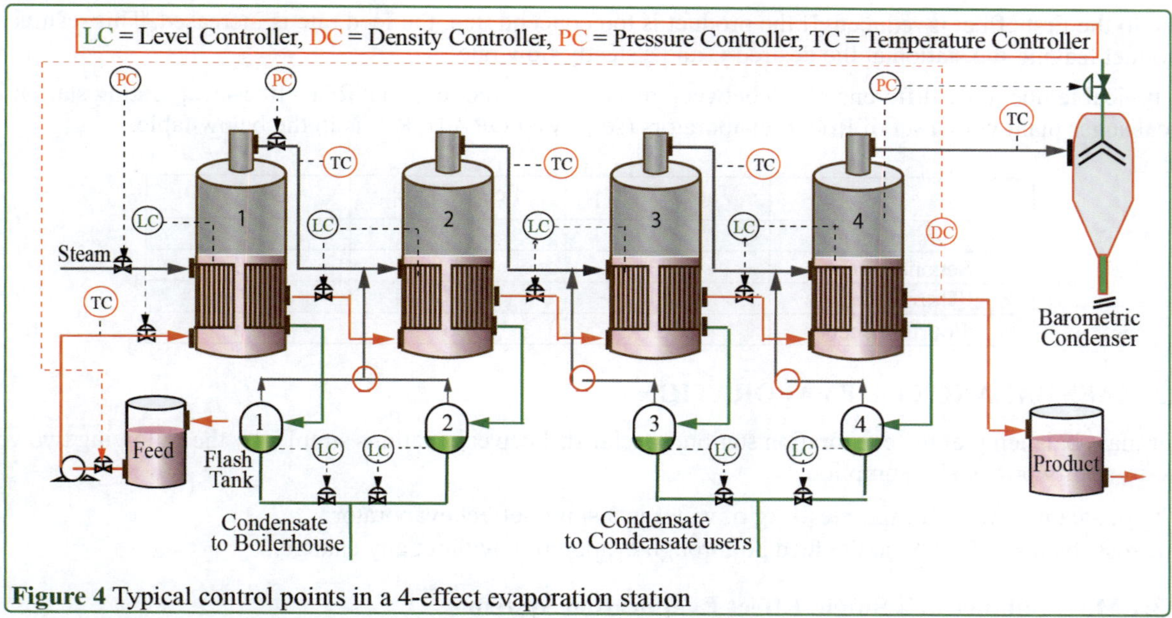

Figure 4 Typical control points in a 4-effect evaporation station

1.2 CONTROL OF MULTIPLE-EFFECT EVAPORATION

The **steady operation** is the most important point in running an evaporation station. Control of a multiple-effect evaporating station is based on the input and output values of the **level controller** (LC), **density controller** (DC), **pressure controller** (PC), and **temperature controller** (TC), as discussed under PROCESS CONTROL OF CHEMICAL ENGINEERING. A steady operation can be achieved by controlling the following parameters:

- **Steam Pressure:** Feeding the first-effect evaporator with the right-pressure steam is one of the main points in running the station steadily. It is *not* recommended to use highly supersaturated steam (simply **super steam** or **live steam**) because it has lower heat transferability than mildly super steam or highly saturated steam. Some chemical plants use high-pressure steam boilers with 1 500 to 3 500 kPa (= 15 to 35 Bar or 220 to 510 Lb/In^2) pressure (P) to produce super steam with T of 200 to 255ºC (= 390 to 490ºF). The live steam above these values is *not* appropriate for the first effect. The plants, which have a steam turbine, use live steam to run the turbine. Then the steam discharged from the turbine's exhaust (so-called the exhaust steam) is used in the first effect. In the plants that are *not* equipped with the turbine, the P of the live steam is reduced to around 230 kPa (= 33 Lb/In^2) by the steam pressure reduction process, and then it is used in the first effect.
- **Pressure Control:** Pressure (P) is usually controlled in the first and last effects. In the last-effect evaporator, the controller adjusts the P by cooling water flow to the barometric condenser. The P in the last effect is usually kept constant by a **direct-contact barometric condenser** (discussed under CONDENSERS). Thus, the cooling water flow to the condenser can keep the last effect at a constant P. The condensate P is typically kept at about 20 kPa (= 0.2 Atm = 2.9 PSI) vacuum pressure (P_{Vac}), a P below P_{Atm} (= 101 kPa = 14.7 PSI).
- **Temperature Control:** Temperature (T) is controlled in some streams, including the feed stream to each effect and the vapor entering and leaving each effect, as shown in Figure 4.
- **Level Control:** The feed level (called the liquid head, h), mainly in the last effect, is kept as low as possible. This reduces the processing solution in each effect and improves the steam economy. In addition, the level control minimizes the effect of h on the solution's boiling point temperature (T_{BP}).
- **Product Concentration:** A density controller (DC) can control the concentration (C) of the product leaving the last effect because there is a direct relationship between a solution's D (density) and DS (dissolved solid content). If the steam P and its flow rate and feed level in each effect are maintained stable, changing the feed rate to the first effect can change the product's C. If the product is *not* concentrated enough, the feed

rate to the first effect is reduced. If the product is too concentrated, the feed rate is increased. This results in a product leaving the station at the desired *C* and a steady flow rate.

A typical temperature difference (ΔT) between the vapor and the feed in a four-effect-evaporating station in a typical sugar plant with a set of Robert evaporators (see EVAPORATORS) is in the below table.

	Vapor *T* [ºC]	Feed *T* [ºC]	ΔT [ºC]
First effect	130	125	5
Second effect	123	113	10
Third effect	111	94	17
Fourth effect	92	66	26

1.3 MASS BALANCE OF EVAPORATION

For mass balancing of the evaporation station, specialists keep calculations simpler by the following two very-close-to-reality practical assumptions:

- 1 kg of steam or vapor evaporates 1 kg of water in a single-effect evaporator,
- The dissolved solids (*DS*) in the feed go through evaporation without any change.

1.3.1 Mass Balance of a Single-Effect Evaporating System

Figure 5 shows a single-effect evaporating system with one Robert evaporator. The feed moves inside the evaporator's tubes while steam moves between the tubes. Steam evaporates part of the water in the feed and moves out as condensate. Vapor, released by evaporation of a portion of the water in feed, is pumped by a vacuum pump to the condenser. After the feed under evaporation reaches the desired concentration, it is pumped out from the bottom of the evaporator. The inflows are feed (*F*) and steam (*S*), and outflows are product (*P*), vapor (*V*), and condensate (*C*). The relationship between the mass flow rate of the feed ($\dot{M}_F$), the product ($\dot{M}_P$), vapor ($\dot{M}_V$), condensate ($\dot{M}_C$), and that of evaporated water ($\dot{M}_W$) can be balanced as

$$\dot{M}_F + \dot{M}_S = \dot{M}_P + \dot{M}_V + \dot{M}_C \quad (3)$$

$$\dot{M}_F = \dot{M}_P + \dot{M}_V \quad (4)$$

$$\dot{M}_W = \dot{M}_V = \dot{M}_F - \dot{M}_P \quad (5)$$

$$\dot{M}_S = \dot{M}_C \quad (6)$$

The mass of the dissolved-solids concentration (C_{DS}) can be balanced as

$$\dot{M}_P . C_{DS.P} = \dot{M}_F . C_{DS.F} \quad \text{or} \quad \dot{M}_P = \dot{M}_F \frac{C_{DS.F}}{C_{DS.P}} \quad (7)$$

Mass flow rate is usually given in t/h, and $C_{DS,F}$, and C_{DS} in mass percentage or mass fraction (X).

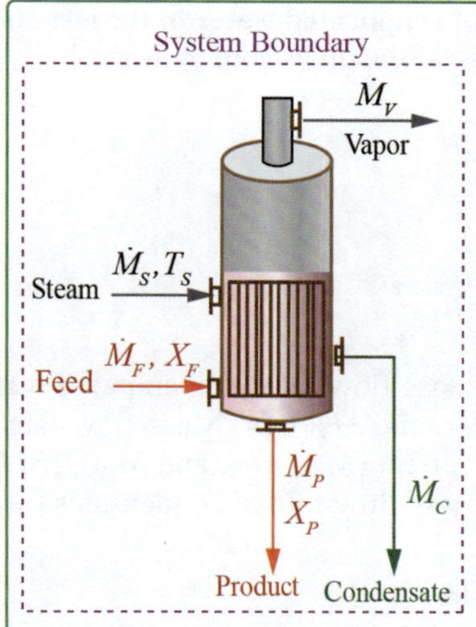

Figure 5 Mass balance on a single-effect evaporating system

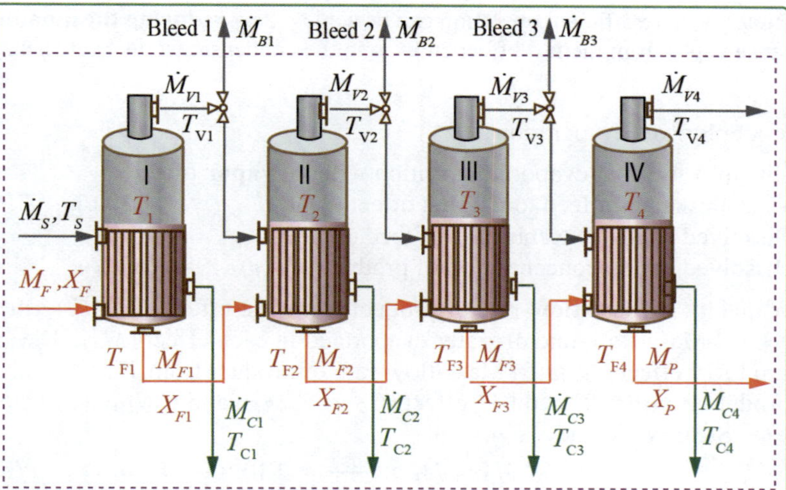

Figure 6 Mass balance on a 4-effect evaporating system with vapor bleed 1, 2, and 3

1.3.2 Mass Balance of a Multiple-Effect Evaporating Station

The mass balance of a multiple-effect evaporating system is almost the same as that of a single-effect system because some calculations for multiple effects are conducted for each effect separately. Here, we consider a four-effect-evaporation station shown in Figure 6. In effect 1, heat from the steam evaporates water in quantity equal to the mass of the vapor produced. This vapor (called **vapor 1**) is then used as the heating medium in 2. And so on. The vapor from 4 enters the condenser to be condensed. The steam fed to 1 becomes the condensate from 1 (condensate from steam, shown with subscript *CS*). The vapor from 1 (*V*1) becomes the condensate from 2 (C_2 or vapor 1 condensate) and so on. Thus, $\dot{M}_S = \dot{M}_{C1} = \dot{M}_{CS}$, $\dot{M}_{V1} = \dot{M}_{C2}$, $\dot{M}_{V2} = \dot{M}_{C3}$ and $\dot{M}_{V3} = \dot{M}_{C4}$. In Figure 6, three **vapor bleeds** (*VB*) are used, with mass flow-rate of $\dot{M}_{VB1}$, $\dot{M}_{VB2}$, and $\dot{M}_{VB3}$. Then, the mass for each effect can be balanced separately, as

$$\dot{M}_F + \dot{M}_S = \dot{M}_{F1} + \dot{M}_{V1} + \dot{M}_{C1} \quad (8)$$

$$\dot{M}_{F1} + \dot{M}_{V1} = \dot{M}_{F2} + \dot{M}_{V2} + \dot{M}_{C2} \quad (9)$$

$$\dot{M}_{F2} + \dot{M}_{V2} = \dot{M}_{F3} + \dot{M}_{V3} + \dot{M}_{C3} \quad (10)$$

$$\dot{M}_{F3} + \dot{M}_{V3} = \dot{M}_{F4} + \dot{M}_{V4} + \dot{M}_{C4} \quad (11)$$

The balance between the feed's flow rate ($\dot{M}_F$) and the product's flow rate ($\dot{M}_P$) is

$$\dot{M}_F = \dot{M}_P + \dot{M}_{V1} + \dot{M}_{V2} + \dot{M}_{V3} + \dot{M}_{V4} \quad (12)$$

Because the vapor from the last effect goes to the condenser, the rate of total condensate produced ($\dot{M}_C$) equates to the sum of the condensed steam in 1st effect and the condensed vapors in 2nd and 3rd effects.

$$\dot{M}_C = \dot{M}_S + \dot{M}_{V2} + \dot{M}_{V3} = \dot{M}_{C1} + \dot{M}_{C2} + \dot{M}_{C3} \quad (13)$$

The mass flow rate of steam ($\dot{M}_S$), which is used in the first effect, is the same as the amount of water evaporated in the first effect, so

$$\dot{M}_S = \dot{M}_{W1} = \dot{M}_{V1} \quad (14)$$

$\dot{M}_S$ can also be calculated from the sum of all **vapor bleeds** (*VB*), taken from individual effects ($\dot{M}_{VB1}$, $\dot{M}_{VB2}$, and $\dot{M}_{VB3}$), and the vapor taken from the last effect ($\dot{M}_{V4}$).

$$\dot{M}_S = \dot{M}_{VB1} + \dot{M}_{VB2} + \dot{M}_{VB3} + \dot{M}_{V4} \quad (15)$$

[Note: A more efficient operation can be achieved by **reducing the amount of evaporated water in the last effect** because vapor from the last effect ends up in the condenser, so its heat energy is wasted in its cooling water.]

Example 1 on Evaporation

Given: A 4-effect-evaporating station without **vapor bleed**

Mass flow rate of feed to the first effect ($\dot{M}_F$)	130 t/h
Dissolved solids concentration of feed ($C_{DS.F}$)	15%
Dissolved-solids-concentration of product ($C_{DS.P}$)	65%

Wanted: (1) Mass-flow-rate of product from last effect ($\dot{M}_P$), (2) Total mass flow rate of evaporated water ($\dot{M}_W$), (3) Mass-flow-rate of water evaporated in each effect ($\dot{M}_{W1}$, $\dot{M}_{W2}$, $\dot{M}_{W3}$, and $\dot{M}_{W4}$), (4) Mass-flow-rate of steam to 1st effect ($\dot{M}_S$), (5) Mass-flow-rate of product from 1st, 2nd, and 3rd effect ($\dot{M}_{P1}$, $\dot{M}_{P2}$, and $\dot{M}_{P3}$), (6) *DS* in product from 1st, 2nd, and 3rd effect ($C_{DS,P1}$, $C_{DS,P2}$, and $C_{DS,P3}$), (7) Total mass-flow-rate of condensates ($\dot{M}_C$), and (8) Steam efficiency (E_S).

$$\dot{M}_P = \dot{M}_F \times \frac{C_{DS.F}}{C_{DS.P}} = 130 \times \frac{15}{65} = 30 \qquad \text{t/h (14 kg/s)}$$

The total mass flow rate of evaporated water ($\dot{M}_W$) is the difference between $\dot{M}_F$ and $\dot{M}_P$.

$$\dot{M}_W = \dot{M}_F - \dot{M}_P = 130 - 30 = 100 \text{ t/h}$$

Mass-flow-rate of water evaporated in each effect is the same, so

$$\dot{M}_{W1} = \dot{M}_{W2} = \dot{M}_{W3} = \dot{M}_{W4} = \frac{100}{4} = 25 \text{ t/h}$$

Because there is *no* vapor bleed, the mass flow rate of steam ($\dot{M}_S$) is also the same as $\dot{M}_{W1}$, so

$$\dot{M}_S = 25 \qquad \text{t/h}$$

$$\dot{M}_{P1} = \dot{M}_F - \dot{M}_{W1} = 130 - 25 = 105 \text{ t/h} \qquad \dot{M}_{P2} = \dot{M}_{P1} - \dot{M}_{W2} = 105 - 25 = 80 \text{ t/h}$$

$$\dot{M}_{P3} = \dot{M}_{P2} - \dot{M}_{W3} = 80 - 25 = 55 \text{ t/h} \qquad \dot{M}_P = \dot{M}_{P3} - \dot{M}_{W2} = 55 - 25 = 30 \text{ t/h}$$

$$C_{DS.P1} = C_{DS.F} \times \frac{\dot{M}_F}{\dot{M}_{P1}} = 15 \times \frac{130}{105} = 18.6\% \qquad C_{DS.P2} = C_{DS.P1} \times \frac{\dot{M}_{P1}}{\dot{M}_{P2}} = 18.6 \times \frac{105}{80} = 24.4\%$$

$$C_{DS.P3} = C_{DS.P2} \times \frac{\dot{M}_{P2}}{\dot{M}_{P3}} = 24.4 \times \frac{80}{55} = 35.5\% \qquad C_{DS.P} = C_{DS.P3} \times \frac{\dot{M}_{P3}}{\dot{M}_P} = 35.5 \times \frac{55}{30} = 65\%$$

Because the last vapor goes to the condenser, the total amount of condensates is

$$\dot{M}_C = \dot{M}_S + \dot{M}_{V2} + \dot{M}_{V3} = 25 + 25 + 25 = 75 \qquad \text{t/h}$$

$$E_S = \frac{\dot{M}_W}{\dot{M}_S} = \frac{100}{25} = 4 \qquad \text{t water/1 t steam}$$

Example 2 on Evaporation

Given: A 4-effect station like the previous example, but with 3 **vapor bleeds**

Total mass-flow-rate of evaporated water in all effects ($\dot{M}_W$)	100 t/h
Mass-flow-rate of bleed 1 (vapor taken from 1st effect), $\dot{M}_{B1}$	8 t/h
Mass-flow-rate of bleed 2 (vapor taken from 2nd effect), $\dot{M}_{B2}$	3 t/h
Mass-flow-rate of bleed 3 (vapor taken from 3rd effect), $\dot{M}_{B3}$	2 t/h
Heat-transfer area of the 4th effect evaporator (A)	1000 m^2

Wanted: (1) Mass-flow-rate of evaporated water in each effect ($\dot{M}_{W1}$, $\dot{M}_{W2}$, $\dot{M}_{W3}$, and $\dot{M}_{W4}$), (2) Mass-flow rate of 4th vapor per A going to the condenser ($\dot{M}_{V4}/A$), (3) Mass-flow-rate of steam used in the first effect ($\dot{M}_S$), (4) Total mass-flow-rate of condensate ($\dot{M}_C$), and (5) Steam efficiency (E_S).

The total amount of evaporated water ($\dot{M}_W$ = 100 t/h) is the same as in the previous example, but the amount evaporated in each effect is different. We have four unknown variables ($\dot{M}_{W1}$, $\dot{M}_{W2}$, $\dot{M}_{W3}$, and $\dot{M}_{W4}$), so four equations are needed to calculate them. Assume that X ton/h water evaporates in the fourth effect. To evaporate this amount of water, we need to produce X ton/h vapor in the 3rd effect, plus additional vapor bleed ($\dot{M}_{VB3} = 2$ t/h, known as the **vapor bleed** 3), so the 3rd effect needs to evaporate

$$\dot{M}_{W3} = \dot{M}_{V3} = X + \dot{M}_{VB3} = X + 2$$

The second effect needs to evaporate $X + 2$ t/h water, plus more water to cover the additional vapor bleed taken from it ($\dot{M}_{VB2} = 3$ t/h, known as the vapor bleed 2), so

$$\dot{M}_{W2} = \dot{M}_{V2} = \dot{M}_{W3} + \dot{M}_{VB2} = X + 2 + 3 = X + 5 \quad \text{t/h}$$

The first effect needs to evaporate $X + 5$ t/h water, plus more water to cover the additional vapor bleed taken from it ($\dot{M}_{VB1} = 8$ t/h, known as the vapor bleed 1), so

$$\dot{M}_{W1} = \dot{M}_{V1} = \dot{M}_{W2} + \dot{M}_{VB1} = X + 5 + 8 = X + 13 \text{ t/h}$$

We know that $\dot{M}_W = \dot{M}_{W1} + \dot{M}_{W2} + \dot{M}_{W3} + \dot{M}_{W4} = 100$ t/h, so

$$(X + 13) + (X + 5) + (X + 2) + (X) = 100 \qquad 4X = 80 \qquad X = 20 \text{ t/h}$$

$$\dot{M}_{W1} = 20 + 13 = 33 \text{ t/h} \quad \dot{M}_{W2} = 20 + 5 = 25 \text{ t/h} \quad \dot{M}_{W3} = 20 + 2 = 22 \text{ t/h} \; \dot{M}_{W4} = 20 \text{ t/h}$$

The mass-low rate of the vapor from the fourth effect going to the condenser ($\dot{M}_{V4}$) is the same as the mass-flow rate of water evaporated in that effect, so $\dot{M}_{V4} = \dot{M}_{W4} = 20$ t/h.

Because heat-transfer area is 1000 m^2, $\dot{M}_{V4}/A$ would be $(20 \times 1000)/1000 = 20$ kg/h.m^2. Note that $\dot{M}_{V4}/A$ is usually between 20 and 40 kg/h per m^2 heating surface area.

$\dot{M}_S$ is the same as the amount of water evaporated in 1st effect, so $\dot{M}_S = 33$ t/h. $\dot{M}_S$ can also be calculated from Equation 15, as $20 + 2 + 3 + 8 = 33$ t/h.

$$\dot{M}_C = \dot{M}_S + \dot{M}_{V2} + \dot{M}_{V3} = 33 + 25 + 22 = 80 \text{ t/h} \qquad E_S = \frac{\dot{M}_W}{\dot{M}_S} = \frac{100}{33} = 3 \text{ t water/1 t steam}$$

Note that E_S (t water evaporated/1 t steam used) is better than in the previous example (because the vapor bleeding process was used in this example).

1.4 ENERGY BALANCE OF EVAPORATION

Again, we base our heat-energy (scientifically enthalpy) balance calculations on the two practical assumptions given previously under the subsection of Mass Balance of Evaporating Station. In addition, we consider the following very-close-to-reality assumptions:

- The eat energy losses are negligibly low.
- The subcooling effect of condensate is negligible.
- The liquid head (h) effect in an evaporator is negligible.
- Noncondensing gases are sufficiently removed from evaporators.
- Steam entering the evaporating station is at saturation temperature.
- Tubes' heat-transfer coefficient (U_Q) is constant during evaporation.
- Specific heat capacity (C_Q) of the feed is constant during evaporation.
- Temperature differences (ΔT) are average, *not* logarithmic mean temperature differences.
- The effect of the feed's T_{BE} (boiling elevation temperature) is negligible, so the feed's T_{BP} (boiling point temperature) can be taken as the T_{BP} of the volatile component (usually water).
- ΔT (the driving force of evaporation) is the difference in the T of the steam (T_S, or vapor, T_V) and the liquid feed under evaporation (T_L, which equates to the T of the vapor above the liquid), so $\Delta T = T_S - T_L$ or $\Delta T = T_V - T_L$. The symbol ΔT denotes the T between steam (or vapor) and the liquid feed, but *no* **temperature change** in a substance.
- The total enthalpy (H) is the sum of sensible enthalpy and latent enthalpy, where sensible enthalpy is the H of the condensate or liquid and latent enthalpy is the H of vapor, and the total H (total enthalpy or total heat-energy content) is the H of the steam.

The second term (subcooling or **undercooling**) assumes that *no* cooling occurs, so when condensate leaves the evaporator, its T is *not* below its condensation temperature (T_C), and its enthalpy of condensation (H_{Con}) corresponds to the H of water at its T_{BP}. [In reality, some subcooling occurs, but it is negligible.]

It helps to mention here that in an evaporator, the temperature drop (generally known as the temperature difference, ΔT) across the heat-transfer area (A_Q) depends on the following:

- ΔP between the heating section (liquid section) and vapor section (above liquid section),
- Dissolved-solids (DS) concentration of the feed entering the evaporator,
- Feed's temperature (T) at the entrance to the evaporator, and
- Liquid head (depth of the feed over the heating area).

It also helps to mention that if we know T or P, the steam table (Table 1 in the Table Section of the book) can provide the following:

- Enthalpy (refers to specific enthalpy, in kJ/kg) of steam or vapor.
- Enthalpy of the liquid feed or condensate produced by evaporation.
- Enthalpy of Evaporation (**H_E**): In the evaporation process, $H_{Lat.S}$ (latent enthalpy of steam) is the difference between the steam enthalpy (H_S) and condensate enthalpy (H_C), so that $H_{Lat.S} = H_S - H_C$. Similarly, $H_{Lat.V}$ (latent enthalpy of vapor) equates to the difference between the vapor enthalpy (H_V) and condensate enthalpy (H_C) or $H_V - H_C$

Another point to be mentioned here is the **overall** (total) **heat transfer rate** ($\dot{E}_Q$, in kJ/h or BTU/ h). The main basic equation for calculating $\dot{E}_Q$ in a single-effect or multi-effect station is

$$\dot{E}_Q = U_{QO}.A_Q.\Delta T = U_{QO}.A_Q(T_2 - T_1) = U_{QO}.A_Q(T_S - T_L) \qquad (16)$$

U_{QO} is the overall heat transfer coefficient [in kJ/(h.m^2.ºC), W/(h.m^2.ºC), or BTU/(h.Ft^2.ºF)], A_Q is the wall's heat transfer area, through which heat transfers (in m^2 or Ft^2), and ΔT is the temperature difference between steam and the liquid feed (in °C or °F). [U_{QO} decreases as the feed under evaporation becomes more concentrated (because of the decrease in the heat transfer at higher DS contents). As mentioned earlier, the feed's T_{BP} increases as its DS content increases.]

With the above-listed simplifying assumptions and comments in mind, let us balance a single-effect and multiple-effect evaporation stations.

1.4.1 Energy Balance on a Single-Effect Evaporator

For heat-energy (enthalpy) balancing of a single-effect evaporator, consider Figure 7. The streams entering and leaving the evaporator are shown with subscript F for feed, S for steam, V for vapor, P for product, and C for condensate. Feed (with a mass flow rate of $\dot{M}_F$ and enthalpy of H_F) and steam (with a mass flow rate of $\dot{M}_S$ and enthalpy of H_S) enter the evaporator. Vapor (with a mass flow rate of $\dot{M}_V$ and enthalpy of H_V), product (with a mass flow rate of $\dot{M}_P$ and enthalpy of H_P), and condensate (with a mass flow rate of $\dot{M}_C$ and enthalpy of H_C) leave the evaporator. Then, the system's enthalpy balance can be started with the following equation:

$$\dot{M}_F.H_F + \dot{M}_S.H_S = \dot{M}_P.H_P + \dot{M}_V.H_V + \dot{M}_C.H_C \qquad (17)$$

In this equation, the multiplication product of a stream's mass flow rate ($\dot{M}$) and its enthalpy (H) gives the stream's heat rate (heat-content rate). For example, the first term ($\dot{M}_F.H_F$) represents the feed's heat rate ($\dot{E}_{Q.F}$, in kJ/h or BTU/h), so $\dot{E}_{Q.F}$ equates to

$$\dot{E}_{Q.F} = \dot{M}_F.H_F \qquad (18)$$

$$\dot{E}_{Q.F} = \dot{M}_F.\lambda_{Q.F}.T_F \qquad (19)$$

$C_{Q.F}$ is the feed's specific heat capacity (simply **heat capacity**), given in kJ/kg.ºC or BTU/Lb.ºF.

From Equations 18 and 19 feed's enthalpy (H_F) and product's enthalpy will be

$$H_F = C_{Q.F}.T_F \tag{20}$$

$$H_P = C_{Q.P}.T_P \tag{21}$$

We know that in a heat transfer process, the product of the mass flow rate ($\dot{M}$) of a heat stream and its enthalpy (H) is the heat-energy content of that stream. Thus, the heat-transfer rate from steam (with subscript S) to the heating area in the heat-transfer section of an evaporator is

$$\dot{E}_Q = \dot{M}_S.H_{ES} = \dot{M}_S(H_S - H_C) \tag{22}$$

H_{ES} (the enthalpy of evaporation of the saturated steam) equates to the difference between H_S (the enthalpy of the steam) and H_C (the enthalpy of the condensate). Similarly, H_{EV} (the enthalpy of evaporation of the saturated vapor) equates to $H_V - H_C$. Generally, H_E (enthalpy of evaporation) is the amount of latent enthalpy required to evaporate 1 kg of a liquid.

At a given T, the enthalpy of a saturated steam (H_S) can be obtained from Table 1. H_C (enthalpy of the condensate) can also be obtained from the same steam table as enthalpy of saturated liquid at that T (so-known as saturated temperature).

The $\dot{E}_Q$ from the solid wall (with subscript S) to the feed (with subscript F) is

$$\dot{E}_Q = (\dot{M}_F - \dot{M}_S)H_S - \dot{M}_F.H_F + \dot{M}_P.H_P \tag{23}$$

And because the amounts of heat transfer in Equations 22 and 23 are the same, we can combine these two to obtain an equation for the system's overall heat balance.

$$\dot{E}_Q = \dot{M}_S.H_S = (\dot{M}_F - \dot{M}_S)H_S - \dot{M}_F.H_F + \dot{M}_P.H_P \tag{24}$$

In the heat-transfer section of the evaporator, the heat transfer rate from the steam to the feed through the heating tubes (with the heat transfer area of A) is given as

$$\dot{E}_Q = U_{QO}.A(T_S - T_V) = \dot{M}_S.H_S - \dot{M}_S.H_C \tag{25}$$

The area through which the heat transfers is calculated from the next equation.

$$A = \frac{\dot{E}_Q}{U_{QO}(T_S - T_V)} \tag{26}$$

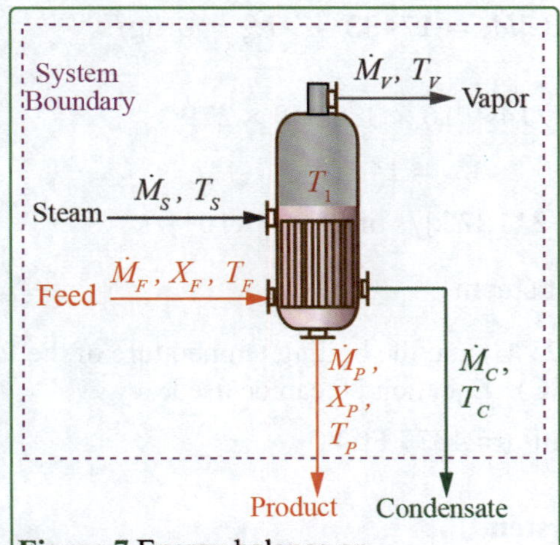

Figure 7 Energy balance on a single-effect evaporation station

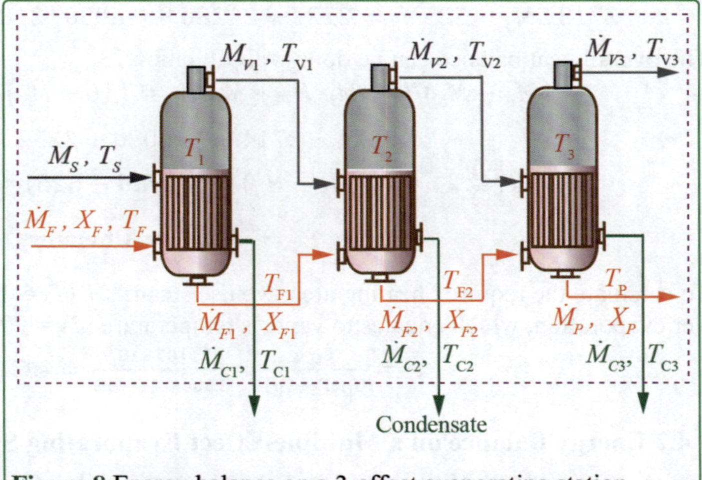

Figure 8 Energy balance on a 3-effect evaporating station

Example 3 on Evaporation: A single-effect evaporator, as shown in Figure 7

Steam's pressure (P_S)	230 kPa (= 33 Lb/In^2)
Feed's mass flow rate, $\dot{M}_F$	16 kg/s
Feed's *DS* concentration, $C_{DS,F}$	15%
Product's *DS* concentration, $C_{DS,P}$	30%
Feed's temperature entering evaporator, T_F	100ºC
Feed's boiling point temperature, $T_{BPF} = T_P$	90ºC
Feed's heat-transfer coefficient (U_Q)	1500 W/h.m^2.ºC (1500 J/s.m^2.ºC)

Wanted: (1) Amount of steam required ($\dot{M}_S$), (2) Steam efficiency (E_S), and (3) Required heating area

The mass flow rate of the product is calculated from Equation 7.

$$\dot{M}_P = \dot{M}_F \times \frac{DS_F}{DS_P} = 16 \times \frac{15}{30} = 8 \text{ kg/s}$$

Because $\dot{M}_W = \dot{M}_V$, the amount of water evaporated from Equation 5 will be

$$\dot{M}_W = \dot{M}_V = \dot{M}_F - \dot{M}_P = 16 - 8 = 8 \quad \text{kg/s}$$

Feed's specific heat capacity ($C_{Q.F}$) and that of the product ($C_{Q.P}$) can be calculated as

$$C_{Q.F} = 4.186(1 - 0.006C_{DS}) = 4.186(1 - 0.006 \times 15) = 3.8 \text{ kJ/kg.°C}$$

$$C_{Q.P} = 4.186(1 - 0.006 \times 45) = 3.1 \text{ kJ/kg.°C}$$

Feed's specific enthalpy (H_F) and that of product from Equations 20 and 21 are

$$H_F = C_{Q.F}.T_F = 3.8 \times 100 = 380 \text{ kJ/kg}$$

$$H_P = C_{Q.P}.T_P = 3.1 \times 90 = 279 \text{ kJ/kg}$$

For steam at 230 kPa, the following can be found from Table 1: (1) Temperature of steam at 230 kPa = 125ºC, (2) Enthalpy of condensate (H_C) at 125ºC = 525 kJ/kg, (3) Enthalpy of saturated steam (H_S) at 125ºC = 2 714 kJ/kg, and (4) Enthalpy of saturated vapor (H_V) at 90ºC = 2 660 kJ/kg

Knowing that $\dot{M}_V = \dot{M}_W$ and $\dot{M}_C = \dot{M}_S$, Equation 17 becomes

$$\dot{M}_F.H_F + \dot{M}_S.H_S = \dot{M}_P.H_P + \dot{M}_W.H_V + \dot{M}_S.H_C$$

$$16 \times 380 + \dot{M}_S \times 2713.5 = 8 \times 279 + 8 \times 2660 + \dot{M}_S \times 525$$

$$2713.5\dot{M}_S - 525\dot{M}_S = 2232 + 21280.8 - 6080 \quad 2188.5\dot{M}_S = 17433 \qquad \dot{M}_S = 8 \text{ kg/s}$$

The overall heat balance can be done with Equation 23.

$$(\dot{M}_F - \dot{M}_S)H_S - \dot{M}_F.H_F + \dot{M}_P.H_P = (16 - \dot{M}_S)2714 - 16 \times 380 + 8 \times 279$$

$$43424 - 2714\dot{M}_S - 6080 + 2232 \qquad \dot{M}_S = 14.6$$

$$\dot{E}_{Q.S} = \dot{M}_S.\lambda_E = \dot{M}_S(H_S - H_C) = 8(2714 - 525) = 21187 \text{ kJ/s or } 21187{\times}10^3 \text{ J/s}$$

$$E_S = \frac{\dot{M}_W}{\dot{M}_S} = \frac{8}{8} = 1 \text{ t water/1 t steam}$$

To calculate the required heating area, we use steam's T (T_S = 125°C) and the boiling temperature of the feed under evaporation, which equates to vapor's temperature (T_V = 90°C). Equation 26 can be used.

$$A = \frac{\dot{E}_{Q.S}}{U_Q(T_S - T_V)} = \frac{21187{\times}10^3}{1500(125-90)} = 403 \text{ m}^2 \ (= 4337 \text{ Ft}^2)$$

1.4.2 Energy Balance on a Multiple-Effect Evaporating System

We consider a three-effect station for balancing a multiple-effect evaporating system (see Figure 8). Using the same symbols as previously used, the enthalpy balance for each effect can be expressed by the next 3 equations:

$$\dot{M}_F.H_F + \dot{M}_S.H_S = \dot{M}_{F1}.H_{F1} + \dot{M}_{V1}.H_{V1} + \dot{M}_S.H_{C1} \qquad (27)$$

$$\dot{M}_{F1}.H_{F1} + \dot{M}_{V1}.H_{V1} = \dot{M}_{F2}.H_{F2} + \dot{M}_{V2}.H_{V2} + \dot{M}_{V1}.H_{C2} \qquad (28)$$

$$\dot{M}_{F2}.H_{F2} + \dot{M}_{V2}.H_{V2} = \dot{M}_P.H_P + \dot{M}_{V3}.H_{V3} + \dot{M}_{V2}.H_{C3} \tag{29}$$

[In some ChemEng books, H_{C1} is shown by the symbol H_{CS} (where subscript C is for condensate and S is for steam) to indicate that the condensate in the first effect is made from steam.]

We can also write the following heat balance:

$$\dot{M}_F.H_F = \dot{M}_P.H_P + \dot{M}_{V1}.H_{V1} + \dot{M}_{V2}.H_{V2} + \dot{M}_{V3}.H_{V3} \tag{30}$$

In the heat-transfer section of each evaporator, the heat transfer rate through the tubes (with the heat transfer area of A) of each effect can be calculated by the heat-transfer coefficient (U_Q) of that effect and ΔT between the heating medium entering the effect and the vapor leaving it.

$$\dot{E}_{Q1} = U_{Q1}.A_1.\Delta T_1 \qquad \dot{E}_{Q2} = U_{Q2}.A_2.\Delta T_2 \qquad \dot{E}_{Q3} = U_{Q3}.A_3.\Delta T_3 \tag{31}$$

In these equations, ΔT_1 is in the first effect ($T_S - T_{V1}$), ΔT_2 is in the second effect ($T_{V1} - T_{V2}$), and ΔT_3 is in the third effect ($T_{V2} - T_{V3}$), where subscript S is for steam and V is for vapor.

ΔT in each effect can be calculated using the U_Q of that effect and the total ΔT between the steam entering the first effect and the vapor leaving the last effect ($\Delta T = T_S - T_{V3}$). For example, the ΔT in the first effect (ΔT_1) of a three-effect evaporating station is

$$\Delta T_1 \approx \Delta T \frac{\frac{1}{U_{Q1}}}{\frac{1}{U_{Q1}} + \frac{1}{U_{Q2}} + \frac{1}{U_{Q3}}} \tag{32}$$

[$\dot{E}_{Q1}$, $\dot{E}_{Q2}$, and $\dot{E}_{Q3}$ are almost equal (because most of the time, the heating areas in all effects in a multiple-effect-evaporating station are almost equal.)]

We can use the station's total heat transfer area (A).

$$U_{Q1}.\Delta T_1 = U_{Q2}.\Delta T_2 = U_{Q3}.\Delta T_3 = \frac{\dot{E}_Q}{A} \tag{33}$$

This equation shows that the ΔT in each effect is approximately inversely proportional to the effect's heat-transfer coefficient (U_Q).

Example 4 on Evaporation: A triple-effect-evaporation station, as shown in Figure 8

Steam temperature to the first effect (T_S)	120°C
Boiling point temperature of the solution in 3rd effect (TBP3)	65°C
Heat-transfer coefficient in 1st effect (U_{Q1})	3 000 W/h.m².°C
Heat-transfer coefficient in 2nd effect (U_{Q2})	2 000 W/h.m².°C
Heat-transfer coefficient in 3rd effect (U_{Q3})	1 000 W/h.m².°C

Wanted: (1) Total temperature change (ΔT), (2) Temperature change in each effect (ΔT_1, ΔT_2, and ΔT_3), and (3) Solution's boiling point temperature in 1st and 2nd effect (T_{BP1} and T_{BP2}).

The total (ΔT) is 120 – 65 = 55°C.

$$\Delta T_1 = \Delta T \frac{\frac{1}{K_{Q1}}}{\frac{1}{U_{Q1}} + \frac{1}{U_{Q2}} + \frac{1}{U_{Q3}}} = 55 \frac{\frac{1}{3000}}{\frac{1}{3000} + \frac{1}{2000} + \frac{1}{1000}} = 55 \frac{3.33 \times 10^{-4}}{18.33 \times 10^{-4}} = 10$$

$$\Delta T_2 = 55 \frac{\frac{1}{2000}}{18.33\times 10^{-4}} = 15 \qquad \Delta T_3 = 55 \frac{\frac{1}{1000}}{18.33\times 10^{-4}} = 30$$

T_{BP} of the solution in 1st, 2nd, and 3rd effects are

$$T_{B1} = 120 - 10 = 110\ ℃ \qquad T_{B2} = 110 - 15 = 95\ ℃ \qquad T_{B3} = 95 - 30 = 65\ °C$$

Example 5 on Evaporation

Given: A triple-effect evaporator

Exhaust steam pressure to 1st effect	230 kPa (= 33 Lb/In^2)
First-vapor pressure	140 kPa (= 20 Lb/In^2)
Amount of first-effect condensate ($\dot{M}_C$)	20000 kg/h
Condensate enthalpy at 230 kPa, H_{230} (from Table 1)	525 kJ/kg (= 226 BTU/Lb)
Condensate enthalpy at 140 kPa, H_{140} (from Table 1)	461 kJ/kg (= 198 BTU/Lb)
Enthalpy of evaporation of vapor (H_E or λ_E) at 140 kPa	2230 kJ/kg (= 959 BTU/Lb)

Wanted: The amount of vapor produced (M_V) from flashing of first-effect condensate to the flashing tank for using in the second effect

$$\dot{E}_Q = M_C(H_{230} - H_{140}) = 20000(525 - 461) = 1280 \times 10^3 \text{ kJ/h}$$

$\dot{M}_V$ is obtained from the amount of heat released from condensate by flashing.

$$\dot{E}_Q = \dot{M}_V . H_E \qquad \dot{M}_V = \frac{1280000}{2230} = 574 \text{ kg/h } (= 1263 \text{ Lb/h})$$

1.5 OPERATING PROBLEMS OF EVAPORATION STATION

As the **heat center** of a chemical process plant, the evaporation station's operation is important (because of the high-energy demand and large amount of water that this station must evaporate.) This station usually supplies the vapor to a few stations, such as the heating station. In addition, it provides condensate to the boilers and other condensate users. Any problem that delays this station's operation will eventually affect the other stations. Calculating the steam efficiency (E_S) of the evaporating station determines if the station is efficient or *not*. However, some operating problems in this station are unavoidable, as discussed next.

- **Deposit in Heating Tubes:** Scale deposits create a resistance to heat transfer and, consequently, reduce the efficiency of the evaporating station considerably.
- **Insufficient Capacity:** When the **station capacity** (the total heat transfer area of the heating tubes of all evaporators) is insufficient, the station operates inefficiently. In this case, try one or more of the following: 1) Feed the station with a more concentrated solution. 2) Increase the steam pressure. 3) Increase the vacuum pressure on the last effect. [The vacuum in the condenser that receives the vapor from the last effect can maintain the pressure of that effect. There is an optimum vacuum P in the condenser (because too low vacuum pressure in an evaporator leads to liquid entrainment problem.)]
- **Low Heat Rate:** Steam supply from the boilerhouse might be low, or the vapor demand (vapor bleed) from the first effect for vapor users might be high.
- **Slow Removal of Noncondensing Gases** (NC gases)**:** Usually, NC gases (air, ammonia, and CO_2) are produced in individual effects by evaporating the feed, so they mix with the vapor and move with it. Because NC gases do *not* condense, they decrease the condensation T and gradually reduce the evaporation efficiency. The NC gases can be removed completely if their discharge points are enough and are located furthest from the vapor inlet. The NC gases are vented to the vapor line of the next effect, to the last-effect condenser, or to the atmosphere (if their P is above P_{Atm}).
- **Wrong Feed Level:** The feed level over the heating surface (known as the liquid head) in a Robert evaporator should be kept at such a height that the top tube's sheet is covered. A very low level reduces the efficiency of the evaporator. Instead, a high feed level decreases the ΔT and heat transfer. As a result, the station efficiency becomes lower.
- **Low Feed Temperature:** When the feed's T entering the first effect is low, the amount of heat usage increases (because the feed must be heated to T_{BP} before any evaporation can start.)
- **Leaks in Heating Tubes:** If there is a leak in the heating tubes, vapor can get to the heating area and dilute the feed. In such cases, pressure testing of the evaporator's steam chest is necessary. The test can be done by pressurizing the steam chest with water and watching for a leak.
- **Wrong Rate of Vapor Bleeds:** The amount of vapor bleeds taken from individual effects is too high.

2. EVAPORATORS

An evaporator is a device (equipment) in which evaporation is performed. It is, actually, a large heat exchanger, which uses heat energy (E_Q, simply heat and scientifically enthalpy) to concentrate a liquid. Usually, water (with relatively high specific heat capacity, C_Q) is the liquid that must be evaporated. In its typical design, an evaporator is a closed-round-vertical vessel, which consists of two (2) sections:

- Heat-transfer section (the section where the liquid is under evaporation), and
- Vapor section (the section above the liquid).

The **heat-transfer section** (also called the **steam section** or **steam chest**) receives steam or vapor as a heating medium to transfer E_Q from the heating medium to the liquid feed through the walls of the heating tubes (in tube evaporators) or heating plates (in plate evaporators). As a result of the heat transfer process, some vapor is produced that goes to the evaporator's **vapor section**.

The multiplying product of U_Q (heat transfer coefficient), A_Q (heat transfer area), and ΔT (temperature difference between steam and the liquid feed) calculates an evaporator's heat transfer rate ($\dot{E}_Q = E_Q/t$).

$$\dot{E}_Q = U_Q.A_Q.\Delta T \tag{34}$$

According to this equation, an evaporator's $\dot{E}_Q$ in kJ/(h.m^2.°C) is the amount of E_Q (in kJ) through a 1 m^2 area of its heating tubes to create a ΔT of 1°C in 1 h.

Therefore, if the feed's T is near or at its T_{BP} (boiling point temperature), almost all the steam's E_Q is used for evaporation, so the evaporator's steam economy (efficiency) is better (lower).

Based on the design, evaporators can be broadly divided into two (2) types:

- Tube evaporators, and
- Plate evaporators.

Tube (tube-and-shell) evaporators are further divided into two (2) types:

- Robert evaporators, and
- Thin-film tube evaporators.

The thin-film tube evaporators are furthermore subdivided into two (2) types:

- Rising-film tube evaporators, and
- Falling-film tube evaporators.

2.1 ROBERT EVAPORATORS

Robert evaporator was first designed in the 1850s by F. Robert (a Czech sugar technologist). The modified Robert evaporators are still the most widely used. As shown in Figure 9, a typical Robert evaporator consists of a closed-cylindrical vessel, typically 5 to 6 m (= 16 to 20 Ft) in diameter and 6 to 10 m (= 20 to 33 Ft) in height, depending on the capacity of the evaporator. The vessel is usually covered with a 5 cm (= 2 In) insulated material with a thin outer layer of aluminum to prevent the loss of heat energy. The vessel consists of two main sections: 1) **Steam Section** (heating section or steam chest)**:** The space that receives steam. 2) **Vapor Section:** The space above the feed (this space is mainly used for releasing vapor).

The main part of the steam section is the **tube bundle** (tube bank), to which many (around 2000 for a typical size evaporator) round tubes, called the **heating tubes**, are fitted. Each heating tube is 2 to 3 m long (the same distance between **tube plates**). The inside diameter of the tubes is 40 to 50 mm (= 1.6 to 2 In). Tubes are placed vertically between two **tube plates** (tube sheets). The bottom plate is placed slightly above the base of the evaporator to allow for liquid feed circulation. The tube plates have the same number of round holes as heating tubes. Each hole has a clearance of 0.25 mm, compared with the heating tube's outside diameter, to allow for rolling the tubes into the holes of the tube plates.

The heating section has a wider tube, called the **circulating pipe** (also called **downtake pipe** or **draft pipe**), which is welded to the middle of the tube plates. Typically, the size of the circulating pipe is about 20% of the diameter of the evaporator. [Today, some suppliers offer Robert evaporators without downtake pipe. In this design, the liquid feed moves down the heating tubes instead of the intake tube.]

The heating section also has a steam trap, which usually operates on a density difference to separate condensate from steam. The condensate runs to a collecting tank, and from there, it is pumped to the condensate users, such as the steam boilers. Some gauge glasses are fitted to the heating section to show the condensate level in that section. [Proper discharge of condensate from an evaporator is important (because its accumulation in the evaporator may cause water hammering.)]

The main vessel and pipes are usually covered with a 5 cm (= 2 In) insulated material with a thin outer layer of aluminum, used for preventing heat loss and providing safety.

Feed (which enters the bottom of the vessel) circulates uniformly **inside** the heating tubes, below and above the tube sheets, and comes down through the intake (circulating) pipe.

Steam (which enters the vessel's side in the middle of the steam section) flows outside the heating tubes without direct contact with the feed. E_Q from the steam transfers through the wall of the tubes to the feed, evaporating its water in quantity equal to the mass of the vapor produced. The amount of heat transfer between the steam and the feed under evaporation depends on the evaporator's heat transfer area (A_Q) in a way that the *greater* the A_Q, the *more* heat transfer occurs. The A_Q of a typical Robert evaporator is around 2 000 m^2 (= 21 530 Ft^2).

Vapor (formed from feed's evaporation) rises toward the upper section of the steam inlet, passes an entrainment separator (to remove the water's droplets), and leaves the evaporator at the very top.

Condensate (formed from steam's condensation) moves toward the bottom and is discharged by a vacuum pump on the other side of the steam inlet, as seen on the right side of Figure 9. Under the evaporator's main vessel, a **condensate flashing tank** (simply flashing tank) is placed to collect the condensate from the evaporator and separate the vapor from the condensate. The flashing tank pressure (P) is lower than the main vessel, so part of the condensate entering the tank is converted to vapor, used in the next-effect evaporator. Flashing evaporation (the sudden conversion of condensate to vapor by lowering the temperature, pressure, or both) reduces steam consumption (because the flashing heat formed in the flashing tank can be used in the next effect of multiple-effect evaporation).

Noncondensing gases (NC gases, such as air, ammonia, and carbon dioxide gas) formed during evaporation are discharged from the side of the vessel by two (or more) independent outlets (ports), which are located furthest from the vapor inlet. If the NC gases are discharged into the atmosphere, a steam trap, activated by temperature, is adjusted *not* to vent more than necessary of these gases into the atmosphere.

The heating tubes are made of mild steel, brass, or copper. Today, however, modern-designed Robert evaporators use tubes made of stainless steel because,

- The heat transfer coefficient (U_Q) of stainless is about 1100 W/h.m^2.°C, almost the same as brass (with U_Q of 1150) and copper (with U_Q of 1200 W/h.m^2.°C),
- The heat resistivity of stainless is *not* great,
- Less tube-replacement requirement, and
- Less scale-cleaning requirement.

Two (2) types of stainless steel used in heating tubes are 304 and 430 grades. The thickness of the tubes is 1.2 to 1.6 mm, depending on the stainless steel's grade. The stainless tubes' thermal conductivity (K_{Th}) is in the range of 20 to 40 W/h.m.°C. And their heat expansion is between 10 and 20 μm/(m.°C).

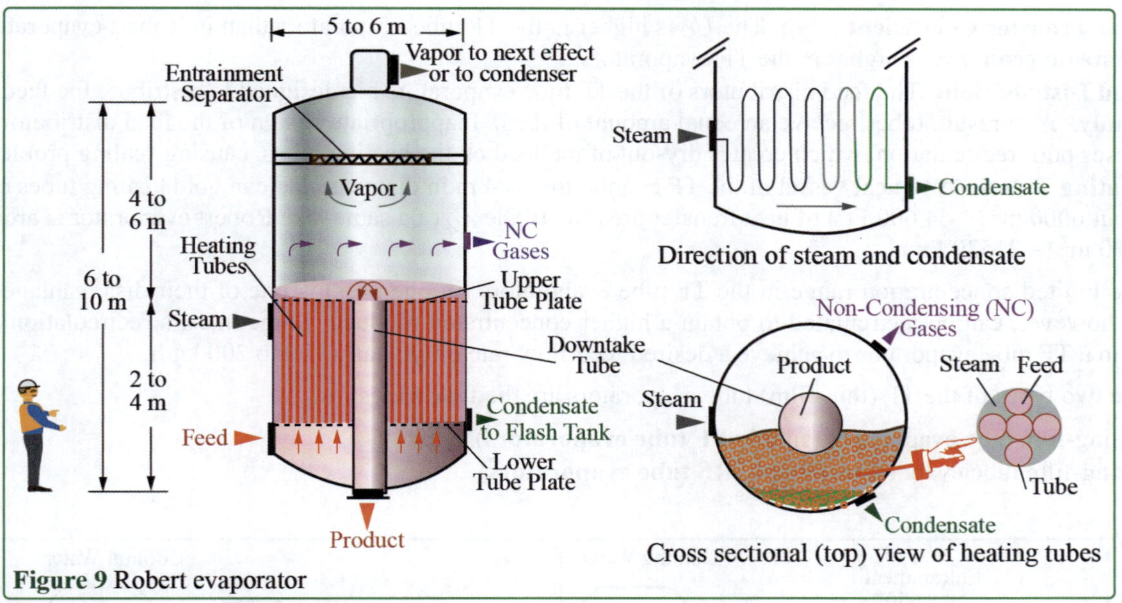

Figure 9 Robert evaporator

2.2 THIN-FILM TUBE EVAPORATORS

The thin-film tube evaporators (the TF tube evaporators) use long heating tubes and compact evaporating vessels, compared with the Robert evaporators. In a TF tube evaporator, depending on the design, the feed moves on the inside (in most designs) or outside surface of the heating tubes as a **thin layer** (thin film), which is in the millimeter range. This is why they are called **thin-film tube** (TF) **evaporators**. The height of the heating tubes is in the range of 5 to 10 m (= 17 to 33 Ft), and their diameter is in the range of 30 to 50 mm (= 1.25 to 2 In). [The height and diameter of the tubes depend on the evaporator's design and capacity.]

To become familiar with creating a thin film on the heating tubes, consider a TF tube evaporator in which feed moves slowly (at about 0.5 to 2 m/s) inside the tubes and steam moves outside the tubes (as is usually the case). Because of heat transfer, the feed starts to boil, so it forms some vapor, whose pressure (P) presses the remaining liquid against the wall of the tubes to form a thin film. [The film's thickness affects the **heat transfer coefficient** (U_Q). A thinner film is favored because the *thinner* the film, the *greater* is the U_Q. This is true because a thinner film decreases the distance between the two heat-transfer surfaces.]

Following are the comparison of the TF tube evaporators and Robert evaporators:

- **Feed and Steam Movement:** In both TF tube and Robert evaporators, feed moves inside the heating tubes and steam outside. [In some falling-film tube evaporators, feed moves outside the tubes and steam inside.]
- **Operability:** Both TF tube and Robert evaporators are operable and controllable easily.
- **Longer Heating Tubes:** The TF tube evaporators have longer tubes than Robert evaporators. The TF evaporators have tubes 8 to 14 m (= 26 to 46 Ft) long, compared with 2 to 3 m (= 6.5 to 9.8 Ft) in Robert evaporators. This comparably gives a greater heat transfer area in the TF evaporators.
- **Inventory:** The feed inventory is much smaller in a TF tube evaporator than in a Robert evaporator. Small inventory, of course, can reach the desired concentration in a single pass.
- **Retention Time:** The retention time (residence time) is lower (typically 2 to 4 minutes) in the TF tube evaporators (an advantage) than in the Robert evaporators (with several minutes).
- **Boiling Point Elevation** (T_{BPE})**:** Unlike in Robert evaporators, there is *no* boiling point elevation (T_{BPE}) in the TF tube evaporators. Because of the short retention time (the *smaller* the T_{BPE}, the *larger* is the ΔT and the *better* is the steam economy).

- **Heat Transfer Coefficient** (U_Q)**:** The U_Q is higher in the TF tube evaporators than in Robert evaporators, so the **steam economy** is higher in the TF evaporators.
- **Feed Distribution:** The feed distributors of the TF tube evaporators are designed to distribute the feed uniformly. As a result, tubes receive an equal amount of feed. Inappropriate design of the feed distributor causes poor recirculation, which creates dry-out of the feed on the heating tubes, causing scaling problems.
- **Heating Tubes:** A typical vessel of the TF evaporators is 4 m in diameter and can hold heating tubes of about 6000 m^2 (= 64 600 Ft^2) of heat transfer area (A_Q). The A_Q of a same-size Robert evaporator is around 2000 m^2 (= 21530 Ft^2).

The limited concentration range in the TF tube evaporators (in one pass) is one of their disadvantages. The feed, however, can be recirculated to obtain a higher concentrated product. Sometimes, a recirculation line is used in a TF tube evaporator to achieve a desired feed flow rate of typically 100 to 200 kg/h.

The two types of the TF (thin-film) tube evaporators are the followings:

- Falling-film tube evaporators (simply **FF tube evaporators**), and
- Rising-film tube evaporators (simply **RF tube evaporators**).

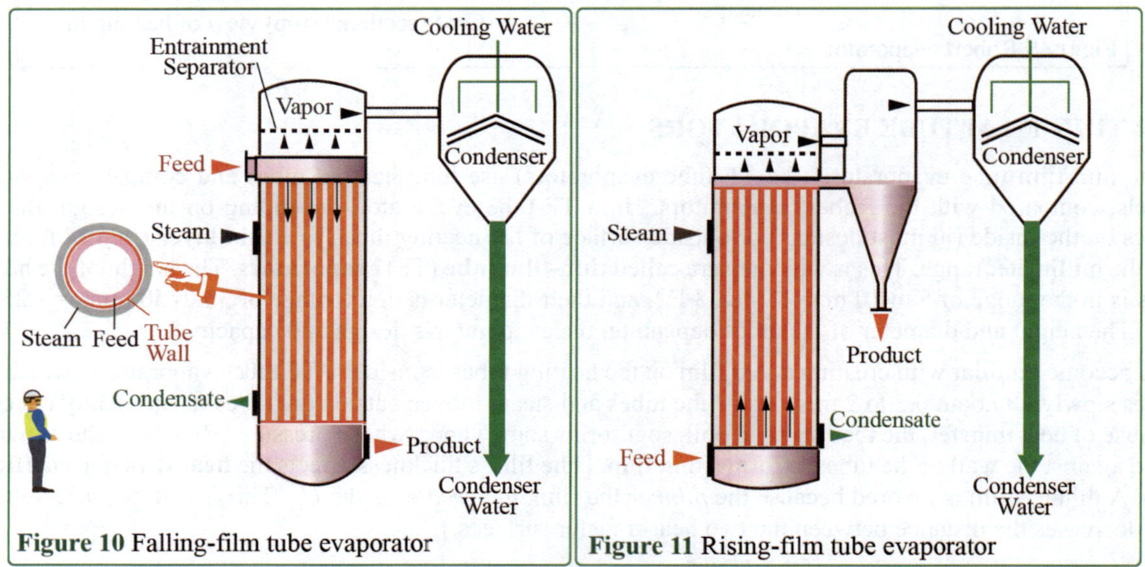

Figure 10 Falling-film tube evaporator

Figure 11 Rising-film tube evaporator

2.3 FALLING-FILM TUBE EVAPORATORS

The falling-film (FF) tube evaporators have round vertical heating tubes, typically 30 to 50 mm (1.25 to 1.5 In) in diameter and 8 to 12 m (26 to 40 Ft) high. Figure 10 shows a typical FF tube evaporator in which **feed**,

- Enters the evaporator at the top,
- Distributes above the upper tube sheet,
- Enters the heating tubes in an equal amount,
- Makes a thin layer (film) inside of the heating tubes,
- Boils in the heating tubes while moving downward by gravity, and
- Enters the product collecting vessel, which is installed next to the evaporator.

Steam,

- Enters the evaporator close to the top,

- Distributes outside of the heating tubes, and
- Moves downward while giving part of its heat value to the feed.

Vapor,

- Enters the collecting vessel, which connects to a barometric condenser,
- Part of the vapor changes to condensate, which exits at the bottom of the evaporator.

Because of falling, the feed's velocity (V) in an FF tube evaporator (with v of about 2 m/s) is greater than that of the feed in an RF tube evaporator (with v of about 0.5 m/s). Because of the falling mechanism, however, controlling a uniform liquid film in the tubes of an FF tube evaporator is more difficult than a rising movement in the tubes of an RF tube evaporator. Special design feed distributors or spray nozzles can solve this problem in FF tube evaporators. The absence of liquid head effect on evaporation in an FF tube evaporator is, on the other hand, one of its advantages. This eliminates boiling the liquid above the tubes, so the feed entering the feed distributor flashes it to form a vapor.

2.4 RISING-FILM TUBE EVAPORATORS

The rising-film (RF) tube evaporators are offered in different designs. Figure 11 shows a typical rising tube evaporator in which **feed**,

- Enters the evaporator at the bottom,
- Distributes below the lower tube sheet,
- Enters the heating tubes in an equal amount,
- Makes a thin layer (film) inside of the heating tubes,
- Boils in the heating tubes while moving upward by vacuum pressure, and
- Enters the product's collecting vessel, which connects to a barometric condenser.

Steam,

- Enters the evaporator close to the top,
- Distributes outside of the heating tubes, and
- Moves downward while giving part of its heat value to the feed.

Vapor,

- Rises and enters the feed's collecting vessel, which connects to a barometric condenser, and
- Part of the vapor changes to condensate, which exits at the bottom of the evaporator.

Some RF tube evaporators, like the **Kestner rising-film evaporator**, consist of two vessels; evaporating vessel and a flashing tank (condensate collecting tank). The evaporating vessel is 3 m in diameter (compared with 5 m in the Robert evaporator with an equivalent capacity). The collecting vessel is smaller than the evaporating vessel and installed on the side and near the top of the collecting vessel. The flash tank, which operates at low negative vacuum pressure (P_{Vac}), separates vapor from the liquid feed. The heating tubes in Kestner are 6 to 8 m long, compared with 2 to 3 m in Robert evaporators. The diameter of heating tubes is the same as in Robert evaporators (50 mm).

The advantages of FF (falling-film) tube evaporators over RF (rising-film) tube evaporators are:

- **Temperature Difference** (ΔT): An FF tube evaporator can operate satisfactorily with a much lower ΔT than an RF tube evaporator, requiring more effects. Consider when the steam has a temperature of 130ºC, and the boiling temperature in the last effect is 70ºC. Only four [(130-70)/14 = 4] effects are achievable in an RF tube evaporator (because it needs a ΔT of 14ºC between the boiling liquid and the heating medium to operate properly). But as many as 8 effects can be operated using an FF tube evaporator (because it needs a ΔT of only 6ºC).
- **Viscosity:** An FF tube evaporator can handle more viscous feed than a rising-film one.

- **Retention Time:** An FF tube evaporator has a lower retention time (typically 2 minutes) than an RF tube evaporator (with a typical retention time of 4 minutes).
- **Feed Movement:** In an FF tube evaporator, the feed moves over the heating surface by gravity but must be pumped in an RF tube evaporator.

Some chemical process plants prefer to use falling-film evaporators because they provide greater efficiency (lower heat economy) than rising-film evaporators (better heat transferability).

2.5 PLATE EVAPORATORS

The plate evaporators are the newest and the most energy-efficient. First, some plants installed them as add-on effects, but later they were used in a much wider range. The plate evaporators are designed for evaporation duties using the thin-film tube evaporators (which have a good heat transferability and short retention time of the feed). The plate evaporators operate in a multiple-pass mode, like Robert evaporators. For the same heat-transfer capacity, the plate evaporators have the following advantages over Robert evaporators:

- They require less energy,
- They need less floor area,
- They have higher flow rates,
- They require less heating-media cleaning,
- They have a higher heat-transfer coefficient (U_Q),
- They create less color increase if the feed is a color-creating solution,
- They have a lower ΔT between the heating medium at the entrance and the product at the exit,
- They are designed in a way that the feed boils on the surface of the plates as a film, allowing good heat transferability and a short retention time of the feed in the evaporator, and
- They typically have a shorter retention time of 1 to 2 minutes (because of smaller feed volume) than 2 to 4 minutes in thin-film tube evaporators and several minutes in the Robert evaporators.

The disadvantages of the plate evaporators, compared with Robert evaporators, are

- They are limited on feed's viscosity, η (maximum η operable is 1.5 Pa.s), and
- They create a greater pressure drop (generally known as pressure difference, ΔP).

Unlike gasketed plate heat exchangers, the plate evaporators do *not* need a rubber gasket between the pressed (corrugated) plates because they are welded. A feed collector is installed inside the bottom or outside the bottom of a welded plate evaporator that functions as a separate feed collecting vessel. The feed collector receives the liquid after passing the plate packs. The vapor from boiling the feed in the packs rises to the top and passes an entrainment separator before leaving the evaporator.

The plate evaporators are of three (3) types: 1) Falling-film plate evaporators, 2) Rising-film plate evaporators, and 3) Rising-falling-film plate evaporators.

2.5.1 Falling-Film Plate Evaporators

In a **falling-film** (FF) **plate evaporator**, feed enters the evaporator at the bottom, pumps by a recirculation pump to the top, passes through the feed distributor, boils while flowing through plate packs, and enters the collecting vessel (which is located at the bottom of the evaporating vessel). FF plate evaporators have up to 6500 m^2 heat transfer area (A_Q). High A_Q makes the FF plate evaporators have a low retention time (typically 4 minutes). The heating section of an FF plate evaporator consists of a bundle (set) of parallel plates (called the **plate packs**), 1 to 2.2 m (= 3 to 7 Ft). The plates are usually made of copper or stainless steel. Two adjacent plates are welded together in a corrugated way to create two vertical tube-shaped passages. One passage (with 10 to 14 mm in diameter) is used for feed and the other for steam (or vapor). Because of the smaller thickness of the plates (compared with the wall of the tube in tube evaporators), the heat transfer efficiency in plate evaporators is higher than in tube evaporators.

2.5.2 Rising-Film Plate Evaporators

The feed and steam movements in a **rising-film** (RF) **plate evaporator** are like the Kestner rising-film tube evaporator. When a capacity expansion is needed, additional plates can be added to the plate packs in the existing frame.

2.5.3 Rising-Falling-Film Plate Evaporators

A typical rising-falling-film (RFF) **plate evaporator** is shown in Figure 12. An RFT plate evaporator uses the advantage of both RF plate and FF plate evaporators to create the shorter possible retention time (typically 1 minute). For this reason, the RFF plate evaporators are used where the feed *cannot* keep its properties at high temperatures, such as the concentration of fruit juices. As the same figure shows, a typical RFF plate evaporator has two sections, in which feed,

- Enters the bottom of the rising section,
- Moves upward through the corrugated plates,
- Enters the falling section at the top of the evaporator, and
- Moves downward under gravity at comparably high velocity (V).

In both sections, the feed moves in the form of a thin film. Toward the bottom of the falling section, some cooling starts to occur. The vapor leaves the system at the top of the collecting tank, while the product leaves at the bottom of the tank.

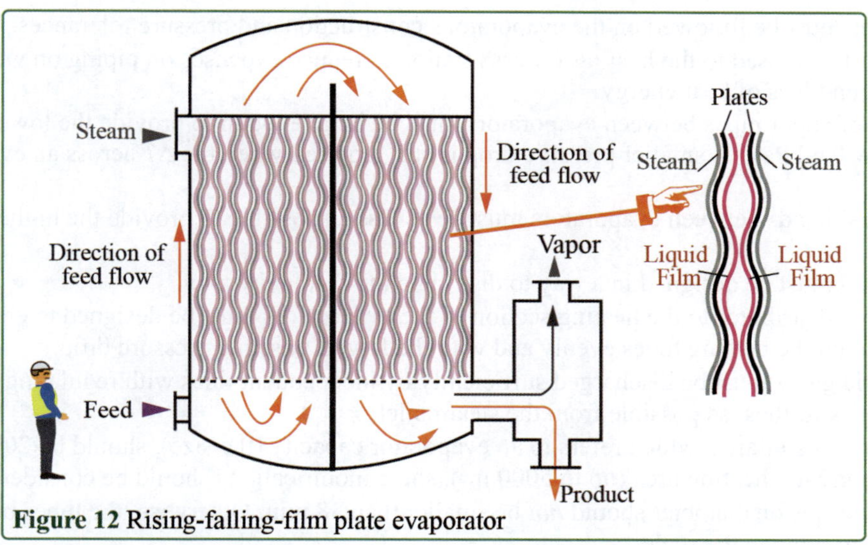

Figure 12 Rising-falling-film plate evaporator

2.6 PRE-EVAPORATORS AND PO-EVAPORATORS

A **pre-evaporator** is used as an add-on evaporator to the existing evaporation station to evaporate the feed before being fed to the first effect of a multiple-effect evaporating station. A pre-evaporator, thus, can improve the vapor-bleeding process of the station. For example, the vapor can be taken from the first effect of the station and used in a heat exchanger. In this case, the vapor is called **vapor bleed 1**. The vapor-bleeding process improves the steam economy of an evaporating station by saving heat energy, particularly when the vapor is taken **from later effects** (study Example, given under VAPOR SHIFTING PROCESS).

A **po-evaporator** (also called the **concentrator**) is used as an add-on evaporator to the existing evaporation station to concentrate more the last effect's product of a multiple-effect evaporating station. Most concentrators are thin-film or plate-type evaporators. In some industries (like the sugar industry), a concentrator is common in modern factories. A concentrator usually uses the second or third vapor at slight vacuum pressure (P_{Vac}) of about 70 kPa (= 10 PSI).

A concentrator is usually used in a sugar factory to concentrate the evaporating station's product (typically with a *DS* of about 65%) to about 73% *DS* concentration, so the feed to the crystallizer is already pre-evaporated before being used in the crystallization station. In this way, the concentrator improves steam economy (because it evaporates part of the water that otherwise must be evaporated in the crystallizers).

2.7 DESIGN AND SIZING OF EVAPORATORS

The sizing of an evaporator is based on the rate of the released vapor ($\dot{M}_V$), which can be easily calculated from the rate of the evaporated water ($\dot{M}_W$), as done in Example 1. Generally, the design and size of an evaporating station require mass and heat balancing and some technical considerations. From mass balances, the amount of the **feed flow rate** ($\dot{M}_F$) to the first effect of the evaporating station and the desired concentration of the product leaving the last effect can be determined. From heat balances, the required **heat flow rate** ($\dot{E}_Q$) and required steam of the station are determined. From the overall heat-transfer coefficient ($U_{Q.O}$) and the average total of ΔT (the) between the steam entering the first effect and the vapor leaving the last effect, the required heat transfer area of tubes (or plates) for the station can be calculated. It is noteworthy that $U_{Q.O}$ values given in some technical books (like Perry R.H. and coauthors, 2008) can be used for estimation purposes. But, they *cannot* be used in main calculations.

As for the technical considerations, the following points are recommended for designing an evaporating station with a set of Robert evaporators:

- Technical codes must be followed on the evaporator's construction and pressure tolerances.
- The station must be closed to the heating-process station to reduce expenses on piping on vapor bleeds to the heating station and loss of heat energy.
- The diameters of vapor pipes between evaporators must be large enough to provide the lowest pressure drop possible (below 0.6 kPa). A smaller pressure drop is still required when the ΔT across an evaporator is low (below 6°C).
- The vapor pipes' bends between evaporators must be as less as possible to provide the highest velocity of vapor flow.
- Feed distributors must be designed in a way to distribute the feed uniformly.
- Steam (or vapor) distributor to the heating section of the evaporators must be designed to ensure that the steam gets through the heating tubes evenly and with the lowest possible pressure drop.
- Noncondensable gases must be discharged sufficiently by independent lines with regulating valves, and their outlets must be as furthest as possible from the steam inlet.
- The tubes' heat transfer area, which refers to an evaporator capacity (the size), should be 2000 to 3000 m^2. In the case of a greater heating area (up to 5000 m^2), some modifications should be considered.
- The heating tubes inside diameter should *not* be smaller than 38 mm. Otherwise, the tubes need more frequent cleaning to remove the scale.
- Downtake tubes should be sized appropriately to allow as-less-as possible pressure drop during circulation of the feed. The recommended size of the downtake tube is about 20% of the diameter of the vessel.
- The size of the line for the product outlet must be about one-third to half the size of the downtake tube.
- It is more efficient to design the downtake tube to allow a portion of the boiling feed to come down through the tubes than through the downtake tube to increase the heat transfer efficiency.
- When the heating tubes are made of stainless steel, type 430 with 1.2 mm wall thickness (18-gauge) is the better choice (because of less tube expansion). When stainless steel and mild steel are connected, special attention is required on the interface between them (because corrosion occurs at the interface).

Viscosity (η) of the liquid and its increase in value when the liquid is undergoing evaporation are important factors affecting the overall heat-transfer coefficient ($U_{Q.O}$). This is more evident in natural-circulation evaporators. ChemEng assumes that $U_{Q.O}$ varies in inverse proportion to viscosity.

Pay attention to the following:

- Some errors in calculations of such magnitudes may occur. The important point is if those errors are within the safe limit or *not*. Say, up to 15% error in sizing of evaporator's heat transfer area is acceptable.
- For achieving the best result in designing a project, the final decision always requires some compromises based on the judgment of the in-charge process engineer.

2.8 EVAPORATOR SCALING

Evaporator scaling is the process of the buildup of a layer (commonly called a **film**) of scale-causing salts (SC salts) on the inside of the tubes (called the **feed side**) of an evaporator. During service, the scale layer gets thicker, so the heat transfer between the heating medium and the feed is decreased. Consequently, the performance of the evaporator becomes reduced because scale deposits have low thermal conductivity (K_{Th}). If, for example, the heat-transfer coefficient (U_Q) of heating tubes is 1000 W/(h.m^2.°C) when the heat-transfer area (A_Q) of the evaporator is clean (at the time zero after cleaning the tubes), the U_Q can decrease to one-third when a scale with 2 mm thickness covers the heating tubes.

Scaling (incrustation) occurs because

- The solubility of the SC salts decreases at higher *DS* (dissolved solids) concentrations, created by evaporation or heating, and
- The solubility of SC salts at the heating wall's temperature (*T*) is lower than at the bulk's *T* (solubility *decreases* at *lower T*).

As a result of gradual scaling, the thickness of the scale layer gets greater, and high thermal resistance to the heat transfer process occurs (because SC salts have low thermal conductivity (K_{Th}). The development of the **scale layer** (scale film) with time is an important point in the operation of evaporators. Usually, the scale-buildup process is fast at the start of operation (when the operating parameters are not maintained yet). But, it gets to a stable state when the process parameters (particularly the feed's flow rate and temperature) are maintained. However, the scale layer gets noticeably thicker to affect an evaporator's heat-transfer ability. At this time, the affected evaporator is removed from service (often by shutting down the process) for cleaning. As the tubes become cleaned, the heat transfer goes back to normal.

The amount of scale formation in an evaporator's tubes depends on 1) The amount of SC salts. 2) The type of SC salts (some precipitate at a faster rate than others).

Because it is impossible to measure the **scale-layer** (scale-film) **thickness**, the chemical engineers use a practical method to judge the time for cleaning. This is based on the daily recording of the temperature difference (ΔT) between an evaporator's steam and the feed sides. For example, if the normal value of the ΔT in the evaporator is 14°C, and it drops to below 12°C, it signifies that its tubes are dirty (deposited by scale). At this time, the evaporator is taken from service for cleaning.

[Note: The effect of the SC salts (scale-causing salts) can be reduced by using scale inhibitors, which minimize the tendency for deposition. The **scale inhibitor** is added to the feed before entering the evaporating station. However, some SC salts still precipitate on the tubes to the point that the evaporator needs to be cleaned. The SC salts can be cleaned chemically, as discussed next.]

2.9 EVAPORATOR CLEANING

Evaporator cleaning (descaling) refers to using some means (like weak acids, special solvents, or high-velocity water jet) to remove the scale layer (scale film) from the heat-transfer area of an evaporator's tubes (or plates of a plate evaporator).

Let us consider a typical Robert tube evaporator to discuss how its tubes are cleaned. Usually, the cleaning is performed without shutting down a multi-evaporator evaporation station. Just the evaporator that must be cleaned is bypassed. Scale *cannot* be removed by using only acid, so it should be treated first with soda ash (Na_2CO_3)

and caustic soda (NaOH) to change the chemical nature of the SC salts so that the acid can then dissolve them. Therefore, a typical cleaning process consists of the next steps.

- The evaporator is rinsed with condensate to remove the feed's leftover.
- The evaporator is filled with 4% soda ash and 1% caustic soda at the same rate and temperature.
- The chemicals are boiled for 5 to 10 hours to convert the calcium sulfate and oxalate into calcium carbonate ($CaCO_3$).

$$CaSO_4 + Na_2CO_3 \rightarrow CaCO_3 + Na_2SO_4$$
$$CaC_2O_4 + Na_2CO_3 \rightarrow CaCO_3 + Na_2C_2O_3$$

- The evaporator is drained from the chemicals and filled with 3 to 5% hydrochloric acid, which usually contains an **inhibitor** to protect the metal against corrosion,
- The evaporator is heated to about 70ºC for about 3 h to decompose the carbonate,

$$CaCO_3 + 2HCl \rightarrow CaCl_2 + CO_2 + H_2O$$

- The solution is drained from the evaporator and rinsed again with condensate.

[Note 1: In multiple-effect evaporation, the precipitation rate of scale causing salts is different in individual effects. Precipitation in the first effect is more than in the second and third effects, and maximum occurs in the last.]

[Note 2: In the case of stainless-steel tubes, weak acid, like **formic acid** (HCOOH) or **sulfamic acid** (H_3NSO_3), is used for tube cleaning.]

E-103

EVAPORATIVE COOLING DEVICES

An evaporative cooling device works on the principle of the evaporative cooling process (when a warm liquid is brought into contact with air, part of the liquid evaporates, and the liquid temperature, T, decreases.) Industrially, a warm process stream (such as condenser water) is cooled by the following cooling devices: 1) Cooling pond, 2) Cooling tower, and 3) Wet surface (WS) air cooler.

The order given here indicates the cooling device with the lowest **cooling effect temperature** (defined in a moment). [For comparison of cooling devices, the cooling tower is usually taken as the standard, and another device (a cooling pond or a wet surface air cooler) is compared.]

Some chemical plants and all power plants have one (or more) cooling devices to process warm process water coming from the condensation station. After cooling, the warm water gets some **makeup water** (usually from a river, lake, or a pond) and is used again in the station's condensers.

Two (2) criteria usually evaluate an evaporative cooling device (such as a cooling tower):

- **Cooling Effect Temperature** (**T_E**)**:** This is the difference between the temperature (T) of the hot process water entering a cooling device and T of the processed cool water leaving the device; that is, $T_E = T_{W1} - T_{W2}$ (see Figure 1). When, $T_{W1} = 40°C$ (= 104°F) and $T_{W2} = 25°C$ (= 77°F), the T_E will equate to 40 – 25 = 15°C.
- **Cooling Approach Temperature** (**T_A**)**:** This is the difference between T of the cool water leaving a cooling device and T of air (refers to air wet-bulb temperature) entering the device; $T_A = T_{W2} - T_{A1}$, as shown in Figure 1. Cooling towers are usually designed for T_A of 3 to 7ºC (= 37 to 43ºF).

COOLING PONDS

A cooling pond (Figure 2) is a large basin used for heat removal from a warm liquid stream (later **process stream**) to bring its T down for using it again in the condensation station. Some chemical process plants and power plants with a large ground area have one (or more) suitable-size cooling pond for cooling the condenser water coming from the condensation station. In addition to a pond, some of these plants also have a cooling tower or a WS air cooler to increase the plant's cooling capacity. Water after cooling in a cooling pond (or other cooling devices) gets some **makeup water** and is used again in the condensers of the condensation station.

Now we compare the performance of a typical cooling tower with a typical cooling pond because usually, a cooling tower is used as a standard to compare the other two devices (cooling pond or wet surface air cooler).

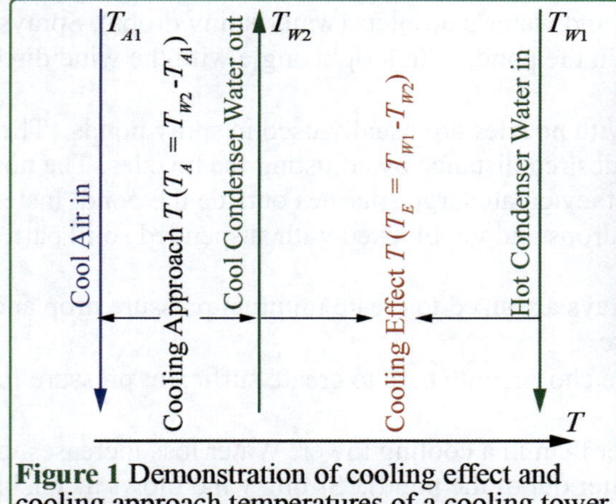

Figure 1 Demonstration of cooling effect and cooling approach temperatures of a cooling tower

Figure 2 A cooling pond

The two (2) major differences between a cooling tower and a cooling pond are: 1) Cooling towers usually have a T_E (cooling effect T) of 7 to 17°C (= 45 to 63°F). It is difficult to give such specific values for cooling ponds because their T_E depends on the climatic air's temperature, moisture content, and wind conditions (wind's velocity and direction). 2) Cooling towers require less makeup water than cooling ponds, as the **condensation rate** in a tower is higher than in a pond. Typically, the amount of makeup water needed for a cooling tower is about 2.5% of the water coming to it, while that in a pond is up to 5%.

The following are other differences between a cooling tower and a cooling pond:

- A cooling tower requires less area to construct than a pond,
- A cooling tower requires a higher investment to be built than a pond,
- A cooling tower requires higher operating costs to operate than a pond,
- A cooling tower requires less makeup water than a cooling pond (because of larger drift loss), and
- A cooling tower produces cleaner cooled water than a pond (because cooled water produced in a pond has more contamination caused by wind-borne debris and ground-nesting birds).

Cooling ponds are built in a flat area. The depth of the ponds is *not* an important factor in sizing a pond. Ponds are usually built 1 to 3 m (= 3 to 10 Ft) deep. Specialists recommend ponds with an area of 1000 to 2000 m^2 (= 10764 to 21528 Ft^2) in long and narrow shapes to provide better heat transfer between the hot water and cooling air. In general, the size of a cooling pond to process a certain amount of water depends on the operating conditions, like the following:

- Climatic air temperature,
- Condenser-water's temperature,
- Condenser-water quantity to be treated,

- Wind's velocity, direction, and frequent blowing,
- Spray-system's type, arrangement, and power requirement.

As a rough indication of the size of a spray pond, specialists use a simple equation that gives the ratio of water's mass-flow rate ($\dot{M}_W$, in t/h) to the area of the pond (A, in m^2) in the unit of t/(h.m^2).

$$\frac{\dot{M}_W}{A} = 0.75 \tag{1}$$

If, for example, a condensation station produces 1 000 t condenser water per day, it needs a cooling pond with an area of 1000/0.75 = 1 333 m^2 (= 14 350 Ft^2).

In designing and operating a spray cooling pond, the following points are important:

- **Sprays Installation:** The sprays must be installed with enough space (typically 8 m apart) as high as possible to create maximum contact time between the air's and water's droplets (water's tiny drops). Sprays are usually installed about 2 m above the water's surface in the pond, with a right angle with the wind direction to minimize splashes to the outside of the pond.
- **Nozzles Opening:** Centrifugal (garden-type) sprays with nozzles are usually used in spray ponds. These sprays use centrifugal force to discharge the water to desired distance by adjusting the nozzles. The nozzles' openings are sized to produce water droplets because they create large splashes outside the pond. Instead, nozzles with too small openings create high-pressure drops and get blocked with suspended solid particles, lowering the cooling effect.
- **Sprays Piping:** The pipes that deliver the water to sprays are sized to create minimal pressure drop and equal water distribution to each spray at equal pressure.
- **Pumping:** Pumps for pumping water to the sprays are chosen with care to create sufficient pressure for each spray. Pumps also must have cleanable strainers.
- **Makeup Water:** Water loss in a cooling pond is larger than in a cooling tower. Water loss increases, particularly in windy climatic conditions (blowing some water out of the pond). Strong wind blows a considerable amount of water out of the pond, creating a high-water loss. Thus, makeup water can reach up to 5% of the warm process water entering a pond. Sometimes the amount of makeup water is minimal because the amount of water produced by condensation in the pond is greater than the total water lost by evaporation and splashing to the outside of the pond.

COOLING TOWERS

A cooling tower gets warm condenser water from a condensation station, cools it, and sends it back to the condensation station to be reused, again, as the cooling water of the **barometric condensers** (discussed under CONDENSERS). In the tower, the condenser water cools by contacting atmospheric air (the cooling medium). The water after cooling gets a small amount (usually about 2.5%) of makeup water before it is reused again as cooling water in the condensation station.

Two types of cooling towers are used: **wet cooling towers** and **wet-dry cooling towers**. Wet cooling towers are usually designed to cool the warm condenser water near the air's wet-bulb temperature. In wet-dry-cooling towers, cooling reaches near the air's dry-bulb temperature in the dry section of the tower. [Most of the discussion here is about wet cooling towers (simply **cooling towers**).]

The evaluation of a tower is usually based on T_E (cooling effect temperature) and T_A (cooling approach temperature). T_A depends on the cooling tower's design and some other variables, including the following:

- **Air Temperature:** At a given air's humidity, the *lower* the air's T, the *cooler* is the outlet water from the tower.
- **Air Humidity:** At a given air's T, the *higher* the humidity, the *cooler* is the outlet water.

In both **crossflow forced tower** and **counterflow forced** tower, hot process water can enter the top and distribute uniformly by the nozzles of a **water distributor** over the **packing** (also called the **fill**). After passing the packing, cool water enters the **water basin** at the bottom of the tower.

In both designs, air flows between the packing bed to cool the process water and goes out of the tower by the force of a fan to release heat into the atmosphere.

Packing, which fills the column, increases the air-water contact area. In a typical medium-size cooling tower, the packing height is about 2 m (= 7 Ft), which occupies a small section of the tower's total height. Generally, the packing height depends on packing and tower design types. Some towers have two or more packing sections to increase the contact area between the process water and cooling air.

Different types of special packing are used in the cooling towers, including the following:

- **Wooden Slates Packing:** It is usually made from redwood and was used in older towers.
- **PVC Bar Packing:** It is made of PVC (polyvinyl chloride) with a bar shape and is used in newer towers.
- **PVC Plate Packing:** It is made from PVC and has a plate-corrugated shape, and is used in most towers.

PVC packing has the following advantages over wooden packing:

- It creates a lower-pressure drop,
- It is easier to be inspected and cleaned, and
- It catches the process-water drops better (because the next layer of packing drops are caught), so less **drift** (water-drop splashing) to the outside occurs.

The plates are corrugated, like metal plates used in the plate heat exchangers. The plates are spaced 20 mm to 25 mm (= 3/4 In to 1 In) apart to provide

- Less microbial contamination,
- Low-pressure drop, and
- High airflow rate.

Comparatively, plate-type packing has the following advantages over bar-type packing:

- It creates a lower pressure drop,
- It requires a lower height of packing bed,
- It creates a higher flow rate of water and air.

In a **forced-draft cooling tower**, a propeller-type fan (or more fans) is installed at the base to provide the air **draft** (the difference in pressure between two points), move the air through the packing, and discharge it from the top of the tower through the drift eliminators. Fans have several blades, which can be adjusted, in some designs, to change the direction of the airflow. In an **induced-draft tower**, the fan is installed at the top to take the air from the bottom through the drift eliminators.

The **drift eliminators**, usually V-shaped, capture water drops (the **drifts**), preventing them from splashing to the outside of the tower. In counter-flow towers, the eliminators are mounted at the top of the towers above the water distributor (see Figure 3). In **crossflow** (counter-flow) **cooling towers**, the drift eliminators are installed along the tower's wall (see Figure 4).

In both designs, a pump with a **pumping head** greater than the tower's head pressure (P_h) pumps the water to the top of the tower to flow through the nozzles and the packing.

The output of a cooling tower's fan is usually expressed by HP (horsepower). Some cooling towers are equipped with a two-speed fan. In such designs, HP decreases considerably as the air's T decreases and the fan operates at half speed. Theoretically, when a fan operates at half speed, its air suction ability reduces by 50%, while its HP is reduced only by 1/8th of full speed.

The fan's speed controls the water temperature leaving the cooling towers. During cold winter days, normally, little change occurs in the air's wet-bulb temperature, so a slight adjustment on the fan's speed may be needed. Otherwise, more adjustments are required.

In some recent-designed cooling towers, the **AVPP** (automatic variable pitch propeller) regulates the fan's speed by changing the fan's blades' pitch when receiving a pneumatic signal from the outlet water's temperature. An inverter changes the fan's speed in some cooling towers.

In addition to the design of a cooling tower, the **cooling effect** per unit mass of air used in a tower depends on the following operating factors:

- **Air Temperature:** At a given air's humidity, the lower the air's *T*, the cooler is the outlet process water from the tower will be.
- **Ais Humidity:** At a given air's *T*, the higher the humidity, the colder the outlet process water from the tower. But the air's humidity has its limitations. In an area with high humidity, cooling-tower operators keep the air's *T* above the air's dew point temperature (the *T* at which water vapor in the air starts to condense).
- **Process Water Quantity:** The amount of process water to be cooled is usually 30 to 40 times the amount of vapor condensed by a barometric condenser.
- **Process Water Temperature:** The *T* of hot process water leaving the condensation station in a chemical plant located in a moderate climatic area is usually 55 to 65°C (= 130 to 150°F). At normal operating conditions, such water can usually be reduced to 15 to 35°C (= 60 to 95°F). After cooling, the water is again used in the condensation station as the cooling water to condense some vapor in the condensers.

In a cooling tower, the heat transfer rate ($\dot{E}_Q$, in kJ/s = kW/h) from process water to cooling air equates to the sum of the water latent enthalpy and the vapor sensible enthalpy. Thus, $\dot{E}_Q$ can be expressed by a simple heat-transfer equation.

$$\dot{E}_Q = U_Q.A(T_{W1} - T_{W2}) \quad (2)$$

In this equation, U_Q is the process water's heat-transfer coefficient (in W/h.m^2.°C), *A* is water-air contact surface area (in m^2), and ($T_{W1} - T_{W2}$) is a **cooling effect** (in °C, where subscript *W* is for wet *T*). The cooling effect is the water temperature drop between entering the tower (T_{W1}) and leaving it when it is cold (T_2); that is, when it reaches T_{WB}, so $T_2 = T_{WB}$. Cooling towers are usually designed to cool the warm process water near the air's wet-bulb temperature. The **cooling tower characteristic** (CTC) is the difference between the cause of the cooling and the cooling effect.

$$\text{CTC} = (H_W - H_A) - (T_{W1} - T_{W2}) \quad (3)$$

The Merkel equation can also formulate CTC.

$$\frac{U_Q.A.V}{J} = \frac{T_{W1}-T_{W2}}{H_W-H_A} \quad (4)$$

U_Q is the water's heat transfer coefficient, *A* is the cooling contact area (in m^2), *V* is the volume of process water that goes to the tower (in m^3), *J* is the water's mass flux rate (mass flow rate per unit area, in kg/s.m^2), H_W is inlet water enthalpy (in kJ/kg), and H_A is the inlet air enthalpy (in kJ/kg). Equation 3 can also be written in relation to the packing's height (*h*, in m) and the water mass flow rate ($\dot{M}$, in kg/s) as

$$\frac{U_Q.A.h}{\dot{M}} = \frac{T_{W1}-T_{W2}}{H_W-H_A} \quad (5)$$

Figure 5 shows the specific enthalpy (H_{Sp}) of air and temperature of water in a **counter-flow cooling tower**. In this figure, AB indicates the water's **operating line** (starting at point A), CD indicates the **air's operating line** (starting at point C), AC indicates **cooling approach temperature** (T_A), and integrating Equation 3 gives the area ABDC, which represents **cooling tower characteristics** (CTC). As shown in the same figure, an increase in entering air's temperature increases its H_{Sp}, and as a result, it changes the origin C, so the line AC shifts to the right to maintain a new T_A for the tower.

[Note: At fixed process water and air conditions and a given T_A (cooling approach temperature), **cooling tower characteristic** (*CTC*, or *K.A.V/L* characteristic) is an important value to evaluate cooling tower specifications and efficiency. At certain conditions, the *lower* the CTC, the *better* is the tower's efficiency.]

For example, the cooling tower characteristic (CTC) of a counter-flow cooling tower, operating under the water temperature to the cooling tower (T_{W1}) of 44°C and that from the tower (T_{W2}) of 30°C is:

$$T_{W1} - T_{W2} = 44 - 30 = 14\ °\text{C}$$

Types of Cooling Towers

Cooling towers vary in size from small units to very large ones. They are usually constructed in rectangular or hyperboloid (quadratic) shapes. In the rectangular shapes, the height can be up to 40 m (= 104 Ft) and the length up to 80 m (= 208 Ft). In the hyperboloid shapes, the tower's height can be up to 200 m (= 520 Ft) and the diameter up to 100 m (= 260 Ft). Smaller towers are normally factory-built, while larger ones are constructed on-site. The hyperboloid cooling towers are mostly used in nuclear power plants and large chemical plants.

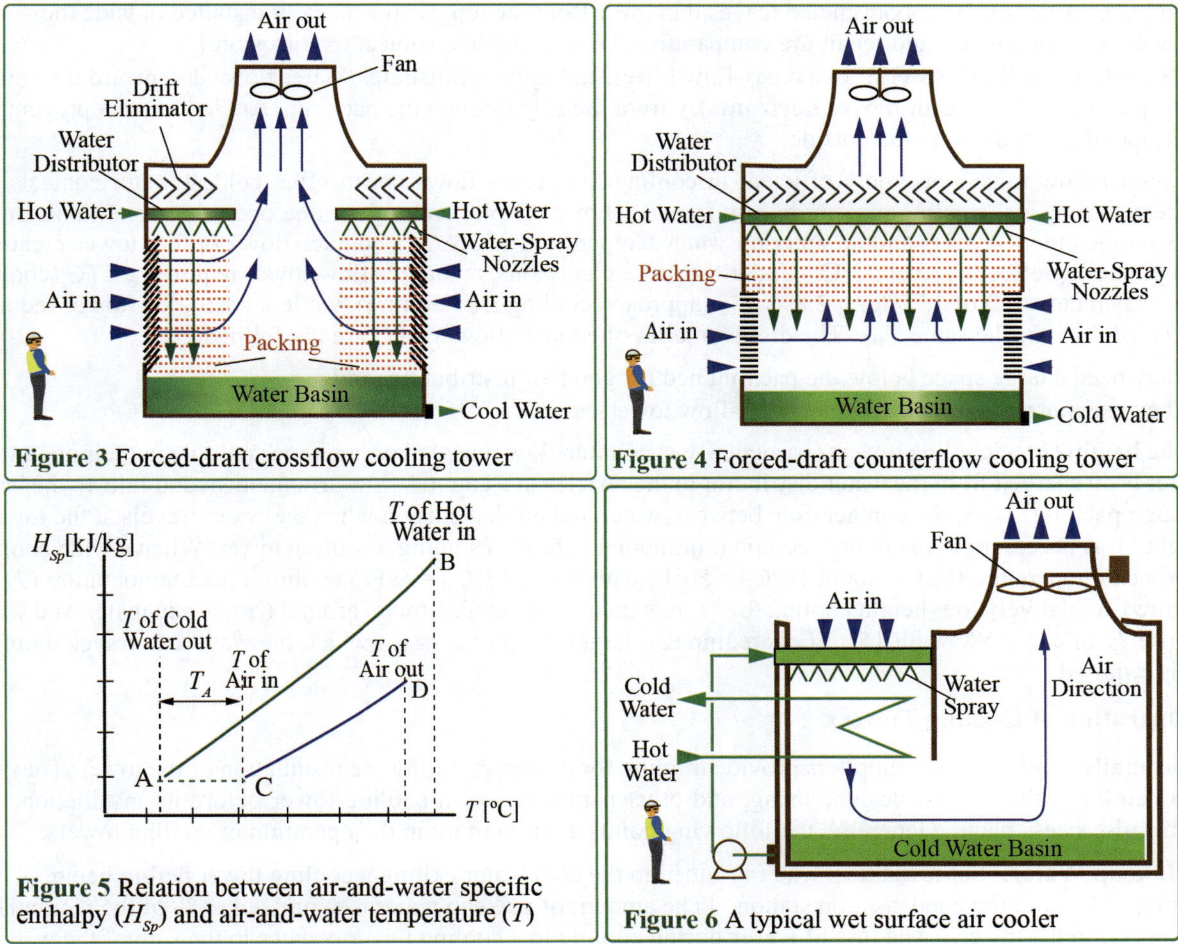

Figure 3 Forced-draft crossflow cooling tower

Figure 4 Forced-draft counterflow cooling tower

Figure 5 Relation between air-and-water specific enthalpy (H_{Sp}) and air-and-water temperature (T)

Figure 6 A typical wet surface air cooler

Based on the P applied to move the cooling air, the cooling towers are divided into the next two (2) types:

- **Natural-Draft Cooling Towers:** In a natural-draft tower, the rising property of warm air (because of the difference in density between the cool input air and warm output air) is enough to create sufficient air draft (the difference in pressure between two points) without the use of fans. This is because warm air has a lower density (*a container filled with heated gas weighs less than a container of the same cool gas*), moving upward. The efficiency of the draft in natural-draft towers depends on the air's temperature and relative humidity (W_R) and the tower's height. At a given air temperature, the draft increases as W_R increases, as the available cooling air per unit mass of water also increases. Thus, the *higher* the W_R, the *cooler* the exit water from the tower will be. This property of natural-draft towers is used to design the cooling towers in areas with high W_R (more than 70%). Today, natural-draft cooling towers are hardly used in areas with normal W_R.

- **Mechanical-Draft Cooling Towers:** A fan with several blades provides the draft in these towers. [Today, most cooling towers are operated mechanically.]

Based on the direction of the air and hot water, mechanical-draft towers are classified as

- **Counterflow Cooling Towers:** In a counterflow (countercurrent) tower, as Figure 3 illustrates, water flows downward through the packing, while air flows parallel but opposite to the direction of water flow. Air is forced by a fan from the bottom and leaves the tower from the top. [Fan is usually installed outside the tower, so maintenance and repair are comparatively easier and less subject to corrosion.]
- **Crossflow Cooling Towers:** In a cross-flow tower, as Figure 4 illustrates, water flows downward through the packing bed while air moves **horizontally** from the side through the packing. Angled louvers prevent the escape of water drops to the outside.

Counter-flow towers are more efficient in cooling than cross flows because the coldest water contacts the coldest cooling air, creating maximum heat transfer. For example, under the same operating conditions, at the air's temperature of 25°C and an entering water temperature of 35°C, a counter-flow cooling tower creates a higher cooling effect by about 2°C. Under the same conditions, a counter-flow tower requires a *CTC* (cooling tower characteristic) of 1.75 for a 2.8°C T_{AC} (approach cooling temperature), while a cross-flow tower requires a *CTC* of 2.25 for the same T_{AC}. The disadvantages of counter-flow towers are the followings:

- They need a large space below the packing bed for good air distribution, and
- They use more electric power than cross-flow towers.

The **height** (*h*) of cooling towers (particularly in counter-flow types) plays an important role in their operation. Water is discharged from the water distributor to the nozzles in a counter-flow arrangement and falls to the basin through packing. Thus, the contact time between water and air depends on when the water travels at the tower's height. It is necessary to maintain a certain minimum height in designing a cooling tower. When a wide cooling approach temperature (T_A) of about 10°C (= 50°F) with about 15°C (= 59F°) cooling effect temperature (T_E) is required, a relatively low-height cooling tower, in which the water can travel around 6 m, is adequate. And when a close T_A of about 5°C with 15°C T_E is required, a larger-height tower (in which the water can travel about 12 m) is required.

Operation of Cooling Towers

Generally, cooling tower suppliers provide training for operators during the installation of the tower. They are also helpful in the general design, sizing, and other parameters of a cooling tower before its installation in a chemical-process plant. Generally, the following points are important in the operation of cooling towers:

- **Makeup Water:** Some makeup water is added to the cool water exiting a cooling tower before being pumped back to the condensation station. [The amount of makeup water is expressed as % of the recirculation rate to the tower.] The **loss of water** during cooling in a cooling tower equates to the sum of the water loss by free evaporation (W_E, which is about 2%), by water drops splashed (the **drift**) to the outside of the tower (W_D, which is about 0.2%), and the water loss by blowdown (W_B, which is about 0.2%). These create a need for total makeup water of about 2.5% of the circulating water to the tower. [Sometimes, there is *no* need for makeup water, as the amount of condensed water to the tower is greater than the total water lost.]
- **Process Water Chemical Treatment:** Chemical treatment of the feed to the cooling tower for PH adjustment is necessary to prevent the growth of bacteria, algae, and slime between the packing. These organisms

slow the flow of water and air through the packing, reducing the tower's efficiency. In addition, low-PH water causes corrosion in the tower's vessel and **fittings** (attached parts). Lime ($CaCO_3$) or another PH increaser can adjust the feed's PH to around a neutral level.

- **Process Water Blowdown:** Blowdown (purging process), which decreases the water suspended solids content, is performed in some chemical plants. [In some plants, a rough filtration of the process water before entering the tower is done when the amount of suspended solids is too high.]
- **Distribution of Process Water:** Uniform water distribution over the packing is necessary. A non-uniform distribution reduces the cooling effect because the process stream does *not* cover the entire parking area. If the tower consists of **multiple-packing cells**, equal water distribution to each cell is also needed.
- **Air Humidity:** The air quality to a cooling tower is an important factor in its operation. The *higher* the cooling air humidity in a natural-draft tower, the *better* is the draft. A higher draft improves airflow against internal resistances.
- **Ground Fog:** Ground fog (ground-level fog), which occurs around a cooling tower on cold winter days, forms from mixing warm, highly-saturated discharged air from the tower with cooler air, which *cannot* fully absorb the vapor in the discharge air. Reducing the moisture content of the discharge stream from the cooling tower will reduce the fogging problem.
- **Icing:** Icing occurs in cold areas. In cold areas, cooling towers are equipped with high stacks and are operated at high loads to minimize icing problems.
- **Air Pressure:** The air *P* in the forced-draft cooling towers is the fan's HP (horsepower) function. Low pressure causes insufficient draft, low air velocity (below 10 m/s), and higher pressure drop in the tower. These reduce the efficiency of the tower. In addition, low pressure causes the leaving air from the tower to be discharged at ground level, increasing the chance of returning the moist air to the tower and creating **ground fog** on cold winter days.

WET SURFACE AIR COOLERS

Wet surface air coolers (wet surface coolers or WS coolers) are the newest and most effective cooling device used for heat removal from a warm fluid stream (later **process stream**) to bring its temperature (*T*) down for using it again in the condensation process.

Figure 6 simply illustrates a typical wet-surface (WS) cooler, which consists of the following:

- **Tube Bundle:** The bundle consists of several round tubes specially designed.
- **Basin:** The basin is on the bottom of the air cooler. It works as a closed-loop to send the cooling water to the tube bundle and receive it back after losing some of its cooling value by cooling the process stream.

The main differences between a WS cooler and a cooling tower are:

- **Less Space:** WS cooler needs less space to be constructed than a tower.
- **Cooling Medium:** A WS cooler uses water and atmospheric air as cooling media.
- **Single Device:** A WS cooler uses the waste heat to evaporate a small portion of the water by using cooling water sensible heat (a phase-change heat).
- **High Efficiency:** In a WS cooler, the process stream flows in an enclosed tube bundle, and cooling water is constantly sprayed on the tubes, so all water's cooling value is used in the cooling process.

The operation of a WS cooler can be briefly outlined as follow:

- A warm process stream is pumped into the tube bundle,
- Air is forced down over the tube bundle along the water,
- Cooling-water stream is sprayed on the tube bundle, also downward,
- The heat from the warm stream is released through the tubes' walls to the cooling water,
- The cooler process stream is pumped out of the tube bundle from the bottom of the cooler, and
- After absorbing some heat from the warm water, the warm air stream is discharged from the top of the air cooler using a strong fan to minimize the warm air recirculation.

During operation, some free evaporation of cooling water occurs on the surface of the tube bundle, causing the following:

- It decreases the cooling water's temperature, and
- It transfers heat from cooling water to the air stream.

So, some water vapor has produced that part of it goes through the condensation process, and the rest is discharged from the cooler into the atmosphere by using a strong fan, which operates at high velocity.

E-104

EVAPORATIVE COOLING PROCESS

As a process unit of ChemEng, evaporative cooling is a heat transfer process performed in an evaporative cooling device (a cooling pond, a cooling tower, or a wet surface cooler) to cool a warm fluid stream (like condenser water) at typically 50 to 65°C (=120 to 150°F). The driving force (cause) of evaporative cooling is the enthalpy difference (ΔH) between the water to be cooled and the air (the cooling medium), as each of them is at a different temperature (T). Each water molecule is assumed to be surrounded by a thin layer (called a thin film or simply **film**) of air, and ΔH provides the cause of heat transfer between the film and the surrounding air.

Evaporative cooling is performed to cool a warm stream by decreasing its T and removing its heat energy (E_Q, simply heat and scientifically enthalpy). And the warm stream is used again in the condensation station.

In evaporative cooling, both of the following heat transfer processes occur:

- Temperature-change process (sensible heat transfer process) because the T of the warm stream decreases during the evaporative cooling process.
- Phase-change process (latent heat transfer process) because a portion of the warm stream evaporates.

Thus, part of the enthalpy change ($\Delta H = E_Q$) that occurs during the evaporative cooling is a temperature change enthalpy (sensible enthalpy), and part is phase change enthalpy (latent enthalpy), known as the enthalpy of condensation.

[Note 1: Because the cooling in an evaporative-cooling device (like a cooling tower) occurs by evaporation, it is called the **evaporative cooling process** to distinguish it from the evaporation process and cooling process.]

[Note 2: The evaporation occurring during the evaporative cooling process is free evaporation, which is a phase-change heat transfer process. Free evaporation occurs because the temperature (T) and enthalpy (H) of a warm stream entering a cooling device are higher than those of the cooling medium (usually, atmospheric air).]

Warm process water is usually cooled in one of the following evaporative cooling devices: 1) Cooling pond, 2) Cooling tower, and 3) Wet surface (WS) air cooler.

The listed devices order is from the lowest cooling-effect temperature to the highest. The cooling effect and cooling approach temperatures can evaluate the operation of an evaporative cooling device, as defined next.

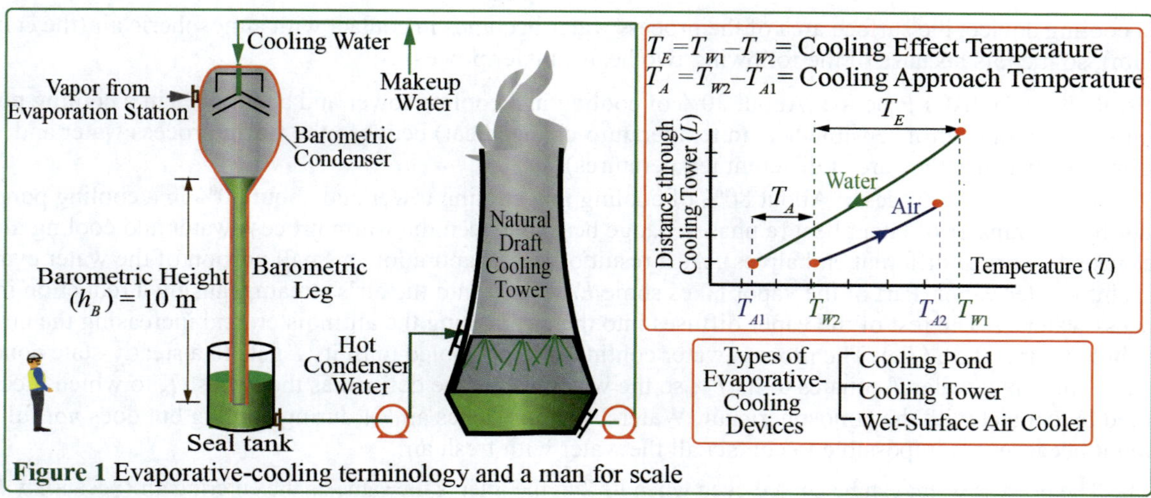

Figure 1 Evaporative-cooling terminology and a man for scale

Cooling Effect Temperature (T_E): The T_E of a cooling device is the difference between the temperature (T) of the hot water to the device (T_{W1}) and cool water from it (T_{W2}); that is, $T_E = T_{W1} - T_{W2}$. When, for example, T_{W1} = 40°C (= 104°F) and T_{W2} = 25°C (= 77°F), the T_E is 15°C (= 59°F). The cooling effect is sometimes expressed as the heat removability of a cooling device per unit mass of air used.

Cooling Approach Temperature (T_A): The T_A of a cooling device is the difference between T of the cool water leaving the device and T of air (refers to air wet-bulb temperature) entering the device; that is $T_A = T_{W2} - T_{A1}$, as shown on right side of Figure 1. Cooling towers are usually designed for T_A of 3 to 7ºC (37 to 43ºF).

When condensation is performed in a barometric condenser (a direct-contact condenser), the condensation product is called the condenser water. The condenser water is hot, so it *cannot* be used again as cooling water (cooling medium) in the barometric condenser. It is, therefore, cooled in the evaporative-cooling station by an evaporative cooling device. After cooling, the cool stream gets some **makeup water** and is used again as cooling water in the condensation station. When a cooling tower is used, the makeup water is small (typically 2.5% of the recirculating-water rate), but this value is high (up to 5%) when a cooling pond is used.

A household's evaporative air conditioner (the evaporative cooler), operating with water as the cooling medium, is a simple example of evaporative cooling. This process occurs in a cooling tower or a spray-cooling pond, but atmospheric air is the cooling medium. The difference in T between cooling water and air causes evaporation of a small portion of water, so some water vapor (vapor) is produced. Part of the vapor condenses, which cools the remaining water, and the rest of the vapor moves (diffuses) into the air, so the surrounding air's **moisture content** (humidity) increases. High air humidity reduces the cooling effect because the *higher* the air humidity, the *lower* is free evaporation rate.

[Note 1: We feel evaporative cooling when our skin is wet and in contact with moving air because evaporation causes a decrease in water's T. Evaporative cooling can be demonstrated with a simple test. Wrap the end of a thermometer in cotton soaked in water. Notice the temperature decrease as part of the water evaporates.]

[Note 2: The other type of cooling is **refrigeration**, which is *not* covered in this book.]

The differences between the evaporative-cooling process and the cooling process are outlined next.

- In evaporative cooling, *no* heat energy, E_Q (the enthalpy, H) is used to cool the cooling liquid; while in the cooling process, E_Q is used,
- In evaporative cooling, both sensible (phase-change) enthalpy and latent (temperature-change) enthalpy are used; while in cooling, just the sensible enthalpy is used, and
- In evaporative cooling, the vapor takes a portion of E_Q, causing the liquid to become cooler, while vapor does *not* play an important role in cooling.

In a cooling device, the surface area of the process water becomes in contact with atmospheric air (the cooling medium), so it cools because of the following two heat-transfer processes:

- Sensible Heat Transfer Process**:** About 20% of cooling in a cooling tower and about 50% in a cooling pond occurs by the transfer of sensible heat (a temperature-change heat) between the warm process water and cooling air (because they are at different temperatures)
- Latent Heat Transfer Process**:** About 80% of cooling in a cooling tower and about 50% in a cooling pond occur by the transfer of latent heat (a phase-change heat) between the warm process water and cooling air (because they are at different enthalpies). As a result of free evaporation, a small portion of the water evaporates into water vapor. Part of the vapor takes some E_Q with it into the air's stream, causing a reduction in the process water *T*. The rest of the vapor diffuses into the air, making the air moister, and increasing the air wet-bulb temperature (T_W). The process water continues to be cooled until its *T* gets to a steady-state condition. At this time, water *T* equates to its T_W, so the water T_W can be defined as the lowest *T*, to which it can be cooled by contact with the atmospheric air. Water TW approaches air T_W during cooling but does *not* fully reach it because it is impossible to contact all the water with fresh air.

[Note: The process water can be cooled even when its *T* at the inlet is the same as the entering air (because water's surface *T* in contact with air is lower than its bulk *T*.)]

The efficiency of an evaporative-cooling device (E_E) can be estimated from the following equation (see right side of Figure 1):

$$E_E = \frac{T_{A2}-T_{A1}}{T_{A2}-T_{W2}} \times 100 \qquad (1)$$

In this equation, T_{A1} is the air's temperature at the entrance to the cooling device, T_{A2} is that at the exit, and T_{W2} is the water's temperature at the exit. If, for example, T_{A1} to an evaporative-cooling tower is 18°C, T_{A2} is 40°C, and T_{W2} is 15°C, the E_E of the tower will be

$$E_E = \frac{40-18}{40-15} \times 100 = 88\%$$

Usually, the efficiency of evaporative cooling towers runs between 80 to 90%.

The air temperature leaving an evaporative cooling device, which is correctly known as the air adiabatic saturation temperature ($T_{Sat.A}$, simply called **air saturation temperature**), can be calculated as

$$T_{Sat.A} = T_{A1} - \frac{H_{E.A}(W_{Sp.A2}-W_{Sp.A1})}{1.005+1.88W_{Sp1}} \qquad (2)$$

In this equation, T_{A1} is the air's *T* at the entrance to the cooling device, $H_{E.A}$ is the air enthalpy of evaporation at the entrance (in kJ/kg), $W_{Sp.A2}$ is the air's specific humidity at the exit from the device (in kg water/kg dry air), and $W_{Sp.A1}$ is the air's specific humidity at the entrance to the device (same unit). The value 1.005 is the dry-air's C_Q (specific heat capacity), and 1.88 is the C_Q of water vapor.

E-105
EVAPORATORS

Study EVAPORATION PROCESS AND EVAPORATORS.

E-106
EXCESS AIR REQUIREMENT

Discussed under COMBUSTION REACTIONS AND COMBUSTION AIR REQUIREMENT.

E-107
EXCESS MASS

The short name for NUCLEAR EXCESS MASS.

E-108
EXCITED ENERGY STATE

Study GROUND AND EXCITED ENERGY STATES.

E-109
EXERGY

Exergy (also called **available work**) is the energy (E) that is available to be used in a thermodynamic system (heat-involving system). More scientifically, exergy is the maximum useful work (W) of a heat-involving system that can be used before the system becomes in equilibrium with its surroundings. After the system and its surroundings reach equilibrium, its exergy becomes zero.

Like energy, exergy is *not* destroyable during a process but can be converted to mass (M), or vice versa, as in nuclear reactions. Exergy, however, can always be destroyed during a reversible process or reversible chemical reaction.

The four important properties of exergy are outlined next.

- Exergy and energy are the same in an isothermic process,
- A heat engine's exergy efficiency is always greater than its energy efficiency,
- A decrease in a system's exergy is proportional to the increase in its entropy (S), and
- Exergy can analyze delicate energy calculations, such as choosing the best use of roof space for solar energy (photon energy).

[Historical Note: The concept of **exergy** was first used by Willard Gibbs (1839–1903, American scientist) in the 1870s to refer to a combination of two Greek words, **ex** and **ergon**, meaning **from work**.]

E-110
EXHAUST STEAM

Discussed under the topic of VAPOR AND STEAM.

E-111
EXOTHERMIC PROCESS

Another name for HEAT RELEASING PROCESS.

E-112

EXOTHERMIC REACTIONS

Another name for HEAT RELEASING REACTIONS.

E-113

EXPLOSIVES

An explosive is a reactive substance with a high amount of energy that can create an **explosion** (a rapid increase in volume and release of energy). Certain substances, such as gases, volatile organic compounds, dust, and powders, are combustible under ordinary conditions but become explosive under specific conditions. Some substances become explosive when mixed with other substances, like when a fuel is mixed with air.

E-114

EXPONENTS

Study LOGARITHMS.

E-115

EXTENSIVE QUANTITY

Study INTENSIVE AND EXTENSIVE QUANTITIES.

E-116

EXTERNAL AND INTERNAL COMBUSTION ENGINE

External Combustion Engines: An external combustion engine (ECE) is a heat engine that gets its driving energy from an outside source in a working fluid (like steam). For example, a steam turbine that gets steam to perform shaft work (W_S) to run an electric generator to produce electric power (simply **power** or **electricity**) is an ECE. An ECE may also get its driving energy from a fuel combustion or other sources (like a nuclear reactor). For example, an ECE is an electric motor that gets its E_E (electric energy) from an outside source and converts it into E_K (kinetic energy). [Combustion, in general, is the process of reacting a fuel with atmospheric oxygen.]

Internal Combustion Engines: An internal combustion engine (ICE) is a heat engine that gets its driving energy from a high-temperature, high-pressure gas, applied as a force, to some of its components (such as a piston, turbine blades, a rotor, or a nozzle). This force moves the engine's component to convert chemical potential energy (E_{CP}) into useful kinetic energy (E_K). An example of an internal combustion engine is a car engine that uses natural gas. In the engine, the gas forces the shaft to convert the E_K into E_Q (heat energy) to create high-T, high-P gas when the gas is compressed inside the cylinder.

E-117
EXTRACT AND RAFFINATE

The **extract** is a general term used in some process units (unit operations) of ChemEng to refer to the product of a separation process. The extract mainly contains the wanted solute (or solutes).

Raffinate is a general term used to refer to the byproduct of a separation process. The raffinate usually contains the unwanted solute (or solutes), so-called impurities.

[Note: The terms **extract** and **raffinate** are mostly used in the extraction, distillation, and ion-exclusion chromatographic process. In the extraction process, the extracted (separated) solute is usually called **component-of-interest** (wanted or desired component), the raffinate is called the **unwanted** (undesired) **component**, and the solvent is called **extracting solvent**. The liquid phase rich in solute and extracting solvent is called the **solvent phase,** and the liquid phase, rich in raffinate, is called the **raffinate phase**.]

E-118
EXTRACTION PROCESS

As a process unit (unit operation) of ChemEng, extraction is a **separation process** performed in an extractor (extracting column) to remove (scientifically **extract**) a liquid from a liquid mixture by contacting the mixture with an **extracting solvent** (simply solvent or **extractant**). By simpler definition, extraction is the removal (extraction) of a solute (called the **solute-of-interest**) from one liquid phase to another one by contacting it with an extractant (solvent). The driving force (the cause) of extraction is the high solubility of the liquid-of-interest in the extractant compared with other liquids in the feed mixture, so the miscibility of the liquid-of-interest with the extractant is an important condition in extraction.

Before going through the detail of extraction, it is helpful to study the following three informative points:

- The term **solute-of-interest** (also called **liquid-of-interest** or **wanted liquid**) is used in extraction to refer to a liquid to be separated (extracted) and used as the **product** of the process.
- Extraction is also called **liquid-liquid extraction** because of contacting two liquid phases.
- A ternary mixture (a three-component system) containing two immiscible liquids and an extractant is usually used in the extraction process.

Usually, the extractant is chosen to be miscible with the liquid-of-interest but fully or partially immiscible with the other liquid (or liquids) of the feed to create a new ternary mixture, which is then processed in an extractor to separate the liquid-of-interest from the mixture.

In the extraction process, the wanted liquid (liquid-of-interest) stays in the extract, and the unwanted liquid stays in the raffinate (also called impurity). To better understand the terms **extract** and **raffinate**, consider a batch type extractor, and assume that it is fed with:

- A quantity of feed with wanted component A and unwanted component B. Assume that A is **heavier** than B, so A (with greater density) moves down the column.
- A quantity of solvent (extractant) with component C (C has greater miscibility with A than with B).]

In the extractor, we, thus, have a mixture of three (3) components ($A + B + C$), known as a **ternary mixture**. After mixing, the mixture can settle to become a two-layer mixture. The heavier portion, which leaves the bottom of the extractor and contains A, C, and a bit of B, is the **extract** (the **product** of the process), and the lighter stream, which leaves the top and contains B, a bit of A, and a bit of C, is the **raffinate** (the **byproduct** of the process), as shown in Figure 1. The extract is processed further (mostly in a distillation column) to separate solvent, which is used again in the extractor, as shown in Figure 2.

[Note 1: Because **removals are never perfect**, always a bit of B (unwanted component) stays in the **extract**, and a bit of A (wanted component) stays in the **raffinate**. Also, note that a small amount of solvent always stays in the raffinate stream.] [Note 2: The terms **light** and **heavy**, used in extraction, refer to density (D), *not* to volatility, as is used in the distillation process.]

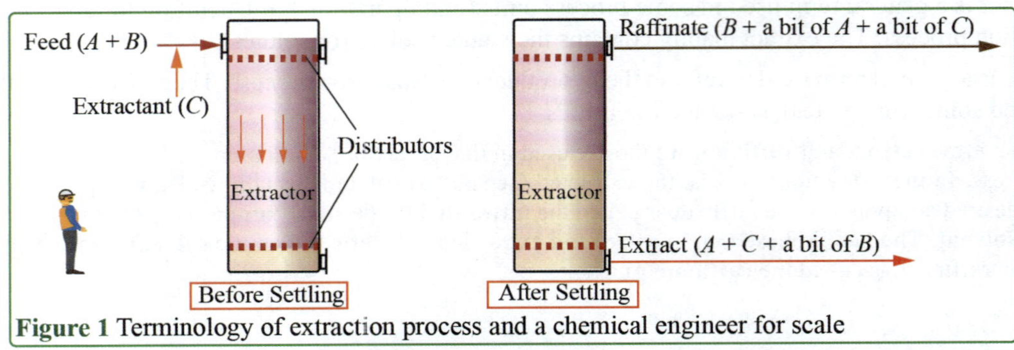

Figure 1 Terminology of extraction process and a chemical engineer for scale

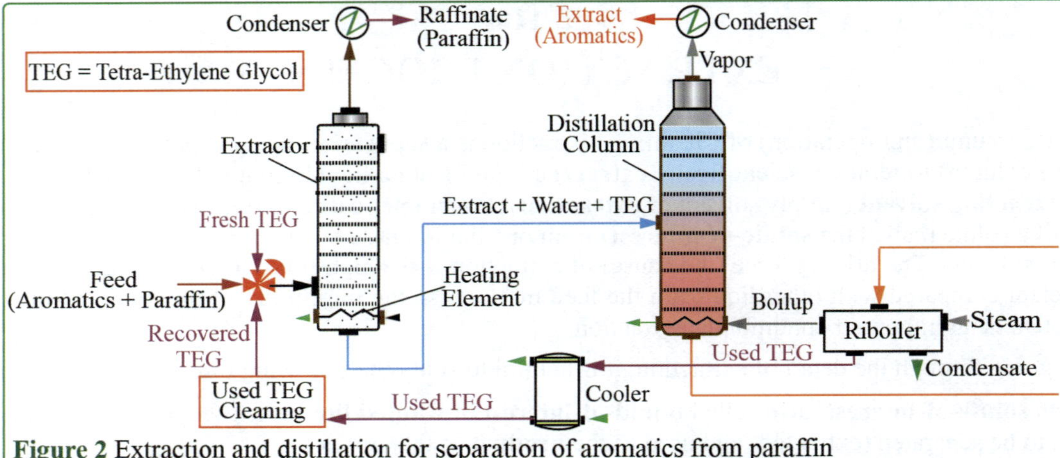

Figure 2 Extraction and distillation for separation of aromatics from paraffin

Extraction Applications

Extraction is mostly used to extract (remove) heat-sensitive compounds. Its largest application is in the **petrochemical industry**, where aromatic compounds (aromatics) are extracted from a hydrocarbon mixture using a polar solvent with high miscibility with aromatics.

The following are some other applications of extraction:

- Removal of penicillin (extract) from the fermentation broth (feed) by using butyl acetate (extracting solvent) after lowering the PH to get a practical distribution coefficient. Only penicillin is dissolved in the butyl acetate, so it can be separated from other components (impurities) by treating the extract with a buffered phosphate solution to extract the penicillin from the mixture. This treatment gives a purified aqueous solution, from which penicillin is produced by drying. Some use distillation to distill extract and produce pure penicillin and then dry it to produce dry penicillin.
- Removal of gasoline spills from water. An organic liquid (like hexane) removes gasoline spills from the water in this process.
- Removal of acetic acid from dilute aqueous solution by using ethyl ether or ethyl acetate.

As a real example, consider a typical and industrially important separation of aromatics from paraffin using an extractive distillation process (combination of extraction and distillation) and **tetra-ethylene glycol** (TEG) as the solvent. Figure 2 shows the schematic diagram of this process. Aromatics and paraffin, which are *not* miscible, enter the extractor bottom as a feed, and TEG (solvent) enters the top. In the column, the flow of the immiscible liquid compounds through each other occurs by density. Because the aromatics dissolve more readily in the TEG than paraffin, the raffinate that leaves the top of the column has fewer aromatics. Instead, the extract leaving the bottom has much more aromatics than the raffinate. The extract stream (with a little paraffin) is fed into a distillation column to separate the remaining aromatics from the solvent. The TEG (solvent) is pumped back to the extractor.

When two immiscible liquids do *not* mix, one of them is dispersed (disorderly distributed) in the other to form a dispersion (with two distinct and separate phases). For example, aqueous (water-based) liquids do *not* mix with oil-based liquids. An immiscibility can be seen when vinegar and olive oil are mixed to make salad dressing. If we want to separate vinegar from oil, a solvent, like water, which mixes better with vinegar than oil, must be added to the mixture. This causes most vinegar to mix with water, so oil becomes a separate phase (because the solubility of the vinegar in water is much greater than in oil). The solubility difference, thus, creates a **driving force** for the extraction (removal) of vinegar from the oil. More scientifically, the driving force causes the mass transfer of vinegar. In this example, water is the extracting solvent, and the liquid-rich in vinegar is the extract (because vinegar is extracted from the oil).

The following two points are important to know about extraction:

- The extract may have a higher or lower density (*D*) than the raffinate. The extract may be shown coming from the bottom of an extractor, in some cases, and from the top, in other cases.
- After extraction, a supplementary process unit is usually used to remove the remaining solvent from the extract for reuse in the extractor. This process improves the extract's purity. When distillation is used after extraction, the combined process is called **distillation extraction**, and when crystallization is used, the combined process is called **crystallization extraction**.

Liquid-liquid extraction (simply extraction) is like gas-liquid extraction, but with some differences, including the following:

- In extraction, the involved phases are two immiscible liquids. The phases (gas and liquid) are usually partially miscible in gas-liquid extraction.
- In extraction, a solvent, which is immiscible or partially miscible with one of the liquid phases, is usually added to the feed for extracting the liquid-of-interest from the mixture. In gas-liquid extraction, the gas phase is partially absorbed by the liquid phase. Say, bubbling carbon-dioxide gas (CO_2) through a sweet solution causes some of the CO_2 molecules to be absorbed by the solution to form a bubbled solution.
- In extraction, the molecules of one liquid phase move (scientifically diffuse) through its phase by convection-diffusion, then through the liquid-liquid boundary by conduction diffusion, and into the other liquid phase, again by convective diffusion. [Both **convection-diffusion** and **conductive-diffusion** are discussed under DIFFUSION PROCESS.] In gas-liquid extraction, the molecules of one phase (usually the gas phase) diffuse through its phase by convective diffusion, then through the gas-liquid boundary by conductive diffusion, and into the liquid phase, again by convection.

The extraction process has some applications in the chemical process industry. Usually, liquids that *cannot* resist the temperature (T) of distillation or when they have close boiling point temperatures (T_{BP}) are processed by extraction to separate component-of-interest (wanted component) from feed liquid. Economically, extraction is more cost-effective than distillation because it requires smaller equipment and less energy.

During extraction, two processes occur at the molecular level: 1) The mass transfer process and 2) The diffusion process. This means that the transferring liquid diffuses through another liquid by diffusion. There are, however, some differences between extraction and diffusion, including the following six (6):

- In extraction, some chemical reactions occur. In diffusion, it does *not*,
- In extraction, the temperature does *not* play an important role. In diffusion, it does,
- In extraction, the solvent is often an organic compound. In diffusion, the solvent is usually water,

- In extraction, the solubility difference of solutes is the driving force. In diffusion, the concentration difference of solutes is the driving force;
- In extraction, mostly one solute is dissolved in a solvent. In diffusion, all solutes are dissolved in a solvent.
- In extraction, a single-component or a two-component process takes place. In diffusion, mostly a multi-component process takes place.

From a diffusion viewpoint, the molecules of the solvent diffuse in the following stepping order:

- **Step 1:** In this step (diffusion on side 1), the molecules diffuse jointly through the bulk of liquid phase 1 toward the **boundary** (the area where the phases are in contact) between the two phases by **convection**.
- **Step 2:** In this step, the molecules diffuse individually through the boundary by **conduction**.
- **Step 3:** In this step, the molecules diffuse collectively through the bulk of liquid phase 2, again by convection. Thus, steps 1 and 3 are similar.

Extraction Types

The following are the types of extraction:

- Liquid-liquid extraction process (simply extraction process or solvent extraction);
- Liquid-solid extraction process (also called the leaching process or solid extraction),
- Gas-liquid extraction process (also called gas absorption process), and
- Gas-solid extraction process (is *not* covered in this book).

Based on the number of feed components, extraction is divided into the following two common types:

- **Standard Extraction:** In standard (single-component) extraction, the component present in a feed is transferred into the extract. As the most widely used, the standard extraction can be performed in batch or continuous, single-stage or multi-stage, and cross-current or counter-current flow.
- **Fractional Extraction:** In fractional extraction, two components in the feed are separated; one leaves the extractor in the extract and the other in the raffinate. In this process, the feed enters the extractor at an intermediate stage, located between the extract and raffinate ends, and the solvent is added to the extract end.

Extraction Solvent Choice

Choosing the right extracting solvent is one of the most important subjects in the extraction process. The four (4) most important criteria in choosing the right solvent are:

- The solvent should selectively dissolve only *A*, the wanted component that has to be extracted (removed).
- The solvent and raffinate phases should have a large density difference to settle easily.
- The solvent remaining in the extract must be easily recoverable from *A* by a process (usually distillation).
- The solvent should be inexpensive, nontoxic, noncorrosive, and nonhazardous.

The first statement can be expressed by a ratio known as **selectivity** (β), so the solvent should have a high selectivity for component *A* (the extracted-and-wanted component). When a binary mixture with *A* and *B* are under extraction and compositions are in mass fractions of *A* relative to *B*, shown as β_{AB}, can be expressed as

$$\beta_{AB} = \frac{\frac{X_{AE}}{X_{BE}}}{\frac{X_{AR}}{X_{BR}}} \quad (1)$$

X_{AE} is the mass fraction of *A* in the extract, X_{BE} is the mass fraction of *B* in the extract, X_{AR} is the mass fraction of *A* in the raffinate, and X_{BR} is the mass fraction of *B* in the raffinate.

[Note: The selectivity used in extraction is like volatility in distillation. In solvent selection, a selectivity value close to one ($\beta_{AB} \approx 1$) is desired. Based on relative selectivity, water, alcohols, esters, and ketone are good solvents. Also, note that in addition to solvent, sometimes a salt (called here a **modifier**) is added to the extractor to make the extraction process easier. In the process of producing uranium yellowcake, a concentrated acid is used as a solvent to extract U_3O_8 (uranium oxide) from the **raw** (natural) **uranium** coming from a mine.]

Mass Balance of a Ternary System in a One-Stage Extractor

To mass-balance a one-stage extractor, shown in Figure 3, we assume a feed with *A* (the **wanted component**), which will end up in the extract, and *B* (the unwanted component), which will end up in the raffinate. As the goal of extraction, we try optimally separate *A* from *B* by adding a solvent to the extractor. After mixing feed and solvent and achieving phase equilibrium in the extractor, the two liquid phases can be separated based on their density differences. We can, thus, remove two liquid streams, the extract, and raffinate, from the extractor.

Our goal in mass balancing is to determine the amount of wanted component *A* in the exiting streams from the system (the extractor). Referring to Figure 3 and expressing the amount of each stream in mass flow rate ($\dot{M}$) and compositions of each stream in **mass fraction** (*X*), we can express the streams entering and leaving the extractor in the following ways:

- **Feed stream:** It has a mass flow rate of $\dot{M}_F$ and mass fractions (compositions) of X_{AF} (where subscript *A* is for component *A* and *F* is for feed) and X_{BF}(where *B* is for component *B*).
- **Solvent stream:** It has a mass flow rate of $\dot{M}_S$ and mass fractions of X_{CS} (if it is pure).
- **Extract stream:** It has a mass flow rate of $\dot{M}_E$ and mass fractions of X_{AE}, X_{BE}, and X_{CE}.
- **Raffinate stream:** It has a mass flow rate of $\dot{M}_R$ and mass fractions of X_{AR}, X_{BR}, and X_{CR}.

The total mass balance of the system can be written as

$$\dot{M}_F + \dot{M}_S = \dot{M}_E + \dot{M}_R \quad (2)$$

The total mass of the material in the system, shown with the symbol *M*, can be given as

$$M = \dot{M}_F + \dot{M}_S = \dot{M}_E + \dot{M}_R \quad (3)$$

Figure 4 shows the system's situation when the feed stream (*F*) and solvent stream (*S*) are mixed and the system is in phase equilibrium. Point *M* in the figure represents the mixing point of feed at phase equilibrium. From the mixing rule, the point M must lie on the straight line that joins points F and S. Figure 4 also shows the coordinates of point *M* (the X_{AM} and X_{CM}) and the **liquid-liquid-equilibrium line** (LLE line), produced by connecting points R_A and E_A. Thus, the two liquid phases leaving the system are in phase equilibrium.

Considering Equation 3, we can express $M.X_{AM}$ (the total balance of extracted component *A*), and $M.X_{CM}$ (the total balance of solvent component *C*).

$$M.X_{AM} = \dot{M}_F.X_{AF} + \dot{M}_S.X_{AS} \quad (4)$$

$$M.X_{CM} = \dot{M}_F.X_{CF} + \dot{M}_S.X_{CS} \quad (5)$$

[Note: For the conciseability reason, this subtopic focuses only on the mass balance of a one-stage system. Readers interested in multistage balancing can refer to Chapter 22 of *Unit Operations of Chemical Engineering*, 7th Edition.]

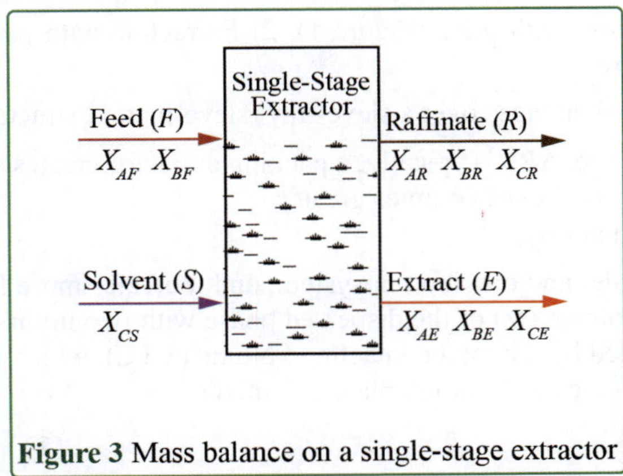

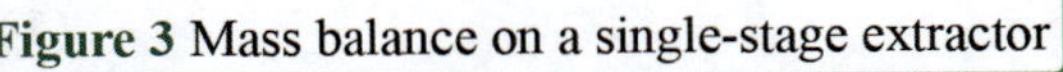
Figure 3 Mass balance on a single-stage extractor

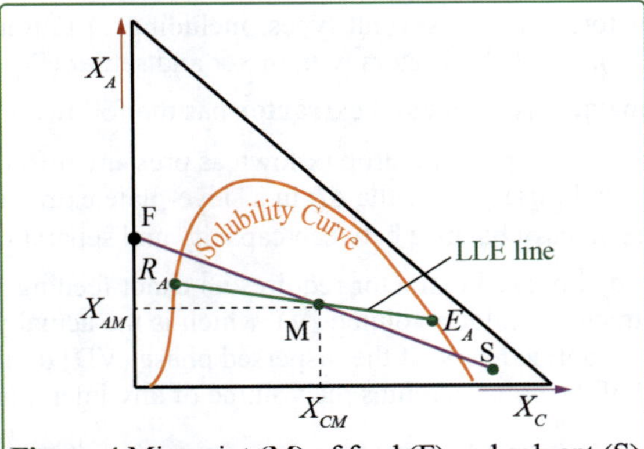

Figure 4 Mix point (M) of feed (F) and solvent (S)

E-119

EXTRACTIVE DISTILLATION

Discussed under the topic of DISTILLATION PROCESS.

E-120

EXTRACTORS

An extractor (also called **extracting column**) is usually a **vertical cylinder** (column) used for performing the extraction process. Extracting columns used for extraction are different in design than those used for the distillation process and leaching process. The four (4) main differences are:

- Most extracting columns are *not* of sieve type, meaning the trays are *not* perforated to allow passage of the liquids. Instead, the trays of distillation and leaching columns are often perforated. Distillation trays, however, allow passage of the liquid and vapor through each other. Perforated leaching trays operate like a filter by keeping the solids and letting the solvent pass.
- The extractors' columns are usually packed with **packing** (solid particles of glass, ceramic, and stainless-steel rings) or have **trays** to better contact the liquids through the column. However, in both types, the number of stages in extracting columns is smaller than in distillation columns. This is because of the larger settling times required for the extraction process (small density differences between the liquids under extraction). Distillation and extraction columns operate with packing or trays, but leaching columns have trays.
- Distillation columns are comparatively taller (with too many trays) than extracting and leaching columns.
- Distillation columns relatively require more energy to be operated (because of high reflux ratios).

In an extractor, two phases must be in a counter-flow contact for a good mass transfer process to maximize the dispersion of one phase in the other phase and minimize back-mixing. A good extractor has a high separation ability to separate the two phases from each other. The phases' separation efficiency depends on the extractor's number of **theoretical stages**, with the next processing abilities:

- It can handle different feeds with high or low solubility,
- It can handle different processing temperatures (T),
- It can handle different processing flow rates, and
- It can handle different retention times (t).

Other factors are relative **capital** and **operating costs** associated with an extractor.

Extractors come in several types, including 1) Extractors with trays (Figure 1), 2) Extractors with packing (Figure 2), and 3) Extractors with mixer and settler (Figure 3).

Comparatively, a **packed extractor** has the following advantages over a sieve-tray (sieve-plate) extractor:

- Creates lower pressure drop (known as pressure difference, ΔP). Typically, a packing extractor creates a ΔP of about 4 mBar, while the ΔP in a sieve-plate extractor is about two times greater.
- Offers an easy balance between capacity and separation ability.

Instead, a packed extractor requires an exact feeding inlet and distribution system, and it creates more foam. The extractor's holdup volume (V), which is the actual volume (V) of the dispersed phase with two immiscible liquids, is defined as V of the dispersed phase (VD) divided by the total contacting volume (VTC), which is the volume of the column minus the volume of any internals (such as packing, plates, or mixers).

$$V = \frac{V_D}{V_{TC}} \tag{1}$$

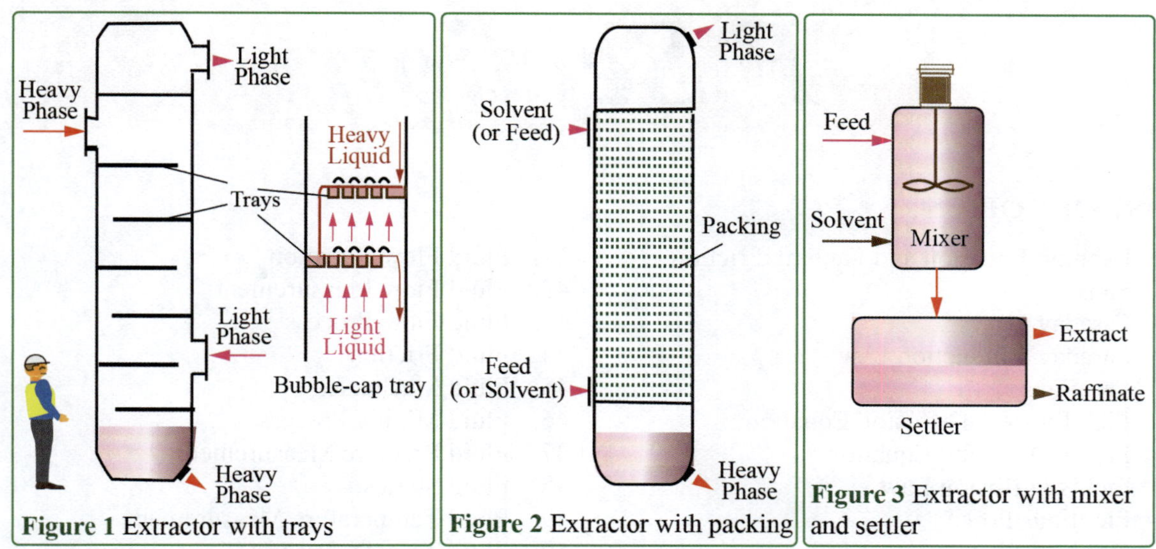

Figure 1 Extractor with trays

Figure 2 Extractor with packing

Figure 3 Extractor with mixer and settler

E-121

EXTRAPOLATION

Study INTERPOLATION AND EXTRAPOLATION.

E-122

EXTRINSIC PROPERTY

Study INTRINSIC AND EXTRINSIC PROPERTIES.

F Section

LIST OF TOPICS

1. Fanning Equation and Fanning Friction
2. Fans
3. Faraday
4. Faraday's Induction Law
5. Fermions
6. Fick Einstein Diffusion Equation
7. Fick's Diffusion Equation
8. Fick's Diffusion Law
9. Fictitious Force
10. Field
11. Filter Aids
12. Filter Cake
13. Filter Cake Resistance
14. Filter Cloths
15. Filter Medium Resistance
16. Filtering Centrifuges
17. Filters
18. Filtration Process
19. Filtration Rate
20. Firing Point Temperature
21. First Order Reaction
22. Fission Process
23. Fitting Friction Factors
24. Fitting Parts
25. Fixed Quantity
26. Flammable Liquids
27. Flashing Evaporation
28. Flashing Heat Energy
29. Flashing Point and Firing Point Temperatures
30. Flashing Tanks
31. Flocculants
32. Flow
33. Flow Measurement
34. Flow Rate
35. Flow Work
36. Flowmeters
37. Flue Gas
38. Fluid and Superfluid
39. Fluid Dynamics
40. Fluid Entrainment
41. Fluid Flow Equation
42. Fluid Flow Measurement
43. Fluid Flow Process
44. Fluid Friction
45. Fluid Mechanics
46. Fluid Mixing Process
47. Fluid Pressure Measurement
48. Fluid Statics
49. Fluid Temperature Measurement
50. Fluid Transfer Process
51. Fluidization Process
52. Flux and Flux Rate
53. Flux Rate
54. Foam and Defoamers
55. Foot
56. Force and Shear Force
57. Force of Gravity
58. Forces of Nature
59. Formaldehyde
60. Fossil Fuels
61. Four-Dimensional System
62. Fourier's Heat Conduction Equation
63. Fourier's Heat Conduction Law
64. Fractional Energy
65. Fractional Distillation
66. Fractionation Process
67. Frame of Reference
68. Free Electrons and Valence Electrons
69. Free Energy
70. Free Evaporation
71. Free Fall Motion
72. Free Surface Energy
73. Freezing Depression Temperature
74. Freezing Elevation Temperature
75. Freezing Point Temperature
76. Freezing Process
77. Frequency and Period
78. Friction
79. Friction Factors, Friction Force, and Friction Coefficient

80. Friction Head Loss
81. Froude Number
82. Fructose
83. Fuels
84. Fuel Oil
85. Fugacity and Fugacity Coefficient
86. Functional Groups
87. Fundamental Constants of Nature
88. Fundamental Fields of Nature
89. Fundamental Forces of Nature
90. Fundamental Interactions of Nature
91. Furnaces
92. Fusion Process

F-1

FANNING EQUATION AND FANNING FRICTION

Discussed under the topic of LIQUID FLOW PROCESS.

F-2

FANS

Discussed under the topic of COMPRESSORS, FANS, AND BLOWERS.

F-3

FARADAY

Michael Faraday (1791−1867) was a British physicist who discovered a close relation between magnetism and electric current (simply **current** or **electricity**) in 1831, known later as Faraday's Induction Law. This law says that an electric field (E-field or E) is produced (induced) by a changing magnetic field (M-field or B). In other words, placing an electric conductor, like a **wire coil** (a wire loop with multiple turns), in a rotating M-field produces (induces) electricity in the conductor. And the amount of the produced electricity depends on the M-field's size (the *larger* the M-field, the *greater* is the electricity). [Soon later (in the early 1860s), Maxwell formulized this law by several equations (later, **Maxwell's equations**) to mathematically describe how electric charges and electric current in an M-field are related.]

Faraday, illustrated for this book

Einstein kept the pictures of Newton, Faraday, and Maxwell in his office to respect them as the pioneers of physics

Rutherford said, when we consider the extent of Faraday's discoveries and the influence of these discoveries on the progress of science and industry, there is *no* honor too great to pay to the memory of Faraday

The SI unit of electric capacitance, Farad (F), is named after Faraday

Some of Faraday's memorable achievements

By researching the M-field around a conductor, Faraday discovered electromagnetic field (EM-field) and the basics of generating electricity. Based on Faraday's and Maxwell's discoveries, other scientists could develop electric generators to generate electricity in the 1880s at a large scale to be distributed to houses and businesses.

First, the problem was that some inventors recommended the AC (alternating current) electricity and some the DC (direct current) electricity through a **commutator**. The disagreements continued for the rest of the 19th century. Toward the end of that period, the idea of multiple-phase generators, generating 50 or 60 Hz frequency AC electricity, became the most practical idea for commercial electricity use. In these efforts, the innovative ideas of Edison and Tesla get some credit.

Faraday also discovered diamagnetism and the principles of electrolysis. He was also a talented chemist and chemical experimentalist, discovering electrolysis and benzene (C_6H_6). He invented oxidation numbers and popularized terminology like ion, anode, cathode, and electrode. We can finish this topic by saying that

- Faraday was one of the two (2) greatest contributors to electricity (the other one was Maxwell).
- Newton, Faraday, and Maxwell can be named as the three (3) top classical physicists. [For the name of top quantum physicists, refer to the topic of QUANTUM PHYSICS.

F-4

FARADAY'S INDUCTION LAW

Faraday's Induction Law (simply **Faraday's Law**) is a discovery of Faraday in 1831 that says placing an electric conductor, like a **wire coil** (a wire loop with multiple turns), in a rotating magnetic field (M-field or B) produces (induces) electricity in the conductor. And the amount of the produced electricity depends on the M-field's size (the *larger* the M-field, the *greater* is the electricity). To Faraday's Law, magnetism and electric current (simply **current** or **electricity**) are closely related. Practically, when a wire coil rotates in an M-field, an alternating current (AC) electricity is induced (produced) in the coil. [This law also works in reverse (moving current generates an M-field).]

The amount of induced AC electricity in the coil mainly depends on the following:

- **Coil's Rotational Velocity:** More current is produced when the wire coil turns *faster* in the M-field, so the M-field *increases* with *increasing* the coil's rotational velocity (ω). This tells us that the number of M-field lines passing through a coil changes as it turns (see Figure 1), as double the ω, double the AC produced.
- **Coil's Rotational Direction:** More current is produced when the wire coil's rotating motion is perpendicular (vertical at 90° angle) to the M-field.

Later, Faraday's discovery was formulized by Maxwell. Their findings were then followed by creative inventors (like Edison and Tesla) to produce electricity for commercial use by using the kinetic energy (E_K) of a steam turbine whose shaft can rotate the M-field of an electric generator. [Electric generators, electric motors, and electric transformers operate based on the induction law. A generator is a device (equipment) that has a rotor (a rotating M-field) in a stator (an electromagnet that creates the M-field) and, therefore, electricity.]

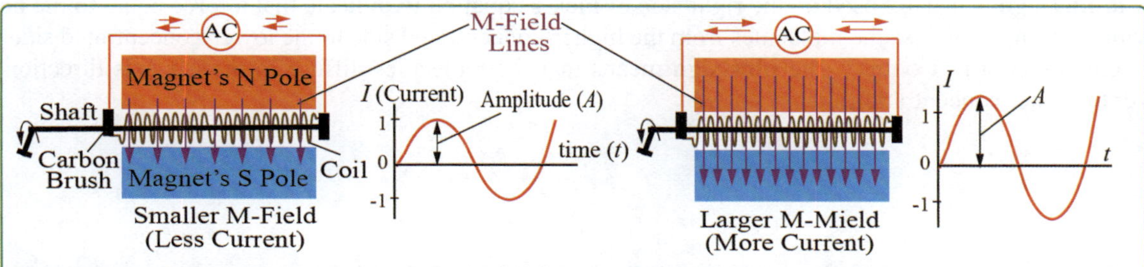

Figure 1 Faraday's Induction Law; turning a coil in a magnetic field creates (induces) electric current, and the amount of current depends on the size of M-field (the *larger* the M-field, the *greater* is the current)

F-5
FERMIONS

Study BOSONS AND FERMIONS.

F-6
FICK-EINSTEIN DIFFUSION EQUATION

Discussed under EINSTEIN'S DIFFUSION EQUATION.

F-7
FICK'S DIFFUSION EQUATION

Fick's diffusion equation (simply **Fick's equation**) is the mathematical expression of Fick's Diffusion Law. It calculates diffusion transfer rate ($\dot{M}_A$), which is the diffusion rate of diffusant A in a binary mixture with components A and B. It calculates $\dot{M}_A$ (the mass of diffusant A diffused in unit time) by knowing the diffusion's driving force for diffusant A, which is the concentration gradient ($\Delta C_A/L$), area (A) through which the diffusion process occurs, and the diffusion coefficient of component A in the mixture, shown as D_{AB}.

$$\dot{M}_A = D_{AB}.A\frac{\Delta C_A}{L} \qquad (1)$$

Usually, diffusants diffuse through an imaginary tiny thin layer in the range of a few nm (known as thin film), through which the diffusion occurs in a certain direction, say, the x-axis (horizontal) direction. Therefore, the diffusion equation should be given in its differential (final-minus-initial) form (d form) to indicate the diffusion applied on a tiny thickness (dx), through which the diffusion occurs in a certain direction (for example, in the positive X-axis direction).

$$\dot{M}_A = D_{AB}.A\frac{\Delta C_A}{dX} \qquad (2)$$

If D_{AB} is in m^2/h, area (A) is in m^2, concentration (C) is in kgmole/m^3, and length (L or X) is in m, the SI unit of $\dot{M}_A$ becomes in kgmole/h. The US unit of $\dot{M}_A$ is Lbmole/h. [Instead of mass transfer rate ($\dot{M}_A$), if we consider the mass transfer (M_A without dot sign over M), which is the mass transfer given in kg mole, then the unit of D_{AB} will be in m^2.]

A **minus sign** is usually used on the right side of Fick's equation to indicate that a force equal to the negative driving force must diffuse the molecules from the higher-concentrated side to the lower-concentrated side (in the + X-axis direction). Contrary, the **plus sign** means that the molecules diffuse in the – x-axis direction (from lower to higher concentration).

F-8

FICK'S DIFFUSION LAW

Fick Diffusion Law (also called **Fick's First Law**), named after Adolf Fick (1829 – 1901, a German scientist), is a concept in physical chemistry that Fick discovered in 1885. It discusses the molecular diffusion process in a multi-component mixture from the higher-concentrated to the lower-concentrated side. Consider a binary (two-component) mixture with components *A* and *B*, where *A* diffuses into *B*, shown in Figure 1 under DIFFUSION PROCESS. According to Fick's Law, the mass transfer rate of diffusant *A* (the mass of diffusant *A* diffused in unit time, shown as $\dot{M}_A$) is the product of the diffusion coefficient (D_{AB}) of *A* in the mixture multiplied by diffusing area (*A*) and concentration gradient ($\Delta C/L$, where ΔC is for concentration difference and *L* is for length).

$$\dot{M}_A = D_{AB}.A\frac{\Delta C_A}{L} \quad (1)$$

This equation, which is known as the Fick's diffusion equation, often gets a **minus sign** on the right side to indicate that a force equal to the negative driving force must be used to diffuse the molecules from the higher-concentrated side to the lower-concentrated side (in the + *X*-axis direction). Instead, the **plus sign** means that the molecules diffuse in the – *X*-axis direction (lower to higher concentration).

F-9

FICTITIOUS FORCE

Another name for INTERNAL FORCE.

F-10

FIELD

A field in Physics is a geometric system that takes a value for every point in space and time (together spacetime). Say, temperature (*T*) is a field because it varies from place to place and changes from time to time. Based on its definition, we can write *T*(*X*, *t*) to express a field, where *X* is for the length coordinate and *t* is for time. Most forces are described as fields to transfer information (energy, force) to a distant point.

F-11

FILTER AIDS

A filter aid is used in some types of filtration to add strength to the suspended solid particles (simply **suspended particles** or **solid particles**) and prevent their breakup. They are usually used when a feed contains slimy or fine suspended particles that, otherwise, can quickly plug the filter pores. Filter aids consist of porous and charged particles. Thus, a filter aid can capture and trap the feed's fine particles to form coarser particles that do *not* pass the pores of a filter's filter cloth.

The two (2) common naturally-occurring filter aids are diatomaceous earth and perlite. Some polymeric compounds and special ground woods have started recently as filter aids. Natural diatomaceous earth (diatomite) is an aquatic plant containing about 85% silicon dioxide (SO_2) and 5% aluminum oxide (Al_2O_3). To be used as a filter aid, it is heated to above 800°C and ground to make powder with a small particle size of 10 to 200 μm. [More suppliers offer diatomite under different trade names.]

Perlite is a volcanic rock consisting of about 75% SO_2 and 15% Al_2O_3. To be used as a filter aid, it is ground to make powder with small particles.

The amount of filter aid used to precoat a filter depends on the nature of the feed's solid particles. For example, a feed containing colloids requires five (5) times more filter aid than a feed with *no* colloid. In operation, a filter is first precoated with the filter aid at a dosage of 0.05 to 0.2% on solids of the feed. This dosage can form a filter cake on the filtering medium with 2 to 3 mm thickness. Usually, the filtrate comes first cloudy but then improves to clear. The cloudy filtrate is returned to the feed tank for refiltration.

F-12

FILTER CAKE

Defined under the topic of CAKE, MUD, SLUDGE, AND SLURRY.

F-13

FILTER CAKE RESISTANCE

Filter cake resistance (shown by R_{FC} in this book and by α in some other reference books) is a resistance (R) that occurs in a filter when the thickness of the filter cake (simply **cake**) exceeds a certain thickness. As the cake becomes thicker, the filter resistance increases, too. When the R_{FC} gets to a certain level in the filtration process, the cake starts to block the filtering medium's pores, so the cake must be removed from the medium, say, by **backflushing**.

F-14

FILTER CLOTHS

A filter cloth is a material with very fine pore size. It is used to cover the surface of a filter's filtering medium. A filter cloth must meet general filtration requirements, such as those outlined next.

- It shouldn't plug easily,
- It shouldn't be expensive,
- It shouldn't get damaged easily,
- It should be thermally resistant,
- It should be chemically resistant,
- It should produce a clear filtrate,
- It should be cleaned conveniently,
- It should handle filter aid easily, and
- It should allow filter cake to be dropped easily.

The following filter cloths meet all, or most, of the listed requirements:

- Canvas filter cloth,
- Polyamide filter cloth,
- Polypropylene filter cloth,
- Monofilament-fiber filter cloth.

Polypropylene and polyamide types are commonly-used filter cloths in the sugar industry. The filter cloths made from polyamide are the strongest ones of all filter cloths.

F-15
FILTER MEDIUM RESISTANCE

Filter medium resistance (R_M) is a resistance (R) that occurs when suspended solid particles pass through the filter medium. This word is used in the filtration process and centrifugal process to indicate the ability of a solid's particles when they pass through a filtering medium of a filter or a centrifuge. During the early stage of filtration, the R_M varies with the pressure difference (ΔP) between each side of the filtering medium. The higher liquid's velocity (V), caused by a large ΔP, may force more particles into the filter-medium pores. The R_M depends on the ΔP, V, and liquid's η (viscosity).

$$R_M = \frac{\Delta P}{\eta . V} \tag{1}$$

When ΔP (pressure drop, generally called pressure difference) is given in kPa, the η in kPa.s, and v in m/s, R_M becomes in 1/m. The typical R_M values range from 10^{-10} to 10^{-11} m.

F-16
FILTERING CENTRIFUGES

Discussed under CENTRIFUGES.

F-17
FILTERS

Study FILTRATION PROCESS AND FILTERS.

F-18

FILTRATION PROCESS AND FILTERS

1. FILTRATION PROCESS

As an important process unit of ChemEng, filtration is the process of separation of suspended solid particles (simply **suspended particles**) from a suspension solution (simply **suspension**, a solution containing suspended particles) by forcing the suspension through a porous **filtering medium** (simply **filter**) on which oversized particles retain. The cause (driving force) of filtration is the pressure difference (ΔP) between each side of a filter. ΔP during filtration is formed mainly because of resistance created by the filter cake (simply **cake** or **deposit**), known as the filter cake resistance. [The **filter cake** is the solid that remains on the filter medium (filter), and the **filtrate** is the liquid that passes through it and is collected during filtration.]

Both filtration and sedimentation are separation processes, so they have the same goal; separation of suspended particles from a suspension solution. Two major differences, however, exist between them:

- Filtration is a fine particle-separation process, while **sedimentation** is a rough particle-separation process.
- Filtration's driving force is ΔP between each side of a filter, while sedimentation is caused by gravity.

[Note: The word **filtration** is generally used for all types of separation that use a filter, but it is particularly used when a filter can remove solid particles larger than a few μm, where 1 micrometer = 1 micron = 10^{-6} m. The word microfiltration process is used when the process can filter fine particles in the range of 0.1 to 10 μm. The ultrafiltration technology filters particles from 0.001 to 0.1 μm (1 nm to 100 nm), where 1 nm (nanometer) = 10^{-9} m. Nanofiltration technology filters particles of 0.1 to 1 nm. Under this topic, we concentrate on liquid-solid filtration when solid particles larger than a few μm are under filtration.]

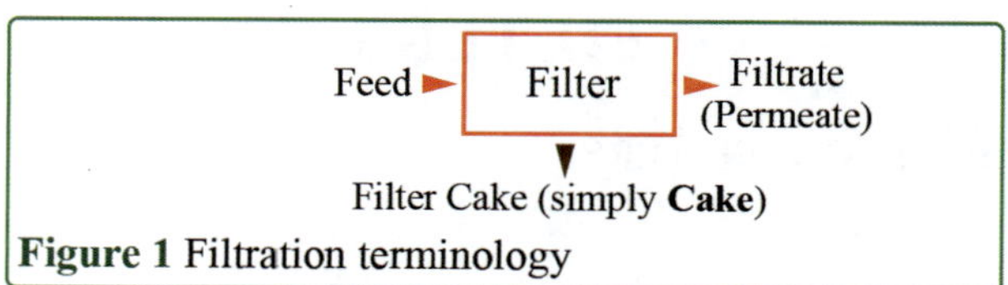

Figure 1 Filtration terminology

The **terms** often used in the filtration process are (see Figure 1):

- **Suspension Feed:** This word is used for the feed entering a filtration system.
- **Filter Cake:** This word is used for suspended particles accumulated on the filter medium.
- **Filtrate** (permeate)**:** This word is used for the liquid leaving the filtration system as the product.

The filtrate, the filter cake (simply **cake**), or both can be the product of a filtration station. When the suspension feed under filtration contains too many suspended particles, it goes first through a pretreatment process, such as sedimentation, to separate the coarse particles and then enters the filtration station. This greatly increases the feed's filtration rate (R_F).

Consider a suspension feed containing suspended solid particles under filtration. At the start, some particles enter the pores of the filter medium, but soon some of them remain on the filter, forming a **precoat layer**. This layer blocks the passage of the remaining particles through the filter. As time passes, the layer gets thicker to make a **filter cake** (wet accumulated solids retained on the filter medium). Then the cake acts as a filter medium, performing most solid-liquid separation. As filtration continues, the thickness of the wet cake increases more until the cake reaches desired thickness. From this point on, the difference in pressure (P) on each side of the filter medium increases, so the process must be stopped to remove the cake from the filter medium. In some modern filters, the cake-removal process is performed automatically without stopping the process, so known as **continuous filtration**.

Some branches of the chemical process industry use simple filtration, and some highly complicated ones. However, based on how particles are separated, filtration is classified into two (2) classes:

- **Cake** (surface) **Filtration:** Suspended particles stay on the surface of the filter to form a cake (Figure 2A). Figure 2B shows the detail of cake filtration. At the beginning of filtration, some small particles escape through the filter's pores and bridge together across the openings to the pores. These bridges then act as a filter medium so that the solution can be filtered through the layers of these buildup particles (which form a cake on the filter medium).
- **Bed** (bulk) **Filtration:** Suspended particles go deep into the filter's pores to form a cake (Figure 3).

With this classification, those filtrations involved with increasing the cake's thickness, such as crossflow filtration, are in the **cake** (surface) **filtration** class. And those that operate based on filter media, such as cartridge filtration, fibrous filtration, and granular filtration, are in **bed** (bulk) **filtration** class. Cake filtration is used when the feed relatively contains a high solid-particle concentration. Numerically, the feeds with particle content of lower than 100 PPM can be treated by bulk filtration. The feeds with more particles form cake, so it is better to be clarified by surface filtration. [Note that today some deep filtrations, such as crossflow filtration, can handle a feed with relatively high particle concentration. At different stages of filtration, however, the cake filtration and bulk filtration cross each other. For example, during the early stage of cake filtration, some particles penetrate deep into the pores of the filter medium, leading to their deposition there. Similarly, after prolonged deep filtration, particles start to settle on the surface of the filter medium, leading to operational problems.]

Cake (surface) filtration can be further divided into two classes:

- **Cake Filtration without Coating:** In this type of filtration, *no* filter aid is used.
- **Cake Filtration with Coating:** In this type of operation, a layer of filter aid is first deposited on the filter cloth at a small dosage. The feed is then pumped through the layer of filter aid (typically 0.1% on the feed's solids), leading to the deposition of a thin layer of solids. For this reason, the filtrate comes through cloudy first and then improves in clarity. The cloudy filtrate is returned to the feed tank for refiltration.

The applied pressure (P) on the filter is provided by

- Pump**:** The P applied by a pump acts in the direction of filtration.
- Centrifugal Force**:** It occurs by a centrifuge and acts away from the basket of the centrifuge.
- Head Pressure**:** It occurs by the feed's weight above the filter medium, acting in the filtration direction.
- Vacuum Pressure**:** It occurs by a vacuum pump and acts in the opposite direction of the filtration process.

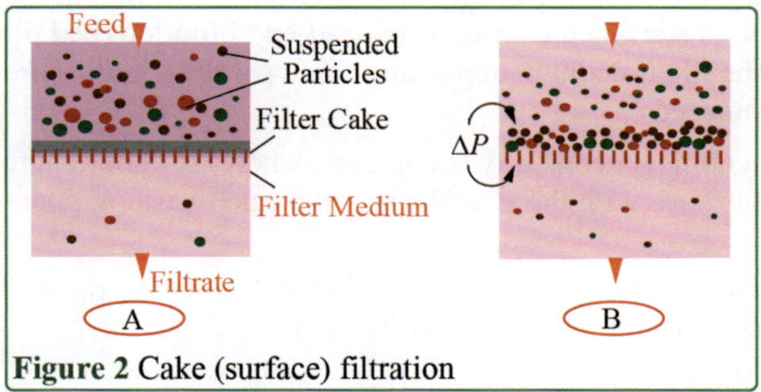

Figure 2 Cake (surface) filtration

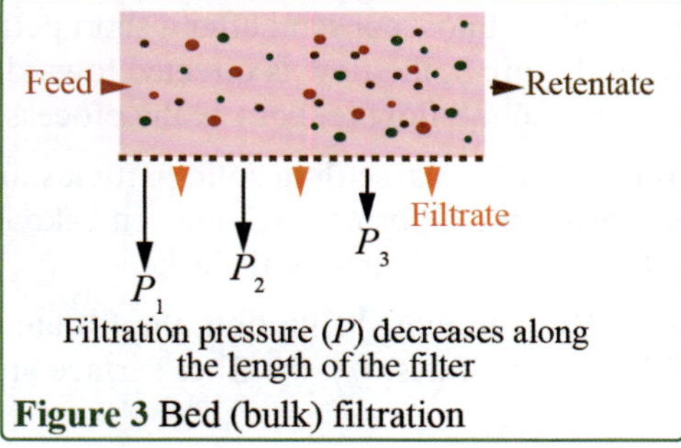

Figure 3 Bed (bulk) filtration

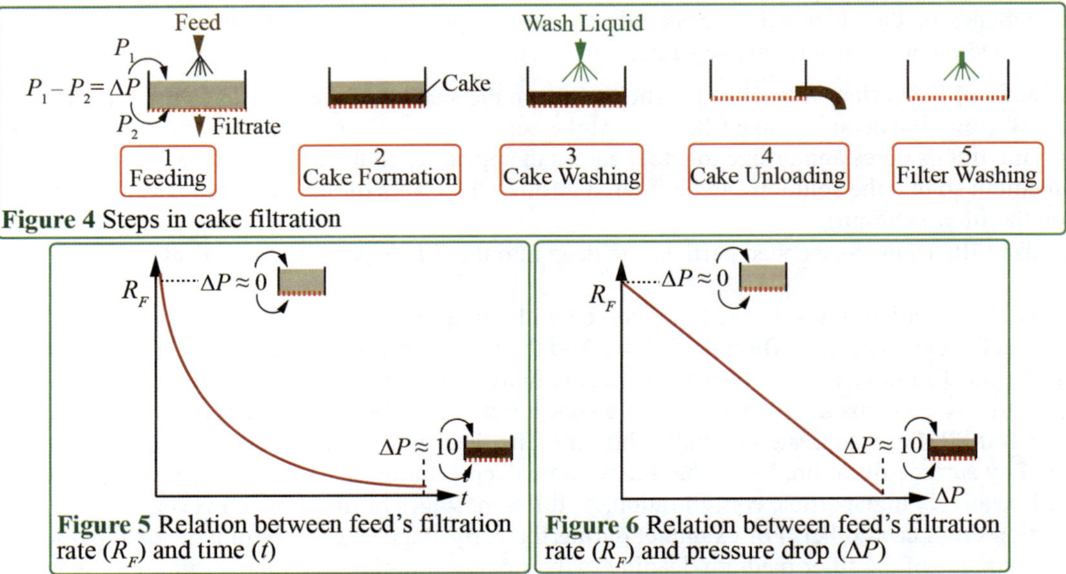

Figure 4 Steps in cake filtration

Figure 5 Relation between feed's filtration rate (R_F) and time (t)

Figure 6 Relation between feed's filtration rate (R_F) and pressure drop (ΔP)

As shown in Figure 4, a cycle of cake filtration consists of five (5) steps:

- **Feeding:** Feed is pumped to the filter medium at a certain P (pressure) and T (temperature).
- **Cake Formation:** Particles grow in thickness to form a **cake** on the surface of the filter.
- **Cake Washing:** The cake is cleaned from the liquid by blowing water or air.
- **Cake Unloading:** Cake is removed from the filter medium automatically.
- **Filter Washing:** The filter medium is washed for the next cycle.

1.1 FILTRATION EQUATIONS

The filtration rate (R_F) *decreases* as the cycle proceeds, and the cake grows. This can be observed from a solid-liquid cake filtration in a laboratory flask at constant vacuum pressure (see Figure 5). As the cake grows, the **cake's resistance** to the feed flow increases.

In crossflow filtration (cake filtration), as shown in Figure 2, the flow is directed across the filter medium, so the cake that forms on the filter moves further by the crossflowing of the feed. In crossflow filtration, the flow is fast and remains almost constant after a short period of starting the process. In dead-end filtration (bed filtration), as shown in Figure 3, the flow is directed toward the filter medium, depositing some particles in the pores of the filter medium, so the flow reduces as the process proceeds.

In a filtration process, settling solid particles in a homogeneous way (same everywhere) is important to ensure that a uniform cake is formed. An uneven cake interferes with the efficiency of the cake-washing process, as it reduces the effective volume of the cake.

In batch (discontinuous) filtration, the filtrate volume (V_F, in m^3) can be calculated using the time (t) during which filtration operates (t_F), the filter surface area (A_F), and filtration velocity (V_F).

$$V_F = t_F . A_F . V_F \quad (1)$$

From here,

$$t_F = \frac{V_F}{A_F . V_F} \quad (2)$$

In continuous filtration, the filtrate's volumetric flux (Q_F, in m^3/m^2 = m) can be calculated as

$$Q_F = \frac{V_F}{A_F} \quad (3)$$

Similarly, the cake's volumetric flux ($Q_{FC} = V_{FC}/A_F$, in m) represents the cake volume (V_C) produced during the same period per A_F. Q_{FC} can also be calculated by using cake resistance (R_C), filtration coefficient K_F (a proportionality constant), and filtrate viscosity (η).

$$Q_{FC} = \frac{V_{FC}}{A_F} = \frac{R_C}{K_F.\eta} \tag{4}$$

This equation can be related to Q_F and Q_{FC} through K_F.

$$t_F = \frac{K_F}{Q_F+Q_{FC}} \tag{5}$$

K_F depends on the total filtration pressure loss ($\Delta P =$), η, and F_C.

$$K_F = \frac{\Delta P_F}{F_C.\eta} \tag{6}$$

If filtration proceeds at constant velocity (or $\Delta V = 0$), t_F is calculated as

$$t_F = \frac{Q_F^2+Q_F.Q_C}{K_F} \tag{7}$$

If filtration proceeds at constant pressure (or $\Delta P = 0$), meaning that the cake is incompressible (properties of the cake do *not* change with P), the t_F is calculated as

$$t_F = \frac{Q_F^2+2Q_F.Q_C}{2K_F} \tag{8}$$

Example 1 on Filtration

Given: A batch filterpress used to filter a suspension at 20ºC at constant velocity. The following data pretended:

Filtration surface area (A_F)	100 m^2
Initial pressure (P_1)	3 Bar (= 3×10^5 N/m^2)
Final pressure (P_2)	6 Bar (= 6×10^5 N/m^2)
Filtrate volume (V_F)	4 m^3
Filtrate viscosity (η)	2×10^{-3} Pa.s (= 2×10^{-3} $N.s/m^2$)
Cake resistance (R_C)	5×10^8 kg/(m^2.s)
Filtration coefficient (K_F)	13×10^{13} 1/m^2

Wanted: 1) Filtrate volume per unit of filter-medium surface area (filtrate volumetric flux, Q_F), 2) Cake volume per unit of filter-medium surface area (cake volumetric flux, Q_C), 3) Filtration coefficient (K_F), and 4) Filtration time (t_F)

Q_F that is produced during $t_F = 0$ to time t_F can be calculated from Equation 3.

$$Q_F = \frac{V_F}{A_F} = \frac{4}{100} = 0.04 \text{ m}$$

Q_C is calculated from Equation 3.

$$Q_C = \frac{R_C}{F_C.\eta} = \frac{5\times10^8}{13\times10^{13}\times2\times10^{-3}} = 2\times10^{-3} \text{ m}$$

Filtration coefficient (K_F) is calculated with Equation 6 and filtration time with Equation 7.

$$K_F = \frac{\Delta P_F}{F_C.\eta} = \frac{(6-3)\times10^5}{13\times10^{13}\times2\times10^{-3}} = 1.1\times10^{-6} \text{ m}^2/\text{s}$$

$$t_F = \frac{Q_F^2+Q_F.Q_C}{K_F} = \frac{0.04^2+0.04\times2\times10^{-3}}{1.1\times10^{-6}} = 1527 \text{ s } (= 26 \text{ min})$$

2. FILTERS

A filter is a device (equipment) used in the filtration process to remove suspended solid particles (simply **suspended particles** or **solid particles**) from a suspension solution (a solution containing solid particles) by forcing it through a porous **filter medium** (simply called **filter**), on which oversize suspended particles retain. Both feed input to the filter and filter cake (simply **cake**) output is continuous in a continuous filter. In a discontinuous filter, feed input is continuous, but the filter's operation is periodically stopped to discharge the accumulated cake.

The three most-used filters in chemical process plants are the following:

- Vacuum filters (for example, rotary drum filters and filterpresses),
- Pressure filters (say, plate filters and candle filters), and
- Centrifugal filters (filtering centrifuges).

In selecting a filter, the following should be considered:

- The content of suspended particles in the feed to be filtered,
- The required thickness of the cake to be produced,
- The required floor space to install the filter, and
- The required filtrate clarity is to be produced.

2.1 ROTARY-DRUM FILTERS

E.L. Oliver designed the first modified **rotary-drum filter** (also called a **rotary-vacuum filter**) in the early 1900s. Since then, the modified types of this filter are the most common type of **continuous mud filters** used in the chemical process industry because:

- They are low-cost relative to other filters (say, membrane-plate filters) with the same capacity,
- Their filter cloths do *not* need to be changed as often as other filters need, and
- They are operable, easily, and conveniently.

The disadvantages of rotary-drum filters, compared with filterpresses, however, are

- Rotary filters *cannot* produce a cake with low moisture content
- Rotary filters use more wash water.

The advantages of rotary filters are that they are low-cost relative to the equivalent capacity of membrane filterpresses, and their filter cloth does *not* need to be changed frequently.

Today's rotary drum filters are of two types: 1) Multiple-compartment rotary-drum filters and 2) Single-compartment rotary-drum filters. Most rotary filters work under vacuum pressure (P_{Vac}), but some operate under pressure (P). A multiple-compartment operating under a vacuum consists of the following (Figure 7):

- An outer drum (a hollow slotted-face drum) 3 to 4 m (= 10 to 13 Ft) in diameter and 4 m in length, rotating horizontally around an axis and partly submerged in the liquid feed to be filtered,
- A smaller inner drum (installed under the outer drum) for solid collection,
- A feed tank for the liquid feed under filtration,
- A vacuum pump for making a vacuum,
- A pump for pumping the filtrate out,
- An ash-water receiving tank, and
- Some connecting pipes.

A filter cloth made from **canvas**, polypropylene, or **polyamide** covers the face of the slotted drum (outer drum), which turns slowly at 1 to 2 R/min and is partly (almost half) submerged in the agitated feed tank. The area between the slotted and the solid-face drums is divided into multiple same-size compartments (usually 24, as shown in Figure 8).

Filter cloth covers the entire slotted-face drum to make 24 independent panels. The panels are connected to a central rotary valve, which connects two vacuum systems (each with different vacuum pressures, P_{Vac}) and one air system, as shown in Figure 9. This arrangement allows vacuum P and air P to be applied alternately to each panel through the rotary valve as the drum rotates.

Rotary filters work continuously and use P_{Vac} during feeding, compressing the cake, cake washing, and low-pressure air during the cake-removal step from the filter cloth. The feed is sucked from the outside of the filter cloth to the middle, where the clear feed (filtrate) is collected. During filtration, the cake layer gradually thickens, increasing the pressure drops across the leaf.

Consider Figure 7 and assume that 50% of the panels are under higher vacuum pressures to suck the **filtrate** (clear liquid), 25% are under lower vacuum pressures to suck the washing water, and 25% are under air pressure to move the cake away from the filter cloth. Further, consider a panel about to enter the liquid feed in the feed tank. As a result of these assumptions, the panel goes through three sections:

- **Filtering Section:** As soon as the panel is in the liquid feed, vacuum pressure is applied from outside the filter cloth through the rotary valve to suck the liquid. As a result, a layer of solids builds on the face of the cloth, and some liquid passes through the cake and cloth into the filtrate section, from where the filtrate is pumped out into the filtrate collecting tank. When the panel is in the feed tank, the layer of the cake gradually thickens, so the pressure drop across the cloth increases.
- **Washing Section:** As soon as the panel enters the washing section, water is sprayed on the cake. A vacuum is applied to the panel from a separate vacuum line through the rotary valve to suck the wash liquid through the filter cake into the wash-liquid tank.
- **Dewatering and Drying Section:** As the panel enters this section, vacuum pressure from the same low-vacuum line sucks the remaining wash liquid from the filter cloth and sends it to the wash-liquid tank. During this period, the air blows through the cake from the air line of the rotary valve to produce the cake with the lowest possible moisture content.

The filter cake is removed continuously from the panel with a scraper and dropped into a screw conveyor. [A little air is blown under the cake to crack the cake to be removed easier from the filter cloth.] Then, the panel enters the liquid again, and the cycle starts again.

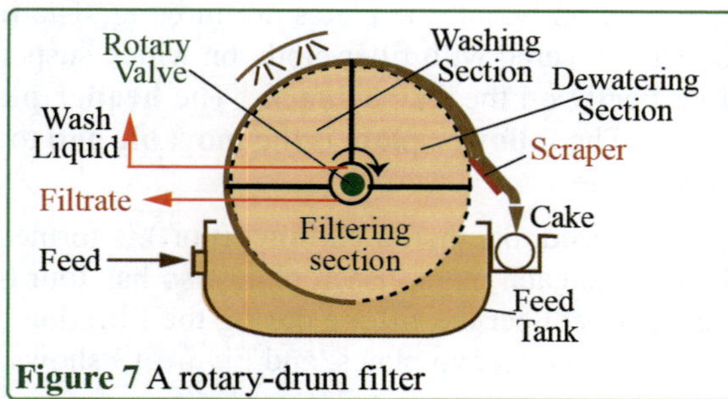

Figure 7 A rotary-drum filter

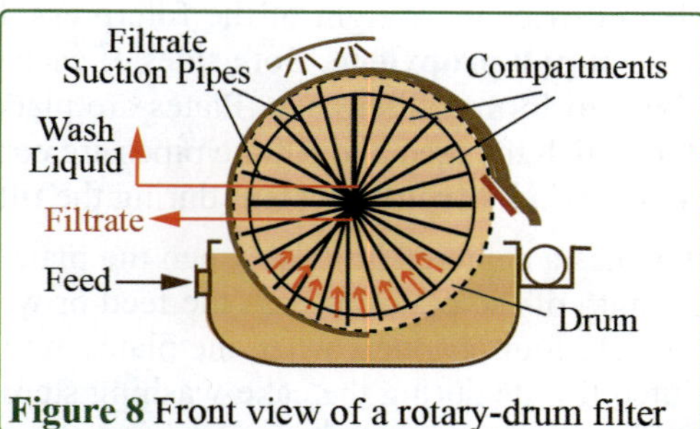

Figure 8 Front view of a rotary-drum filter

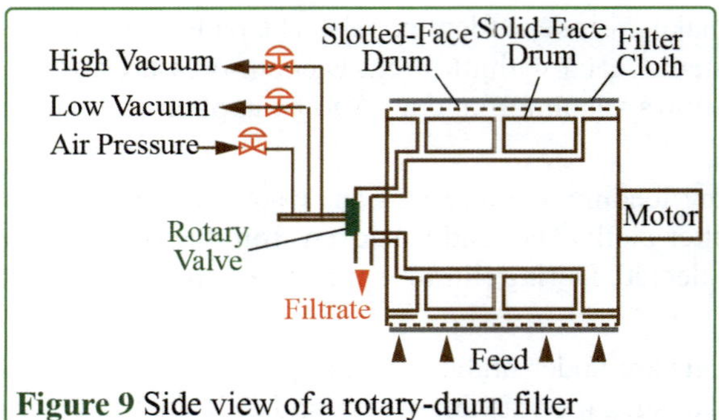

Figure 9 Side view of a rotary-drum filter

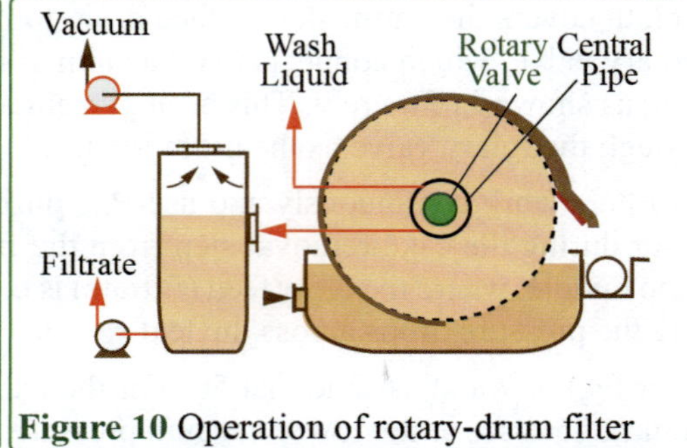

Figure 10 Operation of rotary-drum filter

2.2 MEMBRANE FILTERPRESSES

The original filterpress, called the **plate-and-frame press**, was first designed in the 1860s. The original plate-and-frame presses were batch-operated, space-consuming, and labor-intensive (because of hand washing the plates). About 100 years after its invention, the modified and automated design of filterpress, called **membrane filterpress** or **chamber filterpress**, was introduced.

Membrane filterpresses are used when a load of suspended particles is high (more than 5%). A typical filterpress is semi-continuous and has a high filtration rate (R_F, the volume of the feed to be filtered per filtration area per unit time). It has a capacity of 1 m^3 (= 35 Ft^3) and about 73 m^2 (= 22 Ft^2) filtering surface area, so its R_F is 0.14 $m^3/m^2.s$ = 0.14 m/s.

Filterpresses have the following advantages over the old plate-and-frame presses:

- They require less floor area,
- They produce filter cake with lower moisture content,
- They have less standby time between the operating steps, and
- They are labor savers (because they automatically discharge filter cake and wash the filter cloth).

As shown in Figure 11, a typical filterpress mainly consists of a strong frame and several filtering plates. The **frame**, which carries the weight of the filterpress, has a rack on which the plates are moving. The **plates** are usually made of **polypropylene**. Both sides of each plate are covered with filter cloth, on which suspended particles are built to form a filter cake. Plates are placed vertically on the frame's rack. The **header plate** is the **fixed end** to which the feed and filtrate pipes are connected. The **follower plate** is the **movable end** to press the plates together by a **hydraulic system** during the filtration cycle.

Each plate has a centered hole, so when the plates are squeezed together, a **channel** (port) is formed through the entire length of the plates to pass the feed or wash water to each plate. Each plate also has four (4) corner holes that create four channels when the plates are together to collect the filtrate during the filtration cycle and collect diluted filtrate during the cake-washing step. Figure 12 shows two plates, and Figure 13 shows the same plates in different operating cycles.

The plates made of polypropylene are common because:

- They withstand high temperatures (80 to 85°C),
- They have a high filtration area, and
- They are lightweight.

Filterpresses come in different plate sizes, from 0.5 by 0.5 m (= 20×20 In) to 2 by 2 m (= 80 × 80 In). Depending on the plate size, the thickness of each plate is about 10 to 50 mm (= 0.4 to 2 In). The number of plates is different. The large ones have up to 150 plates, each about 2 by 2 m, with up to 1000 m^2 filtering area and a cake capacity of 20 m^3. Depending on the size and the number of plates, the filterpresses require a hydraulic system of 6 to 12 Bar (= 88 to 176 PSI) to squeeze the plates.

Filterpresses come with different **recess** (empty) **areas** between two plates. The width of recesses is usually 16, 20, or 25 mm, so the thickness of the produced cake is 32, 40, or 50 mm, correspondingly.

A typical operating cycle of a filterpress consists of the following seven automatically-performed steps:

- **Feeding:** The feed slurry enters at the head-end of the assembly and runs lengthwise through the feed channel to another corner of the assembly. The smaller channels carry the feed from the main feed channel into each plate.
- **Filtering:** The suspended particles are evenly deposited on the face of the plates in the form of filter cake. Most of the solid-liquid separation is done by the cake. The filtrate passes through the filter cloth, down the plate face, and runs through a discharge outlet. With the increasing thickness of the cake, the pressure (P) increases, so the flow rate decreases until P reaches its maximum set point. At this point, the feed valve closes, and the cake-washing step starts.
- **Cake Washing:** As the feed valve is closed, the wash-water valve opens to flow water through the space behind the plates to clean the cake from the mother liquid. [In some operations, hot condensate is used for washing the cake.] The diluted filtrate is collected in the **filtrate collecting tank**.
- **Cake Pressing:** The air valve opens to press the plates with high pressure to compress the filter cake toward the frames.
- **Cake Dewatering:** The air blows through the cake to reduce its moisture content to the lowest possible. [In some operations, steam is used for drying the cake.]
- **Cake Discharging:** The assembly opens, and the plates are moved one by one to drop the cake on a belt conveyor. A shaking system vibrates the plates to help the cake-discharging process. [If, however, the process has been done poorly, the cake drops with difficulties.]
- **Cloth Washing:** The hot-water valve opens to wash the filter cloths. At this time, the plates are closed, and the filterpress gets ready for the next cycle.

The operating cycle time of filterpresses is different, from a few minutes to 40 minutes, depending on the following factors:

- Suspended particles content: The cycle time for a feed slurry with 10% suspended particles is about half that of a slurry with 5% (when all other factors are equal). This ratio exists because the process must work on half of the water content coming with the particles.
- The pressure of the feed entering a filtration system.
- The thickness of the filter cake norm.

[The operating cycle time of a filterpress is almost independent of its operating capacity (a filterpress with 1 m^3 capacity has about the same cycle time as a 2 m^3 filter).]

2.3 PRESSURE LEAF FILTERS

Pressure leaf filters (simply **leaf filters**) are used when a load of suspended particles is low to medium (1 to 10%), and the clear filtrate is required. They operate continuously and automatically under high pressure (P) in a closed tank. The space between the leaves (disks covered with filter cloth) for cake accumulation is different, from 20 mm to 80 mm, depending on the ability of the cake to hold on to the filter medium. For a fast-filtering feed, the space between the leaves can be doubled by removing every second leaf. In this case, the cake space doubles, but the filtration area becomes half. Each leaf is covered with a coarse-mesh screen, which supports the filter cloth that retains the cake. Each leaf has a hole at its bottom's center for discharging the filtrate through a valve. The cake discharge valve is chosen for an operating P of about 6 bar (= 88 PSI). Leaf filters are cleaned internally by nozzles mounted on movable arms.

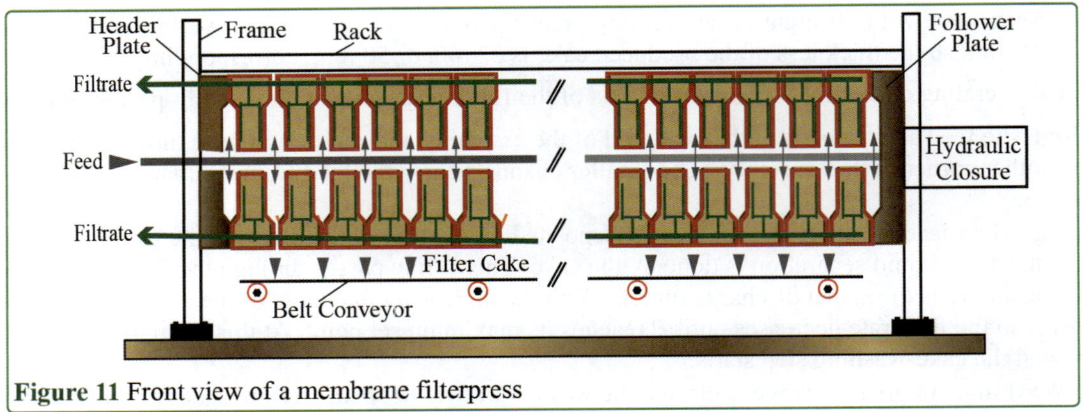

Figure 11 Front view of a membrane filterpress

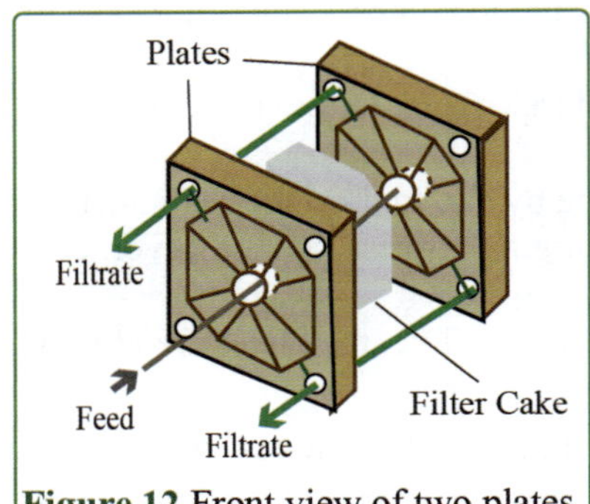

Figure 12 Front view of two plates of a membrane filterpress

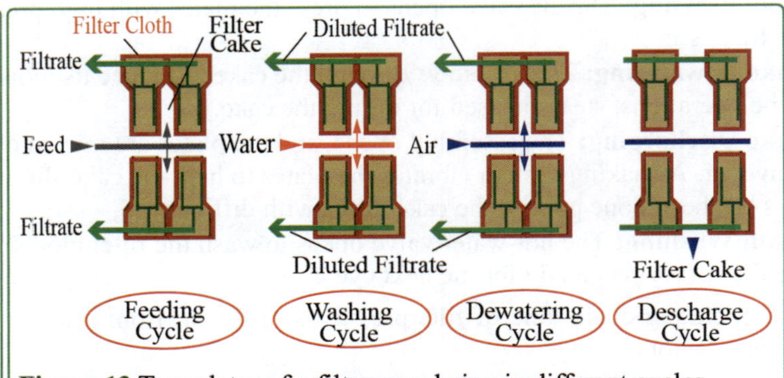

Figure 13 Two plates of a filterpress being in different cycles

A typical operating cycle of a leaf filter consists of the following steps:

- The feed cycle starts by pumping the feed through each leaf and filter cloth.
- The filtrate cycle starts to discharge the filtrate from the discharge end of the filter.
- The cake cycle starts to release the cake (1 to 2 mm thick) from the bottom of the filter.
- The cleaning cycle starts to wash the filter cake by spraying warm water with spray nozzles.

Leaf filters are used for filtration with and without precoating. In the precoating operation, a layer of filter aid at a dosage of about 0.05 to 0.2% on solids of the feed is first deposited on the filter cloth. The feed is then pumped through the layer of the filter aid.

Leaf filters are made in a variety of designs with two body types (most suppliers offer both types):

- **Horizontal Leaf Filters:** A typical horizontal leaf filter has several vertical leaves (Figure 14) installed in a horizontal body. The leaves are held on a retractable rack to move in and out of the body. Horizontal leaf filters have a filtration surface area of up to 300 m^2 (= 3250 Ft^2).
- **Vertical Leaf Filters:** A typical vertical leaf filter has several vertical leaves installed in a vertical body. Vertical leaf filters have a filtration area of up to 100 m^2 (= 1080 Ft^2).

2.4 DISK FILTERS

Disk filters are used when a load of suspended particles is low (1 to 5%) and a clear filtrate is required. Based on the disks (plates) position, the disk filters are divided into two groups:

- **Horizontal Disk Filters:** A horizontal disk filter has parallel filtering disks installed horizontally in a vertical body with a volumetric capacity of 10 to 30 m^3 (353 to 1060 Ft^3). The disks, usually made of stainless steel, are covered with a filter cloth. Typically, these filters have up to 60 m^2 (= 650 Ft^2) filtering area and 4 m^3 (= 140 Ft^3) cake capacity. Horizontal disk filters are used when the load of suspended particles is low (1 to 5%) and a clear filtrate is required. They are also used when contaminated, flammable, and corrosive feeds must be filtered. Figure 15 shows a few disks of a horizontal disk filter, consisting of a stack attached to a hollow shaft used to discharge the filtrate. The feed is pumped at a pressure of about 6 Bar through the filtering disk to form the cake on the filter cloth.
- **Vertical Disk Filters:** Vertical disk filters (vertical leaf filters) have parallel filtering disks installed vertically in a vertical body. The disks, usually made of stainless steel, are covered with a filter cloth. Vertical disk filters are larger than horizontal disk filters. Typically, vertical disk filters have up to 100 m^2 filtering area and 7 m^3 cake capacity. Figure 16 shows the disks of a vertical disk filter. The disks are attached to a hollow shaft to discharge the filtrate.

2.5 CANDLE FILTERS

A typical candle filter has a cylindrical body with a spherical lid, a **conical bottom**, and a **dished bottom** when a thicker slurry is desired. Numbers of vertical tubes (usually made of stainless steel) are installed in the filtering body (Figure 17). The tubes are covered with a filter cloth.

Candle filters operate under *P*, so they are **pressure filters** and, thus, are used when the feed *cannot* be subjected to vacuum pressure. In addition, they are used

- When a filtrate with a high clarity must be produced, and
- When a dryer cake filter or a thickened slurry must be produced.

A candle filter produces a higher filtration rate than a clarifier. Thus, it operates on very short cycle times.

In operation, a pump delivers the feed slurry to the lower part of the filtering body to allow upward flow through the filtering candles at a certain velocity. The upward arrangement ensures that the suspended particles settle homogeneously to produce a uniform filter cake on the filter cloth of each filtering candle. When the cake builds up on the cloths, it is released by pressure to the bottom of the cone and moves out the filter.

The filtrate outlet from each row of candles is connected to a separate horizontal header (see Figure 17). Each header delivers the filtrate through a filtrate discharge valve to the main filtrate outlet.

The large candle filters are 2.5 to 3 m (= 8 to 10 Ft) in width and have up to 200 m^2 (= 2 150 Ft^2) filtering area. They have around 250 filtering candles and operate at a typical pressure of around 6 Bar (= 6 Atm).

Candle filters are used:

- When high filtrate quality is required,
- When minimum floor area for a given filtration area is available,
- When the cake can be discharged as dry cake or as thickened slurry, and
- When the liquid feed is volatile and *cannot* be subjected to vacuum pressure.

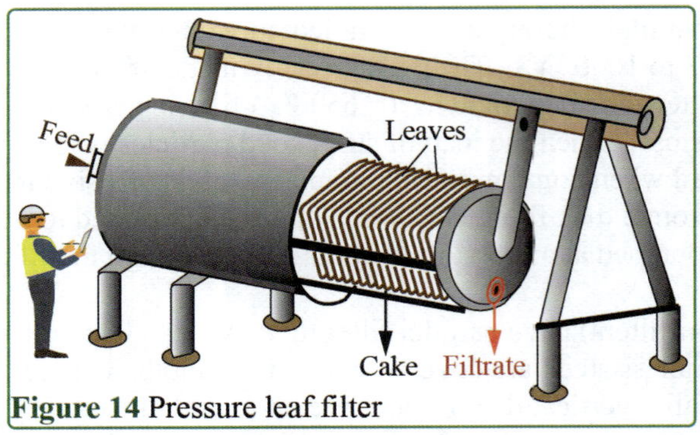

Figure 14 Pressure leaf filter

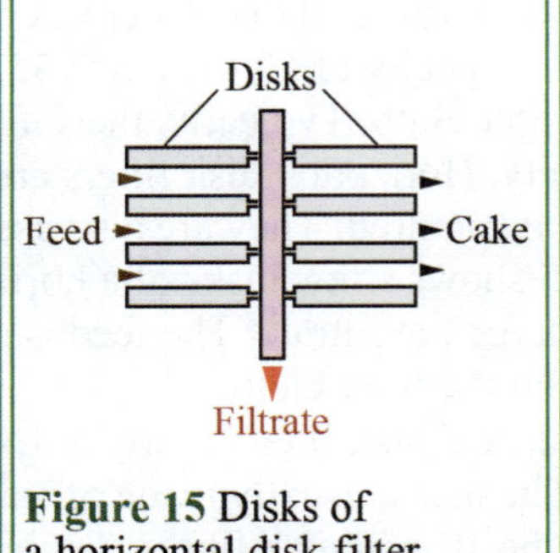

Figure 15 Disks of a horizontal disk filter

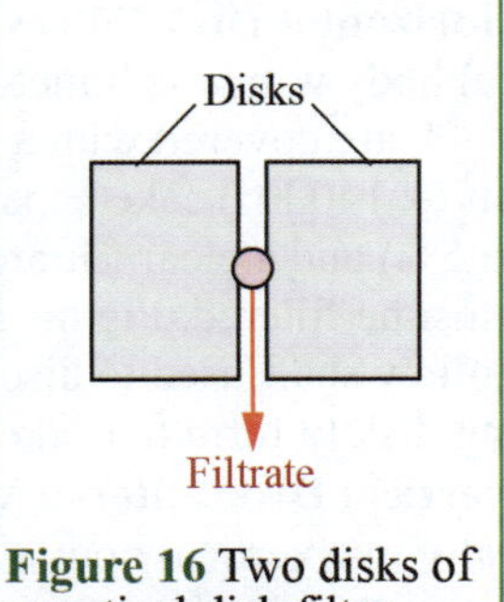

Figure 16 Two disks of a vertical disk filter

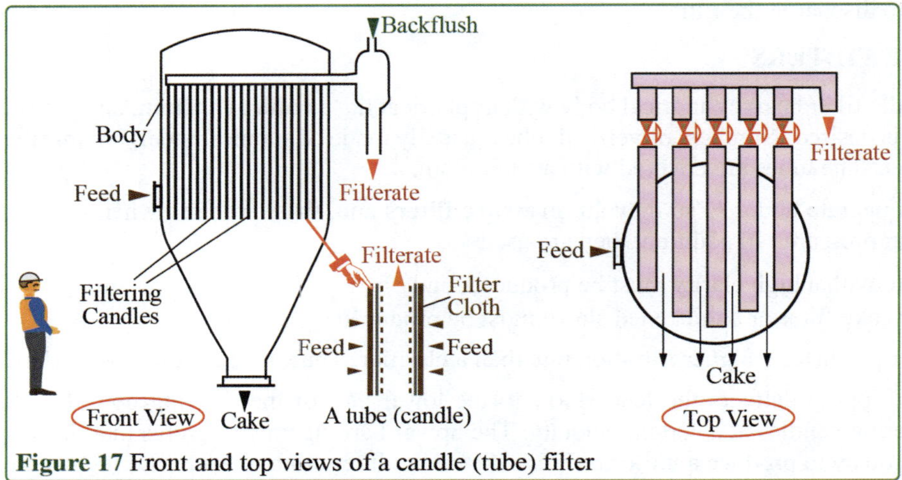

Figure 17 Front and top views of a candle (tube) filter

2.6 CENTRIFUGAL FILTERS

Centrifugal filters (filtering centrifuges) are discussed under CENTRIFUGES.

F-19

FILTRATION RATE

Filtration rate (R_F) is the volume of the feed to be filtered by a filter per filtration area per unit time. It is given in $m^3/m^2.s = m/s$. For example, a typical membrane filterpress (discussed under FILTERS) has a capacity of 1 m^3/s (= 35 Ft^3/s) and about 73 m^2 (= 22 Ft^2) filtering area, so the R_F of this filter is 0.14 m/s.

F-20

FIRING POINT TEMPERATURE

Discussed under FLASHING AND FIRING POINT TEMPERATURES.

F-21

FIRST-ORDER REACTION

Defined under CHEMICAL REACTIONS.

F-22

FISSION PROCESS

Study NUCLEAR FISSION AND NUCLEAR FUSION.

F-23

FITTING FRICTION FACTORS

Discussed under LIQUID FLOW PROCESS.

F-24

FITTING PARTS

Study ATTACHED AND DETACHED PARTS.

F-25

FIXED QUANTITY

Fixed quantity is a physical quantity (simply **quantity** or **variable**) that is *not* dependent on the time (t) that a system (or a process) takes to reach the final (the current) situation. Energy is a fixed quantity.

F-26

FLAMMABLE LIQUIDS

A flammable liquid has a low flashing point temperature (T_{FP}, simply flashing temperature). [The term flammability is primarily used for flammable liquids.] A flammable liquid evaporates at its T_{FP} to form an ignitable vapor, which **suddenly** ignites in the air to cause a **fire**. The test that determines the flammability of a flammable liquid at atmospheric pressure (P_{Atm}) is called the **fire test**.

The flammable liquids with a T_{FP} of lower than 60.5°C (= 141°F) are flammable liquids. In another standardization, the flammable liquids with a T_{FP} of lower than 37.8°C (100°F) are considered flammable liquids.

Acetone (with T_{FP} = – 17°C = –1.4°F), methanol (with T_{FP} of 11°C = – 12°F), and ethanol (with T_{FP} of 16.6°C = 62°F) are examples of liquids with low flammability. Paper, wood, and rubber are solid substances with low flammability. [The values of T_{FP} are used for different purposes, such as for storing and handling a flammable.]

F-27

FLASHING EVAPORATION

Flashing evaporation (simply **flashing**) is an evaporation process that suddenly occurs by a decrease in pressure (P), temperature (T), or both in one medium compared to another medium in which the first medium enters. Flashing can occur in an evaporator or a flashing tank, as shown in Figure 1.

The left side of the same figure shows an evaporator, to which a saturated single-component liquid feed enters. While in the evaporator, a reduction in the liquid feed's P occurs, so a part of the liquid flashes (suddenly cools) to release some flashed vapor. Then both the flashed vapor and the rest of the liquid are cooled to the saturation temperature of the liquid at the new (reduced) P to produce some condensate. The process occurred in the evaporator is commonly called **flashing evaporation**.

As shown on the right side of Figure 1, the condensate produced in an evaporator enters a flashing tank with a lower P and T than those in the evaporator. So, a reduction in the liquid's P and T occurs, causing part of the liquid to flash (sudden cooling with the release of condensate) into vapor. As a result of flashing, some heat energy (E_Q), known as the flashing heat, is released. The released heat equates to the enthalpy change (ΔH) between the liquid's T and the flashing tank's T. If, say, condensate is at 100°C (= 212°F) and enters the flashing tank, which is at 95°C (= 203°F), the condensate cools down to 95°C. Because of losing 5°C, an enthalpy of condensation (H_C), which equates to the difference in enthalpy (H) between these two temperatures, is released.

H of saturated liquid at 95°C	398 kJ/kg (from Steam Table)
H of saturated liquid at100°C	419 kJ/kg (from Steam Table)
Difference (enthalpy of condensation)	21 kJ/kg

The difference in enthalpies is the flashing heat, which can be used elsewhere, such as in an evaporator to perform some evaporation or heat exchanger to perform some heating.

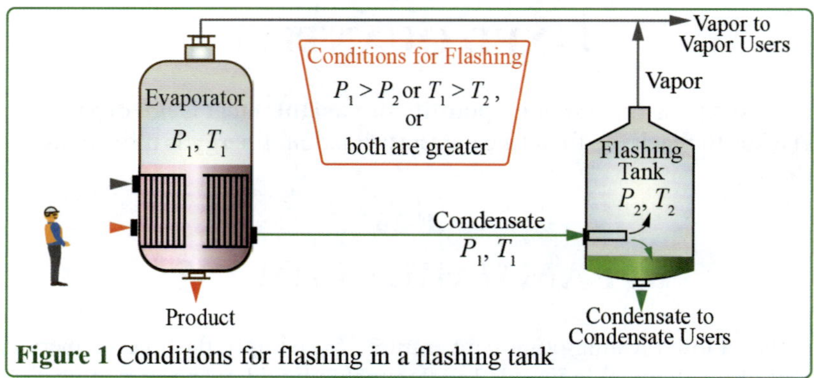

Figure 1 Conditions for flashing in a flashing tank

F-28

FLASHING HEAT ENERGY

Flashing heat energy (simply **flashing heat** or **flashing enthalpy**) is the heat energy (E_Q) that suddenly releases when a liquid feed entering an evaporator flashes (cools suddenly with some condensation). When an evaporation process is performed in a multiple-effect-evaporation station (discussed under EVAPORATION PROCESS), the process uses two sources of E_Q, the E_Q from steam and flashing evaporation.

F-29

FLASHING POINT AND FIRING POINT TEMPERATURES

Flashing Point Temperature: The flashing point temperature (T_{FP}, simply **flashing point** or **flashing temperature**) of a flammable compound (with high flammability) is the temperature (T) at which that compound evaporates to form a gas, which **suddenly** ignites in the air to cause a **fire**. An explosive mixture is formed when enough vapor exists in equilibrium with atmospheric air. The T_{FP} is used in storing and handling flammable liquids, like alcohol. Theoretically, the flashing T of a flammable binary (two-component) mixture consisting of flammable components A and B is determined using the next equation.

$$1 = \frac{X_A.\gamma_A.P_A}{P_{V.A}} = \frac{X_B.\gamma_B.P_B}{P_{V.B}} \quad (1)$$

Here, X_A is the molar fraction of A, γ_A is the activity coefficient of A, and $P_{V.A}$ is vapor pressure at the flashing T of pure A. And X_B, γ_B, and $P_{V.B}$ are defined similarly. If one of the components is nonflammable (water), the second term is eliminated, and the remaining term is used for the flammable component under the test.

Experimentally, a flammable liquid's T_{FP} is determined using either a closed container test (closed-cup test) or an open container test (open-cup test), usually at P_{Atm}. The result of a closed-cup test is usually a few degrees less than that of an open-cup test. The values of flashing temperature are used for different purposes,

In one standardization, the liquids with T_{FP} of lower than 60.5°C (= 141°F) are **flammable**. In the other standardization, flammable liquids have a T_{FP} of lower than 37.8°C (= 100°F). Acetone (with T_{FP} of – 17°C = –1.4°F), methanol (with T_{FP} of 11°C = – 12°F), and ethanol (with T_{FP} of 16.6°C = 62°F) are examples of liquids with low flammability. And paper, wood, and rubber are examples of solid compounds with low flammability.

Firing Point Temperature: The firing point temperature of a liquid is the T, at which the vapor of that liquid starts to burn to create a fire. [At **firing temperature**, which is higher than **flashing temperature**, a compound ignites briefly, but vapor might *not* be produced to the extent that a fire occurs.]

F-30

FLASHING TANKS

Discussed under the topic of TANKS, VESSELS, AND DRUMS.

F-31

FLOCCULANTS

Not scientifically recommended name for COAGULANTS.

F-32

FLOW

Flow is the motion of a fluid (a liquid or gas) in a medium (like a pipe) because of a force (F). Mass flow rate ($\dot{M}$) or volumetric flow rate ($\dot{V}$) of fluid at specified temperature and pressure are used to quantify a fluid flow.

Flow, in electrical engineering, is the motion of electrical current (simply **current**) in a conductor (such as a metal wire). All electrical appliances operate on the flow of current. A motor, for example, uses changing current to create a constant force to turn a rotor.

F-33
FLOW MEASUREMENT

Discussed under the topic of PROCESS CONTROL OF CHEMICAL ENGINEERING.

F-34
FLOW RATE

Flow rate is the quantity of a fluid (liquid or gas) per unit time (t). The flow rate in and out of a system can be steady or unsteady (more information is given under OPEN SYSTEM). The flow rate of a fluid can be expressed in volumetric flow rate ($\dot{V}$) or mass flow rate ($\dot{M}$). In pumping systems, the flow rate with which a liquid flows in a pipe by a pump is known as the pump's **capacity**.

The SI unit of $\dot{V}$ is m^3/h, m^3/min, or m^3/s, and its US unit is Ga/h, Ga/min, or Ga/s. In the US units, $\dot{V}$ is also expressed in Ft^3/min (cubic feet per minute), where 1 m^3/h = 0.59 Ft^3/min. The SI unit of $\dot{M}$ is kg/h, kg/min, or kg/s, and its US unit is Lb/h, Lb/min, or Lb/s.

F-35
FLOW WORK

Flow work (W_F, also called **pressure-volume work** or ***PV* work**) is the work (W) or energy (E) associated with the flow of a fluid into or out of a system. When, for example, a fluid is pumped into a pipe by a pump, flow work is applied **on the system** (on the fluid). Note that when a force (F) does work on a system, the energy of the system increases.

The W_F is related to a system's F, L (length), A (area), P (pressure, where $P = F/A$), and V (volume, where $V = L^3 = A.L$).

$$W_F = F.L = \frac{F}{A}A.L = P.A.L = P.V \quad (1)$$

W_F can be **positive** or **negative**. The following are important:

- If work is done **on the system** by the surroundings (outsides), W_F gets a + sign. For example, when a fluid is pumped into a pipe, some flow work is done **on the system** (the fluid); thus, the flow work is positive.
- If work is done **on the surroundings** by the system, W_F gets a – sign. When a fluid is pumped out of a pipe, the system (the fluid) does some work on the surroundings, so flow work is negative.

The flow work done on a fluid is expressed as (see Figure 1 under the topic of WORK)

$$W_F = -P.V \quad (2)$$

The differential (final-minus-initial) form (d form or derivation form) of a flow work done on a system when the volume is changed by an infinitesimal (tiny) amount is

$$dW_F = -P.dV \quad (3)$$

Flow work can also be given in the integral form to express it within a finite (specified) change in volume. In applying the integral equation to the whole system at constant pressure ($\Delta P = 0$, the usual condition in the laboratory), Equation 3 must be integrated within a specified change in V from initial state 1 to final state 2.

$$W_F = -\int_{V1}^{V2} P.dV = -P\int_{V1}^{V2} dV = -P(V_2 - V_1) \quad (4)$$

This equation tells us that

- The work is done on the system (because of the negative sign in front of the equation).
- When calculating W_F, we must know the volume path (from initial to final). For example, W done on a piston (the system) over a specified change in volume ($dV = V_2 - V_1$) can be obtained by integrating Equation 4 if we know V_1 and V_2. Similarly, suppose a gas is very slowly expanded or compressed. The P throughout the gas will be uniform and equal to external pressure (P_{Ext}), so W of compression (which is **positive**, as shown in Figure 2 under the topic of WORK) or expansion (which is **negative**, as shown in the same figure) can be obtained by an infinitesimal (tiny) amount by using Equation 4. [In this case, P is a function of T (temperature) and V (volume), as seen in the next Example.]

Example 1 on Flow Work

Calculate the flow work (W_F) done by an ideal gas on the piston of an enclosed cylinder when the gas expands (increases its volume) to force the piston. The following data are available:

Gas pressure (P)	3 Atm (= 304 kPa)
Gas temperature (T)	23°C (= 296 K)
Gas volume at no expansion (V_1)	2 L (= 0.2 m^3)
Gas volume at some expansion (V_2)	3 L (= 0.3 m^3)
Gas constant (R)	0.0821 atm.L/mole.K

To find the amount of the gas in mole (n), we use the ideal gas equation.

$$n = \frac{P.V}{R.T} = \frac{3\times2}{0.0821\times296} = 0.25 \text{ mole (or } 2.5\times10^{-4} \text{ kg mole)}$$

The W_F is negative because it is done on the piston (the surroundings) by the gas (the system).

$$W_F = -\int_{V1}^{V2} P.dV = -P(V_2 - V_1) = -304(0.3 - 0.2) = -30.4$$

For converting the unit of W_F from kPa.m^3 to kJ, the conversion factor of (1 N/1 m^2.Pa) and (1 J/1 Nm) is used. Then, the product of (kPa.m^3) (1N/1m^2.Pa) (1J/1Nm) simplifies to kJ. Thus, the answer is −30.4 kJ.

F-36
FLOWMETERS

Discussed under PROCESS CONTROL OF CHEMICAL ENGINEERING.

F-37
FLUE GAS

Flue gas (stack gas) is a hot gas that leaves the stack of a furnace (the main part of a steam boiler). As a numerical example, a typical boiler produces about 2 kg (= 1.5 m^3) of flue gas from evaporating 1 kg of water to steam, where each kg of flue gas has about 150 kJ of E_Q (heat energy). Because flue gases usually contain particulate matters (PM, simply **particulates**), which are pollutants (emissions), they go through a particulate-removing device, like a gas scrubber or gas cyclone, before being released into the atmosphere. Flue gases are usually analyzed by an **Orsat analyzer** (for the percentage of O_2, CO_2, CO, and N_2 on a dry basis). [Historically, the word **flue** meant **stack** or **chimney**.]

A chemical engineer should be aware of the next points on the flue gas **pollutability** (polluting ability):

- A furnace's flue-gas pollutability is its **emission concentration** (mass per unit of fuel used by the furnace).

- Although flue gas is environmentally a pollutant, using a clean fuel (a fuel low in sulfur, nitrogen, and heavy metals) reduces its pollutability.
- Pollution regulations for flue gases are *not* the same in different countries (even in different states in a country). These regulations, however, have become more similar and stricter in recent years.
- Modern boilers usually have a **feedwater economizer**, which saves heat energy (E_Q) use of the boiler by recovering E_Q from the flue gas and heating the boiler feedwater. As said a moment ago, the furnace of a typical boiler discharges about 150 kJ of E_Q to the atmosphere. The boiler's economizer can save most of this amount of E_Q.

The amount, composition, and the particulates content of a flue gas depend on the following factors:

- The fuel type used in a boiler and fuel's ash, SO_2, nitrogen, and moisture contents.
- The type of the boiler's furnace and the furnace's particulates-removing device.

F-38

FLUID AND SUPERFLUID

Fluid: The word **fluid** is generally used for either liquid or gas or when both are addressed collectively. More scientifically, it refers to liquid, gas, and plasma (because these three states of matter flow *freely* from higher to lower elevations by gravity). Defined so, viscosity (η, a force acting against a fluid's flow) is one of the top properties of a fluid. [Liquids and solids, instead, are known collectively as the condensed substances because their molecules are condensed (closer to each other), so they do *not* flow under ordinary conditions.]

Fluids can be classified into two (2) main groups:

- Incompressible Fluids: The D (density) of an incompressible fluid does *not* change considerably when its pressure (P) or temperature (T) changes. Liquids are incompressible fluids.
- Compressible Fluids: The D of a compressible fluid changes considerably when its P or T changes. Gases are compressible fluids.

[Sometimes, the term **fluid** is used in common practice for liquid (incompressible fluid), with *no* implication that a gas could also be present. We say, for example, **brake fluid** to mean a liquid.]

The three (3) main properties of the fluid are the following:

- It takes the shape of its container,
- Its molecular kinetic energy (E_K) increases as the molecules move faster, and
- It flows without a force, but its velocity is affected by a shear force and temperature.

A fluid either works *on* its surroundings or has work (W) done on it *by* its surrounding through a device. Say, the shaft of a steam turbine (the surrounding) turns *by* the falling water (the system) from a dam. The W done *by* the water on the shaft decreases the water's E_K as water turns the shaft. [In such cases, the value of W is *negative* (because the system does work *on* surroundings).] A fluid has W done on it *by* its surrounding (a device). For example, a pump (the surrounding) increases the E_K of water (the system) to flow in a pipe. [In such cases, the value of W is *positive* (because W is done on the system *by* surrounding).]

In fluids, particles (atoms, molecules, or ions) are free to move around in all directions. However, the moving speed of a fluid depends on its temperature, T (the *greater* the T, the *faster* is its average speed). In solids, particles are kept in fixed positions but can vibrate (the *greater* the T, the *faster* is their average vibration).

Consider a container with a fluid. The fluid pressure (P) on the container's wall is expressed as the shear force (F_S) applied on the wall divided by the wall's surface area (A). The term F_S/A, called the shear stress (S_S), is important in a liquid flow process because it acts as the liquid's driving force to flow. Viscosity (η), instead, acts as a liquid flow's opposing force.

[In fluid-flow subjects, it is better to use shear force (F_S), but *not* normal force (F, simply force). The F_S is a force that acts on a system parallelly. The term F_S/A is called shear stress, which defines pressure (F/A).]

Liquids and gases have some similarities, but they are dissimilar in some properties. A liquid's P is an F exerted by its molecules on the wall of its container. Instead, the gas's P is the E_K of its molecules as they collide with the wall of its container. A gas's molecules collide with each other stronger if the volume (V) of the gas is decreased, so the average distance between the molecules is decreased. The increase in V causes the frequency of molecular collision to increase, increasing the gas's P, as proved by the ideal gas law.

Listed next are some differences between liquids and gases:

- Liquids' molecules are larger compared with that of gases.
- Liquids' molecules are held together strongly by the intermolecular forces (F_{Int}), so they are incompressible. Conversely, the F_{Int} is negligible for gases' molecules. This is why gases' molecules move freely, are far apart, and, therefore, compressible.
- Liquids' molecules move in the direction of a force (F) that acts on them. Instead, gases' molecules move continuously in all directions without any force.
- Liquids' molecules have surface tension (S_T), and gases do *not*.
- Liquids' molecules can move by gravity, while gravity is negligible for gases.
- Liquids' molecules do *not* diffuse without any means. In contrast, gas molecules diffuse constantly. If CO_2 gas is released on one side of a tank, it gets throughout until CO_2 molecules occupy the entire tank.
- Liquids' particles **are** composed of molecules, while gas particles can be composed of molecules (like O_2 and CO_2) or atoms (like helium, He).
- Liquids' molecules collide in their container and with the container's walls by losing some energy (because of friction), while gases' molecules collide without any energy loss.
- Liquids' pressure (P) exerted on their container's walls is greater at greater depth (because of gravity). In contrast, gases exert the same pressure on their container's walls regardless of the depth because gravity is negligible for gases.
- Liquids have a greater density (D) than gases. For example, the D of water is 998 kg/m^3 at 20ºC and 1 Atm. The dry air D is 1.18 kg/m^3 under the same conditions. [The densities of gases are about a thousand times smaller than those of solids and liquids.]
- Liquids' D decreases with increasing temperature (T) a little. Say, the density of water at 20ºC is 998 kg/m^3 and decreases to 972 at 80ºC (about a 2.6% decrease). While, gases' D decrease with increasing T, notably. For example, the dry air density is 1.18 kg/m^3 at 20ºC and decreases to 0.97 at 80ºC (an 18% decrease).
- Liquids' D decreases with increasing P. Conversely, gases' D increases with increasing P.
- Liquids' viscosity (η) is considerably greater than that of gases.
- Liquids' η decreases with increasing T (for example, η of water at 0ºC is 1.8 Cp, decreasing to 0.3 Cp at100ºC). Conversely, gases' η slightly increases with increasing T.
- Liquids have smaller entropy (S) than gases because gases move in a more disorderly way than liquids.

Fluids, from a compressibility viewpoint, are divided into two broad classes: 1) Incompressible fluids (liquids) and 2) Compressible fluids (gases).

When an external force does work (W) on a fluid, the fluid's energy increases. When, for example, a pump does work on a fluid, the fluid's potential energy (E_P) and velocity (V) increase. A fluid can also do work on its environment and, therefore, lose energy.

Superfluid: A superfluid has zero viscosity (η) at a cryogenic temperature (T_{Cry} , approximately –150°C = –238°F = 123 K). Supercooled helium-4 (He-4) was the first discovered superfluid. At the T_{Cry}, the superfluid helium atoms lose their colliding ability, so the helium becomes motionless (with zero viscosity). [The word ideal fluid is also used to indicate the fluids that flow smoothly (with *no* resistance) because their viscosity (η) is close to zero. The phrase **perfect fluid** refers to a fluid free of η and is characterized by its D and P.]

F-39

FLUID DYNAMICS

Fluid dynamics studies fluids in motion (flow) when a shear force (F_S) is applied to them. Instead, fluid statics studies the fluids at rest.

F-40

FLUID ENTRAINMENT

Study LIQUID ENTRAINMENT.

F-41

FLUID FLOW EQUATION

The fluid-flow equation relates the shear stress (S_S, the driving force of a flow), the viscosity (η, the opposing force of the flow), and the velocity (V) at which a fluid travels (in the direction of the flow) between two points that are apart by distance L (for length).

$$S_S = \eta \frac{V}{L} \quad (1)$$

Usually, a negative sign is written on the right side of the fluid-flow equation (because viscosity acts in the opposite direction of the flow). The fluid-flow equation defines Newton's Viscosity Law (the greater the η of a liquid, the greater S_S is needed to move it to a distance L at velocity V).

[For more information, study LIQUID FLOW.]

F-42

FLUID FLOW MEASUREMENT

Study FLOW MEASUREMENT.

F-43

FLUID FLOW PROCESS

This topic is divided into two subtopics: LIQUID FLOW PROCESS and GAS FLOW PROCESS.

F-44

FLUID FRICTION

Friction (f_F or f, also called **friction coefficient** or **friction factor**) in a viscous flowing fluid occurs because the fluid's molecules

- Rub against each other,
- Rub against the pipe's wall or pipe's fittings, and
- Pass the solid boundary of that fluid (a liquid or a gas) or other fluid.

For example, when friction occurs in a flowing liquid in a pipe because of a fitting (like a valve) being on the way of the flow, a resistance, known as **friction effect,** to flow occurs. The friction effect decreases

- Fluid pressure is a so-called pressure drop (decrease).
- Fluid mechanical energy (by converting it to heat energy).

A decrease in the fluid's pressure (generally known as the pressure difference or pressure drop) and a decrease in the fluid energies (generally known as the friction energy losses) are important in the liquid flow process, so they are included in the related calculations. Fluid frictions in a pipe are measured by estimating the pressure difference (ΔP) between the beginning and end of the pipe and the same between the suction-end and discharge-end of a pump used to move a liquid.

[Note 1: The symbol f shows both fluid friction and frequency. This must *not* create confusion because these terms are rarely used in one equation, so *no* confusion occurs.] Note 2: More information about fluid friction is given under the topic of LIQUID FLOW PROCESS.]

F-45

FLUID MECHANICS

Fluid mechanics is the study of the motion of fluids (liquids and gases) and their interaction with a solid body. Compressible flow and incompressible flow are the two important subtopics of fluid mechanics.

F-46

FLUID MIXING PROCESS

Study MIXING PROCESS.

F-47

FLUID PRESSURE MEASUREMENT

Study PRESSURE MEASUREMENT.

F-48

FLUID STATICS

Fluid statics (also known as **hydrostatics**) is the study of fluids (liquids and gases) at rest and in stable condition (equilibrium), as opposed to fluid dynamics, which studies fluids in motion.

When studying a static liquid, the following must be considered:

- A static fluid applies a pressure (*P*) on the wall and bottom of its container.
- In the bulk (under-the-surface) of a static fluid, a pressure at every point of the fluid exists that acts in all directions, so it is an isotropic pressure (it acts equally in all directions).
- In the bulk of a static fluid, although the isotropic pressure is constant in all directions (in all horizontal cross-sections) of the fluid, it varies from height to height.

F-49

FLUID TEMPERATURE MEASUREMENT

Study TEMPERATURE MEASUREMENT.

F-50

FLUID TRANSFER PROCESS

Study LIQUID TRANSFER PROCESS and GAS TRANSFER PROCESS.

F-51

FLUIDIZATION PROCESS AND FLUIDIZERS

FLUIDIZATION PROCESS

As a process unit of ChemEng, fluidization is the process of suspending (fluidizing) particles of a solid in a fluid (liquid or gas) to form a solid suspension (a two-phase fluid mix) for a certain purpose, such as drying the solid particles. [Because the particles in a fluidizer are in constant motion and behave like a fluid flowing through the air, the process is known as **fluidization**.]

As shown in Figure 1, when a gas (such as air) enters the bottom of a **fluidizer** at a certain velocity (*V*) and some solid particles enter the top, the solid particles become fluidized (suspended). The created gas-suspended-solid system is known in the fluidization terminology as the **fluidized bed**, which moves in the gas flow direction. The terms **fluidization** and **fluidized bed** are, thus, used to describe the condition of fully fluidized (suspended) particles in a fluidizer. [The solid particles' fluidity is the fluidization's **driving force**.]

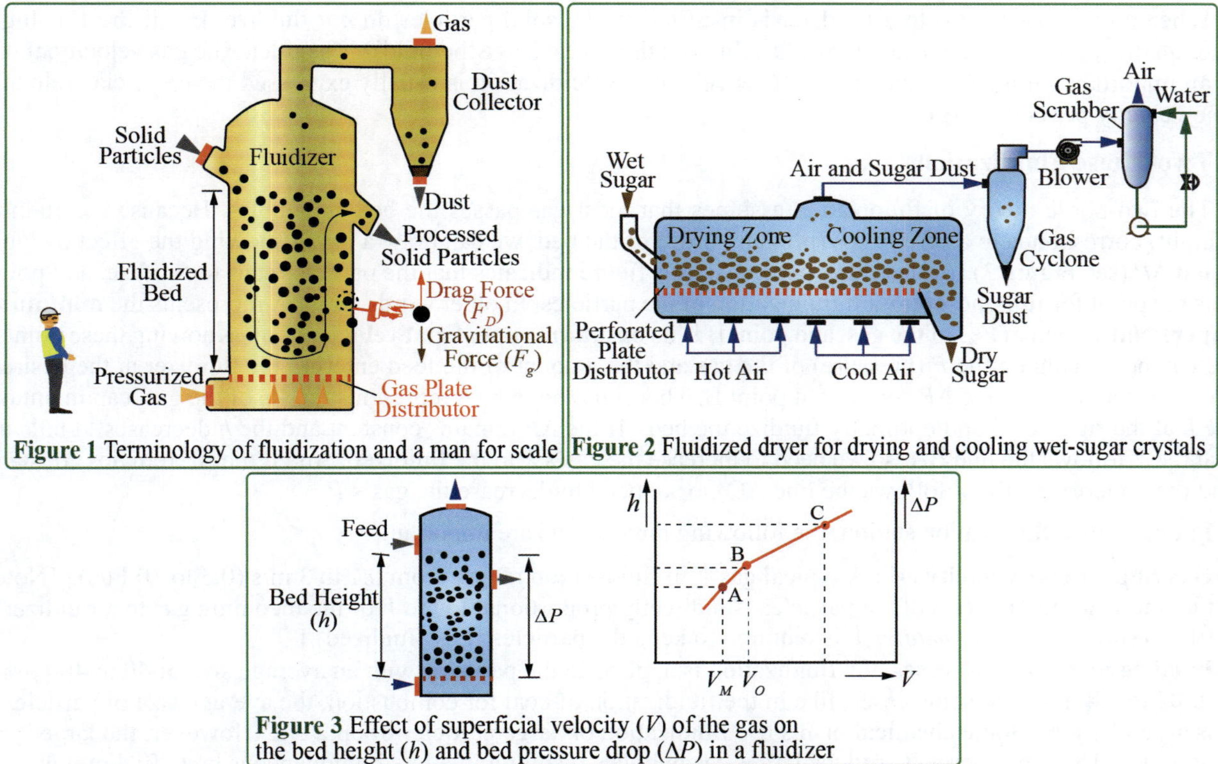

Figure 1 Terminology of fluidization and a man for scale

Figure 2 Fluidized dryer for drying and cooling wet-sugar crystals

Figure 3 Effect of superficial velocity (V) of the gas on the bed height (h) and bed pressure drop (ΔP) in a fluidizer

The fluidization of popcorn kernels in a popcorn popper is a simplified example of fluidization. The hot air forcefully causes the kernels to fluidize and expand (puff up) to make the popcorn particles in the popper's heating chamber.

Applicability of Fluidization

Industrially, fluidization is used in different branches of the chemical process industry, such as

- In the petroleum industry, for catalyst regeneration after the cracking in a reactor,
- In the sugar industry, for drying wet sugar crystals in a fluidized-bed dryer,
- In the coal industry, to reduce pollutants from stack gas (flue gas),
- In the synthetic industry, for the synthesis of acrylonitrile, and
- In the regeneration of ion exchange resin.

To become familiar with fluidization when used to dry fine particles, consider a **fluidized dryer** (discussed under DRYERS), used in the sugar industry for drying wet sugar crystals, as shown in Figure 2. The dryer has an inlet at the top to receive the wet sugar crystals and a perforated distributor plate at the bottom to support the bed of the crystals. Heated drying air enters the dryer below the distributor at a certain velocity (V). It passes the distributor's pores to uniformly fluidize (suspend) the crystals over the entire dryer's cross-section. The intense mixing of the crystals in the dryer causes all crystals' uniform temperature (T). From the top, the air and the very fine crystals go to a dust collector to separate dust from the air.

Suppose the pressure difference (ΔP, commonly known as the **pressure drop**) across the crystal bed overcomes the gravitational force (F_g, a downward force) applied to the crystals. The crystals are said to be fully fluidized. If, in other words, ΔP overcomes the weight (w, the F_g exerted on a system by a mass) of the crystal bed, the crystals are fully fluidized.

When a gas *V* (velocity) to a fluidizer is insufficient, the solid particles do *not* fluidize. But if the *V* is high enough, the particles fluidize and move fast through the bed to leave the fluidizer's outlet. The gas velocity, thus, is an important variable in fluidization. [Gas velocity in fluidization is usually expressed in superficial velocity (the velocity per bed area).]

Two-Phase Fluidization

The two-phase theory of fluidization assumes that most gas passes the bed as bubbles. Because a certain *h* (height) corresponds to a certain ΔP (pressure drop) of the bed, we can draw a graph showing the effect of *V* on *h* and ΔP (see Figure 3). Assume that point A in this figure indicates that the particles start to fluidize, and point B is the point for full-and-optimum fluidization of the particles. In other words, point A represents the **minimum superficial velocity** (V_M) of the gas, and point B is its **optimum superficial velocity** (V_O). Knowing these points, we can now maintain the *P* (pressure) of the gas and the amount of the feed entering the fluidizer at the desired range by maintaining the ΔP constant at point B. This situation, which represents the V_O of the gas, can maintain the *h* at the right level and optimally fluidize the bed. If the ΔP remains constant and the *h* decreases, it tells us that the *V* follows the line BA, so we need to increase the gas's *P* to the fluidizer. And if the ΔP remains constant and the *h* increases, the *V* follows the line AC, so we need to decrease the gas's *P*.

In operating a fluidization station, the following three points are important:

- **Gas Superficial Velocity (*V*):** A typical gas *V* in fluidization ranges from 0.1 to 3 m/s (0.3 to 10 Ft/s). [Note that the void fraction (ε_F) of the particles is indirectly proportional to the *V* of the incoming gas to a fluidizer (the *greater* the ε_F, the *smaller* *V* is required to keep the particles fully fluidized).]
- **Particle Size:** In most cases, the fluidization is applied to the particles with an average size of 40 to 400 μm (0.04 to 0.4 mm). In some cases, like in the fluidization of coal for combustion, the average size of particles is around 1 mm. Some chemical plants use fluidization on large particles of up 2 cm. However, the larger particles (150 μm or larger) produce larger gas bubbles, resulting in a less homogeneous bed. [0.4 mm is about the average size of typical medium-size table sugar crystals, where 1 mm = 0.04 In.]
- **Pressure Drop (ΔP):** The ΔP through the bed mainly varies with the size of solid-feed particles (the *smaller* the particle size, the *greater* is the ΔP through the bed). As a rough estimate, the ΔP varies with the 2 power of the particle size. This means that if the ΔP of particles of 0.6 mm in size is *X* kPa, the ΔP of the particles with 0.3 mm is X^2 kPa.

Types of Fluidization

Fluidization is mainly grouped into three types, based on the velocity of the fluidizing fluid and the size of solid particles under fluidization. Based on the fluid velocity (in the order of flow increasing) and particle size (in the order of size increasing), the three main types of fluidization are listed next.

- **Particulate Fluidization:** Relatively, this fluidization uses the lowest fluid velocity and the finest particles, known as particulate matter. It uses water as the fluidizing fluid to fluidize the fine particles. Because processing small particles, it creates large bed expansion.
- **Bubble Fluidization:** This fluidization uses air at moderate *V* (velocity) to fluidize the medium-size solid particles. As the air passes through the solid particles' empty spaces (voids), the air starts to bubble. The bubbles grow as the air *V* increases. In general, the size of bubbles can be small as a few centimeters in diameter or big as several centimeters, depending on the particles' size and the air's *V*.
- **Fast Fluidization:** This type uses air with *V* (the superficial velocity of the air) above V_M (the minimum superficial velocity). The bed is expanded so much that the air *cannot* make bubbles in this process.
- **Centrifugal Fluidization:** This is fluidization in which the solids are rotated in a centrifuge basket that puts them under centrifugal force (F_C) instead of gravitational force (F_g). F_C is much stronger than F_g. The devices used for the fluidization process are much more complex than those used for conventional fluidization. Thus, centrifugal fluidization is used in some technologies, such as for the absorption of CO_2 from the atmosphere when a spacecraft operates at zero gravity.

In all types of fluidization, the fluidized bed (simply **bed**) expands as the fluid's superficial velocity (V) increases. The quantity of the bed expansion from the highest to the lowest order is in centrifugal, fast, particulate, and bubble fluidizations. [The bed expansion in bubble fluidization is in the range of 20 to 50%, and in fast type, the expansion might get up to three folds.]

FLUIDIZERS

A fluidizer is used for the process of fluidization. Chemical engineers do *not* recommend a specific shape for fluidizers' main vessels because forming a right fluidized bed can occur in any vessel of ordinary shape. In the case of using a vertical fluidizer (see Figure 1), a typical vessel can be as high as 3 m (= 10 Ft) to 15 m (= 60 Ft), from which 2/3 is the fluidized bed, as shown in the same figure.

F-52

FLUX AND FLUX RATE

The **flux** (F_X) of a physical quantity (simply **quantity**) is the amount of that quantity per unit area (A) through which that quantity flows. For example, heat flux (E_q) in a heat exchanger is the amount of heat energy (E_Q, simply heat) that flows through the heat transfer area (A) of that exchanger. E_q (which equates to E_Q/A) is expressed in units of energy per area, such as kJ/m^2 in SI units and BTU/Ft^2 in US units, where 1kJ ≈1 BTU. [The area required to calculate the flux can be a flat surface, curved surface, or cross-sectional.]

ChemEng uses the following six (6) fluxes:

- Energy flux,
- Heat flux (heat energy flux),
- Momentum flux (also called shear stress),
- Mass flux (mass diffusion flux or simply **diffusion flux**),
- Particle flux, and
- Volume flux.

The **flux rate** ($\dot{F}_X$) of a quantity (like mass or heat) is the amount of that quantity per unit area (A) per unit time (t). Flux rate can also be defined in the next two ways:

- Quantity's rate (a quantity per time) per unit area (A), and
- Rate of flux (F_X, a quantity per unit A),

$$\dot{F}_X = \frac{F_X}{t} \tag{1}$$

For example, heat flux rate ($\dot{E}_q$) in a heat exchanger is the amount of heat transfer (E_Q) per exchanger's heat transfer area (A) per time (t) during which the heat transfer process is happening. Thus, the SI unit of heat flux rate is kJ/(m^2.h). Similarly, mass flux rate is the amount of mass transfer of a component per mass-transfer area (A) per unit time (t), expressed in kg/(m^2.h) or Lb/(Ft^2.h).

Fluxes are vector quantities at each point in space, so they have definite quantity and direction. Flux rates, instead, are scalar quantities, so they have quantity but *no* direction.

[Note 1: For simplicity reasons, sometimes the term **flux rate** is abbreviated to just **flux**. In such cases, the given unit of the quantity can determine the writer's purpose because the heat flux is given in kJ/m^2, whereas **the heat flux rate** is given in kJ/m^2.s or kJ/m^2.h.]

[Note 2: In Physics, the term **flux** is used as an imaginary line through which a physical quantity can travel. For example, **magnetic flux** means the number of magnetic field lines passing through a surface. Similarly, **electric flux** means the number of electric fields that pass through a closed surface.]

F-53
FLUX RATE

Study FLUX AND FLUX RATE.

F-54
FOAM AND DEFOAMERS

Foam: Foam is of two kinds with a minor difference between their definitions:

- **Liquid foam** is the gas bubbles separated from a liquid by thin films. Soup foam trapped in water molecules and beer foam trapped in beer molecules are liquid foams.
- **Solid foam** is the gas bubbles separated from a solid by that solid's thin films. Solid foams can be opened-cell foams or closed-cell foams. In an opened-cell foam, gas bubbles are connected, but thin films in closed-cell foam separate them.

[The word **foam** usually refers to a **liquid foam**.]

In the chemical process plants, foams are of many origins, such as polystyrene foam, polyurethane foam, phenolic foam, and more. In the food industry, colloids and saponin are major foam-causing compounds.

Foam can create serious operating problems in a chemical plant by reducing the rate of chemical reactions, preventing the efficient filling of containers, reducing the heat transfer process, and more.

Defoamers: A defoamer (also called **antifoam** or **anti-foaming agent**) is a compound used to prevent foam formation or break an already-formed foam by reducing a liquid's surface tension and preventing the binding of the foam's molecules with the liquid's molecules. A defoamer mainly consists of an insoluble compound, like silicone oil, which does *not* decompose in the foaming medium, and an aqueous solution (water-based solution). Hence, its defoaming effect continues for a longer period. Today's silicone-based defoamers are dispersed in silicone oil and an emulsifier. A typical food-grade defoamer mainly contains a modified **fatty acid** (a carboxylic acid with a long hydrocarbon chain).

F-55
FOOT

Study METER AND FOOT.

F-56
FORCE AND SHEAR FORCE

Several forces are used in ChemEng, such as normal force (F, simply **force**), shear force (F_S), adhesive force (F_A), buoyant force (F_B), centrifugal force (F_C), centripetal force (F_{CP}), cohesive force (F_{Co}), gravitational force (F_g), and intermolecular force (F_{Int}). The Universe, however, is held together by just four (4) forces, called the fundamental forces of nature, from which the other forces originate. Under this topic, we will discuss the normal force and shear force (see Figure 1).

Normal Force

A normal force (F, simply **force**) is a force that pushes or pulls a system (Figure 2), so it can be viewed as an effect that

- Can move a non-moving system,
- Can accelerate a moving system,
- Can change a moving system's direction, and
- Can transfer energy from one system to another.

Newton's Second Law of Motion defines F as the product of a system's mass (M) multiplied by its acceleration (a).

$$F = M.a \tag{1}$$

This equation, which is always valid, tells us that in a moving system with mass M, force (F) is the driving force of the motion, and acceleration (a) is the effect of the motion.

When M is lifted or fallen in the Earth's gravitational field (which has a gravitational acceleration of a_g), this equation is written as

$$F = M.a_g \tag{2}$$

F is a vector quantity, so it has two components: **parallel** and **perpendicular** (vertical or upright) to the motion. A force, thus, can be divided into two components, which are perpendicular to each other. The parallel component (which is in the direction of motion) does work (W), but the perpendicular component does *not* (see Figure 3).

The SI units of F (force) and F_S (shear force) are N (Newton) and their US units are pound force (Lb_F), where 1 N = 1 kg.m/s^2 = 0.225 Lb_F.

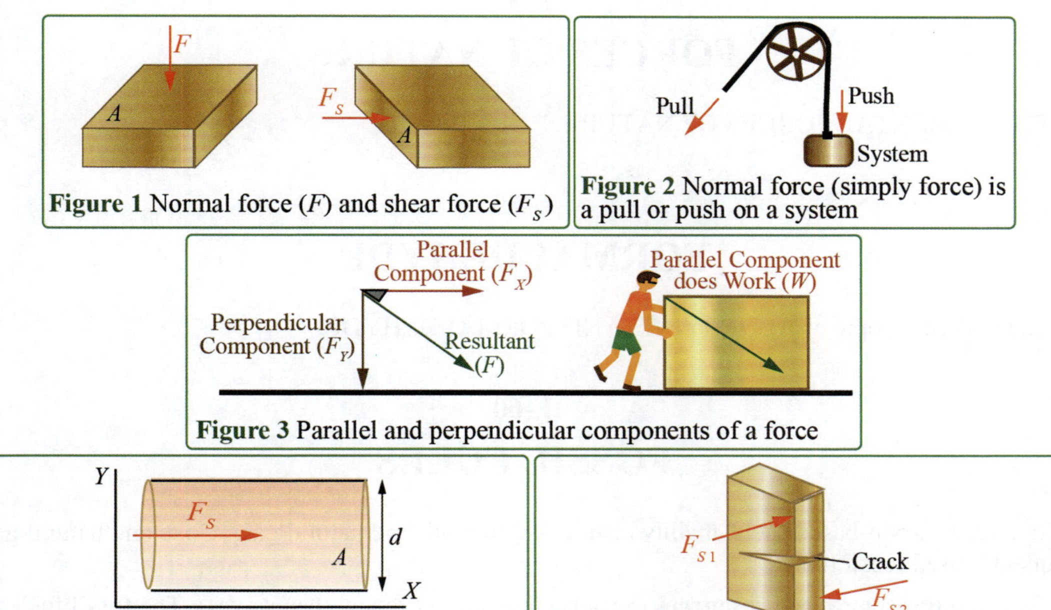

Figure 1 Normal force (F) and shear force (F_S)

Figure 2 Normal force (simply force) is a pull or push on a system

Figure 3 Parallel and perpendicular components of a force

Figure 4 Applying shear force on cross-sectional area of a liquid in a pipe causes the liquid to flow

Figure 5 Applying shear forces on a solid in opposite directions causes a crack on the solid

Shear Force

A shear force (F_S) is a force (F) that acts parallelly on a system's surface. Figure 1 shows the difference between a normal force (F) and shear force (F_S) applied to solid material. [In liquid flow subjects, it is convenient to use F_S, but *not* F.] Mathematically, F_S is the product of S_S (shear stress) multiplied by A (area).

$$F_S = S_S.A \quad (3)$$

$$S_S = \frac{F_S}{A} \quad (4)$$

The term F_S/A in this equation is called shear stress (S_S). This equation tells us that an F_S must act on a liquid to flow. As Figure 4 shows, applying F_S on the cross-sectional area (A) of a liquid in a pipe causes the liquid to flow in the desired direction. F_S acting parallel on A of a liquid in a pipe is the product of the S_S multiplied by the pipe's cross-sectional area ($A = \pi R^2 = \pi d^2/4$), where R is the radius and d is the diameter.

$$F_S = S_S.\pi.R^2 \quad (5)$$

Based on the rules of the strength of material, when parallel shear forces are applied in opposite directions at different points of a solid system, a crack or tear develops in the system (see Figure 5).

F-57
FORCE OF GRAVITY

Another name for **gravitational force**. It is discussed under FUNDAMENTAL FORCES OF NATURE.

F-58
FORCES OF NATURE

Study FUNDAMENTAL FORCES OF NATURE.

F-59
FORMALDEHYDE

Discussed under the topic of ALDEHYDES AND FORMALDEHYDE.

F-60
FOSSIL FUELS

Fossil fuels are carbon-based fuels, mainly coal, coke, fuel oil, and natural gas. [Coke and natural gas are the most frequently used fossil fuels.]

Fossil fuels are **nonrenewable resources** (because they do *not* renew themselves). The fossil fuels that exist today are formed from remains of ancient plants and animals by exposure to high pressure and heat in the absence of oxygen between 300 and 400 million years ago. Many wetlands grew close to the ocean and sea levels, so they periodically became submerged and then buried under the marine sediments and were eventually converted into fossil fuels.

Fossil fuels (oil, coal, and natural gas) are mainly used in different industries to produce a considerable amount of heat energy (E_Q) per unit mass of the fuel. In a rough estimate, about 80% of the world's heat-energy production and electricity production is from fossil fuels. Carbon (C) is the main component of fossil fuels. It reacts with molecular oxygen to produce E_Q and CO_2.

$$1 \text{ kg C} + 2.67 \text{ kg } O_2 \rightarrow 3.67 \text{ kg } CO_2 + 49000 \text{ kJ } E_Q$$

Compared with fossil fuels, biofuels and nuclear fuels produce less CO_2 (carbon dioxide), making them environmentally safer.

[About 21 million tons of CO_2 is produced worldwide by burning fossil fuels. CO_2 acts as a greenhouse gas in the atmosphere by trapping heat, and increasing temperature, known as global warming.]

F-61

FOUR-DIMENSIONAL SYSTEM

Study THREE- AND FOUR-DIMENSIONAL SYSTEMS.

F-62

FOURIER'S HEAT CONDUCTION EQUATION

The Fourier's heat conduction equation (simply **Fourier's equation**) defines Fourier's Law as

$$\dot{E}_Q = K_T.A\frac{\Delta T}{L} = K_T.A\frac{T_2-T_1}{L} \tag{1}$$

When heat transfer occurs perpendicular (vertical at 90° angle) to the X-axis (horizontal-axis) direction, as shown in Figure 1, it is better to replace L (the length through which heat transfers) with X.

$$\dot{E}_Q = K_T.A\frac{\Delta T}{X} \tag{2}$$

When the heat energy rate ($\dot{E}_Q$) flowing into (or out of) a system changes infinitesimally, Fourier's equation is used in its differential (d) form

$$\dot{E}_Q = K_T.A\frac{dT}{dX} \tag{3}$$

$$\dot{E}_Q = \frac{E_Q}{t} = K_T.A\frac{dT}{dX} \tag{4}$$

In these equations, E_Q is heat energy, t is time, A is the heat transfer area, K_T is conductive heat transfer coefficient (thermal conductivity), ΔT is the temperature difference (final-minus-initial), and L is the length (distance) along which heat moves. If we use s (second) for t, J/m.°C for K_T, m^2 for A, °C for T, and m for L (or X), the SI unit of $\dot{E}_Q$ becomes in J/s.

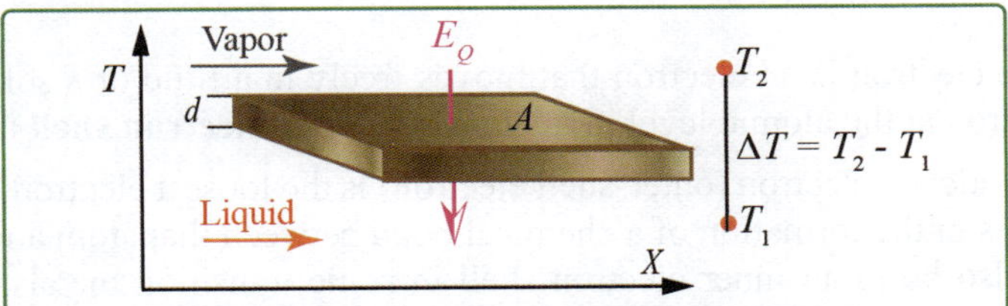

Figure 1 Demonstration of Fourier's heat conduction by showing a conductive heat transfer through a solid plate

F-63

FOURIER'S HEAT CONDUCTION LAW

Fourier's Heat Conduction Law, which is named after Joseph Fourier (1768–1830, French physicist), states that the heat flux ($E_q = E_Q/A_Q$) is proportional to the negative temperature gradient ($\Delta T/L$) through a proportionality constant, named conductive heat transfer coefficient (K_T, also called **thermal conductivity**). Putting these words in the equation form gives Fourier's heat-conduction equation.

$$E_q = \frac{E_Q}{A_Q} = -K_T \frac{dT}{dL} \quad (1)$$

F-64

FRACTIONAL DISTILLATION

Discussed under DISTILLATION PROCESS.

F-65

FRACTIONAL ENERGY

Defined under ENERGY AND ITS FORMS.

F-66

FRACTIONATION PROCESS

This topic is *not* covered in this book.

F-67

FRAME OF REFERENCE

Another name for REFERENCE SYSTEM.

F-68

FREE ELECTRONS AND VALENCE ELECTRONS

Free Electrons: A free electron is an electron that moves freely in a fluid or a solid crystal structure. A free electron is a valance electron at the atomic level if an atom's **valence electron shell** is *not* closed.

Valance Electrons: A valence electron (outer-shell electron) is the loosest electron in the valence (outer) shell of an atom that participates in the formation of a chemical bond between that atom and another atom (or atoms). A valence electron can also be in an inner electron shell in some transition metals. As Figure 1 shows, both valence electrons and electron pairs (pairs of two valance electrons that act together) form a bond. Thus, the valence electrons and electron pairs are the **bonding electrons** (atoms are bonded **electronically**). [The maximum valence electrons in one atom is 8 (4 electron pairs), that is, 2 (1 e^-) + 6 e^- = 8 e^-.]

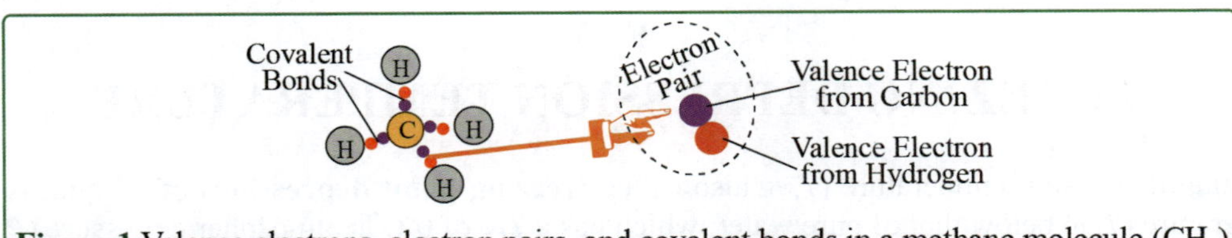

Figure 1 Valance electrons, electron pairs, and covalent bonds in a methane molecule (CH_4)

F-69

FREE ENERGY

See GIBBS FREE ENERGY.

F-70

FREE EVAPORATION

Free evaporation in a liquid occurs at ordinary temperature (T) and pressure (P) without reaching its boiling point temperature (T_{BP}). Water, for example, in a container evaporates to water vapor (vapor phase of water) at ordinary T and P without reaching its T_{BP}. The evaporation occurs because water's partial pressure is decreased to below the atmospheric pressure (P_{Atm} = 1 Atm ≈ 100 kPa ≈ 14.7 PSI).

F-71

FREE-FALL MOTION

A free-fall motion is a motion that is affected by two major forces, the gravitational force (F_g) and the air's drag force (F_D). A skydiver free fall, a space shuttle in space with a turn-off motor, a person jumping off the ground, and an object thrown upward are examples of the free-fall motions.

In a free-fall system and when the air's F_D is small, the F_g cancels the air's F_D, so the system does *not* accelerate, so falls at the constant gravitational acceleration (a_g) of 9.8 m/s^2 (= 32.2 Ft/s^2) and is independent of its mass (M). Because all free-fall systems with different masses fall at the same rate in the absence of other forces, a free-fall system experiences **weightlessness** (with zero gravity). A free-fall skydiver feels weightless when it reaches its **terminal velocity**, around 53 m/s (=190 km/h = 118 Mi/h).

F-72

FREE SURFACE ENERGY

See SURFACE ENERGY.

F-73

FREEZING DEPRESSION TEMPERATURE

The freezing depression temperature (T_{FD}, also called **freezing point depression**) of a liquid is its freezing point temperature (T_{FP}) below that of pure water, which has a T_{FP} of 0°C at atmospheric pressure (P_{Atm}).

In another context, the T_{FD} of a liquid is the difference between its T_{FP} and the T_{FP} of water at the same pressure (P). For example, a 50% sugar solution freezes at –7.6°C, so its T_{FD} is –7.6°C, as shown in Figure 1. Thus, adding a salute to water decreases water's T_{FP} (freezing point temperature).

Besides P, the T_{FD} of a solution is a function of concentration, C (*T_{FD} increases* as *C increases*), so T_{FD} is a colligative property. A simple equation calculates the T_{FD} when an ideal solution's molality (m, moles/1 kg of solution) is known.

$$T_{FD} = K_{FD}.m \tag{1}$$

[The K_{FD} (the freezing depression constant, in °C.kg/mole) for water is –1.86°C.kg solvent/(mole solute).]

An Example on T_{FD}

How much sugar must be added to 1 kg of water to lower the solution's T_{FP} from 0 to – 2°C?

The molality (m) of the solution with T_{FP} (freezing point temperature) of –2°C can be found as

$$m = \frac{T_{FP}}{K_{FD}} = \frac{-2}{-1.86} = 1.1\ (°\text{C})/°\text{C.kg/mole}) = \text{mole/kg}$$

The mass of solute, M_S (here sugar), can be determined from the molality equation when we know the solute's molar mass (M_n = 342 g/mole) and the amount of the solution (kg_{Sol}).

$$m = \frac{M_S}{M_n.kg_{Sol}}$$

$$M_S = m.M_{Mol}.kg_{Sol} = 1.1 \times 342 \times 1 = 376\ (\text{mole/kg})(\text{g/mole})(\text{kg}) = \text{g}$$

Figure 1 Comparison of freezing point temperature (T_{FD}) of water with that of 50% sugar solution and calculation of freezing depression temperature (T_{FD}) of sugar solution

F-74

FREEZING ELEVATION TEMPERATURE

The freezing elevation temperature (T_{FE}, also called **freezing point elevation**) of a liquid is its freezing point temperature (T_{FP}) above that of pure water (the water with *no* dissolved solids), which has a T_{FP} of 0°C at atmospheric pressure (P_{Atm}). Besides P, the T_{FE} of a solution is a function of concentration, C (*T_{FE} increases* as *C increases*), so T_{FE} is a colligative property.

F-75
FREEZING POINT TEMPERATURE

The freezing point temperature (T_{FP}, simply **freezing point** or **freezing temperature**) of a liquid is the temperature (T) at which it changes to solid at the pressure (P) surrounding that liquid. The T_{FP} closely depends on the pressure, P (*for a given P, different liquids freeze at different temperatures*). Differences in the strength of molecular attractions explain why different liquids have different T_{FP} at the same P. For this reason, freezing point temperatures are usually specified at atmospheric pressure (P_{Atm} = 1 Atm ≈ 100 kPa), which is standard. A freezing temperature given for P_{Atm} is usually called a **normal freezing temperature**. At P_{Atm}, T_{FP} is different for different substances. For example, water freezes at 0°C (32°F), ethanol (C_2H_5OH) at 78.3°C (173°F), and 0°C (32°F) in the case of water.

During the freezing process, heat (Q, the simplified term for heat energy, E_Q) is gradually and uniformly released from the liquid until it reaches its T_{FP}. At the T_{FP}, the liquid and solid phases are at equilibrium (stableness).

[Note that T_{FP} and melting point temperature (T_{MP}) are almost the same for most chemical substances. For example, the T_{FP} and T_{MP} of water (in its liquid and solid forms (ice) is 273 K (0°C or – 32°F). And the T_{FP} and T_{MP} of mercury (Hg) are 234 K (– 38.8°C or – 38°F. As related topics, study FREEZING POINT DEPRESSION and FREEZING POINT ELEVATION.]

F-76
FREEZING PROCESS

As a process unit (unit operation) of ChemEng, freezing is changing a liquid into a solid when the liquid's temperature (T) reaches its freezing point temperature (T_{FP}). Freezing, thus, is a phase-change process that releases heat energy (E_Q), so it is a heat releasing process (exothermic process). The enthalpy change ($\Delta H = E_Q$) released in freezing is a phase change enthalpy (latent enthalpy), known as the enthalpy of freezing (H_{FZ}, also known as **enthalpy of crystallization**). We also know from the topic of ENTHALPY that E_Q and change in enthalpy (ΔH) have the same meaning, so E_Q released by freezing ($E_{Q.FZ}$) is

$$E_{Q.FZ} = \Delta H = \Delta H_{FZ} \tag{1}$$

When liquid releases E_Q, its T decreases until it reaches its T_{FP}. At T_{FP}, the solid-liquid system maintains its T until the freezing process is complete. During this period, the enthalpy (H) of the system gradually and uniformly decreases. The relation between T_{FP}, change in enthalpy of freezing (ΔH_{FZ}), and change in **entropy of freezing** (ΔS_{FZ}) is given as:

$$T_F = \frac{\Delta H_{FZ}}{\Delta S_{FZ}} \tag{2}$$

In freezing, a liquid's molecules have some energy (E) in the form of kinetic energy (E_K), and when it is cooled, that energy is released in E_Q. As the result of a decrease in E, the intermolecular forces (F_{Int}) have a chance to draw the molecules closer together, create some chemical bonds, and finally form a solid.

[The freezing process is used in some branches of ChemEng, including the food industry, so more information about this topic can be gained from a general food-engineering book.]

F-77

FREQUENCY

Study AMPLITUDE, FREQUENCY, AND PERIOD.

F-78

FRICTION

Simplified name for FRICTION FORCE.

F-79

FRICTION FACTORS, FRICTION FORCE, AND FRICTION CO-EFFICIENT

Friction Factors: A friction factor is a unitless quantity used to calculate a flowing liquid's head loss in a pipe. The Fanning friction factor and Darcy-Weisbach friction factor are two important friction factors.

Friction Force: Friction force (F_F, simply called **friction** and showed by f) is a force (F) that resists the motion of a system. Usually, three frictions are used in ChemEng:

- **Liquid Friction:** This force occurs when the layers of a liquid robing against each other. Liquid friction is the product of the liquid's viscosity (η) and its velocity (V).
- **Dry Friction**: This force occurs when a solid system is robing against another solid system.
- **Surface Friction:** This force occurs when two (or more) solid surfaces are robing against each other. A lubricant reduces surface friction by adding a material layer between two solid surfaces. This makes the two surfaces slide over each other more easily.

[The symbol f shows both frequency and friction. This must *not* create confusion because these terms are rarely used in one equation.]

Friction Coefficient: The friction coefficient (C_f, also called the coefficient of friction) is a unitless quantity for describing the ratio of a system's friction force (F_F) and the force (F) pressing that system.

[Friction coefficient is shown in this book with C_f to include C for coefficient and f for friction. In other reference books, it is shown with μ (mu) or ξ (xi).]

F-80

FRICTION HEAD LOSS

Study HEAD LOSS.

F-81

FROUDE NUMBER

Froude number (N_F, where N is for number and F is for Froude) is a unitless quantity used in Physics to calculate the velocity-length ratio of a submerged-accelerating system. Thus, velocity (V), characteristic length (L), and gravitational acceleration (a_g = 9.8 m/s^2 = 32.2 Ft/s^2) are used in its calculations.

$$N_F = \frac{u}{\sqrt{a_g.L}} \qquad (1)$$

For example, the N_F of a submerged-accelerating ship moving in a sea can be calculated if the ship's u and L (the ship's length at the waterline level) are known.

The N_F of a mixer's stirrer is calculated based on the stirrer's speed (shown as rotation per second, N), the stirrer's diameter (d), and a_g.

$$N_F = \frac{N^2.d}{a_g} \qquad (2)$$

This is the amount of electric power (P_E) used by the mixer's stirrer to perform a mixing process.

F-82

FRUCTOSE

Discussed under the topic of SUGARS.

F-83

FUELS

A fuel is a chemical compound (simply **compound**) that consists of hydrocarbon molecules, in which energy (E) is generated in the form of chemical potential energy. In combustion reactions (simply combustions), fuels produce heat energy (E_Q, simply heat). Fuel resources can generally be divided into three (3) classes:

- **Fossil Fuels:** Coal, coke, fuel oil, and natural gas are fossil fuels. [Today, natural gas is the most frequently used fuel.]
- **Biofuels:** Bioethanol is an important biofuel. Biofuels are produced from biomasses. In Brazil, about 18% of the fuel comes from bioethanol.
- **Nuclear Fuels:** They are produced mainly from uranium (U) and plutonium (Pu). [Nuclear fuels have the highest energy density of fossil fuels and biofuels.]

In power plants, fuel is combined with oxygen (O_2) from the air to produce carbon dioxide, water, and E_Q. The general formula for combustion of a fuel with O_2 can be written as

$$C_nH_m + O_2 \rightarrow n\ CO_2 + \tfrac{1}{2}\ m\ H_2O + E_Q$$

When, for example, 1 kg of natural gas, which is mainly methane (CH_4: where n = 1 and m = 4), reacts with oxygen, 49 000 kJ of E_Q is released, according to the following reaction:

$$CH_4 + O_2 \rightarrow CO_2 + 2\ H_2O - 49\ 000\ \text{kJ}\ E_Q$$

This reaction tells us that the natural gas's enthalpy of combustion (H_C) is 49000 kJ/kg (= 21070 BTU/Lb).

The H_C of fuel can be calculated if the contents (in percentage) of its carbon (C), hydrogen (H), oxygen (O), and sulfur (S) are available.

$$H_C = 33878 \times \text{C} + 14416 \times \text{O}\left(\text{H} - \frac{\text{O}}{8}\right) + 9436 \times \text{S} \qquad \text{kJ/kg}$$

$$H_C = 14540 \times \text{C} + 6200 \times \text{O}\left(\text{H} - \frac{\text{O}}{8}\right) + 4050 \times \text{S} \qquad \text{BTU/Lb}$$

The value O/8 (oxygen/8) exists because some hydrogen combines with oxygen to form water. The previous equation is based on the amount of H_C released from each component of fuel:

C = 33878 kJ/kg (= 14565 BTU/Lb)

H = 144460 kJ/kg (= 62100 BTU/Lb) – O/8

S = 9436 kJ/kg (= 4060 BTU/Lb)

An Example on Fuel Composition

Calculate the H_C (enthalpy of combustion) of a fuel that contains 80% C, 6 % O, 5 % H, and 1% S.

$$H_C = 33878 \times 0.8 + 14446 \times 0.06\left(0.05 - \frac{0.06}{8}\right) + 9436 \times 0.01 = 27139 \text{ kJ/kg}$$

$$\frac{27139}{2.33} = 11648 \text{ BTU/Lb}$$

F-84

FUEL OIL

Discussed under CRUDE OIL AND FUEL OIL.

F-85

FUGACITY AND FUGACITY COEFFICIENT

Fugacity

Fugacity (f) is the tendency of a component to evaporate from a liquid mixture. The vapor formed above the mixture is richer in the component's molecules evaporated (escaped) from the mixture. Because f is expressed at equilibrium, a component's f is the pressure (P) exerted on the liquid mixture when the vapor and liquid are at phase equilibrium.

Fugacity (f) is usually used in the distillation process instead of chemical potential (μ) to eliminate undesirable properties of μ and make the calculations at vapor liquid equilibrium (VLE) easier. The next equation is used to calculate the f of component A in a binary mixture consisting of similar components A and d.

$$f_A^L = P_V.X \qquad (1)$$

If components are *not* similar, we must use the activity coefficient (K_{Act}) of component A.

$$f_A^L = P_V.X.K_{Act} \qquad (2)$$

In these equations, P_V is the vapor pressure of pure component A, and X is the molar fraction (X, a unitless quantity) of A in the liquid phase.

For calculating component A's fugacity in the vapor phase, the P_V of A and its molar fraction (Y) are used.

$$f_A^V = P_V.Y \qquad (3)$$

This equation is valid if the vapor phase is an ideal gas and follows Raoult's Law of Vapor Pressure, so an activity coefficient must be added if the vapor does *not* follow the ideal-gas rules.

Because fugacity is the P exerted by a component on the liquid mixture when both the vapor and liquid are at phase equilibrium, Equation 1 can be written as

$$P.Y = P_V.X \tag{4}$$

In this equation, P is the total pressure of the mixture under distillation, and P_V is the vapor pressure of A at the mixture's T. Equation 4 can be used for almost any mixture under distillation with some modifications. For example, it can be modified if a mixture consists of dissimilar components.

$$P.Y = P_V.X.K_{Act} \tag{5}$$

When a system is in phase equilibrium, the next equation is valid.

$$f_A^L = f_A^V \quad \text{or} \quad f_A(L) = f_A(g) \tag{6}$$

Fugacity can also be used instead of chemical potential energy (E_{CP}). The relation between the E_{CP} of component A (shown as $E_{CP.A}$) and fugacity of component A (shown as f_A) at a certain T (temperature) when the P approaches zero is expressed as

$$E_{CP.A} = R.T.Lnf_A \tag{7}$$

In this equation, R is the gas constant used in the ideal gas equation, and Ln is the sign for the natural log.

Fugacity Coefficient

The fugacity coefficient (ϕ) is the ratio of the fugacity (f) to the pressure (P).

$$\emptyset = \frac{f}{P} \tag{8}$$

The fugacity coefficient is often used to measure the non-ideal behavior in relation to a gas's phase equilibrium. When PVT data of a gas are available, a graph can be plotted of the difference between the gas's V_n (molar volume) and the V_n of an ideal gas in relation to the gas's P at the T of interest to calculate the ϕ (fugacity coefficient) using the next equation.

$$\emptyset = \frac{f}{P} = exp\left[\frac{1}{R.T}\int_0^P (V - V^{id})dP\right] \tag{9}$$

In this equation, V is the volume of the gas under study, and V^{id} is the volume of an ideal gas.

F-86

FUNCTIONAL GROUPS

A functional group is a group of atoms that acts as a unit to characterize a chemical substance. For example, the HCO group characterizes the aldehydes. Hydroxyl (OH), aldehyde (HCO), carbonyl (CO), carboxyl (COOH), and sulfonic (SO_3H) are examples of functional groups. A molecule's functional group is responsible for its reactions with other molecules. The functional groups attach to other substances (mainly carbon chains) to form new substances with similar properties during a reaction. For example, the attachment of OH to a hydrocarbon creates alcohol. Alcohols have similar properties, such as more polarity than the parent hydrocarbon. [Na (sodium) is the **exchangeable ion** in a cationic ion exchange resin with SO_3Na functional group.]

F-87

FUNDAMENTAL CONSTANTS OF NATURE

Fundamental constants of nature are three (3): Planck's constant (h), gravitational constant (K_G or G), and speed of light constant (c).

F-88

FUNDAMENTAL FIELDS OF NATURE

Fundamental fields of nature (simply **fundamental fields**) are four (4), given next in the order of their strength (from weakest to the strongest to the): 1) Gravitational field, 2) Weak nuclear field, 3) Electromagnetic field, and 4) Strong nuclear field. Study the following:

- The four fundamental fields are related to the four fundamental forces of nature that exist in the Universe. Say, the gravitational field is the space around a system under the gravitational force (the force of gravity).
- A quantum field is a system with a quantity at every point in space at every moment in time. It is a vector quantity (with direction) attached to every point in space and possibly changes with time. Instead, a scalar quantum field is a scalar quantity (a quantity with *no* direction) attached to every spacetime point.
- Although physicists think that the Higgs field exists in the entire Universe, its existence has *not* proved yet unless elevating it to an excited energy state (a state with a greater energy than a reference energy state).

F-89

FUNDAMENTAL FORCES OF NATURE

Fundamental forces of nature (FFN, simply **fundamental forces** or **fundamental interactions**) are the four (4) forces that act in the Universe to hold different systems together. Thus, FFNs, which are gravitational force (F_g), weak nuclear force (F_{WN}), the electromagnetic force (F_{EM}), and strong nuclear force (F_{SN}), have different functionality, strength, and effective range, as shown in Figure 1 (given in the order of their strengths, from weakest to the strongest). Next, a few generalities of FFN are outlined.

- Each fundamental force acts in one of the fundamental fields of nature.
- All other forces operating in the Universe are derived from fundamental forces.
- The strength of fundamental forces is compared with gravitational force (F_g), the weakest FFN.
- At high energy levels, the F_{WN} (weak nuclear force) and F_{EM} (electromagnetic force) combine to form a new force, named **electroweak force**, making the FFN number five (5).

Knowing the meaning of the following three (3) terms helps the reader while reading about FFN:

- The term **nuclear force** is used to refer to both F_{SN} and F_{WN}.
- The term **non-gravitational forces** refers to all fundamental forces, except F_g.
- The terms **interaction** and **force** are often used equally, so **strong interaction** refers to the **strong force**.

Note the following points about the fundamental forces:

- Some physicists theorize that at the Big Bang, just one extremely strong force existed, and then it was divided into four (4) forces over time, as shown in Figure 2.
- **Gravitational force** (F_g) could *not* be described mathematically in relation to other forces because the F_g acts in an infinite range (the Universe).
- **Non-gravitational forces**, unlike F_g, act at the atomic range. [In his last years, Einstein tried to connect his principle of gravity and spacetime with quantum field theory and some of the theories that govern elementary particles to create a unified theory, known as the theory of unification of physics. Unfortunately, he could *not* finish this important work.]

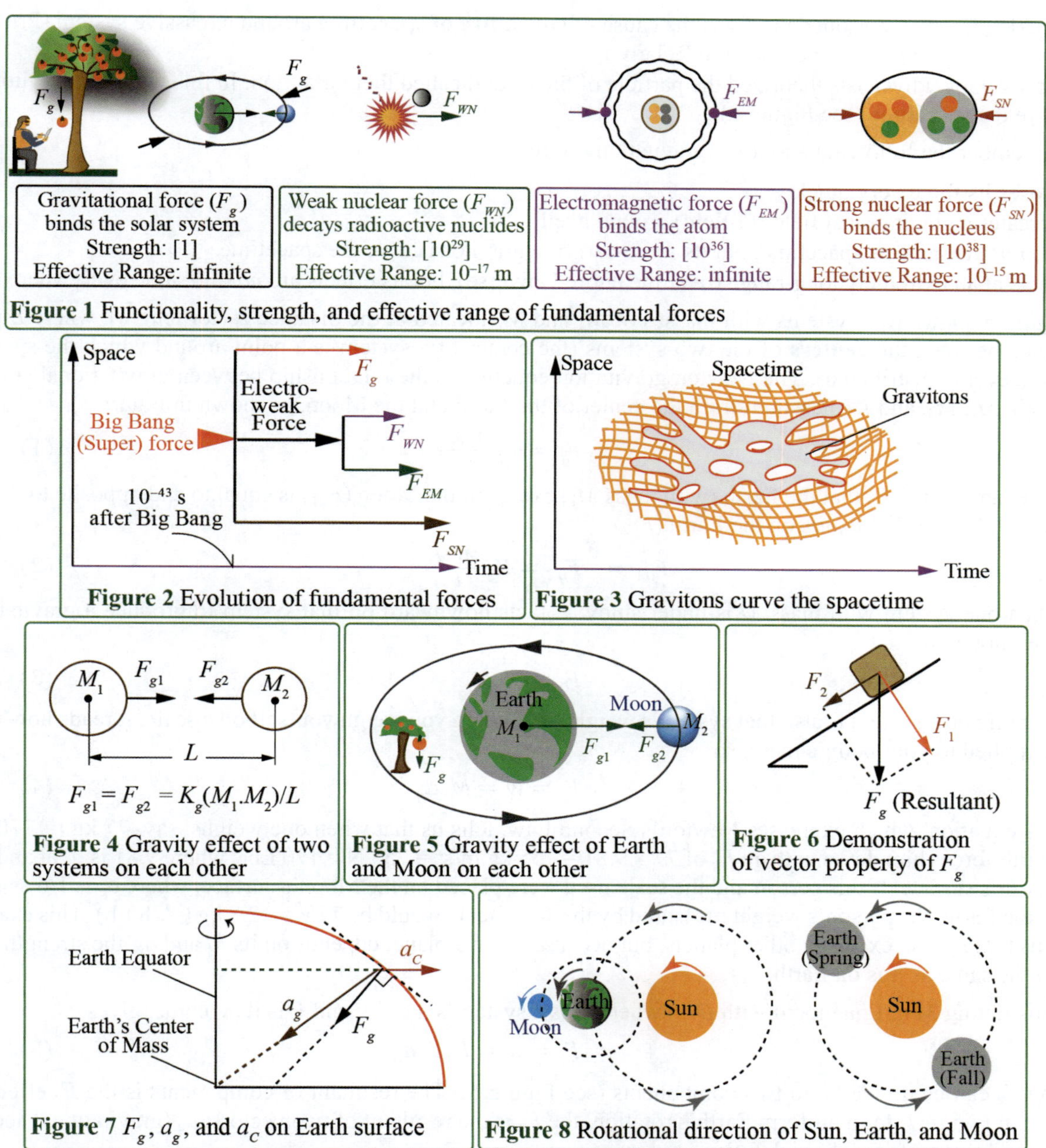

Figure 1 Functionality, strength, and effective range of fundamental forces

Figure 2 Evolution of fundamental forces

Figure 3 Gravitons curve the spacetime

Figure 4 Gravity effect of two systems on each other

Figure 5 Gravity effect of Earth and Moon on each other

Figure 6 Demonstration of vector property of F_g

Figure 7 F_g, a_g, and a_c on Earth surface

Figure 8 Rotational direction of Sun, Earth, and Moon

GRAVITATIONAL FORCE

As the weakest of the four fundamental forces, gravitational force (F_g or g; also called **force of gravity** or simply gravity) is an attractive force around a massive system (a system with a rest mass of M). The F_g is a force (F) that gives a freefalling system near the Earth's surface gravitational acceleration (a_g) of 9.81 m/s^2 (= 32 Ft/s^2), meaning that a falling system's speed near the Earth's surface increases by 9.81 m/s.

The main timelines of F_g can be summarized as

- In 1687: Newton reasoned the F_g as the cause of falling an **apple** downward (a historical event). He proved that all masses in the Universe exert F_g on all other masses (Newton's Law of Gravitation).

- In 1915: Einstein reasoned the F_g as the cause of **curvature of spacetime** around a massive system (Principle of Gravity-Spacetime of General Relativity).
- In the 1930s: Physicists theorized the particle of the F_g and called them graviton. In this way, the gravitons curve the spacetime (see Figure 3).

Remember the following about F_g (gravitational force):

- It loses its force very quickly.
- It creates a gravitational field (G-field) around itself.
- It is *not* the same as spacetime, but its force-carrying gravitons curve the spacetime.
- It acts at an extremely long-range (over the entire Universe), but its effects are *not* the same everywhere.

Figure 4 shows two systems with masses of M_1 and M_2 located at the distance L (for length), where L is the distance between the **centers** of the two systems (the center of a system is a point around which the system's mass is evenly distributed). The Newton gravitation equation is the relationship between gravitational constant (K_g), F_g, M_1, M_2, and L (measured from the center of the Earth and the Moon, as shown in Figure 5).

$$F_g = K_g \frac{M_1.M_2}{L^2} \tag{1}$$

For example, the F_g that the Earth (with mass M_1) exerts on the Moon (F_{g1}) is equal to and opposite to that the Moon (with mass M_2) exerts on the Earth (F_{g2}).

$$F_{g1} = -F_{g2} = K_g \frac{M_1.M_2}{L^2} \tag{2}$$

When one system with mass M is under study, F_g acts downward on that system to produce a gravitational acceleration of a_g.

$$F_g = M.a_g \tag{3}$$

F_g acting on a system is also that system's weight (w). When you weigh yourself on a scale, it reads how much F_g is applied to your body's mass, so

$$F_g = w = M.a_g \tag{4}$$

This equation, which expresses Newton's Second Law, tells us that when one weighs; say, 77 kg (= 170 Lb), the Earth forces him down with an F_g of 77 × 9.81 = 755 kg.m/s^2 = 755 N = 170 Lb$_F$, where 9.81 is a_g at and near the Earth's surface. If this person and the scale used were placed on the Moon's surface, where a_g is 1/6 as much as on the Earth, the person's weight measured by the same scale would be 77/6 = 12.8 kg (= 28 Lb). This example tells us that F_g also exists on other planets, but because F_g on a planet depends on its M and a_g, the strength of F_g is *not* the same as it is on Earth.

Substituting M in Equation 4 with $D.V$, where D is a system's density and V is its volume, gives

$$F_g = w = D.V.a_g \tag{5}$$

The F_g can be divided into two components (see Figure 6). The resultant of components is the F_g effect. As shown in Figure 7, for a uniform Earth's rotation, the F_g is the resultant of two vectors: a_g (gravitational acceleration) and a_C (centrifugal acceleration).

Like force (F), the SI unit of F_g is kg.m/s^2 and its US unit is Lb$_F$ (pound force), where 1 kg.m/s^2 = N (Newton) = 0.225 Lb$_F$ (simply Lb).

To conclude this subtopic, we summarize the properties of F_g as follows:

- It affects all systems in the Universe.
- It keeps all planets in their orbits (orbitals).
- It can give a system gravitational acceleration (a_g).
- It almost does *not* affect the internal properties of a substance.
- It is a downward force applied to a system located near the ground.

- It deforms rotating systems in space-time, known as the curvature of spacetime.
- Its effect on the systems with ordinary mass is negligible (study the next Example). Thus, it is effective when at least one of the systems has a huge mass (like Earth with a mass of 6×10^{21} t).
- Its incorporation with the other three FFN could *not* be done because it acts in infinite ranges of the Universe. In contrast, F_{EM} (electromagnetic force) acts at both atomic and universal scales, and F_{SN} (strong nuclear force) and F_{WN} (weak nuclear force) act only at an atomic scale. The successful incorporation of all four of F_{FN} with the quantum field theory can bring Physics closer to the theory of unification of physics.
- Its classical importance has *not* been reduced since Einstein came up with his new idea, and physicists still use it in many calculations.

An Example on F_g

Given: Two identical systems, which each has a mass of 100 kg, are 10 m away from each other

Wanted: Gravitational force (F_g) that attracts these two systems

$$F_g = k_g \frac{M_1 M_2}{L^2} = 6.67 \times 10^{-11} \times \frac{100\times100}{10^2} = 6.67 \times 10^{-9}\ \text{N}$$

The F_g that attracts these two systems is extremely small (like blowing too gently on one of the systems) so that *no* movement can occur on either system.

WEAK NUCLEAR FORCE

As the second weakest force of the four FFN, the weak nuclear force (F_{WN}, simply **weak force**) with its force-carrying quantum particle (W- and Z-Bosons) is involved in nuclear fission and nuclear decay to convert a particle into one (or more) different particles. For example, in the **beta minus decay** (β^- decay), the F_{WN} converts a neutron in a nucleus into a proton, an electron, and an antineutrino (also called a positron).

Instead, the strong nuclear forces (F_{SN}, the strongest of FFN) act in the nucleus to keep protons and neutrons together and the quarks in a proton or neutron. Thus, F_{SN} holds particles together, while F_{WN} keeps particles apart.

A few important points about F_{WN} are outlined next.

- It was discovered in 1933 by Enrico Fermi (1901–1954, Italian physicist).
- It functions at an extremely short-range (at about 0.1% of the diameter of a proton); beyond that, it rapidly disappears, so it is recognized as "weak.'
- Its force-carrying particles are W- and Z-Bosons. [W- and Z-Bosons were predicted in the 1960s and discovered in 1983 at CERN.]

ELECTROMAGNETIC FORCE

As the second strongest of the FFN, electromagnetic force (F_{EM}, also called **EM force**, **EM interaction**, or **electromagnetism**) is a force (F) that occurs between electrically charged particles (like protons or electrons). In an atom, the F_{EM} is produced by positive electric charges (Q_E or q) of protons. In nature, F_{EM} can be produced by the buildup of electric charges in thunderstorms.

The two important properties of F_{EM} are outlined next.

- Its force-carrying elementary particles are the photons.
- Its effect is an electromagnetic field (EM-field), where the EM-field is the carrying media of F_{EM}.
- It has both the properties of electric force (represented by the term **electro** in **electromagnetic**) and magnetic force (represented by the term **magnetic** in **electromagnetic**).

Other functionalities of F_{EM} are:

- In a molecule, it keeps atoms together,
- In a compound, it acts as an intermolecular force to keep its molecules together, and
- In light, it moves its particles (the photons), so photons are the force-carrying particles of F_{EM}.

At the atomic level, F_{EM} functions in the following ways:

- It keeps away the protons from each other to prevent collision between them, and
- It moves the electrons of an atom around its nucleus.

The following are important to know about electromagnetic force (F_{EM}):

- Its discovery in the 1860s is credited to Maxwell,
- It exists in atoms, molecules, photons, and chemical compounds (simply **compounds**), and
- F_{EM}, like F_g (gravitational force), acts in infinite ranges of the Universe, while F_{SN} (strong nuclear force) and F_{SN} (weak nuclear force) act at the atomic level. [This is why the physicists still could *not* describe these forces in the framework of quantum physics.]

STRONG NUCLEAR FORCE

As the strongest force of the fundamental forces of nature, the strong nuclear force (F_{SN}, simply **strong force**) with its force-carrying particles (the gluons) acts in the nucleus of an atom in the following manners:

- On a larger scale (range), it keeps the nuclei of atoms of a chemical element together,
- On a medium scale, it keeps the protons and neutrons together to form the nucleus,
- On a smaller scale, it keeps the quarks together in a proton or a neutron.

Although F_{SN} is the strongest of all forces, it has the shortest range because it works at a distance like the diameter of a proton (about 10^{-12} mm). This means its gluons must be extremely close before they start to act.

Knowing the following two (2) points about F_{SN} is important:

- The F_{SN} originates in a quantity known as the color charge, unrelated to color (the human eye's visual property). But, it is related to electric charge (q). Just as q is the main source of F_{EM}, a color charge is the main source of F_{SN}.
- F_{SN} between protons and neutrons increases as the distance between them increases. Thus, the F_{SN} between them decreases at a smaller distance, so an unstable situation between attractive F_{SN} and repulsive F_{EM} occurs. And as a result, the nucleus becomes unstable.

A few more important points about F_{SN} are:

- It becomes stronger with distance, unlike other FFNs,
- Its elementary force-carrying particle is a gluon (a meson),
- It does *not* diminish with increasing distance between two particles,
- Its discovery in the 1930s is credited to a few physicists, including Heisenberg, and
- It is 10^2 times stronger than electromagnetic force (F_{EM}), 10^9 times stronger than weak nuclear force (F_{WN}), and 10^{38} times stronger than gravitational force (F_g, the force of gravity). [F_{SN} and F_{SW} act at the atomic level, while F_{EM} and F_g act in infinite ranges of the Universe.]

Quantization of Fundamental Forces of Nature: Physicists could *not* describe all four FFNs together because of their activity ranges. The F_g acts in infinite ranges of the Universe, F_{EM} acts at both atomic and universal levels, and F_{SN} (strong nuclear force) and F_{WN} (weak nuclear force) act only at the atomic scale. The successful inclusion of all four FFNs into the quantum field theory (QF theory) and Einstein's principle of gravity and spacetime (discussed under the topic of Einstein's theories of relativity) can lead to a unified theory known as the theory of unification of physics, which combines all FFNs. Such a yet-unsolved theory can define all FFNs by a limited number of unified equations.

F-90
FUNDAMENTAL INTERACTIONS OF NATURE

Study FUNDAMENTAL FORCES OF NATURE.

F-91
FURNACES

Discussed under the topic of STEAM BOILERS.

F-92
FUSION PROCESS

Study NUCLEAR FISSION AND NUCLEAR FUSION.

G Section

LIST OF TOPICS

1. G Force
2. Gamma Ray
3. Gas
4. Gas Absorption Process
5. Gas Compressibility Factor
6. Gas Constant
7. Gas Cyclones
8. Gas Density
9. Gas Emission
10. Gas Flow Process
11. Gas Laws
12. Gas-Liquid Extraction process
13. Gas Molar Density
14. Gas Molar Mass
15. Gas Partial Pressure
16. Gas Pollutants
17. Gas Scrubbers
18. Gas-Solid Extraction Process
19. Gas Transfer Process
20. Gas Turbines
21. Gas Vapor Mixture
22. Gas Viscosity
23. Gas Volumetric Flow Rate
24. Gasoline
25. Gauge Boson
26. Gauge Pressure
27. Gay-Loussac's Gas Law
28. General Relativity
29. Generators
30. Gibbs Dalton Law
31. Gibbs Donnan Effect
32. Gibbs Free Energy
33. Gibbs Phase Rule
34. Glass
35. Global Warming
36. Glucose
37. Gluon
38. Glycosidic Bond
39. Graham's Law
40. Graphene
41. Gravimetric Analysis
42. Gravitational Acceleration
43. Gravitational Constant
44. Gravitational Field
45. Gravitational Force
46. Gravitational Mass
47. Gravitational Potential
48. Gravitational Potential Energy
49. Gravitational Waves
50. Gravitational Work
51. Graviton
52. Gravity
53. Gravity-Spacetime Principle
54. Greenhouse Effect
55. Greenhouse Gases
56. Ground and Excited Energy States

G-1

G FORCE

Simplified name for GRAVITATIONAL FORCE.

G-2

GAMMA RAY

Discussed under the topic of ELECTROMAGNETIC WAVES.

Gamma Ray

As an invisible wave to the human eye, a gamma ray (gamma wave, gamma particle, or gamma radiation) is one of the seven (7) types of electromagnetic waves (EM waves or EM radiations) with a wavelength (λ) shorter than that of visible light. The λ of gamma waves is between 1 mm to 1 m, and its *f* (frequency) is between 300 GHz and 300 MHz, where G is for Giga (= 10^9), M is for mega (= 10^6), and Hz is for Hertz (the SI unit of *f*).

Gamma rays have a high penetrating ability (because of their short λ) and carry enormous energy (release ionizing radiation).

G-3

GAS

Discussed under the topic of STATES OF MATTER.

G-4

GAS ABSORPTION PROCESS

Study GAS LIQUID EXTRACTION.

G-5

GAS COMPRESSIBILITY FACTOR

See IDEAL GAS COMPRESSIBILITY FACTOR.

G-6

GAS CONSTANT

Study IDEAL GAS CONSTANT.

G-7

GAS CYCLONES

Discussed under the topic of PARTICULATE REMOVING DEVICES.

G-8

GAS DENSITY

Discussed under the topic of DENSITY.

G-9

GAS EMISSION

Gas emission is one of the important properties of the gases. Each gas emits (radiates) light of a particular color. When an electric current passes through a gas, the color of the gas changes because each gas has its **emission spectrum** (a particular set of atomic spectral lines). The neon signs are good examples of this **observing phenomenon** (event).

G-10

GAS FLOW PROCESS

BASICS

As a process unit of ChemEng, gas flow (**gas transfer** or scientifically **compressible flow**) is the process of flowing (transferring) a gas from one point to another. Gas transfer by the pressure difference (ΔP) in pipes to, from, and between tanks and devices is a routine operation in chemical process plants. [Liquid flow (incompressible flow) is used in chemical plants in a relatively larger area than the gas transfer. Thus, we do not go into a great depth of coverage as we have done under LIQUID FLOW PROCESS. It is, however, recommended to study that topic also because most subjects are similar in both liquid flow and gas flow.]

A fluid flow is usually expressed in volumetric flow rate ($\dot{V} = V/t$, in m^3/min or Ft^3/min) at a certain temperature (T) and pressure (P), and *not* often in mass flow rate ($\dot{M} = M/t$, in kg/min or Lb/min).

A gas flows without a force in all directions. When it flows in a pipe, it moves in the direction of the pressure (P) applied to it. Shear stress (S_S, shear force per unit area, F_S/A), which is defined the same as P (force/area), however, can act on a gas in a pipe to affect its direction and velocity (V). In a pipe, the S_S causes a cross-sectional flow of a gas. [In fluid-flow subjects, it is convenient to use shear force (F_S), which acts in a **parallel** direction, instead of normal force (F, simply force), which can act in any direction.]

Gas flows (compressible flows) are classified into 2 classes: 1) Laminar flow (Figure 1) and 2) Turbulent flow (Figure 2).

Consider the smoke coming from a cigarette in a no-breeze area. First, the smoke rises smoothly and vertically for a few centimeters, demonstrating a laminar flow. Then, the smoke starts to widen and becomes unstable, demonstrating a turbulent flow. This classification, however, *cannot* be numerically expressed by Reynolds number (N_R), as it is in liquid flows, but by Mach number (N_M), which is the speed of a gas divided by the speed of sound.

In another classification, which is based on Mach number (N_M, where N is for number and subscript M is for Mach), compressible flows are grouped into

- **Sonic flows** (with N_M of nearly 1),
- **Subsonic flows** (with N_M of less than 1), and
- **Supersonic flows** (with N_M of greater than 1).

An example of a **supersonic** (turbulent) **flow** is when warm and cold air in the atmosphere mix by the wind to form turbulence, which greatly affects the air's V, P, and D (density). Another example is when a gas flows from its **reservoir** (the origin source, such as a tank) to a **receiver** (the ending source, such as a pipe, another tank, or a nozzle). Because the reservoir's cross-sectional area is different from the receiver, **compression** or **expansion** occurs in the gas. As a result of compression or expansion, the gas's V (velocity), P (pressure), and D (density) change. Considering the context of these two examples, the most important subject in the gas-transfer process is the changes (particularly P) that a gas goes through under different conditions when it flows in a pipe. Remember that as V increases for a compressible (gas) flow, its P decreases.

The properties of a fluid (liquid or gas) change when it flows in the following conditions:

- **Adiabatically:** A fluid flows adiabatically when it flows from a receiver to a reservoir with *no* (most correctly almost *no*) change in its heat energy (E_Q), so $\Delta E_Q \approx 0$. A fluid is under the adiabatic condition when it flows through an insulated-wall pipe (Figure 3), so there is almost *no* heat transfer between the fluid and its surrounding environment through the pipe's wall.
- **Isothermally:** A fluid flows isothermally from a receiver to a reservoir with *no* (most correctly almost *no*) change in its temperature, so $\Delta T \approx 0$. A fluid is under the isothermic condition when it flows, say, through a wall-jacketed pipe (Figure 4), so the fluid's T remains constant ($\Delta T = 0$) because of sufficient heat transfer between the fluid and heating (or cooling) medium to keep it steady.
- **Isentropically:** A fluid flows isentropically when it flows from a reservoir to a receiver with *no* change in its entropy (S). The flow is **reversible**, like when the flow goes through compression or expansion. When the cross-sectional area (A) gradually decreases, **compression** occurs. And when the area gradually increases, the **expansion** occurs. In both cases, gas's P and, to some extent, D change. Both compression and expansion occur when a fluid flows through a **converging-diverging nozzle** (Figure 5). Gas P gradually increases through the nozzle's **converging section** (smaller-diameter section, measured from the entrance to the throat). It gradually decreases when it goes to the **diverging section** (larger-diameter section, measured from the throat to the end of the nozzle).

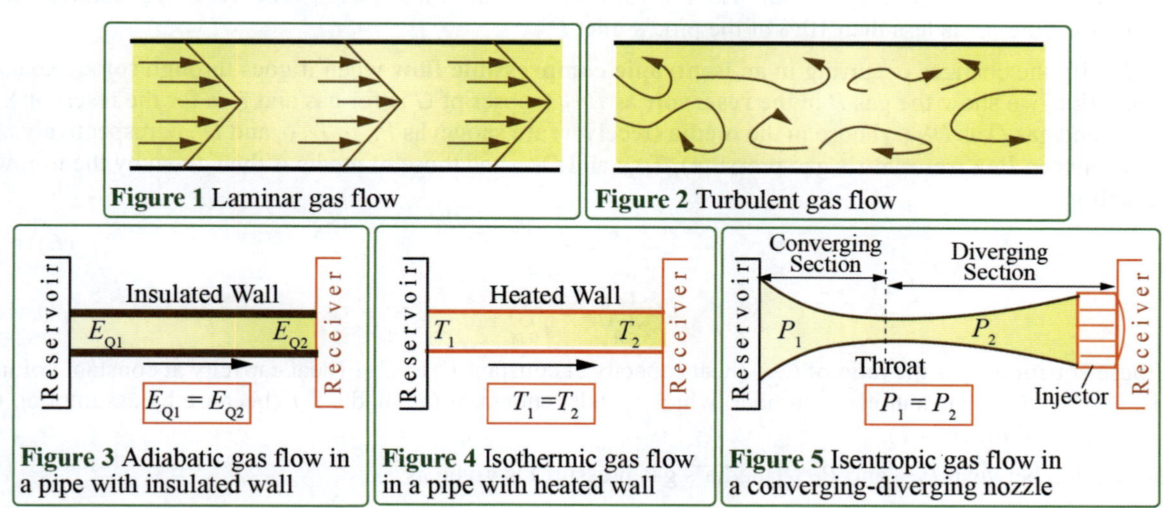

Figure 1 Laminar gas flow

Figure 2 Turbulent gas flow

Figure 3 Adiabatic gas flow in a pipe with insulated wall

Figure 4 Isothermic gas flow in a pipe with heated wall

Figure 5 Isentropic gas flow in a converging-diverging nozzle

FRICTIONLESS ISENTROPIC GAS FLOW IN A PIPE

To derive the equations for a gas that flows under isentropic conditions (when the system's S and D change during the flow) and adiabatic conditions (when *no* heat transfer occurs in a system) in a pipe, we will base our discussions on the following simplifying assumptions:

- The gas behaves as an ideal gas,
- The gas flows smoothly (luminary),
- The pump's shaft work does *not* exist, so $W_S = 0$,
- Gravitational acceleration is negligibly small, so $a_g = 0$,
- Frictions are restricted to the wall frictions and are negligible, and
- Specific heat capacity (C_Q, simply **heat capacity**) of the gas at constant P is independent of its T.

Under these conditions, a modified ideal gas equation that relates P, D, T, and M_n (molar mass) of an ideal gas through a proportionality constant, known as the gas constant (R), is used.

$$\frac{P.M_n}{D.T} = \text{Constant} = R \tag{1}$$

From here, the gas density calculates as

$$D = \frac{P.M_n}{R.T} \tag{2}$$

The gas average velocity ($\bar{V}$) is the product of its density (D_G) multiplied by its velocity (V_G).

$$\bar{V} = D_G.V_G \tag{3}$$

A few methods exist to calculate the pressure drop (ΔP) of compressible flows in pipes. One of the shortcut methods is the use of the following equation in the SI unit:

$$\Delta P = \frac{4150\dot{M}^{1.8}.\mu^{0.2}}{d^{4.8}.D} \tag{4}$$

This equation for the US unit is

$$\Delta P = \frac{\dot{M}^{1.8}.\mu^{0.2}}{20000d^{4.8}.D} \tag{5}$$

The units in Equations 4 are: bar/100m for ΔP, kg/h for $\dot{M}$ (the gas mass flow rate), mPa.s for μ (the gas viscosity), mm for d (the pipe's diameter), and kg/m^3 for D (the gas density). The units in Equation 5 are: PSI/100Ft for ΔP, Lb/h for $\dot{M}$, cP (centipoise; P is for Poise) for μ, In for d, and Lb/Ft^3 for D. [Equations 4 and 5 are used when the ΔP is less than 10% of the pipe's inlet P.]

To identify the changes occurring in an **isentropic compressible flow** when it goes through some expansion or contraction, we show the gas P in the **reservoir** as $P_{G.R}$ (subscript G is for gas and R is for the reservoir), gas T as $T_{G.R}$, and gas D as $D_{G.R}$. Those in the **media** (receiver) are shown as $P_{G.M}$, $T_{G.M}$, and $D_{G.M}$, respectively. The relation between $P_{G.R}$ (reservoir's gas-pressure), $T_{G.R}$, and $D_{G.R}$ and those of media is then given by the following two equations:

$$\frac{P_{G.R}}{D_{G.R}^{1/\gamma}} = \frac{P_{G.M}}{D_{G.M}^{1/\gamma}} \tag{6}$$

$$\frac{T_{G.R}}{P_{G.R}^{1-1/\gamma}} = \frac{T_{G.M}}{P_{G.M}^{1-1/\gamma}} \tag{7}$$

In these equations, γ is the ratio of $C_{Q.P}$ (heat capacity at constant P) to $C_{Q.V}$ (heat capacity at constant volume); that is, $\gamma = C_{Q.P}/C_{Q.V}$.γ is a unitless number, which is independent of the media's T (because by assumption $C_{Q.P}$ is independent of media's T).

The relation between $P_{G.R}$ and $P_{G.M}$ (media's gas pressure) is given as

$$\frac{P_{G.M}}{P_{G.R}} = \frac{1}{\left\{1+\left[\left(\frac{\gamma-1}{2}\right)\right][N_M]^2\right\}^{1/(1-\frac{1}{\gamma})}} \tag{8}$$

$D_{G.M}$ can be calculated from Equation 6 as

$$D_{G.M} = D_{G.R}\left(\frac{P_{G.M}}{P_{G.R}}\right)^{\frac{1}{\gamma}} \quad (9)$$

$T_{G.M}$ can be calculated from Equation 7 as

$$T_{G.M} = T_{G.R}\left(\frac{P_{G.M}}{P_{G.R}}\right)^{1-1/\gamma} \quad (10)$$

FRICTIONLESS ISENTROPIC GAS FLOW IN A NOZZLE

The calculation for an ideal gas that flows isentropically from a reservoir to a converging-diverging nozzle is almost the same as flowing in a pipe. Because the beginning of the nozzle is sufficiently wide relative to its throat, the velocity (V) of the flow at the entrance is minimal, so it can be taken as zero in calculations. And because the length (L) of the converging section (measured from the entrance to the throat) is relatively short, the T and P of the gas at the nozzle entrance can be assumed equal to those in the reservoir.

An Example on Gas Flow

Given: Hot air moves from a straight pipe (a pipe of constant cross-section) to a convergent-divergent nozzle (the media)

Air pressure in the pipe (reservoir, $P_{G.R}$)	22 Atm
Air temperature in the pipe ($T_{G.R}$)	500K (227°C)
Air molar mass (M_n)	29 g/mol
Ratio of $C_{Q.P}$ to $C_{Q.V}$ for air (γ)	1.4
Mach number at the divergent-section of the nozzle (N_M)	0.7
Gas constant (R)	82.05×10^{-3} Atm.m^3/kmole.°C

Wanted: 1) Air density in the pipe (reservoir, $D_{G.R}$); 2) Air pressure in the nozzle (media, $P_{G.M}$); 3) Air density in the nozzle ($D_{G.M}$), and 4) Air temperature in the nozzle ($T_{G.M}$)

The air density in the pipe ($D_{G.R}$) can be calculated from Equation 2.

$$D_{G.R} = \frac{P_{G.R}M_M}{RT} = \frac{22\times29}{82\times10^{-3}\times500} = 15.6\ \text{kg/m}^3$$

The air pressure in the nozzle (media, $P_{G.M}$) is calculated from Equation 8

$$\frac{P_{G.M}}{P_{G.R}} = \frac{P_{G.M}}{22} = \frac{1}{\{1+[(1.4-1)/2]0.7^2\}^{1/(1-\frac{1}{1.4})}} = \frac{1}{(1+0.098)^{3.4965}} = 0.72$$

$$P_{G.M} = 22\times0.72 = 15.9\ \text{Atm}$$

Gas P decreases (from 22 to 15.9 Atm) when it goes from the convergent (smaller-diameter) section of the nozzle to the divergent (larger-diameter) section.

The air density in the nozzle (media, $D_{G.M}$) can be calculated from Equation 9.

$$D_{G.M} = D_{G.R}\left(\frac{P_{G.M}}{P_{G.R}}\right)^{1/\gamma} = 15.6\left(\frac{15.9}{22}\right)^{0.714} = 12.4\ \text{kg/m}^3$$

The air D decreases (from 15.6 to 12.4 kg/m^3) when it enters the nozzle.

The air temperature in the nozzle ($T_{G.M}$) can be calculated from Equation 10.

$$T_{G.M} = T_{G.R}\left(\frac{P_{G.M}}{P_{G.R}}\right)^{1-1/\gamma} = 500\left(\frac{15.9}{22}\right)^{0.286} = 500\times0.911 = 455\ \text{K}\ (-\ 182°\text{C})$$

The air T decreases from 500 (227°C) to 455 K (182°C) when it enters the nozzle.

G-11
GAS LAWS

The Gas Laws are six (6) principles:

- Boyle's Gas Law (1662)
- Charles's Gas Law (1780)
- Gay-Lussac's Gas Law (1808)
- Avogadro's Gas Law (1812)
- Combined Gas Law
- Ideal Gas Law (1834)

The gas laws use the relations between the pressure (*P*), temperature (*T*), volume (*V*), and the amount of a gas (expressed in mole, *n*) under certain conditions and apply to all gases. The proportionality constant that relates these variables is known as the gas constant (*R*). Figure 1 shows the relations between *R* and Boyle's, Charles's, Gay-Lussac's, and Avogadro's Laws.

The first four (4) listed gas laws were combined later to develop the Combined Gas Law, which was further developed into the Ideal Gas Law. The ideal gas law expresses all basic properties of a gas into a single equation, named the ideal gas equation.

$$P.V = n.R.T \tag{1}$$

Boyle's Gas Law

Boyle's Gas Law (*P-V* relation at constant *T*), which is named after Robert Boyle (1627–1691, Irish physical chemist), states that at constant *T* and *n* (amount of a gas in mole), the *V* of a gas decreases as its *P* increases, meaning that the *P* of a gas is **inversely proportional** to its *V*.

$$V \propto \frac{1}{P} \qquad \text{or} \qquad P.V = K \tag{2}$$

The newer expression of Boyle's Gas Law states that the molar volume of any gas at STP (standard temperature and pressure) is 22.4 L/mole, where the value 22.4 is the *V* of one mole of any gas at STP.

The next equation compares a gas's *P* and *V* under two conditions.

$$P_1.V_1 = P_2.V_2 \qquad \text{or} \qquad \frac{P_1}{P_2} = \frac{V_2}{V_1} \tag{3}$$

Figure 2 is a numerical example of Boyle's Gas Law. The example asks for the calculation of a cylinder gas's volume at 4 Atm (or $P_2 = 4$ Atm) if we know that the *V* of that gas at 2 Atm (or $P_1 = 2$ Atm) and the same *T* is 1 m^3 (or $V_1 = 1$ m^3).

$$V_2 = \frac{P_1.V_1}{P_2} = \frac{2\times1}{4} = 0.5 \text{ m}^3$$

Charles's Gas Law

Charles's Gas Law (*V-T* relation at constant *P*), which is named after Jacques Charles (1746–1823, French physical chemist), relates the *V* of a gas to its *T* at constant *P*, meaning that the *V* of a gas is proportional to its *T* at constant *P*. In another context, at constant *P* ($\Delta P = 0$, the usual condition in the laboratory), the *V* of a gas increases or decreases by the same factor as its *T*.

$$V \propto T \quad \text{or} \quad \frac{V}{T} = k \tag{4}$$

The following equations compare a gas under two conditions:

$$\frac{V_1}{V_2} = \frac{T_1}{T_2} \quad \text{or} \quad \frac{P_1}{P_2} = \frac{T_1}{T_2} \tag{5}$$

Figure 3 is an example of Charles's Gas Law. Based on this law, if the *V* of a balloon at atmospheric pressure and 15ºC = 288 K temperature (T_1) is 10 cm^3, its *V* at 25ºC = 298 K (T_2), and the same *P* will be

$$V_2 = \frac{V_1.T_2}{T_1} = \frac{10 \times 298}{288} = 10.3 \text{ cm}^3$$

Similarly, we can calculate the pressure of oxygen (O_2) in a tank at 50ºC if we know that the pressure of O_2 at T_1 = 25ºC is P_1 = 5.8 Atm. The *T* of 25ºC equates to T_1 = 25 + 273 = 298K and that of 50ºC equates to T_2 = 50 + 273 = 323K, thus

$$P_2 = \frac{P_1.T_2}{T_1} = \frac{5.8 \times 323}{298} = 6.3 \text{ Atm}$$

This tells us that the increase of the gas *T* from 25 to 50ºC increases its pressure from 5.8 to 6.3 Atm.

Gay-Lussac's Gas Law

Gay-Lussac's Gas Law (*P-T* relationship at constant *V* and *n*), which is named after Joseph Louis Gay-Lussac, French physical chemist) states that at constant *V* and *n*, the *P* of a gas increases if its *T* increases, meaning that the *P* of a gas is proportional to its *T* (see Figure 4).

$$P \propto T \qquad \text{or} \qquad \frac{P}{T} = K \tag{6}$$

The next equation compares a gas's *P* and *T* under two conditions.

$$\frac{P_1}{P_2} = \frac{T_1}{T_2} \tag{7}$$

Avogadro's Gas Law

Avogadro's Gas Law (*V-n* relationship at constant *T* and *P*), which is named after Amedeo Avogadro (1776–1856, Italian physical chemist), states that at constant *T* and *P*, the *V* of a gas increases if its content increases, meaning that the *V* of a gas is proportional to its *n*.

$$V \propto n \qquad \text{or} \qquad \frac{V}{n} = K \tag{8}$$

The next equation compares a gas's *V* and *n* under two conditions.

$$\frac{V_1}{V_2} = \frac{n_1}{n_2} \tag{9}$$

Figure 5 is a numerical example of Avogadro's Law. According to this law, if 2 moles of molecular hydrogen gas (H_2) react with 1 mole of molecular oxygen gas (O_2), 2 moles of water vapor (H_2O) is produced.

$$2\ H_2 + O_2 \rightarrow 2\ H_2O$$

Combined Gas Law

The Combined Gas Law was introduced later because each of the above-listed laws considers only two variables while holding two constants. Instead, the Combined Gas Law keeps one quantity constant, the amount of gas (in mole, *n*), and studies two conditions (say, the *P* and *V* in points 1 and 2).

$$\frac{P_1.V_1}{T_1} = \frac{P_2.V_2}{T_2} \tag{10}$$

At constant *n* and *T*, this equation becomes

$$P_1.V_1 = P_2.V_2 \tag{11}$$

As a numerical example, consider a tank with a *V* of 10 m^3 (or V_1 = 10 m^2) filled with oxygen (O_2) at T_1 = 25ºC. The example asks for calculating the gas's *V* at 6 Atm pressure (or P_1 = 6 Atm) and STP. First, we convert the 25ºC to Kelvin (K) as T_1 = 25 + 273 = 298K. We know that the temperature at STP is T_2 = 273K, and the pressure at STP is P_2 = 1 Atm. Thus,

$$V_2 = \frac{P_1.V_1.T_2}{P_2.T_1} = \frac{6 \times 10 \times 273}{1 \times 298} = 55 \text{ m}^3$$

So, the P decrease (from 6 to 1 Atm) resulted in a V increase (from 10 to 55 m^3).

The combined-gas-law equation is useful when we want to know, for example, what happens to the V of a given amount of a gas when its P increases at constant T. At constant T and n, if the P of a gas increases, its V decreases. Or, at constant P and n, if the T of a gas increases, its V increases, also.

When we study a particular gas sample under certain conditions, we can write the combined gas law using the proportionality constant of k for the sample's fixed amount (n moles).

$$\frac{P.V}{T} = k \tag{12}$$

The T is in K (Kelvin), where K = °C + 273 in **combined gas law**. [The degree sign (°) is *not* used with the Kelvin scale.] [For the reason that the **combined gas law** must keep one variable constant, it was later developed into a more effective version, named the Ideal Gas Law.]

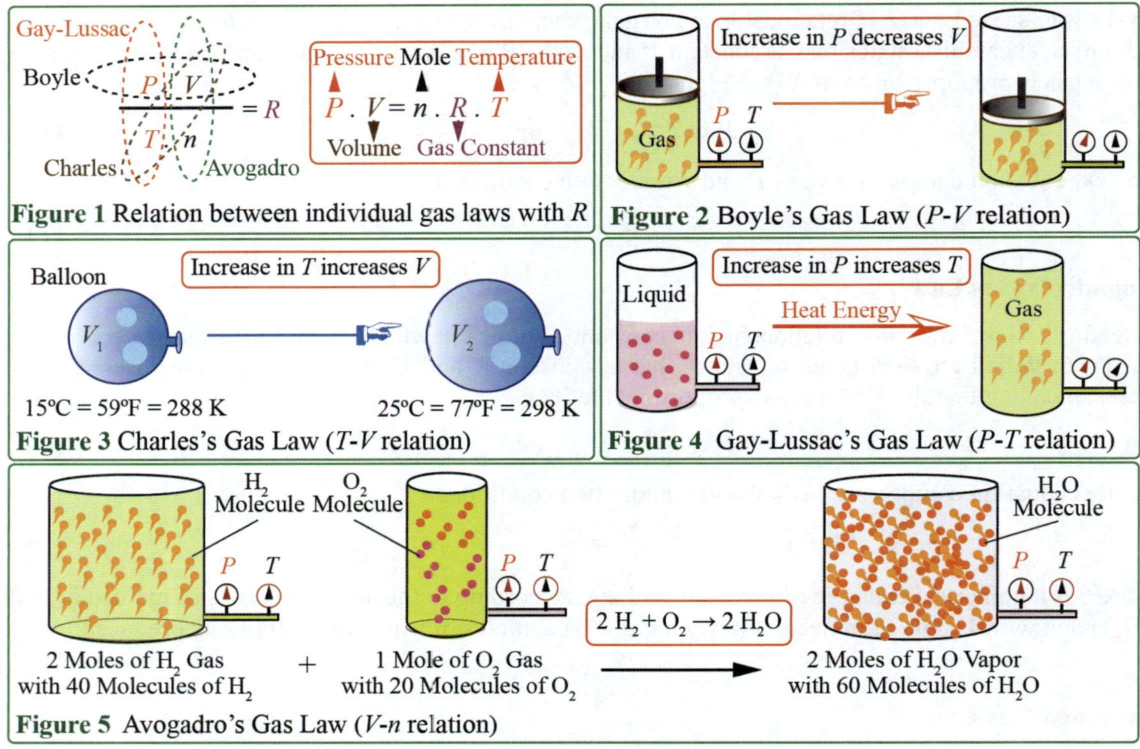

Figure 1 Relation between individual gas laws with R

Figure 2 Boyle's Gas Law (P-V relation)

Figure 3 Charles's Gas Law (T-V relation)

Figure 4 Gay-Lussac's Gas Law (P-T relation)

Figure 5 Avogadro's Gas Law (V-n relation)

Ideal Gas Law

Ideal Gas Law, unlike the other laws, combines all the properties of an ideal gas, which are P, T, V, and the amount of gas (in mole, n), into a single equation, named **ideal gas equation**, through a proportionality constant, known as the ideal gas constant (R, simply gas constant). Based on this law, the n mole of a gas occupies a volume of V when it is kept at a certain P and T.

$$P.V = n.R.T \tag{13}$$

In an ideal gas,

- Particles move in straight lines,
- Particles contact each other randomly,
- Particles do *not* interact when they hit each other,

- Particles do *not* slow down when they hit each other, and
- Particles have the same chemical potential energy as real gas.

Van der Waals Equation for Real Gases: This equation, named after its developer Johannes van der Waals (1837−1923, Dutch physicist), modifies the ideal gas equation ($P.V = n.R.T$) for real gases, which mostly do *not* act ideally. For the non-ideality behavior of real gases, van der Waals applied a two-step modification to the ideal gas equation ($P.V = n.R.T$):

- **First Step:** In this step, which is done for the V that a real gas occupies, V is replaced with $(V_n - b)$, where V_n is the gas's molar volume, and b is the V that is occupied by one mole of the gas's molecules, so $n = 1$.
- **Second Step:** In this step, which is done for interaction between the molecules (attraction at low and repulsion at high pressures), it applies the term $a/(V_n)^2$, where a is a constant that its value depends on the gas.

As the result of the modification, the ideal gas equation, written for a non-ideal gas, becomes

$$\left[P + a\frac{1}{(V_n)^2}\right](V_n - b) = R.T \tag{14}$$

This equation (van der Waals equation) can also be written as

$$\left[P + a\frac{n^2}{V^2}\right](V - n.b) = n.R.T \tag{15}$$

Factor a has typical values of 0.01 to 0.1 Atm(L/mole)^2, and b is 0.01 to 0.1 L/mole. When the V_n (molar volume) of the gas is large, b becomes negligible in comparison with V_n, and $a/(V_n)^2$ becomes negligible in comparison with P, so Equation 14 reduces to $P.V_n = R.T$, and Equation 15 reduces to $P.V = n.R.T$ (the ideal gas equation).

G-12
GAS-LIQUID EXTRACTION PROCESS

As a process unit (unit operation) of ChemEng, gas-liquid extraction (also called **gas absorption**) is the separation of a soluble gas from a mixture by adding a liquid (generally known as the **extracting liquid** or extracting solvent) to the mixture. Usually, the solvent to be added to the mixture is chosen to be miscible with the gas but immiscible with the mixture's liquid (or liquids) to create a second phase. The solvent can then be recovered from the liquid in a packed distillation column. Figure 1 shows a typically packed distillation column for the gas extraction process and two types of packing rings.

[Note: Because of contacting a gas phase with a liquid phase, the process is called **gas-liquid extraction**. This process is also called **gas absorption** because it absorbs a gas from its mixture by coming into contact with a solvent. The **reverse of gas absorption**, which is the separation of a solute from its mixture by adding a gas to the mixture, is called **gas stripping** (gas desorption).]

In general, the gas-liquid extraction process has the following three types:

- **Gas Absorption Process** (gas-liquid extraction)**:** This is a gas-liquid interaction by which a gas is removed from a mixture by adding a liquid to the mixture.
- **Gas Desorption Process** (liquid-gas extraction, also called gas stripping)**:** This is a liquid-gas interaction by which a liquid is removed from a mixture by adding a gas to the mixture. Thus, the **gas desorption process** is the opposite of the **gas absorption process**.
- **Gas Adsorption Process** (gas-solid extraction)**:** This is a gas-solid interaction by which a gas is removed from a mixture by adding a solid to the mixture.

These processes have become more important as environmental agencies have decreased the number of components discharged by the chemical process industry directly into the water or air. The following are three examples of such applications:

- Removal of ammonia (NH_3) from an ammonia-air mixture by adding water (as a solvent). In this process, most NH_3 is absorbed into H_2O.
- Removal of sulfur dioxide (SO_2) from flue gas by passing the flue-gas mixture through calcium hydroxide [$Ca(OH)_2$]. In this process, most SO_2 is absorbed into $Ca(OH)_2$.
- Removal of NOX (NO, NO_2, N_2O_4, and N_2O_5) from flue gas by passing the flue-gas mixture through sodium hydroxide (NaOH). In this process, most of the NO_2 (the main component of NO_x) reacts with water in NaOH to form nitric acid (HNO_3), and the rest of NO_2 reacts with NaOH to form sodium nitrate ($NaNO_3$) and sodium nitrite ($NaNO_2$).

$$3NO_2 + H_2O \rightarrow 2HNO_3 + NO$$

$$2NO_2 + 2NaOH \rightarrow NaNO_3 + NaNO_2 + H_2O$$

[The removal of SO_2 and NO_2 greatly reduces acid rain (the acidification of the atmospheric air).]

Gas-liquid extraction is like liquid-liquid extraction (simply extraction process), but with some differences, such as the following:

- In gas-liquid extraction, the phases (gas and liquid) are usually partially miscible. In liquid-liquid extraction, the involved phases are two immiscible liquids.
- In gas-liquid extraction, the gas phase is partially absorbed by the liquid phase. For example, bubbling carbon-dioxide gas (CO_2) through a sweet solution causes some of the CO_2 molecules to be absorbed by the solution to form a bubbled solution. In liquid-liquid extraction, a solvent, which is immiscible or partially miscible with one of the liquid phases, is usually added to the feed for extracting the liquid-of-interest from the mixture.
- In gas-liquid extraction, the molecules of one phase (usually gas phase) move (diffuse) through its phase by **convective diffusion** (discussed under DIFFUSION PROCESS), then through the gas-liquid boundary by **conductive diffusion** (discussed under the same topic), and into the liquid phase, again by convective diffusion. In liquid-liquid extraction, 1) The molecules of one liquid phase diffuse through conduction, 2) Through the liquid-liquid boundary by conduction, and 3) Into the other liquid phase by convection.

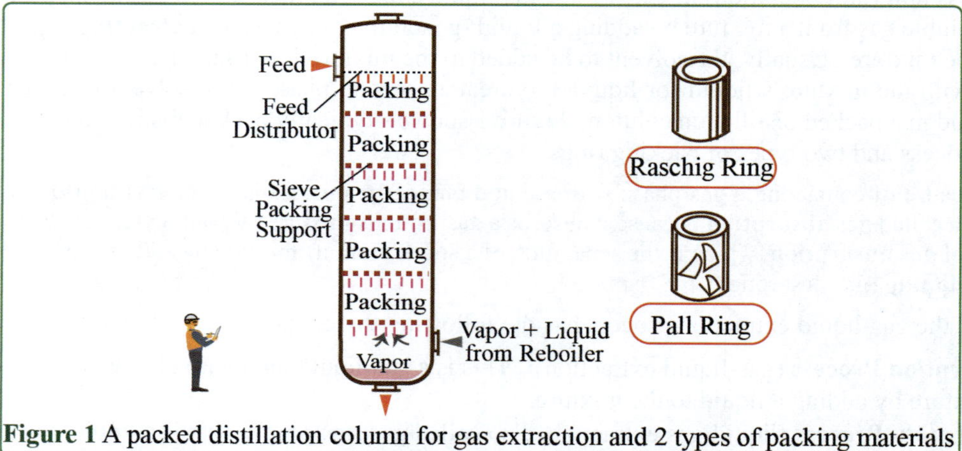

Figure 1 A packed distillation column for gas extraction and 2 types of packing materials

G-13

GAS MOLAR DENSITY

The molar density (D_n) of a gas is its mass of 1 mole (n), which equates to its molecular mass or molar mass) divided by its volume (V).

$$D_n = \frac{n}{V} \tag{1}$$

From here, $n = D_n.V$. Substituting $D_n.V$ for n in the ideal-gas equation ($P.V = n.R.T$),

$$P.V = D_n.V.R.T \qquad D_n = \frac{P}{R.T} \tag{2}$$

In this equation, P is for pressure (in Atm), T is for temperature (in K), and R is for gas constant (which equates to 0.0821 Atm.L/mole.K), giving D_n in mole/L. Then D of the gas is the product of the D_n and molar mass (M_n).

$$D = D_n.M_n \tag{3}$$

G-14

GAS MOLAR MASS

The molar mass is its molar volume (V_n, the volume of one mole) at STP is 22.4 L (10.2 Ft^3). The value 22.4 changes if we change the temperature (T) of the gas from STP to any other value.

G-15

GAS PARTIAL PRESSURE

The partial pressure of a gas is the pressure (P) of that gas that exists in a mixture of gases. In a mixture of gases, each gas applies pressure partially. Thus, the total pressure of the mixture equates to the sum of the partial pressures. This statement is known as Dalton's Law of partial pressures, which applies to mixtures of both ideal gases and **non-ideal gases**. For example, the total pressure (P_T) of a mixture that is composed of two gases of A and B is given as

$$P_T = P_A + P_B \tag{1}$$

According to this equation and as shown in Figure 1, if we connect a tank of oxygen gas (O_2), which is under a pressure of 1.4 Atm, to a tank of nitrogen gas (N_2), which is at 1.2 Atm, the pressure of the mixture would be

$$P_T = P_{O_2} + P_{N_2} = 1.4 + 1.2 = 2.6 \text{ Atm}$$

When there are n_A moles of A component and n_B moles of B component in an ideal-gas mixture, the **total pressure of the gas mixture** (P_T) can be calculated from the ideal gas equation ($P.V = n.R.T$).

$$P_T = P_A + P_B = n_A\left(\frac{R.T}{V}\right) + n_B\left(\frac{R.T}{V}\right) = (n_A + n_B)\left(\frac{R.T}{V}\right)$$

$$P_T = n_T\frac{R.T}{V} \tag{2}$$

It is important to know that each gas behaves independently of other gases in a mixture of ideal gases. Because of this statement, we can relate the amount (in mole, n) of a given component (say, component A) in a gas mixture to its partial pressure (P_A).

$$\frac{P_A}{P_T} = \frac{n_A \frac{R.T}{V}}{n_T \frac{R.T}{V}} = \frac{n_A}{n_T}$$

$$P_A = P_T \frac{n_A}{n_T} \quad (3)$$

The ratio n_A/n_T (mole of gas A to total moles in the mixture) is called molar fraction (X, a unitless quantity). Say, the molar fraction of A in a mixture with A and B components is

$$X_{n.A} = \frac{n_A}{n_A+n_B} = \frac{n_A}{n_T} \quad (4)$$

Combining this equation with Equation 3 gives us the following useful equation:

$$P_A = X_{n.A}.P_A \quad (5)$$

Total volumetric flow rate ($\dot{V}_T$, in m^3/s or m^3/h) of the gas mixture is

$$\dot{V}_T = \dot{V}_A + \dot{V}_B = \dot{V}_A\left(1 + \frac{P_B}{P_A}\right) = \dot{V}_A \frac{P}{P_A} \quad (6)$$

Because density (D) is mass (M) per volume (V), then

$$\dot{V}_T = \frac{\dot{M}_A}{D_A} \times \frac{P}{P_A} \quad (7)$$

At temperature T, this equation becomes

$$\dot{V}_T = \frac{\dot{M}_A}{D_A} \times \frac{P}{P_A} \times \frac{T}{273.2} \quad (8)$$

In this equation, $\dot{M}_A$ is the mass flow rate of component A, D_A is the density of component A, P is the atmospheric pressure (1 Atm = 101.33 kPa), P_A is the partial pressure of component A, T is the temperature of the gas mixture, and the value 273.2 is the conversion factor from °C to Kelvin. Table 8 in the table section of the book gives the Vapor Pressure of Water at Different Temperatures.

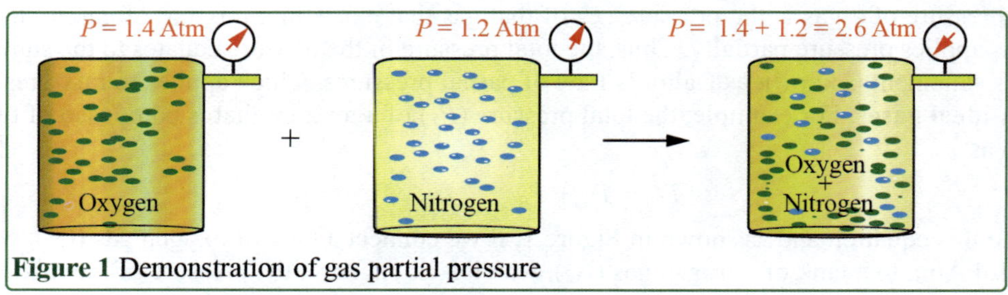

Figure 1 Demonstration of gas partial pressure

G-16

GAS POLLUTANTS

Discussed under POLLUTANTS.

G-17
GAS SCRUBBERS

Discussed under the topic of PARTICULATE REMOVING DEVICES.

G-18
GAS SOLID EXTRACTION PROCESS

This topic is *not* covered in this book.

G-19
GAS TRANSFER PROCESS

Study GAS FLOW.

G-20
GAS TURBINES

Discussed under TURBINES.

G-21
GAS VAPOR MIXTURE

A gas-vapor mixture is a mix of properties that vary with total pressure. Unless otherwise specified, a total pressure of 1 Atm is assumed when discussing a gas-vapor mixture. Also, it is assumed that the gas-vapor mixture follows the ideal-gas law.

G-22
GAS VISCOSITY

The viscosity (η) of gases increases with temperature, unlike liquids. The following equation can be used for approximate calculations of a gas's viscosity at a given temperature (T):

$$\frac{\mu}{\mu_0} = \left(\frac{T}{273}\right)^k \quad (1)$$

Where η is the viscosity at temperature T (in absolute temperature), η_0 is the viscosity at 0ºC (273 K), and exponent k is a constant for a particular gas (for example, k is 0.6 for air, 0.9 for CO_2, and 1 for steam).

[Viscosity of gases is too small (between 0.005 and 0.02 cp at 20ºC). The η of the dry air is 0.014 cp, CO_2 is 0.007 cp, and that of hydrogen is 0.009 cp.]

G-23

GAS VOLUMETRIC FLOW RATE

The volumetric flow rate ($\dot{V}$) of a gas is its molar flow rate ($\dot{M}$) per its molar density (D_n).

An Example on Gas Volumetric Flow

Given: A condenser for condensing water vapor. The vapor contains air (a noncondensable gas). The related data are given below.

Total mass-flow rate of air in the condenser ($\dot{M}_A$)	90 kg/h
Vacuum pressure in the condenser (P)	14 kPa
Temperature of the water vapor (T)	35°C (= 35+273.2 =308 K)

Wanted: 1) Total volumetric flow rate of air ($\dot{V}_T$), 2) Volumetric flow rate of dry air ($\dot{V}_A$), and 3) Volumetric flow rate of water vapor ($\dot{V}_{W.V}$)

From Table 1 (in the table section at the end of the book), the vapor pressure of water at 35°C is 5.6 kPa, so the partial pressure of air (P_A) is

$$P_A = 14 - 5.6 = 8.4 \text{ kPa}$$

The air's mass flow rate can be calculated from Equation 8, given under GAS PARTIAL PRESSURE.

$$\dot{V}_T = \frac{\dot{M}_A}{D_A} \times \frac{P}{P_A} \times \frac{T}{273.2} = \frac{90}{1.2} \times \frac{101.33}{8.4} \times \frac{308}{273.2} = 1020 \text{ m}^3/\text{h}$$

The volumetric flow rate of air ($\dot{V}_A$) can be calculated from Equation 8, given under VOLUMETRIC FLOW RATE. And the volumetric flow rate of water vapor ($\dot{V}_{W.V}$) can be calculated from $\dot{V}_A$.

$$\dot{V}_A = \dot{V}_T \frac{P_A}{P} = 1020 \frac{8.4}{14} = 612 \text{ m}^3/\text{h} \qquad \dot{V}_{W.V} = 1020 - 612 = 408 \text{ m}^3/\text{h}$$

G-24

GASOLINE

Gasoline (in the USA, **gas**) is a colorless, flammable liquid with the next properties:

- It is mainly used as a fuel in cars with combustion engines.
- It mainly consists of hydrocarbons with between 4 and 12 carbon atoms per molecule, so it is usually shown with an approximate chemical formula of C_8H_{18}.

Some other gasoline properties are outlined next.

- Its regular-type's octane rating is 85,
- Its density (D) is 755 kg/m^3 (6.3 Lb/Ga),
- Its enthalpy of combustion (H_C) is 46 700 kJ/kg.

Gasoline is produced from crude oil in oil refineries by the distillation process. In the refining process, from a 160-L (= 42-Ga) barrel of crude oil, 72 L (= 19 Ga) of gasoline is produced, equaling a yield of 45% by volume.

When 2 kg of gasoline is combusted in the engine of a car with 25 kg of oxygen (O_2), 16 kg of carbon dioxide (CO_2) and 18 kg of water (H_2O) are formed. The reaction is a heat-releasing (exothermic) reaction, releasing 46 700 kJ of heat energy (E_Q). This tells us that the heat of combustion (enthalpy of combustion) of gasoline is 46 700 kJ/kg. [When in a reaction, E_Q is released, it is shown, by definition, with a **negative** sign.]

$$2\ C_8H_{18} + 25\ O_2 \rightarrow 16\ CO_2 + 18\ H_2O - 46700 \text{ kJ of } E_Q$$

G-25

GAUGE BOSONS

Discussed under the topic of BOSONS AND FERMIONS.

G-26

GAUGE PRESSURE

Discussed under ABSOLUTE, ATMOSPHERIC, GAUGE, AND VACUUM PRESSURES.

G-27

GAY LUSSAC'S GAS LAW

Discussed under the topic of GAS LAWS.

G-28

GENERAL RELATIVITY

Study EINSTEIN'S THEORIES OF RELATIVITY.

G-29

GENERATORS

Study ELECTRIC GENERATORS.

G-30

GIBBS DALTON LAW

Study DALTON LAW OF PARTIAL PRESSURE.

G-31

GIBBS DONNAN EFFECT

The Gibbs-Donnan effect was suggested first by J. W. Gibbs (1839 – 1903, American physical chemist) and completed by F. G. Donnan (1870 – 1956, Irish chemist). Consider a binary solution with components *A* and *B*, where *A* has greater distribution coefficients (K_D), so with lower attractive energy (E_{At}). And *B* with lower K_D, so with higher E_{At}. Suppose this solution slowly passes through a semipermeable membrane or equivalent (like ion exchange resin). Here, *A* (the non-diffusing component with greater K_D) moves faster through the membrane than *B* (the diffusing component with smaller K_D). As a result, a separation between *A* and *B* occurs (because of their unequal molecular distribution on each side of the membrane). This effect was later named the **Gibbs-Donnan effect**.

The other impression of the Gibbs-Donnan effect is that charged particles near a semi-permeable membrane do *not* distribute evenly across the two sides of the membrane. The reason is that the presence of a different charged substance *cannot* pass through the membrane, so the electric charges on each side of the membrane are different than the other side.

[The Gibbs-Donnan effect plays an important role in some process units of ChemEng, including in membrane separation process and ion-exclusion chromatographic process.]

G-32

GIBBS FREE ENERGY

Discussed under the topic of ENERGY AND ITS FORMS.

G-33

GIBBS PHASE RULE

Study PHASE RULE.

G-34

GLASS

As one type of silicate, a glass is an amorphous solid (non-crystalline solid) whose molecules are *not* arranged in a crystalline way. Glasses are mainly composed of linked base units, the silicon dioxide (SiO_2, simply **silica**). [A glass, however, need *not* contain silicon (Si), but it must be made by cooling a compound from a molten state or dehydration of a solution. The compounds that meet these properties are generally known as glasses.]

Glasses are polar compounds with transparency. The refraction, reflection, and transmission properties of glasses make them suitable for producing optical lenses, prisms (triangular glass blocks), and artificial (manufactured) quartz. The most familiar type of glass, the window glass, is made of about 75% of silicon dioxide (SiO_2, commonly **silica**), and the rest are sodium oxide (Na_2O) and calcium oxide (CaO, lime).

Glasses are made using heating SiO_2 to form a **melt** (a molten state) and then cooling the melt. The two main differences between glasses and crystals are the following:

- Glasses do *not* have a regular-repeating structure, while crystals do.
- Glasses have different X-ray diffraction (spreading) patterns than crystals.

G-35

GLOBAL WARMING

Global warming (also called **global climate warming**) is the increase in the average surface temperature (T) of Earth and oceans as a result of releasing heat energy (E_Q) from the Sun into the Earth's atmosphere. Another consequence of global warming is that the climatic air gets more diverse and extreme. An area that used to be wet enough happens to be mild draught, while a mild-draught area gets wetter. Both warming and diversity of climatic air occur because the greenhouse gasses (mainly water vapor, carbon dioxide, methane, and NOX) prevent the air from sufficiently circulating.

Greenhouse gasses act as a blanket for the atmospheric air, preventing E_Q circulation. The burning of fossil fuels increases the greenhouse gasses and, therefore, the greenhouse effect. [The content of greenhouse gases in atmospheric air gradually increased since humans began large-scale burning of carbon-based fuel, starting the Industrial Revolution around the 1760s in Europe. The environmentalists believe that since the early 20th century, the Earth's average surface T has increased close to 1°C (= 1.8°F), and over half of the increase has occurred since the 1980s. The Earth's average surface T is 15°C (= 59°F).]

In a rough estimate, about 80% of the world's E_Q and E_E (electric energy) production is from fossil fuels. Carbon (C), the main component of fossil fuels, reacts with oxygen in the air to produce E_Q and carbon dioxide.

$$1 \text{ kg C} + 2.67 \text{ kg } O_2 \rightarrow 3.67 \text{ kg } CO_2 + 49\,000 \text{ kJ } E_Q$$

Water and Earth can absorb E_Q, but 1) There is more released than absorbed, and 2) Damage is there before it is absorbed (when the climate gets warmer, more water vapor goes back into the atmosphere).

[There are two ideas about **global warming**, political and scientific. Some politicians think that global warming does *not* exist, and if it exists, it is caused naturally. On the other hand, most environmentalists believe *not* that global warming exists but is caused by industries that pollute the environment unlawfully. Instead, ordinary people and caring politicians think that global warming is a science, but *not* politics.]

G-36
GLUCOSE

Discussed under the topic of SUGARS.

G-37
GLUON

A gluon (the name comes from **glue**) is the force-carrying particle of strong nuclear force (F_{SN}). The gluons functionalities are outlined next.

- They keep the quarks together to form a proton or neutron. Gluons glue together two up-quarks and one down-quark to make a proton, and two down-quarks and one up-quark make a neutron.
- They can change quarks (like up-quarks to down-quarks or vice versa).
- They can change a proton to a neutron or vice versa, changing a chemical element to a different one.

A few other properties of gluon are outlined next.

- It is a Boson,
- Its discovery in 1962 is credited to an American physicist,
- It does *not* carry an electric charge (q) but carries a color charge (a quantity unrelated to color), and
- It is considered a string in string theory. A string behaves like a massive particle (a particle with mass) and is governed by how it vibrates in spacetime (a 4-dimensional system).

A gluon is hard to study because although it always exists all over, it is so small that it requires enormous energy to break away from its quark. For this reason, scientists could be able to study the gluons in the particle accelerator at CERN.

G-38

GLYCOSIDIC BOND

Defined in the subtopic of Covalent Bonds under the topic of CHEMICAL BONDS.

G-39

GRAHAM'S LAW

Graham's Law of Diffusion, named after Thomas Graham (1805 – 1869, British chemist), is a principle in chemistry that says the *lighter* is a gas, the *faster* it diffuses. The gas diffusion rate (R) is directly proportional to its particles' velocity (V) and inversely proportional to its particles' molar mass (M_n) square root. This statement for comparison of two gases is formulized as

$$\frac{R_1}{R_2} = \frac{V_1}{V_2} = \sqrt{\frac{(M_n)_2}{(M_n)_1}} \tag{1}$$

If, for example, we place a few drops of perfume on a table at one end of a room, it can be smelt at the other end of the room. Similarly, if we put a few drops of that same perfume inside a rubber balloon and blow it up, we can smell the perfume outside the balloon (because it diffuses through the balloon's microscopic pores). This process is known as the **gaseous effusion** (the diffusion of a gas through fine openings). This process can be noticed when air escapes from the pores of a rubber balloon.

Graham's equation can be used in the context of the next example. Consider 2 same-size rubber balloons; one filled with hydrogen (H_2, with M_n of 2 g/mole) and the other one with oxygen (O_2, with M_n of 32 g/mole). The hydrogen molecules diffuse through the balloon's pores faster (because it is lighter), but we want to know how much faster to compare their rates.

$$\frac{R_1}{R_2} = \sqrt{\frac{(M_n)_2}{(M_n)_1}} = \sqrt{\frac{32}{2}} = \sqrt{16} = 4$$

G-40

GRAPHENE

Discussed under the topic of CARBON.

G-41

GRAVIMETRIC ANALYSIS

Gravimetric analysis is a quantitative determination of the concentration of a chemical substance (simply **substance**) in a solution sample. It is based on the mass of a solid. The general steps in performing a gravimetric analysis are as follow:

- A reagent is added to a known volume of a solution sample,
- The sample is filtered after precipitation of the substance of interest,
- The precipitate (↓) is washed to remove the traces of the residual impurities, and
- The filtered sample is dried in the oven and weighted to find the amount of the substance of interest.

G-42

GRAVITATIONAL ACCELERATION

Gravitational acceleration (a_g or g, the **acceleration of free fall**) is a system's acceleration (a) associated with its mass (M) and gravitational force (F_g, **force of gravity**, **force of Earth's gravity**, or simply **gravity**). Consider the Earth (a massive system), which is spherical to a good approximation. According to Newton's Law of Gravitation, the F_g at and near the Earth's surface can be calculated by using the Earth's M, its L (distance from its center, which is larger than its radius), and a proportionality constant named gravitational constant (K_g), where $K_g = 6.67\times10^{-11}$ N m^2/ kg^2 on the Earth's surface and N (Newton) = kg.m/s^2).

$$F_g = K_g \frac{M}{L} \tag{1}$$

The a_g that determines a system's motion in the Earth's gravitational field is the differential of this equation.

$$a_g = \frac{dF_g}{dR} = K_g \frac{M}{R^2} \tag{2}$$

Knowing the value of $K_g = 6.67\times10^{-11}$ N m^2/ kg^2 = 6.67×10^{-11} m^3/kg/s^2, $M = 5.972 \times10^{24}$ kg, and $L = 6.371 \times10^6$ m, we can calculate the a_g for a system that is near the Earth's surface.

$$a_g = 6.674 \times 10^{-11} \frac{5.972\times10^{24}}{(6.371\times10^6)^2} = 9.81 \text{ m/s}^2$$

Thus, a_g equates to 9.81 m/s^2 (= 32.2 Ft/s^2) at or near the Earth's surface. If therefore, we neglect drag force (a force acting against a moving system) and buoyant force (an upward force acting against F_g), a freefalling system accelerates near the Earth's surface at 9.81 m/s^2. [For simplicity, physicists approximate a_g to 10 m/s^2, regardless of the system's mass.]

In the Earth's gravitational field, which has a gravitational acceleration of a_g, when a system with a mass of M is falling, the system's a_g can be calculated from Newton's Second Law of Motion ($F_g = M.a_a$).

$$a_g = \frac{F_g}{M} \tag{3}$$

Here, F_g is in kg.m/s^2 = N, and M is in kg, giving a_g the unit of m/s^2, the SI unit of acceleration.

Consider two men with different masses are freefalling from an airplane. At the beginning of the fall, each man has his velocity (because some acceleration exists), but both men continue falling with the same constant velocity and acceleration very soon. The constant falling occurs because the extra F_g, acting on the heavier man, is canceled by his larger M (see Figure 1). Thus, a freefall system, whose weight is the only force acting on it, experiences *no* acceleration. [In 1963, an astronaut of Apollo 15 dropped a hammer and feather on the Moon's surface, where there is *no* air resistance, and both fell at the same velocity, meaning they accelerated equally. This, however, doesn't happen on the Earth because the feather slows down by air resistance.]

A freefalling system from the rest ($V_0 = 0$) has a velocity of 10 m/s at the end of the first second and 20 m/s at the end of the next second. And so on. This effect occurs because a falling system is always acting on by the same force (its weight), making it constantly accelerate (speed up). Assume after time t; a falling system reaches a vertical elevation of h, then the system's velocity (V) related to the a_g and t is

$$V = V_0 + a_g.t = a_g.t \tag{4}$$

Similarly, a system's velocity related to a_g and h will be

$$V = \sqrt{V_0^2 + 2a_g(h - h_0)} = \sqrt{2a_g.h} \tag{5}$$

A falling system, however, has negative V and a_g in relation to positive h, so the vertical distance h traveled by the system during the time t when the initial velocity is V_0 can be calculated as

$$h = V_0.t + \frac{1}{2}a_g.t^2 \tag{6}$$

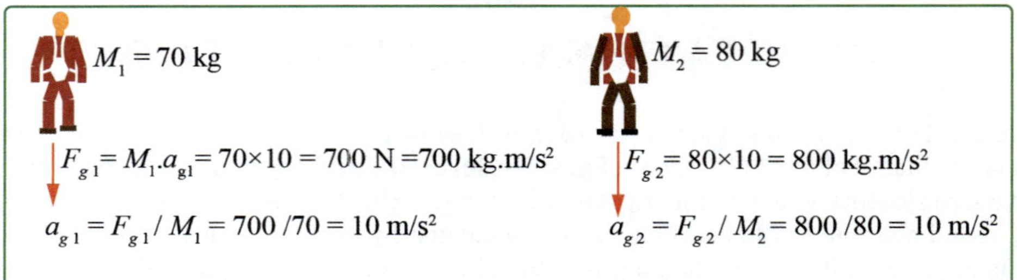

$M_1 = 70$ kg

$M_2 = 80$ kg

$F_{g1} = M_1.a_{g1} = 70\times10 = 700$ N $=700$ kg.m/s^2

$F_{g2} = 80\times10 = 800$ kg.m/s^2

$a_{g1} = F_{g1} / M_1 = 700 / 70 = 10$ m/s^2

$a_{g2} = F_{g2} / M_2 = 800 / 80 = 10$ m/s^2

Figure 1 Two differently-massive skydivers accelerate equally

G-43

GRAVITATIONAL CONSTANT

The gravitational constant (K_G, G, or g_c; also called **Newton's constant**) is used in Newton's Law of Gravitation as a proportionality constant to relate the gravitational force (F_g) between two systems with masses M_1 and M_2, located in the distance L (where L is for length) from the center of each other.

$$F_g = K_G \frac{M_1.M_2}{L^2} \tag{1}$$

If thus, the values of variables in this equation are known, we can calculate K_G, and then this value is constant, equal to 6.67×10^{-11} N.m^2/ kg^2(=3.34×10^{-8} Lb.Ft^2/slug^2). As N=kg.m/s^2, $K_g = 6.67\times10^{-11}$ N.m^2/ kg^2 = 6.67×10^{-11} m^3/kg/s^2. If we put two 1 kg systems 1 m apart, they will attract each other with a force of 6.67×10^{-11} 1 N (Newton). This tiny force is like blowing very gently on one of the systems. Using the mass of the Earth of 6×10^{24} kg and its distance (say, from us) of 6.37×10^6 m, we can calculate F_g for a place on the Earth according to the next equation.

$$F_G = 6.67 \times 10^{-11} \frac{6\times10^{24}}{(6.37\times10^6)^2} = 9.86 \text{ m/s}^2$$

[Note: Therefore, K_G can prove how weak the F_g is, compared to the other three fundamental forces of nature (strong nuclear force, electromagnetic force, and weak nuclear force).]

G-44

GRAVITATIONAL FIELD

A gravitational field (G-field) is the area around a system that is under the effect of the gravitational force (F_g, also called the **force of gravity** or simply gravity) and can carry energy (E) and momentum (p = mass × velocity) from place to place. Thus, its amount is different in different places. In classical physics, G-field can be defined as a **gravitational system** (G-system), which is used as a model to explain the effect of F_g on a system with mass M. In quantum physics, the G-field is defined as a system that has a quantity in spacetime.

A vector G-field is a vector quantity (a quantity with direction) that can be viewed as many little arrows attached to every point in space at every moment in time. And a scalar G-field is a scalar quantity (a quantity with *no* direction) attached to every spacetime point. This is why quantum physics views spacetime as a quantity that its measuring metric is the G-field, but unlike G-field, the spacetime does *not* carry E and p and has *no* measurable properties.

The next important points must be made about G-field:

- It has almost *no* effect on the internal properties of a system.
- It affects any system that goes through it, even the light, by bending its beams.
- A system located on the Earth's G-field can give energy (E), can do work (W), and more.
- Clocks react differently, as Einstein said, to two different G-fields. Consider a clock in a space shuttle at extremely high speed to be compared with the same type of clock on the Earth. Because the first system, which moves very fast, is in a weaker G-field, it has a tiny delay, comparably. This means that the faster a system travels, the more time slows down, relative to a stationary system or to a system that moves slower.

In his gravity-spacetime principle (discussed under Einstein's theories of relativity), Einstein used a G-field model to explain his theory of the curvature of spacetime. Referring to this model, he said that F_g is *not* an attractive force between two systems but the result of those systems that curve the spacetime.

The SI unit of G-field is N (Newton, the unit of force) per kg (the mass unit).

Figure 1 Gravitational field surrounding the Earth

G-45
GRAVITATIONAL FORCE

Discussed under FUNDAMENTAL FORCES OF NATURE.

G-46
GRAVITATIONAL MASS

Defined under MASS.

G-47
GRAVITATIONAL POTENTIAL

The gravitational potential (V) of a system equates to the gravitational potential energy (E_{GP}) of that system per its mass (M)

$$V = \frac{E_{GP}}{M} \tag{1}$$

The V equates (in value, but negative) to work (W) done by the gravitational field moving a system to a given location in space.

G-48

GRAVITATIONAL POTENTIAL ENERGY

Discussed under the topic of ENERGY AND ITS FORMS.

G-49

GRAVITATIONAL WAVES

As theorized and non-detected waves, gravitational waves (G-waves or gravity waves) are produced in the spacetime from movements of massive systems (like a big blackhole). G-waves, like photons (light particles), move at the speed of light in a vacuum, so they have a strong gravitational force (F_g). Some other characteristics of G-waves are outlined next.

- G-waves are detectable if the system under study is extremely massive, such as when two blackholes collide or a star explodes in a supernova (explosion of a star and its slow fading). [The G-waves of two blackholes were indirectly detected in 2015 for a short time (0.2 seconds). G-wave detectors use extremely long light beams to detect curves in spacetime.]
- G-waves are similar to electromagnetic waves (like light waves and radio waves), generated when electric charges oscillate (propagate) in spacetime.
- G-waves are *not* blocked by anything. But they can pass through most systems undisturbed. As an advantage, this property of G-waves can be used to observe places that we normally *cannot*. A lot of research still needs to be done on them to discover their unknowns. When this is complete, it opens the door to a new way of investigating the Universe.

G-50

GRAVITATIONAL WORK

Gravitational work (W_g) is work (W) done to lift (or fall) a system with mass M to a height h (or from the height h). In the Earth's gravitational field, a system can fall from a higher elevation 1 to a lower elevation 2 and give E (energy) and do W (work).

$$W_g = M.a_g.h \quad (1)$$

Here, a_g is a constant (9.81 m/s^2 = 32.2 Ft/s^2), known as gravitational acceleration. For example, a gravitational work needed to lift a system with a mass of 100 kg to the height of 2 m is

$$W_g = 100 \times 9.81 \times 2 = 1960 \text{ kg.m/s}^2\text{.m} = \text{J}$$

G-51

GRAVITON

A graviton (the name comes from gravity) is theorized to be the elementary particle of gravitational force (F_g, the force of gravity), a force (F) that creates a gravitational field (G-field). Confirming the fact that each of the non-gravitational fundamental forces of nature (FFN), the electromagnetic force (EM force), strong nuclear force, and weak nuclear force, has its particles, led physicists to believe that F_g, the weakest of four FFN, must also have its force-carrying particles. They called these the gravitons.

A few important properties of graviton are outlined next.

- It was theorized in the 1930s. It, however, is still a non-confirmed (non-detectable) particle because its existence has *not* been observed yet (because it has insufficient energy).
- It is considered a string in the string theory, so it vibrates in space like a massive particle (a particle with mass, M) with an electric charge.
- It is a Boson (other Bosons are photon, gluon, Z-Boson, W-Boson, Higgs Boson, and gauge Boson.)

According to Einstein, the F_g of a massive system (a system with a rest mass of M) can curve the spacetime (the *more* massive the system, the *greater* is its F_g and, thus, the *more* it curves the spacetime).

G-52

GRAVITY

As a general and outdated term, gravity is an attractive force quantified by gravitational force (F_g, the force of gravity). Based on this definition, the terms **gravity**, **gravitational force**, and **force of gravity** are used equally. Knowing the following two points about gravity is important:

- Instead of gravity, mainly the term **gravitational force**, a self-defining word, is used in this book.
- Often physicists describe gravity as the curvature of spacetime (warping of spacetime). They, however, do *not* mean that gravity (gravitational force) and spacetime are the same things.

G-53

GRAVITY-SPACETIME PRINCIPLE

Discussed under EINSTEIN'S THEORIES OF RELATIVITY.

G-54

GREENHOUSE EFFECT

The greenhouse effect is the process of trapping the heat energy (E_Q) of the Sun by the greenhouse gases (mainly water vapor, carbon dioxide, methane, and NOX) and passing infrared radiation of the Sun to the Earth's surface. The greenhouse effect causes the following two damages to the environment:

- It increases the Earth's average surface temperature (T), so known as global warming, and
- It prevents the climatic air from sufficiently circulating, so an area that used to be wet enough happens to be mild draught, while a mild-draught area gets wetter.

The term **greenhouse** is used because a glass greenhouse traps the heat energy (E_Q) of the Sun inside to keep the plants warm, the way the greenhouse gases act in the atmosphere, causing global warming. The name is from the similar effect that a greenhouse utilizes to increase plant growth.

To better understand the subject, let us first clarify the following two phenomena:

- How the heat energy is absorbed and reflected by the Earth's surface, and
- How the Earth-surface's T is changed from day to night.

Most of the Sun's E_Q is absorbed by the Earth during a sunny day, and some return to the atmosphere. Earth's surface, thus, warms in the sunlight during the day. The Earth's surface cools at night, releasing the E_Q back into the atmosphere. Thus, a noticeable difference in T between day and night exists.

However, a portion of the E_Q is trapped inside the atmosphere by the greenhouse gasses, which keep the Earth's surface warmer. In addition, the greenhouse gases *cannot* reflect the Sun's infrared radiations to the atmosphere, so they are passed to the Earth's surface, causing skin cancer. The greenhouse gases act like a blanket to trap the E_Q, preventing the air from circulation.

The reason for trapping the E_Q of the Sun in the greenhouse zone is that the molecules of greenhouse gases are loosely bonded together, so they can easily absorb E_Q. The molecules of major components of air, nitrogen (N_2) and oxygen (O_2), instead, are tightly bonded, so they *cannot* absorb E_Q as easily as the greenhouse gases do. In addition, the loos-bonding property of greenhouse gases causes them to pass the infrared radiation to the Earth's surface (see Figure 1).

[Note: The environmentalists believe that since the early 20th century, the Earth's average *T* increased about 1°C (= 1.8°F), and over half of the increase has occurred since the 1980s. The Earth's surface average *T* is 15°C (= 59°F). One of the easiest ways to reduce the greenhouse effect is the reduction of fossil fuel usage.]

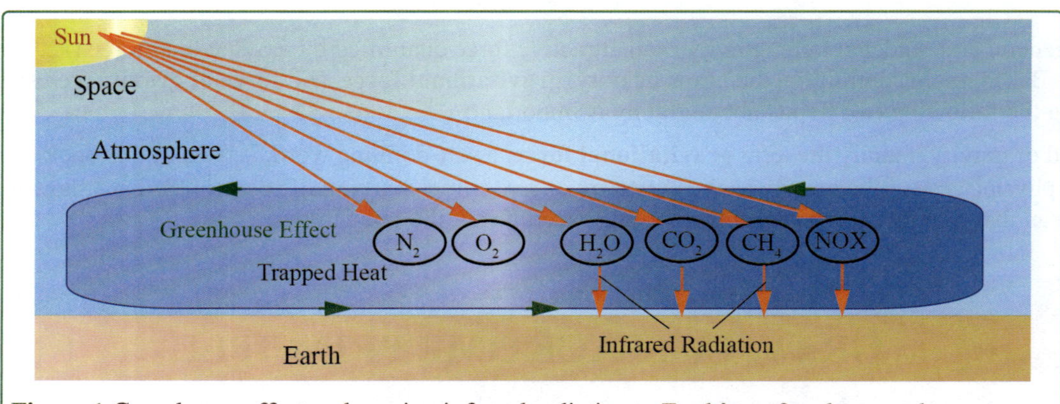

Figure 1 Greenhouse effect and passing infrared radiation to Earth's surface by greenhouse gases

G-55

GREENHOUSE GASES

Greenhouse gases are some gases in the atmosphere that act as a blanket, preventing the climatic air from circulation. This causes heat-trapping in the climatic air, called global warming. By their percentage contribution to the greenhouse gases on Earth, the four major greenhouse gases are: 1) Water vapor (H_2O; 36 to 70%), 2) Carbon dioxide (CO_2; 9 to 26%), 3) Methane (CH_4; 4 to 9%), and 4) NOX (NO and NO_2).

The molecules of these compounds are loosely bonded together to absorb the E_Q of the Sun and pass the infrared radiation to the Earth's surface, as shown in Figure 1 under GREENHOUSE EFFECT. Instead, the molecules of major components of the atmospheric air, nitrogen (N_2) and oxygen (O_2), are tightly bonded, so they *cannot* absorb heat as much as the greenhouse gases do and *can*not get to the Earth's surface.

The CO_2 content in atmospheric air gradually increased since humans began large-scale burning of carbon-based fuel, starting the Industrial Revolution around the 1760s. CO_2 also reacts with water in the air to form carbonic acid (H_2CO_3), one of the causes of acid rain. Fortunately, half of the produced CO_2 is absorbed by vegetation and water in oceans. Scientists think that the greenhouse gases in the air result in global warming.

G-56

GROUND AND EXCITED ENERGY STATES

The words **ground energy state** (simply **ground state**) and **exited energy state** (simply **excited state**) are used in Physics to refer to the energy (E) that an atomic system contains or changes. Specifically, a system at its **ground energy state** has a lower E than the **excited energy state**. In another context, an excited state is an elevation in E level above the ground state (a reference energy state).

When, say, the electron of a hydrogen atom (H with one electron) is in the $n = 1$ **electron shell** (simply **shell**), the electron is in the lowest shell (it is closest to its nucleus), its E (refers to E_P, potential energy) is at the lowest. Thus, it is in the **ground energy state**, as shown in Figure 1. [The symbol n is for **principal quantum number** (simply a **quantum number**), defined under the topic of ATOM.] Instead, when that electron moves up to any shell with n greater than 1 (say, to $n = 2$), it is farther from its nucleus, its E is greater, and thus it is in the **excited energy state** (as shown in the same figure).

When an electron jumps (**leaps** in quantum physics) from an exited-energy shell to a ground-energy shell, an **excess energy** forms in that electron, which is released as photon energy (E_{Ph}) of a photon. Instead, an electron absorbs enough E_{Ph} when it moves up to an excited energy shell. But, it *cannot* act there forever (because electrons prefer to be in the ground energy state) and later returns to a ground-energy shell.

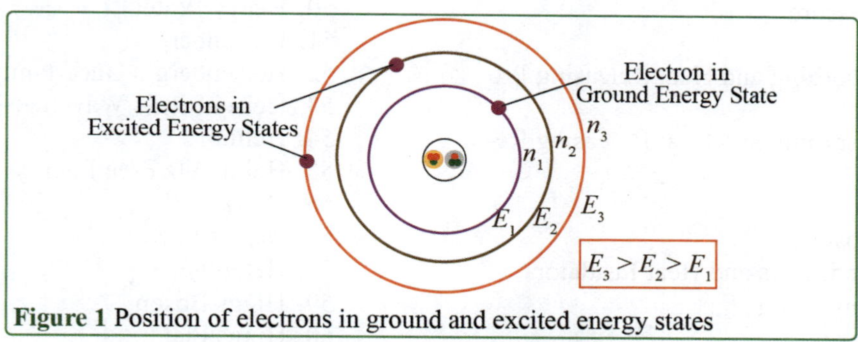

Figure 1 Position of electrons in ground and excited energy states

H Section

LIST OF TOPICS

1. Hadrons
2. Half Lifetime
3. Halftime Reaction
4. Halogens
5. Hard Water
6. Hardness [Chemistry]
7. Hardness of Material
8. Hawking
9. Hazards
10. Head
11. Head Loss
12. Head Pressure
13. Heat
14. Heat Absorbing and Heat Releasing Processes
15. Heat Absorbing and Heat Releasing Reactions
16. Heat Balance
17. Heat Capacity
18. Heat Conductors and Heat Insulators
19. Heat Convection
20. Heat Energy
21. Heat Energy Rate
22. Heat Engines and Heat Pumps
23. Heat Exchangers
24. Heat Expansion
25. Heat Flux and Heat Flux Rate
26. Heat of Combustion
27. Heat of Condensation
28. Heat of Evaporation
29. Heat of Freezing
30. Heat of Melting
31. Heat of Reaction
32. Heat of Sublimation
33. Heat Pumps
34. Heat Reactions
35. Heat Releasing Process
36. Heat Releasing Reactions
37. Heat Reservoir
38. Heat Resistance
39. Heat Transfer Area
40. Heat Transfer by Conduction
41. Heat Transfer by Convection
42. Heat Transfer by Radiation
43. Heat Transfer Coefficients
44. Heat Transfer Process
45. Heat Transfer Rate
46. Heaters
47. Heating Process
48. Heavy Hydrogen
49. Heavy Metals
50. Heavy Water
51. Heisenberg
52. Heisenberg's Uncertainty Principle
53. Heisenberg's Wavematrix Theory
54. Helium
55. Helmholtz Free Energy
56. Hertz
57. Hess's Law
58. Heterogeneity
59. Higgs Boson
60. Higgs Field
61. Homogeneity and Heterogeneity
62. Hooke's Principle
63. Horsepower
64. Hoses
65. Humid Air
66. Humidity and its Measurement
67. Humidity Diagram
68. Humidity Ratio
69. Hydrated Cluster
70. Hydrates
71. Hydration Reaction
72. Hydraulic Head
73. Hydraulic Pressure
74. Hydraulics
75. Hydrides
76. Hydrocarbons
77. Hydrochloric Acid
78. Hydrogen

79. Hydrogen Bond
80. Hydrogen Chloride
81. Hydrogen Peroxide
82. Hydrogen Sulfide
83. Hydrophobes, Hydrophiles, and Hygroscopes
84. Hydrostatic Equilibrium
85. Hydrostatic Pressure
86. Hydrostatic Testing
87. Hydrostatics
88. Hygrometer and Hygrometry
89. Hygrometric Diagram
90. Hygroscopes

H-1
HADRONS

Discussed under BOSONS, FERMIONS, AND HADRONS.

H-2
HALF LIFETIME

The **half lifetime** ($t_{1/2}$, simply **halflife**) of a chemical element is the time when half of its atoms decay (break down). Elements decay at different rates. Highly radioactive elements decay faster than less radioactive and nonradioactive elements. Uranium-238 has a huge halflife (4.46 billion years), close to the age of the Earth (approximately 4.54 billion years). The following give three general properties of the halflife. 1) It is given in units of time (*t*). 2) It is usually measured experimentally. 3) It is an exponential process (it can be decreased or increased as time goes on).

The term **half lifetime** is used in three ways: 1) Biological halflife, 2) Nonradioactive halflife, and 3) Radioactive halflife.

Biological Halflife: The biological halflife of a chemical substance (like a drug) is the time (*t*) it takes for that substance to lose half of its pharmacological activity in a human's body (or in any living organism). It also refers to the half time it takes to eliminate a substance from a human body (or any living organism). This is called the **cleansing process**, which proceeds through kidney and liver functions. For example, the biological halflife of water in our body is 7 to 14 days, and that of lead (Pb) from our blood is 28 to 36 days, depending on the body's internal behavior.

Nonradioactive Halflife: The word **nonradioactive halflife** is usually used in chemistry to describe a halflife reaction.

Radioactive Halflife: The radioactive halflife of a radioactive element (radionuclide or simply **nuclide**) is when it takes to be decayed (decomposed) to its half value. When saying the halflife of carbon-14 (C-14; a nuclide) is 5 730 years, it means that the number of C-14 that exists today will decay (to undergo nuclear decay process) to half of its amount in the next 5 730 years. Similarly, the half-lifetime of Cs-137 (cesium-137 in American-English spelling and ceasium-137 in IUPAC spelling) is 32 years, meaning in 32 years, it loses 50% of its content.

Some radionuclides (simply nuclides) have a very small halflife, while some have very large ones. For example, the halflife of iodine-131 (a strong radionuclide) is 8 days, while that of uranium (U) is 4.5 billion years (close to the age of the Earth; about 4.54 billion years). Radium-226 (R-226; the most stable isotope of radium) has a $t_{1/2}$ of 1 600 years to decay to radon (Rn, a radioactive gas).

The following dots give a few general properties of the radioactive halflife:

- Halflife depends on a radioactive element's atom and isotope.
- Halflife is related to an element's radioactivity (the shorter the $t_{1/2}$, the greater is the radioactivity).
- Halflife is *not* related to a radioactive element's quantity; say, a nuclide decays to half of its quantity, regardless of how big or small its original quantity was.

[The word **lifetime** is also used in chemistry to refer to **mean radioactive lifetime**, which is the time it takes for a radionuclide to decay completely. Both half-lifetime and mean lifetime are in the group of **exponential decay** (λ. lambda), which indicates the decay of a nuclide at a rate proportional to its current value.]

H-3

HALFLIFE REACTION

A halflife reaction is a term used in an oxidation-reduction reaction (simply **redox reaction**) to refer to the time that the concentration (*C*) of a substance is decreased to half its initial value, or half of the time its reaction takes place. Halflife reactions are important in analytical chemistry because they are independent of the initial *C* of the reactant when the reaction behaves as a first-order reaction. This means that the rate of change of a first-order reaction is constant (if *C* decreases by half, the reaction rate is half as fast).

An example is a sugar (sucrose) inversion in acidic solutions. Here, the halflife determines the rate of the sugar inversion, which depends on its **inversion rate constant** (K_I) and is independent of its initial *C*. The $t_{1/2}$ of a first-order reaction is determined as

$$t_{1/2} = \frac{\mathrm{Ln2}}{K_I} = \frac{0.693}{K_I} \qquad (1)$$

The K_I is the inversion rate constant (a temperature-dependent value) and Ln is the natural log. The K_I value for sugar at 70ºC is 1.18/h (this means that in one hour, 1.18 part of the sugar molecules decomposes). The inversion of sugar to invert sugar is an oxidation-reduction reaction, in which two reactions take place simultaneously, representing one reaction, called a **halflife reaction**. Thus, here the halflife is when the *C* of sugar is decreased to half its initial value.

An Example on Halflife

The sugar industry produces **invert sugar liquid** from 70% sugar ($C_{12}H_{22}O_{11}$) solution at 70ºC and a PH of 5 (PH of the solution is reduced by acid). What amount of time is required for 50% of the initial concentration of sugar to be inverted under this acidic condition? $C_{12}H_{22}O_{11} + H_2O \rightarrow C_6H_{12}O_6 + C_6H_{12}O_6$

Because sugar is 100% pure, its inversion to 50% corresponds to the definition of the halflife reaction, so Equation 1 can be used. The K_I for sugar at 70ºC is 1.18/h.

$$t_{1/2} = \frac{0.693}{K_1} = \frac{0.693}{1.18} = 0.59\text{ h } (= 35\text{ min})$$

H-4

HALOGENS

Halogens are fluorine (F), chlorine (Cl), bromine (Br), iodine (I), and astatine (At), located in group 17 of the periodic table of elements. F, Br, Cl, and I are the main halogens. [The term **halogen** comes from Greek words, meaning **salt-former**. When a halogen reacts with a metal, a salt is produced, like sodium chloride (NaCl), calcium fluoride (CaF_2), silver bromide (AgBr), and potassium iodide (KI).]

Fluorine (F) is a pale-yellow gas, chlorine (Cl) is a yellow-greenish gas, bromine (Br) is a dark-red liquid, iodine (I) is a metallic-gray solid, and astatine (At) is an unstable short-lived phase. Fluorine, bromine is Chlorine (Cl) is a yellow-greenish gas, which is extremely reactive and acts strongly as an oxidizing agent.

All of the halogens' atoms have seven valence (outer) electrons. The lack of one electron in a halogen atom's valence electron shell makes it an **electron acceptor** (oxidizing agent). Some other properties of the main four halogens are. 1) They all produce salts when they react with metals. 2) They all form diatomic molecules, shown as F_2, Cl_2, Br_2, and I_2. 3) They all are highly reactive, so they can be harmful to biological organisms. 4) They all produce acids when they react with hydrogen, such as $Cl_2 + H_2 \rightarrow 2\text{ HCl}$. 5) Three (Cl, Br, and I) are frequently used as **disinfectants** (antimicrobial compounds).

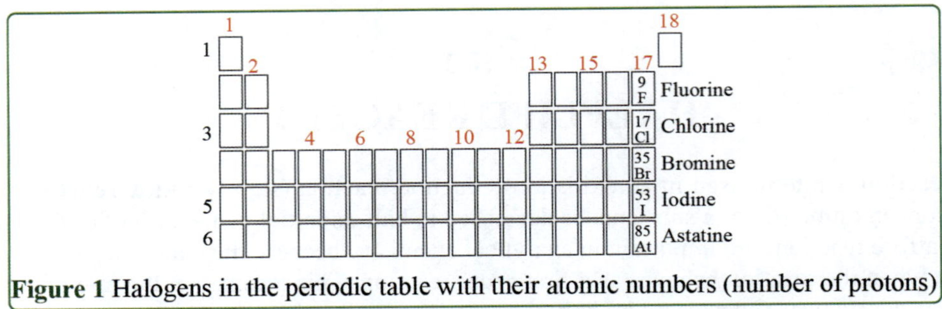

Figure 1 Halogens in the periodic table with their atomic numbers (number of protons)

H-5

HARD WATER AND SOFT WATER

Hard water contains a considerable amount of scale causing salts (hardness), which are soluble (non-filterable) salts of calcium (Ca) and magnesium (Mg), such as $CaCO_3$, $CaSO_4$, $MgSO_4$, and CaC_2O_4. Soft water, instead, is water with minimum or *no* scale-causing salts. A quality soft water has a low specific conductance of 0 to 4 μS/cm, corresponding to 0 to 2 PPM of scale-causing salts.

Typically, hard water is classified into four (4) classes:

- **Slightly Hard Water:** It contains 17 to 60 PPM of limesalts hardness.
- **Moderately Hard Water:** It contains 60 to 120 PPM of hardness.
- **Hard Water:** It contains 120 to 180 PPM of hardness.
- **Extremely Hard Water:** It contains more than 180 PPM of hardness.

In chemical process plants, hard water *cannot* be used as feedwater for the steam boilers. Instead, quality condensate from evaporators is usually used to feed the boilers. If the condensate is *not* enough, hard water is softened by one of the following water-softening processes:

- Water Softening Process by Chemicals: This type of softening is used when the amount of limesalts hardness in water is relatively high and complete (or near-complete) hardness removal is required.
- Water Softening Process by Ion-Exchange Resin: This type of softening is used when the limesalt hardness is relatively low and complete (or near-complete) hardness removal is required.

H-6

HARDNESS [Chemistry]

For definition of hardness, as used in chemistry, study SCALE CAUSING SALTS.

H-7

HARDNESS OF MATERIAL

Study STRENGTH AND HARDNESS OF MATERIAL.

H-8

HAWKING

Stephen Hawking (1942–2018) was a British **cosmophysicists** (a physicist who specialized in the development of the Universe from its origin until now); whose discoveries improved the understanding of the **cosmos** (Universe). Hawking was also an excellent physics writer who could explain difficult scientific subjects to his readers. His books for general readers include *A Brief History of Time* (1988), *Black Holes and Baby Universes* (1993), *The Universe in a Nutshell* (2001), *The Theory of Everything* (2002), *God Created the Integers* (2005), *My Brief History* (2013), and *Brief Answers to the Big Questions* (2018).

Hawking was a professor of mathematics at the University of Cambridge from 1979 to 2009. Before him, Paul Dirac (1902–1995) had this position for about 20 years (and Newton in 1669 for several years).

At 21, Hawking was diagnosed with MND (motor neuron disease), which paralyzed him until his death. After losing speech, he tried talking through a speech-generating computer (synthesizer) using a single cheek muscle. He died at the age of 76 after living with the MND for 55 years.

Hawking has some scientific theories in Physics and cosmology, including the following three:

- **Blackhole Evaporation Theory:** Gradual releasing of blackhole radiation (Hawking radiation) from a blackhole (also written as a black hole) reduces its mass (M) and energy (E), causing it to die in a long time (in billion years). Based on this theory, blackholes that lose more M than they gain are expected to vanish. Hawking calculated that any blackhole formed in the birth of the Universe with an M of less than 10^{12} kg would have evaporated completely by the present time. [**Hawking** (blackhole) **radiation** is produced by **gravitational vacuum polarization** in a blackhole's event horizon (the outer area of a blackhole), where escaping radiation is *not* a problem.]
- Birth of the Universe theory and end of time theory.

Hawking proved by calculation that time, space, energy, and mass originated from a single dense point, the **Big Bang singularity** (BBS). He also proved that radiation (called **Hawking radiation**) is released from a blackhole's event horizon (the surrounding area of a blackhole). [Hawking radiation is produced by **gravitational vacuum polarization** in a blackhole's event horizon, where the transport of radiations is possible.]

[Despite all scientific achievements, some physicists think that Hawking would *not* have been a household name if he had *not* been sitting in a wheelchair and one of the first synthesizer users.]

Stephen Hawking, taken from Wikipedia

Was the first recipient of Medal for Science Communication for writing about fundamental physics in 2016

His book, *A Brief History of Time* stayed on the best-selling list of Sunday Times for a record-braking number of 237 weeks in the early 1990s

His books for the general reader made him a household name in the entire world since 1990s

A few Hawking's recognitions as a physics writer

H-9

HAZARDS

A hazard is a chemical substance that can cause harm or damage to the human's health, environment, or property. An **incident** (an event caused by a hazard) occurs when a **contact** (exposure) with a hazard occurs. Usually, many hazardous substances are in a typical chemical process plant. For example, vapor in an evaporator is a hazard if it is released and somebody is exposed to it. Similarly, carbon dioxide gas (CO_2) produced in a limekiln is a hazard if it is released and somebody is exposed to it.

[Note: Some use the words **hazard** and **risk** equally, while they are different. A hazard creates *no* risk if there is *no* contact with that hazard. Risk is a probable contact with a hazard, and if there is a certain contact with a hazard, it will create an incident (a negative effect).]

Hazards have several kinds, including the following three (3):

- **Industrial Hazards:** An industrial hazard occurs when a disaster in, say, a chemical process plant occurs. For example, a fire explosion (sudden fire) in an insufficiently ventilated tank containing a liquid that releases CO_2 gas can occur because of the exothermic (releasing-heat) property of the CO_2. Removing CO_2 from the tank by airflow reduces the risk of fire explosion. [Nuclear waste can NOT be recycled (because they are single-use materials).]
- **Environmental Hazards:** An environmental hazard occurs when hazardous waste, such as untreated wastewater from a chemical process plant is discharged into a river. Such action can pollute the environment. [**Pollution** is the action of polluting the environment by a pollutant.]
- **Structural Hazards:** A structural hazard occurs when a structural system, like a bridge, fails.

H-10

HEAD

Study LIQUID HEAD AND LIQUID HEAD LOSS.

H-11

HEAD LOSS

Study LIQUID HEAD AND LIQUID HEAD LOSS

H-12

HEAD PRESSURE

Head pressure (P_h, also called **hydrostatic pressure** or **weight pressure**) is a downward pressure (P) caused by the weight (w) of a fluid (liquid or gas) on a reference surface, like the base (bottom) surface of a tank filled with a liquid. [Note: P_h is different from h (liquid head). P_h is expressed in units of P (in Atm, kPa, or PSI), while h is the height of a liquid above a reference level, expressed in units of length (in m or Ft).]

In a column with liquid, P_h increases with h (height) of the liquid head, so it is greater at the bottom of a column than at its top. Consider a tank containing a liquid with density D under P_{Atm}, as shown in Figure 1. Because the system (the tank and the liquid in it) is in the Earth's gravitational field, which has a gravitational acceleration a_g, the P_h acted on the tank's base area equates to the multiplying product of a_g, D, and h.

$$P_h = a_g.D.h \quad (1)$$

In this equation, D is in kg/m^3, a_g is in m/s^2, and h is in m, so P becomes in (kg.m/s^2)/(m/m^3) = (N)/(m^2), where 1 N/m^2 = 1Pa. Because the system is under an a_g of 9.8 m/s^2 (= 32.2 Ft/s^2), Equation 1 can be written as

$$P_h = 9.8D.h \quad (2)$$

As seen from Equation 1,

The P_h depends on h, so it applies to a point located at any depth of a column of fluid.
The P_h does *not* depend on the area of a container's base, so its equation applies to a column of fluid with a base area as small as a test tube or as wide as a large tank.
The P_h is the result of the weight of the liquid above a reference point. This tells us that at greater depth, more liquid acts downward (a swimmer feels more P as he swims deeper underwater).
The term $a_g.D$ in Equation 1 is called specific weight (w_{Sp}), so the P_h equation can be written as

$$P_h = a_g.D.h = w_{Sp}.h \quad (3)$$

Usually, pressure measuring instruments are calibrated relative to vacuum pressure (P_{Vac}) of zero, so P_h is in absolute pressure (P_{Abs}), as shown in Figure 1. Instead, if an instrument is calibrated relative to P_{Atm}, the P_h will be in gauge pressure (P_G), as shown in Figure 2, so we should add P_{Atm} to Equation 2 to obtain P_h in P_{Abs}.

$$P_h = a_g.D.h + P_{Atm} \quad (4)$$

Based on this equation and because both pressures (P_h and P_{Atm}) act downward, a diver 10.3 m underwater experiences 2 Atm pressure; that is, 1 Atm from atmospheric air and 1 Atm from the weight of water at 10.3 height, where the value 10.3 is called the barometric height. In water, for every 10.3 m (= 33 Ft) increase in h, the P_h increases by 1 Atm (14.7 PSI), as shown in Figure 3. Thus, P_h for each m equates to about 0.1 Atm. This equates to about 10 kPa for each m of h or 0.4 PSI for each Ft of h.

The P_h of a liquid can also be estimated by comparing the density (D) of a given liquid with the density of water (with D = 1000 kg/m^3). Considering this, we can face the following three cases:

- **Liquid Denser than Water:** In this case, the P increase in a column caused by P_h is greater than water. In a column containing mercury (with D = 13600 kg/m^3, a liquid 13.6 times denser than water), the P increase in the column caused by P_h is 13.6 times greater than water. Thus, P_h for 0.76 m (= 29.9 In) increase in depth of mercury equates to 1 Atm (because 10.3/13.6 = 0.76), as shown on the right side of Figure 3.
- **Liquid Lighter than Water:** In this case, the P increase in a column caused by P_h is less than water. For example, in gasoline (C_8H_{18}, with D = 740 kg/m^3, a fuel 0.74 times lighter than water), for every 13.9 m increase in depth, P increases by 1 Atm (because 10.3/0.74 = 13.9).
- **Liquid with the same D as water:** In this case, the P increase is the same as in water. Because the D of fuel oil is almost the same as water, the P increase is the same in fuel oil as in water.

Figure 4 illustrates a liquid flow from tank 1 to tank 2 using head pressure (P_h). To formulize this situation, we have to use h_1 (h at point 1) and h_2 (h at point 2). P_h in gauge pressure (P_G) is given as

$$P_h = a_g.D(h_2 - h_1) \quad (5)$$

Figure 5 illustrates the measurement of P_h with three different pressure-measurement devices. These devices are open to the atmosphere, so they measure P_G.

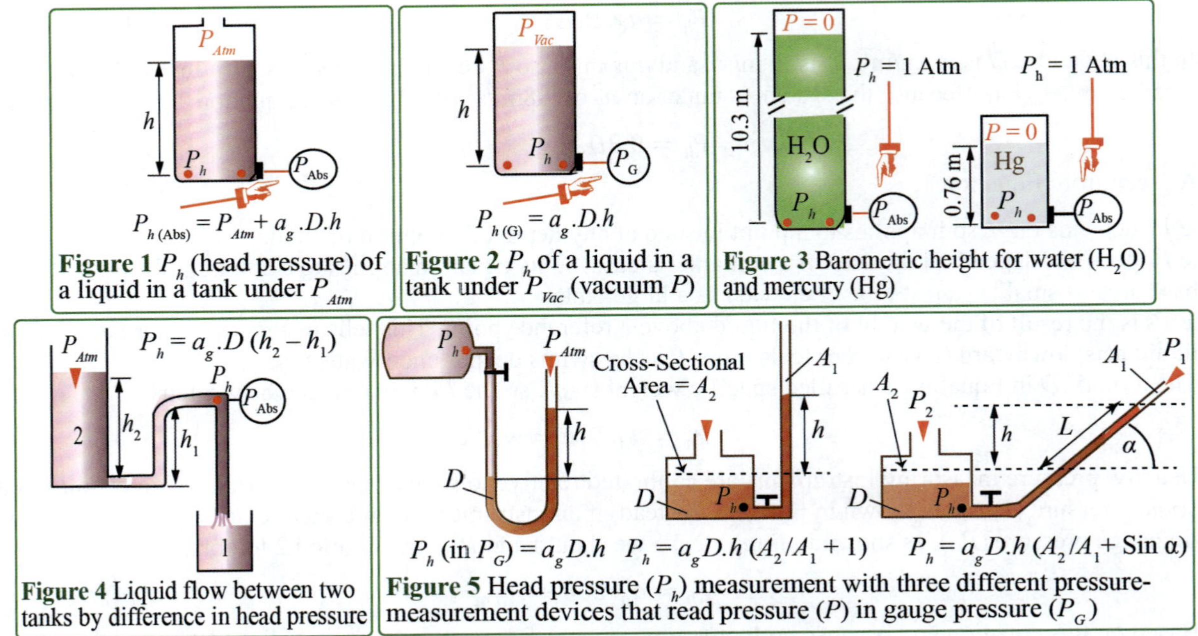

Figure 1 P_h (head pressure) of a liquid in a tank under P_{Atm}

Figure 2 P_h of a liquid in a tank under P_{Vac} (vacuum P)

Figure 3 Barometric height for water (H_2O) and mercury (Hg)

Figure 4 Liquid flow between two tanks by difference in head pressure

Figure 5 Head pressure (P_h) measurement with three different pressure-measurement devices that read pressure (P) in gauge pressure (P_G)

H-13

HEAT

The word heat (Q) is generally used for heat energy (E_Q). Scientists use the word heat to refer to the flow of E_Q from a hotter system to a colder system because of a temperature difference (ΔT) between the systems.

Heat does *not* stay in a system but just flows into or out of it. Defined so, Q is the flow of E_Q, and E_Q is the mover of Q. When heating a substance, its E_Q increases, forcing its molecules to move faster. As a result of an increase in E_Q, heat moves faster. For example, hot water molecules move faster than those in cold water.

It is important to know about the following general terminologies:

- The terms heat (Q) and heat energy (E_Q) are used almost equally in heat transfer processes as enthalpy (H), which numerically gives the **heat value** of, say, steam or vapor at constant pressure ($\Delta P = 0$). Often, however, the term **heat** is used instead of **heat energy**, **enthalpy**, and **enthalpy change**, so $Q \approx E_Q \approx H \approx \Delta H$.
- The terms heat (Q) and temperature (T) are *different*. Heat is a flow of E_Q, whereas T is the measurement of the **hotness** or **coldness** of a system (or a substance), which are that system's molecular properties.

H-14

HEAT ABSORBING AND HEAT-RELEASING PROCESSES

Heat Absorbing Processes

A heat-absorbing process (HA process; also called **endothermic process** or **enthalpy-absorbing process**) is a process during which some heat energy (E_Q, simply heat) is absorbed (taken) from the surroundings (outsides). Evaporation, for instance, is a HA process because the solution under evaporation needs some E_Q to boil to its boiling point temperature (T_{BP}).

Heat Releasing Processes

A heat-releasing process (HR process; **exothermic reaction** or **enthalpy-releasing process**) is when some E_Q is released to the outsides. For example, condensation is a heat-releasing process because when a vapor condenses, some E_Q is released.

The differences between HA (positive or endothermic) and HR (negative or exothermic) processes are:

- In a **HA process**, the entire required E_Q (which has the same meaning as enthalpy change, ΔH) is **added** to the process from an outside source, so E_Q is **positive** (+). When, as said a moment ago, a solution is under evaporation, some E_Q is added to the process from steam, so E_Q is +. Here, the process goes from a lower-energy state to a higher-energy state, resulting in a net positive value ($E_Q > 0$). Therefore, a HA process is also known as the **positive process**. In an **HR process**, instead, some E_Q is **taken** from the process, so E_Q is **negative** (−). When, for example, vapor in a condenser condenses to produce condensate, some E_Q is taken from the vapor under condensation and added to the surroundings, so E_Q is −. Here, the process goes from a higher-energy state to a lower-energy state, resulting in a net negative value ($E_Q < 0$). This is why an HR process is also known as the **negative process**.
- In a **HA process**, the E_Q absorbed by the process from an outside source results in a decrease in the temperature (T) of the surroundings. Instead, in an **HR reaction**, the E_Q released by the process increases the T.

H-15
HEAT ABSORBING AND HEAT-RELEASING REACTIONS

All chemical reactions (simply **reactions**) either absorb or release energy (E), usually in the form of heat energy (E_Q, simply heat). Based on this statement, reactions are classed into two groups, as discussed next.

Heat-Absorbing Reactions

A heat-absorbing reaction (HA reaction; also called **energy-absorbing reaction**, **enthalpy-absorbing reaction**, or **endothermic reaction**) occurs when the reactant (or reactants) absorbs some E_Q from outside. The absorption of E_Q from an outside source tells us that an HA reaction's reactants are at a lower energy state than the products, so the reaction's net result (from the reactant side to the product side) is **positive** ($E_Q > 0$), as E_Q is gradually increasing (see the left side of Figure 1). This is the reason that the HA reactions are also called **positive reactions**. [The change in E_Q, which has the same meaning as enthalpy change (ΔH), is used to form new chemical bonds of the products, where the **new bonds** are *weaker* than the **old bonds**.]

Heat-absorbing (endothermic) reactions are generally written with a **positive** sign as

$$\text{Reactants} + E_Q \rightarrow \text{Products} \quad \text{or} \quad \text{Reactants} \rightarrow \text{Products} + E_Q$$

The decomposition of limestone ($CaCO_3$) in a limekiln is an example of HA (endothermic or positive) reactions, as 1 kg of $CaCO_3$ absorbs 1812 kJ (= 1812 BTU) of E_Q from fuel to be decomposed.

$$1 \text{ kg } CaCO_3 + 1812 \text{ kJ of } E_Q \rightarrow 0.56 \text{ kg } CaO + 0.44 \text{ kg } CO_2$$

Thus, $E_Q = \Delta H = 1812$ kJ/kg (= 780 BTU/Lb), where 1 kJ/kg = 0.43 BTU/Lb.

Heat-Releasing Reactions

A heat-releasing reaction (HR reaction; also called **enthalpy-releasing reaction** or **exothermic reaction**) occurs when the reactant (or reactants) releases some E_Q to the outside. The release of E_Q to an outside source tells us that an HR reaction's reactants are at a higher energy state than the products, so the reaction's net result (from reactant side to product side) is **negative** ($E_Q < 0$), as E_Q is gradually decreasing (see Figure 1). This is the reason that the HR reactions are also called **negative reactions**. [The released E_Q, which has the same meaning as ΔH, is used to form new chemical bonds of the products, where the **new bonds** are *stronger* than the **old bonds**.]

Heat-releasing (exothermic) reactions are generally written with a **negative** sign as

$$\text{Reactants} - E_Q \rightarrow \text{Products} \quad \text{or} \quad \text{Reactants} \rightarrow \text{Products} - E_Q$$

The combustion reaction of hydrogen (H_2) with oxygen (O_2) is an example of HR (exothermic or negative) reactions. When 2 mole of hydrogen reacts with 1 mole of oxygen, 484 kJ (= 208 BTU) of E_Q is released.

$$2\ H_2\ (g) + O_2\ (g) \rightarrow 2\ H_2O\ (g) - 484 \text{ kJ of } E_Q \text{ released per 2 mole of } H_2\ (E_Q = \Delta H = -484 \text{ kJ})$$

Considering the reaction of 1 mole of H_2 with ½ mole of O_2, the released E_Q is half the previous case.

$$H_2\ (g) + \tfrac{1}{2}\ O_2\ (g) \rightarrow H_2O\ (g) - 242 \text{ kJ of } E_Q \text{ per mole of } H_2\ (E_Q = \Delta H = -242 \text{ kJ})$$

[Note that the E_Q released is – 286 kJ if the reaction forms the liquid H_2O, as H_2 (g) + ½ O_2 (g) → H_2O (g)]

As another example of HR reactions, consider the reaction of ethanol (C_2H_5OH) with oxygen (O_2).

$$C_2H_5OH + 3\ O_2 \rightarrow 2\ CO_2 + 3H_2O - 583 \text{ kJ of } E_Q \text{ per mole ethanol}$$

Instead, if we consider the reaction of 1 mole of carbon (C) in ethanol with oxygen (O_2), the released E_Q would be – 1065 kJ/mole of carbon.

$$C + O_2 \rightarrow CO_2 - 1065 \text{ kJ of } E_Q \text{ per mole of carbon}$$

The combustion of a fuel, like natural gas, is another example of HR reactions.

$$CH_4 + 2\ O_2 \rightarrow CO_2 + 2\ H_2O - 890 \text{ KJ/mole}$$

[Note: Both HA and HR reactions only account for a reaction's heat energy (the enthalpy, *H*). The full energy account of a reaction is given by the Gibbs free energy (E_{GF}), which *not* only considers the *H* of the reaction but its *S* (entropy) and *T* (temperature), as well.]

An Example on a Heat-Releasing Reaction

Given: A reaction between two compounds (1 and 2) to form compound 3. The *H* (enthalpy) of the reactants is –1300 kJ, and that of the product is –1500 kJ

Wanted: 1) Enthalpy change (ΔH), 2) Determine if the reaction is a heat-absorbing or heat releasing

$$\Delta H = H_{\text{Products}} - H_{\text{Reactants}} = -1500 - (-1300) = -200 \text{ kJ}$$

Because the result is negative, the reactants have more energy than the products, so the reaction is a heat-releasing (exothermic or negative) reaction.

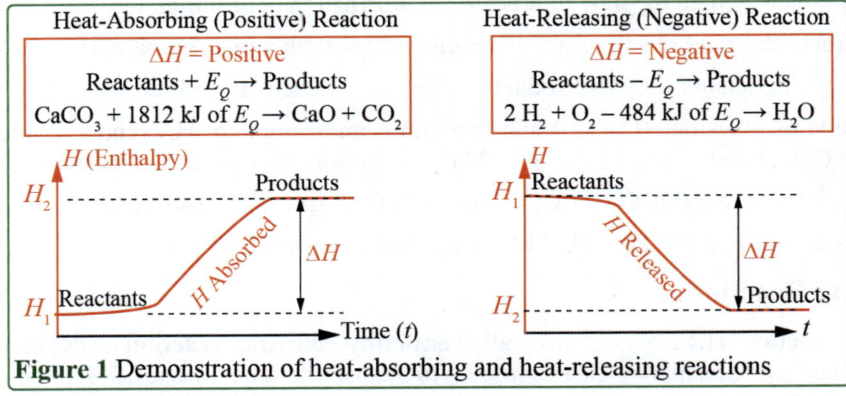

Figure 1 Demonstration of heat-absorbing and heat-releasing reactions

H-16

HEAT BALANCE

Study ENERGY BALANCE.

H-17

HEAT CAPACITY

Study SPECIFIC HEAT CAPACITY.

H-18

HEAT CONDUCTORS AND HEAT INSULATORS

Study THERMAL CONDUCTORS AND THERMAL INSULATORS.

H-19

HEAT CONVECTION

Discussed under the topic HEAT TRANSFER PROCESS.

H-20

HEAT ENERGY

Discussed under the topic of ENERGY AND ITS FORMS.

H-21

HEAT ENERGY RATE

The heat energy rate ($\dot{E}_Q$, simply heat rate) is the amount of heat energy (E_Q, simply heat, Q) per unit time (t, usually in second or hour). The $\dot{E}_Q$ is usually used in heat transfer processes (like evaporation or distillation processes) to refer to the heat energy rate of a warm (or hot) flow, such as steam. The heat energy rates are usually given in kJ/h. [**Specific heat energy rate** is E_Q per unit mass (M) per unit time (t).]

H-22

HEAT ENGINES AND HEAT PUMPS

A heat engine (also called a **steam engine**) and a heat pump operate reversely (see Figures 1, 2, and 3). Both work in the form of a thermodynamic (heat-involving) cycle. If the cycle moves clockwise, it acts as a heat engine to move the heat energy (E_Q) from the hot reservoir to the cold reservoir (see Figure 2). And if the cycle moves counterclockwise, it acts as a heat pump to move the E_Q from the cold reservoir to the hot reservoir (see Figure 3). Both consist of three main elements: 1) Hot reservoir, 2) Working fluid, and 3) Cold reservoir.

The **working fluid** is a fluid that takes the E_Q from the hot reservoir and sends it to the cold reservoir. Most heat engines (like a steam turbine) use steam as the working fluid, while most heat pumps (like a refrigerator) use **refrigerants**. Thus, the behavior of each can be controlled by its working fluid's pressure (P), temperature (T), and volume (V), as indicated by the ideal gas equation.

A heat engine or a heat pump behavior is usually shown in a P-V (pressure-volume) diagram or a T-S (temperature-entropy) diagram. The P-V diagram shown in Figure 4 plots a thermodynamic cycle's P against the cycle's V. The T-S diagram shown in Figure 5 plots T of a hot reservoir T_H and a cold reservoir (T_C) against the cycle S (entropy). The red lines (1 and 3) in the P-V and T-S diagrams show the *isothermic change* (no change in T), the blackline 2 shows isentropic and adiabatic expansion. Blackline 4 shows no change in S. The area in red in the T-S diagram shows the amount of E_Q transferred between the working fluid and cold reservoir (shown as $E_{Q.C}$), and the area in blue shows the amount of work (W)

Heat Engines

A heat engine (also called **steam engine**) converts E_Q (heat energy or simply heat) into E_K (kinetic energy) to perform W_S (shaft work), a useful W (work). A heat engine may get its driving energy from steam, combustion of a fuel, or other sources (like a nuclear reactor). Steam and power production is an example of a heat engine, where a steam boiler gets its E (energy) from the combustion of a fuel to produce steam. A steam turbine converts the steam's E_Q into E_K to perform W_S to run an electric generator, generating electric power (simply **power** or **electricity**).

In a heat engine, the hot reservoir always supplies E_Q, and the cold reservoir always receives E_Q, but *not* the other way round (because the transfer of E_Q is irreversible).

A heat engine's efficiency (E) can be calculated as

$$E = \frac{W}{E_{Q.H}} = \frac{E_{Q.H} - E_{Q.C}}{E_{Q.H}} \quad (1)$$

The W is the engine's useful work (mainly shaft work, W_S), $E_{Q.H}$ is the E_Q of the hot reservoir, and $E_{Q.C}$ is the E_Q of the cold reservoir. The difference in T between the hot and cold reservoirs ($\Delta T = T_H - T_C$) can also determine a heat engine's approximate efficiency (the efficiency is *greater* when the ΔT is *greater*).

$$E = \frac{T_H - T_C}{T_H} \times 100 \quad (2)$$

The efficiency of heat engines is 30% to 90%, depending on their design. Their efficiency is low because they lose some E_Q to their surrounding environment, an effect known as **entropy**.

[Historical Note: When scientists started to use the principles of thermodynamics to develop heat engines in Europe around the 1760s, a scientific event (known as Industrial Revolution) started.]

Heat Pumps

A heat pump (also called a **steam pump**) converts the W_S (shaft work) into the E_K (kinetic energy) to transfer the E_Q (heat energy) from a cold reservoir to a hot reservoir (see Figure 3). While in operation, a heat pump changes the T, phase, or both of a pumping fluid. As a T changer, a heat pump is used in homes to absorb E_Q to decrease T during summer and release E_Q to increase T in winter. As a phase changer, a heat pump is used in a **refrigeration cycle** to evaporate its working fluid (refrigerant) to absorb E_Q from the refrigerator's interior (cold reservoir). And the vapor is then compressed back to the fluid to release E_Q to its exterior (hot reservoir), as shown in the same figure. Thus, a refrigeration cycle is the reverse of a heat-engine cycle.

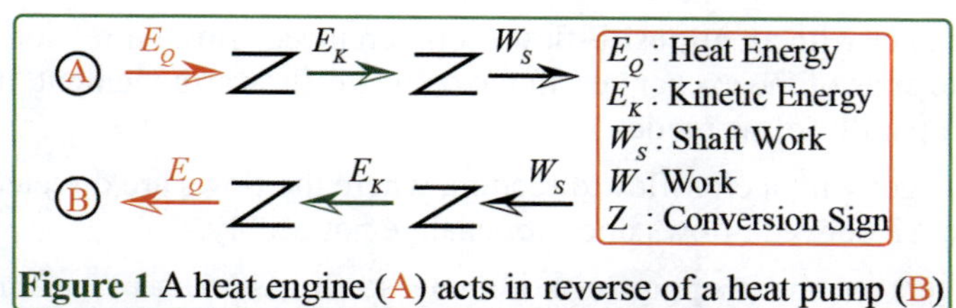

Figure 1 A heat engine (A) acts in reverse of a heat pump (B)

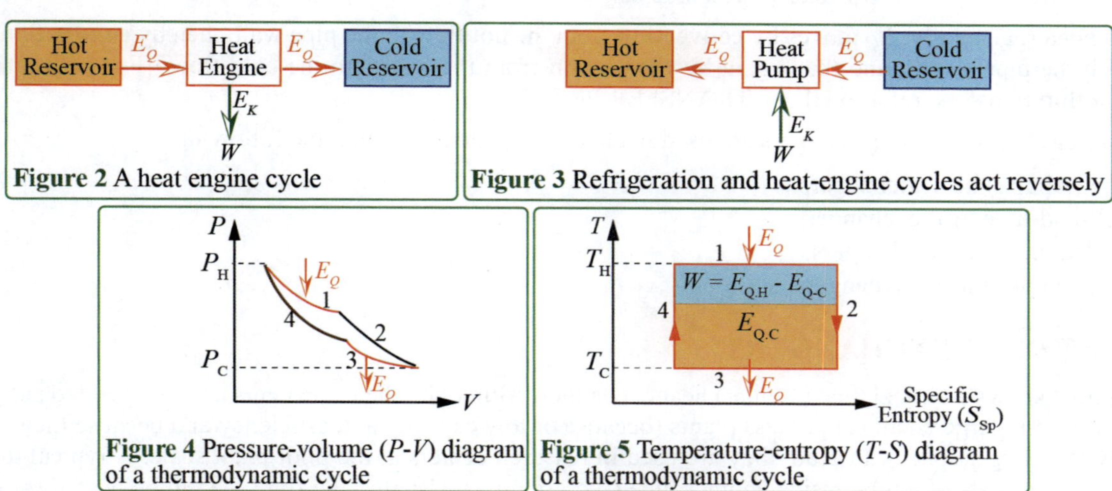

Figure 2 A heat engine cycle

Figure 3 Refrigeration and heat-engine cycles act reversely

Figure 4 Pressure-volume (P-V) diagram of a thermodynamic cycle

Figure 5 Temperature-entropy (T-S) diagram of a thermodynamic cycle

H-23

HEAT EXCHANGERS

A heat exchanger is a device (equipment) for transferring heat energy (E_Q, simply heat and scientifically enthalpy) from a higher-temperature liquid to a lower-temperature liquid or vice versa. Therefore, a heat exchanger can be used for both heating and cooling. A hot medium (usually steam, vapor, or hot condensate) is used as the E_Q source in the heating process, a cold medium in the cooling process, or electric energy in either heating or cooling. [A heat exchanger used in the heating process is generally called the **heater**.]

Knowing the next basic points about heaters is helpful:

- Heaters usually operate under constant pressure ($\Delta P = 0$),
- Heaters are governed by the rules and equations of the heat transfer process,
- Heaters' **capacity** is related to their heat transfer area (A_Q, in m^2), design, and type,
- Heaters with A_Q of 100 to 700 m^2 are usually used in a typical medium-size chemical process plant, and
- In heating a heater, low-pressure steam (or vapor) limits that steam temperature.
- In heaters, the **heat duty** is defined as the heat gained by cold liquid, equating to the heat released by the hot liquid. [For simplicity, heat loss (rather, heat-*not*-used) in a heater is ignored in calculations.]

The direction of the hot and cold flows in a heat exchanger affects its performance (because the heat-transfer process is different when the flows move in parallel or opposite directions). Figure 1 shows an exchanger that operates in a **parallel-flow** (cocurrent-flow) direction, meaning that both cold and hot flows have the same direction. In a parallel flow, the temperature difference (ΔT) between flows is a maximum at their entrance to the exchanger, but it decreases as the flows move forward in the exchanger.

Figure 2 shows an exchanger with an **opposite-flow** (countercurrent-flow) direction, meaning that the hot and cold flows enter at opposite ends of the exchanger. In the opposite-flow arrangement, the ΔT between flows does *not* change as much as in a parallel-flow mode.

Figure 3 shows an exchanger with a crossflow direction, where the flows are directed across the exchanger. In a crossflow exchanger, the ΔT between flows does *not* change noticeably.

[Note: Most heat exchangers operate in **opposite-flow** mode, so we assume here that an exchanger operates in the opposite-flow direction unless otherwise mentioned.]

In a heater, generally, E_Q moves by **convection** from the hot flow to the pipe wall, then by **conduction** moves through the pipe's wall, and then again by **convection** from the wall into the cold flow. [For **convection** and **conduction** transfers, refer to HEAT TRANSFER PROCESS.]

Different types of heat exchangers are used in chemical plants, including the following:

- Tube (tabular) heat exchangers,
- Shell-and-tube heat exchangers,
- Welded plate heat exchangers,
- Gasketed plate heat exchangers.

TUBE HEAT EXCHANGERS

Figure 4 shows a typical tube (tabular) heat exchanger. Although tube exchangers can be operated simply, but are *not* used in large chemical process plants (because of low capacity and efficiency and because they comparatively take larger space). Instead, they are used in research centers at the pilot-plant scale. A typical tube heat exchanger consists of a tube inside another tube (see Figure 4). Usually, the fluid feed to be heated (or cooled) enters the smaller tube, and the heating medium moves between the tubes. However, the location of the target fluid and heating (or cooling) medium can be the opposite.

To become familiar with the value of U_Q (heat transfer coefficient) of heat exchangers, study the following:

- The U_Q of a typical tube exchanger is around 1000 W/(h.m^2°C) = 1000 J/(s.m^2.°C).
- The U_Q of a typical shell-and-tube exchanger is around 1500 W/(h.m^2°C).
- The U_Q of a typical plate exchanger is around 6000 W/(h.m^2°C).

[The typical velocity (V) of the feed in an exchanger can be around 1 m/s.]

SHELL AND TUBE HEAT EXCHANGERS

A typical shell-and-tube heat exchanger (simply **shell exchanger**) consists of a vessel usually 2 to 4 m (= 7.5 to 13 Ft) in diameter and 4 to 7 m in height, depending on its capacity and number of tubes. The vessel can be installed vertically or horizontally. Vertical installation is more common because of lower installation costs and easier tube cleaning. The bottom has a door to make the cleaning or repair easier. The door is sealed with a rubber gasket (above 100°C) and locked with several bolts. The same type of rubber gasket is used for sealing the feed-side header. [The main vessel is usually covered with a 5 cm (= 2 In) insulated material with a thin outer layer of aluminum for preventing heat loss and providing safety.]

The vessel can be considered a large outer pipe (called the **shell**), in which several smaller tubes (called the **tube bundle**) are installed in different rows. Each row consists of an equal number of tubes. For example, a typical tube bundle with 10 rows and 50 tubes in each row has 500 tubes. The distance between centers of adjacent tubes in a tube bundle is called a **pitch**. This arrangement creates longer tube lengths in almost the same space as a tube exchanger. The colder fluid usually flows inside the tubes, and the hotter fluid (usually vapor or condensate) flows outside the tubes, in the shell. In a heater heated with vapor, the target liquid that must be heated flows inside the tubes, and the vapor moves in the shell. This moving arrangement creates a multipass flow for target and heating fluids. While moving, the feed flows from one tube to the next, so its movement changes in each **pass**; for example, two times for an exchanger with two tube passes in a shell. Compared with a single pass mode, the multipass arrangement provides 1) Shorter tube length. 2) Higher heat efficiency. 3) Higher heat transfer coefficient (U_Q). 4) Higher feed velocity. For example, at the same number and size of tubes and feed's flow rate, the velocity (V) of the feed in the tubes of a 2-pass exchanger is almost two times that in a single-pass exchanger (because of the longer tubes length). [Note that high velocity also increases the pressure drop (generally known as pressure difference, ΔP). Note also that feed must be pumped to an exchanger at a moderate velocity (V) of 1 to 2 m/s. This value is about 1 m/s for a typical multipass exchanger.]

Figures 5 and 6 show two heat exchangers with one shell pass and one tube pass (also called **1-1 exchanger**, **single-tube-pass**, or **single-shell pass exchanger**), but one operates in parallel and the other in the counter-flow arrangement. In a 1-1 exchanger, the fluid flowing inside the shell passes from one end to another end of the exchanger only one time. Similarly, the feed flowing inside the tubes passes from one end to the other end, also one time. An 1-1 shell exchanger, thus, may have a limitation because when the tube-side feed flow is divided evenly among all the tubes, as said earlier, U_Q and V on the tube side may be quite low. If the number of tubes is reduced and the length increased so that the V is sufficiently high, the tube length may be too long, which is impractical. Most chemical plants use multipass exchangers with two, four, or more tube passes to use practical tube length while achieving sufficient heat transfer.

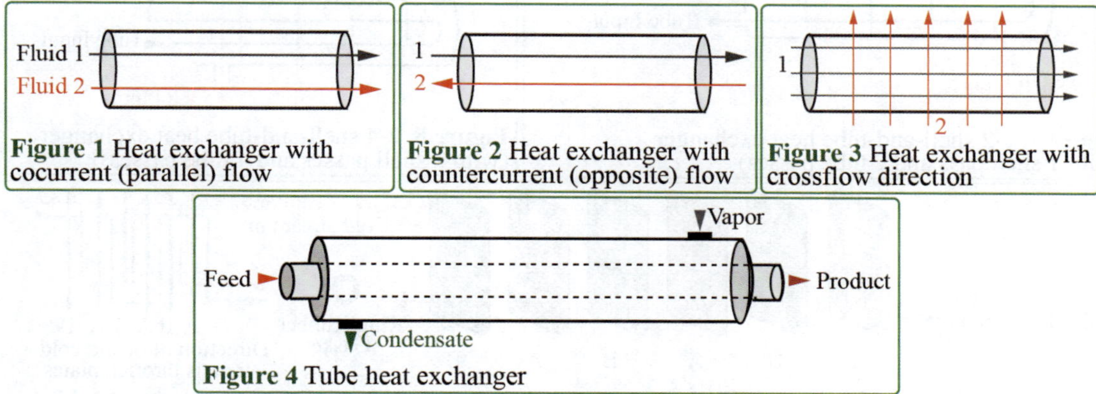

Figure 1 Heat exchanger with cocurrent (parallel) flow

Figure 2 Heat exchanger with countercurrent (opposite) flow

Figure 3 Heat exchanger with crossflow direction

Figure 4 Tube heat exchanger

Figure 7 illustrates a typical **1-2 exchanger** (with one shell pass and two tube passes), and Figure 8 shows a **2-4 exchanger** (with two shell passes and four tube passes). [While more passes provide some advantages, they create higher head pressure drop and higher friction, particularly on exchangers with several tubes per pass. This is, thus, the disadvantage of multipassers.]

The **heating tubes**, with a diameter of 40 to 50 mm (1.6 to 2 In), are placed vertically between two horizontally-placed **plates**. One plate is installed slightly below the top, and the other is placed above the exchanger's base. The areas above and below the tube plates allow the feed to flow. The tube plates have the same number of round holes as the number of the heating tubes. Each hole has a small clearance (about 0.25 mm) with the tubes' outside diameter to allow for rolling the tubes into the plates' holes.

Mostly, the tubes are made of copper brass, but in modern-designed exchangers, stainless steel is used, where the thermal conductivity (K_T) of copper brass is about 110 W/h.m.°C and that of stainless is about 40 W/h.m.°C, where W/h.m.°C = J/s.m.°C. Brass, however, has higher thermal expansion than stainless (with thermal expansion of about 15 µm/m.°C). In addition, brass has the following important advantages:

- Less need for tubes replacement and maintenance,
- Less scaling (incrustation),
- Easier tube cleaning, and
- Low heat resistance.

AISI 430 and 304 are two types of stainless steel used for the tubes. The thickness of the tubes is in the range of 1.2 to 1.6 mm (0.05 to 0.06 In), depending on the type of stainless steel.

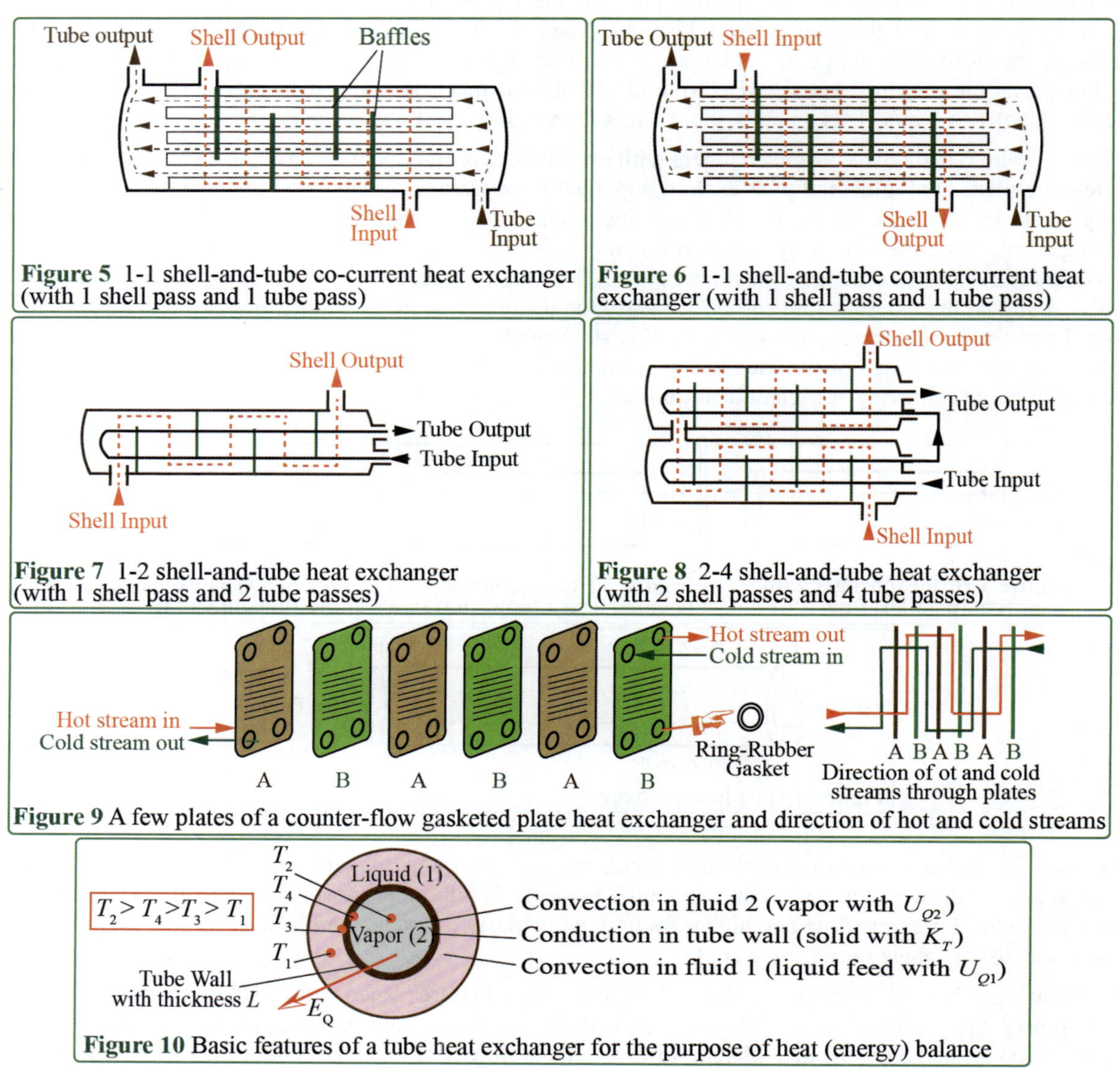

Figure 5 1-1 shell-and-tube co-current heat exchanger (with 1 shell pass and 1 tube pass)

Figure 6 1-1 shell-and-tube countercurrent heat exchanger (with 1 shell pass and 1 tube pass)

Figure 7 1-2 shell-and-tube heat exchanger (with 1 shell pass and 2 tube passes)

Figure 8 2-4 shell-and-tube heat exchanger (with 2 shell passes and 4 tube passes)

Figure 9 A few plates of a counter-flow gasketed plate heat exchanger and direction of hot and cold streams

Figure 10 Basic features of a tube heat exchanger for the purpose of heat (energy) balance

WELDED AND GASKETED PLATE HEAT EXCHANGERS

Heat exchanger manufacturers offer efficient welded and gasketed heat exchangers. The rubber gaskets used to seal the plates of gasketed exchangers are made of different materials to be chosen based on the heating medium's temperature (T). For example, the gaskets made of EPDM (ethylene propylene diene monomer) work satisfactorily up to 150°C. Figure 9 illustrates a typical gasketed plate exchanger consisting of parallel steel plates made of iron or stainless steel. The plates are pressed so that when a set of them are placed next to each other, their corrugations (troughs) create two channels, each having a typical diameter of 10 mm. One channel is used for passing the hot fluid and the other for the cold fluid. A rubber gasket is placed between the flat parts of each corrugated plate, and clamps or bolts tighten the plates to prevent mixing the hot and cold fluids. The groove (corrugation) of the plates improves the following: 1) It moves the feed faster. 2) It creates turbulence flow. 3) It improves the heat transfer. 4) It improves the plates' mechanical strength.

Because placing A and B plates alternately, both cold and hot flows enter different passages. For example, hot fluid between A-B passages and cold fluid between B-A passages, as shown on the right side of Figure 9. The direction of the flow can be in the **parallel** or **opposite** (counter) direction. In an opposite-flow **plate exchanger**, shown in the same figure, the hot and cold flows enter at opposite ends of the exchanger. Narrow spacing between the plates and multiple indirect contacts between the hot and cold flows improves the heat transfer. This makes the plate exchangers have a high heat transfer coefficient (U_Q) of around 6 000 W/(h.m^2°C), about 6 times greater than shell-and-tube exchangers. Other advantages of plate exchangers over shell exchangers are:

- Lower energy use and high processing flow rates (up to 20 t/h),
- Heat transfer area (A_Q) can be increased by adding more plates to the frame,
- Lower weight and less floor area requirement for the same heat-transfer capacity, and
- Lower temperature difference (ΔT) between hot flow at the entrance and cold flow at the exit (this can be as low as 1°C, compared with about 5°C in shell-and-tube heaters).

The disadvantages of plate exchangers, compared with the shell exchangers, are step-outlined next.

- Rubber gaskets are a limiting factor (because they must be replaced occasionally),
- Creation of greater pressure drop (because of narrow space between the plates),
- Limitation on feed's viscosity (maximum viscosity allowed is 1.5 Pa.s), and
- Limitation of high-pressure (high-P uses are *not* recommended).

HEAT BALANCE OF HEAT EXCHANGERS

For the transfer of the heat energy (E_Q, simply heat and scientifically enthalpy) from the hot side to the cold side through the heater's tube wall, the following three steps occur one after the other (see Figure 10):

- Heat transfer by convection (convective heat transfer) from the hot fluid to the tube's wall,
- Heat transfer by conduction (conductive heat transfer) through the tubes' wall, and
- Heat transfer by convection from the tubes' wall to the cold fluid.

The main purposes of heat balancing of a heat exchanger are the calculations of the next quantities.

- Amount of heat energy (E_Q) required for heating a cold fluid,
- Heat transfer area (A_Q) of the exchanger, and
- Mass flow rate ($\dot{M}$) of the feed.

To calculate the rate of heat energy ($\dot{E}_Q$), the following are needed:

- Feed's flow rate and feed's inlet temperature (T_1),
- Product's outlet temperature (T_2), and
- Feed's heat capacity (C_Q).

For heat balancing of a shell-and-tube heater heated with vapor, we consider one of the tubes of a **shell-and-tube heater** and assume that

- The tube is rectangular, and
- The tube outside diameter (d) and length (L) are known.

Further, we assume the following simplifying assumptions:

- Heat-transfer process in the heater involves two separate processes; one process involves the heat transfer of the hot flow, and the other one involves the heat transfer of cold flow;
- Heat capacity (C_Q) is the same for the inlet and outlet flows;
- Heater operates at a steady state (*no* change with time),
- No shaft work is involved in the process,

- No latent heat transfer occurs, and
- No heat loss occurs to outside.

[Because the heat-transfer area (A_Q) of some heat exchangers is made of tubes or pipes, the related calculations are based on either the inside or outside diameter (d) or area (A) of the tubes or pipes. Thus, the choice is usually given because the results of calculations will *not* be the same for both choices. Mostly, outside d is used.]

Now, we can easily apply the heat equation to calculate $\dot{E}_Q$ (rate of heat energy) for the hot and cold flows.

$$\dot{E}_Q = [\dot{M}.\lambda_Q(T_2 - T_1)]_{\text{Hot}} \quad (1)$$

$$\dot{E}_Q = [\dot{M}.\lambda_Q(T_2 - T_1)]_{\text{Cold}} \quad (2)$$

In this equation, $\dot{M}$ is the feed's mass flow rate, C_Q is the specific heat capacity (simply **heat capacity**) of the fluid under heating, T_2 is the product's (output's) temperature, and T_1 is the feed's (input's) temperature. Equations 1 and 2 can be solved together to calculate the $\dot{E}_Q$ (heat-transfer rate).

Calculation of a Heat Exchanger Size

For running a heat exchanger efficiently, its size (heat transfer area, A) is an important factor, where A is the total surface area of the exchanger's tubes. To calculate A, we must know the heat transfer coefficient (U_Q) of the hot fluid and cold fluid entering an exchanger. As shown in Figure 10 and as said a moment ago, the heat transfer in a heater consists of three steps, occurring one after the other. And at a steady-state system, the rates of the total heat transfer must equate to the total of individual steps.

$$\dot{E}_Q = U_{Q2}.A(T_2 - T_4) + K_T.A\frac{T_4 - T_3}{L} + U_{Q1}.A(T_3 - T_1) \quad (3)$$

In this equation, U_{Q2} is the heat transfer coefficient of fluid 2 (vapor), U_{Q1} is fluid 1 (liquid feed), K_T is the thermal conductivity of the solid wall between fluids 1 and 2, and L is the thickness of the tubes.

Equation 3 can be solved to give the next equation.

$$\dot{E}_Q = \frac{T_2 - T_1}{\frac{1}{U_{Q1}.A} + \frac{L}{K_T.A} + \frac{1}{U_{Q2}.A}} \quad (4)$$

The nominator of this equation ($T_2 - T_1$) is the overall **driving force** of the heat-transfer process ($\sum F_D$), and its denominator is the overall heat resistances of the process ($\sum R$).

The overall heat transfer coefficient (U_{QO}) and the **average temperature difference** can be used here to simplify the previous equation.

$$\dot{E}_Q = U_{QO}.A.\Delta T_{Avg} \quad (5)$$

Like U_Q (heat transfer coefficient), the SI unit of U_{QO} is kJ/(s.m^2.ºC), which equates to W/(h.m^2.ºC). The US unit of U_{QO} is Btu/(h.Ft^2.ºF).

SCALING AND SCALE-CLEANING OF HEAT EXCHANGERS

A heat exchanger scaling (also called **fouling**) is a thin layer of **deposits** (scales, incrustation) accumulated during service on its heat transfer area. The substances that cause scaling are generally called the scale-causing salts (SC salts; also called the **limesalt hardness**). Calcium sulfate, magnesium sulfate, and silica dioxide are common examples of the SC salts. They are dissolved at moderate temperatures, staying in the solution even after filtration. During heating, SC salts precipitate (↓) on the heat transfer area because their solubility at the surface temperature (T) is lower than at the bulk (under-the-surface) T. And because they usually have low thermal conductance (K_T), decrease the heat transfer coefficient (U_Q) and, thus, create considerable resistance to the process of heat transfer. During service, the thickness of the **scale layer** (scale-film) gradually increases until the exchanger must be disconnected to clean its tubes (or plates).

The effect of scale-causing salts over time *cannot* be eliminated but can be considerably reduced by using the following actions:

- **Using Scale Inhibitor:** This is usually practiced in different industries at a moderate dosage because a high dosage may create erosion, damaging the heating area.
- **Increasing Velocity of the Feed:** This effectively reduces the scaling, but it is limited because it requires an increase in the heat transfer area. Generally, the heat-exchanger specialists recommend pumping the feed to the exchanger at a moderate velocity of 1 to 2 m/s and *not* lower than 1 m/s.

The development of the **scale layer** (scale film) is an important point. Usually, the scale-buildup process is relatively faster at the start of the operation. But it gets to a stable state when the process parameters (particularly the feed's flow rate and temperature) are maintained. However, the scale layer gets thicker so that the heat-transfer coefficient (U_Q) is affected noticeably. At this time, the following two actions are performed on the affected heat exchanger:

- It is removed from service (often by shutting down the heat-exchanging station), and
- It is cleaned. [Note: The scale-deposit cleaning of the heat exchangers is like the evaporators cleaning, which is discussed, in detail, under the topic of EVAPORATORS.]

H-24

HEAT EXPANSION

Another name for THERMAL EXPANSION.

H-25

HEAT FLUX AND HEAT FLUX RATE

Heat Flux: The heat flux (E_q; in other reference books, q) is the quantity of heat energy (E_Q) that a system transfers with its outside per heat transfer area (A).

$$E_q = \frac{E_Q}{A} \tag{1}$$

For example, heat flux in a heat exchanger is the amount of E_Q (in kJ) per exchanger's A (in m^2), so the SI unit of E_q is kJ/m^2, and its US unit is BTU/Ft^2, where 1 kJ/m^2 ≈ 10.76 BTU/Ft^2.

Heat Flux Rate: The heat flux rate ($\dot{E}_q$, also called **heat-transfer rate**) is defined as the amount of E_Q that a system transfers per heat transfer area (A) per time (t).

$$\dot{E}_q = \frac{E_Q}{A.t} \tag{2}$$

Because heat flux (E_q) equates to E_Q/A, the $\dot{E}_q$ is the time rate of E_q (or E_q/t).

$$\dot{E}_q = \frac{E_Q}{A} \times \frac{1}{t} = \frac{E_q}{t} \tag{3}$$

The SI unit of $\dot{E}_q$ is kJ/s.m^2, equating to W/h.m^2, where W is for watt. The US unit of $\dot{E}_q$ is BTU/s.Ft^2, where 1 BTU/h.Ft^2 = 3.155 = 3.155 kJ/s.m^2 = 3.155 W/h.m^2.

[Note: Some writers abbreviate the term **heat flux rate** to just **heat flux**. In such cases, the given unit of the quantity can determine the writer's purpose. The heat flux is given in kJ/m^2, whereas ***the*** heat flux rate is in kJ/s.m^2 or kJ/h.m^2. Note also that in ChemEng, a dot sign (•) over a symbol indicates a **rate** (time-based) quantity.]

H-26
HEAT OF COMBUSTION

Another name for ENTHALPY OF COMBUSTION.

H-27
HEAT OF CONDENSATION

Another name for ENTHALPY OF CONDENSATION.

H-28
HEAT OF EVAPORATION

Another name for ENTHALPY OF EVAPORATION.

H-29
HEAT OF FREEZING

Another name for ENTHALPY OF FREEZING.

H-30
HEAT OF MELTING

Another name for ENTHALPY OF MELTING.

H-31
HEAT OF REACTION

Another name for ENTHALPY OF REACTION.

H-32
HEAT OF SUBLIMATION

Another name for ENTHALPY OF SUBLIMATION.

H-33
HEAT PUMPS

Discussed under the topic of HEAT ENGINES AND HEAT PUMPS.

H-34
HEAT REACTIONS

A heat (thermal) reaction is a heat-involving chemical reaction (simply **reaction**). Heat reactions are heat absorbing reactions (endothermic reactions) and heat-releasing reactions (exothermic reactions).

H-35
HEAT RELEASING PROCESS

Study HEAT ABSORBING AND HEAT RELEASING PROCESSES.

H-36
HEAT RELEASING REACTIONS

Study HEAT ABSORBING AND HEAT RELEASING REACTIONS.

H-37
HEAT RESERVOIR

A heat reservoir (thermal reservoir) is a thermodynamic (heat-involving) system with a specific heat capacity (C_Q). In industry, a reservoir size does *not* matter to its definition, but in nature, it does. Natural science uses a lake, ocean, or river as a heat reservoir. An ocean is so large that when it is in heat (thermal) contact with another system, its temperature (T) remains unchanged. In another context, an ocean is a source of heat energy (E_Q) that is large enough that when more E_Q is added to it, its T does *not* change, notably.

H-38
HEAT RESISTANCE

Study THERMAL RESISTANCE.

H-39
HEAT TRANSFER AREA

Heat-transfer area (A_Q, where subscript Q is used because heat-transfer area is heat-related) is the total surface area (A), through which the heat (Q, the simplified term for heat energy, E_Q) is transferred from a hotter side to a colder side. For example, in a Robert (tube) evaporator (see EVAPORATORS), A_Q is the total surface area of the tubes. A_Q is particularly important in the performance of an evaporator, a heat exchanger, a crystallizer (refers to a heating crystallizer), or a boiler. In such equipment, A_Q is used to estimate the equipment's capacity. For example, a Robert evaporator's A_Q is around 2000 m^2 (21530 Ft^2). Similarly, in a plate heat exchanger (discussed under Heat Exchangers), A_Q is the total surface area of the plates. [A steam boiler's A_Q can be estimated by its horsepower (HP), where 1 m^2 (= 10 Ft^2) A_Q equates to about 1 HP (0.75 kW).]

In heat-transfer equipment, A_Q is constructed from pipes or plates. In the pipe case, the calculations must be based on its diameter inside or outside area. Thus, the choice is usually given (because the results of calculations will *not* be the same for both choices).

H-40

HEAT TRANSFER BY CONDUCTION

Discussed under the topic of HEAT TRANSFER PROCESS.

H-41

HEAT TRANSFER BY CONVECTION

Discussed under HEAT TRANSFER PROCESS.

H-42

HEAT TRANSFER BY RADIATION

Discussed under the topic of HEAT TRANSFER PROCESS.

H-43

HEAT TRANSFER COEFFICIENTS

A simple name for **convective heat transfer coefficient**, so study CONDUCTIVE AND CONVECTIVE HEAT TRANSFER COEFFICIENTS.

H-44

HEAT TRANSFER PROCESS

BASICS

As an important process unit of ChemEng, heat transfer (thermal transfer) is a heating or cooling process during which the heat energy (E_Q, simply heat) is transferred (absorbed or released) from one part of a system to another part of that system in three ways. 1) By convection in liquids, 2) By conduction in solids, and 3) By radiation in space. The E_Q is transferred between a system's particles (atoms or molecules), caused by the temperature difference (ΔT) between the particles. Instead of ΔT (where T is for temperature), scientists prefer to use $\Delta T/L$ (temperature gradient) as the cause of heat transfer to indicate the length (L) in the direction of heat flow (see Figure 1). So, heat transfer occurs whenever a ΔT exists in a system or between two systems.

[Note: Under this topic, the discussion is about the generalities of the heat transfer process, and under the topic of HEATING PROCESS, the discussion is about the particularities of warming a fluid that is under heating. It is, thus, recommended to study both topics carefully.]

Heat transfer applications are in almost every chemical process plant involved with E_Q. With today's high cost of energy, heat balance (energy balance) on a process in a chemical plant is the only way to judge whether the heat transfers efficiently or *not*.

The heat transfer, in general, has some similarities with the diffusion process because:

- In each of them, the flow moves in a system by convection, conduction, or both.
- Heat transfer occurs by $\Delta T/L$ when one part of a system is at a higher T than another part. Diffusion mostly occurs by $\Delta C/L$ when one part of a phase is at a higher C (concentration) than another part, or one phase is at a higher C than another phase.

For these reasons, heat transfer is also called **heat diffusion**. For the same reasons, some equations related to the heat transfer process and mass diffusion process (simply **diffusion process**) are similar.

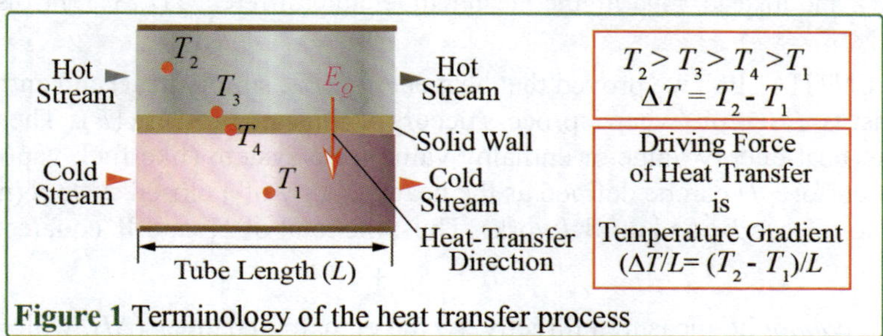

Figure 1 Terminology of the heat transfer process

We will discuss later in detail the three (3) common ways that heat transfers, but for now, let us remember the following brief definition of those heat transfers:

- **Convective heat transfer** (heat transfer by convection)**:** Heat convection transfer the E_Q from one part to another part of a fluid (liquid or gas), so it is a direct (allover) heat transfer by a fluid's molecular movement in the presence of a temperature gradient ($\Delta T/L$).
- **Conductive heat transfer** (heat transfer by conduction)**:** Heat conduction transfers the E_Q from a system's hotter side to the colder side through a heat conductor, so it is an indirect heat transfer that occurs most readily in solids, and to a less extent, in liquids.
- **Radiation heat transfer** (heat transfer by radiation)**:** This is the direct transfer of the E_Q in space from a hotter point to a colder point by electromagnetic radiation. Unlike the other two transfers, radiation is a non-materialistic heat transfer (because it does *not* need a medium to be transferred). The radiation heat travels in a vacuum at the speed of light.

The Sun involves all three ways of heat transfer. Energy comes from its center by conduction, moves to the outer part by convection, and finally moves through space by radiation.

In addition to the change of T, when a heat transfer occurs in a system, the system's E_Q, H (enthalpy), and M (mass) are also changed. Also, the W (work), another type of E (energy), is involved in a heat-transfer process.

How Energy Inverts to Heat Energy: When a fuel (oil, coke, coal, or natural gas) burns, its E (energy) converts to E_Q (heat energy) because the bonds of fuel's molecules break to release E_Q. When, for example, carbon (C) in natural gas reacts with oxygen in the air in the furnace of a boiler, some E_Q is released, which changes the T of the boiler's feedwater by both convection and conduction. This is known as the temperature-change process (sensible heat process). With the continuation of heating, the heated water changes to steam. Thus, a phase-change process (latent heat process) occurs.

When 1 kg carbon in gas burns during the next reaction, 49 000 kJ (= 21 066 BTU/Lb) of E_Q is released (usually shown by a negative sign).

$$1 \text{ kg C} + O_2 \rightarrow CO_2 - 49\ 000 \text{ kJ of } E_Q$$

In general, 1 kg of a substance (say water or stainless steel) needs a different amount of E_Q to raise its T by 1°C. The amount of E_Q needed to raise T of 1 kg of a mass (M) by 1°C at constant P_{Atm} (= 1 Atm), without phase change, is called specific heat capacity (C_Q, simply **heat capacity**). Formulizing M, C_Q, and ΔT (temperature difference between two situations) give us a **heat equation** for a non-phase-change process.

$$E_Q = M.C_Q.\Delta T = M.C_Q(T_2 - T_1) \quad (1)$$

This equation can be written in the rate format as

$$\dot{E}_Q = \dot{M}.C_Q.\Delta T = \dot{M}.C_Q(T_2 - T_1) \quad (2)$$

[Note 1: In a **heat transfer process**, the symbol $\Delta T = T_2 - T_1$ (where $T_2 > T_1$) is generally used to indicate the temperature difference (ΔT) between two fluids (or two systems), like T of the hot flow (T_2) and that of cold flow (T_1), but *not* the temperature change in a single flow.] [Note: In some cases, average temperatures *can*not be used (because T curves are nonlinear), and instead, logarithmic mean temperature difference (LMTD) is used to make the calculations more correct.]

Under the topic of ENTHALPY, we proved that heat energy (E_Q, simply heat) and enthalpy change (ΔH) have the same meaning (that is, $E_Q = \Delta H$) when a process occurs at constant pressure (P). There, we said that enthalpy (H) is the **heat value** (heat-energy value or enthalpy value) of a system (like fuel, vapor, or steam) at constant pressure ($\Delta P = 0$). Therefore, H can be defined as the heat capacity of a closed system (mass *cannot*, but energy can enter or leave it) to release E_Q and do W (work). Thus, the total of E_Q and W equates to the system's total H.

$$H = E_Q + W \quad (3)$$

A system's H or E_Q *cannot* be measured directly, so the enthalpy changes (ΔH, which has the same meaning as the system's E_Q) between two situations (initial state, H_1, and final state, H_2) are measured. For example, a calorimeter can measure the enthalpy change (ΔH, the heat change) of a fuel's combustion reaction.

A closed system's ΔH, which is H in its differential (final-minus-initial) form, in relation to its P and V (volume), is given as

$$\Delta H = H_2 - H_1 = E_Q + W = E_Q + P.V \quad (4)$$

Next, let us answer a question: why in the heat-transfer subjects, the term **enthalpy** (H) is used instead of **heat energy** (E_Q) or **heat** (Q). The answer is that all these three terms have almost the same meaning. But because enthalpy changes (ΔH) of many substances (such as vapor and steam) are determined and given in tables (such as Table 1 in the Table Section of this book), the term **enthalpy** is often used. [This book follows this tradition and uses the words heat energy (simply **heat**) and enthalpy equally to the point that it does *not* conflict with a concept.]

When a closed system's internal energy (E_I), kinetic energy (E_K), and potential energy (E_P) are extensively greater than the other energies, the sum of E_I, E_K, and E_P is usually used as the system's total energy (E_T).

$$E_T = E_I + E_K + E_P \quad (5)$$

At constant pressure ($\Delta P = 0$), the E_K and E_P are negligibly small when a system is in a condensed (liquid or solid), closed, and heat-involving situation, so they can be omitted from the previous equation. We also know that in a thermodynamic system, the E_Q is the greatest energy involved, so the system's total energy is

$$E_T = E_I = E_Q \quad (6)$$

Adding another form of energy, the H (enthalpy), to our discussion, we can write an enthalpy equation for a closed system that is under constant pressure ($\Delta P = 0$).

$$H = E_I + P.V \quad (7)$$

A moment ago, it was said that we *cannot* measure a system's H directly. So, the **changes** (shown by Δ sign) between the **initial enthalpy** (H_1) and **final enthalpy** (H_2) is a more useful quantity than the enthalpy's ordinary value. Thus,

$$\Delta H = H_2 - H_1 = E_I + P.V \quad (8)$$

Considering $E_I = E_Q$ and knowing that the product of $P.V$ is negligible when ΔP or ΔV is too small leads us to the practical form of the Thermodynamic First Law.

$$\Delta H = E_Q \tag{9}$$

As one of the most important equations of heat transfer, this equation tells us the following:

- Energy is conserved, meaning it remains unchanged in a closed system, and
- Change in enthalpy (ΔH) in a closed system equates to the amount of heat transferred (gained or released), shown by E_Q, by that system.

Again, it is helpful to mention that ΔH and E_Q have the same meaning (because it makes the heat-balance calculations much easier).

Equation 9 can also be written for a steady-state open system (M and E can enter or leave the system).

$$E_Q = \Sigma_{Out}\, M.\Delta H - \Sigma_{In}\, M.\Delta H \tag{10}$$

This equation can be written in its rate format.

$$\dot{E}_Q = \Sigma_{Out}\, \dot{M}.\Delta H - \Sigma_{In}\, \dot{M}.\Delta H \tag{11}$$

Here, the $\dot{E}_Q$ is the system's **heat transfer rate** (heat energy per time) that enters (or leaves) the system through its boundary. [Based on Equation 9, if the E_Q of the output flows is greater than that of the input flows, it tells us that E_Q was entered into the system (from outside). And if the E_Q of the output flows is smaller than that of the input flows, E_Q was transferred to the outside (from the system). Thus, the E_Q gets a **positive** sign if heat enters a system and a **negative** sign if heat leaves a system.]

Heat transfer is usually classified into the following four (4) types:

- Convective heat transfer
- Conductive heat transfer
- Combined heat transfer
- Radiation heat transfer

Before discussing the types of heat transfer, it is helpful to mention the main three differences between **convective** and **conductive** heat transfers, as outlined next.

- In convective transfer, the E_Q transfers directly. Instead, in conduction transfer, it does *not* because the heating (or cooling) medium and the fluid to be heated (or cooled) are separated by a solid wall.
- In convective heat transfer, the molecules diffuse much faster than in conductive heat transfer because the molecules of liquids and gases are free to move around. Thus, the fast movement of molecules increases the volume in one part of the liquid, making it less dense, so it rises above denser parts, replacing colder liquid. Repeating this pattern creates **convective** flow.
- In convection, the molecules diffuse collectively, while in conduction, they diffuse individually.

CONVECTIVE HEAT TRANSFER

Convective heat transfer (also called **heat transfer by convection** or simply **heat convection**) is the direct transfer of E_Q from one part of the fluid to the other part of that fluid by the movement of the fluid's molecules. The molecules carry some E_Q that causes heat convection from one place of a phase to another place. If a liquid at T flows along a surface at T_S, heat will transfer to (or away) from that surface.

Listed next are the two major types of heat (thermal) convection:

- **Forced Heat Convection:** It occurs when the movement of a fluid is produced mechanically using a fan or a pump. [A modern boiler station usually uses a draft fan to produce air draft instead of a tall stack.]
- **Natural Heat Convection:** It occurs when temperature difference creates a density difference at different fluid points. Constant changes in the atmospheric air are caused by convection. As air warms up in a region,

its T increases and its D decreases, so the air rises, while cool regions of air fall, so an air draft forms. Natural convection also occurs when a fluid is in contact with a solid surface of different T.

- **Boiling or Condensation:** The heat transfer occurs by convection during boiling or condensation. We can simply observe convection currents when water is heated in a glass pot to boil. As the water warms, its molecules move from the bottom to the top because the temperature difference between the water in the bottom and top of the pot creates the density difference (ΔD) in those points. When the molecules arrive at the top, they cool and go down again. The molecular changes in locations create convection currents, which cause the water's T in the entire pot to become equal.

Consider a simple **tabular heater** (consisting of a tube located inside another tube), as shown in Figure 2, used to heat a liquid using vapor (the heating medium). For transferring the heat from the vapor to the cold liquid through the pipe's wall, the following three steps occur one after the other:

- Transfer of heat (heat energy) from vapor to tube wall by **convection**;
- Transfer of heat through the tube wall by **conduction**, and
- Transfer of heat from tube to liquid by **convection**.

Consider a solid-thin-flat-metal plate to formulize the first step (heat transfer by convection), as shown in Figure 3. Here, the thin plate represents a differential area dA (where d is the differentiation sign) of a small section of a heating plate in a plate heater. Further, assume that the plate at temperature T_1 is in contact with **vapor** at T_2. Because T_2 is greater than T_1, heat flows from the vapor to the plate's surface and the liquid.

The heat transfer rate from vapor to the plate is a function of the plate's surface area (A) and temperature difference between vapor and plate, so $\Delta T = T_2 - T_1$.

When the heat energy (E_Q) transfers from a solid wall to a fluid, the heat transfer rate ($\dot{E}_Q$), heat transfer area (A, the area through which convection occurs), and the driving force of the transfer ($\Delta T = T_2 - T_1$) are related through a proportionality coefficient, known as the **convective heat transfer coefficient** (simply heat transfer coefficient, U_Q).

$$\dot{E}_Q = U_Q.A.\Delta T = U_Q.A(T_2 - T_1) \qquad (12)$$

In this equation (called **convective heat-transfer equation**), T_2 is the T of hot flow (vapor), and T_1 is the T of warm flow (liquid) leaving the heater. Temperatures are in °C, the A (area) is in m^2, and the U_Q (the fluid's heat-transfer coefficient under heating) is in kJ/(s.m^2.°C), so the $\dot{E}_Q$ becomes in kJ/s.

As a numerical example, consider an evaporator. E_Q (the amount of heat transfer) from the steam to the liquid under evaporation depends on the evaporator tubes' U_Q (say, 1400 kJ/m^2.°C), tubes A (say, 2000 m^2), ΔT between the steam (say, 125 °C), and the liquid at boiling (say, 95°C under vacuum), so $\Delta T = 125 - 95 = 30$°C. Substituting these values in the convective heat equation results in an E_Q of 84×10^6 kJ.

As another example, consider a person's body. E_Q from the person (the system) to a room (the outside) depends on U_Q (for a human's body, about 7 kJ/m^2.°C), the total area of the person's body (say, $A = 2$ m^2), and ΔT between the person's body (say, 30°C) and the room temperature (say, 25°C), so $\Delta T = 30 - 25 = 5$°C and E_Q from the person to the outside will be $7\times2\times5 = 70$ kJ.

Example 1 on Heat Transfer

Calculate the heat-transfer rate ($\dot{E}_Q$) from heating medium to the tubes of a small pilot-plant heater for heating a liquid with vapor by convection when knowing the following data:

Vapor temperature (T_2)	110°C
Tubes-surface's temperature (T_1)	30°C
Heat transfer area	1 m^2
Vapor heat-transfer coefficient (U_Q)	10 kW/h.m^2.°C

$$\dot{E}_Q = U_Q.A(T_2 - T_1) = 10(110 - 30) = 800 \text{ kW/h}$$

CONDUCTIVE HEAT TRANSFER

Conduction heat transfer (**heat transfer by conduction** or simply **heat conduction**) is an indirect transfer of heat energy (E_Q) from a hotter side of a system to a colder side of that system (or another system) through a heat conductor by the system's molecular interactions. Heat-transfer equipment, in which E_Q is transferred by conduction, is so built that the colder fluid is separated from the heating medium by a solid wall.

In gases and most liquids, thermal conduction occurs as the molecules transfer E_Q to their neighboring molecules. In conducting solids, conduction occurs by the fast movement of free electrons and collision between them. And in insulating solids, instead, the absence of free electrons notably slows the heat-transfer process.

Unlike heat convection, heat conduction is *not* a direct-contact transfer because the heating (or cooling) medium and the fluid to be heated (or cooled) are separated by a solid wall. Heat transfer from a heating medium to a cold liquid through a heater's solid-metal wall is an example of heat transfer by conduction. [Heat transfer by conduction is *partly* responsible for overall heat transfer in a heater because both convection and conduction participate in its overall heat transfer. Thus, a heat-transfer device (like a heat exchanger, an evaporator, or a condenser) partly operates by conduction and convection.]

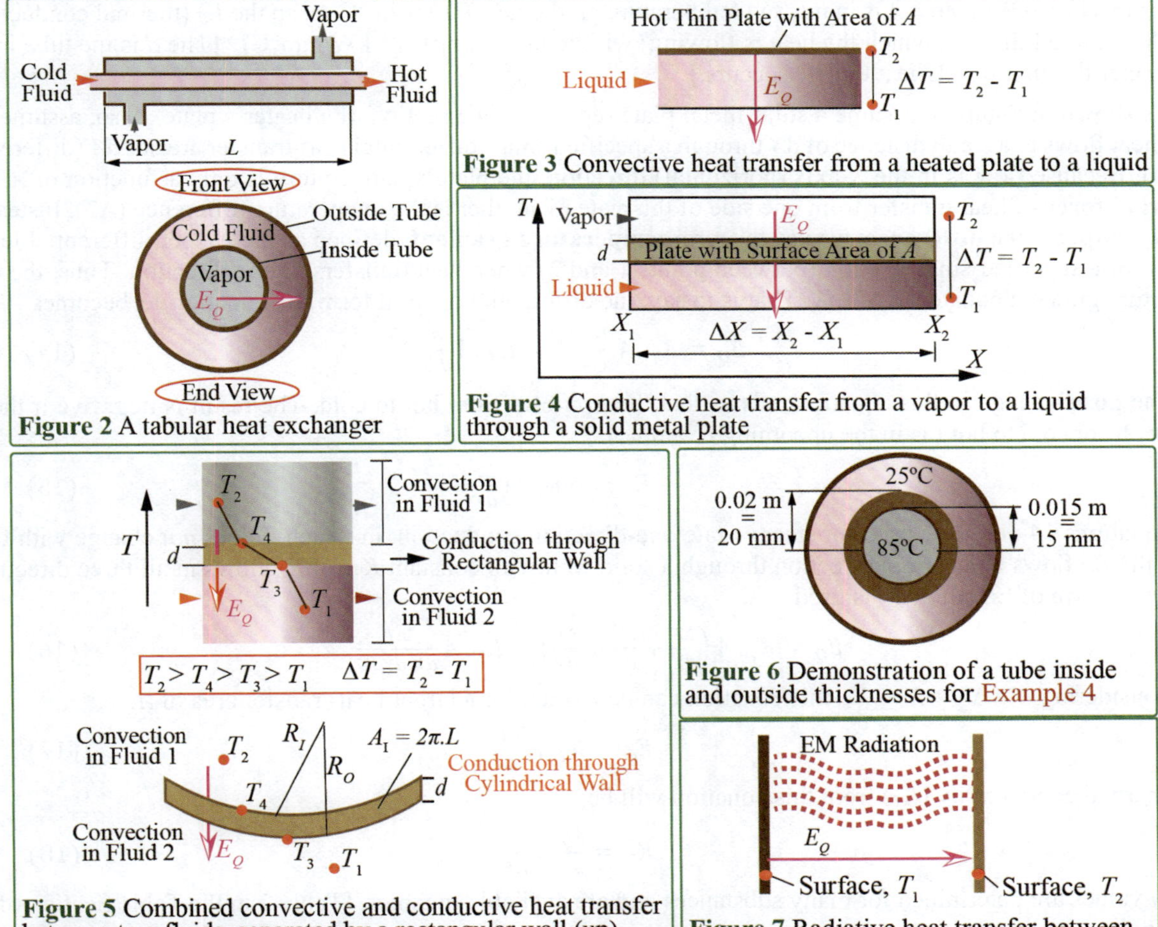

Figure 2 A tabular heat exchanger

Figure 3 Convective heat transfer from a heated plate to a liquid

Figure 4 Conductive heat transfer from a vapor to a liquid through a solid metal plate

Figure 5 Combined convective and conductive heat transfer between two fluids, separated by a rectangular wall (up) and a cylindrical wall (down)

Figure 6 Demonstration of a tube inside and outside thicknesses for Example 4

Figure 7 Radiative heat transfer between two surfaces

The rate at which E_Q is conducted varies from substance to substance. Most metals are good thermal conductors. For example, copper with thermal conductivity (K_T) of about 400 W/h.m.°C (where W/h.m.°C = J/s.m.°C) transfers E_Q better than stainless steel with K_T of about 40 W/h.m.°C. Instead, some materials (like fiberglass with thermal conductivity of almost zero) do *not* transfer the heat, so-called thermal insulators.

During heating a liquid in a heater, the amount of heat transferred by conduction through the tubes depends on the following two:

- **Contact area** (A) between the tube's solid wall and the liquid, and
- **Temperature difference** (ΔT) between the heating medium and the liquid ($\Delta T = T_2 - T_1$), where T_2 is the temperature for the **heating medium** (like vapor), and T_1 is T of liquid at its bulk.

The **conduction heat transfer rate** ($\dot{E}_Q$), the area through which heat conduction occurs (A), and the **driving force** of conduction ($\Delta T/L$ = temperature gradient) are related through a proportionality coefficient, which is called the **conductive heat transfer coefficient** (K_T, simply **thermal conductivity**).

$$\dot{E}_Q = K_T.A\frac{\Delta T}{L} = K_T.A\frac{T_2-T_1}{L} \quad (13)$$

In this equation, known as the Fourier's heat conduction equation or **conductive-heat-transfer equation**, the $\dot{E}_Q$ is in kJ/s = kW/h, area A is in m^2, and temperature gradient ($\Delta T/L$) is in °C/m, so the K_T (thermal conductivity of the material through which the heat is flowing) will be in kJ/s.m.°C (= kW/h.m°C). [The d is the tube inside diameter through which heat transfer occurs.]

As shown in Figure 4, assume a solid-metal plate representing a section of a heater's plate. Also, assume that the heat flows to a small distance of dX through a specified small-differential heat-transfer area of dA (differential area). Because flow is in the X-axis (horizontal) direction, the plate's temperature is only a function of X. The **driving force** of heat transfer from one side of the plate to another is the temperature difference (ΔT). Instead of term **temperature difference**, we use the term **temperature gradient**, defined as the ΔT per differential length (dX) for a specified-small section (between points 1 and 2) when heat transfers in one direction. Thus, the temperature gradient equates to $\Delta T/dX$. That is to say, the differential form (d form) of Equation 13 becomes

$$\dot{E}_Q = K_T.A\frac{T_2-T_1}{X_2-X_1} = K_T.A\frac{\Delta T}{dX} \quad (14)$$

The **positive** sign in this equation tells us that the E_Q flows from hot to cold. The result is **negative** if the E_Q flows from cold to hot (as in the upcoming Example).

$$\dot{E}_Q = -K_T.A\frac{\Delta T}{dX} \quad (15)$$

Equations 14 or 15 are used for steady-state one-direction conduction, in which T does *not* change with time, and the E_Q flows in a certain direction through a solid wall with constant K_T. If E_Q flows in all three directions, the next form of Equation 14 is used.

$$\dot{E}_Q = K_T.A\left(\frac{\Delta T}{dX} + \frac{\Delta T}{dY} + \frac{\Delta T}{dZ}\right) = K_T.A\frac{\Delta T}{dX.dY.dZ} \quad (16)$$

Considering $L = \Delta X = X_2 - X_1$, this equation can be written for a larger heat-transfer area of A.

$$\dot{E}_Q = K_T.A\frac{\Delta T}{L} \quad (17)$$

Thermal conductivity (K_T) from this equation will be

$$K_T = \frac{\dot{E}_Q}{A} \times \frac{L}{\Delta T} \quad (18)$$

K_T values are determined for many substances and are available in tables. [Table 7 in the Table Section of the book gives K_T for some substances.]

Example 2 on Heat Transfer

Calculate the heat transfer rate ($\dot{E}_Q$) per hour (h) of a stainless-steel plate heater, which uses vapor to heat a liquid. The following data are known:

Exchanger's heat-transfer area (A)	100 m^2
Exchanger-plate's thickness (L)	1 mm (= 10^{-3} m = 0.04 In)
Vapor's temperature (T_2)	110°C (= 230°F)
Liquid's temperature (T_1)	40°C (= 104°F)
Stainless-steel's thermal conductivity (K_T)	34 W/(h.m.°C)

$$\dot{E}_Q = -K_T.A\frac{T_2-T_1}{L} = -(34 \times 100)\frac{110-40}{10^{-3}} = (-3400)(70 \times -10^3) = 2.2 \times 10^8 \text{ W/h} = 2.2\times10^5 \text{ kW/h} = 2.2\times10^5 \text{ kJ/s} = 8 \text{ BTU/h}$$

The positive result shows that heat flows from hot to cold (from 110°C to 40°C).

Example 3 on Heat Transfer

Calculate the heat transfer rate ($\dot{E}_Q$) in 1 h of a small distillation column with a copper kettle, placed over a gas flame when we know the following:

Kettle's diameter (d)	200 mm (= 0.2 m = 8 In)
Kettle-wall's thickness (d)	1 mm (= 10^{-3} m = 0.04 In)
Kettle's surface temperature (T_2)	102°C (= 216°F)
Copper's thermal conductivity (K_T)	360 W/(h.m.°C)

$$A = \pi\frac{d^2}{4} = 3.14\frac{0.2^2}{4} = 3.14 \times 10^{-2} \text{ m}^2$$

The temperature in the kettle is the same as boiling water (100°C), so

$$\dot{E}_Q = \frac{E_Q}{t} = \frac{E_Q}{1} = -K_T.A\frac{T_2-T_1}{d} = -(360 \times 3.14 \times 10^{-2})\frac{102-100}{10^{-3}} = 22608 \text{ W/h}$$

COMBINED CONVECTIVE AND CONDUCTIVE HEAT TRANSFER

Combined (multi-step) heat transfer occurs by convection and conduction. During the transfer of the heat from a hot fluid to a cold fluid in a tube heat exchanger through the wall of the tubes, the following **one-after-the-other steps** occur:

- First convective heat transfer from the hot fluid to the tube's wall,
- Conductive heat transfer through the tubes' wall, and
- Second convective heat transfer from the tubes to the cold fluid.

Knowing that "if there is a flow, heat transfer occurs by convection and if there is *no* flow, the transfer occurs by conduction" helps us derive equations for a three-step heat-transfer process. With this statement, the E_Q transfers from fluid 1 (say, vapor) to the solid wall by convection. Then, it moves through the wall by conduction. And finally, it moves from the wall to fluid 2 (cold fluid under heating) by second convection.

Referring to Figure 5 and considering $T_2 > T_4 > T_3 > T_1$, the heat transfer rate at a steady-state flow through a three-step process must equate to each other. We also consider U_{Q1} as the heat transfer coefficient of fluid 1 and U_{Q2} as that of fluid 2, A_I as the area through which the **inside** (first step) **convective transfer** occurs, and A_O as that through which the **outside** (third step) **convective transfer** occurs, and A as the wall's area through which the **conductive transfer** (second step) occurs. We can now add the convective-heat-transfer equation (Equation 12) twice and the conductive-heat-transfer equation (Equation 13) once to obtain the equation for the entire steps.

$$\dot{E}_Q = U_{Q1}.A(T_2 - T_4) + K_T.A\frac{T_4-T_3}{L} + U_{Q2}.A(T_3 - T_1) \qquad (19)$$

After canceling out the same temperatures, the combined heat transfer equation is obtained.

$$\dot{E}_Q = \frac{T_2 - T_1}{\frac{1}{U_{Q1}.A} + \frac{L}{K_T.A} + \frac{1}{U_{Q2}.A}} = \frac{\sum F_D}{\sum R} \quad (20)$$

The nominator of this equation ($T_2 - T_1$) is the overall **driving force** of the process ($\sum F_D$, the sum of the forces for individual steps), and its denominator is the overall resistance of the process ($\sum R$, the sum of the resistances for individual steps).

[Equation 20 is like Equation 8, given under MEMBRANE SEPARATION PROCESS. This tells us that the heat and mass transfer processes have some common generalities.]

Based on Equation 20, when the convective outside transfer through a liquid is very slow, the U_{Q2} is small, and the resistance ($1/U_{Q2}.A$) is large so that the slow rate will limit the heat transfer.

When the wall is **cylindrical** (see the bottom of Figure 5), we must use the next quantities in Equation 2. The tube outside radius (R_O), the tube inside radius (R_I), tube outside surface area (A_O), the tube inside surface area (A_I), and tube wall surface area ($A_W = 2\pi.L$, where L is the heater's length).

$$\dot{E}_Q = \frac{T_2 - T_1}{\frac{1}{U_{Q1}.A_I} + \frac{Ln\frac{R_O}{R_I}}{2K_T.\pi.L} + \frac{1}{U_{Q2}.A_O}} \quad (21)$$

The last three equations show that the heat transfer increases as the overall resistances decrease. For this reason, the following are industrially practiced:

- Tubes of heat exchangers and evaporators are metals with high thermal conductivity.
- Tubes are cleaned when deposited (because scale increases resistance to heat transfer).

We can simplify Equations 20 and 21 and write a general heat-transfer equation based on the overall heat transfer coefficient (U_{QO}, where subscript O is for overall), the tubes' area (A), and the temperature difference (usually in ordinary average).

$$\dot{E}_Q = U_{QO}.A(T_2 - T_1) \quad (22)$$

This equation is the basic heat-transfer equation, which includes U_{QO}, so it can be used to calculate the amount of heat transfer rate ($\dot{E}_Q$) and heat transfer area (A) of a heat exchanger.

From Equation 22, we can write the following equation:

$$\dot{E}_Q = \frac{T_2 - T_1}{\frac{1}{U_{QO}.A}} \quad (23)$$

From this and Equation 21, we obtain an equation for overall resistances (the reciprocal of overall heat transfer coefficients) when the wall is cylindrical, and calculations are based on the wall's **outside area** (A_O).

$$\frac{1}{U_{QO}.A_O} = \frac{1}{U_{Q1}.A_I} + \frac{Ln\frac{R_O}{R_I}}{2K_T.\pi.L} + \frac{1}{U_{Q2}.A_O} \quad (24)$$

Because the selection of area for calculation of U_{QO} is arbitrary, we can write a similar equation when the area is selected based on the wall's **inside area** (A_I), so Equation 23 changes to,

$$\frac{1}{U_{QO}} = \frac{R_O}{U_{Q1}.R_I} + \frac{R_O.Ln\frac{R_O}{R_I}}{K_T} + \frac{1}{U_{Q2}} \quad (25)$$

Study the next Example as an application for this equation.

Example 4 on Heat Transfer: Calculate the overall heat transfer coefficient (U_{QO}) and heat-energy rate ($\dot{E}_Q$) of a small heater with stainless steel tubes (shown in Figure 6) for heating a liquid feed,

Liquid temperature at entrance (T_1)	25°C (= 77 °F)
Liquid desired temperature at exit (T_2)	85°C (= 185 °F)
Liquid first (inside) convective heat transfer coefficient (U_{Q1})	10 W/(h.m^2.°C)
Liquid second (outside) convective heat transfer coefficient (U_{Q2})	100 W/(h.m^2.°C)
Tubes thermal conductivity (K_T)	40 W/(h.m.°C)
Tubes outside radius (R_O)	0.02 m (= 20 mm = 0.8 In)
Tubes inside radius (R_I)	0.015 m (= 15 mm = 0.6 In)
Tubes length (L)	1 m (= 1000 mm = 40 In)

We try here to calculate U_{QO} based on the tube's **outside** area. We cancel area terms from Equation 23, except A_I (area of transfer based on inside area), and substitute A_Q with $2\pi.R_O.L$.

$$\frac{1}{U_{QO}} = \frac{R_O}{U_{Q1}.R_I} + \frac{R_O.Ln\frac{R_O}{R_I}}{K_T} + \frac{1}{U_{Q2}} = \frac{0.02}{10\times0.015} + \frac{0.02Ln\frac{0.02}{0.15}}{40} + \frac{1}{100} = 0.133 + 0.00014 + 0.01 = 0.144$$

$$U_{QO} = \frac{1}{0.144} = 6.94\ \text{W/(h.m.°C)}$$

For calculation of $\dot{E}_Q$, we use the basic heat-transfer equation and outside wall area (A_O).

$$\dot{E}_Q = U_{QO}.A_O(T_2 - T_1) = 6.94 \times 2\pi.L.R_O(85 - 25) = 43.58 \times 1 \times 0.02 \times 60 = 52.3\ \text{W/h}$$

If wanting to calculate the U_{QO} based on the tube's **inside** area, we use Equation 24 and cancel area terms from the equation and substitute A_O with $2\pi.R_I.L$. The modified equation for the outside case is

$$\frac{1}{U_{QO}} = \frac{1}{U_{Q1}} + \frac{R_I.Ln\frac{R_O}{R_I}}{K_T} + \frac{R_I}{U_{Q2}.R_O} = \frac{1}{10} + \frac{0.015\times Ln\frac{0.02}{0.015}}{40} + \frac{0.015}{100\times0.02} = 0.1 + 0.000107 + 0.0075 = 0.108$$

$$U_{QO} = \frac{1}{0.108} = 9.26\ \text{W/(h.m.°C)}$$

$$\dot{E}_Q = U_{QO}.A_I(T_2 - T_1) = 9.26 \times 2\pi.L.R_I(85 - 25) = 58.15 \times 1 \times 0.015 \times 60 = 52.3\ \text{W/h}$$

Note that both ways give the same $\dot{E}_Q$, regardless of whether A_O or A_I is used.

RADIATION HEAT TRANSFER

Heat transfer by radiation (also called **thermal radiation**) transfers heat from one system to another by electromagnetic radiation (EM radiation or EM waves), as shown in Figure 7. The EM waves can travel through a vacuum and a materialistic medium. The Sun's heat energy is transferred to the Earth through outer space (the vacuum) by radiation. Similarly, the heat from a home's fireplace is transferred by radiation.

When EM radiations hit a system's surface, they convert to heat energy (E_Q), so the surface releases thermal radiation. When a surface radiates thermal radiation to the environment around it, the environment also radiates E_Q back to that surface, and the net heat transfer is the difference between these two values. For example, when we are in the Sun, we feel warmer than in the shade because our body (the system) receives more E_Q from sunlight than it gives away. The heat transfer rate by radiation from a given surface to its surroundings can be estimated by the Stefan-Boltzmann equation:

$$\dot{E}_Q = \varepsilon.K_{SB}.A.T^4 \tag{26}$$

In this equation, ε is the emissivity of a given surface (unitless), K_{SB} is the Stefan-Boltzmann constant (a proportionality constant equal to 5.67×10^{-8} W/m^2.K^4 = 5.67×10^{-8} W/m^2.°C^4), A is the cross-sectional area from which radiation occurs (in m^2), and T is the surface's temperature in K (Kelvin) or °C. The fourth power of T tells us that the thermal radiation from a surface is *not* large at low temperatures, such as room temperature (around 25ºC or 77 ºF). We can see the thermal radiation of a hot system with **night glasses**. If the thermal radiation is strong, the system's T increases to a high level, so we can even observe the radiation with our eyes.

H-45

HEAT TRANSFER RATE

The heat transfer rate ($\dot{E}_Q$) of a system is the amount of heat energy (E_Q, or enthalpy change) that the system transfers with its outside per time (t).

$$\dot{E}_q = \frac{E_Q}{t} \quad (1)$$

The SI unit of the $\dot{E}_Q$ is kJ/s (= W/h), where J is for Joule and W is for Watt, and its US unit of the $\dot{E}_Q$ is BTU/s.

H-46

HEATERS

Discussed under HEAT EXCHANGERS.

H-47

HEATING PROCESS

BASICS

As a process unit of ChemEng, heating (warming) is a heat transfer process performed in a **heater** (a heat exchanger used for heating purposes) to increase the temperature (T) of a fluid (a liquid or a gas) using heat energy (E_Q, simply heat) of a heating medium (like vapor). In a chemical process plant, a liquid feed is heated in the heating station using a lower-pressure vapor (water vapor). Although vapor is the main source of E_Q, low-pressure steam or hot condensate is also used in some chemical plants. Choice of heating sources is important because it affects E_Q use of the heating station. In chemical plants with a multiple-effect evaporating station, the vapor bleeds from individual effects are used for heating. [For high-heat-demanding stations, a **two-stage heating method** is used. In the first stage, the feed is heated with a lower-T vapor, and then the output from the first stage is heated in the next step with a higher-T vapor.]

The enthalpy change ($\Delta H = E_Q$) occurring during the heating process is known as the temperature-change enthalpy (sensible enthalpy or non-phase-change enthalpy) because it does *not* change the fluid's phase but just changes its T. Heating, therefore, is a sensible heat process (non-phase change process).

[Note that we talk about the particularities of the heating process under this topic. It is, thus, recommended to study the topic of HEAT TRANSFER PROCESS, which talks about the generalities of heat transfer (absorption or releasing of heat energy). Note also that the terms **heat energy** (E_Q) and **enthalpy change** (ΔH) used here have the same meaning when a process occurs at constant pressure (P). However, the term heat is often used instead of heat energy and enthalpy.]

In chemical plants, the heating process is widely used to transfer heat between two flowing streams (flows) with different temperatures (see Figure 1). For example, it is used in connection with the evaporation process. In this way, the feed, before being pumped to the evaporating station, is heated in the heating station to increase the feed's T to nearly its boiling point temperature (T_{BP}). The feed preheating saves E_Q used in the evaporating station (because all the steam's E_Q is used for evaporation).

Heating differs from evaporation because, in heating, the E_Q only changes the liquid feed's T but *not* its phase. In evaporation, instead, the E_Q *not* only changes the feed's T but converts a portion of it to vapor, so evaporation is both the T change process and phase change process.

To transfer E_Q from the vapor to the liquid feed under heating through the tubes' wall, a driving force, namely a temperature difference (ΔT), between the vapor and the feed ($\Delta T = T_V - T_L$) must exist. When this is met, the following three steps take place one after the other:

- Transfer of heat (heat transfer) from vapor to pipe's solid wall by convection,
- Transfer of heat through the pipe's solid wall by conduction, and
- Transfer of heat from pipe to liquid feed by convection.

[Heat transfer by convection and conduction are discussed under HEAT TRANSFER PROCESS.]

TEMPERATURE PROFILE IN A HEATER

Heat transfer in a **heater** (a heat exchanger used for heating) can be defined as the transfer of E_Q (heat energy) between a heating medium (like vapor) and a liquid feed through the heater tubes' wall. During heating, the E_Q constantly transfers (flows) in the vapor by **convection**, through the wall by **conduction**, and in the cold feed by **convection**, so a combined heat transfer occurs (see Figure 1).

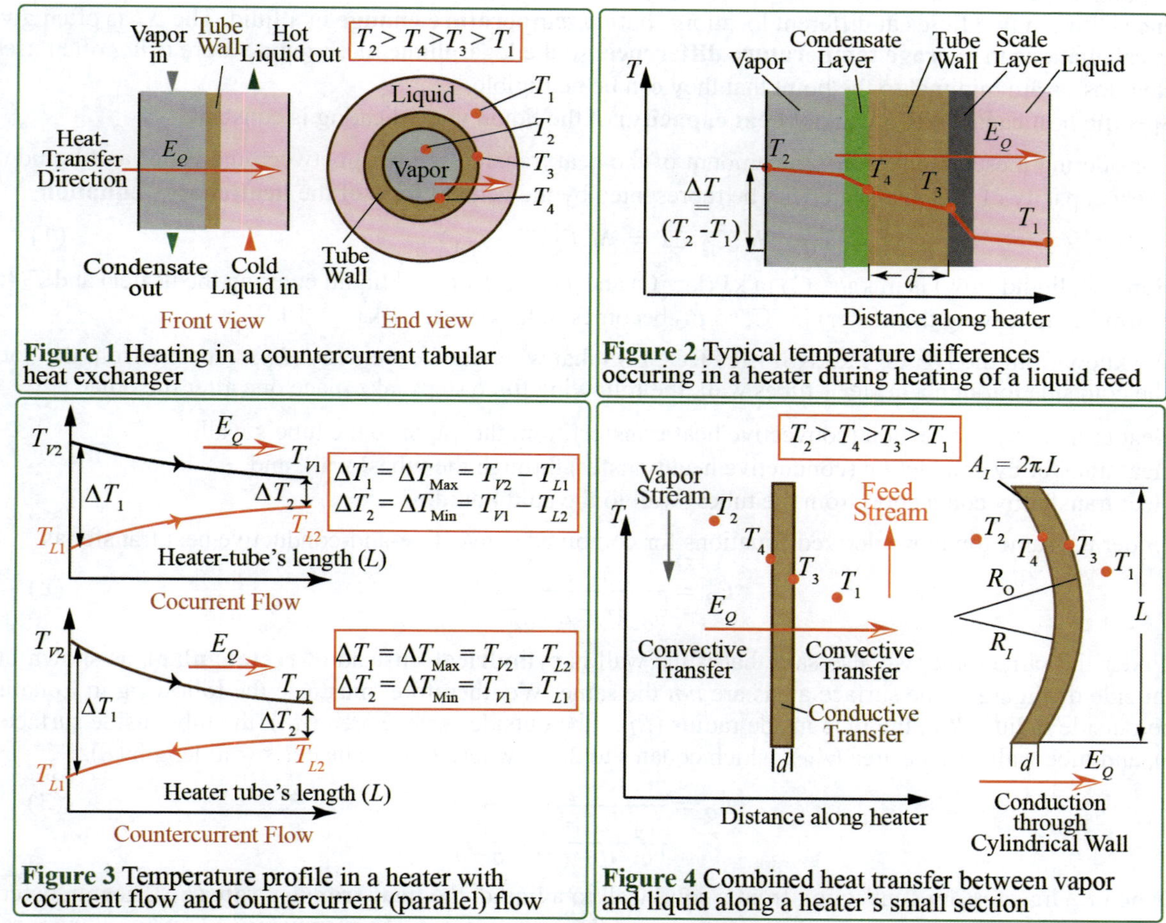

Figure 1 Heating in a countercurrent tabular heat exchanger

Figure 2 Typical temperature differences occuring in a heater during heating of a liquid feed

Figure 3 Temperature profile in a heater with cocurrent flow and countercurrent (parallel) flow

Figure 4 Combined heat transfer between vapor and liquid along a heater's small section

To become familiar with the temperature (T) profile (pattern) in a heater, assume a vapor at T_2 is flowing on one side of a solid-thin-metal plate (simply **solid plate** or **solid wall**) and a cold liquid at T_1 flowing on the other side of the plate. Further, assume that the plate is covered by two thin layers (see Figure 2):

- **Condensate Layer** (condensate film)**:** This represents a layer of liquid created on the surface of the heater's tube by condensation of the vapor (because the surface is colder than the vapor).
- **Scale Layer** (scale film)**:** This is a layer of scale (incrustation) deposited on the surface of the heater's tube by **scale-causing salts** (discussed later) when the heater is in service over time.

Both layers change the feed's T profile under heating. [Note that each layer creates a certain amount of resistance to heat transfer. We will talk later in this section about individual resistances.] Figure 3 shows the temperature profile in a heater with cocurrent flow and parallel flow.

ENERGY BALANCE OF A HEAT EXCHANGER

To generalize the energy balance of a heat exchanger, we consider a counter-current tabular heater and base our calculations on the following assumptions:

- Vapor is the heating medium. The vapor's temperature (T) at the entrance to the heater is shown as T_{V2} and at the exit (in the form of condensate) as T_{V1}, where $\Delta T_V = T_{V2} - T_{V1}$. The liquid feed at the entrance is shown as T_{L1} and at the exit as T_{L2}, where $\Delta T_L = T_{L2} - T_{L1}$. [Note that the symbol ΔT is used for the temperature difference between two fluids at different locations, but *no* **temperature change** in a fluid. The ΔT is often given in calculations in **average temperature difference**, so the logarithmic mean temperature is *not* often used.]
- Heat losses are minimal to the point that they can be negligible.
- Specific heat capacity (C_Q, simply **heat capacity**) of the liquid under heating is constant.

Considering these assumptions, the amount of the heat transfer rate ($\dot{E}_Q$) between the vapor and liquid (with the heat capacity of C_Q) in a heater can be represented by the general form of the **heat-energy equation**.

$$\dot{E}_Q = \dot{M}.C_Q.\Delta T = \dot{M}.C_Q(T_2 - T_1) \qquad (1)$$

Here, $\dot{M}$ (liquid flow) is in kg/s, C_Q in kJ/(kg.°C) and T_1 (the T of cold liquid entering the heater) and T_2 (the T of warm liquid leaving the heater) in °C, so $\dot{E}_Q$ becomes in kJ/s, where 1 kJ/s = 1 kW/h.

We know from the HEAT TRANSFER PROCESS that when the heat energy (E_Q) transfers from the hot side to the cold side through a heater's tubes wall, the following three steps take place one after the other:

- Heat transfer by convection (convective heat transfer) from the vapor to the tube's wall,
- Heat transfer by conduction (conductive heat transfer) through the tubes' wall, and
- Heat transfer by convection from the tubes' wall to the cold liquid.

Under the same topic, we derived equations for combined convective-and-conductive heat transfer as

$$\dot{E}_Q = \frac{T_2 - T_1}{\frac{1}{U_{Q1}.A} + \frac{L}{K_T.A} + \frac{1}{U_{Q2}.A}} \qquad (2)$$

Under the same topic, we also said that if the wall is **cylindrical** (instead of **rectangular**), as shown on the right side of Figure 4, the surface areas are *not* the same. We, therefore, must use the following in Equation 2: tube outside radius (R_O), the tube inside radius (R_I), tube outside surface area (A_O), the tube inside surface area (A_I), and tube wall surface area (A_W), which equates to $2\pi.L$, where L is the heater's wall length (L).

$$\dot{E}_Q = \frac{T_2 - T_1}{\frac{1}{U_{Q1}.A_I} + \frac{Ln\frac{R_O}{R_I}}{2K_T.\pi.L} + \frac{1}{U_{Q2}.A_O}} \qquad (3)$$

When E_Q transfers by convection from a solid wall to a liquid, the **heat-transfer rate** ($\dot{E}_Q$), heat transfer area (A, the area through which convection occurs), and the driving force of the transfer ($\Delta T = T_2 - T_1$) are related through a proportionality constant, known as the **convective heat transfer coefficient** (known as the heat transfer coefficient, U_Q, in kJ/(m^2.°C) or BTU/(Ft^2.°F).

$$\dot{E}_Q = U_Q.A(T_2 - T_1) \qquad (4)$$

In this **convective heat-transfer equation**, the T_2 is the T of hot flow (vapor), and the T_1 is the T of warm liquid feed leaving the heater. The conductive heat-transfer equation can be calculated using the K_T (thermal conductivity) of the solid walls (in W/h.m.°C) and the heater length (L, in m).

$$\dot{E}_Q = K_T . A \frac{T_2 - T_1}{L} \quad (5)$$

An Example of Heating: A countercurrent tabular heater for heating a liquid with hot condensate

Liquid's temperature at entrance (T_{L1})	22°C
Liquid's temperature at exit (T_{L2})	62°C
Liquid's flow rate to heater ($\dot{M}_L$)	1.5 kg/s
Liquid's specific heat capacity (C_{QL})	5 kJ/(kg.°C)
Condensate's temperature at entrance (T_{C2})	88°C
Condensate's flow rate to heater ($\dot{M}_C$)	0.5 kg/s
Condensate's specific heat capacity (C_{QC})	4.18 kJ/(kg.°C)
Process's overall heat transfer coefficient (U_{QO})	2.5 kW/(m^2.°C) = 2500 W//(m^2.°C)
Heater-tube's inside diameter (d)	6 cm (= 0.06 m = 2.4 In)

Wanted: 1) Condensate's temperature at exit (T_{C1}), 2) LMTD (logarithmic mean temperature difference) between condensate and liquid under heating, 3) Length of heater (L)

The condensate outlet T can be calculated from a heat balance between hot condensate and cold liquid.

$$\dot{E}_Q = \dot{M}_C . \lambda_{QC} \Delta T_C \qquad 1.5 \times 5(62 - 22) = 0.5 \times 4.18(88 - T_{C1}) \qquad T_{C1} = 56°\text{C}$$

$$\dot{E}_Q = \dot{M}_L . C_{QL}(T_{L2} - T_{L1}) = 0.5 \times 4.18(62 - 22) = 83.6 \text{ kJ/s}$$

The LMTD can be calculated from its equation for a countercurrent heat transfer.

$$\Delta T_{LM} = \frac{\Delta T_2 - \Delta T_1}{Ln \frac{\Delta T_2}{\Delta T_1}} = \frac{(T_{C2} - T_{L2}) - (T_{C1} - T_{L1})}{Ln \frac{(T_{C2} - T_{L2})}{(T_{C1} - T_{L1})}} = \frac{(88 - 62) - (56 - 22)}{Ln \frac{(88 - 62)}{(56 - 22)}} = 28°\text{C}$$

$$\dot{E}_Q = U_Q . A . \Delta T_{LM} = U . \pi . d . L . \Delta T_{LM} \qquad L = \frac{E_Q}{U . \pi . d . \Delta T_{LM}} = \frac{83.6 \times 1000}{2500 \times 3.14 \times 0.06 \times 28} = 6.3 \text{ m}$$

H-48

HEAVY HYDROGEN

Discussed under HYDROGEN.

H-49

HEAVY METALS

Heavy metals are elements with high density (D), high atomic mass (M_A), or high atomic mass number (N_Z). Some differences exist in classifying these metals in the periodic table, depending on the author and context. Some authors include the metalloids (the elements between metals and nonmetals) in the heavy-metals group.

H-50

HEAVY WATER

Discussed under WATER.

H-51

HEISENBERG

Werner Heisenberg (1901–1976) was a German physicist who received the Nobel Prize in Physics in 1932 for his contribution to quantum theories, known later as Heisenberg's wave matrix equation. The following are memorable years of Heisenberg's scientific activities in the field of physics:

- 1924: He started to work as Bohr's research assistant at the University of Copenhagen in Denmark.
- 1924–1927: He had some scientific debates (in face-to-face and written conversations) with Bohr. [These scientific conversations became known later as Copenhagen Interpretation.]
- 1925: He published his atomic theory. He treated electrons as a wave (but *not* a particle) to formulate his matrix equation, later known as Heisenberg's wave matrix equation.
- 1927: He published his uncertainty theory, later called Heisenberg's uncertainty principle, explaining uncertainty, one of the most important properties of quantum particles (particles with *no* subparticle).
- 1927: He was appointed as the head of the physics department at the University of Leipzig.
- 1932: He described the functionalities of the protons and neutrons in the nucleus through quantum physics.
- 1933: He was frequently attacked in the press as a Jew by the Nazis elements of the German Physics Movement. The attack issues were finally finished in the early1940s.
- 1938: He and two German physicists discovered nuclear fission. He later defended his involvement in the project by saying that he did it for self-protection against the Nazi's threat.
- 1954: He and Broglie played a leading role in establishing the European Organization for Nuclear Research (known by its French abbreviation, CERN) in Switzerland.
- 1976: Died of kidney cancer and was buried in Munich.
- 1999: Was chosen as one of the ten (10) greatest physicists by Physics World magazine.

[Planck, Einstein, Rutherford, Bohr, Heisenberg, Schrodinger, and Broglie can be named as the top seven (7) quantum physicists. And Newton, Faraday, and Maxwell as the three (3) top classical physicists. The ten (10) pioneers contributed to Physics more than all physicists.]

Heisenberg explaining the math of his wave-matrix theory [Illustrated specifically for this book]

Heisenberg sculpture at the Max Planck Society [Copied from the Wikipedia site]]

H-52

HEISENBERG'S WAVEMATRIX THEORY

Discussed under the topic of ATOMIC MODELS AND ATOMIC THEORIES.

H-53

HEISENBERG'S UNCERTAINTY PRINCIPLE

In 1926, Heisenberg offered his uncertainty principle, one of the fundamental quantum theories. This theory talks about the uncertain properties of quantum particles (particles with *no* subparticles, like electrons) in a quantum system. He said that it is impossible to measure accurately two properties of an electron (say, the electron's energy and velocity) at the same moment. Once one property (say, the energy) is measured precisely, the other (the velocity, *V*) becomes a less-precise measurement (because the measurement of the first property affects the other property). If, for example, a beam of light is used to measure the amount of an electron's energy (*E*), its *V* changes notably by that amount of *E*, making the *V* measurement *incorrect*.

Heisenberg came to the idea of uncertainty when he was trying to measure an electron's position (see the next Note) and its *V* at the same time, and the results were uncertain (the *more* accurately the position of the electron was measured, the *less* accurately its *V* could be measured, and conversely.) Thus, he said we must accept an approximate result by considering the volume in which an electron is positioned and functioning. So, it is more accurate to use the word **electron cloud** instead of the exact location of the electron.

[Note: In the case of an electron (a quantum particle, a particle with *no* subparticle), it is correct to use the word **position of an electron** instead of the **energy of an electron** (because the amount of an electron's energy tells us in what **electron shell** (energy level) it is positioned).]

To simplify the uncertainty principle, let us compare the functionality of a car with an electron. It is easy to measure the car's position and speed simultaneously (because its **uncertainty effect** is extremely small) because the car's location and speed are known at any given time. Such certainty, however, *cannot* be applied to an electron because its uncertainty effect is extremely large (as it acts all over and at a very high velocity).

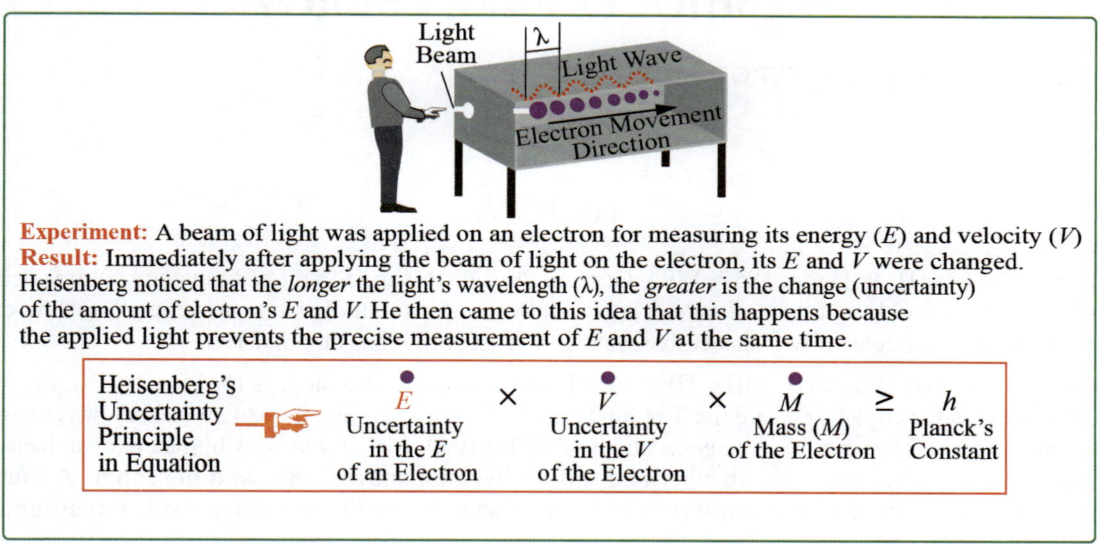

Experiment: A beam of light was applied on an electron for measuring its energy (*E*) and velocity (*V*)
Result: Immediately after applying the beam of light on the electron, its *E* and *V* were changed. Heisenberg noticed that the *longer* the light's wavelength (λ), the *greater* is the change (uncertainty) of the amount of electron's *E* and *V*. He then came to this idea that this happens because the applied light prevents the precise measurement of *E* and *V* at the same time.

To measure the position (energy) and velocity of an electron at the same time, Heisenberg applied a beam of light, with a known short wavelength (λ), to that electron (see Figure 1). He then measured the electron's position by comparing the λ of the applying beam with that of the returned beam (because part of the light beam returns by the electron). He repeated the same test with a tiny beam of light and noticed that the subject of uncertainty remains notable. Then he came to the idea that the *more* accurately an electron's position is measured, the *less* accurately its velocity can be measured, and vice versa.

The cause of uncertainty, as he said, is *not* the faultiness of the measuring method or laboratory instruments. But it is because an electron can be at two positions at the same time, as shown in the same figure. Thus, once we measure its E, the electron might be in another shell with a different E. This uncertainty proves that the measurement of an electron's energy and velocity *cannot* be accurately done at the same time. Heisenberg went further and formulated his principle, as given in Figure 1.

H-54

HELIUM

As the element two and as a Noble gas in the periodic table of elements, helium (He) is a colorless, odorless, tasteless, and non-toxic noble gas with an atomic mass number (the total number of protons and neutrons) of 4, atomic number (the total number of protons) of 2, atomic mass (M_A) of 2 AMU (simply 2 g), and molar mass (M_n) of 2 g/mole.

Some properties of atomic helium (He) are:

- It has two protons, two neutrons, and two electrons.
- Its electron acts as a chemical bonding in chemical reactions.
- Its atoms are extremely small, typically 100 pm (picometer), where 1 pm = 10^{-9}m.
- It is the second (after hydrogen, H) lightest and second most abundant element in the Universe.

[The word **helium** is from the Greek word *helios*, the Sun.]

H-55

HELMHOLTZ FREE ENERGY

Discussed under the topic of ENERGY AND ITS FORMS.

H-56

HERTZ

The Hertz (Hz, after H. R. Hertz, 1857–1894, German Physicist) is the SI unit of frequency (f). It is defined as one cycle per second or 1 cycle per minute (1/s or 1/min). If a wave moves one wavelength (λ, the distance between the peaks or troughs of two successive waves) in a second, it has an f of 1 Hz.

Because Hz is a small unit, kHz, MHz, GHz, and THz are used, where the k is for kilo (= 10^3), the M is for mega (10^6), the G is for Giga (10^9), and the T is for Tera (10^{12}). For example, the f of an ocean's wave can be 0.2 Hz, and that of a light wave can be as huge as about 430 THz (with λ of 700 nm). A human ear can hear sounds with frequencies in the hearing range (between 20 and 20 000 Hz), known as the **audible range**. A sound with the f below this range is called **infrasound** (like earthquake sound), and the one above this is **ultrasound**.

H-57

HESS'S LAW

Hess's Law (also called Hess's Law of Constant Enthalpy) is a physical chemistry concept published in 1840 by its inventor, Germain Hess (a Swiss-born Russian scientist).

The law says that the total enthalpy change ($\Delta H = E_Q$, heat energy) during a chemical reaction is independent of the number of steps taken from the initial to the final state. It confirms that enthalpy (H) is a state quantity and obeys the Thermodynamic First Law (the H, or E_Q, of a closed system is conserved, so it remains unchanged). Say, the amount of H of 100 kg of a liquid (a system) is independent of how the heating process proceeds, say, 30 to 60°C. This means that the amount of H used is the same if we heat first the liquid from 30 to 40°C and then from 40 to 60°C, or heat it with *no* delay from 30 to 60°C. But, the time during which the heating process occurs is *not* the same. [Hess's Law can be used to determine the overall required H of a reaction by the initial and final states of the reactant (or reactants) and product (or products), as they are the same (see Figure 1).]

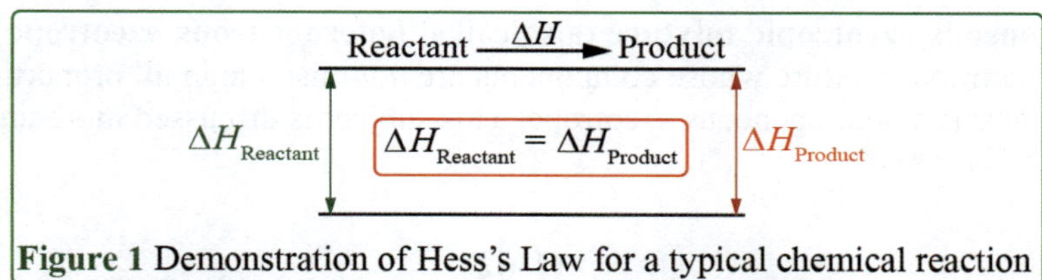

Figure 1 Demonstration of Hess's Law for a typical chemical reaction

H-58

HETEROGENEITY

Study HOMOGENITY AND HETEROGENEITY.

H-59

HIGGS BOSON

Discussed under the topic of BOSONS, FERMIONS, AND HADRONS.

H-60

HIGGS FIELD

Defined under FUNDAMENTAL FIELDS OF NATURE.

H-61

HOMOGENEITY AND HETEROGENEITY

Homogeneity: The word **homogeneity** refers to a homogeneous system. A homogeneous mixture is in a single phase with uniform chemical composition. Thus, if dividing the volume of a homogeneous system in half, we get two equal portions, uniform in composition, and stay in the same phase. If dividing a solution (a homogeneous mixture) into two tanks, both will have a solution with the same composition and properties.

Study the following useful points about homogeneity:

- The definition of homogeneity, however, strongly depends on the context used. Sometimes, it is used when a system is made from one or more compounds combined chemically, so its chemical components *cannot* be separated through a physical change.
- The word **homogenous azeotropic mixture** (also called **homogenous azeotrope**) is also used in ChemEng to refer to an azeotropic liquid mixture (simply **azeotrope**) that its components are miscible with each other in all proportions. [For example, the ethanol-water mixture is a homogeneous azeotrope because any amount of ethanol (C_2H_5OH) can be mixed with any amount of water (H_2O).]

Heterogeneity: The word **heterogeneity** refers to a heterogeneous system that is *not* uniform and is *not* in a single phase. By another definition, a heterogeneous system comprises one or more compounds mixed but are *not* combined chemically, so its components **can be** separated physically. A mixture of oil and water and sand and water are heterogeneous mixtures.

[The word **heterogeneous azeotropic mixture** (also called **heterogeneous azeotrope**) is also used in ChemEng to refer to an azeotropic mixture whose components are *not* miscible in all proportions. For example, the chloroform-water mixture is a heterogeneous azeotrope. This subject is discussed more under the topic of AZEOTROPIC LIQUID MIXTURE.]

H-62

HOOKE'S PRINCIPLE

Hooke's principle (also called Hooke's Law), named after Robert Hooke (1635–1703, British physicist), is a principle in Physics that says stress (load in the form of force) is proportional to strain. In the case of a **spring**, the force (F) applied to the spring is proportional to the spring's extension. In other words, it is proportional to the length (L) that the spring is extended from its rest position (see Figure 1). If, say, F is doubled, L will also double.

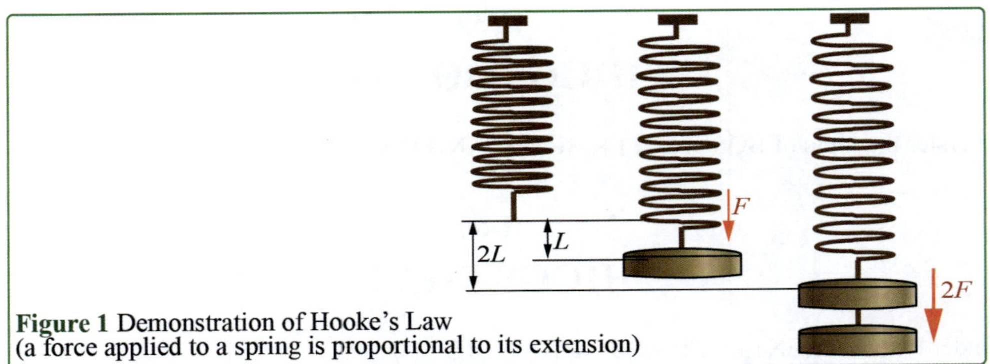

Figure 1 Demonstration of Hooke's Law
(a force applied to a spring is proportional to its extension)

Mathematically, this principle is expressed as

$$F = K.L \quad (1)$$

The K is a proportionality coefficient, called the **deformation coefficient**, which depends on the spring's **rigidity** (stiffness or resistance to deformation), depending on the material from which a spring is made. For example, if an F of 6 N (where N is for Newton, the unit of force) is applied to a spring, it stretches 2 cm, and if F is 12 N, the spring stretches 4 cm. We can then express this test using the quantity of 3 as the **spring coefficient**.

$$6 = 3 \times 2 \qquad 12 = 3 \times 4 \qquad F = 3L$$

[The theory of elasticity generalizes Hooke's principle that the strain (deformation) of many elastic materials is proportional to the stress applied to them. In ChemEng, this principle is used in pressure measurement by a strain gauge and other instruments.]

H-63

HORSEPOWER

Horsepower (HP) is the unit of measurement of electric power (P_E, energy/time), where 1 HP = 745.7 W/h (also written as W.h or just W) or 1 HP = 550 Ft.Lb$_F$/s (foot-pound per second). The unit of power came into the picture when in 1781, **James Watt** (1736–1819, Scottish scientist) wanted to compare the output of his invented steam engine with the output of a strong horse. He found that such a horse can produce about 750 W of work in 8 hours (1 working day). And a strong man can generate about 75 W in 8 hours, which equates to 75 × 1.34 = 100 HP. [In SI units, one HP is the power needed to lift 75 kg by 1 m in 1 s time (see Figure 1).] The HP is used to rate some devices, like steam boilers and steam turbines. The HP of a boiler can be roughly estimated by its heat transfer area, where 1 m^2 (= 10 Ft^2) heating area equates to about 1 HP (≈ 0.75 kW/h).

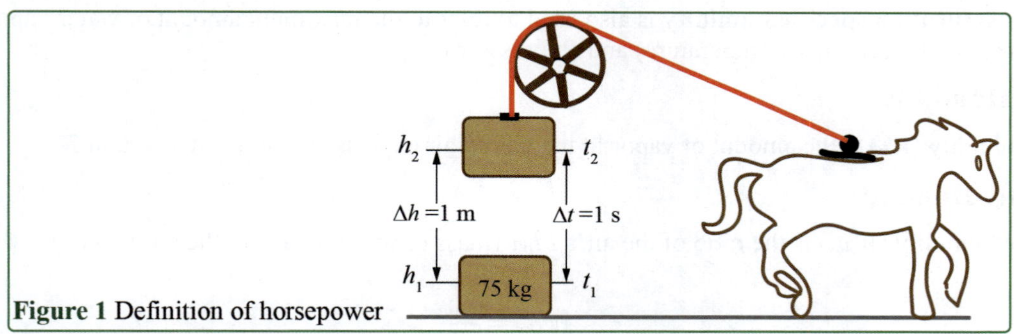

Figure 1 Definition of horsepower

H-64

HOSES

A hose is a cylindrical hollow shape device made from a plastic (flexible) material and is mainly used to transport fluids (liquids and gases). Rubber hoses are produced from vulcanized rubber, waterproof, elastic (see ELASTICITY), and resilient (see RESILIENCE). Some hoses are made from PVC (polyvinyl chloride).

[The term **hose** is usually used when the pipe or tube is flexible.]

H-65

HUMID AIR

Discussed under AIR.

H-66

HUMIDITY AND ITS MEASUREMENT

Humidity

Humidity (W) is the amount of water vapor (simply **vapor**) in the humid air (the atmospheric air). In a similar definition, the W is the air's moisture because moisture is the amount of water in moist air. Thus, air humidity is the amount of the air's moisture content. [Note that the symbol W is used for humidity and moisture.]

The air humidity is usually measured in one of the following ways:

- **Absolute Humidity** (W_{Abs}): It is expressed in g water vapor/m^3 of humid (moist) air.
- **Molar Humidity** (W_n): It is expressed in mole (n) of water vapor/mole dry air.
- **Relative Humidity** (W_R): It is given in percentage or molar fraction (% X).
- **Specific Humidity** (W_{Sp}): It is given in g water vapor/kg dry air.

It is important to know the following points about humidity:

- The relative humidity is the most common way of expressing air humidity.
- The term **saturation specific humidity** is also used to refer to the maximum amount of water vapor that can exist in the air at a certain T (temperature) and P (pressure).

Molar Humidity

Molar humidity (W_n) is the amount of vapor in the humid air expressed in mole at a certain T.

Absolute Humidity

Absolute humidity (W_{Abs}) is the ratio of the air's M_{WV} (mass of water vapor) to the air's V_A (air's volume) at a certain T.

$$W_{Abs} = \frac{M_{WV}}{V_A} \qquad (1)$$

Defined so, W_{Abs} (absolute humidity) is the maximum amount of water vapor in the humid air at a certain T. Thus, the air's W_{Abs} and saturated air at the same T have the same meaning. The air's W_{Abs} ranges from zero to about 30 g/m^3 when **saturated** at room temperature (around 25°C = 77 °F).

The relation between W_{Abs} and W_n (molar humidity) can be expressed as

$$W_{Abs} = \left(\frac{(M_n)_{W.V}}{(M_n)_{D.A}}\right) W_n = \frac{18}{29} W_n = 0.62 W_n \qquad (2)$$

In this equation, $(M_n)_{W.V}$ is the molar mass of water vapor (18 g/mole) and $(M_n)_{D.A}$ is that of dry air (29 g/mole).

Figure 1 shows the relation between the air's W_{Abs} and saturated air's T (the T_S). Figure 2 shows a section of an air psychrometric diagram to indicate the W_{Abs} versus T. The **green** curve in the same figure represents the saturation curve that divides the diagram into two sections. The section to the left of the curve represents the air-water mixture, and the section to the right represents the air-vapor mixture.

Relative Humidity

Relative humidity (W_R, commonly **humidity**) is unitless. It is defined as the percentage of molar fraction (X, a unitless quantity) of water vapor (simply vapor) in an air sample (X_{VA}, where subscript V is for water vapor and A is for air) divided by the X of saturated air (fully humid air), both at the same T and P.

$$W_R = \frac{X_{VA}}{X_{VS}} \times 100 \qquad (3)$$

Defined, 0% humidity (W_R) means complete dry air (vapor-free air), and 100% humidity means saturated air. Thus, humidity is a function of the air's T and its vapor content (the *greater* the air's T, the *greater* is its ability to absorb and hold vapor).

The molar fractions in Equation 4 can be given as partial pressures.

$$W_R = \frac{P_{VA}}{P_{VS}} \times 100 \qquad (4)$$

High air's relative humidity (W_R) increases the apparent T (felt air T). For example, 32°C (= 90°F) would feel like 38°C (= 100°F) if W_R were 60% (high humidity). High air's W_R also reduces the cooling effect of the human body because the *higher* the W_R of air, the *lower* is the rate of evaporation of moisture (created by sweating) from the human skin.

The relation between W_R and W_A is given as

$$W_R = \frac{W_{Abs}}{0.62} \qquad (6)$$

The value of 0.62 is the ratio of the water molar mass (M_n = 18 g/mole) to the air molar mass (M_n = 29 g/mole).

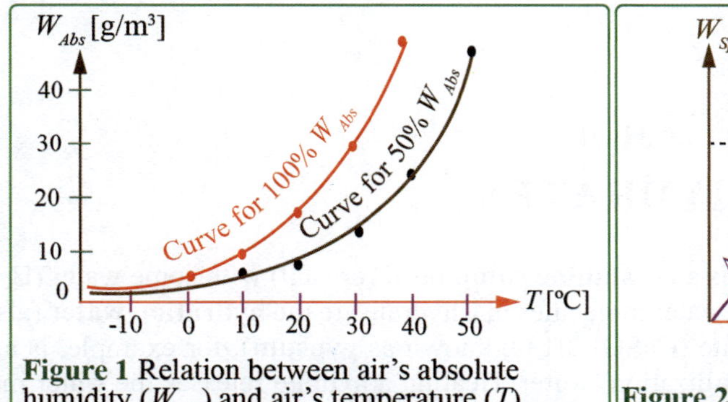

Figure 1 Relation between air's absolute humidity (W_{Abs}) and air's temperature (T)

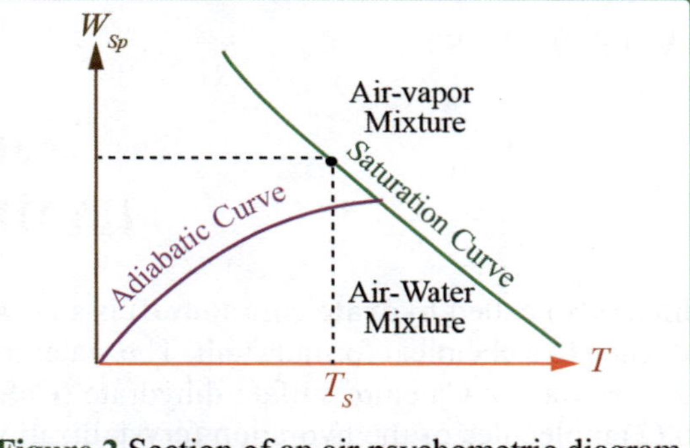

Figure 2 Section of an air psychometric diagram

Specific Humidity

Specific humidity (W_{Sp} or W, also called **humidity ratio** or **moisture content**) is the mass of water vapor ($M_{W.V}$) per unit mass of dry air ($M_{D.A}$) at a certain T.

$$W_{Sp} = \frac{M_{WV}}{M_{D.A}} \qquad (7)$$

The common unit of specific humidity (W_{Sp}) is kg water/kg dry air, but it is also given in g/g, g/100 g, or g/kg. W_{Sp} can also be expressed as

$$W_{Sp} = \frac{M_{WV}}{M_{D.A}} = \left(\frac{(M_n)_{W.V}}{(M_n)_{D.A}}\right)\left(\frac{X_{W.V}}{X_{D.A}}\right) = \left(\frac{18}{29}\right)\left(\frac{X_{W.V}}{X_{DA}}\right) = 0.62\,\frac{X_{W.V}}{X_{D.A}} \qquad (8)$$

The M_n is for molar mass, and X is for the molar fraction (a unitless quantity). The molar fractions of water vapor and dry air in the previous equation can be given as partial pressures (P_P) of water vapor and dry air.

$$W_{Sp} = 0.62\,\frac{(P_P)_{W.V}}{(P_P)_{D.A}} \qquad (9)$$

[Specific humidity (W_{Sp}) is determined experimentally using a hygrometer or theoretically using an air psychrometric diagram.]

H-67

HUMIDITY DIAGRAM

Study AIR PSYCHROMETRIC DIAGRAM.

H-68

HUMIDITY RATIO

Another name for **specific humidity**, so study HUMIDITY AND ITS WAYS OF MEASUREMENT.

H-69

HYDRATED CLUSTER

Study WATER CLUSTER.

H-70

HYDRATES

A hydrate (also called **hydrate compound**) is a **crystalline compound** (crystal) with some water (H_2O) molecules attached to a chemical formula unit. The water molecules in a hydrate are the **hydration water** (also called crystallization water). Calcium sulfate dihydrate ($CaSO_4.2H_2O$, known as **gypsum**), for example, is a hydrate with two (2) molecules of the hydration (crystallization) water. Heating a hydrate releases the water molecules from the hydrated compound. Say, heating $CaSO_4.2H_2O$ releases the water molecules to produce $CaSO_4$ (called **anhydrous** calcium sulfate).

The formula of hydrates is written with a centered **dot** that separates the two parts of the formula, as in $CaSO_4.2H_2O$ (calcium sulfate dihydrate), $CuSO_4.5H_2O$ (copper sulfate pentahydrate), and $CaCl_2.6H_2O$ (calcium chloride hexahydrate).

H-71

HYDRATION REACTION

Defined under CHEMICAL REACTIONS.

H-72

HYDRAULIC HEAD

Another name for LIQUID HEAD.

H-73
HYDRAULIC PRESSURE

Another name for LIQUID HEAD PRESSURE.

H-74
HYDRAULICS

Hydraulics (hydrostatics) is a branch of Physics that studies the properties of fluids and their mechanics and applications in engineering. Hydraulics often uses water as its basic liquid. Pascal (1623–1662, a French physicist) laid the foundation of hydraulics in the 17th century, known as Pascal's principle. His principle states that "a change in pressure (*P*) at any point in a liquid at rest in a closed container is transferred without loss to every portion of the fluid and the wall of the container."

The other hydraulic basic principles are the following:

- A small quantity of liquid can be made to lift a much larger mass,
- A pressure applied on a liquid is proportional to its depth below the surface,
- A pressure exerted by a liquid on a surface is proportional to its surface's area (*A*), and
- A liquid rises to the same level in each arm of a U-tube when its temperature is the same in each arm, and it rises to different levels when the *T* is different in each arm.

H-75
HYDROCARBONS

Hydrocarbons are organic compounds that contain only carbon (C) and hydrogen (H). Alkanes, alkenes, and aromatic hydrocarbons are the main hydrocarbons that differ by the number of C and H atoms they contain and the bonding number. Alkanes (with a chemical formula of C_nH_{2n+2}) have one carbon double bond (C=C) in their molecular structures, while **alkenes** (with the general formula of C_nH_{2n}) have one carbon triple bond (C≡C).

Hydrocarbons differ from one another in the way the carbon atoms connect. [Because C has 4 electrons in its outer shell and each covalent bond needs one electron per atom, C has 4 bonds when combined with another atom. And it is only stable if all 4 bonds are used. For example, consider methane (CH_4), the simplest hydrocarbon with 1 carbon per molecule. Therefore in a CH_4 molecule, 4 single covalent bonds exist between the carbon and each hydrogen atom.]

Figure 1 shows the molecular structure of three hydrocarbons; methane (CH_4, the main component of natural gas), ethane (C_2H_6, also called **ethylene**) with 2 carbon atoms per molecule, and propane (C_3H_8) with 3 carbons per molecule. Butane (C_4H_{10}), pentane (C_5H_{12}), hexane (C_6H_{14}), heptane (C_7H_{16}), and octane (C_8H_{18}, the main component of gasoline) are other hydrocarbons. Some hydrocarbons, like polyethylene (PE), are polymers with hundreds of carbons connected by a hydrocarbon group (CH_3). Some hydrocarbons are the components of crude oil and coal.

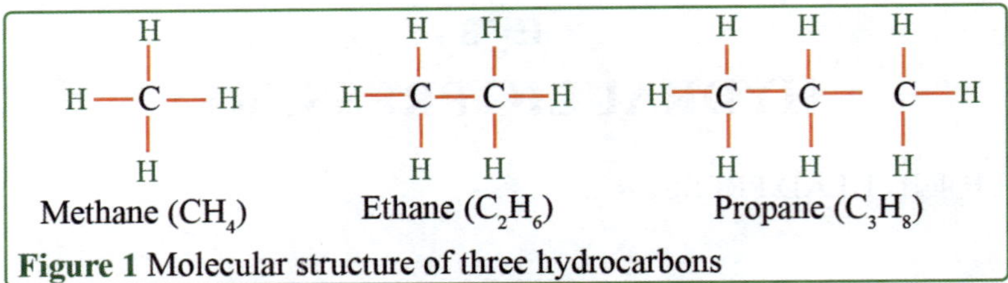

Methane (CH_4) Ethane (C_2H_6) Propane (C_3H_8)

Figure 1 Molecular structure of three hydrocarbons

H-76

HYDRIDES

A hydride, in chemistry, is the anion of hydrogen, shown as H^-. Chemical compounds containing hydrogen-bonded to a metal are also hydrides. For example, ammonia (NH_3), methane (CH_4), and ethane (C_2H_6) are hydrides. In a compound, a hydride is usually bonded to a more electronegative element.

H-77

HYDROCHLORIC ACID

Hydrochloric acid (HCl, also called **hydrogen chloride** or **muriatic acid**) is a strong, water-soluble, colorless acid with a distinctive odor. It is one of the four strongest inorganic acids; the other ones are nitric acid (HNO_3), sulfuric acid (H_2SO_4), and perchloric acid ($HClO_4$). Because of its low reactivity, HCl is one of the least hazardous in the class of strong inorganic acids.

When its concentration is more than 40%, it is called **fuming hydrochloric acid**. HCl usually comes with a concentration of 36% (by mass), with density (D) of 1180 kg/m^3 (= 73.6 Lb/Ft^3). A few other properties of HCl are outlined next.

- Its molar mass (M_n) is 36.5 g/mole.
- Its specific heat capacity (C_Q) is 2.46 kJ(kg.°C).
- Its boiling point temperature (T_{BP}) is 48°C (= 118°F).

Because of its complete dissociation in aqueous solutions (water-based solutions) burns the skin in different concentrations. HCl completely dissociates in water as a strong acid to form hydronium cation (H_3O^+) and chloride anion (Cl^-).

$$HCl + H_2O \rightarrow H_3O^+ + Cl^-$$

Because releasing chloride ion (Cl^-) can produce salts, when salt (NaCl) is added to the aqueous HCl, the PH change of the resulting solution is *not* noticeable, indicating that Cl^- is a very weak base and non-reactive.

The HCl has many uses in both industry and laboratory (as a reagent), with about 20 Mt per year worldwide. For example, it produces polyvinyl chloride (PVC) and descales the evaporators' tubes (usually at 3 to 5% concentrations). It is also used in the labs in titration. [In general, using a strong acid as a **titrant** gives a better result than a weak acid because a strong acid creates a wider distinct endpoint.]

H-78
HYDROGEN

Hydrogen (H) is a chemical element in group 1 and period 1 of the periodic table of elements. Its atomic mass number (the total number of protons and neutrons) is 1, and its atomic number (the total number of protons) is 1, so it has *no* neutron (that is, $1 - 1 = 0$). Its atomic mass (M_A, the actual mass of one atom of an element) is 1.008 AMU (simply 1 g), and molar mass (M_n) is 1 g/mole. It is a colorless, odorless, and highly flammable gas.

Atomic hydrogen (H, also called **natural hydrogen**), under normal conditions, combines with another hydrogen atom to form **molecular hydrogen** (H_2) or combines with an oxygen atom (O) to form water (H_2O). Unlike oxygen, hydrogen is *not* found in the atmospheric air in large quantities (air has only 0.00005% H_2). Hydrogen can be produced by changing a fossil fuel into its elemental components. This takes a lot of energy, so it is quite expensive. The separation of water molecules can also produce hydrogen by using electrolysis. This is even more expensive.

Some other properties of atomic hydrogen are outlined next.

- It has one proton (p^+), one electron (e^-), and *no* neutron,
- Its electron acts as a chemical bonding in chemical reactions, and
- Its atoms are extremely small, typically 100 pm, where 1 pm (picometer) = 10^{-12} m;
- It is the lightest and the most abundant element in the Universe (as its content in nature counts for more than 90% of the total atoms).
- Molecular hydrogen (H_2) has the greatest explosive-ignition mix range with the air of all gasses except acetylene. Listed next are some other properties of H_2:
- Its content in atmospheric air is low (in trace amount),
- Its density (D) is too low (0.09 kg/m^3 = 5.6×10^{-3} Lb/Ft^3),
- Its boiling point temperature (T_{BP}) is very low (–252.9°C),
- Its melting point temperature (T_{MP}) is also low (–259.2°C),
- Its triple point occurs at –38.8°C and pressure (P) of 0.07 Atm.

As Figure 1 illustrates, atomic (natural) hydrogen (H) has three (3) isotopes:

- **Protium** (H-1 or H_1)**:** The nucleus of protium (normal hydrogen) has one proton and, therefore, N_A of 1. Its content in natural hydrogen is about 99.985%. It is the most stable form of hydrogen.
- **Deuterium** (H-2, H_2, or D; also called **heavy hydrogen**)**:** The deuterium nucleus has one proton, one neutron, and, thus, the N_A of 2. Its structure makes a deuterium atom about twice as heavy as a protium atom. Its content in natural hydrogen is about 0.015%.
- **Tritium** (H-3 or H_3)**:** The nucleus of tritium has one proton, two neutrons, and, thus, N_A of 3.

All three isotopes of hydrogen have one electron. Deuterium and tritium are rare in nature. Deuterium can be extracted from seawater.

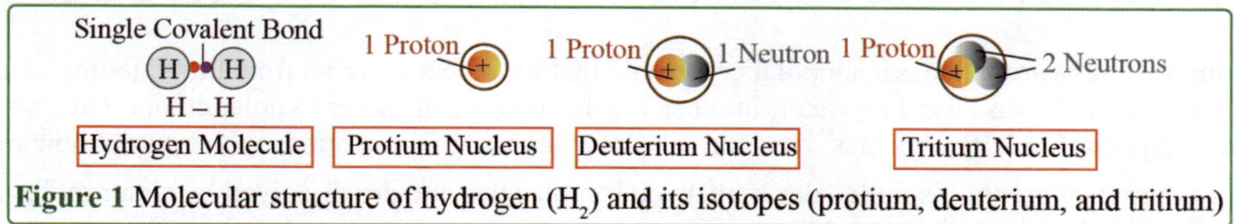

Figure 1 Molecular structure of hydrogen (H_2) and its isotopes (protium, deuterium, and tritium)

H-79

HYDROGEN BOND

Discussed under CHEMICAL BONDS.

H-80

HYDROGEN CHLORIDE

Chemical name for HYDROCHLORIC ACID.

H-81

HYDROGEN PEROXIDE

Hydrogen peroxide (H_2O_2) is a chemical compound (simply compound) in a liquid form and slightly more viscous than water (H_2O). It is a common oxidizing agent, bleaching agent, and antiseptic (usually in a dilute solution in water for antibacterial and disinfecting purposes).

H-82

HYDROGEN SULFIDE

Hydrogen sulfide (H_2S) is a colorless, flammable, toxic, and corrosive gas with a strong odor of rotten egg. In chemical plants, it is formed from the breakdown of organic compounds by anaerobic bacteria without oxygen when wastewater is processed in an anaerobic reactor. This process is commonly known as **anaerobic digestion**. Methane (CH_4) is the main product of the digestion process.

Some properties of H_2S are outlined next.

- Its molar mass is 34 g/mole,
- Its solubility in water is 4 g/L (at 20°C),
- It burns in oxygen to form SO_2 and H_2O, and
- Its boiling point temperature (T_{BP}) is – 60°C (= – 76°F).

H-83

HYDROPHOBES, HYDROPHILES, AND HYGROSCOPES

Hydrophobes: A hydrophobe is a nonpolar compound that its molecules repel from the water molecules. Thus, a hydrophobe *cannot* be dissolved by water; in other words, mixed with water (a polar compound). Such a property is called **hydrophobicity**. Alkanes, fats, and oils are examples of compounds with hydrophobic molecules.

Hydrophyles: A hydrophile's molecules attract water molecules and are dissolved by water molecules. Such a property is called **hydrophilicity**.

Hygroscopes: A hygroscope's molecules attract and hold water molecules but are *not* dissolved by water molecules.

H-84

HYDROSTATIC EQUILIBRIUM

Hydrostatic equilibrium (also known as **hydrostatic stability**) is the stability condition in a **hydrostatic system** (a static pressure-involving system) when the sum of all forces acting on the system is zero. According to the first law of Newton's Motion Laws, a volume (V) of a fluid, which is *not* in motion, has a zero-net force ($\sum F$, the sum of all forces acting on a system) on it. Consider a liquid in a column shown in Figure 1. The three forces applied to a given volume of the liquid are: 1) A downward F related to the pressure (P) from the fluid above, 2) An upward F related to the P from the fluid below the given volume of the fluid, and 3) A downward F is related to the weight (w) of the fluid that exists in the given volume of the fluid.

According to Newton's Law, the sum of the forces in each direction equates to the sum of the forces in the opposite direction.

Consider Figure 2, which shows a vertical column with the cross-sectional area of A containing a liquid with density D. Although, P remains constant in any cross-section parallel to the base surface of this column but varies from height (h, head) to the column's height. Assume that at the height h above the base of the column, the pressure equates to P, then the net force on the small volume (shown as dV) of height dh must be zero, where d is the differential sign. Again, the three forces applied to this small volume of the liquid are: 1) A downward F from pressure $P + dP$, which equates to $(P + dP)A$, 2) An upward F from pressure P, which equates to the product of pressure and area or PA, and 3) A downward F or gravitational force (F_g) equates to $w = D.V.a_g = D.A.dh.a_g$, where a_g is the gravitational acceleration.

If we take the upward acting forces as positive and those downward acting as negative, their sum is zero.

$$-(P + dP)A + P.A - D.A.dh.a_g = 0 \tag{1}$$

After division by A and canceling out the P, we obtain

$$dP + D.dh.a_g = 0 \tag{2}$$

We can integrate this equation if density (D) is constant (in the case of incompressible fluids because their D remains constant (and when D of a compressible fluid does *not* change appreciably) to obtain

$$\frac{P}{D} + h.a_g = \text{constant} \tag{3}$$

Mathematically, this equation expresses the condition of **hydrostatic equilibrium**. Similarly, such an equation can be written for any two definite heights in a liquid column. For example, by integrating Equation 3 for P_1, P_2, h_1, and h_2, shown in Figure 2, we obtain

$$\frac{P_2}{D} - \frac{P_1}{D} = (h_1 - h_2)a_g \tag{4}$$

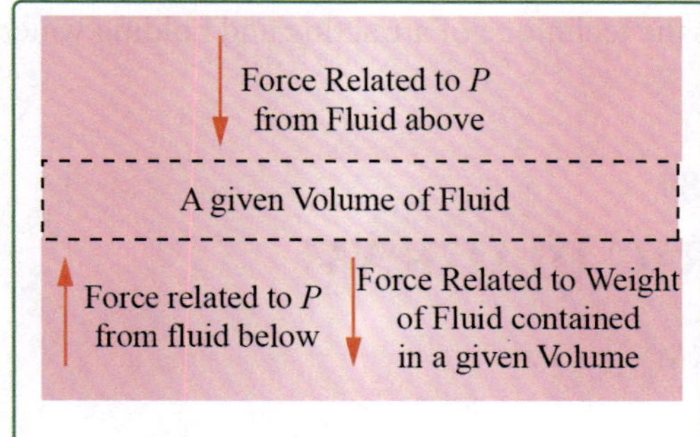

Figure 1 Forces applied on a given volume of a liquid

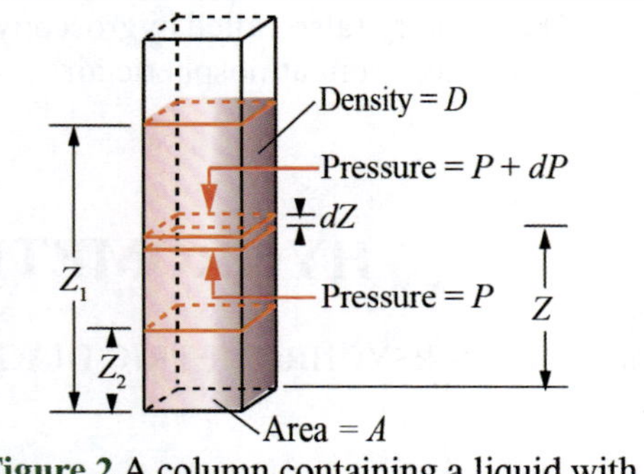

Figure 2 A column containing a liquid with cross-sectional area of A

H-85

HYDROSTATIC PRESSURE

Another name for LIQUID HEAD PRESSURE.

H-86

HYDROSTATIC TESTING

Another name for PRESSURE TESTING.

H-87

HYDROSTATICS

Hydrostatics is a branch of Physics that mainly studies the pressure (P) of fluids (liquids and gases) at equilibrium. Head pressure (hydrostatic pressure), hydrostatic equilibrium, liquid head, static lift, and hydrostatic balance (Archimedes' principle) are examples of the topics under study in hydrostatics. Water is the fluid most often used in hydrostatics, but other fluids are also used.

H-88

HYGROMETER AND HYGROMETRY

Hygrometer: A hygrometer is an instrument for measuring the air's relative humidity (W_R). In old hygrometers, an organic material expands and contracts with the air's humidity changes. In a **dew hygrometer** (dew-point hygrometer), a polished surface's temperature (T) is reduced until water vapor from air forms on it. The dew temperature enables the W_R of the air to be calculated. Tension-dial hygrometers and chilled-mirror dew hygrometers are precise instruments commonly used for measuring W_R.

A **wet-and-dry bulb hygrometer** has a wet-bulb thermometer and a dry-bulb thermometer (an ordinary thermometer) to measure the air's W_R. A wet-bulb thermometer reads a lower T than an ordinary thermometer (because of the evaporating water's cooling effect). The temperature difference (ΔT) is then used to measure the W_R.

[Only the **dew hygrometer** (dew-point hygrometer) can work as an absolute hygrometer. Thus, all other hygrometers are calibrated against a dew hygrometer.]

Hygrometry: Hygrometry (also called hygroscopy) is the technique of attracting and holding water molecules by absorption or adsorption from atmospheric air.

H-89

HYGROMETERIC DIAGRAM

Another name for AIR PSYCHROMETRIC DIAGRAM.

H-90
HYGROSCOPES

Defined under HYDROPHOBES, HYDROPHILES, AND HYGROSCOPES.

I Section

LIST OF TOPICS

I-1
IAEA

IAEA (the **I**nternational **A**tomic **E**nergy **A**gency) was established in 1957 in Vienna, Austria. With 171 member countries, it oversees its member states' scientific and technical activities for peaceful use of the nuclear industry, including nuclear power plants and nuclear medicine. The IAEA reports to both the United Nations General Assembly and Security Council. In 2004, the IAEA established a program called Program of Action for Cancer Therapy (PACT) to respond to the needs of research programs in the nuclear treatment of patients with cancer. The IAEA has three (3) main missions:

- To assure that the nuclear energy (E_N) is used in peaceful programs,
- To verify and safeguard that the E_N is *not* used for military purposes, and
- To provide nuclear safety by promoting high safety standards for peaceful nuclear programs.

I-2
IDEAL FLUID AND IDEAL FLOW

Ideal Fluid

An ideal fluid is a fluid (liquid or gas) that has the next properties:

- Its viscosity (η) is very close to zero; therefore, it has *no* shear force (F_S).
- It creates *no* resistance; therefore, it flows smoothly at a constant velocity (V).
- Its molecules indicate *no* intermolecular forces to pull them close to each other.

Additionally, and importantly, we can say the following about the properties of ideal fluids:

- In reality, *no* fluid has the listed properties to behave ideally. Thus, when talking about an ideal fluid, we mean a fluid that behaves as an ideal-like fluid at low pressures (P) and high temperatures (T). If, however, high pressures are used, the molecules of an ideal fluid are forced to be closer to each other (because its volume decreases until the intermolecular forces become active). If low temperatures are used, the same situations occur. Again, the molecules are forced to be closer to each other (because the molecular movement slows at low temperatures), making the fluid's V (volume) smaller. Thus, under conditions of high pressures and low temperatures, **deviation** from ideality occurs.
- In the fluid flow process and Gas Laws, the ideal condition is assumed in water and highly diluted solutions.
- A **non-ideal fluid** in a medium (such as a pipe), instead, is the resulting motion of a non-ideal fluid, so it moves roughly in a pipe at a high and inconsistent V.

Ideal Flow

An ideal flow is the resulting motion of an ideal fluid and has the next properties.

- It flows smoothly at a constant mass flow rate ($\dot{M}$).
- It flows at a constant velocity (V) in a medium (like a pipe). And,
- Its pressure (P) and temperature (T) do *not* change appreciably with time (t).

Conversely, a **non-ideal flow** (turbulent flow or unsteady flow) is the resulting motion of a non-ideal fluid, so it moves roughly in a pipe at a high and inconsistent V (velocity).

I-3

IDEAL GAS COMPRESSIBILITY FACTOR

The ideal gas compressibility factor (the *Z* factor) is a convenient way to determine the deviation from ideal gas behavior. The *Z* factor is a unitless number and is calculated based on the *P* (pressure) of the gas under the test, its *T* (temperature), its V_n (molar volume), and *R* (the ideal gas constant).

$$Z = \frac{P.V_n}{R.T} \quad (1)$$

The *Z* factor of an ideal gas equates to one (Z = 1). When a gas is compressed, its molecules get closer together, causing it to behave non-ideally. In Figure 1, which shows the deviation of oxygen gas (O_2, a real gas) from ideality, the oxygen's *Z* factor is shown as a function of its *P* at 25°C (= 298 K). As the oxygen's *P* is reduced to zero Atm, its *Z* factor approaches one (as expected from an ideal gas). As *P* increases to around 400 Atm, the *Z* factor stays below one. At a very high *P* (above 400 Atm), it becomes greater than one (Z > 1). This pattern continues to the point that at 800 Atm, it gets to 1.5. [The high *Z* factor at high pressures is related to the distance of the gas molecules (the *smaller* the intermolecular distance, the *higher* is the effect of intermolecular forces and, thus, the *higher* is the Z factor). Instead, the effect of the intermolecular forces disappears as *P* gets closer to zero (because of the extreme distance between the molecules). That is to say, the *greater* the *P* of a gas, the *smaller* is its *V* (volume) and, thus, the *greater* is its Z factor.]

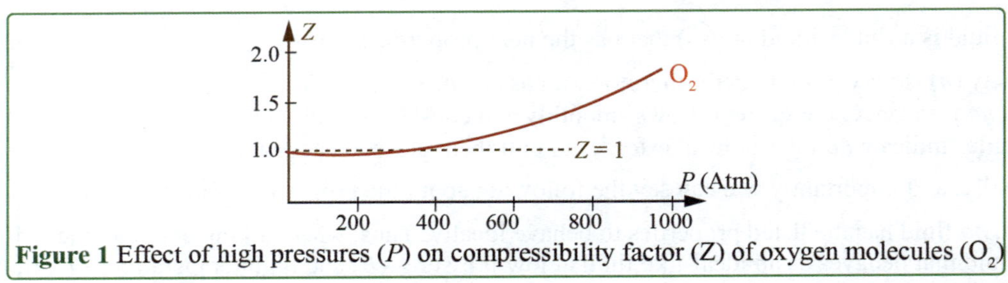

Figure 1 Effect of high pressures (*P*) on compressibility factor (Z) of oxygen molecules (O_2)

I-4

IDEAL GAS CONSTANT

The ideal gas constant (*R*, simply **gas constant**; also called **molar gas constant**) is a proportionality constant that relates the pressure (*P*), volume (*V*), quantity (in mole, *n*), and temperature (*T*) of an ideal gas or a mixture of gases. The ideal gas equation defines the *R*.

$$\frac{P.V}{n.T} = \text{Constant} = R \quad (1)$$

Therefore, if the variables of this equation are known, we can calculate *R*, a constant equal to 0.0821 (Atm.L)/(mole.°C) for an ideal gas. This value is obtained at gas *P* of 1 Atm (the *P* at STP), gas *V* of 22.4 L (the *V* of one mole of any gas at STP), its quantity of one mole (*n* = 1), and its *T* of 0°C. Thus, the SI unit of *R* becomes (1×22.4)/(273×1) = 0.0821 (Atm.L)/(mole.°C). This equates to 82.1 (Atm.L)/(kmole.°C) = 8.314 (N.m)/(mole.°C) = 8.314 (Pa.m^3)/(mole.°C), where the N is for Newton, m is for meter, Pa is for Pascal, °C is for degrees centigrade, and the L is for liter. The *R* is usually expressed as (Pa.m^3)/(kg.°C). For example, the *R* for dry air is 287 (Pa.m^3)/(kg.°C).

Since *P* is force (*F*) per area (*A*), *R* can also be expressed as

$$R = \frac{\frac{F}{A}.V}{n.T} \qquad [(N.m^3)/m^2]/(mole.^{o}C) = (N.m)/(mole.^{o}C) = J/(mole.^{o}C) \quad (2)$$

Specific Ideal Gas Constant: The specific ideal gas constant (R_{Sp}, simply **specific gas constant**) is R (ideal gas constant) to M_n (molar mass) of a gas or mixture of gases.

$$R_{Sp} = \frac{R}{M_n} \tag{3}$$

Considering the unit kJ/(kgmole.°C) for R, the unit for R_{Sp} will be kJ/[(kgmole.°C)/(kg/kgmole)] = kJ/(kg.°C). In this case, R_{Sp} for an ideal gas is 8.314 kJ/(kg.°C), so that for dry air (with M_n of 29 kg/kgmole) will be 8.314/29 = 0.287 kJ/(kg.°C). Similarly, the R_{Sp} of water vapor (with M_n of 18 kg/kgmole) is 0.462 kJ/(kg.°C).

Considering the unit (N.m)/(mole.°C) for R and knowing that 1 N = 1 kg.m/s^2, the unit for R_{Sp} will be (kg.m^2)/(mole.°C.s^2). In this case, the R_{Sp} for an ideal gas is 8.314 kg.m^2/(mole.°C. s^2), where s is for second.

I-5
IDEAL GAS EQUATION

The ideal gas equation interrelates four quantities: pressure (P), temperature (T, which refers to absolute temperature), volume (V, which refers to molar volume), and the mole (n) of a gas (either a pure or a mixture gas) through a proportionality constant, known as the ideal gas constant (R).

$$\frac{P.V}{n.T} = R \tag{1}$$

This equation tells us that P varies linearly with T, V, and n (the amount of gas expressed in moles). For one mole of an ideal gas (n = 1) and at all pressures, the equation becomes

$$\frac{P.V}{R.T} = 1 \tag{2}$$

The term $P.V/R.T$ is called the ideal gas compressibility factor (Z factor), which is used to measure the deviation behavior of a gas from ideality.

The **modified ideal gas equation** interrelates a gas's D (density), P, T, and M_n (molar mass) through R.

$$\frac{P.M_n}{D.T} = R \tag{3}$$

I-6
IDEAL GAS LAW

Discussed under the topic of GAS LAWS.

I-7
IDEAL LIQUIDS

Study IDEAL SOLUTIONS.

I-8
IDEAL LIQUID-VAPOR EQUILIBRIUM MIXTURE

An ideal liquid-vapor equilibrium mixture (ideal VLE mixture) is a liquid-vapor mixture in which the liquid phase behaves as an ideal liquid, and the phases are in equilibrium.

Instead, the term **non-ideal LVE mixture** refers to a liquid-vapor mixture in which the liquid phase behaves as a non-ideal liquid, and the phases are in equilibrium.

I-9
IDEAL LVE MIXTURE

Short name for IDEAL LIQUID-VAPOR EQUILIBRIUM MIXTURE.

I-10
IDEAL SOLUTIONS

An ideal solution is a homogenous solution whose components' molecules act similarly. The molecules of most pure liquids and highly diluted solutions act ideally. In addition, ideal solutions

- Obey Raoult's Law of Vapor Pressure,
- Flow at a steady and constant velocity,
- Perform identically at any given pressure,
- No **circulation** occurs in their stream flows,
- No eddy current occurs in their stream flows,
- No friction occurs between their stream flows and their stream boundaries, and
- No considerable repulsive and attractive forces are applied by their molecules to each other.

Ideal solutions have other important properties, including the following three:

- A linear function of their compositions expresses their vapor pressures,
- Their **enthalpies of mixing** are zero, so there is *no* heat transfer when they are mixed, and
- Their molecules have a similar structure.

Generally, the components' molecules of ideal solutions 1) Have a **repulsive effect** on each other, 2) Exert greater pressure (*P*) than if they were pure, and 3) Behave almost similarly at different pressures with no considerable non-ideality.

The **repulsion effect** (also called a **positive deviation from ideality**) between the components' molecules of a mixture exists because of their similarities and concentration (*C*). Suppose the *C* of ethanol in an ethanol-water mixture is low (below 15%). Then the ethanol molecules behave ideally by repulsing the water molecules (the *lower* the mixture's ethanol content, the *more* ideally its molecules behave). This is different when ethanol *C* is high (talk in a moment).

Non-ideal solutions, instead, do *not* obey the above-listed points given for ideal solutions because their components' molecules, 1) Have an **attractive effect** on each other, 2) Exert lower pressure than if they were pure, and 3) Behave unexpectedly at different pressures or even at the same pressures.

The **attraction effect** (the **negative deviation from ideality**) between the components' molecules of a mixture exists because of their dissimilarities and *C*. If, say, the ethanol *C* in an ethanol-water mixture is high (above 15% and particularly above 95%), the ethanol molecules behave nonideally by attracting the water molecules. In this way, the *higher* the mixture's ethanol content, the *more* the ethanol molecules attract the water molecules, and consequently, the *more* nonideally the ethanol molecules behave.

A mixture of nitric acid (HNO_3) and water is another attraction effect. The *higher* the mixture's HNO_3 content, the *more* the HNO_3 molecules attract the water molecules. Consequently, the *more* the mixture behaves nonideally, meaning the *more* the mixture deviates from ideality.

I-11

IDEAL, REAL, AND PERFECT GASES

Ideal Gasses: An ideal gas is a gas that obeys the Ideal Gas Law and Raoult's Law of Partial Pressure, and its particles (atoms, molecules, or ions) act as if they are all the same at any pressure (P) and temperature (T). The ideal gas equation, which solves the relations between P, T, V (volume), and n (amount of gas expressed as mole) through R (ideal gas constant), is valid for an ideal gas.

$$P.V = n.R.T \tag{1}$$

In an ideal gas: 1) Particles move in straight lines, 2) Particles contact each other randomly, 3) Particles do *not* interact when they hit each other, and 4) Particles do *not* slow down when they hit each other.

[Note: Ideal gas is a theoretical gas (because *no* gas acts exactly like an ideal gas). When, therefore, talking about an ideal gas, it means a gas that behaves like an **ideal-like gas** at atmospheric pressure (P_{Atm} = 1 Atm ≈ 100 kPa) and at room temperature (T_R ≈ 22 to 24°C or 72 to 75°F). The ideal gas compressibility factor (the Z factor) is a convenient way to determine the deviation from ideal gas behavior. However, at high P and low T, some gases begin to behave non-ideally. Under such conditions, for example, oxygen and nitrogen form liquids. The deviation of oxygen gas (O_2, a real gas) from ideality is discussed under IDEAL GAS COMPRESSIBILITY FACTOR.]

Real Gasses: A real gas is a gas that behaves almost ideally like an ideal gas at low pressures (P) and high temperatures (T), but it behaves non-ideally at high pressures and low temperatures. Unlike an ideal gas, a real gas does *not* obey the Ideal Gas Law and ideal gas equation, so the van der Waals equation is used to solve the relations between its P, T, V, and n.

Perfect Gases: The term **perfect gas** is used in chemistry and ChemEng to refer to a gas that obeys the ideal gas equation and has a low viscosity at P_{Atm} (atmospheric pressure) and T_R (room temperature).

I-12

IGNITION TEMPERATURE

The ignition temperature (T_{Ig}, also called **ignition point**) of a chemical compound is the lowest temperature (T), at which that compound starts to ignite by itself (without an external source). An ignition occurs because of heat-releasing reactions (exothermic reactions) that start to occur in a compound. The released heat energy (E_Q) is then used to supply activation energy (E_A) needed for combustion reactions.

Study the following important points about the T_{Ig} (ignition temperature):

- The T_{Ig} decreases with increasing pressure (P) or oxygen content of the surrounding environment.
- The T_{Ig} increases with the increased thermal conductivity of the substance under study.
- The T_{Ig} is usually applied to combustible fuels like coal, coke, or oil.

Ignition temperature (T_{Ig}) of some chemical compounds

Compound	T_{Ig} [°C]	T_{Ig} [°F]	
Calcium (Ca)	790–800	1454–1472	
Ethanol (C_2H_5OH)	365	690	
Gasoline	247–280	477–536	
Hydrogen (H_2)	535	995	
Iron (Fe)	1315	2400	
Paper	218–246	424–475	

I-13
IMMISCIBLE LIQUIDS

Study MISCIBLE AND IMMISCIBLE LIQUIDS.

I-14
IMPURE SOLUTIONS

Study PURE AND IMPURE SOLUTIONS.

I-15
IMPURITY

Study PURITY AND IMPURITY.

I-16
INCOMPRESSIBLE FLOW

Study COMPRESSIBLE AND INCOMPRESSIBLE FLOWS.

I-17
INCOMPRESSIBLE FLUIDS

Study COMPRESSIBLE AND INCOMPRESSIBLE FLUIDS.

I-18
INDEX OF REFRACTION

Study REFRACTIVE INDEX.

I-19
INDICATORS

Study ACID BASE INDICATORS.

I-20

INDUSTRIAL REVOLUTION

The Industrial Revolution was a transitional period that started in Britain around the 1760s and continued in most European countries until the 1840s. Starting this period, Europe switched from small to large production using coal, steam engine, and advanced machines to produce machine-made mass products. The industrial revolution went through the following two (2) periods:

- **First Industrial Revolution** (from the 1760s to the 1840s).
- **Second Industrial Revolution** (from the 1840s to the 1914s).

During the second revolution, some industries improved and expanded greatly, such as steel, petroleum, electricity, textile, and sugar productions.

I-21

INERT GASES

Another name for noble gases, so study NOBLE GASES.

I-22

INERTIA, INERTIAL FORCE, AND INERTIAL MASS

Inertia: The term **inertia** is used in Physics to refer to a system resisting motion and maintaining a constant velocity (V). Thus, unless acted by a force (F), a system remains at rest, and a system in motion remains in motion with uniform V. In this way, a system's inertial mass is its stationary (at-rest) mass. In Physics, therefore, inertia has the following properties:

- A non-moving system remains still (motionless) until a force (F) acts on it, and
- A moving system keeps moving until a force stops it.

Einstein used the term **inertia** (resistance) in his theories of relativity to characterize a system's mass (M) to relate its R (resistance) to M (mass). He said that a heavy system (like a tractor) takes more effort to accelerate than a lighter system (like a bicycle). Thus, the *greater* a system's M, the *greater* is its resistance (inertia) to acceleration (a), so the *more* chance for the system to move at a steady V. Defined so, an inertial reference system (also called **inertial reference frame**) is a nonaccelerating moving reference system. [Einstein, in his theories of relativity, talks only about one type of mass and calls it the **inertial mass**, which moves when an F (force) applies to it. Such a force is called an **inertial force**.]

Inertial Force: Inertial force (F_I, also called **fictitious force**) is a force (F) that acts on a mass (M) that its motion acts as an accelerating reference system (noninertial reference system), such as a rotating system. An F_I overcomes a moving system's inertial mass (M_I) to accelerate it. For example, the force acting on a system in the rotating basket of a centrifuge is an inertial force, as it is proportional to the centrifugal acceleration. Consider a space shuttle that is accelerating relative to a fixed star. The astronauts in the shuttle feel an F_I equivalent to F_g (gravitational force) on Earth. Applying an inertial force to a system creates an **inertial motion**. [In Physics, four (4) inertial forces are used; the most important of them is centrifugal force.]

Inertial Mass: Inertial mass (M_I) is an inertial (nonaccelerating) mass, so mass = inertia (resistance to motion). In this way, a system mass (inertia) is stationary. It is difficult to change an inertia's state of motion (because it resists motion and, thus, resists acceleration) when it is affected by an inertial force.

I-23

INERTIAL FORCE

Defined under the topic of INERTIA, INERTIAL FORCE, AND INERTIAL MASS.

I-24

INERTIAL MASS

Defined under the topics of MASS and INERTIA, INERTIAL FORCE, AND INERTIAL MASS.

I-25

INERTIAL REFERENCE SYSTEM

Study ACCELERATING AND NONACCELERATING REFERENCE SYSTEMS.

I-26

INFRARED WAVE

As an invisible wave to the human eye, an **infrared wave** (IR wave or IR radiation) is one of the seven (7) types of electromagnetic waves (EM waves or EM radiations), with a wavelength (λ) longer than that of visible light. The λ of IR waves is between 750 nm and 1 mm, and its *f* (frequency) is between 400 THz and 300 GHz, where T is for Tera (= 10^{12}), G is for Giga (= 10^9), and Hz is for Hertz (the SI unit of *f*).

As a type of EM wave, the IR exhibits similar properties as EM waves, including the following:

- It heats a surface that absorbs its waves,
- It exhibits the properties of both waves and particles,
- It is distinguished by its frequency (*f*) and wavelength (λ),
- It is the movement of a photon (because an electron releases a photon),
- It can travel at the speed of light in space without the need for a medium, and
- It has wave-particle property by moving like a wave and releasing energy as a particle, but never together.

Some other properties of IR are outlined next.

- It carries photon energy and behaves like a wave and like its quantum particle (the photon);
- It contains more than half of the total energy of the Sun,
- It affects Earth's climate considerably, and
- It is used in medicine and industry.

[Note: The **EM waves** include radio wave, microwave, infrared, visible light, ultraviolet, X-ray, and gamma ray, given in the longest to shortest wavelengths. The *smaller* the λ of an EM wave's length, the *smaller* its *f*.]

I-27
INHERENT MOISTURE

Defined under MOISTURE AND ITS KINDS.

I-28
INJECTORS

I-29
INORGANIC COMPOUNDS

Study ORGANIC AND INORGANIC COMPOUNDS.

I-30
INSTRUMENTATION

Instrumentation, in ChemEng, is a technique that uses instruments (measuring devices) to monitor and control a process (like evaporation process) or a laboratory device (like PH meter) in the desired range.

I-31
INSTRUMENTS

An instrument (also called a **measuring instrument**) is a delicate device used to measure and control a physical quantity, such as temperature (T), pressure (P), flow, or voltage. Some instruments, like thermometer (for measuring T), manometer (for measuring P), flowmeter (for measuring flow), voltmeter (for measuring voltage), and controllers, are the key parts of control loops in the field of process control.

Laboratory devices, like PH meter (for measuring a solution PH), polarimeter (for measuring the concentration of a solution), microscope, and even balances are instruments.

I-32
INSULATORS

Study ELECTRIC INSULATORS and THERMAL INSULATORS.

I-33
INTEGRATION

Study DERIVATION AND INTEGRATION.

I-34

INTENSITY

Intensity (I, also called **radiant power**) is a physical quantity that is used in Physics as a rate to express:

- **Light Intensity:** The light intensity (I_L, also called **brightness**) indicates the amount of light transferred per unit area (A). The I_L is given in **candela** to represent a light's brightness as an observer sees it.
- **Electric Intensity:** The electric intensity ($I_E = P_E / A$) expresses the P_E (electric power) transferred per A (unit area). The I_E is given in $W/h.m^2$, where W is for Watt, the h is for hour, and m is for meter.
- **Sound Intensity:** The sound intensity (I_E) indicates the sound traveled per unit time (t). Because sound travels as waves, the I_E is given in Hz (Hertz, the SI unit of frequency), where 1 Hz = 1 cycle/s.

I-35

INTENSIVE AND EXTENSIVE QUANTITIES

Intensive Quantity: An intensive quantity (intensive variable) is a physical quantity that is *not* **addable**, so the value of a system's intensive quantity does *not* depend on its size. Temperature (T), pressure (P), density (D), energy (E), enthalpy (H), and entropy (S) are examples of intensive quantities. For example, if a system at T_1 is combined with another system at T_2, the resulting system will *not* have the sum of the temperatures.

Extensive Quantity: An extensive quantity (extensive variable) is an addable quantity, so its quantity depends on its size–that is, how much there is. Mass (M), energy (E), volume (V), and length (L) are examples of extensive quantities. If, for example, a system with mass M_1 is combined with another system with mass M_2, then the resulting system will have the sum of the masses ($M_1 + M_2$).

[Note: The **ratio** of two extensive quantities is an intensive quantity. Both mass (M) and volume (V), for example, are extensive quantities, but their ratio (M/V) is density, which is an intensive quantity.]

I-36

INTERACTION ENERGY

Discussed under ENERGY AND ITS FORMS.

I-37

INTERIOR MOISTURE

Defined under MOISTURE AND ITS TYPES.

I-38
INTERMOLECULAR FORCE

An intermolecular force (F_{IM}) is a force (F) that holds the adjacent molecules of a solid, liquid, or gas phase together. The F_{IM} between the molecules can be expressed as the interaction energy (E_{IN}, also called **potential-interaction energy**) and the intermolecular distance (d_{IM}) between the molecules.

$$F_{IM} = \frac{E_{IN}}{d_{IM}} \quad (1)$$

Consider a water-based solution in an evaporator under the evaporation process. The solution is affected by F_{IM} and the evaporator's P (pressure), so two (2) conditions are needed for water molecules to evaporate:

- Molecules must have higher-than-average E_K (kinetic energy) to overcome F_{IM}, and
- Molecules must overcome the evaporator's P to move to the vapor phase.

At a small intermolecular distance, where the E_{IN} is positive, the molecules repel each other. At a medium intermolecular distance, where the E_{IN} is negative, the molecules attract each other weakly. And at a very large intermolecular distance, where the E_{IN} approaches zero, the molecules do *not* influence each other. Therefore, when drawing the E_{IN} versus d_{IM}, a typical graph such as the one shown in Figure 1 is obtained.

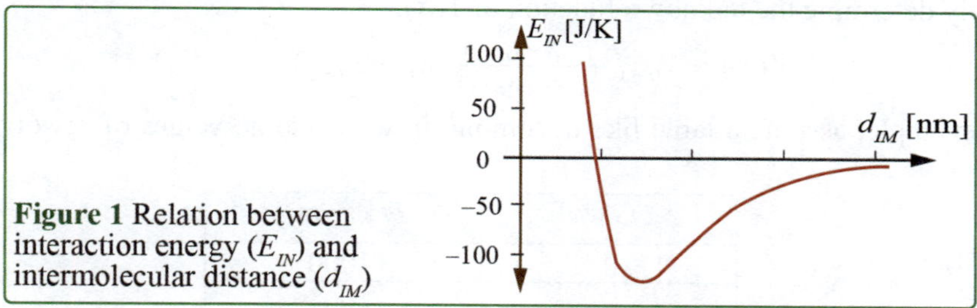

Figure 1 Relation between interaction energy (E_{IN}) and intermolecular distance (d_{IM})

I-39
INTERNAL COMBUSTION ENGINE

An internal combustion engine (ICE) is an engine in which a combustion reaction occurs. A combustion reaction is a rapid chemical reaction (simply **reaction**) between the combustible carbon atoms of a fuel and oxygen atoms of air to produce carbon dioxide (CO_2) and water (H_2O), and some heat energy (E_Q) is released (by definition, shown by a negative sign).

$$C + O_2 \rightarrow CO_2 - E_Q$$

$$2\ H_2 + O_2 \rightarrow 2\ H_2O - E_Q$$

The gasses produced by combustion create a high-pressure, high-temperature situation that can apply a strong force on some attached parts of an engine. The force can be applied, say, to the piston of a car's engine (an internal combustion engine) or the blades of a turbine.

I-40
INTERNAL ENERGY

Discussed under the topic of ENERGY AND ITS FORMS.

I-41

INTERNATIONAL ATOMIC ENERGY AGENCY

See IAEA.

I-42

INTERPOLATION AND EXTRAPOLATION OF DATA

Interpolation and extrapolation are mathematical methods used to estimate a value (a variable). **Interpolation** is used to estimate a value **between** two known values. And **extrapolation** is used to estimate a value **beyond** the range of some known values. [The result of interpolation is far more reliable than extrapolation.]

Interpolation

To formulize the interpolation, consider the values $f(X_1)$, $f(X_2)$, …., $f(X_n)$ of function f are known, where $X_1 < X_2 < \ldots < X_n$. We can interpolate to determine an unknown $f(X)$ for X, where X is between two known values. If the two values to be interpolated, nearest to the value X, are (X_{n-1}, Y_{n-1}) and (X_n, Y_n), then the **linear interpolation equation** can closely determine the unknown function of $Y(X)$.

$$Y(X) \approx Y_{n-1} + \frac{(X-X_{n-1})}{(X_n-X_{n-1})}(Y_n - Y_{n-1}) \quad (1)$$

As a numerical example, assume a table like upcoming, in which some values of dissolved solids (DS) and density (D) are given.

DS [%]	D [kg/m³]
1	1000
2	1004
3	1008
4	1012
5	1016
6	1018

If we want to find D for; say, $DS = 3.5$, which lies between $DS = 3$ and $DS = 4$, we must write the interpolation equation in the following form:

$$Y_{3.5} \approx Y_3 + \frac{(X - X_4)}{(X_4 - X_3)}(Y_4 - Y_3) \approx 1008 + \frac{3.5 - 3}{4 - 3}(1012 - 1008) = 1010$$

[In another interpolation method, the values of the function with more than two (2) values are used. This method uses complicated math, which is beyond the scope of this book.]

An Example of Interpolation

Calculate the specific enthalpy (H) of a saturated steam at 133°C. According to Table 1 (Steam table in the book's table section), the H of saturated steam at 130°C is 2721 kJ/kg, and that of steam at 135°C is 2727 kJ/kg.

The lower values are (130, 2721), and the higher values are (135, 2727), so we must interpolate between the values that bracket the desired value (H for 133°C or H_{133}).

$$H_{133} \approx Y_1 + \frac{(X-X_1)}{(X_2-X_1)}(Y_2 - Y_1) \approx 2721 + \frac{(133-130)}{(135-130)}(2727 - 2721) \approx 2721 + 3.6 \approx 2725 \text{ kJ/kg}$$

Extrapolation

To formulize the extrapolation, assume that the values $f(X_1), f(X_2), \ldots, f(X_n)$ of function f are known, where $X_1 < X_2 < \ldots < X_n$. An extrapolation can determine an unknown $f(X)$ for X, where X is beyond the known range of known values. If the two values nearest the value x to be extrapolated are (X_{n-1}, Y_{n-1}) and (X_n, Y_n), the **linear extrapolation equation** can closely determine the unknown function of $Y(X)$.

$$Y(X) \approx Y_{n-1} + \frac{(X-X_{n-1})}{(X_n-X_{n-1})}(Y_n - Y_{n-1}) \qquad (2)$$

Assume having the same *DS-D* table previously used. If we want to find *D* for *DS* = 15, which lies beyond the range of values in this table, we must write the equation in the following form:

$$Y_{15} \approx Y_5 + \frac{(X - X_6)}{(X_6 - X_5)}(Y_6 - Y_5) \approx 1016 + \frac{15-6}{6-5}(1018 - 1016) \approx 1034$$

Under ABSOLUTE TEMPERATURE, we said it is *not* easy to obtain absolute temperature (T_{Abs} = – 273°C). If, however, we want to extrapolate the graph of volume (*V*) versus temperature (*T*) of an ideal gas to zero volume, the temperature axis reads – 273°C, as shown in Figure 1.

An Example of Extrapolation

Given: A layer of isolated material for which we have the following data:

Material's thermal conductivity (K_{Th}) at 0°C 0.04 W/h.m.°C

Material's thermal conductivity at 40°C 0.05 W/h.m.°C

Wanted: Isolated material's thermal conductivity (K_{Th}) at 90°C

Our data points for the first case are (0.04, 0) and for the second case are (0.05, 40), so K_{Th} at 90°C, according to Equation 2, will be

$$(K_{Th})_{90} \approx 0.04 + \frac{(90-0)}{(40-0)}(0.05 - 0.04) \approx 0.04 + 0.02 \approx 0.06 \quad \text{W/h.m.°C}$$

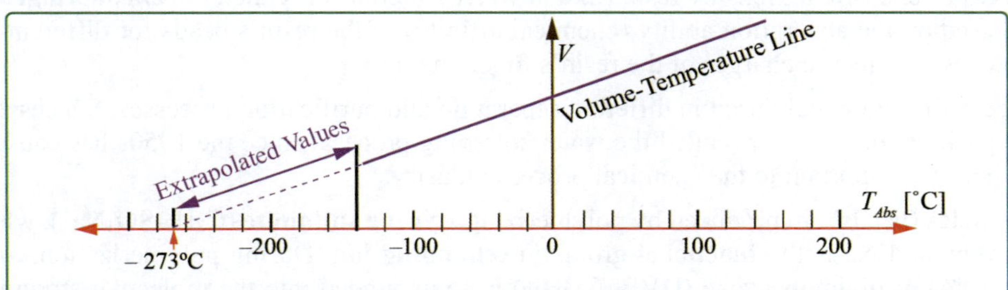

Figure 1 Extrapolating the graph of volume (*V*) versus temperature (*T*) of an ideal gas

I-43

INTRINSIC AND EXTRINSIC PROPERTIES

Intrinsic Property: An intrinsic property is the property of a physical quantity (simply **quantity**) that does *not* depend on the amount of that quantity in a system. Density (*D*), for example, is an intrinsic property of a system (because it does *not* change when the amount of that quantity changes in the system).

Extrinsic Property: Instead, an extrinsic property is the property of a quantity that depends on the amount of that quantity in a system. Weight (w), for instance, is an extrinsic property (because it changes when the amount of that quantity changes in the system).

[In Physics, **extrinsic quantity** refers to a quantity that is observer-dependent. Say, the wavelength (λ) of a photon is an extrinsic quantity because an observer moving fast in the photon's direction will see a longer λ. An observer moving fast in the photon's opposite direction will see a shorter λ. In this example, what is changed is *not* the photon's λ but the reference system.]

I-44

ION EXCHANGE CHROMATOGRAPHIC PROCESS

Study CHROMATOGRAPHIC PROCESSES.

I-45

ION EXCHANGE RESINS

BASICS

Natural resin is a gummy juice taken from some trees. **Synthetic resin**, instead, is produced by the polymerization of **styrene** molecules (C_8H_8, a monomer). Synthetic resin is called **ion-exchange resin** (simply **resin**) because it can exchange ions for other ions in a solution. Resin is a porous-insoluble polymer in the form of small (0.2 to 0.8 mm in diameter) round particles (called **beads**), usually yellowish (see Figure 1). The holes of the resin's beads are like those of a hard sponge but are too small to be seen by our eyes. Because of the small pore size (porosity), the beads have a large surface area, so they can selectively exchange ions in a solution for other ions. The process of exchanging ions by resin (like in water softening) is called the **chromatographic process**, which works based on the absorption ability (chemical affinity) of the resin's beads for different ions. [The affinity exists because of electric charges of the resin's functional group.]

Ion-exchange resins are widely used in different separation and purification processes. Successful application of resin in the purification of water (called the water softening process) since the 1950s has caused resin-based technology to become important to the chemical process industry.

The resin particles (beads) are produced by polymerizing **styrene sulfonate** (C_8H_7-SO_3Na^+), where SO_3Na^+ is a functional group, and Na is the functional group's **exchanging ion**. During polymerization, a small amount (typically 2 to 10%) of divinylbenzene (DVB, $C_{10}H_{10}$) is compounded into the molecular structure (matrix) of the styrene to crosslink (to bind covalently) its molecules (see Figure 2). Because of the high boiling point temperature (T_{BP}) of DVB, resin beads can operate at high temperatures and different pH ranges. In addition, the DVB affects the following operating parameters:

- **Operating temperature** (the *higher* the DVB content, the *higher* is the operating temperature of the resin),
- **Moisture absorption** (the *higher* the DVB content, the *higher* is the moisture-absorption ability),
- **Expandability** (the *higher* the DVB content, the *lower* is the resin expansion during operation),
- **Exchanging Capacity** (the *higher* the DVB content, the *higher* is the capacity of the resin),
- **Crosslinking** (the *higher* the DVB content, the *stronger* is the crosslinks), and
- **Porosity** (the *higher* the DVB content, the *larger* is the pore size).

Furthermore, the DVB content affects the resin's expansion during operation (the *higher* the DVB content, the *smaller* is the resin expansion).

The chemical process industry mainly uses the following two resin-based processes:

- Ion-Exchange Chromatographic Process: This is an exchanging process in which the resin's anionic ions are selectively exchanged with the cationic ions of the solution under process or vice versa. [The exchangeability between ions occurs (because of electric charges in the resin's particles).]
- Ion-Exclusion Chromatographic Process: This is an absorbing-excluding process in which the resin's particles absorb the molecules of some nonionic compounds (nonionics) of the solution (because of having opposite charges) while excluding (do *not* absorb) its molecules of ionic compounds (ionics). As a result, the ionic compounds appear first in the effluent (output solution from the column). In contrast, the nonionic compounds appear after the elution water is applied to the particles.

In both listed processes, the resin's particle (bead) size plays an important role, as smaller particles have a larger outer surface area, creating greater head pressure loss in the column.

TERMINOLOGY OF ION-EXCHANGE RESIN

Resin technology has its special terms. Below, several of them are defined and discussed.

Resin Regeneration: This is the process of contacting the resin with a regenerant to be converted back to its original exchanging capability (capacity) when its active part is exhausted (filled) and needs to be regenerated (reactivated or refreshed) with a **regenerant**. When regeneration is complete, the resin gains its exchange capacity and becomes ready for operation again. If, for example, the resin was originally in sodium form (Na form) and during the exchanging step, its Na ions were replaced by calcium ions (Ca^{2+} ions) from the solution under the softening process, the resin becomes exhausted with Ca ions. It needs regeneration with a regenerant that contains Na ions. This action, in resin technology, is called **regeneration of the resin.**

Na^+ Form and H^+ Form: Assume that a cationic resin (catex) with the sulfonic functional group $(SO_3)^-$, as shown in Figure 2, is exhausted with calcium cations (Ca^{2+}), so the resin needs to be regenerated with a regenerant. Further, assume that sodium hydroxide (NaOH) is used for the resin's regeneration. As the NaOH solution passes through the resin particles, some exchanges occur, chemically shown as

$$R_2\text{-}SO_3Ca + 2\ NaOH \leftrightarrow 2\ R\text{-}SO_3Na^+ + Ca(OH)_2$$

The R indicates the resin's matrix (structure), SO_3Na is its functional group, and Na is the exchanging ion. And the two-way arrow (↔) is used because ion-exchange reactions are **reversible**.

When the exchanging reaction is complete, the resin is said to be in the **sodium form** (Na^+ form), regenerated, and ready for a new batch of feed. If now, the column containing the refreshed resin is fed again with the solution with calcium cations (Ca^{2+}), the resin replaces its sodium cations (Na^+) for Ca cations (Ca^{2+}).

$$2\ R\text{-}SO_3Na^+ + Ca^{2+} \leftrightarrow R_2\text{-}SO_3Ca + 2Na$$

This reaction keeps continuing until the resin gets exhausted again. At that time, the resin needs to be regenerated again.

The above-exchanging reactions are based on the higher chemical affinity of the cationic resin for divalent cations (Ca cations) in the solution than monovalent cations (Na cations) in the resin. Thus, sodium ions (Na^+) from the resin are replaced by calcium ions (Ca^{2+}) in the solution. [This process is very similar to the water softening process by ion exchange resin.]

Resin Capacity: Resin exchange capacity (simply **resin capacity**) is the ability of resin to remove ions. Resin capacity is usually expressed as gram per liter of resin (g/L). For example, if a resin's capacity is 25 g/L and is in Na^+ form, 1 L of this resin can displace 25 g cations for sodium. The **theoretical column capacity** (loading) is defined as the **hardness removal efficiency** (hardness in feed minus hardness in the soft product) multiplied by the theoretical capacity of the resin. [The limesalt hardness is expressed as CaO or as $CaCO_3$ (as $CaCO_3$ = CaO ×1.8).]

Resin Life Expectancy: The life expectancy of resin is a period during which it can function effectively. The life expectancy of the resin is affected by its stability against thermal shock, pressure shock, the way it was regenerated, PH of the solution, and microbial growth, as well as treatment of the resin when it is *not* used between usages. Microbial growth is more active if the resin is kept untreated between usages.

Resin Fouling: This term is used when the resin feeds with a feed with a high impurity content. Resin capacity decreases faster than normal when the feed contains high-molecular compounds, such as colorants.

Resin Leakage: This term refers to the partial elimination of separating ions by the resin. To make the ion-exchange process economically feasible, an optimum balance must be reached between the factors affecting the ion-exchange process, such as resin-capacity usage and regenerant-level usage. This means that some ion leakage is allowed because it is too costly to remove all removable ions.

Resin Expansion: When the resin is placed in a solution, it expands. The expansion depends on the percentage of DVB used for crosslinking of the resin (the *greater* the percentage of *DVB*, the *less* is the resin expansion). Unlike strong-cationic resin, weak-cationic resin expands significantly at the beginning of the exchanging (exhaustion) step. Resin also expands at the backwashing step. For weak-cationic resins, the optimum expansion is about 200% of resin volume. [Columns must be partially filled to allow for expansion during operation.]

Resin Particle Size: Resin particle size and particle uniformity considerably affect separation efficiency (E_S). Resins with small particles have a higher exchanging capacity, but the particles must *not* be smaller than 0.25 mm to avoid a high-pressure drop. Usually, a resin size between 0.3 and 0.4 mm is desirable. The density (*D*) of such resin particles is about 1.3 g/mL, and its bulk density usually varies between 0.5 and 0.7 g/mL.

Resin Preparation: Resins used in food processing require careful preparation before being used. The resin bed should be flushed with at least three-bed volumes of soft water until the effluent is clear.

SELECTIVITY COEFFICIENT OF ION-EXCHANGE RESIN

The resin selectivity coefficient (K_S, also called resin affinity) numerically determines a resin's chemical affinity for an ion (the *larger* the K_S value, the *greater* is the affinity of the resin for the ion). K_S for $R_2\text{-}SO_3Ca + 2\ NaOH \leftrightarrow 2\ R\text{-}SO_3Na^+ + Ca(OH)_2$ (simply $R\text{-}Ca^{2+} \leftrightarrow 2\ R\text{-}Na^+$) at equilibrium (at the end of reaction with NaOH) can be given as

$$K_S = \frac{[Ca^{2+}]_R \times [Na]_S}{[Na^+]_R \times [Ca^{2+}]_S} \qquad (1)$$

The *R* subscript indicates the resin phase, *S* indicates the solution phase, and the bracket indicates an ion concentration (*C*). The *C* of the resin phase is usually expressed in mmole/g, and that of the solution phase is expressed in mmole/mL, where mmole is for millimole and mL is for milliliter.

The displacement of ions under process is based on the resin selectivity for those ions. If, say, the resin is in sodium form (Na^+ form) and is surrounded by a solution with calcium ions (Ca^{2+}), the resin displaces its sodium ion for calcium ion (because the resin has a greater affinity for Ca^{2+} than for Na^+). The next table gives the K_S (selectivity coefficient) of cationic resins with different DVB contents for various ions, compared with the standard hydrogen ion (H^+). [The K_S of other resins can be different.]

Cation	K_S (at 4% DVB)	K_S (at 8% DVB)	K_S (at 10% DVB)
H^+	1.0	1.0	1.0
Na^+	1.2	1.6	1.6
K^+	1.7	2.3	2.5
Mg^{2+}	2.2	2.6	2.6
Ca^{2+}	3.1	4.1	4.4
Ba^{2+}	5.7	9.1	9.4

TYPES OF ION-EXCHANGE RESINS

Ion-exchange resins are generally divided into the following two (2) main groups:

- **Cationic Resins** (catex): These resins are electro-negatively charged so that they can remove cations.
- **Anionic Resins** (anex): These resins are electro-positively charged so that they can remove anions.

In the cationic resins, the exchanging ion of the functional group (like Na in SO_3Na) can be exchanged for divalent cations present in the solution sample because of the resin's high attractive affinity for divalent cations. For example, the Na+ ions in the resin can be exchanged with calcium ions (Ca^{2+}) in the solution when it passes through a resin bed in a small or large column. Figure 2 shows the exchange of Ca ions with Na ions by a cationic-exchange resin (catex) with the sulfonate functional group $[(SO_3)^-]$.

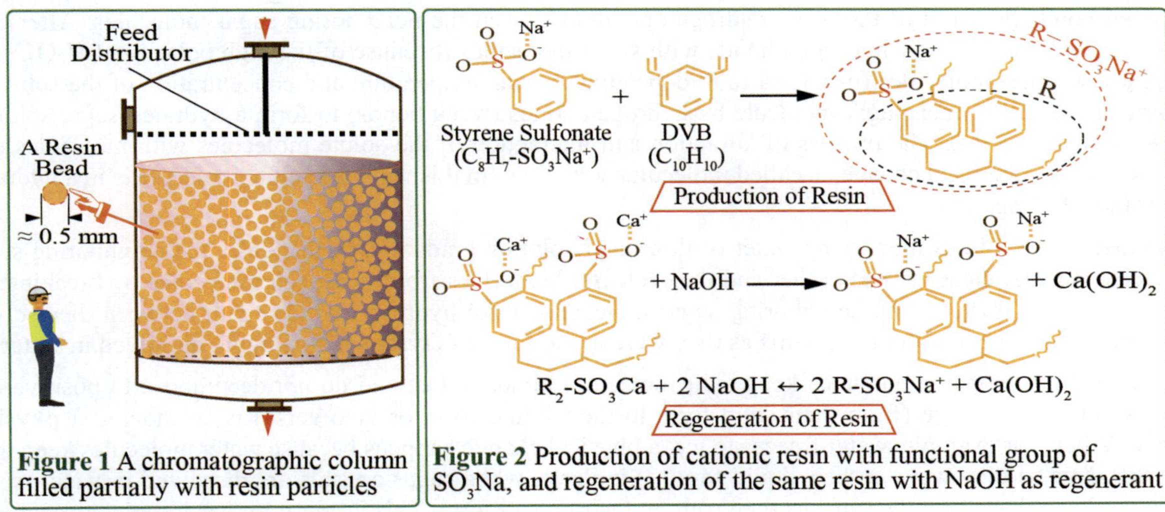

Figure 1 A chromatographic column filled partially with resin particles

Figure 2 Production of cationic resin with functional group of SO_3Na, and regeneration of the same resin with NaOH as regenerant

I-46

ION EXCLUSION CHROMATOGRAPHIC PROCESS

Discussed under the topic of CHROMATOGRAPHIC PROCESSES.

I-47

IONIC BONDS

Defined under CHEMICAL BONDS.

I-48

IONIC AND NONIONIC COMPOUNDS

An ionic compound can be ionized (decomposed) in a solution into cations and anions. Instead, a **nonionic compound** *cannot* be ionized in a solution. Salt (NaCl) and some organic compounds are examples of ionic compounds. Sugar (sucrose, $C_{12}H_{22}O_{11}$), water (H_2O), and ethanol (C_2H_5OH) are common examples of nonionic compounds (see Figure 1).

When an ionic compound is dissolved in water, an **ionic solution** is formed. Similarly, when a nonionic compound is dissolved in water, a **nonionic solution** is formed. Since ionic compounds deionize to ions, their solutions conduct electricity, just like metals conduct electricity by their free electrons.

An ionic compound consists of oppositely charged ions (cations or anions). For example, in a salt solution, the bonds in each NaCl molecule are broken to form a positive sodium ion (Na^+) and a negative chloride ion (Cl^-). Here, none of the ions has properties of the original compound (because Na and Cl are different from NaCl). Thus, the change in an ionic compound from its solid form to its liquid form is a chemical change. Instead, a **nonionic compound** change from solid to liquid form is a physical change.

Let us find out what happens when sugar (a typical **nonionic compound**) is dissolved in water. In the sugar solution (a nonionic solution), the covalent bonds in each sugar molecule are *not* broken and stay intact (because of the strength of covalent bonds). But water molecules penetrate between the sugar molecules and break the hydrogen bonds (because of the weak hydrogen bonds) between the neighboring sugar molecules. After that, water molecules create new hydrogen bonds with sugar molecules (because of the high polarity of H_2O). As a result, a few water molecules (usually 4 to 8, depending on the temperature and concentration of the solution) become connected to each sugar molecule by hydrogen bonds (weak bonds) to form a hydrated sugar solution ($H_2O–C_{12}H_{22}O_{11}–H_2O$). The process of attraction and interaction of the solute molecules with molecules of a solvent, with *no* chemical change, is called molecular solvation. In this way, the solute molecule is in a hydrated cluster (solvent cage).

Suppose we start to evaporate the water of this sugar solution gradually. In that case, the neighboring sugar molecules get first closer to each other and then release themselves from hydrogen molecules by breaking the hydrogen bonds. Instead, the neighboring sugar molecules make hydrogen bonds again between themselves. Thus, the sugar molecules look the same as they were in the form of crystals before being dissolved in water.

Because the nonionic compounds keep their molecules almost intact and do *not* decompose to positive and negative ions, the change (from their solid form to their liquid form or vice versa) is considered a **physical change**. When, for example, water freezes to ice, a physical change happens because water molecules keep their form the same as they were in their liquid form. Similarly, when sugar crystals are dissolved in water, sugar molecules keep their form the same as they were in their crystal form. This is contrary to salt molecules when it is dissolved in water. In the salt solution, thus, the change is a **chemical change**.

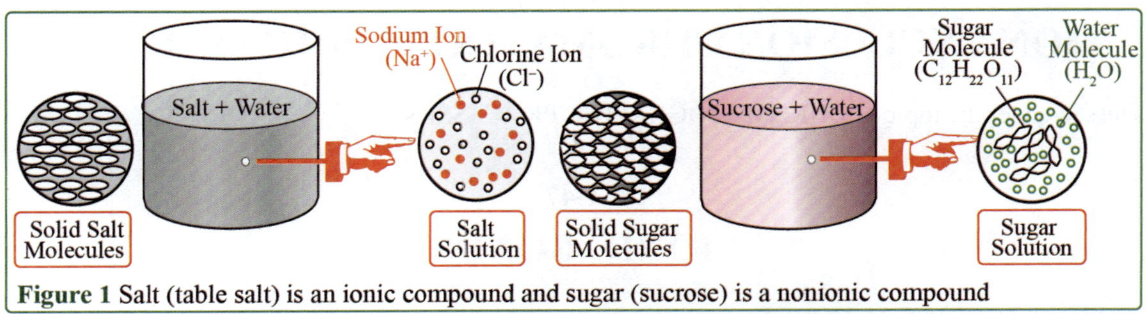

Figure 1 Salt (table salt) is an ionic compound and sugar (sucrose) is a nonionic compound

I-49

IONIZATION AND DEIONIZATION

Ionization: Ionization, in chemistry, is the process of dissociation of a chemical element (simply **element**) to anions (electro-negatively-charged ions) and cations (electro-positively-charged ions) by gaining or losing electron (or electrons). The ionization in an element's atom occurs if it has two electrons in its **valance** (outer) **shell**, known as the electron pair. The valance electrons are the most weakly-bound electrons.

During an ionization process, one of the following can happen to an atom: 1) It absorbs (takes) an electron from another atom to become an anion, or 2) It releases (gives) an electron to another atom to become a cation.

The following are four of the many ways that ionization can occur:

- It can occur in a chemical reaction, leading to an ionic bond between two oppositely-charged particles in a solution. In this way, acids can be ionized into their ions.
- It can occur by the light of a specific frequency. Light causes electrons to be released (given), creating cations. This process is known as the photoelectric effect (discovered by Einstein).
- It can occur by an electromagnetic field absorbing (taking) electrons from an element, creating cations.
- It can occur if a gas is extremely heated, creating plasma (the fourth state of matter).

Deionization: Deionization, which is the reverse of ionization, is the process of separating dissolved ions, such as cations (like calcium, sodium, iron, and copper) and anions (like chloride and sulfide), from hard water. Water deionization uses special ion-exchange resin (simply **resin**) to exchange hydrogen and hydroxide ions for dissolved ions in hard water to produce soft water. Deionization of hard water can be performed continuously using ion-exchange resin, ion-exchange membrane, and electricity. [This technology does *not* treat water chemically and is often used as a polishing treatment for water softening by reverse osmosis process.]

I-50

IONIZATION ENERGY

Study ELECTRONEGATIVITY, ELECTRON AFFINITY, AND IONIZATION ENERGY (as these are electron-energy-related subjects).

I-51

IONIZATION REACTION

Defined under the topic of CHEMICAL REACTIONS.

I-52

IONIZING RADIATION

Ionizing radiation is radiation composed of particles with a lot of kinetic energy (E_K). This huge energy can release an electron from an atom and fire it into its nucleus. This causes the split of the atom's nucleus. During splitting, a small amount of mass (M) of the ionizing nucleus is converted to a large amount of energy (E). Radioactive elements (also called **radioactive isotopes** or **radioactive nuclides**, such as isotope of uranium-235) simultaneously emit ionizing radiation.

I-53

IONS, CATIONS, AND ANIONS

Ions: An ion is an atom or molecule with a net electric charge (simply **charge**). A cation is an electro-positively charged ion, and an anion is an electro-negatively charged ion. [The process of dissociating an atom (here, it is also correct to say an element) to anions and cations by gaining or losing electrons is called deionization.] We know from the topic of HYDROGEN that a hydrogen atom (H) contains a proton and an electron (e^-), with *no* neutron. If, however, a neutral H atom releases an electron, a cation (X^+) is formed, and if it absorbs an electron, an anion (X^-) is formed.

$$H + e^- \rightarrow H^+ \qquad H - e^- \rightarrow H^-$$

Three important properties of ions are outlined next.

- They are electrically charged,
- They have different numbers of electrons and protons, and
- Their net charge is non-zero (because an ion's number of electrons is unequal to its number of protons).

Consider the formation of an ionic bond between a sodium atom (Na) and a chlorine atom (Cl) to form sodium chloride (NaCl, salt). As Figure 1 shows, the Cl atom absorbs one of the valence electrons of the Na atom, so both atoms become electrically charged; the Cl atom becomes an electro-negatively-charged ion (Cl^-), and the Na atom becomes an electro-positively-charged ion (Na^+). Then, an ionic bond is formed between Na^+ and Cl^- to create a NaCl molecule.

Cations: A cation (X^+) is an atom or molecule with a positive charge, like Na^+ and Fe^{+2}. If thus, an atom releases one (or more) electrons, it becomes an electro-positively charged, so it is a cation. Thus, a cation has fewer electrons than protons, giving it a net positive charge. Instead, if a cation (X^+) absorbs an electron (e^-), it becomes a neutral atom (X^0).

$$X^+ + e^- \rightarrow X^0$$

Anions: An anion (X^-) is an atom or molecule with a negative charge, like Cl^-. Because the electron's charge is negative when an atom absorbs one (or more) electrons, it becomes an electro-negatively charged, becoming an anion. Thus, an anion has fewer protons than electrons, giving it a negative charge. When, instead, an anion (X^-) releases one of its valence electrons (e^-), it becomes a neutral atom (X^0).

$$X^- \rightarrow X^0 + e^-$$

According to IUPAC, the process of naming cations and anions proceeds in the following ways:

- A **cation** is named by using its parent metal, followed by the word **ion**. Na^+ is sodium ion, Ca^{2+} is calcium ion, and Al^{3+} is aluminum ion. If, however, a metal has more than one ionic charge, each of its charges is specified by a Roman numeral. Consider Cu (copper), which has two forms, Cu^+ and Cu^{2+}. The Cu^+ is named copper (I) ion, and Cu^{2+} is named copper (II) ion. Fe (iron) also has two forms, Fe^{2+} and Fe^{3+}. The Fe^{2+} is named iron (II) ion, and Fe^{3+} is named iron (III) ion.
- An **anion** is named using its parent nonmetal, followed by the word **ide**. Cl^- is a chloride ion, S^{2-} is a sulfide ion, and P^{3-} is a phosphide ion.

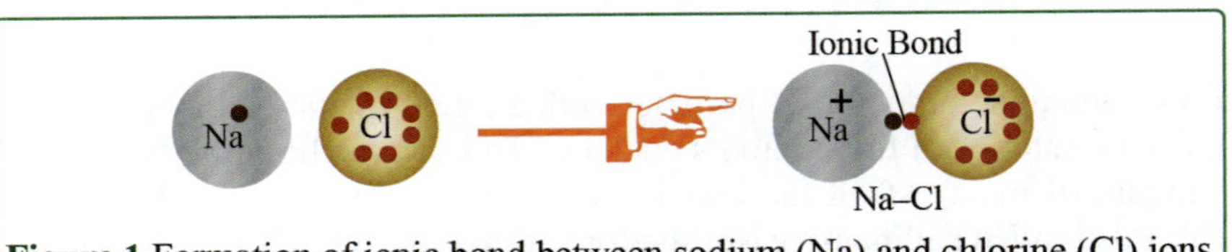

Figure 1 Formation of ionic bond between sodium (Na) and chlorine (Cl) ions

I-54

IRON

As the most abundant element on the Earth, iron (Fe) is a chemical element in group 8 and period 4 of the periodic table of elements. Its atomic mass number (N_A or A; the total number of protons and neutrons of an atom) is 26, and its atomic mass (M_A, the actual mass of one atom of an element) is 56. Iron is a metal with a ferromagnetic (permanent magnetic) property. At its Curie temperature (T_C) of 770°C, it changes to **paramagnetic** (with *no* magnetic property because of having two unpaired electrons per molecule). Some other properties of iron are given next.

- Its density (D) is 7874 kg/m^3(= 491 Lb/Ft^3),
- Its thermal expansion (X_L) is 12 µm/(m.°C),
- Its specific heat capacity (C_Q) is 0.45 kJ/kg.°C,
- Its molar heat capacity ($C_{Q.n}$) is 25100 kJ/mole.°C,
- Its boiling point temperature is 2862°C (= 5182°F),
- Its melting point temperature is 1538°C (= 2000°F),
- Its specific thermal conductivity ($K_{T.Sp}$) is 80 W/(m.°C).

Iron acts as a reducing agent in an oxidation-reduction reaction. Iron-containing ores consist of impurities, so the ores need to be heated in an iron kiln at around 1500°C to separate impurities from iron.

I-55

IRREVERSIBLE PROCESSES

Discussed under the topic of CHEMICAL PROCESSES.

I-56

ISENTROPIC AND ISOBARIC CONDITIONS

Study ADIABATIC, ISENTROPIC, ISOBARIC, ISOMETRIC, AND ISOTHERMIC CONDITIONS.

I-57

ISOCHORIC CONDITION

Another name for the **isometric condition**. It is discussed under ADIABATIC, ISENTROPIC, ISOBARIC, ISOMETRIC, AND ISOTHERMIC CONDITIONS.

I-58

ISOLATED SYSTEMS

Discussed under the topic of OPEN, CLOSED, AND ISOLATED SYSTEMS.

I-59

ISOMERS AND STEREOISOMERS

Isomers: Two chemical compounds (simply compounds) are isomers with the same composition (chemical formula) but different molecular structures, like A–B–C and B–A–C. Two isomers have different chemical properties and physical properties.

For example, glucose and fructose are isomers, as both have the same formula of $C_6H_{12}O_6$, but glucose has an aldehyde group (H–C=O) bonded to carbon 1 (C–1), and fructose has a ketone group (–C=O) bonded to C–2. Thus, glucose is aldohexose, and fructose is ketohexose, as shown in Figure 1.

Stereoisomers: Two compounds are stereoisomers with the same composition, but their functional group is in different geometric positions. Two stereoisomers have different chemical and physical properties.

For example, 1-propanol (propyl alcohol) and 2-propanol (isopropyl alcohol) are stereoisomers, as both have the same formula of C_3H_7OH. But in 1-propanol, the OH (hydroxyl functional group) is on C-1, while in 2-propanol, that is positioned on C-2, as shown in Figure 2.

Cis butane (called **cis-2-butene**) and **trans** butane (called **trans-2-butene**) are also stereoisomers, as their methyl functional groups (CH_3) are in different positions (see Figure 3). [The notation **cis** (in Latin means the **same side**) indicates that the functional groups are on the carbon chain's side, while **trans** (in Latin means **across**) tells us that the functional groups are on opposing sides of the carbon chain. As seen in the same figure, both CH_3 groups are on the same side in cis-butene structure while on different sides in trans butene.]

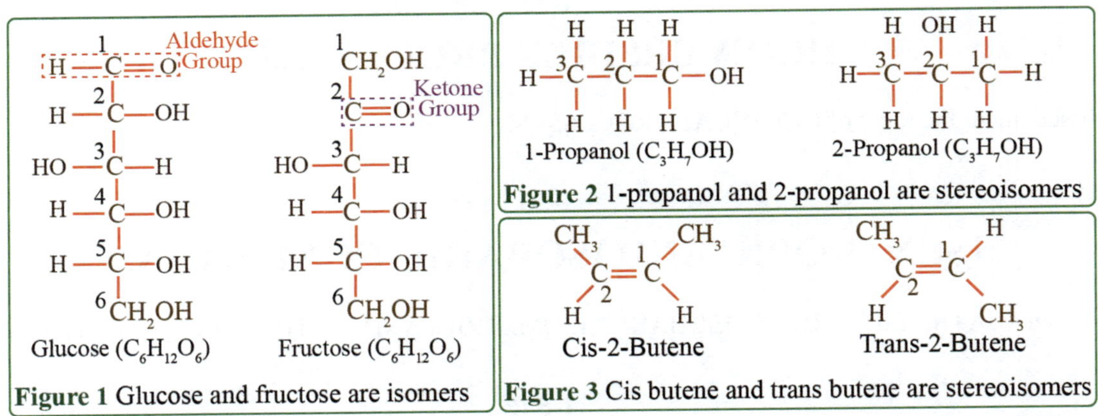

Figure 1 Glucose and fructose are isomers

Figure 2 1-propanol and 2-propanol are stereoisomers

Figure 3 Cis butene and trans butene are stereoisomers

I-60

ISOMETRIC AND ISOTHERMIC CONDITIONS

Study ADIABATIC, ISENTROPIC, ISOBARIC, ISOMETRIC, AND ISOTHERMIC CONDITIONS.

I-61

ISOTHERMIC FLASHING CALCULATIONS

Study BUBBLE POINT, DEW POINT, AND ISOTHERMIC FLASHING CALCULATIONS.

I-62

ISOTOPES

Isotopes are different forms of an element with the same number of protons but different neutrons. For example, the element hydrogen has three isotopes with different atomic mass numbers (N_A or A; the total number of protons and neutrons in the nucleus of an atom). The three (3) hydrogen isotopes are:

- Protium (H or H-1; with one proton, *no* neutron, and, therefore, N_A of 1)
- Deuterium (D or H-2; with one proton, one neutron, and, thus, N_A of 2)
- Tritium (H-3; with one proton, two neutrons, and, therefore, N_A of 3)

Unlike hydrogen, most isotopes have *no* special names, so they are recognized by their N_A. For example, carbon (C) has two isotopes (C-12 and C-14, shown in Figure 1) but *no* special names. [Note: The atomic mass (M_A) of an element's isotopes is based on the weighted average of the atomic masses of its isotopes. For example, the hydrogen M_A is the weighted average of its isotopes (protium, deuterium, and tritium).]

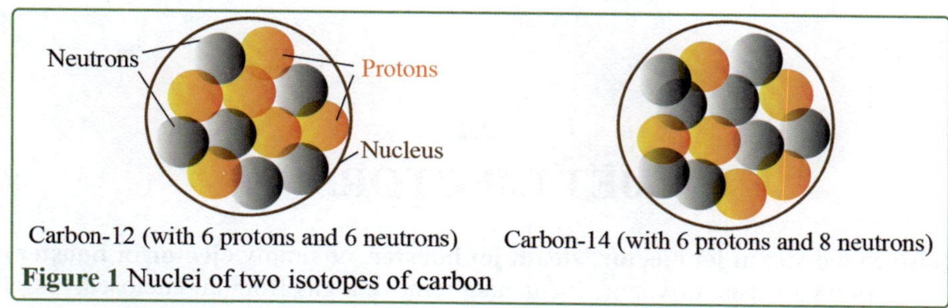

Figure 1 Nuclei of two isotopes of carbon

I-63

ISOTROPIC CONDITION

Study ADIABATIC, ISOTHERMIC, ISENTROPIC, AND ISOMETRIC CONDITIONS.

I-64

ISOTROPIC PRESSURE

Isotropic pressure is a pressure (P) that acts equally in all directions. The pressure present at every point in the bulk (under-the-surface) of a static fluid is isotropic and constant, so P = constant or $\Delta P = 0$.

I-65

IUPAC

IUPAC (International Union of Pure and Applied Chemistry) is an international organization that represents **chemists** in different countries. It was established in 1919 in Zurich, Switzerland and its administrative office is in Research Triangle Park, North Carolina, USA. IUPAC has published four rules for naming (nomenclature) chemical elements and chemical compounds in systematic, unambiguous, and internationally accepted ways.

J Section

LIST OF TOPICS

1. Jet Boosters
2. Jet Ejectors
3. Joule

J.1
JET BOOSTERS

Study JET EJECTORS.

J.2
JET EJECTORS

A jet ejector (also called **steam jet ejector**, **steam jet booster**, or simply **ejector** or **booster**) is installed in a piping system to compress air, gas, or vapor. It can also remove a gas from an enclosed vessel under negative pressure. For example, a jet ejector can remove the noncondensing gasses (such as ammonia, air, and carbon dioxide gas) from a condenser.

Jet ejectors work based on the Venturi effect (the pressure of a flowing fluid decreases, and its velocity increases as the fluid go from a **Venturi tube**'s wider section to its narrower section.) A steam ejector uses a fluid's momentum (mass × velocity) to move other fluid. An ejector uses a second fluid (the **motive fluid**) to move the main fluid at a high V (velocity). In most cases, the main fluid and the motive fluid are *not* the same, but in some cases, they are when compressed air is used as a motive fluid to move the air. In an ejector, the pressure energy (E_{Pr}) of the motive fluid (generally steam) converts into kinetic energy (E_K) to push the mixed fluids. Typically, the pressure (P) of steam used as the motive fluid in an ejector is 7 to 14 Atm.

Based on the functionality, the jet ejectors are divided into three types:

- **Steam Jet Ejectors** (simply **ejectors**)**:** They can be used on all kinds of evaporators, crystallizers, condensers, distillation columns, vacuum filters, flashing coolers, and more. Figure 1 shows a typical steam jet ejector, consisting of a converging section and diverging section (also called **diffuser**), connected by a short and narrow section (called the **throat**). In Figure 2, a low-pressure vapor's pressure (P) is increased by passing through a steam jet ejector, where the motive fluid is high-pressure steam. This process is called the vapor compression process.
- **Liquid Jet Ejectors:** These are designed to pump liquids, agitate, or mix liquid solutions.
- **Air Jet Ejectors:** These are designed to supply compressed air, particularly in hazardous areas! In Figure 3, an air jet ejector is used instead of a vacuum pump to remove a gas from an enclosed vessel, which operates under a vacuum (such as a condenser). Here compressed air is used as the motive fluid. The listed processes are two of the main applications of the ejectors.

Steam jet ejectors are classified into 1) Single Stage Ejectors and 2) Multistage Ejectors (usually, the multistage ejectors are a two-stage type, as shown in Figure 4).

Steam jet ejectors have some advantages over vacuum pumps, including 1) Ejectors have *no* moving parts and are therefore maintenance-free, and 2) Ejectors require very little space for installation.

Steam ejectors, however, are *not* as popular as they once were because, 1) They mostly need steam as motive fluid, and steam is costly to produce 2) They must be used at steady loads, pressure, and vacuum, and 3) They are more corrosive than vacuum pumps.

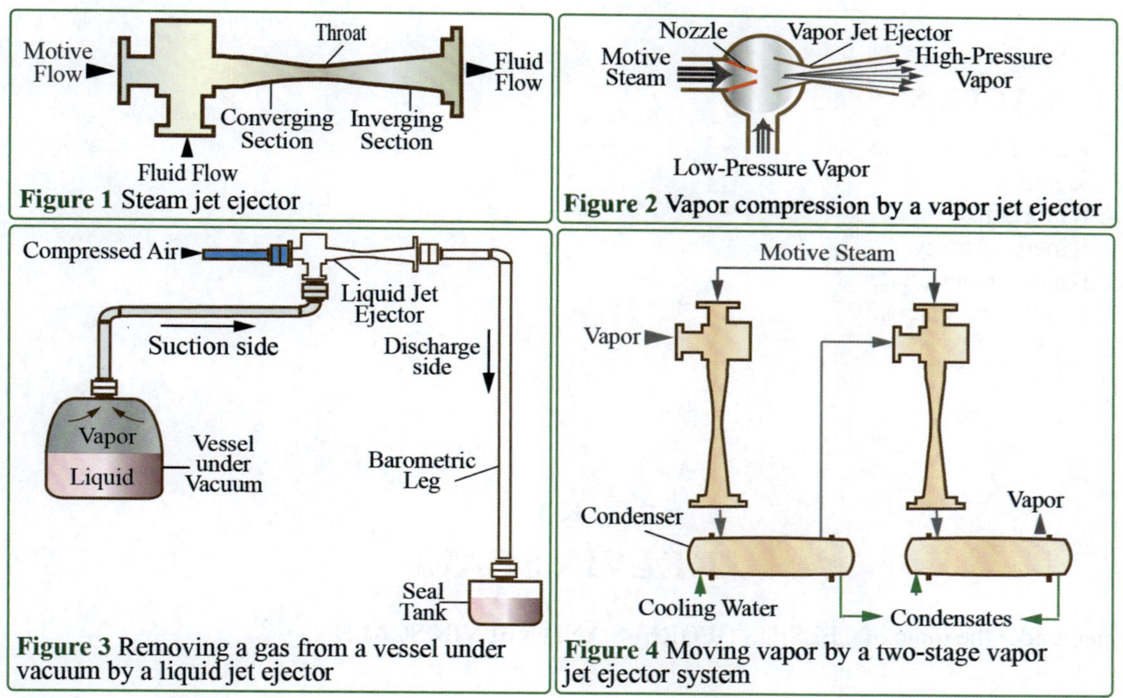

Figure 1 Steam jet ejector

Figure 2 Vapor compression by a vapor jet ejector

Figure 3 Removing a gas from a vessel under vacuum by a liquid jet ejector

Figure 4 Moving vapor by a two-stage vapor jet ejector system

J.3
JOULE

Joule (J, rhymes with the **tool**; named after the British physicist James Joule, 1818–1889) is the SI unit of energy (E) and work (W). One J is the amount of energy released from a candle, burning for one second. When 1 kg of natural gas burns, about 49 000 kJ (= 21 300 BTU/Lb) of heat energy (E_Q) is released. Joule is the product of the unit of force (in N, for Newton) and distance (in m), or N.m, where 1 N.m = 1 (kg.m/s^2)(m) = 1 kg.m^2/s^2 = 1 J. [For having a sense of the amount of one Joule, it can be viewed as the amount of force that an apple falling from a one-meter branch of an apple tree, would have had on your head.]

As for the work (W), Joule is defined in the following ways: 1) One J is the work done by applying a force of 1 N (Newton) through a one-meter length. 2) One J is the work needed to produce 1 W (Watt) of electric power (P_E) in 1 s (second). Such work is known as Watt-second work, expressed in W/s (wrongly Ws).

$$\frac{J}{s} = \frac{W}{h} = \frac{N.m}{s} \tag{1}$$

3) The amount of work needed to move 1 coulomb (C) of electric charge through a voltage of 1 volt (V). This type of work is known as Coulomb-volt work (the CV work). 4) The amount of electric current (I) of one ampere (A) passing through a resistance (R) of one ohm (Ω) in one second (s). This type of work is known as ampere/second work (the A/s work).

K Section

LIST OF TOPICS

1. Kelvin Scale
2. Ketones
3. Kilogram
4. Kinetic Energy
5. Kinetic Friction
6. Kinematic Viscosity

K-1

KELVIN SCALE

Defined under the topic of CELSIUS DEGREES AND KELVIN SCALE.

K-2

KETONES

Ketones are organic compounds that contain the carbonyl group (C=O), linked to two hydrocarbon groups (CH_3). A ketone's name ends with the suffix "one." Propanone (CH_3COCH_3, also called acetone) and butanone ($CH_3COC_2H_5$ or $CH_3COCH_2CH_3$), also called methyl ethyl ketone) are ketones.

K-3

KILOGRAM

As the SI unit of mass (*M*), kilogram (kg) is officially defined by the meter (m), the second (s), and the Planck's constant (*h*), which is exactly 6.62607×10^{-34} kg.m^2/s.

K-4

KINETIC ENERGY

Discussed under the topic of ENERGY AND ITS FORMS.

K-5
KINETIC FRICTION

Kinetic friction (f_K, also called **dynamic friction**) is the resistance to motion between one moving system and one static system or between two moving systems. Because of friction, conversion of mechanical energy (E_M) to heat energy (E_Q) occurs, so some energy losses, generally known as the **friction energy losses** (rather **friction energy used**, because energy is *not* losable), occur.

K-6
KINEMATIC VISCOSITY

Defined under the topic of VISCOSITY.

L Section

LIST OF TOPICS

1. Laminar Flow
2. Lanthanides
3. Latent Enthalpy
4. Latent Enthalpy of Evaporation
5. Latent Heat of Evaporation
6. Law (Physics)
7. Law of Gravitation
8. Law of Mass Action
9. Laws of Conservation
10. Laws of Definite Composition and Multiple Composition
11. Laws of Motion
12. Leaching Process
13. Length and Characteristic Length
14. Level Measurement
15. Light and Speed of Light Constant
16. Light Absorbance, Transmittance, and Intensity
17. Light Energy
18. Light Hydrogen
19. Light Theory
20. Light Water
21. Limesalt Hardness
22. Limestone
23. Linear Momentum
24. Liquefied Natural Gas
25. Liquefied Petroleum Gas
26. Liquid
27. Liquid Entrainment
28. Liquid Flow Equation
29. Liquid Flow Process
30. Liquid Head and Liquid Head Loss
31. Liquid Head Loss
32. Liquid Head Pressure
33. Liquid-Liquid Equilibrium
34. Liquid-Liquid Extraction
35. Liter
36. Logarithm and Antilogarithm
37. Logarithmic Mean Temperature Difference

L-1
LAMINAR FLOW

Discussed under the topic of REYNOLDS NUMBER.

L-2
LANTHANIDES

Lanthanides are 15 chemical elements (simply **elements**), starting from lanthanum (La) through lutetium (Lu), as shown in Figure 1, with atomic number (N_Z) of 57 through 71. They are customarily shown as an additional row below the main body of the periodic table of elements. These elements are called lanthanides because they fall after the lanthanum (La).

The lanthanides and actinides have similar chemical and physical properties known as **rare earth metals**.

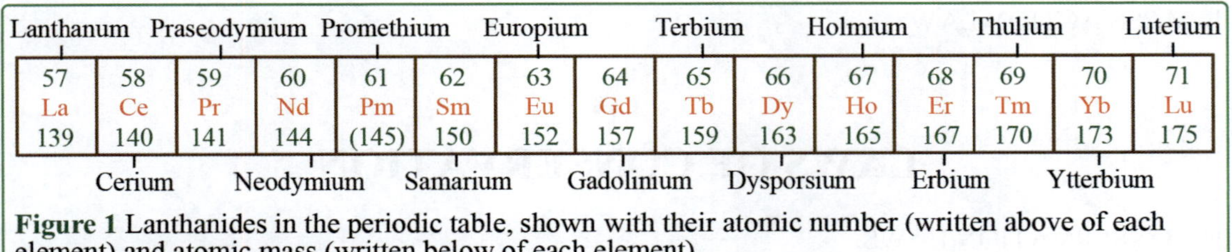

Lanthanum	Cerium	Praseodymium	Neodymium	Promethium	Samarium	Europium	Gadolinium	Terbium	Dysporsium	Holmium	Erbium	Thulium	Ytterbium	Lutetium
57	58	59	60	61	62	63	64	65	66	67	68	69	70	71
La	Ce	Pr	Nd	Pm	Sm	Eu	Gd	Tb	Dy	Ho	Er	Tm	Yb	Lu
139	140	141	144	(145)	150	152	157	159	163	165	167	170	173	175

Figure 1 Lanthanides in the periodic table, shown with their atomic number (written above of each element) and atomic mass (written below of each element)

L-3
LATENT ENTHALPY

Study SENSIBLE AND LATENT ENTHALPIES.

L-4
LATENT ENTHALPY OF EVAPORATION

See ENTHALPY OF EVAPORATION.

L-5
LATENT HEAT OF EVAPORATION

See ENTHALPY OF EVAPORATION.

L-6

LAW (Physics)

Study THEORY AND LAW (Physics).

L-7

LAW OF GRAVITATION

Study NEWTON'S GRAVITATION LAW.

L-8

LAW OF MASS ACTION

Study MASS ACTION LAW.

L-9

LAWS OF CONSERVATION

Study CONSERVATION LAWS.

L-10

LAWS OF DEFINITE COMPOSITION AND MULTIPLE COMPOSITION

Law of Definite Composition: The Law of Definite Composition (also called **Law of Definite Proportion** or **Law of Constant Composition**) states that " atoms combine in fixed ratios (whole-number ratios) to produce one (or more) compound, which is independent of its source." In another expression, this law says that "atoms of two, or more, elements combine in a definite mass ratio to form one, or more, compound)."

Consider a drop of water (H_2O), a glass of water, and a lake of water, as shown in Figure 1. A molecule of H_2O (with a molecular mass of 18 g) from each source consists of 2 atoms of H (hydrogen) and 1 atom of O (oxygen). In other words, 11.1 g of H atoms [that is $(2\times1)/18 = 11.1$ g] and 88.9 g of O atoms [that is $(1\times16)/18 = 88.9$ g] combine to form 100 g of H_2O molecules. We can, thus, express this equation in the following fixed mass ratios and mass percentage ratios:

$$11.1 \text{ g H} + 88.9 \text{ g O} \rightarrow 100 \text{ g } H_2O$$

$$11.1\% \text{ H} + 88.9\% \text{ O} \rightarrow 100\% \; H_2O$$

[Many other compounds contain H and O, but only H_2O has a mass ratio of 1 to 8 (11.1/11.1= 1 hydrogen and 88.9/11.1= 8 oxygen), as shown on the left side of Figure 2. Thus, a sample of H_2O, taken from any source and analyzed properly, the result is always 11.1% (by mass) of H and 88.9% of O. This, thus, proves the Law of Definite Composition.] According to this law, C (carbon) and O also always react in the same mass ratio (one-to-two) to produce CO_2 (carbon dioxide).

Law of Multiple Composition: The Law of Multiple Composition (also called **Law of Multiple Proportion**) states that "because certain elements can combine in 2 (or more) mass ratios to produce different compounds, these elements must, therefore, combine in 2 (or more) mass ratios." Consider the reaction of C and O to produce CO (carbon monoxide) and CO_2. The masses of C and O required to produce 100 g of these gases equates to:

$$42.9 \text{ g C} + 57.1 \text{ g O} \rightarrow 100 \text{ g CO} \qquad 27.3 \text{ g C} + 72.7 \text{ g O} \rightarrow 100 \text{ g } CO_2$$

As the numbers on the right side of Figure 2 describe, if a sample of CO contains 27.3 g of C, 36.3 g of O is needed to keep the ratio of 42.9%C-to-57.1%O the same in the sample. A comparison of these numbers with the amount of each element in the original CO_2 sample above shows that when a sample of CO contains the same amount of C as the sample of CO_2 (that is, 27.3 g C), the ratio of the amounts of O present in each sample reduces to a small whole number (that is, 72.7 g of O in the CO_2 sample is 2 times the amount of O in the CO sample, 36.3 g when each sample contains the same amount of C). This confirms the Law of Multiple Composition.

Figure 1 Based on the Law of Definite Composition, a drop of water, a beaker of water, and a lake of water all contain hydrogen and oxygen in the same mass ratio of 1 to 8

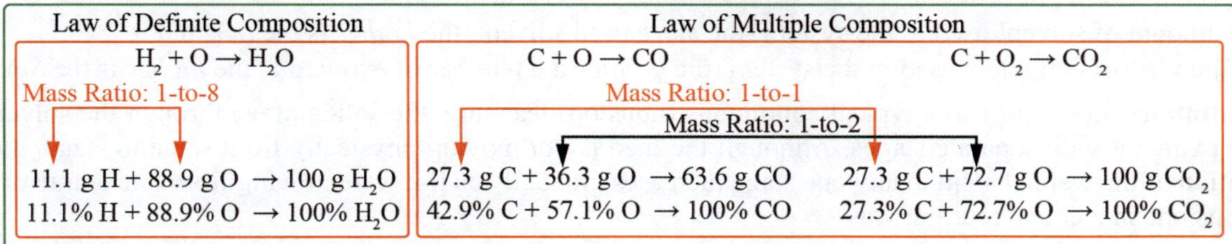

Figure 2 Proving the Law of Definite Composition (left) and Law of Multiple Composition (right)

L-11
LAWS OF MOTION

Study NEWTON'S MOTION LAWS.

L-12
LEACHING PROCESS

As a process unit (unit operation) of ChemEng, the leaching process (also called **solid-liquid extraction process**) is the separation (leaching) of a feed's wanted solute (or solutes) by mixing the feed with a solvent (called **feed solvent**, **extraction solvent**, **leaching**, or **extractant**), in which the feed's wanted solute is dissolved. The device in which the leaching process is performed is called an extractor. It is important to know the following:

- The word **leaching process** is used when the process involves **solid-liquid extraction**, and the word extraction process is used when the process involves **liquid-liquid extraction**. In leaching, therefore, an **insoluble solid** is in contact with a **multi-component liquid**, while in extraction, an **immiscible solvent** (a liquid) is in contact with a multicomponent liquid.

- In leaching, the solvent is usually chosen so that it selectively dissolves only the feed's wanted solute. So, the driving force of the process is the high solubility of the soluble solid.
- The leaching process resembles the **cake-washing step** of the filtration process. In leaching, however, the amount of the wanted solute removed is much greater than in the washing step of an ordinary filtration.

Leaching systems are classed into 1) Batch leaching and 2) Continuous (nonstop) leaching.

Batch Leaching: In batch leaching, the solids move through the solvent in a few extractors (4 in Figure 1). The feed solvent (the feed with fresh solvent) enters the first extractor, and the solute feed (the feed with a few solids) enters the last extractor. The leaching then proceeds in the next treatment order:

- The mixture of solvent and solids in the feed settles in each extractor.
- The overflow solution with solvent from each extractor enters the next extractor.
- The underflow slurry, washed in each extractor with the recirculated solution from the next extractor, enters the previous extractor.

This treatment order causes the slurry, which leaves one end of the system, to be strong in the wanted solid and the solvent, which leaves the other end, to be strong in unwanted solids. As the overflow solution moves from extractor to extractor, it becomes stronger in unwanted solids. As the underflow slurry recirculates backward from extractor to extractor, it becomes stronger in the wanted solid.

The piping-and-pumping system can be arranged to enter solvent into any extractor. And the used solvent can be left from any extractor, making it possible to charge and discharge one extractor at a time.

The separating efficiency (S_E) of the leaching process depends on the following:

- The amount of solvent used in the system (the *more* used solvent, the *higher* is the S_E), and
- The number of extractors used in the system (the *greater* the number of extractors, the *higher* is the S_E).

Continuous Leaching: In a typical continuous (nonstop) leaching, the solids move through the solvent in a single extractor with separate stages. Although the feed is *not* moving physically from stage to stage, the concentration of the wanted solid in any one stage increases gradually as if it were moving from one extractor to the previous one in a countercurrent way.

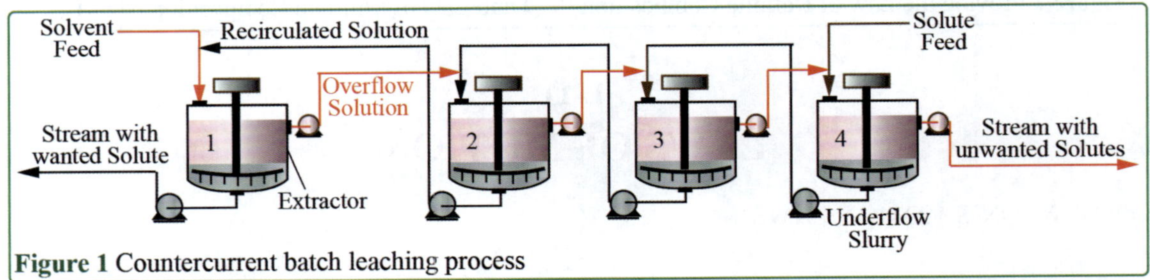

Figure 1 Countercurrent batch leaching process

L-13

LENGTH AND CHARACTERISTIC LENGTH

Length

Length (L) is a physical quantity used to measure a distance in space. [The words **length** and **distance** are usually used in Physics and ChemEng equally, and both are shown by the symbol L. Physics defines the **length** (L) as the longest dimension of a system and **distance** (L) as the length of a straight line between two points. We say, for example, the length of a tank is larger than its diameter, and the distance from point A to B is 1 m.] The SI unit of L is m (meter), and its US unit is Ft (foot).

In ChemEng, the length is also used to express the liquid head (h, a liquid's pressure expressed in unit of length). For example, we say the h of a liquid between a tank and a pump is 2 m, meaning that the distance between the liquid's surface level and the centerline of a pipe that connects the tank to the pump is 2 m.

[In calculus, the word **infinitesimal length** (dL) is used to refer to an extremely small length, where d is the sign for differential, L (length) is the variable of integral, and dL means that we are integrating over L in a specified (infinite) change in L from situation 1 to situation 2.]

Characteristic Length

The word **characteristic length** (L_C) is used in engineering to define the character and scale of a physical system (simply **system**). For example, for fluid flow through a pipe, the pipe's L_C is its area ($A = \pi d^2$) per its circumference ($C = \pi d$).

$$L_C = \frac{\pi d^2}{\pi d} = d \tag{1}$$

Similarly, in the flow of a fluid through a square tube with a length of a, the tube L_C is its area ($A = 4a^2$) per its perimeter ($4a$).

$$L_C = \frac{4a^2}{4a} = a \tag{2}$$

L-14
LEVEL MEASUREMENT

Discussed under the topic of PROCESS CONTROL OF CHEMICAL ENGINEERING.

L-15
LIGHT AND SPEED OF LIGHT CONSTANT

Light

As one of the seven electromagnetic waves (EM waves or EM radiations), light (the **visible light** or **light energy**) consists of elementary particles known as photons. Figure 1 compares the classical (non-quantum) and quantum perceptions of light, which are important in knowing how light acts. Let us first talk about the next two important light timelines:

- Planck's Quantum Theory: In 1900, Planck proved that when the light moves, its particles become quantized (accumulated) into tiny-separated packets, called the quanta (the plural of quantum), as seen in Figure 1. He also proved that the light energy is carried by its elementary particles (quanta later photons).
- Einstein's Theory of Light Duality: In 1905, Einstein proved that the light's quanta (he called them light's **photons**, as reasoned in a moment) *could not* be described as particles or as waves but as a combination of both (see right side of Figure 1). [Note: Einstein used the word **photon** instead of the **quantum** because an electron creates a photon, so both have similar properties, and the names rhyme.]

Considering these two theories, we can say the following important points about the light's properties:

- Light consists of individual energy packets (quanta), each consisting of extreme numbers of photons,
- Photons (light particles) have wave-and-particle properties, called wave-particle duality,
- Light packets deliver their photon energy at the lightspeed and different paths,
- Light packets behave collectively like a single-and-large particle, and
- Light packets travel individually (like discontinuous waves).

In the subjects of light, the following phrases have the same meanings:

An Elementary Particle of Light = A Quantum of Light = A Photon of Light

[In quantum physics, the word **photon** is used for elementary particles of light and other types of electromagnetic radiation, and the word **quantum** is used for elementary particles of any other physical quantity, so the terms **photon** and **quantum** can be used equally when talking about light and other EM radiations.]

It took over three (3) centuries for physicists to define the light's concept correctly, as were outlined a moment ago. A more detailed timeline of this advancement will be discussed next.

From 1704 when Newton published his second book (*Opticks*) until the early 1900s when Planck and Einstein published their articles, the exact nature of light was *not* proved with certainty. During these two centuries, a few physicists, including Newton, thought of light as a particle, while most physicists, including Tomas Young (1773–1829, British physicist), considered it continuous waves. But, both classes thought that light creates an electromagnetic field (EM field) around itself while moving (see left-side of Figure 2). This can be taken as the light's **classical definition**, which is *not* complete as its **quantum definition**.

Double-Slit Experiment: Tomas Young, in 1803, performed an experiment known as a **double-slit experiment** (Figure 3) to prove the wavelike property of the light. In this experiment, a beam of light goes through two slits. As the light goes through a slit or another, the waves' patterns change by interfering with each other, as seen on a viewing screen. The interference indicates that light consists of waves. But as the waves go further, some dots gather on the screen that seems like particles. Young could *not* answer the particle issue, so physicists could *not* believe that light is waves, particles, or both.

This situation continued until 1900 when Planck published his light quantum theory to prove that light consists of particles (quanta) that travel in many packets of energy. And the energy of these packets directly relates to their wavelengths (the *shorter* the λ of the light's waves, the *greater* is its E_{PH}, photon energy). Instead of wavelength, Planck used the wave's frequency (the *greater* the f of the light's waves, the *greater* its E_{PH}), as seen in Figure 4.

In 1905, Einstein approved Planck's discovery and proved that light has **particlelike** and **wavelike** properties. It travels as a wave and releases its energy as particles, known as the **wave-particle duality**.

Some light's other properties are outlined next.

- Its effect can be given by its wavelength (λ) or frequency (f).
- Its energy (E) can be calculated by Planck's equation ($E_{Ph} = h.f$).
- It follows the path of the shortest time between two points while traveling.
- It travels at a constant speed of 300 000 km/s in a vacuum or a homogeneous medium.
- Its particles disperse by a **prism** into different components with different wavelengths (Figures 5 and 6).
- Its beams are bent in a heterogeneous (inhomogeneous) medium, most evident on the boundary of two mediums with different refractive indices (IR), such as the boundary between air and water.
- It originates from electrons as they jump (leap) from one energy-level shell to another one.
- It has a photoelectric effect (releases electrons as it emits on the surface of most metals).
- It travels discontinuously, although it looks continuous (because of its high speed).
- It consists of packets of photons (the quanta of light or the particles of light).
- Its packets have dual (wavelike and sometimes particle-like) properties.
- Its particles have energy, although the energy of a photon is very tiny.

Light absorption is the penetrability (penetration ability) of its waves (radiations) to a medium. Light passing a medium can be absorbed, reflected, or transmitted (if the medium is transparent). When visible light passes through a red filter, all its waves are absorbed except the red waves, which pass through.

Based on wavelength (λ), light is divided into two general groups: (1) **Visible light** (with λ of 400 to 700 nm) and (2) **Invisible light** (with λ below 400 and above 700 nm). [Some physicists use the value of 400 to 800 nm for visible light.] Different regions correspond to different colors. **Blue** light has λ between 420 and 450 nm, and **red** light has λ between 680 and 700 nm.

The **invisible light** subdivides into two groups: 1) Infrared light (IR light) with λ of 700 to 1000 nm (longer than visible light), 2) Ultraviolet light (UV light) with λ of 10 to 400 nm (shorter than visible light).

[Note 1: Anything with mass *cannot* reach the **speed of light constant** (c) exactly but only can approach it. Light can reach this speed limit because it is made of massless photons (having *no* mass when at rest).]

[Note 2: The Universe gets its light from the Sun, which generates its enormous energy by turning mass (M) into energy (E) through the fusion process of hydrogen molecules (H_2).]

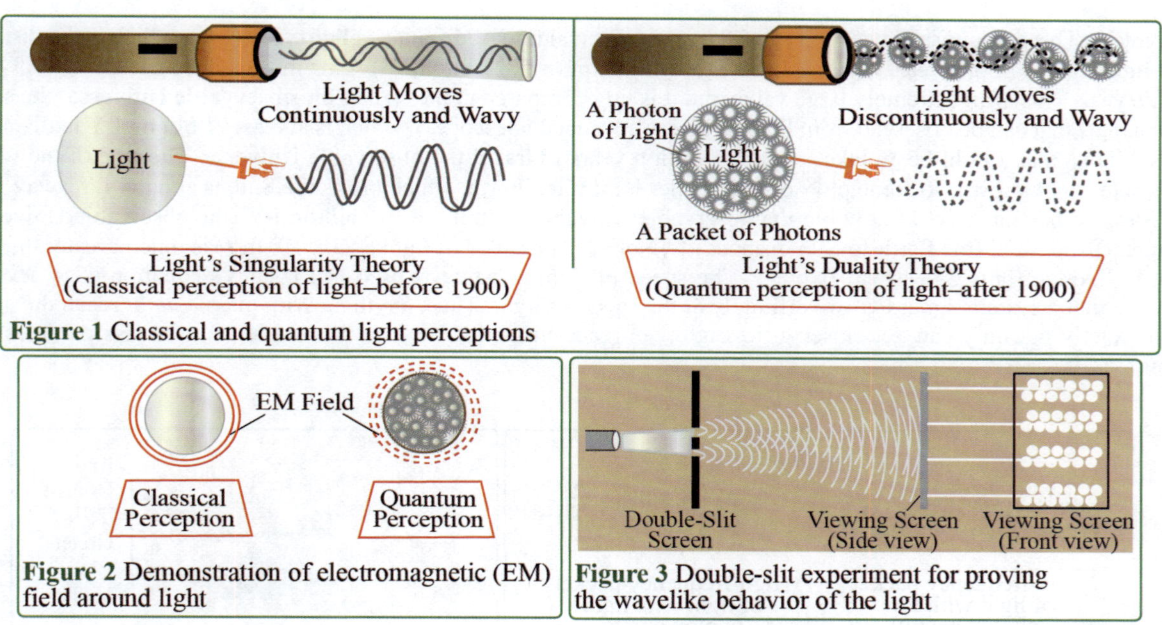

Figure 1 Classical and quantum light perceptions

Figure 2 Demonstration of electromagnetic (EM) field around light

Figure 3 Double-slit experiment for proving the wavelike behavior of the light

Speed of Light Constant

The speed of light constant (symbol c, from the Latin word *celeritas* = speed) is a proportionality constant, which relates the distance (L, for length) that a light beam travels in a vacuum to the unit of time (t). The speed of light in a vacuum is 299 792 km/s (≈ 300 000 km/s ≈ 186 000 Mi/s), the maximum speed any system can travel. [It is important to mention here that the speed of light of 3×10^5 km/s is only valid in a vacuum medium, as light travels differently in different mediums or when it hits an obstacle in its way. Light travels in water at around 225 000 km/s and glass at around 200 000 km/s.]

It is helpful to know the following about the speed of light constant (simply **speed of light**):

- The vacuum speed of light is **independent** of the reference's (observer's) speed. But, the speed of all moving systems is always **dependent** on a reference's speed (because speed is a **relative** quantity). This means that light travels at the same speed if released (emitted) by a non-moving source, a fast-moving car, a faster-moving airplane, or a very fast-moving space shuttle (see Figure 6). This is why physicists use the phrase **invariant speed of light** to refer to the **vacuum speed of light**.
- At the vacuum speed of light of 300 000 km/s, it takes 8 minutes and 20 seconds for Sun's light to travel 150×10^6 km (= 93×10^6 Mi) to reach the Earth. [The distance between the Sun and Earth varies because the Earth orbits the Sun, from a maximum to a minimum, and back again once a year.]

The following are also important to know about the speed of light constant:

- Massless particles, like photons, are the only ones that can reach the speed of light constant.
- Massive particles (the particles with mass), like electrons, can get close to the speed of light but need an extreme amount of energy (E) to exactly reach it. The closer a system gets to the light's speed, the more massive it gets, making it more difficult to accelerate without using an infinite amount of E. [It needs an infinite amount of energy to accelerate a moving system to move at c, and this is impossible.]

Before Einstein, Maxwell (in 1863) proved that when the light travels through a vacuum, it is under the effect of two physical quantities, permittivity and permeability. And because these quantities are constant in a vacuum, the speed of light is also a constant value. Therefore, to believe anything can move faster than light is to believe something exists with permittivity and permeability less than a vacuum.

[Note 1: The vacuum speed of light is used as the universal unit of distance, a **lightyear** (LY), which is the distance that light travels in one year, where 1 LY = 9.5 trillion km (= 5.8 trillion Mi). This means that light travels 9.5 Tkm in one year. This is an extremely large value, but it is tiny compared to the size of the **observable Universe** (the space and planets that can be observed from Earth with the advanced telescopes), which is at least 91 billion LY in diameter. This tells us that a light beam takes about 91 billion years to travel the observable Universe. The size of the whole Universe is *not* known, so some physicists consider it infinite. Earth, which orbits the Sun, is about 4 LY away from the Sun. To have a sense of how big the observable Universe is, think of 91 billion LY (the observable Universe's diameter) and 4 LY (the Earth-to-Sun distance).] [Note 2: The speed of light (= 3×10^8 m/s) is much greater than the speed of sound (only 343 m/s).] [Note 3: The speed of light constant is used in Einstein's equation ($E = M.c^2$) to indicate that a system's mass grows infinitely at the speed of light. Thus, anything with mass *cannot* reach the speed limit exactly but only can get closer to it. Light can reach this limit because it is made of mass-less particles (the photons).]

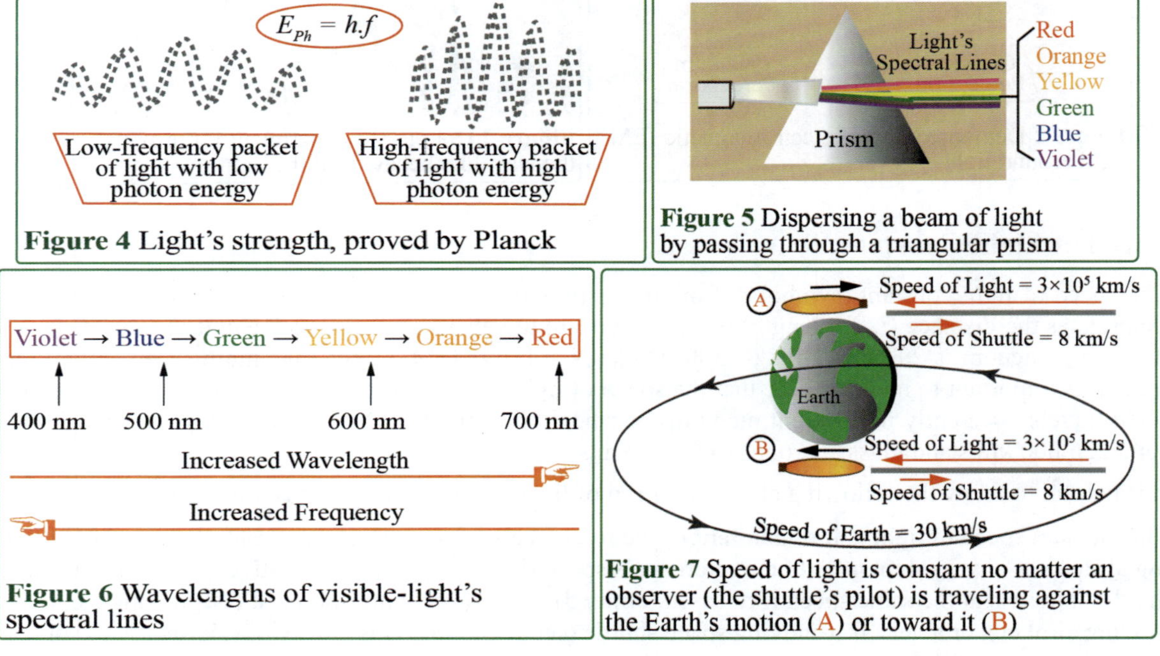

Figure 4 Light's strength, proved by Planck

Figure 5 Dispersing a beam of light by passing through a triangular prism

Figure 6 Wavelengths of visible-light's spectral lines

Figure 7 Speed of light is constant no matter an observer (the shuttle's pilot) is traveling against the Earth's motion (A) or toward it (B)

L-16

LIGHT ABSORBANCE, TRANSMITTANCE, AND INTENSITY

When light passes a medium (like a solution), it can be absorbed, transmitted, or reflected.

Light Absorbance: The light absorbance (A, simply absorbance) is a **unitless** (dimensionless) quantity that expresses the light's absorbing ability (absorbency) by a colored medium.

Light Transmittance: The light transmittance (T, simply **transmittance**) is a unitless quantity that expresses the light's transmitting ability by a transparent medium. [Note: In Physics, the symbol T is used for both the temperature and **transmittance**, but they are *not* used in the same equation so that *no* confusion can occur.]

Light Intensity: The light intensity (I, also called **light brightness**) is a quantity with unit **candela** that expresses its brightness as an observer sees it. The I is the amount of light transferred per unit area.

Both absorbance (A) and transmittance (T) can be measured by using the intensity (I) of a light's **thin beam** (a good approximation of a light's **ray**) when it passes a solution sample (the *darker* the color of a sample, the *more* of the light's beam is absorbed by the sample). Assume that 3 light beams with the same intensity (I) enter 3 different samples. The next 3 cases occur:

- If the sample absorbs *no* light, then $I_2 = I_1$, $A = 0$, and $T = 100\%$ (see the left side of Figure 1).
- If the sample absorbs *part* of the light, then $I_2 < I_1$, $A > 0$, and $T < 100\%$ (see the middle of Figure 1).
- If the sample absorbs *all* the light, then $I_2 = 0$, $A =$ infinite (∞), and $T = 0$ (see the right side of Figure 1).

The ratio of leaving intensity (I_2) and entering intensity (I_1) is transmittance (T).

$$T = \frac{I_2}{I_1} \qquad \text{Or} \qquad \%T = \frac{I_2}{I_1} \times 100 \tag{1}$$

Absorbance (A) can be given with the help of a logarithm to the base of 10 (shown as Log).

$$A = \text{Log}\frac{I_2}{I_1} = \text{Log}\frac{1}{T} = \text{Log}\frac{1}{\%T} = -\text{Log}\%T = -(\text{Log}T - \text{Log}100) = 2 - \text{Log}T \tag{2}$$

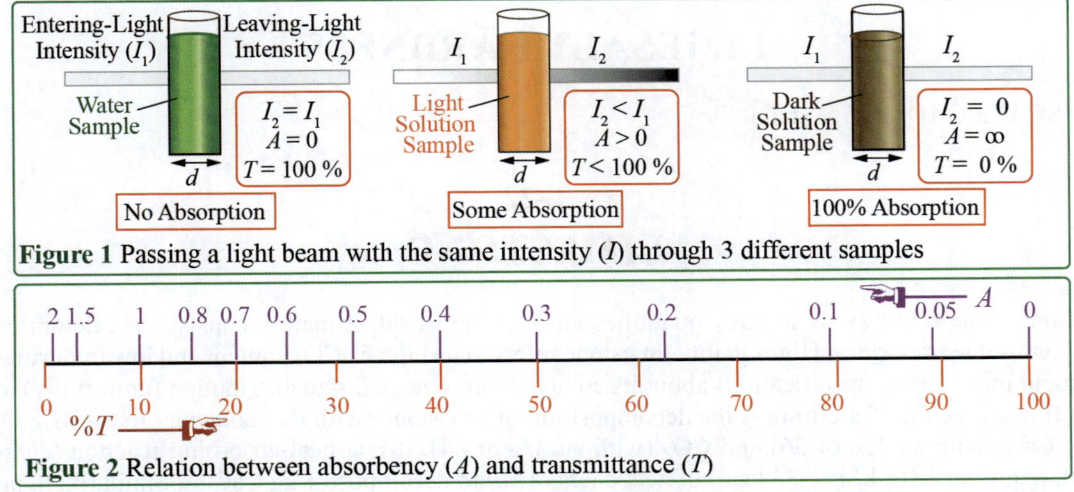

Figure 1 Passing a light beam with the same intensity (I) through 3 different samples

Figure 2 Relation between absorbency (A) and transmittance (T)

Because of **Beer-Lambert Law** (the amount of light transmitted through a medium gets weaker **exponentially** as it passes the medium) and because a sample's absorbance (A) is measured as a **logarithm**, the light's A is directly proportional to the sample's **thickness** (shown by symbol d in Figure 1) and to the sample's concentration (C). This statement applies to the light's T (transmittance), too. [Light's A and T properties have some applications in analytical chemistry, mainly in spectrophotometry for measuring the color of a solution sample (the *darker* the color of a sample, the *greater* is its A).]

L-17

LIGHT ENERGY

Study PHOTON ENERGY.

L-18

LIGHT HYDROGEN

Discussed under the topic of HYDROGEN.

L-19

LIGHT THEORY

Study EINSTEIN'S THEORY OF LIGHT DUALITY, EINSTEIN'S THEORY OF PHOTOELECTRIC EFFECT, and PLANCK'S QUANTUM THEORY.

L-20

LIGHT WATER

Discussed under HYDROGEN.

L-21

LIMESALT HARDNESS

Study SCALE CAUSING SALTS.

L-22

LIMESTONE

Limestone (lime rock) exists in large quantities all over the world. It mainly consists of calcium carbonate ($CaCO_3$) and some impurities. High-quality limestone refers to its high $CaCO_3$ content and low impurities. Limestone should meet certain specifications about its composition, size, and size distribution (uniformity) to be calcined well in a limekiln. **Calcining** is the decomposition of limestone (with the molecular mass, M_M, of 100) in a kiln to CaO (with an M_M of 56) and CO_2 (with an M_M of 44). It is a heat-absorbing reaction (endothermic reaction), requiring 1812 kJ (= 433 kcal) of heat energy (E_Q) to decompose 1 kg $CaCO_3$. Similarly, to produce 1 kg CaO, 3236 kJ E_Q is required (1812×100/56 = 3236).

$$1 \text{ kg } CaCO_3 \leftrightarrow 0.56 \text{ kg } CaO + 0.44 \text{ kg } CO_2 + 1812 \text{ kJ of } E_Q$$

$$1.79 \text{ kg } CaCO_3 \leftrightarrow 1 \text{ kg } CaO + 0.79 \text{ kg } CO_2 + 3236 \text{ kJ of } E_Q$$

Limestone containing $CaCO_3$ lower than 94% is *not* suitable for the limekiln. Limestone with high silicon dioxide (SiO_2, simply **silica**) content (more than 2%) creates **clinker** (hard and cement-like material) in the kiln, which can block the kiln. In addition, it prevents complete slaking. Limestone with high alkali (Na_2O and K_2O) content damages the refractory brick lining of the kiln. The following table indicates the composition and bulk density of a typical limestone:

$CaCO_3$	95.0% min
$MgCO_3$	2.0% max
SiO_2	2.0% max
Al_2O_3	0.4% max
$Na_2O + K_2O$	0.2% max
SO_4	0.2% max
Bulk density	1500 kg/m^3 (= 94 Lb/Ft^3)

On size, uniformed limestone particles 60 to 160 mm (2.4 to 6.4 In) across are suitable for calcining. This size of limestone weighs about 2 kg per piece. Large pieces require a longer burning time, and too-small pieces increase resistance to the flow of CO_2 gas in the kiln.

L-23

LINEAR MOMENTUM AND ROTATIONAL MOMENTUM

Linear Momentum: A moving system's linear momentum (p, simply **momentum**) is the amount of its motion (Figure 1). A moving system's p is given as the product of its M (mass) multiplied by its V (velocity).

$$p = M.V \tag{1}$$

A heavier (more massive) car has more p than a lighter car. When, similarly, a car moves at 100 km/h, it has more p than when it moves at 70 km/h, while its mass stays the same. If the driver tries to stop the car when it moves at 100 km/h by applying the brake, it takes a longer time to stop than when it moves at 70 km/h, assuming the driver applies the break with the same force. And when the car stops, its p is zero. Thus, the p of a system changes if its V changes, assuming its M stays constant.

As another example, consider a game of billiard. If one ball stops moving after hitting the other ball, the other ball starts moving with all the momentum from the first ball. And if both balls continue moving after hitting, each ball carries a portion of momentum. Both balls' sum of momenta (the plural of momentum) equates to the first ball's momentum (p).

$$p = p_1 + p_2 = M_1.V_1 + M_2.V_2 \tag{2}$$

The SI unit of linear momentum (p) is kg.m/s (according to Equation 1), and its US unit is Lb.Ft/s.

Rotational Momentum: The rotational momentum (L, also called **angular momentum**) of a rotating system can bring that system to rest. A rotating system's L is the product of its moment of inertia (I, the ability to change a system's rotational motion) multiplied by its rotational velocity (ω), as shown in Figure 2.

$$L = I.\omega \tag{3}$$

The L of a system with mass M rotating in a circle of radius R at a rotational velocity of ω is given as

$$L = M.\omega.R = p.R \tag{4}$$

For example, the L of the Earth rotating around the Sun in a circular orbit would be the product of the Earth's M multiplied by its ω and R (the distance between the center of the Earth and the center of the Sun).

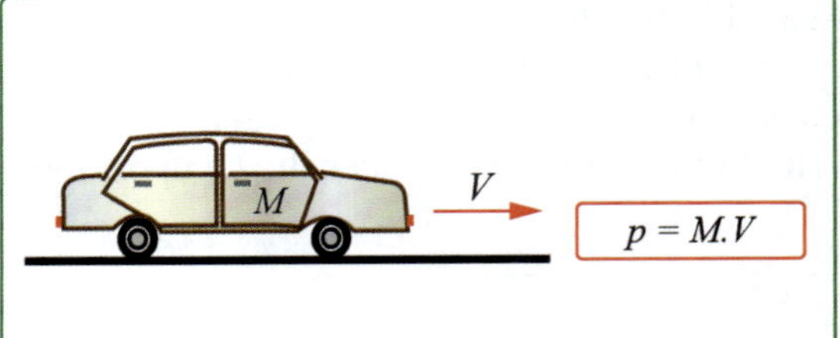

Figure 1 Linear momentum (*p*) of a moving system with mass of *M* and velocity of *V*

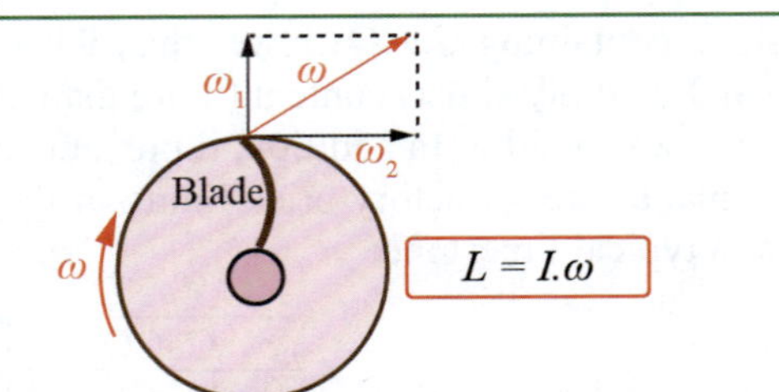

Figure 2 Rotational momentum (*L*) of a liquid moment of inertia of *I* and rotational velocity of *ω* at outlet of a centrifugal pump

The right-hand rule can determine the direction of *L*. If you curl the fingers of your right hand along the direction of rotation, then your right thumb points along the axis of rotation in the direction of *L* (see Figure 1 under RIGHT-HAND RULE).

Both *p* (linear momentum) and *L* (angular momentum) obey the next conservation rules.

- Conservation of rotational momentum states, "the *L* of an isothermic system remains constant in quantity and direction if *no* external torque affects the system."
- Conservation of linear momentum, which states "the *p* of an isothermic system (*no* temperature change occurs in it) does *not* change (remains constant) in both quantity and direction if *no* torque (a twisting effect of a force applied to a rotating system) affects the system."

Based on the two listed points, *L* is a conserved quantity (because it takes the same value before and after an event) and a vector quantity (because its value does *not* change in quantity and direction in an isothermic system.)

The SI unit of rotational momentum (*L*) is $kg.m^2/s$ (according to Equation 4).

[Note 1: The word **momentum** refers to **linear momentum** (because there are more momenta in Physics, such as **translational momentum** (momentum along a path).] [Note 2: The term **momentum diffusivity** (diffusion) is also used to refer to the diffusion coefficient.] [Note 3: In quantum physics, *L* (rotational momentum) also refers to the quantum spin (simply **spin**) of a subatomic particle, such as an electron, when turning around its nucleus.]

L-24

LIQUEFIED NATURAL GAS

Liquefied natural gas (LNG) is a liquefied gas, mainly methane and ethane, while liquefied petroleum gas (LPG) mainly consists of propane and butane. LNG is produced by cooling natural gas at low temperatures (−162°C = − 260°F) and atmospheric pressure. The liquefication process involves the removal of some components, such as water (H_2O), hydrogen (H), and carbon dioxide gas (CO_2).

The following are three (3) advantages of LNG (liquefied natural gas) over natural gas:

- It is safer to store but requires cryogenic (low-temperature) storage to keep it in liquid form.
- It is easier to transport but requires a cryogenic road trucker, and cryogenic see a container to be carried.
- It occupies 1600 times less volume (*V*) than natural gas. [It even needs less *V* than compressed natural gas.]

Listed next are some properties of liquefied natural gas:

- Its heat energy (E_Q), 38 MJ/m^3, is lower than LPG (46 MJ/m^3).
- It is flammable, odorless, colorless, non-toxic, and non-corrosive.
- It is mainly used to simplify the transport of natural gas from source to destination.

L-25

LIQUEFIED PETROLEUM GAS

Liquefied petroleum gas (LPG) is a fuel produced during crude oil (petroleum) distillation in an oil refinery or natural gas during extraction from the ground. The LPG mainly consists of propane (C_3H_8) and butane (C_4H_{10}), while liquefied natural gas (LNG) mainly consists of methane (CH_4) and ethane (C_2H_6). A full LPG container contains about 85% liquid. The LPG's octane rating is high, typically 105 RON (research octane number). Some other properties of the LPG are listed next.

- It is flammable, odorless, colorless, non-toxic, and non-corrosive,
- Its boiling point temperature (T_{BP}) is low (below room temperature),
- Its heat energy (E_Q), 46 MJ/m^3, is higher than the LNG (38 MJ/m^3), and
- It can be used in internal combustion engines, heating, and cooking appliances.

L-26

LIQUID

Discussed under the topic of STATES OF MATTER.

L-27

LIQUID ENTRAINMENT

Liquid entrainment (simply **entrainment**) is the movement of a fluid (liquid or gas) by another. For example, in an evaporator, the liquid entrainment is the movement of liquid under evaporation with the vapor (a gas) into the evaporator's vapor section. The sources of entrainment are many, including boiling a liquid in an evaporator, condensing a vapor in a condenser, cooling a saturated vapor in a distillation column, bubbling a gas with a liquid, and spraying a liquid from a spray nozzle.

In general, liquid entrainment is an undesired process that creates negative results, such as the following:

- It decreases the efficiency of a process.
- It causes the loss of a valuable processing liquid.

In an evaporator, entrainment occurs by some operating problems, such as

- Too high or too low liquid level,
- Too much foam above the liquid level,
- Sudden pressure changes in the evaporator, and
- Blockage in the entrainment separator's return line.

Another important cause of entrainment in an evaporator is when the velocity (V) of the water's droplets (water's tiny drops) in the evaporator is less than the velocity of the vapor stream. The main causes of this problem are high-pressure drop through the entrainment separator and low vacuum P in the evaporator.

Entrainment Separators: An entrainment separator prevents the negative effect of a liquid entrainment in a device, like an evaporator, which usually uses one of the separators shown in Figure 1.

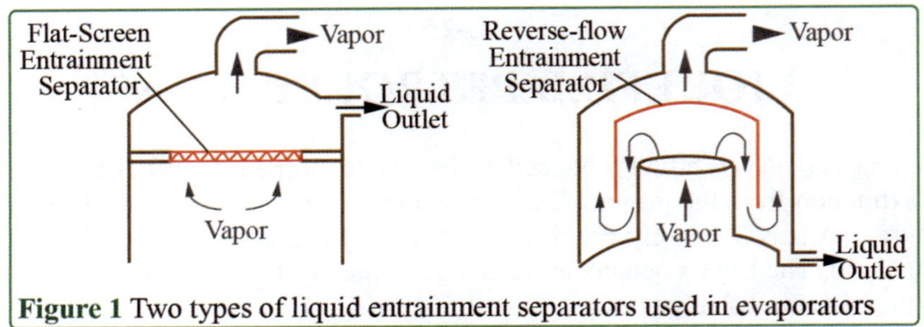

Figure 1 Two types of liquid entrainment separators used in evaporators

L-28
LIQUID FLOW EQUATION

The liquid flow equation (also called **Newton's viscosity equation** or simply **viscosity equation**) formulizes Newton's Viscosity Law (the *greater* the viscosity, η, of a liquid, the *greater* the shear stress (S_S) is needed to move it to a distance L at velocity V).

$$\eta = S_S \frac{L}{V} \quad (1)$$

Here, η is in Pa.s, L is in m, and V is in m/s, so S_S will become in N/m^2 = Pa, which is the unit of pressure (P). Similarly, if the η is given in N.s/m^2, the L in m, and the V in m/s, the S_S will again become in N/m^2 = Pa.

L-29
LIQUID FLOW PROCESS

BASICS

As a widely-used process unit of ChemEng, liquid flow (scientifically incompressible flow) is the process of flowing (transferring) a liquid from one point to another. Liquid transfer by the pressure difference (ΔP) in pipes to, from, and between tanks and systems is a routine operation in chemical process plants. Instead, gas transfer (compressible flow) is used in chemical process plants in a relatively smaller area than liquid transfer. We, thus, go here into a greater depth of coverage as we have done under the GAS FLOW PROCESS.

[Note: Although both fluid flow and diffusion are **mass transfer processes**, but are *not* the same. When mass flows by the pressure difference (ΔP) between two points, it is called a **fluid flow process**, but when it diffuses between molecules by concentration difference (ΔC), it is a **diffusion process**.]

The liquid flow is usually expressed in mass flow rate ($\dot{M} = M/t$, in kg/min or Lb/min) or volumetric flow rate ($\dot{V} = V/t$, in m^3/min or Ft^3/min) at certain T (temperature) and P (pressure).

Liquids flow freely. When a liquid (like water) flows in a pipe, it moves in the direction of P applied to it. When a shear stress (S_S), which is defined as shear force per unit area (F_S/A), is applied to a liquid in a pipe, the following actions occur:

- The liquid's velocity (V) changes.
- The liquid's flow direction changes.
- The liquid's flow pattern also changes.

When a liquid's flow pattern changes, it causes some time until the flow returns to its original steady pattern. And when the flow becomes steady, the S_S starts to disappear, so a steady flow is free from S_S.

When a liquid is flowing in a pipe, the flow next to the pipe's wall is slower than in the middle of the pipe. This occurs because the liquid molecules next to the wall *stick* to the wall. Liquids flow from a higher-P point to a lower-P point, so ΔP (pressure difference) is the flow's **driving force** (cause). [Scientists, equally, consider shear force (F_S), or shear stress (S_S, shear force/area) as the driving force of a liquid flow and viscosity (η) as its opposing force. S_S and η, thus, work against each other to form a flow pattern if, of course, S_S is *greater* than η.]

The upper section of Figure 1 shows the flow of a liquid in a pipe when an S_S (the cause of the flow) and F_g (gravitational force) are applied to the flow. And the lower section of the same figure shows that a flow's V in a pipe is *not* uniform across the pipe in a way that the V next to the pipe wall (boundary) is almost zero (because the liquid's molecules closest to the wall **stick** to the wall).

Before going further, it is important to pay attention to the following three points:

- **Shear stress** (S_S) is the liquid flow's **driving force**, and **viscosity** is its **opposing force**.
- **Shear force** (F_S), which acts in a **parallel** direction, is used in liquid-flow subjects instead of normal force (F, simply force), which acts in all directions.
- In the liquid flow subjects, in most cases of interest to chemical engineers, when talking about velocity (V), the average velocity ($\bar{V}$), which is half of the maximum velocity (V_{Max}), is meant.

A liquid is **flowless** (motionless or static) when one (or both) of the next applies to the flow.

- S_S (shear stress) applied on the flow is lower or equal to viscosity (η),
- P (pressure) applied on the flow is an isotropic pressure (acts equally in all directions).

When a liquid is **stagnant** (non-flowing), like water in a tank (Figure 2), pressure (P) is the result of the mass of the liquid above a reference point, so at a *greater* depth, *more* liquid acts downward (a swimmer feels more P when swims deeper under the water).

In the Earth's gravitational field with a gravitational acceleration of a_g, the ΔP can be defined by the head pressure (P_h) equation. This equation uses a_g (a constant = 9.8 m/s^2), D (liquid's density), h_1 (liquid head at point 1), and h_2 (liquid head at point 2), as seen in Figure 2.

$$\Delta P = P_h = P_2 - P_1 = a_g.D(h_2 - h_1) \quad (1)$$

In this equation, a_g is in m/s^2, D is in kg/m^3, and h is in m, so P becomes in (kg.m/s^2)/(m/m^3) = N/m^2, where 1 N/m^2 = 1Pa = 0.145×10^{-3} Lb/In^2.

The shear stress (S_S) applied to a liquid to make it moving can be created by the following:

- Pressure (P): When P is the cause, the liquid flows in the direction of P.
- Shear force (F_S): When F_S is the cause, the liquid flows in the direction of the force.
- Gravitational force (F_g): When F_g is the cause, the liquid flows toward the lower level.
- Heat energy (E_Q): When E_Q is the cause, the liquid keeps flowing in different directions because lighter molecules rise and denser ones take their place (heat affects the density).

Incompressible (liquid) flows can be classed by the Reynolds number (N_R) to laminar flow (smooth flow), transitional flow (in-between flow), and turbulent flow (rough flow). In other classifications, liquid flows can be further classified into a steady flow and unsteady flow.

In general, a proportionality constant (K_P) can relate the flux (F_X, a quantity per unit area) to its driving force (F_D), as given next.

$$F_X = K_P.F_D \quad (2)$$

We talk now more about the **driving force** (F_D) of a liquid flow. In a steady flow, a velocity gradient (velocity per distance, V/L, or $\Delta V/L$; also called **shear rate**) is the F_D of the S_S (shear stress). S_S is the flux (quantity) of a flow, given as the shear force (F_S) per unit area (A). Based on Equation 2, the K_P relates the S_S to the F_D as F_D =

V/L. The K_P for a liquid flow is called the **viscosity coefficient** (simply **viscosity**, η). Putting these words in Equation 2 gives us the liquid flow equation, which expresses Newton's Viscosity Law (the *greater* the η of a liquid, the *greater* S_S is needed to move it to a distance L at velocity V).

$$S_S = \frac{F_S}{A} = \eta \frac{V}{L} \quad (3)$$

The liquid-flow equation tells us that when the velocity gradient (V/L) in a liquid flow *increases* (by increasing F_S), S_S also *increases* in direct proportion. We, therefore, can say that V/L is the cause (the driving force) of the S_S, and the S_S is the cause of the flow of a liquid.

Usually, the liquids move (flow) like extremely thin layers in a certain direction, say, in the X-axis (horizontal) direction. Visualize two imaginary layers of a liquid, like two parallel razor-thin blades, as shown in the upper section of Figure 3. To move the upper layer by a small distance dL (d is for differential and L is for length) from point 1 to point 2 at a velocity of V in the X-axis direction, a S_S must be applied toward that direction. The driving force for the flow between two points is the difference in velocity (dV) per a specified-small unit length (dX; it is the same as dL, but dX indicates the direction of the flow). Thus, it is better to give Equation 3 in its differential form when the flow moves by a tiny distance of dL.

$$S_S = \eta \frac{dV}{dL} \quad (4)$$

From this equation, η (viscosity) can be defined as

$$\eta = S_S \frac{dL}{dV} \quad (5)$$

Either Equation 3, 4, or 5 defines Newton's Viscosity Law. Note that the SI unit of S_S is N/m^2 and that of V/L (velocity gradient) is (m/s)/m = 1/s, so η becomes in N.s/m^2 = Pa.s.

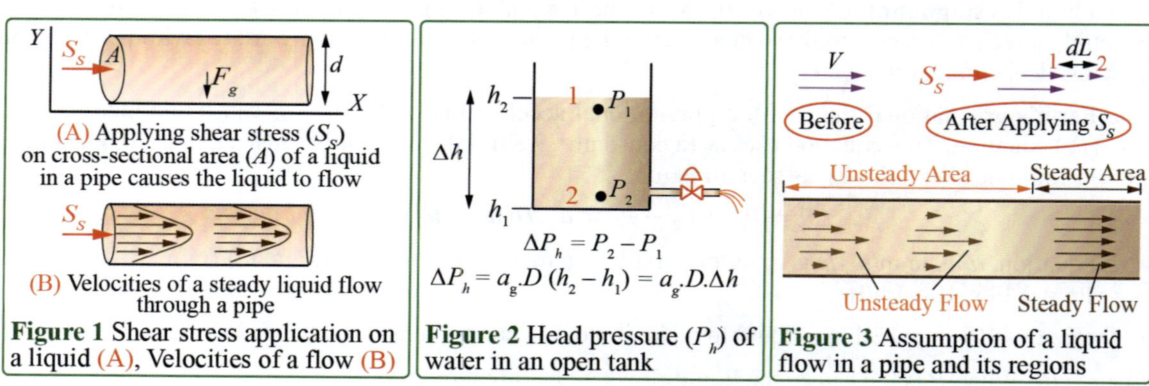

Figure 1 Shear stress application on a liquid (A), Velocities of a flow (B)

Figure 2 Head pressure (P_h) of water in an open tank

Figure 3 Assumption of a liquid flow in a pipe and its regions

LIQUID FLOW IN A PIPE

The Reynolds number (N_R, where N is for number and subscript R is for Reynolds) considers all four (4) quantities that affect the flow of a liquid in a pipe. These quantities, which are the liquid's density (D), liquid's average velocity (V), liquid's viscosity (η), and the pipe inside diameter (d), are used in an equation known as the Reynolds equation.

$$N_R = \frac{D.V.d}{\eta} \quad (6)$$

The units in Reynolds equation are [(kg/m^3)(m/s)(m)]/[(kg/m.s)] = (~~kg.m^3.s~~)/(~~kg.m^3.s~~) = 1, where we used the unit for viscosity (η) as kg/m.s = Pa.s. As seen, the units cancel out, so N_R becomes a **unitless quantity**. The mass flow rate ($\dot{M}$ in kg/time) of a liquid in a pipe is the product of the liquid's density (D) multiplied by its volumetric flow rate ($\dot{V}$).

$$\dot{M} = D.\dot{V} = D.V.A = D.V.\pi\frac{d^2}{4} \quad (7)$$

In this equation, A is the pipe's cross-sectional area ($= \pi R^2 = \pi d^2/4$, where R is the pipe inside radius). Because the product of $V.A$ is $\dot{V}$ (volumetric flow rate, in m^3/time), this equation can be written as

$$\dot{V} = V.\pi\frac{d^2}{4} \tag{8}$$

From Equation 7, $D.V = 4\dot{M}/\pi d^2$. Substituting Equation 7 into Equation 6 gives us N_R (Reynolds number).

$$N_R = \frac{D.V.d}{\eta} = \frac{4\dot{M}.d}{\eta.\pi.d^2} = \frac{4\dot{M}}{\eta.\pi.d} \tag{9}$$

This equation can only calculate N_R for Newtonian liquids. For nonNewtonian liquids, N_R is calculated as

$$N_R = 2^{3-n}\left(\frac{n}{3n+1}\right)^n \frac{D.V^{2-n}.d}{\eta} \tag{10}$$

[For Newtonian liquids (when $n = 1$), this equation changes to the simple form of the Reynolds equation (Equation 6).]

Example 1 on Liquid Flow

Given: A solution with 15% dissolved solids is pumped at 20°C through a pipe to a higher-level tank with assumptions that *no* friction exists in the flow.

Reynolds number of the flow (N_R)	2000
Tank's height (h)	5 m
Tank's diameter (dT)	3 m
Pipe's inside diameter (d)	0.2 m (200 mm = 8 In)
Solution's viscosity (η)	3×10–3 Pa.s (3 Cp)
Solution's density (D)	1055 Kg/m^3

Wanted: 1) Tank's volume, 2) Solution's average velocity (V), 3) The time needed to fill the tank.

$$V = \pi\left(\frac{d_T}{2}\right)^2 h = 3.14\left(\frac{3}{2}\right)^2 5 = 35.3 \text{ m}^3 \ (= 1246 \text{ Ft}^3)$$

$$V = \frac{N_R.\eta}{d.D} = \frac{2000\times3\times10^{-3}}{0.2\times1055} = 0.03\ [\text{Pa.s}]/[(\text{m})(\text{kg/m}^3)] = [\text{Pa.s}]/[\text{kg/m}^2] =$$

$$[(\text{N/m}^2)\text{s}]/[\text{kg/m}^2] = \text{s}.[(\text{kg.m/s}^2)/\text{m}^2]/[\text{kg/m}^2] = [\text{kg/m.s}]/[\text{kg/m}^2] = \text{m/s}$$

To calculate the time needed to fill the tank, we need the solution's volumetric flow rate ($\dot{V}$).

$$\dot{V} = V.\pi\frac{d^2}{4} = 0.03 \times 3.14 \times \frac{0.2^2}{4} = 9.4 \times 10^{-4} \text{ m}^3/\text{s} \ (= 3.4 \text{ m}^3/\text{h})$$

$$t = \frac{V}{\dot{V}} = \frac{35.3}{3.4} = 10.4 \text{ h}$$

Visualization of a Liquid Flow in a Pipe

A liquid flow in a pipe can be visualized as many imaginary stream layers (S-layers), which slide over each other (like playing cards) when the liquid moves from one point to another. When a fitting (attached part like a tee or elbow) exists in the flow stream, the velocity (V) of the flow changes, so the liquid starts moving in an unsteady way. As a result, all (or some) stream layers change their shape to boundary layers (B-layers), which flow in the following ways:

- They flow in a slow and unsteady way close to the pipe's wall,
- They flow at considerably lower velocity than stream layers.

From what has been said, we can say that boundary layers are deformed stream layers.

[Note 1: For more information about boundary and stream layers' shapes, refer to STREAM AND BOUNDARY LAYERS.] [Note 2: The length of a piping system (pipes, pumps, valves, and more) to move a liquid from point 1 to 2 in a chemical process plant is different. Thus, our study here applies to piping systems, which are as small as a short length of a pipe or as large as a long pipeline that carries a liquid from one side of a chemical plant to the other side and has several attached and detached parts.]

Entrance and Developed Region in a Pipe

A pressure change (pressure drop) occurs when a liquid with a steady flow enters a pipe. The P change increases slowly at a low flow rate, but at high rates, it increases rapidly (as the square of the liquid's velocity). P change, which creates frictions (obstructions), generally occurs because liquid molecules 1) Rub along the pipe's wall and 2) Hit some fittings that usually exist in a pipeline.

On the deformation of a steady flow when it enters a pipe, **stream layers** (S-layers) go through two regions with different characteristics. Listed next are the regions.

- **Unsteady Region:** Unsteady (entrance) region is a short distance of unsteady flow immediately at the pipe entrance, shown in the lower section of Figure 3 with **unequal arrows** (for unequal velocities). At this distance, **boundary layers** form and gradually develop until they reach the pipe center. They start to move at a uniform velocity in the form of stream layers, so the flow at the center behaves as a steady flow. The length of the entrance region is necessary for the boundary layers to reach the center of the pipe to establish a steady flow is known as the **entrance length** (L_E).
- **Steady Region:** Steady (developed) region is the following pipe length after the entrance, the unsteady region, shown in Figure 3 with **equal arrows** (for equal velocity vectors). At the start of this distance, boundary layers occupy the main portion of the cross-section of the pipe. But, gradually become stream layers when they reach the pipe center to occupy the entire stream flow and move steadily at a uniform velocity. The point that the layers start to move in a steady-flow way is the beginning of the steady region. From this point on, the flow remains unchanged during the remaining length of the pipe unless there is an object (like a pipe fitting) on the way of the flow.

[Here and then, we deal with steady flows, which move with uniform velocity in fully-filled pipes. A flow in a partially-filled pipe almost has the same rules and equations.]

The ratio (a unitless quantity) of the **entrance length** (L_E in m) to the **pipe's inside diameter** (d_P in m) for a liquid with a laminar flow depends on the Reynolds number (N_R).

$$\frac{L_E}{d_P} = 0.05N_R \tag{11}$$

According to this equation, for example, the L_E for a 100-mm (0.1 m = 4 In) d_P, in which a liquid with N_R of 1400 is flowing, is 7 m (= 23 Ft). For a **turbulent flow**, however, L_E is almost independent of the N_R, and can be estimated by using the following simple equation:

$$L_E = 50d_P \tag{12}$$

ENERGY BALANCE OF A LIQUID FLOW

Bernoulli's equation, in its different forms, is usually used to balance the energy (E) required to pump a liquid in a pipe. Consider a pumping system in which a pump elevates a liquid at a constant $\dot{V}$ (volumetric flow rate). The energies that the pump uses to elevate the liquid from location 1 to 2 are the following:

- Pressure Energy**:** The E_{Pr} is used to overcome the liquid's change in density (ΔD).
- Kinetic Energy**:** The E_K is used to overcome the liquid's change in velocity (ΔV).
- Potential Energy**:** The E_P is used to overcome the elevation change (Δh), where h is for the liquid head (liquid's height above a reference level). [The E_P is related to gravitational acceleration (a_g, a constant = 9.8 m/s^2 on the Earth).]
- Frictional Energy**:** The E_f (also called **frictional work**) is used to overcome the pipe's frictions, pump's frictions (because of pump's fittings), and liquid's friction (because of liquid's viscosity). The E_f is the energy spent in the pumping system to overcome the pipe's friction, pump's friction, and liquid's friction. [The value of E_f is always **positive** (because it represents the E given to frictions. Also, note that the frictional effect decreases the liquid's mechanical energy by converting it to heat energy. That is why the word **frictional energy loss** is also used.]

- Shaft Work: The W_S (also called **pump work**) is the E in the form of W (work), used on the pump's shaft. [The value of the W_S is **negative** when the system (here the liquid) does work on its surrounding (here the pump's shaft) and **positive** when work is done on the system by its outside. The W_S is also **negative** in a turbine because falling water (the system) from a dam turns the turbine's shaft (the surrounding). Also, note that W_S done by water *decreases* the energy of water as it turns the turbine shaft.]

Using all five terms gives us the complete form of the Bernoulli equation that states, "the net result of all energies applied on a flow is zero."

$$\frac{P_2-P_1}{D}+\frac{V_2^2-V_1^2}{2}+a_g(h_2-h_1)+E_f-W_S=0 \tag{13}$$

[Although each of the energy terms used in Bernoulli equations represents different functions, all of them are in the unit of specific energy (J/kg), which is the energy (in J) per unit mass (in kg) of the liquid to be pumped. The unit of the first term is $(N/m^2)/(kg/m^3) = (N.m)/kg = J/kg$. The unit of the second term is $m^2/s^2 = (N.m)/kg = J/kg$. And the unit of the third term is $(m/s^2).m = m^2/s^2 = (N.m)/kg = J/kg$. And those of the fourth and fifth terms are also in J/kg. Thus, the overall result will be in J/kg, also.]

When using the Bernoulli equation, remembering the following two (2) brief points is helpful:

- If a pipe connects two tanks under P_{Atm}, and the liquid moves from one tank to another, there is *no* pressure change, so $P_1 = P_2$ and $P_1 - P_2 = \Delta P = 0$. The first term drops, so it does *not* need to be included in calculations. If, however, the tanks are under different P, the first term must be included.
- If the liquid is *not* viscous, its average velocity from 1 to 2 does *not* change ($\Delta V = 0$), so the second term of the Bernoulli equation drops.

For deriving the related balance equations, three simplifying assumptions are usually used:

- The flow in a pipe proceeds by gravity or by a pump,
- The flow proceeds in a steady-and-laminar way (called developed flow), and
- The flow from point 1 to 2 proceeds with *no* change in the liquid's **density** ($\Delta D = 0$).

Based on the Bernoulli equation and assumptions, we will discuss energy balance and ΔP on

- A flowing liquid in a pipe without friction (f) and pump's shaft work (W_S), and
- A flowing liquid in a pipe with friction and pump shaft work.

Energy Balance on a Liquid Flow without Shaft Work and Friction

Figure 4 shows a non-viscous (frictionless) steady liquid flow in an inclined pipe with a constant cross-sectional area (A) by gravity (without the pump's shaft work, $W_S = 0$). When the changes in D are *not* considerable (incompressible flow), the resultant of all energies applied to the flow is 0, and the Bernoulli equation becomes simpler.

$$\frac{P}{D}+\frac{1}{2}V^2+a_g.h=0 \tag{14}$$

The flow's **pressure drop** (ΔP) between points 1 and 2 inside a pipe can be calculated as

$$\frac{\Delta P}{D}+\frac{1}{2}\Delta V^2+a_g.\Delta h=\frac{P_2-P_1}{D}+\frac{1}{2}(V_2^2-V_1^2)+a_g(h_2-h_1)=0 \tag{15}$$

The last two equations are applicable when

- The liquid flows by gravity (without the pump's shaft work),
- The liquid flows without appreciable change in density ($\Delta D = 0$),
- The liquid flows in a laminar and steady (fully developed) manner,
- The liquid flows in a pipe with *no* fitting, so there is *no* pipe fitting friction, and
- The liquid is *not* viscous; therefore, *no* liquid friction occurs in the pipe's wall.

Consider a small section of a liquid flowing from point 1 to 2. In this case, Equation 15 must be given in the integral form.

$$\int_{P_1}^{P_2} \frac{dP}{D} + \frac{1}{2}\int_{v_1}^{v_2} V.dv + a_g \int_{h_1}^{h_2} dh = 0 \quad (16)$$

When a flow's pressure change is zero ($\Delta P = 0$), the first term in Equation 15 drops, becoming a two-item equation known as the Torricelli equation.

$$\frac{1}{2}V^2 + a_g.h = 0 \quad (17)$$

The Torricelli equation can calculate a moving liquid's velocity (V).

$$V = \sqrt{2a_g(h_2 - h_1)} \quad (18)$$

If the liquid flows frictionless in a pipe with a constant diameter ($d_1 = d_2$), the expression becomes

$$\frac{P_1 - P_2}{D} = 0 \quad (19)$$

This equation is the expression of the **liquid-flow principle**; in a steady flow through a constant-diameter pipe, the following are valid:

- The liquid flows through a pipe because P is greater at the pipe inlet, and
- The friction produced by the flow can be specified by $\dot{V}$ (volumetric flow rate of the flowing liquid), D_{Sp} (specific density of the liquid relative to water), and ΔP.

The friction factor (f_f, a unitless quantity, which is specific to a particular fitting like a valve) in a pipe can be calculated when we know $\dot{V}$, D_{Sp}, and ΔP.

$$f_f = \dot{V}\sqrt{\frac{D_{Sp}}{\Delta P}} \quad (20)$$

In practice, liquids are usually moved in pipes by pumps. Thus most of the time, some pipe shaft work (W_S) and pump friction energy losses (friction energy uses) are associated with the flow of liquids. We will study these frictions after studying the upcoming two Examples of the energy balance of a flowing liquid in a piping system without a pump (a flow under gravity).

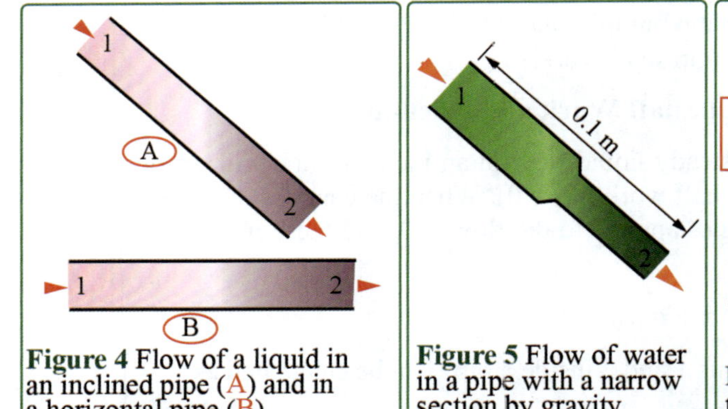

Figure 4 Flow of a liquid in an inclined pipe (A) and in a horizontal pipe (B)

Figure 5 Flow of water in a pipe with a narrow section by gravity

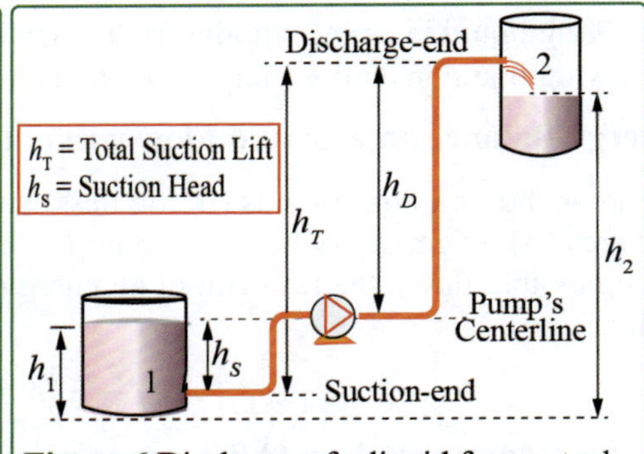

Figure 6 Discharge of a liquid from a tank to another tank by a pump

Example 2 on Liquid Flow

Calculate water pressure at point 2 (P_2, as shown in Figure 5) when water flows downward by gravity in a vertical pipe whose diameter reduces by almost one-half at a certain point (so its velocity increases). We know the following data:

Water density (D)	1000 kg/m³ (= 62.4 Lb/Ft³)
Water pressure at point 1 (P_1)	700 Pa (= 0.1 PSI)
Water average velocity at point 1, V_1	0.25 m/s (= 10 In/s)
Water average velocity at point 2, V_2	1 m/s (= 3.3 Ft/s)
Distance between 1 and 2 (Δh)	0.1 m (= 4 In)

We choose point 1 as the point we know its P and point 2 (the starting of the reduced section) as the point we want to calculate its P. To calculate P_2, we use Equation 14.

$$\frac{P_2 - P_1}{D} + \frac{1}{2}(V_2^2 - V_1^2) + a_g.\Delta h = 0$$

$$P_2 - P_1 = \frac{1}{2}D(V_1^2 - V_2^2) + D.a_g.\Delta h = \frac{1}{2}1000(0.25^2 - 1^2) + 1000 \times 9.81 \times 0.1$$

$$P_2 - P_1 = -469 + 981 = 512 \text{ kg.m/(m}^2\text{.s}^2) = 512 \text{ (kg.m/s}^2\text{)/m}^2 \text{ (= 512 N/m}^2\text{= 512 Pa)}$$

$$P_2 - 700 = 512 P_2 = 512 + 700 = 1212 \text{ Pa (= 1.2 kPa = 0.2 PSI)}$$

Example 3 on Liquid Flow

Given: A valve at the bottom of a tank under atmospheric pressure discharges a liquid to a long pipe with negligible friction.

Tank's diameter (d_T)	4 m (= 12 Ft)
Liquid's height in the tank (liquid head, h)	3 m (= 9 Ft)
Pipe's inside diameter (d_P)	0.125 m (= 125 mm = 5 In)

Wanted: 1) Liquid's volume in the tank (V), 2) Liquid's average velocity in the discharge pipe (V), 3) Volumetric flow rate in the discharge pipe ($\dot{V}$), and 4) Time required to empty the tank (t).

$$V = \pi\left(\frac{d_T}{2}\right)^2 h = 3.14\left(\frac{4}{2}\right)^2 \times 3 = 37.7 \text{ m}^3$$

The liquid average velocity in the discharge pipe is calculated from the Torricelli equation (Equation 17).

$$V = \sqrt{2a_g.h} = \sqrt{2 \times 9.81 \times 3} = 7.7 \text{ m/s}$$

Volumetric flow rate ($\dot{V}$) in the discharge pipe is calculated from Equation 7.

$$\dot{V} = V.A = v.\pi\frac{d_P^2}{4} = 7.7 \times 3.14 \times \frac{0.125^2}{4} = 0.09 \text{ m}^3\text{/s}$$

$$t = \frac{V}{\dot{V}} = \frac{37.7}{0.09} = 419 \text{ s (= 7 min)}$$

Energy Balance on a Liquid Flow with Shaft Work and Friction

In any flowing liquid, some energy is used to overcome the friction (f), which is a resistance to flow when the liquid molecules rub against the pipe wall (or its fittings). As a result of friction, conversion of mechanical energy (E_M) to heat energy (E_Q) occurs, so some non-useful energy, generally known as **friction energy losses**, occurs, which must be included in the related calculations. Pipe friction related to fittings must also be included in calculating the ΔP (pressure drop) of a flowing liquid in a pipe.

[Note: The term **energy loss** is incorrect because **energy** is *not* losable. Some scientists, therefore, use the word **friction energy use** (frictional energy use).]

Consider a liquid flowing in a pipe from point 1 to 2 by a pump, as seen in Figure 6. In this figure, h_1 is for the liquid head in tank 1, h_2 is in tank 2, h_S is the pump suction head, and h_D is the pump discharge head. Assume that *no* heat transfer with the surroundings occurs, so $\Delta E_Q = 0$ (an adiabatic flow). To balance such a system, we must use the complete form of the Bernoulli equation (Equation 13), which can be rearranged to calculate a pump's shaft work.

$$W_S = \frac{P_2-P_1}{D} + \frac{1}{2}(V_2^2 - V_1^2) + a_g(h_2 - h_1) + E_f \qquad (21)$$

If we show the pump's **suction head** by h_1 (or h_S) and its **discharge head** by h_2 (or h_D) and using the pump efficiency (E_P), we can write the Bernoulli equation in a simple form to relate the pump shaft work to the differential change in the total net head ($\Delta h_T = h_2 - h_1$).

$$W_S.E_P = h_2 - h_1 = \Delta h_T \qquad (21)$$

Consider a flowing system in which a liquid goes through a pipe of non-constant diameter. If $W_S = 0$ (*no* pump between points 1 and 2) and $E_f = 0$ (the frictions are negligible), Bernoulli equation for this system is

$$\frac{P_2-P_1}{D} + \frac{1}{2}(V_2^2 - V_1^2) + a_g(h_2 - h_1) = 0 \qquad (22)$$

Example 4 on Liquid Flow

Given: A pumping system in which a liquid flows in a pipe horizontally (point 1) by a pump to another reduced-diameter pipe (point 2) through a 45° reducer with negligible frictions.

Liquid's flow rate ($\dot{V}$)	1×10^{-3} m³/s (1 L/s = 60 L/min = 15.9 Ga/min)
Elevation ($h_2 - h_1$) = Δh	10 m
Liquid's density (D)	1100 kg/m³
Pipe 1 inside diameter (d_1)	0.025 m (= 25 mm = 1 In)
Pipe 2 inside diameter (d_2)	0.05 m (= 50 mm = 2 In)
Gauge pressure in pipe 2 (P_2)	1 Atm (= 101×10^3 N/m² = 101 kPa)
Gravitational acceleration (a_g)	9.8 m/s² (= 32.2 Ft/s²)

Wanted: 1) Liquid velocity in pipe 1 (V_1), 2) Liquid velocity in pipe 2 (V_2), and 3) Liquid pressure in pipe 1 (P_1).

The cross-sectional area of pipes 1 and 2 are calculated as

$$A_1 = \pi\frac{d_1^2}{4} = 3.14\frac{0.025^2}{4} = 4.9\times10^{-4}\ \text{m}^2 \quad A_2 = 3.14\frac{0.05^2}{4} = 19.6\times10^{-4}\ \text{m}^2$$

The average velocity of the liquid in both pipes ($\bar{V}_1$ and $\bar{V}_2$) can be obtained from the volumetric flow rate ($\dot{V}$) flowing through pipes 1 and 2 with a cross-sectional area of A_1 and A_2

$$V_1 = \frac{\dot{V}}{A_1} = \frac{1\times10^{-3}}{4.9\times10^{-4}} = 2\ \text{m/s} \qquad V_2 = \frac{\dot{V}}{A_2} = \frac{1\times10^{-3}}{19.6\times10^{-4}} = 0.5\ \text{m/s}$$

$$\Delta V^2 = V_2^2 - V_1^2 = 0.5^2 - 2^2 = -3.8\ \text{m}^2/\text{s}^2$$

At $P_2 = 101\times10^3$ N/m², P_1 (in gauge pressure) can be calculated from Equation 22.

$$\frac{P_2 - P_1}{D} + \frac{1}{2}\Delta V^2 + a_g.\Delta h = \frac{101\times10^3 - P_1}{1100} + \frac{1}{2}(-3.8) + 9.8\times10 = 0$$

$$P_1 = 4.7\times10^3\ \text{N/m}^2\ (\text{or } 4.7\ \text{kN/m}^2 = 4.7\ \text{kPa} = 0.7\ \text{PSI})$$

FRICTION HEAD LOSS AND FRICTION ENERGY LOSSES

Frictions (also called **friction forces**), in the liquid-flow subjects, are the forces (F) that resist the motion of a flowing liquid. The main **effects** of frictions on a flowing liquid are the following:

- Some liquid head loss (h_L) in the flow, and
- Some energy loss in the flow.

The overall friction head loss (h_L, also called **friction pressure drop**), happening in a liquid flow, can be calculated from the **Fanning equation** (also called **Fanning head-loss equation**).

$$h_L = \frac{2f_F.L.V^2}{d.a_g} \qquad (23)$$

In this equation, f_F is the Fanning friction factor (a unitless quantity), L is the pipe's length (in m), V is the liquid's **average velocity** (it is ½ of maximum **velocity**, in m/s), d is the pipe's diameter (in m), and a_g is gravitational acceleration (= 9.81 m/s^2 = 32.2 Ft/s^2 on the Earth surface), so the h_L becomes in m. [The f_F (Fanning friction factor) quantifies resistance caused by the wall of a pipe when a viscous liquid flows through it.]

As seen from the same equation, d is conversely related to the h_L (the *smaller* is the d, the *greater* is the h_L). We know from basic plumbing that 12-mm (= 1/2-In) moves water to arrive at our kitchen's faucet at a lower pressure than a 20-mm (= ¾-In) pipe. This is because of the higher h_L that occurs in the lower-diameter pipe.

The f_F (Fanning's friction factor) in the fanning equation is related to the Reynolds number (N_R) and can be calculated for a **laminar flow** as

$$f_F = \frac{16}{N_R} \tag{24}$$

[Note: **Darcy's friction factor** (f_D) equates to 4 times f_F (Fanning's friction factor), so $f_D = 64/N_R$.]

When the flow is turbulent (when its N_R is above 4000), the f_F is a function of N_R and the **pipe's relative roughness** (k/d, see Figure 1 under ROUGHNESS), where k is the pipe's roughness (the height of a single unit of roughness, expressed in m) and d is pipe's diameter (in m). Thus, k/d is unitless. When the flow is turbulent, f_F can be calculated from Moody's chart when k is known or can be estimated as

$$f_F = \frac{0.125}{{N_R}^{0.3}} + 0.0014 \tag{25}$$

For calculation of friction energy losses (rather uses), ChemEng divides the uses into two groups:

- Major friction energy uses ($E_{F.Maj}$), and
- Minor friction energy uses ($E_{F.Min}$).

Major friction energy uses ($E_{F.Maj}$) can be calculated as

$$E_{F.Maj} = \frac{2f_F.L.D.V^2}{d} \tag{26}$$

In this equation, L and d are in m, D is in kg/m^3, and V is in m/s, so $E_{F.Maj}$ becomes in kg.m/s^2 = J, which is SI unit of energy.

Minor friction energy uses ($E_{F.Min}$) consist of the following:

- Friction energy-use by pipe's fittings ($E_{f.Fit}$),
- Friction energy-use by contraction ($E_{f.Con}$),
- Friction energy-use by expansion ($E_{f.Exp}$).

$$E_{f.Min} = E_{f.Fit} + E_{f.Con} + E_{f.Exp} \tag{27}$$

Friction Energy-Use by Pipe's Fittings ($E_{f.Fit}$)**:** The $E_{f.Fit}$ occurs because of the pipe fittings (valves, elbows, or measuring instruments). A pipe fittings contribute strongly to the pressure drop, so the $E_{f.Fit}$ often is the main part of the minor friction uses. The $E_{f.Fit}$ can be calculated from the liquid's **average velocity** (V).

$$E_{f.Fit} = \frac{\Delta P}{D} = f_{Fit}\frac{V^2}{2} \tag{28}$$

The term f_{Fit} in this equation is the **fitting friction factor**, which is specific to a particular fitting, meaning that the factor, say, used for a valve has a different value than that used for an elbow. Table 1 below gives fitting factors for some common fittings used in piping systems.

[Note: Three friction factors are used in ChemEng: Fanning, Darcy, and Moody friction factors. In this book, we use Fanning friction factors. Also, note that the fitting friction factors of individual fittings must sum up when there is more than one fitting in the pipe, as seen in Example 5.]

Table 1 Fitting Friction Factors (f_{Fit})

Open-angle valve	2.0
Open ball valve	2.3
Half-open ball valve	1.5
Open diaphragm valve	2.3
Half-open diaphragm valve	4.2
Quarter-open diaphragm valve	2.1
45° flanged elbow	0.2
45° threaded elbow	0.4
90° flanged elbow	0.3
90° threaded elbow	1.5
180° flanged return bend	0.5
Medium-size heat exchanger	12

Friction Energy-Use by Contraction ($E_{f.Con}$)**:** The $E_{f.Con}$ happens when a flowing liquid in a pipe enters a smaller-diameter pipe (Figure 5). The $E_{f.Con}$ is calculated as

$$E_{f.Con} = \frac{\Delta P}{D} = f_{Con}\frac{V^2}{2} \tag{29}$$

The f_{Con} is the contraction friction factor, and V is the average velocity in the pipe's smaller-diameter section. For a laminar flow and $f_{Con} < 0.1$, $E_{f.Con}$ is negligibly small. The f_{Con} depends on the pipe cross-sectional area (A). If A_2/A_1 is smaller than 0.7, the f_{Con} can be calculated as

$$f_{Con} = 0.4\left[1 - \left(\frac{A_2}{A_1}\right)\right] \tag{30}$$

If the diameter of point 1 (like a tank) is much larger than the diameter of point 2 (say, a pipe), contraction occurs (see Figure 7), so $A_2/A_1 = 0$ and $f_{Con} = 0.4$. If A_2/A_1 is larger than 0.7, f_{Con} is calculated as

$$f_{Con} = 0.8\left[1 - \left(\frac{A_2}{A_1}\right)\right] \tag{31}$$

Friction Energy-Use by Expansion ($E_{F.Exp}$): The $E_{F.Exp}$ happens when a flowing liquid in a pipe enters a larger-diameter container (like a tank, as seen in Figure 8). The $E_{F.Exp}$ is calculated as

$$E_{F.Exp} = \frac{\Delta P}{D} = f_{Exp}\frac{V^2}{2} \tag{32}$$

The f_{Exp} is the **expansion friction factor**, which can be calculated as

$$f_{Exp} = \left(1 - \frac{A_1}{A_2}\right)^2 \tag{33}$$

If the diameter of point 1 is much smaller than 2, expansion occurs, so $A_1/A_2 = 0$ and $f_{Exp} = 1$.

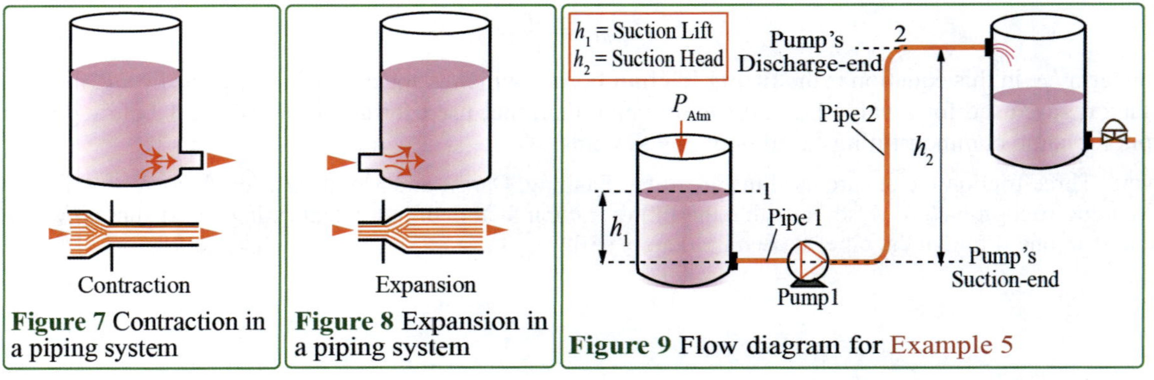

Figure 7 Contraction in a piping system

Figure 8 Expansion in a piping system

Figure 9 Flow diagram for Example 5

Example 5: A piping system like Figure 9, in which a liquid is pumped from tank 1 to tank 2 through two pipes with the same-sized inside diameter. One fully-open diaphragm valve and two 90° elbows are in the second pipe. Both tanks are under P_{Atm}, meaning $P_1 = P_2$, so $\Delta P = P_1 - P_2 = 0$. The following data are known:

Liquid's mass flow rate ($\dot{M}$)	10 kg/s
Liquid's density (D)	1060 kg/m^3
Liquid's viscosity (η)	8×10^{-3} (= 8 cp)
Liquid's level in tank 1 from ground (h_1)	4 m
Liquid's level in tank 2 from ground (h_2)	16 m
Pipe's inside diameter (d_P)	0.05 m (= 50 mm = 2 In)
Pipe's length (L_P)	20 m (= 66 Ft)
Gravitational acceleration (a_g)	9.8 m/s^2 (= 32.2 Ft/s^2)

Calculate: 1) Liquid's average velocity in pipe 2 (V_2), 2) Reynolds number of the flow (N_R), 3) Total frictional energy losses (E_F), 4) Total head loss in the system (h_L), and 5) Pump's shaft work (W_S).

The average velocity of the liquid in pipe 2 and the Reynolds number (N_R) can be calculated as

$$V_2 = \frac{\dot{M}}{D.A_P} = \frac{\dot{M}}{D\left[\pi\left(\frac{d^2}{4}\right)\right]} = \frac{20}{1060\left[3.14\left(\frac{0.05^2}{4}\right)\right]} = \frac{20}{2.08} = 9.6 \text{ m/s}$$

$$N_R = \frac{D.V.d_P}{\mu} = \frac{1060 \times 9.6 \times 0.05}{8 \times 10^{-3}} = 63600$$

Such N_R represents a turbulent flow that its fitting friction factor (f_{Fit}) can be calculated as

$$f_{Fit} = \frac{0.125}{N_R{}^{0.3}} + 0.0014 = \frac{0.125}{63600^{0.3}} + 0.0014 = 0.006$$

To calculate **total friction energy uses** (E_F), we need to calculate the energy used due to the liquid's viscosity, the pipe's fittings, and contraction caused by the liquid discharge from a tank to a pipe. Fanning equation calculates the friction energy loss due to viscosity ($E_{F.Maj}$) in the pipe with diameter $d_P = 0.05$ and length $L_P = 20$ m.

$$E_{F.Maj} = \frac{2f_{Fit}.L_P.V^2}{d_P} = \frac{2\times0.006\times20\times9.6^2}{0.05} = 442\ (\text{m/s}^2)(\text{m}) = 442 \text{ N.m} = 442 \text{ J}$$

To calculate **friction energy use by pipe's fittings** ($E_{f.Fit}$), we use Equation 28 and consider two **pipe fitting factors** (f_{Fit}) for two elbows in the pipe. The value for f_{Fit} for the fully-open-diaphragm valve is 2.3 and for 90° elbow is 0.3 (from Table 1).

$$E_{f.Fit} = f_{Fit}\frac{V^2}{2} = (2.3 + 2 \times 0.3)\frac{9.6^2}{2} = 134 \text{ m}^2/\text{s}^2 = \text{N.m} = 134 \text{ J}$$

To calculate **friction energy use by contraction** ($E_{f.Con}$), we must remember that a contraction occurs when the liquid is discharged from tank 1 to the pipe. To calculate the $E_{f.Con}$, we need to know the **contraction-friction factor** (f_{Con}), which equates to 0.4 because the diameter of the tank (point 1) is much larger than the diameter of the pipe (point 2), $A_2/A_1 = 0$. The $E_{f.Con}$ can be calculated from Equation 29.

$$E_{f.Con} = f_{Con}\frac{V^2}{2} = (0.4)\frac{9.6^2}{2} = 18 \text{ J}$$

Then, the total friction energy losses (E_f) would be $E_f = 442 + 134 + 18 = 594$ J (= 0.6 kJ). The total head loss in the system (h_L) can be calculated from Equation 23.

$$h_L = \frac{2f_{Fit}.L.V^2}{d.a_g} = \frac{2\times0.006\times20\times9.6^2}{0.05\times9.8} = 45 \text{ m}$$

To calculate the pump shaft work (W_S), we use Equation 20 because point 1 is the upper level of the liquid in the supply tank (tank 1), and point 2 is the end of the pipe, where the liquid is discharged to the tank 2. [Note that $P_1 = P_2$ and $P_1 - P_2 = 0$, so the first term of the equation becomes zero. Also, note that V_1 is minimally negligible because of the large diameter of tank 1 in comparison with that of pipe 1.] Thus,

$$W_S = \frac{V_2^2}{2} + a_g(h_2 - h_1) + E_f = \frac{9.6^2}{2} + 9.81(16 - 4) + 594 = 757 \text{ J}$$

L-30

LIQUID HEAD AND LIQUID HEAD LOSS

Liquid Head: Liquid head (*h*; also called the **static head**, **pressure head**, **hydraulic head**, or simply **head**) is a liquid's height (head or elevation) above a reference level. The *h* indicates a liquid's pressure (*P*) in a column in the unit of length (*L*, usually in m or Ft) instead of a unit of *P*. For example, the *h* of water in a tank is its height that would exert some amount of *P* at the tank's base, where the tank's base is taken here as the reference level. Thus, a change in *h* indicates a change in tank level.

[Note 1: Liquid head (*h*) is different from head pressure (P_h). The P_h is given in unit *P* (like in kPa or PSI), while the *h* is expressed in the height unit (in m or Ft). The P_h is defined as the *P*, caused by the mass of a liquid on a certain reference surface, such as a tank's base.]

[Note 2: The use of liquid head is approximate because the *P* exerted by a column of a liquid is *not* a constant but depends on the temperature (which affects the liquid's density).]

Consider a tank shown on the left side of Figure 1. The *h* is measured vertically between ground level, where $h = 0$, and the liquid surface level in the tank. In the tank shown on the right side of the same figure, the *h* is measured from below the ground level. In Figure 2, which shows a liquid flow between two tanks, the liquid heads of h_1, h_2, and h_3 are measured as shown in the figure. Similarly, in a hydraulic dam, the liquid (hydraulic) head is the distance from a river's surface to the top of the dam's reservoir, as shown in Figure 3.

In evaporator tubes, the *h* is the height of the solution from the heating tubes' surface to the solution's surface (the solution's level above the surface of the heating tubes). In evaporators, the *h* is important because the solution boils at a higher *T* (temperature) in the heating section than in the liquid-head area. When the *h* becomes higher, the heat transfer rate becomes lower. This occurs because the temperature difference (ΔT) between the steam and the solution under evaporation above the heating surface is lower than the heating section, so the solution boils at a higher *T*. Thus, the **evaporation efficiency** becomes lower.

In pumping systems, the following three (3) words are used to express a pump's liquid heads: 1) Pump's suction head (h_S), 2) Pump's discharge head (h_D), and 3) Pump's total head (h_T). [These quantities are expressed in the height unit (m or Ft).]

Liquid Head Loss: The liquid head loss (h_L, simply **head loss** or **hydraulic loss**) in a piping system indicates a pressure loss caused by friction (*f*), happening in a flowing liquid in a pipe. Like *h* (liquid head), the h_L (liquid head loss) is given in the unit of length (*L*) and can be calculated by the Fanning equation (head-loss equation).

$$h_L = \frac{2f_F.L.V^2}{d.a_g} \qquad (1)$$

In this equation, f_F is the **Fanning friction factor** (a unitless quantity), *L* is the pipe's length (in m), *V* is the liquid's **average velocity** (it is ½ of maximum **velocity**, in m/s), *d* is the pipe's diameter (in m), and a_g is gravitational acceleration (= 9.81 m/s^2 = 32.2 Ft/s^2 on the Earth surface), so the h_L becomes in m. [The f_F (Fanning friction factor) quantifies resistance caused by the wall of a pipe when a viscous liquid flows through it.]

When *L* (the pipe's length) is in m, *V* (the liquid's average velocity, which is ½ of maximum velocity) is in m/s, *d* (the pipe's diameter) is in m, and a_g (gravitational acceleration) is in m/s^2, h_L becomes in m.

The Darcy-Weisbach equation can also calculate the head loss (h_L). [The term liquid head (simply **head**), which is expressed in unit length (m or Ft), is generally used to refer to a liquid's pressure at a certain level.]

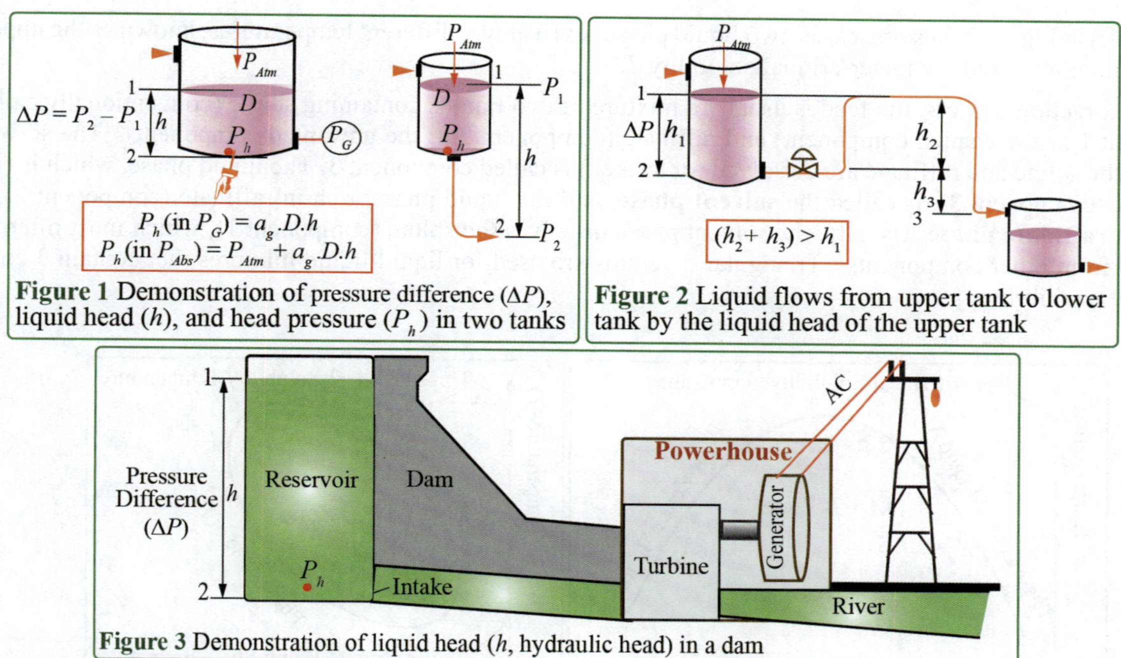

Figure 1 Demonstration of pressure difference (ΔP), liquid head (h), and head pressure (P_h) in two tanks

Figure 2 Liquid flows from upper tank to lower tank by the liquid head of the upper tank

Figure 3 Demonstration of liquid head (h, hydraulic head) in a dam

L-31
LIQUID HEAD LOSS

Discussed under the topic of LIQUID HEAD AND LIQUID HEAD LOSS.

L-32
LIQUID HEAD PRESSURE

Study HEAD PRESSURE.

L-33
LIQUID-LIQUID EQUILIBRIUM

Liquid-liquid equilibrium (LLE), which is used in the extraction process, is a condition under which equilibrium (stability) between two liquid phases of a mixture occurs at a certain temperature (T) and pressure (P). The mixture can consist of one of the following:

- Two partly miscible liquids,
- Two miscible liquids (like ethanol in water), and
- Two immiscible liquids (like oil-in-water or water-in-oil).

The LLE and VLE (vapor-liquid equilibrium) diagrams look like phase diagrams. Figure 1 shows two typical LLE diagrams for one mole of a binary (two-component) mixture with components A and B at different temperatures. The same figure shows the solubility increases as T increases until the two liquid phases disappear at the upper liquid-liquid (LL) solubility line. As T increases above this line, only one liquid phase exists in the mixture.

As shown in Figure 2, in some cases, two liquid phases exist at two different temperatures, known as the upper-critical-solubility T and the lower-critical-solubility T.

In the extraction process, the feed is usually a mixture of two liquids containing solute (conventionally called component 1 or the wanted component) and raffinate (component 2 or the unwanted component). The solvent in which the solute and raffinate are dissolved (or soaked) is called component 3. The liquid phase, which is rich in solvent (component 3), is called the **solvent phase**, and the liquid phase, rich in raffinate (component 2), is called the **raffinate phase**. Usually, the solvent phase dissolves the solute (component 1), which must often be separated from other components. [Triangular diagrams are used for liquid-liquid mixtures that contain 3 components at equilibrium.]

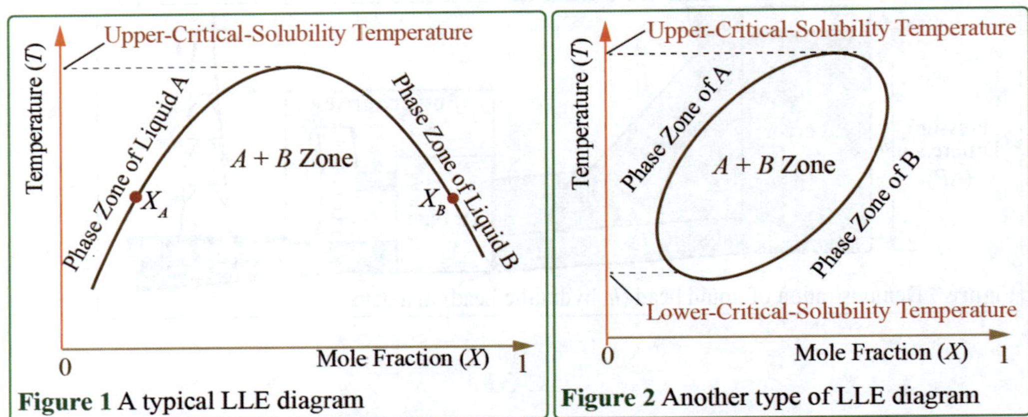

Figure 1 A typical LLE diagram

Figure 2 Another type of LLE diagram

L-34
LIQUID-LIQUID EXTRACTION

Another name for EXTRACTION PROCESS.

L-35
LITER

The liter (in British spelling, **litre**) is one of the SI units of volume (V). It is defined as one cubic decimeter (dm^3), where 1 dm = 0.1 m (meter) = 10 cm = 3.937 In. In this way, 1 L = 10 cm × 10 cm × 10 cm = 1000 cm^3 = 0.001 m^3, as shown in Figure 1. [Although the liter is *not* an official SI unit, it is accepted by the CGPM (the General Conferences on Weights and Measures), as was defined here,]

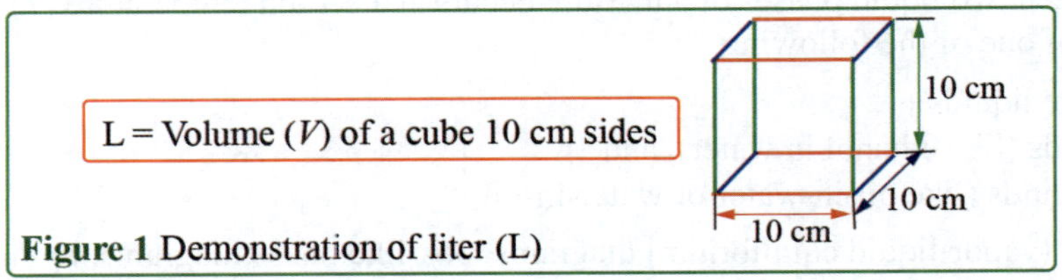

Figure 1 Demonstration of liter (L)

L-36

LOGARITHMS AND ANTILOGARITHMS

Logarithms: A logarithm (simply written **log** or **Log** and called **common log**, **log to the base of 10** or **log10**) is the exponent of 10 when the number is written in the base 10. Thus, a number's Log is the power to which 10 must be raised to give that number. For example, Log 1 = 0 (because $1 = 10^0$), Log 10 = 1 (because $10 = 10^1$), Log 100 = 2 (because $100 = 10^2$), Log 0.1 = –1 (because $0.1 = 10^{-1}$), and Log 0.01 = –2 (because $0.01 = 10^{-2}$). These examples tell us that the log is the inverse of the exponent, so the relation of the log to the exponent is like the relation of division to multiplication, as shown in Figure 1 for $Y = \log_2 X$ (often written as $Y = \log X$) and $Y = 2^X$. Figure 2 shows the graphs of the exponential equations of $Y = A^X$ and $Y = A^{-X}$.

The general rules of the common logs are outlined next.

- The log of a number greater than 1 is positive; for example, Log 1.3 = 0.11,
- The log of a number lesser than 1 is negative; say, Log 0.3 = – 0.52,
- Negative numbers do *not* have logs.

Log Exponent Rule:

$$(A^X)^Y = A^{XY}$$
$$A^X A^Y = A^{X+Y}$$
$$A^X / A^Y = A^{X-Y}$$
$$\text{Log } A^n = n\text{Log } A$$

The exponent of 10 for a number between 1 and 10 will be between 0 and 1. For example, $2 = 10^{0..30103}$ and log 2 = 0.30103. The exponent of 10 for a number between 10 and 100 will be between 1 and 2, so $20 = 10^{1.30103}$ and log 20 = 1.30103. The exponent of 10 for a number between 100 and 1000 will be between 2 and 3, so $222 = 10^{2.346353}$ and log 222 = 2.346353.

To convert the exponential statement $100 = 10^2$ to a logarithmic statement, we must think that $Y = A^X$ is the same as $X = \text{Log}_a y$, so $100 = 10^2$ is $2 = \text{Log}_{10} 100$.

Log Multiplication Rule: Log A.B = Log A + Log B

Log Division Rule: Log A/B = Log A – Log B

Natural Log: As another form of the log, the natural log (Ln, natural logarithm) is a Log to the base of 2.71828. Ln can be solved according to the next general rule.

$$\text{Ln } X = Y \qquad X = 2.71828^Y$$

The following formula can be used to convert a Log to Ln or vice versa:

$$\text{Ln } X = 2.303\text{Log } X$$

Antilog, instead, is the same as an exponent, meaning raising the base to a power equal to the log, so the antilog of N can be solved as

$$N = 10^N \qquad \text{Log N} = 2 \qquad \text{N} = 10^2 = 100$$

Antilogs: An antilog (antilogarithm) is the same as exponentiation, meaning raising the base to a power equal to the log, so the antilog of N can be solved as $\text{N} = 10^{\text{N}}$.

$$\text{Log N} = 2 \qquad \text{N} = 10^2 = 100$$
$$\text{Log N} = 1.5 \qquad \text{N} = 10^{1.5} = 31.6$$

[The most common way for performing the antilog operation on a calculator is to enter the value and press the 10^x key. For example, the antilog of 1.234 is 17.14. Some calculators have the INV (inverse) function instead. In this case, enter the value, press INV, and then press the "Log" key or "Ln" key.]

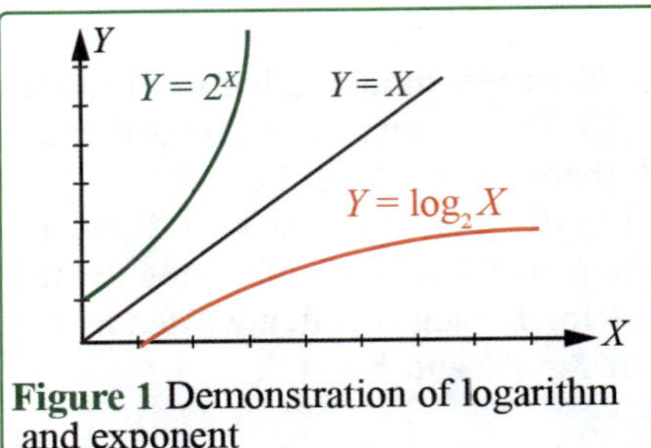

Figure 1 Demonstration of logarithm and exponent

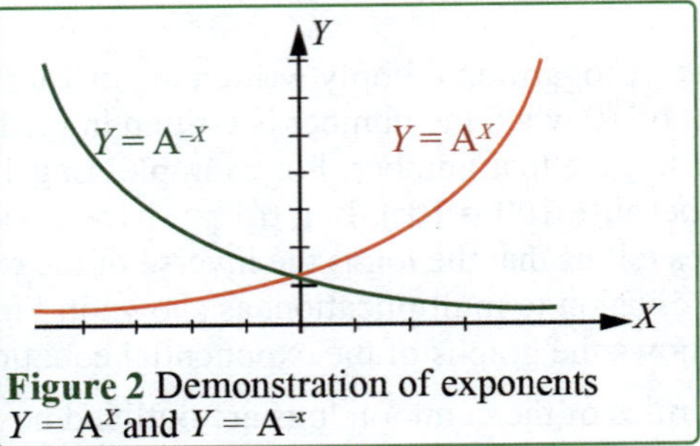

Figure 2 Demonstration of exponents $Y = A^X$ and $Y = A^{-x}$

L-37

LOGARITHMIC MEAN TEMPERATURE DIFFERENCE

Logarithmic mean temperature difference (LMTD or ΔT_{LM}, where subscript LM is for the logarithmic mean; simply called **mean temperature difference**, MTD or ΔT_M) is a correct way of expressing the temperature difference (ΔT) between the heating medium and the fluid (mainly a liquid) under heating. The LMTD is important in the delicate calculations of heat transfer processes. For example, we might need to use the LMTD to design a heater (a heat exchanger used for heating) because its temperature (T) may vary from point to point, so its curve is *not* linear. This situation occurs because the liquid under heating is at maximum T at the wall of the heating surface, but it decreases toward the center of the flow. For these reasons, the ordinary average temperature difference [$\Delta T_{Avg} = (T_2 - T_2)/2$] does *not* work correctly, so the LMTD is used. Here, the LMTD can be viewed as the T achieved if the entire liquid in a heater were withdrawn and mixed **adiabatically** (with *no* heat loss) to a uniform T. The following equation is used to find the ΔT_{LM} between two points of a heater (usually feed inlet and product outlet), where $T_2 > T_1$:

$$\Delta T_{LM} = \frac{\Delta T_2 - \Delta T_1}{Ln\frac{\Delta T_2}{\Delta T_1}} \quad (1)$$

In this equation, Ln is the symbol for the natural log.

[In a **cocurrent** (parallel) **tube heater**, the ΔT between the two fluid streams is maximum when the two streams enter the heater, but ΔT decreases greatly as the streams move through the heater. Instead, the tube is reversed for one of the streams in a **countercurrent heater**, so the fluid streams flow in opposite directions.]

Figure 1 shows a flow diagram of the heat transfer in a tabular heater with cocurrent flow and its T profile by plotting the T of the vapor (T_V, the heating medium) and T of the liquid under heating (T_L) against the flow path (the length of the heater's tubes). Figure 2 shows the same graph but for a tabular heater with a **countercurrent flow**. In both figures, the inlet vapor (with higher T) is indicated with T_{V2}, the outlet vapor (with lower T) from the heater with T_{V1}, the inlet liquid (with lower T) with T_{L1}, and the outlet liquid (with higher T) from the heater with T_{L2}. Referring to Figure 1, the ΔT_1 (the ΔT at the vapor-inlet side) and ΔT_2 (the ΔT at the vapor-outlet side) in a tabular heater with **cocurrent flow** can be defined as

$$\Delta T_1 = \Delta T_{Max} = (T_{V2} - T_{L1}) \qquad \Delta T_2 = \Delta T_{Min} = (T_{V1} - T_{L2}) \quad (2)$$

Referring to Figure 2, ΔT_1 and ΔT_2 in a tabular heater with **countercurrent flow** can be defined as

$$\Delta T_1 = \Delta T_{Max} = (T_{V2} - T_{L2}) \qquad \Delta T_2 = \Delta T_{Min} = (T_{V1} - T_{L1}) \quad (3)$$

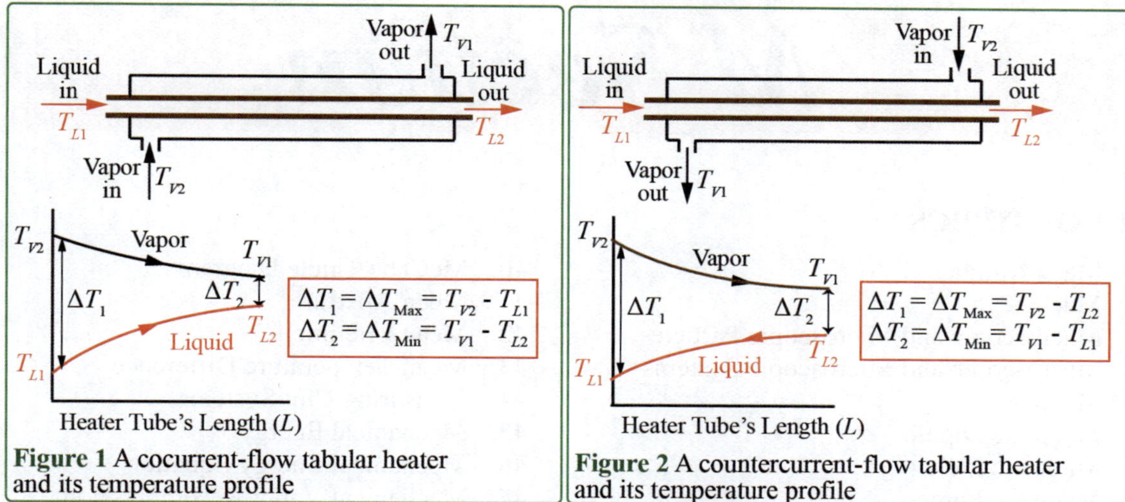

Figure 1 A cocurrent-flow tabular heater and its temperature profile

Figure 2 A countercurrent-flow tabular heater and its temperature profile

An Example on LMTD

Calculate the ΔT_{LM} between vapor and liquid under heating at each end of a counter-flow shell-and-tube heater for heating a liquid when the liquid's temperature in (T_{L1}) is 32°C, the liquid's temperature out (T_{L2}) is 98°C, the vapor's temperature in (T_{V2}) is 108°C, and the vapor's temperature out of heater (T_{V1}) is 36°C.

ΔT_{Max} at shell inlet is $\Delta T_{Max} = (T_{V2} - T_{L2}) = 108 - 98 = 10°C$

ΔT_{Min} at shell outlet is $\Delta T_{Min} = (T_{V1} - T_{L1}) = 36 - 32 = 4°C$

$$\Delta T_{LM} = \frac{\Delta T_{Max} - \Delta T_{Min}}{Ln\dfrac{\Delta T_{Max}}{\Delta T_{Min}}} = \frac{10-4}{ln\dfrac{10}{4}} = \frac{6}{0.9} = 6.7°C$$

[If we use **arithmetic average temperature difference**, the average temperature would be $(\Delta T_{Max} + \Delta T_{Min})/2 = (10 + 4)/2 = 7°C$. The arithmetic formula can be used for thin-walled tubes (or plates) without error.]

M Section

LIST OF TOPICS

1. Mach Number
2. Machines
3. Macroscopic and Microscopic Particles
4. Macroscopic and Microscopic Systems
5. Magma
6. Magnetic Dipole
7. Magnetic Field
8. Magnetic Force
9. Magnetic Moment and Magnetic Dipole
10. Magnetic Potential Energy
11. Magnetic Resonance Imaging
12. Magnetism and Magnets
13. Manometers
14. Margules Activity Coefficients
15. Mass
16. Mass Action Law
17. Mass Balance
18. Mass Defect
19. Mass Diffusion Coefficient
20. Mass Diffusion Process
21. Mass Energy and Mass-Energy Equation
22. Mass Energy Equality
23. Mass Excess
24. Mass Flow Process
25. Mass Flow Rate
26. Mass Flux and Mass Flux Rate
27. Mass Flux Rate
28. Mass Fraction, Molar Fraction, and Volume Fraction
29. Mass Number
30. Mass Spectrometry
31. Mass Transfer by Diffusion
32. Mass Transfer Process
33. Mass Velocity
34. Mass, Weight, and Specific Weight
35. Massive and Massless Particles
36. Material and Matter
37. Material Balance
38. Matter
39. Maxwell
40. McCabe Thiele Diagram
41. Mean Aperture
42. Mean Lifetime
43. Mean Temperature Difference
44. Measuring Unit Systems
45. Mechanical Energy
46. Mechanical Energy Equation
47. Mechanical Vapor Recompression
48. Mechanical Work
49. Melt Crystallization
50. Melting Point Temperature
51. Melting Process
52. Membrane Separation Process
53. Meniscus
54. Mesons
55. Metallic Bonds
56. Metalloids
57. Metals, Nonmetals, and Metalloids
58. Meter
59. Methane
60. Methanol
61. Metric System
62. Microfiltration Process
63. Microscopes
64. Microscopic Size
65. Microwave
66. Miscibility
67. Miscible and Immiscible Liquids
68. Mixers
69. Mixing Process
70. Mixtures
71. Modulus
72. Moist air
73. Moisture and its Types
74. Molal Concentration
75. Molality
76. Molar Concentration
77. Molar Density
78. Molar Diffusion Flux
79. Molar Diffusion Flux Rate

80. Molar Enthalpy of Evaporation
81. Molar Enthalpy of Formation
82. Molar Enthalpy of Reaction
83. Molar Flow Rate
84. Molar Flux
85. Molar Flux Rate
86. Molar Fraction
87. Molar Gas Constant
88. Molar Heat Capacity
89. Molar Heat of Evaporation
90. Molar Heat of Formation
91. Molar Heat of Reaction
92. Molar Humidity
93. Molar Mass
94. Molar Volume
95. Molarity
96. Mold and Yeast
97. Mole and Molar Mass
98. Mole Fraction
99. Molecular Diffusion Process
100. Molecular Mass
101. Molecular Sieve and Molecular-Sieve Process
102. Molecular Solvation
103. Molecular Structure
104. Molecule
105. Mollier Diagram
106. Moment of Inertia
107. Momentum and Rotational Momentum
108. Momentum Diffusivity
109. Momentum Flux
110. Monomers
111. Mother Liquid
112. Motion
113. Motors
114. Mud

M-1
MACH NUMBER

Mach number (N_M, pronounced *ma:k*) is a unitless quantity that is used in the gas flow process to compare a **gas velocity** (V_G) with the speed of sound constant (U_S).

$$N_M = \frac{V_G}{U_S} \quad (1)$$

In the N_M equation (where N is for number and subscript M is for Mach), the V_G is evaluated by comparing it with a solid boundary (like a pipe's wall) and the U_S is measured at room temperature (around 25ºC = 77 ºF) and local pressure (P). So, when $N_M = 1$, the gas V equals the sound speed.

Based on the N_M, a gas flow can take one of the following classes:

- **Sonic flow** (with N_M of nearly 1),
- **Subsonic flow** (with N_M of less than 1), and
- **Supersonic flow** (with N_M of greater than 1).

[For more information on Mach number, study GAS FLOW PROCESS.]

M-2
MACHINES

Study ENGINES, MACHINES, AND MOTORS.

M-3

MACROSCOPIC AND MICROSCOPIC PARTICLES

Discussed under PARTICLE AND ITS TYPES.

M-4

MACROSCOPIC AND MICROSCOPIC SYSTEMS

Macroscopic Systems: A macroscopic system (also called **macroscopic-size system, macro-size system**, or **at-large system**) is a system that is **visible** to the naked eye, so there is *no* need for a microscope to investigate the properties of a macro-size system.

Microscopic Systems: A microscopic system (also called **microscopic-size system**, **micro-size system**, or **quantum-size system**) is a system that is **invisible** to the naked eye and needs a microscope to investigate. Usually, the atomic, subatomic, and molecular studies are considered micro-size investigations. For example, nuclear magnetic resonance spectroscopy (NMR spectroscopy) can study an atom's electron (or electrons) to determine in what electron shell an electron is acting at a certain time, as Bohr used while developing his atomic model. Physics considers a system with a length of some hundreds of **micrometers** (μm) as a micro-size system. Most of the phenomena under study in quantum physics are microscopic systems.

M-5

MAGMA

The word **magma** is used in the crystallization and centrifugal processes to refer to a two-phase thick suspension solution consisting of the mother liquid and crystals. Say, magma is the mixture of a saturated solution (the liquid phase) and sugar crystals (the solid phase) in sugar crystallization. In sugar factories, a mild washing of the magma removes the retained mother liquid from the crystals during the centrifugal process.

M-6

MAGNETIC DIPOLE

Study MAGNETIC MOMENT AND MAGNETIC DIPOLE.

M-7

MAGNETIC FIELD

Discussed under ELECTRIC FIELD, MAGNETIC FIELD, AND ELECTROMAGNETIC FIELD.

M-8

MAGNETIC FORCE

Study ELECTRIC FORCE AND MAGNETIC FORCE.

M-9

MAGNETIC MOMENT AND MAGNETIC DIPOLE

Magnetic moment (M-moment) and **magnetic dipole** (M-dipole) are almost similarly defined, but each has its unit of measurement. The SI unit of M-moment is N.m/T (= J/T), and M-dipole is A.m^2, where N is for Newton, m for meter, T is for Tesla, J is for Joule, and A is for Ampere.

Magnetic Moment: A magnetic moment (*m*, also called **M-moment** or **field strength**) is a vector quantity (a quantity with value and direction) that represents the strength and orientation of a magnetic field (simply M-field, B-field, or just *B*). At the atomic level, the M-field of an M-moment can be viewed as a tiny imaginary magnet that dictates the spin of a subatomic particle like an electron (see Figure 1).

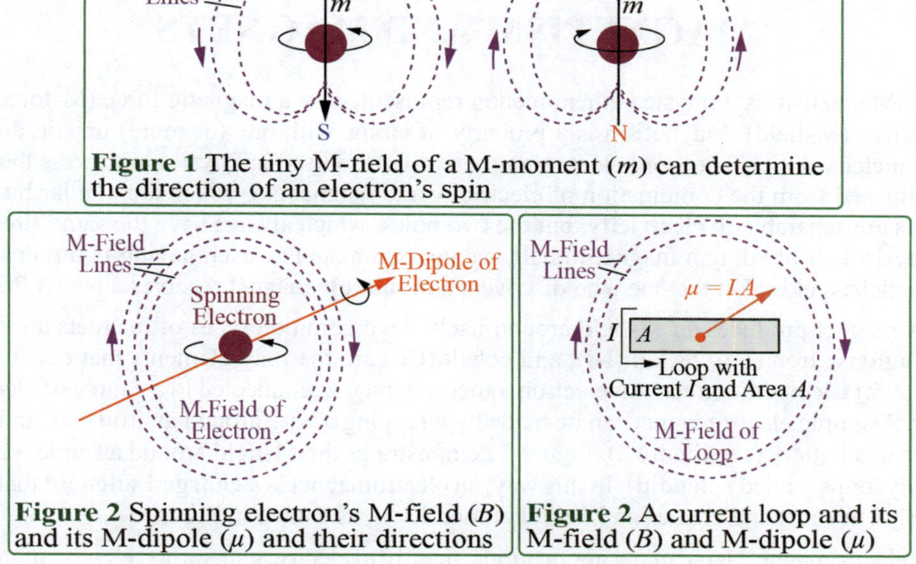

Figure 1 The tiny M-field of a M-moment (*m*) can determine the direction of an electron's spin

Figure 2 Spinning electron's M-field (*B*) and its M-dipole (*μ*) and their directions

Figure 2 A current loop and its M-field (*B*) and M-dipole (*μ*)

Magnetic Dipole: A magnetic dipole (*μ*, also called **M-dipole, dipole moment,** or **magnetic dipole moment**) is a vector quantity representing the strength and orientation of an M-field created by a loop of an electric current (simply **current loop**). A wire coil with current, an electron, and a planet are examples of moving systems with M-moment and M-dipole.

If a magnet is placed in the M-field of *B*, it experiences a torque (T_R or τ), which is determined as

$$T_R = B.\mu \tag{1}$$

Figure 2 shows an electron's M-field and M-dipole and its M-field direction. As shown in Figure 3, the M-dipole of a current loop with current *I* is a vector quantity with a direction perpendicular (vertical) to the loop. The quantity of the loop's M-dipole (*μ*) is the product of current *I* multiply by the loop area (*A*).

$$\mu = I.A \tag{2}$$

The T_R that the current loop experiences in the M-field *B* will be

$$T_R = I.A.B \tag{3}$$

The potential energy (E_P) of a system's M-dipole (*μ*) in the M-field of *B* is given as

$$\Delta E_P = -\mu.B \tag{4}$$

M-10

MAGNETIC POTENTIAL ENERGY

Defined in the subtopic of Potential Energy under ENERGY AND ITS TYPES.

M-11

MAGNETIC RESONANCE IMAGING

Discussed under NUCLEAR MAGNETIC RESONANCE AND MAGNETIC RESONANCE IMAGING.

M-12

MAGNETISM AND MAGNETS

Magnetism: Magnetism is a physical phenomenon represented by a magnetic force (M-force or F_M) carried by a magnetic field (M-field). Magnetism is a property of atoms with one (or more) unpaired electron, which spins around a nucleus alone. [The word **electromagnetism** is also used in Physics to express the same phenomenon, but it is formed from the combination of electricity and magnetism, which are similar but *not* the same.] The two charges are separable in **electricity**, but the two poles, which always have the same strength, are inseparable in **magnetism**. If dividing a magnet in half, we get two magnets, each having two poles (see Figure 1). This is why physicists jokes that the one who discovers a **monopole** magnet receives a Nobel Prize.

Magnets: A magnet produces an M-field around itself. Two common types of magnets are defined next. 1) **Permanent Magnets:** Iron (Fe), nickel (Ni), and cobalt (Co) are the only elements that occur naturally in the magnetized state. 2) **Electromagnets:** An electromagnet is a magnet connected to a source of electricity (usually DC electricity). A simple electromagnet can be made by wrapping a wire around an iron core and connecting the ends of the wire to a battery (see Figure 2). Figure 3 demonstrates the M-field around a single wire loop and in a wire coil of many loops (called **solenoid**). In this way, an electromagnet is a **charged solenoid** that carries electric current (*I*, simply **current**) and creates an M-field around itself, as shown in Figure 3.

Magnets and electromagnets have many applications, mainly in electric generators, electric motors, and electric transformers. The three key phenomena that use the concept of electromagnetism (F_{EM}) are:

- **Electromagnet:** If a current passes through a metal wire, the movement of charged electrons creates an electromagnetic field (EM field). This is the idea behind making an electromagnet.
- **Electric Power:** If a metal wire moves in an EM field, an electric current occurs in the wire. This is the idea behind the generation of electric power (electricity).
- **Electric Motor:** If an electric current passes through a metal wire in a magnetic field, the wire will move. This is the idea behind making an electric motor, such as an electric drill.

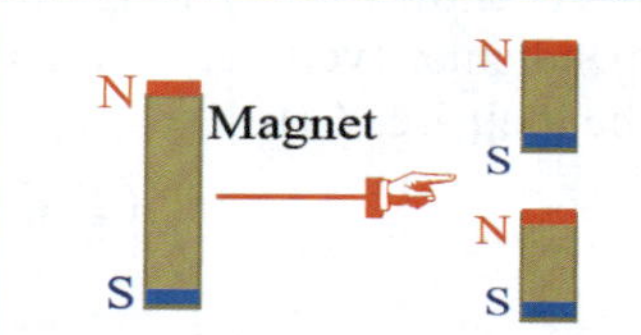

Figure 1 Dividing a magnet into two magnets, each with both north and south poles

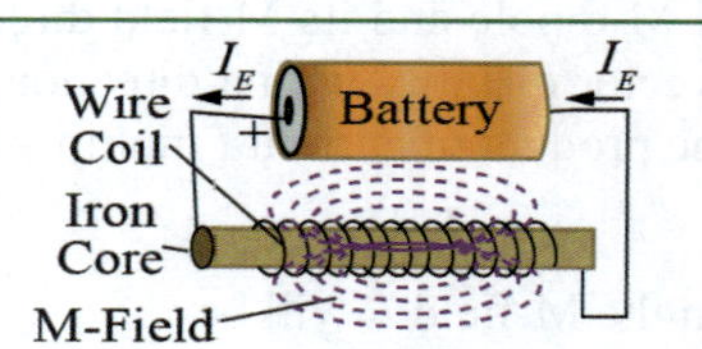

Figure 2 A simple electromagnet, consisting of a wire coil connected to a battery

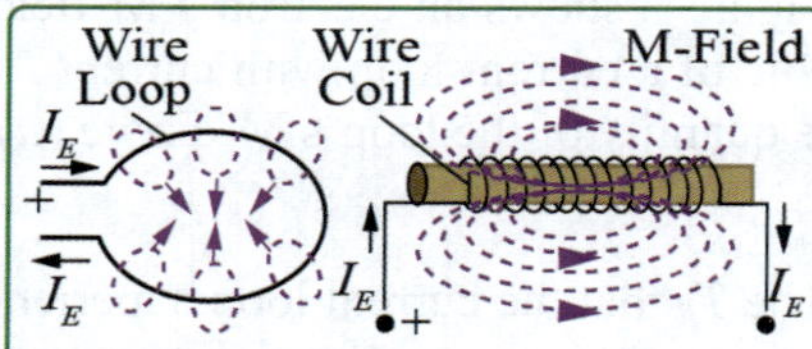

Figure 3 An M-field around a wire loop and a wire coil (a wire with many loops)

M-13
MANOMETERS

Discussed under the subtopic of Pressure Measurement and Control in PROCESS CONTROL OF CHEMICAL ENGINEERING.

M-14
MARGULES MODEL AND COEFFICIENTS

Discussed under ACTIVITY EQUATIONS, MODELS, AND COEFFICIENTS.

M-15
MASS

Discussed under MASS, WEIGHT, AND SPECIFIC WEIGHT.

M-16
MASS ACTION LAW

The Mass Action Law talks about the concentrations of the reactants and reaction rate (R_R) of a chemical reaction at a given temperature (T). Consider the next reversible reaction: a.A + b.B ↔ c.C + d.D. As for this reaction, this law says that its forward reaction rate (R_{R1}) is a function of the concentrations of the reactants (A and B), raised to their corresponding exponents (a and b).

$$R_{R1} = K_1[A]^a[B]^b \tag{1}$$

And the backward (reverse) reaction rate (R_{R2}) is related to the concentration of the products (C and D).

$$R_{R2} = K_2[C]^c[D]^d \tag{2}$$

In these equations, the sign [ ] is for concentration, and K_1 and K_2 are proportionality constants, called **reaction rate constants** (simply **rate constant**), for forward and backward reactions.

M-17
MASS BALANCE

Mass balance (also called **material balance**; study the Note below) is a series of calculations on the flows of mass (M) entering and leaving a system to evaluate if the material (or materials) is used efficiently or *not* in a chemical process plant. Mass balancing is widely used to keep account of raw material used in a process plant or in a particular station of a process plant (facility) and how much product (or products) is produced. This evaluation can be used as the base for comparison of the day-to-day operation of the plant. Mass balancing is also important in designing a new efficient process unit of ChemEng.

[Note: The word **mass balance** is a better word to be used because **mass** is a well-defined word, while the word **material** is used in a broad sense (because it is *not* specifically defined.)]

Mass-balance calculations are usually based on the **mass rate** (mass per unit time; M/t), conveniently in kg/s, t/h, or Lb/s). And it is like balancing a checking account at a bank. What goes into the account (deposits) are added, and what is taken out of the account (withdrawals) are subtracted. The result (the balance) is what is left in the account. Mass balancing is based on the conservation of mass (mass *cannot* be created or destroyed in a process), what enters a process (called **inputs** or **inflows**) are added, and what leaves the process (called **outputs** or **outflows**) subtracted. And the result (called **accumulation**) is what is left in the process. [Instead of **accumulation**, some use the term **unaccounted** or **loss**, which are incorrect words (because mass is a conserved quantity).] However, accumulation (in its negative or positive way) is a sign of an **unsteady process**. If we choose a unit time, for example, 1 h (hour), the accumulation equates to the sum of all the masses built up in the process during 1 h. In a **steady process**, the mass remains unchanged ($\Delta M = 0$), so accumulation = 0.

We start with a simple mass balance.

$$M_{\text{In}} = M_{\text{Out}} + M_{\text{Ac}} \qquad \text{Or} \qquad M_{\text{Ac}} = M_{\text{In}} - M_{\text{Out}} \tag{1}$$

In mass balancing, the assumption is that the process under balance operates under **steady-state conditions**, meaning that *no* accumulation (shown by subscript Ac) and consumption occur. But, the total mass of the process remains unchanged ($\Delta M = 0$). As shown in Figure 1, if a liquid inflow rate to a tank is 5 m^3/h, its outflow rate must also be 5 m^3/h, so $M_{\text{In}} = M_{\text{Out}}$, meaning *no* accumulation.

Consider a chemical plant's limekiln, in which limestone (mainly $CaCO_3$) is decomposed by the E_Q (heat energy) of coke to produce quicklime (CaO) and carbon dioxide gas (CO_2).

$$CaCO_3 \rightarrow CaO + CO_2$$

$$100\ \text{kg} \rightarrow 56\ \text{kg} + 44\ \text{kg}$$

$$100\ \text{kg} \rightarrow 100\ \text{kg}$$

Considering the molecular mass (M_M) of the participating compounds, we can say that for every 100 kg of $CaCO_3$ (where the M_M of $CaCO_3$ is 100), 56 kg of CaO and 44 kg of CO_2 are produced. [Instead of taking kg (or Lb) as the unit of mass, we can base our calculations on t or mole.] According to the conservation of mass applied to a chemical reaction, the M (mass) of the **reactant** ($CaCO_3$) equates to the total M of the **products** (CaO and CO_2). So said, if instead of 56 kg of CaO, the process produces 50 kg, the process involves some unaccountability, which is normal in many cases (because almost *no* process is 100% efficient).

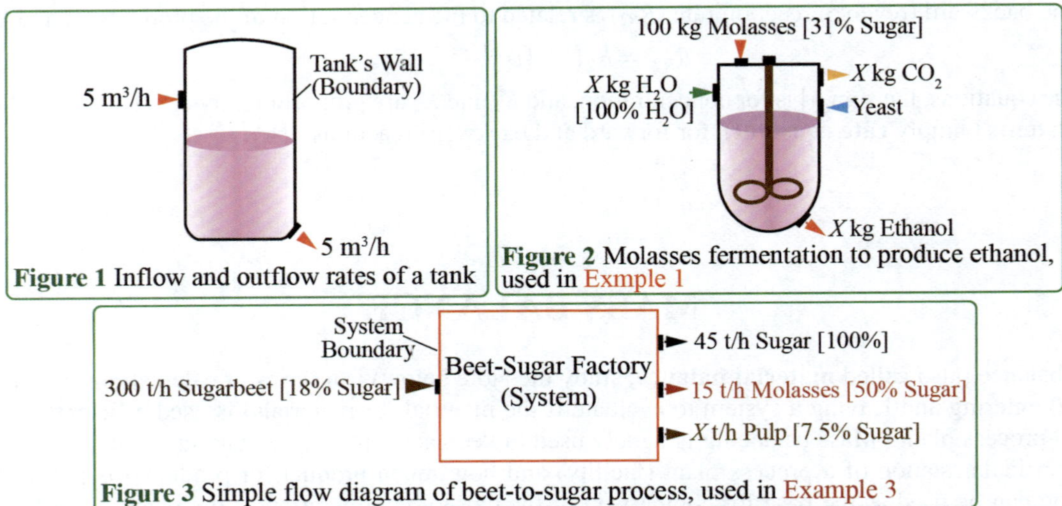

Figure 1 Inflow and outflow rates of a tank

Figure 2 Molasses fermentation to produce ethanol, used in Exmple 1

Figure 3 Simple flow diagram of beet-to-sugar process, used in Example 3

Flow rate, a flow per unit time (t), is usually used in mass balances. For example, mass flow rate ($\dot{M}$) is M (mass) per t (time) or $\dot{M} = M/t$, and volumetric flow rate ($\dot{V}$) is V (volume) per t.

Using $\dot{M}$ (mass flow rate), we can express a mass balance as $\dot{M}_{In} = \dot{M}_{Out}$. A process can have more than one inflow and outflow, so the symbol $\sum$ (sigma, for summation) indicates the **sum**.

$$\sum_{In} \dot{M} = \sum_{Out} \dot{M} \tag{2}$$

Component Balance

A component balance can determine the components present in the inflows and outflows so that the previous equation can balance component *A*.

$$\sum_{In}(\dot{M}_A) = \sum_{Out}(\dot{M}_A) \tag{3}$$

If a flow consists of 2 components, *A* and *B*, the relation between concentrations of components *A* and *B* is given based on their molar fraction (*X*, a unitless quantity) as $X_A + X_B = 1$ or $X_A = 1 - X_B$. Similarly, if a flow has 3 components with X_A, X_B, and X_C concentrations, the relation among the variables is $X_A + X_B + X_C = 1$.

The flow rate of *A* is the product of the mass rate and concentration of *A* in that flow. If; say, the $\dot{M}$ of *A* is 300 kg/h and the amount of *A* in the inflow is 18% (or $C_A = 0.18$, where C_A is the concentration of component *A*), the mass flow rate of *A* in the inflow is

$$\dot{M}.C_A = 300 \times 0.18 = 54 \text{ kg/h}$$

Similarly, we can balance the amount of solid as a component, so a **solid balance** determines the amount of dissolved solids (*DS*) present in the inflows and outflows.

Scaling in Mass Balancing

Scaling in mass balancing is the decreasing (or increasing) the value of all flows by a convenient proportional amount to ease a mass balance's calculations. It is called **scaling-down** when the values of flows are decreased and **scaling-up** when the values are increased. Usually, the values of industrial mass balancing are scaled down to a convenient proportion. The results, afterward, can be scaled up to real values. Consider a feed flowing to a process at 1 200 kmole/h (kilo moles per hour). If during the process, the feed is separated into two fractions of *A* = 600 kmole/h and *B* = 600 kmole/h, we can choose the feed rate as the basis of calculation and scale down all flows by 12 times. So, 100 kmole/h of inflow is separated into 600/12 = 50 kmole/h of *A* and 50 kmole/h of *B*.

In some cases, the values are scaled down from a ton (t) to a kilogram (kg). If, say, a plant processes raw material at 300 t/h, the value is scaled down to 300 kg/h. [Compared with day-to-day operations of chemical process plants, all examples given under this topic are scaled-down.]

MASS BALANCING OF A BATCH PROCESS

In a batch process, a certain amount of feed enters a system at once (*not* at a constant rate), and the product is taken from the system later. A batch process, thus, is considered a closed system (energy can enter or leave the system, but **mass** *cannot*) because, during the process, *no* mass enters or leaves the system. [In the mass balancing of a **batch process**, the amount of mass flow (*M*) is considered. This is contrary to a continuous process that considers the mass flow rate ($\dot{M}$).]

To practice, we start with a simple example of batch mass balancing, the mass balancing of ethanol (C_2H_5OH) production by fermentation of sugars in molasses in a bench (laboratory) test. [Note that this is called bioethanol production because molasses is biomass. Also, note that the ethanol and bioethanol's chemical formula and chemical properties are the same.]

Example 1 on Mass Balancing

Given: A bench test for fermentation of diluted molasses in a batch fermenter with the help of a yeast, simply shown in Figure 2, to produce ethanol (C_2H_5OH) according to the following equations:

$$C_{12}H_{22}O_{11} + H_2O \rightarrow 4\ C_2H_5OH + 4\ CO_2$$

$$342 \text{ kg} + 18 \text{ kg} \rightarrow 4 \times 46 \text{ kg} + 4 \times 44 \text{ kg}$$

$$360 \text{ kg} \rightarrow 360 \text{ kg}$$

Diluted molasses processed, $M_{Molasses}$	100 kg
Diluted-molasses sugar (*S*) content, $C_{S.Mol}$	31%
Sugar molar mass, $M_{n.S}$	342 kg/kmole
Ethanol molar mass, $M_{n.E}$	46 kg/kmole
Ethanol density, *D*	807 kg/m^3
CO_2 gas density, D_G	1.56 kg/m^3

Wanted: 1) Ethanol's theoretical yield (Y_E), 2) Ethanol production (M_E) from molasses in kg and m^3, 3) Ethanol production from 100 kg sugar, 4) Water consumption (M_W), and 5) CO_2 gas production (M_G)

The given equation tells us that 1 mole of sugar produces 4 moles of ethanol, so the ethanol yield (Y_E) can be calculated using the ratio of the molar mass of ethanol (46 kg/kmole) to that of sugar (342 kg/kmole).

$$Y_E = 4 \times \frac{M_{n.E}}{M_{n.S}} = 4 \times \frac{46}{342} = 0.538 \text{ kg ethanol/kg molasses or } 53.8\%$$

The mass of sugar (M_S) in 100 kg of molasses will be

$$M_S = M_{n.S} \times C_{S.Mol} = 100 \times 0.31 = 31 \text{ kg sugar}$$

Ethanol production (M_E) from 100 kg molasses will be

$$M_E = M_S \times \frac{M_{n.E}}{M_{n.S}} = 31 \times 4 \times \frac{46}{342} = 16.7 \text{ kg ethanol/100 kg molasses}$$

The ethanol mass (16.7 kg) and its density (807 kg/m^3) can calculate its volumetric production (V_E).

$$V_E = \frac{M_E}{D} = \frac{16.7}{807} = 0.02 \text{ m}^3 \text{ ethanol}$$

Ethanol production from 100 kg of sugar can be similarly calculated.

$$M_E = M_S \times \frac{M_{n.E}}{M_{n.S}} = 100 \times 4 \times \frac{46}{342} = 53.8 \text{ kg ethanol/100 kg sugar}$$

Water consumption (M_W) can be calculated from the mass of sugar in molasses (31 kg) and the ratio of the molar mass of water ($M_{M.W}$) to sugar ($M_{M.S}$).

$$M_W = M_S \times \frac{M_{n.W}}{M_{n.S}} = 31 \times \frac{18}{342} = 1.6 \text{ kg water}$$

The mass of produced CO_2 gas (M_G) and its volumetric production (V_G) will be

$$M_G = M_S \times \frac{M_{n.G}}{M_{n.S}} = 31 \times 4 \times \frac{44}{342} = 16 \text{ kg} \qquad V_G = \frac{M_G}{D_G} = \frac{16}{1.56} = 10.3 \text{ m}^3$$

Example 2

Given: A tank for mixing two syrups

Purity of the first syrup (P_1)	88%
Purity of the second syrup (P_2)	77%

Wanted: How much of the first syrup (V_1) and the second syrup (V_2) must be mixed to produce 50 m^3 ($V_P = 50$ m^3) of syrup of 86% purity ($P_P = 86\%$).

We have two unknown variables (V_1 and V_2), so we need two equations to calculate them. Because *no* reaction occurs when we mix two syrups, the generation and consumption can be omitted from the general mass balance. Thus, the total of V_1 and V_2 equates to 50 m^3.

$$V_1 + V_2 = 50 \text{ m}^3 \qquad V_1 = 50 - V_2$$

For the second equation, we use the total mass balance

$$V_1.P_1 + V_2.P_2 = V_P.P_P \quad V_1 \times 0.88 + V_2 \times 0.77 = 50 \times 0.86$$

$$V_2 = \frac{43}{0.77} - \frac{0.88V_1}{0.77} \qquad V_2 = 55.8 - 1.14V_1$$

From the first equation, we found that $V_1 = 50 - V_2$, thus

$$V_1 = 50 - 55.8 - 1.14V_1 \qquad V_1 - 1.14V_1 = -5.8$$

$$-0.14V_1 = -5.8 \qquad V_1 = \frac{5.8}{0.14} = 41.4 \text{ m}^3$$

$$V_2 = 50 - V_1 = 50 - 41.4 = 8.6 \text{ m}^3$$

So, we must mix 41.4 m^3 of the first syrup with 8.6 m^3 of the second syrup to produce 50 m^3 of the desired syrup of 86% purity. To find the percentage of the syrups, we can proceed as

$$V_1 = \frac{41.4}{50} \times 100 = 82.8\% \qquad V_2 = \frac{8.6}{50} \times 100 = 17.2\%$$

MASS BALANCING OF A CONTINUOUS PROCESS

In a continuous (nonstop) process, the inputs continuously enter the system, and the outputs continuously leave the system, so mass (or masses) continuously crosses (enters and leaves) the system's boundary. So said, a continuous process is an open system (**mass** and **energy** can enter or leave the system). As a result, we talk about mass flow rate ($\dot{M}$) rather than the amount of mass flow (M). For example, pumping a liquid at a constant rate to and from a tank is a continuous process representing an open-and-steady process. [Continuous processes are used in mass productions and are usually run as steady as possible.]

As a numerical example, we mass balance a **beet-sugar factory** in its simplest way. As Figure 3 shows, a beet factory has one inflow (sugarbeet) and three outflows, sugar (product), molasses (a byproduct), and beet pulp (a byproduct). [Beet-sugar factories use weighing scales for weighing sliced beet, sugar produced, and molasses but do *not* use the weighing scale for pulp (because of untrustworthiness results created by fluctuations in the pulp's moisture content.) Instead, the amount of pulp is determined from mass-balance calculations.] We introduce the data in the context of the next example.

Example 3

Given: A beet-sugar factory that processes sugarbeet with the following data:

Mass flow rate of beet processed, $\dot{M}_B$	300 t/h
Sugar content of beet, $C_{S,B}$	18 %
Mass flow rate of sugar (S) production, $\dot{M}_S$	45 t/h
Mass flow rate of molasses production, $\dot{M}_{Mol}$	15 t/h
Sugar content in molasses, $C_{S,Mol}$	50 %
Sugar content in dry pulp, $C_{S,DP}$	7.5 %

Wanted: Mass balance of the process to find the dry pulp's mass flow rate ($\dot{M}_{DP}$) and sugar left in it ($\dot{M}_{S,DP}$) because the crystallized-refined sugar is almost 100% pure ($C_S = 1$).

As Figure 3 shows, we have one inflow and three (3) outflows, so

$$(\dot{M}.C)_{In} = \Sigma_{Out}(\dot{M}.C) \qquad \dot{M}_B.C_{S.B} = \dot{M}_S.C_S + \dot{M}_{Mol}.C_{S.Mol} + \dot{M}_{DP}.C_{S.DP}$$

$$300 \times 0.18 = 45 \times 1 + 15 \times 0.5 + \dot{M}_{DP} \times 0.075$$

$$54 = 45 + 7.5 + \dot{M}_{DP} \times 0.075 \qquad 0.075\dot{M}_{DP} = 54 - 52.5 = 1.5$$

$$\dot{M}_{DP} = 20 \text{ t/h Dry pulp production}$$

$$\dot{M}_{S.DP} = \dot{M}_{DP}.C_{S.DP} = 20 \times 0.075 = 1.5 \text{ t/h Sugar left in the dry pulp}$$

Thus, inflow rate of sugar (54 t/h) equates to the total of outflows of sugar (45 + 7.5 + 1.5 = 54 t/h).

MASS BALANCING OF A MULTIPLE-UNIT PROCESS

Almost all industrial processes are multiple units because two or more flows are usually mixed, or one flow is split into fractions. The *more* units in a mass balance, the *more* difficult is its calculations.

In multiple-unit mass balancing, we must choose the boundary in a way that completely encloses the units on which we want to calculate a mass balance. We can subdivide the system into subsystems if it makes the calculations easier. Figure 4 indicates a two-unit system with an imaginary boundary of A, which encloses the entire system. This system has 3 inputs, shown as feed 1 (F_1), feed 2 (F_2), and feed 3 (F_3), and 2 outputs, shown as product 1 (P_1) and product 2 (P_2). We subdivide this system into a few subsystems to make the calculations easier. Boundary B encloses subsystem B, which mixes feed 1 and feed 2. Boundary C encloses subsystem C, which consists of unit 1 (with 1 input and 2 outputs). Boundary D encloses subsystem D, consisting of unit 2 (with 2 inputs and 1 output). Follow this mass balance in the context of the next example.

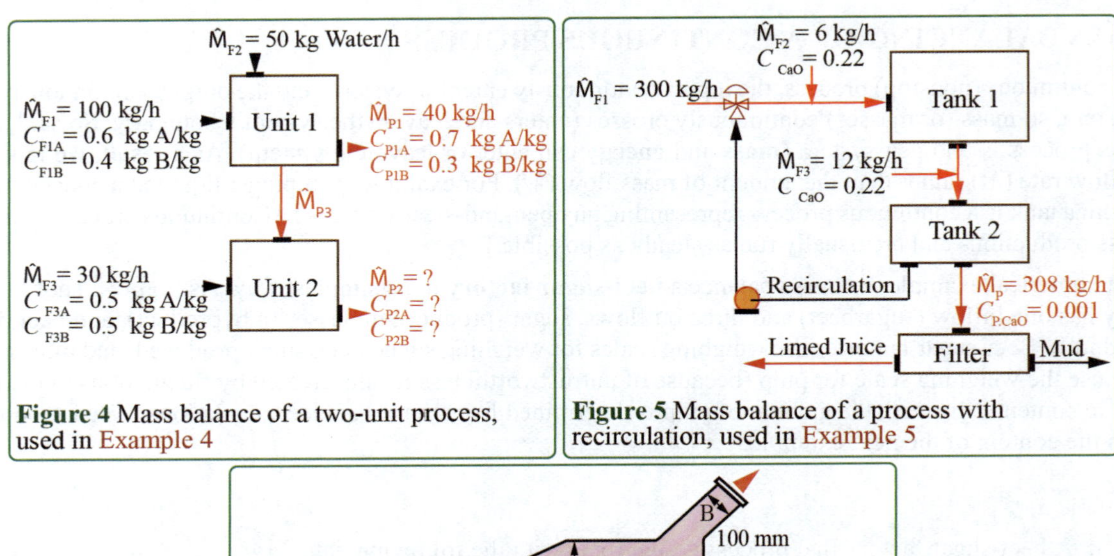

Figure 4 Mass balance of a two-unit process, used in Example 4

Figure 5 Mass balance of a process with recirculation, used in Example 5

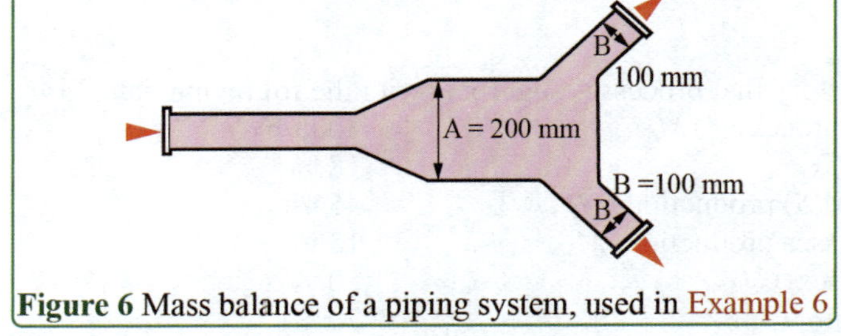

Figure 6 Mass balance of a piping system, used in Example 6

Example 4 on Mass Balancing

Given: A two-units continuous process with 3 inputs and 2 outputs (see Figure 4).

Mass flow rate of feed 1, $\dot{M}_{F1}$	100 kg/h
Concentration of component A of feed 1, C_{F1A}	0.6kg of A/kg
Concentration of component B of feed 1, C_{F1B}	0.4kg of B/kg
Mass flow rate of feed 2 (which is water), $\dot{M}_{F2}$	50 kg/h
Mass flow rate of feed 3, $\dot{M}_{F3}$	30 kg/h
Concentration of component A of feed 3, C_{F3A}	0.5kg of A/kg
Concentration of component B of feed 3, C_{F3B}	0.5kg of B/kg
Mass flow rate of product 1, $\dot{M}_{P1}$	40kg/h
Concentration of component A of product 1, C_{P1A}	0.7kg of A/kg
Concentration of component B of product 1, C_{P1B}	0.3kg of B/kg

Wanted: 1) Mass flow rate of product 2 ($\dot{M}_{P2}$); 2) Concentration (C) of component A of product 2 (C_{P2A}); 3) C of component B of product 2 ($C_{P2.B}$); 4) Mass flow rate of product 3 ($\dot{M}_{P3}$); 5) C of component A of product 3 ($C_{P3.A}$), and 6) C of component B of product 3 ($C_{P3.B}$)

Product 3 is an in-between product that feeds into unit 2, producing 2 products (P_1 and P_2). The balance of unit 1 is

$$\dot{M}_{F1} + \dot{M}_{F2} = \dot{M}_{P1} + \dot{M}_{P3} \qquad 100 + 50 = 40 + \dot{M}_{P3} \quad \dot{M}_{P3} = 110 \text{ kg/h}$$

Concentration (C) of A of product 2, shown as C_{P2A}, can be found from the solid balance of unit 1

$$\dot{M}_{F1}.C_{F1.A} = \dot{M}_{P1}.C_{P1.A} + \dot{M}_{P2}.C_{P2.A} \qquad 100 \times 0.6 = 40 \times 0.7 + 40C_{P2.A}$$

$$C_{P2.A} = 0.8 \text{ kg/kg}$$

C of component B of product 2, shown as $C_{P2.B}$, is

$$C_{P2.B} = 1 - 0.8 = 0.2 \text{ kg/kg}$$

The mass flow rate of product 2, shown as $\dot{M}_{P2}$, can be calculated from the overall mass balance

$$\dot{M}_{F1} + \dot{M}_{F2} + \dot{M}_{F3} = \dot{M}_{P1} + \dot{M}_{P2}$$

$$100 + 50 + 30 = 40 + \dot{M}_{P2} \qquad \dot{M}_{P2} = 140 \text{ kg/h}$$

The C of A of product 2, shown as $C_{P2.A}$, can be found from the overall solid balance on component A

$$\dot{M}_{F1}.C_{F1.A} + \dot{M}_{F3}.C_{F3.A} = \dot{M}_{P1}.C_{P1.A} + \dot{M}_{P2}.C_{P2.A}$$

$$100 \times 0.6 + 30 \times 0.5 = 40 \times 0.7 + 140C_{P2.A} \qquad C_{P2.A} = 0.3 \text{ kg/kg}$$

The C of component B of product 2, shown as $C_{P2.B}$, is

$$C_{P2.B} = (1 - 0.3) = 0.7 \text{ kg/kg}$$

MASS BALANCING OF A PROCESS WITH RECIRCULATION

In ChemEng, recirculation is the continuous pumping of a portion of a container's content to the same container (or to another container) for some operating purposes. Consider a process in which feed flow that consists of 2 components, A and B, enters an ion-exchange chromatographic separator. Because the separation of components A and B in the separator is *not* complete, part of the outflow of the separator is recirculated to the feed stream.

It is convenient to draw recirculated lines as a separate system for mass balancing of a recirculated system. We consider this situation in the context of the next example.

Example 5 on Mass Balancing

Given: A recirculation process is performed between 2 tanks (see Figure 5). Tank 1 receives feed (a juice), recirculated juice, and fresh lime [CaO in water or $Ca(OH)_2$]. Tank 2 gets the product of tank 1, which is partially limed. The following values are available:

Mass flow rate of the feed to tank 1, $\dot{M}_{F1}$	300 kg/h
Mass flow rate of the lime to tank 1, $\dot{M}_{F2}$	6 kg/h
Mass flow rate of the lime to tank 2, $\dot{M}_{F3}$	12 kg/h
Mass fraction of CaO in lime to tank 1 and tank 2, C_{CaO}	0.22
Mass flow rate of the product (limed juice), $\dot{M}_P$	308 kg/h
Mass fraction of CaO in the product, $C_{P.CaO}$	0.001
Mass fraction of CaO in the mud, $C_{M.CaO}$	0.2

Wanted: 1) Mass flow rate of the mud to the mud filter ($\dot{M}_M$), 2) Mass flow rate of the recirculated mud ($\dot{M}_{RM}$), 3) Percent of recirculated mud, and 4) Percent of recirculated mud on feed

The simple flow diagram of this process is given in Figure 5. The mass flow rate of the unreturned mud that goes to the mud filter ($\dot{M}_M$) can be calculated from the overall mass balance

$$\dot{M}_{F1} + \dot{M}_{F2} + \dot{M}_{F3} = \dot{M}_P + \dot{M}_M$$

$$300 + 6 + 12 = 308 + \dot{M}_M \qquad \dot{M}_M = 10 \text{ kg/kg}$$

The mass flow rate of the recirculated mud ($\dot{M}_{RM}$) can be calculated from the overall CaO balance

$$\dot{M}_{F2} + \dot{M}_{F3} = \dot{M}_P + \dot{M}_M$$

$$\dot{M}_{F2}.C_{F.CaO} + \dot{M}_{F3}.C_{F.CaO} = \dot{M}_P.C_{PCaO} + \dot{M}_M.C_{M.CaO} + \dot{M}_{RM}.C_{M.CaO}$$

$$6 \times 0.22 + 12 \times 0.22 = 308 \times 0.001 + 10 \times 0.2 + \dot{M}_{RM} \times 0.2$$

$$\dot{M}_{RM} = 8.3 \qquad \text{kg/h}$$

Total mud is the sum of the recirculated mud and the mud that goes to the mud filter: 8.3 + 10 = 18.3 kg/h, so the percentages of the recirculated mud and recirculated mud on the feed will be

$$\frac{8.3}{18.3} \times 100 = 45.4\% \qquad\qquad 8.3 \times \frac{100}{300} = 2.8\%$$

MASS BALANCING OF A FLOWING LIQUID IN A PIPE

In the mass balancing of a flowing liquid in a pipe, we assume dealing with incompressible fluids with a constant density (D). However, when a liquid is heated or cooled, its density varies, but usually, the variation is small and negligible. Under these conditions, a liquid's mass flow rate ($\dot{M}$) through a pipe is the product of its density (D) and velocity (V), and the cross-sectional area (A) of the pipe. The volumetric flow rate ($\dot{V}$) of a liquid in a pipe is the product of the liquid's V multiplied by the pipe's cross-sectional area ($A = \pi R^2 = \pi d^2/4$, where d is for the pipe's inside diameter).

$$\dot{V} = \frac{\dot{M}}{D} = \frac{D.V.A}{D} = V.A \tag{4}$$

Thus, the $\dot{V}$ remains constant if the liquid flows under steady-state (uniform) velocity. Because $\dot{V}$ is the product of the v and A, the mass flow rate ($\dot{M}$) becomes

$$\dot{M} = D.V.A = D.\dot{V} = D.V\frac{\pi.d^2}{4} \tag{5}$$

When D (the liquid's density) is in kg/m^3 and $\dot{V}$ is in m^3/s, $\dot{M}$ becomes in kg/s.

As Figure 6 shows, according to the Conservation Law of Mass, the mass of the liquid in section A_1A_2 equates to the mass in the B_1B_2 section. And the mass in section A_1B_1 equates to that of A_2B_2. Thus, the **mass flow rate** at location A_1 (that is, $\dot{M}_{A1}$) equates to $\dot{M}_{B3}$ (so, $\dot{M} = \dot{M}_{A1} = \dot{M}_{B1}$).

The average velocity ($\bar{V}$) of the flow equates to the volumetric flow rate ($\dot{V}$) of the liquid divided by the cross-sectional area of the pipe (A) through which the liquid flows.

$$\bar{V} = \frac{\dot{V}}{A} \tag{6}$$

Substituting v into Equation 5, we obtain the same conclusion.

$$\dot{M} = D.\bar{V}.A = D \times \frac{\dot{V}}{A} \times A = D.\dot{V} \tag{7}$$

Mass velocity (V_M) is a liquid's mass flow rate ($\dot{M}$) per pipe's cross-sectional area (A, where $A = \pi R^2 = \pi d^2/4$).

$$V_M = \frac{\dot{M}}{A} = \frac{\dot{M}}{\pi\frac{d^2}{4}} = \frac{4\dot{M}}{\pi.d^2} \tag{8}$$

When $\dot{M}$ is given in kg/s, and A is in m^2, V_M becomes kg/m^2.s. In US units, it is in Lb/Ft^2.s.

Volumetric velocity (V_V) is a liquid's volumetric flow rate ($\dot{V}$) per pipe's A.

$$V_V = \frac{\dot{V}}{A} = \frac{\frac{\dot{M}}{D}}{A} = \frac{\dot{M}}{D} \times \frac{4}{\pi.d^2} \tag{9}$$

When $\dot{M}$ is given in m^3/s, and A is in m^2, V_V becomes in m/s.

Example 6 on Mass Balancing

Given: Crude oil is pumped through pipe *A*, which branched to two same-size pipes *B* to carry the oil equally, as shown in Figure 6. The following data are available:

Density of oil, *D*	900 kg/m^3 (= 56.2 Lb/Ft^3)
Diameter of pipe in section *A* (shown as d_A)	200 mm (= 8 In)
Inside sectional area of pipe *A* (shown as A_A)	0.032 m^2 (= 0.345 Ft^2)
Diameter of pipe in section *B* (shown as d_B)	100 mm (= 4 In)
Inside sectional area of pipe *B* (shown as A_B)	0.008 m^2 (= 0.086 Ft^2)
Volumetric flow rate in pipe *A* (shown as $\dot{V}_{FA}$)	22 m^3/h (= 777 Ft^3/h)
Density of oil, *D*	900 kg/m^3 (= 56.2 Lb/Ft^3)

Wanted: 1) Total volumetric flow rate ($\dot{V}$), 2) Volumetric flow rate in pipe *B* (shown as $\dot{V}_B$), 3) Mass flow rate in pipe *A* (shown by $\dot{M}_A$) and *B* (shown by $\dot{M}_B$), and 4) Velocity in pipe *A* (shown by V_A) and pipe *B* (or V_A)

The total volumetric flow rate ($\dot{V}$) equates to $\dot{V}_A$ (22 m^3/h) + $\dot{V}_B$ (22/2 = 11 m^3/h) = 33 m^3/h.

The total mass flow rate in pipe *A* is

$$\dot{M}_A = D.\dot{V}_F = 900 \times 22 = 19800\ (\text{kg/m}^3)(\text{m}^3/\text{h}) = \text{kg/h}$$

The mass flow rate in each of pipe *B* is half of the total mass flow in pipe *A*, so $\dot{M}_B$ = 19800/2 = 9900 kg/h

The velocity (*V*) in pipe *A* is

$$V_A = \frac{\dot{V}_A}{A_A} = \frac{22}{0.032 \times 3600} = 0.2\ (\text{m}^3/\text{h})/[(\text{m}^2)(\text{s/h})] = \text{m/s}$$

The velocity in pipe *B* is

$$V_B = \frac{\dot{V}_B}{A_B} = \frac{11}{0.008 \times 3600} = 0.4\ \text{m/s}$$

Example 7 on Mass Balancing

Given: Ethanol at 30ºC flows through a piping system whose pipes are of Schedule 40.

Ethanol's density (*D*) at 80% purity and 30ºC	0.83 kg/m^3
Pipe 1 inside diameter (d_1)	0.15 m (= 150 mm = 6 In)
Pipe 2 inside diameter (d_2)	0.2 m (= 200 mm = 8 In)
Pipe 3 inside diameter (d_3)	0.1 m (= 100 mm = 4 In)
Pipe 4 inside diameter (d_4)	0.1 m (= 100 mm = 4 In)
Volumetric flow rate in pipe 1 ($\dot{V}_1$)	0.2 m^3/s (= 7 Ft^3/s)

Wanted: 1) Average velocity (*v*) in each pipe; 2) Mass flow rate ($\dot{M}$) in each pipe, and 3) Mass velocity (V_M) in each pipe

The cross-sectional area of pipes 1, 2, 3, and 4 are

$$A_{P1} = \pi \frac{d_1^2}{4} = 3.14 \frac{0.15^2}{4} = 1.77 \times 10^{-2}\ \text{m}^2$$

$$A_{P2} = 3.14 \frac{0.2^2}{4} = 3.14 \times 10^{-2}\ \text{m}^2$$

$$A_{P3} = A_{P4} = 3.14 \frac{0.1^2}{4} = 0.78 \times 10^{-2}\ \text{m}^2$$

The average linear velocity (*V*) of ethanol in pipes 1, 2, 3, and 4 can be calculated from Equation 9.

$$V_1 = \frac{\dot{V}}{A_{P1}} = \frac{0.2}{1.77 \times 10^{-2}} = 11.3\ \text{m/s}\ (= 37.1\ \text{Ft/s})$$

$$V_2 = \frac{\dot{V}}{A_{P2}} = \frac{0.2}{3.14 \times 10^{-2}} = 6.4\ \text{m/s}\ (= 21\ \text{Ft/s})$$

$$V = V_4 = \frac{0.2}{0.78 \times 10^{-2}} = 25.6 \text{ m/s } (= 84 \text{ Ft/s})$$

The mass flow rate ($\dot{M}$) in pipe 1 and 2 is the same and represent the total mass flow. $\dot{M}$ can be calculated from Equation 7.

$$\dot{M}_{Total} = \dot{M}_1 = \dot{M}_2 = D.\dot{V} = 0.83 \times 0.2 = 0.166 \text{ kg/s } (= 0.37 \text{ Lb/s})$$

The mass flow rate in pipes 3 or 4 is half of the total, so

$$\dot{M}_3 = \dot{M}_4 = \frac{\dot{M}_{Total}}{2} = \frac{0.166}{2} = 0.83 \text{ kg/s } (= 0.19 \text{ Lb/s})$$

The mass velocity (V_M) in each pipe is calculated from Equation 8.

$$V_{M1} = \frac{\dot{M}}{A_{P1}} = \frac{0.166}{1.77 \times 10^{-2}} = 9.4 \text{ kg/m}^2\text{.s} \qquad V_{M2} = \frac{0.166}{3.14 \times 10^{-2}} = 5.3 \text{ kg/m}^2\text{.s}$$

$$V_{M3} = V_{M4} = \frac{0.166}{0.78 \times 10^{-2}} = 21.3 \text{ kg/m}^2\text{.s}$$

MASS BALANCING OF A PROCESS WITH REACTIONS

Mass balancing of combustion reactions, like the next example, is the most-used type of these balances.

Example 8 on Mass Balancing

Given: A fuel oil with the formula of $C_{16}H_{32}$ and molar mass (M_n) of 224 kg/kmole burns in a furnace with excess dry air above the theoretical air required for complete combustion to CO_2 and H_2O

$$C_{16}H_{32} + 24\ O_2 \rightarrow 16\ CO_2 + 16\ H_2O$$

Mass flow rate of oil burned ($\dot{M}$)	1000 kg/h
Excess air requirement (*EAR*)	40%
Molar ratio of CO_2 to CO in the flue gas	3
Temperature (*T*) at combustion	150°C
Pressure (*P*) at combustion	110 kPa (= 16 Lb/In^2)

Wanted: 1) Amount of fuel used in kmole/h, 2) Amount of O_2 used, 3) Amount of N_2 used, 4) Amount of O_2 used to produce CO_2, 4) Amount of O_2 used to produce CO, 5) Amount of O_2 unused, 6) Amount of CO_2 in flue gas, 7) Amount of CO in flue gas, 8) Amount of flue gas, 9) Molar density (D_n) of flue gas at 144°C (= 306°F) and 1 Atm, and 10) Volumetric flow rate ($\dot{V}$) of flue gas at T=140°C and P = 1 Atm

The amount of the fuel in kmole/h is calculated from its $\dot{M}$ (mass flow rate) and M_n (molar mass)

$$M = \frac{\dot{M}}{M_n} = \frac{1000}{224} = 4.5 \text{ kmole/h}$$

Based on the above equation, 24 moles of O_2 were used to burn 1 mole of gas, so the amount of O_2 used is

$$4.5 \times 24 = 108 \text{ kmole/h}$$

Actual O_2 used at 40% *EAR* is

$$108 \times 1.4 = 151 \text{ kmole/h}$$

Under the topic of air, we say that 78% of the dry air is N_2 and 21% is O_2, so the amount of N_2 in the air, which will be ended in the flue gas, can be calculated as

$$151 \times \frac{78}{21} = 561 \text{ kmole/h}$$

Being CO in the flue gas tells us that complete combustion did *not* occur, meaning that besides the CO_2 reaction (given above), another reaction also occurred that produced CO.

$$C_{16}H_{32} + 16\ O_2 \rightarrow 16\ CO + 16\ H_2O$$

Because the flue gas has 3 moles of CO_2 per mole of CO, the CO_2 reaction uses three-fourths of the fuel, and the CO reaction uses the other one-fourth. So, the amount of O_2 used by the CO_2 reaction is

$$\frac{3}{4} \times 4.5 \times 24 = 81 \text{ kmole/h}$$

The amount of O_2 used by the CO reaction is

$$\frac{1}{4} \times 4.5 \times 16 = 18 \text{ kmole/h}$$

The total O_2 used by CO_2 and CO is 81 + 18 = 98 kmole/h. We know that the actual O_2 used was 151 kmole/h, so the unreacted O_2 in the flue gas would be 151 – 98 = 53 kmole/h.

The amount of CO_2 and CO in the flue gas will be

$$\frac{3}{4} \times 4.5 \times 16 = 54 \text{ kmole } CO_2/h \qquad \frac{1}{4} \times 4.5 \times 16 = 18 \text{ kmole } CO/h$$

The gases in the flue gas consist of N_2 (in the amount of 561 kmole/h), unburned O_2 (81 kmole/h), CO_2 (54 kmole/h), and CO (18 kmole/h), so the total mass flow of the flue gas is 714 kmole/h. To find the molar density (D_n) of the flue gas at 140°C and 1 Atm, we consider it an ideal gas and use the ideal gas equation.

$$D_n = \frac{P}{R.T} = \frac{1}{0.0821 \times (140+273)} = 0.003 \text{ mole/m}^3 \text{ (3.2 mole/Ft}^3)$$

And because one mole of any gas at STP is 22.4 L (= 10.2 Ft^3), the volume of one mole of the flue gas at 144°C and 1 Atm will be

$$V = \frac{nRT}{P} = \frac{1 \times 0.0821(140+273)}{1} = 34 \text{ L/mole (- 0.034 m}^3\text{/mole or 34 m}^3\text{/kmole)}$$

Volumetric flow rate ($\dot{V}$) is the gas's molar flow rate ($\dot{M}$) per its molar density (D_n)

$$\dot{V} = \frac{\dot{M}}{D_n} = \frac{714 \times 34}{0.003} = 8092 \times 10^3$$

M-18

MASS DEFECT

Study NUCLEAR MASS DEFECT.

M-19

MASS DIFFUSION COEFFICIENT

Another name for **conductive diffusion coefficient**. Study CONDUCTIVE AND CONVECTIVE DIFFUSION COEFFICIENTS.

M-20

MASS DIFFUSION PROCESS

Another name for DIFFUSION PROCESS.

M-21

MASS ENERGY AND MASS ENERGY EQUATION

The word **mass energy** is abbreviated for **rest mass energy**, discussed under ENERGY AND ITS FORMS. For the mass-energy equation, study EINSTEIN'S THEORY OF MASS-ENERGY EQUALITY.

M-22

MASS ENERGY EQUALITY

Study EINSTEIN'S THEORY OF MASS-ENERGY EQUALITY.

M-23

MASS EXCESS

Short name for NUCLEAR CRITICAL AND NUCLEAR EXCESS MASSES.

M-24

MASS FLOW PROCESS

Another name for MASS TRANSFER PROCESS.

M-25

MASS FLOW RATE

As a physical quantity, mass flow rate ($\dot{M}$) is the mass (M) of a fluid that passes a reference plane (flat) in a unit of time (t).

$$\dot{M} = \frac{M}{t} \qquad (1)$$

Consider a liquid flow through a valve. Putting this equation into action, if $\dot{M}$ of the liquid is 1 kg/min (= 2.2 Lb/min), we can collect 4 kg of liquid in 4 minutes. Conversion between $\dot{M}$ and $\dot{V}$ (volumetric flow rate; volume/t) requires the fluid D (density).

$$\dot{M} = D.\dot{V} \qquad (2)$$

Differentially (infinitesimally), $\dot{M}$ (the M rate) is the time differential of M.

$$\dot{M} = \lim_{\Delta t \to 0} \frac{\Delta M}{\Delta t} = \frac{dM}{dt} \qquad (3)$$

Consider a flowing liquid in a pipe. The liquid's $\dot{M}$ in the pipe is the product of its density (D), average velocity ($\bar{V}$), and the pipe's cross-sectional area ($A = \pi R^2 = \pi d^2/4$, where d is for the pipe's inside diameter).

$$\dot{M} = D.\bar{V}.A = D.\bar{V}.\pi\frac{d^2}{4} \qquad (4)$$

The term $\bar{V}.A$ is the definition of volumetric flow rate ($\dot{V}$), so

$$\dot{M} = D.\dot{V} \qquad (5)$$

When the liquid's D is given in kg/m^3, its $\bar{V}$ in m/s, and the pipe's A in m^2, the $\dot{M}$ becomes in kg/s. Similarly, when D is in kg/m^3 and $\dot{V}$ in m^3/s, $\dot{M}$ also becomes in kg/s.

The mass flow rate through a differential area (dA) is given as

$$\dot{M} = D.\bar{V}.dA \qquad (6)$$

[The SI unit of $\dot{M}$ is kg/h, kg/min, or kg/s, and its US unit is Lb/h, Lb/min, or Lb/s. In some practices, the mass flow rate of a device, such as an evaporator, is taken as its **capacity**.]

M-26

MASS FLUX AND MASS FLUX RATE

Mass Flux

The mass flux (J, also called **mass diffusion flux** or **diffusivity flux**) of a physical quantity (like mass or heat) is its mass (M) per unit area (A).

$$J = \frac{M}{A} \tag{1}$$

For example, in the diffusion process, the mass flux of diffusing component A is the amount of A per diffusing area. The usual SI unit of mass flux is kg/m^2, and its US unit is Lb/Ft^2. In some processes, like the diffusion process, J is expressed in kgmole/m^2 or Lbmole/Ft^2. [Because the amount of component A is given here in **mole**, often the term **molar flux** is used instead of **mass flux**.]

Mass Flux Rate

The mass flux rate ($\dot{J}$, also called **mass diffusion flux rate**, or **diffusivity flux rate**) of a physical quantity (like mass or heat) is its mass flow rate ($\dot{M}$) per unit area (A) or its mass (M) per A (area) per t (time).

$$\dot{J} = \frac{\dot{M}}{A} = \frac{M}{A.t} \tag{2}$$

In the diffusion process, for example, the mass flux rate of diffusing component A is proportional to the driving force of diffusion (C/L) through a proportionality constant, named diffusion coefficient of component A in a mixture with components A and B (shown by D_{AB}).

$$\dot{J}_A = \frac{\dot{M}_A}{A} = D_{AB}\frac{C}{L} \tag{3}$$

Usually, a minus sign is used on the right side of this equation to indicate that a force (F) equal to the negative driving force must diffuse the molecules from the higher-concentrated side to the lower-concentrated side (in the + X-axis direction). Instead, the **plus sign** means that the molecules diffuse in the – X-axis direction (lower to higher concentration). The force that must be applied to the flow determines the diffusion direction

If we use m^2 for the area (A), m^2/h for D_{AB}, kgmole/m^3 for C (concentration), and m (meter) for diffusing length (L), the SI unit of $\dot{J}_A$ (mass flux rate of A) becomes kgmole/(m^2.h). The US unit of $\dot{J}_A$ is Lbmole/(Ft^2.h).

[Note: When the amount of component A is given in mole, the term **molar flux rate** is used instead of **mass flux rate**. For simplicity, sometimes, **mass flux rate** is abbreviated to just **mass flux**. In such cases, the given unit of the quantity can determine the writer's purpose because the **mass flux rate** is usually given in kmole/m^2.h, whereas **mass flux** is given in kmole/m^2.]

M-27

MASS FLUX RATE

Study MASS FLUX AND MASS FLUX RATE.

M-28

MASS FRACTION, MOLAR FRACTION, AND VOLUME FRACTION

Mass fraction (X_M), molar fraction (X_n), and volume fraction (X_V) are different ways of expressing the concentration (C) of a mixture's component in relation to all components in that mixture when it is in a liquid phase or gas phase. As ratios, these quantities are **unitless**.

Mass Fraction

The mass fraction (X_M, also called **solid fraction**) is the mass (M) of a component in a mixture in relation to the total masses of all components in that mixture. We can say, for instance, that the X_M of component A in a solution is 0.4. The X_M of component A (shown as $X_{M.A}$) in a binary solution with components A and B when M_A amount of A component and M_B amount of B component is in the solution can be expressed as

$$X_{M.A} = \frac{M_A}{M_A+M_B} = \frac{M_A}{M_T} \quad (1)$$

Because the total (sum) of all mass fractions of a mixture equates to one, the $X_{M.A}$ and $X_{M.B}$ of a liquid phase are related as

$$X_{M.A} + X_{M.B} = 1 \quad (2)$$

Similarly, when N components are in a liquid phase, the $X_{M.A}$, $X_{M.B}$, and $X_{M.N}$ are related as

$$X_{M.A} + X_{M.B} + \cdots X_{M.N} = 1 \quad (3)$$

Similar equation can be written for the mass fractions of components A and B in the vapor phase, where the mass fraction of A in the vapor phase is shown as $Y_{M.A}$ and that of B as $Y_{M.B}$.

$$Y_{M.A} + Y_{M.B} = 1 \quad (4)$$

[The same concept as a **mass fraction** with a denominator of 100 is called the **mass percent concentration** (% by mass), which is defined under PERCENTAGES). For instance, a binary solution containing 95% by mass of ethanol and 5% by mass of water means that the ethanol's X_M in the solution ($X_{M.A}$) is 0.95 and water's X_M in the solution ($X_{M.B}$) is 0.05.]

Molar Fraction

The molar fraction (X_n or X: also called **mole fraction**) of a component in a solution mixture is its number of moles (n) divided by the total moles of all components in that mixture. In the case of a liquid phase or gas phase, X_n is one way of expressing a mixture's concentration. We say, for instance, that the X_n of component A in a solution is 0.2.

The X_n of component A (shown as $X_{n.A}$) in a binary solution with components A and B, when n_A moles of A component and n_B moles of B component are in the solution, can be expressed as

$$X_{n.A} = \frac{n_A}{n_A+n_B} = \frac{n_A}{n_T} \quad (5)$$

Because a mixture's total of all molar fractions equates to one, the $X_{n.A}$ and $X_{n.B}$ of a liquid phase are related as

$$X_{n.A} + X_{n.B} = 1 \quad (6)$$

Similarly, the $X_{n.A}$, $X_{n.B}$, and $X_{n.N}$ of a liquid phase with N components are related as

$$X_{n.A} + X_{n.B} + \cdots X_{n.N} = 1 \quad (7)$$

Similar equation can be written for the molar fractions of components A and B in the vapor phase, where the molar fraction of A in the vapor phase is shown as $Y_{n.A}$ and that of B as $Y_{n.B}$.

$$Y_{n.A} + Y_{n.B} = 1 \quad (8)$$

The same concept with a denominator of 100 is the **molar percentage** (mole percentage). For instance, a binary solution of 60 molar percent of ethanol and 40 molar percent of water means that the solution's X_{nA} is 0.6 and its $X_{n.B}$ is 0.4. [Molar fraction (X_n) is a ratio of moles to moles, while molarity (M, molar concentration) is a ratio of moles to a liter (mole/L).]

Volume Fraction

The volume fraction (X_V) is the volume (V) of a component in a solution mixture in relation to the total volumes of all components in that mixture. Saying, for instance, the X_V of component A in a solution is 0.2. The X_V of component A (shown as $X_{V.A}$) in a binary solution with components A and B, when V_A is the volume of A component and V_B is the volume of B component are in the solution, can be expressed as

$$X_{V.A} = \frac{V_A}{V_A+V_B} = \frac{V_A}{V_T} \quad (9)$$

Because the total (sum) of all volume fractions of a mixture equals unity (1), the $X_{V.A}$ and $X_{V.B}$ of a liquid phase with N components are related as

$$X_{V.A} + X_{V.B} = 1 \quad (10)$$

[The same concept with a denominator of 100 is the **volume percentage**. When we say, for example, a solution of 90% by volume of ethanol in water, we mean that the solution's $X_{V.A}$ is 0.9, and its $X_{V.B}$ is 0.1.]

M-29
MASS NUMBER

This is the simplified name for the **atomic mass number,** and it is discussed under ATOMIC NUMBER AND ATOMIC MASS NUMBER.

M-30
MASS SPECTROMETRY

Study SPECTROMETRY AND MASS SPECTROMETRY.

M-31
MASS TRANSFER PROCESS

As one of the widely-used process units (unit operations) of ChemEng, mass transfer (mass flow) is the process of diffusion (transformation of mass at the **molecular level**) in a phase (or from one phase to another) by using differences in diffusivity, solubility, concentration difference (ΔC), or pressure difference (ΔP).

[Mass transfer acts in most of the process units. Because of the active participation of mass transfer in the diffusion process, fluid flow process, and membrane separation process, mass-transfer-related subjects are mostly discussed under those topics. The diffusion process studies the mass transfer of a diffusing component (or components) at the **molecular level**. The fluid-flow process studies the mass transfer of a fluid (liquid or gas) at the **bulk level**. And membrane separation process studies the separation of larger molecules from smaller molecules in a solution by ΔP between the two sides of a **semipermeable membrane**.]

M-32

MASS TRANSFER BY DIFFUSION

Study DIFFUSION PROCESS.

M-33

MASS VELOCITY

Mass velocity (V_M or G) is the mass flow rate ($\dot{M}$) of a fluid (liquid or gas) divided by the cross-sectional area (A) of a pipe in which the fluid flows.

$$V_M = \frac{\dot{M}}{A} = \frac{D.\bar{V}.A}{A} = D.\bar{V} \quad (1)$$

Or

$$V_M = \frac{\dot{M}}{\pi\frac{d^2}{4}} = \frac{4\dot{M}}{\pi.d^2} \quad (2)$$

In these equations, the D is the fluid's density, $\bar{V}$ is the fluid's average velocity, and d is the pipe's diameter. [The SI unit of mass velocity is kg/m^2.s, and its US unit is Lb/Ft^2.s.]

The following are the two advantages of using mass velocity (V_M):

- It is independent of a fluid's temperature (T) and pressure (P), and
- It is considered the fluid's mass flow rate ($\dot{M}$).

[The term **mass velocity** is *not* the same as **mass averaged velocity**. Mass velocity is the velocity of a fluid, taken in relation to its mass flow rate ($\dot{M}$). Mass average velocity, instead, is the average velocity ($\bar{V}$) of a mixture consisting of individual liquids that flow together with consideration of their masses.]

M-34

MASS, WEIGHT, AND SPECIFIC WEIGHT

The words **mass** (M) and **weight** (w) are usually used equally. This is incorrect because 1) Mass, like energy, is *not* creatable, but weight is. 2) Mass is force (F) per acceleration (a), but weight is the product of multiplication of mass and gravitational acceleration (a_g = 9.8 m/s^2 = 32.2 Ft/s^2).

$$w = M.a_g \quad (1)$$

Because a_g is constant on and near the Earth's surface, the words **mass** and **weight** can be used equally under those conditions. However, other differences exist between the mass and weight, as discussed next.

- The SI unit of mass is kg, and its US unit is the pound (Lb). The SI unit of weight is Newton (1 N = 1 kg.m/s^2), and its US unit is Lb.Ft/s^2 (rather Lb_F.Ft/s^2, where subscript F is for force and Lb_F is for pound-force). Thus, "weight in kg" is a measure of mass, and "weight in Lb" is a measure of force.
- Mass is a constant quantity (because it depends on how many atoms a system contains), but weight is *not*. Thus, a system's mass remains the same *no* matter where it is in the Universe. For example, the mass of an astronaut is the same on the moon and the Earth, but his weight would be 1/6 on the Moon than on the Earth (because a_g on the Moon acting on him is 1/6 that of the Earth).

- Mass is a scalar quantity (with *no* direction), but weight is a vector quantity (with a downward direction). For this reason, say, 5 kg of water plus 3 kg of water always makes 8 kg of water, while two weights must be added together with consideration of their force direction (shown by their vectors).

Mass: Mass (M) is a system's quantity (amount), expressed in kg or Lb. Below, three types of mass are discussed.

- **Gravitational Mass (M_g):** The M_g characterizes the strength by which a system responds to gravitational force, F_g (the *greater* the M_g, the *grater* is the F_g, with which a system attracts another system). M_g is defined as an F_g needed to accelerate a system, so it is the ratio of F_g to a (acceleration).

$$M_g = \frac{F_g}{a} \tag{2}$$

- **Inertial Mass (M_I):** The M_I refers to the mass used in Physics, so mass = inertia (resistance to motion). In this way, a system mass (inertia) is stationary. It is difficult to change its state of motion (because it resists motion and, thus, resists acceleration) when it is affected by an inertial force. Based on what has been said, M_I is used in Physics to refer to the inertial (nonaccelerating) mass.
- **Effective Mass (M_E):** The M_E is the M of a system minus the M of the liquid it displaces. In Physics, the M_E of a massive particle is the M when a force (F) acts on it.

You should be aware of the following about the M_g (gravitational mass) and M_I (inertial mass):

- M_I is identical in size to M_g.
- M_I was used as the more specific name for M by Einstein to express a system's resistance to motion and acceleration. He also used M_I as a system's energy content and proved that M and E (energy) are related through $E = M.c^2$ (where c is the speed of light constant). We can, thus, think of M as concentrated E, as in the Sun, where M is converted to E. When, however, oil burns, E comes from changes in chemical bonds.

Weight: Weight (w) is the gravitational force (F_g, the **force of gravity**) applied to a system by a mass M. Thus, F_g gives weight to a system with mass M, so $F_g = w$. The weight of a system is the product of its M and a_g.

$$w = F_g = M.a_g = D.V.a_g \tag{3}$$

Here, D is for density, and V is for volume. According to this equation, a system with a mass of 1 kg (= 2.2 Lb) has a weight of 10 kg.m/s^2 = 10 N = 10 × 0.225 = 2.2 Lb$_F$ (simply Lb). When, for example, a man weighs 77 kg (= 170 Lb), the Earth pulls him down with F_g of 77 × 10 = 770 N. Thus, the weight of the man, whose mass was measured at 77 kg, would be 770 N. Interesting to know that if this man were transported to the Moon, where the a_g is 1/6 as much as on the Earth, his weight measured by the same scale would be 12.8 kg. Thus, weight depends on a_g what one feels.

Because weight is an acceleration-dependent quantity, if a system undergoes rapid acceleration, its weight *increases*. A pilot in a fighter jet can experience up to 12 F_g, so his weight *increases* and, therefore, feels more pushed into the seat. This is why pilots need specific training to cope with such extra force.

[Note 1: Usually, the word **weight** is used in ChemEng to the extent that it does *not* create any confusion. We say a system's weight is so and so, although we think about its mass.] [Note 2: It is recommended to use **mass** instead of matter because the matter is *not* a well-defined word.]

Specific Weight: The specific weight (w_{Sp} or by Greek letter gamma, γ) of a substance is its weight (w) to its volume (V) at a certain temperature (T). The SI unit of w_{Sp} is N/m^3 and its US unit is Lb$_F$/Ft^3 (simply Lb/Ft^3). For example, w_{Sp} of water at 4°C (= 39°) is 9.81 kN/m^3 (= 62.4 Lb/Ft^3), and that of mercury is 133 kN/m^3 (848 Lb/Ft^3). The ratio between these two is 133/9.81 = 13.6.

The relation between w_{Sp} of a substance, gravitational acceleration (a_g = 9.81 m/s^2 = 32.2 Ft/s^2 on Earth), and the substance's density (D) is given as

$$w_{Sp} = a_g.D \tag{4}$$

[The T of a substance considerably affects its w_{sp}, but the P (pressure) effect is *not* great.]

M-35

MASSIVE AND MASSLESS PARTICLES

Discussed under PARTICLES AND ITS TYPES.

M-36

MATERIAL AND MATTER

Both **material** and **matter** are not well-defined in physical chemistry (because of their broad and general use in different subjects). We, however, define them here as generally used. [The word **matter** is *not* used in this book often, and instead, the word system is used.]

Material: Material is a chemical substance (simply **substance**) or a mixture of manufactured substances. Materials can exist in different states of matter. The word **raw material** is used in ChemEng as the input (or inputs) to produce a product (or products). [In material engineering, materials are tested for strength by a strength test in a **strength tester** when a force (F) is applied to them.]

Matter: Matter is a quantity with mass (M), but unlike mass,

- Matter does *not* have a universally-accepted definition in scientific subjects.
- Matter is *not* a **conserved quantity** (because it can be created or destroyed, say, in a process).

The following are three (3) general uses of the word **matter**:

- In **chemistry**, it is used as a chemical compound (simply **compound**) that has mass, occupies space, and can be touched, heard, tasted, or smelled.
- In **physics**, it is used as the states of matter (solid, liquid, gas, and plasma) or as anything that exhibits inertia (the tendency to maintain a constant velocity). In its broadest possible sense, matter means everything, including gravitation force, electromagnetic radiation, and even gravitation field that carries energy and momentum (mass × velocity). [Broglie used the word **matter** in his atomic theory (Broglie's theory of duality of matter) as the particles of all matter.]
- In **cosmology**, it is used as everything that is *not* spacetime.

In relation to purity, chemistry classifies matter in the following ways:

- **Pure Matter:** It consists only of a single element (like gold) or compound (like water).
- **Impure Matter:** An impure matter is a mixture of two (or more) elements or compounds.

In other classification, chemistry divides matter based on its size, as

- **Macroscopic Matter:** It can be physically observed, like a few grams of sugar or salt.
- **Microscopic Matter:** It needs a microscope to be observed, or even impossible to observe it clearly with a microscope, like the structure of an atom, so we must raise our imagination to study such a matter.

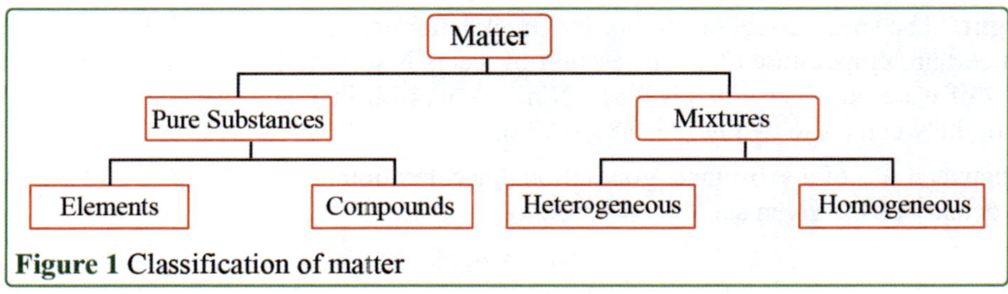

Figure 1 Classification of matter

M-37

MATERIAL BALANCE

Another name for MASS BALANCE.

M-38

MATTER

Study MATERIAL AND MATTER.

M-39

MAXWELL

Maxwell, James Clerk (1831−1879) was a British physicist who greatly contributed to Physics by following the discoveries of Faraday about the close relationship between magnetism and electricity (later called **Maxwell's theory**). In the early 1860s, Maxwell formulated this relationship by several equations (later, **Maxwell's equations**) to describe Faraday's Induction Law (the relation between electric charges and electric current in a magnetic field). In the same year, Maxwell proposed the existence of electromagnetic waves (EM-waves). He also discovered the following:

- An electromagnetic field (EM field) has the properties of electric field (E-field, represented by the term **electro** in **electromagnetic**) and M-field (represented by the term **magnetic** in **electromagnetic**).
- M-field, created by a magnet, acts like a wave, and based on this, he used the velocity (V) of the EM-waves to fully describe the relation between M-field and E-field in his equations.

Maxwell proved that when the light travels through a vacuum medium, it is under the influence of two physical quantities, the permittivity and permeability of the vacuum. And because these two values in a vacuum medium are constants, the speed of light is also a constant value, named the speed of light constant ($c = 2.998 \times 10^5$ km/s).

Maxwell also proved that the light must consist of EM fields, each made of an E-field and M-field. This tells us that many EM waves that travel at light speed are in a conducting loop.

After the discoveries of Faraday and Maxwell about generating electricity, experimental inventors tried to develop electric generators to produce electricity. The problem was that every inventor said his version of work to be superior, whether that be AC (alternating current) or DC (direct current), low or high voltage, and low or high frequency. These efforts continued until the end of the 19th century when generating 50 or 60 Hz AC electricity became the most practical idea for commercial electricity use. In these efforts, the innovative ideas of Edison and Tesla in the field of electricity get the most credit.

It is interesting to know the way two top physicists, Einstein and Hawking, thought about Maxwell:

- Einstein kept a picture of Newton, Faraday, and Maxwell in his office to respect them as the pioneers of Physics (see the portrait under the topic of EINSTEIN). Einstein also said, "Maxwell was the most profound and the most fruitful that physics has experienced since the time of Newton." He also said, "One scientific time ended, and another began with Maxwell."
- Hawking said, "Maxwell is the physicist's physicist and the unsung hero of British science."

And we can add the following:

- Maxwell was one of the two top theoretic contributors to electricity (the other one was Faraday).

- Newton, Faraday, and Maxwell are the three top classical physicists and the three of the ten top physicists (classical and quantum) of all time. [For the name of top quantum physicists, see QUANTUM PHYSICS.]

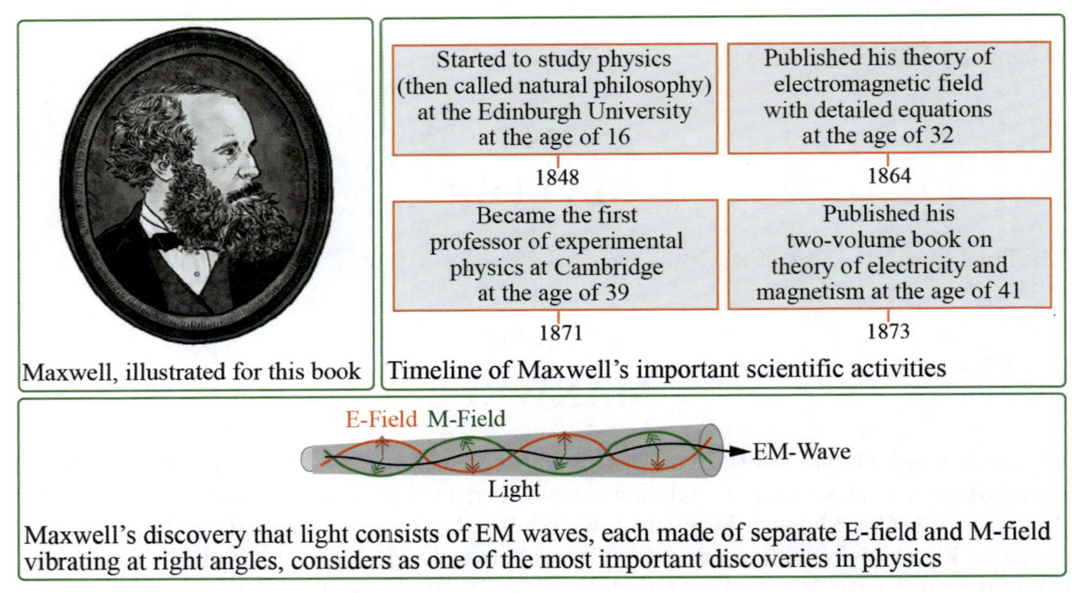

Maxwell, illustrated for this book

Timeline of Maxwell's important scientific activities

Maxwell's discovery that light consists of EM waves, each made of separate E-field and M-field vibrating at right angles, considers as one of the most important discoveries in physics

M-40

MCCABE THIELE DIAGRAM

Discussed under DISTILLATION PROCESS.

M-41

MEAN APERTURE

Mean aperture (M_A) is a value used to express the average size of the crystals or the aperture corresponding to 50% of the crystals. Say, M_A of 0.4 mm (400 micrometers, μm) means that 50% (one-half) of the sample crystals fall through the screen with 0.4 mm opening and 50% retain on it. [0.4 mm is approximately the mean size of typical medium-size table sugar crystals, where 1 mm = 10^{-3} m = 0.04 In, and 1 μm = 10^{-6} m.]

M-42

MEAN LIFETIME

Study RADIOACTIVE HALF LIFETIME AND MEAN LIFETIME.

M-43

MEAN TEMPERATURE DIFFERENCE

Simplified name for LOGARITHMIC MEAN TEMPERATURE DIFFERENCE.

M-44

MEASURING UNIT SYSTEMS

Measuring unit systems (simply **unit systems**) measure standards used in science and engineering. The SI unit system (SI is for **Systeme International** in French) and the US unit system (also called **US customary system**, simply **US units** or **US system**) are the two most used systems of units in the world. The SI unit system is adapted from the **metric system** (meter-kilogram-second, MKS, system), introduced in the 1750s. The SI units were standardized in 1799 and 1960, both in France. It is now used in most countries except the USA, UK, Liberia, and Myanmar. In the UK, the **imperial unit system** is used. [Because the US of America is the only advanced country that still uses the US system, it is often called the **United States Customary Units** (simply **US Units**). This book uses this tradition.]

SI Unit System

The SI unit system is based on the following seven base units:

- Meter (m) for length (*L*),
- Kilogram (kg) for mass (*M*),
- Second (s) for time (*t*),
- Ampere (A) for current (*I*),
- Kelvin (K) for temperature (*T*),
- Candela (cd) for luminous intensity (*I*), and
- Mole for the amount of a chemical substance.

Unlike the US unit system, the SI unit system is easy to work with (because most values are based on a multiple or division of 10). This means that conversion measurements can be multiplied or divided by 10. A meter (m) divided into 100 is a centimeter (cm). Each centimeter consists of 10 millimeters (mm). And so on. However, because the main SI units are *not* always convenient (for example, expressing the mass of a filter paper in kg is difficult), the following **prefixes** are used to convert the SI units:

Prefix	Symbol	Name	Multiplier
Tera-	T	Trillion	1 000 000 000 000 = 10^{12}
Giga-	G	Milliard	1 000 000 000 = 10^{9}
Mega-	M	Million	1 000 000 = 10^{6}
Kilo-	k	Thousand	1 000 = 10^{3}
Hecto-	h	Hundred	100 = 10^{2}
Deca-	da	Ten	10 = 10^{1}
No Prefix		One	1 = 10^{0}
Deci-	d	Tenth	0.1 = 10^{-1}
Centi-	c	Hundredth	0.01 = 10^{-2}
Milli-	m	Thousandth	0.001 = 10^{-3}
Micro-	µ	Millionth	0.000 001 = 10^{-6}
Nano-	n	Milliardth	0.000 000 001 = 10^{-9}
Pico-	p	Trillionth	0.000 000 000 001 = 10^{-12}

Prefixes, symbols, names, and multipliers for conversion of SI Units

US Unit System

The US unit system is the modified English measurement unit system used in the USA. The US units are based on Ft (foot), Lb (pound), and s (second).

Knowing the following about the US unit system and SI unit system is helpful:

- In 1959, some of the US units were redefined.
- Unlike the SI unit system (most values are based on a multiple or division of 10), it is difficult to work with the US unit system.
- The SI unit system is used in chemistry, physics, and engineering in the USA. The US armed forces, government, and some industries (like pharmaceutical) have already switched to the SI unit system.
- In ChemEng (particularly in this book), the calculations are solved in SI units, and the results are converted to the US units.

[Note 1: In 2019, CODATA suggested that the SI units be based on physical constants. For example, a **meter** (the SI unit of length) is defined as the length of the path traveled by light in a vacuum in 1/299 792 458 of a second, where the value 1/299 792 458 is the speed of light constant in a vacuum.]

[Note 2: Thomas Jefferson and a few other American presidents tried without success to change the system of units in the United States. However, some industries in the USA, such as the chemical process industry, have already started to use the metric system (SI units).]

[Note 3: This book gives the SI unit, followed by the US unit in parentheses.]

[Note 4: In **long calculations**, it is much easier to do basic calculations in SI units and convert the result to the US unit. This is done in this book.]

M-45
MECHANICAL ENERGY

Discussed under the topic of ENERGY AND ITS FORMS.

M-46
MECHANICAL ENERGY EQUATION

Another name for BERNOULLI EQUATION.

M-47
MECHANICAL VAPOR RECOMPRESSION

Discussed under VAPOR RECOMPRESSION.

M-48
MECHANICAL WORK

Discussed under WORK.

M-49

MELT CRYSTALLIZATION

In melt crystallization, the crystals are formed from a molten feed without using seed particles. In solution crystallization, discussed under CRYSTALLIZATION PROCESS, the crystals are formed from a solution feed using seed particles.

M-50

MELTING POINT TEMPERATURE

The melting point temperature (T_{MP}, simply **melting point** or **melting temperature**) of a solid is the temperature (T) at which its molecular structure changes from a solid phase to the liquid phase at the pressure (P) surrounding that solid. [The T_{MP} of a substance closely depends on the applied P. For this reason, melting temperatures are usually specified at atmospheric pressure (P_{Atm} = 1 Atm ≈ 100 kPa), which is standard. A T_{MP} given at P_{Atm} is sometimes called **normal melting temperature**. At P_{Atm}, the T_{MP} is different for different substances. For example, ice melts at 0°C, sugar ($C_{12}H_{22}O_{11}$) at about 185°C, and salt (NaCl) at about 800°C (1474°F).]

During the melting process, heat (Q, heat energy, or enthalpy) is gradually and uniformly added to a solid to increase its T until it reaches its T_{MP}. At this point, the solid-liquid phase maintains its T equal to T_{MP} until melting is complete. At the T_{MP}, the solid and liquid phases are at equilibrium (stableness).

At T_{MP}, the solid and liquid phases are at equilibrium (stableness). The T_{MP} of a substance closely depends on the surroundings' pressure (P). T_{MP} is usually specified at P_{Atm}.

[Note 1: If heat is gradually and uniformly applied to a solid, the temperature increase stops at the T_{MP} until the melting process is complete. For example, when ice is melting, the T remains constant ($\Delta T = 0$) at 0°C until all the ice is converted to water.] [Note 2: For most substances, melting point temperature (T_{MP}) and freezing point temperature (T_{FP}) are almost the same. For example, the T_{MP} and T_{FP} of water in its liquid form and solid form (ice) is 0°C (– 32°F or 273 K).]

M-51

MELTING PROCESS

As a process unit of ChemEng, melting (fusion) is a phase-change process by which a solid melts into a liquid when its temperature (T) reaches its melting point temperature (T_{MP}). The solid that has melted is called **melt** (a molten state). Melting, the reverse of crystallization, can occur by pressure (P), but industrially it is performed by absorbing heat energy (E_Q), so melting is a heat-absorbing process (endothermic process). The E_Q (rather enthalpy, H) absorbed in melting is a latent enthalpy (phase-change enthalpy), known as the enthalpy of melting (H_M). We also know from the topic of ENTHALPY that E_Q and ΔH (the enthalpy change) have the same meaning, so the E_Q absorbed by the melting = $\Delta H = \Delta H_M$.

When a solid absorbs heat energy, its T increases until it reaches its T_{MP}, at which the solid's chemical bonds break, causing it to be liquefied. Then, the solid-liquid system maintains its T equal to its T_{MP} until the melting process is complete. However, during this period, the system's enthalpy (H) gradually and uniformly increases. The relation between the T_{MP}, change in enthalpy of melting (ΔH_M), and change in entropy of melting (ΔS_M) can be given as

$$T_{MP} = \frac{\Delta H_M}{\Delta S_M} \tag{1}$$

M-52

MEMBRANE SEPARATION PROCESS

As one of the process units (unit operations) of ChemEng, **membrane separation** (MS) is a mass transfer process at the molecular level for separating a solution's larger molecules from smaller ones by the pressure difference (ΔP) between the two sides of a semipermeable membrane. [A **semipermeable membrane** has fine pores (0.1 to 10 μ) **permeable** to the solvent with smaller molecules but nearly **impermeable** to the solute with larger molecules.] As shown in Figure 1, the separation of a component (or components) in a solution occurs by the movement (scientifically, diffusion) of that component's molecules through a membrane. Thus, the MS (membrane separation) is a multi-step diffusion process in which the molecules that are smaller than the membrane's pores penetrate the membrane, and the larger molecules retain on the membrane.

The following are two membrane-based separation processes:

- In the dialysis process, the molecular separation can be performed just by differences in diffusivity, where aqueous solutions at PAtm are on both sides of the membrane.
- In the liquid-liquid extraction (simply **extraction process**), the membrane separates the immiscible extract and raffinate phases.

  Membranes can be used for homogeneous solutions of macromolecules (like proteins, polymers, or suspended solid particles) larger than the membrane's pores.

  The following two feeding arrangements are used in MS operations:

- Dead-end feeding, in which the feed flows straight toward a dead point (Figure 2), and
- Crossflow feeding, in which feed flows tangentially to the membrane's surface (Figure 3).

The arrangement's advantages and disadvantages depend on the feed's characteristics. Crossflow feeding has an advantage because a feed with high suspended particles accumulates much *less* on the membrane's feed side than on the membrane's dead-end side. In both arrangements, the feed's smaller molecules permeate (diffuse or penetrate) through the membrane (because of applying high pressure on the **feed**, F, side) to form the **permeate** (P, the product). The larger molecules that *cannot* permeate through the membrane retain to form the **retentate** (R, the byproduct of the process).

Based on the membrane's pore size, the MS (membrane-separation) process classifies into three classes:

- **Microfiltration** (MF) **Process:** The pore size of the membranes used for MF is usually in the range of 0.1 to 10 μm, where 1 μm (1 micrometer = 1 micron = 10^{-6} m). The MF separates larger molecules, like colloids and some microorganisms.
- **Ultrafiltration** (UF) **Process:** The pore size of the membranes used for UF is usually in the range of 0.001 to 0.1 μm (1 nm to 100 nm), where 1 nm (nanometer) = 10^{-9} m. The UF separates medium-size molecules, like proteins, RNA, and DNA.
- **Nanofiltration** (NF) **Process:** The pore size of the membranes used for NF is usually 0.1 to 1 nm. The NF separates the extremely small molecules (like peptides).

  A membrane for a particular MS duty is usually chosen based on one of the next criteria:

- **Membrane's Pore Size:** It is usually a bit smaller than the larger molecules to be separated. The pore size is particularly important in MF, UF, NF, and RO (reverse osmosis).
- **Membrane's Material:** It is chosen to match the solubility of the solution under the process. A **hydrophilic** (water-like) **membrane**, for example, is used when a water-based solution is under the process, or a **hydrophobic** (oil-like) membrane is used for an oil-like solution.
- **Molecular Diffusivity:** The diffusion coefficient of the diffusing component is important in all types of MS processes, particularly in osmosis, pervaporation, and membrane distillation.

  Based on the **driving force** (the cause) of the process, the MS process is divided into:

- Processes that operate based on the pressure gradient ($\Delta P/L$) between the two sides of a membrane. MF, UF, NF, and RO are in this group.
- Processes that operate based on the concentration gradient ($\Delta C/L$) between the two sides of a membrane. Osmosis, RO, pervaporation, and dialysis are the main examples of this group.
- Processes that operate based on the temperature gradient ($\Delta T/L$) between the two sides of a membrane. The membrane distillation is an example of this group.
- Processes that operate based on the electric potential (voltage) between the two sides of a membrane. Membrane electrolysis and membrane electrodialysis are examples of this group.

In all listed four groups, the way the molecules diffuse from one side of the membrane to the other is the same.

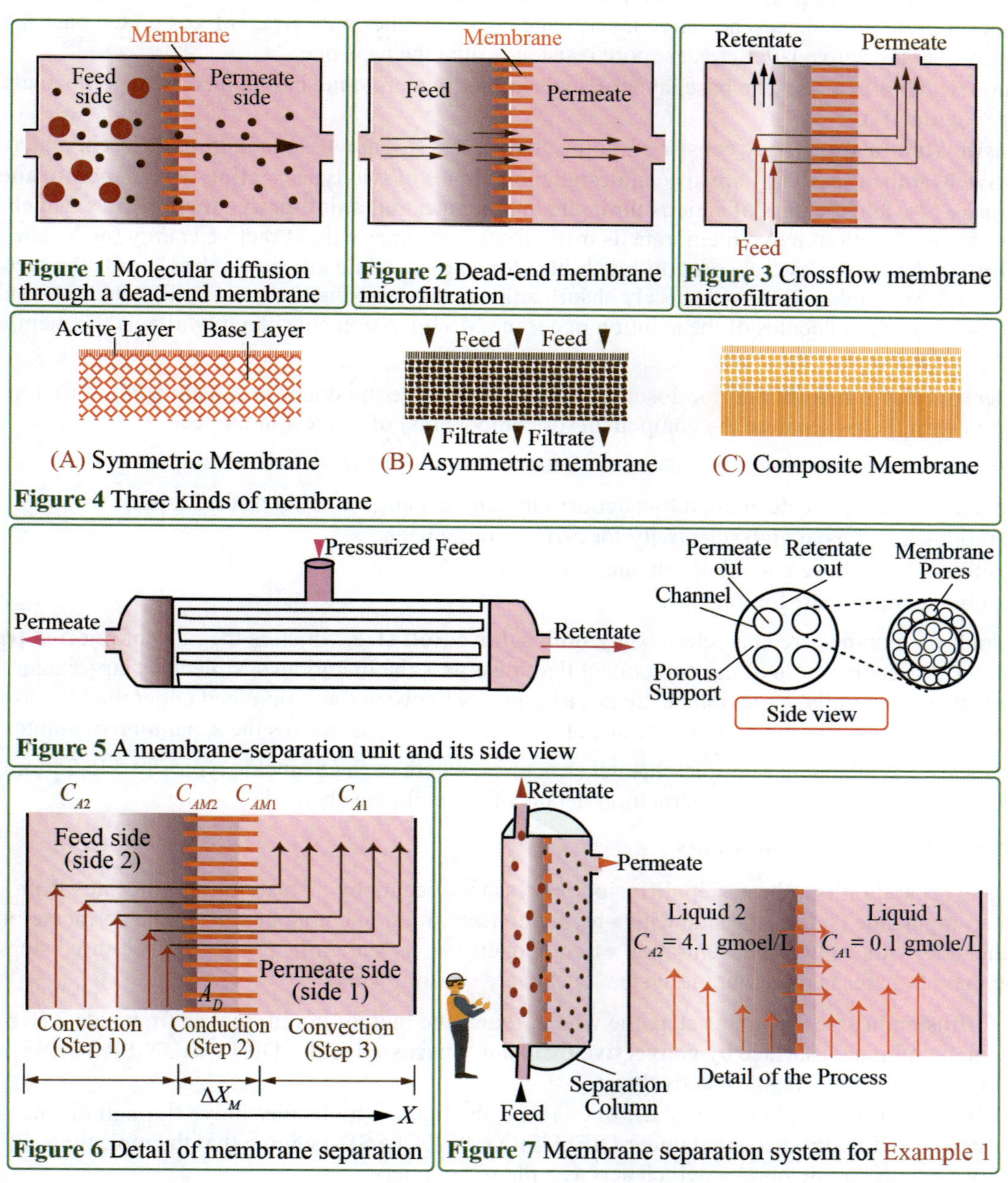

Figure 1 Molecular diffusion through a dead-end membrane

Figure 2 Dead-end membrane microfiltration

Figure 3 Crossflow membrane microfiltration

Figure 4 Three kinds of membrane

Figure 5 A membrane-separation unit and its side view

Figure 6 Detail of membrane separation

Figure 7 Membrane separation system for Example 1

Membranes

The membranes used for the MS process are usually made from polymer, ceramic, or stainless steel. The application of polymeric membranes has increased in recent years by using special polymers, like polyamide, polysulphone, polyethersulphone, and polyvinylidene fluoride. These membranes comparatively indicate more strength against organic solvents, pH, and high temperatures. Ceramic membranes, made from aluminum oxide, zirconium oxide, and titanium oxide, are used because of their hardness and strength.

To control the diffusivity, membranes are made with different molecular structures, such as

- **Symmetric Membranes:** The asymmetric membrane's base layer (under the thin active layer) has a consistent molecular structure, as shown in Figure 4A. Both active and base layers are made from the same material but different pore sizes. The active layer, which has a smaller pore size, is fixed on the base layer with larger pores, so the active layer creates more resistance than the base one.
- **Asymmetric Membranes:** The base layer of an asymmetric membrane has an inconsistent molecular structure (see Figure 4B).
- **Composite Membranes:** They consist of more active layers (Figure 4C) made from different materials.
- **Ion-active Membranes:** They are special design membranes of two types, **cation-active membranes**, which make possible the pass of cations through a membrane, and **anion-active membranes**, which make that for anions. A cation-active membrane is made from a polymer with attractive energy (also called **chemical affinity**, which expresses absorption capability) for cations, while anions can freely pass the membrane. An anion-active membrane can selectively absorb anions while passing the cations. The electric conductivity (K_E) of the charged molecules of the solution under the MS operation considerably affects the membrane's attraction (affinity).

The **selectivity of a membrane** for absorption of a particular component in a feed, applied to a membrane-separation system, helps separate the component (or components) of interest in the feed.

In the selection of a membrane for a particular process, the following criteria are important:

- The membrane must provide enough transfer area to handle a large amount of feed input,
- The membrane must have high selectivity for certain components,
- The membrane must have enough mechanical stability, and
- The membrane must resist fouling.

Sometimes, membranes are characterized by **molecular cutoff size**, which is the ratio of rejected (**retentate**) fraction to the molecular mass of the component that must pass the membrane. Molecules larger than the cutoff size are rejected. Generally, a membrane creates a boundary between a solution feed under the MS, so the feed's solutes and solvent flow through the membrane at different rates. This makes the separation of solutes easier.

Membranes are available in multiple-channel structures, where each channel is typically 5 to 25 mm (= 0.2 to 1 In) in diameter. Figure 5 shows the structural details of a membrane channel.

Membrane Separation Equations

Membrane separation is a three-step diffusion process that occurs by diffusivity of molecules from the membrane's feed-input side (side 2, the side with a higher concentration of component A) to the permeate-output side (side 1, the side with a lower concentration of component A), as shown in Figure 6. The three steps through which the mass transfer in a membrane system occurs are the following:

- **Step 1** (diffusion in side 2)**:** In this step, the whole liquid (the bulk of liquid) moves from side 2 (feed side) toward the membrane's surface by **convective diffusion** (discussed under DIFFUSION PROCESS), meaning that the molecules diffuse collectively.
- **Step 2** (diffusion through the membrane)**:** In this step, the liquid's molecules move through the membrane by **conductive diffusion** (discussed under DIFFUSION PROCESS), meaning that the molecules diffuse individually through the membrane, which acts as a phase boundary.

- **Step 3** (diffusion in side 1)**:** This step is like step 1 by moving the whole liquid from the membrane's surface area toward side 1 (permeate side), again, by convection.

Knowing that "if there is a flow, diffusion occurs by convection and if there is *no* flow, diffusion occurs by conduction" helps us derive the diffusion equations for a three-step diffusion process. Assuming that component A is the diffusing component, we can relate the concentration difference (ΔC) for each step to determine an equation for the overall process. Concentration (C) of A in different steps are as given in Figure 6, where C_{A2} is the concentration of A on side 2 (the feed side), C_{AM2} is that on the membrane's surface on side 2, C_{AM1} is that on the other side of the membrane, and C_{A1} is the concentration on side 1(the permeate side). Because of mass-transfer rate (mass-diffusivity rate) of all three steps are equal when the system is in a steady-state, we show all three of them by the same symbol of $\dot{M}_A$ (the rate of M_A), which is the amount of mass transfer of A in unit time or diffusion rate of A (actually, the mass flow rate of A).

For step 1 (feed side), ΔC can be given in relation to $\dot{M}_A$ diffused by **convection**, K_{A1} (convective diffusion coefficient of A on feed side), and A (diffusing area).

$$\Delta C_2 = C_{A2} - C_{AM2} = \frac{\dot{M}_A}{K_{A2}.A} \tag{1}$$

For step 2, we must realize that A-molecules diffuse through the membrane's pores, so a fraction of the total area of the membrane is called the **membrane porosity** (ε_p, where subscript p is for porosity), is involved in diffusion. Thus, the membrane's diffusing area for the second step (A_D) must be given based on the membrane's A (total membrane's diffusing area) and ε_p (which can be in the range of 0.2 to 0.8, meaning 20 to 80% porosity)

$$A_D = A.\varepsilon_p \tag{2}$$

Considering this, the ΔC in step 2 can be given in relation to $\dot{M}_A$ (diffusion rate of A), D_{AB} (diffusion coefficient of A into B for the membrane's surface), x (membrane thickness), and $A\varepsilon_P$.

$$\Delta C_2 = C_{AM2} - C_{AM1} = \frac{\dot{M}_A x}{D_{AB}.A.\varepsilon_p} \tag{3}$$

For step 3, ΔC can be given like step 1, but with a different diffusion coefficient.

$$\Delta C_3 = C_{AM1} - C_{A1} = \frac{\dot{M}_A}{K_{A1}.A} \tag{4}$$

We can now add Equations 1, 3, and 4 together and factor $\dot{M}_A$ to obtain the equation for the entire process (step 1 + step 2 + step 3).

$$(C_{A2} - C_{AM2}) + (C_{AM2} - C_{AM1}) + (C_{AM1} - C_{A1}) = \dot{M}_A\left(\frac{1}{K_{A2}.A} + \frac{x}{D_{AB}.A\varepsilon_p} + \frac{1}{K_{A1}.A}\right) \tag{5}$$

After canceling out the same concentrations, we obtain

$$C_{A2} - C_{A1} = \dot{M}_A\left(\frac{1}{K_{A2}.A} + \frac{x}{D_{AB}.A.\varepsilon_p} + \frac{1}{K_{A1}.A}\right) \tag{6}$$

After solving this equation for $\dot{M}_A$, we obtain

$$\dot{M}_A = \frac{C_{A2} - C_{A1}}{\frac{1}{K_{A2}.A} + \frac{x}{D_{AB}.A.\varepsilon_p} + \frac{1}{K_{A1}.A}} \tag{7}$$

The nominator of this equation ($C_{A2} - C_{A1}$) is the overall **driving force** of the process ($\sum F_D$, the sum of the forces for individual steps), and its denominator is the overall **resistance** of the process ($\sum R$, the sum of the resistances for individual steps), so

$$\dot{M}_A = \frac{C_{A2} - C_{A1}}{\frac{1}{K_{A2}.A} + \frac{x}{D_{AB}.A.\varepsilon_p} + \frac{1}{K_{A1}.A}} = \frac{\sum F_D}{\sum R} \tag{8}$$

This equation is like Equation 20, given under HEAT TRANSFER PROCESS.

Because the membrane creates the greatest **resistance** to the diffusion rate ($\dot{M}_A$, the amount of mass transfer of component A), the membrane's thickness has the greatest effect on the diffusion rate of component A. Study the upcoming Example, which is the application of Equation 8.

Example 1 on Membrane Separation

Given: Consider a membrane-separation system, in which two liquids (feed and permeate) flow on each side of its membrane, as shown in Figure 7. Component A, which exists in both liquids, diffuses from side 2 to side 1. The following values are given:

C_{A2} (concentration of A in feed)	4.1 mole/L (liter)
C_{A1} (concentration of A in permeate)	0.1 mole/L
D_{AB} (diffusion coefficient of A through membrane)	2×10^{-6} cm²/s = 2×10^{-10} m²/s
K_{A2} (convective diffusion coefficient on side 2)	6×10^{-2} cm/s = 6×10^{-4} m/s
K_{A1} (convective diffusion coefficient on side 1)	3×10^{-2} cm/s = 3×10^{-4} m/s
x (membrane's thickness)	100 μm = 100×10^{-6} m
A (membrane's diffusing area)	2 m²
ε_p (membrane's porosity)	80%

Wanted: 1) The $\dot{M}_A$ (mass-transfer rate or diffusivity rate of A from side 1 to side, and 2) Resistances (R) in each stage

$$\dot{M}_A = \frac{C_{A2} - C_{A1}}{\frac{1}{K_{A2}.A} + \frac{x}{D_{AB}.A.\varepsilon_p} + \frac{1}{K_{A1}.A}} = \frac{4.1 - 0.1}{\frac{1}{6\times10^{-4}\times2} + \frac{100\times10^{-6}}{2\times10^{-10}\times2\times0.8} + \frac{1}{3\times10^{-4}\times2}}$$

$$\dot{M}_A = \frac{4\ \text{mole/L}}{833\frac{s}{m^3}+312500\times\frac{s}{m^3}+1667\frac{s}{m^3}} \times 1000\frac{L}{m^3} \times 60\frac{s}{min} = \frac{240000}{315000} = 0.8\ \text{mole/min}$$

Resistance in each stage is calculated from the denominator of the above equation as

$$R_2 = \frac{1}{K_{A2}.A} = 833\ \text{s/m}^3 \quad R_1 = \frac{x}{D_{AB}.A.\varepsilon_p} = 312500\ \text{s/m}^3 \quad R_3 = \frac{1}{K_{A1}.A} = 1667\ \text{s/m}^3$$

M-53

MENISCUS

Meniscus (a **liquid meniscus** in a chemistry lab) is the curving of a liquid at its surface in a narrow container. [The plural of the meniscus is **menisci**.]

Consider two narrow laboratory glass cylinders. One filled with water (H_2O, a polar compound with high molecular adhesive force, F_A) and one with mercury (Hg, a nonpolar compound with high molecular cohesive force, F_{Co}), as shown in Figure 1. This example can show us the two types of the meniscus:

- **Concave Meniscus:** A concave meniscus (an **inward curving** at a liquid's surface in a narrow container) in water is formed because its molecules are attracted to the glass molecules with stronger F_A than its molecules (adhesion). As the result of adhesion, the water molecules on its surface stick (adheres) to the glass molecules and move up along the wall to form a concave meniscus.
- **Convex Meniscus:** A convex meniscus (an **upward curving** at a liquid's surface in a narrow container) in mercury is formed because its molecules are attracted to each other with stronger F_{Co} than the glass molecules (cohesion). As the result of cohesion, the mercury molecules on its surface stick to its molecules (but *not* to the glass molecules) and move down along the wall to form a convex meniscus.

The following rules must be followed in laboratory practices when reading a meniscus:

- Level the line of your sight with the center of the meniscus, and

- Read the scale where it lines with the bottom of a concave meniscus (for example, the volume is 7.3 mL in Figure 1) and the top of a convex meniscus (for example, 5.9 mL in the same figure).

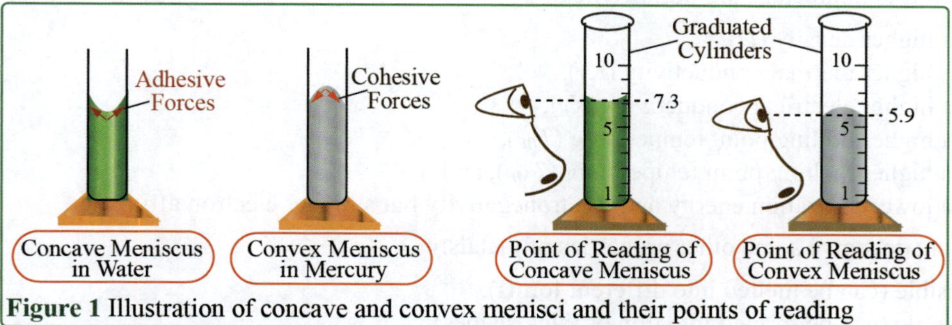

Figure 1 Illustration of concave and convex menisci and their points of reading

M-54
MESONS

Discussed under the topic of BOSONS, FERMIONS, AND HADRONS.

M-55
METALLIC BONDS

Discussed under CHEMICAL BONDS.

M-56
METALLOIDS

Discussed under the topic of METALS, NONMETALS, AND METALLOIDS.

M-57
METALS, NONMETALS, AND METALLOIDS

In the periodic table of elements, 91 of the 118 chemical elements (simply **elements**) are metals, and 27 are nonmetals. Some of these have properties between metals and nonmetals, so-known as metalloids. [No specific definition and an exact number of metalloids exist. Six (6) elements are recognized as common metalloids: boron (B), silicon (Si), germanium (Ga), arsenic (As), antimony (Sb), and tellurium (Te). Two (2) elements are recognized as less-common metalloids; polonium (Po) and astatine (At). And aluminum (Al) is a rarely-recognized metalloid.]

Metals: Metal is an electro-positively-charged element that needs to **absorb** (or share) an electro-negatively-charged electron (or electrons) from its binding partner to be converted to a neutral metal atom (M^0), so it must be reduced.

$$M^+ + e^- \rightarrow M^0$$

The best-known metals are iron (Fe), copper (Cu), and aluminum (Al). Metals share many similarities. They conduct heat energy and electric energy strongly, while nonmetals conduct poorly. Some other properties of metals, compared to nonmetals, are outlined next.

- They have a higher density (*D*),
- They have a higher thermal conductivity (K_T),
- They have a higher electrical conductivity (K_E),
- They have a higher boiling point temperature (T_{BP}),
- They have a higher melting point temperature (T_{MP}), and
- They have a lower ionization energy and electronegativity but a higher electron affinity.

The following dots give some other properties of metals:

- They are fusible (can be melted into different forms),
- They are ductile (can be formed into thin or thick shapes),
- They (except mercury) are **malleable** (can be hammered or pressed),
- They (except mercury) are solids at room temperature of about 25ºC (= 77 ºF),
- Most of them can easily undergo the corrosion process in atmospheric air (disadvantage),
- Most of them are mixed easily when melted (the mixture of metals is called alloy steel), and
- They do *not* look like crystals, but their structures look similar. Their atoms are closely positioned to the neighboring atoms in the form of **face-centered cubic** (each atom is positioned at the center of 6 other atoms) or **body-centered cubic** (each atom is positioned at the center of 8 other atoms).

Nonmetals: A nonmetal is an electro-negatively-charged element that needs to **release** an electron (or more) to its bonding partner to be converted to a neutral nonmetal atom (N^0), so it must be oxidized.

$$N^- - e^- \rightarrow N^0$$

The best-known nonmetals are carbon (C), hydrogen (H), oxygen (O), nitrogen (N), helium (He), fluorine (F), chlorine (Cl), bromine (Br), iodine (I), silicon (Si), phosphorus (P), sulfur (S), and argon (Ar).

Metalloids: A metalloid is an element with properties between metals and nonmetals. About the appearance and properties of the six (6) common metalloids (B, Si, Ge, Se, Po, and At), we can say the following:

- They are sometimes called **semimetals** (but *not* scientifically recommended).
- They have a metallic appearance but are brittle (fragile).
- They chemically behave mostly as nonmetals.
- They are only fair electric conductors.
- They can form alloys with metals.

[In another classification, halogens are also metalloids.]

M-58

METER AND FOOT

Meter: The meter is the SI unit of length (*L*). In 2019, CODATA defined the meter as the *L* of the path traveled by light in a vacuum in 1/299 792 458 of a second. One meter equates to 3.2808 Ft (feet).

Foot: The foot (Ft, the plural is **feet**) is the US unit of length (*L*). It is defined as 0.3048 meters. One foot equates to 12 **inches,** and 3 feet equates to one **yard**.

M-59
METHANE

Methane (CH_4) is the simplest hydrocarbon (1 carbon atom per molecule). It is a highly flammable gas when it mixes with the air. It is the main component of natural gas (about 85% of natural gas is methane). In a methane molecule, a pair of electrons is shared between each carbon (C) and each of the four (4) hydrogen atoms. [Carbon is only stable if all its 4 bonds are used, so in a CH_4 molecule, four covalent bonds connect a carbon atom to each hydrogen atom.]

Some properties of methane are outlined next.

- Molar mass (M_n) = 16 g/mole,
- Density (D) = 0.66 kg/m^3 at 25°C,
- Specific gas constant (R_{Sp}) = 518 J/(kg.°C),
- Molar heat capacity ($C_{Q.n}$) = 35.7 kJ/kmole.°C,
- Boiling point temperature (T_{BP}) = –161.5°C (= –258.7°F),
- Melting point temperature (T_{MP}) = –182.5°C (= –296.4°F).

The following are some other properties of methane:

- It is a major greenhouse gas,
- It is soluble in water in the amount of 22.7 g/L,
- It is soluble in acetone, ethanol, methanol, diethyl ether, and toluene,
- It is colorless, odorless, explosive (when mixed with air), toxic, and corrosive,
- Its T_{BP} is too low, so it must be cooled to below its T_{BP} before it can be liquefied, and
- It exists in nature below ground and under the seafloor and enters and leaves the atmospheric air at about 500 million tons a year worldwide.

[Globally, methane (CH_4) enters the atmosphere at a rate of about 500 Mt (million tons) a year. Assuming that its retention time is 10 years, so $500 \times 10^6 \times 10 = 5 \times 10^9$ = 5 billion tons of CH_4 is in the atmosphere at a given time. Interesting to know that each cow produces about 37 kg (= 77 Lb) of CH_4 per year.]

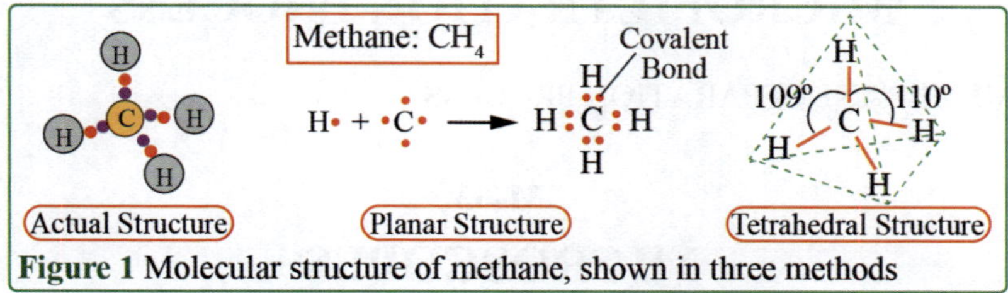

Figure 1 Molecular structure of methane, shown in three methods

M-60
METHANOL

Methanol (CH_3OH, also known as **methyl alcohol**) is the simplest alcohol with a functional group of OH (hydroxyl group). In the human body, methanol forms formic acid (H–COOH, also called methanoic acid), which is poisonous to the nerve system, so it may cause **blindness** if consumed in a large quantity.

Methanol is a colorless, low-density, volatile, and highly flammable liquid. It is miscible in water. It is poisonous (drinking 10 mL of pure methanol can cause blindness).

Some other properties of methanol are:

- Molar mass (M_n) = 32 g/mole,
- Density (D) = 792 kg/m^3 at 20°C,
- Flashing point temperature (T_{FP}) = 11°C (52°F),
- Boiling point temperature (T_{BP}) = 64.6°C (149°F),
- Freezing point temperature (T_{FP}) = – 97.6°C (– 143.7°F),
- Vapor pressure (P_V) = 13 kPa at 20°C,
- Viscosity (η) = 5.9×10^{-4} Pa.s at 20°C, and
- Refractive index = 1.331.

The chemical bond between CH_3 and OH in methanol (CH_3OH) is a hydrogen bond (see Figure 1).

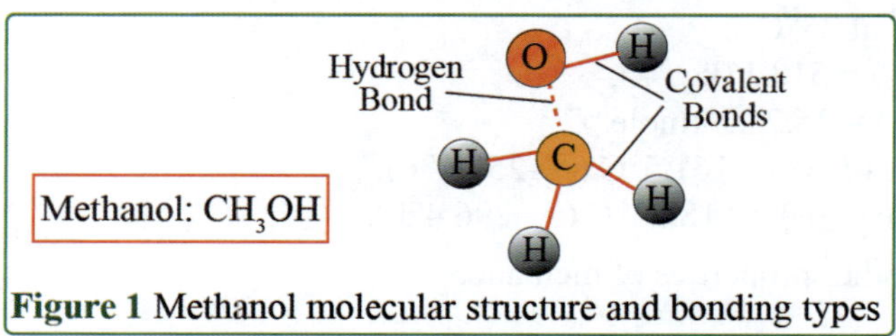

Figure 1 Methanol molecular structure and bonding types

M-61
METRIC SYSTEM

The term **metric system** is often used as a synonym for the **SI unit**, discussed under MEASURING UNIT SYSTEMS.

M-62
MICROFILTRATION PROCESS

Discussed under MEMBRANE SEPARATION PROCESS.

M-63
MICROSCOPES

A microscope is a laboratory instrument that uses a magnifying lens (or lenses) to increase the size of a tiny object that is too small for the naked eye. The technique of studying tiny objects using a microscope is called **microscopy**. Microscopes are of many types, including **optical microscopes**, **compound optical microscopes**, **scanning electron microscopes**, and **scanning tunneling microscopes**.

Optical Microscopes: A typical optical microscope uses a beam of visible light and one (or more lenses) to increase the image of the sample under study through angular magnification. Figure 1 shows a schematic view of a simple optical microscope with one **converging** (convex or eyepiece) **lens** that refracts visible light through a thinly sectional sample for magnification. A transparent sample can be lit with a light coming from below, and a solid sample can be lit with a light coming through the lens. A polarized light can be used to view the crystal structure. A set of lenses with different magnifications is usually used on a turret, allowing the lenses to be rotated to provide different zooms.

Compound Optical Microscopes: As seen in Figure 2, a typical compound microscope uses visible light and two lenses (eyepiece and objective lenses) to increase the size of a sample more than an optical microscope. The sample is placed below the objective lens, which the eyepiece lens magnifies its image (image 1). The eyepiece lens gives the viewer a more magnified image (image 2). Compound microscopes can magnify a sample up to 2 000 times.

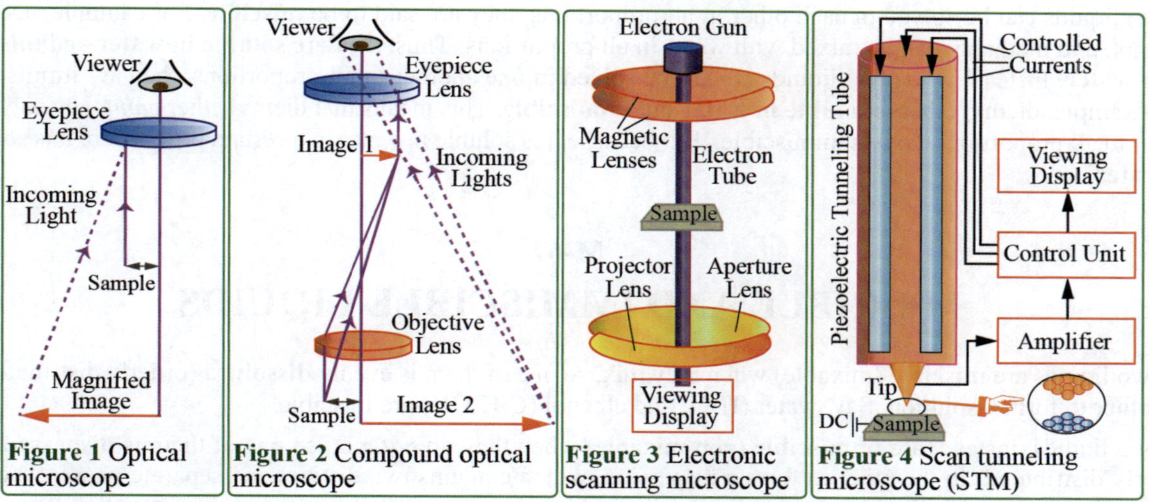

Figure 1 Optical microscope

Figure 2 Compound optical microscope

Figure 3 Electronic scanning microscope

Figure 4 Scan tunneling microscope (STM)

Electronic Scanning Microscopes: An electronic scanning microscope (ESM), developed in the 1930s, uses a beam of electrons instead of a light beam to scan the sample's surface. High magnification is achieved because the wavelength of an electron beam is typically thousands of times shorter than that of a light beam.

As shown in Figure 3, an ESM sends a focused stream of electrons through a thin sample and from there to a viewing screen below. As seen from the same figure, an ESM, contrary to an optical microscope, acts downward. An ESM can magnify a sample up to 10 million times and even see inside a human cell.

Scan Tunneling Microscopes: A scan tunneling microscope (STM) developed in the mid-1980s uses a beam of electrons and a tiny electric conducting tip. The conducting tip measures the electric current between the tip and the sample's surface and sends the result to a control unit, which sends the signals to a viewing display (see Figure 4). An STM can see objects that are 0.1 nm across–that is, the size of the helium atom (He, the second smallest atom), so the hydrogen atom (H, the smallest atom) *cannot* be viewed yet.

M-64
MICROSCOPIC SIZE

Study MACROSCOPIC AND MICROSCOPIC SIZES.

M-65
MICROWAVE

Discussed under the topic of ELECTROMAGNETIC WAVES.

M-66
MISCIBILITY

Miscibility is a property of liquids to mix in all proportions to form homogeneous solutions. When two (or more) liquids can be solved in each other in all proportions, they are said to be **miscible**. For example, acetone, ethanol, and methanol can be mixed with water in all proportions. Thus, they are **soluble in water** and **miscible with water**. Instead, when two liquids *cannot* be solved in one another in all proportions, they are **immiscible**. For example, diethyl ether is **soluble in water** but **immiscible**. This means that diethyl ether *cannot* be solved in water in all proportions, so it is immiscible. But because it is soluble in water in a certain proportion, it is **soluble in water**.

M-67
MISCIBLE AND IMMISCIBLE LIQUIDS

Two liquids are **miscible** (mixable) when they mix, so one of them is evenly **dissolved** (orderly distributed) in the other to form a solution. Say, water (H_2O) and ethanol (C_2H_5OH) are miscible.

Two liquids, instead, are **immiscible** (non-mixable) when they do *not* mix, so one of them is **dispersed** (disorderly distributed) in the other to form a dispersion, which contains two distinct and separate phases. For example, the mixture of oil and water forms an immiscible mix, in which oil sits above the water (because of the lower density of oil) in a separate phase. [The listed definitions show that solutions are homogeneous, and dispersions are heterogeneous.]

From the **like-dissolves-like rule** (discussed under POLAR AND NONPOLAT COMPOUNDS), we can say that a polar solvent and a nonpolar solvent are immiscible. Say, both water and methanol (CH_3OH) are polar molecules, so they are miscible. Instead, toluene (C_7H_8) is nonpolar and almost immiscible with water.

Two immiscible liquids can be separated with the help of a solvent, called **extraction solvent** or **extractant**, by the extraction process. The extractant is more miscible with one of the two immiscible liquids.

M-68
MIXERS

A mixer is a device (equipment) that performs the mixing process. Because many chemical process plants require mixing, many mixers are on the market. A typical mixer (see Figure 1), which can handle different mixing duties, has some attached parts (like a turbine-type stirrer) and detached parts (like a motor to drive the stirrer's shaft, pumps for input and output streams, and some instruments for measuring flow rate, temperature, or more). The mixing tank is usually cylindrical. However, the shape of the tank varies (depending on the mixing goals).

In most cases, the tank bottom is rounded to eliminate sharp spots and better movement of the liquid mix. The top of the tank is usually closed with a flat, heavy metal to support the weight of the stirrer's motor. The stirrer's shaft, which is driven from the top of the tank, is connected from one side to the motor and from the other side to the stirrer through a speed-adjusting gearbox

Mixing Tanks: The following are the main types of mixing tanks: 1) Simple mixing tanks (with *no* baffles and draft tubes), 2) Baffled mixing tanks (with two or more baffles), and 3) Draft-tube mixing tanks.

Baffles: A baffle is a flat metal strip (often 2 to 4) mounted vertically to the mixer's mixing tank wall. The width of the baffles is 1/10 to 1/12 the tank's diameter, depending on the viscosity (η) of the liquid (the *more* dense the liquid, the *narrower* baffles are needed). For mixing slurry, the baffles are mounted one-half of their width from the tank's wall to minimize solid accumulation on or behind them.

Figure 1 shows a typical **baffled mixing tank**, allowing large top-to-bottom and moderate toward-the-wall flows with the slow swirling flow (undesired). In general, baffles greatly improve the mixing process, particularly when a low-viscosity liquid mix is under strong mixing. Such mixing creates a turbulent mixing with a high Reynolds number ($N_{Re} > 10\,000$). In such cases, however, baffles can minimize undesired flowability.

Baffled tanks are *not* used for viscous liquid mixes (with $\mu > 10$ Pa.s). Baffles are also *not* needed with inclined-mounting and when helical stirrers.

Draft tubes are used in the mixing tank of some mixers to create friction in the liquid mix to reduce the velocity (V) of the flow to the discharge section of the mixer. Draft tubes, however, are used in the mixers that serve a special-duty mixing, such as when solid particles are to be kept on the surface of a liquid mix.

Figure 2 illustrates a continuous mixer, in which the mix is a continuously mixed turbine-type stirrer in a single pass. Generally, the weighing, feeding, and discharge steps occur simultaneously in a continuous mixing process. In the mixer, radial and axial mixing occur in the entire mixing tank, so the right retention time is important in operating continuous mixers.

Figure 3 shows two types of **static mixers**. In contrast to dynamic mixers, the static mixers mix the feed without moving parts. Instead, they use the flow energy of the streams. In an in-line mixer, some mixing elements are inserted axially into a straight length of pipe.

The ways the stirrers mix a liquid mix in a mixer are different. Marine-type stirrers mainly push the liquid mix in the vertical (axial) direction parallel to the axis of rotation (the stirrer's shaft), as shown in Figure 1. Turbine-type stirrers with flat blades mainly move the mix in a circular (radial) direction, so the flow moves outward toward the tank's wall and then downward toward the bottom of the tank, as shown in Figure 2. [For more discussion about stirrers, see STIRRERS.]

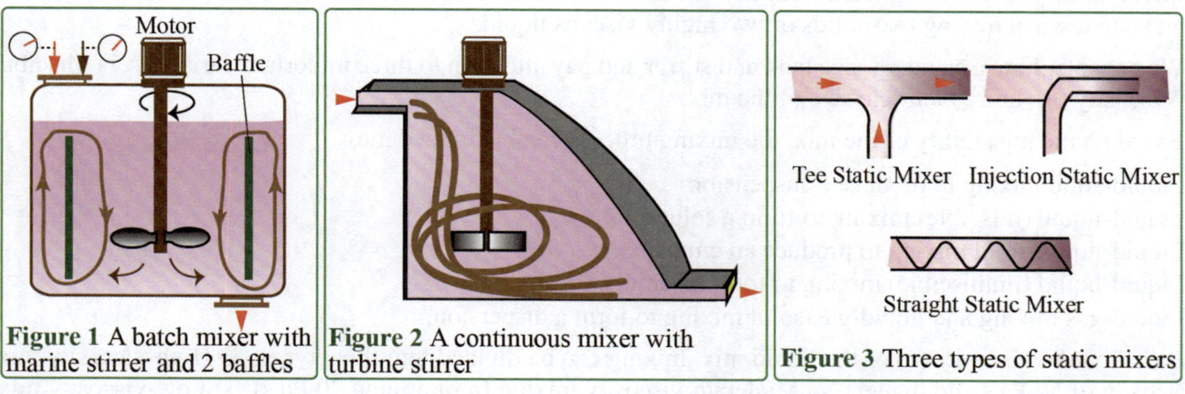

Figure 1 A batch mixer with marine stirrer and 2 baffles

Figure 2 A continuous mixer with turbine stirrer

Figure 3 Three types of static mixers

M-69
MIXING PROCESS

As one of the process units of ChemEng, mixing is a homogenization process performed in a mixer, such as the following four (4) examples:

- A gas (like CO2 gas) is added to the water and stirred in a mixer,
- A soluble solid (like salt) is added to the water and stirred in a mixer,

- An insoluble solid (like sand) is added to the water and stirred in a mixer, and
- An immiscible liquid (for example, oil) is added to the water and stirred in a mixer.

The general definition of all four examples is **mixing**, although the product of the first case is a dispersion solution. And of the second is a homogeneous solution. And of the third is a heterogeneous mixture. And finally, the last case is a suspension solution. Study first the next two Notes.

[Note 1: In the mixing process, the general term of the **mix** (fluid mix or liquid mix) is used to refer to all components to be mixed. A mix (mixture) can be a system consisting of two or more components or two or more phases of different components, with *no* regard to their miscibility and solubility.] [Note 2: The terms **mixing** (blending) and **stirring** (agitation) are *not* the same, although some use them equally. Mixing is performed with two (or more) components or phases of the same component, while stirring is performed with only one component. For example, a hot water tank can be stirred but *cannot* be mixed until another component is added to it and stirred to be mixed.]

Generally, mixing helps the chemical plants as

- Improving the rate of dispersing one fluid in another,
- Improving the rate of chemical reactions in a liquid mix,
- Blending a heterogeneous solution with a homogeneous solution,
- Blending two (or more) phases to produce a homogeneous solution,
- Blending two (or more) components of the same or different phases,
- Dispersing a gas's particles in a solution (like carbonation of beverages),
- Dispersing two (2) miscible liquids in each other or two immiscible liquids,
- Constant moving of a solid-liquid mix to keep its particles in suspension, and
- Random distribution of two (2) or more initially separate phases into one another.

Mixing also increases heat and mass transferability. The mixing process is used routinely in almost any chemical plant. Mixing operations vary in complexity. Simple operations deal with one phase of two miscible liquids, whereas some deal with multiple phases. The phases involved can be two miscible liquids, two immiscible liquids, liquid-solid, liquid-gas, or combinations. However, the degree of uniformity of the mix varies. For example, it is easy to achieve good homogeneity when two miscible liquids are under mixing. But, it is difficult to achieve that when mixing two solids or two highly viscous liquids.

We consider here a standard-size tank and stirrer and pay attention to three important variables: 1) Miscibility, 2) Viscosity (η), and 3) Particle size of the mix.

Based on the miscibility of the mix, the mixing process can be divided into:

- Liquid-solid mixing to produce a suspension,
- Liquid-liquid (miscible) mixing to form a solution,
- Liquid-liquid-solid mixing to produce an emulsion,
- Liquid-liquid (immiscible) mixing to form an emulsion, and
- Liquid-gas mixing and liquid-gas-solid mixing to form a dispersion.

Based on the viscosity (η) of the liquid mix, mixing can be divided into three types: 1) High-viscosity mixing (viscosity of 50 Pa.s and higher). 2) Moderate-viscosity mixing (η of around 20 Pa.s). 3) Low-viscosity mixing (with η below 20 Pa.s).

Based on the average particles size of the solids in the liquid mix, the mixing process can be divided into the following classes:

- **Macro-particle mixing:** The average particle size is greater than 1000 μm.
- **Micro-particle mixing:** The average particle size is less than 50 μm.

[The particle-size numbers are rough to give an approximate idea about the size involved.]

Depending on the types of the mix, mixing can be performed in

- **Batch Operation:** Although it relatively requires more labor and energy, it is easy to modify simply by changing the type of the mixer's stirrer and (or) its speed.
- **Continuous Operation:** Although it requires an appropriate mix, it eliminates the variations between the batch process runs. A continuous mixer is constantly fed with a certain amount of feed at one end, and the mixed feed is discharged from the opposite end.

Mixing of fluids can be used in one or both of the following ways:

- As the main process, mixing improves the suspendability of solid particles in a liquid, dispersity of a solid or gas particles in a liquid, or heat transferability. [Often, one mixer may simultaneously serve more than one of the listed improvements.]
- As a supplementary process, mixing is used in the crystallization process to improve the suspendability of the crystals, homogeneity of the magma, and transferability of the heat. As a result, the crystallization efficiency increases greatly.

The mixing operation depends on the following:

- Enough mixing time is needed to achieve a specific level of homogeneity. A complete mixing can be achieved if the feed mix in a mixer circulates five (5) times.
- The right stirrer's type with size, diameter, and speed are required.
- The number of stirrer blades and their shape must be sufficient.
- A mixing vessel's geometry and design must be used.
- The liquid mix's viscosity (η) must be right.

Mixing Flow Pattern: Stirrers generally form three **flow patterns** (a flow's flowing behavior, which is often visual): 1) Axial (vertical, longitudinal, or top-to-bottom) flow, 2) Radial (horizontal, center-to-wall, or toward-the-wall) flow, and 3) Tangential (rotational with angle) flow is *not* desirable in the mixing process.

However, most chemical plants use stirrers that create axial (vertical or top-to-bottom) **flow** or **radial** (horizontal or center-to-wall) **flow** patterns. Propeller stirrers create an axial flow, and turbine stirrers create a radial flow. In some special cases, helical stirrers are also used. [Generally, all axial flows become radial flow as the flow approaches the dense region.]

Consider a stirrer that creates axial flow; one rotation (R) of the stirrer would move the mix vertically to a certain distance, depending on the shape of the stirrer's blades. The ratio of the moving distance of the mix resulting from one full rotation to the stirrer diameter is called the stirrer **pitch** (pitch ratio). A stirrer with a pitch ratio of 1 is said to have a **square pitch**.

A stirrer's **mixing rate** (R_M, also called **circulation flow rate**) is the volume (V) of the flow, leaving the tip of its blades to a certain distance. The mixing rate must be great enough to move the entire mix to the farthest sections of the mixer's tank in the shortest possible time. A stirrer's R_M (in m^3/min) can be calculated from its power number (N_P, a constant for each type of stirrer, given by the AIChE), speed (n, in R/min), and diameter (d, in m).

$$R_M = N_P . n . d^2 \quad (1)$$

When a mixer mixes a liquid mixture with a certain viscosity (η) by its rotating **stirrer** (impeller), the stirrer blades act shear stress (S_S, shear force per unit area; F_S/A) on the mixture. When the S_S is greater than the liquid mixture's viscosity (η), the mixture is in flow (in motion). Thus, the S_S (the driving force of a liquid flow) and η

(the opposing force of the liquid flow) work against each other to form a **mixing flow pattern**. The pattern is a combination of **flow** (motion) and **shear** (cut). Flow occurs by the mixer's stirrer, and shear occurs when the mix contacts the stirrer blades and tank wall. The mixture becomes more and more randomly ordered over a certain mixing time, so an evenly flow pattern is developed. The developed flow pattern depends on the following: 1) Liquid's viscosity (η), 2) Liquid's Reynolds number (N_R), 3) Tank's type (baffled or unbaffled), and 4) Stirrer's type (paddle-, marine-, or turbine-type stirrers).

[Note: The Reynolds number values for liquid mixes used in the **mixing process** are different from those used in the liquid flow process. For example, N_R of 10 000 or above represents a turbulent mix flow in a mixer, while N_R of 4 000 or above indicates a liquid turbulent flow in a pipe.]

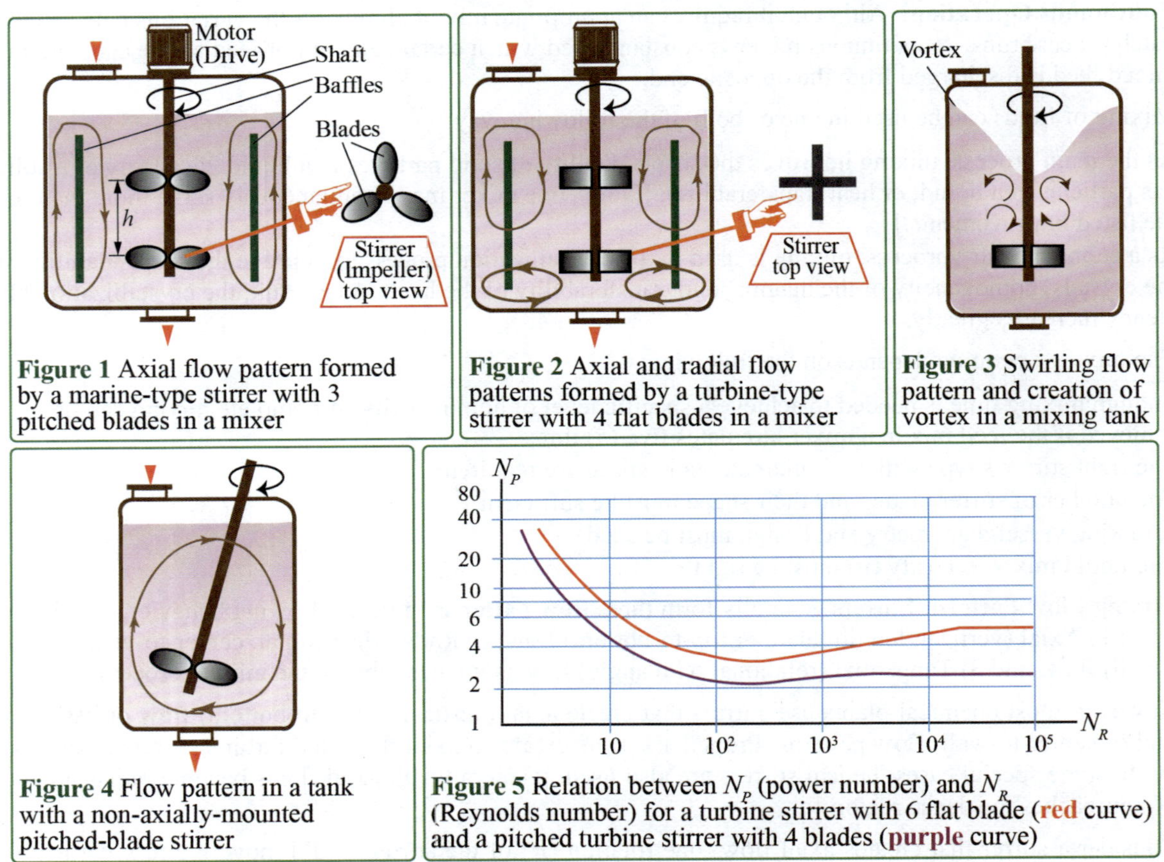

Figure 1 Axial flow pattern formed by a marine-type stirrer with 3 pitched blades in a mixer

Figure 2 Axial and radial flow patterns formed by a turbine-type stirrer with 4 flat blades in a mixer

Figure 3 Swirling flow pattern and creation of vortex in a mixing tank

Figure 4 Flow pattern in a tank with a non-axially-mounted pitched-blade stirrer

Figure 5 Relation between N_p (power number) and N_R (Reynolds number) for a turbine stirrer with 6 flat blade (red curve) and a pitched turbine stirrer with 4 blades (purple curve)

We now consider two same-size baffled mixing tanks to study two main flow patterns. For both cases, we assume a vertical shaft stirrer, centrally mounted. Further, we assume that a similar medium-viscosity mix containing some solid particles is mixing in both tanks. We have assumed all the variables are the same up to this point. We, however, further assume that each mixer is equipped with different stirrers to create different mixing patterns at the same rotational speed. The chosen stirrers are 1) A propeller stirrer with 3 pitched blades (known as a marine propeller) and 2) A turbine stirrer with 6 flat blades.

We now consider the moving behavior of a single particle of the mix in each tank. In general, the particle's vector velocity (V) at any point can be described by three components. The particle flow pattern depends on these velocity components' fluctuations (moving from one point to another). The components are:

- **Axial Component** (V_Y)**:** It acts axially (vertically), parallel to the shaft.

- **Radial Component** (V_X)**:** It acts radially (horizontally) perpendicular to the shaft.
- **Tangential Component** (V_Z)**:** It acts circularly (with changing its angles) around the shaft.

Under normal conditions, V_Y and V_X are the components of interest, and V_Z is negligible. If V_Z becomes too strong, a vortex (eddy current) is formed (discussed in a moment).

In a mixer with a **marine stirrer** (propeller), an **axial** (vertical) **flow** is formed, so propeller stirrers are also called **axial-flow stirrers**. As shown in Figure 1, the mix moves down toward the bottom of the tank, where the flow spreads in all directions toward the wall. From there, it moves upward along the wall and then down along the stirrer's shaft to the center of the tank, known as the **suction section of the stirrer**. As for the N_R, when it is above 500, an axial flow occurs, and as it decreases to below 500, the flow changes to radial.

A radial flow (center-to-wall flow) is formed in a mixer with a **turbine stirrer**, so the turbine stirrers are also called the **radial-flow stirrers**. As shown in Figure 2, the mix moves in the plane of the stirrer toward the tank's wall. At the wall, the flow divides to form two separate circulations. One portion moves downward along the wall and back to the center of the stirrer (the suction section). The other portion moves upward toward the surface and then downward along the shaft to the center of the stirrer.

Swirling Flow and Vortex

As said earlier, the flow direction acted by the tangential component (V_Z) is disadvantageous simply because it creates a circulatory (swirling) flow, which turns horizontally around the shaft (which is vertically mounted) in the direction of the stirrer blades. At high-speed mixing in a tank with no baffle and with a stirrer rotating in the center of the tank, the diameter of each circulatory flow becomes smaller as it gets closer to the stirrer's blade, so a V-shaped channel is created around the shaft. A circulatory flow is formed owing to centrifugal force (F_C), which acts on the liquid mix raising its level at the wall and lowering it at the shaft. Such a special circulatory movement is generally called the **swirling flow** (twisting flow). In a low-viscosity liquid mix, the swirling flow becomes stronger to the extent that the bottom of the channel reaches the level of the stirrer's blade. Such flow pattern, created by a strong swirling flow, is known as the vortex (eddy or rough swirls), as shown in Figure 3. Vortex reduces mixing efficiency, so it is *not* desirable.

The depth and shape of a vortex are related to the following:

- Tank's dimensions,
- Stirrer's type and shape,
- Stirrer's rotational speed, and
- Liquid-mix's viscosity and density.

The vortex greatly affects mixing efficiency (the *deeper* the vortex, the *lower* is the mixing efficiency). As a result of the vortex, the particles' **segregation** (the reverse of mixing) occurs instead of mixing. That is why vortex is *not* desired in mixing.

Vortex formation can be prevented by one or more of the followings:

- **Using Baffled Tank:** Baffles greatly slow down tangential flow (undesired), which is the cause of vortex and swirling. [More talk about baffled tanks later.]
- **Using Right Stirrer:** In a non-swirling flow, the flow pattern depends on the shape of the stirrer. Marine-type stirrers are usually used when a low-viscosity mix is stirred.
- **Installing Stirrer Non-Vertically:** Some mixes require the stirrer to be mounted non-axially (inclined), about 15° from the vertical position (see Figure 4). Inclined stirrers create a strong vertical circulation without creating a vortex.

Fluctuations in the mixing rate (velocity per unit time) that may occur during mixing, particularly in a macro-particle mixing, are *not* desired. Large fluctuations can be observed visually as changing flow patterns, creating swirls (vortexes). The main causes of the fluctuation in flow are the following:

- Running the stirrer at the wrong speed,

- Using a stirrer with the wrong number of blades, and
- The difference in property of the liquid mix in various parts of the mixer.

Shape Factors

Shape factors are various dimensionless ratios used in the mixing process. The diameter of the stirrer (d_S) and the mixing tank (d_T) is chosen as the base, and the remaining values are divided by these two quantities. The six important shape factors ($S_1 \ldots . S_6$) and their approximate ratios are the following:

- $S_1 = d_S/d_T$, where d_S is the stirrer's diameter, d_T is tank diameter, and $S_1 \approx 1/3$
- $S_2 = H_S/d_T$, where H_S is the height of stirrer above tank bottom and $S_2 \approx 1/12$
- $S_3 = W_B/d_T$, where W_B is the baffles' width and $S_3 \approx 1/12$
- $S_4 = H_T/d_T$, where H_T is the tank's height and $S_4 \approx 1$
- $S_5 = W_S/d_S$, where W_s is the stirrer's width and $S_5 \approx 1/5$
- $S_6 = L_{SB}/d_S$, where L_{SB} is the blades length and $S_6 \approx 1/4$

[Note: The listed shape factors are widely accepted in almost all mixing duties. However, it may be helpful to use different proportions when a particular liquid mix must be mixed. For example, choosing a deeper mixing tank or placing the stirrer higher or lower in the tank might help the mixing duty in particular cases.]

Power Requirement of Mixers

The required electric power (P_E, simply **power**) to drive a mixer's stirrer is important in the mixer's design and evaluating its operating cost for a particular mixing duty. Almost entire energy absorbed by the stirrer is converted to heat known as the enthalpy of mixing (H_{Mix}, also called the **heat of mixing**).

In a shortcut approach and by using some simplifying assumptions, the power used by a stirrer of diameter d rotating at N revolution per second in a liquid mix of density D can be calculated as

$$P_E = N_P . N^3 . d^5 . D \tag{2}$$

The N_P (a dimensionless number) is the power number that expresses the stirrer's power usage. It is based on the stirrer's speed and size and the liquid mix's density. The N_P is determined from Equation 1.

$$N_P = \frac{P}{N^3 . d^5 . D} \tag{3}$$

Before discussing the conditions under which Equation 2 can be used, it is helpful to discuss the dependability of the electric power usage (P_E). In general, a mixer's P_E is a function (f) of some factors as

$$P_E = f(N, d, D, \eta, a_g, S_1 \ldots . S_6) \tag{4}$$

In this equation, η is for viscosity, a_g is gravitational acceleration, and S_1 through S_6 are shape factors (discussed a moment ago). To formulize Equation 3, scientists have used dimensional analysis on some experimentally verified data and came up with the following expression:

$$\frac{P_E}{N^3 . d^5 . D} = f\left(\frac{N . d^2 . D}{\eta}, \frac{N^2 . d}{a_g}, S_1 \ldots . S_6\right) \tag{5}$$

The first term in this equation, the power number (N_P), was discussed a moment ago. The second term is known as the Reynolds number (N_R), which depends on the liquid mix's viscosity (η, in Pa.s = kg/m.s), stirrer's speed (N, in R/s), stirrer's diameter (d, in m), and the mix's density (D, in kg/m^3).

$$N_R = \frac{N . d^2 . D}{\mu} \tag{6}$$

The third term in Equation 5 (that is, $N^2 . d/a_g$) is the Froude number (N_F), which is based on the stirrer's speed (N, in R/s), stirrer's diameter (d, in m), and the gravitational acceleration ($a_g = 9.8$ m/s^2).

$$N_F = \frac{N^2 . d}{a_g} \tag{7}$$

Since the rotating stirrer can be considered a noninertial reference system (a system in which the effect of a_g is zero), N_F is negligible. Thus, the relationship between the other two terms, N_P and N_R, must be specified before calculating the power use (P_E). After this is done, the P_E can be calculated from Equation 2.

Reynolds number (N_R) is an important value in the mixing process. The following values have been experimentally verified for N_R in mixing:

- N_R less than 10 indicates laminar flow,
- N_R greater than 10^5 indicates turbulent flow, and
- N_R between 10 and 10^5 indicates transitional flow.

Scientists have set up a typical log-log graph on some experimentally verified data for baffled mixing tanks with the centrally located shaft to relate the N_P to N_R. Figure 5 shows such a graph for two different types of stirrers. The figure has two curves, each showing N_P for one stirrer on the vertical axis (*y*-axis) and related N_R on the horizontal axis (*x*-axis). Such graphs assist one in calculating the required electric power (P_E) from Equation 1 and knowing the following:

- Stirrer's diameter (d_S) and its rotational speed (N), and
- Liquid-mix's density (D) and its viscosity (η).

[Note: The data obtained from Figure 5 can be used only for the type of stirrers for which this graph was made. You, thus, must first ensure that the type of stirrer and its number of blades, and the type of the tank used in a mixing duty is like the ones shown in the figure. There are, of course, other graphs in other literature that are made for other types of stirrers. Study the upcoming real-process example for a better understanding of the subject.]

An Example on Mixer's Power Usage

Given: A baffled-tank mixer with turbine stirrer with 6 flat blades is used to mix a sugar factory's syrup

Syrup's viscosity (η) at 40°C	0.02 Pa.s (200 cp)
Syrup density (D)	1067 kg/m3
Tank's diameter (d_T)	2 m (= 79 In)
Stirrer's diameter (d_S)	0.5 m (= 27 In)
Height of stirrer above tank's bottom (h_S)	0.2 m (= 8 In)
Stirrer's width (W_s)	0.1 m (= 4 In)
Stirrer's speed (N)	1.5 R/s (= 90 R/min)

Wanted: 1) Syrup's Reynolds number (N_R), 2) Stirrer's electric power use (P_E), and 3) P_E use if molasses (with a viscosity of 25 Pa.s at 40°C and density of 1350 kg/m^3) is mixed in the mixer instead of syrup.

If we look carefully at the given data and make quick math on the tank and stirrer measurements, we will find that the shape factors are standard and like the ones shown in Figure 5. So, we first determine the N_R.

$$N_R = \frac{N.d_S^2.D}{\eta} = \frac{1.5 \times 0.5^2 \times 1067}{0.02} = 20\,000$$

This N_R is in the range of turbulent flow, so a simple (un-baffled) mixer can do the mixing process. We use the red curve in Figure 5, set for a turbine stirrer with 6 flat blades, to determine N_P. For $N_R = 2\times10^4$, the N_P is 5.5. Then we use Equation 2 to calculate the power requirement.

$$P_E = N_P n^3 d^5 D = 5.5 \times 1.5^3 \times 0.5^5 \times 1067 = 620\text{ J/s} = 620\text{ W/h} = 0.6\text{ kW/h}$$

The N_R for molasses is calculated the same way.

$$N_R = \frac{1.5 \times 0.5^2 \times 1350}{25} = 20$$

This N_R is in the range of transitional flow. Similarly, for $N_R = 20$, the N_Φ is 5.8, so

$$P_E = 5.8 \times 1.5^3 \times 0.5^5 \times 1350 = 826\text{ J/s} = 826\text{ W/h} = 0.8\text{ kW/h}$$

Because the power requirement is independent of the mixing tank baffling, molasses with such high viscosity (25 Pa.s) and low N_R of 20 do *not* need to be mixed in a baffled tank, as a vortex does *not* occur under these conditions. Note that a 1250–fold increase in viscosity (25/0.02) increases the power usage by only 33% over that required in a baffled mixer used to mix the syrup.

OPERATING PROBLEMS OF MIXING

A few problems can occur in the operation of industrial mixers. The formation of a vortex (a strong swirling flow) caused by the strong swirling of the liquid mix in the mixing tank is the most important problem because a vortex reduces mixing efficiency greatly.

The creation of a mild swirling at the surface of the mixing material can generally happen in any tank, regardless of the tank design and stirrer type. But, strong swirling, which forms a vortex, is undesirable and must be prevented in any possible way. The following are the causes of the fluctuations in the flow and, consequently, the formation of the vortex:

- **Wrong Mixing Tank:** In an unbaffled tank, particularly when a low-viscosity liquid mix is under mixing, the tangential flow (undesired) becomes strong, so the normal flow pattern changes to a swirling flow, consequently, to a vortex. Baffles slow down the tangential flow without interfering with radial and axial flows. Thus, an effective mixing can be achieved by mounting a few (usually 2 to 4) baffles vertically along the wall of an unbaffled mixing tank.
- **Wrong Stirrer:** For a mixer to be effective in a particular mixing duty and *not* to form a vortex, once a suitable tank is chosen, the type of stirrer and its number of blades must be chosen right. For example, marine-type stirrers form a vortex when a high-viscosity mix is stirred at high speed.
- **Wrongly Mounted Stirrer:** Some mixings require the stirrer to be mounted off the center (inclined) instead of on the center. The incline is about 15° from the vertical position to prevent vortex formation.
- **Wrong Stirrer's Level:** It may be advantageous to mount the stirrer higher or lower in the tank.
- **Wrong-Size Tank:** A deeper tank may be needed to achieve the best mixing result.
- **Wrong Mix Depth:** In a vertical tank, the liquid mix's depth must be equal to or somewhat greater than the tank's diameter. Two or more stirrers are installed on the same shaft if a greater depth is desired. The bottom stirrer is usually a radial-flow stirrer (like a turbine stirrer with flat blades). The top ones are usually axial-flow stirrers (like propeller stirrers with pitched blades).

M-70

MIXTURES

A mixture (simply a **mix**) is made of two or more chemical substances (simply **substances**) mixed but are *not* bonded chemically. A mixture is an impure substance (because it consists of more than one substance). Sand (mainly silicon dioxide, SO_2) is a common example of a mixture.

A mixture can be in one of the following types:

- In the form of heterogeneity (its substances can be separated through a physical change),
- In the form of homogeneity (its substances *cannot* be separated through a physical change), and
- In the form of a solution, suspension, or colloid (a solution containing ethanol and water is a mixture).

M-71

MODULUS

Study ELASTIC FORCE, MODULUS, AND STRAIN OF MATERIAL.

M-72

MOIST AIR

Discussed under the topic of AIR.

M-73

MOISTURE AND ITS TYPES

Moisture: Moisture (W) is the amount of a liquid (usually water) in the particles of a moist (wet) solid. It is mostly expressed in percentage by mass. [The word **moisture** also indicates the amount of water in the air. Thus, the word humidity is often used instead of **moisture** when talking about the air's water content. Also, note that the symbol W is used for moisture and humidity.]

In chemical process plants, moisture in the particles of a moist-solid product is removed by the drying process in a dryer. Moisture in moist-solid particles exists in the following three (3) forms:

- **Surface** (free) **Moisture:** This moisture, which exists on the surface of the moist solid particles in a high amount, escapes fast from the particles during drying.
- **Interior** (bound) **Moisture:** This moisture, which exists near the surface of the moist solid particles, escapes from the particles during drying slowly. It creates problems in packing, storing, or shipping a dry product if it remains in the product after the drying and conditioning processes.
- **Inherent** (permanent) **Moisture**: This moisture, which exists in the middle of the moist solid particles in a tiny amount, does *not* escape from the particles during drying. [However, it does *not* create any problem in packing, storing, or shipping a dry product.]

Critical Moisture: The critical moisture (w_C, also called **critical moisture content**) is the moisture at which the constant rate period in a drying process ends. It is often *not* identifiable (because it is an approximate value).

Equilibrium Moisture Content: Equilibrium moisture (W_E) is the lowest and optimum moisture content that a product can have without creating any problem during packing, storing, and shipping. Sugar (table sugar or sucrose), for example, has a W_E of about 0.03%. At this moisture level, the sugar crystals do *not* absorb or lose moisture in the sugar silo and during packing in a bag and shipping to customers unless exposed to a high air humidity or temperature.

M-74

MOLAL CONCENTRATION

Another name for MOLALITY.

M-75

MOLALITY

Study MOLARITY, NORMALITY, AND MOLALITY.

M-76

MOLAR CONCENTRATION

Another name for MOLARITY.

M-77

MOLAR DENSITY

Discussed under the topic of DENSITY.

M-78

MOLAR DIFFUSION FLUX

Study MASS FLUX.

M-79

MOLAR DIFFUSION FLUX RATE

Study MASS FLUX RATE.

M-80

MOLAR ENTHALPY OF EVAPORATION

Molar enthalpy of evaporation ($H_{n.E}$ or $\lambda_{.E.n}$, also called **molar heat of evaporation**) is the ΔH (enthalpy change) needed to evaporate one mole of a liquid to vapor. The liquids $H_{n.E}$ (rather $\Delta H_{n.E}$) is usually determined at atmospheric pressure (P_{Atm}) and their boiling point temperature (T_{BP}). For example, at 1 Atm and 100ºC, the $H_{n.E}$ of water is 40.6 kJ/mole (= 39 BTU/mole), where 100ºC is T_{BP} of water at 1 Atm. And ethanol (C_2H_5OH) at 78.4°C is 39 kJ/mole (= 37 BTU/mole), where 78.4°C is the T_{BP} of ethanol at 1 Atm. A liquid's $H_{n.E}$ can be calculated using its enthalpy of evaporation (H_E) and molar mass (M_n).

$$H_{n.E} = \frac{H_E . M_n}{1000} \quad (1)$$

For example, $H_{n.E}$ of ethanol (with an H_E of 848 kJ/kg and M_n of 46 g/mole) at 78.4°C and 1 Atm is

$$H_{n.E} = \frac{848 \times 46}{1000} = 39 \text{ kJ/mole}$$

[Because $H_{n.E}$ is determined at standard conditions, it is also called **standard molar enthalpy of formation**.]

M-81

MOLAR ENTHALPY OF FORMATION

Molar enthalpy of formation ($H_{n.F}$ or $\lambda_{n.F}$, **molar heat of formation**) is the ΔH (enthalpy change = heat energy) that occurs during the formation of one mole of a chemical substance (simply **substance**) during a reaction.

The $H_{n.F}$ (rather $\Delta H_{n.F}$) of a substance is usually determined at atmospheric pressure (P_{Atm} = 1 Atm ≈ 100 kPa) or at standard conditions (25°C and 1 Atm). [Because $H_{n.F}$ is determined at standard conditions, it is also called **standard molar enthalpy of formation**.]

A substance $H_{n.F}$ can be calculated using its H_F (enthalpy of formation) and M_n (molar mass).

$$H_{n.F} = \frac{H_F.M_n}{1000} \quad (1)$$

Say, the $H_{n.F}$ of carbon dioxide gas (with H_F = 8943 kJ/kg and M_n = 44 g/mole) is the enthalpy of the next heat-releasing reaction: C (solid, graphite) + O_2 (gas) → CO_2 (gas). So, the reaction releases the heat energy (E_Q) of:

$$H_{n.F} = \frac{8943 \times 44}{1000} = 393.5 \text{ kJ/mole}$$

Similarly, the $H_{n.F}$ of ethanol (with H_F = 6022 kJ/kg and M_n = 46 g/mole) is

$$H_{n.F} = \frac{6022 \times 46}{1000} = 277 \text{ kJ/mole}$$

[Note that CO_2 or ethanol *cannot* be formed by combining their elements in the laboratory.] [The molar enthalpy of formation of some substances is given in Table 5 in the Table Section at the end of the book.]

M-82

MOLAR ENTHALPY OF REACTION

Molar enthalpy of reaction ($H_{n.R}$ or $\lambda_{n.R}$, also called **molar heat of reaction**) is the ΔH (enthalpy change) that occurs (produced or consumed) when one mole of a reactant (or reactants) is converted to product (or products) during a chemical reaction (simply **reaction**). Usually, $H_{n.R}$ is expressed at standard conditions (25°C and 1 Atm). [Because $H_{n.R}$ is determined at standard condition, it is also called **standard molar enthalpy of reaction**.]

Consider the reaction of glucose ($C_6H_{12}O_6$) with oxygen (O_2) in our body. When 1 mole of glucose (with a molar mass of 180 g/mole) reacts with oxygen, 2 800 kJ (672 kcal = 672 Cal) of enthalpy (heat energy, E_Q) is released, so its $H_{R.n}$ = 2 800 kJ/mole, most correctly – 2 800 (because the reaction is a heat-releasing reaction).

1 mole $C_6H_{12}O_6$ + 6 mole O_2 → 6 mole CO_2 + 6 mole H_2O – 2800 kJ of E_Q

[Because this energy is released by combustion of 1 mole of glucose, it is also called **molar enthalpy of combustion** of glucose. In general, the term **molar enthalpy of combustion** is usually used instead of **molar enthalpy of reaction** when talking about the combustion reaction of a fuel.]

The enthalpy of reaction (H_R) of glucose can be simply calculated from its $H_{n.R}$ as 2800/180 = 15.5 kJ/g or 15 500 kJ/kg (= 6665 BTU/Lb = 3 720 kcal/kg = 3.72 kcal/g).

Under the topic of ENTHALPY, we said that the enthalpy (H) of a system *cannot* be measured directly, so the enthalpy change ($\Delta H = E_Q$) between two situations (initial state, H_1, and final state, H_2) is measured. Based on this statement, the $\Delta H_{R.Mol}$ of a reaction equates to the sum of enthalpies of reaction of the products, shown by $\Delta H_{R.n}$ (P), minus the sum of enthalpies of the reactants, shown by $\Delta H_{R.n}$ (R).

$$\Delta H_{nR} = \sum \Delta H_{n.R}(P) - \sum \Delta H_{n.R}(R) \quad (1)$$

Consider the general expression for a reversible reaction (↔).

$$A + B \leftrightarrow C$$

Assume that $\Delta H_{n.R}$ [A] = 444, $\Delta H_{n.R}$ [B] = –333, and $\Delta H_{R.n}$ [C] = 555, all in kJ/mole, then the general equation can be written as

$$\Delta H_{n.R} = \{\Delta H_{n.R}[C]\} - \{\Delta H_{R.n}[A] + \Delta H_{n.R}[B]\} \quad (2)$$

$$\Delta H_{n.R} = (1\text{mole})\left(\frac{555\text{kJ}}{\text{mole}}\right) - \left\{(1\text{mole})\left(\frac{444\text{kJ}}{\text{mole}}\right) + (1\text{mole})\left(\frac{-333\text{kJ}}{\text{mole}}\right)\right\}$$

$$\Delta H_{\text{n.R}} = 555 - 444 + 333 = 444 \text{ kJ}$$

Because we have 1 mole each of *A*, *B*, and *C*, the $H_{n.R}$ of each reactant and product is multiplied by 1 mole to eliminate the mole in the denominator.

M-83

MOLAR FLOW RATE

The molar flow rate ($\dot{n}$) of a fluid is its number of moles (n) that pass a reference plane (flat surface) in a unit of time (t).

$$\dot{n} = \frac{n}{t} \tag{1}$$

The SI unit of molar flow rate is mole/h (mole per hour) or kmole/h (kilo mole/h). [In distillation and similar processes, a molar flow rate is usually shown with an alphabetic letter instead of $\dot{n}$. For example, the molar flow rate of a feed entering a distillation column is shown with *F* and distillate with *D*.]

M-84

MOLAR FLUX

The abbreviated name for **molar diffusion flux**. It is discussed under MASS DIFFUSION FLUX.

M-85

MOLAR FLUX RATE

The abbreviated name for **molar diffusion flux rate** (see MASS DIFFUSION FLUX RATE).

M-86

MOLAR FRACTION

Discussed under MASS FRACTION, MOLAR FRACTION, AND VOLUME FRACTION.

M-87

MOLAR GAS CONSTANT

Study GAS CONSTANT.

M-88

MOLAR HEAT CAPACITY

The molar heat capacity ($C_{Q.n}$) of a chemical substance is its ability to absorb heat energy (E_Q which has the same meaning as enthalpy change, ΔH). The $C_{Q.n}$ is defined as the amount of E_Q (= ΔH) needed to raise the temperature (T) of 1 mole (n) of a substance by 1°C at constant atmospheric pressure, without phase change.

$$C_{Q.n} = \frac{E_Q}{n.\Delta T} = \frac{\Delta H}{n.\Delta T} \qquad (1)$$

In this equation, ΔH (change in enthalpy) is the enthalpy transferred (absorbed or released) by a substance (in kJ), and ΔT is its temperature difference (in °C). These give $\lambda_{Q.n}$ to be in kJ/mole.°C, the unit of energy per unit mole per unit T. The US unit of the $C_{Q.Mol}$ is BTU/mole.°F.

[Specific heat capacity (C_Q, simply **heat capacity**) is defined as the amount of E_Q (= ΔH) needed to raise the T of 1 kg of a substance by 1°C at constant P_{Atm} of 1 Atm, without phase change.]

M-89

MOLAR HEAT OF EVAPORATION

Study MOLAR ENTHALPY OF EVAPORATION.

M-90

MOLAR HEAT OF FORMATION

Study MOLAR ENTHALPY OF FORMATION.

M-91

MOLAR HEAT OF REACTION

Study MOLAR ENTHALPY OF REACTION.

M-92

MOLAR HUMIDITY

Discussed under HUMIDITY AND ITS WAYS OF MEASUREMENT.

M-93

MOLAR MASS

Study MOLE AND MOLAR MASS.

M-94

MOLAR VOLUME

The molar volume (V_n) of a chemical substance is the volume (V) occupied by one mole of that substance at a given temperature (T) and pressure (P). A substance's V_n is its molar mass (M_n) divided by its density (D).

$$V_n = \frac{M_n}{D} \quad (1)$$

In this equation, M_n is in kg/mole, and D is in kg/m^3, giving V_n the unit of m^3/mole. [The V_n of one mole of any gas at STP is 22.4 L.] The V_n is an intensive quantity (is *not* **addable**).

M-95

MOLARITY, NORMALITY, AND MOLALITY

Molarity (M), normality (N), and molality (m) are important ways of expressing a solution's concentration (C) in chemistry. M (molarity) and N (normality) are useful in laboratory practices when preparing a **standard solution** (a solution with known and exact C) and in the titrimetric analysis (titration of a solution with unknown C with a standard solution). And m (molality) is useful for calculating physical properties, such as a solution's boiling point temperature or freezing point temperature. M, N, and m are defined next.

Molarity

Molarity (M, also called **molar concentration**) is the number of moles of a solute dissolved in 1 liter (L) of a solution (the solvent), so it is expressed in the mole of solute per liter (L) of solution; that is mole/L. [A solution of a given M is prepared by dissolving the solute in enough water to give a volume of 1 L (*not* by dissolving it in an initial volume of 1 L).]

[Note 1: Both mass and molarity are symbolized with M; of course, with notification of what the M stands for.]

[Note 2: Molarity (M) and molar fraction (X_n) are different. M is a mole-to-L ratio, but X_n is a mole-to-mole ratio.]

The M of a solute in a solution is given in relation to the solute's number of moles (n), the amount of that solution (L_{Sol}, in L), the solute's mass (M_S, in g), and the solute's molar mass (M_n, in g/mole).

$$M = n \times \frac{1}{L_{Sol}} = \frac{M_S}{M_n} \times \frac{1}{L_{Sol}} \quad (1)$$

The solute's mass (M_S) needed to prepare a solution with the desired molarity is calculated using the next equation, derived from the previous equation.

$$M_S = M . M_n . L_{Sol} \quad (2)$$

Molarity can be related to normality (N) by using the solute's charge number (N_C).

$$M = \frac{N}{N_C} \quad (3)$$

For example, a solution containing 58.5 g of salt (NaCl, with M_n of 58.5 g/mole) in 1 L is a 1 M solution of NaCl. Similarly, the M of a solution containing 58 g of NaCl in 200 mL (= 0.2 L) of water is

$$M = \frac{M_S}{M_n} \times \frac{1}{L_{Sol}} = \frac{58}{58.5} \times \frac{1}{0.2} = 5 \text{ mole/L (or 5 } M\text{)}$$

As another example of molarity, 1 mole of sulfuric acid (H_2SO_4, the solute, with M_n of 98 g/mol), dissolved in water (the solvent) to prepare a 1 L solution is one molar (1 M) solution of H_2SO_4.

Normality

Normality (N, also called **normal concentration**) is the equivalent number (N_{Eq}, also called the **number of equivalents**) of a solute per liter (L) of a solution, so it is expressed in Eq/L.

$$N = \frac{N_{Eq}}{L_{Sol}} \tag{4}$$

For example, a solution made from 1 Eq of sulfuric acid (H_2SO_4, the solute) dissolved in water (the solvent) to prepare a 1 L solution is a 1 normal (1 N) solution of H_2SO_4. Thus, the Eq of the H_2SO_4 solution is 1.

By substituting the N_{Eq} equation ($N_{Eq} = M_S/M_{Eq}$), where M_S is the solute's mass and M_{Eq} is the equivalent mass (given in g), into the previous equation, we get a useful equation.

$$N = \frac{M_S}{M_{Eq}} \times \frac{1}{L_{Sol}} \tag{5}$$

The solute's mass (M_S) needed to prepare a certain amount of solution (L_{Sol}, in L) with the desired normality can be calculated using the following equation (which is derived from the previous equation):

$$M_S = N.M_{Eq}.L_{Sol} \tag{6}$$

By substituting the M_{Eq} equation ($M_{Eq} = M_M/N_C$, where M_M is molecular mass and N_C is charge number), into the previous equation, we get another useful equation.

$$M_S = N \times \frac{M_M}{N_C} \times L_{Sol} \tag{7}$$

N (normality) can be related to M (molarity) by using the solute's N_C (charge number).

$$N = N_C.M \tag{8}$$

For example, the normality (N) of 3 L of EDTA.2H_2O (ethylenediamine-tetraacetic acid dihydrate, with M_M of 372 g and N_C of 2), containing 20 g EDTA.2H_2O, can be calculated with Equation 7.

$$N = \frac{M_S.N_C}{M_M.L_{Sol}} = \frac{20\times2}{372\times3} = 0.036 \text{ N}$$

We can calculate this solution's M (molarity) with Equation 8.

$$M = \frac{N}{N_C} = \frac{0.036}{2} = 0.018$$

Molality

Molarity (m, also called **molal concentration**) is the number of moles (n) of a solute dissolved in 1 kilogram (kg) of a solution, so it is expressed in the mole of solute per kg of solution (mole/kg). For example, a solution made from 1 mole of sulfuric acid (the solute; H_2SO_4, with M_n of 98 g/mole)dissolved in water (the solvent) to prepare a 1 kg solution is a 1 mole/kg or 1 molal (1 m) solution of H_2SO_4.

The m of a solute in a solution is given in relation to the solute's number of moles (n), the amount of the solution (M_{Sol}, in kg), the solute's mass (M_S, in g), and the solute's M_n (in g/mol).

$$m = n \times \frac{1}{M_{Sol}} = \frac{M_S}{M_n} \times \frac{1}{M_{Sol}} \tag{9}$$

The M_S needed to prepare a solution with a given molality is calculated using the following equation (derived from the previous equation):

$$M_S = m.M_n.M_{Sol} \tag{10}$$

For example, the molality (m) of a solution sample containing 25.5 g of NaCl (with M_n = 58.5 g/mole) in 135 g (= 0.135 kg) of water can be calculated as

$$m = \frac{M_S}{M_{Mol}} \times \frac{1}{M_{Sol}} = \frac{25.5}{58.5} \times \frac{1}{0.135} = 3.2 \text{ mole/kg (or 3.2 m)}$$

M-96

MOLDS AND YEASTS

Mold is a multicellular microorganism (a microbe that grows in a colony), while yeast is a monocellular microbe. Both mold and yeast are in the family of **fungus**. Molds do *not* need sunlight to grow and cause discoloration and fuzzy appearance in the food products. [Both molds and yeast are in the **aerobic group** (organisms that grow in the presence of oxygen).]

M-97

MOLE AND MOLAR MASS

Mole: Mole (n or mole, also called **mole concentration**) is a basic unit for expressing the mass (M) of a chemical substance (simply **substance**). In 2019, CODATA defined mole as the mass (in grams) of 6.02×10^{23} **particles** (atoms, molecules, or ions) of a substance (element or compound), where the number 6.0×10^{23} is the Avogadro's number (Avogadro's constant, the number of atoms in exactly 12 g of carbon-12). Thus, 6.02×10^{23} particles are in 1 mole. Previously, the mole was defined as the molar mass (M_n) of a substance. If thus, weighing a quantity of an **element** equal to its M_n, we have 1 mole of that element.

Because 1 mole of any substance always contains 6.0×10^{23} particles, the mole is used for chemical reactions (simply **reactions**). Consider equation $C + O_2 \rightarrow CO_2$, in which 1 mole of carbon atoms (12 g of C) reacts with 1 mole of molecular oxygen (32 g of O_2) to produce 1 mole of carbon dioxide (44 g of CO_2). There are, therefore, 6.02×10^{23} atoms in 12 g of carbon (C), 6.02×10^{23} molecules in 32 g of oxygen (O_2), and 6.02×10^{23} molecules in 56 g of carbon dioxide (CO_2).

Most of the time, the term **number of moles** is used instead of the **mole** to refer to the molar quantity. The number of mole (n) of a substance in a solution can be calculated from that substance's M (mass) and M_n.

$$n = \frac{M}{M_n} \quad (1)$$

Next is the relationship between the mole, the M_n (molar mass), the M_M (molecular mass), and Avogadro's number (the number of molecules in 1 mole) for water (H_2O).

1 mole of H_2O (18 g) = M_n of H_2O (18 g/mole)= M_M of H_2O (18 g) = 6.02×10^{23} molecules of H_2O (18 g)

An Example on Mole

Given: The concentration of a glucose ($C_6H_{12}O_6$) solution is 0.15 M (where M is for molarity), and the molar mass (M_n) of glucose is 180 g/mole.

Wanted: 1) Molar quantity of glucose (n) in the solution, and 2) Volume (V, in liter) of 0.15 M glucose solution to provide 55 g of glucose

n of glucose in 55 g glucose (M_S = mass of glucose = 55 g) is

$$n = \frac{M_S}{M_n} = \frac{55}{180} = 0.3 \text{ mole}$$

The molarity equation can calculate the volume (in L) of the 0.15 M glucose solution.

$$V_{Sol} = \frac{M_S}{M.M_n} = \frac{55}{0.15\times180} = 2 \text{ L}$$

Molar Mass: Molar mass (M_n, also known as **molecular weight**, M_W) is the mass (M) of one mole (n) of a substance, expressed in g/mole. Numerically, M_n equates to the M_M (molecular mass), usually expressed in g.

For example, for water, $M_n = M_M = 18$ g/mole, meaning that one mole of H_2O masses 18 g. Similarly, for sulfuric acid (H_2SO_4), $M_n = M_M = 98$ g/mole.

Consider dry air, which mainly consists of about 78% molecular nitrogen (N_2, at 28 g/mole) and about 21% of molecular oxygen (O_2, at 32 g/mole), so the air's molar mass is $0.78 \times 28 + 0.21 \times 32 = 28$ g/mole.

Next are the relations between the M_n (molar mass), M_M (molecular mass), mole, and Avogadro's number (the number of molecules in 1 mole).

M_n of Water (= 18 g/mole) = M_M of water (= 18 g) = 1 Mole of Water (= 18 g) = 6.02×10^{23} Molecules of Water (= 18 g)

M-98
MOLE FRACTION

Another name for MOLAR FRACTION.

M-99
MOLECULAR DIFFUSION PROCESS

Study DIFFUSION PROCESS.

M-100
MOLECULAR MASS

Study ATOMIC MASS AND MOLECULAR MASS.

M-101
MOLECULAR SIEVE AND MOLECULAR-SIEVE PROCESS

Molecular Sieve: A molecular sieve is a desiccant with a porous and orderly organized molecular structure. It has a large surface area per unit mass (M) and a small pore size (almost the same size as a typical molecule). **Zeolite** (with the general formula of $Na_2Al_2Si_3O_{10}.2H_2O$) and **silica gel** (silicon dioxide, SiO_2) are common desiccants.

To be more effective in discussing this topic, consider separating water from hydrous ethanol (with about 5% water content) using **zeolite** to produce anhydrous ethanol (with below 0.3% water content). Zeolite effectively absorbs, separating the smaller water molecules from the larger ethanol molecules. Because of different molecular sizes, the larger molecules of ethanol (with a diameter of about 0.44 nm) *cannot* enter the zeolite's pores, while smaller molecules of water (about 0.28 nm) can. Thus, as the ethanol-water mixture passes through the stationary bed of porous zeolite, the molecules of ethanol (the component with the greatest M_M), which *cannot* enter the zeolite's pores, leave the zeolite bed first. And the water molecules appear in the effluent later.

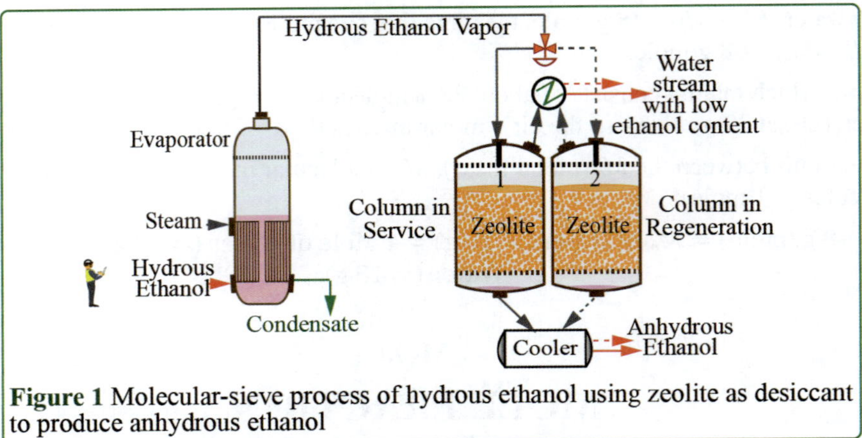

Figure 1 Molecular-sieve process of hydrous ethanol using zeolite as desiccant to produce anhydrous ethanol

Molecular-Sieve Process: Molecular-sieve is the process of passing a hydrous feed through a column filled with a desiccant, like zeolite, to remove water from the feed and produce an anhydrous product. [The name **molecular-sieve process** is used because of using a desiccant that its molecular structure is orderly organized like a sieve. Also, note that the name **molecular-sieve process** is used in a large column in a chemical process plant. And the name desiccation process is used when it is performed in a desiccator in a lab.]

Figure 1 shows a molecular-sieve station for dewatering hydrous ethanol. The station has two columns, filled partially with zeolite, from which one column is usually in service mode (column 1 in the same figure), and the other one is in regeneration mode (column 2). The outlines of the process follow:

- The hydrous ethanol produced by ordinary distillation is vaporized in an evaporator, which operates at a steam with *P* (pressure) of about 200 kPa and *T* (temperature) of about 120°C.
- The vapor from the evaporator is sent to the serving column 1, where the water-vapor molecules penetrate the zeolite pores, and the ethanol molecules continue moving through the zeolite bed.
- The water-vapor fraction with a low amount of ethanol is discharged from the top of column 1, going to a condenser. And the ethanol-vapor fraction free of water is discharged from the bottom of 1, going to a condenser to form the anhydrous ethanol product.

M-102

MOLECULAR SOLVATION

Molecular solvation is the attraction and interaction abilities of a solute's molecules with a solvent's molecules, with *no* chemical change between them.

Let us see how sugar ($C_{12}H_{22}O_{11}$, a typical nonionic compound) goes through the solvation process. When the sugar is dissolved in the water (H_2O), its molecules do *not* react chemically with the water molecules, so *no* chemical change happens (because the sugar molecules are *not* decomposed to their components). Instead, several water molecules surround a sugar molecule to build a water cluster (known as the **hydrated cluster**, **hydrated water**, or **solvent cage**) around that sugar molecule (see Figure 1 under WATER CLUSTER). Thus, a **hydrated sugar solution** (H_2O-$C_{12}H_{22}O_{11}$-H_2O) is formed that has many water clusters. At this point, chemists say that the sugar molecule is in the form of molecular solvation.

M-103

MOLECULAR STRUCTURE

Molecular structure (also called **molecular geometry**, **molecular configuration**, or simply **configuration** or **matrix**) is a three-dimensional drawing of a molecule's atoms. We know that the atoms of a molecule join by chemical bonds, so a molecular structure mainly shows the bonding types of that molecule. In addition, it shows the atomic bond angles, atomic lengths, and any other geometric parameters that determine the position of a molecule's atoms. A molecular structure influences some properties of a chemical substance (simply **substance**), including its chemical polarity. Figures 1 and 2 show the molecular structure of water (H_2O) and methane (CH_4) in three different ways (actual, planar, and tetrahedral).

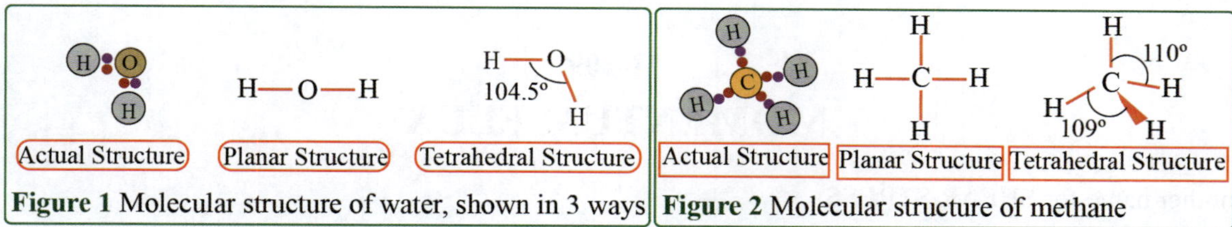

Figure 1 Molecular structure of water, shown in 3 ways **Figure 2** Molecular structure of methane

M-104

MOLECULES

Discussed under the topic of ATOMS.

M-105

MOLLIER DIAGRAM

Study ENTHALPY-ENTROPY DIAGRAM.

M-106

MOMENT OF INERTIA

The moment of inertia (I, also called **inertial moment**) is associated with a system rotating around a central point. The I measures how easy or difficult it is to change a system's rotational motion. Numerically, it is defined as a system's rotational momentum (L) per its rotational velocity (ω).

$$I = \frac{L}{\omega} \tag{1}$$

For a pendulum (a weight suspended from a pivot so that it can swing freely), the I equates to the product of the mass (M) of the pendulum multiplied by its squared distance R from the pivot (the axis of rotation).

$$I = M.R^2 \tag{2}$$

The kinetic energy (E_K) of a rotating system with the inertial moment of I and rotational velocity of ω is

$$E_K = \frac{1}{2} I.\omega^2 \tag{3}$$

M-107

MOMENTUM

Study LINEAR MOMENTUM AND ROTATIONAL MOMENTUM.

M-108

MOMENTUM DIFFUSIVITY

Another name for DIFFUSION COEFFICIENT.

M-109

MOMENTUM FLUX

Another name for SHEAR STRESS.

M-110

MONOMERS

A monomer is a molecular unit that can be connected to another unit. When two monomers are connected, a **dimer** is formed. And a **trimer** is formed when three monomers are connected. Similarly, many monomers can connect to other molecular units to form a polymer. [The term **polymer** is from **poly**, meaning many, and **mer** means units.]

Glucose ($C_6H_{12}O_6$, reads *gloo'kos*), for example, is a monomer because many (up to 1 million) of its molecules can be connected by glycosidic bonds (oxygen bonds) to produce starch [$(C_6H_{10}O_5)_n$], a polysaccharide. Starch is produced by consecutive dehydration reactions (losing-water reactions) of monosaccharides (monomers). Under suitable conditions, the polymerization reactions can continue indefinitely because the terminal units always have one or more unreacted OH groups. Polymerization of glucose occurs according to the following approximate equation: $n\ C_6H_{12}O_6 \rightarrow (C_6H_{10}O_5)_n + n\ H_2O$

M-111

MOTHER LIQUID

The term mother liquid (also called **mother liquor**) is mostly used in the crystallization process to refer to a liquid containing seeded particles and crystals. The mother liquid stays with the crystals in the crystallizer until the end of the process. After crystallization, the crystals are separated by the centrifugal process or filtration process. A mild washing of the crystals is used during centrifugation or filtration to remove the retained mother liquid from the crystals.

Mother liquid is the carrier of almost all impurities, so it has much lower purity than crystals, as crystallization only occurs on the **crystalable solid** (the solid of interest), which has the highest crystallization ability compared to other solutes in the mother liquid. Thus, impurities stay in the mother liquid with *no* changes.

M-112

MOTION

In physics, motion is the change of position of a system in space in relation to time (t) and a reference system. When a system moves, its position in space changes as time passes. If a system's position is *not* changing in relation to a reference (an observer), that system is at rest (motionless or stationary). [Because motion is **relative** to a reference, some physicists say **relative motion** instead of **motion**.]

You should also be aware of the following four (4) brief points about motion:

- Motion's rules, known as Newton's Motion Laws, were first proved by Newton.
- Motion is *not* touchable but is measurable by determining how far a system is moved.
- Position, acceleration, momentum, speed, velocity, and more quantities result from motion.
- A system *cannot* be in motion unless a force (F) acts on it, so F is the **driving force** (cause) of a system's motion with mass M, and acceleration (a) is the effect of that motion. Thus

$$F = M.a \tag{1}$$

Figure 1 shows a sports car's velocity (V) in relation to time (t). The graph in the figure shows the total distance that the car travels (total area under the graph, shown as shaded **orange**) and the car's acceleration (a), which equates to the slope (the rise-to-run ratio) of the curve at any point on the curve.

Elementary particles in any phase (solid, liquid, or gas) have one, two, or all the following motions. 1) **Rotational Motion:** It occurs when a moving system rotates in a circle around an axis, like the rotating basket of a centrifuge. 2) **Translational Motion:** It occurs when a system's center of mass changes its location along a path, like a car moving on a highway. 3) **Vibrational Motion:** It occurs when a system moves in a non-oriented (periodic) direction; like a wave.

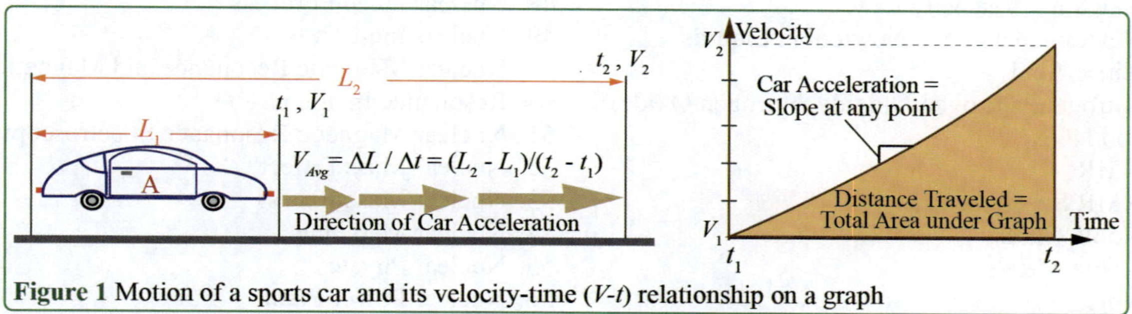

Figure 1 Motion of a sports car and its velocity-time (V-t) relationship on a graph

M-113

MOTORS

Mechanical motors are discussed under ENGINES, MACHINES, AND MOTORS. And electric motors are discussed under the topic of ELECTRIC GENERATORS AND MOTORS.

M-114

MUD

Defined under CAKE, MUD, SLUDGE, AND SLURRY.

N Section

LIST OF TOPICS

1. Nanofiltration Process
2. Nanotechnology
3. Natural Gas
4. Natural Log
5. Negative Pressure
6. Net Positive Suction Head
7. Neutrino
8. Neutron
9. Neutron Emission
10. Newton (Force Unit)
11. Newton (Scientist)
12. Newton's Gravitation Law
13. Newton's Motion Laws
14. Newton's Number
15. Newton's Viscosity Law
16. Newtonian and NonNewtonian Liquids
17. Nitric Acid
18. Nitrogen, Nitrogen Dioxide, Nitrogen Oxide, and NOX
19. NMR
20. NMR Spectroscopy
21. Noble Gases
22. Noble Metals
23. Noise
24. Nonaccelerating Reference System
25. Noncondensing Gases
26. Noninertial reference System
27. Nonionic Compounds
28. Nonmetals
29. NonNewtonian Liquids
30. Nonpolar Compounds
31. Normal Boiling Point Temperature
32. Normality
33. NOX
34. Nozzles
35. Nuclear Binding Energy
36. Nuclear Bombs
37. Nuclear Chain Reactions
38. Nuclear Chemistry
39. Nuclear Critical Mass
40. Nuclear Decay Process
41. Nuclear Defect Mass
42. Nuclear Emission Process
43. Nuclear Energy
44. Nuclear Excess Mass
45. Nuclear Fission and Nuclear Fusion
46. Nuclear Force
47. Nuclear Fuel
48. Nuclear Fusion Process
49. Nuclear Industry
50. Nuclear Magnetic Resonance and Magnetic Resonance Imaging
51. Nuclear Magnetic Resonance Spectroscopy
52. Nuclear Mass Defect
53. Nuclear Mass Excess
54. Nuclear Medicine
55. Nuclear Physics
56. Nuclear Power Plant
57. Nuclear Reactions
58. Nuclear Reactors
59. Nuclear Waste
60. Nuclear Weapons
61. Nucleon and Nucleon Number
62. Nuclides
63. Number of Degrees of Freedom
64. Number of Distillation Plates
65. Nusselt Number

N- 1

NANOFILTRATION PROCESS

Discussed under MEMBRANE SEPARATION PROCESS.

N- 2

NANOTECHNOLOGY

Nanotechnology is a modern technique (started in the 1980s) to manufacture products at the nanoscale, called **nanomanufacturing**. It deals with developing devices at the scale of around 100 nanometers (nm), where 1 nm = 10^{-9} m (one billionth of a meter, m). The properties of nano products are maybe even better than their similar ordinary-size products. Some, for example, can relatively better conduct the electric current, some may be relatively more chemically effective, and some may be better programmable.

There are already many nanoproducts on the market. Scientists believe that soon nanotechnology will affect almost any aspect of modern technologies. For example, in the medical field, a nanocomputer the size of a cell can control the heart rate. Likewise, a few drops of bactericide can disinfect a large amount of water.

A nanomachine (nanosized machine) with a motor, gear, and rotor can be smaller than a hair's width and move like an inchworm. The user of such a machine would see it using a video screen and feel it using special gloves, capable of intensifying and transmitting tiny forces to the user's hands.

A nanotube long enough to stretch to the Moon can roll into a small bundle (coil). Some nanotubes are produced from graphene (a strong form of carbon), so they can conduct electricity more than 1 000 times as a copper wire. With these interesting properties, nanotubes may replace, in the future, metal wires and even optical fiber telecommunication cables.

As a difficult job, nanomanufacturing can be done in one of the following methods:

- Top-down Method: In this method, a product's components are reduced down to the nanoscale.
- Bottom-up Method: In this method, a product is built from atomic- and molecular scale components.

[In recent years, some governments have invested a lot of money in developing nanotechnology. The US of America has invested 3.7 billion dollars, followed by the EU (European Union) with 1.2 billion and Japan with 750 million. The US National Nanotechnology Initiative was established in 2000 to fund and support the R&D in many fields of nanotechnology.]

N-3

NATURAL GAS

Natural gas is a hydrocarbon-based gas containing methane (CH_4, around 85%), ethane (C_2H_6), propane (C_3H_8), carbon dioxide (CO_2), and some impurities (such as a small amount of nitrogen and carbon monoxide). Natural gas is low in sulfur, but its content is high in some areas. Natural gas is found near crude oil (petroleum) deposits and coal fields.

Oil, coal, and natural gas are the world's main fossil fuels, while renewable energy has rapidly increased. Natural gas is widely used for combustion reactions and producing compressed natural gas (CNG) and liquefied natural gas (LNG).

The combustion reaction of natural gas and oxygen is a heat-releasing (exothermic) reaction, so the enthalpy of combustion (H_C or λ_C, the heat-energy content) of natural gas is 890 kJ/mole.

$$CH_4 + 2\ O_2 \rightarrow CO_2 + H_2O - 890\ \text{KJ/mole}$$

Expressing in kJ/kg, the H_C of natural gas is about 49 000 kJ/kg (= 21 300 BTU/Lb). Because about 92.5% of natural gas is carbon (C), when 1 kg of carbon in the gas burns, 49 000 × 100/92.5 = 53 000 kJ of heat energy (E_Q) is released. Thus, the H_C of carbon is 53 000 kJ/kg (= 23 000 BTU/Lb).

Theoretically, 10.2 m^3 of dry air is needed for each cubic meter of natural gas. [The practical air calculations are based on **dry air**, assuming *no* water is in it.]

Excess oxygen above the theoretical air requirement (TAR) is required to complete fuel combustion. Without sufficient oxygen, the combustion is incomplete, producing carbon monoxide (CO), which is hazardous! Therefore, the practical air requirement (PAR), by applying a factor of 1.4, is used. The factor of 1.4 increases the air usage from 10.2 to 14.3 m^3 of air per kg of natural gas.

N-4

NATURAL LOG

Defined under LOGARITHM AND ANTILOGARITHM.

N-5

NEGATIVE PRESSURE

See PRESSURE, PRESSURE DIFFERENCE, PRESSURE GRADIENT, AND NEGATIVE PRESSURE.

N-6

NET POSITIVE SUCTION HEAD

Study PUMP NET POSITIVE SUCTION HEAD.

N-7

NEUTRINO

Neutrino (so named because it is electrically neutral) is a quantum particle (a particle with *no* subparticle) with *no* electric charge (simply **charge**) and almost *no* mass (M), but with energy (E). [Neutrino was predicted in the 1930s by Wolfgang Pauli (1900–1958, an Austrian physicist) but *not* detected because it has low interaction (forcing) ability until 1956 by two American particle physicists.]

The **neutrino theory of light** says that a photon is equivalent to two neutrinos' fusion (joining), and a neutrino has the following properties:

- It is hard to be detected, yet,
- It has a quantum spin of ½ (half),
- It is a Fermion because it obeys Fermi-Dirac statistics,
- It moves close to the speed of light because its E_K is much more than its M,
- It is *not* affected by the electromagnetic force because it has *no* electric charge,
- It has an antiparticle, known as an **antineutrino** (also with *no* charge but opposite spin), and
- Many neutrinos exist in nature, passing our bodies all the time (because of their fast-moving ability).

N-8

NEUTRON

Discussed under ATOM.

N-9

NEUTRON EMISSION

Study NUCLEAR EMISSION PROCESS.

N-10

NEWTON (Force Unit)

The Newton (N) is the SI unit of force, where 1 N = 1 kg.m/s^2, as shown in Figure 1. The name is in honor of the contributions of Newton.

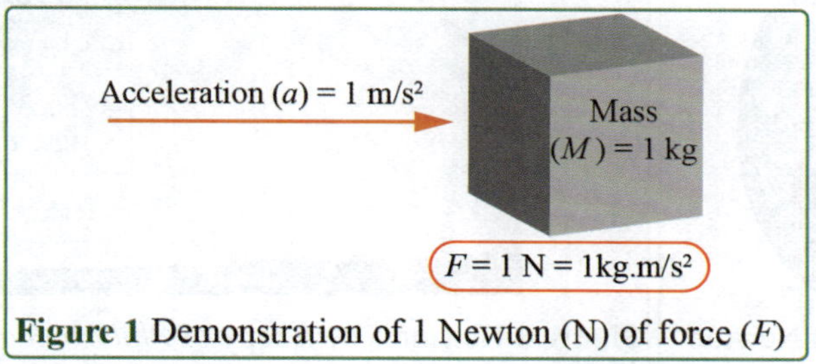

Figure 1 Demonstration of 1 Newton (N) of force (F)

N-11

NEWTON (Scientist)

As one of the two most talented physicists ever lived (the other was Einstein), Isaac Newton (1642–1727) was a British scientist. He established the foundation of **classical physics** by publishing his first book in 1687 written in Latin, the *Philosophiae Naturalis Principia Mathematica* (Mathematical Principles of Natural Philosophy), where **natural philosophy** is the old name for **Physics**. In his book, Newton described his discoveries about motion and its three (3) basic rules (later Newton's Motion Laws). In his book, he also wrote about gravitational force (F_g, simply **gravity**) and its formulation (later Newton's Law of Gravitation) by saying for the first time that F_g is a force that all systems exert on each other (see Figure 1).

In 1704, Newton published his second book, the *Optiks* (**Optics** in English), to discuss the light and its particle nature while moving and proved that white light consists of seven (7) colors, as shown in Figure 2.

Newton's father was a farmer. His mother was from a family with some university-educated priests. In 1669 when he was only 26, Newton was appointed as a math professor at the University of Cambridge. He invented **Calculus** (more or less simultaneously with Leibniz, a German mathematician).

Usually, Newton studied, experimented, and took notes for about 16 hours a day in his library room (with about 1 600 books) and laboratory (with his many hand-made experimental devices).

Newton had never been married. It is also interesting to know the following about Newton:

- In 1999, he was voted the second greatest physicist of all time (after Einstein) by *Physics World*.
- In 2013, a copy of the first edition of *Principia Mathematica* was sold at an auction for about $0.5 million.
- Einstein kept a picture of Newton, Faraday, and Maxwell in his office to respect them as the key pioneers of Physics (see the portrait under EINSTEIN).

Figure 1 In 1666, Newton discovered that the reason an apple falls downward from a tree to the ground is gravitational force

Figure 2 In 1704, Newton discovered that white light splits into a band of colors by passing through a triangular prism

Figure 1 A portrait of Newton [Illustrated for this book]

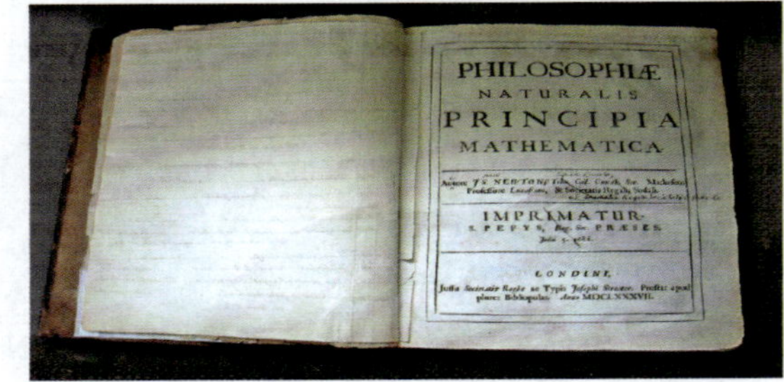

Figure 2 Newton's own copy of *Philosophiae Naturalis Principia Mathematica* with hand-written corrections, kept in Trinity College

N-12

NEWTON'S GRAVITATION LAW

Newton's Gravitation Law (also called **Newton's Gravity Law**), which was named by Newton as the **rule of gravitation** in his 1687's book (*Principia Mathematica*), states that any system that has mass (M) attracts every other system that has M. The attraction force between two massive systems was called by Newton the gravitational force (F_g, simply gravity). In this way, all masses in the Universe exert an attractive force on all other masses. If an apple falls from a tree, the F_g causes it to move toward the Earth. But, at the same time, the apple also exerts its own tiny F_g on the Earth.

Newton used his gravitation principle to calculate the F_g as an attractive force between any two systems with masses of M_1 and M_2, located in the distance L from each other. He proved that the quantity of F_g on each system is directly proportional to the product of the masses of the systems (M_1 and M_2) and inversely proportional to the square of the distance between their centers (L^2) through a proportionality constant named the gravitational constant (K_G or G).

$$F_g = K_G \frac{M_1.M_2}{L^2} \tag{1}$$

Here, L (for length) is the distance between the **centers of masses** (the **center of geometry** of a spherically symmetric system like a planet).

If thus, the values of variables in the NG equation are known, we can calculate K_G, which is constant, equal to 6.67×10^{-11} N m²/ kg² in the SI units and 3.34×10^{-8} Lb.Ft²/slug² in the US units. In the SI units, F_g is in Newton (N, the unit for force), M is in kg, and L is in m, so the K_G becomes in Nm²/ kg².

When Newton developed his gravitational equation, he assumed that space and time are independent, therefore absolute quantities. But later, Einstein, in his gravitational equation (study EINSTEIN'S GRAVITATIONAL FIELD EQUATION), proved that

- Spacetime is *not* an absolute quantity (because space and time are dependent on each other).
- Spacetime can go through a transition from one condition to another without a sudden change.

[Although Newton's gravitational equation (NG equation) has been completed by Einstein's gravitational equation (EG equation), most gravity-related calculations are still solved using the NG equation, as it is simpler and gives enough accuracy for most systems with ordinary mass, energy, and speed.]

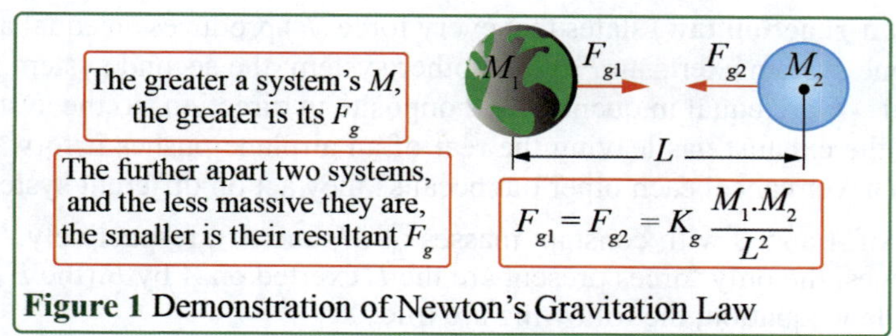

Figure 1 Demonstration of Newton's Gravitation Law

N-13

NEWTON'S MOTION LAWS

Newton's theories of motion, which became laws later, describe how a system moves when a force (F) acts on it. These laws, which were first published by Newton in 1687, can be applied to both a translational motion and a rotational motion.

Newton's First Motion Law

The first law (the **force-motion** or **inertial law**) states the following:

- A non-moving (at-rest or stationary) system will stay at rest unless a force (F) acts on it.
- A moving system does *not* change its velocity (does *not* accelerate) unless a force acts on it.

Each system's motion is affected differently when a force is acted on it. The measure of how easy or difficult it is to change a system's motion is called inertia (resistance to motion). Based on the first law, a system's mass (M) is directly related to its inertia. For this reason, the first law is also called the **inertial law**.

Mathematically, the first law can be expressed using a system's velocity (V).

$$\sum F = 0 \Rightarrow \frac{dV}{dt} = 0 \tag{1}$$

This equation (the first-law equation) tells us that if the net force ($\sum F$, the sum of all forces) acting on a system is zero, then the system's V remains constant (do *not* accelerate). As an example of the first law, a spacecraft, which was sent to space with *no* friction (f) and resistance (R) in 1997, is still moving through space today (see Figure 1).

The first law also proves that a system with a large M needs a larger F to change its motion than a smaller system (because a large M means large inertia).

Newton used the first law as a reference system to explain his other laws, as we will see later.

Newton's Second Motion Law

The second law (the **force law**) states that a net force acting on a system equates to that system's M multiplied by its acceleration (a),

$$F = M.a \quad (2)$$

This equation, which is the mathematical definition of force (F), tells us that

- For a given F, the *larger* a system M, the smaller is its acceleration (a), as shown in Figure 2.
- In a moving system with mass M, the F is the driving force of the motion, and a is the effect of the motion.

Equation 2 is consistent with the first law because if there is *no* F acting on M, then the left-hand side of this equation is zero, and, thus, the acceleration (a) must also be zero, as we would expect from the first law.

Newton's Third Motion Law

The third law (the **action-reaction law**) states that every force (F) produces an equal and opposite reaction. In other words, whenever one system exerts an F on the other system, the second system then exerts a negative F on the first system. F and $-F$ are equal in quantity and opposite in direction, so the system that exerts F will go backward. For example, the exhaust gas leaving the rear of an airplane pushes it forward. [**Action force** (F_{AB}) and **reaction force** (F_{BA}) never cancel each other out because they act on different systems.]

Consider two systems of A and B with constant masses of M_1 and M_2, respectively. If we isolate them from all other physical influences, the only forces present are the F exerted on A by B (the F_{AB}) and B by A (the F_{BA}). According to the second-law equation, the following are true:

$$F_{AB} = M_A.a_A \qquad F_{BA} = M_B.a_B \quad (3)$$

$$M_A.a_A = -M_B.a_B \quad (4)$$

In these equations, α_A and α_B are the accelerations of A and B, respectively. And according to the third law,

$$F_{AB} = -F_{BA} \quad (5)$$

A proportionality constant, named gravitational constant ($K_G = 6.67\times10^{-11}$ N m^2/ kg^2), can relate gravitational force (F_g), which acts between M_A and M_B, and the distance between the centers of the two systems (L).

$$F_g = K_G \frac{M_A.M_B}{L^2} \quad (6)$$

Newton's laws, however, have the following weaknesses: 1) They are valid only in a nonaccelerating moving system (an inertial reference system). Instead, the Einstein principle of gravity and spacetime can be applied to nonaccelerating and accelerating systems. 2) They do *not* talk about the types of forces because in 1687 when Newton published his book, only F_g (the weakest of four fundamental forces of nature) was known. Newton, however, knew that the F_g affects each motion in the entire Universe.

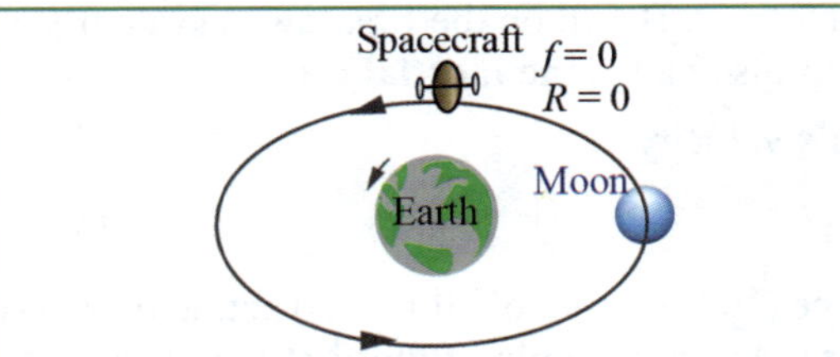

Figure 1 A spacecraft sent to space in 1997 with no friction (f) and resistance (R) is still moving in space

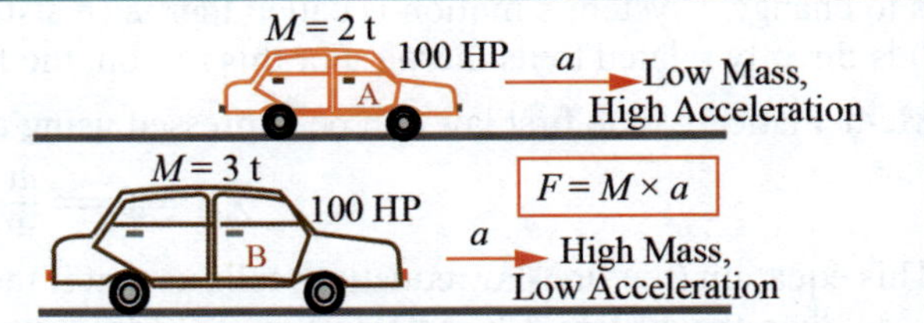

Figure 2 Demonstration of the second law by comparison of two cars with the same HP, but different masses

N-14
NEWTON'S NUMBER

Another name for POWER NUMBER.

N-15
NEWTON'S VISCOSITY LAW

Newton's Viscosity Law (simply **viscosity law**) is expressed by the liquid flow equation (also called **viscosity equation**), which relates the viscosity (η) of a flowing liquid, the distance (L, for length) between two points that the liquid flows, velocity (V) of the flow, and shear stress (S_S) applied on the flow.

$$\eta = S_S \frac{L}{V} \quad (1)$$

The η is in Pa.s, L is in m, and V is in m/s, so S_S becomes in N/m^2 = Pa, which is the unit of pressure (P). Similarly, if η is given in $N.s/m^2$, L in m, and V in m/s, the unit for S_S will again become N/m^2 = Pa.

The viscosity law has the following expressions:

- The *greater* is the viscosity of a liquid; the *greater* shear stress is needed to move it,
- The viscosity of a Newtonian liquid depends only on its P and T (temperature),
- The viscosity of a liquid is constant if its P and T are kept constant.

[The liquids that do *not* follow the viscosity equation (liquid flow equation) are nonNewtonian liquids.]

N-16
NEWTONIAN AND NONNEWTONIAN LIQUIDS

NEWTONIAN LIQUIDS

A Newtonian liquid is a liquid with a low molecular mass (M_M), and its η (viscosity) depends only on the P (pressure) and T (temperature) of that liquid. In addition,

- Its viscosity is dependent on shear stress (S_S),
- Its viscosity *cannot* influence the behavior of its flow,
- Its viscosity remains constant if its P and T are kept constant, and
- When flows, the relation between its velocity gradient and S_S applied is linear.

Velocity gradient (shear rate) is V/L, where V is for velocity and L is for length. For these reasons, a Newtonian liquid follows Newton's Viscosity Law and liquid flow equation (Newton viscosity equation), which formulizes the relation between η of a flowing liquid, L between two points that the liquid moves, V of the flow, and S_S applied on the flow.

$$\eta = S_S \frac{L}{V} \quad (1)$$

Water, ethanol, and some food products (like fruit juices, tea, and coffee) are examples of Newtonian liquids. All gases also behave like Newtonian fluids, but most liquids are non-Newtonians.

A Newtonian liquid behaves like a series of imaginary layers (like thin plates) in motion when it flows. Each layer moves with a velocity proportional to its distance from the lower layer. Thus, S_S (shear stress) is directly proportional to the rate at which V changes over distance. This means that the relation between the S_S and V/L (velocity gradient) in a Newtonian liquid is linear, like line A in Figure 1.

The linearity line starts from the **origin**, the point the axes (the plural for axis) intersect. Curve B in the same figure shows the relation between S_S and v/L of a non-Newtonian liquid (like a viscoelastic liquid). As shown in Figure 2, if we stir a Newtonian liquid with a rod, the liquid does *not* climb the rod, but when a Non-Newtonian liquid is stirred, the liquid climbs the rod (see Figure 3).

NONNEWTONIAN LIQUIDS

NonNewtonian liquids are highly viscous liquids with a high M_M and indicate complicated flow behavior. A nonNewtonian liquid indicates the next properties when it flows:

- Its viscosity is *not* a function of shear stress (S_S),
- Its viscosity (η) can influence the behavior of its flow,
- Its viscosity does *not* remain constant if its P and T are kept constant,
- Its viscosity does *not* depend only on its P (pressure) and T (temperature), and
- The relation between the V/L (velocity gradient) and S_S applied to its flow is nonlinear.

For these reasons, nonNewtonian liquids indicate different properties than Newtonian liquids. This is why nonNewtonian liquids do *not* follow Newton's Viscosity Law.

Curve B in Figure 1 shows the relationship between S_S and v/L in a **pseudoplastic liquid** (one of a few types of nonNewtonian liquids.) Solutions of long molecules (like starch solution) and suspension solutions (like mayonnaise, mustard, and sludge) are examples of pseudoplastic nonNewtonian liquids. As shown in Figure 2, if we stir a NonNewtonian liquid with a rod, the liquid climbs the rod.

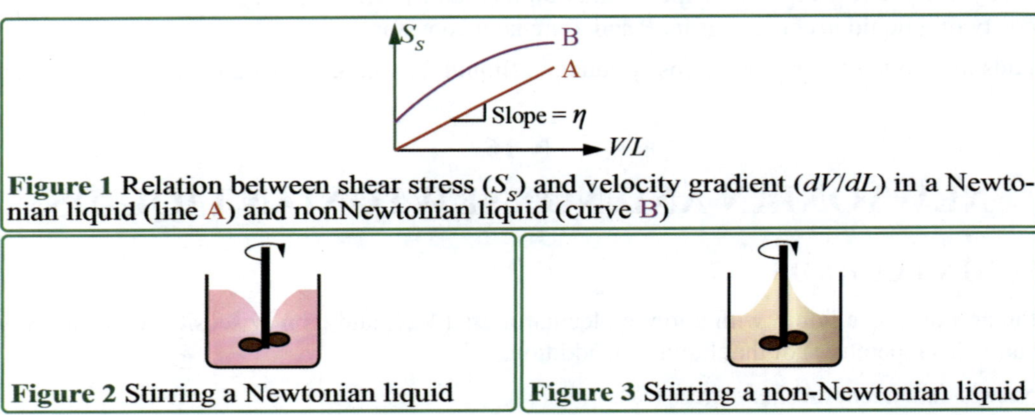

Figure 1 Relation between shear stress (S_S) and velocity gradient (dV/dL) in a Newtonian liquid (line A) and nonNewtonian liquid (curve B)

Figure 2 Stirring a Newtonian liquid

Figure 3 Stirring a non-Newtonian liquid

N-17

NITRIC ACID

Nitric acid (HNO_3) is a water-soluble-and-colorless strong acid with a molar mass (M_n) of 63 g/mole. It is one of the four strongest inorganic acids; the other ones are hydrochloric acid (HCl), sulfuric acid (H_2SO_4), and perchloric acid ($HClO_4$). When its concentration is more than 86%, it is called **fuming nitric acid**. For industrial use, nitric acid usually comes in a concentration of 68% (by mass) in water. To prevent its corrosive activity (because of its dissolved NO_2 content) to a metal tank, the HNO_3 is mixed with 0.6% hydrogen fluoride (HF) to create a fluoride coating on the tank's surface to protect the metal. For laboratory use as a reagent, it usually comes in 70.6% and density (D) of 1420 kg/m^3 (88.6 Lb/Ft^3).

Next, three properties of HNO are outlined.

- It is miscible with water in all proportions.

- It is one and half times as dense as water.
- Its boiling point temperature is 86ºC.

One way of nitric acid production is the Oswald process, in which anhydrous ammonia (NH_3) is oxidized by oxygen (O_2) in the air to produce NO (nitrogen monoxide) and NO_2 (nitrogen dioxide).

$$4\ NH_3 + 5O_2 \rightarrow 4\ NO + 6\ H_2O$$

$$2\ NO + O_2 \rightarrow 2\ NO_2$$

Then NO_2 reacts with H_2O to produce HNO_3.

$$3\ NO_2 + H_2O \rightarrow 2\ HNO_3 + NO$$

The aqueous HNO_3 produced can be concentrated by the distillation process up to about 68% (by mass). To further increase its concentration to 98% (called **anhydrous nitric acid**), the dehydration process with concentrated sulfuric acid (H_2SO_4) is used.

Nitric acid has many uses, mainly in the production of **fertilizers**. Its other application is in the production of explosives. It is also used as a strong oxidizing agent.

N-18

NITROGEN, NITROGEN DIOXIDE, NITROGEN OXIDE, AND NOX

Nitrogen: Nitrogen (N) is a chemical element in group 15 and period 2 of the periodic table of elements. Its atomic mass number (the total number of protons and neutrons) is 14, and its atomic number (the total number of protons) is 7, so it has 7 neutrons (that is 14 – 7 = 7). Its atomic mass (M_A, the actual mass of one atom of an element) is 14 AMU (simply 16 g), and its molar mass (M_n) is 14 g/mole.

Nitrogen (N) is a colorless and odorless gas with an atomic mass number (the total number of protons and neutrons) of 7, atomic mass (M_A) of 7 AMU (simply 7 g), and molar mass (M_n) of 7 g/mole. Under normal conditions, nitrogen combines with another nitrogen atom to form **diatomic nitrogen** (N_2; called the **molecular nitrogen**) or to combine with other atoms, like hydrogen (H), to form NH_3 (ammonia).

Some properties of molecular nitrogen (N_2) are outlined next.

- It forms 78% of the air,
- Its electronegativity is 3,
- Its molecular mass (M_M) is 14,
- Its liquid form is used as a coolant,
- Its density (D) is 1.25 g/L (= 1250 kg/m^3 = 78 Lb/Ft^3), and
- Its boiling point temperature (T_{BP}) is – 196°C, which equates to – 320°F.

Nitrogen Dioxide: Nitrogen dioxide (NO_2) is a brownish gas that can be fatal (if inhaled in large quantities). It is a pollutant by contributes to acid rain formation.

$$3\ NO_2 + H_2O \rightarrow 2\ HNO_3 + NO$$

Nitrogen Oxide: Nitrogen oxide (NO, **nitrogen monoxide** or **nitric oxide**) is a colorless gas with high toxicity (if NO is breathed, it is absorbed by the blood and reduces oxygen uptake, causing serious health problems, even death). It forms in the combustion reaction of a fuel. It is a pollutant by contributes to acid rain formation.

$$2\ NO + H_2O \rightarrow 2\ HNO_3$$

It reacts with oxygen (O_2) in the air to form NO_2.

$$2\ NO + O_2 \rightarrow 2\ NO_2$$

It reacts with oxygen (O_2) in the presence of water (H_2O) to form nitrous acid (HNO_2).

$$4\ NO + O_2 + 2\ H_2O \rightarrow 4\ HNO_2$$

It reacts with chlorine (Cl), fluorine (F), and bromine (Br) to form the nitrosyl halides, such as nitrosyl chloride (NOCl).

$$2\ NO + Cl_2 \rightarrow 4\ NOCl$$

NOX: NOX (rhymes with ***box***) is a simplified word used in the environmental field to refer to nitrogen oxides, NO, NO_2, N_2O_4, and N_2O_5. The NO and NO_2, which are the most important components of NOX, harm the environment as toxic pollutants in the next ways:

- They contribute to global warming,
- They contribute to the greenhouse effect,
- They contribute to formation of smog (smoky fog),
- They react with airborne chemicals to form toxic chemicals,
- They form nitric acid (HNO_3) in the atmosphere, causing acid rain in the air, and
- They harm humans, animals, and plants directly and through the above-mentioned factors.

The gas-liquid extraction process can considerably reduce the NOX in a flue gas (a hot gas leaving a furnace stack). In the extraction process, the flue gas passes through sodium hydroxide (NaOH) as the extracting solvent, causing most NO_2 to react with water in NaOH to form nitric acid (HNO_3). The rest of NO_2 reacts with NaOH to form sodium nitrate ($NaNO_3$) and sodium nitrite ($NaNO_2$).

$$3NO_2 + H_2O \rightarrow 2HNO_3 + NO$$

$$2NO_2 + 2NaOH \rightarrow NaNO_3 + NaNO_2 + H_2O$$

[NOX, carbon dioxide (CO_2), and sulfur dioxide (SO_2) are the strongest air pollutants.]

N-19
NMR

Study NUCLEAR MAGNETIC RESONANCE.

N-20
NMR SPECTROSCOPY

Study NUCLEAR MAGNETIC RESONANCE SPECTROSCOPY.

N-21
NOBLE GASES

Noble gases (also called **inert gases**) are inactive gases with resistive characteristics against chemical reactions, as they do *not* react with almost any chemical substance (simply **substance**) under certain conditions. This non-reactivity exists because a Noble gas atom's valance electron shell (the outer shell containing valance electrons) is completely occupied, so it has little (or *no*) tendency to participate in a reaction. Noble gases are helium (He), neon (Ne), argon (Ar), krypton (Kr), xenon (Xe), and radon (Rn), the six (6) elements that are located in group 18 of the periodic table of elements (see Figure 1).

Some other properties of noble gases are:

- They all exist as monoatomic gaseous atoms.
- Their inert property is used in chemical reactions that are *not* wanted.
- About 1% of the Earth's atmosphere is Ar, and the other ones are present in only trace amounts.
- They are produced from the liquification of the air, except Ar, which is extracted from natural gas.
- Helium is used to fill balloons, and helium and argon are used in welding and metallurgical processes.

[In science and engineering, the term **inert** is used to describe a chemically inactive substance. In general English, **inert** is the state of doing little or nothing.]

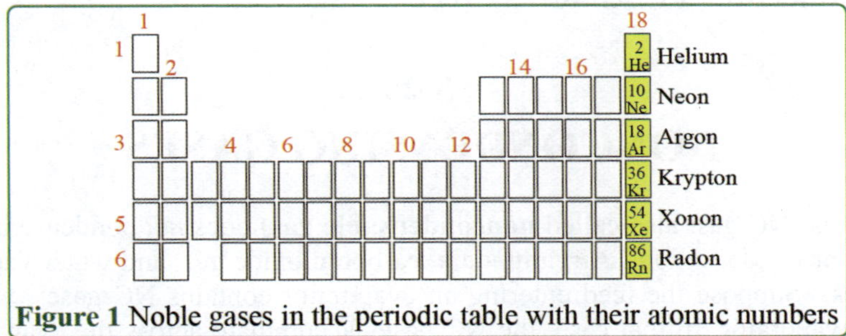

Figure 1 Noble gases in the periodic table with their atomic numbers

N-22

NOBLE METALS

Noble metals are metallic elements with resistive characteristics against chemical reactions, even at high temperatures. Noble metals are ruthenium (Ru), rhodium (Rh), palladium (Pd), osmium (Os), iridium (Ir), platinum (Pt), gold (Au), and silver (Ag), the eight (8) elements that are located in the group 8, 9, 10, and 11 of the periodic table of elements (see Figure 1). [In some classification, copper (Cu), rhenium (Re), and mercury (Hg) are also considered noble metals.]

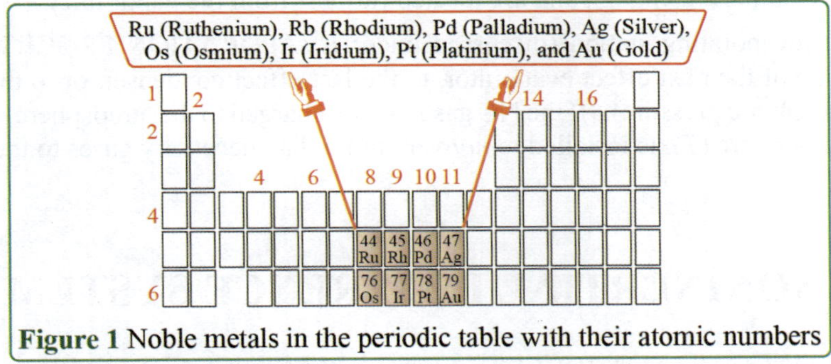

Figure 1 Noble metals in the periodic table with their atomic numbers

N-23

NOISE

Noise is a disturbing, unwanted, and unsafe sound. Loud noise (like heavy equipment in an industrial facility and frequently listening to loud music in close areas) can cause permanent hearing damage.

The strength of noise is expressed by decibel (dB). Daily exposure to noises louder than 100 dB in an industrial facility can damage employees hearing over time. Thus, the related regulations should be followed by that facility for its employees, who expose to loud noise. Wearing ear-protection devices, like an ear-banded cap, earmuff, and earplug, can quiet the noise and protect the ear.

N-24

NONACCELERATING REFERENCE SYSTEMS

Another name for INERTIAL REFERENCE SYSTEMS.

N-25

NONCONDENSING GASES

A non-condensing gas (NC gas; also called **noncondensable gas**) does *not* condense in a heat-involved process, like evaporation or condensation. Air, ammonia, carbon dioxide gas, and water vapor mixed with air are examples of NC gases. Suppose the feed entering an evaporator contains NC gases, which are not properly discharged from the evaporator. In that case, the NC gases accumulate across the evaporator's heating tubes, causing the temperature difference (ΔT) across the heating tubes to be decreased. This causes the following problems:

- It decreases the T_{Con} of the condensing gases,
- It decreases the steam economy of the evaporators, and
- It decreases the evaporation rate (R_E) of the evaporators.

The NC gases are usually removed from an evaporator before their concentration becomes too great (more than 10% of existing vapor). Typically, the NC gases are discharged at about 1% of the vapor entering an evaporator. This is achievable if the following conditions are met:

- A positive vapor-flow path from inlet to vent outlet exists, and
- The vent's discharge points are enough and are located furthest from the vapor inlet.

In a multiple-effect evaporating station (discussed under EVAPORATION PROCESS), the NC gases are vented to the vapor line of the next effect evaporator, to the last-effect condenser, or to the atmosphere (if their pressure is above atmospheric pressure). [If the NC gases are discharged to the atmosphere, a **thermostatic steam trap**, activated by temperature (T), is installed to *not* vent more than necessary gases to the atmosphere.]

N-26

NONINERTIAL REFERENCE SYSTEM

Study ACCELERATING AND NONACCELERATING REFERENCE SYSTEMS.

N-27

NONIONIC COMPOUNDS

Study IONIC AND NONIONIC COMPOUNDS.

N-28

NONMETALS

Study METALS AND NONMETALS.

N-29

NONNEWTONIAN LIQUIDS

Study NEWTONIAN AND NONNEWTONIAN LIQUIDS.

N-30

NONPOLAR COMPOUNDS

Discussed under POLAR AND NONPOLAR COMPOUNDS.

N-31

NORMAL BOILING POINT TEMPERATURE

Discussed under the topic of BOILING POINT TEMPERATURE.

N-32

NORMALITY

Study MOLARITY, NORMALITY, AND MOLALITY.

N-33

NOX

Study NITROGEN AND NOX.

N-34

NOZZLES

A nozzle is a cylindrical device, usually installed at the end of a pipe, tube, or hose, to discharge a fluid (liquid or gas) at high velocity (V) and pressure (P). A typical nozzle has a compression section and minimum wall friction to increase the flowing fluid's V and P.

Figure 1 illustrates a typical converging-diverging nozzle, which consists of three sections:

- **Converging Section:** This section starts from the entrance of the nozzle to its throat. In this section, the fluid's V *increases* to its maximum, and its P *decreases* slightly.

- **Throat:** This small section connects the converging section to the diverging section. At the throat, the fluid's *v* reaches its maximum.
- **Diverging Section:** This section starts from the throat to the end of the nozzle. In this section, the fluid's *P* *increases* to its maximum, and its *v* *decreases* slightly.

Remember the following brief helpful points about nozzles:

- In nozzles, the volumetric flow rate ($\dot{V}$) follows the pressure trend (the $\dot{V}$ *increases* with *increasing P*).
- Nozzles can produce a strong isentropic flow (a flow that goes through pressure change, ΔP) because the fluid in a nozzle goes through expansion and compression.
- Nozzles can also produce **turbulent flow** (defined under REYNOLDS NUMBER) for a liquid or **supersonic flow** (defined under MACH NUMBER) for a gas.

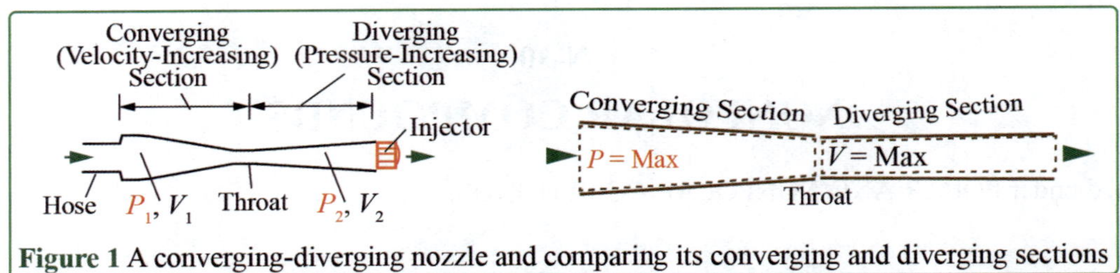

Figure 1 A converging-diverging nozzle and comparing its converging and diverging sections

N-35
NUCLEAR BINDING ENERGY

Study NUCLEAR ENERGY.

N-36
NUCLEAR BOMBS

Discussed under NUCLEAR WEAPON.

N-37
NUCLEAR CHAIN REACTIONS

Discussed under the topic of NUCLEAR REACTIONS.

N-38
NUCLEAR CHEMISTRY

As a branch (subfield) of chemistry, nuclear chemistry (NC) studies nuclear processes that occur in the nucleus of an atom, such as nuclear reactions, nuclear chain reactions, nuclear decay, nuclear fission, nuclear fusion, and more.

[Note: Nuclear chemistry and nuclear physics are somewhat similar, particularly those given in this book. Thus, **nuclear topics**, such as nuclear reactions or nuclear decay, can be used in both fields.]

N-39
NUCLEAR CRITICAL MASS

Study CRITICAL AND EXCESS MASSES.

N-40
NUCLEAR DECAY PROCESS

A nuclear decay (also called **radioactive decay** or simply **decay**) is the process of decaying (decomposing or splitting) the nucleus of a radioactive element (simply **radionuclide** or **nuclide**), causing the release of radioactive radiation (like alpha particles, beta particles, and gamma particles). In a decay process, a radionuclide's nucleus decays (decomposes) into two or more new nuclei.

When a decay process occurs, the created element (or elements) can be as unstable as its parent or stable as a non-radionuclide. When, for example, uranium-235 (U-231, a radionuclide) decays, its initial products are protactinium-231 (Pa-231) and actinium-227 (Ac-227), both being radionuclides. [In this example, U-235 is said to be the **parent nuclide,** and Pa and Ac are the **daughter nuclides** (the products of the decay).] On the other hand, consider the decay of carbon-14 (with 6 protons and 8 neutrons, so an atomic mass number of 14), a beta-ray-emitter radionuclide. The C-14 naturally decays over time to nitrogen (N-14, with 7 protons and 7 neutrons), a non-radionuclide, by gaining one electron and changing one of its neutrons to a proton.

$$ {}_{14}^{8}\mathrm{C} + 1\mathrm{e} \rightarrow {}_{14}^{7}\mathrm{N} $$

During the decay, the C-14 (with a half lifetime of 5730 years) emits β-rays, so it is a beta-ray emitter.

Decay always starts at the level of a single atom. Consider uranium (U, refers to U-238; with 92 protons, so-called element 92, and 146 neutrons), a radionuclide. The decay starts with one of its atoms splitting its nucleus into another kind of nucleus with a different N_A. [The atom that splits is said to be **radioactively decayed** (degraded).] The decay process continues over time until all atoms of uranium have decayed. And because the uranium's halflife ($t_{1/2}$) is extremely large (about 4.46 billion years), it decays slowly. During the long decaying period, uranium constantly (but sometimes less and sometimes more) emits alpha particles.

The decay of a radionuclide can occur naturally over time or in a particle accelerator over a shorter time. It is possible to measure the decay process's rate by the element's halflife in a natural decay. [Depending on the structure of the nucleus, halflife can vary from a fraction of a second to billions of years.]

The three (3) most common decays are the following:

- **Alpha Decay** (α-decay)**:** This decay emits alpha particles (rays). For example, when helium (a nuclide consisting of two protons and two neutrons) decays, it emits alpha particles. An alpha particle consists of two protons and two neutrons and is therefore identical to the nucleus of the helium-4 isotope.
- **Beta Decay** (β-decay)**:** This lengthy decay occurs by weak nuclear force, emitting beta particles. For example, the beta decay of a neutron changes it into a proton and releases an electron. Because the released electron moves at high speed, this radiation is dangerous. However, in a controlled instrument, beta decay is used to treat certain cancers. [In **beta minus decay** (β^- decay), the weak nuclear force acts to convert a neutron into a proton, an electron, and an antineutrino. In **beta plus decay** (β^+ decay), which is a rare process, a proton in a nuclide (like carbon-14) changes into a neutron, a neutrino, and a positron.]
- **Gamma Decay** (γ-decay)**:** This decay emits gamma particles.

The SI unit for measuring nuclear decay is Becquerel (Bq). If a quantity of a nuclide produces one decay per second, it has an activity of one Bq.

A nuclear decay (radioactive) process is the opposite of a nuclear emission process because the neutrons are released. But, during **nuclear emission**, the neutrons are absorbed.

The following points are important to know about nuclear decay and nuclear emission:

- When decay occurs on a nuclide, its nucleus loses some of its mass (because of releasing neutrons), while in emission, the nucleus gains mass (because of absorbing neutrons).
- When decay occurs on a nuclide, its nucleus loses its stability, while when a nuclear emission occurs, its nucleus reaches stability (by releasing its excess neutrons).

Radioactive decay is a random (accidental) process at the level of a single atom, so it is impossible to predict when a given atom will start to decay.

[Note 1: Inside the Earth, naturally slow decay of some nuclides constantly occurs to provide the Earth's heat energy (E_Q).] [Note 2: A difference exists between **nuclear fission** and **nuclear decay**. Fission is splitting a nucleus into two nuclei (the fission's products), while decay releases particles (like alpha particles, beta particles, or gamma particles). When the nucleus of U-235 absorbs a neutron and becomes U-236, it most likely fissions (splits), but a chance also exists to be decayed to release gamma particles.]

N-41

NUCLEAR DEFECT MASS

Another name for NUCLEAR EXCESS MASS.

N-42

NUCLEAR EMISSION PROCESS

Nuclear emission (also called **neutron emission**) is the process of emission (release) of a neutron (or neutrons) from an atom's nucleus with an excess neutron (or neutrons). The nuclear emission process is the opposite of a nuclear decay process because:

- In nuclear emission, the neutrons are absorbed, while neutrons are released in decay.
- When a nuclear emission occurs, the nucleus reaches its stability (by releasing its excess neutrons), while when a nuclear decay occurs, the nucleus loses its stability (by absorbing extra neutrons).
- When a nuclear emission occurs, the nucleus gains some mass, while in decay, the nucleus loses some of its mass (because of releasing some neutrons).

N-43

NUCLEAR ENERGY

Discussed under the topic of ENERGY AND ITS FORMS.

N-44

NUCLEAR EXCESS MASS

Study CRITICAL NUCLEAR AND EXCESS NUCLEAR MASSES.

N-45

NUCLEAR FISSION AND NUCLEAR FUSION

Nuclear fission is the process of **splitting** (fission) the nucleus of a heavy nuclide (like uranium-235) to create lighter nuclei (like barium-141and krypton-92) and a great amount of nuclear energy (E_N), which is specifically called **fission energy**.

Nuclear fusion is **joining** (fusing) two or more nuclei of light nuclides together to create larger nuclei and E_N (specifically, **fusion energy**).

The fission and fusion processes occur during self-sustaining reactions, called nuclear chain reactions. Further, both are energy-releasing reactions. Some, however, major differences exist between them, including the following two (2):

- Unlike fission, fusion needs extreme conditions (high pressure and temperature).
- A large nucleus splits into smaller nuclei in fission, while in fusion, small nuclei join to form a larger nucleus. Fission occurs only on heavier elements (heavier than iron, Fe) to produce lighter elements, while fusion occurs on lighter elements (lighter than Fe) to produce heavier elements.

Next, we discuss these two important processes in more detail.

NUCLEAR FISSION PROCESS

The nuclear fission process, which was discovered in 1938 by Heisenberg and two other German physicists, is a series of nuclear chain reactions during which the nucleus of a heavy nuclide absorbs a neutron and splits (fissions) in half to create smaller nuclei (called **fission products**, **fission fragments**, or simply **fragments**) and a great amount of E_N in the form of E_Q (heat energy). According to Einstein's equation ($E = M.c^2$), the E_N is released by converting excess nuclear mass (M_{EN}, simply **excess mass**) into E_N,

Consider a nuclear power plant that uses a nuclear fuel, containing 4% uranium-235 (U-235) and 96% uranium-238 (U-238) in its nuclear reactor. The nucleus of U-235 (with 92 protons and 143 neutrons) is much more unstable than that of U-238, meaning that U-235 atoms are much more fissile (splittable) than U-238 atoms. [The U-238 atoms *cannot* split because it needs neutron with much more energy (E) than U-235 atoms. Thus, U-235 atoms are the only ones that split and release E_N.]

The split of U-235 starts by absorbing a neutron (shown here as ${}^{1}_{0}\mathrm{N}$) to become U-236, which then splits into smaller nuclei of Ba-141 (barium-141 with 56 protons and 85 neutrons) and Kr-92 (krypton-92 with 36 protons and 56 neutrons). Then the reaction releases 3 neutrons and some E_N (nuclear energy).

$${}^{235}_{92}\mathrm{U} + {}^{1}_{0}\mathrm{N} \rightarrow {}^{236}_{92}\mathrm{U} \rightarrow {}^{141}_{56}\mathrm{Ba} + {}^{92}_{36}\mathrm{Kr} + 3({}^{1}_{0}\mathrm{N}) + E_N$$

Understanding this chain reaction requires two (2) explanations, as given next.

- As calculated under EXCESS NUCLEAR MASS, the difference between the reactants' M_{EN} (excess nuclear mass) is slightly greater than the products. Anytime a nucleus splits into two new smaller nuclei (fission fragments), such tiny M_{EE}, which accounts for about 0.1% of the original mass of the participating reactants, is converted into E_N, according to Einstein's equation ($E = M.c^2$). [An atom produces a tiny amount of E_N, but when an enormous number of atoms (in trillions) split, the produced E_N is huge. For example, when 1 kg of U-235 splits, it produces 57.4×10^9 kJ of E_N. This is about 2.2 million times more than the E_Q released from burning 1 kg of coal (with the enthalpy of combustion of about 26 000 kJ/kg).]
- If at least one neutron hits the atom of U-235 to split its nucleus, the fission occurs, and the chain reaction continues. This is a **critical condition** for the fission process. [The mass (M) of U-235 needed to produce the critical condition is called the nuclear critical mass (simply **critical mass**).]

The following are the detailed explanation of how the nucleus of U-235 splits (see Figure 1):

- A U-235 atom is hit (technically **bombarded**) by a **thermal neutron** (a high-energetic and slow-moving neutron), and its nucleus splits into two lighter nuclei (fragments) of Ba-141 and Kr-92. In addition, 2 (or 3) new thermal neutrons and some E_N are released. Thus Ba-141, Kr-92, and neutrons are the products of each fission stage.
- One of the released neutrons hits a U-235 atom to split its nucleus and release 2 (or 3) new neutrons and more E_N. [One (or more) gamma particle is also released (*not* shown in Figure 1) in each stage of fission.]
- The process of absorbing a neutron, splitting the atoms, and releasing neutrons and E_N continues in the further stages.

The explanations given so far tell us that the E_N is released when a U-235 atom splits other U-235 atoms split, so fission is a self-sustaining reaction, during which each stage creates more neutrons and E_N.

[The self-sustaining reaction, called **fission chain reaction**, can be controlled in a nuclear power plant's reactor but is *not* controllable in a nuclear weapon.]

The fissionability (capability to fission) of a nuclide depends on the following:

- **Released Neutrons:** Some of the released neutrons randomly leave the process, so *none* are available for the next stage. Assume that each atom of U-235 releases 2 neutrons in each stage, and then the number of neutrons exponentially increases in each stage. In the second stage, 4 neutrons are released. In the third stage, 8 neutrons. And in the tenth stage, the number of released neutrons is 1024 (because $2^{10} = 1024$). If, however, the condition is such that the rate of neutrons that leave the process is faster than the rate of new neutrons released, the chain reaction will *not* sustain. To prevent this from occurring in an **atomic bomb**, two (or more) **subcritical masses** are getting together to make a nuclear mass excess (a mass in excess of the nuclear critical mass) to assure that the explosion will occur.
- **Released Energy:** When U-235 absorbs a neutron to form U-236, the E_N of the neutron in the U-236 is about 6.4 MeV (mega electron volts), where 1 MeV = 1.6×10^{-13} Joules (J). But the energy required for the fission process is only 5.3 MeV, so when U-235 absorbs a neutron, the resulting U-236 has excess energy of 1.1 MeV above the critical energy required to cause the fission.

A good question here is, "Why is it easier to bombard a nucleus with neutron than with proton?" The answer is that the neutron has *no* electric charge, so when it approaches an electro-positively charged nucleus, it will *not* face any repulsion. Thus, it easily breaks the nucleus to be incorporated into it.

The released E_Q in a nuclear reactor heats the reactor's cooling water to reach its boiling point temperature to generate pressurized steam that drives a steam turbine to produce the AC electricity.

NUCLEAR FUSION PROCESS

The nuclear fusion process, which was discovered in 1939 by a German physicist, is a series of nuclear chain reactions during which the nuclei of two (or more) light nuclides fusion (join) to create heavier nuclei. During fusion, a great amount of E_N (nuclear energy) in the form of E_Q (heat energy), specifically the **fission nuclear energy**, is released by converting mass (M) into energy (E), according to $E = M.c^2$. The fusion process occurs on light elements (lighter than Fe) to produce heavier elements. [Like in fission, an atom produces a tiny amount of E_N, but when an enormous number of atoms (in trillions) fusion, the produced E_N is huge.]

The fusion process occurs naturally in some stars, like the Sun, in which hydrogen molecules (H_2, with 1 proton in each H) fuse into helium-3 (He-3, with 2 protons and 1 neutron) atoms. The reactions occurring in the Sun create a great amount of E_N by converting M (mass) into E (energy), according to $E = M.c^2$. Figure 2 shows the initial stages of hydrogen fusion in the Sun. One of the hydrogen molecule's protons changes into a neutron to form deuterium (a heavy isotope of hydrogen, H-2, or D), and another joins the deuterium to form a He-3 nucleus. When two He-3 nuclei combine, they form helium-4 (He-4, a nuclide with 2 protons and 2 neutrons), the non-pollutant end-product of the Sun fusion process. The nucleus of He-4 weighs less than its nucleus's components (the protons and neutrons). This affects the mass balance of each He-4 to create a small amount of nuclear excess mass (simply **excess mass**).

According to $E = M.c^2$, the conversion of the excess mass of He-4 in the amount of 4.4×10^6 t/s creates a large amount of photon energy (E_{Ph}), which shines on the Universe and keeps us warm. Sun fuses about 620×10^6 t/s of hydrogen to produce:

- About 4.4×10^6 t helium-4 (He-4),
- Approximately 4×10^{20} MJ/s of photon energy (E_{Ph}), and
- A temperature (T) of about 5 777K (= 5 500°C = 9 940°F) at its surface, while its interior T is 10^6 °C.

While these numbers are huge, they indicate that the rate of the Sun's fusion is small (about 0.6%). At this rate, physicists estimate that the Sun is roughly halfway through its active life (it takes about 5 billion years to die).

It is helpful to note the following two points about the fission process: 1) To fuse two protons, they must get extremely close to each other in the range of the strong nuclear force. This is extremely unlikely. But because approximately 10^{32} protons exist in each cm^3, just a few of them are enough to hit each other to fuse. 2) Difficulties in controlling the release of E_N during the fusion process prevent it from being used in nuclear power plants. Fusion, however, is used in the production of **fusion bombs** (also called **hydrogen bombs** or H-bombs), such as the one that used plutonium-235 and was dropped on Hiroshima in August 1945.

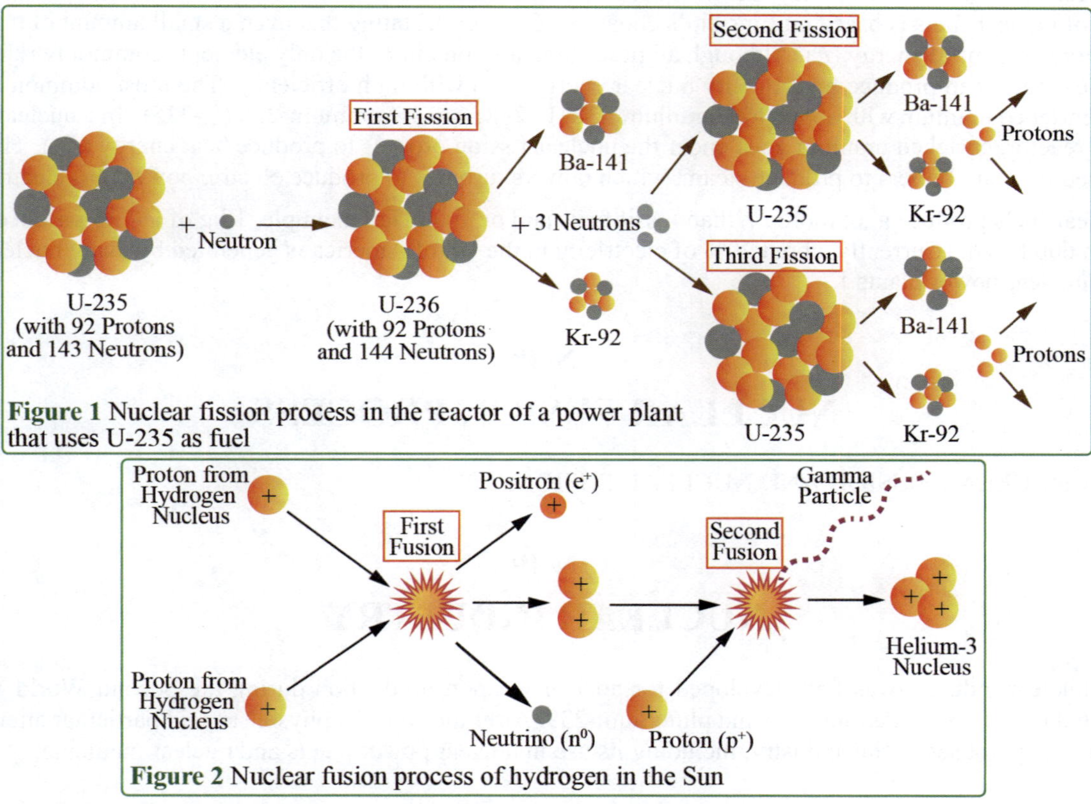

Figure 1 Nuclear fission process in the reactor of a power plant that uses U-235 as fuel

Figure 2 Nuclear fusion process of hydrogen in the Sun

Fusion physicists think that one possible solution to the shortage of electricity is to generate it by fusion, the way the Sun does. They think that we *cannot* create the huge amount of temperature (around 1 million ºC) that the Sun uses to trigger the proton-proton fusion of hydrogen. But, we can combine (fuse) its isotopes (deuterium and tritium) to create neutrons and helium. The neutrons can then react with water in a reactor to change it to pressurized steam to drive the steam turbines to generate electricity,. Physicists successfully tried this process at the Culham Center for Fusion Energy in England. The downside was that the research needed more input energy than it produced (because fusion needs a high-temperature medium to continue). The International Thermonuclear Experimental Reactor (ITER) in France produces 500 MW of E_N (about the same as a small nuclear power plant that uses the fission process).

N-46

NUCLEAR FORCE

Study FUNDAMENTAL FORCES OF NATURE.

N-47

NUCLEAR FUELS

Nuclear fuel is a high-efficiency fuel produced mainly from uranium (U) and plutonium (Pu). The high efficiency of nuclear fuels is based on Einstein's equation ($E = M.c^2$), stating that even a small amount of mass (M) has a large amount of energy (E). Although all pure elements contain E, the only elements commonly referred to as nuclear fuels can produce high-quality nuclear energy (E_N) with high efficiency. The most common nuclear fuel is enriched uranium with about 96% uranium-238 (U-238) and 4% uranium-235 (U-235). In a nuclear power plant's reactor, enriched uranium goes under the nuclear fission process to produce heat energy (E_Q). The E_Q is then used in steam boilers to produce steam, which powers turbines to produce electric power (P_E, electricity).

Nuclear fuels produce a lot more E_Q than fossil fuels and biofuels. For example, 1 kg of U-235 produces more E_Q than 600 t coal. [Currently, about 20% of electricity in the US of America is generated by using nuclear fuels in five nuclear power plants.]

N-48

NUCLEAR FUSION PROCESS

Study NUCLEAR FISSION AND NUCLEAR FUSION.

N-49

NUCLEAR INDUSTRY

The nuclear industry was first developed for nuclear weapon production during the Second World War by splitting the nucleus of uranium-235 and plutonium-239. After the war, the physicists paid particular attention to the peaceful purposes of this industry, including its use in nuclear power plants and nuclear medicine.

N-50

NUCLEAR MAGNETIC RESONANCE AND MAGNETIC RESONANCE IMAGING

Nuclear Magnetic Resonance

Nuclear magnetic resonance (NMR) is the **resonance** of an atom's nucleus to a magnetic field (simply M-field) created by radioactive radiation (wave), where the word **resonance** used here is the rotational response (spin) of an atom's nucleus around its axis (like the spin of an electron around its axis). A nucleus spin changes when an external M-field is applied to it. This nucleus behavior is used in magnetic resonance imaging (MRI) in medicine to create images of a human organ. It is also used in nuclear magnetic resonance spectroscopy (NMR spectroscopy) for investigating the structure and chemical composition of a chemical substance at micro (atomic and molecular) size, even over an astronomical distance.

When an atom receives enough radioactive waves, its nucleus resonates (response) to the created M-field by changing its moving direction (called a **net magnetic vector**, NMV) away from the direction of the applied M-field. And the angle to which the NMV moves out of alignment is called the **flip angle**, shown by the symbol alpha (*a*) in Figure 1. The NMV can be separated into two magnetic components of **X-magnetic component** (simply X-axis or transversal axis) and **Y-magnetic component** (simply Y-axis or longitudinal axis), as shown in the middle of Figure 2. The NMR spectroscopy is usually used as the radiation source. The strength of a given RF pulse and, thus, the M-field's strength (represented by magnetic moment, M-moment) determines the quantity of the flip angle (*a*). When the RF pulse is sufficient, the flip angle relative to the NMV is 90°, as shown on the right side of the same figure.

A human tissue, like **fat** (lipid) and **muscle**, has a large **resonance** if it has a large X-axis. In this case, the frequency (*f*) of the RF pulse (signal) received by the **pulse receiver** of the NMR spectroscope is large, resulting in a bright area on the image. If a tissue sends a low signal instead, it has a small X-axis (a small *f*), resulting in a dark image.

In general, three (3) nucleus-related processes participate in NMR and NMR spectroscopy:

- **Resonance Process:** This is the nucleus's response to the applied radiation (usually in RF pulse with a certain *f*), so resonance is a **radiation process**.
- **Relaxation Process:** This is the reverse of **resonance**, causing the nucleus to return from the excited energy state to the ground energy state by releasing photons. Thus, relaxation, instead, is a **non-radiation process**. [To produce detectable signals, the relaxation time, particularly the excited step, should be fast.]
- **Precession Process:** This is the nucleus's rotational movement on a **circular path**, caused by the applied RF pulse to the nucleus, as shown in the middle of Figure 2. [**Precession**, in Physics, is a change in the spinning direction of a rotating system, measured by the flip angle (*a*). The precession's rotational velocity (ω, omega) of the nucleus is directly proportional to the applied RF pulse and, thus, to the created M-field, and inversely proportional to the rotational momentum (L) of the spinning nucleus (right side of Figure 2).

In an NMR spectroscope, a liquid sample is placed in an M-field, an RF (radio-frequency) pulse is applied to the sample, and the decrease in strength of the pulse, caused by the absorbing sample, is measured.

Magnetic Resonance Imaging

Magnetic resonance imaging (MRI) is a medical technique that uses the properties of the NMR (nuclear magnetic resonance) to create images of a human body's organs. An MRI scanner forms a strong M-field and applies it around the area to be imaged. Unlike **CT** (computer tomography) **scan**, an MRI scanner does *not* use an X-ray. Instead, it uses **radiofrequency** (RF) **pulse** as the radiation source to form a strong M-field.

[MRI was originally named NMRI (nuclear magnetic resonance imaging), but the word **nuclear** was dropped to avoid negative perception.]

To generate an image. MRI relies on the resonance (response) of a hydrogen atom (H) in the human body for the following two (2) reasons:

- The H atoms are abundance in our body, and
- An H nucleus's magnetic moment (M-moment, an indication of an M-field's strength) is comparatively strong (because the H nucleus has only 1 proton).

As said under the subtopic of NMR, the **net magnetic vector** (NMV) can be separated into **X-component of magnetization** (simply X-axis or transverse axis) and **Y-component of magnetization** (simply Y-axis or longitudinal axis) for different body tissues, such as fat (lipid) and muscle. A human's tissue has a large **resonance** if it has a large X-axis. Said that the frequency (*f*) of the RF (radio frequency) pulse received by the **pulse receiver** of the NMR scanner is large, resulting in a bright area on the MRI image. If a tissue sends a small signal instead, it has a small X-axis (with a signal of a small *f*), resulting in a dark image.

The amount of hydrogen atoms in water (H_2O) and **fat** (lipid) molecules are the two thresholds of imaging contrast in MRI. The H atoms in water molecules are linked to oxygen atoms, while those in fat molecules are linked to carbon atoms. Removing an electron from around the H nucleus in a water molecule causes the nucleus to be less protected and, therefore, to interact more strongly with the applied M-field (and absorb more RF waves). Instead, the carbon molecules in fat are less electron-removing, so their H atoms do *not* interact with the M-field as strongly (and absorb fewer RF waves). As a result, the *f* of the RF pulse passed the water molecules and sent to the **pulse receiver** is smaller than those sent by the fat molecules (Figure 3). The result is an MRI image with sufficient contrast between dark and bright areas.

In NMR spectroscopy (Figure 4), a liquid sample is placed in an M-field, an RF pulse is applied to the sample, and the *decrease* in strength of the pulse, caused by the absorbing sample, is measured.

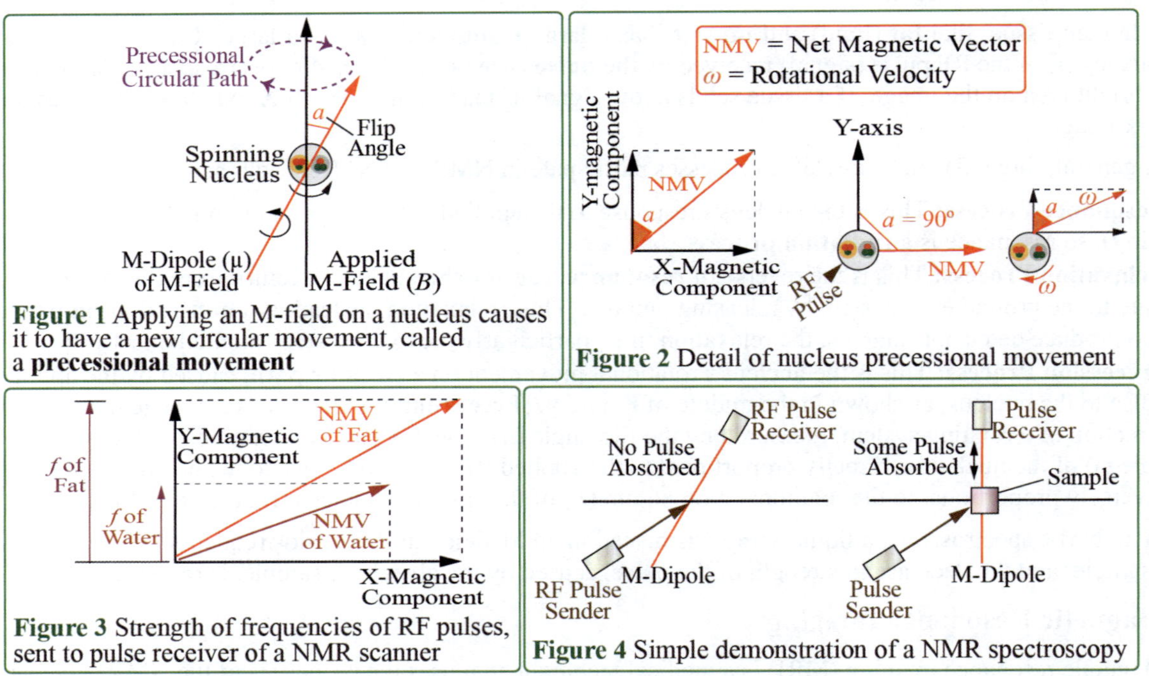

Figure 1 Applying an M-field on a nucleus causes it to have a new circular movement, called a **precessional movement**

Figure 2 Detail of nucleus precessional movement

Figure 3 Strength of frequencies of RF pulses, sent to pulse receiver of a NMR scanner

Figure 4 Simple demonstration of a NMR spectroscopy

N-51

NUCLEAR MAGNETIC RESONANCE SPECTROSCOPY

As one kind of spectroscopies, nuclear magnetic resonance spectroscopy (NMR spectroscopy) is a technique that uses the properties of nuclear magnetic resonance (NMR). NMR spectroscopy has many applications. It can study, for example, the energy (E) of electrons in different electron shells of an atom to determine in what shell an electron is acting at a certain time, as Bohr used while developing his atomic model. It is also used in astronomy to determine the light's spectral lines coming from stars. [Light is our only means of studying faraway stars.]

[Note: The basics of NMR spectroscopy and its simple graphical demonstration are given under NUCLEAR MAGNETIC RESONANCE AND MAGNETIC RESONANCE IMAGING.]

N-52

NUCLEAR MASS DEFECT

Another name for NUCLEAR DEFECT MASS.

N-53

NUCLEAR MASS EXCESS

Another name for EXCESS NUCLEAR EXCESS.

N-54

NUCLEAR MEDICINE

Nuclear medicine is a medical specialty involved with the application of radioactive elements (nuclides) in the **diagnosis** and **therapy** of different diseases, including some types of cancers, heart diseases, and gastrointestinal conditions. The nuclides used in nuclear medicine are called **tracers** (radiotracers). The dose of a tracer used in nuclear medicine is extremely small.

In traditional medicine, oral medication (called a **tracer**) passes through the digestive system and enters the bloodstream. It is then transported to the relevant location in the body (say, a bacterial infection). There, the tracer bonds chemically to a receptor. In nuclear medicine, the tracer is carried directly by a **special chemical** to a particular organ in the body. Therefore, the tracer travels only a short distance, minimizing damage to noninvolved organs and unwanted side effects. The other advantages of nuclear medicine over traditional medicine are the following:

- It uses fewer doses,
- It is more accurate,
- It is less expensive,
- It has fewer side effects,
- It has fewer allergic reactions, and
- It acts from inside the body toward the outside.

The most important applications of nuclear medicine are:

- **Medical Imaging:** This technique is used for the diagnosis of internal disorders. To produce a nuclear image, first, a small (but measurable amount) of a tracer, such as sodium iodide (NaI), which contains the radioactive element iodine-131, is injected into the patient's bloodstream. The tracer's radiation is traced through the body with a detector (like a gamma camera) and developed to produce an image. Nuclear images give physicians molecular information to recognize the patients' medical conditions. Nuclear images work well because the tracer's path is from inside the body outward. In addition, the tracer acts based on its chemical properties but *not* its nuclear radioactivity. In traditional medicine, in contrast, radiation (such as X-rays) is applied from outside to pass through the body to form an image.
- **Medical Therapy:** For patient treatment, the tracer doses are taken orally, intravenously, or by inhalation of a gas. But the tracer is carried, by a special carrier chemical, to a particular type of organ in the body. The tracer's location can be followed by its released radiation (energy in the form of gamma rays). The amount taken by the body can be measured with a radiation detector.

N-55

NUCLEAR PHYSICS

As a branch (subfield) of classical physics (CP) and quantum physics (QP), nuclear physics (NP) mainly deals with the atomic nucleus and its nuclear energy (E_N), the complicated subjects that have been under study and research for many years. The NP had started with the discovery of the nuclear fission process (1938) and nuclear fusion process (1939) and established itself when the first atomic bomb successfully exploded in Hiroshima in August 1945.

Before studying the rest of this topic, it is helpful to study the next Note.

[Note: Nuclear physics and nuclear chemistry are somewhat similar, particularly those given in this book. Thus, **nuclear topics**, such as nuclear reactions or nuclear decay, can be used in both fields.]

Other applications of NP include the following:

- Nuclides and their Properties
- Nuclear Chain Reactions
- Nuclear Power Plants
- Nuclear Processes
- Nuclear Medicine
- Nuclear Emission
- Nuclear Decay
- Nuclear Waste
- Nuclear Fuels
- Nuclear weapons

[All these, and more, topics are discussed in this book.]

N-56

NUCLEAR POWER PLANT

A nuclear power plant is a facility that uses nuclear fuel and a nuclear fission process to produce electric power (P_E, simply **power** or **electricity**). Although it is more difficult to run a nuclear power plant than a fossil power plant, the way of generating electricity in those plants is almost the same. The main differences are the following:

- **Type and Amount of Fuel:** The amount of fuel used in a nuclear plant is much less than in a fossil-fuel power plant. 1 kg of low-enriched uranium, consisting of 3 to 5% uranium-235 (U-235) and 95 to 97% uranium-238 (U-238), yields more electricity than 30 carloads of coal.
- **Operability:** The way the water is heated to produce pressurized steam in a nuclear plant is different from in a fossil-fuel plant. In a fossil-fuel plant, water is heated in steam boilers to produce high-pressure steam, then used to drive the steam turbines to generate electricity. Nuclear plants use the heat created by nuclear fission to heat the water.
- **Cleanness:** Nuclear fuels are clean.

As the nucleus of a nuclide splits during a fission chain reaction, the following are released:

- Nuclear energy (E_N, the energy in the nucleus of an atom),
- Heat energy (E_Q, the energy in transfer), and
- Radioactive radiation (simply **radiation**).

A typical nuclear power plant mainly consists of 1) Nuclear reactor, 2) Steam pressurizer, 3) Steam turbine, 4) Electric generator, 5) Condenser, and 6) Cooling tower.

The released E_Q in the reactor of a nuclear plant heats the cooling water of the nuclear reactor to produce steam, which goes to a steam-pressure regulator. From this point on, generating electricity is the same as in a fossil-fuel power plant. That is to say that the pressurized steam goes to a steam turbine to drive its shaft, which drives a steam generator to produce electricity (Figure 1).

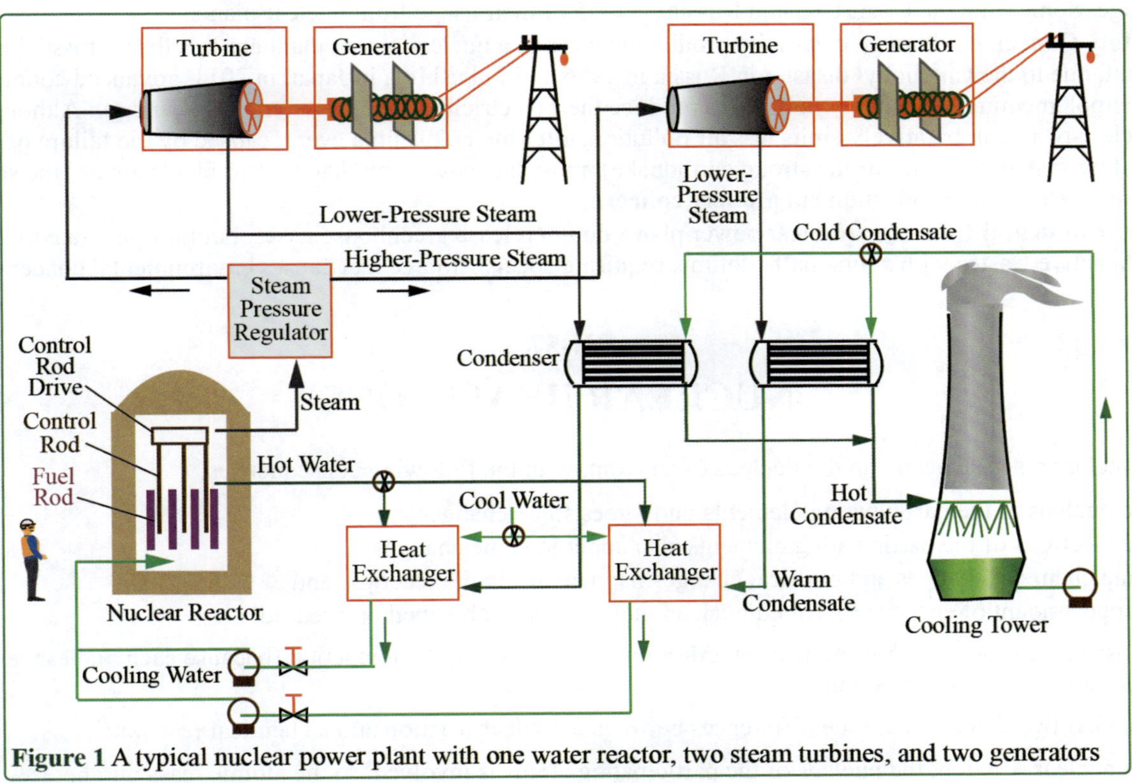

Figure 1 A typical nuclear power plant with one water reactor, two steam turbines, and two generators

A nuclear reactor mainly consists of the following three (3) elements:

- **Control Rods:** The rods are grouped by the hundreds in bundles. Each rod, which has a diameter of 1 to 2 cm and a height of about 4 m, has several cylindrical fuel pellets of nuclear fuel. [The rods' material is a neutron-absorbing element (usually cadmium or boron).]
- **Fuel Rods:** Fuel rods are the place for nuclear fuel, usually low-enriched uranium, consisting of 3 to 5% U-235 and 95 to 97% U-238. This ratio prevents extreme explosion, like that in a nuclear weapon. The explosion rate also depends on the number of neutrons available in the rods to initiate the fission process.
- **Cooling Water System:** Mostly, water (in some cases air) is used as the carrier of E_Q created by the fission process in the nuclear reactor. The hot water surrounding the fuel rods is kept under a high pressure (P) to keep it at a high temperature (T) without boiling.

Some important information about nuclear power plants is outlined next.

- **Power Production:** A typical coal-fired power plant produces about 500 megawatts per hour (MW/h) of electricity. A typical nuclear power plant can produce about 1500 MW/h of electricity, while a typical hydroelectric dam produces electricity at 10 000 MW/h.
- **Number of Power Plants:** As of 2014, according to the IAEA (the International Atomic Energy Agency), 450 nuclear power plants are in operation in 31 countries, with a total production capacity of about 370 000 MW/h. This is about 11.5% of global electricity production. And about 71 nuclear power plants are under construction (including 5 in the USA). France gets three-quarters of its electricity from nuclear energy. Some countries (like Belgium, Czech Republic, Sweden, and Switzerland) get around one-third of their electricity usage. Some (like the USA, UK, and Russia) get 1/5 of their usage from nuclear plants.
- **Safety Concern:** Although electricity production costs in a nuclear power plant are less than a fossil-fuel plant, due to the Chernobyl disaster in Russia in 1986 and Fukushima in Japan in 2011, advanced countries are implementing new energy policies to produce their electricity usage from renewable energy. Although a nuclear plant comparatively emits less air pollution, after the Fukushima event, caused by the failure of the cooling system (because of the strong earthquake), most Japanese think that nuclear plants are *not* the **solutions** to electricity production but a **safety concern**.
- **Environmental Concern:** Nuclear power plants do *not* release greenhouse gases, but they generate toxic radioactive wastes with a long half-lifetime, requiring special storage that causes environmental concerns.

N-57

NUCLEAR REACTIONS

A nuclear reaction occurs in the nucleus of an atom, with the following consequences:

- The nucleus of the participating elements undergoes some changes,
- The electrons of the participating elements also undergo some changes,
- Some chemical changes and physical changes happen during the reaction, and
- A huge amount of energy (E), called nuclear energy (E_N), is absorbed or released.

[Most of the time, the term **nuclear reaction** refers to a nuclear chain reaction (because each nuclear reaction causes more subsequent reactions.)]

The next two dotes explain the differences between a nuclear reaction and a chemical reaction:

- In a nuclear reaction, the nucleus of the participating atoms is involved, so the atomic mass number (N_A, the number of protons and neutrons) of the atoms changes to form new atoms of different N_A. In a chemical reaction, the nucleus of the participating atoms is *not* involved in the reaction, and the atoms' electrons are the only ones involved, so the atoms' N_A does *not* change.

- In a nuclear reaction, many million times more E per reaction is released than in an energy-releasing chemical reaction.

Nuclear reactions are of two (2) types:

- Nuclear Fission: During fission, a large nucleus absorbs a neutron and splits into smaller fragments. Fission occurs only on heavier elements (the elements heavier than iron, Fe) to produce heavier elements.
- Nuclear Fusion: During fusion, small nuclei join to form a larger nucleus. Unlike fission, fusion needs extreme conditions (high pressure and temperature) to form heavier elements from elements (lighter than Fe).

Nuclear Chain Reactions: A nuclear chain reaction is a series of complex **nuclear reactions** occurring when a nuclear reaction causes subsequent reactions. So, a chain nuclear reaction is a self-sustaining series of nuclear reactions. [Most of the time, the term **nuclear reaction** refers to the **nuclear chain reaction** because each nuclear reaction causes more subsequent reactions.]

Consider a typical nuclear power plant. Nuclear fuel in the reactor of the plant causes many nuclear reactions. During this so-called **chain nuclear reaction**, uranium-238 (U-238) and uranium-235 (U-235) undergo nuclear fission. During the fission process, some minor changes occur in the nucleus of U-238, but the changes occurring in the nucleus of U-235 are a lot. As a result of changes in the U-235, some E_N in the form of E_Q (heat energy) is released. According to Einstein's equation ($E = M.c^2$), the released energy equates to the amount of nuclear excess mass of the U-235 because E and M are equivalent.

[Note: The discovery of nuclear chain reactions contributed to creating atomic bombs and nuclear reactors.]

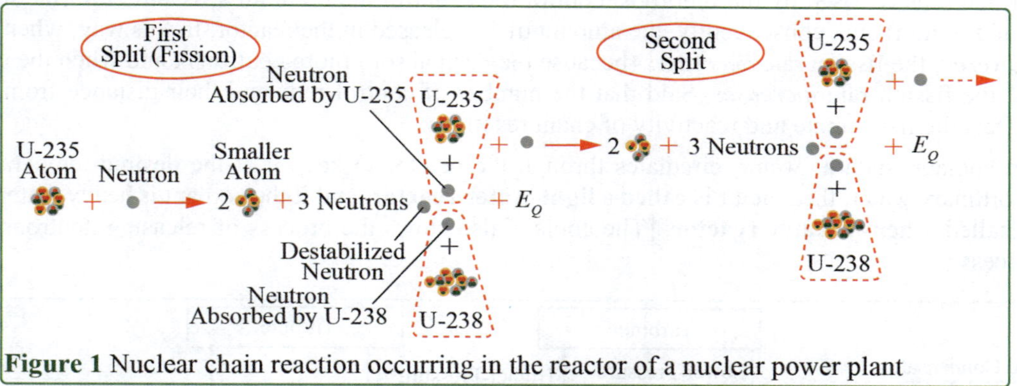

Figure 1 Nuclear chain reaction occurring in the reactor of a nuclear power plant

Consider a reactor with many (in trillions) of U-235 atoms and assume that one of them is under our study for a **chain nuclear reaction**. We can then summarize this process in the following ways (see Figure 1):

- A U-235 atom absorbs a neutron, and its nucleus splits (fissions) into 2 smaller nuclei (called **fission fragments**) and releases 2 or 3 neutrons and some amount of E_{NB} (nuclear energy).
- If 3 neutrons are released, one leaves the system without being absorbed, so it becomes destabilized. The other neutron becomes absorbed by a U-238 atom. And the third one hits a U-235 atom and splits it into 2 new smaller nuclei, releasing 3 new neutrons and more E_{NB}.
- Each new neutron hits a U-235 atom and splits its atom the same way explained.
- Releasing-and-absorbing neutrons, splitting U-235 atoms, and releasing the E_{NB} keep continuing.

NUCLEAR REACTORS

A nuclear reactor (also called **nuclear fission reactor**) is a large device (equipment) with complicated auxiliaries (attached and detached parts) that is used in a nuclear power plant for producing nuclear energy (E_N). A reactor's main function is to control the self-sustained nuclear chain reactions of nuclear fuel, such as U-235 or Pu-239, used in that reactor. Typically, nuclear reactors use a mix of 3% U-235 and 97% U-238 to produce E_N in the form of E_Q (heat energy), which is then used in turbines to generate electric power (simply **power** or **electricity**), as shown in Figure 1.

A nuclear reactor acts as a steam boiler to produce steam, with enough E_Q to run the turbines. The main difference is in the amount of fuel used. In this way, 1 kg of U-235 generates approximately 3 million times more E_Q than 1 kg of coal.

Nuclear power plants usually use the nuclear fission process as one of their two choices (the other one is the nuclear fusion process). Here a typical reactor, which uses a fission process and the mix of U-235 and U-238 as its fuel, is described. The split of U-235 starts by absorbing a neutron to become U-236. Then the U-236 splits into smaller nuclei to produce E_N. [The control of released neutrons in a reactor is important.]

A reactor's main parts are **fuel rods** and **control rods** (see Figure 1). Control rods, which are installed between the fuel rods, are made of boron (B) or cadmium (Cd) because these elements can easily absorb many neutrons. Each fuel rod is filled with solid-rod fuel, which goes through the chain reactions. By absorbing the desired number of neutrons released by the fuel rods, control rods control the uranium's **fission rate** (the rate of chain reactions of uranium) and, consequently, the amount of E_Q released in the reactor. In this way, when the control rods are *lowered*, the fission rate *decreases* (because they can absorb more neutrons), and when the control rods are *raised*, the fission rate *increases*. Said that the number of control rods and their distance from each other strongly affect the fission rate and reactivity of chain reactions.

A liquid coolant, such as water, circulates through the reactor to keep it at the desired temperature. If the coolant is ordinary water, the reactor is called a **light-water reactor**, and if the coolant is heavy water (D_2O), the reactor is called a **heavy-water reactor**. [The coolant also slows the process of releasing neutrons during the fission process.]

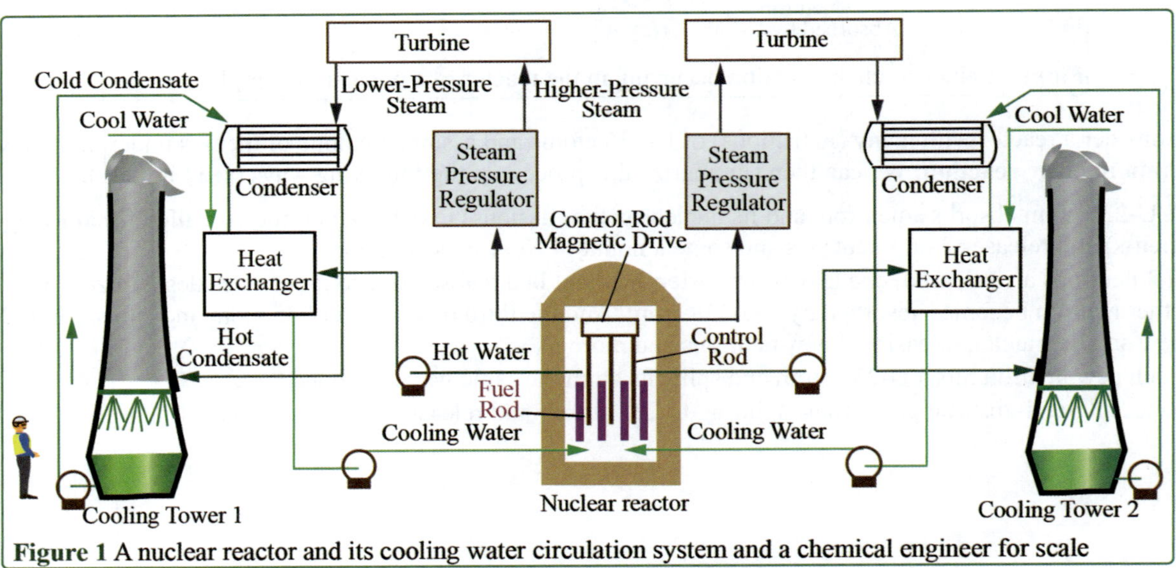

Figure 1 A nuclear reactor and its cooling water circulation system and a chemical engineer for scale

The following are some basic must-know brief points about nuclear reactors:

- They are built in a dome-shaped containment structure that prevents the release of radioactive elements in the event of an accident.
- The control rods fall instantly, under gravity, into the fuel pile to stop the chain reaction in the event of power failure.
- The fuel rods get exhausted after some operations. The exhausted rods are still highly radioactive, so they must be stored and recycled safely.
- They do *not* create an explosion like that of a nuclear bomb (because the U-235 atoms are greatly diluted with U-238 atoms), while the content of U-235 is much higher (above 80%) in a nuclear bomb, so the fuel is less diluted.
- As of 2014, according to the IAEA (the International Atomic Energy Agency), 450 nuclear power plants are in operation in 31 countries.

N-59

NUCLEAR WASTES

Another name for RADIOACTIVE WASTES.

N-60

NUCLEAR WEAPONS

A nuclear weapon acts based on nuclear chain reactions (like those that occur during nuclear fission, nuclear fusion, or a combination of both). All three cases cause a huge explosion (typically expressed in kilo tones), which releases a lot of nuclear energy (E_E) in the form of heat energy (E_Q). The explosion also creates a high temperature (T). [While nuclear power plants can use uranium with 4 to 40% uranium 235 (U-235), nuclear weapons need uranium with at least 80% U-235, so a complicated uranium enrichment process is needed to *increase* the purity of the U-238 before it can be used to produce a nuclear weapon.]

Atomic Bomb: Figure 1 shows a simplified drawing of a **uranium atomic bomb** (also called **uranium fission bomb**), in which a highly-enriched U-235 or a mixture of U-235 and Pu-239 (plutonium-239) is used as nuclear fuel (in this case called the **fissile fuel**). In a typical uranium atomic bomb (see the same figure), two small pieces of U-235 are used, each having a mass (M) smaller than nuclear critical mass (M_{NC}, simply **critical mass**). Thus, each piece has a **subcritical mass**. The reason for using two pieces with subcritical masses is that the total surface area of two smaller pieces is greater than that of just one larger piece, so the neutrons escape through the surface of each small piece before a sustained chain reaction can occur.

If now (at the right time), the two fuel pieces are suddenly pushed together in the bomb's barrel by a small explosive, a nuclear excess mass (a mass greater than the nuclear critical mass) is formed, so the bomb explodes violently. Thus, three cases can occur:

- If a supercritical M of nuclear fuel is used, the reactions are self-sustaining, and the bomb will explode.
- If the M of the fuel is less than the critical M of fuel, too many neutrons escape during the chain reaction, so the reaction becomes non-self-sustaining, and the bomb will *not* explode.
- If the M of fuel equates to the critical M of fuel, the reaction may be (or may *not* be) self-sustaining, and the bomb will (or will *not*) explode.

[Note 1: In the first atomic bomb (the Fat Man), dropped on Hiroshima in August 1945, the excess mass (supercritical mass) of the fuel was produced by the **gun method** (shooting one subcritical mass into another). [**Excess mass** (refers to nuclear excess mass) is a mass (M) greater than the critical mass (refers to nuclear critical mass), which is the minimum M needed to sustain a nuclear chain reaction.]

[Note 2: Constructing a fission bomb is difficult because enough U-235 must be enriched from the abundant U-238. It took more than two years to prepare enough U-235 to build the bomb used in Hiroshima in 1945.]

Hydrogen Bomb: In producing a hydrogen bomb, a hydrogenous substance, such as deuterium (D), lithium deuteride (Li_6H_2 or Li_6D), is used. The first hydrogen bomb was tested in 1952, releasing energy equivalent to 10.4 megatons of TNT, a large amount of energy.

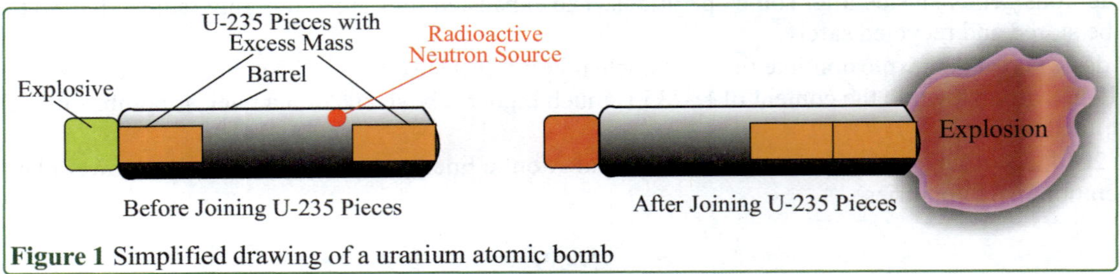

Figure 1 Simplified drawing of a uranium atomic bomb

N-61

NUCLEON AND NUCLEON NUMBER

The term **nucleon** is used in physics and chemistry as a collective name for proton and neutron in the nucleus of an atom. Thus, a nucleon is surrounded by one (or more) electrons.

A **nucleon number** is the total number of protons and neutrons in the nucleus of an atom. Remember the following two (2) helpful brief points:

- The number of protons in the nucleus of an atom is called the atomic number (N_Z), that of neutrons is called **neutron number** (N_N), and the collective name for protons and neutrons is called the nucleon.
- The term **nucleon number** sometimes is used instead of more common name atomic mass number (N_A), where $N_A = N_Z + N_N$. According to this equation, the N_A of hydrogen (H) becomes 1 + 0 = 1; for oxygen (O), 8 + 8 = 16; for carbon (C), 6 + 6 =12; and for uranium-238 (U-238), the N_A becomes 92 + 146 = 238.

N-62

NUCLIDES

Another name for RADIOACTIVE ELEMENTS.

N-63

NUMBER OF DEGREES OF FREEDOM

Discussed under PHASE RULE.

N-64

NUMBER OF DISTILLATION PLATES

Discussed in the subtopic of Theory of Distillation Plates under DISTILLATION PROCESS.

N-65

NUSSELT NUMBER

Nusselt number (N_N, where N is for number and subscript N is for Nusselt) is a unitless number used to express the ratio of **convective heat transfer** to **conductive heat transfer** across a boundary of a heat transfer system. So, the $N_N = 1$ indicates heat convection and heat conduction of a similar quantity. [**Convective heat transfer** and **conductive heat transfer** are discussed under HEAT TRANSFER PROCESS.]

N_N considers three quantities that affect the heat transfer process in, for instance, a pipe. These quantities are heat transfer coefficient (U_Q, in W/h.m^2.°C), inside pipe's diameter (d, in m), and thermal conductivity (K_{Th}, in W/h.m.°C).

$$N_N = \frac{U_Q.d}{K_{Th}} \quad (1)$$

O Section

LIST OF TOPICS

1. Octane Rating
2. Odor
3. Ohm
4. Ohm Law
5. Oil
6. Opacity
7. Open, Closed, and Isolated Systems
8. Organic and Inorganic Compounds
9. Orifice Flowmeter
10. OSHA
11. Osmosis and Reverse Osmosis Processes
12. Osmotic Pressure
13. Overall Heat Transfer Coefficient
14. Oxidants
15. Oxidation Reactions
16. Oxidation-Reduction Reactions
17. Oxidation State
18. Oxidizing Agents
19. Oxygen
20. Ozone and Ozone-Depleting Compounds

O-1

OCTANE RATING

Octane rating is a quantity used in the USA to evaluate the combustive strength of a gasoline (C_8H_{18}, a fuel) or other combustive engine fuels (like ethanol). [In Europe, the **RON** (research octane number) system is used.] In the USA, an octane number of 100 is arbitrarily assigned to *iso*-octane, and zero is assigned to *n*-hexane. The performance of a gasoline is then compared with various mixtures of these two compounds, and an octane number is assigned for that gasoline. In the USA, the octane rating of regular gasoline is 86 (= 95 RON), that of super gasoline is 91, and that of ethanol is 108. This tells us that the *greater* a gasoline octane rating, the *more* compression it withstands before ignition temperature (T_{Ig}). [Note that the octane rating is *not* an indication of the energy content of a fuel.]

O-2

ODOR

The word **odor** generally refers to a noticeable unpleasant smell. Many receptors are at the back of the nasal cavity in humans and animals for feeling the odors. The receptors are in direct contact with the air that contains the odor. [The words **fragrance** and **aroma** are, instead, used by the food and cosmetic industries to describe a pleasant odor. By this definition, the odor is the pleasant and unpleasant smells.]

It is difficult to deal with odor-related air pollutants because odor formation and reactions are too complex to indicate with simple chemical equations. In chemical process plants, volatile organic compounds and hydrogen sulfide (H_2S) are the main sources of unpleasant odor.

O-3

OHM AND OHM'S LAW

Ohm: As the SI unit of electric resistance (R_E), the Ohm (Ω, omega), which is named after German physicist George Ohm (1789–1854), is defined as the R_E between two points of an electric conductor. 1 Ω = 1/S = 1 V/A = 1 W/h.A^2 = 1 V^2.h/W, where S is for Siemens, V is for Volt (the SI unit of), A is for Ampere (the SI unit of electric current, W is for Watt, h for hour, and W/h (the SI unit of electric power).

Ohm's Law: Ohm's Law, which is the relation between electric current (I_E, simply **current**), electric voltage (V_E, simply **voltage**), and electric resistance (R_E), states that the current that passes through an electric conductor (simply **conductor**) between two points is directly proportional to the V_E across those points through a proportionality constant, named the electric resistance (R_E), as simply illustrated in Figure 1. Formulizing this expression gives Ohm's equation.

$$I_E = \frac{V_E}{R_E} \tag{1}$$

In this equation, I (the current through the conductor) is in Ampere (A), V_E (the voltage measured across the conductor) is in Volt (V), and R_E (the conductor's resistance) is in Ohm (Ω).

Some show the parameters of Ohm's equation in a triangle (see Figure 1), in which the line that divides the left and right sections indicates multiplication. The divider in the middle indicates the division.

Some materials are **ohmic** (obey Ohm's Law to be conductive), while others are **non-ohmic**.

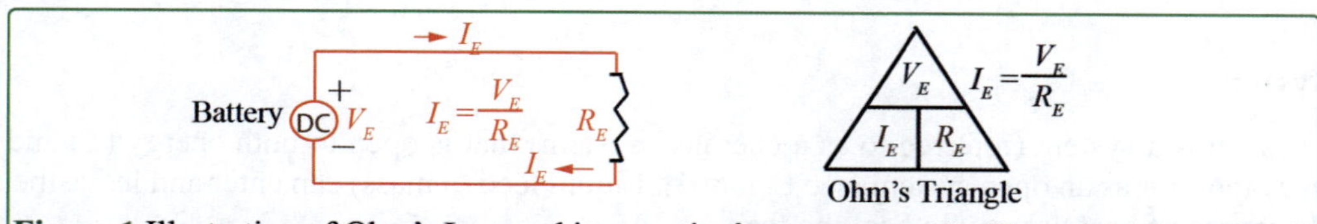

Figure 1 Illustration of Ohm's Law and its equation's parameters (I_E, V_E, and R_E) in a triangle

O-4

OHM'S LAW

Study OHM AND OHM'S LAW.

O-5

OILS

Oil is a nonpolar compound that is composed mainly of hydrocarbons. Oils are hydrophobic (they do *not* mix with water) and lipophilic (they mix with other oils). They are usually flammable and surface-active (they are surfactants, they lower the surface tension between two liquids).

[Note: The word **oil** (in the singular) is used as a simplified name for **fuel oil**, discussed under CRUDE OIL AND FUEL OIL.]

O-6

OPACITY

As a physical property, opacity is the haziness ability of a medium. It is used in the environmental field to express an opaque medium's intensity. Stack flue gas consisting of particulate matter (PM) in the air is an example for an opaque medium. Opacity partially prevents the spread of the light.

O-7

OPEN, CLOSED, AND ISOLATED SYSTEMS

Figures 1, 2, and 3 illustrate the main differences between open, closed, and isolated systems. These differences are particularly important when a mass balance or energy balance is performed on a system. Remembering the following three (3) general points about systems is helpful:

- Open systems are *not* limited to process control (automation), while closed systems and isolated systems are. For this reason, chemical engineers mostly concentrate on balancing the open systems.
- Open systems, by definition, characterize continuous processes because of continuous entering and leaving both M and E to and from them. In contrast, batch processes fall into closed systems (because of constant mass during a batch process operation).
- Most of the systems (small or large) dealt with in ChemEng are open systems. [Physicists consider all systems as open systems because of Einstein's equation ($E = M.c^2$). Any E that enters a system carries a certain amount of M. And we know that this property characterizes an open system (both M and E can enter an open system.)]

Open Systems

An open system is a system (referred to as a chemical system) that is open to both energy (E) and mass (M). Consider an evaporator as an open system (see Figure 4). Liquid feed (a mass) can enter and leave the evaporator and steam (a source of heat energy) to heat the feed.

Open systems can be grouped into the following two classes:

- **Steady Open System:** In such a system, the amount of feed (or feeds) entering the system (such as a tank or reactor) equates to the product (or products) leaving the system, as shown in Figure 5. As the result of an equal amount of flow-in and flow-out, the amount of feed in the system remains unchanged with time (t); in other words, *no* **accumulation** occurs in the system. Because the amount of the material in the system does *not* change with time, the system under study is a **steady-state system** (simply a **steady system**), and the process in the system is steady. And because mass flows to the system and out of the system are the same, all the process conditions (like temperature and pressure) remain constant (unchanged) with time.

- **Unsteady Open System:** In such a system, the amount of feed (or feeds) entering the system is *not* equal to the product (or products) leaving the system. Figure 6 shows the initial condition of a tank for storing water. Assume that water enters the tank at a constant rate of 50 kg/min and leaves it at 40 kg/min, so it accumulates at the rate of 10 kg/min (= 50 – 40 = 10 kg/min). Because the amount of water in the tank changes with time, the system is **unsteady,** and the process in the tank is unsteady. And because the mass flows to and out of the tank are *not* the same, *not* all the process conditions remain constant.

Positive Accumulation

Figure 7 shows the tank after 50 minutes of 10 kg/min positive accumulation. This makes 500 kg more accumulation, so the amount of water in the tank after 50 more min is 1000 kg. Comparing Figure 6 with Figure 7, we find that a **positive accumulation** exists in the tank (because the amount of water in the tank increases with time at 10 kg/min).

Negative Accumulation

If now changing the amount of water in the tank to 40 kg/min and leave the tank at 50 kg/min, we will face a **negative accumulation** in the tank (because the amount of water in the tank decreases with time at a rate of 10 kg/min). Figure 8 shows an unsteady open system after 50 minutes of negative (–) accumulation.

Now we can generalize the rules of steady and unsteady systems to obtain a simple-but-important equation, which is used in mass balance calculations for a single-component process.

Accumulation in a system = Flow rate into the system – Flow rate out of the system

$$M_{Ac} = \dot{M}_{In} - \dot{M}_{Out} \tag{1}$$

In this equation, $\dot{M}$ is the mass flow rate (M per unit of t).

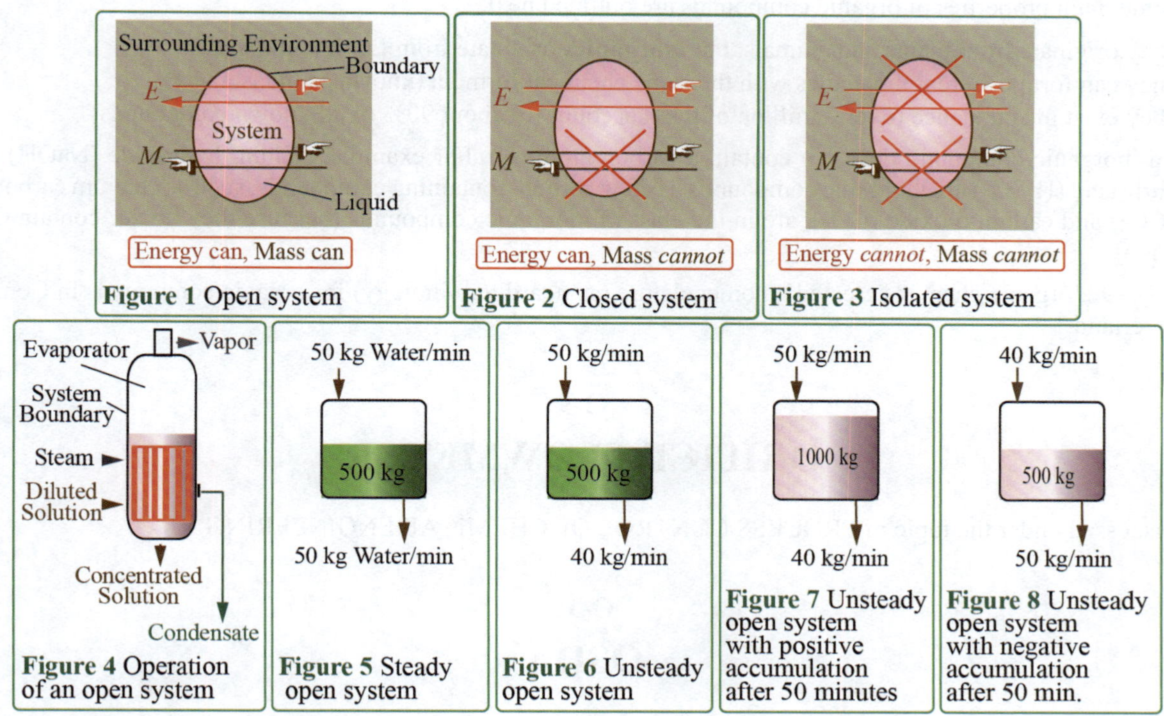

Figure 1 Open system

Figure 2 Closed system

Figure 3 Isolated system

Figure 4 Operation of an open system

Figure 5 Steady open system

Figure 6 Unsteady open system

Figure 7 Unsteady open system with positive accumulation after 50 minutes

Figure 8 Unsteady open system with negative accumulation after 50 min.

Closed Systems

A closed system (refers to the chemical system) is open to E but is closed to M. It is also defined as a fixed system with *no* streams entering or leaving it. Consider a closed tank containing a warm liquid.

Mass *cannot* enter or leave through the wall (the boundary) of the tank (the system), but energy can be transferred (absorbed or released) through the tank's wall as heat energy (E_Q, simply heat). A batch process, by this definition, falls into the group of closed systems because of constant mass ($\Delta M = 0$) during the operation of such a process. [No system can be considered completely closed because it *cannot* be perfectly separated from its surroundings (outsides). Also, we know that because of the relation of E and M as $E = M.c^2$, when E enters a system carries a certain amount of M, so scientists consider **near-to-perfect closed systems.**]

Isolated Systems

An isolated system is closed to both E and M, as shown in Figure 3.

O-8

ORGANIC AND INORGANIC COMPOUNDS

An organic compound (also called **organic**) is made of carbon atoms (C), bonded (connected) to each other, and atoms of other elements. For example, hydrocarbons consist of carbon and hydrogen atoms. Sugar ($C_{12}H_{22}O_{11}$), an organic compound and hydrocarbon, consists of carbon atoms bonded to oxygen and hydrogen atoms. Acetone (CH_3CH_3CO), methanol (CH_3OH), and ethanol (C_2H_5OH) are organic compounds, too. Most organic compounds are nonpolar compounds.

Some main properties of organic compounds are outlined next.

- They originate from plants and animals, but **inorganics** originate from Earth's minerals.
- They can form different molecules with the same chemical formula (known as the isomers).
- They exist in abundance (over 7 million of them account for about 90% of all known compounds).

An inorganic compound does *not* contain a carbon atom (C). For example, sodium hydroxide (NaOH) and sulfuric acid (H_2SO_4) are inorganic compounds. [A few carbon-containing compounds, such as calcium carbonate ($CaCO_3$) and carbon dioxide (CO_2), are in the class of inorganic compounds (because they do *not* contain C–H bonds.)]

[In 1892, organic chemists created a nomenclature (standard terminology) for organic compounds in Geneva, Switzerland.]

O-9

ORIFICE FLOWMETER

Discussed under the topic of PROCESS CONTROL OF CHEMICAL ENGINEERING.

O-10

OSHA

OSHA (Occupational Safety and Health Administration) is a US governmental organization responsible for ensuring that each employer has a safe working environment for its workers. OSHA has many responsibilities, including investigations of work-related injuries, illnesses, and fatalities. OSHA also prepares the rate of injuries, illnesses, and fatalities for a fixed number of workers per certain time (usually per year).

The OSHA incidence rate (R_{OI}) is calculated from the number of injuries per year (N_I) and the total facility's number of hours worked by all employees per year (N_T) as

$$R_{OI} = \frac{N_I}{N_T} \times 200000 \quad (1)$$

The value 200 000 is calculated as follows. The number of incidences is usually based on cases per 100 work years. A **work year** has 2 000 hours, calculated as 50 workweeks × 40 hours/week. The R_{OI}, therefore, will be based on 100 × 2 000 = 200 000 work years.

The same equation can calculate the R_{OI} based on **lost workdays**. Instead of N_I (number of injuries), the term **number of lost workdays** is also used.

O-11

OSMOSIS AND REVERSE OSMOSIS PROCESSES

As two process units of ChemEng, osmosis and reverse osmosis are special diffusion processes that are used to separate a solvent (mostly water) from its solutes (dissolved particles) through a semipermeable membrane (later **SP membrane**). An SP membrane is **permeable** to the solvent with smaller molecules but nearly **impermeable** to the solute, which has larger molecules. Under atmospheric pressure (P_{Atm}), the solute molecules move (scientifically **diffuse**) from an area of higher concentration (C) to areas of lower C. [For simplicity, it is better to name the side with lower solute C "side 1" and the side with higher C "side 2".]

Osmosis Process

Osmosis uses an SP membrane with a microscopic pore size (0.1 to 1 nm, where 1 nm = 10^{-9} m) to diffuse the molecules from side 1 (the side with lower C) to side 2 (the side with higher C), as shown in Figure 1. In addition to water (a typical solvent), osmosis can occur in some non-water-based solutions.

Figure 1 illustrates a typical osmosis process at the start (A) and end (B) in a container with two compartments separated by an SP membrane. Side 1 contains a less concentrated salt (NaCl) solution, and side 2 is a more concentrated salt solution. Initially, both sides are at the same level, but the goal of osmosis is to decrease the volume (V) of the fresh water on side 1 and increase the V of the salt water on side 2, as shown in Figure 1B. The changes in V cause a buildup pressure, known as the osmotic pressure (P_O), which naturally occurs in side 1 (because of lower solute concentration there). Osmosis stops when side 2 becomes high enough in solvent molecules to exert sufficient P_O at the membrane to stop the net movement of the solvent's molecules. The solution on side 2 has become more dilute, but some differences in concentration between the two sides exist. But after a while, the level on side 1 drops. This occurs because the rate at which water molecules pass from side 1 to side 2 is greater than the rate at which they pass from side 2 to side 1. The reasons are given as

- Water prefers to contain solute molecules, if they are present, rather than to be in its pure state, and
- The P_O created during the process becomes greater than the atmospheric pressure (P_{Atm}).

However, the tendency of the diffusion process through the membrane decreases as the concentration difference (ΔC) in water molecules between two sides decreases. When the rate at which water molecules move from either side becomes equal, the diffusing action becomes stable (at equilibrium).

If an external pressure P greater than P_O is now applied on 2, the system becomes unstable again and starts to act as the reverse osmosis (RO), as seen in Figure 2. In RO, the external P does the next two functions:

- To overcome the P_O (osmotic P), which naturally occurred in side 1, and
- To force the water molecules from side 2 to side 1.

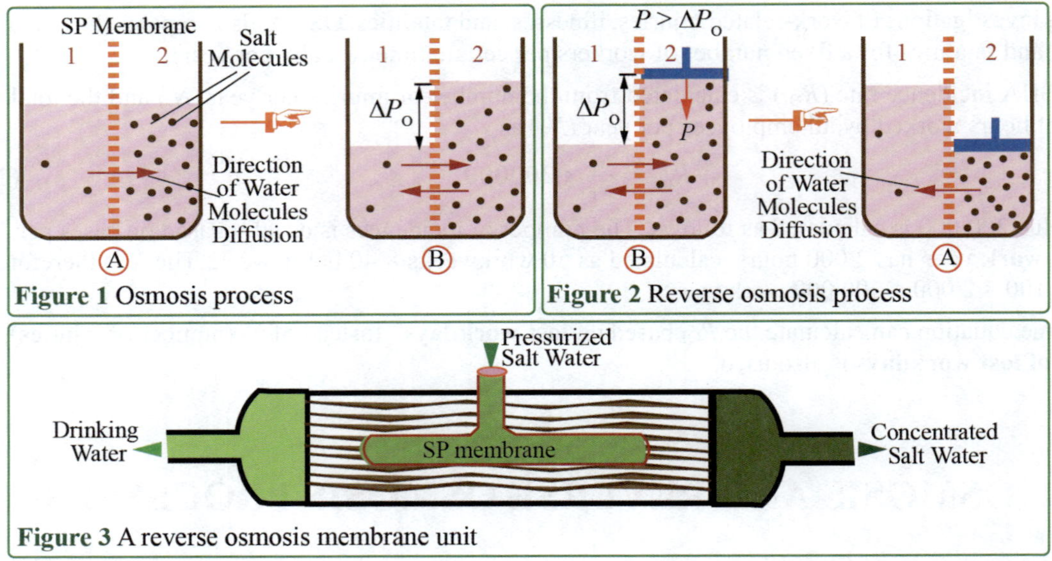

Figure 1 Osmosis process
Figure 2 Reverse osmosis process
Figure 3 A reverse osmosis membrane unit

Reverse Osmosis

In reverse osmosis (RO), a solvent's molecules diffuse through an SP membrane from side 2 to side 1 by applying an external *P*. Comparing this definition with osmosis; we realize that RO is the opposite of osmosis (because osmosis occurs from 1 to 2, but RO acts from 2 to 1). Some other differences between them are:

- RO is based on solute's concentration, while osmosis is based on solute's molecular size, and
- In RO, an external *P* is used to diffuse the molecules, while in osmosis, the diffusion occurs by P_O, which naturally occurs in 1 because of lower solute molecules in 1 than 2.

Today, reverse osmosis (RO) is the preferred method for producing drinking water from hard water or salty seawater, generally called the **water softening by RO**. The goal of the RO is to force the water molecules from side 2, where the level is higher, to side 1 (the lower level) to increase the drinking water's *V* in 1. This *cannot* happen unless an external *P* greater than P_O is applied on side 2 for two reasons:

- To overcome the P_O occurred naturally on side 1, and
- To force the water molecules from side 2 to side 1.

The desalting process is important because of a shortage of drinking water (about 98% of the World's water is salty). This process, which can remove up to 98% of salts in the seawater, currently supplies only about 0.1% of the drinking water because of its high operational costs. The energy demand of RO (about 3 kW/h per m^3 of water processed) is *not* as high as the evaporation process, which can also produce pure water.

[RO is also used in some labs to prepare **deionized water** (DI water) and in some households to improve the drinking water quality.]

Figure 3 simply illustrates an industrial RO unit. Industrially, many RO units, which operate parallelly, are used as a RO system to produce a lot of fresh water per day from salt water or hard water. [An RO unit needs regeneration with soft water when it is exhausted with minerals.]

O-12
OSMOTIC PRESSURE

Osmotic pressure (P_O) is the pressure (P) that occurs naturally in a region with a lower solute concentration (side 1), which is separated from a region with a higher solute concentration (side 2) by a **selective semipermeable membrane** (**permeable** to the molecules of solvent and **impermeable** to those of solute). The P_O occurs because the solute's molecules try to become equally concentrated on each membrane side.

To visualize a solution's P_O, consider a U-shaped tube with an equal amount of water on each side of a water-permeable membrane, placed in the middle of the tube, as shown in Figure 1. If we add a little bit (about half a teaspoon) of salt (NaCl) to the tube's right arm (side 2), the concentration of solute (NaCl) increases on that side. Because of the unequal concentration distribution of salt molecules on each side of the membrane, a P_O on the tube's left arm (side 1) occurs, forcing the water molecules to diffuse through the membrane into side 2 (the region with high solute concentration). The transfer of the solute molecules continues until osmotic stability (equilibrium) occurs on both sides. A process like this occurs in the osmosis process.

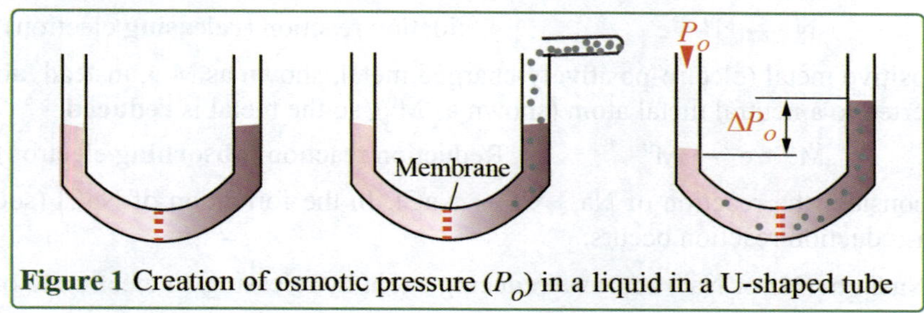

Figure 1 Creation of osmotic pressure (P_o) in a liquid in a U-shaped tube

O-13
OVERALL HEAT TRANSFER COEFFICIENT

Discussed under HEAT TRANSFER COEFFICIENT.

O-14
OXIDANTS

Another name for OXIDIZING AGENTS.

O-15
OXIDATION REACTIONS

Study OXIDATION-REDUCTION REACTIONS.

O-16

OXIDATION-REDUCTION REACTIONS

An oxidation-reduction reaction (simply **redox reaction**) is a two-part chemical reaction (simply **reaction**), which occurs at the same time by transfer (release or absorb) of electron (or more electrons) from one atom to another. The reactant that **releases** the electron is **oxidized**, and the one that **absorbs** the electron is **reduced**. An oxidation-reduction reaction consists of two reactions:

- **Oxidation Reaction:** Oxidation reaction (simply **oxidation**), which is the first half of the reaction, is the **release** of electron (e^-) by a reactant (or **increase** in the oxidation state of a reactant).
- **Reduction Reaction:** A reduction reaction (simply **reduction**), which is the second half of the reaction, is the **absorption** (gain) of an electron by another reactant (or **decrease** in the oxidation state of a reactant).

In the oxidation-reduction reaction of a nonmetal and metal, the electronegative nonmetal (the electro-negatively-charged nonmetal, shown as N^-) **releases** an electronegative electron to be converted to a neutral nonmetal atom (shown as N^0), so the nonmetal is **oxidized**.

$N^- \rightarrow N^0 + e^-$ Oxidation reaction (**releasing** electron)

And the electropositive metal (electro-positively-charged metal, shown as M^+), instead, **absorbs** the released electron to be converted to a neutral metal atom (shown as M^0), so the metal is **reduced**.

$M^+ + e^- \rightarrow M^0$ Reduction reaction (**absorbing** electron)

As an example, consider the reaction of Na + Cl → NaCl. In the formation of NaCl (sodium chloride), the following oxidation-reduction reaction occurs:

- **Oxidation:** The Na atom (Na or Na^0) acts as a reducing agent by releasing an electron to oxidize to sodium cation (Na^+).
- **Reduction:** The Cl atom (Cl or Cl^0) acts as an oxidizing agent by absorbing the released electron to become reduced to chlorine anion (Cl^-).

Thus, Na is the oxidized element (reducing agent), while Cl is the reduced element (oxidizing agent).

Combustion reactions, which involve oxygen (O_2, a strong oxidizing agent), are in the class of oxidation-reduction reactions. For example, the combustion of carbon (C) and hydrogen (H_2) in a fuel with O_2 from the air occurs in the following ways:

- **Oxidation:** C (the reducing agent) releases four (4) electrons to react with O_2 to form CO_2.
- **Reduction:** O_2 (the oxidizing agent) absorbs the electrons to react with H_2 to form H_2O.

$C + O_2 \rightarrow CO_2 + 4\,e^-$ Oxidation reaction

$2\,H_2 + O_2 + 4\,e^- \rightarrow 2\,H_2O$ Reduction reaction

Thus, C is the reducing agent (the oxidized element), while O is the oxidizing agent (the reduced element).

Rusting is also in the class of oxidation-reduction reactions. For example, rusting of iron (Fe) occurs as

- **Oxidation:** Fe (the reducing agent) releases one electron to be oxidized to iron cation (Fe^{2+}).
- **Reduction:** O_2 (the oxidizing agent) absorbs the electron to be reduced and reacts with H_2O to form a hydroxide anion (OH^-).

Then Fe^{2+} and OH^- combine to produce an iron hydroxide molecule [$Fe(OH)_2$], which reacts with OH^- to produce a rust molecule ($Fe_2O_3 .3H_2O$, iron oxide trihydrate).

$2\,Fe \rightarrow 2\,Fe^{2+} + 4\,e^-$ Oxidation reaction

$O_2 + 4\,e^- + 2\,H_2O \rightarrow 4\,OH^-$ Reduction reaction

$$2\,Fe^{2+} + 4\,OH^- \rightarrow 2\,Fe(OH)_2$$

$$2\ Fe(OH)_2 + 2\ OH^- \rightarrow Fe_2O_3.3H_2O$$

The listed reactions can be combined into one reaction.

$$4\ Fe + 3\ O_2 + 3\ H_2O \rightarrow 2\ Fe_2O_3\ .3\ H_2O$$

O-17

OXIDATION STATE

The oxidation state (OS, also called **oxidation number**) of an atom or ion is the number of oxidation (**release** of electron or electrons) or reduction (**absorb** of electron or electrons) of that atom or ion in an oxidation-reduction reaction. In such a reaction, the **increase** in OS of an atom (or ion) is called **oxidation**, and the **decrease** in OS of another atom is called **reduction**. Defined so, an OS can be positive, negative, or zero.

For simplicity, chemistry uses an ion's electric charge (q) as its OS. According to this close-to-reality assumption, chemistry recognizes the following oxidation states (OS) in the periodic table of elements:

- The OS of an element in a free form is 0; for example, the OS of Na is 0 (shown as Na^0).
- The OS of metals in group 1 of the periodic table is +1, and those in group 2 are +2.
- The OS of halogens (bromine, Br, chlorine, Cl, and fluorine, F) is – 1.

[The OS of hydrogen ion (H^+) is + 1 but becomes – 1 when bonded as a hydride to a metal.]

O-18

OXIDIZING AND REDUCING AGENTS

An **oxidizing agent** (also **oxidant**, **oxidizer**, or **electron absorber**) is a chemical substance that absorbs an electron (or more electrons) from a reducing agent in an oxidation-reduction reaction, so its oxidation state decreases. Oxygen (O_2), hydrogen peroxide (H_2O_2), and halogens (F, Cl, Br, and I) are common oxidants.

A **reducing agent** (also **reductant**, **reducer**, **electron releaser**, or **electron donor**) is a substance that releases an electron (or electrons) to an oxidizing agent during an oxidation-reduction reaction, so its oxidation state increases. For example, in the oxidation-reduction reaction of $Ca + Cl_2 \rightarrow CaCl_2$, the calcium atom ($Ca^0$) acts as a reducing agent by releasing two electrons to be oxidized to calcium cation (Ca^+). Instead, the Cl atom (Cl^0) acts as an oxidizing agent by absorbing the released electrons to be reduced to chlorine anion (Cl^-). Thus, Ca is the oxidized element (reducing agent), while Cl is the reduced element (oxidizing agent).

O-19

OXYGEN

Oxygen (O) is a chemical element in group 16 and period 2 of the periodic table of elements. Its atomic mass number (the total number of protons and neutrons) is 16, and its atomic number (the total number of protons) is 8, so it has 8 neutrons (that is 16 – 8 = 8). Its atomic mass (M_A, the actual mass of one atom of an element) is 16 AMU (simply 16 g), and its molar mass (M_n) is 16 g/mole.

Under normal conditions, two oxygen atoms bind to form **molecular oxygen** (O_2; also called **dioxygen**), as shown on the left side of Figure 1. Molecular oxygen can combine with hydrogen to form H_2O (water), as shown on the right side of the same figure.

Molecular oxygen (O_2) is a colorless, odorless, and highly flammable gas that an adult human at rest inhales about 2 g per minute (for free!). It is a cryogenic gas with a boiling point temperature (T_{BP}) of − 219ºC. Listed next are some other properties of molecular oxygen (O_2):

- It remarkably participates in the photosynthetic process,
- It dissolves more readily in water than nitrogen,
- It forms 21% (by volume) of atmospheric air,
- Its condenses at 90ºC and freezes at − 219ºC,
- Its specific gas constant is 260 J/(kg.ºC),
- Its electronegativity (E_{Neg}) is 3.5,
- Its molecular mass (M_M) is 14,
- It is a nonpolar molecule.

The solubility of oxygen in water depends on temperature (T), and roughly twice as much (14.6 mg/L) dissolves at 0ºC than at 20ºC (7.2 mg/L). At 25ºC and P_{Atm} (atmospheric pressure), 1 L of water contains about 6 mL of O_2, while its solubility increases to 9 mL/L at 5ºC and the same P (pressure).

Naturally-occurring oxygen consists of three (3) isotopes, O^{16}, O^{17}, and O^{18}, where O^{16} is the most abundant (over 99%).

Industrially, oxygen is produced from liquefied air by the distillation process. [The world yearly production of O_2 is about 100 million tons.]

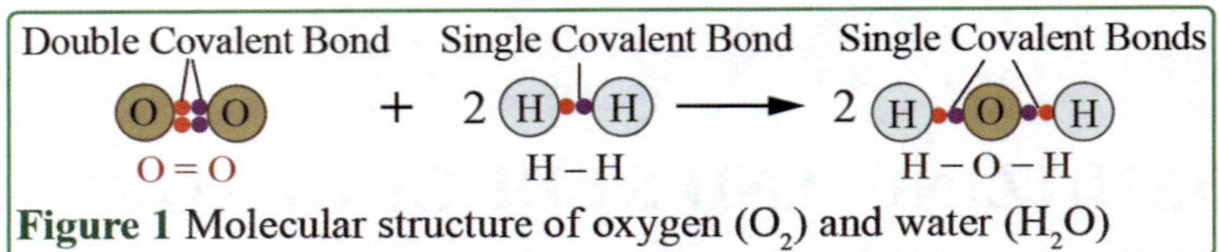

Figure 1 Molecular structure of oxygen (O_2) and water (H_2O)

O-20
OZONE AND OZONE-DEPLETING COMPOUNDS

Ozone

Ozone (O_3, also called **trioxygen**) is a gas with blue color and a specific smell. It is a strong oxidizing agent, even more than oxygen (O_2, also called **dioxygen**). Some other properties of ozone are outlined next.

- It is formed from atmospheric oxygen by ultraviolet (UV) light. Its lifetime, however, is short, as it is *not* stable and breaks again into oxygen ($2\ O_3 \rightarrow 3\ O_2$). [Ozone's half lifetime is short (about 30 minutes).]
- Its content in the **ozone layer** (the atmospheric layer near the Earth that absorbs most of the Sun's UV radiation) is the highest.
- Although it is a hazard to the respiratory system, its normal content (from 2 to 8 PPM) in the ozone layer is beneficial (as it prevents the Sun's UV radiation from reaching the Earth's surface).

Ozone-Depleting Compounds

An ozone-depleting compound is a chemical compound with a low boiling point temperature (T_{BP}). Ozone-depleting compounds, like chlorofluorocarbon and carbon monoxide, destruct the **ozone layer** (part of the atmosphere containing ozone, O_3). Chlorofluorocarbons, such as $CFCl_3$, were used as a refrigerant but *not* now (because of their ozone-depleting effect).

P Section

LIST OF TOPICS

P-1

PARTIAL AIR REQUIREMENT

Discussed under COMBUSTION AIR REQUIREMENT.

P-2

PARTIAL PRESSURE AND DALTON'S LAW OF PARTIAL PRESSURE

Partial Pressure

The partial pressure (P_P) of a gas (or vapor) in a closed vessel (like a tank) is a pressure (P) that the gas would exert on that vessel if it alone would present in the vessel. This means that the sum of the partial pressures of all gases (or vapors) present in the vessel equates to the mixture's **total pressure** (P_T). According to Dalton's Law of Partial Pressure, the P_T of a mixture composed of two non-reacting gases of A and B can be given using the gas's partial pressures.

$$P_T = P_{P.A} + P_{P.B} \tag{1}$$

Figure 1 illustrates Dalton's Law for the dry air, a theoretic air used in calculations and assumed to be zero moisture and consist of only nitrogen (N_2) and oxygen (O_2). Using Equation 1, if we connect a tank of N_2, which is at 1 Atm, to a tank of O_2, which is at 2 Atm, the P_T of the mixture ($N_2 + O_2$) becomes

$$P_T = P_{N_2} + P_{O_2} = 1 + 2 = 3 \text{ Atm}$$

Equation 1 for a multicomponent gas is

$$P_T = P_{P.A} + P_{P.B} + \cdots P_{P.I} \qquad \text{or} \qquad P_T = \textstyle\sum_{I=A}^{N} P_{P.I} \tag{2}$$

If n_A moles of A and n_B moles of B are in an ideal gas mixture, the mixture's P_T can be calculated from the ideal gas equation ($P.V = n.R.T$), where V is for volume, R is for the gas constant, and T is for temperature.

$$P_T = P_{P.A} + P_{P.B} = n_A\left(\frac{RT}{V}\right) + n_B\left(\frac{RT}{V}\right) = (n_A + n_B)\left(\frac{RT}{V}\right) = n_T\left(\frac{RT}{V}\right) \quad (3)$$

Because in a mixture of ideal gases, each gas behaves independently of other gases, we can relate the mole (n, the molar amount) of a given component (say, component A) in a gas mixture to its P_P and mixture's P_T.

$$\frac{P_{P.A}}{P_T} = \frac{n_A\left(\frac{RT}{V}\right)}{n_T\left(\frac{RT}{V}\right)} = \frac{n_A}{n_T} \qquad P_{P.A} = P_T\frac{n_A}{n_T} \quad (4)$$

The ratio n_A/n_T (mole of gas A to the mixture's total moles) is the molar fraction (a unitless quantity) of A and is shown as $X_{n.A}$. The molar fraction of A (shown as $X_{n.A}$) in a mixture with A and B is given as

$$X_{n.A} = \frac{n_A}{n_A + n_B} = \frac{n_A}{n_T} \quad (5)$$

Combining this equation with the previous one gives us the following useful equation for an ideal gas:

$$P_{P.A} = X_{n.A}.P_T \quad (6)$$

In a mixture of two gases, vapor pressure (P_V) of gas A (shown as $P_{V.A}$) can be used instead of P_T, so

$$P_{P.A} = X_{n.A}.P_{V.A} \quad (7)$$

Similarly, $P_{P.A}$ can be calculated from its vapor pressure ($P_{V.A}$) and P_T.

$$P_{P.A} = \frac{P_{V.A}}{P_T} \quad (8)$$

Remember the following two brief points about partial pressure (P_P): 1) A gas's partial pressure indicates its molecular activities. When dissimilar molecules are mixed, a greater P_P is exerted, resulting in a **positive deviation from ideality**. 2) Gases dissolve, react, and diffuse in a gas or liquid mixture based on their partial pressures but *not* based on their concentrations.

Dalton's Law of Partial Pressure

Dalton's Law of partial pressure (also called **Gibbs-Dalton Law** or simply **Dalton's Law**), which was named after John Dalton (1766–1844, British chemist), is a principle in physical chemistry published in 1802 that talks about partial pressure (P_P) of non-reacting gases in a gaseous mixture. Mathematically, it states that the total gas pressure (P_T) of a gaseous mixture equates to the sum of the partial pressures of the gases in that mixture. The general expression for the P_T of a mixture of two gases is Equation 1, and for a mixture of n gases is Equation 2.

[Dalton's Law can be combined with Raoult's Law of Vapor Pressure to state that a gaseous mixture's total vapor pressure (P_V) equates to the sum of the components' vapor pressures in that mixture.]

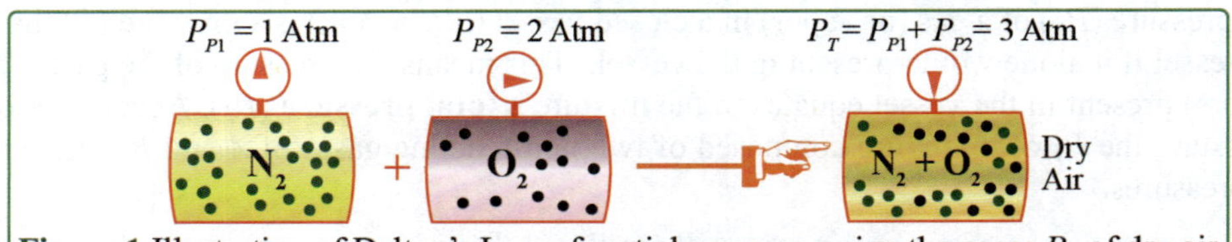

Figure 1 Illustration of Dalton's Law of partial pressure, using the gases P_p of dry air

P-3
PARTICLE ACCELERATORS

A particle accelerator (simply **accelerator** or **collider**) is a very-long device (up to 30 kilometers) that is mainly used to keep the charged quantum particles (particles with *no* subparticle), such as electrons and positrons, in well-defined **beams** that move at an extremely high speed (up to 99.99% of the speed of light). Such highly energetic particles (with high kinetic energy, E_K) in an accelerator can collide to form other quantum particles. [The energy (E) used in an accelerator is extremely high, in a thousand trillion GeV), where G is for Giga (= 10^9) and eV is for electron volt, where 1 GeV = 1.6×10^{-16} Joules (J).]

A collider is a long-and-complicated accelerator in a nuclear research facility to study the collision theory. The biggest collider is the Large Hadron Collider (LHC) at the European Organization for Nuclear Research (known by its French abbreviation, CERN) in Switzerland, founded in 1954. This collider, a 27 km (= 17 Mi) long tunnel located on the Swiss-French border, can hugely accelerate particles in opposite directions before colliding.

An accelerator can be used in many ways, including the following research programs:

- Nuclear Reactions: An accelerator can discover new particles by collision and reactions of differently charged particles.
- Nuclear Decay: An accelerator can be used in the nuclear decay process, in which the nucleus of a radioactive element (a nuclide) splits into two or more new nuclei.
- Quantum Entanglement: An accelerator can accelerate electrons to move close to the speed of light to produce **quantumly twin electrons** used in entanglement experiments.
- Modeling: An accelerator can create high-energy particle collisions to form conditions like those after the Big Bang.

[Linear and cyclic accelerators are two important types of accelerators.]

P-4
PARTICLES

The word **particle** is used as a tiny elementary system in which some physical properties and chemical properties can be described. Based on the size, particles can be grouped into the following four (4) groups:

- **Macroscopic particles:** The word **macroscopic particle** (simply **particle**) is used in general writing and conversation to refer to something too tiny, like powders and crystals. The size of, for example, one grain of sand is too tiny compared to a beach full of sand, so a grain of sand is considered here as a particle. If sand is compared with an atom of sand, then an atom of sand is a particle of sand.
- **Atomic particles** (atoms, molecules, and ions).
- **Subatomic particles** (protons, neutrons, and electron study Note 1).
- **Quantum particles** (like quarks, which make protons and neutrons).

The last three groups are the **atomic elementary particles** (the smallest building units of the Universe), each at a certain time. During **classical** (Newtonian) **physics**, the atom was the only elementary particle. After discovering **atomic components** (electron in 1897, proton in 1920, and neutron in 1932), the consideration of atom as elementary *no* longer could be valid, so the word elementary particle was used for these three particles (electron, proton, and neutron). And after the discovery of **atomic subcomponents** (like quark in 1964), atomic components are *not* elementary particles anymore, but quark is.

In relation to what has been discussed so far, it is important to know the upcoming three (3) notes.

[Note 1: Unlike proton and neutron, which are composed of quantum particles (particles with *no* subparticle), *no* quantum particle has been discovered for electron yet, so it is a non-composite particle. Physics, thus, consider electron as both subatomic particle and quantum (non-composite) particle. Another reason that electron can be considered a quantum particle is that its mass is negligibly small (about 1% of a nucleus mass) to the extent that it can be considered **massless**. These properties seem to be true for a quark because its mass (about 1% of a proton's mass) is even smaller than an electron (because a quark originated from an electron).]

[Note 2: Most technical writers do *not* pay attention to the listed changes yet use the word "**particle**" and let their readers determine their purpose. When using the word **particle** in this book, I mean a system consisting of many molecules, such as particles of powdered sugar. When using the word **atomic particle**, it means an atom, a molecule, or an ion. The word subatomic particle refers to a proton, neutron, or electron. And finally, the word **quantum particle** means a photon (the particle or quantum of light), a quark (the particle of proton and neutron), a gluon (the particle that glues two quarks together), or a graviton (the particle that carries the gravitational force).]

Quantum Particles

Besides *not* having a subparticle and being almost massless, a **quantum** (non-composite) **particle** typically has the next 10 properties:

- It can have an uncertain location,
- It can (or *cannot*) have an electric charge,
- It can be in a quantum superposition state,
- It can only carry discrete (separate) values of E,
- It can follow Heisenberg's uncertainty principle,
- It can be quantumly entangled (Quantum Entanglement),
- It can carry its own energy, so its E is a particle self-energy,
- It can carry EM force. thus it is a Boson (a force-carrier particle),
- It can take any possible path when traveling from one place to another,
- It can behave as a wave in a moment and as a particle in another moment, and
- It can move at different speeds, including at the speed of light constant in a vacuum.

Instead, an **atomic** (composite) **particle**, which is massive (with M of 10^{-12} g), has the next properties:

- It has a certain location,
- It can have an electric charge (q),
- It can move at different speeds (U),
- It can carry any type of energy (E), except photon energy (E_{Ph}),
- It can take multiple paths when traveling from one place to another place, and
- It can carry electromagnetic force (EM force, a force in atoms, molecules, and elements).

In particle physics, quantum particles are classified into the following two classes:

- Bosons**:** They are the force-carrying elementary particles that characteristically obey Bose-Einstein statistics (defined under BOSONS AND FERMIONS). The seven currently known Bosons are photon, gluon, graviton, Z-Boson, W-Boson, Higgs Boson, and gauge Boson.
- Fermions**:** These are the energy-carrying particles that characteristically obey Fermi-Dirac statistics. The five Fermions are proton, neutron, electron, quark, and neutrino.

[Note 3: The four quantum particles of gluon, photon, Boson, and graviton are also called **field particles** (because each is the cause of one of four fundamental fields of nature). Gluons are the carrier particles for the strong nuclear force (F_{SN}), photons are those for the electromagnetic force (F_{EM}), W and Z Bosons are those for the weak nuclear force (F_{WN}), and gravitons are the carrier particles for the gravitational force (F_g). All these particles are detected, except for the graviton. Notably, the F_{SN}, F_{EM}, F_{WN}, and F_g are the four (4) fundamental forces of nature.] [Note 4: All quantum particles (about 60, including the Higgs Boson) can be classified into two broad classes: hadrons and leptons.] [Note 5: Quantum physics considers all quantum particles as waves with different energy (the *smaller* the particle's wavelength, the *greater* is its energy). Particle physics considers a quantum particle's mass due to how fast it moves in the Higgs field (the *faster* a particle moves through the Higgs field, the *lighter* it is). The **Higgs field** is a fundamental field that is predicted to occupy all the space. In this way, photons and gluons are the lightest, so they can move masslessly in the Higgs field as birds move in the air. Electrons move a bit slower, quarks move even slower, and the W and Z Bosons move the slowest of all (because they are heavy particles).]

P-5
PARTICLE DENSITY

Discussed under the topic of DENSITY.

P-6
PARTICLE FLUX

Particle flux is the quantity of transfer of atomic particles (atoms, molecules, or ions) of a diffusing component (or components) across a unit area (*A*). It is given in many particles per m^2.

In the same way, **particle flux rate** (rate of particle flux) is the particle flux per unit time (*t*). Particle flux rate is given in the number of particles per m^2 per s (second) or h (hour).

P-7
PARTICLE PHYSICS

As the expanded version of quantum physics (QPhy), the particle physics (PPhy) standard model describes 17 known quantum particles, mainly bosonic particles (photon, gluon, graviton, Z-Boson, W-Boson, Higgs Boson, and gauge Boson) and fermionic particles (proton, neutron, electron, quark, and neutrino). PPhy started in the early 1970s, after most Bosons and Fermions were discovered.

Some of the differences between PPhy and QPhy are outlined next.

- The PPhy deals with a system of very many particles, while QPhy deals with a system with a single or a few particles.
- The PPhy deals with the **Higgs field** as its fundamental field, while QPhy deals with all four fundamental fields of nature. Unlike fundamental fields of nature, the Higgs field takes a non-zero constant value almost everywhere, permeating all of space.
- Comparatively, the PPhy is closer than QPhy to reaching a theory of unification of physics. [Many physicists, however, think that a combination of the PPhy, QPhy, and string theory is the closest way to get to a reasonable theory of unification.]

P-8
PARTICLE SELF ENERGY

Discussed under the topic of ENERGY AND ITS FORMS.

P-9

PARTICLE SIZE DISTRIBUTION

Particle size distribution (PSD) is a set of values that express the average size of a product's particles or crystals and their uniformity (distribution). The average size of crystals and their uniformity are important to customers and, therefore, the producers must meet the PSD specifications of their products. In practice, the size of the crystals is indicated by the mean aperture (M_A) and the uniformity of the crystals by the coefficient of variation (K_V). The next two bullets give some generalities about the M_A and K_V:

- **Mean Aperture** (M_A)**:** The M_A value indicates the crystals' average size (the aperture corresponding to 50%). For example, the M_A of 0.4 mm (400 microns or 400 μm) means that 50% (one-half) of the sample crystals fall through the screen with 0.4 mm opening (aperture) and 50% retain on it. [0.4 mm is approximately the size of typical sugar crystals (table sugar).]
- **Coefficient of Variation** (K_V)**:** Statistically, the K_V describes the precision of measurements (the *lower* the K_V value, the *more* precise the measurements are). In crystallization, K_V expresses the size uniformity of the crystals (the *lower* the K_V value, the *more* uniformed the crystals). So, a minimum possible value in size variation is desired. A high K_V value, on the other side, is an indication of a wide and poor distribution size. Lower K_V can be achieved with a larger M_A. K_V requirements are different in different industries. For example, a K_V of less than 35% is required in the sugar industry.

The PSD control starts with a screen (sieve) test, in which a certain amount of dry crystals (usually 100 g) is screened in a set of screens (usually 4 to 6 screens). After shaking the screens in a shaker for a few minutes and reweighing the screens containing the sample, the cumulative percentages retained on the screens are plotted in the graphic paper against the corresponding screen **aperture** (the opening size of the screen). As shown in Figure 1, the result is a straight line, as the data are linear. From the graph, the size of the apertures corresponding to 16% (or M_A16), 50% (or M_A50), and 81% (or M_A81) can be read. These values are then used to calculate K_V as

$$K_V = \frac{M_A16 - M_A81}{2M_A50} \times 100 \qquad (1)$$

Consider a screen test on 100 g of medium-size sugar crystals and assume that the result of the test tells us that the aperture corresponding to 16% is 630 μm (1micrometer = 10^{-6} m or 10^{-3} mm), that of 50% is 510 μm, and that of 81% is 330 μm, as shown in Figure 1. The K_V of the sugar crystals will be

$$K_V = \frac{630 - 330}{2 \times 510} \times 100 = 29\%$$

This tells us the following information: 1) 50% of crystals pass through the screen with a 510 μm (0.5 mm) opening, and 50% retain on it. 2) 30% of the crystals are either smaller than 330 μm or larger than 630 μm. 3) 70% of the crystals are between 330 and 630 μm.

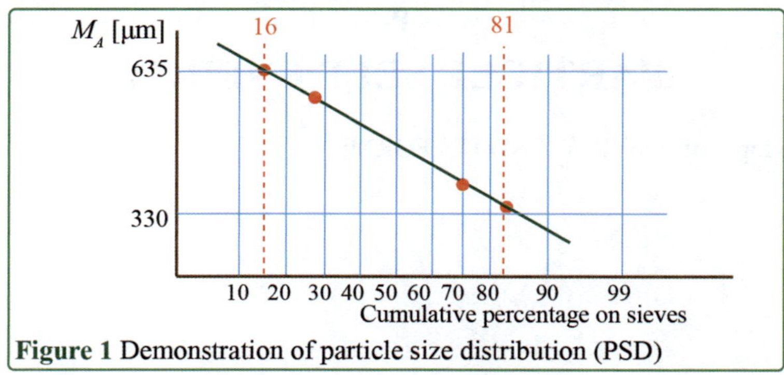

Figure 1 Demonstration of particle size distribution (PSD)

P-10

PARTICULATE MATTERS

Particulate matters (simply PM, **particulates**, or **aerosols**) are fine suspended solid particles or liquid droplets (tiny drops) in a gas or air stream. Because particulates are fine and always in suspension, they are considered gas pollutants. Dust, smoke, smog, and sooth (a general name for particles resulting from incomplete combustion) contain particulates.

In furnace operations, particulates are in the flue gas that leaves the furnace stack. The pollutability (pollution ability) of a flue gas mainly depends on the following:

- **Fuel:** Using a clean fuel (low in ash, sulfur, and nitrogen contents) reduces pollution.
- **Scrubbing Device:** Using an efficient scrubbing device reduces pollution.

In chemical process plants, the following scrubbing (removing) devices are used to remove particulates:

- Gas cyclones,
- Gas scrubbers, and
- Electrostatic collectors.

[Note: Environmental field has classified particulate matter smaller than 10 microns (10 micrometers, μm) as PM_{10} and particulates smaller than 2.5 μm as $PM_{2.5}$. The *smaller* the PM, the *more* hazardous it is to humans and animals. When non-soluble PM_{10} is inhaled, it becomes permanently embedded in the lungs, causing irritation and possible disease. $PM_{2.5}$ is so small that it can pass directly from the lungs to the bloodstream, which transports any hazardous materials it contains to all parts of the body.]

P-11

PARTICULATE REMOVING DEVICES

Gas cyclones, gas scrubbers (also called **wet gas scrubbers**), and electrostatic precipitators are three important devices used for scrubbing (removing) particulates (particulate matters) from a gas stream, like a flue gas (a hot gas leaving the stack of a furnace). [These devices are also used as **dust collectors** to collect dust, which their particles are larger than the particles of particulate matter. For example, they are used in a sugar dryer to collect sugar dust (with particles smaller than 0.2 mm) created by the abrasion of sugar crystals. Not only sugar dust particles are harmful to a human's lungs, but they are also combustible under ordinary conditions and become highly explosive under specific conditions.]

Gas Cyclones

A gas cyclone (simply **cyclone**) is a device (equipment) with a cylindrical body and cone-shaped bottom for separating solid particulates from a gas stream (flow). A clear gas is a product, and a thickened particulate stream is the waste of a cyclone, as shown in Figure 1.

Once in a cyclone, a gas stream starts spinning through its body. The **driving force** (cause) for spinning is the centrifugal force (F_C), which is a strong force compared to F_g (gravitational force). The F_C, created by the fast gas movement in a cyclone, acts radially to move particulates toward the cyclone's wall. And from there, they move downward. Assuming that the particulates have a spherical shape with an average diameter of d, then the **settling efficiency** (E_S, also called **settling rate** or **settling velocity**) of particles directly depends on d and a_C (centrifugal acceleration, in m/s^2).

$$E_S = d.\,a_C \quad (1)$$

This equation, which uses the a_C because the settling in a cyclone is caused by a centrifugal force (F_C), tells us that the *larger* the particles, the *greater* are their settling efficiency.

The volumetric flow rate ($\dot{V}$, the rate of V) of a suspension in a cyclone can be calculated from its particles' average velocity (V) in the cyclone and the cyclone's active cross-sectional area ($A = \pi R^2 = \pi d^2/4$, where d is for the cyclone's active diameter as shown in Figure 1).

$$\dot{V} = V.A.h = V.\pi.R^2.h = V.\pi\frac{d^2.h}{4} \quad (2)$$

In addition to their size, the following are also affect the particles' E_S to the bottom of a cyclone:

- **Pressure Drop:** A cyclone E_S is **directly proportional** to the pressure drop, known as the pressure difference (ΔP), between the inlet gas and outlet gas (the *greater* the ΔP across a cyclone, the *greater* is its E_S).
- **Cyclone Diameter:** A cyclone's E_S is **inversely proportional** to its diameter (the *smaller* its diameter, the *greater* is its E_S). [For this reason, some cyclones are built with a small diameter of 0.25 to 0.35 m with multiple cells, mostly mounted vertically next to each other.]
- **Friction** (f): A cyclone E_S is **inversely proportional** to the friction (f) of particles with the cyclone wall (the *greater* the f, the *smaller* is the E_S).

A unitless ratio, called **C-factor** (C_F), can compare the created F_C in a cyclone with F_g, where $F_g = M.a_g$, M is for mass, and a_g is the gravitational acceleration (in m/s^2).

$$C_F = \frac{F_C}{F_g} = \frac{F_C}{M.a_g} \quad (3)$$

Under the topic of CENTRIFUGAL PROCESS, the equations for F_C were derived as

$$F_C = M.a_C = M\frac{2V^2}{d} \quad (4)$$

Substituting F_C (usually in kg.m/s^2 = N) into Equation 3 yields

$$C_F = \frac{F_C}{M.a_g} = \frac{2M.V^2}{M.d.a_g} = \frac{2V^2}{d.a_g} \quad (5)$$

According to this equation, a gas that enters a cyclone with 0.5 m diameter (d) and its velocity (V) increases to 20 m/s creates a C_F (C-factor, a unitless quantity) equal to

$$C_F = \frac{2V^2}{d.a_g} = \frac{2 \times 20^2}{0.5 \times 9.81} = \frac{800}{4.9} = 163$$

Small-diameter cyclones have a C_F as high as 2 500. [In cyclones, a velocity above 15 m/s (= 50 Ft/s) is usually impractical because of the next reasons: 1) It increases the pressure drop, and 2) It increases the abrasive wear.]

Like the one shown on the left of Figure 1, a typical cyclone consists of a vertical cylindrical body with a cone shape at the bottom. The feed (usually a gas with dusty particles) enters near the top of the body and moves spirally downward toward the bottom. The spiral movement creates an F_C that moves the particles radially toward the wall of the cylinder. Here, the particulates slow down (because of **friction** with the wall), falling to the bottom and leaving the cyclone. And the gas leaves the body at the top. [Some cyclones have one circulator (or two), which draws a portion of the gas flow and returns it to the cyclone, as shown in the middle of Figure 1.]

Gas Scrubbers

A gas scrubber (also called a **wet gas scrubber**) is a device with a cylindrical body for separating solid particulates from a gas stream by using a scrubbing (removing) liquid, mostly water. Scrubbers work based on the sedimentation (settling) of the particulates. [Scrubbers can also remove gas pollutants from flue gas, like sulfur dioxide (SO2). When a scrubber is used to remove SO_2, calcium hydroxide [$Ca(OH)_2$] is added to the scrubbing water. Part of SO_2 reacts with water to form sulfurous acid (H_2SO_3), which then reacts with $Ca(OH)_2$ to precipitate calcium sulfite ($CaSO_3$). The rest of SO_2 reacts with $Ca(OH)_2$ to precipitate $CaSO_3$.]

Scrubbers with entrainer, Venturi scrubbers, fixed-vane scrubbers, and perforated (sieve) scrubbers are common gas scrubbers. The left side of Figure 2 shows a typical gas scrubber with an entrainer (entrainment separator). A gas stream with particulates passes through water sprayed on the gas through a set of nozzles to create water droplets (water's tiny drops) for collecting the particulates. On the scrubber's upper part, an entrainment separator (entrainer), which contains Raschig rings, separates more particulates from the gas, so the clean gas leaving the upper section of the scrubber is almost free of solid particles.

When the η (viscosity) of a suspension (water droplets and particulates) in a scrubber is negligible, Equation 1 can be used to determine the particulates' **settling efficiency** (E_S) if the term a_C is replaced by the term a_g.

$$E_S = d.\, a_g \tag{6}$$

This equation, which uses the a_g (because the F_g causes the settling in a scrubber), tells us that the *larger* the particulates, the *easier* it is to remove them, so the *more* efficiently the scrubber operates.

In operating a gas scrubber, the following three generalities are important:

- **Electricity Usage:** A typical scrubber uses 400 to 500 kW/h (= 536 to 670 HP).
- **Water Usage:** A typical scrubber consumes about 1 L of water/m^3 of the process gas.
- **Critical Factors:** Gas and water volumetric flow rates and gas pressure are important parameters.

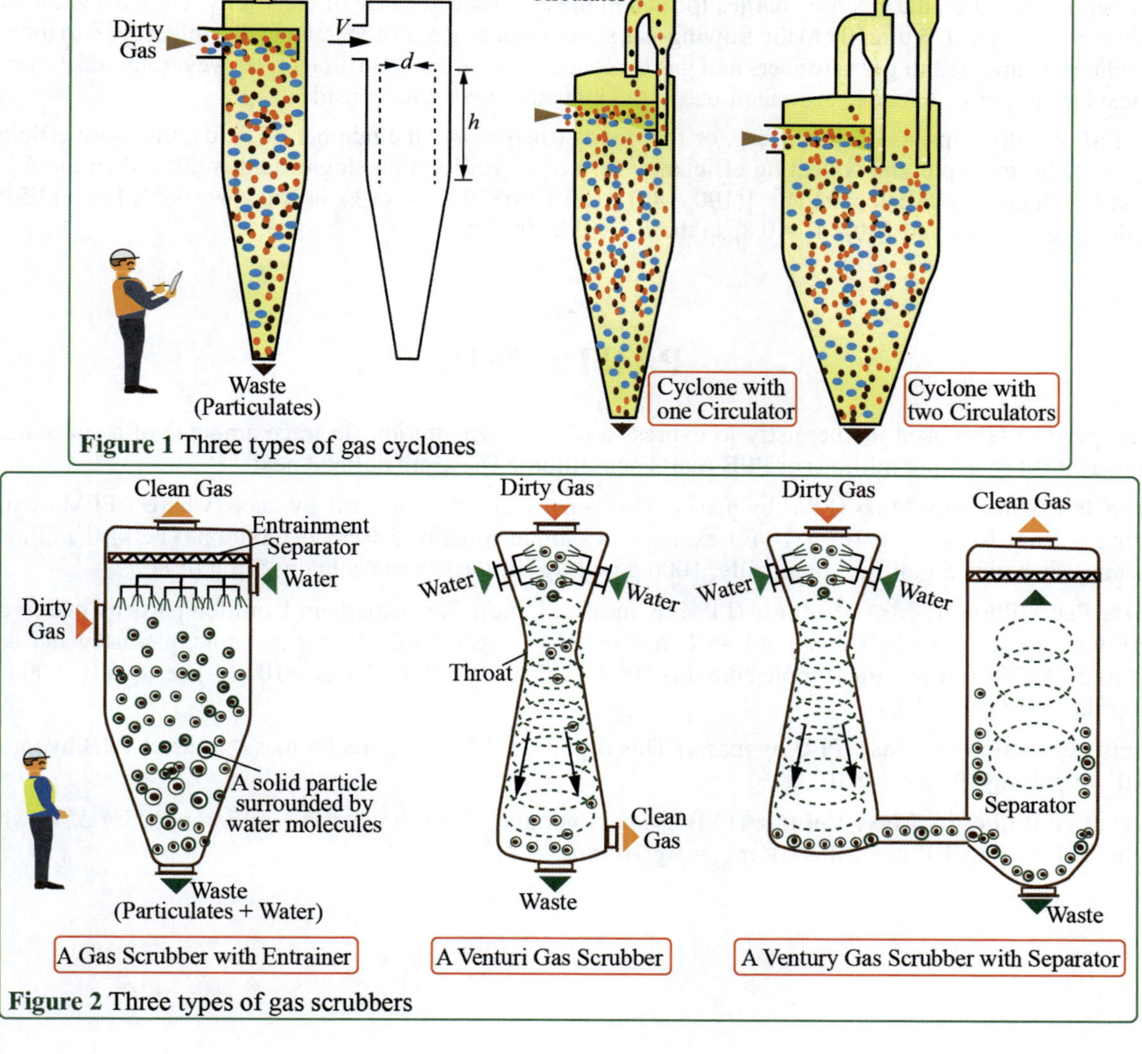

Figure 1 Three types of gas cyclones

Figure 2 Three types of gas scrubbers

Venturi Gas Scrubbers

A typical Venturi gas scrubber (see the middle of Figure 2) looks like a Venturi tube with a converging section connected to the diverging section through a throat (a short narrow section in a Venturi device). In the scrubber, the scrubbing water is injected at a slight angle into the gas stream. The gas stream goes from the narrower section of the tube to the wider section. As particulates get to the wider section, their speed decreases to be removed from the bottom of the scrubber. The **driving force** of separation particulates in a Venturi scrubber is the F_C (centrifugal force), created by the movement of the gas flow. The F_C, a stronger force than F_g (gravitational force), acts radially to move the particulates toward the scrubber wall. Here, the particulates slow down (because of friction with the wall), falling to the bottom and leaving the scrubber.

The right side of Figure 2 shows a Venturi scrubber that operates with a separator to remove particulates and leave the gas clean completely.

Electrostatic Precipitator

A typical electrostatic precipitator (ESP) is a dust-collecting device with two sets of **electrodes**, one being insulated from the other. The electrodes operate securely grounded at a high direct current (DC) electricity. An ESP operates based on the electric charges formed in the electrode because of electricity. Unlike a gas scrubber, which applies energy (E) directly to the flowing-gas stream entering a scrubber, an ESP applies the E to individual particulates. Compared to gas scrubbers and gas cyclones, EPSs are more efficient. However, the ESPs are bulkier (heavier) and more expensive, so their use in the industry is *not* widespread.

An ESP usually consists of three, four, or five fields (the *greater* the number of fields, the *more* efficient an ESP is). If, for example, the collecting efficiency (E_C) of an ESP with a single field is 80%, then the E_C of an ESP with 2 fields can be calculated as: $[(100 - 80) - (80/100)\times20] = 4$, so E_C is $100 - 4 = 96\%$. For an ESP with 3 fields, $[(100 - 96) - (80/100)\times4] = 0.8$, so the E_C will be 99.2%.

P-12

PARTS PER

Parts per is a term used in chemistry to express a small concentration (in trace amount) of a substance in a sample as PPM (parts per million) or PPB (parts per billion). These are defined next.

Parts Per Million by Mass (PPM by mass)**:** This is parts in 1 million parts by mass, where 1 PPM by mass = 1 mg/kg = 1 mg/10^3 g = 1 g/10^6 g. If, for example, a sample contains 5 PPM of iron ions (Fe^{2+}), 1 million g of this sample contains 5 g of Fe^{2+} or equally, 1000 g (= 1 kg) of the sample contains 5 mg of Fe^{2+}.

Parts Per Million by Mass-Volume (PPM by mass/volume)**:** This is parts in 1 million parts by mass/volume (M/V), where 1 PPM by M/V = 1 mg/L = 1 mg/10^3 mL = 1 g/10^6 mL. If, for example, a wastewater sample contains 500 PPM of Ca^{2+}, the sample contains 500 g Ca^{2+} in 10^6 mL (= 10^3 L = 1000 L) or equally, 500 mg Ca in 10^3 mL (= 10^3 mL = 1 L).

Parts Per Billion by Mass (PPB by mass)**:** This is parts in 1 billion parts by mass, where 1 PPB by mass = 1 mg/10^3 kg = 1 mg/10^6 g = 1 g/10^9 g.

Parts Per Billion by Mass-Volume (PPB by mass/volume)**:** This is parts in 1 billion parts by M/V, where 1 PPB by M/V = 1 mg/10^3 L = 1 mg/10^6 mL = 1 g/10^9 mL.

P-13

PASCAL AND PASCAL'S PRINCIPLE

Pascal

Pascal is the SI unit of pressure (P), where 1 Pa = 1 N/m^2 = 1.45×10^{-4} PSI (Lb$_F$/In^2) = 10^{-5} Bar. This name was given in honor of Blaise Pascal's (1623 – 1662, French physicist) scientific contributions. [Because Pa is a small unit, usually kPa is used.]

Pascal's Principle

Pascal's principle (also called **Pascal's Law**) is a concept in hydraulics named after Blaise Pascal (1623 – 1662, a French scientist). This principle states that a change in pressure (P) at any point in a liquid at rest (equilibrium) transfers without loss to every portion of the liquid and the wall of the container. In a short expression, P in a liquid acts equally in all directions.

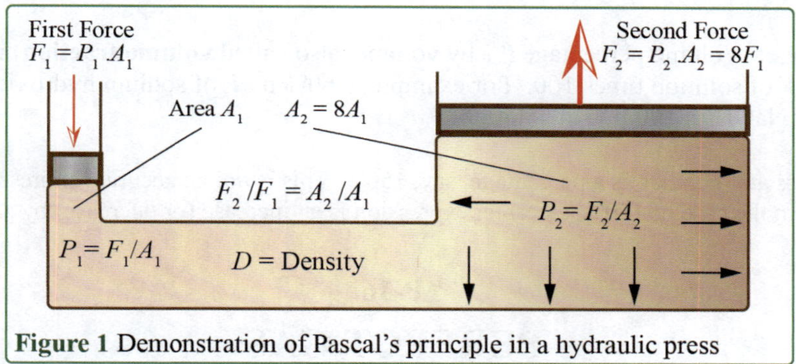

Figure 1 Demonstration of Pascal's principle in a hydraulic press

P-14

PATH AND STATE QUANTITIES

The path and state quantities are reversely related. A **path quantity** (also known as **path variable** or **path function**) depends on its path from point 1 to point 2. Instead, a **state quantity** (also known as the state variable or state function) is independent of its path to move from 1 to 2.

Distance (L for length) and work (W) are examples of **path quantities**. For instance, the resulting distance from traveling a system (like a car) from point 1 to point 2 depends on the system's path when it goes directly from point 1 to 2 or indirectly to point 3 and from there to point 2.

Pressure (P), temperature (T), volume (V), mass (M), energy (E), enthalpy (H), and entropy (S) are examples of **state quantities**. As for the H (a state quantity), we can say that the amount of H of 100 kg of a liquid (a system) is independent of how the heating process proceeds from, say, 30 to 60°C. This means that the amount of H used is the same if we heat first the liquid from 30 to 40°C and then from 40 to 60°C, or heat it with *no* delay from 30 to 60°C. The required time to achieve the heating process is *not* the same.

Based on what has been said here, we *cannot* calculate a **path quantity** of a system unless its path (from initial to final, shown usually by the symbol Δ) is known to us. While we, instead, can calculate a **state quantity** of a system without knowing its path. We can calculate a state quantity irrespective of how the system gets to its final state in another context.

P-15

PERCENTAGES

Percentage (%) is a way of expressing a quantity in a fraction of 100. Percentages express how large (or small) one quantity is relative to another quantity. For example, an increase of 2°C today compared with yesterday of 22°C is an increase of (2/22) × 100 = 9.1%. And a decrease in today's stock price of $0.50 compared to yesterday's price of $20.50 is a decrease of (0.50/20.50) × 100= 2.4%.

The following are the definitions of percentages used in chemistry:

- **Mass Percentage:** Mass percentage (% by mass, % by *M*, % by weight, or mass fraction) is the *M* (mass) of solute divided by the total *M* of solution times 100. For example, a solution with 25% by *M* of NaCl contains 25 g of NaCl in 100 g of solution (solute + solvent).
- **Mass-Volume Percentage:** Mass-volume percentage (% by mass volume, *M*/*V*) is the *M* of solute divided by the total *V* (volume) of solution times 100. Say, a solution with 50% *M*/*V* of calcium chloride ($CaCl_2$) has 50 g of $CaCl_2$ in 100 mL of solution. In context, 50 g of $CaCl_2$ is mixed with water to form 100 mL of $CaCl_2$ solution.
- **Volume Percentage:** Volume percentage (% by volume, also called **volume fraction**) is the *V* of solute divided by the total *V* of solution times 100. For example, a 60% by *V* of sodium hydroxide (NaOH) solution contains 60 mL of NaOH in 100 mL of solution.

[Note: Some express any number as a percentage, say, 150%. This is *not* an accurate expression based on the definition of percentage. In the case of 150%, a correct expression is an increase (or decrease) by a factor of 1.5.]

P-16

PERFECT GAS

Study IDEAL, REAL, AND PERFECT GASES.

P-17

PERFECT VACUUM

See VACUUM.

P-18

PERIOD

Study AMPLITUDE, FREQUENCY, AND PERIOD.

P-19

PERIODIC TABLE OF ELEMENTS

The periodic table of the elements, arranged in 1869 by D. I. Mendeleev (1834–1907, a Russian chemist), is organized by increasing the atomic number (N_Z, proton numbers). [As of 2020, 118 chemical elements exist. Scientists even gave names and symbols to a few elements that have *not* been discovered yet but are in the table. However, the table is *not* finished, as more elements might be discovered synthetically.]

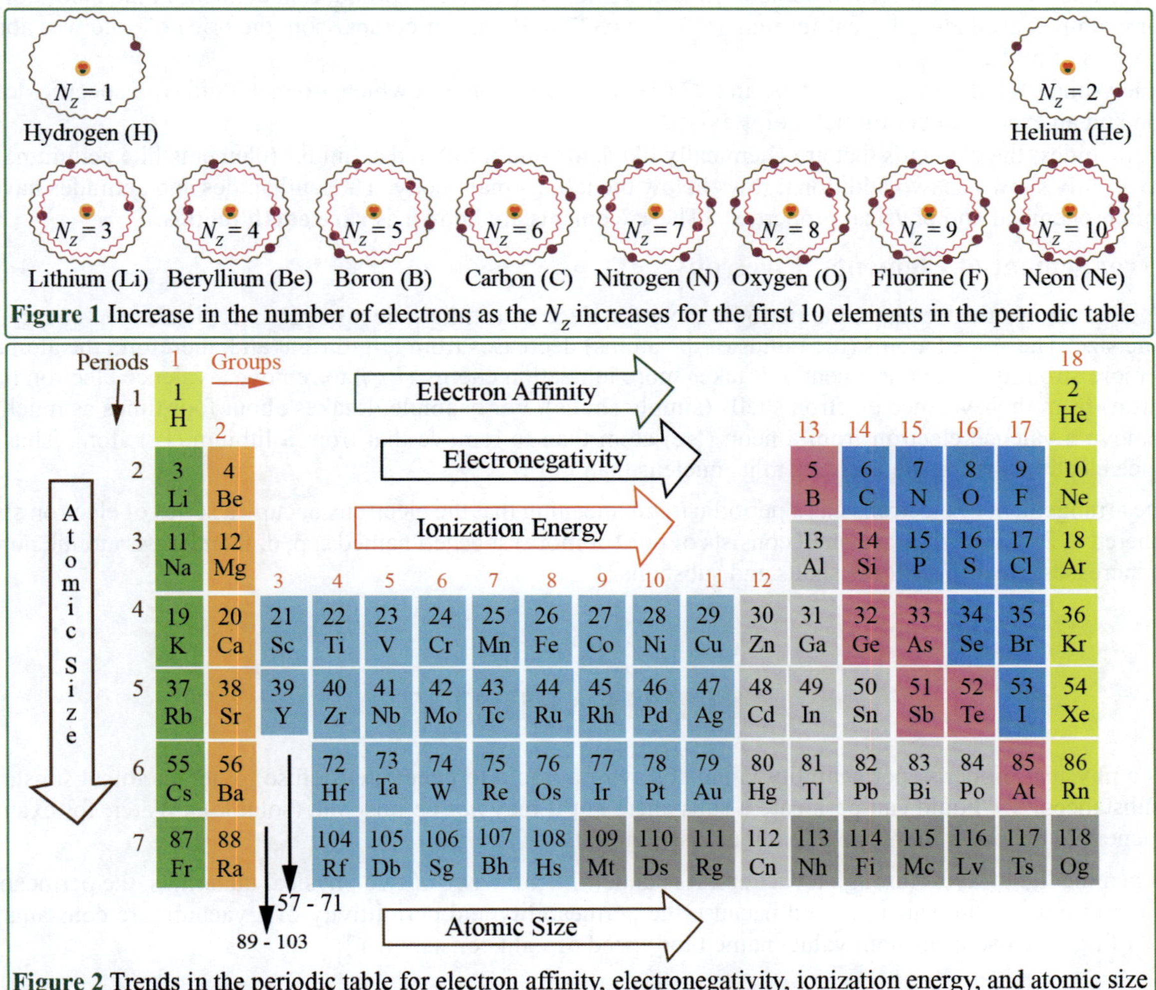

Figure 1 Increase in the number of electrons as the N_z increases for the first 10 elements in the periodic table

Figure 2 Trends in the periodic table for electron affinity, electronegativity, ionization energy, and atomic size

In the table (given on this book's inside front cover), the chemical symbol of each element is written in the middle, the atomic number (N_Z) above each element's symbol, and the atomic mass (M_A, the mass of an atom) is written below the element. For example, carbon (C) is shown as C^{6}_{12}. [Another way of showing an element is to use its atomic mass number (N_A, the total number of protons and neutrons) before its symbol, like C-12.]

Every element has a specific proton number (N_Z). Hydrogen has one proton ($N_Z = 1$), helium two ($N_Z = 2$), carbon 6, oxygen 8, and so on. Figure 1 shows the increase in the number of electrons as the number of protons increases for the periodic table's first ten (10) elements.

Some other characteristics of the table are outlined next.

- It has 7 rows (periods) and 18 columns (groups). The rows are organized based on the increasing atomic number (N_Z) of the elements from $N_Z = 1$ (hydrogen, H), $N_Z = 2$ (helium, He), and finally $N_Z = 118$ (oganesson, Og). The columns are organized based on the atomic structure of the outer electron shells (the electrons that determine the properties of an element's atom), so the elements in each column have similar chemical properties and physical properties.
- Some groups have traditional names, such as alkaline earth metals, which are in group 2 and contain Beryllium (Be), magnesium (Mg), calcium (Ca), strontium (Sr), barium (Ba), and radium (Rd).
- About 95 of the elements are found in nature. Elements from the N_Z of 95 to 118 are produced synthetically by the nuclear decay process in the lab. [It is extremely expensive to produce an element in the laboratory. For example, producing 1 g californium (Cf) costs $27 million. For comparison, the price of gold was about $56/g as of mid-2021.]
- Ninety-one (91) elements are metals, and 27 are nonmetals, some of which are metalloids (*no* specific definition and an exact number of metalloids exist).
- Lanthanides (the elements that are chemically like lanthanum, La) and actinides (elements like actinium, Ac) are usually shown as two additional rows below the table's main body. The lanthanides and actinides have similar chemical and physical properties. [These elements are known as **rare earth metals**.]

Arrangement of Elements' Electrons

Figure 2 shows the trends in the periodic table for electron affinity, electronegativity, ionization energy, and atomic size. The size of atoms (the radius of the atoms) decreases from left to right and, therefore, the atoms are held more strongly and, consequently, it takes more ionization energy (E_{Ion}) to remove a valence electron (outer electron) from their valence electron shells (simply **shells**). For example, it takes about four times as much E_{Ion} to remove a valence electron from a neon (Ne) atom than to remove that from a lithium (Li) atom. Thus, the valence electron shell in Ne is closer to its nucleus than in Li.

The arrangement of electrons has a periodic trend, meaning that the electrons occupy a series of electron shells, numbered 1, 2, and so on. Each shell consists of one (or more) subshell named s, p, d, f, and g. As atomic number (N_Z) increases, electrons fill the shells and subshells.

P-20
PERMEABILITY

As a physical property, permeability is the ability of a liquid to penetrate (defuse) other chemical substances (or substances). A liquid can permeate a substance, but it may *not* be miscible (soluble). Water, for example, can penetrate the pores of a sponge without dissolving it.

[When the light travels through a vacuum, it is under the influence of two physical quantities, the permeability and permittivity of the vacuum. And because the permeability and permittivity of a vacuum are constants, the speed of light is also a constant value, named the speed of light constant (*c*).]

P-21
PERMITTIVITY

As a physical quantity, permittivity (ε, epsilon) is the ability of light to move through a medium. Light travels through a vacuum medium faster than water (1.333 times), where the value of 1.333 is the water refractive index. [When the light travels through a vacuum, it is under the influence of two physical quantities, the permittivity and permeability of the vacuum. And because the permeability and permittivity of a vacuum are constants, the speed of light is also a constant value, named the speed of light constant (*c*).]

P-22
PERVAPORATION PROCESS

As one of the process units (unit operations) of ChemEng, pervaporation is a separation process consisting of two simultaneous steps: (1) Permeation of a liquid mixture through a **membrane** by the pressure difference (ΔP) between the membrane's sides to separate the permeate. (2) Evaporation of the liquid permeate to its vapor phase.

The membrane allows the liquid feed's wanted (desired) components to pass its pores, so its separation efficiency is based on a difference in diffusing rate of individual components through its pores. Therefore, the membrane acts as a selective barrier between the components of two phases: the liquid-phase feed and the vapor-phase permeate.

P-23
PETROLEUM

Another name for CRUDE OIL.

P-24
PH AND PH METERS

PH: The PH (mostly written pH, where P is for **power** and H for **hydrogen ion**) is a unitless quantity (a value with *no* unit) that indicates a solution sample's acidity or alkalinity (basicity). A solution's PH equates to the negative log (logarithm) to the base 10 of the solution's **hydrogen-ion concentration** (H^+).

$$PH = -\log[H^+] \quad (1)$$

Here, the brackets indicate that the concentration is in moles (mole)per liter (L), which is the definition of molarity (M). And the log is the exponent of 10 when the number is written in the base 10. For example, $100 = 10^2$, so the log of 100 is 2. If, for example, the molarity of hydrochloric acid (HCl) is 0.1 mole/L, its PH is $-\log 10^{-1} = -(-1) = 1$. And if the molarity of a solution is 10^{-8} mole/L, its PH is $-\log 10^{-8} = 8$.

A solution's PH is measured by a PH meter and expressed on a scale of 1 to 14, with 7 as the neutral value. Acids have a PH from 1 to 7 (the *greater* the PH value, the *weaker* the acid is). Bases (alkalis) have a PH from 7 to 14 (the *greater* the PH value, the *stronger* is the base). Some acids, like acetic (HCH_3COO) and boric (H_3BO_3), are weak. Other acids, such as sulfuric acid (H_2SO_4) and nitric acid (HNO_3), are strong. Likewise, bases can be weak, such as ammonia (NH_3), or strong (sodium hydroxide, NaOH).

PH is a temperature-related quantity (it *decreases* with *increasing* temperature). For example, pure water (the water with *no* dissolved solids) has a PH of 7 at 25ºC, but at 50ºC, it decreases to 6.6, and at 100ºC, it decreases to 6. Thus, PH measurements must be compared only on tests performed at the same temperature.

In an aqueous solution at 25ºC, *no* matter what it contains, the products of (H^+) and (OH^-) must equate to 1×10^{-14}, so three situations are possible:

- A neutral solution, where (H^+) = (OH^-),
- An acidic solution, where (H^+) > (OH^-),
- A basic solution, where (H^+) < (OH^-).

PH Meters: A PH meter is an instrument that uses the **potentiometric principle** to measure a solution sample's PH. A typical PH meter consists of two cells and a voltmeter that measures the cell's small electric voltage (V, simply **voltage**) difference.

Figure 1 shows the detail of a PH-meter's glass electrode and has a **reference cell** and **a measuring** (responsive) **cell**, both made of glass and placed in an electrode tube. The reference cell has a long conductive wire made of silver-silver chloride (Ag-AgCl) for creating a voltage, and the measuring cell has a wire of the same material and a bulb shape at the bottom. Both cells are filled with a **filling solution**, usually neutral potassium chloride (KCl) solution with PH 7. Usually, the measuring cell is placed in the reference cell, and a ceramic junction keeps the electric conduction between them (see the same figure). When the electrode, consisting of both cells, is placed in a solution sample, the PH value is calculated from the difference in the voltages between the **reference cell** and the **measuring cell**.

When a PH electrode is placed, for example, in a diluted hydrochloric acid (HCl), which consists of electro-negatively-charged chloride ions (Cl^-) and electro-positively-charged hydrogen ions (H^+), the Cl^- ions spread in the solution, while the H^+ ions move toward the outside of the measuring cell. The same process occurs inside the measuring cell, with constant H^+ ions, as shown on the right side of Figure 1. Then the voltmeter reads the voltages coming from the cells (reference and measuring cells) and shows the difference between them as the PH of the HCl solution sample.

Indicating the voltage coming from the reference cell by the symbol V_R and that coming from the measuring cell by the symbol V_M, three situations are possible:

- If V_R is the same as the V_M, the sample is neutral (PH value = 7).
- If V_R is lower than V_M, the sample is acidic (PH value is lower than 7).
- If V_R is greater than V_M, the sample is basic (PH value is greater than 7).

PH meters are calibrated by using standard buffer solutions. [Commercially prepared buffer solutions with PH values of 4, 7, and 10 are usually used to calibrate the PH meters.]

[Historical Note: In 1906, Danish chemist, **Soren Sorensen**, introduced hydrogen ion exponent, which became the base for potentiometric PH measurement. In 1936, Arnold Beckman (a professor at the California Institute of Technology) built the first commercial PH meter. Later, he started the Beckman Instruments Company.]

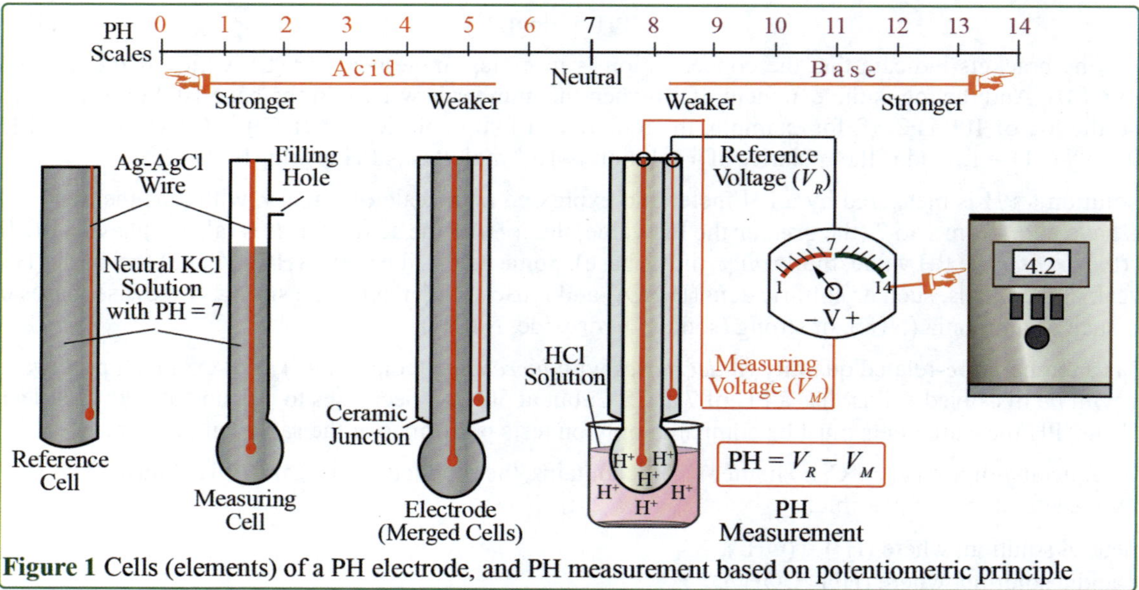

Figure 1 Cells (elements) of a PH electrode, and PH measurement based on potentiometric principle

P-25

PH INDICATORS

A PH indicator (also called a **color indicator**, **acid-base indicator**, or simply **indicator**) is a PH-sensitive chemical compound that changes a solution sample's color, so the sample's PH (acidity or basicity) can be determined visually. PH indicators are often used in analytical chemistry. Usually, a few drops of a PH indicator are used to do the job.

Phenolphthalein, methyl red, and bromothymol blue are common indicators. Phenolphthalein, which acts in a PH range of 8 to 10, is colorless in acidic solutions and **pink** in basic solutions. Methyl red is **yellow** in samples with a PH above 5. It is **red** in samples with a PH above 5. And it is **orange** at a PH of 5 (because only a portion of the indicator has been converted from yellow to red).

Knowing the following about PH indicators is helpful:

- Sometimes, a mix of two (or more) indicators is used to achieve a few smooth color changes over a wide range of PH values.
- Sometimes, **indicator PH papers** (like Hydrion paper) are used in quick PH tests. The operator matches the dominant color of the blocks on the tester box.

P-26

PHASE DIAGRAMS

A phase diagram (refers to **pressure-temperature phase diagram**) of a chemical substance shows the conditions under which equilibrium between the three (3) phases (solid, liquid, or gas) of that substance occurs at different pressures and temperatures. Figure 1 shows a pure substance's phase diagram. As seen, the substance's temperature (*T*) is usually plotted on *X*-axis and its pressure (*P*) on *Y*-axis, and phases are separated by boundary curves (or lines). Each curve represents a phase situation. And the curve between the liquid and gas phases represents a two-phase situation under which liquid and gas are in equilibrium at a given *T*. In the same figure, point T, which is located at the intersection of all three curves, is called the triple point (T-point), representing *T* and *P*, at which all three phases of a pure substance under study are at equilibrium. For example, the T-point in water (H_2O) occurs at $T = 0°C$ (= 32°F = 273 K) and $P = 0.006$ Atm (= 0.6 kPa, small *P*), as shown in Figure 2.

The solid-liquid phase situation occurs at the highest *P*, the solid-gas phase situation occurs at the lowest *T*, and the liquid-gas phase situation occurs at the highest *T* and ends at a point known as the critical point (C-point), where there is *no* distinction between the liquid and gas phases. Thus, the C-point represents the T_C (critical temperature) and P_C (critical pressure), the *T* and *P*, at which the liquid phase and vapor phase of a pure substance approach each other, resulting in only one phase. The C-point occurs at high temperatures and pressures. For example, the C-point in water occurs at T_C of 374°C and P_C of 218 Atm, as shown in Figure 2.

At C-point, therefore:

- No phase boundary exists between liquid and vapor phases.
- Liquid and vapor phases are at equilibrium (stable) conditions.
- The liquid phase and gaseous phase become indistinguishable.

When the substance under study moves from liquid to gas, the process is called evaporation, and as it moves from gas to liquid, it is called condensation. As the substance moves from liquid to solid, the process is called freezing, and as it moves from solid to liquid, the process is known as the melting process. The curve between the liquid and solid phases corresponds to a two-phase situation in which the liquid and solid phases of the substance are in equilibrium. Similarly, the curve between the gas and solid phases corresponds to these phases' situation in equilibrium.

[Water (H_2O) and carbon dioxide (CO_2) are usually chosen in textbooks for general discussion of phase diagrams. This tradition is followed here, as well. Also, note that the axes in their phase diagrams (Figures 2 and 3) are *not* illustrated to scale.]

As shown in Figure 2 (phase diagram of H_2O) and Figure 3 (phase diagram of CO_2), three (3) lines exist (TA, TB, and TC), each showing the situation under which two (2) phases are at equilibrium. Each line represents a situation, as explained next.

- Line TA represents situations of T and P for solid-gas equilibrium,
- Line TB represents situations of T and P for solid-liquid equilibrium, and
- Line TC represents situations of T and P for liquid-gas equilibrium (stability).

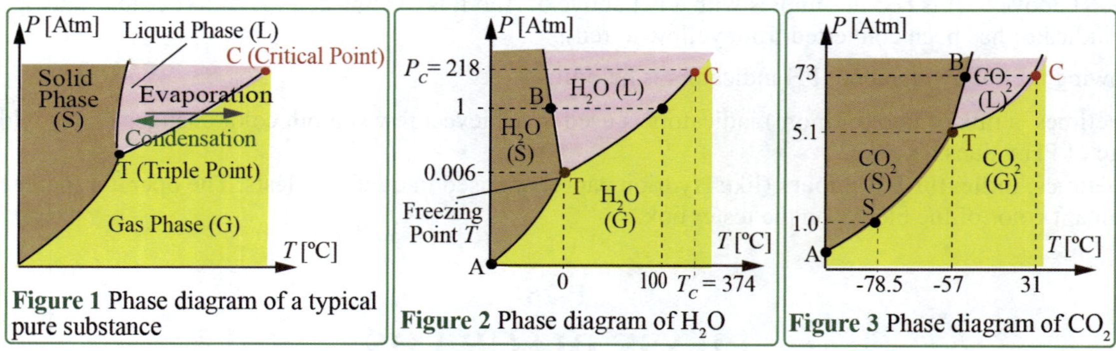

Figure 1 Phase diagram of a typical pure substance

Figure 2 Phase diagram of H_2O

Figure 3 Phase diagram of CO_2

These lines in a phase diagram identify the conditions under which two (2) phases exist at equilibrium. Instead, all points that do *not* fall on the lines represent conditions under which only one phase exists.

The following points can be said by comparing the phase diagrams of H_2O and CO_2:

- The basic features of the phase diagram for H_2O and CO_2 are similar, except that the water's solid-liquid equilibrium line (TB) has a negative slope, meaning that the higher the P, the lower is the water's T_{MP} (melting point temperature). This is because the water is denser than solid water (the ice).
- Solid CO_2 sublimes directly to CO_2 gas, escaping the liquid phase as it warms to room temperature (around 25ºC or 77 ºF) at P_{Atm} (atmospheric pressure). It goes through the sublimation process (shown with symbol S in Figure 3).
- The T-point of H_2O is 0°C (= 32°F) and 6×10^{-3} Atm. And the T-point of CO_2 is –57°C (= –71F°) and 5.1 Atm. [As seen, the T-point of H_2O occurs at a much lower P than CO_2.]
- The C-point of H_2O is 374°C (= 705°F) and 218 Atm. And those of CO_2 are 31°C (= 87°F) and 73 Atm. Therefore, for H_2O to exist as a liquid, P must exceed 1 Atm, and for CO_2, the P must exceed 5.1 Atm.
- At 0°C and 1 Atm, solid H_2O melts. At –78.5°C (= –109.3°F) and 1 Atm, solid CO_2 goes through the sublimation process. [The value –78.5°C is called the sublimation point temperature (T_{SP}) for dry CO_2.]
- At 1 Atm, both the T_{MP} and T_{FP} (freezing point temperature) of H_2O is 0°C, and the T_{SP} of CO_2 is –78.5°C.
- At 1 Atm, liquid water and ice are in equilibrium at the T_{MP} (0°C). Liquid water and water vapor are in equilibrium at T_{BP} (that is100°C). At 1 Atm, solid CO_2 and gas CO_2 are in equilibrium at the T_{SP} (–78.5°C).

P-27

PHASE EQUILIBRIUM

Discussed under the topic of EQUILIBRIUM.

P-28

PHASE RULE

The phase rule (also called the **Gibbs phase rule**) determines the required number of independent intensive variables (which do *not* depend on a system's size) to control a fluid system in an equilibrium condition. In association with a system's phase rule is the **number of degrees of freedom** (D_N), which is the number of independent variables, such as *T* (temperature), *P* (pressure), and *C* (concentration), that is used to control the equilibrium state of a system. If thus, more (or less) D_N is used, the system will be over-specified (or under-specified). D_N can be calculated from a system's number of components (C_N) and its number of phases (P_N).

$$D_N = C_N - P_N + 2 \tag{1}$$

This equation (called the phase-rule equation) applies to non-reactive fluid systems. If, however, the system involves one (or more) chemical reactions, a modified phase-rule equation, which includes the system's **number of independent reactions** (R_N), must be used.

$$D_N = C_N - P_N + 2 - R_N \tag{2}$$

The phase-rule equation has some applications in heat-involving (thermodynamic) systems. Consider a fluid system that contains one component and one phase. Based on Equation 1, D_N of this system equates to 2. This means that the system's equilibrium state can be controlled if two (2) intensive variables (like *T* and *P*) are controlled. Say, in a binary feed, which is under the distillation process and contains two components and two phases, as is usually the case, two phases can keep at equilibrium by *T* and *P* (because D_N is 2).

As another example, consider a fluid system that contains one component and two phases. From the phase-rule equation, the D_N of this system equates to 1. Either *T* or *P* can control the system's equilibrium state (because its D_N equates to 1). Similarly, the equilibrium state of a fluid system that contains two components and one phase can be controlled by three (3) intensive variables: *T*, *P*, and *C* of one of the components, where *C* can be expressed, say, in several moles (*n*).

Further, consider a fluid system that contains water in three different phases (water, water vapor, and ice). Here, the number of components (C_N) is one. That would give us a D_N of $1 - 3 + 2 = 0$. There is, thus, *no* variable required to control the three-phase water system because the system can be controlled by the water's triple point, which is specified at a particular *T* and *P*. [The **triple point** (T-point) of a pure substance is the only *T* and *P*, at which the solid, liquid, and gas phases of that substance can coexist in equilibrium.]

Consider water (H_2O) in the liquid state that has three (3) independent constituents ($C_{N1} = 3$), water, hydronium cations (H_3O^+), and hydroxyl anions (OH^-). In the system, one chemical reaction occurs.

$$2\ H_2O \rightleftharpoons (H_3O)^+ + (OH)^-$$

The C_N of this system can be calculated based on Equation 1, given under the topic of CHEMICAL COMPONENTS.

$$C_N = C_{N1} - R_N - C_{N2} \tag{3}$$

Because only one reaction occurs in the water, the system's R_N equates to 1. The number of constraints (C_{N2}) of the system is one (because of neutrality in electric charges). Thus, C_N will be $3 - 1 - 1 = 1$.

We can now calculate the number of independent variables (number of degrees of freedom, D_N) of the water system using the phase-rule equation (Equation 2).

$$D_N = C_N - P_N + 2 - R_N = 1 - 1 + 2 - 1 = 1$$

Thus, only one variable is needed to control the water system.

P-29

PHASE, PHASE BOUNDARY, AND PHASE CHANGE

Phase: A phase is the state (solid, liquid, or gas) of a substance. In other definition, it is a homogeneous portion of a system that has uniform chemical and physical properties. And it is separated from other parts of that system by a **phase boundary**. For example, a carbonated beverage contains two (2) phases; a homogeneous liquid phase and a gas phase (bubbles) separated by a very thin boundary.

Depending on molecular structure, some substances can exist in all three phases. This happens when the intermolecular forces that hold the molecules of a substance together are strong. For example, water (H_2O), which consists of hydrogen (H) and oxygen (O), can exist in all three phases because H and O are strongly bonded. Instead, sugar (sucrose, $C_{12}H_{22}O_{11}$) exists only in solid and liquid phases. At a high temperature of about 185°C, sugar molecules first change to liquid form and then decompose to the invert sugar and coloring substances. Although these substances turn into gaseous forms, they are *no* longer in the form of sugar molecules.

[Note: The terms **phase** and state of matter are often used equally. This is incorrect because a system can contain two (or more) immiscible phases of the same state of matter. Say, a cup of water (a liquid) with a piece of ice (a solid) contains two phases of the same state of matter, the water.]

Phase Boundary: A phase boundary (phase interface) is an enclosing surface or contacting surface that separates two different phases. The left side of Figure 1 shows a mix of oil in water. The surface where water and oil meet is a liquid-liquid **boundary** (interface). We see a sugar crystal in water in the middle of the same figure. Here the surface of the sugar crystal in water is a solid-liquid boundary. The right side of the same figure shows a container containing water and water vapor. Here the surface of the water is a gas-liquid boundary.

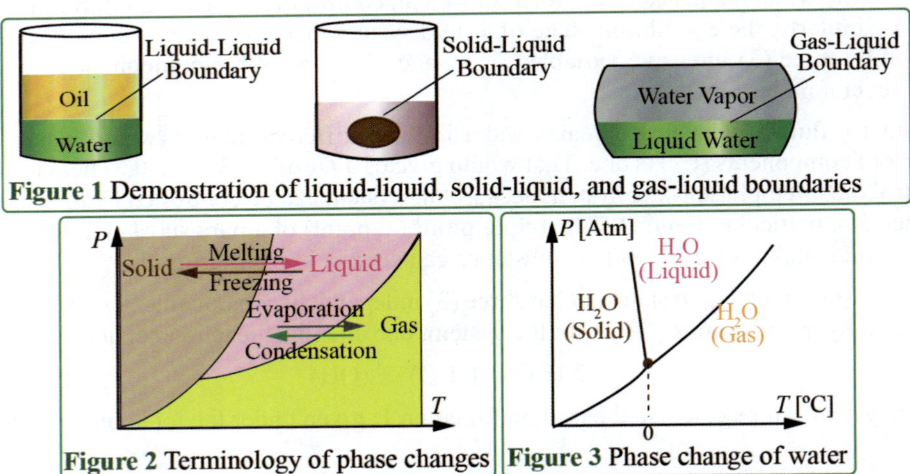

Figure 1 Demonstration of liquid-liquid, solid-liquid, and gas-liquid boundaries

Figure 2 Terminology of phase changes

Figure 3 Phase change of water

Phase Change: Phase change (phase transition) is a change in the phase (the state) of a substance (an element or a compound) when it goes through its upper or lower temperature (T) limit. During a phase change, heat and mass transfer. A phase change is a physical change (because only physical properties of the substance are changed, but *not* its composition).

Phase changes occur between solid, liquid, gas, and, in rare cases, plasma. As shown in Figure 2, when a solid substance goes through its upper limit of T, the melting process (a change from solid to liquid phase) and then the evaporation process (a change from liquid to gaseous phase) occurs. When a gas goes through its lower T limit, the condensation and the freezing processes occur. Some substances, such as carbon dioxide (CO_2), skip a phase, so the sublimation occurs.

Figure 3 illustrates the phase change of water (H_2O). As the figure shows, the water vapor's *T* remains constant at 0C° when condensing to liquid water. The liquid water's *T* also remains constant at 0C° when freezing to form solid water (the ice).

When, for example, ice (a solid) melts into water (a liquid), a physical change occurs because the composition of water has *not* changed. Instead, a chemical change occurs when water reacts with salt because the composition of the involved compounds (the water and salt) was changed.

P-30

PHOTOELECTRIC EFFECT

Study EINSTEIN'S THEORY OF PHOTOELECTRIC EFFECT.

P-31

PHOTON

As the first massless particle discovered, a photon is the quantum particle (a particle with *no* subparticle) of light and other electromagnetic radiations (EM radiations or EM waves). [The term **photon** (rhymes with **electron**) was used by Einstein to indicate that it originates from an electron, and both have similar properties. Instead, the term quantum was first used by Planck for light particles. Said so, the photon is the quantum of light (the quantum particle of light).]

The five top properties of a photon are the following:

- It *cannot* be subdivided anymore, so it is a quantum particle,
- It has a tiny amount of energy (*E*), called photon energy (E_{Ph}),
- It moves at the speed of light constant in a vacuum (because it is massless),
- It does *not* experience time (because it is moving at the speed of light or close to it),
- It has *no* mass (*M*) because it does *not* affect an electric field (E_{ε}), and so *no* electric charge.

When saying a photon has *no* mass (massless), it is *not* the same as having *no* energy (*E*). And this contradicts Einstein equation ($E = M.c^2$). The next explanations try to remove this confusion.

- **First:** When a packet (bundle) consisting of only **one** photon (a rare case) moves in one direction, the packet does *not* have rest *M*. When, instead, a packet consisting of **many** photons (the usual case, shown in Figure 1) is moving in different directions, the packet has *M*. A single photon, however, has a small amount of *E* if it moves at *c* (or close to *c*).
- **Second:** When, in physics, the term "a particle has *no* mass" is used, it means that the mass of that particle is negligible to the extent that it can be approximately considered a massless particle. For example, a single electron is massless, although it has a tiny mass of 9.11×10^{-28} g.
- **Third:** Einstein's equation in the form of $E = M.c^2$ is *not* the full equation. The whole equation considers the particle's momentum (*p*), which is related to the particle's moving velocity (*V*), so $E = M.c^2 + p.c$. If we consider photon as a massless particle, then $M = 0$, so the equation becomes $E = p.c$. Under the topic of PLANCK EINSTEIN EQUATION, we said that a photon's *c*, λ (wavelength), and *f* (frequency) are related by $c = \lambda.f$, and the equation for calculation of photon energy becomes $E_{Ph} = h.c/\lambda$, where *h* is the Planck's constant. To calculate, thus, a photon's energy, we must use $E_{Ph} = h.c/\lambda$, but *not* $E = M.c^2$.

Einstein's contribution to the understanding of light can be briefly outlined as

- He proved that light has a photoelectric effect (when it shines on a metal, it emits electrons).

- He proved that light particles move discontinuously (but look continuous because of their high speed).
- He proved that light moves as individual large packets (bundles) of energy, where each packet consists of many photons that behave like a single-and-large particle.
- He proved that light acts like waves when moving and particles when emitting energy. This dual property was later known as Einstein's theory of light duality. Physicists think low-energy photons (like radiowaves) behave like waves, while high-energy photons (like X-rays) behave more like particles. This behavior is called **wave-particle duality**.

The following are some other properties of the photon:

- It is unstable,
- It has a spin of one,
- It travels in different directions,
- It obeys Bose-Einstein statistics, so it is a Boson,
- It carries *no* electric charge, so it does *not* feel the electromagnetic force (F_{EM}),
- It releases radiation (the release of electromagnetic waves from the atoms of an element),
- It has energy (the photon energy), but it is so tiny that we *cannot* see a photon in a dark room, and

Photon carries energy, which can be calculated by Planck's equation ($E_{Ph} = h.f$), where h is Planck's constant and f is the frequency of a photon's wave. Bohr proved that when an electron falls from a higher-energy shell (orbit) to a lower-energy shell, some energy, which equates to the difference in potential energy between the two shells, is released. The released energy from the electron is then emitted (radiated) in the form of a **packet of light**, known as a **photon** (see Figure 2 under ATOM). Similarly, an electron absorbs energy by colliding with another atom when it jumps from a lower-energy shell to a higher-energy shell (see Figure 3 under ATOM). An electron, in other words, can move between two shells by absorbing or releasing a photon.

The amount of energy that a photon has mainly depends on the number of shell levels (because shells have different amounts of energy). [According to Einstein's theory of special relativity, the time stands unmoved for a photon traveling at the speed of light constant, so the space shrinks to zero. A photon is, therefore, everywhere, at the same time.]

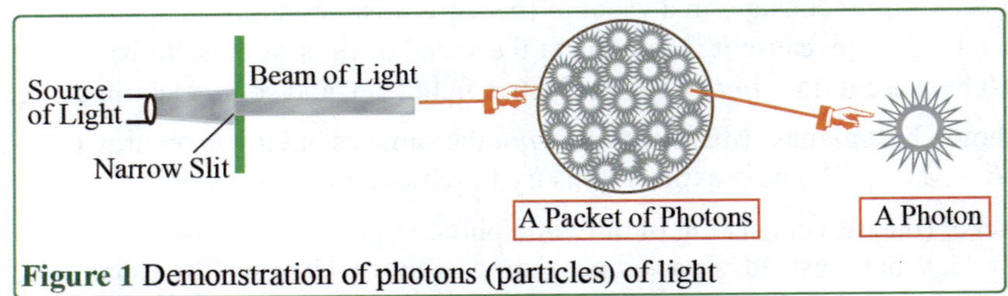

Figure 1 Demonstration of photons (particles) of light

P-32
PHOTON ENERGY

Discussed under the topic of ENERGY AND ITS FORMS.

P-33

PHOTOSYNTHETIC PROCESS

A photosynthetic process (simply **photosynthesis**) is a series of complex reactions during which a plant takes carbon dioxide (CO_2) from the air through the leaves' pores, absorbs water (H_2O) from the soil through its root, and gets the heat energy (E_Q) from the Sun through its leaves to form different sugars (saccharides). A simplified formula for the photosynthetic process is

$$6\ CO_2 + 6\ H_2O + E_Q \rightarrow C_6H_{12}O_6 + 6O_2$$

Carbon dioxide + water + light energy → glucose + oxygen

During this heat-absorbing reaction, the E_Q breaks the chemical bonds between the carbon atom and oxygen atoms in CO_2 molecules and hydrogen and oxygen atoms in H_2O molecules.

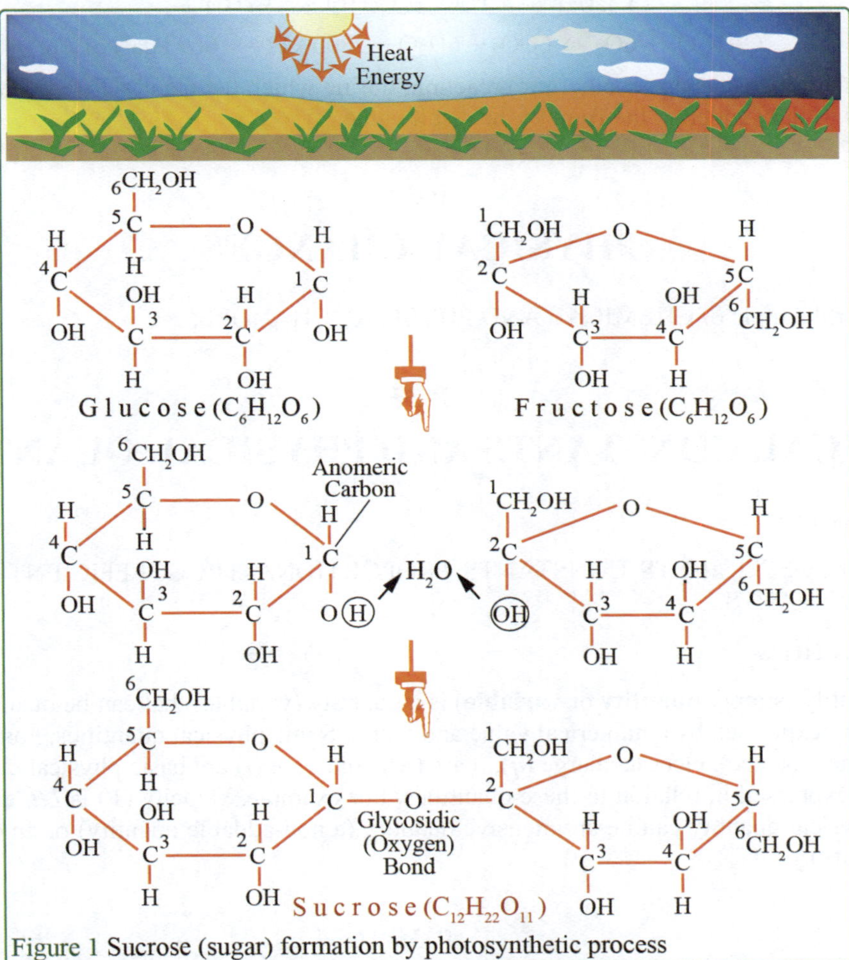

Figure 1 Sucrose (sugar) formation by photosynthetic process

Specifically, let us consider the process of sucrose (sugar) formation in sugarbeet by the photosynthetic process, as shown in Figure 1. First, the monosaccharides of glucose ($C_6H_{12}O_6$) and fructose ($C_6H_{12}O_6$), which are isomers, are produced, as formulized earlier. Then, the two monosaccharides combine with the help of an enzyme called **sucrase** (*not* to be confused with **sucrose**) to form sucrose ($C_{12}H_{22}O_{11}$).

$$C_6H_{12}O_6 + C_6H_{12}O_6 + \text{Enzyme} \rightarrow C_{12}H_{22}O_{11} + H_2O + E_Q$$

This reaction has two characteristics:

- It is a energy-releasing reaction (exothermic reaction).
- It is a dehydration reaction (water-releasing or condensation reaction) because, during the process, one molecule of water is formed by the combining H group on C-1 (reads carbon 1) of the glucose unit (ring) and the OH group of C-2 on the fructose unit. The remaining oxygen then makes a 1:2 oxygen bond (–O–, called glycoside bond when the bond is between sugar molecules), connecting glucose and fructose molecules to form a sucrose molecule ($C_{12}H_{22}O_{11}$). [In general, energy (E) is released to form a chemical bond and absorbed to break a bond.]

The reverse of the photosynthetic reaction is the **respiration reaction**. Sugar and other carbohydrates convert to carbon dioxide and water to produce the energy required for the plant's growth. During growth, particularly at night, the plant respires, and sugar is decomposed to produce E_Q for growth.

$$C_{12}H_{22}O_{11} + H_2O \rightarrow C_6H_{12}O_6 + C_6H_{12}O_6$$

$$C_6H_{12}O_6 + 6O_2 \rightarrow 6CO_2 + 6H_2O - 2800\text{ kJ } (= -669\text{ kcal}) \text{ of } E_Q$$

This reaction is a heat-releasing (exothermic) reaction, during which the plant's T (temperature) is increased, so a minus sign is usually added to the front of the result value.

P-34

PHYSICAL CHANGES

Discussed under the topic of CHEMICAL AND PHYSICAL CHANGES.

P-35

PHYSICAL CONSTANTS AND PHYSICAL QUANTITIES

Physical Constants

Discussed under COEFFICIENTS, CONSTANTS, PROPORTIONALITY COEFFICIENTS, AND PROPORTIONALITY CONSTANTS.

Physical Quantities

A physical quantity (simply **quantity** or **variable**) is a quantity (variable) that can be quantified by measurement and is usually expressed by a numerical value and a unit. Some physical quantities, however, are unitless. Area, length (L, the distance), electric charge (q), mass (M), and time (t) are basic physical quantities. All other quantities can be expressed in relation to these quantities. For example, velocity (V) is L/t, and electric current (I_E) is q/t. [A physical quantity can be an intensive quantity (a non-addable quantity) or an extensive quantity (an addable quantity).]

P-36

PHYSICAL PROPERTIES

Study CHEMICAL AND PHYSICAL PROPERTIES.

P-37

PHYSICS, CHEMISTRY, AND PHYSICAL CHEMISTRY

Physics

Physics studies the physical properties of the universal phenomena, from the tiny quantum particles, which act at atomic and subatomic scales, to the gravitational force (F_g, the force of gravity, or simply **gravity**), which acts in the entire Universe. Based on its definition, physics studies many subjects, like atoms, energy, electricity, magnetism, light, fundamental forces, and many more discussed in this book.

Chemistry

Chemistry studies the chemical properties of the universal phenomena, such as chemical elements and chemical compounds, and their structures, properties, and behavior when undergoing a chemical reaction. This book covers many more chemistry topics.

Physical Chemistry

As a subject study, physical chemistry studies both physical and chemical properties of the universal phenomena using the generalities of central sciences, thermodynamics, and electrochemistry. Dalton's Law of Partial Pressure, Raoult's Law of Vapor Pressure, Thermodynamic Laws, Gas Laws, phase equilibrium, phase diagrams, chemical reactions, energy, entropy, and many more key physical chemistry topics are discussed in this book.

[In this book, the word **physical chemistry** is sometimes used to mean both physics and chemistry. When, for example, saying the Universe acts by a set of supersmart physical chemistry rules, it means that it acts based on the physics and chemistry rules. Similarly, when saying Archimedes' principle is a physical chemistry concept, it is used in physics and chemistry. And when saying Bohr was a great physical chemist, it means he was greatly specialized in physics, chemistry, and physical chemistry.]

P-38

PIEZOELECTRICITY

Piezoelectricity (also called **piezoelectric effect**) is a property of piezoelectric crystals with asymmetric unit cells. [The word **asymmetric unit cell** used here refers to when a crystal's **unit cell** (the smallest unit of atoms, or molecules, that are repeated to form a crystal) is **body-centered** (the unit cell has an extra atom in its center), as discussed under the topic of CRYSTALS.] While each unit cell of a piezoelectric crystal is electronically neutral, when the crystal is compressed (by a tensile, compressive, or shear force), its shape changes, which also changes the distribution of electric charge (simply **charge**) in each of its unit cells. The charged alteration creates a voltage (V, also called **electric voltage** or **potential difference**) across the crystal from one side to the other, as shown in Figure 1. If connected to an electric circuit, the voltage causes an electric current (electricity) that a voltmeter can measure. This effect tells us that the conversion of mechanical energy (E_M) to electric energy (E_E) occurs in the crystal at a microscopic level.

The piezoelectric effect is used in some measuring instruments, such as **ultrasound piezoelectric level probes** and **vibrating piezoelectric level probes**. Both are discussed under the topic of PROCESS CONTROL OF CHEMICAL ENGINEERING. Piezoelectric sensors (transducers) are also used in **microphones**.

[In 1880, Pierre Curie (1859–1906, a French physicist) demonstrated that electricity (alteration of charges) was produced when certain crystals are compressed–a phenomenon now called piezoelectricity.]

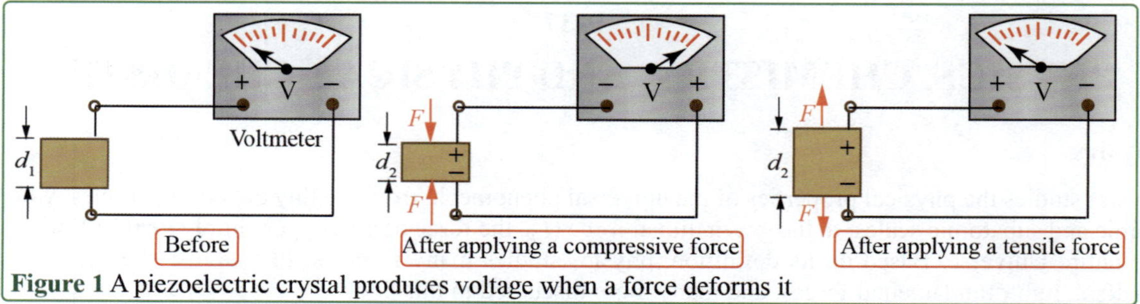

Figure 1 A piezoelectric crystal produces voltage when a force deforms it

P-39

PIPES

A pipe is a cylindrical-hollow shape device (equipment) mainly used to transport a fluid (liquid and gas). Pipes can also carry slurries, powders, granular materials, and more. They are made from metals, ceramics, plastics, fiberglass, or concrete. A pipe is generally specified by its inside diameter (nominal diameter) and a **schedule** that defines its wall thickness.

Fluid flow in the **piping systems** (with pipes, pumps, and valves) is common in chemical plants to carry a fluid from one point to another. The length of the piping systems to move a fluid from point 1 to point 2 is different. In ChemEng, a piping system can be as small as a short pipe or as large as a long pipeline that carries a fluid to a long distance and has several attached and detached parts.

[The terms **pipe** and tube are usually used equally, although minor differences exist. For differences between pipe and tube, refer to the topic of TUBES.]

PIPE SIZING

The simplest way to estimate the length (L) of a pipe follows (see Figure 1):

- Sketch **plan** and **elevation** from a process flow diagram,
- Mark the measurements in XYZ coordinates,
- Estimate the L of each pipe segment,
- Add a factor of 25% for errors, and
- Add 50% to it for fittings.

Referring to Figure 1, the L of line A is: 3m + 1m = 4m and the L of line 11 is: 6m + 3m + 7m + 5m + 3m = 24m. Considering 75% addition for errors and fittings, the total L of the line will be 4m + 1m = 5m and the total L of line 11 will be 24 + 18 = 42m.

A pipe diameter (usually inside diameter) is also necessary for pipe sizing. Assume a liquid flows through a pipe with some fittings and creates a pressure drop of ΔP. Then, the liquid's average velocity ($\bar{V}$) in the pipe can be determined from the liquid's volumetric flow rate ($\dot{V}$) and pipe's diameter (d).

$$\bar{V} = \frac{4\dot{V}}{\pi . d^2} \tag{1}$$

We can calculate the pipe's diameter (d) by substituting this equation into Fanning's equation.

$$d^5 = 32f \frac{\dot{V}^2}{E_{F.Maj}} \times \frac{L}{\pi^2} \tag{2}$$

The f is Fanning's friction factor (unitless), the $\dot{V}$ is the liquid's volumetric flow rate (in m^3/h), L is the pipe's length (in m), and $E_{F.Maj}$ is the major friction energy uses (unitless, discussed under LIQUID FLOW PROCESS).

PIPING SYSTEM DESIGN

The next topics are important in designing a piping system for a liquid flow.

- Mass balance on the flowing liquid,
- Energy balance on the flowing liquid,
- Energy losses (E_L) occurring in the system,
- Size of the system (say, the diameter of the pipe), and
- Average velocity ($\bar{V}$) and pressure drop (ΔP) of the flowing liquid.

The mass balancing of a liquid flow is discussed under MASS BALANCE, and energy balancing and energy losses are discussed under LIQUID FLOW PROCESS. Here, we talk about the velocity (V) and pressure drop (generally pressure difference, ΔP) of a liquid flow in the piping systems.

Consider a horizontal pipe and assume a liquid with a certain viscosity (η) is flowing through the pipe under fully-developed conditions, meaning that the velocity (V) of the flow does *not* change along the flow's direction, which is assumed to be along the X-axis (horizontal) direction. Further, visualize a **cylindrical, small liquid element** (used for coordination purposes) with a radius R and length dL (**differential length** or **tiny length**) moving along the flow's direction (see Figure 2). At the time zero, the liquid element is in AB location, and after a short period, it moves to A_1B_1. Because of the liquid's viscosity and the pipe's wall and attached parts (fittings), the pressure (P) of the liquid element changes from one location to another, so a ΔP will be created in the element. If we indicate the P of the liquid element at points A and B as P_A and P_B and the difference in P between A and B as ΔP, then $\Delta P = P_A - P_B$.

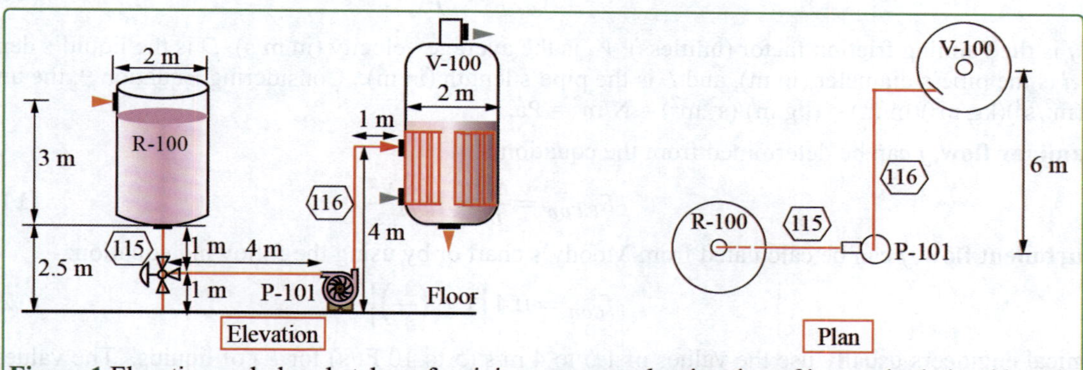

Figure 1 Elevation and plan sketches of a piping system and estimation of its required pipes' length

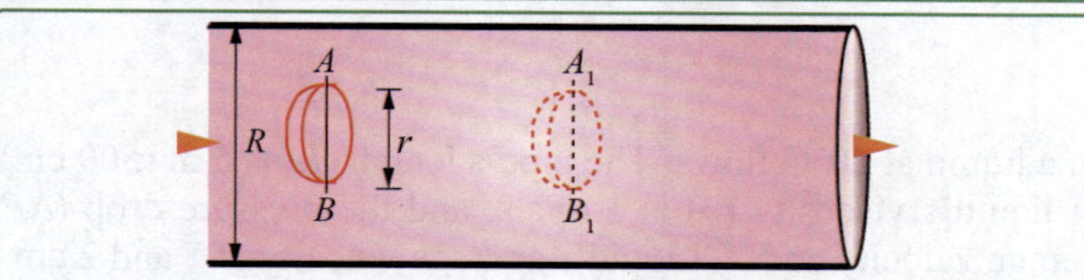

Figure 2 Demonstration of a liquid coordinate element in a pipe for calculation of V (velocity) and ΔP (pressure difference)

Because the pipe is horizontal, F_g (gravitational force, F_g) is zero. The important subject here is the ratio of ΔP (liquid element's pressure drop) to dL (liquid element's length), representing the ΔP over dL per certain time. After some mathematical operations, we can reach an equation that expresses the $\Delta P/dL$ in relation to the liquid's **average velocity** ($\bar{V}$), liquid's viscosity (η), pipe's radius (R), and element's radius (r).

$$\frac{\Delta P}{dL} = \frac{8\bar{V}.\eta}{R^2 - r^2} \qquad (3)$$

This equation can be written for the entire cross-section of the pipe when r is almost zero.

$$\frac{\Delta P}{L} = \frac{8\bar{V}.\eta}{R^2} \tag{4}$$

From this equation, ΔP and $\bar{V}$ can be calculated.

$$\Delta P = 48\eta \frac{L}{R^2} \tag{5}$$

$$\bar{V} = \frac{\Delta P}{8\eta} \times \frac{R^2}{L} \tag{6}$$

If we want to calculate $\bar{V}$ at two different radial locations in the pipe, we must use the radius of the pipe at those locations, that is, R_1 and R_2.

$$\bar{V} = \frac{\Delta P}{8\eta} \times \frac{(R_1^2 - R_2^2)}{L} \tag{7}$$

If we want to calculate V_{max} (the liquid's **maximum velocity**, which is double of $\bar{V}$), we must multiply Equation 6 by two (2).

$$V_{max} = \frac{\Delta P}{4\eta} \times \frac{R^2}{L} \tag{8}$$

The liquid's ΔP and $\bar{V}$ can also be calculated from Fanning's equation.

$$\Delta P = 2f.\bar{V}^2.D\frac{L}{d} \tag{9}$$

$$\bar{V} = \left(\frac{\Delta P}{2f.D} \times \frac{d}{L}\right)^{1/2} \tag{10}$$

Here, f is the Fanning friction factor (unitless), V_A is the average velocity (in m/s), D is the liquid's density (in kg/m^3), d is the pipe's diameter (in m), and L is the pipe's length (in m). Considering Equation 9, the unit for P will be (m^2/s^2)(kg/m^3)(m/m) = (kg.m)/(s^2.m^2) = N/m^2 = Pa.

In a **laminar flow**, f can be determined from the equation,

$$E_{F.Con} = \frac{\Delta P}{D} = f_{Con}\frac{V^2}{2} \tag{11}$$

In a **turbulent flow**, f can be calculated from Moody's chart or by using the following equation:

$$f_{Con} = 0.4\left[1 - \left(\frac{A_2}{A_1}\right)\right] \tag{12}$$

[Chemical engineers usually use the values of 1.5 to 4 m/s (5 to 10 Ft/s) for V_A of liquids. The values are 15 to 40 m/s (50 to 120 Ft/s) for gasses.]

An Example on Pipes:

Given: A pipe in which a liquid at 20°C flows. The pipe's length (L) is 5 m (500 cm), and its inside diameter (d) is 4 cm. The flowing liquid's viscosity (η) is 10 Pa.s, and the pressure drop (ΔP) in the pipe is 500 Pa. Calculate: 1) Liquid's average velocity and 2) Liquid's average velocity at 1 and 2 cm of the pipe's radius

Liquid's average velocity can be calculated from Equation 6.

$$V_A = \frac{\Delta P}{4\eta} \times \frac{R^2}{L} = \frac{500}{4\times10} \times \frac{\left(\frac{4}{2}\right)^2}{500} = 0.1 \text{ m/s}$$

Average velocity at 1 cm and 2 cm radial points can be calculated from Equation 7.

$$V_A = \frac{\Delta P}{4\eta} \times \frac{(R^2 - r^2)}{L} = \frac{500}{4\times10} \times \frac{\left(\frac{4}{2}\right)^2 - \left(\frac{1}{2}\right)^2}{500} = 0.09 \text{ m/s} \qquad V_A = \frac{500}{4\times10} \times \frac{\left(\frac{4}{2}\right)^2 - \left(\frac{2}{2}\right)^2}{500} = 0.075 \text{ m/s}$$

P-40

PLANCK

Max Planck (1858−1947) was an excellent German theoretical physicist and teacher (he taught physics at Berlin University for 39 years). He received the Noble Prize in physics in 1918 for the discovery of blackbody radiation (later Planck's theory of blackbody radiation) and proving that when a blackbody is heated, it radiates energy in the form of electromagnetic waves (EM waves).

Planck made several other contributions to physics, including the following:

- He was the first physicist who appropriately used the word **quanta** (see quantum) in his theory (later Planck's quantum theory. In his theory, he proved that a beam of light (light energy) moves in small-separate (quantized) packets (called them **quanta**). His theory laid the foundation for the general concept of quantum and quantization and later quantum physics.
- Besides his quantum theory and theory of blackbody radiation, he is known for Planck's constant, Planck's length, and some other discoveries.

Planck was the president of a research institute, later the Max Planck Society. In his honor, Germany named all government-funded research centers the Max Planck institutes and founded the Max Planck medal.

In his life, Planck went through some personal tragedies. Two of his daughters died in childbirth. One of his sons was killed in action in World War I, and the Nazi's hardliners executed another son after being accused of planning to assassinate Hitler.

[Planck, Einstein, Rutherford, Bohr, Heisenberg, Schrodinger, and Broglie can be named as the top seven (7) quantum physicists. And Newton, Faraday, and Maxwell as the three (3) top classical physicists. The ten (10) pioneers contributed to physics more than all other physicists combined.]

Planck and Einstein receive the first Max Planck medals in 1929 (illustrated for this book)

1900 — Presented his quantum theory that established the concept of quantization of light by proving that light particles travel in fixed packets, called by Planck "quanta"

1918 — Received the Nobel Prize in physics for discovery of blackbody radiation and proving that when a blackbody is heated, it radiates energy in the form of EM waves

1947 — Nominated many times for the Nobel Prize in physics during his life, but won once

2020 — 83 International research institutes involved in physics are named Max Planck Institutes in Planck's honor

Some of Planck's scientific and honorary achievements

P-41

PLANCK EINSTEIN EQUATION

The Planck-Einstein equation relates Planck's equation ($E_{Ph} = h.f$) with the speed of light constant (c) used in Einstein's equation ($E = M.c^2$). In 1905, Einstein proposed that light consists of photons, whose energy, known as photon energy (E_{Ph}), is related to the wavelength (λ) of the photons' waves in just the way Planck had described in 1900.

Because the speed of light constant (c) and light's wavelength (λ), and the light's frequency (f) are related by $c = \lambda.f$, the equation for calculation of E_{Ph} (photon energy) becomes

$$E_{Ph} = \frac{h.c}{\lambda} \qquad (1)$$

This equation (called the Planck-Einstein equation) expresses the E_{Ph} (in J) in relation to the Planck's constant ($h = 6.63{\times}10^{-34}$ J.s), the speed-of-light constant (in m/s), and light's wavelength (λ, in m).

The Planck-Einstein equation says that higher-frequency photons (shorter-wave photons) carry more energy. And because Planck's constant (h) has a very tiny value, a single photon has a small amount of energy. Say, the energy carried by a photon of red light with $\lambda = 650$ nm (or 6.5×10^{-7} m) is small, as shown here.

$$E_{PH} = \frac{h.c}{\lambda} = \frac{6.63{\times}10^{-34}{\times}3{\times}10^{8}}{6.5{\times}10^{-7}} = 3 \times 10^{-19} \qquad \text{(J.s)(m/s)/m} = \text{J}$$

P-42

PLANCK'S CONSTANT

Planck constant (h) is a proportionality constant that relates photon energy (E_{Ph}) to the frequency (f) of a photon's wave.

$$h = \frac{E_{Ph}}{f} \qquad (1)$$

Heisenberg, in his quantum theory (Heisenberg's uncertainty principle), proved that the uncertainty in the amount of energy (E) of a quantum particle (a particle with *no* subparticle like an electron) times the uncertainty in its velocity (V) times the mass (M) of it *cannot* be smaller than h.

The h is usually expressed in J.s (energy multiplied by time), equating to N.m.s or kg.m^2/s. The h of a photon has a very tiny value of $6.626\,070 \times 10^{-34}$ J.s ($= 6.626\,070 \times 10^{-34}$ kg.m^2/s), as given by CODATA in 2019. To have a sense of the tininess of h, note that 1 J is the amount of energy released from a candle for 1 s. When the h is expressed in J.s, Planck's constant (h) is one of the smallest constants used in physics. Considering Equation 1 as $E_{Ph} = h.f$ and green light with a wavelength of 555 nm (a wavelength that the human's eye can notice), each photon has an energy of 3.58×10^{-38} J, which is too tiny.

[Defining his constant h let Planck formulate a new set of quantities, such as Planck's length (L_P), $1.616{\times}10^{-35}$ m, the smallest unit of measurement possible. The amount of time it takes for a photon to travel a Planck's length at the speed of light is one unit of **Planck's time** (the smallest measurable unit of time, 5×10^{-43} seconds).]

[Sometimes, physicists use **reduced Planck's constant**, which equates to $h/2\pi$.]

P-43

PLANCK'S EQUATION

Planck published a paper in 1900 to mathematically express the photon energy (E_{Ph}) of a photon in relation to the frequency (f) of the photon's wave through a proportionality constant, named later Planck's constant (h = 6.63×10^{-34} J.s/photon).

$$E_{Ph} = h.f \quad (1)$$

The term f (frequency) in this equation equates to c/λ, where c is the speed of light constant ($\approx 3\times10^5$ km/s = 3×10^8 m/s) and λ (lambda) is the wavelength of the photon's wave. Thus,

$$E_{Ph} = h.f = \frac{h.c}{\lambda} \quad (2)$$

This equation tells us as f increases, E_{Ph} increases, and as λ decreases, E_{Ph} increases. In these equations, the h is in J.s, frequency (f) is in 1/s, so E_{Ph} becomes in J. In the upcoming Example, we try to calculate the photon energy of one mole of photons, where there are always 6.02×10^{23} particles in 1 mole of any substance (where the value 6.02×10^{23} is Avogadro's number).

An Example on Planck's Equation

Given: A source of laser that releases blue light (like a disk player) with a wavelength (λ) of 400 nm, where 1 nm = 10^{-9} m (one billionth of a meter, m).

Wanted: The energy of 1 mole of photons of blue light, knowing $h = 6.63\times10^{-34}$ J.s/photon)

We first convert λ from nm to m (400 nm $\times$ 10^{-9} = 4×10^{-7} m) and then find the wave's f (frequency).

$$f = \frac{c}{\lambda} = \frac{3\times10^{8}\ \text{m/s}}{4\times10^{-7}\text{m}} = 7.5 \times 10^{14}\ \ 1/\text{s}$$

$$E_{Ph} = h.f = 6.63 \times 10^{-34} \times 7.5 \times 10^{14} = 5 \times 10^{-19}\ \ \text{J/photon}$$

To find the E_{Ph} for 1 mole of photons, we must multiply the E_{PH} of 1 photon by the Avogadro's number.

$$E_{Ph} = 5 \times 10^{-19} \times 6.02 \times 10^{23} = 3 \times 10^{5}\ \ \text{J/mole photons or 300 kJ/mole photons}$$

P-44

PLANCK'S LENGTH

Planck's length is the shortest measurable length (L), equal to 1.616×10^{-35} m (practically 10^{-35} m), which is used as a subatomic scale for length (distance). It is a scale at which the effect of quantum gravity is believed to become significant. Planck's length is related to the quantization of light and mass. That is to say, the *smaller* the length between two systems, the *more* those systems are ruled by quantum physics. This, however, has a limit (because making a distance too small causes impossible correct measurement). And this occurs around the Planck's length.

Planck's length can be calculated from three (3) fundamental constants of nature, Planck's constant (h), gravitational constant (K_G or G), and the speed of light constant (c).

$$L_P = \sqrt{\frac{h.K_G}{C^3}} = 1.616199(97) \times 10^{-35} \quad (1)$$

The Planck's constant used in this equation is **reduced Planck's constant**, which equates to h/2л.

P-45

PLANCK'S QUANTUM THEORY

Planck published his quantum theory in 1900 to say that light (refers to light energy) travels and emits (releases) its energy (the light or photon energy) in quantized (individual-and-discontinuous) units called **energy packets**. Planck called the light's packets the **quanta** (the plural of quantum). Soon later (in 1905), Einstein called the energy packets the photons, which coincide with electrons (a photon originates from an electron).

The idea of light's quantization came to Planck when he experimented with making **light bulbs** more efficient. Then he became interested in finding an equation for calculating the wavelength (λ) of light and infrared light emitted by a blackbody at a given temperature (T). He tried everything that classical physics could offer at that time, but with *no* success, until he came to the following two important ideas:

- The radiation from a hot body is *not* released continuously, like water running from a faucet, but rather like a dripping faucet, in tiny packets (quanta or photons). This is known as the **quantization of energy**.
- The energy of these packets is related to their wavelengths, and the packets with the shortest wavelengths have the greatest energy.

In his theory, Planck said that the energy of each quantum can be specified by its wavelength (λ) and the distance between two quanta, which was known later as Planck's constant (h). Because λ and f (frequency) are related, he used f and h (as a proportionality constant) to calculate quantum energy (photon energy, E_{Ph}).

$$E_{Ph} = h.f \tag{1}$$

This important equation was then called Planck's equation, which tells us the *greater* the f (or, the *shorter* the λ of the light's waves, the *greater* is the light's E_{Ph}).

P-46

PLANCK'S THEORY OF BLACKBODY RADIATION

Study BLACKBODY RADIATION.

P-47

PLASMA

Discussed under the topic of STATES OF MATTER.

P-48

PLASTICITY

Discussed under the topic of ELASTICITY AND PLASTICITY.

P-49

PLASTICS

Discussed under the topic of ELASTICS AND PLASTICS.

P-50
PLC

Abbreviated word for PROGRAMMABLE LOGIC CONTROLLER.

P.51
PLUTONIUM

Plutonium (Pu) is a radioactive element (radionuclide). As element 94 in the periodic table of elements, the Pu has an atomic mass number (N_A, the total number of protons and neutrons) of 244 and an atomic number (N_Z; the total number of protons) of 94, so it has 150 neutrons. Plutonium 244 (Pu-244) has a short half lifetime (24 000 years), so it has high radioactivity (it releases radiation at a high rate).

Pu-239, an isotope of Pu-244, was first synthesized in the USA in late 1940 by a nuclear chain reaction performed on a uranium-238 (U-238).

$$^{238}_{92}\text{U} + 1\text{ n} \rightarrow {}^{239}_{92}\text{U}$$

$$^{239}_{92}\text{U} \rightarrow {}^{239}_{93}\text{Np} + {}^{0}_{-1}\beta$$

$$^{239}_{93}\text{Np} \rightarrow {}^{239}_{94}\text{Pu} + {}^{0}_{-1}\beta$$

In the first reaction, the U-238 absorbs a neutron (n^0) to become U-239. In the second reaction, the U-239 changes to Np (neptunium, the element 93) and beta particle. In the final reaction, the Np-239 changes to the Pu-239 and releases another beta particle.

As a fissile element, Pu-239 (simply **plutonium**) can release an enormous amount of energy used in nuclear power plants and nuclear weapons. For the first time, Pu-239 was used in a bomb, which was dropped on the Japanese city of Nagasaki on August 9, 1945. Three days earlier, another bomb was dropped on the same city, which used uranium-235. These two bombs ended the Second World War.

Some nuclear power plants use Pu-based fuels, including Pu-239, PuO_2 (plutonium dioxide), and UO_2 (uranium dioxide). This compound is known as the MOX.

The following are two properties of Pu-244

- Its boiling point temperature (T_{BP}) = 3228°C (5842°F), and
- Its melting point temperature (T_M) = 639°C (1183°F).

P-52
POISE

The Poise (P) is one of two SI units of viscosity (η), the other one is Pascal-second (Pa.s), where 1 P = 100 cP (centipoise), 1 cP = 10^{-3} Pa.s = 1 mPa.s (milli Pa,s), and 1 Pa.s = 1 (N.s)/m^2 = 10 P. Here, Pa is for Pascal (the SI unit of pressure), N is for Newton (the SI unit of force), and m is for meter. [The name Poise is after J. L. M. Poiseuille (1797−1869), French physicist.]

P-53

POLAR AND NONPOLAR COMPOUNDS

A **polar compound** (also called **polar covalent compound** because of being a covalent compound) is a compound whose molecules carry a positive electric charge (simply **charge**) on one side and a negative charge on the other side. Thus, a chemical polarity (simply polarity) exists on both sides of a polar molecule. Polarity exists in a molecule as an **electric dipole** (simply dipole), so the molecule has different charges on either side. It, therefore, depends on the amount of electronegativity (E_{Neg}) between a molecule's atoms that share electron pair (two valence electrons that act together as a chemical bond).

Water, ammonia (NH_3), hydrogen fluoride (HF), and glass are examples of polar compounds. In a water molecule (H_2O), a negative polarity exists on the oxygen (O) atom (because the E_{Neg} of the O atom is greater than that of H), and a positive polarity exists on the hydrogen (H) atom. As a result, the oxygen atom pulls the electron pairs (which act as covalent bonds between O and each H atom) toward itself. In a molecule of ammonia (NH_3), similarly, a negative polarity exists on the nitrogen (N) atom (because E_{Neg} of the N atom is greater than that of H). In an ozone molecule (O_3), the two oxygen bonds are nonpolar (because *no* E_{Neg} difference exists between atoms of the same element). Because of, however, a bent molecular shape, the ozone molecule is polar. In relation to polarity, the ozone's central O atom has a charge of + 1, and each side O atom has a charge of – ½. This is because the central O atom must share its electron pair with other atoms, but each of the side O atoms must share its electrons with only one other atom, so the central O atom pulls the side's electrons toward itself. Figure 1 illustrates the concept of polarity in H_2O, NH_3, and O_3 molecules.

A **nonpolar compound** (also called a **nonpolar covalent compound**) is a compound whose molecules do *not* carry charges, so *no* polarity exists on its sides. Molecular hydrogen (H_2 or H–H), molecular fluorine (F_2 or F–F), and boron trifluoride (BF_3) are examples of nonpolar compounds.

A diatomic molecule consisting of the same atoms is a nonpolar molecule (because there is *no* difference in E_{Neg} between the atoms of the same element). An oxygen molecule (O_2, a diatomic molecule of the same element), for example, is a nonpolar molecule (see Figure 2).

Carbon dioxide (CO_2) has 2 polar C = O bonds, but its geometry is linear (straight), so that the two bond dipoles cancel and, therefore, *no* net dipole remains, so the CO_2 molecule is nonpolar (Figure 2).

Study the following:

- If two solvents are both polar, they dissolve in one another. Water and ethanol (C_2H_5OH), both polar solvents, dissolve in one another.
- If two solvents are both nonpolar, they also dissolve in one another. For example, hexane (C_6H_{14}) and chloroform (CCl_4), both being nonpolar, dissolve in each other.

The listed statements are the subject of a principle known as the **like-dissolves-like rule**, which simply says two liquids dissolve in one another if their molecules are similar in polarity.

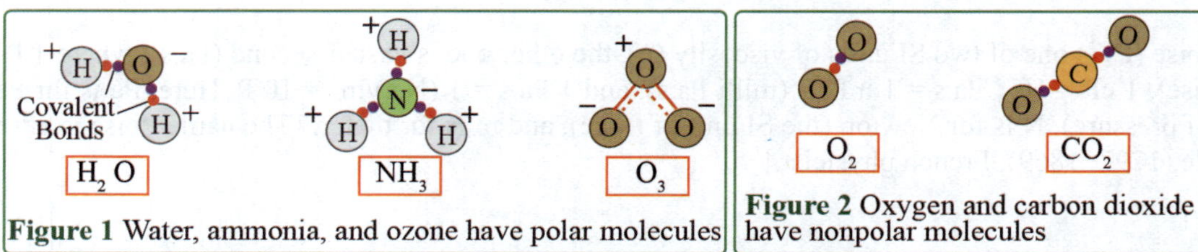

Figure 1 Water, ammonia, and ozone have polar molecules

Figure 2 Oxygen and carbon dioxide have nonpolar molecules

P-54

POLAR COVALENT BONDS

Discussed under CHEMICAL BONDS.

P-55

POLARIMETRY AND POLARIZABILITY

Polarimetry

Polarimetry is a laboratory technique that uses a **polarimeter** (polaroscope, see Figure 1) to measure the concentration (C) of an optically-active substance, like sucrose (sugar), in a solution sample. When light moves, it spreads in all directions (planes). And when it passes through a polarizer, it forms a **polarized light** (a straight one-direction light with a narrow band). Polarimetry uses the polarized light and its **rotation** (bending) when passing through an optically-active substance by measuring the light's rotation angle, which is proportional to the C of that substance in the sample. The degree of rotation of the polarized light is called the **degree of polarization** (polarization or simply **pol**).

The following factors affect the degree of polarization:

- The temperature (T) of the sample,
- The wavelength (λ) of the polarimeter,
- The length (L) of the polarimeter tube (tube's path length), and
- The concentration of optically-active substances in the sample.

The degree of polarization increases with increasing T. In the labs, the T, the λ, and the L of the polarimeter tube are kept constant, so the degree of polarization relates directly to the C of the solution sample.

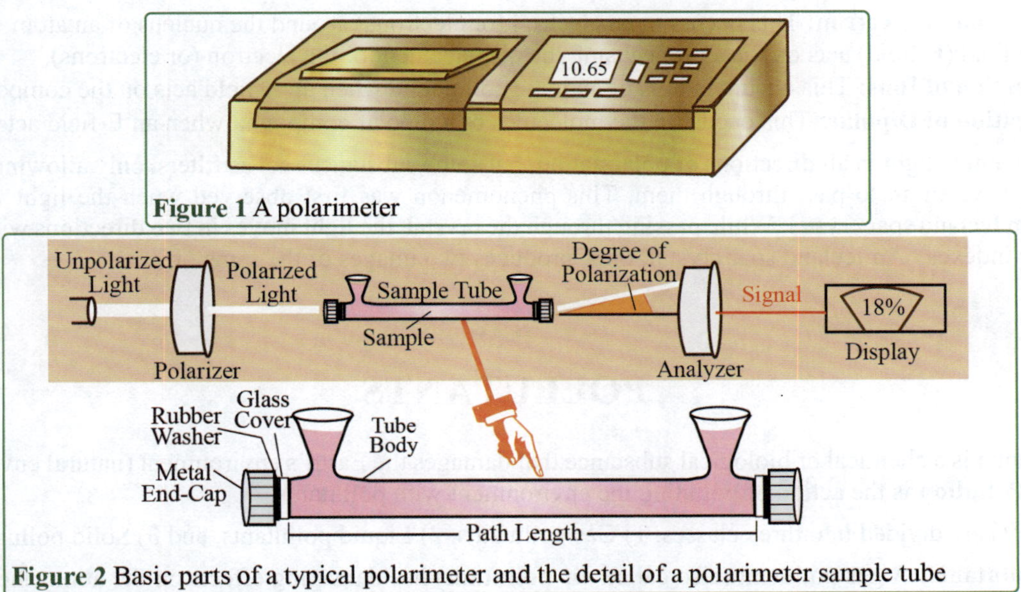

Figure 1 A polarimeter

Figure 2 Basic parts of a typical polarimeter and the detail of a polarimeter sample tube

The following are the main parts of a polarimeter (see Figures 2):

- A polarizer for creating a cross-polarized light,
- A sample tube for holding the sample in the way of the polarized light,
- A prism-type analyzer for finding out if the incoming light is polarized or plane, and
- A scale (calibrated 0 to 360º) for measuring the degree of polarization (simply **polarization** or **pol**).

Polarizability

Polarizability (∝) is a term used in polarimetry to refer to the ability of an optically-active substance (like a sugar solution) to change the angle of polarized light (a light with a narrow band in one direction). A polarized light is formed as light passes through a polarizer, like a **prism** (a triangular glass block). [The term polarizability can also refer to the electrical property of an electrically charged material.]

P-56
POLARITY

See CHEMICAL POLARITY.

P-57
POLARIZATION

Polarization, in science, has different definitions, depending on the context and field. Mostly, it is followed by a defining word, which makes the distinction clearer, as given next.

- **Polarization of Light:** This occurs as a polarized light passes through a polarizer. Conventional linear polarization is in a fixed direction, while **circular polarization** is in a rotational direction
- **Polarization of Electron:** This occurs in an electron (or electrons) around the nucleus of an atom when an electric field (E-field) acts on the atom, causing the displacement of the electron (or electrons).
- **Polarization of Ions:** This occurs in ions of an ionic compound when an E-field acts on the compound.
- **Polarization of Dipolar:** This occurs in the molecules of a dipolar compound when an E-field acts on it.

The Sun emits light in all directions of polarization, but some substances act as filters, only allowing light with a certain wavelength to pass through them. This phenomenon was first observed when the light was passed through an Iceland spar crystal. While passing through the crystal, the light moves in two directions with different refractive indexes. An Iceland spar crystal, thus, produces two images of the same object.

P-58
POLLUTANTS

A pollutant is a chemical or biological substance that damages the Earth's environment (natural environmental system). **Pollution** is the action of polluting the environment with pollutants.

Pollutants are divided into three classes: 1) Gas pollutants, 2) Liquid pollutants, and 3) Solid pollutants.

Gas Pollutants: A gas pollutant (also called **air pollutant**) has damaging effects on the atmospheric air (the air surrounding the Earth's surface) and, consequently, affects the health of humans, animals, and plants. The following two groups of pollutants are in the subclass of gas pollutants:

- Particulate Matters: Particulates are in the class of gas pollutants (because they consist of fine particles and are always in motion in the air).
- Odors, dust, smoke, and smog in the air.

Gas pollutants generated from combustion include sulfur dioxide (SO_2), carbon monoxide (CO), carbon dioxide (CO_2), oxides of nitrogen (collectively called NOX), unburned fuel, and air toxics (like mercury and hydrochloric acid). Other gas pollutants include ammonia (NH_3), hydrogen sulfide (H_2S), and chlorofluorocarbons (CFC). Some gas pollutants (like SO_2, CO_2, NO_2, and NO) can react with water in the air to form acid rain. SO_2 can react with water in the air to form H_2SO_3 (sulfurous acid), a component of acid rain.

$$SO_2 + H_2O \rightarrow H_2SO_3$$

Liquid Pollutants: Wastewater is the major liquid waste of a chemical process plant. After being treated in the plant's wastewater treatment station, most of the wastewater is returned to the facility's water-cycle system to be reused again. The wastewater reuse reduces the amount of water discharged and the plant's operating cost. However, a chemical plant's remaining wastewater, after being carefully treated, is disposed to a natural water source (mostly a river or a lake),

Solid Pollutants: The solid pollutants of chemical facilities are either solid or semi-solid and can be divided into invaluable and valuable solid wastes. Some of the invaluable solid wastes can be discharged into the environment, and the valuable ones can be used as raw material to produce other products.

P-59

POLYETHYLENE, POLYPROPYLENE, AND POLYVINYL CHLORIDE

Polyethylene, polypropylene, and polyvinyl chloride are three of the world's most-used synthetic polymers, each with different properties, which will be discussed next.

Polyethylene

Polyethylene (PE) is a lightweight, inexpensive, and the world's most-used polymer (with about 100 Mt each year). PE's chemical formula is $(C_2H_4)_n$, which is the composition of many repeating units (**monomers** in polymerization) of ethylene (C_2H_4), connected by the methylene group (CH_2).

$$n\ CH_2 = CH_2\ \text{(gas)} \rightarrow [-CH_2 - CH_2 -]_n\ \text{(solid)}$$

In the polymerization of ethylene, T (temperature) and P (pressure) play important roles, as they affect the physical properties of PE. After polymerization, the liquid PE is formed by **extrusion**, a process in which the liquid PE is pressed into long sheets by P or by molding.

The two main types of PE (polyethylene) are the following:

- **Low-Density PE:** It has a low density (D) and is used in making pipes. It is made by extrusion at high T (247ºC) and P (1000 to 5000 Atm).
- **High-Density PE:** It has a high D and is used when greater hardness is required, such as water, detergent, and milk bottles. Extrusion produces low P (6 to 8 Atm) and low T (70ºC).

Some of PE's properties are listed next.

- Its density (D) is low (880 to 960 kg/m^3 or 55 to 60 Lb/Ft^3).
- Its melting point temperature (T_{MP}) is 120 to 130ºC (= 250 to 266ºF).
- Its strength is $4{\times}10^5$ N/m^2 = $0.6{\times}10^5$ Lb/In^2), where Lb is for pound-force and In is for inch.

Polypropylene

Polypropylene (PP) is the world's second-used polymer. PP's formula is $(C_3H_6)_n$ and consists of many monomers of propylene (C_3H_6), connected by

Polyvinyl Chloride

Polyvinyl chloride [$(C_2H_3Cl)_n$, abbreviated PVC) is the world's third-used polymer (with the production of about 40 Mt each year). PVC's formula is $(C_2H_4)_n$ and consists of many monomers of vinyl chloride (C_2H_3Cl), connected by methylene group (CH_2).

$$n\, C_2H_3Cl \rightarrow [CH_2-CH-Cl]_n$$

This reaction is a heat-releasing (exothermic) reaction, so it needs cooling. As the volume (V) is reduced during the polymerization reaction (because PVC is denser than C_2H_3Cl), water is continually added to the mixture to maintain the V. At the start of the reaction, usually, one (or two) initiators, such as hydrogen peroxide (H_2O_2), is added to the mixture to increase the reaction rate.

PVC is produced in two types: inflexible (rigid) and flexible. The rigid type produces pipes, bottles, doors, windows, and more. The T_{MP} of rigid PVC is 100 to 260ºC (= 212 to 500ºF).

P-60

POLYMERS AND POLYMERIZATION PROCESS

Polymers

A polymer (**poly** means many and **mer** means units) is a long-chain (polymeric) molecule with many repeating units and a high molecular mass (M_M). [Monomers are a polymer's repeating units.] In the production of polymers, temperature (T) and pressure (P) play important roles because of changing their physical properties, such as strength.

Plants use glucose ($C_6H_{12}O_6$) as a monomer to produce starch [$(C_6H_{10}O_5)_n$, a polymer] by consecutive dehydration reactions (losing-water reactions). Under suitable conditions, the polymerization of glucose monomers can continue up to one million, as the final units always have one (or more) unreacted hydroxyl functional group (OH).

$$n\, C_6H_{12}O_6 \rightarrow (C_6H_{10}O_5)_n + n\, H_2O$$

For example, monomer ethylene (C_2H_4) is polymerized to produce polyethylene (PE). Similarly, propylene (C_3H_6), vinyl chloride (C_2H_3Cl), styrene (C_8H_8), and tetrafluoroethylene (C_2F_4, also called tetrafluoroethylene) is polymerized to produce the following polymers: polypropylene (PP), polyvinyl chloride (PVC), polystyrene, and polytetrafluoroethylene (PTFE). These polymers are then used to produce different synthetic plastics. Say, PE is used to make plastic bags and other products, PVC is used to make plastic pipes, tubes, and hoses, polystyrene is used to produce ion-exchange resin, and PTFE is used to produce Teflon (C_2F_4).

Because of many applications, the waste disposal of synthetic plastics to the environment is becoming a major concern, so their recycling continuously increases.

Polymers have specific physical properties, including the following:

- They all have the formability to be formed into different shapes with different hardness.
- In their production, T and P play important roles. After polymerization, the liquid polymer is processed by **extrusion**, a process in which the liquid polymer is pressed into long sheets by pressure or molding.

The following are two specific groups of polymers:

- Elastomers are polymers with more than 200% elastic elongation (three times the original length) and can be returned to their original length.
- Plastics are polymers with a minor difference. [For general purposes, scientists recommend distinguishing between the two terms of **plastics** and **polymers** is unnecessary.]

Polymerization Process

Polymerization is the reacting and binding (connecting) the unsaturated molecules of a monomer (a molecular unit connected to another unit) together to produce a polymer. For example, the polymerization of ethylene (C_2H_4) occurs by connecting many of its molecules (**monomers** in polymerization) by methylene group (CH_2).

$$n\,CH_2 = CH_2 \text{ (gas)} \rightarrow [-CH_2 - CH_2 -]_n \text{ (solid)}$$

The T (temperature) and P (pressure) play important roles in polymerization. After polymerization, the liquid polymer is usually formed by **extrusion**, a process in which the liquid polymer is pressed into long sheets by P or by molding.

Polymerization of monomers occurs through some reactions that vary in complexity, as different functional groups exist in the monomers that undergo the polymerization process. This makes the formability of polymers to be shaped difficult. For this reason, some additives are added during the polymerization of plastics to improve their formability. For example, the ion-exchange resin is produced by polymerization (crosslinking) of **styrene** molecules (C_8H_8, a monomer).

P-61
POLYPROPYLENE

Discussed under the topic of POLYETHYLENE, POLYPROPYLENE, AND POLYVINYL CHLORIDE.

P-62
POLYSACCHARIDES

Study SACCHARIDES AND POLYSACCHARIDES.

P-63
POLYVINYL CHLORIDE

Discussed under the topic of POLYETHYLENE, POLYPROPYLENE, AND POLYVINYL CHLORIDE.

P-64
POSITION

Position (R, also called **position vector**) is a single point (symbol P) in space that can be defined by three coordinates in relation to a reference point, called **origin** (symbol O), as shown in Figure 1. It is, therefore, a vector quantity (a quantity with both magnitude and direction) that can be used to define the location of a point in space. In other words, R is a displacement (a vector quantity) of point O to P, so R = OP.

In physics, the time rate of the position is the velocity (V), and the time rate of velocity is acceleration (a).

$$V = \frac{dR}{dt} \tag{1}$$

$$a = \frac{dV}{dt} = \frac{d^2R}{d^2t} \tag{2}$$

The right side of Figure 1 illustrates the derivation of V and a of a particle with mass M.

[In the case of an electron (a quantum particle, a particle with *no* subparticle), it is correct to use the word **position of an electron** instead of the **energy of an electron** (since the amount of an electron's energy tells us in what **electron shell** it is positioned).]

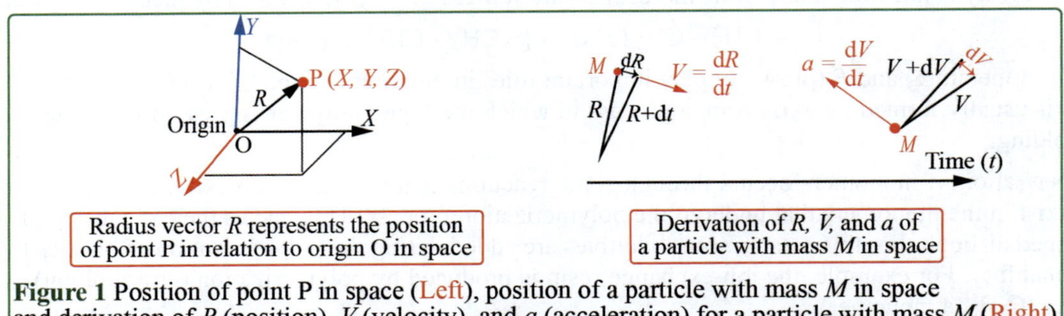

Figure 1 Position of point P in space (Left), position of a particle with mass M in space and derivation of R (position), V (velocity), and a (acceleration) for a particle with mass M (Right)

P-65
POSITRON

A positron (also called **antielectron**) is the antiparticle of an electron (e^-) because it has an equal but opposite electric charge. A positron is an electro-positively charged version of an electron.

A positron is produced when a proton in the nucleus of a radioactive element (nuclide) goes under the process of **beta plus decay** (β^+ decay). As a result, the proton instantly changes into a neutron so that the nuclide can reach a more stable shape.

Positron has the next properties.

- It has low energy (E),
- It has a spin of half (½),
- It has the same mass (M) as an electron,
- It can be produced in a nuclear fusion process or nuclear decay process, and
- It can produce two or more gamma particles when colliding (hitting) with an electron. Thus, its M converts directly into E by Einstein's equation ($E = M.c^2$).

P-66
POTENTIAL ENERGY

Discussed under the topic of ENERGY AND ITS FORMS.

P-67
POTENTIAL ENERGY SURFACE

Another name for surface potential energy. It is discussed under the subtopic of Potential Energy under ENERGY AND ITS FORMS.

P-68
POTENTIOMETERS

A potentiometer is an instrument that measures the voltage (V, also called **electric voltage** or **potential difference**) of an electric current. A PH meter is a potentiometer that operates based on the V between two electrodes placed in a solution sample to measure that solution's **hydrogen ion concentration** (the PH).

P-69
POWDERS

A powder is a dry bulk solid composed of fine, free-flowing particles. Both powders and crystals are in the class of **granular materials**, but powder particles are much smaller than crystal particles. In addition, some other properties differentiate powders from crystals, as outlined next.

- Powder molecules are usually arranged in an unorganized and disorderly-repeating pattern, while those of crystals are arranged in an organized and orderly-repeating pattern.
- Powder particles tend to form clumps when flowing, while crystals are free-flowing unless wet. In other words, the moisture absorbability of powder particles is much greater than those of crystals.

In most cases, powered products are produced by grinding. For example, powdered sugar is produced by grinding crystalline sugar, powdered coffee is produced by grinding coffee bins, and diatomaceous filter aid is produced by heating natural diatomaceous earth (diatomite) to above 800ºC and ground to make powder filter aid with a small particle size of 10 to 200 µm.

P-70
POWER

Simplified name for ELECTRIC POWER.

P-71
POWER NUMBER

Power number (N_{PE}, also called **Newton's number**) is a unitless quantity that relates the resistance force (F_R) to the inertial force (F_I). N_{PE} has different definitions, depending on its application in a concept. For example, the N_{PE} for the stirrer (impeller) of a mixer is defined as

$$N_{PE} = \frac{P_E}{D.N^3.d^5} \qquad (1)$$

Here, P_E is for the electric power (simply **power**), D is the density of the mix under mixing, N is the rotational velocity (known as RPM, rotation per minute), and d is the diameter of the stirrer. If P_E is given in $(kg.m^2)/s^3$, N in 1/s. and d in m, the dimensions cancel. Note that 1 $kg.m^2/s^3$ = 1 W/h.

[Note 1: Power number values for stirrers with different shapes are *not* calculated but experimental values.] [Note 2: For more information on the N_{PE} of different-shaped stirrers, refer to STIRRERS.]

P-72

POWER PRODUCTION

Discussed under STEAM AND POWER PRODUCTION.

P-73

PRESSURE ENERGY

Discussed under the topic of ENERGY AND ITS FORMS.

C.74

PRESSURE EQUILIBRIUM

Discussed under the topic of EQUILIBRIUM.

P-75

PRESSURE GAUGE

A pressure gauge is an instrument for measuring the pressure (P) of a fluid (liquid or gas) in relation to gauge pressure (P_G). [Pressure gauge (for measuring the P_G) differs from P_G (the P relative to P_{Atm}).]

The relation between P_G, P_{Abs} (absolute pressure), and $P_{Atm.}$ (atmospheric pressure) is given as

$$P_G = P_{Abs} - P_{Atm} \quad (1)$$

According to this equation,

- A pressure gauge measures the difference between the P of a fluid and that of the atmosphere,
- A pressure gauge indicates a zero P if a fluid is open to the atmosphere, and
- A pressure-gauge reading is a positive P_G (gauge pressure).

The following are important to know:

- P_{Atm} is usually measured by using a barometer,
- P_G is usually measured by using an open-end manometer, and
- P_{Abs} (absolute pressure) is usually measured by using a closed-end manometer.

Bourdon pressure gauges are the most used gauges (see Figure 1). Spring-and-piston tire pressure gauges (simply tire pressure gauges) are used to check the tires P. Compound gauges measure both positive P_G and P_{Vac} (vacuum pressure).

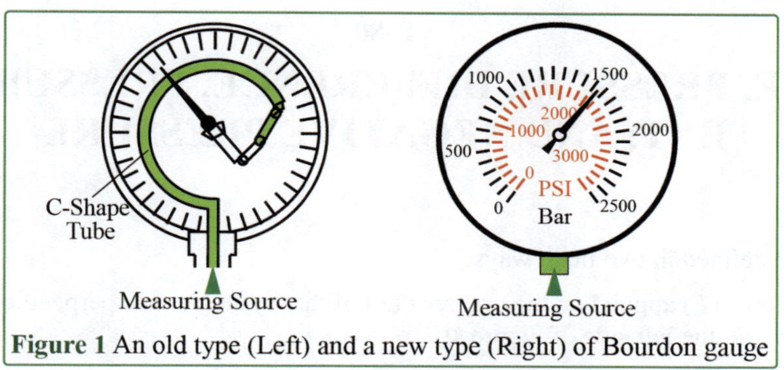

Figure 1 An old type (Left) and a new type (Right) of Bourdon gauge

P-76
PRESSURE GRADIENT

Study PRESSURE DIFFERENCE AND PRESSURE GRADIENT.

P-77
PRESSURE HEAD

Another name for LIQUID HEAD.

P-78
PRESSURE MEASUREMENT AND CONTROL

Discussed under the topic of PROCESS CONTROL OF CHEMICAL ENGINEERING.

P-79
PRESSURE TESTING

Pressure testing (also called **hydrostatic testing** or **hydrostatic pressure testing**) is a common test for leak and safety in a newly-built vessel, a tank, pipeline, gas cylinder, a boiler, or other devices. This test can be done by pressurizing the device with water and observing a leak. The test can then be repeated at regular intervals to re-qualify the device. The test pressure (*P*) is always higher (by about 80%) than the operating *P* of the device under the pressure test.

A tank for liquid storing, for example, can be tested for a leak in the following order:

- Fill the tank with water (maybe dyed to help in the visual observation of the leak's location),
- Shut the supply valve and measure *P* in the tank with a pressure tester, and
- Observe the pressure to see if any loss in its values occurs.

A pressure test is also used for the **strength** of the material used in constructing a device (when the strength is low, a shape deformation occurs in the device).

P-80

PRESSURE, PRESSURE DIFFERENCE, PRESSURE GRADIENT, AND NEGATIVE PRESSURE

Pressure

Pressure (P) can be defined in two main ways:

- P on a system is a force (F) applied on the unit area (A) of that system's face perpendicularly (vertically at 90° angle), as shown on the left side of Figure 1.

$$P = \frac{F}{A} = \frac{F.L}{A.L} = \frac{W}{V} = \frac{E}{V} \tag{1}$$

- P of a liquid in a column is the product of the liquid's density (D), liquid head (h), and gravitational acceleration (a_g = 9.81 m/s^2 = 32.2 Ft/s^2 on the Earth surface).

$$P = a_g.D.h \tag{2}$$

If P is measured against P_{Atm} (atmospheric pressure = 1 Atm ≈ 100 kPa) instead of P_{Vac} (vacuum pressure), we should add P_{Atm} to Equation 2.

$$P = a_g.D.h + P_{Atm} \tag{3}$$

In Equation 1, L is for length, W is for work, V is for volume, and E is for energy. Equation 1 is based on the E and W similarities, like having the same SI unit of J (Joule) and US unit of BTU (British thermal unit).

[A force that perpendicularly acts on a system is the normal force (simply force, F). A force that acts parallelly is the shear force (F_S), as shown on the right side of Figure 1. The result of F_S on the unit area (A) of a system's face is shear stress (S_S).]

Under the topic of FORCE, we said that Newton's Second Law of Motion defines F (force) as the product of M (mass) multiplied by a (acceleration).

$$F = M.a \tag{4}$$

Substituting F into Equation 1, yields

$$P = \frac{M.a}{A} \tag{5}$$

Consider a closed cubic container filled with a gas, as shown on the left side of Figure 2. Further, assume that the size of the container is shrunk to a small cube by applying uniform forces on the container, as shown on the right side of the same figure. The P of the gas will still have a value equal to dP (simply because we also shrunk the unit area of the container from A to dA). Thus, Equation 1 can be expressed in the differential form (d form) to calculate the pressure change when a force is applied on an infinitesimal (tiny) surface area, known as the differential area (dA).

$$dP = \frac{F}{dA} \tag{6}$$

When P is applied to an area (A) during a limited (finite) change from situation 1 to 2, it can also be expressed in integral form.

$$P = \frac{F}{\int_1^2 dA} = \frac{F}{A_2 - A_1} \tag{7}$$

The SI unit of F is Newton (N), and that of A is m^2, giving P the unit of N/m^2, which equates to 1 Pa (for Pascal). Because the Pa unit is so small (like a dollar bill being flat on a table applies roughly 1 Pa pressure), kPa is often used. For example, the P of a car's tire is about 240 kPa (35 PSI). The US unit of F is pound-force (Lb_F), and that of A is square inch (In^2), giving P the unit of pounds per square inch (Lb/In^2 or PSI). If 1 Lb of force is applied to a surface area of 1 In^2, the P is 1 Lb/In^2, where In^2 is for PSI.

Other common P units are atmosphere (Atm), Bar, mm of mercury, In (inch) of mercury, and torr. [For conversion of pressure units, refer to the Conversion Table given in this book's inside backcover.]

Because P has *no* specified direction, it is a scalar quantity (a quantity with magnitude but *not* direction).

Pressure (P) has different types, including the following:

- Absolute pressure (P_{Abs}),
- Atmospheric pressure (P_{Atm}),
- Gauge pressure (P_G),
- Head pressure (P_h),
- Dynamic pressure (P_D),
- Kinetic pressure (P_K), and
- Static pressure (P_S).

It is helpful to know the following about pressure:

- It is usually given in P_{Abs}. When it is given in P_G, its value may be negative. For example, P_{Abs} of 60 kPa may be given as P_G of – 41 kPa; that is, 41 kPa below the P_{Atm} of 101 kPa. Figure 3 shows two ways of expressing the P of liquids, when P is greater than P_{Atm} and when P is smaller than P_{Atm}.
- It is measured by the ability to displace a column of liquid in a manometer. In these cases, P is expressed as the height of mercury (Hg) or water (H_2O); for example, mm of Hg or cm of H_2O.

An Example on Pressure

Given: A system weighing 800 N

Wanted: P exerted by the system on the surface of 2 cm^2 (= 0.0002 m^2) and 200 cm^2 (= 0.02 m^2)

$$P_1 = \frac{F}{A} = \frac{800}{0{,}02} = 40 \text{ kPa (5.8 PSI)} \quad P_2 = \frac{800}{0.0002} = 4000 \text{ kPa (580 PSI)}$$

The pressures are greatly different, although the force in both cases is the same. The first case reminds us of a woman who wears flat-bottomed shoes, and her weight applies a P of 800 N to a linoleum floor. In this case, the exerted P on the floor is small (because of a large surface area). But the second case is when the same woman wears shoes with small heels, so the P is large enough to make a hole in the linoleum.

Pressure Difference

The pressure difference (ΔP, also called **pressure differential** or **pressure drop**) is the difference in pressure (P) between two points or two systems.

$$\Delta P = P_{\text{System 2}} - P_{\text{System 1}} = P_2 - P_1$$

ΔP is the cause (driving force) of some phenomena, such as the flow of a liquid (Figure 4) in a pipe, air draft in the furnace of a boiler, and the discharge of flue gas from the stack of a furnace. It is, thus, used in ChemEng in several calculations, such as

- Sizing of pipes,
- Performance of pumps and compressors,
- Measurement of liquid heads in tanks or vessels, and
- Specification of control valves and measuring instruments.

In fluid-flow subjects, ΔP is used to indicate the **pressure drop** between two points that occurs during the flow of a fluid (a liquid or gas).

ΔP is given as P, usually in N/m^2 = Pa and PSI (Lb/In^2).

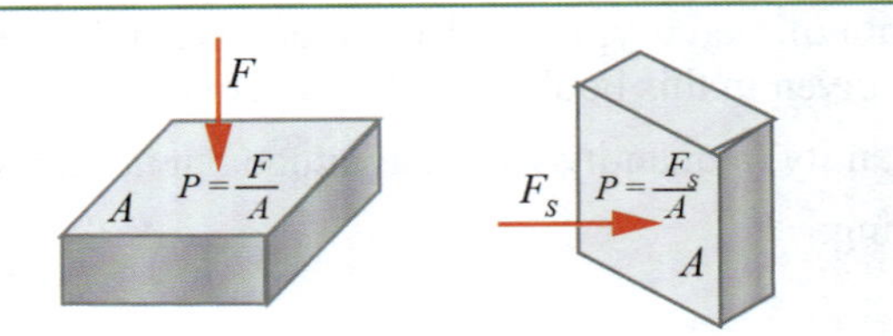

Figure 1 Pressure (P) applied on a solid system by normal force (F) and by shear force (F_S)

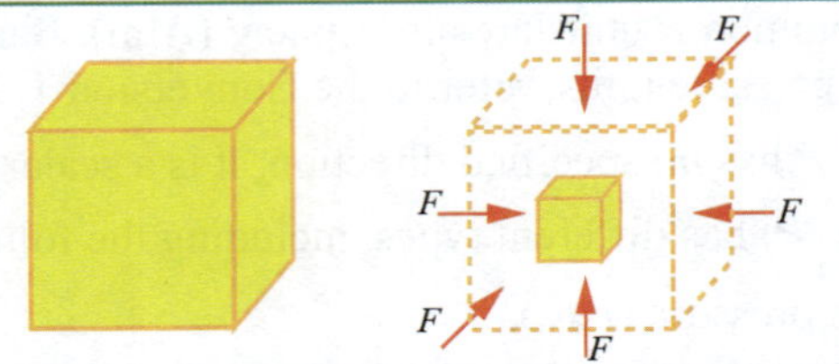

Figure 2 Uniform compression of a cubic container containing a gas

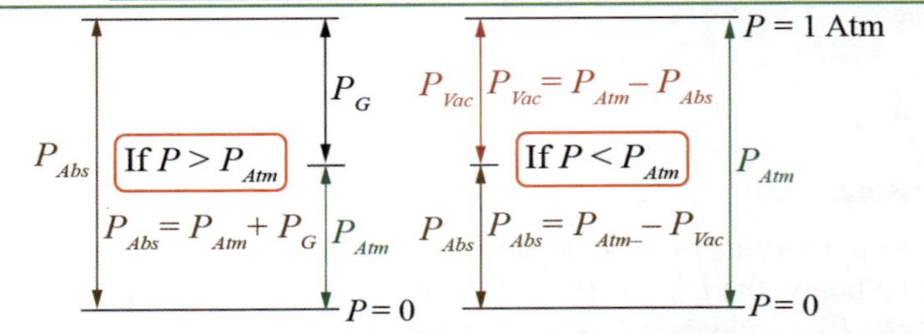

Figure 3 Expressing pressure (P) of a liquid when P is greater than P_{Atm} (atmospheric pressure) and when P is smaller than P_{Atm}

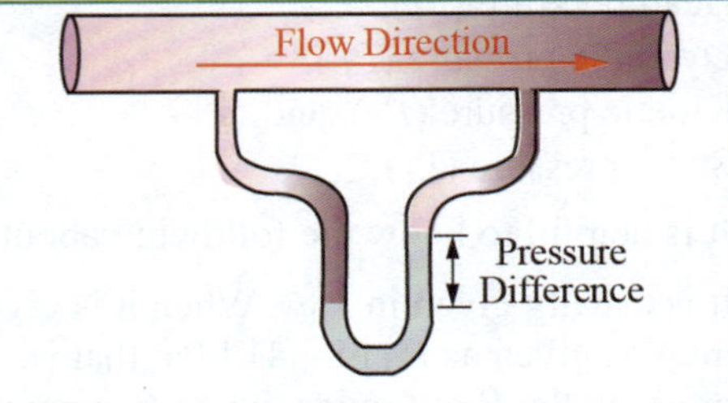

Figure 4 Pressure difference, shown by the difference in height of a manometer

Pressure Gradient

Pressure gradient ($\Delta P/L$) is the pressure difference (ΔP) per unit length (L) or per differential (final-minus-initial) length, shown as dL or dx. When using dx, we mean that P (pressure) changes only along the x-axis direction, so it is only a function of x. $\Delta P/L$, in other words, describes how fast and in which direction P of a fluid changes around a given point. [**Gradient**, in physics, is a change in the value of a quantity (like pressure) per change in L.]

The SI unit of the pressure gradient is kPa/m, and its US unit is Lb/In or Lb/Ft.

[Note 1: Instead of **pressure difference** (ΔP), scientists use the word pressure gradient as the driving force of a fluid flow process. So speaking, ΔP (pressure difference) does *not* mean the $\Delta P/L$ (pressure gradient).] [Note 2: ΔP is also the cause of lift of airplanes because the air passing a plane's wing produces ΔP.]

Negative Pressure

The term **negative pressure** is used when a system's pressure (P) is **below zero** (at below P_{Atm}). When we say a condenser operates at negative P, it means that its P is below P_{Atm} (= 1 Atm = 101 kPa = 14.7 PSI). For example, the P of 0.2 Atm (= 20 kPa) is a negative P because it is below 1 Atm (= 101 kPa).

P-81

PRINCIPLE OF GRAVITY SPACETIME

Discussed under the topic of EINSTEIN'S THEORIES OF RELATIVITY.

P-82

PRINCIPLE OF LENGTH CONTRACTION

Discussed under the topic of EINSTEIN'S THEORIES OF RELATIVITY.

P-83

PRINCIPLE OF MASS-ENERGY EQUALITY

Discussed under the topic of EINSTEIN'S THEORIES OF RELATIVITY.

P-84

PRINCIPLE OF MASS EXPANSION

Discussed under the topic of EINSTEIN'S THEORIES OF RELATIVITY.

P-85

PRINCIPLE OF SPEED OF LIGHT

Discussed under the topic of EINSTEIN'S THEORIES OF RELATIVITY.

P-86

PRINCIPLE OF TIME DILATION

Discussed under the topic of EINSTEIN'S THEORIES OF RELATIVITY.

P-87

PROCESS

Study CHEMICAL PROCESS.

P-88

PROCESS BLOCK DIAGRAMS

Discussed under PROCESS DIAGRAMS.

P-89

PROCESS BYPASS

Process bypass (simply **bypass**), in ChemEng, is skipping one or more subsequent steps of a process unit of ChemEng (unit operation of ChemEng). A bypass system usually has a few valves, pipes, pumps, and sometimes a tank. The valves open when the bypass is needed to allow some of the feed to run through the bypass system instead of going directly through the main process.

P-90

PROCESS BYPRODUCT

A process byproduct (simply **byproduct**) is a secondary product of a production process that usually has less value than its product. Study the following three (3) brief points:

- The byproduct of a production process can be useful and marketable or can be considered waste.
- The byproduct of a production process can be more valuable than its product. Say, in a petroleum refinery, the value of some distillates (like airplane gasoline) exceeds the value of the main product (car gasoline).
- The byproduct of a production process can be processed to increase its value. For example, a gas mixture containing a high amount of hydrogen released from a chemical reaction can be processed to separate the hydrogen gas to be used as a fuel supply in the same facility.

[The word **side-product** is also used in ChemEng to refer to a product formed from a chemical reaction by optimizing the reaction's conditions.]

P-91

PROCESS CONTROL OF CHEMICAL ENGINEERING

Process control of ChemEng is a technique used in chemical process plants for controlling a **process variable** (simply **variable**) in the desired **setpoint value** (simply **setpoint**) with minimal human assistance. The following are some examples of variables that need to be controlled to operate a typical chemical plant efficiently

- Control of a liquid's temperature (T) in a chemical reactor by a temperature controller (TC),
- Control of a liquid's pressure (P) in a heat exchanger by a pressure controller (PC),
- Control of a liquid's density (D) in an evaporator by a density controller (DC),
- Control of a liquid's height (h) in a tank by a level controller (LC),
- Control of a fluid's flow in a pipe by a flow controller (FC), and
- Control of a centrifuge's speed (U) by a speed controller (SC).

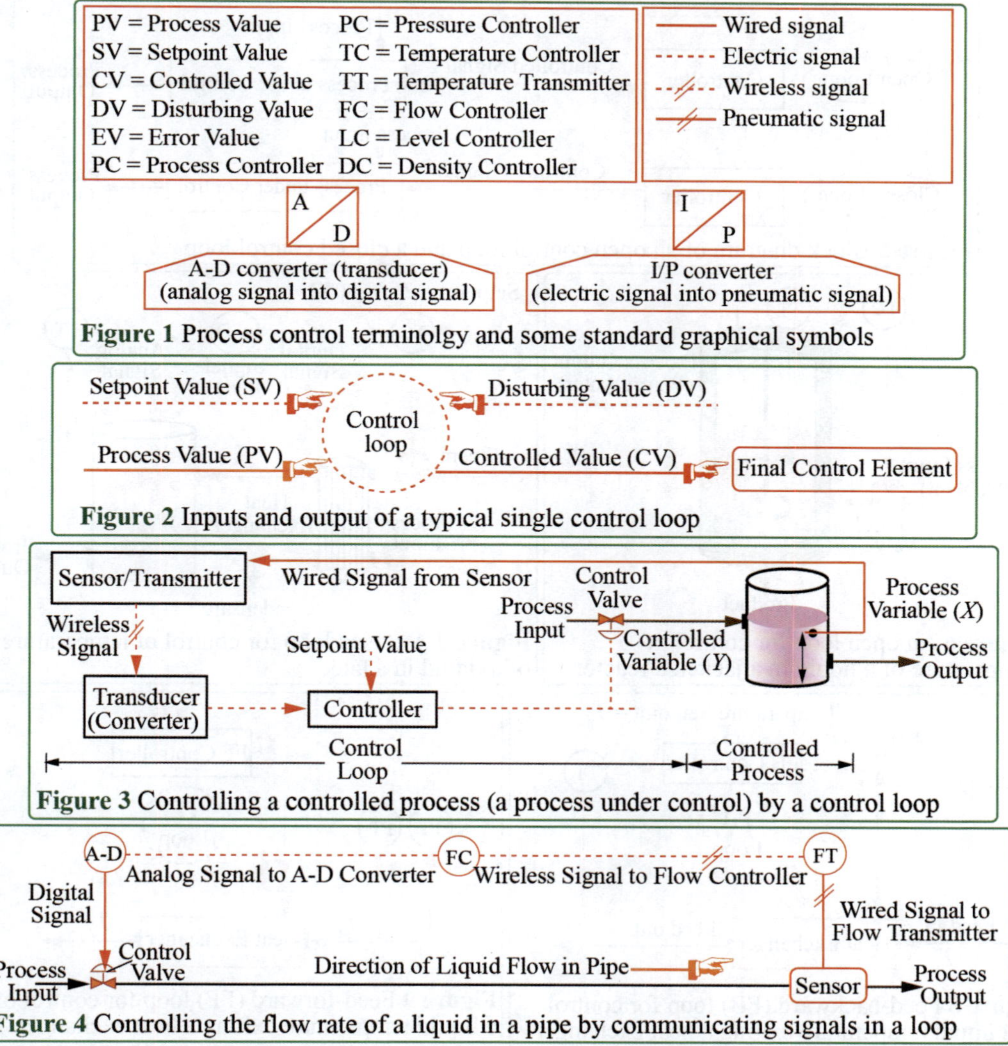

Figure 1 Process control terminolgy and some standard graphical symbols

Figure 2 Inputs and output of a typical single control loop

Figure 3 Controlling a controlled process (a process under control) by a control loop

Figure 4 Controlling the flow rate of a liquid in a pipe by communicating signals in a loop

The process-control field has many special terms, symbols, and abbreviations. Furthermore, different control-system specialists and manufacturers use different names, symbols, and abbreviations to describe the same action in a control loop. Figure 1 shows standard names and abbreviations used in this book. [Table 12 in the Table Section at the end of the book also gives more graphical symbols for process control.]

1. CONTROL LOOPS

A **process-control loop** (simply a **control loop** or just a **loop**) is the foundation of a process control system (see Figure 2). [Because the discussions under this topic are about the loops that control only one variable, we use the term **control loop** (simply **loop**) to refer to a **single control loop**.]

A loop with its elements monitors a **process variable** (PV or X, simply **variable**), such as T or P. It brings the variable back to its **setpoint value** (SV, also called **reference value** or simply **setpoint**) if PV deviates from SV. As Figure 3 shows, a PV continuously enters a loop, gets adjusted (if needed), and leaves the loop as the CV (**controlled value** or **controller's value**).

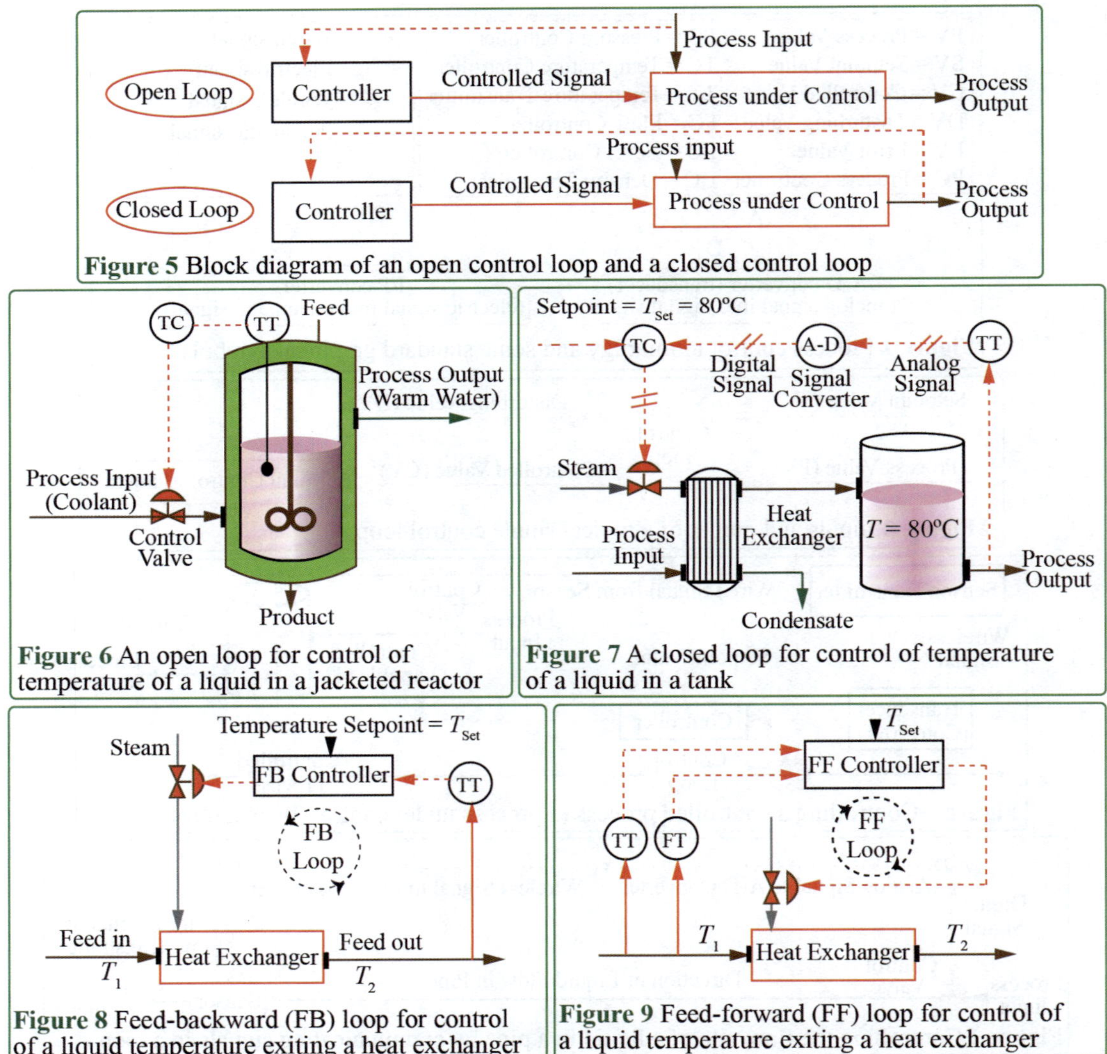

Figure 5 Block diagram of an open control loop and a closed control loop

Figure 6 An open loop for control of temperature of a liquid in a jacketed reactor

Figure 7 A closed loop for control of temperature of a liquid in a tank

Figure 8 Feed-backward (FB) loop for control of a liquid temperature exiting a heat exchanger

Figure 9 Feed-forward (FF) loop for control of a liquid temperature exiting a heat exchanger

A typical-simple loop usually consists of the next **elements** (components):

- **Sensor:** For measuring a process variable and sending it to the transmitter.
- **Transmitter:** To convert measured value to an analog output and send it to the controller.
- **Controller:** To adjust deviation from setpoint value and send its output value to an actuator.
- **Actuator** (final element): To adjust itself to the controller-output value. Say, a valve (an actuator) is used for adjusting its position according to the controller's value.

Study the following points about the elements of a loop:

- An actuator and the process under control are parts of the loop.
- A sensor usually acts as both sensor and transmitter, as shown in Figure 3.
- Output from an A-D (also shown as A/D for analog-digital) converter (transducer) has a unified signal, which is in a defined range; say, 4 to 20 mA (milli Ampere).

In Figure 3, a process variable (*X*) enters the control loop, and a controlled variable (*Y*) exits the loop to control a process. Figure 4 shows a simple control loop for controlling a liquid's flow rate in a pipe by a control valve and the input and output signals to and from the loop's elements.

A **disturbance** (*D*, a disturbing variable), such as a sudden change in weather, a variation in feed, or both, affects the loop undesirably. A disturbance, as a result, can cause the *Y* (**controlled variable** or **controller output**) away from the setpoint. Because any loop can be affected by some disturbances, a process filter (simply filter or buffer) is usually used on the loop before the controller to minimize the disturbances' effects. Over time, however, the controller may need a **tuning process** to optimize itself, as discussed later.

Control Loop Types

Open Control Loop: In an open loop (top of Figure 5), the CV (controlled value) is controlled by adjusting the process's **input** under control, and **output** from the process does *not* affect the control action of the loop. For instance, in a jacketed reactor (the process under control), shown in Figure 6, the controller adjusts the temperature (*T*) of the reactor by decreasing or increasing the coolant flow (the process input) in proportion to the difference between the desired reactor's *T* (setpoint) and the measured *T* (process variable). Because the control in an open-loop system is done without monitoring the output, an open-control loop is called a **non-feedback control loop**. The major disadvantage of open loops, compared with closed loops, is that the open loops can poorly handle a disturbance. Thus, an **open-loop system** can control a process with *no* disturbance.

Closed Control Loop: In a closed loop (bottom of Figure 5), CV is controlled by adjusting the **output** of the process under control. Unlike an open loop, which does *not* check if the process output has achieved its desired goal, a closed-loop continuously adjusts its output by comparing CV with RV (reference variable or generally **setpoint**) and, depending on the result of this comparison; it makes some adjustment on the controller. Such adjustments continue until the difference between CV and RV, called the **error** (*E*), is zero.

The closed-loop in Figure 7, which controls the *T* (temperature) of a liquid in a tank by a heat exchanger, consists of a sensor, a *T* transmitter (TT), an A-D (analog-digital) transducer (converter), a *T* controller (TC), and a control valve. The sensor measures the *T* of the liquid in the pipe and transmits its measuring value, through a **wire**, to TT. The TT sends its value to the A-D transducer, which changes the controller-output analog signal to a useable digital signal and sends its signal **wirelessly** to the *T* controller (TC), which is usually installed in the control room of a chemical factory. TC compares process value (T_1) with setpoint (T_2) and chooses one of the following actions:

- If $T_1 = T_2$, the TC does *not* take any action, and
- If $T_1 \neq T_2$, the TC calculates the **error** (the difference between T_1 and T_2) and creates a corrected value. The controller then sends its corrected value (called the **controller output** or **adjusted variable**) to a pneumatic control valve to adjust the amount of steam entering the heat exchanger, to keep the liquid's *T* in the tank constant, as desired.

A closed-loop can operate backward, known as the **feedback** (FB) **control loop**, in a forward way, known as the **feed-forward** (FF) **control loop**, or both. More info about these loops is given next.

- **Feedback** (FB) **Control Loop:** Figure 8 shows an FB loop for controlling the temperature (T) of the outlet liquid from a heat exchanger by keeping the liquid at a preset T. As the figure shows, the controller must maintain T_2 (the T of the outlet liquid-feed from the exchanger) at the desired value (T_{Set}, the T setpoint). This can be done by installing a FB controller in the loop to measure T_2 and applying its corrected values (the controller output) to the control valve, installed in the steam line, going to the exchanger, as shown in the figure. [**Single loop feedback control** is the most common type of control used in chemical plants.]
- **Feed-Forward** (FF) **Control Loop:** Figure 9 shows an FF loop controlling a heat exchanger. The FF loop's objective, contrary to the FB loop, is to maintain T_1 (the T of the inlet liquid feed to the exchanger) at the desired value. This can be done by installing an FF controller in the loop to measure T and $\dot{V}$ (volumetric flow rate) of the inlet liquid and apply its corrected values to the control valve.

Because the concept of the FB (feedback) control loops is relatively simple and the loops function satisfactorily in many control systems, the FB loops are used universally. An FB control loop, however, has the following disadvantages over an FF control loop:

- In the FB loop, each value is calculated based on the error, so the variable must deviate from its setpoint before the controller can take corrective action.
- FB loop is based on the steady-state flow of the incoming feed, and as such, it neglects how fast the variable responds to the flow's changes.
- FB loop *cannot* achieve **perfect control** because a deviation from the setpoint must occur before the controller can take any action. As such, it does *not* wait for deviations to accumulate, so the effect of each disturbance on the process variable is minimized.

If, as a result, a process system provides frequent disturbances, a process engineer prefers to use an FF control system to get the best possible performance from the control system. An experienced process engineer, however, chooses the best choice based on the following:

- Reviews the dynamic behavior of the process to be controlled,
- Draws PFD (process flow diagram) in both choices, FB and FF systems,
- Provides a simple response test (discussed in a moment) on both systems of choice, and
- Enters the new settings into the controller and tests them to ensure the process under control acts properly.

In addition, the process-control technique identifies the following five (5) control loops:

- Computer-Controlled Loop: A loop that uses a computer instead of a controller.
- Cascade Loop: A control loop that needs a minimum of two controllers.
- Continuous Loop: A loop with frequent repetition of identical actions.
- Fixed-Set Loop: A loop that its setpoint remains constant with time.
- Follow-up Loop: A loop that its setpoint changes with time.

2. CONTROLLERS

A controller is a microprocessor installed in a control loop to correct a deviation from the setpoint (the desired value) by constantly monitoring a process value (feedback) to keep itself in the setpoint range. A controller continuously calculates the **process error** (simply an **error**, E) and accordingly applies its corrected value to a control element (such as a control valve) to adjust itself.

As said earlier, the input to a controller is PV (process value or process variable), which is continuously compared with RV (reference variable or setpoint value) by the controller to determine the error (E), which is the difference between RV and PV. In Figure 10, which shows an open-loop for control of a liquid in a tank, a level controller (LC) compares measured height (h_1) with the desired height (h_{Set}, the setpoint value; say, 3 m) and chooses one of the following actions:

- If $h_1 = h_{Set}$, the LC does *not* take any action.
- If $h_1 \neq h_{Set}$, the LC calculates the **error** (the difference between h_1 and h_{Set}) and creates a correct value (the **output**) that can keep the level in the tank constant, as desired.

A controller calculates its output based on the following:

- Process Error,
- Control procedure, and
- Controller-Tuning Parameter.

In the process-control field, the term **programmable logic controller** (PLC) is generally used to mean a control software that receives data from a sensor, processes the data, and creates outputs based on pre-programmed parameters. A PLC acts as a **real-time system** because its outputs are quickly produced in response to inputs. Depending on the inputs, a PLC can control and record data automatically, such as the start or stop of a process, control the temperature (T) of a process, or generate an alarm if a system (like a centrifugal system) starts to malfunction. Controllers have different types, including the following:

- On-off Controllers
- Proportional Controllers
- Proportional + Integral (PI) Controllers
- Proportional + Derivative (PD) Controllers
- Proportional + Integral + Derivative (PID) Controllers

On-and-off Controllers

An on-and-off controller is used when the process variable has two choices. For example, refrigerators and water heaters operate with on-and-off controllers to control temperature. An on-and-off controller is often used for controlling the level of a liquid in a tank equipped with a pump. Every on-and-off controller has a dead time, which prevents sudden switching.

Proportional Controllers

A proportional controller is a linear feedback (FB) control system that corrects the controlled value, which is proportional to the difference between the setpoint (the desired value) and the process value (measured value). A ball valve used to control the flushing water is a simple example of a proportional controller. The valve is connected to a hollow float (ball) by a lever in the sink. The lever opens and closes the valve connected to the incoming water supply. As the water level rises to a preset level, the float also rises (because the speed of the water increases). This forces the lever to close the valve. This is a simple example of a proportional controller working based on **negative feedback** (feedback with a negative **gain value**), as shown in Figure 11.

PID Controllers

PID (proportional + integral + derivative) controllers are the most-used controllers because of their simplicity in conception and reliability in operation. A PID controller acts in three different modes (Figure 12):

- **Proportional** (P) **Mode**: P mode adjusts the **error** (E) proportionally until the **offset** (the result) is zero. To do so, it multiplies the E value by the **proportional gain value** (K_P). The result will be the **proportional-output value** (the P-value) compared with E. If $E = 0$, the P mode takes *no* action. If $E > 0$, the P mode increases its output, and if $E < 0$, the P mode decreases its output.
- **Integral** (I) **Mode:** I mode adjusts E integrally until zero offsets. To do this, it multiplies E by the **integral gain value** (K_I). The result will be the **integral-output value** (I value) applied to E.
- **Derivative** (D) **Mode:** D mode adjusts E differentially until zero offsets. To do so, it multiplies E by the **derivative gain value** (K_D). The result is the **derivative-output value** (D value) applied to E.

P, I, and D process gains are then summed together and deducted from the setpoint value to get the error value to zero. The following two (2) brief points are important to know about controllers:

- The total of P-value and I-value accelerates the movement of the process toward the setpoint and eliminates E that occurs with a P controller.
- Most PID controllers in service have only their **P mode** and **I mod** active, so D mode is zero and, therefore, they operate like **PI controllers**.

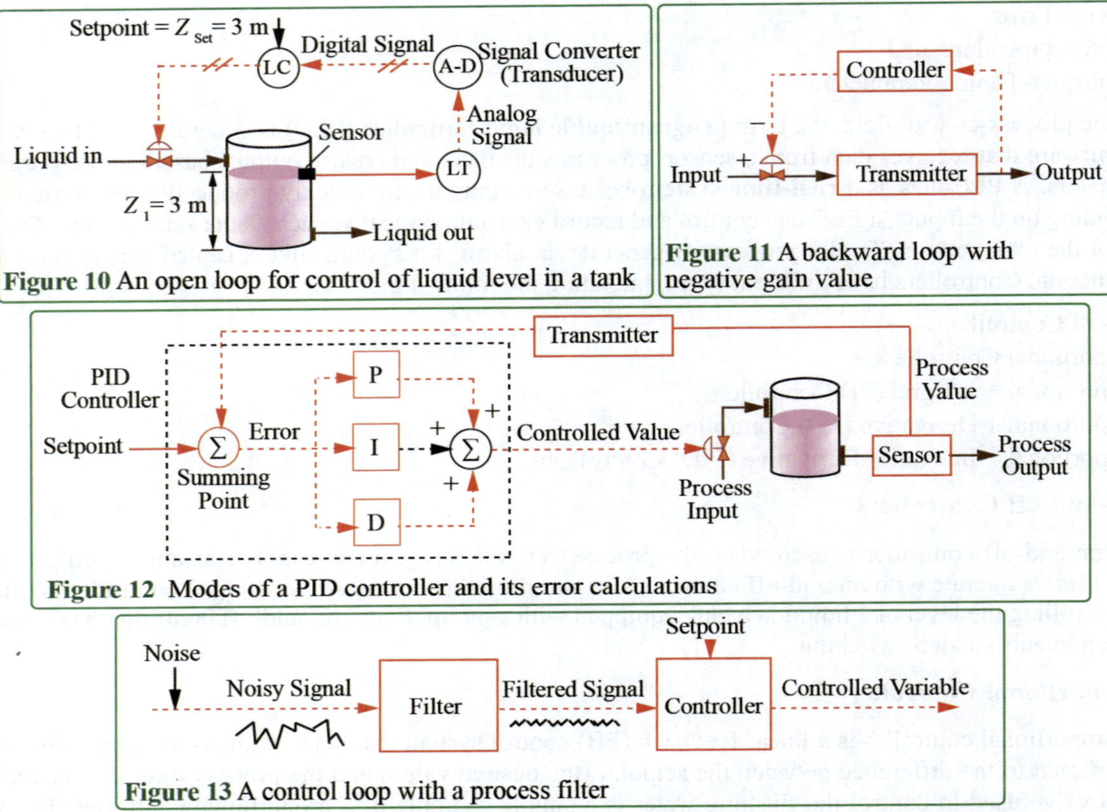

Figure 10 An open loop for control of liquid level in a tank

Figure 11 A backward loop with negative gain value

Figure 12 Modes of a PID controller and its error calculations

Figure 13 A control loop with a process filter

3. PROCESS ERRORS

Process error (E, simply **error**) is the difference between the **reference value** (RV, setpoint value) and **process value** (PV, measured value, or controller input), as shown in Figure 12.

$$E = RV - PV \tag{1}$$

The error value (E) is calculated inside the controller. In a PID controller, P, I, and D **process gains** are summed together and deducted from RV to get the error to zero.

An error occurs in a control loop when the loop is subjected to a disturbance, noise, or other factors.

A **disturbance** can have some causes, such as

- Changing a system into service (or out of service),
- Starting or shutting a device, like a pump or a compressor,
- Changing a loop, which is in interaction with the original loop, and
- Changing the feed's flow rate, temperature (T), pressure (P), or consistency.

[If, in general, the magnitude of a disturbance is small, E is also small, so a controller can handle it easily by subtracting PV from RV to result in a new CV (controlled value). If a disturbance keeps happening frequently, the controller *cannot* handle it, so a correction action, known as the **controller tuning process**, is required. The tuning process is discussed in a moment.]

A **noise** (process noise) occurs when some changes in a process's external conditions happen, like sudden changes in the surrounding weather. A **process filter** (simply **filter** or **buffer**) is used in the control loop when the noise is notably great in quantity. As shown in Figure 13, the filter receives the noisy signal, reduces its quantity, and sends the filtered signal to the controller in a control loop with a filter.

4. TUNING PID CONTROLLERS

Controller tuning optimizes a controller to get the best possible performance from a control loop. Thus, a controller that does *not* properly answer a **step-response test** must be tuned. Tuning can be done manually (by an experienced operator) or automatically (by a computer program). We will talk here about manual tuning. Before starting a tuning process on a controller, an operator needs to do some pre-tuning steps: 1) Visual inspection, 2) Step-response test, and 3) Process identification (modeling).

The operator visually inspects the control loop during these steps to ensure the loop's elements are in good shape. Say, to check the condition of the loop's control valve, the operator checks to see if it is *not* rusty.

Step-Response Test

To do a step-response test (simply **step test**), the operator does the following:

- Puts the controller in the manual position,
- Makes a step change to the controller input, and
- Checks how the controller responds to the step-response change.

The term **step change** is used in the tuning process for injecting energy into a loop's actuator (usually a control valve) to open the valve in small increments (in a fraction of a percent). R**esponse change** refers to the controller's response when a step change (the input to a controller) is made. The test based on the **step-change** (the controller input) and **response-change** (the controller output) is called the **step-response test**, which is used to verify if a controller operates properly.

To perform a step-response test on a loop's controller, given in Figure 14, the operator does the next.

- Puts the controller in manual mode.
- Waits for the controller to become stable (free-of-load).
- Applies a small step change on the flow by opening the control valve in a small proportion (say, 2%) and watches the controller's response. Thus, the pipe's flow rate increases and stabilizes at a new set value.
- Records the controller reading (the controller-output value) after it is stabilized.

[When a controller is in manual mode for tuning, we are dealing with a new process, called **process model** (simply **process**). As shown in Figure 14, the **input** to the process model is a controlled value (CV), and its **output** is the process value (PV). Later, we simply use the terms **process input** and **process output**.]

The step test results can be plotted with time to get two trends: the **process input time-trend** and **process output time-trend**, as shown in Figure 14.

The result of a step-response test may fall into one of the following three classes:

- The controller responses properly to step changes,
- The controller responses too much to step changes, so the loop overshoots its setpoint, and
- The controller responds too little to step changes, so it takes too long for the controller to get its input variable to the setpoint variable.

Obviously, in the second and third cases, the controller needs tuning.

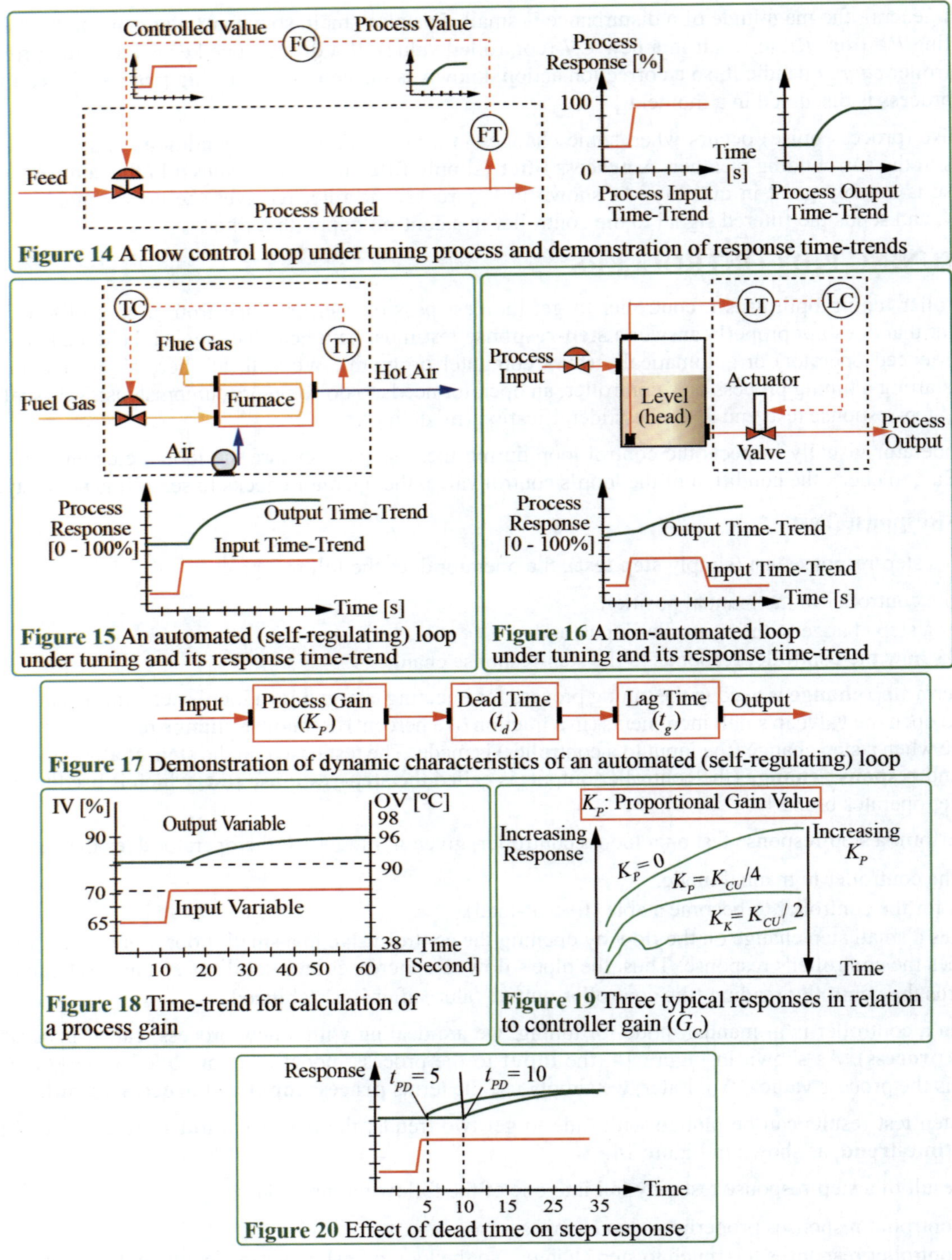

Figure 14 A flow control loop under tuning process and demonstration of response time-trends

Figure 15 An automated (self-regulating) loop under tuning and its response time-trend

Figure 16 A non-automated loop under tuning and its response time-trend

Figure 17 Demonstration of dynamic characteristics of an automated (self-regulating) loop

Figure 18 Time-trend for calculation of a process gain

Figure 19 Three typical responses in relation to controller gain (G_c)

Figure 20 Effect of dead time on step response

Process Identification

The process under control can be identified by its step-response test and step-response time trend. When a process is identified, its **dynamic response behavior** becomes known. A dynamic response represents how a process behaves during the step change. Based on its response time trend, a process can be classified as

- **Automated** (Self-Regulating) **Process:** Figure 15 shows the response time trends of an automated process. This process **output** slows down and becomes steady at a new value when a step change is applied to its **input**. Say, controlling the temperature (T) of a furnace by adjusting the T of the hot air leaving the furnace is an automated process. If, for example, opening the control valve by a few percent, the T of the hot air increases and then becomes stable at a new value. Controlling the T of a liquid, leaving a heat exchanger by a valve installed in the steam line going to the exchanger, is also an automated process. Most pressure processes are also automated. In general, 80 to 90% of the processes behave self-regulating.

Non-Regulated Process: Figure 16 shows the response time trends of a non-regulated process (also called the **integrating process**). As seen from the same figure, the output of such a process keeps changing at a steady rate when a step change is applied to its input. For example, controlling a liquid's head level in a tank is a non-self-regulating process.

Parameters of a Self-Regulating Process

An automated (self-regulating () process can be described (modeled) using three parameters (also called the **dynamic responses**), which affect the tuning of a controller. A controller can be tuned according to the dynamic responses of the process under tuning. This can be better understood if you think of taking a shower. You turn the faucet (the controller) in the shower and then wait to feel its effect before making additional changes. And you keep changing until the temperature of the water reaches your desire. In the same way, a controller can be tuned until it correctly responds to the setpoint. The three dynamic responses of an automated process are: 1) Process gain (K_C), 2) Process time constant (τ_P), and 3) Process dead time (t_{PD}).

These parameters can tell us how much and how fast the output value from a process model responds to a change in input value to the process during tuning. Figure 17 shows a block diagram representing the dynamic responses of an automated process. We can measure the responses from a step-response test and use them to tune a controller. In the tuning process, we must perform several response tests on the loop and determine average values for K_P, τ_P, and t_P, as discussed next.

Process Gain and Process Time Constant

The term **process gain** (K_P) is used in the tuning process to describe how much output from a process model changes for a given change in its input (the *higher* the gain, the *more* the output changes for a given change in input). Thus, K_P is a proportionality constant, which tells us how much output value (OV) is changed in a step-response test for a given change in input value (IV).

$$K_P = \frac{\Delta OV}{\Delta IV} \times 100 \tag{2}$$

The **process time constant** (τ_P) indicates how long it takes for a process's step-response test.

[When the change (Δ) in output value (OV) is *not* in %, it can be converted using the final output value (OV_F), the initial output value (OV_I), the upper-range output value (OV_{UR}), and the lower-range output value (OV_{LR}).]

$$\Delta OV = \frac{OV_F - OV_I}{OV_{UR} - OV_{LR}} \tag{3}$$

An Example on Process Gain

Calculate the process gain (K_P) when the results of a step-response test, conducted on a control loop for controlling the temperature (T) of the output liquid feed from a heat exchanger, are given in Figure 18. Process input values (IV) are scaled in %, and process output values (OV) are calibrated in the range of 38 to 98°C.

As seen in Figure 18, OV_{Final} is 96°C, $OV_{Initial}$ is 90°C, $OV_{Upper\text{-}Range}$ is 98°C, and $OV_{Lower\text{-}Range}$ is 38°C, so

$$\Delta OV = \frac{96-90}{98-38} \times 100 = 10\% \qquad \Delta IV = 70 - 65 = 5\% \quad K_P = \frac{\Delta OV}{\Delta IV} = \frac{10}{5} = 2\%$$

As an example of the act that the K_P on a process under control performs, consider a **closed control loop**, shown in Figure 15, which adjusts the temperature (T) of a furnace by decreasing or increasing the fuel gas flow rate in relation to the difference between the desired T and the measured T of the hot air leaving the system. Thus, the proportionality constant here is K_P. If a small change in the control-valve position of the gas occurs, then, depending on the value of K_P, we can observe T responses in a way that is shown in Figure 19. The top curve shows the case with $K_P = 0$. This is called an **open control loop** (with *no* output control). As K_P increases, we notice that the furnace T responds faster and faster. This effect is desirable because it tells us that the disturbances from normal operation have a small effect on the process under control.

Controller gain (K_C) is used in relation to K_P (process gain) in a way that the K_C is proportional (shown as ∝) to the reverse of K_P (a *high* K_P requires a *low* K_C, and vice versa).

$$K_C \propto \frac{1}{K_P} \tag{4}$$

Because of reverse proportionality, K_C is used to cancel K_P. Some practical limitations, however, exist in canceling K_P with K_C. If a controller has a low K_P, a high K_C will be required to cancel K_P. Any process **noise**, as a result, will be increased by a high K_C and could, consequently result in large changes in the output value from the process model. It is, thus, *not* a good practice to use a high K_C (greater than 10) unless the controller's output signal is smooth and free of noise.

On K_P, the following may occur:

- If K_P is too high (> 10), we must make some changes in the input. The step-change, as said earlier, should be only in small increments at a time. This, however, is *not* easy because the limited resolution of, say, a valve makes it difficult to manipulate it in small increments at a time.
- If K_P is too small (< 0.2), we must question the design of the control loop. One of the causes can be that the final control element (say, a pump) operates close to its maximum capacity.

Process Dead Time

The term **process dead time** (t_{PD}) is used in the tuning process to refer to a time delay between a step change in input value and the response of the output value (the *longer* the process t_{PD}, the *longer* it takes to notice the result of a change in the input value). This can be seen in Figure 20.

In the shower example, as said earlier, it takes some time to feel the effect of a change in the position of the faucet (the controller). When, thus, making a small change in the water flow rate, we must wait until feeling its effect before making another small change. The waiting time here is the **dead time**. We can expect the same dead time behavior from an industrial process controller. The controller should make only small changes to its output and allow enough time for changes to make their way through the loop's final control element. If everything else stays the same but t_{PD} (process dead time) increases, K_C (controller gain) should be decreased to keep the loop stable. A process with a long t_{PD} takes longer to respond to a change in its input.

K_C is proportional (shown as ∝) to the reverse of t_{PD} (a *high* K_P creates a *low* t_{PD}, and vice versa).

$$K_C \propto \frac{1}{t_{PD}} \tag{5}$$

The following points are important to know when tuning a PID controller:

- All PID controller manufacturers do *not* offer the same units of measure for their controllers' P, I, and D tuning parameters. The three popular tuning methods (Ziegler-Nichols, Cohen-Coon, and Lambda) use **controller gain**, **integral time**, and **derivative time**.
- Each tuning method assumes that you have calculated all time measurements (**process gain**, **time constant**, and **lag time**) in the same units your controller uses (while a factor can convert one unit to another.

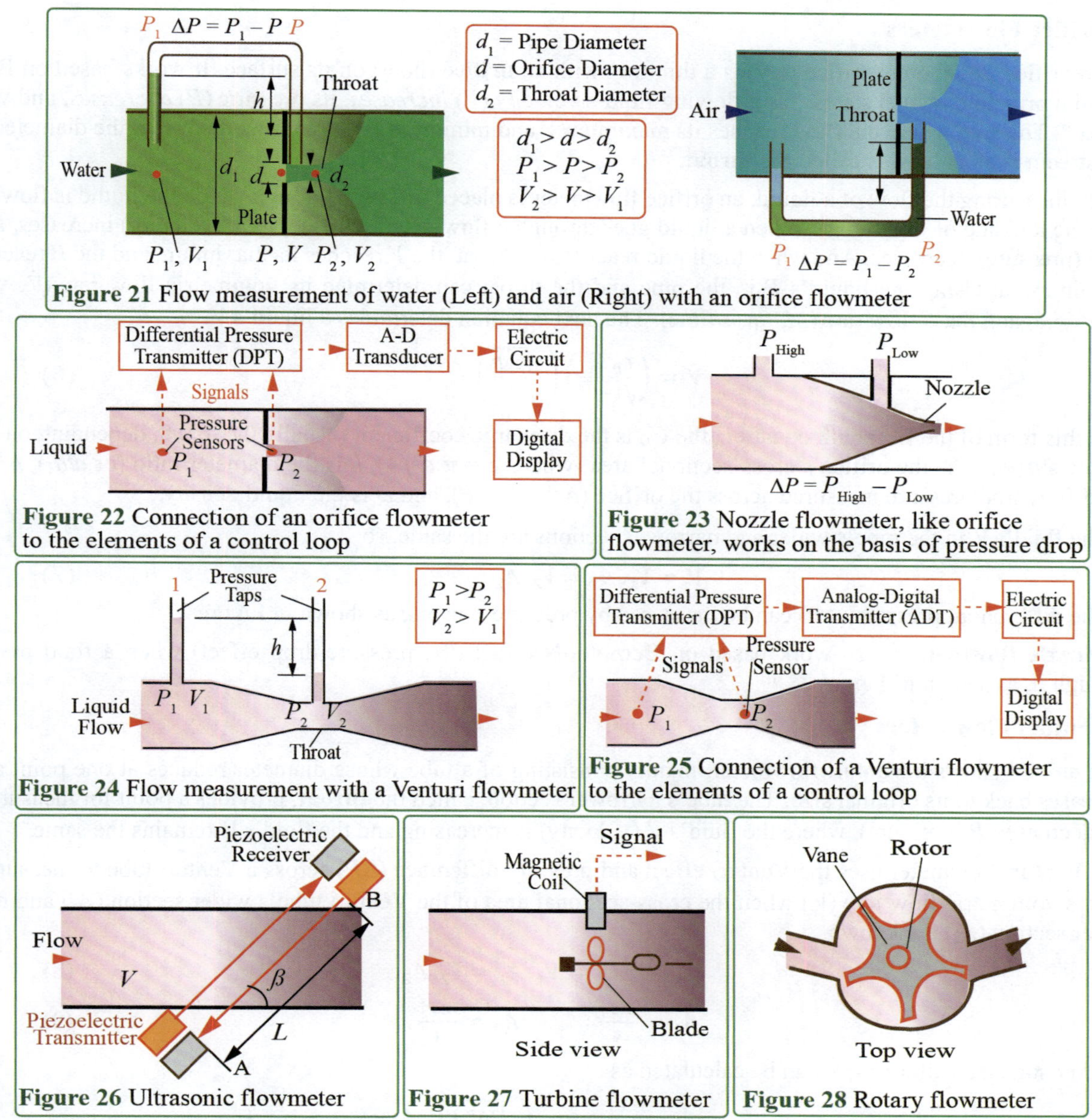

Figure 21 Flow measurement of water (Left) and air (Right) with an orifice flowmeter

Figure 22 Connection of an orifice flowmeter to the elements of a control loop

Figure 23 Nozzle flowmeter, like orifice flowmeter, works on the basis of pressure drop

Figure 24 Flow measurement with a Venturi flowmeter

Figure 25 Connection of a Venturi flowmeter to the elements of a control loop

Figure 26 Ultrasonic flowmeter

Figure 27 Turbine flowmeter

Figure 28 Rotary flowmeter

5. FLOW MEASUREMENT AND CONTROL

Different instruments are used in the chemical process industry for measuring the mass flow rate ($\dot{M}$) or volumetric flow rate ($\dot{V}$, simply **flow rate**) of a fluid (liquid or gas). These instruments, which are generally known as the **flowmeters**, can be classified into two main groups:

- Mechanical flowmeters, and
- Optical flowmeters.

The main types of mechanical flowmeters are orifice flowmeters, Venturi flowmeters, ultrasonic flowmeters, turbine flowmeters, rotary flowmeters, and pitot flowmeters.

Orifice Flowmeters

An orifice flowmeter (orifice tray) is a thin tray with an **orifice** (hole) on its surface. It works based on Bernoulli's principle, which states, "as a flowing fluid's velocity (V) *increases*, its pressure (P) *decreases*, and vice versa." The area where the fluid reaches its maximum V and minimum P. In other words, when the diameter of the stream is at its least is called the **throat**.

For measuring the flow of a liquid, an orifice flowmeter is placed in a pipe through which the liquid is flowing (see the left side of Figure 22). When a liquid goes through a flowmeter's orifice, its V (velocity) increases, and its P (pressure) decreases. And when the liquid reaches the throat, the V reaches its maximum, and the P reaches its minimum. Using the liquid's P in the pipe and the throat can determine its volumetric flow rate ($\dot{V}$, volume/time) and mass flow rate ($\dot{M}$, mass/time). The next equation determines a liquid's $\dot{V}$.

$$\dot{V} = \left(\frac{C_D.A^2}{\sqrt{1-\beta^4}}\right)\left(\sqrt{\frac{2\Delta P}{D}}\right) \quad (6)$$

In this form of the Bernoulli equation, the C_D is the discharge coefficient (usually 0.6 to 0.8, depending on the orifice shape), A is the orifice's cross-sectional area (where $A = \pi.d^2/4$), β is the diameter ratio (or d/d_1), ΔP is the differential pressure measured across the orifice ($\Delta P = P_1 - P$), and D is the liquid density.

The fluid's $\dot{V}$ in the pipe's wider and narrower sections are the same, so

$$\dot{V} = V_1.A_1 = V_2.A_2 \quad (7)$$

The differential pressure (ΔP) can be measured by pressure sensors, as shown in Figure 22.

[**Nozzle flowmeters** also work based on Bernoulli's effect (the pressure-drop effect) when a fluid passes through it, as shown in Figure 23.]

Venturi Flowmeters

Figure 24 shows a Venturi flowmeter, mainly consisting of a tube whose diameter reduces at one point and increases back to its original size. The tube's narrower section, called the **throat**, provides a point for measuring the decreased P (pressure), where the fluid's V (velocity) is increasing and the fluid's $\dot{V}$ remains the same.

A Venturi flowmeter uses the Venturi effect and pressure difference (ΔP) across a Venturi tube to measure a fluid's volumetric flow rate ($\dot{V}$) when the cross-sectional area of the Venturi tube's wider section (A_1) and narrower section (A_2) are known.

$$\dot{V} = V_1.A_1 = V_2.A_2 \quad (8)$$

$$A_1 = \frac{\pi.d_1^2}{4} \qquad A_2 = \frac{\pi.d_2^2}{4} \quad (9)$$

After some substitutions, $\dot{V}$ can be calculated as

$$\dot{V} = V_2.A_2 = \left(\sqrt{\frac{2\Delta P}{D}}\right)\left(\frac{A_2}{\sqrt{1-\beta^2}}\right) \quad (10)$$

In this equation, which is a form of the Bernoulli equation, V_2 is the fluid's velocity in the narrower section (the section with higher V and lower P), A_2 is the cross-sectional area of the narrower section, ΔP is the differential P measured across the orifice (that is $P_1 - P_2$), D is the fluid's density, and β is the diameter ratio (in this case d_2/d_1). [Note that the fluid's $\dot{V}$ (volumetric flow rate) in the tube's wider and narrower sections are the same, as shown in Figure 24.]

For simplification of the formulation, Equation 8 is usually given as a relationship between $\dot{V}$ and the pressure drop (ΔP) through the proportionality constant of K.

$$\dot{V} = K\sqrt{\Delta P} \quad (11)$$

K depends on D, A_1, A_2, P_1, and P_2. The measuring fluid's D and the Venturi tube's A_1 and A_2 are known. A **pressure sensor** can measure the differential pressure (ΔP), as shown in Figure 25. [According to Equation 11, $\dot{V}$ depends on the square root of ΔP, meaning that if ΔP across the measuring points increases by a factor of 2, the $\dot{V}$ increases by a factor of 1.41 (the square root of 2).]

Ultrasonic Flowmeters

An ultrasonic (ultrasound) flowmeter measures the speed of an ultrasound wave when it passes through a flowing fluid in a pipe. Figure 26 shows an ultrasonic flowmeter with a piezoelectric crystal (made from barium titanate) that works as an ultrasound transmitter to send an acoustic signal through a flowing fluid. A piezoelectric crystal also receives the signal.

If the distance between the transducer A and receiver B is L (for length), the sound wave's path is an angle β from the pipe's wall. Then, the sound velocity (V_S) from A to B increases by the fluid velocity (V), so $V_S + V\cos\beta$. Then the frequency (f) of the sound wave, received by the piezoelectric receiver, from A to B (caused by fluid's velocity) can be given as

$$f = \frac{V_S + V.Cos\beta}{L} \tag{12}$$

Similarly, the frequency of the sound wave from B to A (decreased by fluid's velocity) is

$$f = \frac{V_S - V.Cos\beta}{L} \tag{13}$$

And the difference in frequency (Δf) will be

$$\Delta f = \frac{2V.Cos\beta}{L} \tag{14}$$

Solving this equation for a fluid velocity (V) gives

$$V = \frac{\Delta f.L}{2cos\beta} \tag{15}$$

If then we have the pipe's cross-sectional area (A), we can calculate the liquid's $\dot{V}$.

$$\dot{V} = V.A = \frac{\Delta f.L}{2Cos\beta} \times A \tag{16}$$

The sound wave frequency can be measured by a device known as an **electronic mixer**. If, for example, Δf is 80 cycle/s, the angle β is 45°, the sound path L is 0.2 m, and A is 0.01 m², $\dot{V}$ becomes

$$\dot{V} = \frac{80\times0.2}{2Cos45} \times 0.01 = \frac{0.16}{2\times0.7} = 0.1 \text{ m}^3/\text{s}$$

The following two brief points are important to know about ultrasonic flowmeters:

- They are usually installed outside the measuring liquid pipe because their measuring elements are nonintrusive (non-contacting). Thus, an ultrasonic flowmeter can be installed without the process being stopped.
- They are mostly used for wastewater applications, which have suspended particles. [Ultrasonic technology requires the liquid under the flow measurement to contain at least 100 PPM (parts per million) of 100 microns or larger suspended particles.]

Turbine Flowmeters

A turbine flowmeter provides a rotational velocity that changes linearly with the flow rate of the measuring fluid. Figure 27 shows a typical turbine flowmeter consisting of a rotating turbine on a center shaft (axis of rotation). The measuring fluid enters the flowmeter and passes the turbine blades, which rotate the flowmeter's rotor. When a rotor's steady rotation is reached, the frequency (f, pulse) of rotation is linearly proportional to the fluid's flow rate ($\dot{V}$).

$$\dot{V} = \frac{f}{K} \tag{17}$$

For example, if a turbine flowmeter produces 5 pulses/L (pulses/length) when a measuring liquid passes through it, the flowmeter's coefficient K is 5 pulses/L. Thus, this meter reads 50 pulses/L, meaning that the liquid's flow rate is 10 times greater.

Rotary Flowmeters

A rotary flowmeter works almost the same way as a turbine flowmeter (because it converts the rotational velocity to a measuring liquid's flow rate). Figure 28 shows a typical rotary flowmeter consisting of a vane-type float inside a tapered tube (usually made of glass). The float is pushed up by fluid flow and pulled down by gravitational force so that it can spin on the meter's shaft. As the flow rate of the measuring fluid increases, the fluid's pressure (P) increases, causing the float to rotate faster. When a steady rotation is reached, the velocity (V) of rotation is linearly proportional to the fluid's volumetric flow rate ($\dot{V}$). Rotary flowmeters are mainly used for measuring water flow or air flow.

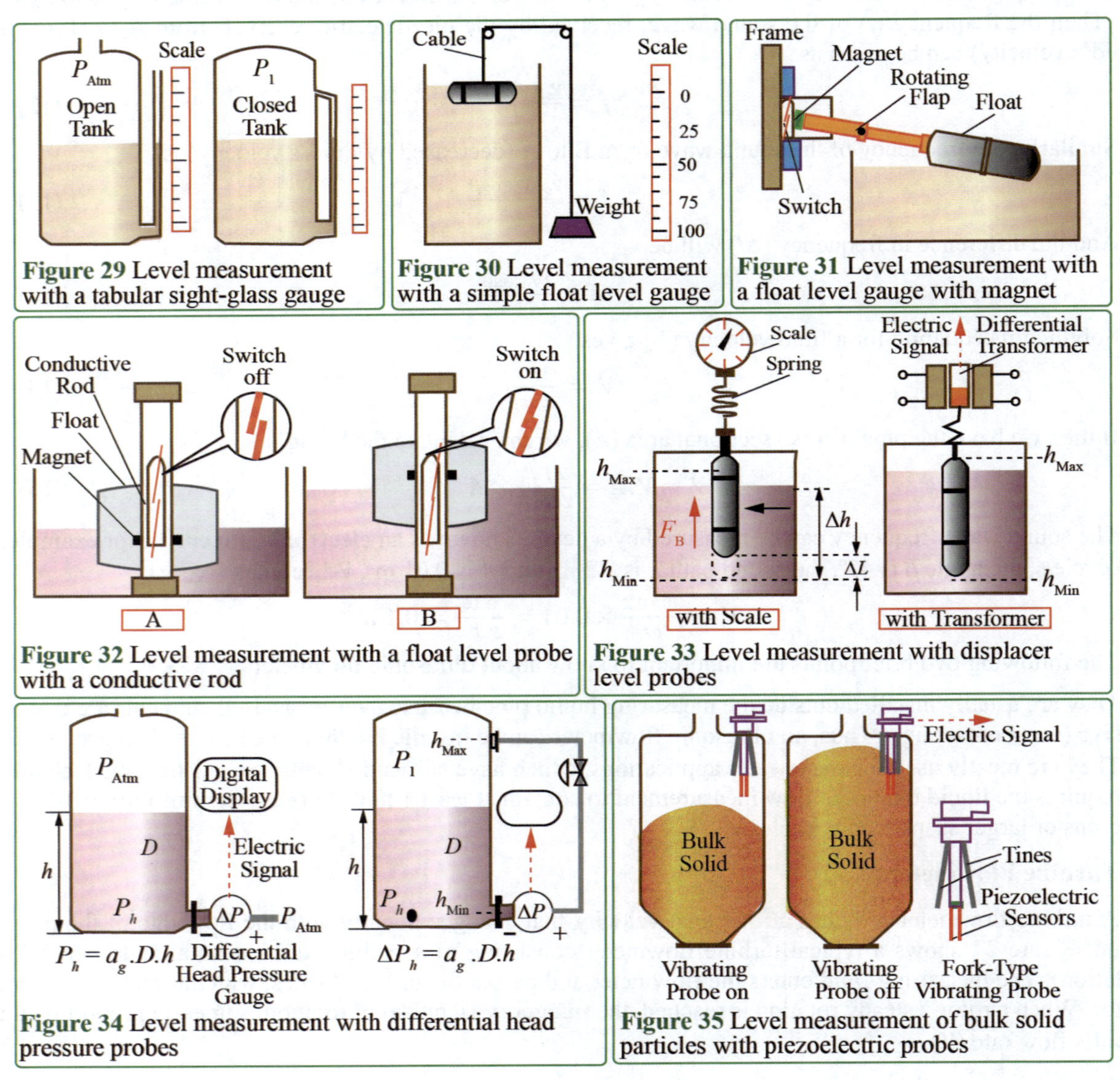

Figure 29 Level measurement with a tabular sight-glass gauge

Figure 30 Level measurement with a simple float level gauge

Figure 31 Level measurement with a float level gauge with magnet

Figure 32 Level measurement with a float level probe with a conductive rod

Figure 33 Level measurement with displacer level probes

Figure 34 Level measurement with differential head pressure probes

Figure 35 Level measurement of bulk solid particles with piezoelectric probes

Level Measurement with a Float Level Gauge

A simple float level gauge is shown in Figure 30. One cable (tape) end is connected to a float and the other end to a counterweight, which keeps the cable under constant pull (tension). As a change in the level of a liquid occurs, the float moves and the counterweight moves up and down across a direct-reading scale. The scale is calibrated to indicate the liquid level in its tank.

Figure 31 shows a float level sensor containing a float, a magnet, and a switch. The magnet regulates the switch so that as the liquid level increases, the magnet gets the switch's connectors closer to each other and turns the switch on. As the liquid level decreases, the magnet gets the switch's connectors farther from each other and shuts the switch off.

Figure 32 shows a float level probe (sensor) with a float, a conductive rod, and a round magnet. Such a sensor works the same way as the previously-explained sensor. The sensor operates in two different forms:

- For a low level of the liquid in the tank, the switch is on, and as the float starts to move up. In other words, as the level increases, it shuts off, as shown on the left side of Figure 32.
- The switch is on for a high level of the liquid, and as the float starts to move down, it turns on (as shown on the right side of the same figure).

Level Measurement with a Displacer Gauge

A displacer level gauge works based on Archimedes' principle. It uses the change in buoyant force (F_B, an upward force exerted on a system by a fluid), acting on a partially submerged displacer. Referring to Figure 33, we can say that changing the liquid level by Δh changes F_B, and a new equilibrium in a different level occurs. At equilibrium, F_B can be given as

$$F_B = a_g . D . V = a_g . D . A(\Delta h - \Delta L) \tag{18}$$

Knowing the fact that a_g is constant and most of the time, the liquid D is also constant, Equation 18 can be written as

$$F_B = K . \Delta L \tag{19}$$

This equation tells us that we can determine a liquid's level in a container by measuring F_B produced by a displacer. In other words, if the liquid's D is constant, then a unit change in the displacer level will result in a certain change in the liquid level.

The left side of Figure 31 shows a simple level displacer, in which the displacer's lift (ΔL) for maximum liquid level can relatively be small (a few mm). This affects the accuracy of the measurement. However, a level displacer with a **differential transformer** (shown on the right side of the same figure) can solve this problem. The transformer's **primary winding** and **secondary winding** are made of non-magnetic material. Because a metal cell is connected to the spring, a change in the spring length changes the metal-cell position, and this causes the change in the voltage (V, also called **electric voltage** or **potential difference**) between the primary and secondary windings. The transformer's output is an electric signal proportional to the liquid level in the tank. The signal value can be viewed on a digital display.

Level Measurement with a Head-Pressure Sensor

Based on the Pascal principle, pressure (P) in a liquid acts equally in all directions, so a head-pressure sensor (probe) can measure its level at any point in the liquid. It is recommended to be installed on the tank's wall close to its bottom (to prevent scale buildup on the sensor). From the topic of HEAD PRESSURE, we know that a direct relationship exists between the head pressure (P_h), gravitational acceleration (a_g), the liquid's density (D), and its height in the container (h, known as liquid head or simply **head**).

$$P_h = a_g . D . h \tag{20}$$

The term a_g is constant, and in most cases, D is also constant (if sudden-and-considerable changes in the liquid's temperature do *not* occur), so P_h can be written as

$$P_h = K.h \quad (21)$$

In this equation, K is a proportionality constant. For water at 20ºC, K equates to

$$K = a_g.D = 9.8 \times 1000 = 9800 \text{ Kg/(s}^2\text{.m}^2\text{)}$$

In an **open** (non-pressurized) tank, where the liquid is under P_{Atm} (see the left side of Figure 34), a differential head pressure (DP) probe can measure the liquid level in the tank. One side of the probe is connected to the measuring source and the other side to the atmosphere. The probe's (transmitter's) output is an **electric signal** proportional to the liquid level in the tank. The signal value can be viewed on a digital display.

A DP sensor can also be used in a **closed** (pressurized) tank, where the liquid is under P_1 (see the right side of Figure 34). Here, the other side of the DP sensor is connected to the tank (*not* to the atmosphere), so a change in P_1 will *not* change the output of the DP sensor because the sensor responds only to changes in pressure difference (ΔP), in other words, to changes in liquid-level values.

Level Measurement with a Vibrating Probe

A vibrating level probe works based on the principle of harmonic vibration in free space and a measuring medium (a liquid or bulk solid), as shown in Figure 35. **Fork type** and **rod type** are the two most-used vibrating level probes.

The right side of the same figure shows a fork-type vibrating level probe, which mainly has

- Two **piezoelectric sensors** (PIEZOELECTRICITY), one for producing vibration (vibrating sensor) and the other one for generating an electric signal (measuring sensor).
- Two tines (teeth) vibrate with high frequency (f) in free space, but they slow down notably when they are in touch with the measuring medium (liquid or bulk solid particles).
- An electric circuit evaluates the frequency of vibration and sends an electric signal.

When the vibrating sensor (probe) vibrates fast in the air, the measuring sensor sees this as the presence of free space (with *no* measuring medium). And when the measuring medium compresses the sensor, it creates an electric signal (as the result of the piezoelectric effect) that its voltage (V) is proportional to the compressed force (load) applied to it. When the V reaches the setpoint, it orders the switch to change its position.

Level Measurement with a Capacitance Probe

The electrodes of a capacitance level probe (usually called capacitor) can contact a measuring substance (liquid or bulk solid). As discussed under CAPACITORS, the total capacitance (C) of capacitors, connected in parallel, equates to the total of the capacitors' capacitances.

$$C = C_0 + C_1 + C_2 = K_1.h + K_2 \quad (22)$$

In this equation, K_1 is the dielectric constant of the liquid, K_2 is the dielectric constant of the vapor above the liquid, and h is the liquid head of the measuring liquid. As seen in Figure 36A, when a **conductive liquid** (like water or aqueous solution) is under measurement, the whole length of the capacitor's **primary electrode** is covered with an insulator (with low conductivity, like Teflon). And when a **nonconductive liquid** (such as oil or gasoline) is under measurement, only the top part of the primary electrode is covered with the insulator (because the nonconductive liquid acts as an insulator), as shown in Figure 36B. In both cases, the metal wall of the tank acts as the **second electrode**.

The capacitance (C) of the second electrode is negligible compared with the C of the primary electrode. Similarly, C of the vapor (with a low dielectric constant of K_2) and C of the air (with a low dielectric constant of K_0) are also negligible, so Equation 10.22 becomes

$$C = K_1.h \quad (23)$$

As the liquid head (h) in the tank rises, the vapor is displaced by the measuring liquid (with a known dielectric constant of K_1), so a level transmitter (LT), which is calibrated in the unit of length, can detect the C changes of the primary electrode, which changes with h in the tank.

Level Measurement with Ultrasound Probes

Ultrasound (ultrasonic) is a sound with waves of a high frequency (f) greater than 20 kHz (= 20 000 cycles/s), which the human ear *cannot* detect. An ultrasound probe acts based on the following:

- A piezoelectric generator can generate ultrasound waves.
- Ultrasound waves can be spread in solids, liquids, and gases but *cannot* in a vacuum (because of a low P). Thus, an ultrasound probe *cannot* be used in a medium with P less than 60 kPa (= 0.6 Atm).
- When ultrasound waves strike the surface of a liquid or a solid medium, a large percentage of the waves reflect, and only a small portion of them penetrate the medium.

An ultrasound probe measures the time it takes ultrasound waves with known speed to move through a measuring substance until it returns to the probe. Figure 37 shows the sending ultrasound pulse waves in a measuring liquid and their reflected sound (the **echo**). The symbols t_1 and t_2 in the figure are time intervals for getting the waves to the liquid's surface and returning to the probe. A level transducer senses the reflected sound, converts it into an electrical signal, and sends it to a receiving controller that measures the total time ($t_T = t_1 + t_2$). The t_T is proportional to the level of the liquid under measurement.

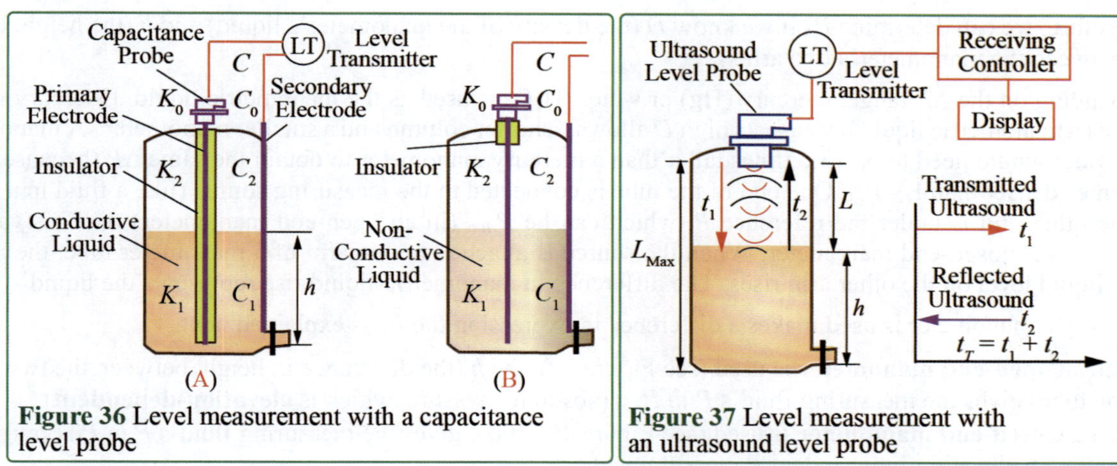

Figure 36 Level measurement with a capacitance level probe

Figure 37 Level measurement with an ultrasound level probe

6. PRESSURE MEASUREMENT AND CONTROL

Different instruments are used in the chemical process industry to measure the pressure (P) of a fluid (liquid or gas) in a vessel (like a tank) or a pipe. These instruments, which are generally known as the **pressure measuring sensors** or **pressure measuring transducers**, come in different types, including the following:

- **Gauges:** These instruments convert the P of a fluid into a physical movement, and the amount of movement, which is proportional to P, can be measured by a scale (gauge). The scale is calibrated for known pressures, so the P of an unknown measuring source can be determined. Examples of this group include **Bourdon gauges, membrane gauges, piston gauges, strain gauges**, and **pressure bellows**.
- **Sensors** (transmitters): These instruments measure the P of a fluid and usually send their signals to some distance (such as to a factory's central control room), where the signal is converted into a usable P reading. **Ionization sensors** and **thermal sensors** are examples of this group.

We discuss here a few instruments from each of the two listed groups.

Pressure Measurement with a Manometer Gauge

A typical manometer is a glass U-tube, which is about half full with a liquid of a certain density (D) and is used for measuring the P of a fluid in a container. A manometer works based on the height difference of the manometric liquid between its two arms (h). [Manometers are calibrated in units of length (usually in mm or In) or in units of pressure (usually in absolute pressure or gauge pressure).]

Relating to Figure 38, in the Earth's gravitational field, which has a gravitational acceleration a_g, the P_A (the P of a liquid at location A), equates to the pressure difference (ΔP) in a manometer's tube that is filled with a liquid of density D. P_A depends on ΔP, which is a function of a_g, D, and h.

$$P_A = \Delta P = a_g.D.h \tag{24}$$

If a_g is in m/s^2, D is in kg/m^3, and h is in m, P becomes in kg/m.s^2 = N/m^2 = 1 Pa, where N is for Newton (the force unit) and Pa is for Pascal (the pressure unit). The term $a_g.D$ is the specific weight of the liquid. Equation 24 is valid if the D of the manometric liquid is much greater than that of the measuring liquid. If the densities are numerically close to each other, Equation 24 becomes

$$P_A = \Delta P = a_g.D_1.h_1 - a_g.D.h \tag{25}$$

Therefore, we can determine P_A if we know D (the density of the manometer's liquid) and h (the height difference between the manometer's two arms).

Depending on the ΔP range, mercury (Hg) or water (H_2O) is used as the manometric liquid. [Mercury is preferred as a manometric liquid because its high D allows a shorter column and a smaller manometer. A manometer using water would need to be 13.6 times taller than a mercury manometer to obtain the same ΔP (because Hg is 13.6 times denser than H_2O).] One end of the tube is connected to the measuring source (like a fluid in a tank), and the other end is under the reference P, which can be P_{Atm} (in an open-end manometer) or P_{Vac} (vacuum pressure) in a closed-end manometer. When the source is attached to one arm of a manometer tube, the manometric liquid level on the other arm rises. The difference in manometric-liquid rise represents the liquid's P.

The way a manometer is used makes a difference in expressing the P, as explained next.

- When an **open-end manometer** is used (see Figure 39), the h (the difference in height between the two arms of the tube) gives the measuring fluid's P in P_{Abs} (absolute pressure, which is **elevation-dependent**).
- When a **closed-end manometer** is used (see Figure 40), the h gives the measuring fluid's P in P_G (gauge pressure, an elevation-independent P measurement).

Pressure Measurement with a Bourdon Gauge

The original Bourdon gauge was patented by E. Bourdon (a French physicist) in 1849. [Although the **android gauges** are modern Bourdon gauges, the term **Bourdon gauge** is still used.] Generally, a Bourdon gauge works based on some metals' elasticity (elastic response). A thin piece of elastic metal is used to form a hollow C-shaped tube (see Figure 41). The tube has the property of expanding and contracting with changing P. One end of the tube is open to a process line for measuring a fluid's P. The other end, which is closed, is attached to a pointer (placed on a calibrated dial). As the open end is exposed to a fluid, the P exerted on the tube causes it to be straightened. This moves a lever that transfers the movement to the pointer, which moves against the dial on the gauge's face. Thus, the dial shows the fluid's P_G (gauge pressure).

Bourdon gauges can measure pressures from nearly zero to 7000 Atm (= 70 kPa = 102×10^2 PSI), depending on the metal used to make the tube. The industrial gauges offer high accuracy of ±1%.

Bourdon gauges are mostly calibrated on P_G, which is elevation-dependent. In vacuum systems, which operate at pressures less than P_{Atm}, Bourdon gauges are calibrated on the P_{Abs} (an elevation-independent P).

Pressure Measurement with a Head-Pressure Gauge

This measuring gauge is discussed under the subtopic of Level Measurement and Control under this topic.

Pressure Measurement with a Membrane Pressure Sensor

Figure 42 shows a membrane (diaphragm) gauge, which is a common instrument that converts *P* into a physical movement. It has a flexible metal membrane, an enclosed capsule that contains air at a certain *P*, and a scale. One side of the gauge (the measuring side) is connected to the capsule, and the other side (the reference side) can be sealed to measure P_{Abs} or open to the atmosphere to measure P_G. The membrane bends and extends when a measuring fluid enters the gauge and pushes the membrane, as shown on the right side of the figure. The membrane is attached to a pointer placed on a calibrated scale. The amount of bending, proportional to the *P* of an unknown measuring source, is measured by the scale.

Pressure Measurement with a Capacitive Pressure Sensor

Figure 43 shows a capacitive pressure sensor that applies differential pressure to a membrane. The sensor has one moving and two non-moving electrodes connected to a measuring bridge. Because the solid electrodes are in an insulating material (called a **dielectric**, like glass), the *P* of the measuring sample does *not* affect them, so the changes in the electrodes' capacitance are high. The sensor is filled with a filling liquid (like silicon oil), moving between isolating and sensing membranes. Thus, the sensing membrane moves toward one of the non-moving capacitors and away from the other, changing the membrane's capacitance (*C*). Because the electrodes act like capacitors (conductors) and *C* is directly proportional to the capacitor's length (*L*), the *P* applied to the sensor is related to the change in *C*. A measuring bridge connected to an electric circuit can measure the change in *C*. The *C* change is then converted into an electric signal to a transmitter (calibrated in *P* units). The output voltage of the measuring bridge is directly proportional to the $C_1 - C_2 = \Delta C$.

Pressure Measurement with an Electric Resistance Pressure Sensor

A pressure sensor (also called a **strain gauge**) works based on the electric resistance (R_E, simply **resistance**) of an **electric resistor** (simply **resistor**, a system that resists the flow of electric current). It works based on Hooke's principle and strain (deformation) of a resistor (a wire) with a length of *L* (Figure 44). [An instrument that uses a resistor's R_E (electric resistance) is commonly called a **strain gauge**.]

The resistor (which has a current running through it) is attached to a metal diaphragm that bends, causing some stretch in the resistor's length (*L*). This causes an increase in the diaphragm's *L* (the *more* the diaphragm bends by the current, the *more* increase occurs in the resistor). By measuring the current, the gauge can determine how much the diaphragm has bent and, therefore, how much *P* the measuring source creates.

Strain gauges come in many types for measuring P_{Abs}, P_G, and P_{Vac}. Modern strain gauges have a silicon wafer connected to one surface of the metal diaphragm. The diaphragm bends when pressure is applied to it, causing the diaphragm to be bent. As a result, some changes in the current of the silicon wafer occur. The changes in the current through the wafer are then converted to a pressure reading.

Pressure Measurement with a Piezoelectric Pressure Sensor

A piezoelectric pressure sensor (simply **piezosensor**) works based on piezoelectricity (the formation of electricity in a piezoelectric crystal by applying a force or pressure). Figure 45 shows a piezosensor, which can produce an electric signal when it is mechanically deformed by *P*. The signal's voltage (*V*) is proportional to the amount of *P* that causes the deformation in the piezosensor.

A ceramic piezosensor is connected to a voltmeter through an electric circuit to measure the signal's voltage in the pressure sensor. Because the output voltage signal from the sensor is usually small, an **amplifier** with a high input is used. The amplifier is placed a few meters from the sensor to prevent signal loss.

Piezoelectric sensors can only measure the *P* of clean-dry air or nonreactive gases (water and vapor affect the sensor, causing corrosion). To prevent the corrosion problem, the piezoelectric ceramic sensors are usually covered with a layer of aluminum (Al).

[Note: More pressure sensors are used in the chemical process industry, such as semiconductor pressure sensors (Figure 46) and resonance pressure sensors (Figure 47). Because of conciseability reasons, it is impossible to discuss all of the sensors in this book.]

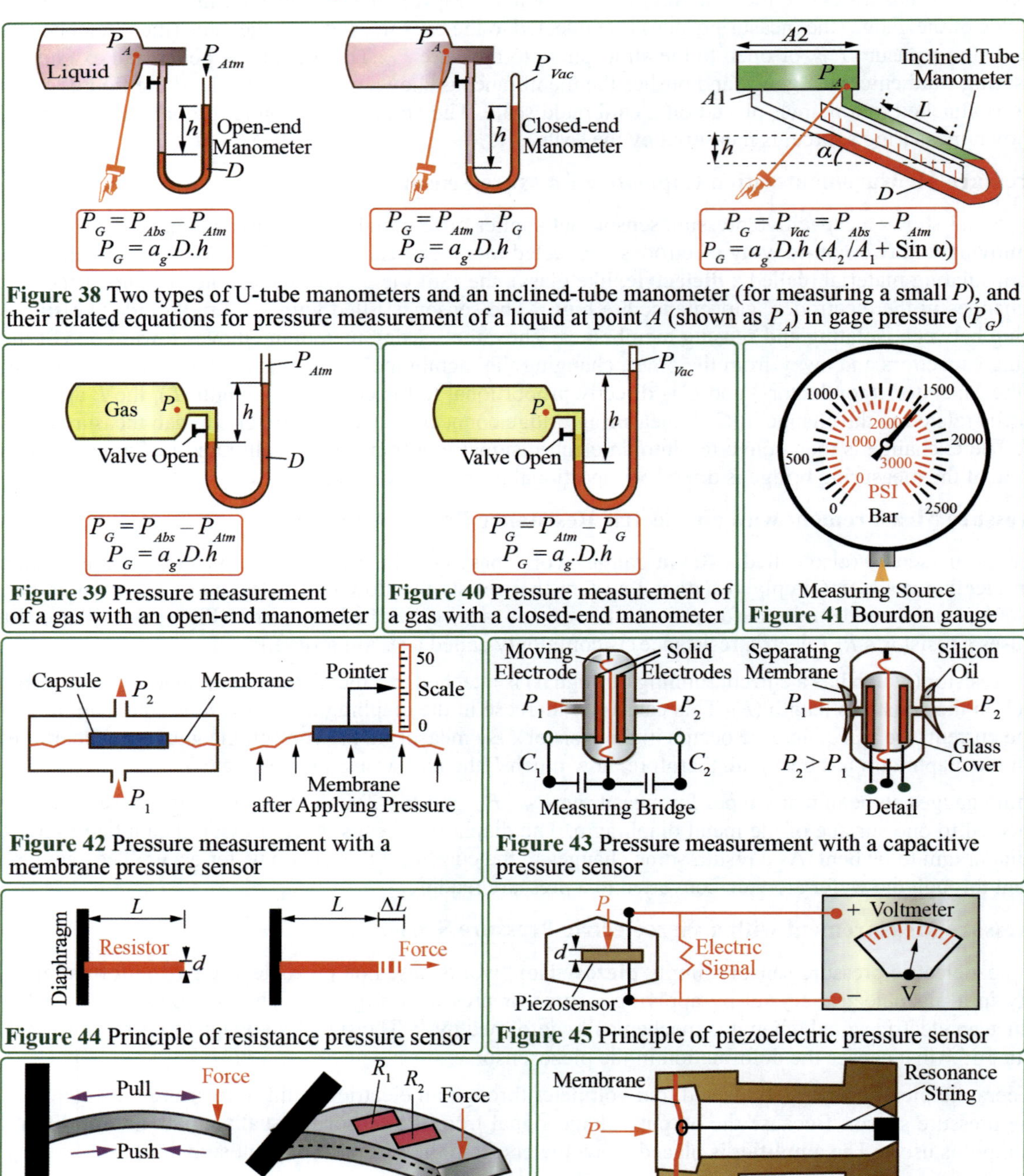

Figure 38 Two types of U-tube manometers and an inclined-tube manometer (for measuring a small P), and their related equations for pressure measurement of a liquid at point A (shown as P_A) in gage pressure (P_G)

Figure 39 Pressure measurement of a gas with an open-end manometer

Figure 40 Pressure measurement of a gas with a closed-end manometer

Figure 41 Bourdon gauge

Figure 42 Pressure measurement with a membrane pressure sensor

Figure 43 Pressure measurement with a capacitive pressure sensor

Figure 44 Principle of resistance pressure sensor

Figure 45 Principle of piezoelectric pressure sensor

Figure 46 Principle of semiconductive pressure sensor

Figure 47 Principle of resonance pressure sensor

7. TEMPERATURE MEASUREMENT AND CONTROL

Different instruments are used in the chemical process industry to measure a fluid or solid's temperature (T). These instruments, generally known as **thermometers**, measure the T by some changes in the physical properties of the measuring source. The physical properties that change with T include the L (length) of a metal rod, the V (volume) of a liquid, the P (pressure) of a gas kept at constant V, the V of a gas kept at constant P, and the R_E (electric resistance) of a conductor. Some of these instruments are invasive (contacting), and some are noninvasive (non-contacting or remote). [Under THERMOMETERS, some of the traditional thermometers were explained. Here, the talk will be about advanced and more accurate instruments used for temperature measurement.]

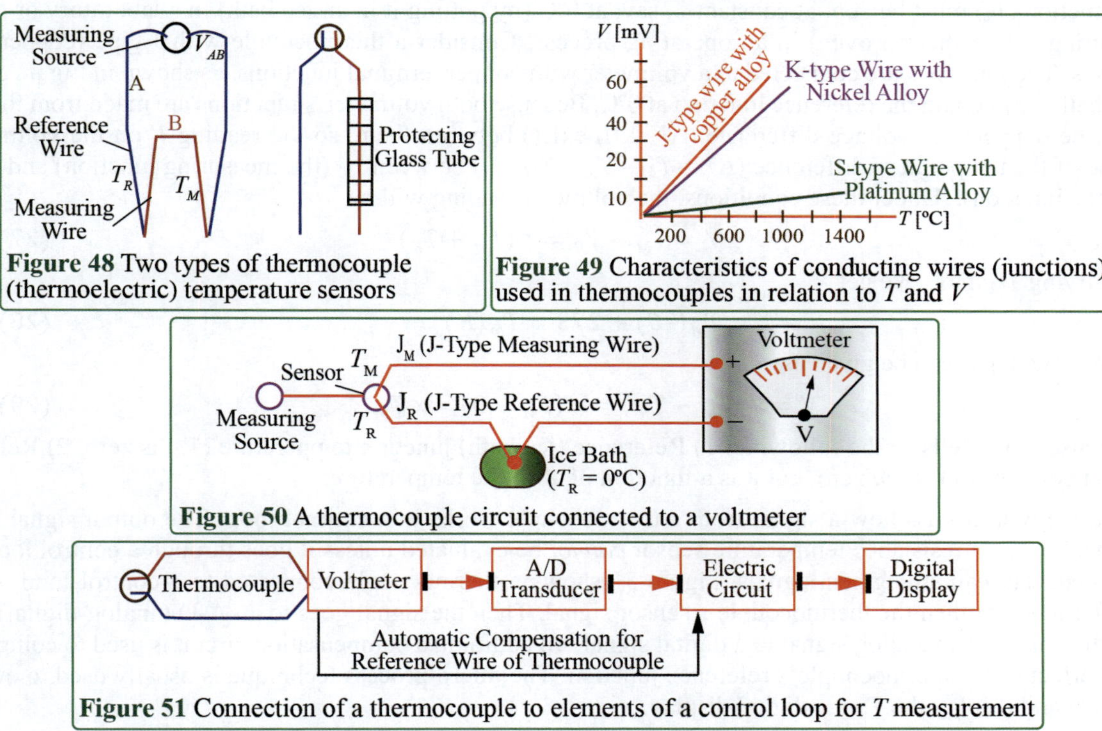

Figure 48 Two types of thermocouple (thermoelectric) temperature sensors

Figure 49 Characteristics of conducting wires (junctions) used in thermocouples in relation to T and V

Figure 50 A thermocouple circuit connected to a voltmeter

Figure 51 Connection of a thermocouple to elements of a control loop for T measurement

Thermocouple Temperature Sensors

A thermocouple (thermoelectric) sensor is a contacting (invasive) thermometer. Figure 48 is a thermocouple circuit that works based on the **Seebeck effect**. This effect says that an electric current (I, simply **current**) flows in two different metal conductors (A and B) if they are connected at both ends, and the junctions are at different temperatures. Let T_R be the T of the **reference junction** and T_M be the T of the **measuring junction**. Changes in T_M create a change in an electric voltage (V or V_E), known as the **Seebeck voltage** (V_{AB}), between the thermocouple's two junctions (J_R and J_M). As T_M increases, V_{AB} increases almost linearly (see Figure 49). A linear equation can express the relationship between the V_{AB} of a thermocouple and T.

$$\mathrm{V_{AB}} = \propto_{\mathrm{AB}} (\mathrm{T_M} - \mathrm{T_R}) \tag{26}$$

$\propto_{AB}$ is the Seebeck coefficient (also called **electric resistance coefficient**) that depends on the conducting metal junctions used in a thermocouple. If, for example, the measuring junction's T is 85ºC and the reference junction's T is 25ºC, the V_{AB} for a thermocouple with $\propto_{AB}$ = 45 µV/ºC will be

$$V_{AB} = 45(85 - 25) = 2700\ \mu\text{V or } 2.7\ \text{mV}$$

The conducting junctions used in a thermocouple are chosen based on the measuring source's T range. This provides a linear V_{AB} in relation to the measuring T. Based on the measuring T range, the junctions are typed as:

- The J type has copper-nickel alloy for measuring T in the range of – 200 to + 600ºC,
- The K type contains nickel-chrome alloy for T in the range of – 50ºC to + 1000ºC, and
- The S type contains platinum-rhodium alloy for measuring T in the range of 0 to 1300ºC.

The linear relationship of these junctions in relation to T is shown in Figure 49.

For measuring a thermocouple electric voltage (the V of a measuring sample), a voltmeter is connected to the thermocouple to create a new thermoelectric circuit. Suppose we want Equation 26 to be applicable. The reference junction (J_R) must be kept at constant T, say, at 0ºC (by putting it in an ice bath) in a laboratory or at 50ºC (by putting it in a thermo oven) in an operating process. Consider a thermocouple with J-type (copper-alloy) junctions. The junctions are connected to a voltmeter with copper terminal junctions, as shown in Figure 50, and an ice bath for keeping the reference junction at 0ºC. Because both voltmeter's junctions are made from the same metal (the copper), *no* voltage difference ($\Delta V = 0$) exists between them, so the reading V on the voltmeter is because of the temperature difference ($\Delta T = T_M - T_R = T_M - 0$) between J_M (the measuring junction) and J_R (the reference junction). Under these conditions, the voltmeter reading will be

$$V = V_M - V_R = \propto (T_M + T_R) \tag{27}$$

Specifying T_M in ºC, we get

$$T_M(ºC) + 273 = T_M(K) \tag{28}$$

Then V (voltage) can be given as

$$V = \propto (T_M - T_R) = \propto (T_M - 0) = \propto T_M \tag{29}$$

This discussion tells us the following: 1) Reference (ice bath) junction temperature (T_R) is zero, 2) Reference junction voltage (V_R) is *not* zero, but it is a function of absolute temperature.

Next, we will discuss how a signal from a thermocouple works in a **control loop**. The output signal from a thermocouple or a resistance temperature sensor *cannot* be evaluated unless it goes through a control loop with an element that can strengthen signals. Figure 51 shows a thermocouple connected to a control loop with an amplifier to strengthen the thermocouple's sensor signal. Then the signal goes to an A-D (analog-digital) transducer that changes an analog signal to a digital signal. In addition, a compensation circuit is used to compensate for the effect of the thermocouple's reference junction. The micro-process technique is usually used to evaluate the signal and display the T on a digital display.

Resistance Temperature Sensors

As a contacting thermometer, a resistance temperature sensor (RTS, also called **resistance temperature detector**, RTD) uses a conductor's R_E (electric resistance) and the change of its R_E to measure a sample's T. An RTS measures R_E, which is calibrated in units T, instead of units R_E (ohm, Ω).

The two main types of resistance sensors are the following:

- **Resistance Temperature Detectors** (RTDs)**:** Platinum (Pt) is used as the most common metal in RTDs because its electric resistance (R_E) considerably and linearly changes with T. Other metals, like nickel and copper, also have high R_E. Platinum has a highly useful range of – 200 to 800ºC, while nickel (– 60 to 200ºC) and copper (– 100 to 100ºC) have lower useful ranges. Usually, the measuring metal of an RTD is placed in a ceramic tube for protection (see Figure 52). The diameter of the ceramic tube is 4 to 5 mm, and its height is 30 to 90 mm. An RTD can be placed on a processing device or in a pipe, while the measuring circuit can be located up to 100 m (330 Ft) from it in a control room of the factory. The most common measuring circuit for RTDs is a **two-wire measuring bridge** (Figure 53), through which an electric current (in the range of a few mA) is passing. The bridge's output voltage (V) indicates the RTD's electric resistance (R_E) in two-wire connectivity, proportional to the measuring-source T.

- **Thermistor Temperature Sensors:** Germanium (Ge) or gallium (Ga) is used as a metal for **semiconductor thermistors** (short word for **thermally sensitive resistors**). Such a metal's R_E decreases nonlinearly with increasing T, as shown in Figure 54. A thermistor mainly consists of two metal wires with 0.2 to 3 mm diameter. The measuring wires are placed in a glass tube for protection. Thermistors are used for applications that require high sensitivity and good accuracy. Their disadvantages, compared with thermocouples, are a nonlinear response to T and a low useful range.

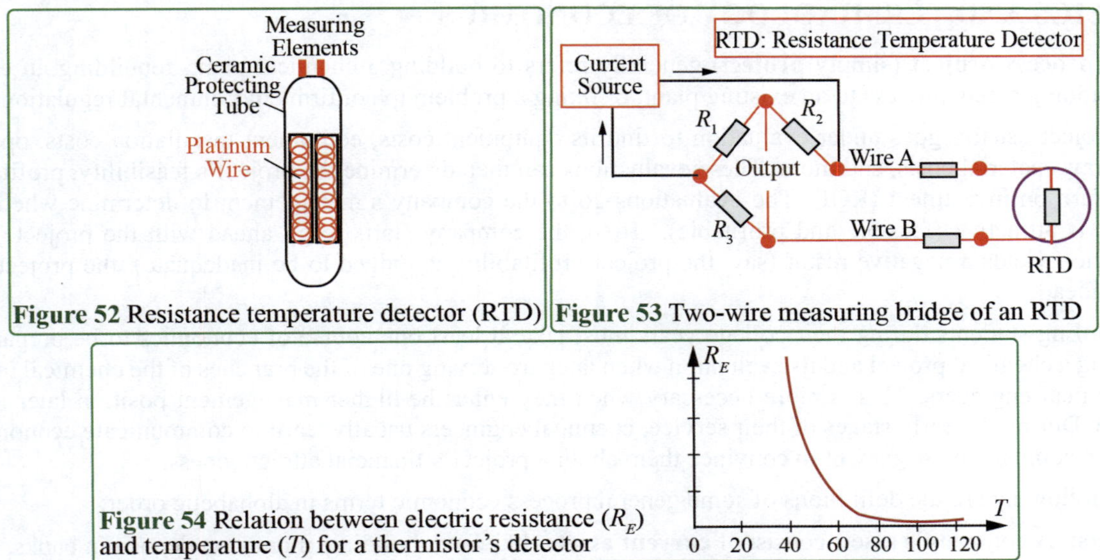

Figure 52 Resistance temperature detector (RTD)

Figure 53 Two-wire measuring bridge of an RTD

Figure 54 Relation between electric resistance (R_E) and temperature (T) for a thermistor's detector

Infrared Temperature Sensors

An infrared temperature sensor (also called **infrared pyrometer**) is a noninvasive (non-contacting) thermometer that can measure the T remotely (from a distance). An infrared pyrometer measures T by the wavelength (λ) of the infrared radiation (simply **infrared**) released from the measuring source. The useful temperature range of infrared pyrometers is from about 700 to 2 000°C.

Photoelectric pyrometers are other pyrometers used to measure the T of a measuring source that its T changes rapidly. Photoelectric pyrometers are glass trays with a thin film coating of PbS or CdS.

P.92

PROCESS DESIGN OF CHEMICAL ENGINEERING

This topic is *not* covered in this book.

P-93

PROCESS ECONOMICS OF CHEMICAL ENGINEERING

Process economics of ChemEng (also called **ChemEng economics**) is the study of economic basics, theories, and equations used in the chemical process industry to evaluate **chemical process projects**.

BASICS AND TERMINOLOGY OF ECONOMICS

The **process project** (simply **project**) generally refers to building a chemical plant, rebuilding an existing plant, adding a new process to an existing plant, or fixing a problem to confirm environmental regulations.

A project usually goes under evaluation to find its equipment costs, equipment installation costs, operating costs, raw-material costs, and more. These evaluations can then determine the project's feasibility, profitability, and return on investment (ROI). The evaluations go to the company's management to determine whether the project is attractive (feasible and profitable). If so, the company starts to go ahead with the project. If the evaluation yields a negative result (say, the project profitability is judged to be inadequate), the project is *not* going ahead.

ChemEng students during their college years must take at least one course of economics to be prepared for planning a chemical project and its evaluation when later are serving one of the branches of the chemical industry as chemical engineers. This is more necessary when they enter the higher management position later in their service. During the early stages of their service, chemical engineers usually learn to communicate economically with top company management to convince them about a project's financial attractiveness.

The following are the definitions of some general process economic terms in alphabetic order:

- **Assets:** A company's assets consist of **current assets** (like land, building, money on deposit in banks, and marketable securities—like bonds) and **intangible assets** (like patents and licenses).
- **Capital Costs:** These costs mainly consist of feasibility cost, land cost, design cost, construction cost, equipment cost, and installation cost. **Feasibility cost** is the cost involved with the study of a project to determine whether it is an efficient project or *not*). **Land cost** is buying the land and paying the real estate agents as a commission). **Design cost** is the expenses associated with pilot-plant tests to decide if the project is worthy of continuation. **Construction costs** include the expenses paid for structuring underground piping, foundation, electrical lines, in-plant roads, different buildings (such as the main operating building, laboratory, warehouse, and boilerhouse), platforms for heavy equipment, and more. **Equipment cost**, which accounts for the highest capital cost, is the total cost of equipment the project needs, such as conveyors, in-plant piping, electrical wiring, instrument wiring, and required devices (such as boilers, furnaces, evaporators, cooling towers, and so on). Usually, other capital costs are given as percentages of the equipment cost. For example, the installation cost can be 50 to 150% of the equipment cost. **Installation cost** is the expenses paid for the installation of equipment. For each piece of equipment, the installation cost is usually a different multiple of its purchased price. The two main factors that affect the installation cost of a piece of equipment are its size and its installation complexity. The total installation cost includes the equipment freight cost from different suppliers, unloading cost, foundations cost, piping cost, electrical wiring cost, instrumentation cost, insulation cost, and more.
- **Depreciation:** This is a fraction of the initial cost of a project that the government allows to be subtracted from the actual gross profit of that project for income tax calculations. It can be considered as a credit that government allows for outdating (obsoleting) the process equipment and the building (but *not* the **land**) of a project with time. Depreciation depends on equipment life expectancy and the building of a project. The depreciation allowance by the US government is 5 to 15 years on the equipment and 25 to 45 years on most buildings. Depreciation credit stops when the total government-allowed useful life period has been used up, even if the equipment or building is still in service.

- **Gross Income** (also called **gross revenue** or **gross sales**): This is the difference between the amount of before-tax money received for a product's sales and the operating costs of that product. [The term **before-tax money** refers to the total tax money that a company must pay to the government and certain expenses (like shipping costs, the money paid for returned products, and allowances for a reduction in prices).]
- **Net Income** (also called **net revenue** or **net sales**): This is the difference between the amount of after-tax money received for a product's sales and certain expenses (like shipping costs, the amount for returned products, and allowances for a reduction in prices).
- **Operating Costs:** These costs mainly consist of **labor**, **raw-material**, and **maintenance costs**. [Note 1: **Labor cost**, which is usually the largest operating cost, also include **overhead cost** (for Social Security, disability insurance, pension, and the company's health insurance), **supervisory costs** (for assisting the operation), and **laboratory costs** (for providing analytical tests). Also, note that shift increased pay also exists for the graveyard-shift (such as 11 PM to 7 AM) workers and sometimes for swing-shift (such as 3 to 11 PM) workers.] [Note 2: **Raw-material cost**, which is usually the second largest operating cost, is for buying the raw materials to produce the product (or products) and byproduct (or byproducts) in a chemical plant. Raw-material costs are usually charged at cost. Some online sites provide the current list price of most chemicals, such as Chemical Buyer's Directory and ICIS Chemical Business.] [Note 3: The **maintenance cost**, which is the total costs of material and labor spent to maintain the devices (equipment), can widely vary from one plant to other, mainly because of the **life expectancy** and **preventive maintenance** (in advance of actual breakdown) of the devices. Maintenance cost per year can be estimated from 2 to 10% (with an average of about 6%) of the equipment cost.]
- **Return on Investment** (ROI): This value determines a project's investment attractiveness. ROI is determined by dividing the project's income per year by the project's total investment (TI). Usually, ROI is calculated based on gross income (before-tax income). [The ROI can be compared with alternative investments (such as investing in bonds) to find how attractive a project can be.]
- **Useful Workdays** (UW): This is the ratio of the days a plant operates to the entire days per year, expressed in percentage. Assume that a plant operates 346 days a year and 19 days is *not* operating, so its UW is (346/365)100 = 95%. [Maintenance, mechanical breakage, and cleaning are the main causes of *not* operating a plant. During downtime, most operating costs (such as labor cost) continue as usual, but some (such as raw-material cost and fuel cost) do *not* continue.]

ECONOMIC EVALUATION OF A PROJECT

Assume that a chemical plant needs to incorporate (add) a medium-size project, like a water softening process, to remove excess minerals, such as calcium (Ca) and magnesium (Mg), from the process water, typically referred to as **hard water**, to produce **soft water** for the cooling tower station of the plant. The first factor that the project manager must be taken understudy to design a water-softening station is the determination of the **operating capacity** of the station. Under the topic of WATER SOFTENING PROCESS BY ION-EXCHANGE RESIN, we calculated the capacity of such a station. Here, we evaluate this project economically by calculating its ROI (return of investment).

Required Devices

To determine the required devices (equipment) for a chemical process project, we should completely familiarize ourselves with the project technology and engineering.

To incorporate a medium-size water-softening process with a capacity of 30 000 m^3/day (= 8 MGa/day) into an existing chemical plant, we need to calculate the approximate equipment costs for a water-softening station. This requires a rough estimate of the capacity of the columns that are filled to a certain level with ion-exchange resin. The water hardness and salt dosage must also be known.

Process Equipment Costs

Process equipment costs can be estimated by one (or both) of the following ways: vendor quotations and chart quotations.

Quotation from Vendors: We can obtain quotations directly from a few vendors that manufacture the same equipment. In the past, directories were the best way of obtaining quotations. But, today, the easiest way to obtain quotations is through the **internet** and direct talk to the representative of a vendor. [Some software programs are on the markets that assist with cost estimation.] [In addition to equipment costs, we must consider the shipping costs of the equipment.]

Quotations from Charts: The equipment costs can be obtained from estimating charts that most equipment sellers prepare. Although chart estimations are *not* as accurate as of the vendor ones, they are almost accurate. It also takes a shorter time to obtain a quotation from charts than directly from the vendors.

P-94

PROCESS FLOW DIAGRAM OF CHEMICAL ENGINEERING

A process flow diagram (PFD; also called **chemical process flow diagram**) is a simplified method to show the flow streams to and from a chemical process (simply **process**). A PDF is used in the chemical process industry to orient and design a particular process. Typically, a PDF illustrates the following:

- All major devices (equipment) and their arrangement, and
- All flow streams and their interconnections.

A process flow diagram (PFD) generally gives more information than a **schematic** (block) **diagram**, which provides a simple process representation. A PFD, instead, shows devices by using standard symbols that look like the actual devices. For example, Figure 1 under NUCLEAR REACTOR illustrates a PFD of a nuclear reactor. This PFD shows different streams back and forth in the system. The PFD of a large system usually includes a few more-detailed diagrams, each showing the sequence of one of the flow streams. In addition, it includes the following:

- One (or more) process control diagram shows how the system is controlled.
- One (or more) **piping and instrumentation diagram** (P&ID) that gives more details, particularly on piping systems (pipes, valves, and fittings) and instrumentation.

[The International Standardization Organization (ISO) provides standard symbols for frequently used devices in chemical process plants. Some countries (and even some companies) have their symbols. Some frequently used symbols used in flow diagrams are given at the end of this book.]

P-95

PROCESS SAFETY OF CHEMICAL ENGINEERING

Process safety of ChemEng (also called **chemical process safety**) is a series of actions taken in a chemical process plant (simply **chemical plant**) against hazards (risks) that can give harmful damage to the health of,

- Workers working in that plant,
- Public affected by the operation of that plant,
- Customers using the productions of that plant, and
- Persons who provide services and raw materials to that plant.

[The word **loss prevention** sometimes replaces the term **safety**.]

Hazards (like an uneven floor, steam leaks, or unsafe devices) can injure workers, create lost workdays, and even cause fatality (death). Say, working with a pump is always associated with safety concerns because blocking a pump's outlet flow can lead to the generation of unsafe pressure (P), which can cause the break of pipes and release the toxic chemicals, thus causing health risks to the workers around the event. Toxic chemicals (hazards) may also damage the property of a chemical plant, causing notable economic disadvantages. Thus, preventive steps must be the priority of both a company's leadership and its workers, simply because the workers' health and the company's economics are important matters.

The three prerequisites for every new project are 1) Process safety, 2) Technology, and 3) Cost. So, a consistent balance must be established between them. It is important to mention that a difference exists between a good and an excellent safety program. A good safety program is a curative preparation by identifying hazards and eliminating them before they occur.

The European Directives on Safety and Health at Work in EU countries manage safety in each workplace. In addition, EU member states can also adopt stricter rules for the protection of workers.

In the USA, OSHA (Occupational Safety and Health Administration) manages the safety of workplaces. It also prepares the PSM (Process Safety Management) for different industries. Say, compliance with the OSHA's PSM regulations is mandatory for every chemical facility that meets one of the following conditions:

- When the quantity of the highly hazardous chemicals used in a facility is greater than the quantity listed in the PSM's regulation. If, for example, a chemical facility uses 500 Lb (or more) of 94.5% (by mass) nitric acid, or 1 500 Lb (or more) of chlorine gas, or 15 000 Lb (or more) of chloromethane (CH_3Cl).
- When the quantity of the flammable liquids present in a facility exceeds 10 000 Lb, except flammable liquids stored in open tanks or transferred below their boiling point temperature (T_{BP}).

OSHA prepares MSDS (Material Data Safety Sheet, later Data Safety Sheet, SDS) for each compound.

On the leadership-side safety responsibilities, the following are important:

- Frequent training classes for workers,
- Issuing safety rules and implementing them, and
- Identification of risks and elimination of them before an accident occurs.

On the worker side, the following three are their most important responsibilities:

- Participation in safety classes to familiarize with safety regulations,
- Paying close attention to safety rules and obeying them, and
- Preventing unsafe actions and conditions.

The safety specialists proved that 96% of all accidents in DuPont (a US chemical company with excellent safety records) are caused by avoidable unsafe acts. It is also reported from DuPont's facilities that one fatal accident occurred for every 30 000 unsafe acts.

For safety measures in a chemical plant, the following are required:

- **Inter-Workplace Measures:** These are rules, regulations, and strategies determined by the safety management of a particular chemical plant. The use of safety glasses, hard hats, safety shoes, and earplugs are examples of these rules.
- **Inter-Industry Measures:** These are rules, regulations, and strategies determined by the state and federal institutions for different industries.

For the **risk-to-benefit ratio** (R/B), consider the following two equations:

$$\frac{R}{B} = 20 \quad \frac{R}{B} = 0.01$$

The first equation represents a large R-B ratio of 20, while the second one expresses a small 0.01 with only a little risk. In both cases, the management must take care of these risks, obviously in the order of higher to lower risk. Instead, the workers must avoid these risks from higher to lower order.

The number of safety-related events per certain number of workers working in a chemical plant is reported by different **evaluation rates**, including the following:

- **Incident Rate** (R_I)**:** It reports the number of incidences (accidents and illnesses) in relation to a given number of workers and given time (usually 1 year).
- **Fatality Rate** (R_F)**:** It reports the proportion of fatalities (deaths) per number of workers.

OSHA calculates R_I based on worker year, where a worker-year has 2 000 hours, which is (50 work weeks/year)×(40 hours/week), and gives it based on 100 worker years, which is 2000×100 = 200 000 worker-years. R_I, thus, is related to N_I (the number of incidences that occurred in 200 000 working hours) and H_T (the total hours/year that all workers work).

$$R_I = 200000\frac{N_I}{H_T} \quad (1)$$

R_I can also be given based on the number of lost workdays (N_{LW}) instead of accidences.

$$R_I = 200000\frac{N_{LW}}{H_T} \quad (2)$$

R_F (fatality rate) equates to N_F (the number of fatalities per year) divided by P_T (total number of designated population).

$$R_F = \frac{N_F}{P_T} \quad (3)$$

P-96

PROCESS SIMULATION PROGRAMS

Process simulation programs, as used in ChemEng, are computer-aided programs that facilitate complicated calculations of ChemEng processes. For example, programs from Aspen Plus® from Aspen Technology, ChemCAD® from Chemstations, HYSYS® from Honewell, PRO/II® from SimSci, and a few more can perform difficult calculations, such as the number of theoretical stages in the distillation process or extraction process, to shorter and simpler calculations.

P-97

PROCESS SUPPLEMENTS OF CHEMICAL ENGINEERING

Process supplements of ChemEng are those processes used in chemical process plants to improve the operating efficiency and economy of the plants. The most important process supplements of ChemEng are the following four (4):

- Process control of chemical engineering,
- Process design of chemical engineering,
- Process economics of chemical engineering, and
- Process safety of chemical engineering.

[Process control, process economics, and process safety of ChemEng are discussed in this book.]

P-98

PROCESS UNITS OF CHEMICAL ENGINEERING

Process units (unit operations) of ChemEng are the processing techniques used in chemical process plants for performing a particular duty. A chemical plant has several process stations (simply **stations**), and each station consists of one or more process units. [The list of process units is given at the end of this topic.] When a feed (or feeds) enters a process unit, one, two, three, four, or all the next five changes occur to that feed (or feeds): 1) Chemical change, 2) Enthalpy change, 3) Physical change, 4) Phase change, 5) Mass change.

We know that chemical changes result from chemical reactions (simply **reactions**). Based on whether a one (or more) reaction occurs on the feed (or feeds) in a process, the process units can be divided into the following two (2) major groups:

- **Process Units without Chemical Reaction:** No chemical reaction or chemical change occurs on the feed (or feeds) during such a process. The changes, therefore, these processes can cause are only physical changes. During, for example, filtration, *no* chemical reaction and *no* chemical change occur. Looking at the list of the process units given in a moment at the end of this topic, you will notice that most of the processes are in this group.
- **Process Units with Chemical Reaction:** One (or more) reaction occurs in such a process, resulting in some chemical changes on the feeds entering the process. During the extraction process, say, one (or more) reaction and, thus, some chemical changes occur between the solute-of-interest and the solvent.

In other classification, the process units can be classed into 2 groups:

- **Main Process Units:** The main process unit (such as crystallization, distillation, and evaporation) serves the main purpose of that process.
- **Supporting** (supplementary) **Process Units:** A supporting process (such as pumping, mixing, and condensation) supports the main process units in completing their duties. [Sometimes, the main process unit is used as a supplementary process to complete another process unit.]

Usually, *not* all but some process units are used in a chemical plant to process raw materials into the product (or products) or separate wanted component (or components) from the raw materials. For example, a beet-sugar plant with a distillery that produces sugar ($C_{12}H_{22}O_{11}$) and bioethanol (a biofuel with the same formula as ethanol) uses the following 16 major process units (unit operations):

- **Fluid Pumping:** It serves as a supporting process unit (unit operation).
- **Fluid Mixing:** It serves as a supporting process to help the main processes.
- **Diffusion:** It separates sugarcane pulp from sugarcane juice in a cane diffuser.
- **Sedimentation:** It separates large particles from the juice to prepare it for filtration.
- **Filtration:** It separates fine particles from the juice to prepare it for heating.
- **Heating:** It increases the temperature of the juice to prepare it for evaporation.
- **Evaporation:** It removes a portion of water from the juice to concentrate it.
- **Condensation:** It serves as a supporting process to condense vapor from the evaporating station.
- **Evaporative Cooling:** It cools condenser water coming from the condensation station.
- **Crystallization:** It separates and solidifies sugar molecules to desired-size sugar crystals.
- **Centrifugation:** It separates crystals from the mother liquid in the magma.
- **Drying:** It separates water from crystals to produce market-quality sugar.
- **Screening:** It separates right-size crystals from out-of-size crystals.
- **Packing:** It serves as a supporting process to pack the sugar.
- **Fermentation:** It converts sugars in molasses to ethanol.
- **Distillation:** It separates ethanol from other volatile components.

This author has *not* yet seen a reference book that gives a complete list of process units (unit operations) of ChemEng. To eliminate the confusability of this book's readers about the number of the process units, 38 of them, which are discussed in this book, are listed here (based on this author's familiarity with the subject).

1. Boiling Process
2. Bulk Material Handling Process
3. Centrifugal Process
4. Chromatographic Processes (Ion-Exchange Chromatography and Ion-Exclusion Chromatography)
5. Condensation Process
6. Cryogenic Process
7. Crystallization Process
8. Distillation Process
9. Drying Process
10. Evaporation Process
11. Evaporative Cooling Process
12. Extraction Process (Liquid-Liquid Extraction Process)
13. Filtration Process
14. Fluid Mixing Process
15. Fluidization Process
16. Freezing Process
17. Gas-Liquid Extraction Process
18. Gas Transfer Process
19. Heat Transfer Process
20. Heating Process
21. Ion Exchange Process
22. Ion Exclusion Process
23. Leaching Process
24. Liquid Transfer Process
25. Mass Diffusion by Convection Process
26. Mass Diffusion Process
27. Membrane Separation Process
28. Mixing process
29. Molecular-Sieve Process
30. Osmosis Process
31. Pervaporation Process
32. Reverse Osmosis Process
33. Screening Process
34. Sedimentation Process
35. Solid Mixing Process
36. Steam-and-Power Production Process
37. Stirring Process
38. Water Softening Process (includes Water Softening by Chemicals and Water Softening by Ion-Exchange Resin)

Some other processes are *not* covered in this book, including the following:

1. Gas-Solid Extraction Process
2. Humidification Process
3. Membrane Distillation Process
4. Solid Mixing Process

5. Phase Separation Process
6. Solid Transfer Process

[Note 1: All the listed process units written in orange color are moderately discussed in this book.]

[Note 2: Some process units are used in a certain branch of ChemEng, like refrigeration, mainly used in the food industry. Such processes are *not* discussed in this book and can be gained from a food-engineering book.]

[Note 3: Some process units subdivide into two (or more) types. Crystallization, for example, divides into solution crystallization (generally called crystallization process), melt crystallization, and membrane crystallization. Similarly, extraction classifies into liquid-liquid extraction (simply extraction process), gas-liquid extraction, and solid-liquid extraction (leaching process).]

P-99

PROGRAMMABLE LOGIC CONTROLLERS

A programmable logic controller (PLC) is software used in process controls to automatically control a device (equipment) by following the instructions of a programmable source. A PLC contains a central processing unit (CPU), input and output modules, and a programming device. A PLC provides the following functions:

- It can receive data from a programmed source, process it, and activate its outputs based on programmed instruction.
- It can act as a real-time system because its outputs are produced in response to input conditions in the shortest time, depending on the inputs and outputs.
- It can monitor and record data automatically, such as the start or stop of a process, control the temperature, or generate an alarm if a device starts to malfunction.

P-100

PROPORTIONALITY CONSTANT

Study COEFFICIENT, CONSTANT, AND PROPORTIONALITY CONSTANT.

P-101

PROTEINS

A protein is a large-molecule chemical compound consisting of one (or more) long chain of amino acids. An amino acid contains an amino group (NH_2) and a carboxylic group (COOH, also called the **carboxyl group**). A protein is formed when the carboxylic group of one amino acid reacts with the amino group on another molecule in a condensation reaction, creating one molecule of water and a CO–NH–CH–R bond (linkage) called a **peptide bond**. Proteins are in the structure of almost all living organisms. In our body, proteins perform a lot of functions, including the following:

- They are important parts of bones, muscles, and skin,
- They act as enzymes to accelerate metabolic reactions, and
- They act as test receptors at the tip of the tongue to sense tastes (like sweetness) and transfer them to the brain, which compares the power of each taste.

P-102

PROTIUM

Discussed under HYDROGEN.

P-103

PROTON

Discussed under ATOM.

P-104

PROTON NUMBER

Another name for ATOMIC NUMBER.

P-105

PSI, PSIA, AND PSIG

PSI: The symbol PSI stands for **pounds per square inch**, the US unit for pressure (P). 1 PSI = PSIG + 14.7, where 14.7 is P_{Atm} at sea level in the US units.

PSIA: The symbol PSIA (PSI absolute or PSI Abs) stands for **pounds per square inch absolute**, which is the US unit of absolute pressure (P_{Abs}) when it is measured relative to absolute vacuum pressure (simply vacuum pressure, P_{Vac}, or vacuum). 1 PSIA = PSIG + 14.7.

PSIG: The symbol PSIG (PSI gauge) stands for **pounds per square inch gauge**, the US unit of gauge pressure (P_G) when P is measured relative to P_{Atm}. PSI = PSIG + 14.7.

Remember the following points that are used (or are *not*) in this book:

- The symbol Lb/In^2 is used instead of PSI, where Lb is for pounds and In is for inch.
- We say, for example, P_{Abs} = 6.9 kPa = 1 PSIA (or 1 PSI absolute).
- We say, for instance, P_G = 13.8 kPa = 2 PSIG (or 2 PSI gauge).

P-106

PSYCHROMETRIC DIAGRAM

Study AIR PSYCHROMETRIC DIAGRAM.

P-107

PSYCHROMETRICS

Psychrometrics (also called **hygrometry**) studies the physical and thermodynamic properties of moist air, dry air, and air-water-vapor systems. Knowing these systems' properties is imperative in designing many systems, such as dryers, cooling towers, and wet surface air coolers.

Many substances are water-absorbing (hygroscopic), a phenomenon related to the air's humidity. Psychrometrics, thus, also discusses types of humidity, air psychrometric diagram, and more.

Psychrometric Data and Equations: Psychrometrics has special air-related expressions and equations to calculate air-involved mass and heat transfers. It is, therefore, helpful to know the following expressions used in psychrometric calculations:

- The molar mass (M_n) of dry air is 29 g/mole,
- The molar mass of moist air leaving the dryer is 18 g/mole,
- The reference temperature (T) is 0ºC, and reference pressure (P) is 1 Atm, and
- The relation between W_{Abs} (absolute humidity) and W_n (molar humidity) is $W_{Abs} = 0.62W_n$.

P-108

PUMP CAVITATION

Pump cavitation (**vapor cavitation** or simply **cavitation**) is the formation of vapor bubbles in a pump by the evaporation part of the liquid to vapor in the pump's suction-end (where the liquid enters the pump). Vapor usually starts to bubble at the pump's suction end and moves through its casing to its discharge end, where the bubbles breakdown. The bubbles (vapor pockets) usually hit the pump impeller's blades (vanes), causing loud noise known as water hammering (also called **cracking**). In relation to pressure, cavitation occurs when the liquid's head pressure (P_h) is less than the liquid's vapor pressure (P_V), as is discussed under Vapor Pressure.

If severe cavitation occurs, *no* liquid can be pumped anymore. Cavitation usually occurs in a pump when

- Net positive suction head (h_{NPS}) on the liquid surface is *not* chosen correctly,
- A pump is *not* installed in the right place in the piping system, and
- A liquid with high volatility is pumped.

One of the most important ways to prevent cavitation is applying necessary h_{NPS}. Before installation of a pump, its h_{NPS} is usually calculated to indicate how much h_{NPS} is available to prevent cavitation in the pump. [A fast way of measuring the h_{NPSA} (available h_{NPS}) is given under NET PRESSURE SUCTION HEAD.]

Cavitation can also occur in the suction line when the h_{NPS} is less than the liquid's P_V. Because of cavitation,

- The pump's efficiency (E_P, also called **pump's capacity**) is reduced considerably,
- Water hammering sound as vapor bubbles strike the impeller's blades, and
- Corrosion may occur in the metallic parts of the pump and pipes.

To prevent cavitation, the following is recommended:

- **Applying Necessary h_{NPS} on the Liquid Surface:** This prevents vapor molecules from escaping the pumping liquid, so the liquid's P_h should *not* be decreased to P_V at the pump's operation T (temperature).
- **Correct Connection of the Discharge Pipe to a Pump:** This prevents vapor pockets in the pump and acts as a seal. The pump's discharge pipe should be extended upward through a riser at least five (5) times the pipe's diameter (see Figure 1). The same figure shows that installing a valve in the riser also helps (because it acts as a vent to discharge vapor bubbles to prevent cavitation).

- **Replacing Pump:** Cavitation can be prevented by replacing a pump with a larger one. Consider a typical pump that pumps 400 L/min (105 Ga/min) of water at 780 RPM, and according to its manufacturer, it has a net positive suction head (h_{NPSA}) of 3 m (= 9 Ft) of water. If we replace it with a larger pump that pumps the same 400 L/min at 340 RPM, the h_{NPSA} drops to about 1 m (= 3 Ft), so slowing a pump allows it to operate without any cavitation problem.

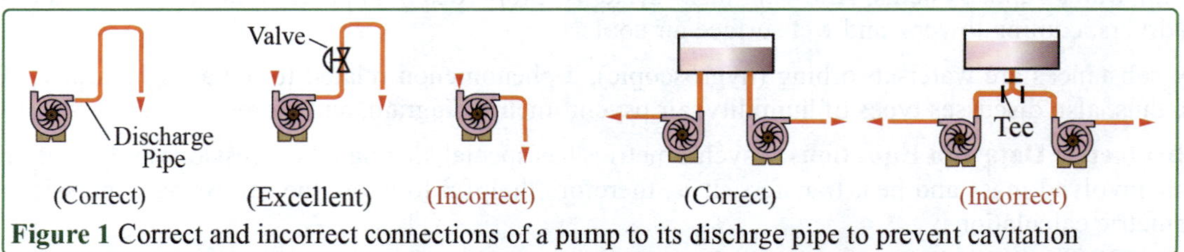

Figure 1 Correct and incorrect connections of a pump to its dischrge pipe to prevent cavitation

P-109

PUMP LIQUID HEADS

The pump liquid heads (simply **pump's heads** or **heads**) are three (3):

- Pump's suction head (h_S),
- Pump's discharge head (h_S), and
- Pump's total head (the total of h_S and h_D).

These heads express the pressure (P) of a liquid in the unit of length (usually in m or Ft) instead of the unit of P when the liquid is under the pumping process by a pump. The liquid heads are defined next.

Pump Suction Head: A pump suction head (h_S, simply **suction head** or **static lift**) is a vertical elevation through which the pumping liquid must be elevated. It represents a pump's required pressure (given in unit of length) to elevate a liquid in a pipe from the pump suction-end to its centerline and overcome all friction forces (simply **frictions**) that act against the liquid flow in that pipe. Numerically, h_S is the height between a pump's centerline and its suction-end. [The term **pump's centerline** is a reference line (the measurement line).]

Pump Discharge Head: A pump discharge head (h_D, simply **discharge head**) is the **height** (head or elevation) between a pump's centerline and its discharge-end (discharge-point). It represents a pump's P (given in m or Ft) to elevate a liquid in a pipe from the pump's centerline to the pump discharge end and overcome all frictions that act against the flow of the liquid in that pipe.

Pump Total Head: A pump's total head (h_T, also called **total liquid head, total dynamic head, total lift head**, or **total pressure head**) is the maximum **height** to pump a liquid in a pipe. Numerically, h_T is the **net** total of a pump's h_S (suction head) and h_D (discharge head).

$$h_T = \Delta h = h_S \pm h_D \quad (1)$$

A pump's suction head (h_S) can be calculated using the Bernoulli equation simple form.

$$h_S = \frac{P_S}{D.a_g} + \frac{V_S^2}{2a_g} \quad (2)$$

In this equation, P_S is for pressure at pump's suction-end (in Pa = kg/m.s^2), D is for the liquid's density (in kg/m^3), V_S is for the liquid's velocity at suction-end (in m/s), and a_g is for gravitational acceleration (a constant equal to 9.81 m/s^2 = 32.2 Ft/s^2 on the Earth surface), so h_S becomes in m (meter).

Figures 1 and 2 demonstrate suction head (h_S), discharge head (h_D), and total head (h_T) in a pumping system, and Figure 3 shows the correct way of discharge from a sump. [Also review the figures under LIQUID HEAD AND LIQUID HEAD LOSS.]

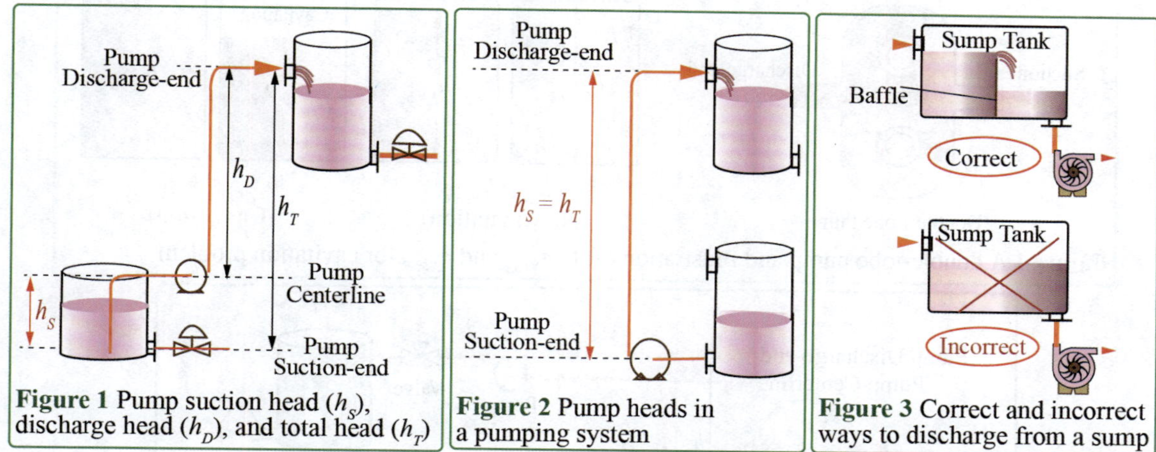

Figure 1 Pump suction head (h_S), discharge head (h_D), and total head (h_T)

Figure 2 Pump heads in a pumping system

Figure 3 Correct and incorrect ways to discharge from a sump

P-110

PUMP NET POSITIVE SUCTION HEAD

A pump's net positive suction head (see the Note) is the necessary pressure (P), expressed in m or Ft, which it must apply on a liquid to prevent pumping problems, like pump cavitation (vapor bubble formation in a pump). [The term **net positive suction head** is usually symbolized in other reference books as NPSH. Here, its equation-friendly format, h_{NPS}, is used, where h is always used in this book for the **head** (or height).]

The pump manufacturer usually provides the required h_{NPS} (shown as h_{NPSR}, where subscript R is **required**. Available (or actual) h_{NPS} (shown as h_{NPSA} (where A is for **available** or **actual**) is recommended to be calculated by pump users to make sure that enough suction head (h_S) is available to prevent pump cavitation.

The h_{NPSR} (the required h_{NPS} or manufacturer h_{NPS}) of a pump can be calculated as

$$h_{NPSR} = \frac{1}{a_g}\left(\frac{P_S - P_V}{D} + \frac{V^2}{2}\right) \tag{1}$$

In this equation, a_g is gravitational acceleration (= 9.81 m/s^2 on the Earth's surface), P_S is the pressure at the suction point (in Pa = kg/m.s^2), P_V is the vapor pressure of the liquid under pumping (in Pa), and V is the liquid velocity in the suction pipe (in m/s). So, the h_{NPSR} becomes in m (meter). [The P_V can be obtained by the liquid's temperature (T) and a steam table.] A pump's h_{NPSA} (the available h_{NPH}) can be calculated as

$$h_{NPSA} = \frac{1}{a_g}\left(\frac{P_S - P_V}{D}\right) - h_S - h_{Fit} \tag{2}$$

The h_S is the suction head (in m), and h_{Fit} is the **fitting friction factor** (also called the **fitting head**), which is friction losses in the suction-piping line. The h_{Fit} is determined as

$$h_{Fit} = f_{Fit}\frac{\overline{V}^2}{2a_g} \tag{3}$$

The f_{Fit} is different for different fittings, as discussed under LIQUID FLOW PROCESS.

The shortest way of measuring the h_{NPSA} is to use a compound pressure gauge to measure gauge pressure (P_G) and vacuum pressure (P_{Vac}). The compound gauge that can be installed on the pump suction end provides:

- It obtains the P_V of the liquid under piping based on the liquid T from a steam table.
- It deducts the P_V value from the pressure gauge reading; the result is the h_{NPSA}. If this value is less than the h_{NPSR} given by the pump manufacturer, you can expect some cavitation problems (as shown in Figure 1).

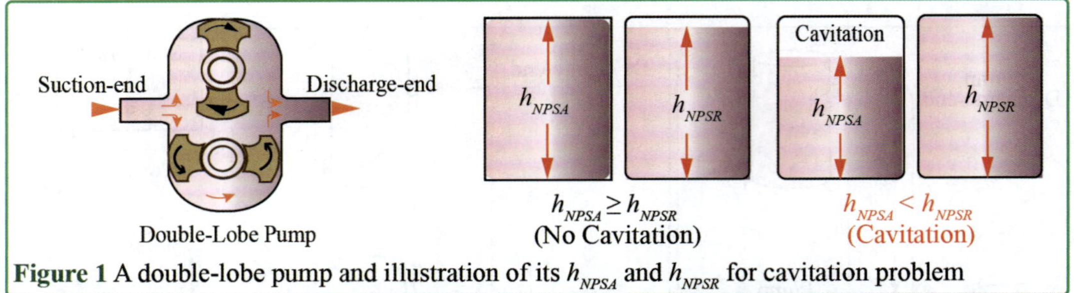

Figure 1 A double-lobe pump and illustration of its h_{NPSA} and h_{NPSR} for cavitation problem

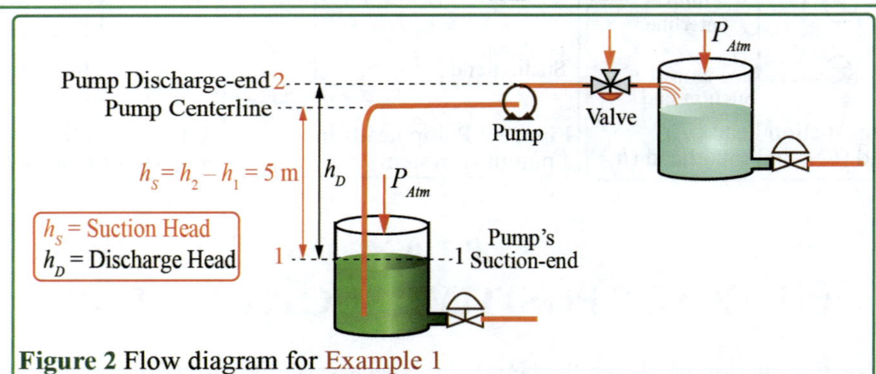

Figure 2 Flow diagram for Example 1

An Example on h_{NPSH}

Given: A pump that pumps water at 33°C (with the D of 993 kg/m^3) to a higher-level tank under 1 Atm pressure. One open valve with the f_{Fit} of 2 is in the suction line (see Figure 2).

Pump's h_{NPSR} (required head, given by manufacturer)	4 m (= 13.2 Ft)
Height between water level in tank 1 and pump centerline (h_S)	5 m (= 16.4 Ft)
Pump's volumetric flow rate ($\dot{V}$)	1.8 m^3/min (= 0.03 m^3/s or 8 Ga/s)
Pipe's inside diameter (d)	0.1 m (= 100 mm = 4 In)
Water's temperature (T)	33°C (= 91°F)

Wanted: The h_{NPSA} (available h_{NPS}) to see if this pump is suitable for the given condition

The liquid's average velocity (V) can be calculated from the continuity equation.

$$\dot{V} = V.A \qquad V = \frac{\dot{V}}{A} = \frac{\dot{V}}{\pi\frac{d^2}{4}} = \frac{0.03\left[\frac{m^3}{s}\right]}{\pi\frac{0.1^2}{4}[m^2]} = 3.8 \text{ m/s}$$

Friction head by the pipe's fittings (shown as $E_{f.Fit}$) can be calculated from Equation 3.

$$h_{Fit} = f_{Fit}\frac{V^2}{2a_g} = 2\frac{3.8^2\left[\frac{m^2}{s^2}\right]}{2\times 9.81\left[\frac{m}{s^2}\right]} = 1.5 \text{ m}$$

According to Table 1, given at the end of this book, the vapor pressure (P_V) of water at 33°C is 5.947 kPa, where 1 kPa = 1000 kg/(m.s^2), so the P_V of water is 5947 kg/(m.s^2). Water in the tank is under 1 Atm pressure, where 1 Atm = 101.33 kPa = 101330 kg/(m.s^2), the pressure at the suction point (P_S). Substituting these values in Equation 2 calculates h_{NPSHA}.

$$h_{NPSA} = \frac{1}{9.81}\left(\frac{101330-5947}{993}\right) - 5\text{m} - 1.5\text{m} \qquad h_{NPSA} = 9.8 \text{ m} - 5 \text{ m} - 1.5 \text{ m} = 3.3 \text{ m}$$

Comparing this value with h_{NPSHR} = 4 m, given by the manufacturer, tell us that $h_{NPSA} < h_{NPSR}$, so the pump is *not* sufficient for its duty, and as a result, cavitation may occur.

P-111
PUMPS

A **pump** is a device (equipment) installed in a **piping system** (pipes, pumps, valves, and more) to move a liquid or slurry through a pipe from one point to another at a certain pressure (P) and a constant flow rate. The flow rate with which a liquid flows in a pipe by a pump is known as the pump's **capacity** (or efficiency).

High P in a pumping liquid is formed by decreasing the intake liquid's volume (V) to the pump. This occurs according to the ideal gas equation. [Some solids are suspended in a liquid to form a pumpable slurry because it is more economical to transport liquids than solids.]

The following are about the terminology of pumps:

- The word **pump** is used when a liquid is pumped and **compressor** when a gas must be moved.
- While the word pump is generally used to move a liquid, the word **vacuum pump** is used when a pump removes a gas from an under-vacuum vessel.

During the transport of a liquid, a typical pump uses one of the following effects:

- **Ram Effect:** A pump, operating based on the ram principle, moves the pumping liquid into its **suction-end** by its high-speed impeller's blades. Then it rams (pushes) the liquid into a space with constant volume (V), from where the liquid is discharged through the pump's **discharge end**. A pump that operates based on this principle is called a **centrifugal pump**.
- **Trapping Principle:** A pump that operates on the trapping principle traps (holds) the liquid into its suction-end by its impeller, squeezes it into a smaller V until a desired P is reached, and discharges it from its discharged end. A pump that operates based on this principle is called a **positive displacement pump**.

For moving a liquid, a pump uses electric energy or steam as a source of energy to perform shaft work (W_S) to perform the following:

- To increase the liquid's V (velocity) and P (pressure), and
- To overcome the liquid's friction (because of liquid's viscosity), pipe's and pump's frictions (both occurring because of their attached parts).

During pumping, part of E (energy) is converted to E_Q (heat energy), causing a decrease in the **pump efficiency** (E_P, pump's capacity). [Because part of E used by a pump is converted (generally speaking, lost), the liquid flow and heat transfer processes must be considered in pumps' calculations.]

Pump's Calculations

In pumps' calculations, we must know the following three (3) properties of the pumping liquid:

- Liquid's $\dot{V}$(volumetric flow rate),
- Liquid's T (temperature), and
- Liquid's η (viscosity).

A liquid's properties usually determine the characteristics of the pump to be used, such as

- Pump's net positive suction head (h_{NPS}),
- Pump's total head (h_T), and
- Pump's capacity.

In a pumping system, a pump sucks a liquid at a constant $\dot{V}$ at its suction end and discharges it at the discharge end. The energies the pump uses to elevate the liquid from point 1 to point 2 are listed next.

- **Pressure Energy:** This is the E used to overcome a liquid density change (ΔD) when pumped from 1 to 2.
- **Kinetic Energy (E_K):** This is the E used to overcome the change in the liquid's velocity (ΔV).

- **Potential Energy** (E_P)**:** This is the E used to overcome the elevation change (Δh), where h is for the liquid head (liquid's height above a reference level). [E_P is related to the gravitational acceleration (a_g, a constant equal to 9.8 m/s^2 on Earth).]
- **Frictional Energy** (E_f, also called **frictional work**)**:** This is the E used to overcome the pipe's frictions, pump's frictions (because of pump's fittings), and liquid's friction (because of liquid's viscosity). E_f is the energy spent in the pumping system to overcome the pipe's friction, pump's friction, and liquid's friction. [The value of E_f is always *positive* (because it represents the E given to frictions.]
- **Shaft Work** (W_S, also called **pump work**)**:** This is the E used in the form of W (work) on the pump's shaft. [The value of W_S is *negative* when the system (here the liquid) does work on its surrounding (here the pump's shaft) and *positive* when work is done on the system by its outside.]

Using all five terms in the Bernoulli equation, the net result of all energies applied to a liquid flow is zero.

$$\frac{P_2-P_1}{D}+\frac{V_2^2-V_1^2}{2}+a_g(h_2-h_1)+E_f-W_S=0 \quad (1)$$

As proved under the topic of LIQUID FLOW PROCESS, all items in this equation are in the unit of specific energy (J/kg), in other words, energy per mass (M) of the liquid to be pumped.

Rearranging the previous equation, an equation for expressing the pump's shaft work is obtained.

$$W_S=\frac{P_2-P_1}{D}+\frac{V_2^2-V_1^2}{2}+a_g(h_2-h_1)+E_f \quad (2)$$

Showing the pump's suction head by h_S (or h_1) and the discharge head by h_D (or h_2) and using the **pump's efficiency** (E_P), we can write Equation 2 in a simple form to relate the pump's shaft work to the differential change in the total net head ($\Delta h_T = h_2 - h_1$).

$$W_S.E_P=h_2-h_1=\Delta h_T \quad (3)$$

$$W_S=\frac{\Delta h_T}{E_P} \quad (4)$$

E_P, given in fraction, is

$$E_P=\frac{W_S-W_f}{W_S} \quad (5)$$

[Note: Because considerable frictions (for example, pipe and liquid frictions) exist, a pump's E_P is low (usually in the range of 0.5 to 0.8 or 50 to 80%).]

A pump's electric power (P_E, in kJ/s = kW/h) requirement for pumping a liquid with a mass flow rate of $\dot{M}$ (in kg/s) and shaft work of W_S (in kPa) is given as

$$P_E=\dot{M}.W_S=\dot{M}\frac{h_T}{E_P} \quad (6)$$

Types of Pumps

In a broad range, pumps are classified into **centrifugal pumps** and **positive-displacement** (PD) **pumps**.

Centrifugal Pumps: Figures 1A and 1B show two different centrifugal pumps, which create a centrifugal force (F_C) by the pump's rotating blades (vanes). Because of F_C, the liquid velocity at the inlet (V_1) increases to V_2 at the outlet, and the decrease in V increases the liquid's P to P_2. As shown in Figure 1C, the liquid enters the pump's center with a 90º incline to the **plane** (flat surface) of the **impeller** (wheel or propeller), flows radially (outwardly) between the rotating **blades**, and exits the pump's outlet at the impeller's velocity. The blades are raised to increase the liquid velocity to V_2, as shown in Figure 2. The symbol F_{CP} (centripetal force) in the same figure represents the tangential component of V_1, and F_C represents that of V_2.

Centrifugal pumps come in different sizes, from a low **capacity** (volumetric flow rate, $\dot{V}$) of 0.5 m^3/h (≈ 130 Ga/h) up to 2×10^4 m^3/h (≈ 5×10^6 Ga/h), and discharge head pressure (P_h, simply **head**) of up to 50 000 kPa (≈ 7 000 Lb/In^2). Advanced models, called **multistage centrifugal pumps**, have more impellers on a single shaft to develop a high h_T (total head) of 200 m (= 650 Ft) in a single stage. Multistage pumps are, by far, the most widely used pumps in chemical process plants.

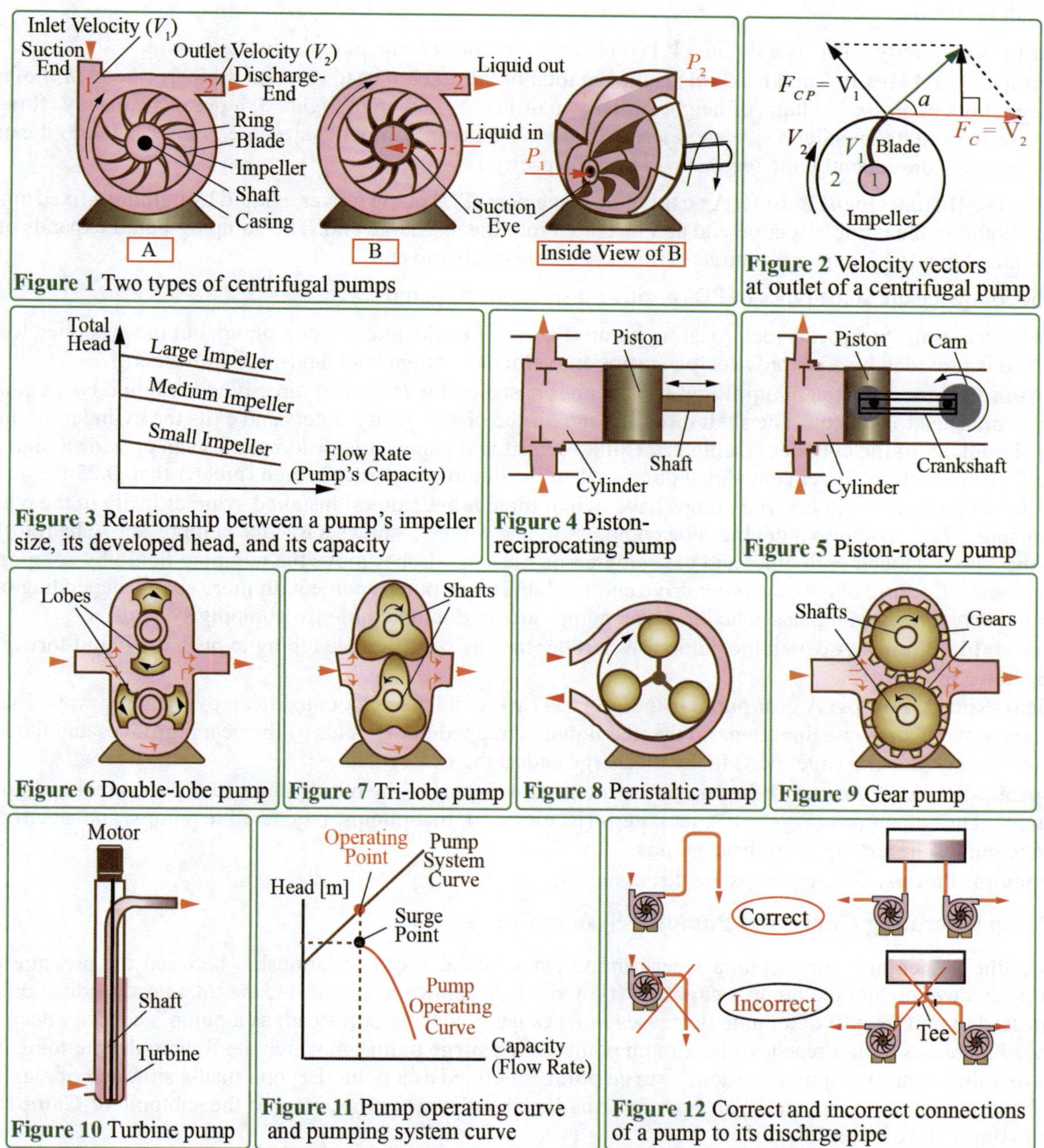

Figure 1 Two types of centrifugal pumps

Figure 2 Velocity vectors at outlet of a centrifugal pump

Figure 3 Relationship between a pump's impeller size, its developed head, and its capacity

Figure 4 Piston-reciprocating pump

Figure 5 Piston-rotary pump

Figure 6 Double-lobe pump

Figure 7 Tri-lobe pump

Figure 8 Peristaltic pump

Figure 9 Gear pump

Figure 10 Turbine pump

Figure 11 Pump operating curve and pumping system curve

Figure 12 Correct and incorrect connections of a pump to its dischrge pipe

A simple-and-typical **centrifugal pump** mainly consists of

- A **casing** (an enclosed protective covering),
- An **impeller** (wheel), which is attached to the blades,
- A **shaft**, which is installed at the center of the impeller,
- Several **blades** (also called **vanes**) are fixed to the impeller, and

- A **drive** (like an electric motor or steam engine) to rotate the shaft.

Shaft work (W_S) must be performed on a liquid to move through a pipe. Either of the following can express the strength of a pump's W_S:

- **Pump's Capacity:** This is a liquid's $\dot{V}$ (volumetric flow rate) at the pump's discharge end.
- **Pump's Total Head:** Total head (h_T) is the net total of the suction head (h_S) and discharge head (h_D) of a pump, both expressed in units of height (usually m or Ft). As shown in Figure 3, a pump's capacity (flow rate or h_T) and its impeller's size are related (the *larger* a pump's impeller size, the *greater* is the h_T it can create and, consequently, the *greater* will be its capacity.)

Positive-Displacement Pumps: A positive-displacement (PD) pump moves a liquid by holding a fixed amount of the liquid in the pump's suction end and forcing it into the discharge end. The pumping liquid expands on the suction end in a PD pump and contracts (shrinks) on the discharge end.

The following are some types of PD (positive-displacement) pumps:

- **Reciprocating Pumps:** A reciprocating pump (Figure 4) works like a piston pump, but the *P* applied to the liquid is provided by a piston's **reciprocating movement** (straight back-and-forth movement).
- **Piston Pumps:** A piston pump (Figure 5) operates based on the *P* applied directly to the liquid by a crankshaft attached to a piston. The shaft turns and moves the piston, which enters and exits the cylinder to move the liquid out of the cylinder at a high *P*. Unlike centrifugal pumps, the piston pumps can provide a high *P*, so they are preferred over centrifugal pumps when the liquid's viscosity is high (greater than 0.25 Pa.s).
- **Lobe-Type Pumps:** Lobe-type pumps have two or three **lobes** (rotors) installed symmetrically in the pump's housing. Figure 6 shows a double-lobe compressor, and Figure 7 shows a tri-lobe compressor. The rotors (lobes) do *not* touch each other and the compressor's casing. Lobes move the pumping liquid by compressing them. Because one lobe *cannot* drive another lobe, these pumps come with more shafts, depending on how many lobes a pump has. The lobe-type pumps are used in medium-size pumping systems.
- **Peristaltic Pumps:** A peristaltic pump uses a roller to squeeze a flexible tubing to push the liquid forward, as shown in Figure 8.
- **Gear-Rotary Pumps:** A gear pump (Figure 9) has two round gears mounted in an overlapping way. The gears move in opposite directions so that the liquid is trapped in the voids of the gears' grooves and moved from the suction end (inlet port) to the discharge end as the gears rotate.
- **Special-Service Pumps:** These pumps are modified versions of the other pumps to serve special operating duties. Turbine pumps (Figure 10), jet pumps (jet ejectors), rota pumps, regenerative pumps, and electromagnetic pumps are examples of these pumps.
- **Vacuum Pumps:** These pumps are discussed later.

Pump Operating Curve and Pumping System Curve

A pump's operating curve (pump's performing curve) indicates the relationship between the pressure (*P*) a pump can develop and the pump's **capacity** (flow rate). As shown in Figure 11, the total head (indication of *P*, expressed in unit length) of a pump decreases as its capacity increases. Instead, as a pump's capacity decreases, its head increases until it reaches a maximum point (called **surge point**), at which the flow of the pumping liquid is at its **minimum**. In pump operation, a **surge point** is defined as a point. Beyond that, a situation of maximum head and minimum flow occur. For more information about surge points, refer to the subtopic of **Compressor Operating Curve** under this topic.

A **pump system curve** shows the head needed at different flow rates to pump a liquid to a certain distance. [In both curves, the pressures are given in the **head**, as shown in the same figure.]

The pump-system head consists of the following two heads:

- **Suction Head:** This is a vertical elevation through which the pumping liquid must be lifted.
- **Friction Head:** This is the head needed to overcome the friction head losses.

A change in the liquid head (like a change in a tank level) and friction head (like a valve in a pipe) cause a change in the pumping system curve. A change in the pump's speed, a change in the impeller diameter, or a change in the pumping liquids viscosity, on the other hand, causes a change in the pump operating curve.

Operation of Pumps

In the operation of a pump, it is important to pay attention to the following points:

- **Pump Cavitation:** Wrong connection of a discharge pipe to a pump causes vapor pockets in the pump, which results in pump cavitation (simply **cavitation**). The pump's discharge pipe should be extended upward through a riser at least five (5) times the pipe's diameter (see Figure 12). The same figure shows that installing a valve in the riser also helps (it acts as a vent to discharge vapor bubbles to prevent cavitation).
- **Airbound:** A pump with air in its casing is airbound, so it *cannot* pump unless the air is sucked out of it. Air can be taken out by priming the pump from a priming tank connected to the suction line or connecting the line to a vacuum source. [Some pumps are in the market that is self-primed.]
- **Pump Net Positive Suction Head:** A pump's net positive suction head (h_{NPS}) is the necessary pressure (P) that must be applied by that the pump must apply on the pumping liquid to prevent cavitation. Required h_{NPS} of a pump, shown as h_{NPSR}, where R is **required**, is usually provided by the pump manufacturer. Available (or actual) h_{NPSH}, which is symbolized as h_{NPSA}, where A is for **available** (or actual), is recommended to be calculated by the pump users to ensure that enough suction head is available to prevent pump cavitation. For h_{NPS} calculation, see the Example given under PUMP NET POSITIVE SUCTION HEAD.
- **Rise in Temperature of Pumping Liquid:** In a piping system, part of the energy put into the pumping liquid is converted to heat energy (E_Q), causing a rise in T of the pumping liquid. The liquid's temperature rise (ΔT) depends on the pumping liquid's specific heat capacity (C_Q, simply **heat capacity**), pump's liquid head (h, simply **head**), and pump's efficiency (E_P). During normal and continuous operation of the pump, ΔT does *not* affect the piping system. But if the pump is running while a blockage is in the piping system, the T of the pumping liquid may increase above the liquid's bubble point temperature, which causes cavitation. In such cases, a **recirculation line** circulates the liquid to its source to prevent an unusual ΔT rise.

P-112

PURE AND IMPURE SOLUTIONS

Pure Solutions: A pure solution consists of a solute and a solvent. For example, sugar (the solute) in water (the solvent) makes a pure sugar solution.

Impure Solutions: An impure solution contains a solvent and two (or more) solutes. Say, beet juice, which contains water (the solvent) and some solutes (sugar, minerals, and more), is an impure solution. The major solute under consideration in an impure solution is the **solute of interest**. In beet juice, sugar (sucrose) is the solute of interest because a beet-sugar plant processes the juice to make table sugar, which is pure.

P-113

PURGING PROCESS

Purging (also called **blowdown**) is the periodic removal of the unwanted suspended solid particles from a device (like a steam boiler or a cooling tower). In boiler operation, purging is done by opening the boiler's blowdown valve for a short period to remove suspended particles from the boiler's feed water. The suspended particles removed from the bottom of the boiler are then pumped to a purge storage tank.

P-114

PURITY AND IMPURITY

Purity: The term **purity** (*P*) is used in chemistry and ChemEng to indicate how pure a solution is. Thus, a solution containing only one solute is a pure substance. Higher purity in one product as compared to another is an indication of a higher quality.

Impurity: Impurity (*I*) is the opposite of purity, indicating how a solution is impure. Thus, a solution with more than one solute is an impure solution.

Mathematically, purity (*P*) is defined as the percentage (by mass) of a solute (*S*) in the total dissolved solids (*DS*) of a solution. And the impurity (*I*) is 100 minus P.

$$P = \frac{S}{DS} \times 100 \quad (1)$$

$$I = 100 - P \quad (2)$$

For example, a cane juice with 13% sugar and 15% *DS* has purity (sugar content as % of *DS*) of

$$P = \frac{13}{15} \times 100 = 86.7 \text{ \% on } DS$$

This means that 100 g *DS* of this juice contains 86.7 g of sugar, assuming all its water is evaporated. And the amount of impurities (*I*) in this juice is 100 – 86.5 = 13.3 % on *DS*. Based on these definitions and examples, impurities are the percentages of all solutes, except the major one under consideration (called the **solute-of-interest** or **wanted solute**), in the total *DS* of a solution. In cane juice, for example, minerals and amino acids are impurities (nonsugars).

[Note 1: A solution's **purity** and **impurity** values do *not* change by **concentration** or **dilution** of that solution because both are expressed on a dry basis (on *DS*), so they are *not* relevant to water content.] [Note 2: The symbol *P* is usually used for pressure and purity, but with *no* confusion because these terms are rarely used together.]

Q Section

LIST OF TOPICS

1. Quantitative Analyses
2. Quantum and Quantization
3. Quantum Atomic Model
4. Quantum Chemistry
5. Quantum Chromodynamics
6. Quantum Computer
7. Quantum Cryptography
8. Quantum Elementary Particles
9. Quantum Entanglement of Particles
10. Quantum Field and Quantum Field Theories
11. Quantum Fundamental Theories
12. Quantum Gravity Theory
13. Quantum Leap
14. Quantum Mechanics
15. Quantum Number
16. Quantum Particles
17. Quantum Physics and Classical Physics
18. Quantum Superposition
19. Quantum System
20. Quantum Teleportation of Particles
21. Quantum Theories
22. Quantum Theories of Duality
23. Quantum Uncertainty Principle
24. Quantum Unified Theory
25. Quantum Vacuum
26. Quantum Wavefunction
27. Quark

Q-1
QUANTITATIVE ANALYSES

A quantitative analysis is a laboratory technique for determining the chemical concentration of an analyte (like a solution sample). It is based on the sample's chemical properties, such as chemical reactivity or solubility. Some analyses are performed based on the sample's physical properties, like boiling point temperature (T_{BP}) or molar mass (M_n). The determination is performed by different methods, like titrimetric analysis, gravimetric analysis, polarimetry, spectrometry, spectrophotometry, and more.

Q-2
QUANTUM AND QUANTIZATION

Quantum (its plural is **quanta**) and **quantization** are the keywords in understanding the basics of quantum physics (QP). [Historical Note: In 1900, Planck used quantum in his light theory (Planck's quantum theory) as an elementary particle of light. Soon later, in 1905, Einstein suggested the word photon be used instead of quantum in his light theory (Einstein's theory of light duality) because 1) A photon originates from an electron (as discussed under ATOM) and 2) The word **photon** rhymes with electron.]

Quantum: Quantum, in general science, is the smallest (quantized) unit of a physical quantity that *cannot* be subdivided. In quantum physics, quantum is generally used for any quantum elementary particle (simply **quantum particle**). And the photon is used only for the particle of light and other electromagnetic radiations (EM radiations). Therefore, the term **a quantum of light** has the same meaning as **a photon of light**:

A Quantum Elementary Particle of Light = A Quantum of Light = A Photon of Light

Quantization: Quantization, in general science, is the process of breaking a physical quantity (simply **quantity**) into its smallest units. In quantum physics, "light quantization" means separating the light particles into tiny-separate units (packets), called quanta, with a certain amount of energy (E), called light energy (photon energy). In simple words, light quantization is the study of the light particle (quantum or photon) when that particle is limited to the next three (3) conditions:

- A quantum of light (photon) *cannot* be subdivided anymore, so it is the smallest unit of that kind,
- A photon contains a small-but-fixed amount of E (energy), and
- Quanta (photons) are the ones that make the light.

Analogical Examples of Quantization: To better understand the difficult subject of quantization, consider an analogical example (a simple example for better understanding a difficult subject); the subject of "dollar quantization to pennies" in the context of "light quantization to photons (quanta)."

- A penny (photon) *cannot* be subdivided anymore, so it is the smallest unit of the dollar (light),
- A penny contains a small-but-fixed amount of E (buying ability), and
- Pennies (photons) are the ones that make the dollar (light).

As another example, assume that you are watching the drops of water from a faucet. If you say a drop of water is the quantum (the smallest unit) of water, you would have only seen a part of a picture (because one drop of water consists of extreme numbers of molecules). Here, thus, we better use the term "molecular quantization of water," which means the following:

- A molecule of water (quantum) is the smallest unit of water,
- A molecule of water contains a small-but-fixed amount of E, and
- Molecules of water are the ones that make water.

Quantization of Electron: In quantum physics, the quantization of an **electron** to a **photon** means:

- An electron *cannot* be subdivided into subparticles, so it is a quantum (non-composite) particle.
- An electron has a small but known amount of E when it stays on a certain electron shell. In this way, a given atom's electron in a shell has a different amount of E than the same electron when it jumps to another shell, as Bohr proved in 1913 in his theory (Bohr's atomic theory).
- When an electron jumps down from a higher-energy shell (E_2) to a lower-energy shell (E_1), say, by cooling its atom, the difference between E_2 and E_1 is released in the form of a photon with known photon energy.

[Note that quantum physicists use the next three (3) phrases equally; "quantization of an electron to a photon," "a photon is a quantized form of an electron," and "a photon is the creature of an electron."]

Quantization of Gravitational Force: The quantization of gravitational force (F_g, simply gravity), which is called quantum gravity, means the description, formulation, and application of F_g at its microscopic (atomic) and macroscopic (universal) levels.

Although top physicists (including Einstein) have tried to quantize the Fg (to express the F_g in the context of quantum physics, QP), so far, their attempts have been unsuccessful (because F_g acts universally). However, similar attempts on the other three fundamental forces of nature (FFN) have been successful (because those forces act at the atomic level). [Incorporating the F_g into the QP (the quantization of F_g) in connection with the other three FFN can bring physics one step closer to the theory of unification of physics (TUP or theory of everything). And the connection of quantized F_g with the other three FFN completes the TUP.]

Q-3
QUANTUM ATOMIC MODELS

Discussed under ATOMIC MODELS.

Q-4
QUANTUM CHEMISTRY

As a modern branch (subfield) of classical chemistry, quantum chemistry (QC) has been gradually established along with quantum physics (QP) during the first quarter of the 20th century. The QC focuses on applying quantum theories in chemical reactions and the phenomena that occur at atomic and molecular levels. Quantum chemists heavily use laboratory methods, such as spectroscopy (molecular spectroscopy), which work based on the quantization of energy at a molecular scale.

[Note: The QC and QP are somewhat similar, particularly those quantum-related topics given in this book. Thus, this book's **quantum topics**, such as quantum entanglement, quantum superposition, or quantum theories, can be used by both a chemical engineer and a chemist. It is, thus, helping to study QUANTUM AND QUANTIZATION and QUANTUM PHYSICS before studying any quantum topic.]

Q-5
QUANTUM CHROMODYNAMICS

Quantum chromodynamics (QCD) is a quantum field theory (see Note 1) describing strong nuclear force (F_{SN}), which originates in a quantity called color charge, from where the name QCD comes (see Note 2).

Knowing the following points about the QCD (quantum chromodynamics) is helpful:

- The F_{SN} (strong nuclear force), F_{EM} (electromagnetic force), F_{WN} (weak nuclear force), and F_g (gravitational force) are the four (4) fundamental forces of nature, given here from strongest to the weakest.
- The **color charge** is *not* related to color (the visual observation property of the human eye). But, it is like an electric charge (q), resulting from the flow of electrons through an electric conductor.
- Only the fourth force of nature, the gravitational force (F_g), has *not*, thus far, been quantized (formulized based on quantum-physics rules).

Q-6

QUANTUM COMPUTER

Discussed under the topic of COMPUTER AND QUANTUM COMPUTER.

Q-7

QUANTUM CRYPTOGRAPHY

As one of the important consequences of quantum physics (QP), quantum cryptography (QC, **cryptography**, or **data encryption**) is the process of hiding data from a third party (**adversary** or **eavesdropper**) when some data are sent from sending location to receiving location. Cryptography (from Greek **kryptos**, meaning **hiding**) uses quantum entanglement (QE) and quantum superposition (QS) to hide data from an adversary. Because any quantum elementary particle is in QS, an adversary *cannot* access real data.

[Note: In quantum computing, qubits replace the **bits** (basic storage units in a classical computer). A bit has a value of 0 or 1. The presence of an electric charge corresponds to 1, and its absence corresponds to 0.]

Q-8

QUANTUM ELEMENTARY PARTICLES

It is discussed under ELEMENTARY PARTICLES.

Q-9

QUANTUM ENTANGLEMENT OF PARTICLES

Quantum entanglement of particles (simply **quantum entanglement**, QE) is the interaction property of entangled (paired) quantum particles (a particle with *no* subparticle like an electron) at a distance (remote). [Note: Schrodinger used the word **quantum entanglement** (QE) for the first time in a paper published in 1935. In this paper, he said it is better *not* to consider QE as an instant-local-to-local interaction but rather an **instant nonlocal interaction** by sharing a similar quantum wavefunction (simply **wavefunction**) at a distance. The Schrodinger explanation, however, conflicted with Einstein's speed-of-light theory.]

According to this theory, placing one of the two quantumly entangled particles at a distance under certain conditions affects the other instantly (at no time), even if they are too far (many kilometers) away from each other. Figure 1 shows two quantumly entangled electrons placed at a distance. If observing (measuring) the spin direction of one of the electrons, the other instantly spins in the opposite direction. This occurs because they obey the spin rule (two electrons in the same electron shell do *not* spin in the same direction). The action of two quantumly entangled electrons can be viewed as two motherly entangled brothers with the same DNAs, one right-handed and one left-handed, who eat similarly. But one with his right hand and the other with his left hand even though they live far away (see Figure 2).

Complicated techniques produce quantumly entangled particles. Say, two electrons can be quantumly entangled while both moving at close to the speed of light constant in a particle accelerator (collider) and collide (see Figure 3). Similarly, two photons can be entangled into photon pairs while going through the narrow slit of a **light-beam splitter** at extremely high speed (see Figure 4).

It is helpful to be aware of the next points about the entanglement of two quantumly paired electrons.

- When talking about a pair of entangled electrons, they are only paired with each other but *not* with others.
- It is probably correct to think that when a pair of electrons are entangled, they are isolated from their environment, so they carry a permanent property that stays with them and controls them (*no* matter how far away they are from each other). It is, instead, incorrect to think that the entangled property of one of the paired electrons travels to the next one at a speed greater than the speed of light constant.
- It is probably correct to think that the entangled electrons are in two quantum superposition states, meaning they are in the more-than-one states. Once an observer **observes** (well-measures) one of the entangled electrons, the **observed** (well-measured) one is *not* in superposition anymore (because its observation forces the other entangled electron to make the opposite choice). If, say, one of the electrons is observed to be spinning **clockwise** (CW) on a certain electron shell and axis, then the other one is spinning **counterclockwise** (CCW) on the same shell and axis (see Figure 1).

Knowing the next four (4) points about QE is also important.

- Although it is hard to reason the QE, its understanding concept is *not* too difficult.
- It is one of the main properties distinguishing quantum physics from classical physics.
- If two particles are paired together at a time, their properties will remain connected at future times.
- The QE has *not* been proved theoretically but experimented successfully about 25 years after Einstein's death (1955), who called it "a spooky action at a distance" because it lacks scientific support.

The following are the experimental timelines of the QE theory:

- In1980, Alain Aspect managed a group of physicists at the Paris Institute of Technology to perform a successful QE experiment on two entangled photons.
- In 2004, an Austrian physicist also proved it by setting up a 500-m (1600-Ft) link between the Vienna University and City Hall and used an entanglement-encrypted message to teleport (with permission) an order to transfer some money from the City-Hall's account to the University's account.
- In 2016, physicists of the University of Calgary in Canada successfully performed the quantum teleportation of entangled particles at 8.2 km (= 5 Mi) apart.
- As of 2020, QE has been performed experimentally between two entangled electrons and entangled photons but has *not* yet been performed between anything larger (say between two molecules).

Based on what has been said so far, we can conclude this interesting topic by saying the following:

- If one of the quantumly entangled electrons is well (observed) measured by an observer, the result instantly affects the quantum state of the other. If, say, one of them is found to have the CW spin on its axis, then the other one's spin, measured on the same axis, is found to have the CCW spin, as shown in Figure 1. Schrodinger said that two entangled particles are in a **quantum superposition of two probabilities**. Interestingly, he tried to highlight this theory with his famous cat (see the figure under the topic of SCHRODINGER).
- Although the entangled particles interact instantly and accordingly, they can change their directions millions of times a second.
- Entangled particles have energy, known as particle self-energy, the energy that a particle has due to changes in a system in which that particle acts.

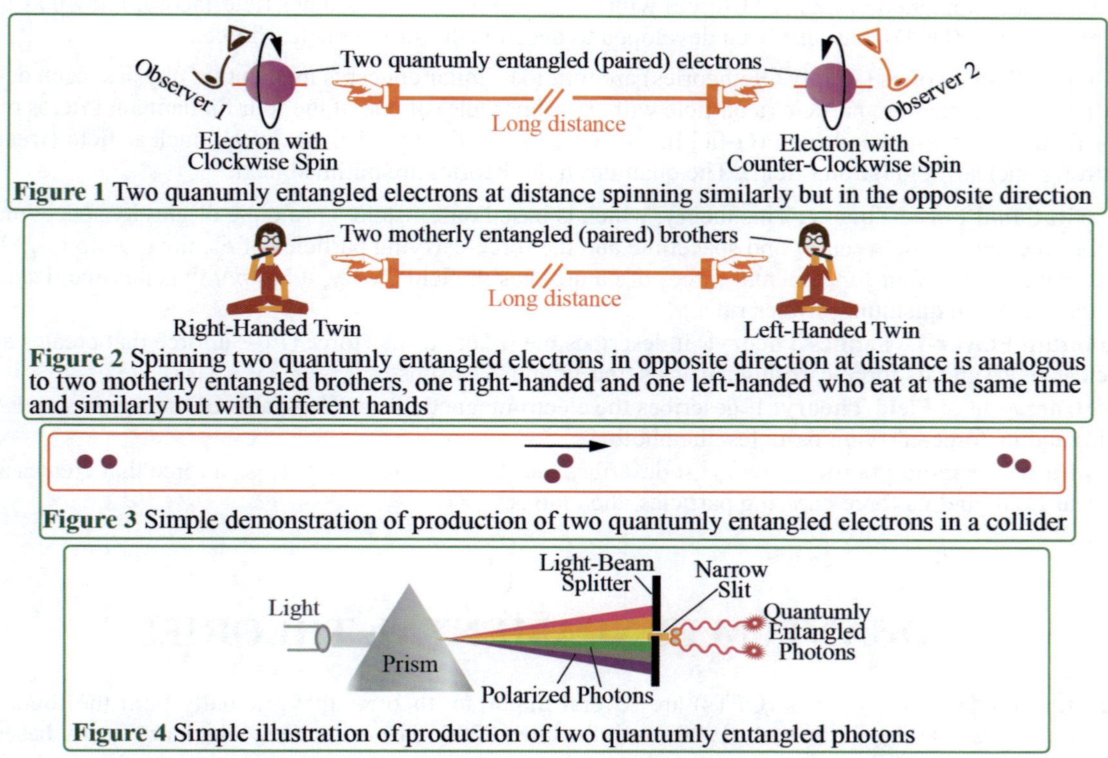

Figure 1 Two quanumly entangled electrons at distance spinning similarly but in the opposite direction

Figure 2 Spinning two quantumly entangled electrons in opposite direction at distance is analogous to two motherly entangled brothers, one right-handed and one left-handed who eat at the same time and similarly but with different hands

Figure 3 Simple demonstration of production of two quantumly entangled electrons in a collider

Figure 4 Simple illustration of production of two quantumly entangled photons

Q-10

QUANTUM FIELD AND QUANTUM FIELD THEORIES

A field, in physics, is an invisible space around a system. A field theory explains how a field interacts with a system when placed in that field and changes that system's physical properties. Examples include electric field (E-field) and magnetic field (M-field), together electromagnetic field (EM field).

Quantum Field

A quantum field is an invisible space around a quantum system that has a quantity (value) at each point in spacetime (space at a moment in time). A vector quantum field is a field with a direction assigned to each point of space and can be changed with time. Instead, a scalar quantum field has *no* direction in space and *cannot* be changed with time, so it is *not* an absolute quantity.

Remember the following points about a quantum field:

- It can be in its so-called ground energy state or excited energy state (a state that carries excess energy above the ground energy state), and
- It is quantized to tiny-separated quantities, called the quanta (the plural of quantum).

Quantum Field Theories

The quantum field theory was advanced in the 1930s by Paul Dirac (1902–1995, a British physicist) and a few physicists in the 1940s. Then Richard Feynman (1918–1988, an American physicist) completed the mathematical difficulties of the field theory in 1949 and called it **quantum electrodynamics** (QED). Later, the field theory combined electromagnetic force (EM-force) with weak nuclear force. Another field theory, known as quantum chromodynamics (QCD), has also been developed to describe the strong nuclear force.

Quantum field theories (simply QF theories) are four (4) similar concepts in quantum physics, each describing the behavior of a quantum particle (a particle with *no* subparticle) of one of the four fundamental fields of nature. These fields are gravitational field (G-field), electromagnetic field (EM field), weak nuclear field (weak field), and strong nuclear field (strong field). The quantum field theories are outlined next.

- **Gravitational Force Theory:** This theory, which is based on Einstein's principle of gravity spacetime, describes the relation between F_g and spacetime and the force-carrying particles of F_g, the gravitons. [Although F_g (the weakest of four fundamental forces of nature) has its field theory, it has *not* thus far quantized (described based on quantum-physics rules).]
- **Quantum Flavor-Dynamics Theory:** It describes the weak nuclear force (F_{WN}, a force that creates a weak nuclear field) and its force-carrying particles, the W and Z Bosons.
- **Electromagnetic Field Theory:** It describes the electromagnetic force (F_{EM}, a force that creates an EM field) and its force-carrying particles, the photons.
- **Quantum Chromodynamics Theory:** It describes the strong nuclear force (F_{SN}, a force that creates a strong nuclear field) and its force-carrying particles, the gluons.

Q-11

QUANTUM FUNDAMENTAL THEORIES

Quantum fundamental theories (QFTs) are several important theories that gradually built the foundation of quantum physics, starting in the early 1900s until the late 1920s. These theories, which are firmly based on the previous theory (or theories), are more. But this book considers the seven most important of them, in the order of the oldest to the newest, to make the subject easier for its readers.

- Planck's Quantum Theory (1900)**:** Planck, for the first time, proved that light (refers to light energy) travels discontinuously in the form of separate set units (packets), called by him the **quanta of light**, where the word **quanta** is the plural of quantum. He also proved that each quantum of light (the particle of light) carries a tiny amount of energy (*E*) equal to *h.f*, where *h* is the Planck's constant and *f* is the frequency of the light's wave. Planck, thus, was the first physicist who proved that energy is quantizable, meaning that it travels in the form of separate packets; in other words, it is quantized to individual packets when traveling.
- Einstein's Theory of Light Duality (1905)**:** Einstein, for the first time, proved that light (light energy) and other electromagnetic radiations *cannot* be described as particles or as waves but as a combination of both. Based on this theory, the light's particle (the photon) acts like wave when moving and acts like a particle when releasing (emitting) energy.
- Bohr's Atomic Theory (1913)**:** For the first time, Bohr proved that the *E* of an electron moving around the nucleus corresponds to a certain electron shell (energy shell or simply **shell**). Also, he discovered how an electron releases (emits) energy in the form of a photon when it jumps from a higher-energy shell to a lower-energy shell and vice versa.
- Heisenberg's Wavematrix Theory (1925)**:** In his atomic theory, Heisenberg treated the electron as a wave (but *not* as a particle) to mathematically determine its location in the electron shells of an atom at a certain time. Based on this assumption, he formulized an equation, which became later known as Heisenberg's wavematrix equation, to determine the energy (*E*) of an electron in the electron shells, with some degree of probability (around 90%). [Here, it is better to use the term position (location) instead of energy because the amount of the electron's *E* tells us in what electron shell it is positioned.]
- Schrodinger's Wavefunction Theory (1926)**:** Schrodinger, independently from Heisenberg, used the wave property of the electrons to mathematically determine the location of an electron in the electron shells. He developed a function called electron's quantum wavefunction, which determines the electron's location in the

electron shells with a high probability (the *greater* the wavefunction, the *more* likely the electron is in that location).

- Heisenberg's Uncertainty Principle (1927)**:** Heisenberg proved that it is impossible to simultaneously measure two properties of an electron (or any other quantum elementary particle, like a photon). We, he said, *cannot* measure, say, the energy and velocity of an electron with accuracy, as the measurement of one quantity changes the other quantity's situation. Thus, the more precisely an electron's property is measured, the less precisely can its other property be measured. He solved this problem by using a probability effect by saying that we *cannot* predict a single definite result for a measurement. We can, instead, predict a few different possible results that tell us how likely each of these is the right one. If, say, we run the same measurement on similar quantum systems, and each of them gives us two results (X and Y), we can find that the result of the measurement would be X, in some cases and Y, in other cases. Although we can predict the approximate number of times that the result was X or Y, we *cannot* predict the specific result of an individual measurement.
- Broglie's Theory of Duality of Matter (1927)**:** In his theory, Broglie extends Einstein's theory of wave-particle duality of light's particles (the photons) to the particles of all matter. To prove his theory, Broglie conducted some experiments on the electron to express his three important ideas: (1) Electrons have a rotating (oscillating) behavior while moving, (2) The *faster* an electron rotates, the *more* its behavior is like a wave of energy, and (3) The *slower* an electron rotates, the *more* its behavior is like a particle.

With certainty, all quantum theories use one, two, or all the next main properties of quantum particles (particles with *no* subparticle):

- Quantum superposition
- Quantum entanglement
- Quantum uncertainty

It is helpful to finish this important topic with the following two (2) notes:

- The quantum theories have proven to be sufficient to explain most of the phenomena that occur in the observable Universe. But they are still insufficient to incorporate all the fundamental forces of nature to reach a unified theory (called the theory of unification of physics) to describe the Universe fully.
- We live in a world surrounded by advanced technologies (like semiconductor technology); almost none of them would have been possible without a full understanding of quantum theories.

Q-12

QUANTUM GRAVITY THEORY

As the quantum version of Newton's gravitation theory and Einstein's principle of gravity spacetime, quantum gravity theory discusses the effect of the gravitons (the quantum elementary particles of the gravitational force, F_g) in the context of quantum physics (QP). In other words, this theory discusses the quantization of the F_g (the weakest of four fundamental forces of nature) and its application at its microscopic (atomic) and macroscopic (universal) levels, known to quantum physicists as the quantization of F_g. The formulation of the F_g quantization with the other three forces is one of the challenges physicists have ever faced because the F_g acts in the entire Universe. But, the other forces act at a much smaller level, the atomic level. For this reason, top physicists, including Einstein, have tried to express the F_g in the context of QP, but, so far, their attempts have been unsuccessful. However, similar attempts on the three non-gravitational forces have been successful (because those forces act at the atomic level). [Incorporating the F_g into the QP can bring physics one step closer to the theory of unification of physics (theory of everything).]

Q-13

QUANTUM LEAP

A quantum leap is the rapid jump of an electron from an electron shell (simply **shell**) to another. Jumping (leaping) an electron from a higher energy-level shell to a lower energy-level shell creates some excess energy, which is released in the form of the photon energy of a photon. Jumping an electron from a lower energy-level shell to a higher energy-level shell, instead, requires some energy absorbed in the form of the photon energy of a photon. [Both releasing and absorbing photons by electrons are discussed and graphically shown under the topic of ATOM.]

Q-14

QUANTUM MECHANICS

The word quantum mechanics, in general, is mostly used equally to quantum physics, and it is used as the foundation of quantum physics, quantum chemistry, quantum field, quantum field theory, and more. In this book, this word is *not* used.

Q-15

QUANTUM NUMBER

Defined under ATOM.

Q-16

QUANTUM PARTICLES

Discussed under the topic of PARTICLE AND ITS TYPES.

Q-17

QUANTUM PHYSICS

Quantum physics (QPhy) is a modern branch (subfield) of classical physics (CPhy or Newtonian physics). It was developed gradually between 1900 and 1930 to study mainly the quantum elementary particles (like electrons and photons), their subparticles (like quarks), and their energy. Let us, first, remember the following fundamental brief points about CPhy and QPhys:

- Although some limitations exist in CPhy, the QPhy does *not* invalidate the CPhy, but adds more to it and modifies some of its subjects.
- Quantum physics and quantum chemistry are somewhat similar, particularly those topics given in this book. Thus, the **quantum topics**, such as quantum entanglement or quantum superposition, can also be used in quantum chemistry.

Under this topic, you will find answers to the next questions:

- When, why, and how the QPhy start?
- What are the main differences between QPhy and CPhy?
- What are the quantum theories, and what are their contributions?
- Who are the key founding physicists of the QPhy (quantum physics)?

Start of Quantum Physics and its Reasons: The quantum era started in 1900 when Planck published his light theory (Planck's quantum theory) to prove that light consists of elementary particles (quanta to him and later photons to Einstein) that travel in individual units (packets) and deliver their energy in a quantized (individual) manner. Soon after (in 1905), Einstein published his light duality theory (see Einstein's theory of light duality) to prove that light acts in both ways, the wavelike and particlelike. As discussed next, both Planck and Einstein could *not* fully express their theories in the CPhy (classical physics). When in the 1860s, Maxwell calculated the speed of light as 300 000 km/s (= 186 000 Mi/s), one key question remained unanswered "why does light *not* behave like other waves? This question remained unanswered until Einstein, in one of his 1905's papers, proved that light does *not* behave exactly like a wave because it has both **wavelike** and **particlelike** properties, together known as the **wave-particle duality**.

In addition to this important point, the CPhy (classical physics) had the next three (3) major shortages:

- **Atom and its Components:** CPhy was insufficient in talking about the atom and its components because when Newton, in his 1687's book (*Principia Mathematica*), talked about the atom, the atomic components were *not* discovered. Thus, the discovery of the electron (1897), proton (1920), and neutron (1932) made the explanation of the atom in the context of CPhy impossible.
- **Space and Time:** CPhy was insufficient in talking about space and time because when Newton, in his book, discussed gravitation (see Newton's Law of Gravitation), he assumed that space is a non-absolute quantity and time is an absolute quantity, so they are independent of each other. If, according to this idea, a beam of light is sent from one point to another, different observers, moving at different speeds, would agree on the time that the beam of light traveled (because time is absolute) but would *not* agree on how far the beam traveled (because space is *not* absolute). According to Newton's idea, different observers measure different light speeds. This treatment seemed **wrong** to Einstein. Thus, Einstein tried to prove that: 1) Space and time are dependent on each other, so *none* of them can be absolute. 2) All observers measure the same speed for the light, regardless of their speed.
- **Gravitational Force:** CPhy was insufficient in talking about gravitational force (F_g, force of gravity). When Newton developed his Laws of Motion around 1687, he considered the F_g as the result of attraction between the massive systems (systems with a rest mass of M). Einstein, in his relativity theories, goes further to say that: 1) F_g of a massive system can curve the spacetime (called the **curvature of spacetime**) by applying its particles (called the gravitons since the 1930s) to the spacetime. That is to say, the *more* massive the system,

the *greater* is its F_g, and, thus, the *more* it curves the spacetime. Thus, F_g can be viewed as a curved spacetime around a massive system. 2) F_g can be created by all forms of E (energy), including E_{Ph} (photon energy), because, as Einstein proved, E and M are equivalent. In this way, any form of E can curve the spacetime. [The problem of F_g, however, is *not* completely solved yet because its mathematical unification with other fundamental forces of nature is *not* solved yet either.]

Differences Between Quantum Physics and Classical Physics: Some differences between quantum physics (QPhy) and classical physics (CPhy) have been discussed. Next, some other differences are outlined.

- The QPhy works on a complicated math basis, while the CPhy works on an ordinary one.
- The QPhy assumes that systems travel in a four-dimensional spacetime, while the CPhy assumes that the systems travel in a three-dimensional space.
- The QPhy is more difficult to understand than CPhy. It is difficult for a student to understand if his physics teacher talks about the detail of how the nuclear fusion process occurs in the Sun to create the light energy than to say that "the Sun rises in the east and sets in the west because the Earth spins toward the east."
- The QPhy studies physical events (phenomena) at atomic and subatomic levels, while the CPhy studies these at atomic and molecular levels. The QPhy, in other words, is based on quantum elementary particles, while the CPhy is based on elementary particles (atoms and molecules).
- The QPhy considers space as a quantity, dependent on M (spacetime becomes curved by a massive system to create F_g), as Einstein proved in his theory of special relativity. When a mass moves through space, it simultaneously influences space and time. Unlike space that started when Big Bang started, the time has *no* known starting or ending point, so it can only be measured on a **relative scale**, set to a defined zero point, like BC (**before Christ**). Thus, as Einstein suggested, space and time are combined in QPhys in such a way as to keep the speed of light as a constant quantity for moving and non-moving observers.
- The QPhy studies the energy (E) of particles, known as the quantum energy (E_Q), at locations and under different conditions, while the CPhy studies energy and its ordinary types.

The seven top quantum physicists and the three top classical physicists behind them. [All of quantum physicists did not participate in the 5th Solvay Conference on Physics in 1927, but this author thought of a non-happening gathering to illustrate these great physicists together for this book. The physicists order of sitting around the table is based on their important contributions to quantum physics: Planck (1900), Einstein (1905), Rutherford (1911), Bohr (1913), Heisenberg (1925), Schrodinger (1926), and Broglie (1927).]

Questionability of Quantum Physics: Although the QPhy has revolutionized the 20th century of science and achieved notable success, some of its basics have remained questionable, such as the following:

- How exactly a quantum system works?
- Why do quantum particles (like an electron) behave strangely?
- Why can one particle exist in more than one place at the same time?
- How does an electron spin around both its nucleus and its axis at the same time?
- How exactly quantum wavefunction works, and what can we do with its probable results?
- How 2 particles at a distance communicate faster than the speed of light (refers to quantum entanglement)?
- Why does an electron choose any possible paths while turning around the nucleus (Einstein said *God does not play dice*)?
- Why quantum measured values are uncertain (see Heisenberg's uncertainty principle). Why, for example, the product of $E.V - V.E$ is *not* equal to zero (in quantum language $E.V - V.E \# 0$), where the value E and V can represent any measurable quantities, but in common notation, E is the energy of a system; say, an electron, and V is its velocity.

These and many other questions make QPhy an incomplete science that works perfectly but questionably.

Quantum Theories: Since 1900, different physicists have offered some quantum theories to cover the limitations of the CPhy. But we can say that the seven most important theories that answered the unknowns of the atom and its components' quantization and laid the foundation of QPhy are:

- 1900: Planck's quantum theory
- 1905: Einstein's theory of wave-particle duality of light
- 1911: Rutherford's atomic theory
- 1913: Bohr's atomic theory
- 1925: Heisenberg's atomic theory and soon later, his uncertainty principle
- 1926: Schrodinger's wavefunction theory
- 1927: Broglie's theory of wave-particle duality of matter

These theories advanced physics from a classical explanation to a quantum explanation. Today, QPhy is the building block of most modern technologies, which use the properties of quantum particles. Without QPhy, scientists could *not* use electron properties and design the electronics that run today's computers, semiconductors, transistors, electronic microscopes, smartphones, smart TVs, tablets, digital cameras, MRI scanners, life-saving medical instruments, and more. In addition, quantum physicists have been developing other technologies, including quantum computing, quantum cryptography, and quantum teleportation.

Founders of Quantum Physics: Planck, Einstein, Rutherford, Bohr, Heisenberg, Schrodinger, and Broglie can be named the top seven (7) quantum physicists. And Newton, Faraday, and Maxwell the three top classical physicists. Together, these pioneers contributed to physics more than all other physicists together.]

Q-18

QUANTUM SUPERPOSITION

As one of the main properties of quantum particles (particles with *no* subparticle like electron or photon), quantum superposition (QS) means that a quantum particle is in a superposition (more-than-one) state, like being in two opposite states at the same time. A quantum particle can have one value or the other, but neither is an actual value until it is well (observed) measured. Therefore, the superposition is the probability of being in two (or more) states until it is well observed. And the moment it is observed, it is in one state, so it has its actual value. Say, an electron can be in a superposition state by being in either of the following states:

- In the state of orbiting its nucleus and having a fixed amount of energy,

- In the state of absorbing energy and moving to a higher-level shell (orbit), and
- In the state of releasing some of its energy and moving to a lower-level energy shell.

Thus, the triple-position **probability** of the electron remains until it is collapsed (observed). After it is observed, it is *not* anymore in a superposition state because it has a single state with a certain amount of energy. [Quantum physicists use the word **collapse** to refer to a system after being **measured** (simply, **observed**)]

Although quantum superposition can only be applied to quantum particles, let us use an **analogical example** (a simple example for understanding a concept) by comparing it with a tossed coin. While tossing, the coin is in two states; one has a 50% probability of being in the **head** position. And one has a 50% probability of being in the **tail** position. But it has just one state when it is on the ground (with one of its sides face up).

Consider a pair of entangled electrons. None of them have a definite state (in two superposed states). Once an observer looks at one of them, the observed electron is *no longer* in a superposition (more-than-one) state (because its observation forces the other entangled electron to make the opposite choice). If, say, one of the electrons is observed to be spinning **clockwise** (CW) on a certain axis, the other is spinning **counterclockwise** (CCW) on the same axis, as shown in Figure 1 under QUANTUM ENTANGLEMENT.

[Although physicists do *not* believe in faster-than-light action, the result of QS is instant, even though *no* physicists YET know why.]

Schrodinger, in 1935, proposed an example, later known as the **Schrodinger's cat analogy** (also called **Schrodinger's cat paradox**), whose illustration, **a cat in a box**, became the most famous analogical example for describing the **paradox** (contradiction) of quantum superposition. He assumed that a cat, a flask with a cat-killing poison, a radioactive source, and a radioactive detector are in a box, as shown in the figure under the topic of SCHRODINGER. He further assumed that in the box, the test is designed so that even the decay of a single atom can cause the release of the poison and kill the cat. Before observation by an observer, the cat (the system) is in both **dead-AND-alive** positions simultaneously. And when the box is opened, the observer forces the system (the cat) into one or another position (**dead-OR-alive**).

In this experiment, the cat is said to be entangled with the nucleus of the decaying atom, so both the cat and the decaying atom are in a superposition (double) state. This means that the atom may be at the same time in both decayed-and-*not*-decayed states, and the cat may be in killed-and-*not*-killed states. When observing the box, we find the cat either dead or alive, so the cat is *not* in a superposition state anymore but in one state. By this analogy, Schrodinger wanted to prove that a quantum system is in a superposition of states, so it has *no* fixed value; it just has the probabilities.

In a quantum world, say, the quantum spin of an electron has two possible values, **up** or **down**. Thus, the spin has *no* actual value but has a probability of being in one state or the other until it is measured (scientifically collapsed) to see in what state it is. Before measurement, it is in a superposition (more-than-one) state, so it has a probability of being in one state or the other. Once, however, it collapses, it has one actual value (with *no* probability), so it is *no longer* in a superposition state. Thus, after collapsing (observation), a quantum system is *not* in a superposition state.

Either of the listed cases tells us that the system is collapsed (observed), so after opening the Schrodinger's box, we find the cat in one state (dead) or the other (alive), meaning that the cat is *not* anymore in a superposition (more-than-one) state. However, the matter of the cat being **dead or alive** does *not* tell us in what state the cat was before we opened the box. Thus, we are facing probabilities while the cat is in superposition.

We must remember that it is *not* possible to put a macro system, like a cat, in a superposition condition. But, like a virus, a micro system can be isolated and put into the superposition state. Lately, German Physicists have performed an experiment in which a virus trapped by laser light was placed in a superposition state.

Q-19

QUANTUM SYSTEM

A quantum system is a micro-size system in which a quantum particle (a particle with *no* subparticle like an electron) changes to a state with more energy (*E*). Such a system is in the excited energy state. Instead, when a quantum particle changes to a state with less *E*, it is in the ground energy state.

Q-20

QUANTUM TELEPORTATION OF PARTICLES

Quantum teleportation of particles (simply **Quantum teleportation** or QT) is the process of instant-and-distant (remote) teleportation of information between entangled (paired) particles from the sending location to the receiving location. [The word **teleportation** can be defined as an instant transfer of entangled particles with *no* physical space between them.]

Teleportation of particles is based on the quantum entanglement of particles (simply **Quantum entanglement** or QE), which is instant signaling between two entangled particles (like photon or electron). Although physics does *not* believe in faster-than-light interaction, the result of both QE and QT is instant (faster-than speed of light constant), even though *no* physicists know why.

In quantum teleportation (QT),

- A particle is converted to energy,
- The energy is teleported to a long distance, and
- The teleported energy is converted again to a particle at that distance.

Unlike classical teleportation, which can teleport **classical bits**, the QT can teleport **quantum bits** (called **qubits**) of information between two locations. Although QT can, so far, teleport entangled particles, physicists also think that it is possible to apply this technology to molecules in the future. [This, however, does *not* mean that human teleportation, as we watch in fiction movies, is possible.]

[An ordinary computer has millions of tiny transistors that use electric charges to store data as **bits** (binary digits). A **bit** (which can have a value of 0 or 1) is the basic storage unit in computers. The presence of a charge corresponds to 1, and its absence means 0. **Qubits** (*kju bits*) replace the bits in a quantum computer.]

[Entangled particles can also be used to teleport coded messages so that only the receiver can read them. Any eavesdropper would break the entanglement state, causing the message corruption.]

Q-21

QUANTUM THEORIES

Study QUANTUM FUNDAMENTAL THEORIES.

Q-22

QUANTUM THEORIES OF DUALITY

Quantum theories of duality refer to the following two (2) theories:

- Einstein's Theory of Light Duality (1905): Einstein, for the first time, proved that light (light energy) and other electromagnetic radiations *cannot* be described as particles or waves but a combination of both. Based on this theory, the light's particle (the photon) acts like waves when moving and particles when releasing (emitting) energy.
- Broglie's Theory of Duality of Matter (1927): In his theory, Broglie extends Einstein's theory of light particles (the photons) to the particles of all matter. To prove his theory, Broglie conducted some experiments on the electron (a particle) to express his two important ideas: (1) The *faster* an electron rotates, the *more* it behaves like a wave of energy, and (2) The *slower* an electron rotates, the *more* it behaves like a particle. [Because of the all-inclusivity of this theory, it is called **Broglie's theory of matter duality**.]

Q-23
QUANTUM UNCERTAINTY PRINCIPLE

Study HEISENBERG'S UNCERTAINTY PRINCIPLE.

Q-24
QUANTUM UNIFIED THEORY

Study THEORY OF UNIFICATION OF PHYSICS.

Q-25
QUANTUM VACUUM

A quantum vacuum (also called a **vacuum state**) is a quantum state that has the lowest possible energy (E); in other words, it has zero-point energy (E_Z).

Q-26
QUANTUM WAVEFUNCTION

Quantum wavefunction (simply **wavefunction**) is a mathematical theory that was formulated in 1926 by Schrodinger to mathematically describe the location and energy (E) of an electron in the electron shells (simply **shells**) of an atom. He used the wave property of an electron and its wavelength (λ) to make its location in a shell calculable. He showed the wavefunction by the Greek letter Ψ (psi) and developed a differential equation, known later as Schrodinger's wavefunction equation, to determine an electron's E. Knowing the amount of an electron's E can determine its probable location in electron shells. For example, solving wavefunction square (ψ^2) and using two real variables of x (position) and t (time) for a hydrogen atom gives the probability of finding the hydrogen's electron at a certain shell (Figure 1), so the *greater* the wavefunction, the *more* likely the electron is in that location (shell).

$$\psi^2(x, t)$$

The ψ^2 of an electron is a positive real number that gives the electron density (called **electron cloud**; see Note below), in which it is located, with some degree of certainty (about 90%). Thus, Schrodinger's wavefunction equation involves the same probability as Heisenberg's wavematrix equation.

[Note: In both Heisenberg's and Schrodinger's quantum atomic models, the word **electron cloud** refers to the paths of an electron in an irregular volume of space, while Bohr's atomic model uses the paths of an electron as an individual (separate) regular shells.]

In his theory, Schrodinger said **wavefunction collapse** is a physical chemistry process and tried to highlight it with his famous cat (see the figure under the topic of SCHRODINGER).

Even though wavefunction usually produces probable answers, it is especially useful in quantum physics because it predicts various physical phenomena, including the nuclear decay process.

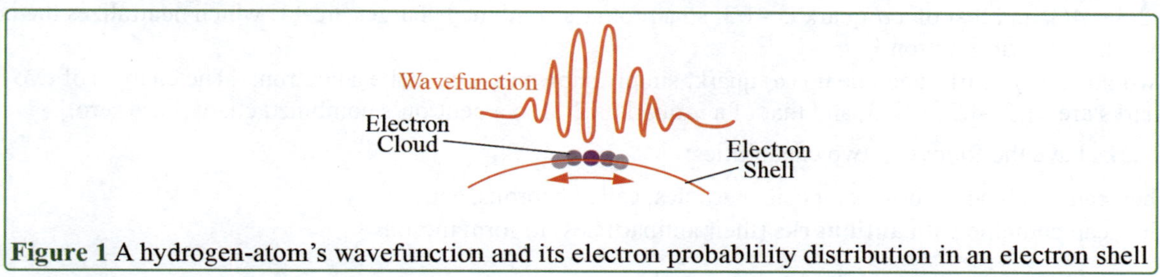

Figure 1 A hydrogen-atom's wavefunction and its electron probablility distribution in an electron shell

Q-27
QUARKS

As a quantum particle (a particle with *no* subparticle) that its existence was proposed in 1964 independently by two physicists (Gell-Man M. and Zweig G), a quark is the component of an atom's proton and neutron so that it is the tiniest system that exists in the Universe. Six important properties of quarks are outlined next.

- Quarks can exist in 6 forms: up-quark (shown as u), down-quark (d), top quark (t), bottom quark (b), strange quark (s), and charmed quark (c), in rising order by mass. The last four quarks are just heavy carbon copies of the first two, which are unstable, decaying into lighter particles. Figure 1 shows a proton with 2 up-quarks and 1 down-quark. Figure 2 shows a neutron consisting of 1 up-quark and 2 down-quarks.
- A quark can change its type; for example, from u-quark to d-quark. As the result of this change, a proton changes to a neutron, or a neutron changes to a proton, causing the change of a chemical element to a different element, a process called nuclear decay. This is what causes nuclear fusion in stars, like the Sun.]
- Two up-quarks (or two down-quarks) are strongly attracted to each other by strong nuclear force (F_{SN}), which acts as an **attractive force**. More to the point, they are attracted to each other by the strings of gluons (the force-carrying particles of F_{SN}) and spin opposite each other.
- Two up-quarks (or two down-quarks) are repulsed (kept away) from each other to prevent collision between them by electromagnetic force (F_{EM}), which acts as a **repulsive force**. [At a distance like the diameter of a proton ($\approx 10^{-12}$ mm), the attractive F_{SN} is about 100 times greater than repulsive F_{EM}. Such a ratio creates a stable situation between two quarks.
- Quarks are responsible for two-thirds proton's electric charge and one-third of an electron.
- Quarks are estimated to comprise 99.9% of the ordinary mass in the Universe (because protons and neutrons consist of quarks). The remaining 0.1% of the mass in the Universe is in the form of electrons.

A quark has some other properties, including the following:

- It is made of tiny vibrating strings that enable it to interact with other quarks.
- It is a Fermion (obeys Fermi-Dirac statistics; defined under BOSONS, FERMIONS, AND HADRONS).
- It is considered a string in the string theory, where a string behaves like a massive particle (a particle with mass) and is governed by how it vibrates in space.

- Its mass (M) is too tiny (almost **massless**), even lighter than an electron (because a quark originated from an electron). [According to Einstein's equation ($E = Mc^2$), the remaining mass of a proton (M of proton − M of quark) is in the form of energy (E). This tells us that the energies associated with the quark, such as the energy that glues the quarks together and the quark's kinetic energy (E_K), contribute greatly to the proton's mass. A quark's E, which is in the form of E_K, is too tiny (as the E of a photon).]
- It *cannot* be separated from its parent group (hadrons) because it *cannot* be observed individually. Much of what physicists know about quarks has been taken from observing their parent groups.
- Two up-quarks (u) and one down quark (d), simply shown as *uud*, make a proton. [An u-quark's charge is 2 × 2/3 = 4/3, and that of a d-quark is –1/3, so a proton's combined charges are +1, which neutralizes the negative charge of an electron.]
- Two down (d) quarks and one up (u) quark, simply shown as *ddu*, make a neutron. [The charges of two d-quarks are –1/3 –1/3 = –2/3, and that of a u-quark is 2/3, so a neutron's combined charges are zero.]

Quarks have the following two capabilities:

- They can combine to form composite particles, called hadrons, and
- They can combine with **antiquarks** (their antiparticles) to form mesons.

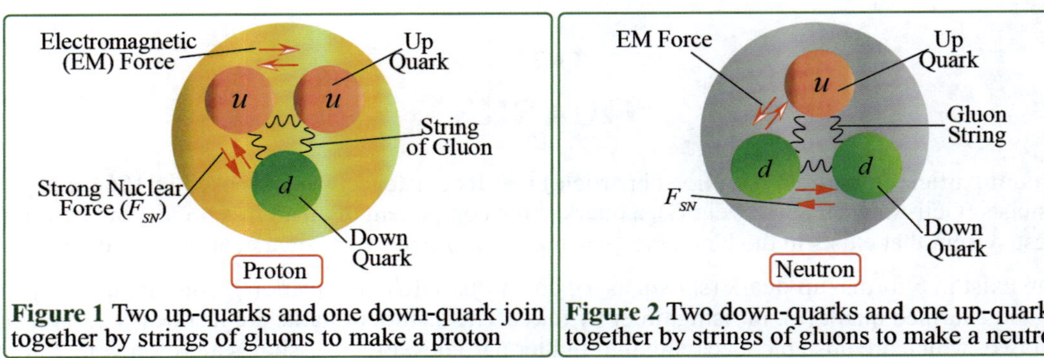

Figure 1 Two up-quarks and one down-quark join together by strings of gluons to make a proton

Figure 2 Two down-quarks and one up-quark join together by strings of gluons to make a neutron

R Section

LIST OF TOPICS

1. Radian and Rotational Angle
2. Radiant Energy
3. Radiant Power
4. Radiation
5. Radio Wave
6. Radioactive Decay
7. Radioactive Elements
8. Radioactive Half Lifetime
9. Radioactive Isotopes
10. Radioactive Radiation
11. Radioactive Wastes
12. Radioactivity
13. Radionuclide
14. Raffinate
15. Raoult's Law of Vapor
16. Rate
17. Raschig Rings
18. Reaction Order
19. Reactions
20. Reaction Rate
21. Reactivity
22. Reactors
23. Reagents
24. Real Gases
25. Reboilers
26. Recirculation Process
27. Recycling Process
28. Reducing Reactions
29. Reference System
30. Reflection
31. Reflux
32. Refraction, Reflection, and Diffraction of Light
33. Refractive Index
34. Refractometric Dissolved Solids
35. Refractometry
36. Regeneration Reaction
37. Regenerative Braking System
38. Regression (Mathematics)
39. Relative Atomic Mass
40. Relative Density
41. Relative Humidity
42. Relative Viscosity
43. Relative Volatility
44. Relaxing Time
45. Renewable and Nonrenewable Energies
46. Repulsive Energy
47. Resilience
48. Resin
49. Resistance
50. Resistance Force
51. Rest Energy
52. Rest Mass
53. Reverse Osmosis Process
54. Reversible Processes
55. Reynolds Equation
56. Reynolds Number
57. Rheology
58. Right-Hand Rule
59. Room Temperature
60. Rotational Momentum
61. Rotational Velocity
62. Roughness
63. Rounding Numbers
64. Rubbers
65. Rusting and Rust
66. Rutherford
67. Rutherford's Atomic Theory

R-1
RADIAN AND ROTATIONAL ANGLE

Radian: Radian (Rad) is the SI unit for rotational angle (α, alpha). Considering Figure 1 and a complete rotation (R = 360°), the following are the relations between Rad, rotation (R), degree, and π (pi):

$$1 \text{ Rad} = R/2\pi = 360°/2\pi = 180°/\pi \approx 57.3°$$

Radian has some uses, such as in calculating a rotating system's rotational velocity (ω).

Rotational Angle: Rotational angle (α, also called the **angle of rotation**) is an angle through which a system rotates circularly around its axis of rotation, as shown in the same figure. It is measured in degree or radian. Considering a circle with a circumference of C, then angle α equates to 90° = ¼ C = 1.57 Rad.

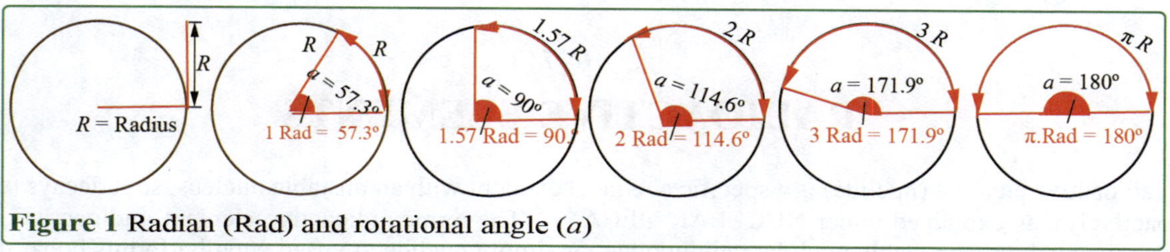

Figure 1 Radian (Rad) and rotational angle (α)

R-2
RADIANT ENERGY

Another name for PHOTON ENERGY.

R-3
RADIANT POWER

Another name for INTENSITY.

R-4
RADIATION

Study RADIOACTIVE RADIATION.

R-5
RADIO WAVE

As an invisible wave to the human eye, radio wave (radio radiation) was discovered by Heinrich Hertz, a German physicist. The radio wave is one of the seven (7) types of electromagnetic waves (EM waves or EM radiations), with a wavelength (λ) longer than that of visible light.

The radio wave λ is between 10 000 km and 1 mm, and its *f* (frequency) is between 30 Hz and 300 GHz, where G is for Giga (= 10^9), and Hz is for Hertz (the SI unit of *f*). Because of their long wavelengths, radio waves can pass through most obstacles, unaffected. This property makes radio waves ideal for carrying broadcast signals.

[Note: Radio waves are the longest, and micro waves are the second-longest EM waves. The **EM waves** include radio wave, micro wave, infrared, visible light, ultraviolet, X-ray, and gamma ray, given in the longest to shortest wavelengths (the *longer* the λ of a wave, the *smaller* is its *f*).]

R-6

RADIOACTIVE DECAY

Another name for NUCLEAR DECAY.

R-7

RADIOACTIVE ELEMENTS

A radioactive element (nuclide) is a specific chemical element with an unstable nucleus, so it decays (changes radioactively), as explained under NUCLEAR DECAY. [The terms radioactive element, radioactive isotope, radioactive nuclide, non-stable nuclide, radionuclide, or simply nuclide are used equally. In this book, the term **radionuclide** (simply **nuclide**) is used mostly.]

Some properties of nuclides are listed next.

- They decay radioactively over time to release radioactive radiation (such as alpha particles, beta particles, and gamma particles) and energy (E) in the form of heat energy (E_Q).
- Most of them undergo an extremely long period of decay before reaching stability and harmlessness.
- It takes time for them to decay into stable and harmless elements. Their decay time determines how long their nuclear waste remains radioactive.
- They are expressed by their atomic mass (M_A). For example, the M_A of U-235 is 235 (92 protons and 143 neutrons), and the M_A of plutonium (Pu) is 244, so-called Pu-244.
- Some are found in nature, but some are made artificially in the lab.
- Some, like uranium-235 (U-235), can cause nuclear fission.

While most elements' nucleus is stable (some for billion years), the nuclides' nucleus is *not*. The main reason for this instability is that too many (or too few) neutrons are present in the nucleus of a nuclide compared to the nucleus of an ordinary element (with a fixed number of neutrons). And because a neutron, by itself (*not* being near a proton), is unstable, it changes (decays) to a proton by absorbing an electron. This change creates instability in a nuclide, causing its nucleus to decay. In addition, it differentiates between two opposing forces (strong nuclear force, F_{SN}, and electromagnetic force, F_{EM}) inside a nuclide's nucleus. The instability in these two forces causes a fission chain reaction, which splits the nucleus. [The F_{SN} acts as an **attractive force** to keep protons and neutrons together, while F_{EM} acts as a **repulsive force** to keep protons away from each other.]

Almost all the elements heavier than bismuth (Bi with atomic mass number, N_A, of 209 and atomic number, N_Z, of 83) have an unstable nucleus, so-called **heavy nuclides**. Some heavy radionuclides exist that fission (split) better, so they are used in nuclear medicine, nuclear power plant, and nuclear weapons. Plutonium-209 (Pu-209; with N_A of 209 and N_Z of 84) and uranium-235 (U-235; with N_A of 235 and N_Z of 92) are common examples of heavy radionuclides. Consider U-235 with N_A of 235 (it has 235 protons and neutrons) and N_Z (the number of protons) of 92. Thus, the number of its neutrons will be 235 – 92 = 143. This is too many neutrons compared with protons, making U-235 a strong (unstable) nuclide.

The strength of radioactivity in a radionuclide is related to the following:

- The size of its nucleus (the *larger* the nucleus, the *less* stable it is, so it has more desire to split).
- The half-life of the radionuclide (the *shorter* the half-life, the *greater* is its radioactivity). [For a radionuclide, half-life ($t_{1/2}$) is the time (t) it takes for half of it to decay.]

When U-235 decays, it produces protactinium-231 (Pa-231) and actinium-227 (Ac-227). Here, U-235 is the **parent nuclide** (the decay origin), and Pa and Ac are the **daughter nuclides** (the decay products).

R-8

RADIOACTIVE HALFLIFE

Discussed under HALF LIFETIME.

R-9

RADIOACTIVE ISOTOPES

Another name for RADIOACTIVE ELEMENTS.

R-10

RADIOACTIVE RADIATION

Radioactive radiation (simply **radiation**) is the process of releasing (emitting) electromagnetic radiations (EM radiations or EM waves) from the atoms of a radioactive element (simply **radionuclide**). Because radionuclides have an unstable nucleus, they decay and cause the release of radioactive radiation (such as alpha particles, beta particles, and gamma particles) and energy. [The term **non-radioactive radiation** is also used in physics to refer to the transfer of light energy, heat energy, and radio waves.]

The following are important to know about radiation:

- It is released when a nuclear decay (splitting the nucleus of an atom) occurs,
- Nuclear decay is splitting the nucleus of an atom, causing the release of radioactive radiation. The rays (beams) of radioactive particles may be visible or invisible to a human's eye.

Unlike cathode rays (electro-negatively-charged electrons), radioactive rays (electro-negatively-charged particles) have the following properties:

- They are *not* deflected by either an electric field or a magnetic field, and
- They can pass through an opaque medium (because of their high penetration ability).

Radiations are of two types:

- **Ionizing Radiation:** This type of radiation creates a considerable amount of ionizing radiation and heat energy (E_Q). For example, when radium (Ra) decays, ionizing radiation and E_Q are its products.
- **Nonionizing Radiation:** It creates *no* ionizing radiation and releases much less E_Q, comparatively, during its decay, and is less damaging to living organisms per unit of energy. For example, the Sun's rays (which release nonionizing radiations) can also damage a living organism. **Sunburn** on a human face is the effect of mild nonionizing radiation, although nearly the entire Sun's ultraviolet rays are absorbed by the atmosphere. [Blackbody radiation is also radiation emitted (radiated) by a perfect absorber of EM radiation.]

R-11

RADIOACTIVE WASTES

A radioactive waste (also called **nuclear waste**) is a radioactive element (radionuclide or simply **nuclide**) discharged after primary use in a nuclear facility, such as a nuclear power plant, a nuclear medicine plant, and a uranium enrichment plant.

Four (4) brief but important points about radioactive wastes are step-outlined next.

- They are hazardous to all life forms and the environment (because they decay over a long period).
- They are regulated by government agencies to protect life and the environment.
- They can NOT be recycled (because they are single-use materials).
- Their handling management requires enormous care and skill.

[Note: In the US of America, Yucca Mountain in Nevada was selected for the centralized disposal of high-level nuclear wastes. In that country, the Office of Health, Safety, and Security of the Department of Energy can be contacted at www.hss.energy.gov/NuclearSafety/techstds/standard/standard.html for information about the safety of nuclear wastes.]

Most radionuclides undergo a long period of decay before reaching stability and harmlessness. The time for a radionuclide to decay into a stable and harmless element determines how long nuclear waste remains radioactive. Some radionuclides (such as plutonium) remain hazardous to all forms of life for many years (the half lifetime of Pu-239 is 24 000 years).

It is possible to separate residual radioactive elements from non-radioactive ones and reuse them as fuel in a nuclear facility (like a nuclear power plant). This helps to reduce the amount of nuclear waste.

R-12

RADIOACTIVITY

Radioactivity is the decayed product of a radioactive element (also called a **radioactive isotope**, **radioactive nuclide**, or simply **nuclide**). When a radioactive element (an element with an unstable nucleus) decays (breaks apart), it creates radioactivity. In nature, most radioactive elements undergo (go under) a long period of decay before reaching stability and harmlessness. The time (t) it takes for a nuclide (a radioactive element) to fall to its half value is called radioactive half lifetime ($t_{1/2}$, simply **halflife**). The time for a nuclide to decay into a stable and harmless element determines how long nuclear waste remains radioactive.

As a nuclide undergoes a nuclear decay (simply **decay**), its nucleus releases energy in the form of alpha particles, beta particles, and gamma particles. Alpha particles have the weakest **penetrability** of the three, so they can be stopped by a sheet of paper. A thin aluminum plate stops beta particles. Gamma particles partly stop and partly penetrate a thick lead plate, so they are strong hazards!

[Historical Note: Radioactivity was discovered in the 1880s by Henry Becquerel (1852–1908, French physicist), Marie Curie (1867–1934, Polish-French physicist and chemist), and Pierre Curie (1859–1906, French physicist). Pierre and Marie Curie lived moderately to fund their research.]

R-13

RADIONUCLIDES

Another name for RADIOACTIVE ELEMENTS.

R-14

RAFFINATE

Study EXTRACT AND RAFFINATE.

R-15

RAOULT'S LAW OF VAPOR PRESSURE

Discussed under VAPOR PRESSURE AND RAOULT'S LAW OF VAPOR PRESSURE.

R-16

RATE

The word rate in ChemEng is used when a physical quantity (simply **quantity**) is expressed per unit time (*t*). Speed (distance per time) and flux rate (a quantity per unit area per unit time) are examples of rates.

R-17

RASCHIG RINGS

A Raschig ring (after its inventor F. Raschig, a German chemist) is a small piece of a round tube made of ceramic or metal, approximately 25 mm (= 1 In) in length and diameter. The Raschig rings are mostly used as random packing in a packed distillation column, in the entrainment separator of a gas scrubber, or in some other equipment. [Figure 5 under DISTILLATION COLUMNS shows the Raschig rings.]

R-18

REACTIONS

See CHEMICAL REACTIONS.

R-19

REACTION ORDER

See CHEMICAL REACTION ORDER.

R-20

REACTION RATE

See CHEMICAL REACTION RATE.

R-21
REACTIVITY

Reactivity (refers to chemical reactivity) is the tendency of a chemical substance to undergo a chemical reaction (simply **reaction**), either by itself or with other substances. A substance's chemical reactivity depends on some conditions, including the following: 1) Type of the substance (or substances) it reacts, 2) Chemical reaction rate it goes through, and 3) Temperature (*T*) of the reaction.

R-22
REACTORS

Study CHEMICAL REACTORS.

R-23
REAGENTS

Study CHEMICAL REAGENTS.

R-24
REAL GASES

Study IDEAL, REAL, AND PERFECT GASES.

R-25
REBOILERS

Discussed under STEAM BOILERS AND STEAM REBOILERS.

R-26
RECIRCULATION PROCESS

Study CIRCULATION, RECIRCULATION, AND RECYCLING PROCESSES.

R-27
RECYCLING PROCESS

Study CIRCULATION, RECIRCULATION, AND RECYCLING PROCESSES.

R-28

REDUCING REACTIONS

Study OXIDATION REDUCTION REACTIONS.

R-29

REFERENCE SYSTEM

A reference system (also called **reference frame** or **frame of reference**) is a coordinating system used to express the properties of a moving system. For example, when measuring a moving system's speed (U), we need to specify a reference system according to the speed measurement. In this case, a motionless observer on the ground is the best reference to be chosen because

- Earth does *not* move relative to a moving system, and
- Earth does *not* accelerate by force (F) other than gravitational force (F_g).

To express why we need to choose a reference system, assume that

- A train is traveling at a steady speed of 80 km/h (50 Mi/h),
- Lexi walks inside the train at 3 km/h (about 2 Mi/h),
- Betty seats on a seat inside the train, and
- Caleb stands on the ground observing the train, Lexi, and Betty.

Referring to these assumptions, we can say,

- Lexi's speed relative to Betty is 3 km/h,
- Lexi's speed relative to the train is 3 km/h,
- Lexi's speed relative to Caleb is 83 km/h,
- Betty's speed relative to Caleb is 80 km/h.

Based on these assumptions, we can say

- The train is the reference system when expressing Lexi's speed relative to Betty,
- Betty is the reference system when expressing Lexi's speed relative to the train,
- The ground is the reference system when expressing Lexi's speed relative to Caleb,
- The ground is the reference system when expressing Betty's speed relative to Caleb, and
- Lexi, Betty, and Caleb are in a nonaccelerating reference system, which is under the F_g effect.

R-30

REFLECTION

Study REFRACTION AND REFLECTION.

R-31

REFLUX

Study DISTILLATE REFLUX.

REFRACTION, REFLECTION, AND DIFFRACTION OF LIGHT

When a light ray (a thin beam of light or several waves of light) hits (strikes) the surface of a medium, it can be refracted (if the surface of the medium is a boundary between two fluids), reflected (if the surface of the medium is solid), or both (if the surface of the medium is transparent). During transmission, both refraction and reflection occur because the speed of light is different in different media (light travels through water *slower* than through air). The next explanations make the differences between these three words easier.

Refraction of Light: Light refraction is the bending of a light ray when it passes from one medium to another. Light refraction (light bending) usually happens at the boundary between two media (see Figure 1). For example, a light ray slightly bends when it passes from air to water (see the same figure). Here, the ray's **refraction angle** is *smaller* than its **incident** (incoming) **angle** (because light moves in the air *faster* than in water). When, instead, the ray passes from water to air, the angle of refraction is *larger* than the angle of incidence (because light moves in water *slower* than in air). Thus, the light's refraction angle is *not* equal to its incident angle (angle of incidence) unless a light ray moves from a medium to the same medium. [When a light ray hits a medium, the amount it refracts can be determined by the refractive index (R_I) of that medium. The R_I of a medium is determined by the speed of light constant (c, speed of light in a vacuum) divided by the light's speed in that medium.]

Reflection of Light: Light reflection is the returning (bouncing back) of a light ray at the same angle as the ray hits the surface of a solid medium. For example, when a light ray shines at 35 degrees to the surface of a mirror, it also reflects at that angle. Thus, the light's reflection angle equals its incoming (incident) angle (see Figure 2). Figure 3 shows both the refraction and reflection of a light ray through a transparent boundary.

Diffraction of Light: Light diffraction is the spreading of the light rays when they pass through an aperture (opening), as shown in Figure 4, or when they pass around an obstacle (barrier or blockade).

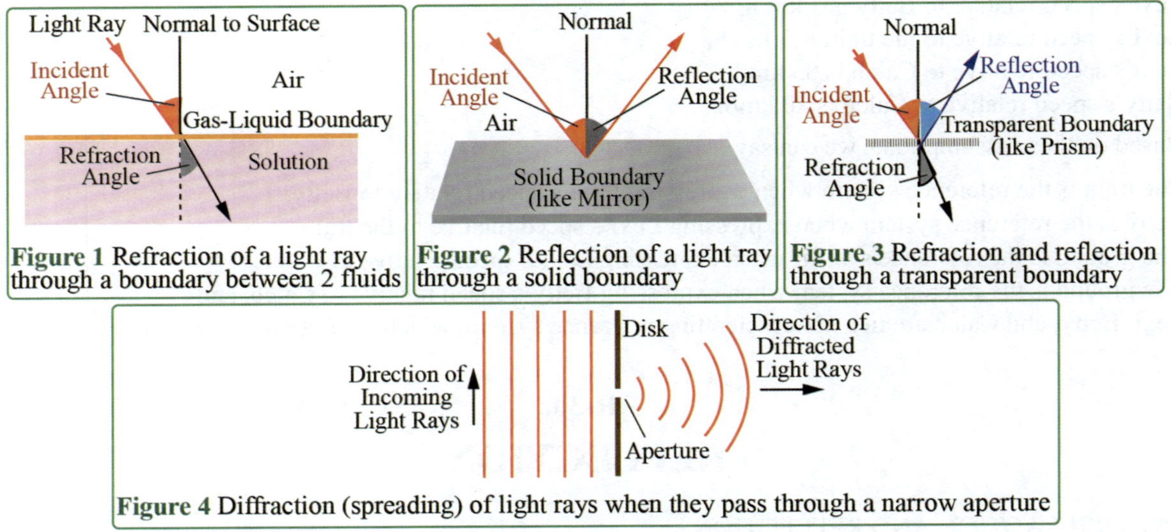

Figure 1 Refraction of a light ray through a boundary between 2 fluids

Figure 2 Reflection of a light ray through a solid boundary

Figure 3 Refraction and reflection through a transparent boundary

Figure 4 Diffraction (spreading) of light rays when they pass through a narrow aperture

R-33

REFRACTIVE INDEX

The refractive index (R_I, also called the **index of refraction**) of a medium is the ratio of the speed of light in a vacuum to that in that medium (see Figure 1). When a beam (ray) of light hits a different medium, the amount it bends (refracts) can be determined by the R_I of both media. Since the speed of light in a vacuum is constant, the R_I of a medium is determined by the speed of light constant (c, the speed of light in a vacuum) divided by the light's speed (U_L) in that medium.

$$R_I = \frac{c}{U_L} \qquad (1)$$

The R_I is greater than 1 for all normal substances. For example, the R_I of water is 1.333, meaning that light travels 1.333 times faster in a vacuum than in water. And the R_I of glass is about 1.5.

[Note: The term refraction is used when a light ray (a thin beam of light) is refracted (bent). And the term reflection is used when a light's beam hits the surface of a medium.]

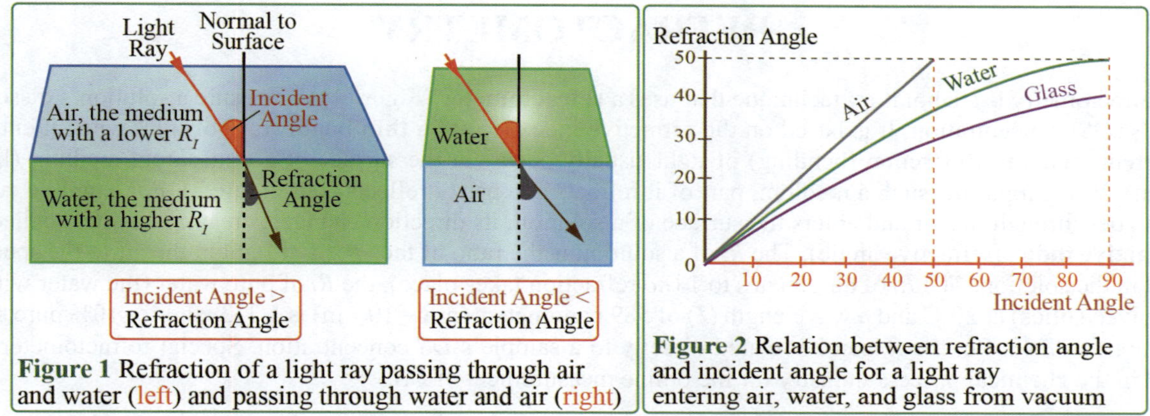

Figure 1 Refraction of a light ray passing through air and water (left) and passing through water and air (right)

Figure 2 Relation between refraction angle and incident angle for a light ray entering air, water, and glass from vacuum

As seen in Figure 1, the R_I is measured in relation to a **normal-to-the-surface** (simply **normal**). Light always bends toward the normal when it enters a medium with a higher R_I and bends away when it enters a medium with a lower R_I. When the light's **angle of incidence** relative to the normal is zero, the amount of bending is zero (*no* refraction), so $R_I = 1$. As the angle of incidence *increases* relative to the normal, the amount of bending *increases*, so the R_I *increases*. Figure 2 shows the relation between the **angle of incidence** (incident angle) and the **angle of refraction** (refractive angle) when a ray of light enters the air, water, or glass from a vacuum medium.

[Refractometry, a laboratory method for measuring the amount of dissolved solids in a solution, is based on the R_I of solutions.]

R-34

REFRACTOMETRIC DISSOLVED SOLIDS

A refractometric dissolved solid (*RDS*, also called refractometric dissolved solid) consists of soluble (non-filterable) and insoluble (filterable) molecules in a solution. Because solution samples are usually tested for dissolved solids by refractometry, the dissolved solids are called the refractometric dissolved solids (*RDS*). In refractometric tests, samples are filtered to remove suspended solids (filterable solids) before being tested by the refractometer. The *RDS* is expressed in mass percentage (see PERCENTAGES).

[Note: Instead of the term **refractometric dissolved solids** (*RDS*), the term Brix is still used incorrectly by some authors. The term Brix is *not* recommended because it is *not* a self-defined word. Although the three terms *RDS*, soluble solid, dissolved solid, and dry substance are used equally to indicate the same meaning but are different. *RDS*, **soluble solid**, and **dissolved solid** are correct terms when referring to just **nonfilterable solids** of a solution. The **dry substance** refers to a solution's **nonfilterable-and-filterable solids**.]

R-35

REFRACTOMETRY

Refractometry is a laboratory technique that uses a **refractometer** (Figure 1) to measure a solution's dissolved solids (*DS*) concentration. It is based on the refractive index (R_I) of a **thin beam** (ray) of light when it enters a different medium. Refraction (bending) of light usually occurs at the surface of a transparent medium (like a prism). When light hits such a medium, part of it refracts and partly reflects (see Figure 2). For example, as the light goes through the air and enters the surface of a solution, its direction changes, creating an angle called the **refractive index** (refractive angle). The R_I of a solution is the ratio of the speed of light in the air to the speed of light in the solution. The R_I of air equates to 1 (*no* refraction takes place), the R_I of pure water (the water with *no* dissolved solids) at 20°C and a wavelength (λ) of 589 nanometers (nm = 10^{-9} m) is 1.333, and for 10% pure sugar solution is 1.348. So, the R_I can be related directly to a sample's *DS* concentration. Special refractometers are used in the chemical process industry for the online measurement of *DS*.

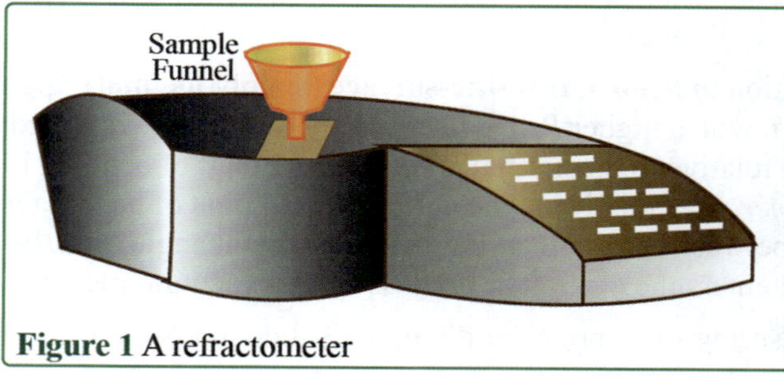

Figure 1 A refractometer

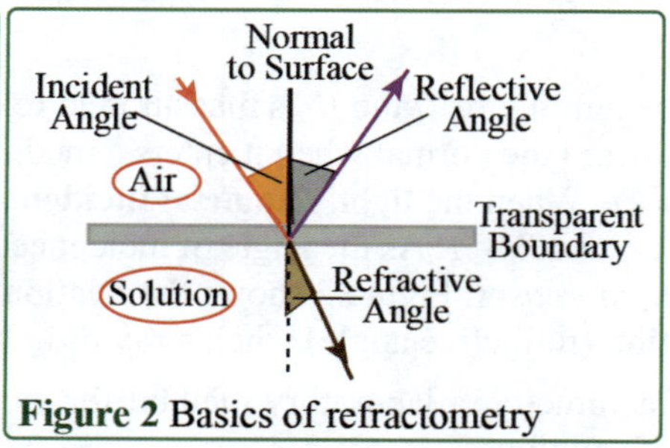

Figure 2 Basics of refractometry

The following affect the R_I:

- Temperature (*T*) of the sample
- Concentration (*C*) of the sample, and
- Wavelength (λ) of the light that strikes the solution.

In refractometry, the *T* and λ are usually kept constant, so the R_I can be calibrated to indicate a sample's dissolved solid content.

R-36
REGENERATION REACTION

Defined under CHEMICAL REACTIONS.

R-37
REGENERATIVE BRAKING SYSTEM

A regenerative braking system is a technique that can recover part of the energy (E) of a motor (like an electric vehicle) by converting the system's mechanical energy (E_M) into E that can be either used immediately or stored until needed. Most of today's **battery electric vehicles** (BEVs) are equipped with a regenerative braking system that uses the vehicle's momentum ($p = M.V$, where M is mass and V is velocity) to recover E that would be, otherwise, lost (dissipated), as heat energy (E_Q), in a conventional vehicle with a disc-braking system. In a vehicle with a **dynamic braking system**, the excess E is recovered but is immediately lost as E_Q in resistors. And in a BEV with a regenerative braking system, the excess E is recovered as its basket's rotational velocity (ω) slows and is stored in the electric batteries. In addition to reducing the net electricity usage, a regenerative braking system can extend the parts' lifetime, as parts do *not* wear as quickly as in a non-regenerative braking system. Similarly, the E is recovered in a batch centrifuge as its basket's ω slows.

R-38
REGRESSION OF DATA

Regression of data (simply **regression**) is a mathematical method used to estimate the value of a dependent variable from the independent variable. A **regression equation** determines the **relationship** (correlation) between two (or more) variables. It is used in many mathematical applications, such as changing a table's data (variables) to a **computer-workable format** when the variables have a **linear** (proportional) **relationship**.

A regression equation can be **linear** or **nonlinear** with **positive** or **negative** correlation, depending on the relationship between the variables. When a linear (straight) line can show the relationship between two variables, Y (dependent variable) is a linear function of X (independent variable). A **linear regression** (when two variables have a linear relationship with each other) can be solved by common linear equation:

$$Y = aX + b$$

This equation tells us that

- The Y (dependent variable) is a linear function of X (independent variable).
- The a is the slope (steepness, the rise-to-run ratio or $\Delta Y/\Delta X$) of the regression line.
- The b is the line's **intercept** (the point of intersection); when $X = 0$, then Y equates to b.

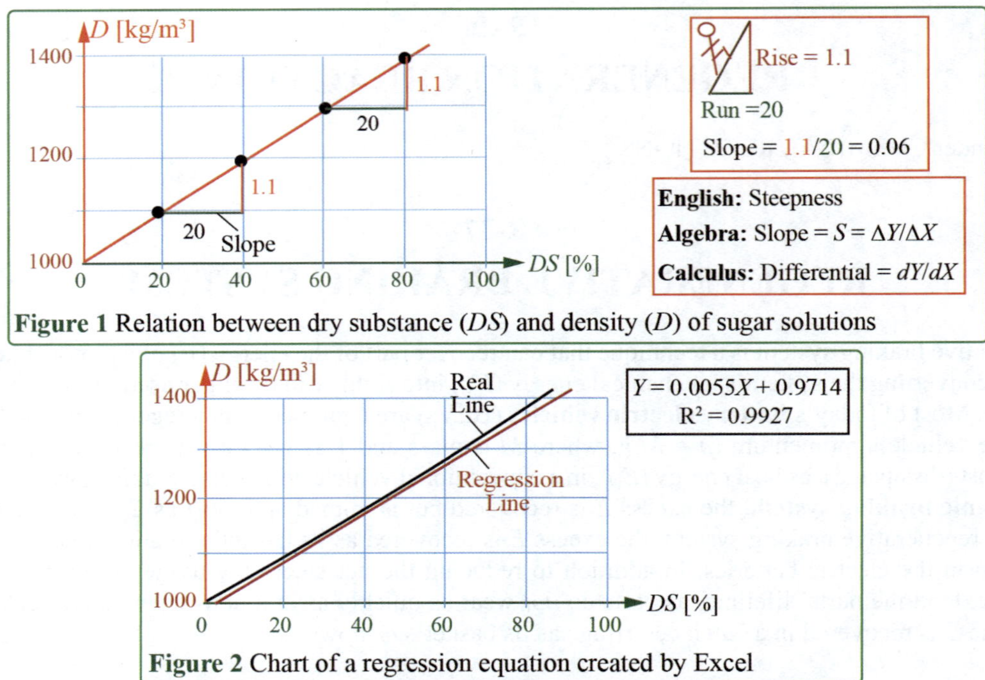

Figure 1 Relation between dry substance (*DS*) and density (*D*) of sugar solutions

Figure 2 Chart of a regression equation created by Excel

As an example, the amount of the dissolved solids (*DS*) of an ideal solution (like a sugar solution) has a linear relationship with its density (*D*) with high **linearity** (proportionality or correlation), as seen in Figure 1. Thus, we can determine the value of one variable by substituting the value of another variable into the linear regression equation. As a result, we are *no* longer dependent on the table to indicate the values related to these two variables.

Using Excel is the easiest way to determine a regression equation to indicate the related values (in our example, *DS* and *D*). For drawing a regression line in Excel, first create a **chart** (graph) of values on an Excel worksheet in the following way:

- Click "Chart Wizard" on the toolbar (the set of icons below the menus).
- Choose the "Chart type" options (say, bar, line, or *XY*) and then click "Next."
- Choose the "Chart source" by clicking the table, highlighting the data you want in the chart, and clicking "Next."
- Chose the Chart type, and then click "Next." [In such a situation, a scatter (*X*–*Y*) chart is one of the best ways to graph the data.]
- Choose the Chart location, and then click "Finish."

Then Excel can determine **R-squared** (R^2) value and **regression equation** as follow:

- Click the Trendline for which you want to display the equation and R-squared.
- On the Chart menu, click "Add Trendline."
- On the Options tab, select "Display Equation" and "Display R-squared."

The R^2 value indicates the linearity between the variables (the *closer* the value of R^2 to 1, the *stronger* is the linearity between the variables), so when $R^2 = 1$, the two variables have a perfect (absolute) linearity.

R-39

RELATIVE ATOMIC MASS

Discussed under ATOMIC MASS.

R-40

RELATIVE DENSITY

Discussed under DENSITY AND ITS TYPES.

R-41

RELATIVE HUMIDITY

Discussed under HUMIDITY AND ITS WAYS OF MEASUREMENT.

R-42

RELATIVE VISCOSITY

Defined under VISCOSITY.

R-43

RELATIVE VOLATILITY

Study VOLATILITY AND RELATIVE VOLATILITY.

R-44

RELAXING TIME

Relaxing time (t_R) is a term used in material and chemical engineering to indicate the time (t) needed for components of a chemical compound (such as glass or polymer) to adjust to the deformation forces resulting from a viscous flow. A relation between a compound's structural units and t_R exists (the *smaller* the structural units and the *less* strongly the units interact, the *shorter* the t_R). The t_R for glasses near their softening points is about 100 s. [Not giving enough relaxing time to a glass product during its production will cause it to break later.]

R-45

RENEWABLE AND NONRENEWABLE ENERGIES

Discussed under ENERGY AND ITS FORMS.

R-46

REPULSIVE ENERGY

It is discussed under Attractive and Repulsive Energies of ENERGY AND ITS FORMS.

R-47

RESILIENCE

R-48

RESIN

Short name for ION EXCHANGE RESIN.

R-49

RESISTANCE

A resistance (R, also called **resistivity**) is the ability of a system to resist its motion. It can also be defined as a physical property that acts as an opposing force (F) applied to a system's motion. For example, friction caused by a valve in a pipe is a resistance to the flow (motion) of a liquid flowing in that pipe. When the word **resistance** is used, the following three (3) impressions may occur in a reader's mind:

- Electric Resistance (R_E): It occurs in a system when an electric current passes through it.
- Thermal Resistance (R_Q): It occurs in a system when heat energy (E_Q) passes through it.
- Chemical Resistance (R_C): It occurs in a system when some of its chemical (or physical) properties (like color) are changed by a chemical substance.

To eliminate the confusion, it is recommended to use a **qualifying** (determining) **word** of **electric**, **thermal**, or **chemical** before **resistance**, such as electric resistance or thermal resistance.

R-50

RESISTANCE FORCE

Resistance force (F_R, simply **resistance**) is an opposing force (F) that is applied to a system by a machine for moving the system to a distance (L for length). Defined so, F_R is a force that can perform work (W) on a system. For an ideal (frictionless) system, in which *no* energy is lost, F_R obeys the following relation:

$$F_R . L_R = F_E . L_E \qquad (1)$$

Here, L_R is resistance length (distance), F_E is effort force, and L_E is effort distance.

Like most other forces, F_R is expressed in N (Newton) or pound-force (Lb_F).

R-51

REST MASS-ENERGY

Discussed under the topic of ENERGY AND ITS FORMS.

R-52

REST MASS

Rest mass is the mass (M) of an at-rest system. Because of mass-energy equivalency, some physicists use **rest mass** to refer to the rest mass energy (the energy of an at-rest system). All forms of energy act as rest mass energy when they are at rest.

R-53

REVERSE OSMOSIS PROCESS

Discussed under OSMOSIS AND REVERSE OSMOSIS PROCESSES and WATER SOFTENING PROCESSES.

R-54

REVERSIBLE PROCESSES

Discussed under the topic of CHEMICAL PROCESSES.

R-55

REYNOLDS EQUATION

Reynolds equation is used to calculate Reynolds number (N_R) or one of its dependents: liquid's density (D), liquid's average velocity ($\bar{V}$), liquid viscosity (η), and pipe diameter (d, usually inside diameter).

$$N_R = \frac{D.V.d}{\mu} \quad (1)$$

[The units in this equation are [(kg/m^3)(m/s)(m)]/[(kg/m.s)] = (~~kg.m^3.s~~)/(~~kg.m^3.s~~) = 1. As you see, the units cancel out, so N_R is a **unitless quantity**. Note also that the unit for viscosity is kg/m.s = Pa.s.]

Reynolds equation, as seen from Equation 1, is a ratio (a unitless quantity) of two forces, 1) The inertial force, which is a function of D (density), $\bar{V}$ (average velocity), and d () and 2) Viscous force (a function of η).

As was derived under the topic of LIQUID FLOW PROCESS, the mass flow rate ($\dot{M}$) of a liquid in a pipe is the product of the liquid's D multiplied by its volumetric flow rate ($\dot{V}$) or the product of the D, $\bar{V}$, and A (the pipe cross-sectional area = $\pi R^2 = \pi d^2/4$, where d is the pipe inside diameter)

$$\dot{M} = D.\dot{V} = D.\bar{V}.A = D.\bar{V}\frac{\pi.d^2}{4} \quad (2)$$

Substituting Equation 1 into 2 gives

$$N_R = \frac{D.\bar{V}.d}{\mu} = \frac{4\dot{M}.d}{\mu.\pi.d^2} = \frac{4\dot{M}}{\mu.\pi.d} \quad (3)$$

The units in this equation are cancel out: (kg/s)/[(kg/m.s)(m)] = ~~kg.s/kg.s~~ = 1

Notice that Equation 1 can be used for Newtonian liquids. For nonNewtonian liquids, the N_R can be calculated from the following equation:

$$N_R = 2^{3-n}\left(\frac{n}{3n+1}\right)^n \frac{D.V^{2-n}.d}{\mu} \qquad (4)$$

For Newtonian liquids (n =1), Equation 4 changes to a simple form of the Reynolds equation (Equation 1).

R-56

REYNOLDS NUMBER

Reynolds number (N_R, where N is for number and subscript R is for Reynolds) is a unitless number used to express the way a fluid (liquid or gas) flows in a system (say, in a pipe or a mixing body of a mixer). Because of using the N_R (a numerical value), we do *not* need to express a flow by qualifying words, such as smooth, intermediate, or rough. [The N_R has much more applications in the liquid flow (incompressible flow) than in the gas flow (compressible flow).] Based on the definition of N_R, incompressible flows (liquid flows) are classed into the next three (3) groups:

- **Laminar Flow:** This is a flow that moves smoothly at a steady velocity (V). In such a flow, a layer slides smoothly over another layer, so a low P (pressure) and V variations can occur. When the V of a laminar flow is great enough, a turbulent flow develops. A liquid that flows in a long pipe with a constant cross-sectional area, with *no* object on the flow stream, behaves laminarly. For example, a liquid laminar flow in a pipe has an N_R of 2100 or below.
- **Turbulent Flow:** This is a flow that moves roughly at a high and inconsistent V. A turbulent flow of a liquid in a pipe has an N_R above 4000. [This is a typical value, as some give the value of 5000.] Turbulent flow usually occurs in places where an object is in the way of the flow. When, for example, some fittings (like a partially-open valve, an elbow, or a tee) exist in the pipe, the flow behaves turbulently. An example of a turbulent gas flow is when wind mixes warm and cold air in the atmosphere. This effect, called **turbulence**, affects the airplane's movement during flight. In a turbulent flow, high variations of P and V occur. Thus, high circulations and eddies (see EDDY CURRENT) are formed in the flow stream.
- **Transitional Flow:** This is a flow between laminar and turbulent flow with the N_R between 2100 and 4000.

[The equation for defining N_R and the Reynolds values used for the flow of liquids in pipes are different than those used for liquid mixes in the fluid mixing process. For example, an N_R of 4000 or above indicates a turbulent flow in a pipe, while an N_R of 10^5 or greater indicates a turbulent flow in a mixer. The following values have been experimentally verified for N_R in the fluid mixing process:

- N_R less than 10 indicates laminar flow,
- N_R greater than 10^5 indicates turbulent flow, and
- N_R between 10 and 10^5 indicates transitional (in-between) flow.]

To demonstrate the laminar, transitional, and turbulent liquid flow in a pipe, consider Figure 1, which shows a smaller glass tube connected to a larger one. The smaller tube can discharge a fine stream of colored water to the larger tube, filled with just water. The valve for discharging colored water is adjusted during the test to change the flow rate. The colored water stream moves at a low flow rate, a straight-line-and-smooth way with *no* cross mixing, demonstrating a **laminar flow**. If we increase the flow rate of the stream, the dye starts to haze after reaching the water, showing that the stream now moves in a bit rough-and-circulated pattern, displaying a **transitional flow**. And at a higher flow rate, the dye starts to haze immediately after injection and spreads uniformly throughout the cross-section. The flow now moves in a rough-and-circulated way, displaying a **turbulent flow**. Reynolds equation considers two main forces affecting a flowing liquid in a pipe, the drag force (F_D) and the friction force (F_F, simply friction).

$$N_R = \frac{F_D}{F_F} = \frac{D.V^2.d}{\eta.v} = \frac{D.V.d}{\eta} \quad (1)$$

In more detail, N_R considers all four quantities that affect the behavior of a liquid flow process in a pipe. These quantities are the liquid's density (D), liquid's velocity (V), liquid viscosity (η), and pipe's diameter (d, usually inside diameter). Equation 1 tells us that the lower the F_D, the lower is the N_R, meaning that the flow moves more smoothly, such as when liquid moves in a pipe without being a solid object (like a valve) in the pipe. Figure 2 indicates the contribution of F_D and F_F of a flowing liquid in a pipe.

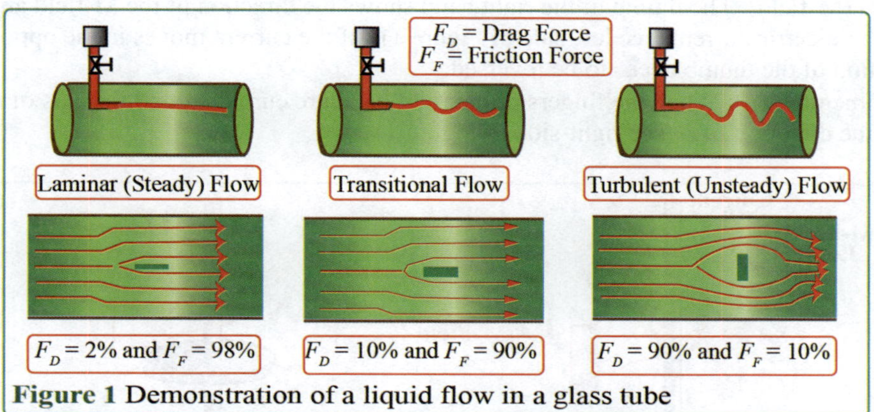

Figure 1 Demonstration of a liquid flow in a glass tube

An Example on N_R

Determine the type of a flow (laminar or turbulent) when it is a low-density liquid (with a density of 1050 kg/m^3 = 66 Lb/Ft^3) pumped from an open tank to another open tank located at a higher level.

Average velocity of the flow (V)	0.5 m/s
Liquid's viscosity (η)	2×10^{-3} Pa.s (2 Cp)
Pipe's inside diameter (d)	0.1 m (100 mm = 4 In)

$$N_R = \frac{D.V.d}{\eta} = \frac{1050\times0.5\times0.1}{2\times10^{-3}} = 26250 \text{ (turbulent flow)}$$

R-57

RHEOLOGY

Rheology is a branch of fluid mechanics. It studies the flow of fluids, particularly the liquids, and the relations between shear stress (S_S), which is the driving force of a liquid flow, and liquid viscosity (η), which acts as the opposing force of the flow.

R-58

RIGHT-HAND RULE

The right-hand rule (RH rule) shows the **direction** of a specific quantity by the thumb and fingers of the RH. A few versions of the RH rules are used in physics to indicate the directions of different quantities.

- Magnetic Field (M-field): The thumb of the right hand shows the direction of the M-field around a straight wire carrying an electric current (see left-side of Figure 1). [If the current moves in the opposite direction, then the direction of the thumb needs to be reversed.]
- Rotational Momentum (L): When the fingers of the right hand are curled around the axis of rotation, the thumb shows the direction of L (see right-side of Figure 1).

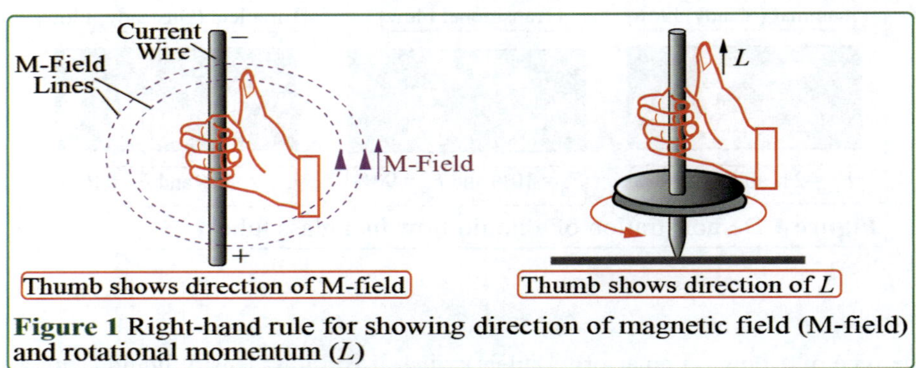

Figure 1 Right-hand rule for showing direction of magnetic field (M-field) and rotational momentum (L)

R-59

ROOM TEMPERATURE

The term **room temperature** (T_R) is used in science and engineering to refer to a temperature (T) of 25ºC (= 77 ºF or 300 K) or slightly less or more. The T_R refers to 22 to 24°C (= 72 to 75°F), a comfortable T for humans living at home.

Most of the time, scientific values are given as the standard temperature (T_S), which is, by definition, 0ºC (= 32ºF = 273K). [Sometimes, however, scientific values are given at 20ºC and considered at T_R.]

R-60

ROTATIONAL MOMENTUM

Study LINEAR MOMENTUM AND ROTATIONAL MOMENTUM.

R-61

ROTATIONAL VELOCITY

Discussed under the topic of SPEED, VELOCITY, AND ROTATIONAL VELOCITY.

R-62

ROUGHNESS

The term roughness (k, also called **roughness parameter**) is used in ChemEng to refer to the cleanliness of the inside wall of a pipe. A pipe whose inside wall is covered by a scale causing salt is called a rough pipe.

In general, even new-and-clean pipes have some roughness. Mathematically, roughness in a pipe is expressed by the **relative roughness** (k/d), where k is the pipe roughness (the height of a single unit of roughness expressed in m) and d is the pipe diameter (in m). Thus, k/d is a unitless quantity.

Figure 1 compares a smooth (clean) pipe with a rough (unclean) pipe. If a rough pipe is smoothed, the friction (f) is decreased. But, this limits because the further smoothing brings about *no* further decrease in f. New-and-clean pipes have close values of k. For example, the k of steel pipe is 4.5×10^{-5}, that of cast-iron pipe is 3×10^{-4}, and the k of galvanized-iron pipe is 1.5×10^{-4}. Old pipes and pipes covered with scale are rough.

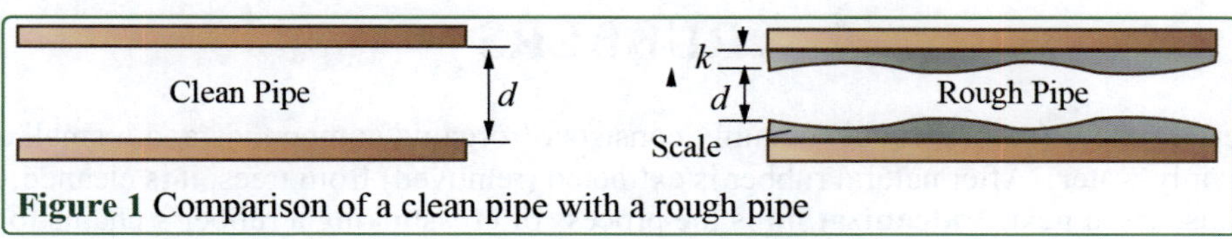

Figure 1 Comparison of a clean pipe with a rough pipe

R-63

ROUNDING NUMBERS

Rounding numbers (rounding figures) is the process of leaving the **significant** (meaningful) **numbers** and eliminating **insignificant** (meaningless) **numbers** in a set of numbers. Numbers (digits) are 0 to 9 (making all the numbers).

Significant numbers (significant figures) are the numbers of **certain digits** plus one **uncertain digit**. Assume that you are asked to determine a solution sample's density (D). To find this sample's D of, you need to measure its mass (M) and volume (V) and divide M by V. Further, assume that the sample's M, measured by an analytical balance, is 52.0022 g. And the sample's V, measured by a graduated cylinder, is 49.0 milliliter (mL). Here, M represents six (6) significant numbers, and V represents three (3) significant numbers, meaning the V value lies between 48.95 and 49.05 mL, but, by guessing, it is closer to 49. We, therefore, report the V as 49.0. [For right reading a liquid V in a cylinder, refer to the topic of MENISCUS.]

To find the sample's D, you usually use your calculator to divide 52.0022 by 49.0. The result is 1.0612694 (with 8 significant numbers, 7 certain, and 1 uncertain digit). Now, you want to know "how the result has to be reported?" The calculator knows nothing about **certainty**, but you know that even if you had an analytical balance and a graduated cylinder accurate to the seventh decimal place (there are *not* any), trying to measure a sample to that accuracy would be impossible. That's why the rule of **rounding numbers** must be used

Let us talk more about this example. Because the least accurate number in this measurement is 49.0 with three (3) significant numbers, the answer (1.0612694) should be rounded to four (4) significant numbers (or 3 decimal places). Thus, the sample's D must be reported as 1.061 g/mL (or g/cm^3).

Now, you need to know the irregularities of the number 0 in different places in a set of numbers and how to treat them. The following examples clarify these irregularities:

- Zeros between two nonzero digits are significant (508 has 3 significant numbers).
- Zeros after a nonzero digit are significant (say, 500 and 50.8 are 3 significant numbers).
- Zeros to the right of a decimal are significant (114.0; 11.40; and 0.**1100** all have 4 significant numbers).

- Zeros to the left of a nonzero digit are insignificant (0.0**45** has 2 and 0.000**408** has 3 significant numbers).

The rounding rules for scientific notations follow; 3×10^3 has one significant number, 3.0×10^3 has two significant numbers, and 3.00×10^3 has three significant numbers.

You must follow certain rules when rounding. Following are examples of rounding numbers to the nearest 0.01 number (to 2 decimal places): (1) 82.3436 rounds to 82.34, (2) 82.3466 rounds to 82.35, (3) 82.3450 rounds to 82.35, and (4) 82.3455 rounds to 82.35.

[Note 1: Rounding should be performed after all other calculations have been made: $12.3 \times 123.4 \times 0.012 = 18.21384$ rounds to 18 because 0.012 has only two significant numbers. In the same way, 123.456/48 = 2.572 rounds to 2.6.] [Note 2: To avoid mistakes, some scientific calculators have a **FIX** button that allows you to set the number of digits displayed.]

R-64

RUBBERS

As a polymer, a rubber (natural rubber) mainly consists of organic compounds and a small amount of other compounds (mainly water). After natural rubber is extracted (removed) from trees, it is cleaned, dried, and often vulcanized, as discussed next. **Vulcanization** is the process of crosslinking a rubber's chains together. It is performed by adding heat and sulfur (S), creating crosslinks (bonds) between the chains. [Vulcanization was invented by Charles Goodyear (1800–1860, a self-taught American chemist) in 1839.]

Vulcanized rubber exhibits unique chemical properties and physical properties. It is waterproof, with high elasticity and resilience. Vulcanized rubbers are mainly used in the production of tires for different vehicles. They are also used in rubber hoses, rubber belts, and more.

[Vulcanized rubber production in 2018 was around 30 million tons, from which about 74% was produced in Thailand, Indonesia, and Malaysia (which are the world's largest natural-rubber producers).]

R-65

RUSTING AND RUST

Discussed under the topic of CORROSION AND RUSTING.

R-66

RUTHERFORD

Ernest Rutherford (1871–1937) was a British physicist born in New Zealand. He won the Nobel Prize in chemistry in 1908 for the discovery of radioactive elements and radioactive half-lifetime. Rutherford, however, was *not* satisfied with the type of his prize and jokingly once said, "any prize other than in physics is like stamp collecting." As a Nobel Prize winner, he was given the title of Knight in 1914 and then Baron in 1931, which gave him a seat in the House of Lords in Britain. In 1919, Rutherford was appointed professor of physics at Cambridge and taught there until his sudden death at 65.

Rutherford was one of the two best experimentalists on atomic subjects to reach first-hand results (the other was Bohr). His gold-foil experiment discovered the atom's nucleus (see Rutherford's gold-foil experiment).

[Planck, Einstein, Rutherford, Bohr, Heisenberg, Schrodinger, and Broglie can be named as the top seven (7) quantum physicists. And Newton, Faraday, and Maxwell as the three (3) top classical physicists. The ten (10) pioneers contributed to physics more than all physicists combined.]

Rutherford explaining his gold-foil experiment, resulting in discovery of atom's nucleus in 1911 (illustrated for this book)

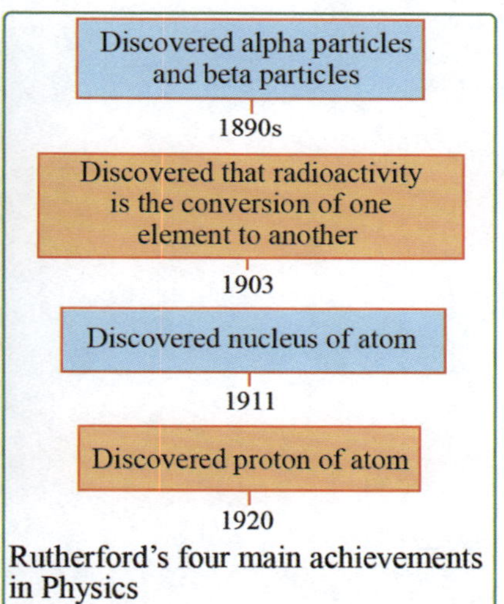

Rutherford's four main achievements in Physics

R-67

RUTHERFORD'S GOLD FOIL EXPERIMENT AND ATOMIC THEORY

Rutherford's Gold-Foil Experiment: In 1911, Rutherford discovered the **atomic nucleus**. Under the direction of Rutherford, two of his students pointed a beam of electro-positively-charged alpha particles at a thin gold foil. They observed the particles' reflection (bounce back) on a transparent screen when they hit the gold foil atoms. Because many particles passed through the foil with *no* reflection and only a few reflected notably (see Figure 1), Rutherford thought that a tiny dense point must be in the center of each atom. He called the atom's tiny dense center the nucleus. Based on his discovery of nucleus, Rutherford proved a few important points:

- Most of the atom's mass (M) is in its nucleus,
- Most of the atom's volume (V) is just space, and
- The atom's positive electric charge (simply **charge**) is in its nucleus.

He also determined, by calculations, the speed of the alpha particles by measuring their reflections in a known magnetic field. These data led Rutherford to calculate the approximate diameter of the gold's nucleus (almost 100 000 times smaller than its atom, meaning that an atom is an almost empty space.

[Note: The term refraction is used when a beam (ray) of light is refracted (bent). And the term reflection is used when a light's beam hits the surface of a medium. For example, a light ray refracts (bends) when it enters the water from a vacuum, while a light ray reflects (bounces back or scatters) when it hits a mirror's surface.]

Rutherford Atomic Theory: Rutherford suggested an atomic model based on his discoveries. [This theory is discussed under ATOMIC MODELS AND ATOMIC THEORIES.]

S Section

LIST OF TOPICS

1. Saccharides
2. Safety in ChemEng
3. Salt
4. Salvation Process
5. SATP
6. Saturated Air
7. Saturated Dry Steam
8. Saturated Gas
9. Saturated Liquid
10. Saturated Pressure
11. Saturated Steam
12. Saturated Temperature
13. Saturated Vapor
14. Saturated. Undersaturated, and Supersaturated Solutions
15. Saturation Coefficient
16. Saturation Pressure
17. Saturation Temperature
18. Saturation, Undersaturation, and Supersaturation
19. Scalar Quantity
20. Scale Causing Salts
21. Schrodinger
22. Schrodinger's Wave-Function Theory
23. Screening Devices
24. Screening Process
25. Scrubbers
26. Second-Order Reaction
27. Sedimentation Process
28. Self-Energy
29. Semiconductors
30. Sensible and Latent Enthalpies
31. Sensible and Latent Heats
32. Sensible and Latent Heat Transfer Processes
33. Separation Efficiency
34. Separation Factor
35. Settling Process and Settling Aides
36. Shaft Work
37. Shear Force and Shear Stress
38. SI Unit System and US Unit System
39. Siemens
40. Significant Numbers
41. Silicates
42. Silicones
43. Silos and Bins
44. Slope
45. Sludge and Slurry
46. Smog
47. Smoke and Smog
48. Sodium Carbonate, Sodium Chloride, and Sodium Hydroxide
49. Soft Water
50. Softening Process by Chromatographic Process
51. Solar Energy
52. Solid
53. Solid-Liquid Extraction Process
54. Solid Transfer Process
55. Solubility
56. Solubility Coefficient
57. Soluble Solids
58. Solutes and Solvents
59. Solution Crystallization
60. Solutions
61. Solvation Process
62. Solvent Cage
63. Solvent Extraction Process
64. Solvents
65. Soot
66. Sound and Sound Intensity
67. Sound Velocity
68. Space, Time, and Spacetime
69. Spacetime
70. Spacetime Principle
71. Special Relativity
72. Specific Conductance
73. Specific Density
74. Specific Energy
75. Specific Enthalpy
76. Specific Enthalpy of Evaporation
77. Specific Ideal Gas Constant

78. Specific Gravity
79. Specific Heat
80. Specific Heat Capacity
81. Specific Humidity
82. Specific Thermal Conductance
83. Specific Volume
84. Specific Weight
85. Spectral Lines
86. Spectrometry and Mass Spectrometry
87. Spectrophotometry
88. Spectroscopy and Mass Spectroscopy
89. Speed of Light Constant
90. Speed of Light Theory
91. Speed of Sound Constant
92. Speed, Velocity, and Rotational Velocity
93. Spin
94. Spin Number
95. Spin Quantum Number
96. Stable and Unstable Systems
97. Stainless Steel
98. Standard Ambient Temperature and Pressure
99. Standard Conditions
100. Standard Pressure
101. Standard Temperature
102. Standard Temperature and Pressure
103. Starches
104. State Quantities
105. States of Matter
106. Static Head
107. Static Pressure
108. Station
109. Steady and Unsteady Flows
110. Steam
111. Steam and Electricity Production Process
112. Steam Boilers and Steam Reboilers
113. Steam Economy
114. Steam Engines
115. Steam Ejectors
116. Steam Recompression and Vapor Compression
117. Steam Tables
118. Steam Traps
119. Steam Turbines
120. Steel
121. Stefan Boltzmann's Constant
122. Stereoisomers
123. Stirrers
124. Stirring Process
125. Stoichiometry
126. Stokes's Law
127. STP
128. Stream Layers and Stream Lines in Fluid Flow
129. Strength and Hardness of Material
130. Stress, Modulus, and Strain of Material
131. String Theories
132. Strong Nuclear Force
133. Subatomic Particles
134. Subcooling
135. Sublimation Point Temperature
136. Sublimation Process
137. Substance
138. Sucrose
139. Suction Head
140. Sugars and Sugar
141. Sulfur and Sulfur Dioxide
142. Sulfuric Acid
143. Supercritical Fluids
144. Superficial Velocity
145. Superfluids
146. Supersaturated Solutions
147. Supersaturated Steam
148. Supersaturation
149. Supersaturation Coefficient
150. Surface Energy
151. Surface Force
152. Surface Moisture
153. Surface Tension and Surfactants
154. Suspended Solid Particles
155. Suspension Solutions
156. Symmetrical System
157. Syngas
158. Synthetic Elements
159. Synthetic Natural Gas
160. Systems

S-1

SACCHARIDES

Scientific names for SUGARS.

S-2

SAFETY IN CHEMICAL ENGINEERING

Study PROCESS SAFETY OF CHEMICAL ENGINEERING.

S-3

SALT

Salt (also called **table salt**, with the chemical name of **sodium chloride** and chemical formula of NaCl) is a chemical compound consisting of 97 to 99% NaCl and usually some anticaking agents (like magnesium carbonate), which are added to make it free-flowing. Some other properties of table salt are:

- Its elements are connected by ionic bonds,
- It is an ionic compound (separates into ions),
- Its melting point temperature (T_{MP}) is about 800°C,
- Its particle density (D_P) is 2 165 kg/m^3 (= 135 Lb/Ft^3), and
- Its bulk density (D_P) is approximately 1 154 kg/m^3 (= 72 Lb/Ft^3).

[Note: Although both **table salt** and table sugar have some similarities, their chemical properties are opposite in most cases. Their opposite properties have some educational applications, as they are usually used as examples to simplify complicated topics. This author also followed this trend For instance, salt (an ionic compound) and sugar (a nonionic compound) are used in this book to compare their different behavior when they are dissolved in water.]

S-4

SALVATION PROCESS

The salvation process is the formation of a water cluster when several water molecules surround a nonionic compound molecule.

S-5

SATP

Abbreviated form of STANDARD AMBIENT TEMPERATURE AND PRESSURE.

S-6

SATURATED AIR

Defined under the topic of AIR, DRY AIR, AND SATURATED AIR.

S-7

SATURATED DRY STEAM

Discussed under the topic of VAPOR AND STEAM.

S-8

SATURATED GAS

Saturated gas is a gas that has the maximum (highest) amount of moisture content (the water vapor content, simply **vapor**) at a certain temperature (*T*). For example, a gas with 100% relative humidity at room temperature (around 25ºC = 77 ºF) is maximally saturated, reaching its limit at that *T*.

S-9

SATURATED LIQUID

The saturated liquid is a pure liquid at its boiling point temperature (T_{BP}) and has *no* vapor. [Although some use the terms saturated liquid and **saturated solution** equally, they are scientifically defined differently. A saturated liquid contains only one solute, while a saturated solution can have two (or more) solutes.]

S-10

SATURATED PRESSURE

Saturated pressure (also called **saturation pressure**) is the pressure (*P*) at which a phase has reached its **maximum limit** at a given temperature (*T*). At saturated *P*, a phase is saturated (at saturation), so a liquid starts to evaporate, or a vapor condenses.

S-11

SATURATED STEAM

Discussed under the topic of VAPOR AND STEAM.

S-12

SATURATED TEMPERATURE

Saturated temperature (also called **saturation temperature**) is the temperature (*T*) at which a phase has reached its **maximum limit** at a given pressure (*P*). At saturated *T*, a phase is saturated (at saturation), so a liquid starts to evaporate, or a vapor condenses. In other words, the liquid is at its boiling point temperature (T_{BP}), and the vapor is at its condensation point temperature (T_{CP}).

S-13

SATURATED VAPOR

The saturated vapor is a vapor that is cooled to its boiling point temperature (T_{BP}). The term saturated vapor commonly refers to saturated water vapor and is used in the same way as saturated steam (both terms are usually used equally). For example, saying a feed enters a distillation column as a saturated vapor means the feed is at its T_{BP} (boiling point temperature).

The enthalpy (H) of saturated vapor at a certain temperature (T) equates to the difference between the vapor's enthalpy (H_V) and the condensate's enthalpy (H_C). Both can be obtained from a steam table.

S-14

SATURATED, UNDERSATURATED, AND SUPERSATURATED SOLUTIONS

The words saturated solution, undersaturated solution, and supersaturated solution are often used in the crystallization process to refer to solutions with different solubility conditions, as defined next.

Saturated Solutions: A saturated solution is a solution whose solute solubility has reached its maximum (limit) at a certain temperature (T). At 20ºC, a saturated sugar solution contains 200 g of sugar (the solute) in 100 g of water (the solvent), as the maximum amount of sugar that can be dissolved in 100 g of water at 20ºC is 200 g (a two-to-one ratio). See Figure 1 under SOLUBILITY. At this T, the sugar molecules will neither crystallize nor dissolve, known as the **solubility-equilibrium condition**. If the sugar molecules crystallize or dissolve slowly, the crystallization rate is the same as that of dissolving in the solution.

Unsaturated Solutions: An unsaturated solution is that its solute's solubility has *not* reached its maximum yet, at a given T (see the same figure). For example, a solution containing 150 g of sugar in 100 g of water at 20ºC has *not* reached its solubility limit, so it is unsaturated (see the same figure).

Supersaturated Solutions: A supersaturated (oversaturated) solution is that its solute's solubility has passed its maximum at a certain T (see the same figure). Thus, a supersaturated solution contains more crystalable solute than normally dissolved in a **saturated solution**.

A supersaturated solution is *not* in equilibrium (refers to solubility-equilibrium) condition, so it is *not* stable. When stability has reached its saturation point, the solution remains the same until the T of the solution changes. If T is decreased, the solute will crystallize until the solution becomes saturated again at the new T. And if T is increased, more solute will be dissolved in the solution until a saturated solution is formed again. Say, sugar solubility at 30ºC is 215 g of sugar in 100 g of water, making a 68.3% sugar solution.

In summary, the main difference between undersaturated, saturated, and supersaturated solutions is their main solute concentration. An unsaturated solution contains the least amount of solute, and a supersaturated solution contains the highest.

[Note: Although some use the terms saturated solution and saturated liquid equally, they are scientifically defined differently. A saturated solution can have two (or more) solutes, while a saturated liquid contains only one solute; in other words, a saturated liquid is a purer solution.]

S-15
SATURATION COEFFICIENT

Discussed under the topic of CRYSTALLIZATION COEFFICIENTS.

S-16
SATURATION PRESSURE

See SATURATED PRESSURE.

S-17
SATURATION TEMPERATURE

See SATURATED TEMPERATURE.

S-18
SATURATION, UNDERSATURATION, AND SUPERSATURATION

Saturation, undersaturation, and supersaturation are general names mostly used in the crystallization process to refer to conditions (situations) at which a phase (or a system) has reached a certain limit at a certain temperature (*T*). These terms are individually defined next.

Saturation: Saturation (saturability) is a condition (situation) at which a phase (or a system) has been reached its maximum limit at a certain *T*. When saying, for example, a steam is at saturation, we mean it is saturated, so heating it to a certain *T* will produce supersaturated steam (simply **super steam**), and cooling it to a certain *T* will produce condensate. **Partial saturation**, instead, is the condition at which a phase is *not* completely saturated. At saturation, the main variables (temperature, pressure, volume, and flow rate) of a phase do *not* change with time, appreciably. Saturation, thus, is a stable condition.

Depending on the context, the term saturation is also used to indicate

- A condition at which a phase equilibrium occurs between a system's liquid and vapor phases at a given *T*.
- A condition at which maximum solubility of a solute in a solution occurs at a given *T*. Similarly, when air is at saturation, it contains the maximum amount of water at a given *T*. Thus, the water in the air evaporates into water vapor (simply **vapor**) at the same rate, at which the vapor condenses to water.

Undersaturation: Undersaturation is a condition at which a phase (or a system) has *not* reached its saturation limit yet, at a certain *T*. When saying, for example, a vapor is at undersaturation, we mean it has *not* reached its maximum saturation limit.

Supersaturation: Supersaturation (supersaturity action) is a condition at which a phase (or a system) has passed its saturation limit at a certain *T*. The word **supersaturation** is mostly used in the crystallization process to refer to the driving force (the cause) of the initiation of that process (crystallization *does not* initiate if supersaturation *is not* properly maintained). Instead, the viscosity (η) is the opposing force of crystallization (because it acts as a resistance against supersaturation).

In crystallization-related subjects, supersaturation can be specifically defined as the concentration difference (ΔC) of the solute between the supersaturated mother liquid (the liquid around crystals), in which a crystal (or a seed particle) is growing and the saturated mother liquid around the crystal. When a system is at supersaturation, its main variables (temperature, pressure, volume, and flow rate) change with time greatly. When, therefore, the term **supersaturation** is used, an **unstable condition** is meant.

[Note: A solution's **supersaturation** is the cause of crystallization in that solution, while the supersaturation coefficient is a numerical value that represents supersaturation.]

S-19

SCALAR QUANTITY

Study VECTOR AND SCALAR QUANTITIES.

S-20

SCALE CAUSING SALTS

Scale causing salts (SC salts) is a term used in this book (see the Note) instead of **limesalts**, **hardness**, or **limesalt hardness** to refer to the Ca and Mg salts present in a solution that can partly precipitate (↓) on a medium, such as a pipe or heating tubes of an evaporator. These salts cause the scale on a medium during service, particularly at high temperatures (T).

[Because mostly the soluble (non-filterable) salts of calcium (Ca) and magnesium (Mg) cause scaling (incrustation), these salts are known as scale-causing salts (limesalts hardness). Calcium sulfate ($CaSO_4$), magnesium sulfate ($MgSO_4$), and silicon dioxide (SiO_2) are common examples of SC salts.]

The SC salts are dissolved at moderate temperatures, staying in the solution even after filtration. In an evaporator or heat exchanger, SC salts precipitate (↓) on the heat transfer area because their solubility at the surface T is lower than at the bulk (under-the-surface) T. Because of low thermal conductivity (k_{Th}), the SC salts decrease the heat transfer coefficient (U_Q); in other words, they create resistance to the heat transfer process. During service, the thickness of the **scale layer** (scale-film) gradually increases until the evaporator or heat exchanger must be taken off the operation to clean their tubes (or plates). The scaling rate depends on the composition of the SC salts, T, and PH of the solution, containing these salts.

The SC salts can be generally divided into two groups:

- **Temporary SC Salts:** They mainly consist of carbonate (CO_3^{2-}), bicarbonate (HCO_3^-), phosphate (PO_4^{3-}), and hydroxide (OH^-) of Ca and Mg.
- **Permanent SC Salts:** They mainly consist of oxalate ($C_2O_4^{2-}$) and sulfate (SO_4^{2-}) of Ca, Mg, and Si.

The first group is the most-present components of SC salts (hardness) in the hard water (like the city or well water). Typically, **soft water** contains less than 17 PPM (or mg/L) of hardness (expressed as mg $CaCO_3$ per liter or PPM of $CaCO_3$).

Typically, hard water is classified into four (4) classes:

- **Slightly Hard Water:** It contains 17 to 60 PPM of hardness.
- **Moderately Hard Water:** It contains 60 to 120 PPM of hardness.
- **Hard Water:** It contains 120 to 180 PPM of hardness.
- **Extremely Hard Water:** It contains more than 180 PPM of hardness.

Although **hard water**, according to WHO (World Health Organization), has *no* known adverse health effects, its content (sometimes in a small quantity) creates some operating problems, such as in the operation of a boiler. The scale caused by SC salts can be removed from evaporators' or exchangers' tubes by regular acid cleaning. A special cleaning procedure is required to clean the SC salts from heating tubes. This subject is discussed under the topic of EVAPORATORS. SC salts can be reduced by using a **scale inhibitor** and increasing the velocity of the feed. If, however, the amount of the SC salts is high, their content can be almost removed from the hard water by one of the following methods:

- Water Softening Process by Chemicals, and
- Water Softening Process by Ion-Exchange Resin.

S-21

SCHRODINGER

Ervin Schrodinger (1887–1961) was an Austrian physicist who became an Irish citizen in 1948. He was the Nobel Prize winner in physics with Paul Dirac (1902–1995, British physicist) in 1933 for his work on quantum theory, known later as Schrodinger's wavefunction theory.

Schrodinger was a simple man (often dressed casually) but a genius physicist to be able to formulize the complicated subject of the wave-particle duality of the electron. In 1926, he published an article about his wavefunction theory to formulize the wave property of electrons, known later as **Schrodinger's wave equation** (Schrodinger's wave mechanics). This equation can numerically describe 1) The probability of an electron's location in a shell and 2) The relation of the electron's energy to its wave's wavelength (λ).

Schrodinger explains his cat analogy [illustrated for this book]

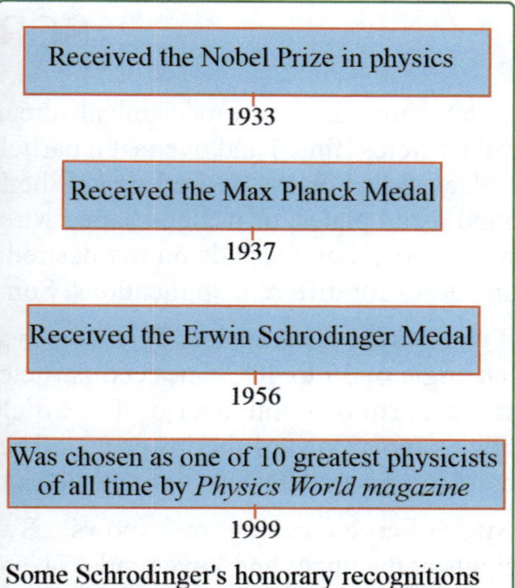

Some Schrodinger's honorary recognitions

In 1935, Schrodinger published an article to support his quantum theory and quantum superposition (simply **superposition**). To effectively explain the **paradox** (contradiction) of the superposition, he proposed a cat-and-decay analogy, whose illustration, a cat (known as the **Schrodinger's cat**) enclosed in a box, became famous. This thoughtful example became known as **Schrodinger's cat analogy** or **Schrodinger's cat paradox**. He assumed that a cat, a flask with a cat-killing poison, a radioactive source, and a radioactive detector (like a Geiger counter), are in an enclosed box (see the upcoming portrait). By these assumptions, he put a cat in a superposition of the following two (2) possible positions:

- **Alive Position:** If *no* atom decays, the detector does *not* detect any radioactivity, so the cat remains **alive**.
- **Dead Position:** If even a single atom decays, the detector detects the radioactivity and sends a signal to a small hammer to move and break the flask, releasing the poison to kill the cat.

Before observation, the system (the cat) remains in a double position, both alive-AND-dead at the same time. After observation, the system is in a single position; alive-OR-dead. Here, the observer's observation acts as a display to tell us the system's final position. In the real world, the observation works like a poison in the cat example by telling us when exactly a system's superposition ends, and reality collapses into one position (alive-OR-dead). [The word **collapse** used here refers to after being observed (measured).]

An electron is in a superposition condition until it is measured to see if it is in a higher-energy or a lower-energy shell. Schrodinger then used the cat analogy one step further in his wavefunction theory. [The Schrodinger's cat analogy is considered an effective example in quantum physics.]

[Planck, Einstein, Rutherford, Bohr, Heisenberg, Schrodinger, and Broglie can be named as the top seven (7) quantum physicists. And Newton, Faraday, and Maxwell as the three (3) top classical physicists. The ten (10) pioneers contributed to physics more than all physicists combined.]

S-22

SCHRODINGER'S WAVEFUNCTION THEORY

Discussed under the topic of ATOMIC MODELS AND ATOMIC THEORIES.

S-23

SCREENING DEVICES

A screening device (a mechanical screener) is used in the screening process to mechanically separate undersized particles (fines) and oversized particles (tails) from a **granulated feed** with different sizes, like sugar crystals. Depending on the desired size of the feed under screening, the screener screens are made from woven wire, slotted metal plates, or wedge-shaped wires. Some screeners use plastic cloth for fine screening. The size of the screen's openings depends on the desired size of the feed particles under screening. Screening devices are of many types for different applications. Some vibrate, some rotate, and some both.

Tyler Screener: A typical Tyler screener (Figure 1) creates vibrating movement, and its screen can be adjusted to an angle of 35 to 40º. The feed particles are fed at the screen's higher-end and spread over the entire screen surface, creating a thin layer of the particles. The screen's incline and speed (vibration rate) determine how the particles move toward the lower end. The screen is usually adjusted to move the particles at 1.0 to 1.4 m per second to pass undersized (fine) particles through the screen openings.

Sweco Screener: Figure 2 shows a Sweco screener that operates on a vibrating mechanism formed by two weights at the upper and lower ends. The top weight creates a horizontal-vibrating movement, and the lower one causes a vertical-vibrating movement, resulting in a two-direction movement.

In some screening devices, rotation occurs at one end and shaking at another. These types of screens are called **eccentric screens**.

Sifters (such as Rotex or Sweco types) are also used to screen granules. The **Rotex** screening machine consists of two screens and operates by a rotating movement. The screens, made from a special cloth, sit on an inclined frame. Several balls are located under the screens and bump against the frame to prevent blocking of the screens. The screens are replaced, cleaned by blowing air, and frequently checked for possible holes.

In general, the next three factors should be considered for the effective operation of a screening machine:

- **Inclined Screen Angle:** The screen must be adjusted to achieve a suitable rate of movement of the granules on the screen.
- **Vibration Speed:** The vibration must be adjusted to prevent the fast movement of under-sized particles because they *cannot* pass through the screen when the screen vibrates too fast.
- **Screen Cleanness:** The screen must be kept clean to prevent blocking of the openings.

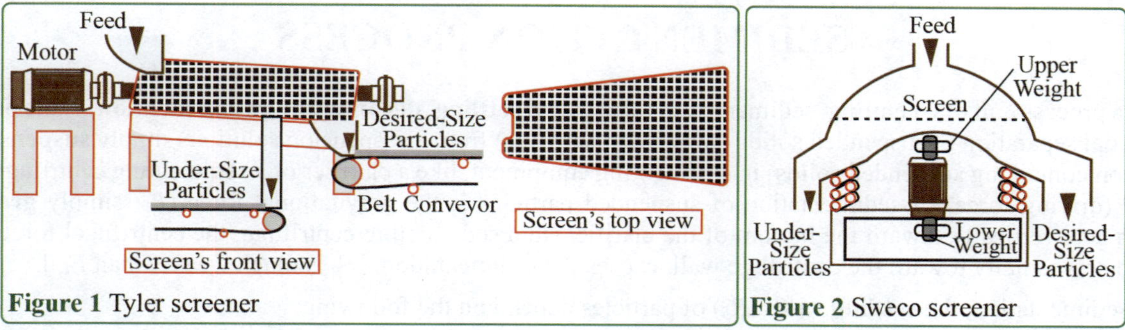

Figure 1 Tyler screener

Figure 2 Sweco screener

S-24
SCREENING PROCESS

Screening is of two (2) types: dry and wet screening. Under this topic, we will talk just about dry screening, so the word screening used here refers to dry screening.

As a process unit of ChemEng, screening (also called **mechanical screening**) is a physical separation process that uses a screening device (screener) to separate undersized particles (fines) and oversized particles (tails) from a **granulated feed** consisting of different granular size.

[A **granule** is defined differently in different branches of the chemical process industry, depending on the average size of the granules. For example, a granule is a sugar crystal of 200 μm (= 0.2 mm) to 1000 μm (= 1 mm) in the sugar industry. Granules are generally larger than sand and smaller than pebbles (gravels).]

The size of the screen's openings depends on the desired size of the coarse feed under screening.

Screening Efficiency: A screening operation can be evaluated by the screening efficiency (E_S), which can be calculated by using the feed's mass percentage of the undersized particles ($\%M_1$) and the product's undersized particles ($\%M_2$).

$$E_S = \frac{(\%M_1 - \%M_2)}{\%M_1(100 - \%M_2)} \times 100 \qquad (1)$$

The E_S and the laboratory screen test on the granulated-feed sample can comfortably determine the amount of out-of-specification (out-of-spec) of the screening process. The screen test on the 24-hour composite sample is usually performed in the laboratory of a chemical process plant.

S-25
SCRUBBERS

Study WET SCRUBBERS.

S-26

SECOND ORDER REACTIONS

Discussed under CHEMICAL REACTION ORDER.

S-27

SEDIMENTATION PROCESS

As a process unit of ChemEng, sedimentation (also called **settling**, **decantation**, or **clarification**) is the process of partial separation of suspended solids (suspended particles) from a suspension solution (simply **suspension**, a solution containing suspended solids) in sedimenting equipment, like a clarifier or a sedimenting centrifuge. The cause (driving force) of sedimentation of suspended particles is the gravitational force (F_g, simply **gravity**), which acts vertically toward the bottom of the clarifier. In a sedimenting centrifuge, the centrifugal force (F_C), which acts radially toward the centrifuge wall, causes the sedimentation. [F_g is much weaker than F_C.].

In sedimentation, the **settling rates** (R_S) of particles depend on the following:

- **Particle Density:** R_S is directly proportional to the density (D) of the suspended particles and the **density difference** (ΔD) between the particles and the suspension (the *greater* the D of the particles and the *greater* the ΔD between the particles and suspension, the *faster* the particles settle).
- **Particle Size:** R_S is directly proportional to particle size (the *larger* the particles, the *faster* they settle).

In addition, the input to a clarifier is directly proportional to its **settling area** (the *larger* is a clarifier's settling area, the *more* feed can be put in it and, consequently, the *more* particles can be settled).

A clear solution, which still contains fine suspended particles and a thickened liquid mixture (called mud or sludge, depending on the mixture's moisture content), is a clarifier or centrifuge (see Figure 1). [**Mud** is thicker than **sludge** and lighter than cake. Mud and sludge are flowable (pumpable), while the cake is *not*.]

Both sedimentation and filtration are particle-separation processes, so they have the same goal; separation of suspended particles from a suspension solution. Two major differences, however, exist between them:

- Sedimentation is a rough particle-separation process, while filtration removes finer particles.
- Sedimentation is caused by F_g, while filtration's driving force is the ΔP (pressure difference) between each side of a filtering medium.

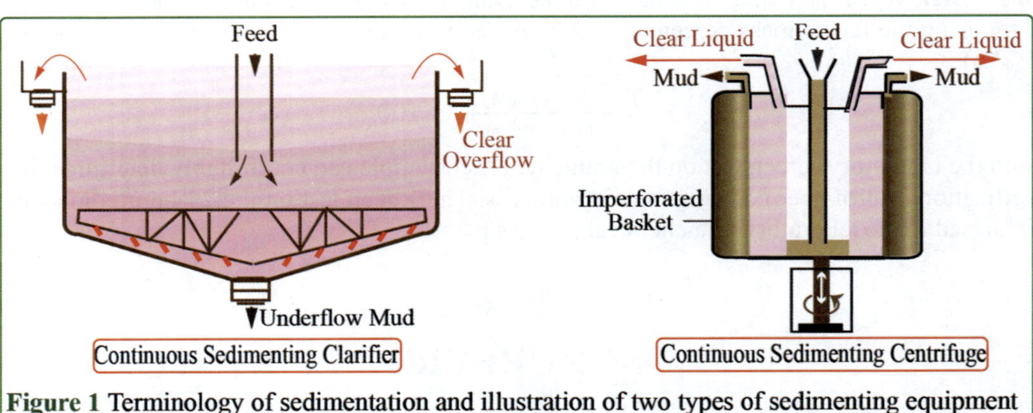

Figure 1 Terminology of sedimentation and illustration of two types of sedimenting equipment

Based on the type of settling equipment that is used, the sedimentation process can be classified into the following two major classes:

- **Gravitational Sedimentation:** This is performed in a sedimenting decanter (simply **decanter**), where particles are under F_g. In sedimentation under F_g, particles **settling** (sedimentation) **rates** are different (the *heavier* the particles, the *faster* they settle).
- **Centrifugal Sedimentation:** This is performed in a sedimenting centrifuge (discussed under CENTRIFUGES); suspended particles are under F_C. In this type of sedimentation, particles are under the same F_C, so their settling rates are fixed (settle at the same velocity). Comparatively, suspended particles under F_C settle much faster than those under F_g. In addition, centrifuges are more effective in separating the fine particles and are smaller in size for a given capacity. For these reasons, to a large extent, the sedimenting centrifuges have replaced the clarifiers in some chemical plants.

Sedimentation has different applications, including removing suspended particles from a wastewater stream. It is also used to separate two immiscible liquids. In general, sedimentation is performed for the following main purposes:

- **Clarification** of a suspension in a clarifier for removal of most of the particles, and
- **Classification** of a suspension in a classifier for separating particles into two fractions.

In a clarifier, the following three forces apply to particles to move them through a solution:

- Gravitational force (F_g, it acts downward),
- Buoyant force (F_B, it acts in the upward direction), and
- Drag force (F_D, it acts opposite to the direction of settling).

To better understand the movement (settling) of the suspended particles in a clarifier, consider Figure 2. At first, particles are distributed in the entire slurry to form one zone (the original zone). After some time, particles start to settle to the bottom to form a settled zone (the bottom zone) and a zone of clear solution on the top (the top zone). Above the bottom zone is a zone of unclear solution (the middle zone), in which the concentration of suspended particles is *not* like the top or bottom zone but still contains some particles. As settling continues, the top and bottom zones increase in depth, and the middle zone gradually disappears. Finally, almost all particles are in the bottom zone in a concentrated-and-compact form, generally known as **mud**.

A settling-rate test is required if we want to indicate the settling behavior of a sample graphically. Such a test is outlined next.

- Use a 1 L graduated cylinder, which is marked in cm (or inch) increments (see the left section of Figure 2),
- Fill the cylinder with a suspension sample,
- Mix the sample and let settle,
- Start timing the settling rate as soon as the sample shows the first sign of settling (a thin layer of the clear solution starts to occur at the top), and
- Record the height of the clear solution (the boundary between clear and unclear solution) in increments; say, at 2, 4, 6, and 8 minutes (depending on how fast the sample settles).

The graph, shown in Figure 3, indicates the clear liquid's height (h) in relation to the sample's settling time. As seen, the curve showing the rate of the early stages of settling is almost fast and constant. But, it starts to decrease when the middle zone disappears gradually. This slow pattern in the settling rate continues until the final height of the clear liquid is reached. At this point, the settling rate becomes almost zero. [Different suspension solutions have different settling rates, to the extent that the rates greatly vary. While some suspensions take a few minutes to settle, the others might take several hours to be settled. A coagulant (flocculent) can decrease the settling rate, notably. A coagulant is used in the sedimentation process to coagulate (to get together) particles. As a result of coagulation, the densities of particles become greater, so they settle at a faster rate.]

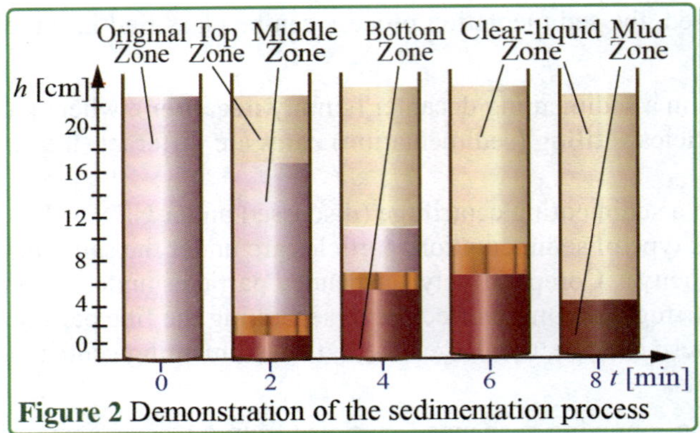

Figure 2 Demonstration of the sedimentation process

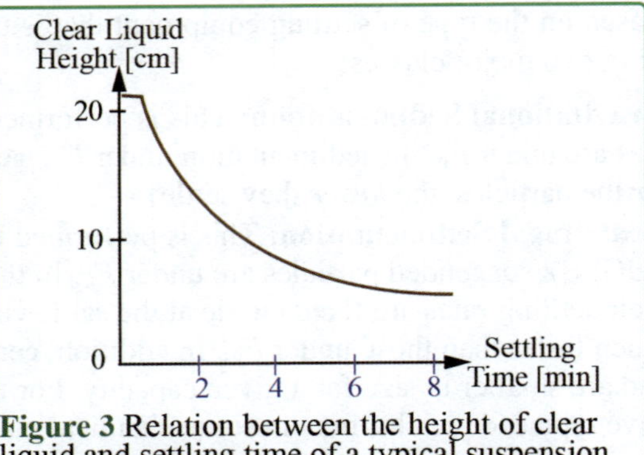

Figure 3 Relation between the height of clear liquid and settling time of a typical suspension

Consider a **gravitational sedimentation process** performed in a **clarifier** under F_g, and assume that suspended particles have a spherical shape with an average diameter of d. The **settling rate** (settling velocity, V) of particles, according to Stokes' Law, directly depends on d, D_P (the average density of particles), D_S (density of the suspension), a_g (gravitational acceleration, in m/s^2), and indirectly on the suspension feed's η (viscosity).

$$V = \frac{d^2(D_P - D_L)a_g}{18\eta} \qquad (1)$$

This equation tells us that V is proportional to d^2 (the *larger* are the particles, the *higher* are their settling rates). This equation can be applied to a particle settling in a suspension, where the suspension flow is quiet, meaning that its Reynolds number (R_N) is too small (less than 1). Such a flow is called **creeping** (extremely smooth) **flow**.

Equation 1 is also valid for calculating V for settling particles in a **sedimenting centrifuge** if the term a_g is replaced by the term a_C (centrifugal acceleration, in m/s^2), where $a_C = R.\omega^2$. Here R is the radius of the centrifuge's basket, and ω (omega) is the rotational velocity of the basket.

$$V = \frac{d^2(D_P - D_L)a_C}{18\eta} = \frac{d^2(D_P - D_L)R.\omega^2}{18\mu} \qquad (2)$$

In addition to the factors mentioned above, the following also affect the particles' settling rate:

- Feed's temperature (T),
- Clarifier's operating capacity, and
- Amount and type of coagulant that was used.

To control the operation of a given sedimentation process, the amount of the mud (X) and clear solution (Y), both in percentages, can be calculated. The X to Y ratio is called the **thickening ratio** (R_T). For this calculation, the density of the feed under sedimentation (D_1), the density of the clear solution (D_2, the product), and the density of the collected mud (D_3) are used.

$$X = \frac{D_3(D_1 - D_2)}{D_1(D_3 - D_2)} \times 100 \qquad Y = 100 - X \qquad (3)$$

S-28

SELF ENERGY

Study PARTICLE SELF ENERGY.

S-29

SEMICONDUCTORS

Study ELECTRIC CONDUCTORS, INSULATORS, AND SEMICONDUCTORS.

S-30

SENSIBLE AND LATENT ENTHALPIES

Sensible Enthalpy: Sensible enthalpy (H_{Sen}, also called **sensible heat** or **temperature-change heat**) is the enthalpy (*H*) of a heat source (like vapor) that is used in a sensible heat transfer process to change the temperature (*T*) of a substance but *not* its phase. Simply defined, H_{Sen} is the temperature-change enthalpy of a heat source. The heat coming from a home heating radiator is an example of sensible heat.

Latent Enthalpy: Latent enthalpy (H_{Lat}, also called **latent heat** or **phase-change heat**) is the *H* of a heat source (like steam) that is used to change the phase of a substance, but *not* its *T*. Thus, H_{Lat} is the phase-change enthalpy that is used to change a substance's phase during a temperature-constant period ($\Delta T = 0$).

Heat energy (E_Q, see Note 1) can change a system's *T* and phase (say, from liquid to vapor). Consider evaporation of a water-based solution (aqueous solution) in an evaporator that uses steam as the source of E_Q. First, a steam H_{Sen} increases the *T* of water until it reaches its boiling point temperature (T_{BP}), which is 100ºC at 1 Atm. From then on, this is the latent enthalpy of the steam that evaporates water to vapor. Here, part of the water in the solution changes to the vapor phase. At 100ºC and 1 Atm, the H_{Lat} required to evaporate 1 kg of water to vapor is about 2255 kJ. This means that the water's enthalpy of evaporation (H_E, also called **heat of evaporation** or **latent heat of evaporation**) is 2255 kJ/kg (or 970 BTU/Lb), where J is for joule and BTU is for the British thermal unit. This means we need 2255 kJ of E_Q to boil 1 kg of water. If, however, we decrease the *P*, less E_Q is required to boil 1 kg of water.

[Note 1: The term **enthalpy** (*H*) used here refers to the enthalpy change (ΔH), which has the same meaning as **heat energy** (E_Q) when a process occurs at constant pressure (*P*).]

[Note 2: Sometimes (say, in the evaporation process), the word **total enthalpy** (total heat-energy content) is also used to mean the sum of sensible and latent enthalpies when steam is used. In such a case, sensible enthalpy is the condensate's enthalpy, latent enthalpy is the vapor's enthalpy, and the **total enthalpy** is the system's enthalpy.]

In a latent (phase-change) process, latent enthalpy change (ΔH_{Lat}) is given as

$$\Delta H_{Lat} = M.C_Q = M(H_V - H_C) \quad (1)$$

In this equation, *M* is the mass of a liquid, C_Q is its specific heat capacity, H_V is the enthalpy of vapor, and H_C is the enthalpy of condensate. For example, in a heat exchanger that uses vapor to heat a liquid, H_E (enthalpy of evaporation) is the difference between the vapor enthalpy (H_V) and condensate enthalpy (H_C). Sometimes (for example, in the evaporation process), the **total enthalpy** is the sum of sensible and latent enthalpies. In evaporation, sensible enthalpy is the condensate or liquid's enthalpy, latent enthalpy is vapor's enthalpy, and **total enthalpy** is the steam's enthalpy.

S-31

SENSIBLE AND LATENT HEATS

Study SENSIBLE AND LTENT ENTHALPIES.

S-32

SENSIBLE AND LATENT HEAT TRANSFER PROCESSES

Sensible Heat Transfer Process: A sensible heat transfer process (temperature-change process) is a heating or cooling process during which the temperature (T) of a substance under the heat transfer changes, but its phase remains unchanged (Figure 1). Thus, a sensible process occurs under a non-constant-temperature period (ΔT # 0), where ΔT is for temperature change. Consider the heating process (a sensible heat-transfer process) in a heat exchanger that uses vapor to warmup a solution from 30 to 90ºC (= 86 to 194ºF), the portion of the enthalpy (H, simply heat energy), which is used to increase the solution's T is the vapor's sensible enthalpy. As another example, consider the evaporation of a water-based (aqueous) solution in an evaporator that uses steam. First, a portion of the steam H is used to increase the solution T until the water reaches its boiling point temperature (T_{BP}) of 100ºC at 1 Atm. This H is the steam's sensible enthalpy (a temperature-change enthalpy). And the portion of the H used to evaporate water to vapor is the steam's latent enthalpy (a phase-change enthalpy).

In a sensible heat transfer occurring in a closed system (energy can enter or leave the system, but mass *cannot*), sensible enthalpy change (ΔH_{Sen}) between points 1 and 2 with a tiny distance from each other can be calculated by integration.

$$\Delta H_{Sen} = H_2 - H_1 = \int_{H1}^{H2} dH = C_Q.\Delta T = C_Q \int_{T1}^{T2} dT \quad (1)$$

Here, T is for liquid's temperature, dT is a tiny change in liquid's T, dH is a tiny change in liquid's enthalpy, and C_Q is the liquid's specific heat capacity (simply **heat capacity**).

In a sensible heat transfer occurring in an open system (mass and energy can enter or leave the system), the liquid's mass (M) must be included in the previous equation.

$$\Delta H_{Sen} = M.C_Q.dT = M.C_Q \int_{T1}^{T2} dT \quad (2)$$

Latent Heat Transfer Process: The latent heat transfer (phase-change) process is a heating or cooling process during which the phase of a substance under the heat transfer changes, but its T remains unchanged (Figure 1). Thus, a latent process occurs under a constant-temperature period ($\Delta T = 0$). Condensation, crystallization, evaporation, distillation, and evaporative-cooling are involved in both T change and phase change.

In a latent process on a certain amount of mass (M), latent enthalpy change (ΔH_{Lat}) is calculated as

$$\Delta H_{Lat} = M.H_E = M(H_V - H_C) \quad (3)$$

In this equation, H_E is the enthalpy of evaporation, which is the difference between the vapor's enthalpy (H_V) and condensate's enthalpy (H_C).

Following are the three-phase changes caused by the latent enthalpy:

- Liquid phase to vapor phase (evaporation) or vapor phase to liquid phase (condensation),
- Solid phase to liquid phase (melting process) or liquid phase to solid phase (freezing), and
- Solid phase to vapor phase (sublimation) or vapor phase to solid phase (solid condensation).

Each of these processes occurs at a specific T. Evaporation occurs at the liquid's boiling point temperature (T_{BP}), melting occurs at the solid's melting point temperature (T_{MP}), and sublimation occurs at the solid's sublimation point temperature (T_{SP}). In evaporation, heat energy increases a liquid's T (sensible heating) until it reaches T_{BP}. Once T_{BP} has been reached, the liquid T remains constant until the addition of heat starts to evaporate a portion of the liquid to vapor (latent heating), as shown in the same figure.

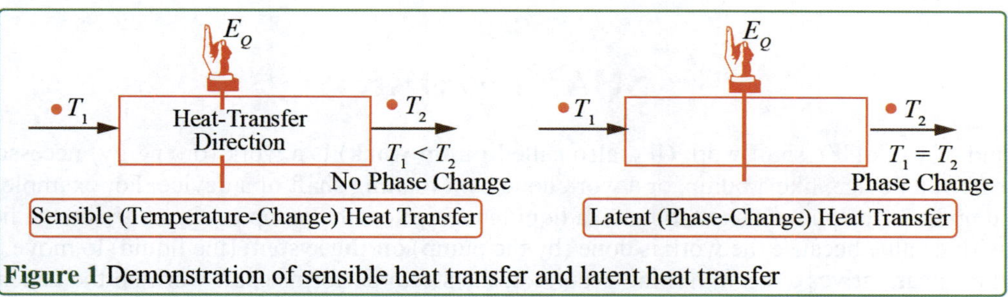

Figure 1 Demonstration of sensible heat transfer and latent heat transfer

S-33

SEPARATION EFFICIENCY

Separation efficiency (S_E, also called **separation factor**) expresses a separation process's efficiency (the *greater* the S_E, the *more* efficient is the separation process). In the distillation process (a separation process), S_E is defined to be the ratio of the concentration of a **lower-boiling component** (LBC, the component with lower boiling point temperature, T_{BP}, and higher volatility) to the **higher-boiling component** (HBC, the component with higher T_{BP} and lower volatility) in the **distillate** (the overhead product). When a binary liquid mixture containing LBC and HBC) is under distillation and the concentration of the components is expressed in molar fraction (a unitless quantity), the S_E is given as

$$S_E = \left(\frac{X_D}{X_B}\right)_{\text{LBC}} \left(\frac{X_B}{X_D}\right)_{\text{HBC}} \tag{1}$$

Here, $(X_D/X_B)_{\text{LBC}}$ is the molar fraction of the LBC in the **distillate** product (D) to that in the **bottom** product (B), and $(X_B/X_D)_{\text{HBC}}$ is the molar fraction of HBC in the bottom product to that in the distillate product.

S_E can be determined by the K_D (contribution coefficient) of a component from another component (the *greater* is the K_D, the *greater* is the S_E and, thus, the *easier* the components can be separated from each other).

Typically, S_E is in the range of 500 to 2 000. And S_E above this range indicates a sharp separation. [In distillation practices, the log of S_E is used, which is roughly proportional to the number of plates (N_P).]

S-34

SEPARATION FACTOR

Another name for SEPARATION EFFICIENCY.

S-35

SETTLING PROCESS AND SETTLING AIDS

The settling process is another name for the sedimentation process, so study SEDIMENTATION PROCESS. And coagulant is another name for settling aid, discussed under COAGULANTS-

S-36

SHAFT WORK

As one kind of work (W), shaft work (W_S, also called **pump work**) is a work (or energy) necessary to rotate (turn) the shaft of a device, like a pump, or a work done by a rotating shaft of a device. For example, the energy given to a pump turns the pump's shaft to move a liquid in a pipe, so the pump performs W_S on the liquid. Here, W_S has a **positive** value because the work is done (by the pump) **on the system** (the liquid) to move the liquid in the pipe. When steam drives a steam turbine generator, the steam performs shaft work on the generator. In this case, the shaft work has a **negative** value because W is done **by the system** (the steam) to drive the turbine's generator. Shaft work can be calculated as

$$W_S = 2T_R.\pi.n \qquad (1)$$

The T_R is the torque (a twisting effect of a force applied to a rotating system), and n is the number of rotations per time (t), known as RPM (rotation per minute or R/min).

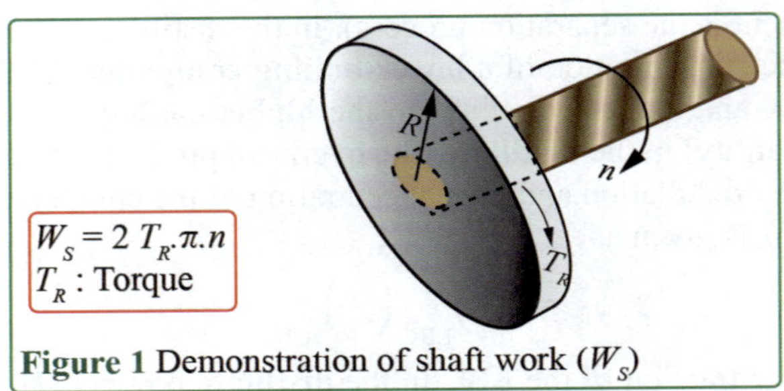

Figure 1 Demonstration of shaft work (W_S)

S-37

SHEAR FORCE AND SHEAR STRESS

Shear Force: It is discussed under FORCE AND SHEAR FORCE.

Shear Stress: Shear stress (S_S, in other references τ, Greek tau; simply called **stress;** also called **shear load** or **momentum flux**) is a force (F) that acts on the unit area (A) of a system's surface in a **parallel** way, as shown in Figure 1. [In physics, a force that applies in a parallel way is called shear force.]

In addition to F, stress can be occurred by other causes, such as pressure (P) or friction (f). When, for instance, a liquid is under an external P, each of its molecules is stressed by all the neighboring molecules. Like F, the stress can occur in any direction relative to a reference surface.

Numerically, S_S is expressed as a shear force (F_S, which acts parallelly) per unit area (A).

$$S_S = \frac{F_S}{A} \qquad (1)$$

The following are two main stresses:

- **Normal Stress** (simply **stress**)**:** This occurs when a system is under a **perpendicular force** (called **normal force** or simply **force**).
- **Shear Stress** (S_S)**:** This occurs when a system's face is under a parallel force (shear force).

[Note 1: Shear stress is usually symbolized by the Greek letter τ (tau) or σ (sigma). In this book, the symbol SS (one S for shear and one for stress) is consistently used to make it easier to remember.]

[Note 2: In the liquid flow process, scientists do *not* use normal force (F, simply force) but shear force (FS).]

Shear stress must act on a liquid to force it to flow, as shown in Figure 2. In a flowing liquid that moves in a laminar (smooth) way in a pipe, the S_S (which acts as the driving force of the flow) causes the liquid to move cross-sectionally (laterally, in XY direction). The S_S is proportional to the V/L through a proportionality constant called viscosity (η), which acts as an opposing force to the flow.

$$S_S = \frac{F_S}{A} = \eta \frac{V}{L} \tag{2}$$

In these equations, the F_S is the shear force applied to the flow, A is the cross-sectional of the pipe (the face area on which F_S is applied), η is the liquid's viscosity, V is the liquid's velocity, and L is the length between two points. Equation 2 tells us when the velocity gradient (V/L, velocity per length; also called **shear rate**) in a liquid flow is increased (by increasing F_S), S_S is increased in direct proportion (see Figure 3). So, we can say the velocity gradient is the cause of the shear stress, and shear stress is the cause of a liquid's flow.

The shear-stress equation can be written in the differential form (d form) to calculate a tiny change in S_S when applied on an infinitesimal length (the differential length, dL).

$$S_S = \eta \frac{dV}{dL} \tag{3}$$

[Usually, a negative sign is written on the right side of the shear-stress equation because viscosity acts in the opposite direction of the flow. S_S equation is the mathematical definition of Newton's Viscosity Law. Liquids that do *not* follow this equation are nonNewtonian liquids.]

In the S_S equation, if η is given in Pa.s, V in m/s, and L in m, the SI unit of S_S becomes in N/m^2 = Pa, which is the unit of P. If, similarly, η is in N.s/m^2, V in m/s, and L in m, the unit of S_S will again become N/m^2 = Pa. Thus, S_S is usually expressed in kPa (kilo Pascal). The US unit of S_S is pound-force (Lb_F)/In^2, usually abbreviated to PSI (pound per square inch).

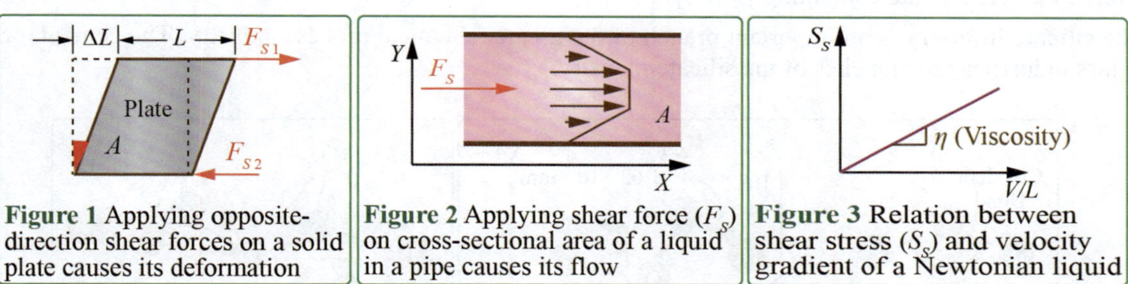

Figure 1 Applying opposite-direction shear forces on a solid plate causes its deformation

Figure 2 Applying shear force (F_S) on cross-sectional area of a liquid in a pipe causes its flow

Figure 3 Relation between shear stress (S_S) and velocity gradient of a Newtonian liquid

S-38

SI UNIT SYSTEM AND US UNIT SYSTEM

Discussed under the topic of MEASURING UNIT SYSTEMS.

S-39

SIEMENS

As the SI unit of electric conductance (K_E), the Siemens (S), which is named after German physicist Ernest Siemens (1816–1892), is defined as the reciprocal (inverse) unit of the electric resistance (R_E). S = 1/Ω = A/V, where Ω (omega) is for Ohm (the SI unit of R_E), A is for Ampere (the SI unit of electric current), and V is Volt (the SI unit of voltage).

S-40

SIGNIFICANT NUMBERS

Defined under the topic of ROUNDING NUMBERS.

S-41

SILICATES

A silicate is a chemical compound consisting mainly of mineral silicon (Si) and oxygen (O_2), with a general formula of $[SiO_{4-X}^{(4-2X)-}]_n$. For example, in an orthosilicate (SiO_4^{4-}), $X = 1$. Different silicate minerals are formed on Earth by melting or crystallizing the crust (topsoil). Figure 1 shows the molecular structure of silicon dioxide (SiO_2, commonly **silica**, a nonionic compound) and orthosilicate tetrahedral $[(SiO_4)^{-4}$, an ionic compound], the two main base units in most silicates. In addition to SiO_2 or SiO_4, some silicate products contain hexafluorosilicate $[(SiF_6)^{-6}]$, other silicates, or some elements, such as Na, Mg, K, and more.

Some other properties of silicates are outlined next.

- They can be either in the form of crystalline solids or amorphous solids.
- They generally have different molecular structures with specific names. For example, Al_2O_3 has the **corundum** structure, TiO_2 has the **rutile** structure, and CaF_2 (a ceramic) has the **fluorite** structure.

Silicates are of several types: cyclic silicates, orthosilicates, and pyrosilicates. Figure 2 shows the molecular structure of a pyro silicate containing $]Si_2O_7]^{6-}$.

[The **silicate industry** is an important branch of the greater chemical process industry. The cement, ceramic, and glass industries are branches of the silicate industry.]

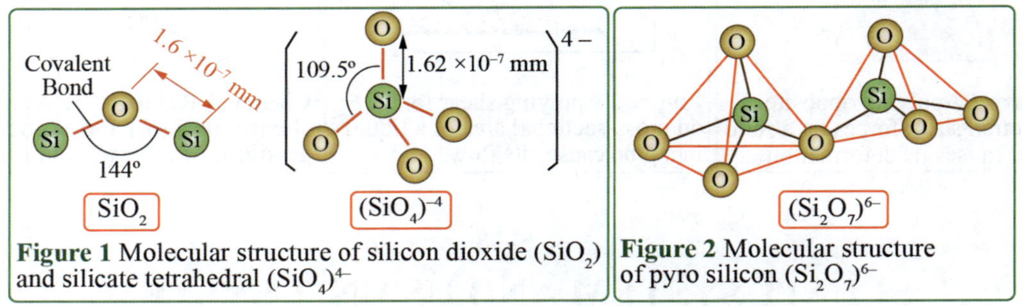

Figure 1 Molecular structure of silicon dioxide (SiO_2) and silicate tetrahedral $(SiO_4)^{4-}$

Figure 2 Molecular structure of pyro silicon $(Si_2O_7)^{6-}$

S-42

SILICONES

Silicone is a rubber-like or oil-like compound made from siloxane (a compound with a functional group of -Si-O-Si-), usually with two organic groups attached to each functional group. By attaching functional groups and crosslinking (bonding between the monomers of a polymer), silicones can be used to produce a wide variety of compounds with different compositions and properties. Examples of silicone-based compounds are **adhesives** (generally known as **glues**), **lubricants** (like silicone grease and silicone oil), **sealants** (generally known as **caulks**), defoamers, and more.

S-43

SILOS AND BINS

A silo is a large and well-designed container for storing bulk materials for a long period. The term **bin** is also used in the process of storing bulk material, but some essential differences exist between silos and bins:

- Silos have a larger capacity (from 20 000 to 80 000 t) than bins (from 1 000 to 3 000 t).
- Silos are much more equipped than bins.

Silos

A typical silo is usually well-equipped with air-conditioning, bulk material handling, a process control system, and more. Silos are used in different branches of the chemical process industry to store bulk materials, such as coal, cement, sugar, and much more. For example, sugar factories use large sugar silos to store dried sugar crystals. The sugar is gradually withdrawn from the silo for packing in small packages or sending to the customers in mobile bins, truckers, or railcars. Under optimum storing conditions in the silo, sugar with moisture (water) content below 0.05% is in the equilibrium (stable) condition, so *no* caking and hardening is expected. During the holding period in the silo, the temperature (T) and relative humidity (W_R) of the **circulation air** are controlled to remove moisture released from the bulk material during storage. After some period, the material becomes conditioned to practice discontinuous air circulation.

Type of Silos

Several silo suppliers in the world offer special silos for the storage of bulk storage, such as Silver-Weibull (Sweden), Abay-ABR (Belgium), Lucks (Germany), Niro-DDS (Denmark), ACMB (France), Spaans (Holland), and more. Silos are usually constructed of concrete floor and reinforced concrete wall (0.2 to 0.3 m thickness) or steel-panel wall.

Figure 1 shows two common Weibull type silos used in the chemical plants; a **top-load-top-unload silo** and a **top-load-bottom-unload silo**. Both silos have similar designs and equipment but differ in discharge design and equipment. Therefore, the similarities of these two silos are outlined first.

- Both silos have a concrete floor and double-jacketed steel wall (mostly mild steel since they last longer).
- Both silos have a conical roof at an angle that almost matches the stored material's angle of repose.
- Both silos have a storing container of 30 to 50 m (= 90 to 150 Ft) in diameter and 30 to 50 m in height with different storing capacities, depending on the material density. For example, a silo with such dimensions can store 20 000 to 80 000 t of sugar.
- Both silos consist of three stories. The first story is below the ground level and contains conveyors for bulk material transport. The second floor, the main **and** largest one, stores the bulk material. The third floor is for conveyors to receive the material and its delivery to the storing area.
- Both silos have a center column in the middle, starting from the first floor and continuing to the third floor. [The diameter of the column in the top-load-top-discharge silo is about 4 m (= 12 Ft), and in the top-load-bottom-discharge silo is about 2 m (because there is *no* bucket elevator in the column).]
- Both silos have an interior ventilation system. The ventilation air is recirculated to the silo after being reconditioned (filtered to remove dust, dehumidified by cooling or with a desiccant to below 60% relative humidity, W_R, and reheated to about 25°C). [Often, the air does *not* need to be reheated, as the increase in temperature (T) across the blowers is enough to reach the required T. Ventilation, which is particularly important in cold or hot climates, creates a uniform T across the silo and prevents condensation and moisture movement through the bulk material.]
- Both silos have a dust-collecting system for collecting and filtering the generated dust.
- Both silos have an elevator to transport the silo's supervisors from one story to the next.

Loading and Unloading of Material to and from a Top-load-Top-Unload Silo

The **feeding system** of a top-loading-top-unloading silo (see the left side of Figure 1) has a bucket conveyor (elevator) that moves the bulk material to the top of the silo. The material moves down to a rotating screw conveyor connected to a rotating feeding crane (bridge) by a steel cable, and the cable is connected to the center column. The conveyor and its feeding crane can rotate around the center column and be raised or lowered automatically over the entire height of the silo, so it moves up as the silo fills. The material is discharged and spread evenly over the storing area, minimizing its classification to different sizes.

The **unloading system** has a discharge funnel at the bottom of the center column, to which the bulk material is moved by gravity. A bucket conveyor moves the material to the top of the silo from the channel. A belt conveyor discharges the material from the silo, and a bucket conveyor moves it down. Once out of the silo, the material is distributed to the packinghouse or loading truckers or railcars to be sent to the customers.

Loading and Unloading of Material to and from a Top-load-Bottom-Unload Silo

The feeding system of a top-loading-bottom-unloading silo (right side of Figure 1) is the same as the previous silo. But, the bulk material is discharged from the bottom by gravity through a discharge funnel. A belt conveyor moves the material out of the silo, and a bucket conveyor moves it up for distribution.

In the operation of a silo, the following generalities are recommended:

- Ventilation of the entire silo and stored material with conditioned air is the key point in the operation of a silo. Air recirculation removes the moisture from the silo and stored material, preventing problems associated with localized moisture concentration, such as mold and yeast activities.
- Bulk material in the silo, if it is possible, can be kept in rotation by transferring the stored material from one silo to another. The material rotation is particularly helpful when *no* discharge occurs for a long period because some dead zones may occur during long storage that the air *cannot* get there.

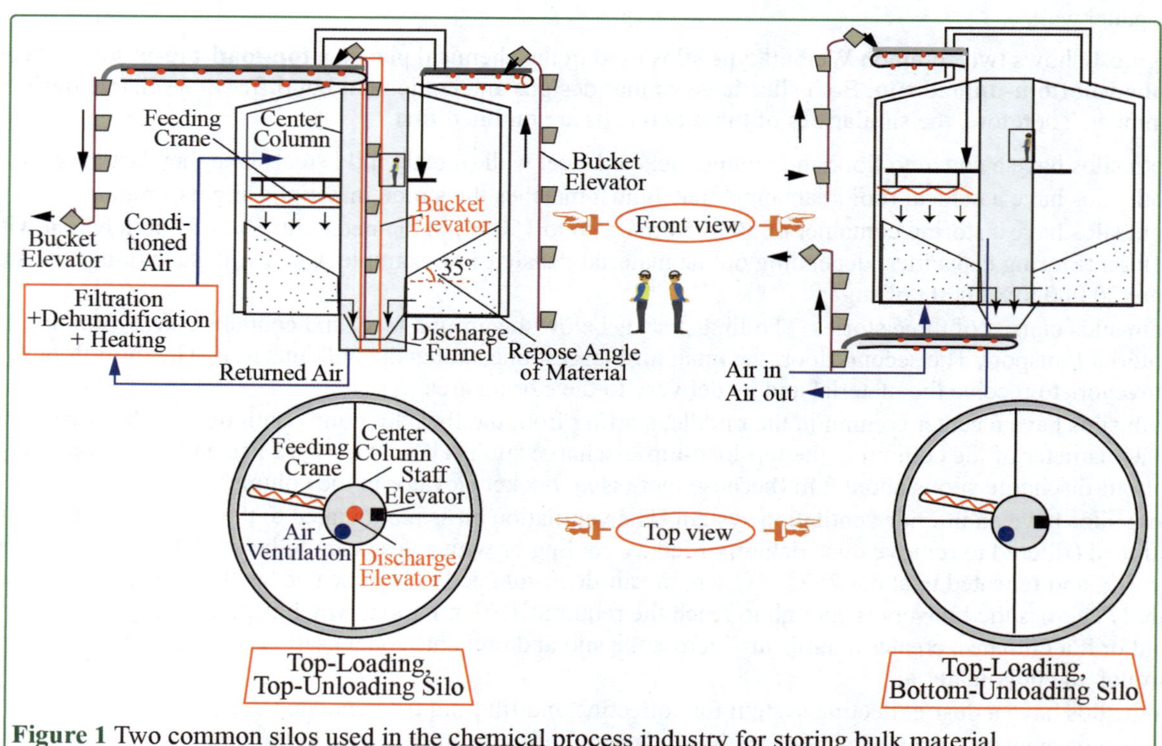

Figure 1 Two common silos used in the chemical process industry for storing bulk material

S-44

SLOPE

Slope (S, steepness) is the rise-to-run ratio of a linear line (straight line or simply **line**) or a curved line (simply **curve**). Rise (shown usually by Y) is a slope's vertical part, and run (shown usually by X) is its horizontal part (see Figure 1).

In **algebra**, the slope is the ratio of final-minus-initial of the rise (ΔY) to final-minus-initial of the run (ΔX), where ΔY (delta Y) means a **normal change**, a small or large change, but *not* a tiny (infinitesimal) one. ΔX (delta X) is defined similarly.

$$S = \frac{Y_2 - Y_1}{X_2 - X_1} = \frac{\Delta Y}{\Delta X} \tag{1}$$

In **calculus**, the slope is the derivative of rising (dY) to the derivative of the run (dX), where dY (the derivative of Y or d form of Y) means a **tiny change** but *not* a normal change. dX (the derivative of X) is defined similarly.

$$S = Y' = \frac{dY}{dX} \tag{2}$$

The symbol Y' has the same meaning as dY/dX (*dee Y dee X*), the derivative (slope or rate change) of Y to X. Generally, a slope tells us the rate at which Y (the dependent variable) changes relative to X (the independent variable). If we draw the quantities of X and Y in a diagram in relation to each other, a slope shows the rate of changes of Y relative to X. In the linear line of $Y = 2X$ in Figure 1, Y increases 2 units for each X unit.

A slope can be applied to any function. Assume that the feed's molar flow rate (F) to a distillation column is 2 kg.mole/h and that of the distillate (D) produced by the column is 1 kg.mole/h. Then the slope of the **operating** (OP) **line** (discussed under DISTILLATION PROCESS) of the column is $D/F = Y/X = 1/2 = 0.5$. This means that the D increases by 0.5 units for each increase in F, so we must increase F by 1 unit to increase D by 0.5.

Slope of a Line: The slope of a **linear line** (straight line or simply **line**) does *not* change if we choose different points on that line. [Thus, the linear lines have **unchanging slopes**.] Figure 2 shows the diagram and value table for the line $Y = 2X$. To draw this line, we simply find points by plugging numbers into X and calculating Y. For example, $X = 1$, then $Y = 2 \times 1 = 2$. To algebraically find the slope (S) of this line, we must use the general slope equation (Equation 1) for any two points, like (X_1, Y_1) and (X_2, Y_2), on this line.

As said a moment ago, the slope of $Y = 2X$ stays the same *no* matter what two points we choose on the line. If, for example, we choose points (1, 2) and (2, 4), the slope of this line according to the slope equation is $(4 - 2)/(2 - 1) = 2$. Similarly, for points (2, 4) and (4, 8), the slope is again $(8 - 4)/(4 - 2) = 2$. This means that Y increases by 2 units for each unit of X.

Likewise, the answer will be the same if we calculate slope differentially ($S = dY/dX$) because the derivative of $2X$ is 2. This means that the derivative of $2X$ at any point on the line gives us the slope of $Y = 2X$. In another context, the slope or the rate of change of Y to X is 2.

[We can also simply realize that $Y = 2X + 1$ has the general form of $Y = aX + b$, and because the derivative of a constant is zero, the slope of the line $2X + 1$ is also 2. This can be noticed by comparison of Figure 1 (which shows the slope of $Y = 2X$) with Figure 2 (which shows the slope of $Y = 2X + 1$.)]

Slope of a Curve: The slope of a **curved line** (tangent line; simply **curve** or **parabola**) changes if we choose different points on that curve. Thus, the curves have **changing slopes**, while lines have **unchanging slopes**. Figure 3 shows the diagram and value table for the curve $Y = X^2$. As shown in the table, the slope of this curve gets greater as it goes to the right because the curve gets steeper as it moves to the right.

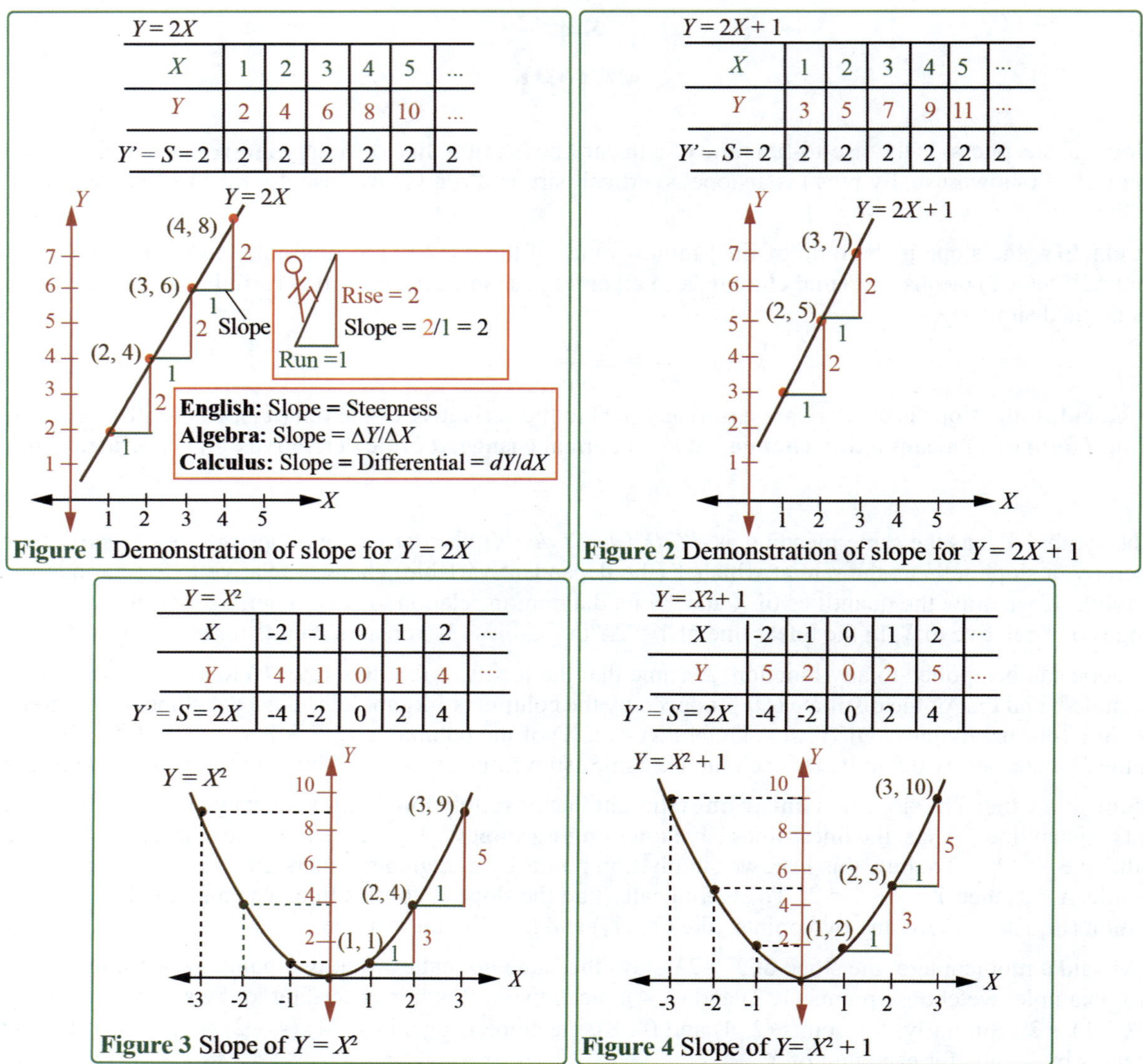

X	1	2	3	4	5	...
Y	2	4	6	8	10	...
$Y' = S = 2$	2	2	2	2	2	2

Figure 1 Demonstration of slope for $Y = 2X$

X	1	2	3	4	5	...
Y	3	5	7	9	11	...
$Y' = S = 2$	2	2	2	2	2	2

Figure 2 Demonstration of slope for $Y = 2X + 1$

X	-2	-1	0	1	2	...
Y	4	1	0	1	4	...
$Y' = S = 2X$	-4	-2	0	2	4	

Figure 3 Slope of $Y = X^2$

X	-2	-1	0	1	2	...
Y	5	2	0	2	5	...
$Y' = S = 2X$	-4	-2	0	2	4	

Figure 4 Slope of $Y = X^2 + 1$

To **algebraically** find the slopes of $Y = X^2$, we can proceed the same way as explained earlier for a line. If, for example, choosing points (1, 1) and (2, 4), the slope of this curve according to the slope equation is (4 – 1)/(2 – 1) = 3. If, choosing points (2, 4) and (3, 9), the slope is (9 – 4)/(3 – 2) = 5.

To **differentially** (infinitesimally) calculate a slope at a certain point on a curve, the X of the point is plugged into the curve's derivative. For example, the slope of $Y = X^2$ at the point (X =1, Y = 1) can be obtained by plugging the X of the point (which is 1) into the derivative of the curve (which is 2X), so, the slope at that point will be 2 × 1 = 2. Similarly, the slope at the point (X = 2, Y = 4) will be 2 × 2 = 4.

[We know that $Y = X^2 + 1$ has the general form of $Y = aX^2 + b$ and because the derivative of a constant (like b) is zero, the derivative of the line $X^2 + 1$ is the same as the derivative of $Y = X^2$. This can be noticed by comparison of Figure 3 (with a slope of $Y = X^2$) with Figure 4 (with a slope of $Y = X^2 + 1$.)]

By comparison, you can see that finding a slope differentially

- It needs one point while finding that algebraically needs two points, and
- It is more accurate and precise and less time consuming than finding it algebraically,

S-45

SLUDGE AND SLURRY

Defined under the topic of CAKE, MUD, SLUDGE, AND SLURRY.

S-46

SMOG

Defined under the topic of SMOKE AND SMOG.

S-47

SMOKE AND SMOG

Smoke: Smoke is a gaseous mixture released from a car, a furnace stack, a wood fireplace, or a cigarette. The composition of smoke depends on its source. Smoke from the fire is mainly composed of ash, and smoke from combustion mainly consists of carbon dioxide (CO_2) and carbon monoxide (CO). Nitrite and sulfite in smoke produce nitrogen dioxide (NO_2), nitrogen monoxide (NO), and sulfur dioxide (SO_2). [Smoke is an air pollutant and **deadly** when its CO content is high.]

Smog: Smog is a smoky fog (smoke and fog) in the air. It creates opacity (haziness or lack of transparency) in the air. Smog can be classed into the next groups.

- **Old Smog:** This is caused by burning a large amount of coal in some cities, like Eastern European cities, until the late years of the 20th century. Sulfur dioxide (SO_2) and soot are the main compounds of the old smog.
- **Modern Smog:** This is caused by the combustion engines of the vehicles in populated cities, the furnace of steam boilers, and likes. This type of smog traps other air pollutants.

S-48

SODIUM CARBONATE, SODIUM CHLORIDE, AND SODIUM HYDROXIDE

Sodium Carbonate: Sodium carbonate (Na_2CO_3, commonly called **soda ash** or simply **soda**) is a colorless (white), inorganic base (soluble in water). Soda ash is produced from sodium chloride (NaCl) and limestone (mostly calcium carbonate). It is a water-softening agent, so used in the production of detergents. As a water-softening agent, its negative carbonate ion [$(CO_3)^{2-}$] binds with positive calcium and magnesium of hard water, freeing the detergent's molecules to combine with grim (dirt plus grease) to be washed with water.

The following are some other properties of Na_2CO_3 (sodium carbonate):

- Its melting point temperature (T_{MP}) is 851ºC (=1564ºF),
- Its solubility in water at 25ºC is 320 g/L,
- Its density (D) at 25ºC is 2540 kg/m^3,
- Its molar mass (M_n) is 106 g/mole.

Washing soda ($Na_2CO_3.10H_2O$) is the most common hydrate of sodium carbonate. It is alkaline (with a PH of 11) and has detergent properties, so it is used as a cleaning chemical because it absorbs grime (dirt plus grease) to form water-soluble products, which are then washed with water. It is produced by dissolving Na_2CO_3 in H_2O.

Sodium Chloride: Sodium chloride (NaCl, commonly known as **table salt** or simply **salt**) is a crystalline solid with the following properties:

- It is an ionic compound,
- Its M_n is 58.4 g/mole,
- Its D is 2170 kg/m^3,
- Its solubility in water is 360 g/L,
- Its solubility in methanol is 14.9 g/L.

Sodium Hydroxide: Sodium hydroxide (NaOH, commonly called **caustic soda** or **caustic**) is a colorless, hazardous, ionic, strong inorganic base with high water solubility. Its reaction with water is a heat-releasing (exothermic) reaction, so it should be handled cautiously. Some other properties of NaOH are outlined next.

- Its D (density) is 2130 kg/m^3,
- Its M_n (molar mass) is 40 g/mole,
- Its solubility in water at 25ºC is 1000 g/L,
- Its T_{BP} (boiling point temperature) is 1388°C (= 2530°F),
- Its T_{MP} (melting point temperature) is 318°C (= 604°F), and
- Its viscosity (η), in a liquid state, is 78 mPa.s (milli Pascal second).

NaOH has many uses, including in paper, pulp, and hygienic industries. It is also used in the plumbing industry for unclogging drains. It has been mixed with animal fat (lipid) for centuries to produce detergents and soaps. [As one of the most produced chemicals, about 80 Mt of NaOH is produced worldwide.]

S-49
SOFT WATER

Study HARD WATER AND SOFT WATER.

S-50
SOFTENING BY CHROMATOGRAPHIC PROCESS

Study WATER SOFTENING PROCESS.

S-51
SOLAR ENERGY

Another name for PHOTON ENERGY.

S-52
SOLID

Discussed under the topic of STATES OF MATTER.

S-53

SOLID-LIQUID EXTRACTION PROCESS

The other name for LEACHING PROCESS.

S-54

SOLID TRANSFER PROCESS

This topic is *not* covered in this book.

S-55

SOLUBILITY

As a physical property, solubility is the maximum ability of a salute to be dissolved in a certain amount of a solvent at a certain temperature (T). Insolubility, instead, is the inability of a solute to be dissolved in a solvent. While a solute is usually a solid, it can also be a liquid or a gas. While similarly, a solvent is usually a liquid, it can also be a solid or a gas. When the solute is a solid and the solvent is a liquid, the product is a solution. [Hereafter, our concentration is only on the solubility of a solid in a liquid.]

We now consider a sugar solution (sugar + water) and define the solubility in its context. The maximum amount of the solute (here sugar) that can be dissolved in a certain amount of the solvent (here water) at a certain T is called the **solubility** of that solute (sugar) in that solvent (water).

When a solute is maximally dissolved in a solvent at a given T, the produced solution is saturated. At saturation, a stability (equilibrium) state is established in the solution, so *no* exchange of molecules between the solute and solvent occurs. Or, if the exchange occurs slowly, the rates on the solute and solvent sides are the same.

Solubility is an important factor in the crystallization process as its driving force. Viscosity (η), instead, acts as an opposing force of crystallization.

A solute solubility in a pure solution depends only on the solution's T. Instead, a solute solubility in an impure solution depends on the solution's T and solution's I (impurity) contents and characteristics.

Solubility is usually expressed as g (gram) of anhydrous solute in 100 g of solvent; this is, g solute/g solvent. Sometimes, it is given in molar fraction (X, a unitless quantity).

On the solubility of solids in solvents, knowing the following is important:

- Solubility of a solid in a solvent *increases* with *increasing* T. The sugar solubility in water at 20ºC is about 2 to 1 (that is, a solubility coefficient, K_S, of 2), while at 100ºC, this ratio increases to about 5 to 1 ($K_S = 5$).
- Solubility of a solid in a solvent increases with decreasing molecular size at the same T. Thus, the solubility of smaller crystals is greater than that of larger crystals. This is because of differences in the surface energy (E_S) between small and large crystals during dissolving. Per unit mass, smaller crystals have larger E_S than the larger crystals, so their amount of E_S per unit mass is relatively greater and, therefore, they dissolve faster. [In crystallization, solubility data are usually given based on the medium-size crystals.]

On the solubility of gases in solutions, knowing the following is important:

- A gas solubility in a solution *decreases* with *increasing* T. Say, at 20ºC and 1 Atm, 9.2×10^{-4} g oxygen dissolves in 100 g water, while at 40ºC, its solubility decreases to 6.5×10^{-4} g/100 g H_2O.
- A gas solubility in a solution, in addition to the T, depends on the pressure (P) of the gas above the solution (the *greater* the gas pressure above a solution, the *more* of the gas dissolves in the solution). For example, in

an unopened soft-drink bottle, the carbon dioxide gas (CO_2) above the solution forces CO_2 gas into the solution. The *P* is released when the bottle is opened, so CO_2 molecules originally dissolved in the solution will escape into the air.

- A gas solubility in a solution also depends on the **surface area** between the liquid and the gas phases. In the soft-drink example, shaking the bottle increases the surface area, causing some CO_2 molecules from the solution to escape into the air.

Figure 1 compares the solubility of sugar and salt (given in g solute/g solvent) in relation to *T* (given in °C). Most solutes have **solubility curves** like sugar (its solubility increases with increasing *T*). At 20°C, 2 parts of sugar are dissolved in 1 part of water to produce a saturated solution, while at 100°C, this ratio is 4.77 to 1. With salt and a few more solutes, the solubility changes slightly with *T*. With some solutes (like $MnSO_4.H_2O$), solubility decreases with increasing *T*, so they have **inverted solubility curves**.

From a solubility viewpoint, solutions are divided into 1) unsaturated solutions, 2) Saturated solutions, and 3) Supersaturated solutions. The solubility concepts are shown in the context of sugar in Figure 2.

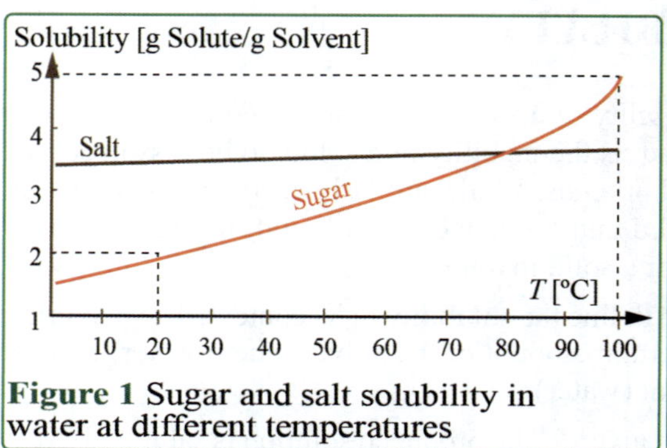

Figure 1 Sugar and salt solubility in water at different temperatures

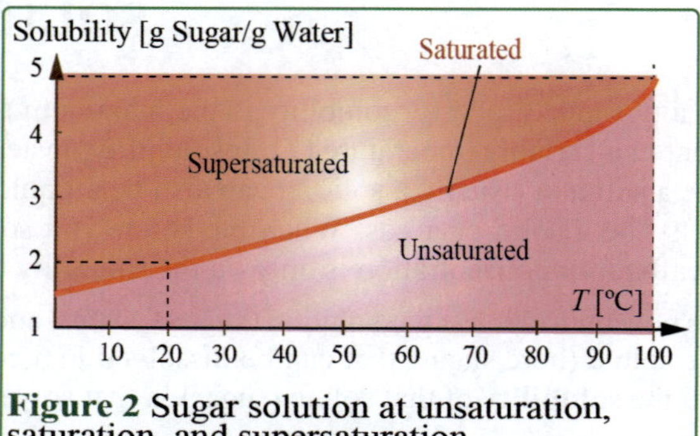

Figure 2 Sugar solution at unsaturation, saturation, and supersaturation

S-56
SOLUBILITY COEFFICIENT

Discussed under the topic of CRYSTALLIZATION COEFFICIENTS.

S-57
SOLUBLE SOLIDS

A soluble solid consists of soluble (non-filterable) molecules in a solution, expressed in mass percentage (see PERCENTAGES). The scale-causing salts in hard water are soluble salts of calcium (Ca) and magnesium (Mg), such as $CaCO_3$, $CaSO_4$, $MgSO_4$, and CaC_2O_4.

[Note: Although the **terms soluble solid**, dissolved solid, dry substance, and Brix are used equally to indicate the same meaning but are different. **Soluble solid** and **dissolved solid** are correct terms when talking about nonfilterable solids. A **dry substance** is correct when talking about both filterable solids (suspended solids) and nonfilterable solids of a solution. Brix (also called refractometric dissolved substance) is a correct term when referring to nonfilterable solids of a solution measured by a refractometer because in refractometric tests, a liquid sample is filtered to remove suspended solids before being tested by a refractometer.]

S-58

SOLUTES AND SOLVENTS

A **solute** is the dissolved solids of a **solvent** (solution). The following are important to know about solutes and solvents:

- A solvent can have more than one solute.
- A solute is usually a solid, but it can also be a liquid or a gas.
- A solvent is usually a liquid, but it can also be a solid or a gas. When the solute is a solid and the solvent is a liquid, the mixture is a solution. In this case, the solute is the solution's dissolved solids (*DS*).

Also, study the following:

- The solute under consideration (study) is the **solute of interest** in a multiple-solutes solvent.
- The maximum amount of a solute dissolved in a certain amount of the solvent at a certain temperature is called the solubility of that solute in that solvent.
- The solute's and solvent's temperature, pressure, pH, and the presence of other solutes in the solvent, determine the solubility of a solute in a solvent.
- In some process units of ChemEng, such as in the extraction process, the term solvent is used as the liquid that soaks the solute (or solutes) but does *not* dissolve it.

S-59

SOLUTION CRYSTALLIZATION

Study CRYSTALLIZATION PROCESS.

S-60

SOLUTIONS

Solutions are in the large group of dispersion solutions, so it is discussed under DISPERSIONS.

S-61

SOLVATION PROCESS

Solvation, in chemistry, is the process of the interaction of molecules of a solvent with those of a solute (or solutes) in a mixture. It can be viewed as a solute and solvent molecular reorganization. Assuming that the solute is a solid and the solvent is a liquid, their molecular interaction forms a solution. The solute properties that can be changed during the solvation process include solubility and reactivity, and those of the solution can be viscosity and density.

The term solvation is mostly used when several molecules of water surround a molecule of a nonionic compound to form a water cluster (hydrated cluster or hydrated cage). The formation of a water cluster involves some bonding processes, mostly hydrogen bonds and van der Waals bonds (weak chemical bonds). The solvation process is quantified by its rate, mostly in mole/s (mole per second).

S-62
SOLVENT CAGE

Another name for WATER CLUSTER.

S-63
SOLVENT EXTRACTION PROCESS

Study EXTRACTION PROCESS.

S-64
SOLVENTS

Discussed under the topic of SOLUTES AND SOLVENTS.

S-65
SOOT

Soot is the impure carbon particles resulting from the incomplete combustion of hydrocarbons. Some scientists theorize that soot is one of the major causes of global warming. Before the late 20th century, in some cities, soot was created by burning coal.

S-66
SOUND AND SPEED OF SOUND

Sound: Sound is a vibration that moves longitudinally as waves by vibrating the air. Sound is expressed with its wave's frequency (f), whose SI unit is Hz (Hertz), where 1 Hz = 1 cycle/s and 1 kHz = 1000 cycles/s. Sound waves vibrate our eardrums, the ear sends the signals to the brain, and the brain evaluates the sound intensity. A human's ear can hear sounds with frequencies in the **audible range** (the range of a human hearing = 20 and 20 000 Hz). [The **sound intensity** (I_E) indicates the sound traveled per unit time (t) in Hz.]

The following are some of sound's properties:

- The sound waves, like all waves, carry energy (E).
- The sound waves disturb a medium when traveling (called **disturbance**).
- When sound waves move through the air, they make the particles in the air vibrate back and forth. This creates high-air and low-air concentration regions with different pressures (P) than atmospheric pressure (P_{Atm}). The difference in P, known as the **acoustic pressure**, vibrates our eardrums to hear that sound.
- Sound needs a medium to travel, unlike light which travels in any medium, including a vacuum.

Speed of Sound Constant: The speed of sound constant (U_S, simply **speed of sound** or **sound velocity**) is a proportionality constant that relates the distance (L, for length) traveled by sound waves to unit time (t, in second) when sound moves in a medium with *no* obstacles and under adiabatic condition (with *no* heat transfer).

The speed of sound constant in dry air at 20ºC (68 ºF) is 343 m/s (1125 Ft/s), which is extremely smaller than the speed of light, which travels at 300 000 km/s. In water at 20ºC, sound moves at 1482 m/s (4861 Ft/s). [The speed of sound in the air is considered a constant value.]

S-67
SOUND VELOCITY

Another name for SPEED OF SOUND.

S-68
SPACE, TIME, AND SPACETIME

Unlike Newton, who assumed that **space** and **time** are **independent** of each other and, therefore, are absolute quantities, Einstein considered them **dependent** and **non-absolute**. Space and time are dependent because both are *not* the same for all observers, and both have directions. The dependency of space and time on each other was the main reason Einstein, in his 1905's principle of gravity spacetime, suggested that it makes more sense if we combine them into one word and call it the **spacetime**.

Space

Space is a three-dimensional (3-D) quantity, with three directions, length (up-and-down), width (right-and-left), and depth (back-and-forth). The size of the space is unknown. Some other properties of space are:

- It is non-visible and non-measurable, known to us as the Universe.
- It locates all masses and energies in certain quantities and all systems and events with relative positions and directions.

It is also important to know the following about space:

- **Unknown Size:** Space can be the entire Universe or part of it that consists of the Earth and its surrounding atmosphere, depending on the context.
- **Unlimited Speed:** Space can move limitless, even much faster than the speed of light (because the light's speed limit is valid as a system moves through the space, but *not* the space itself that has *no* speed limit).
- **Direction:** Space has three directions: length, width, and depth, while time has one direction (forward). Together, spacetime is a four-dimensional system (4-D). In a three-dimensional system (3-D), which we are used to, the dimensions are up/down, left/right, and back/front, each at right angles.
- In 4-D spacetime, the dimensions are those listed and time (Figure 1). Because it is hard to imagine a 4-D shape, physicists show the shape of spacetime as a 2-D blanket, in which a mass curves its shape (Figure 2).]

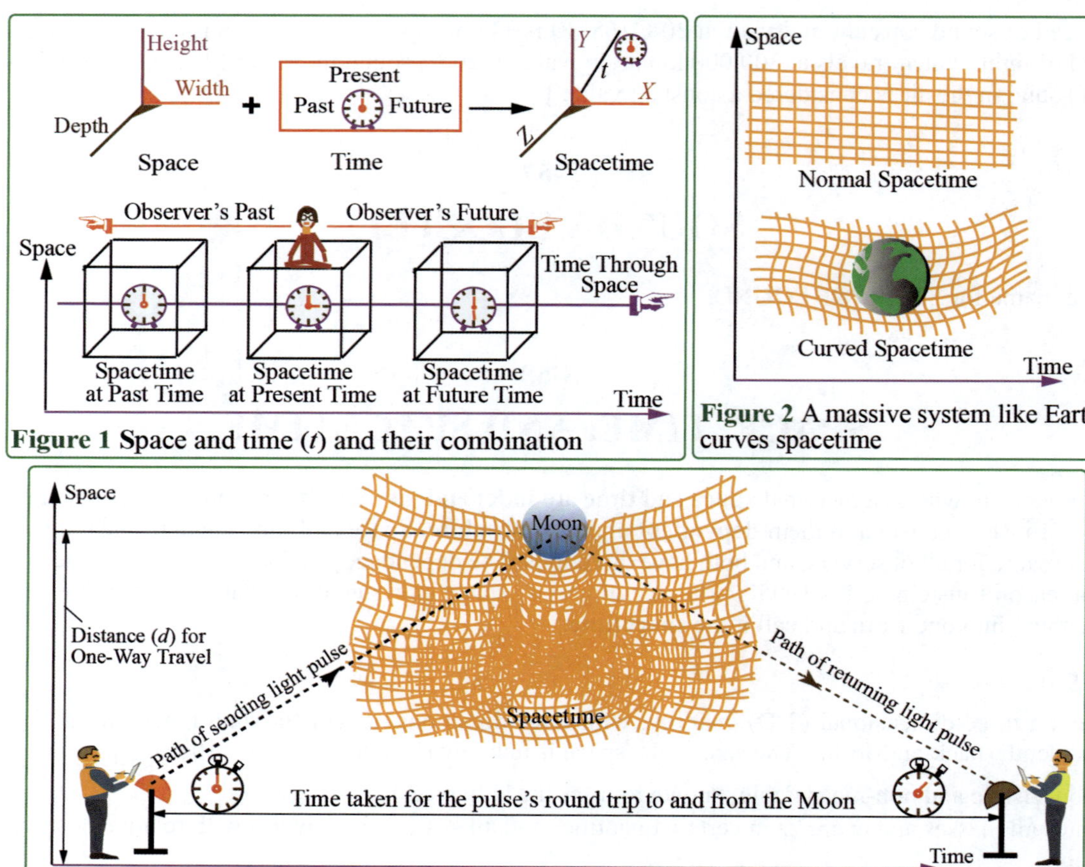

Figure 1 Space and time (*t*) and their combination

Figure 2 A massive system like Earth curves spacetime

Figure 3 Measuring spacetime by sending light pulse to and from the Moon

Time

Time (*t*) is motion from one moment to the next. Time is a one-dimensional (1-D) quantity measured with a clock (in seconds, hours, days, and more). Time tells us that a certain event happened in the past (behind us), now (in front of us), or will happen in the future (ahead of us).

The following are the two key properties of time:

- It has only one direction, from the past to the future.
- It is *not* touchable but measurable by determining how far a system times.

According to Einstein, our experience of time depends on how fast we are traveling (the *faster* we travel, the *more* time slows down for us), known as Einstein's theory of time dilation.

The two important differences between **space** and **time** can be expressed in the next ways:

- Time (*t*) has *no* known starting and ending points, while space started when Big Bang started.
- Time can only be measured **relative** to a reference system, while space does *not* need that. [BC (before Christ) is a relatively backward time scale that ends the year that Christ was put to death. AD (for *anno domini*, meaning after Christ) is a forward time scale that starts the year that Jesus was born.]

The term **arrow of time** is used in physics to give direction to time, from the past to the future (we can go from the past to the future, but *not* the other way round). Physics recognizes at least 3 arrows of time.

- **Thermodynamic Arrow of Time:** This tells us the direction of time in which entropy (S) increases. A glass cup on the table is in a high order state (with a low S), but a broken cup on the floor is in a disordered state (with a high S). We can go from the unbroken cup to the broken cup, but *not* the other way round.
- **Psychological Arrow of Time:** This tells us the direction we remember. We remember the past, but we do *not* know about the future.
- **Cosmological Arrow of Time:** This tells us the direction of time in which the Universe is expanding, telling us that the Universe expands but does *not* contract.

Spacetime

Spacetime (also written as **space and time**, **space-time**, **space of time**, **space at a time**, or **space at a specified time**) is a four-dimensional (4-D) quantity combined with space (a three-dimensional quantity with dimensions of height, depth, and width) and time (a 1-dimensional quantity) as shown in Figure 1.

Physicists think of spacetime as a **transformation** of space to time (or vice versa), but *not* their conversion to each other. In this way, spacetime is a set of all possible points in space at all possible moments in time.

Simply, combining space (3-D) and time (1-D) creates spacetime (4-D) that

- It can be measured like any other quantity (such as mass),
- It can go through a gradual change from one condition to another, and
- It can keep the speed of light as a constant quantity for moving and non-moving observers.

In general relativity, Einstein went further by saying that M (mass), E (energy), and F_g (gravitational force, simply gravity) are related to each other from one side and related to spacetime in the following ways:

- **Spacetime is Related to Mass and Energy:** Spacetime is **flat** in the absence of an M (mass) and **curved** in the presence of an M, so M causes a curve (warp) in spacetime (known as the curvature of spacetime or warping of spacetime). In other words, M tells spacetime how to cure, like a ball that makes a dip in a pulled-out blanket. Because spacetime is related to M and M is related to E (energy), spacetime is related to both. like a heavy ball that makes a dip in a pulled-out blanket. This tells us that spacetime is related to M, and because M is related to E (energy), spacetime is related to both M and E.
- **Spacetime is Related to Gravitational Force (F_g):** Spacetime is the cause of F_g around a massive system. In this way, spacetime curves the space and alters the time to create F_g. [Because physicists often describe gravity (gravitational force) as the curvature of spacetime, some think they are the same things, which are *not*, really.]

In his principle of gravity spacetime, Einstein predicted that spacetime started at the **origin singularity** (later Big Bang singularity, a tiny, high-dense, high-energy, dimensionless system) when the Universe originated (study BIG BANG THEORY).

Figure 3 shows the measurement of spacetime by sending a light pulse to the Moon by observer 1 and receiving the reflected pulse back by observer 2. Both observers can record the time when an event (pulse-sending-and-returning) occurs. For calculation, the **time of the event** is ½ the time for the light pulse to make a trip from observer 1 to the Moon and from there to observer 2. And the **event's distance** is ½ $d.c$, where d is for the distance as shown in the same figure, and c is the speed of light constant.

S-69
SPACETIME

Study SPACE, TIME, AND SPACETIME.

S-70
SPACETIME-GRAVITY PRINCIPLE

Discussed under EINSTEIN'S THEORIES OF RELATIVITY.

S-71
SPECIAL RELATIVITY

Study EINSTEIN'S THEORIES OF RELATIVITY.

S-72
SPECIFIC CONDUCTANCE

Defined under ELECTRIC CONDUCTANCE.

S-73
SPECIFIC DENSITY

Discussed under the topic of DENSITY.

S-74
SPECIFIC ENERGY

Discussed under the topic of ENERGY AND ITS FORMS.

S-75
SPECIFIC ENTHALPY

Study ENTHALPY AND SPECIFIC ENTHALPY.

S-76
SPECIFIC ENTHALPY OF EVAPORATION

See ENTHALPY OF EVAPORATION.

S-77

SPECIFIC IDEAL GAS CONSTANT

Defined under the topic of IDEAL GAS CONSTANT.

S-78

SPECIFIC GRAVITY

Study RELATIVE DENSITY.

S-79

SPECIFIC HEAT

Another name for Specific Enthalpy. It is discussed under ENTHALPY AND SPECIFIC ENTHALPY.

S-80

SPECIFIC HEAT CAPACITY

The specific heat capacity (C_Q or λ, simply **heat capacity** or **specific heat**) of a system is the ability of that system to transfer (absorb or release) heat energy (E_Q). In physics, C_Q is the amount of E_Q added to or removed from a system's unit mass (M) to raise its temperature (T) by 1ºC at P_{Atm} without phase change.

$$C_Q = \frac{E_Q}{M.\Delta T} = \frac{\Delta H}{M.\Delta T} \qquad (1)$$

In this equation, ΔH (change in enthalpy) is in kJ, M is in kg, and ΔT (temperature difference) is in ºC. These give C_Q the SI unit of kJ/kg.ºC. The US unit of C_Q is BTU/Lb.ºF, where kJ/kg.ºC × 0.24 = BTU/Lb.ºF. [Because C_Q is usually given per unit M (mass), it is called **specific heat capacity** (simply **heat capacity**).]

Different substances have different C_Q, meaning 1 kg of each substance (like water, dry air, moist air, or stainless steel) needs a different amount of E_Q to raise its T by 1°C (the *greater* is the C_Q, the *more* E_Q is required to change its T). This means that substances with large heat capacities (like most solids and liquids) need more E_Q to raise their T, while less heat is needed when a substance with small C_Q (like most gases) is under heating. As a numerical example, Figure 1 compares the C_Q of water and sands in the same sunlight.

The specific heat capacities of some substances are listed in Table 7 in the Table Section at the end of the book.

As seen from the table, some substances' C_Q is relatively high. Water's C_Q at 25ºC is 4.186 kJ/kg.ºC (= 1 BTU/Lb.ºF), one of the highest values. This means that 1 kg of water needs 4.186 kJ of E_Q to increase its T by 1ºC (25 to 26ºC). This also means that 1 kg water vapor at 100ºC releases 4.186 kJ of E_Q when it condenses to water at 99ºC. [High C_Q makes water a good coolant.]

At 1 Atm and temperatures below 66ºC, an average value of 1.005 kJ/kg.ºC for C_Q of dry air and 1.88 for C_Q of water vapor are used in calculations. Using the value of 1.005 and W_{Sp} (specific humidity of moist air, given in kg/kg dry air), we can calculate C_{QMA} (moist-air specific heat capacity).

$$C_{QMA} = 1.005 + 1.88W_{Sp} \qquad (2)$$

According to this equation, the C_Q of a moist air with, say, W_{Sp} of 0.02 kg/(1kg dry air) will be

$$C_{QMA} = 1.005 + 1.88 \times 0.02 = 1.04 \text{ kJ/(kg dry air)ºC}$$

Such a moist air with a C_Q of about 1 kJ/(kg.°C) is a good coolant. This is why air is used as a cooling medium in the evaporative cooling process.

[Note 1: In the unit of heat capacity (C_Q), the T unit in the denominator of Equation 1 is a temperature change, so it can be handled as discussed under the topic of TEMPERATURE AND TEMPERATURE DIFFERENCE.]

[Note 2: C_Q can be obtained from tables if they are published. If *not*, they can be calculated to a close estimate from practical equations, such as Equation 1.

Figure 1 In the same sunlight, the sand's temperature (T) increases more than the water's T because sands' specific heat capacity (0.8 kJ/kg.°C) is smaller than that of water (4.184 kJ/kg.°C)

S-81

SPECIFIC HUMIDITY

Discussed under the topic of HUMIDITY AND ITS WAYS OF MEASUREMENT.

S-82

SPECIFIC THERMAL CONDUCTANCE

The complete name for **thermal conductance** or another name for **conductive heat transfer**. It is discussed under CONVECTIVE AND CONDUCTIVE HEAT TRANSFER COEFFICIENTS.

S-83

SPECIFIC VOLUME

The specific volume (V_{Sp}) of a substance is the ratio of its volume (V) to its mass (M) at a certain temperature (T). Mathematically, it is the V occupied by a unit M (1 kg or 1 Lb). The V_{Sp} of a substance is inversely proportional to its D (density). If a substance's D doubles, its V_{Sp} becomes half of the original value.

$$V_{Sp} = \frac{V}{M} = \frac{1}{D} \tag{1}$$

The SI unit of V_{Sp} is m^3/kg, and its US unit is Ft^3/ Lb. The V_{Sp} of an ideal gas is defined using the gas constant (R), gas T, and gas pressure (P).

$$V_{Sp} = \frac{V}{M} = \frac{RT}{P} \tag{2}$$

S-84

SPECIFIC WEIGHT

Discussed under the topic of MASS, WEIGHT, AND SPECIFIC WEIGHT.

S-85

SPECTRAL LINES

Short name for ATOMIC SPECTRAL LINES.

S-86

SPECTROMETRY AND MASS SPECTROMETRY

Spectrometry (also called **spectroscopy**) and mass spectrometry are laboratory techniques for identifying a chemical element. In simpler words, spectrometry is the precise study of color. The instrument used in spectrometry is called a **spectrometer** (spectroscope), and the one used for mass spectrometry is called a **mass spectrometer**. A mass spectrometer is so-named as it separates a gas into a spectrum arranged by electric charge and mass.

Spectrometry: Spectrometry is based on the atomic spectral lines (narrow-colored lines) of elements in a solution sample, as the spectral lines of each element are a characteristic property of that element. Thus, the wavelengths (or frequencies) of a sample's spectral lines can identify the type of a sample.

In a spectrometer, as shown in Figure 1, light from a flame, in which a heated sample passes through a narrow slit for making a light's thin beam, which passes through a prism, from there some spectral lines, instead of the continuous spectral lines when white light passes through a prism. The specific pattern of spectral lines and the intensity of the wavelengths released by each element can identify the sample.

Mass Spectrometry: Mass spectrometry is based on bombarding a solid, liquid, or gas sample with a beam of electrons (by, say, subjecting them to an electric field) to convert the sample's molecules into charged ions. The ions then separate according to their mass-to-charge ratio of ions. Figure 2 shows the mass-to-charge ratio of ions in relation to the ions signals.

In a mass spectrometer, the following steps are followed to identify a solution sample:

- A beam of positive ions is produced from the sample as it enters the spectrometer.
- The positive ions are then accelerated through two slits in an electric field, produced by a voltage.
- The sample is heated by the electric arc of the spectrometer, so its atoms' electrons release (emit) electromagnetic waves (EM waves, like light waves).
- The sample's EM waves are polarized by a prism into its spectral lines. Because each element absorbs or releases (reflects) the EM wave over a certain range of wavelengths (λ). Each element has its specific spectral lines, which are used in the spectrometer's detector to measure the intensity of their wavelengths.
- A signal corresponding to the wavelengths' intensity is sent to the spectrometer's digital display to identify that element numerically.

[Over time, spectroscopy was developed to include the interaction of an atom's nucleus with a magnetic field, known as nuclear magnetic resonance spectroscopy (NMR spectroscopy), which is used in magnetic resonance imaging (MNR).]

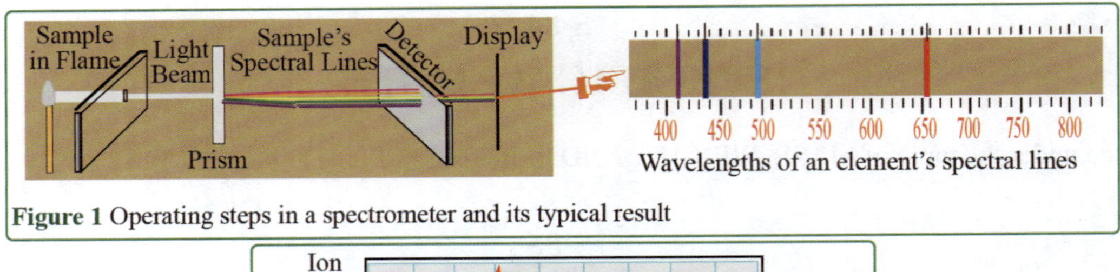

Figure 1 Operating steps in a spectrometer and its typical result

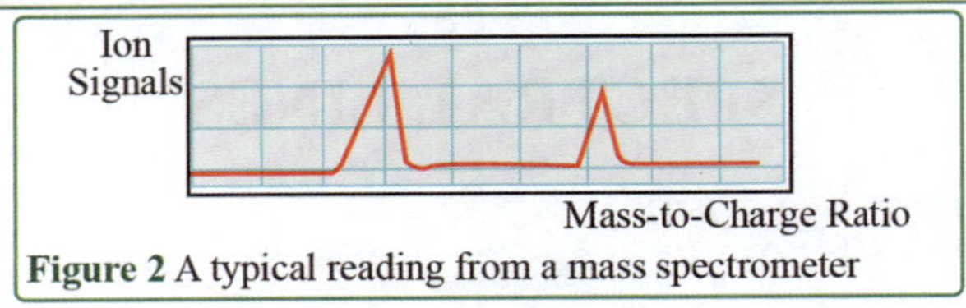

Figure 2 A typical reading from a mass spectrometer

S-87
SPECTROPHOTOMETRY

Study COLOR AND COLORIMETRY.

S-88
SPECTROSCOPY AND MASS SPECTROSCOPY

Study SPECTROMETRY AND MASS SPECTROMETRY.

S-89
SPEED OF LIGHT CONSTANT

Study LIGHT AND SPEED OF LIGHT CONSTANT.

S-90
SPEED OF LIGHT THEORY

Discussed under EINSTEIN'S THEORIES OF RELATIVITY.

S-91
SPEED OF SOUND CONSTANT

Study SOUND AND SPEED OF SOUND.

S-92

SPEED, VELOCITY, AND ROTATIONAL VELOCITY

Speed and Velocity

Speed (U) and velocity (V) have the same definition (distance traveled by a moving system in space per unit time), but three (3) major differences exist between them:

- Speed is a scalar quantity (a quantity without direction), while velocity is a vector quantity (a quantity with direction), so velocity expresses a system's speed and direction. When we say a car moves at 60 km/h, we talk about its speed, but when the direction is mentioned (say, 60 km/h **north**), its velocity is meant.
- Because speed is a scalar quantity, we can add, subtract, or average its quantities. When, for example, a car moves at 50 km/h in the first hour and 70 km/h in the second hour on a straight road, its average speed is (50 + 70)/2 = 60 km/h. Instead, when the car's velocity is 50 km/h north in the first hour and 70 km/h west in the second hour, we *cannot* estimate its velocity unless considering its directions.
- Speed is always positive, while velocity can be positive or negative. Going up (or right) is a positive velocity and going down (or left) is negative. Distance traveled up (or right) is always a positive displacement, but going down (or left) counts as negative. Assume that your college is 2 km (= 1.25 Mi) away from your home. If you take a different road and your car's odometer shows 3 km after setting it to zero, your **distance** traveled is 3 km, but your **displacement** is 2 km.

Speed and velocity are always relative, regardless of where a system travels (on the ground or in space). Thus, different observers record different speeds. Observers traveling alongside a moving system will see the system as motionless.

Both speed (U) and velocity (V), as said a moment ago, are defined the same; that is, the distance (L, for length) per unit time (t, usually in seconds or hours).

$$U = V = \frac{L}{t} \tag{1}$$

The SI unit of speed and velocity is m/s and Ft/s in the US unit. A ball moving at 10 m/s expresses the ball's speed, while a liquid flowing at 4 m/s in a pipe in a certain direction expresses the liquid's velocity.

The symbol ΔU (differential speed, read delta U) is used to calculate the change in speed, where ΔU is the speed at the end of the time interval minus speed at the beginning ($\Delta U = U_2 - U_1$). When, say, a car starts from rest ($U = 0$ km/h) and in a few seconds reaches a speed of 80 km/h, its **average speed** will be,

$$\Delta U = 80 - 0 = 80 \text{ Mi/h}$$

Remember the following useful data:

- The speed of light constant is 300 000 km/s (= 186,282 Mi/s).
- The speed-of-sound constant is 343 m/s (= 1234 km/h = 767 Mi/h).
- The speed of our planet Earth around the Sun is 29.6 km/s (= 18.4 Mi/s).

The velocity equation (Equation 1) is used when the system moves at constant velocity. Instead, when the system does *not* move at constant V; in other words, it moves faster and sometimes slower than average V, the equation for differential form (d form) of velocity is used.

$$dV = \frac{dL}{dt} = \frac{L_2 - L_1}{t_2 - t_1} \tag{2}$$

This equation tells us that velocity is a differential of distance over time. The dL is the differential length, the tiny (infinitesimal) distance a moving system travels in a tiny time of dt.

In a free-fall motion, a skydiver falls fast until he reaches the **terminal velocity** of around 190 km/h (= 118 Mi/h). Then the terminal velocity reduces because the F_g (gravitational force) on the skydiver's body reduces. And when the air's F_D (drag force) is small, the F_g cancels the air's F_D, so the skydiver falls at a constant gravitational acceleration ($a_g = 9.8\ m/s^2 = 32.2\ Ft/s^2$) and independent of its mass (M).

In a free-fall motion, a falling system's velocity from rest ($V_0 = 0$), related to a_g and t, will be

$$V = V_0 + a_g.t = a_g.t \tag{3}$$

And the system's V, in relation to a_g and height (h), will be

$$V = \sqrt{V_0^2 + 2a_g(h - h_0)} = \sqrt{2a_g.h} \tag{4}$$

In some applications (such as when a liquid flows in a pipe), a system's average velocity (V_{Avg}) is needed for calculations. Considering Figure 1, V_{Avg} can be calculated as

$$V_{Avg} = \frac{\Delta L}{\Delta t} = \frac{L_2 - L_1}{t_2 - t_1} \tag{5}$$

Example 1 on Velocity

Calculate the average velocity (ΔV) of a car relative to its start when the driver starts at $t_1 = 0$ to drive north with a velocity of $V_1 = 70$ km/h (= 44 Mi/h). After 1 minute ($t_2 = 1$ min), the driver moves east at a velocity of $V_2 = 90$ km/h (= 56 Mi/h).

Wanted: Average

The two movements are perpendicular because the car's velocity is 70 km/h in the north direction and 90 km/h in the east direction. Thus, the resultant velocity can be found by adding the two velocity components, called the Pythagorean Theorem.

$$\Delta V = \sqrt{V_1^2 + V_2^2} = \sqrt{70^2 + 90^2} = 86\ \text{km/h}\ (53\ \text{Mi/h})$$

Example 2 on Velocity

Given: A ball throwing upward, with a constant acceleration of $a_g = 9.8\ m/s^2$, to reach a vertical height of 10 m in 2 s.

Wanted: The ball's velocity (V) in relation to a_g and t, and in relation to a_g and h

Because of constant gravitational acceleration, the ball's upward velocity must equate to the ball's downward velocity. So, the ball velocity in relation to a_g and t is

$$V = a_g.t = 9.8 \times 2 = 19.6\ \text{m/s}$$

And the ball V in relation to a_g and h will be

$$V = \sqrt{2a_g.h} = \sqrt{2 \times 9.8 \times 10} = 14\ \text{m/s}$$

Rotational Velocity

Rotational velocity (ω, also called **angular velocity** or **circular velocity**) is the velocity (V) of a system that is rotating circularly around its **axis of rotation** per unit time (t), as shown in Figure 2. Like velocity, it is a vector quantity, as it also has a direction (clockwise or counterclockwise).

Unlike ordinary motion, in which the V of a motion is measured in the distance per time (t), in a rotational motion, the ω is measured in one of the following ways:

- In **degrees** per second (°/s).
- In **rotations** (revolutions) per minute, known as RPM (rotation per minute or R/min),
- In radian (Rad) per second (Rad/s), where 1 Rad = $R/2\pi = 360°/2\pi = 180°/\pi \approx 57.3°$, and
- In the unit of frequency (f), which is one rotation/second (s) or one cycle/s (known as Hertz, Hz).

[When ω is expressed in rotation/min, shown as RPM = rotation (revolution) per minute, some use the symbol N (or n) instead of ω.]

Systems that are rotating are constantly changing their V. Assume a material in the basket of a centrifuge, which is rotating at high-but-constant V. Here, we can talk about two (2) rotational velocities:

- **Particle Rotational Velocity** (shown as V)**:** This is a single suspended particle's settling velocity, given in distance per time (t), usually in m/s. [In a centrifuge's basket, all solid-settling particles are under an F_C. But, in calculations, a single spherical particle is considered the only particle in the feed that settles at V under F_C.]
- **Basket Rotational Velocity** (shown as ω, omega)**:** This is the velocity of the basket, given in RPM or rad/s. The basket of ordinary centrifuges operates at 1000 to 2000 RPM.

Figure 2 shows a rotational system's rotational velocity (ω), velocity (V), and rotational acceleration (a, the rate at which the ω changes).

In a centrifuge, the next relation exists between V (the particle's settling velocity), R (the basket's radius), and ω (the basket's rotational velocity).

$$V = R.\omega \tag{6}$$

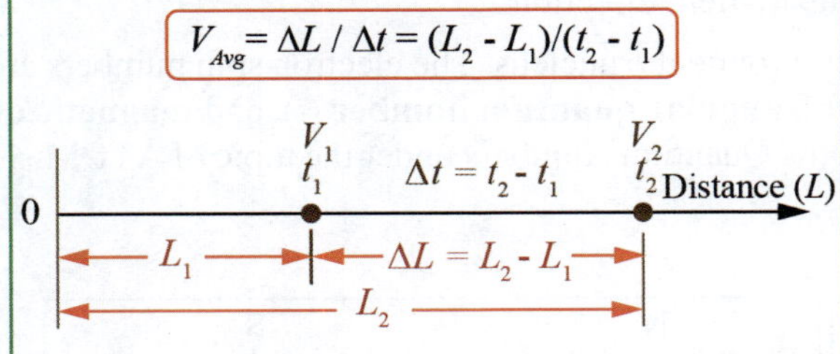

Figure 1 Velocity (V) as a function of distance (L)

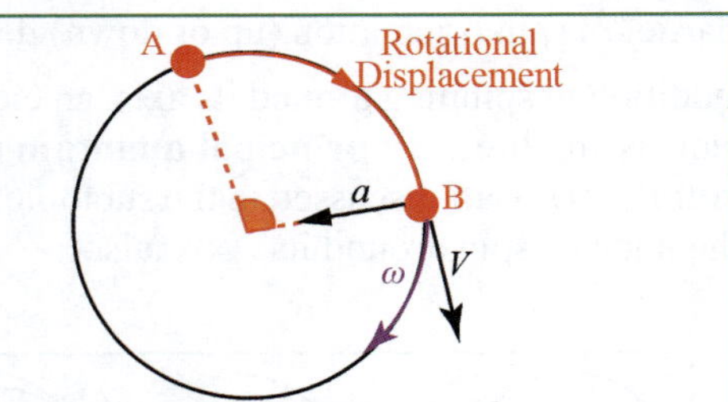

Figure 2 Rotational velocity (ω), velocity (V), and acceleration (a) of a rotating system

S-93
SPIN

Study SPIN QUANTUM NUMBER.

S-94

SPIN NUMBER

Study SPIN QUANTUM NUMBER.

S-95

SPIN QUANTUM NUMBER

As a property of quantum particles (like an electron), the spin quantum number (simply a **spin number** or **spin**) is a unitless number that gives the spinning direction of a quantum particle around its axis. While spinning fast around its axis, an electron creates a magnetic field (M-field) around itself (so, it spins in its M-field).

Quantum particles spin differently. A particle with spin 1 looks the same when it rotates through a full 360º (case A in Figure 1), a particle with spin 2 looks the same when it rotates 180º (case B in the same figure), and a particle with spin ½ must rotate two complete rotations before it looks the same (case C).

Electrons spin **clockwise** (CW) or **counterclockwise** (CCW), giving them magnetic orientation (north and south; also called **up** and **down**).

The following properties of electrons are important:

- In an **electron shell**, the spin orientation of two electrons is always the opposite of each other; one has an **up** (north) orientation (shown as + ½), and the other one has a **down** (south) orientation (shown as – ½). Thus, the values of spin numbers are + ½ and – ½ (see Figure 2). This rule also applies to **electron subshells**. Each subshell can have only two electrons, one with a spin of + ½ and another with – ½.
- In the case of the electron pair in the same shell, their opposite spin directions create oppositely-directed M-fields that are mutually attractive and partly make up for the repulsive force between the electrons.

Two other properties of an electron's spin number are listed next.

- A particle's spin is related to its angular (rotational) momentum, a property of a rotating system.
- A particle's spin orientation (up or down) determines its M-field direction.

In addition to spinning around its axis, an electron spins around the nucleus. The electron spin numbers around the nucleus are three (3); **principal quantum number** (n), **angular quantum number** (l), and **magnetic quantum number** (m), all discussed in the subtopic of Electron's Quantum Numbers under the topic of ATOM. [Note that the nucleus spin around its Axis, also.]

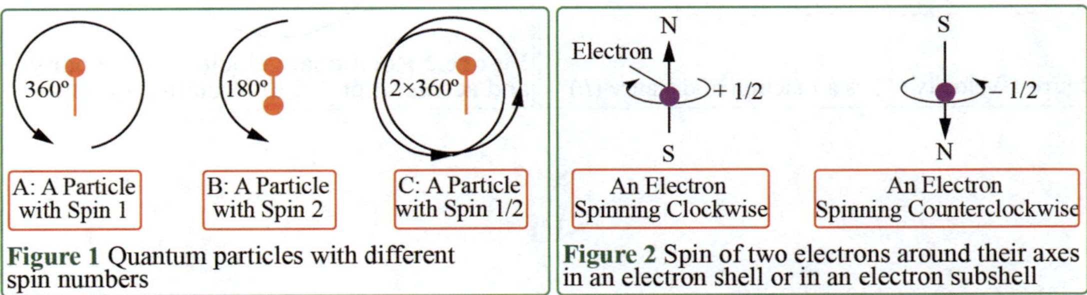

Figure 1 Quantum particles with different spin numbers

Figure 2 Spin of two electrons around their axes in an electron shell or in an electron subshell

S-96

STABLE AND UNSTABLE SYSTEMS

A **stable system** (also called a **steady system** or **equilibrium system**) is one whose variables (like temperature, pressure, concentration, or flow rate) do *not* change greatly with time.

Instead, an **unstable system** (also called a **transient system**) is one whose variables change greatly with time. The content of a winery vessel is an example of an unstable system. Grape juice, water, and yeast are combined in the vessel. As the wine ferments over time, the volume of the juice decreases while the concentration of its alcohol and carbon dioxide increases. In this system, two variables are in an unsteady-state situation, so the system is said to be unsteady. Some stable systems are discussed next.

- **A System with Mass Stability** (also known as a **steady system**)**:** This system's mass (M) remains constant (unchanged) with time. To mathematically express such a system, we can say that $M =$ constant, so $\Delta M = 0$. Here, Δ (read delta) is for the difference. For example, when the rate of addition of a liquid to a tank is equal to the rate of removal of the liquid from the tank, the mass of the liquid in the tank remains constant, so there is no change in mass ($M =$ constant) in the tank over the time. If changing the liquid rate to (or from) the tank, its mass does *not* remain constant; thus, the system becomes unstable. From the mass viewpoint, such a system is an unsteady system. [Some use the term **diffusive stability** when a system remains in a constant mass transferability. A system with diffusive stability can be expressed by its diffusing components' mass (M) or concentration (C). When, for example, in a beet diffuser, the concentration of the sugar and other dissolved solids (DS) on the inside and outside of the sliced-beet cells becomes equal and remains unchanged ($\Delta C = 0$), the system is in diffusive stability. At this point, no more diffusion process occurs because the system is stable.]
- **A System with Pressure Stability:** This system's pressure (P) remains unchanged with time (when the variation in P related to different elevations is ignored in stable systems).
- **A System with Thermal Stability:** This system's T (temperature) remains constant with time, so $T =$ constant and $\Delta T = 0$. Consider a liquid in a tank at 40ºC. If the liquid's T is constant, the system is in thermal stability, so $\Delta T = 40 - 40 = 0$.
- **A System with Phase Stability:** The mass of this system's components' phases remains constant with time, so $M =$ constant and $\Delta M = 0$. Consider a system with sugar crystals and mother liquid (the liquid around the crystals) in a crystallizer. When sugar molecules from the liquid phase do *not* move toward the solid phase (the sugar crystals) to increase the size of the existing crystals and the existing crystals do *not* dissolve (their mass remains unchanged), we say the system is in phase stability.

S-97

STAINLESS STEEL

Stainless steel is ferrous alloy steel (simply **steel**) that mainly consists of iron (Fe), 10 to 11% chromium (Cr), and a small amount of carbon (C, about 0.1 to 0.2%) alloyed (mixed by melting) to Fe. Cr is added to prevent corrosion, and C increases the hardness. The chromium prevents corrosive reactions by forming a passive thin layer of chromium oxide (Cr_2O_3) when exposed to atmospheric oxygen and moisture. Another advantage of the passive layer is that it reforms when the surface of the steel is scratched. This property is called **passivation**.

Stainless steel differs from carbon steel by the amount of chromium. Carbon steel corrodes when exposed to atmospheric oxygen. Properties like resistivity to corrosion, shininess, and low maintenance have made stainless steel an ideal metal for industries and households. Following are other properties of stainless steel:

- Its heat-transfer coefficient (U_Q) is 1 100 to 1 150 W/(h.m^2.°C),
- Its thermal expansion is in the range of 10 to 20 µm/°C, and

- Its thermal conductivity (K_{Th}) is 20 to 40 W/(h.m.°C).

Different types of stainless steel are in the market, including the following:

- **Austenitic Stainless Steel** (also known as 300 grades)**:** It contains a minimum of 16% Cr, 0.15% carbon, and a small nickel (Ni). It makes up about 70% of today's stainless-steel market. Austenitic steels (also called **austenite steels**) of the 304 and 316 grades are used in chemical plants, mostly for heating tubes and heating plates of evaporators and heat exchangers.
- **Ferritic Stainless Steel:** It has a better hardness but less corrosion resistance than austenitic stainless steel. It is also less expensive, comparably. Depending on the type, steels have 11 to 27% Cr and a small amount of Ni. 18/2 stainless steel (sometimes shown as 18-2) consists of 18% Cr and 2% Mo, 18/10, 26/1, 29/4, and 29Cr-4Mo-2Ni are common ferritic types.

Another type of stainless steel, **martensitic stainless steel**, is *not* comparably as corrosion-resistant as the other two types. However, they are extremely hard because of the high amount of carbon (up to 1%).

S-98

STANDARD AMBIENT TEMPERATURE AND PRESSURE

Standard ambient temperature and pressure (SATP) is an unofficial (but commonly used) standard for temperature (T) and pressure (P). SATP, by definition, is room temperature (around 25ºC or 77 ºF) and atmospheric pressure (P_{Atm} = 1 Atm = 760 mm Hg = 101 kPa). A system that is under SATP is called a system under **standard conditions**.

[Note: While both SATP and STP (standard temperature and pressure) are expressed at P_{Atm}, but are different (because SATP is measured at room temperature (T_R) and STP at 0°C.]

S-99

STANDARD CONDITIONS

Another name for STANDARD AMBIENT TEMPERATURE AND PRESSURE.

S-100

STANDARD PRESSURE

See STANDARD TEMPERATURE AND PRESSURE.

S-101

STANDARD TEMPERATURE

See STANDARD TEMPERATURE AND PRESSURE.

S-102

STANDARD TEMPERATURE AND PRESSURE

Standard temperature and pressure (STP) is a standard for temperature (T) and pressure (P). STP, by definition, is 0ºC = 32ºF = 273K and atmospheric pressure is P_{Atm} = 1 Atm = 760 mm Hg = 101 kPa. [Note: In measurements, mostly room temperature, which refers to the temperature of 25ºC (= 77ºF = 288 K) or slightly less or more, is used instead of 0ºC. Most of the time, the measurements are performed at 20ºC.]

Remember the following brief-but-important points:

- The enthalpies (rather specific enthalpies, H_{Sp}), given in steam tables, are measured at STP, and the close-to-reality assumption is that at 0ºC, the H_{Sp} of water is zero.
- At sea level, the standard air pressure is 1×10^5 N/m^2, also called one atmosphere (1 Atm).
- The molar volume (V_n) of any gas at STP is 22.4 L.

S-103

STARCH

Starch is a polysaccharide consisting of many glucose units, joined by glycosidic bonds (oxygen bonds), as shown in Figure 1. It is the most common carbohydrate in human diets. Potatoes, wheat, rice, and beans are the major starch sources. Some other properties of starch are outlined next.

- It is *not* sweet, but if we hold a piece of bread in our mouth for a few minutes, it tastes sweet, indicating that digestion has begun and glucose is formed. In the body, starch is broken down into glucose and enters the bloodstream to become available to generate energy.
- It is produced in plants in two forms: **amylopectin** and **amylose**. Starch contains about 80% amylopectin and 20% amylose. [Amylopectin has larger molecules than amylose and is *not* water-soluble. Amylose is soluble in hot water. When starch is mixed with warm water, the dough is formed.]
- It is converted, in industry, into sugars by fermentation to produce ethanol (C_2H_5OH).
- It can be detected by the **iodine test**, in which a drop of potassium-iodide solution added to a sample containing starch changes the solution to **purple** color.

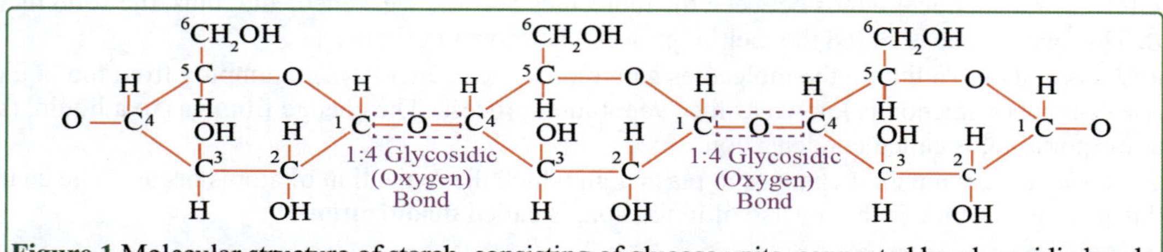

Figure 1 Molecular structure of starch, consisting of glucose units, connected by glycosidic bonds

S-104

STATE QUANTITIES

Study PATH AND STATE QUANTITIES.

S-105

STATES OF MATTER

States of matter are solid, liquid, gas, and plasma (see Figure 1). Before getting further, a chemical engineer should be aware of the following:

- Liquids, gases, and plasma are collectively referred to as fluids.
- Some less-common states are also known, such as the Bose-Einstein condensate state (phase). These states, however, only occur under extreme conditions, such as ultra-cold or ultra-dense conditions.
- Some use the terms **state of matter** and phase equally. This is incorrect because a system can contain some immiscible phases of the same matter. A cup of water (a liquid) with a piece of ice (a solid) contains two phases of the same matter, the water.

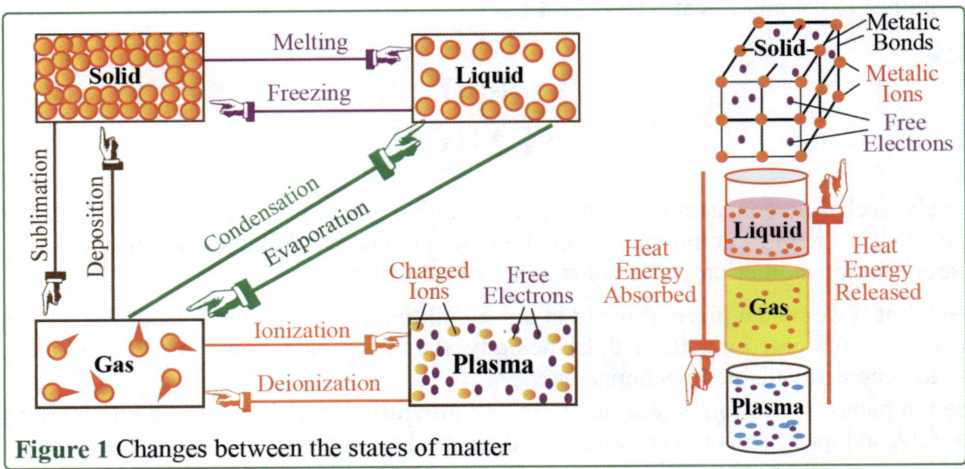

Figure 1 Changes between the states of matter

Each matter has its distinct properties, which will be discussed in a moment. It is, however, helpful to first explain how the matters change to one another.

- As heat energy (E_Q) is added to a solid, its molecules vibrate more rapidly. And, if E_Q is kept adding, the attractive forces and chemical bonds between the molecules become weakened, and, thus, the solid melts into a liquid. This occurrence is called the melting process, as shown in Figure 1.
- As more E_Q is added to a liquid, the molecules gain more kinetic energy (E_K), jumping from the liquid to the gas phase. This phenomenon is known as the evaporation process. The change from gas to a liquid, the reverse of evaporation, is called condensation.
- As a gas is heated very much, it changes to plasma, in which the ionization of atoms occurs. The change from plasma to gas, which is the reverse of ionization, is called **deionization**.

Solids

A solid is rigid and has a definite shape and definite volume. A solid's molecules are packed closely together, so they do *not* move around freely (because of strong attractive forces between their atoms). [Solids are also **condensed substances** (because their molecules are compressed.]

The other general properties of solids are outlined next.

- Solids are denser than liquids and gases,
- Solids have definite (constant) shape and volume,
- Solids do *not* easily deform or flow (a fluid's motion),

- Solids are resistant to a shape change or volume change,
- Solids' molecules are fixed but can vibrate in a certain direction,
- Solids can be in the form of crystalline solid or amorphous solid,
- Solids' density does *not* change greatly when their *P* or *T* changes,
- Solids' molecules *cannot* be compressed because they are close together,
- Solids' *V* does *not* change considerably when their pressure (*P*) or temperature (*T*) changes,
- Solids melt at a certain *T*, called T_{MP} (melting point temperature), at which their molecular structures break down and become liquids at the *P* surrounding them,
- Some solids are soft (because their molecules are weakly bonded), and some are rigid.
- Some solids are conductors (because their atoms contain mobile electrons), and some are insulators (because their atoms do *not* contain mobile electrons).

Liquids

A liquid is *not* rigid and has *no* definite shape but definite volume. A liquid's molecules are:

- They are neither orderly like a solid *nor* disorderly like a gas (because the molecules are bonded mildly).
- They are very close to each other (because of high intermolecular forces between them), and
- They collide as they move (the *higher* is a liquid's *T*, the *greater* is its collision rate).

So, 1) Little compression is possible between liquid molecules, and 2) Small spacing exists between liquid molecules compared with gas molecules. [To numerically visualize the listed concepts, study Example 1.]

The following terminology applies to liquids:

- Liquids are also known as fluids (liquids, gases, and plasma) because their molecules flow freely.
- Liquids are also known as incompressible fluids because their molecules *cannot* be compressed by *P* (pressure) to a much lower *V* (volume).
- When one (or more) compound is dissolved in a liquid, it is *not* a liquid anymore but a solution.

The other general properties of liquids are:

- Liquids are denser than gases and lighter than solids,
- Liquids can be Newtonian liquids or non-Newtonian liquids, and
- They can be formed by melting solids to their melting point temperature (T_{MP}).

Liquids can be further discussed in the following ways:

- Liquids' density (*D*) is great versus gases (water's *D* is 1000 and dry-air's *D* is 1.2 kg/m3),
- Liquids' volume (*V*) does *not* change considerably when their *P* or *T* changes,
- Perfect liquids are non-viscous, therefore can flow by minimal force,
- Liquids' *D* does *not* change considerably with *P* and *T*, and
- Simple liquids obey Newton's Viscosity Law.

Example 1 on Liquids and Gases

Given: Two same-size tanks, each with a volume (*V*) of 22.4 L, where tank 1 is filled with water and tank 2 with water vapor (a gas) at STP

Wanted: Comparison of the number of molecules in tank 1 and tank 2 and comparison of molecular spacing between water and water vapor

We know one mole of a substance contains 6.02×10^{23} particles (atoms or molecules). Also, we know that one mole of water masses18 g (because the molecular mass of water is 18). Furthermore, we know that 22.4 L of water masses $22.4\times1000 = 22400$ g, where the value 1000 is the density (*D* in g/L) of water at STP. We can calculate the number of molecules in one mole of water in the first tank with these values.

$$\frac{22400}{18} \times 6.02 \times 10^{23} = 7.5 \times 10^{26}$$

According to Boyle's Law, at STP, 22.4 L of any gas contains 1 mole of that gas, so the number of water vapor molecules in tank 2 is 6.02×10^{23}. If dividing the number of molecules in tank 1 by the number of molecules in tank 2, we realize that there are 1246 times as many liquid molecules as gas in the same volume.

$$\frac{7.5 \times 10^{26}}{6.02 \times 10^{23}} = 1246$$

Gases

Gas is *not* rigid and has *no* definite shape and volume. A gas's molecules are disordered, so they move around freely and much faster than a liquid's molecules. The molecules of air (a gas) at room temperature (T_R, 22 to 24°C or 72 to 75°F) move at about 500 m/s (= 1640 Ft/s), but because air's M_M (molecular mass) is small, its molecules' E_K (kinetic energy) is also small. Some notes can be made about general names of gases:

- Gases are also known as **fluids** (because their molecules flow freely).
- Gases are also known as compressible fluids (because their molecules are much farther apart than they are in liquid form, so they can be compressed by P to a much lower V). Example 1 proved this statement.

The other general properties of gases are listed next.

- Gases are much lighter than solids and liquids,
- Gases produce a force on a barrier, which is felt like pressure (P).
- Gases have *no* definite (constant) shape and *no* definite volume (V).
- Gases are formed by boiling liquids to their boiling point temperature (T_{BP}).
- Gases' P times gases' V remain constant, a relationship known as Boyle's Law.
- Gases occupy whatever V is available to them. If, for instance, water boils in a lab, the released water vapor spreads over until the entire lab is filled with the same vapor.
- Gases condense at a certain T, at which their molecular structure breaks and they become liquids.

Gases can be further discussed in the following ways:

- Gases' density (D) is small versus liquids (D of dry air is 1.2 and D of water is 1000 kg/m^3),
- Gases' volume (V) changes greatly when compressed, heated, or cooled,
- Gases' molecules move in all directions with different velocities (V),
- Gases' density (D) changes considerably with P (pressure) and T,
- Gases' density change from one point to another when they move,
- Gases' molecules move freely and hit randomly each other,
- Gases' kinetic energy (E_K) is the same at a given T,
- Gases' solubility is higher at high P and lower T,
- Gases obey Newton's Viscosity Law.

[Note: To visualize the volume expandability of a gas, let us consider the evaporation of one mole of water (18 g) to water vapor (a gas). The volume (V) increases from 18 mL (in water) to 30 600 mL (in water vapor). This is an increase in V by 1 700 times. The number of water molecules did *not* change (because each mole of any substance contains 6.02×10^{23} particles), but its V did. This huge expansion in V tells us a large space between gas molecules. Despite large spaces between a gas molecules, its molecules move fast at high V. It takes a notable time for gas molecules to move from one side of a room to the other, as the molecules constantly collide (contact) each other. Interesting to know that 1) Gas particles have about 8 billion collisions every second, and 2) The air's average velocity at STP is about 1 800 km/h, and that of hydrogen is 6120 km/s.]

Plasma

As the fourth state of matter, plasma occurs as a gas is heated to extreme temperatures or subjected to a strong electromagnetic field. In plasmas, the ionization of atoms occurs so that the valance (outer) electrons are so energized that they leave their parent atoms to become free electrons. Because of containing ions, the plasmas carry electric charges, so electrically are conductive, producing electric current. Neon signs, which carry current, are in the plasma state. Plasma is the most abundant state of matter in the Universe (because the Sun and stars are made of plasma and a thin layer of plasma exists in the space between galaxies).

Other general properties of plasma are outlined next.

- Plasma has *no* definite (constant) shape and *no* definite volume,
- Plasma is very opaque; therefore, *nothing* can be seen through it,
- Plasma's particles are neither close together nor move around freely, and
- Plasma heat energy (E_Q) is the highest of all other states of matter (see Figure 1).

[Note: Some scientists think that at high temperatures and pressures, such as in the interior of some planets, water exists in the plasma state, known as **ionic water**. This occurs when water molecules break down into hydrogen and oxygen ions. And at even higher temperatures, water exists as **superionic water**, in which the released O ions crystallize and H ions float around the oxygen crystals. Knowing that plasma is hot and very opaque, the Universe can be seen when it cools down so much that plasma can become atoms.]

S-106

STATIC HEAD

Another name for LIQUID HEAD.

S-107

STATIC PRESSURE

The term **static pressure** is used in the following few ways:

- In fluid dynamics, the word **static** is omitted, so the pressure has the same meaning as **static pressure**.
- In fluid statics, it is used as **hydrostatic pressure** to refer to the liquid head (*h*), the *P* of a non-moving liquid in a container (like in a tank), given by the liquid's height. So defined, *h* is a measure of *P*, expressed in length units (*L*, usually in m or Ft). [The terms **static pressure**, **hydrostatic pressure**, and **liquid head** have the same meanings.]
- It is used as air's static pressure (simply pressure) in an airplane or a space shuttle in the space industry.

S-108

STATION

Simplified name for CHEMICAL PROCESS STATION.

S-109

STEADY AND UNSTEADY FLOWS

Steady Flows: A steady (fully-developed or uniform) flow is an ideal liquid flow with the next characteristics.

- It flows smoothly at a constant mass flow rate ($\dot{M}$),
- It flows at a constant velocity (V) in the direction of an applying force, and
- It usually exists where stream layers (S-layers, the layers toward the center of a pipe) are.

In addition, a steady flow has three (3) more properties:

- No friction occurs between the stream of the flow and its boundary (say, the wall of the pipe),
- No eddy (vortex or whirlpool) occurs in the stream of the flow, and
- No **circulation** occurs in the stream of the flow.

Unsteady Flow: An unsteady (unstable) flow (**interrupted flow**) refers to a non-ideal liquid flow with the following characteristics:

- It flows roughly at a varying $\dot{M}$ (mass flow rate),
- It flows at a varying V (velocity) in the direction of an acting force, and
- It usually exists where boundary layers (the layers toward the wall of a pipe) are.

To become familiar with steady and unsteady flows, consider Figure 1, which shows a liquid flow in a pipe. Usually, liquids flow in a pipe as extremely thin layers in a certain direction. A complete, steady flow exists in the pipe's middle parts, where S-layers exist. Instead, a flow occurring in the areas next to the pipe's wall, where B-layers exist or where an object (such as a valve) exists in the flow, is an **unsteady flow**. As seen from the same figure, the velocities of the S-layers in the pipe's middle area are shown with equal arrows (for equal velocity vectors). Note that the lengths of arrows are *not* the same; the arrows indicating S-layers in the middle of the flow are shown larger and ahead of the arrows of B-layers to indicate that a steady flow with maximum velocity exists at the flow's *center*.

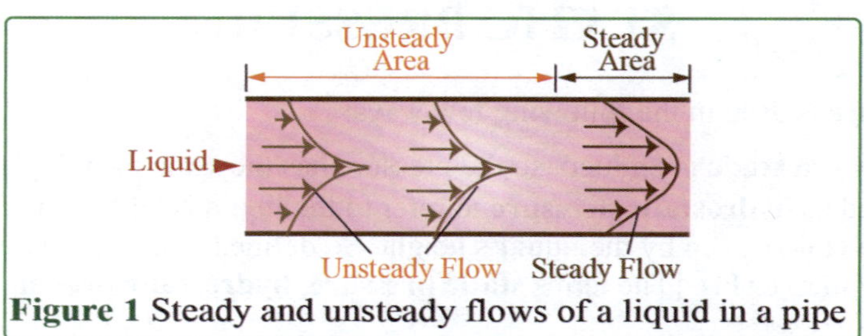

Figure 1 Steady and unsteady flows of a liquid in a pipe

S-110

STEAM

Study VAPOR AND STEAM.

S-111

STEAM AND ELECTRICITY PRODUCTION PROCESS

The steam-and-electricity production (SAEP; also called **steam-and-power production**, SAPP) in a chemical process plant is the process of producing supersaturated steam (simply **super steam** or live steam) in a steam boiler (simply **boiler**), converting the steam's heat energy (E_Q) into kinetic energy (E_K) in an electric turbine (simply **turbine**), and using the turbine's E_K in an electric generator (simply **generator**) turning its rotor to generate **power** (electricity). [Terminology: The terms **power** and **electricity** are usually used equally, while electric power (P_E, simply **power**) is defined as electric energy (E_E, simply **electricity**) per time (t). The reason for doing so is that the produced electricity is usually expressed in the P_E units, mainly in megawatt/hour (MW/h) instead of the E_E units.]

The steam discharged from the turbine, called exhaust steam, is used in a chemical plant's steam-user stations (like the evaporation station). [Steam production in the boilerhouse and its efficient use in the turbines and steam users are very important to the economy of a chemical plant.]

Before going further, it is helpful to study the following:

- **Boilerhouse and Powerhouse:** A boilerhouse is a process station (simply **station**) where one (or more) boiler and its attached and detached parts are located. A powerhouse is a station where one (or more) turbine and one (or more) generator are located. The boilerhouse is operated by the boilerhouse operator, the powerhouse by the powerhouse operator, and the plant's **chief engineer** supervises both. The person in charge must be fully familiar with the boilerhouse and powerhouse operations and devices. [There is *no* time for on-the-job training, reviewing layouts, or tracing pipelines in an emergency.]
- **Safety:** Safety is important in operating the boilerhouse, powerhouse, and steam-and-electricity distribution systems. Thus, sufficient training of the operators on the safety issues is a must.

Based on operations, a chemical process plant can be classified into the following two types:

- **Electricity-Producer Plant:** Such a plant produces both steam and electricity (see the left side of Figure 2), so **super** (live) **steam** is produced more than needed for the process. The entire steam is used to drive the turbines to produce electricity, and exhaust steam from the turbines is used by steam users (like evaporation station). [Some factories are designed to sell some surplus electricity to a near power plant.]
- **Electricity-Buyer Plant:** Such a plant produces only steam and buys its entire electricity need from a near power plant (see Figure 2).

[The interest in chemical plants of the first type has increased recently, as the cost of fuel and electricity has steadily gone up.]

A steam-and electricity-production (SAEP) operations of a chemical plant consist of the next four steps:

- **Step 1:** The boiler uses feedwater to produce supersaturated steam (simply **super steam** or **live steam**).
- **Step 2:** The turbine expands the super steam to increase its pressure (P) to rotate its shaft at high speed (U).
- **Step 3:** The steam discharged from the turbine (exhaust steam) is used in the steam-user stations to cover their heat energy (E_Q) needs and produce condensate that returns to the boiler as feedwater.
- **Step 4:** The generator uses the turbine's shaft work (W_S) to rotate its magnetic field (M-field), created by its electromagnet, to generate alternating current (AC) electricity.

The first three steps make a **thermodynamic** (heat-involving) **cycle** (Figure 3), which can be represented by the Rankine cycle (also called the **temperature-entropy diagram** or ***T-S* diagram**). The Rankine cycle uses the Thermodynamic Second Law, which says E_Q in a closed system is the product of the system's T (temperature) multiplied by its change in S (entropy); that is, $E_Q = T.\Delta S$. In the theoretical T-S diagram shown in Figure 4, the liquid phase is on the left, the vapor phase is on the right, and the peak of the curve shows the water's critical temperature ($T_C = 374$°C). The figure also shows a small T increase line that represents pumping.

We can learn the following important points from the *T-S* diagram and *T-S* equation ($E_Q = T.\Delta S$):

- The *higher* a super steam's *T* and the *lower* the exhaust-steam *T*, the *more* W_S (shaft work) can be obtained from its SAEP cycle. Similarly, the *higher* the super steam's *P*, the *greater* is the W_S. This means that the *greater* the steam's *T* and *P*, the *greater* is the turbine's W_S and, thus, the *more* electricity is produced.
- The *lower* a condenser's *P*, the *more* W_S can be obtained from its cycle. This is because the turbine-exhaust steam's *T* is a function of the condenser's *P* (the turbine's condenser or an evaporator's condenser). Thus, the lower the condenser's *P*, the *greater* the W_S. Therefore, *more* AC electricity is generated in the generator (**alternator** because it produces AC electricity).

What was shown in Figure 4 represents a theoretical *T-S* diagram under the assumption that the steam expansion in the turbine behaves like an isentropic flow (a *P*-change flow). The cycle's expansion line (black) is shown vertically in the same figure, but it generally slopes to the right, as shown in Figure 5. This slope (the rise-to-run ratio) indicates that the *S* (entropy) increases, and the amount of its increase indicates the turbine's **inefficiency** compared with an ideal theoretical cycle efficiency.

As seen in Figure 6 (*T-P* relation of steam at saturation), the curve's slope is *greater* at *lower* pressures than at *higher* pressures. This tells us that a larger *P* increase is required to get the same *T* to increase in the areas with higher *P*. We know that increasing *P* directly affects the wear of devices (equipment), which is a disadvantage, so it must be chosen appropriately.

Boiler Operation and Efficiency

When pressure (*P*) in a boiler increases, the following also increase:

- The enthalpy (*H*) of steam,
- The temperature (*T*) of steam, and
- The boiling point temperature (T_{BP}) of water.

While super (live) steam is the best steam that can be used in a steam turbine but is *not* the right steam to be used directly in some heat-user stations (like an evaporating or heating station) of a chemical plant because:

- It has high pressure (*P*), which is inappropriate for some steam users.
- It has low heat transferability compared with saturated steam.

Thus, an electricity-buyer chemical plant with *no* turbine must adjust the steam *P* at the required level by the steam recompression process before entering a steam-user station. And an electricity-producer plant uses exhaust steam, which is well above the saturated condition, to feed its steam-user stations.

[Note 1: If the *T* or *P* of steam is known, its *H* (enthalpy) can be found from the steam tables (such as Table 1 at the end of this book). Then *H* can be used to calculate the amount of steam required for a process.]

Boiler Size and Type: Steam boilers come in different sizes. A typical small electricity-buyer plant (without a steam turbine and generator) uses low-pressure boilers that operate at 400 to 600 kPa (= 4 to 6 Bar or 58 to 87 PSI) to produce super steam with 145 to 150ºC. An electricity-buyer plant (with turbine and generator), instead, uses high-pressure boilers with 1500 to 3500 kPa (= 15 to 35 Bar or 220 to 510 PSI) *P* to produce super steam with 200 to 255ºC (= 390 to 490ºF). Today, some plants use extra high-pressure boilers to produce super steam with up to 8 000 kPa (= 80 Bar = 1180 PSI) at 500ºC (= 932ºF). A modern steam turbine, which uses super steam, can discharge exhaust steam at about 145ºC and 415 kPa. Such steam is well above the saturated state for high steam users, such as an evaporation station.

Steam boilers come in different types that can use different fuels (natural gas, fuel oil, or coal). When fuel reacts with atmospheric oxygen, the chemical bonds of its molecules break to release energy (in the form of chemical-potential energy, E_{CP}). The E_{CP} then converts to E_Q (heat energy) absorbed by the water in a boiler to produce steam. When, say, 1 kg of natural gas in a boiler's furnace reacts with molecular oxygen (O_2), 49 000 kJ of E_Q is released. Or, more precisely, when 1 kg of carbon (C) in natural gas reacts with O_2, 53 000 kJ of E_Q is released (because 92.5% of natural gas is C).

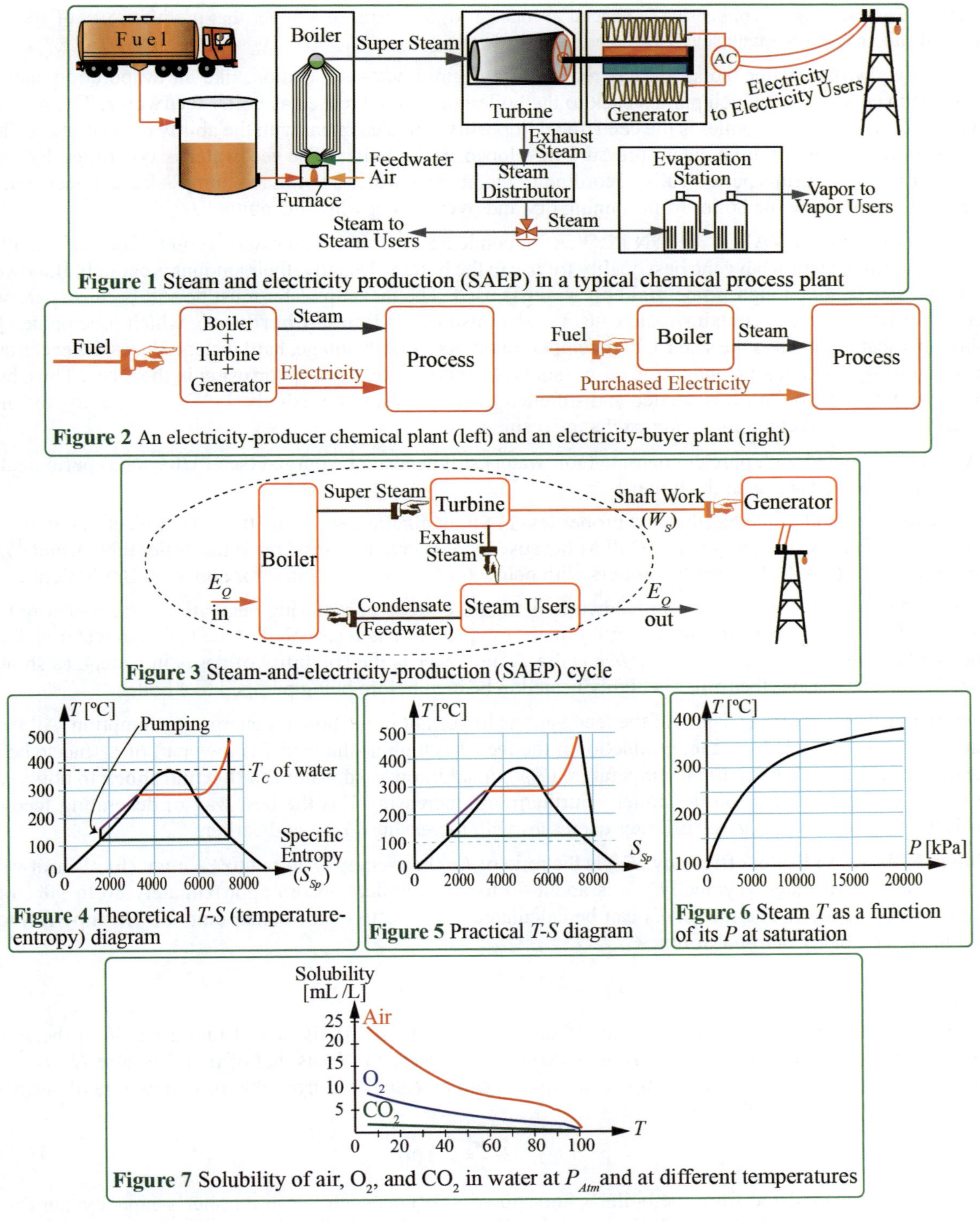

Figure 1 Steam and electricity production (SAEP) in a typical chemical process plant

Figure 2 An electricity-producer chemical plant (left) and an electricity-buyer plant (right)

Figure 3 Steam-and-electricity-production (SAEP) cycle

Figure 4 Theoretical *T-S* (temperature-entropy) diagram

Figure 5 Practical *T-S* diagram

Figure 6 Steam *T* as a function of its *P* at saturation

Figure 7 Solubility of air, O_2, and CO_2 in water at P_{Atm} and at different temperatures

[Note 2: Enough air, with about 21% O_2 mixed with fuel in a boiler's furnace, is important in the efficiency of steam production. This subject is sufficiently discussed under combustion air requirement and furnace.]

[Note 3: Almost 1 kg of condensate is needed to make 1 kg of steam, so a boiler that produces 80 t of steam per hour needs about 80 t of condensate/h as the boiler's feedwater.]

Boiler Feedwater: After the steam has released its E_Q in a heat-user station, like an evaporation station, it condenses to condensate, which pumps back to the boilerhouse to be reused as boiler **feedwater**. The pump that moves the feedwater to the boiler is the centrifugal or positive-displacement with the ability to generate sufficient pressure to overcome the high steam pressure developed in the boiler. The feedwater is controlled by a **level controller** (LC), so it runs periodically according to the boiler's water level. Each pump's LC connects with the boiler's LC, preventing the boiler from running dry and overheating when the pump has failed.

As discussed under EVAPORATION PROCESS, condensates from the first and second effects of a multiple-effect evaporation station have the best quality for use in the boilers. Usually, their amount is enough. If, however, the condensate is *not* enough, some **makeup water** is used. The makeup water must be soft because hard water (well water or city water) contains scale-causing salts (also called **limesalt hardness**), which precipitate (↓) on the boiler's heating tubes as the scale at high temperatures. As a disadvantage, hard water reduces the heat transfer and contains oxygen and noncondensing gases (such as ammonia) that create corrosion in the tubes. Thus, before hard water enters the boiler, it is aerated and softened by one of the two methods: 1) Water softening by chemicals, and 2) Water softening by an ion-exchange resin.

[A boiler that is fed with pure condensate (soft water) still needs to be purged (see PURGING) periodically to remove the dissolved solids in the boiler.]

A typical pure condensate has the next properties: 1) Slight alkaline PH (8 to 10), 2) Low electric conductivity (almost zero), 3) Low oxygen (max 0.02 PPM because oxygen creates corrosion in the boiler tubes), and 4) Low limesalt hardness (1 to 2 PPM for the boilers with below 60 Bar pressure and 0 for above 60 Bar boilers).

Feedwater Deaeration: Oxygen in feedwater is highly corrosive, requiring deaeration. The best way to deaerate water is to boil it because the solubility of air, oxygen (O_2), and carbon dioxide (CO_2) in water is directly related to the water temperature (the *higher* is the *T*, the *lower* is the solubility of gases in water), as shown in Figure 7. For this reason, feedwater is highly heated in heaters before being pumped to a boiler.

Feedwater Temperature: The *T* of the feedwater is important in the boiler's energy consumption. All the EQ (heat energy) is available for steam production if the feed *T* is high. If the feed *T* is low, part of E_Q has to be used to heat the water to its boiling point temperature (T_{BP}). In addition, cold water is a **thermal shock** to boiler metal that increases wear and tear on the boiler. Furthermore, increasing *T* is the best way of deaerating feedwater (generally, the solubility of gases in water decreases with increasing *T*), as said earlier.

Boiler Efficiency: Boiler efficiency (E_B) is the ratio of E_Q (heat-energy) output to E_Q input (fuel's heat value), expressed as a percentage. Typically, E_B is about 80 to 90% (boilers absorb approximately 80 to 90% of the enthalpy value of fuel). The rate of E_B can be calculated as the ratio of the steam output's enthalpy (*H*) to the steam input's enthalpy per unit of time.

$$E_B = \frac{\dot{M}_S(H_S - H_{F.W})}{\dot{M}_F . H_F} \times 100 \qquad (1)$$

In this equation, $\dot{M}_S$ is the mass flow rate of steam produced, and $\dot{M}_F$ is that of fuel used. H_S is the specific enthalpy of steam produced (in kJ/kg), $H_{F.W}$ is that of feed water, and H_F is that of fuel. Because H_S, $H_{F.W}$, and H_F in a chemical process plant are almost constant, E_B can be calculated from the mass flow rate of steam produced ($\dot{M}_S$) and the fuel used ($\dot{M}_F$).

$$E_B = \frac{\dot{M}_S}{\dot{M}_F} \times 100 \qquad (2)$$

The $\dot{M}_S$ can be calculated from the boiler's horsepower (HP), as each HP in a boiler's capacity can roughly evaporate 15.7 kg (= 34.5 Lb) of feedwater per hour (h), so a boiler with 2 000 HP can produce:

$$\dot{M}_S = 2000 \times 15.7 = 31400 \text{ kg of steam/h}$$

This tells us that such a boiler needs 31 400 kg of water/h, equating to 2000 × 34.5 = 69000 Lb /h.

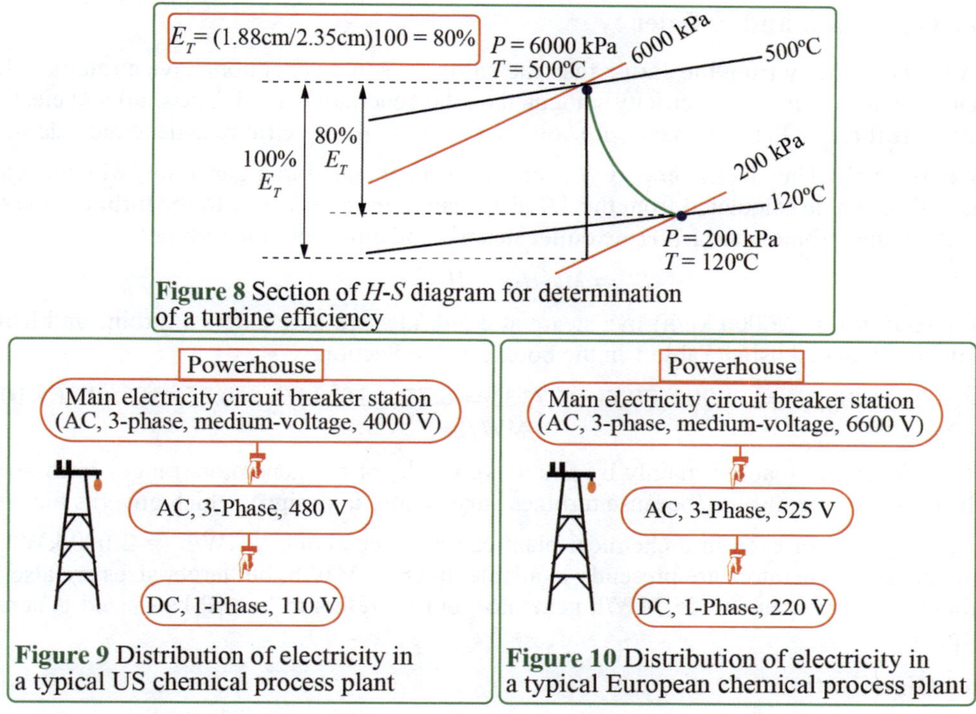

Figure 8 Section of *H-S* diagram for determination of a turbine efficiency

Figure 9 Distribution of electricity in a typical US chemical process plant

Figure 10 Distribution of electricity in a typical European chemical process plant

Turbine Operation and Efficiency

A turbine's main function is to convert as high as possible the E_Q (heat energy) used in that turbine to convert into E_K (kinetic energy) to produce a high amount of W_S (shaft work). This depends on the following parameters:

- **Turbine Design:** A right-designed turbine with the right blades that turn at the right speed (same as the steam's speed) can expand the steam sufficiently to increase its *P* (pressure).
- **Steam Quality:** The super steam entering a turbine must be high in *H* (enthalpy), *T* (temperature), and *P* (pressure) with *no* traces of water.
- **Steam Quantity:** The amount of steam depends on its entering mass flow rate ($\dot{M}$) to the turbine.

In a typical chemical process plant, **super** (live) **steam** from boilers, usually at *P* of about 8 000 kPa (= 80 Bar = 1 180 PSI) and *T* of about 500ºC (= 932ºF), enters the turbine. [Super-steam *P* of around 8 500 kPa (with *T* of around 525ºC) is the maximum *P* that can be allowed to be used in a turbine (because greater *P* than this causes steam expansion and creates corrosion problems.] The high-pressure steam, which enters the turbine through many narrow nozzles, forces the turbine's shaft to turn at a high RPM of up to 10 000. Several (in thousands) **moving blades** (rotors) are attached to the turbine's shaft. Several **stationary blades** (stators) also direct the steam across the moving blades. The **hydraulic governor** of the turbine maintains a constant speed of the blades, which drive the generator. After turning the turbine's shaft, the steam leaves the turbine as the exhaust steam, which has lower energy than the super (live) steam entering the turbine.

Turbine Efficiency: A turbine's efficiency (E_T) can be determined graphically on an enthalpy-entropy diagram (*H-S* diagram, also known as the Mollier diagram), such as the one shown under ENTHALPY ENTROPY DIAGRAM. For orientation, Figure 8 shows a section of an *H-S* diagram to determine a turbine's E_T (efficiency). If the turbine were reversibly operable, the efficiency line would be 100%, shown by a vertical black line. But it intersects the steam-exhaust *P* below the saturation line. As the detailed situations are given in the same figure, the E_T is shown to be 80%, which means the turbine converts 80% of the enthalpy (*H*) in steam to the shaft work (W_S). The operating line (green) is a curve line because the E_T is higher at higher steam conditions.

Generator Operation and Efficiency

It is easier to get electricity from the **stator** than the **rotor**, so some generators have a rotating electromagnet (a magnet connected to a source of electricity) mounted on the generator's shaft. The shaft and electromagnet act as the generator's **rotor**, and the stationary wire coil, in which the AC electricity is generated, acts as its **stator**.

Generator Efficiency: The electric energy (E_E, electricity) generated in a generator, which is called generator's efficiency (E_G), can be calculated from the $\dot{M}_S$ (the steam's mass flow rate to the turbine), the H_{In} (the inlet steam's enthalpy to the turbine), and H_{Out} (the outlet steam's enthalpy from the turbine).

$$E_E = \dot{M}_S(H_{In} - H_{Out}) \tag{3}$$

If, for example, 75 t/h (= 75 000 kg/h) live steam at 2 548 kPa pressure enters a turbine and leaves it at 232 kPa, the E_E can be calculated using Table 1 in the book's Table Section.

$$E_E = \dot{M}_S\,(H_{In} - H_{Out}) = 75000(2803 - 2713) = 6.75 \times 10^6 \text{ kJ/h} = 6.75\times10^6\times0.36\times10^{-6} = 2.4 \text{ MW/h}$$

Because of inefficiencies (caused mainly by frictions), the E_E of the generators ranges from 30 to 90%, depending on the design of the turbine (because turbines vary greatly in design), which governs the generator.

A small electric generator used in a chemical plant can produce about 2 MW/h (= 2 000 kW/h) of electric power (E_E, electricity). Generators are presently available up to 25 MW/h, but larger sizes are also built. A medium-sized chemical plant uses one 25 MW/h generator, but it prefers to have 2 half-sized generators, should one unit be repaired.

Electricity Distribution

Typical today's chemical plants use electricity (power) in the following three forms:

- Three-phase medium-voltage is for main electric distribution and selected large motors.
- Three-phase low-voltage is used in electric motors, pumps, compressors, conveyors, and more.
- Single-phase low-voltage is used for control rooms, instruments, lighting, office equipment, and more.

In a typical US chemical plant, AC electricity is distributed from the main circuit-breaker station at the 3-phase, the medium voltage of 4000 V, to the electric users of the plant, as shown in Figure 9. Then it is reduced by a transformer at strategic points to 3-phase, low-voltage of 480 V to be used in AC motors with 250 HP (= 184 kW/h) or less, while larger motors (about 680HP = 500 KW/h), like the motor of a centrifuge, may use 4000 V to save electricity cost. Finally, the 480-V is reduced to single-phase low-voltage DC electricity of 110 V for users, such as lighting and control rooms. [Sometimes, a voltage of 50 V is also used in the plant for process-control purposes.]

In a typical European chemical process plant, AC is distributed from the main station at 3-phase, 6600 V, then is reduced to 3-phase, 525 V, AC electricity, and finally to 1-phase, 220 V, DC (as shown in Figure 10). [European variable-speed motors use AC up to 690V.]

You should also be aware of the next points about this subtopic:

- 6600 V was high-voltage electricity in the past, but 11000 V is now.
- The electricity cost depends on the voltage (the *higher* the voltage, the *less* electricity cost).
- A 3-phase, 3-wire electricity is usually more economical than an equivalent single-phase, 2-wire one.
- Almost all electric motors (simply **motors** or **drives**) in modern chemical plants are AC motors.
- Chemical facilities use variable frequency motors (also called **variable speed drives**) and direct-current (DC) motors. The disadvantages of the DC motors are their high initial cost, maintenance, and the need for the device to transform variable DC electricity to AC electricity used in the facility.

S-112
STEAM BOILERS AND STEAM REBOILERS

Steam Boilers

A steam boiler (simply **boiler**) is a closed vessel in which heat energy (E_Q, simply heat) from a fuel (or from nuclear reactions) is used to convert pure water (usually condensate) to supersaturated steam (simply **super steam**). The produced super (live) steam has high pressure (P) and temperature (T) because steam occupies more volume (V) than water. The steam with a high P from the boiler of a chemical process plant can be used in a steam turbine (simply **turbine**), which converts the heat energy (E_Q, simply heat) of steam to kinetic energy (E_K). The E_K then turns the shaft of an electric generator to produce electric power (simply **power** or **electricity**). And the exhaust steam from the turbine can be used by the steam users of the plant.

Boiler Attached Parts: The main attached parts (fittings) of a boiler are the following (see Figure 1):

- **Furnace:** Furnace is discussed in detail in a moment.
- **Burner:** It mixes fuel and air in oil-fired or gas-fired boilers.
- **Bunker** (stocker): It mixes coal and combustion air in coal-fired boilers.
- **Feedwater Valve:** It is used for controlling the flow of feedwater to the boiler.
- **Safety Valve:** It protects the boiler from maximum allowable working pressure (MAWP).
- **Blowdown Valve:** It is for **blowdown** (opening the boiler's blowdown valve for a short period and removing the suspended solids from the boiler).
- **Steam Stop Valve:** It takes the boiler out of the operating cycle.
- **Pressure Gauge:** It is used for showing steam gauge pressure.
- **Vacuum Gauge:** It shows the boiler's vacuum pressure.
- **Water Indicator:** It shows the boiler's water level.

Boiler Detached Parts: The main detached parts (accessories) of a boiler are the following:

- **Condensate Tank:** It holds the boiler's condensate (a boiler's feedwater).
- **Feedwater Pump:** It pumps feedwater to the boiler (reciprocating or centrifugal pumps are usually used).
- **Feedwater Regulator:** It maintains the amount of feedwater in the boiler (common types are thermo expansion, thermohydraulic, and float feedwater regulators).
- **Feedwater Heater:** It heats feedwater (feedwater is mostly heated by using heat from the boiler flue gas).
- **Air Heater:** It heats combustion air to the ignition temperature by using the heat of the flue gas.
- **Fuel-Oil Heater:** It is used to heat oil (particularly No. 5 and 6 oil) in oil-fired boilers.
- **Fuel Oil Strainer:** It is used for removing impurities from oil in oil-fired boilers.
- **Feedwater Economizer:** It is used to recover E_Q from a boiler's flue gas to heat its feedwater. [A typical boiler produces about 2 kg (= 1.5 m^3) of flue gas from evaporating 1 kg of water to steam, where each kg of flue gas has about 150 kJ of E_Q.]

Boiler Furnace: As the main attached part of a boiler, a furnace is a device for combustion reaction between the combustible components of a fuel and oxygen (O_2) in the air to create E_Q (heat energy). The released E_Q is then used in the boiler's tubes to convert soft water (usually quality condensate) to high-pressure super steam.

Furnaces can use natural gas, oil, or coal as fuel. Natural gas is the cleanest and the least polluting fuel to use in a furnace. It is, however, more subject to the explosion (sudden fire) than oil or coal.

For a furnace to operate efficiently, it must have enough blowing capacity to supply enough air to complete combustion and to remove the flue gas from the furnace. For the blowing process, air blowers or fans are used, depending on the required air pressure (P), as blowers' can blow air with a higher discharge P (3.5 to 55 kPa) than fans do (0.5 to 25 kPa). [Furnaces are kept under a slight negative vacuum pressure (P_{Vac}) because a positive pressure causes the flue gas to come back to the boilerhouse and possibly harm boiler operators.]

Fuel flows into a burner mixed with the air and burns in the furnace. The flame from the burner then heats the boiler's heating tubes. The water to be steamed flows inside the tubes. The flue gas, produced by the combustion of fuel and air, goes to the furnace's heat recovering (breaching) section, from where it leaves the furnace's stack to the atmosphere. Some E_Q is recovered from the flue gas before venting to the atmosphere in the furnace's recovering section to heat the combustion air.

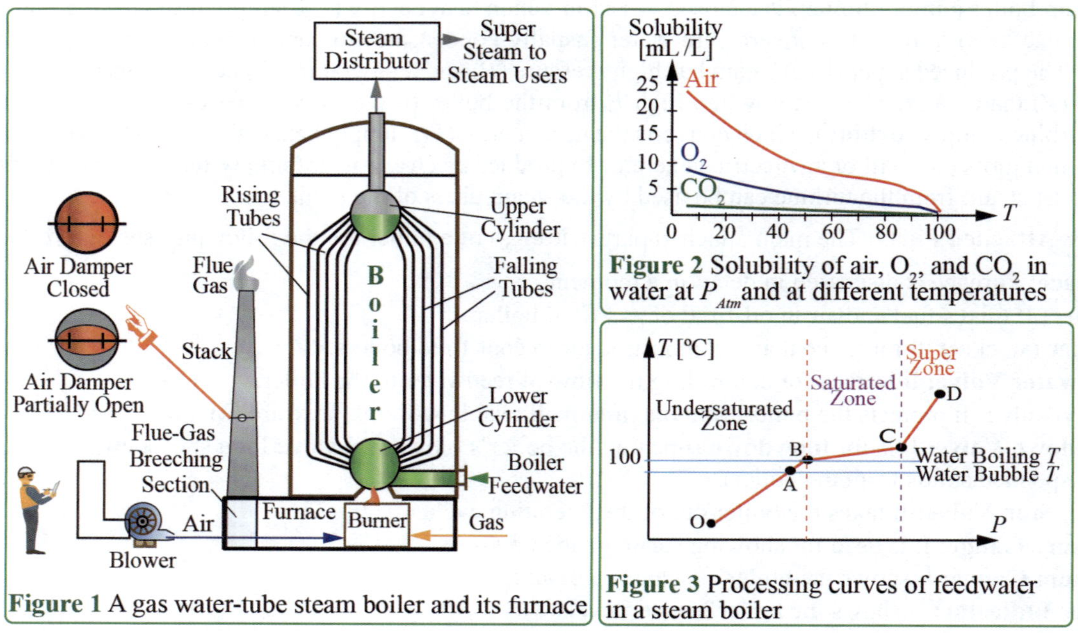

Figure 1 A gas water-tube steam boiler and its furnace

Figure 2 Solubility of air, O_2, and CO_2 in water at P_{Atm} and at different temperatures

Figure 3 Processing curves of feedwater in a steam boiler

Furnace Combustion Heat Requirement: Combustion air requirement (CAR) for the furnace is usually expressed as kg (or Lb) of air required for combustion of one kg (or one Lb) of fuel. Usually, the term **excess air factor** (EAF) indicates the amount of air above the theoretical air requirement (TAR). Often, an EAF of 1.3 to 1.5 (which equates to 30 to 50% excess air) is used. The excess air increases the combustibility of fuel at the expense of using extra air (which is free!). Enough air mixed with fuel is important in furnace operation. The use of the right amount of air can be evaluated based on the composition of the flue gas because,

- High carbon monoxide (CO) in the flue gas is an indication of **insufficient** air, and
- High oxygen (O_2) in the flue gas (more than 4%) indicates **excess** air.

Furnaces can be classified into two (2) classes:

- **Liquid-Fuel Furnaces:** A fluid-fuel furnace has a fuel pump to inject oil (fuel oil). These boilers are used in oil-fired boilers.
- **Solid-Fuel Furnaces:** A solid-fuel furnace has a bunker to feed the coal to the furnace. These furnaces are used in coal-fired boilers.

A pressure difference (ΔP) is required to create an air draft (simply **draft**) to get the air into the furnace's burner and discharge the flue gas from the combustion chamber to the furnace's recovering section and from there to the stack. Based on how the **draft** is supplied, furnaces are classed into two (2) groups:

- **Natural-Draft Furnaces:** A natural-draft furnace uses a chimney effect to create a draft. Because the density (D) of a gas is directly proportional to its pressure (P) and the P of the hot air inside the stack is different than that of the cold air outside the stack, it creates a difference in the D of the air in these areas, creating the air draft in the furnace. In addition, the temperature difference (ΔT) between the inside and outside of the stack affects the draft (the *greater* the ΔT, the *stronger* is the draft). Furthermore, the stack height is also a factor (the *higher* the stack's height, the *stronger* the draft is). The outlet and the inlet air dampers can control the draft quantity in a natural-draft furnace. A damper supplies air to the furnace and discharges the flue gas from the stack.

- **Forced-Draft Furnaces:** To create a draft, a forced-draft furnace uses fans. The draft quantity is controlled by the speed of the fans and the adjustment of the **air dampers**. Fans are located either in front of the furnace or between the furnace and stack to force air to the furnace and discharge the flue gas from the stack.

Boiler Types: The two important types of boilers are the following:

- **Water-Tube Boilers:** Water flows inside the tubes in a water-tube boiler (Figure 1), and heat (heat energy) flows outside the tubes. Water-tube boilers equipped with natural or mechanical draft are the most common boilers used in chemical facilities. A water-tube boiler can produce steam with higher steam pressure than a fire-tube boiler. The tubes in a water-tube boiler are straight or mildly bent. Boilers with bent tubes have more heating surfaces and provide better energy efficiency.
- **Fire-Tube Boilers:** Water flows outside the tubes in a fire-tube boiler, and heat flows inside the tubes.

[Note: Packaged (shop-assembled) boilers are built at the boiler-manufacturing shop and shipped to the facility for installation. The production cost of packaged boilers is lower than that of facility-assembled boilers. Today, most new chemical facilities use packaged boilers.]

Boiler Size: A typical chemical process plant with *no* steam turbine uses low-pressure boilers, operating at 400 to 600 kPa (= 4 to 6 Bar or 58 to 87 PSI) to produce super steam with 145 to 150ºC. Instead, chemical facilities with turbines use high-pressure boilers with 1500 to 3500 kPa (= 15 to 35 Bar or 220 to 510 PSI) *P* to produce super steam with 200 to 255ºC (= 390 to 490ºF). Today, some facilities use extra high-pressure boilers to produce super steam with up to 8 000 kPa (= 80 Bar = 1180 PSI) at 500ºC (= 932ºF). A modern steam turbine, which uses such steam, can discharge exhaust steam at about 145ºC and 415 kPa. Such steam is well above the saturated state for high-steam users, like an evaporation station.

Boiler Rating: Horsepower (HP) is used to rate a steam boiler or steam turbine. HP of a boiler can be roughly estimated by its heat transfer area, where 1 m^2 (= 10 Ft^2) heating area equates to about 1 HP ($\approx$ 0.75 kW.h). Similarly, HP equates to the evaporation of 15.7 kg (= 34.5 Lb) of water/h (per hour). This equates to 15.7 × 2 256 = 35 420 kJ/h (= 34.5 × 970 = 33 465 BTU/h), where 2 256 and 970 are the latent heat of the water in kJ (kilo Joules) and BTU (British thermal units). This means that a boiler with 2 000 HP can produce 2 000 × 15.7 = 31 400 kg (= 2 000 × 34.5 = 69 000 Lb) of steam/h.]

Boiler Feedwater: The industrial boilers use condensate (pure water) as feedwater. But all produced condensates are *not* suitable for use as feedwater in boilers (because of impurities that deposit on the boiler's tubes). In a chemical facility with a multiple-effect evaporation station, feedwater is usually supplied mainly from the condensate produced from the condensation of the exhaust steam in the first effect of the station. This condensate (the exhaust condensate) is the highest quality for boilers. The balance is covered by the condensate produced from the condensation of the first vapor in the second effect. When there is *not* enough suitable condensate, **makeup water** (usually softened city or well water) is added to the boiler after being softened. Water softening is required because the limesalt hardness of **raw water** (hard water from well or city water) is often high and would lead to excessive tube scaling.

Feedwater Deaeration: Oxygen in feedwater is highly corrosive, and the best way to deaerate water is to boil it. This can be proved by Figure 2, which indicates that the solubility of air, oxygen (O_2), and carbon dioxide (CO_2) in water is directly related to the water temperature (*T*). For this reason, feedwater is heated in a heater to near its T_{BP} (boiling point temperature) before being pumped to the boiler.

Feedwater Pump: A feedwater pump pumps condensate from the feedwater tank into the boiler. These pumps are centrifugal or positive-displacement types that can generate sufficient pressure to overcome the high steam pressure developed in the boiler. Pumps are controlled by a **level controller** (LC) to control the water level in the boiler, so they run periodically according to the boiler's water level. Each pump's level controller connects with the boiler control system, preventing the boiler from running dry and overheating when the pump has failed, its feed has been cut off, or its discharge is blocked.

Boiler Operation: A boiler operates in a circulation process, meaning that the condensate periodically returns to the boiler. Consider a boiler that operates in connection with a condensate tank, a turbine, an evaporator, and a condenser. In such a combined operation, the circulation process consists of six (6) steps:

- Pumping condensate from the boiler's feedwater tank into the boiler.
- Converting condensate to steam with high T and P by getting the E_Q from the fuel.
- Converting the steam's E_Q to shaft work (W_S) to turn the turbine's shaft. As a result of W_S, the steam expands in the turbine, causing the stem's T and P to be *decreased*.
- Sending turbine exhaust steam to the evaporator gives part of its E_Q to the liquid under evaporation.
- Condensation part of steam and vapor into condensate in the evaporator.
- Returning the condensate to the boiler's feedwater tank (the beginning of the cycle) to be used again as the boiler feedwater.

As shown in Figure 3, the processing curves of the boiler's feedwater go through three (3) zones:

- **Undersaturated** (unsaturated) **Zone:** This zone is represented by line OA, which indicates the heating of the condensate to A, which is the water's bubble point temperature, and from there to point B, which is the boiling point temperature (T_{BP}) of the condensate.
- **Saturated Zone:** This zone is represented by line BC, during which the vapor's T gradually *increases* to produce saturated steam.
- **Super Zone:** This zone is represented by line CD, during which the steam's T still *increases* to produce super (supersaturated) steam with the highest T and P.

Boiler Fuel: The fuel cost for producing steam is second to raw material operating costs for most chemical process facilities. Therefore, efficient fuel consumption for steam production and efficient steam and vapor used in the process is important to the economy of every chemical facility.

Common fuels used in the boiler are coal, fuel oil, and natural gas are fossil fuels. When a boiler can operate with different types of fuel, the type of fuel used depends on the following:

- Fuel's environmental emissions,
- Fuel's resource availability,
- Fuel's price.

Boiler Air Draft: The air draft refers to atmospheric air's pressure difference (ΔP) between two points. In boiler operation, air draft is needed to perform the following:

- Supplying air to the combustion chamber of the furnace for the combustion of fuel, and
- Moving the flue gas (stack gas) out of the furnace's stack.

The pressure required for air draft can be applied naturally (known as the **natural air draft**) or by force of fans (known as the **forced air draft**).

In a **natural-draft furnace**, a chimney effect provides the air draft. As air warms in a furnace, it becomes lighter and moves upward. Colder air is heavier and moves below the warmer air. This process, called the **chimney effect**, occurs in the chimney of a natural-draft furnace. In a natural-draft furnace, the outlet and the inlet **air dampers** control draft to supply air to the furnace and discharge the flue gas from the stack.

The efficiency of air draft produced in a natural-draft furnace depends mainly on the following two factors: 1) Temperature difference (ΔT) between the inside and outside of the stack (the *greater* is the ΔT, the *stronger* is the *draft*), and 2) Stack height (the greater is the stack's height, the stronger is the draft).

The ΔT creates a density difference (ΔD) between the air and higher and lower-pressure points. This also helps the draft (the *greater* is the ΔD, the *stronger* is the draft).

A fan (or more fans) provides the air draft in a forced-draft furnace. Modern chemical plants *no* longer use tall stacks. Instead, the furnace is equipped with a draft fan whose speed controls the draft, supplies air to the furnace, and discharges the flue gas from the stack. Fans are located either in front of the furnace to force air into the furnace or between the furnace and stack to discharge the flue gas into the atmosphere.

Boiler Efficiency: Boiler efficiency (E_B) is the ratio of heat-energy output to heat-energy input, expressed as a percentage. In sugar factories, E_B is about 80 to 90% (boilers absorb approximately 80 to 90% of the heat value of fuel). E_B can be calculated as the ratio of energy output to the energy input per unit of time.

$$E_B = \frac{\dot{M}_S(H_S - H_{F.W})}{\dot{M}_F.H_F} \times 100 \quad (1)$$

In this equation, $\dot{M}_S$ is the mass flow rate of steam produced, $\dot{M}_F$ is fuel burned, H_S is the specific enthalpy of steam produced (in kJ/kg), $H_{F.W}$ is the specific enthalpy of feed water, and H_F is that of fuel.

Because H_S, $H_{F.W}$, and H_F in a chemical process plant are almost constant, the E_B can be calculated from the amounts of steam produced (M_S) and the fuel burned (M_F).

$$E_B = \frac{M_S}{M_F} \times 100 \quad (2)$$

Preparing data to calculate E_B is easy because chemical plants usually have two flowmeters; one for recording steam production and the other for fuel consumption (for oil-fired or gas-fired boilers) or a scale (for coal-fired boilers). Knowing the following two points about E_B (boiler efficiency) is helpful: 1) Typically, the accuracy of E_B calculations is in the range of ±3%. 2) The main portion of E_Q losses in boilers is stack loss. Other losses occur because of incomplete combustion, moisture in the air, low-temperature feedwater, low-temperature combustion air, and heat loss during steam transportation (poor insulation of the pipes).

Boiler Stack Emissions: Boiler stack emissions are gases, particulate matters (PM, simply **particulates**), and odor released from the furnace stack. In general, a gas that contains particulate matter (PM) and leaves a furnace stack is called flue gas or stack gas. The amount and composition of these emissions (pollutants) depend on the type of the fuel (and its amount of ash, SO_2, nitrogen, and moisture) and the design of the boiler and particulate-collecting devices. Using clean fuels (fuels low in sulfur, nitrogen, sodium, and heavy metals) reduces pollution. Stack emission regulations are *not* the same in different countries (even in different states in a country). However, these regulations have become stricter in recent years. Stack emission concentrations are usually expressed in mass per unit energy used by the furnace or mass per unit volume of the flue gas. [A wet scrubber, **cyclone collector**, or **electrostatic precipitator** can remove the particulates from the boiler's furnace. A typical wet scrubber uses about 0.8 L of water per m^3 of gas to fluidize the particulates.]

Steam Reboilers

A steam reboiler (simply **reboiler**) is a steam-heated heat exchanger. Reboilers are often used in the distillation process to bring the temperature (T) of a liquid feed to near its boiling point temperature (T_{BP}) to produce a vapor-liquid mixture, which enters the distillation column. As a source of heat energy (E_Q), a reboiler receives steam from the boilerhouse, or a steam-pressure regulator, at P of 150 to 475 kPa and T of 110 to 150ºC, depending on its duties. In the reboiler, steam flows inside the tubes, and feed flows outside (the shell-side) the tubes.

The reboilers are divided into the following two types:

- **Partial Reboilers:** In a partial reboiler, a portion of the liquid feed evaporates, so the reboiler's product is a mixture of vapor and liquid. [Partial reboilers are the most used ones in the distillation industry.]
- **Total Reboilers:** In a total reboiler, all the feed evaporates. [Total reboilers are rarely used in the industry.]

Reboilers come in different designs, such as kettle, thermosyphon, and forced-circulation reboilers. Figure 4 shows a typical cattle-reboiler, a horizontal heat exchanger consisting of a heating section in which several round **heating tubes** are installed. Steam flows inside the heating tubes, and the liquid feed flows outside (the shell side) of the tubes. A weir (the retaining plate) makes the liquid section of the reboiler into two sections. The deeper-but-narrower section is where the residual re-boiled liquid (the **bottom product**) is withdrawn.

Figure 5 shows a vertical reboiler in which the liquid feed circulates naturally by its decrease in density (D). The feed enters the bottom of the reboiler and is partially evaporated, causing the decrease of D. The decrease in D causes the vapor-liquid mixture to rise to the top of the reboiler. Both liquid and vapor leave the unit's top and enter the distillation column.

Figure 6 shows two reboilers connected in parallel, and Figure 5 shows those in series for increasing the capacity of a distillation column. Figure 8 shows an extra reboiler installed at an upper section of a distillation column to achieve the distillation rate at the top of the column.

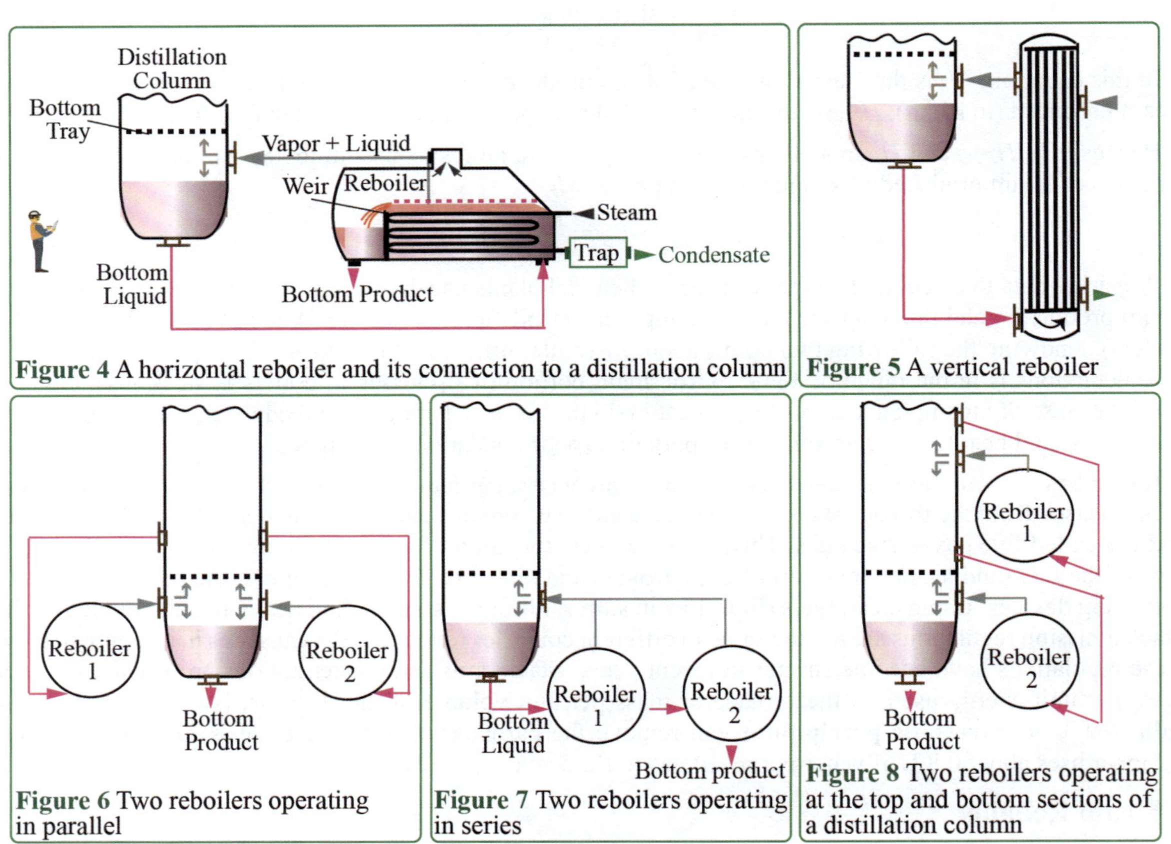

Figure 4 A horizontal reboiler and its connection to a distillation column

Figure 5 A vertical reboiler

Figure 6 Two reboilers operating in parallel

Figure 7 Two reboilers operating in series

Figure 8 Two reboilers operating at the top and bottom sections of a distillation column

S-113

STEAM ECONOMY

Another name for evaporation efficiency. It is discussed under the EVAPORATION PROCESS.

S-114

STEAM ENGINES

Another name for HEAT ENGINES.

S-115

STEAM JET EJECTORS

Discussed under JET EJECTORS.

S-116

STEAM RECOMPRESSION AND VAPOR COMPRESSION

Steam recompression (steam pressure decrease) and vapor compression (vapor pressure increase) are the processes for adjusting a steam's pressure (*P*) and a vapor's pressure to required levels.

Steam Recompression

Steam recompression is the process of decreasing the *P* of a high-pressure steam to a required level. As the result of steam-pressure decrease (steam-*P* reduction), the next two changes occur on a high-pressure steam.

- Its volume (*V*) is increased, and
- Its heat value (heat-energy value or enthalpy value) is decreased.

In chemical process plants, steam is often produced at high *P,* so its *P* is reduced before entering a steam user (like an evaporation station) to achieve the following benefits:

- It downsizes the steam distribution piping system (pipes, valves, and more),
- It improves the steam economy of each steam user, such as evaporation station,
- It keeps steam *P* at the required level, so steam users are *not* affected by fluctuating steam *P*, and
- It improves the heat transferability of supersaturated steam (simply **super steam** or **live steam**) because it has lower heat transferability than saturated steam.

The process of steam recompression is usually done by passing the high-pressure steam through a **steam-pressure reducer**, such as a **pressure-reducing valve** (also called a **recompression valve**). Figure 1 shows a steam-recompression system with a typical recompression valve. Such a system automatically adjusts the level of the valve piston by a pressure controller (PC), so the outlet steam stays at the desired *P*, even when the inlet steam pressure fluctuates. Figure 2 shows a direct-acting (non-piloted) recompression valve used for smaller steam loads. Figure 3 shows a pilot-operated recompression valve used for larger loads, requiring more precise pressure control. The pilot-operated valve has an extra valve (called **pilot valve**) that loads the second piston, increasing the downward force used to open the main valve.

Vapor Compression

Vapor compression (also called vapor pressure compression) increases the pressure (*P*) of a low-pressure vapor to a higher level. As the result of compression of a low-pressure vapor, the next 2 occur on the vapor:

- Its volume (*V*) is decreased, and
- Its **heat value** (heat-energy value or enthalpy value) is increased.

In chemical plants, vapor compression is mainly performed in an evaporation station or distillation station to increase the station's efficiency (because the compressed vapor can evaporate more liquid). For example, in a multiple-effect evaporation station (discussed under EVAPORATION PROCESS), the temperature drop (known generally as temperature difference, ΔT) in individual effects occurs as a result of decreasing the boiling point temperature (T_{BP}) of the liquid feed. Thus, the *P* of the vapor of the individual effects is decreased to the extent that it becomes a low-value vapor and, therefore, *cannot* be used in the next effect evaporator. By compression, a low-pressure vapor becomes a high-pressure vapor, so it can be used in the next effect evaporator or the evaporator from which it came.

Vapor compression is performed by using one (or both) of the following:

- A mechanical device (like a compressor or jet ejector), and
- A high-pressure makeup steam.

Figure 4 illustrates the compression of a low-pressure vapor using a compressor and high-pressure makeup steam, and Figure 5 shows the same process using a steam jet ejector and high-pressure makeup steam.

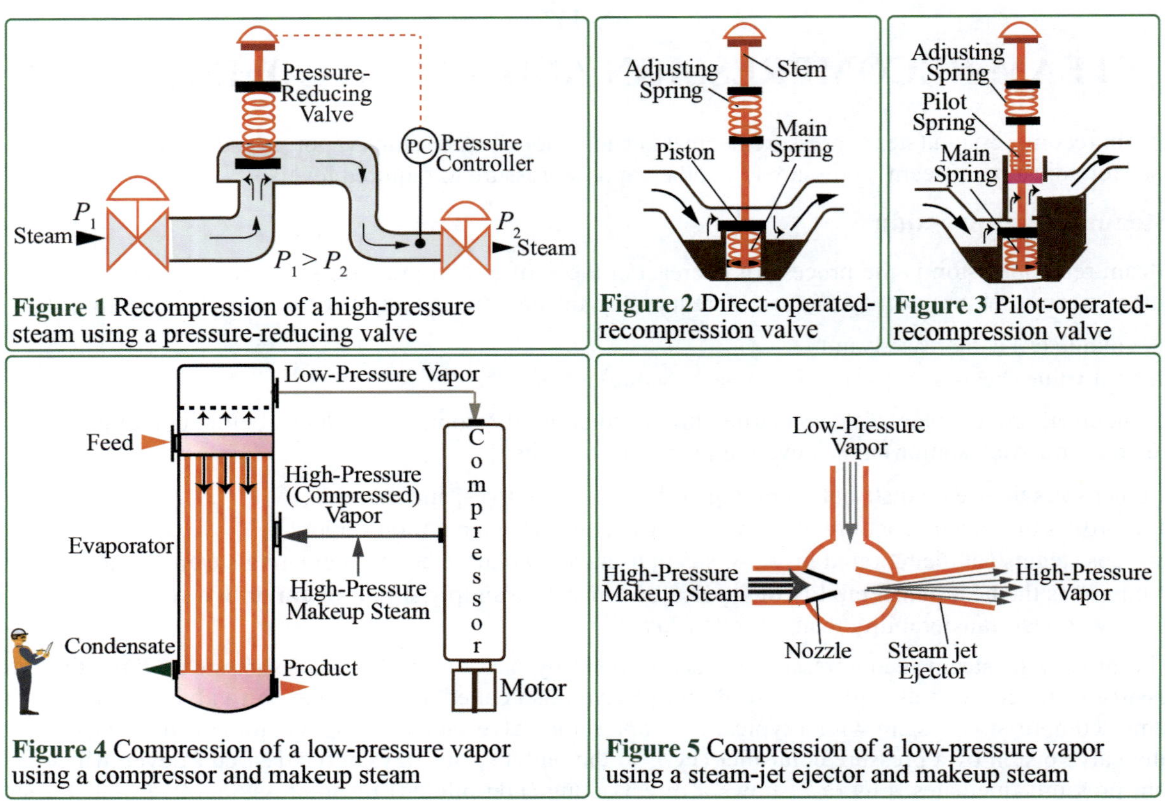

Figure 1 Recompression of a high-pressure steam using a pressure-reducing valve

Figure 2 Direct-operated-recompression valve

Figure 3 Pilot-operated-recompression valve

Figure 4 Compression of a low-pressure vapor using a compressor and makeup steam

Figure 5 Compression of a low-pressure vapor using a steam-jet ejector and makeup steam

S-117
STEAM TABLES

Discussed under the topic of VAPOR AND STEAM.

S-118
STEAM TRAPS

A steam trap is used in a piping system, which carries steam (or vapor) for removing the condensate and air (a noncondensing gas, NC gas) from steam (or vapor). The separation of condensate and air from steam is based on the differential density. On the other hand, a condensate trap is used in a piping system, which carries condensate for removing the air from the condensate.

Steam traps come in different types. Figure 1 illustrates a typical **bucket steam trap** consisting of a cylindrical body. A bucket is placed in the trap's body in an upside-down position, so it can act as a float when it is filled with condensate to about 2/3 of its volume.

The bucket is attached to a lever connected to the air vent and a valve from the other side. During operation, the trap's body is always filled with condensate to a level above the top of the bucket. The condensate provides a water seal above and around the bucket, so the steam *cannot* escape (trapped between the top of the bucket and the water seal below). A space exists on the top of the body above the water seal, where the air is collected while the valve is closed. As the amount of condensate increases, the bucket becomes heavy enough to pull the valve, so the condensate is discharged from the bucket through the condensate port, and the air is released from the top through the air vent.

The steam enters the trap from one side, goes down to move the bucket up, and leaves the bucket from its top. The condensate, formed in the bucket by steam condensation, moves down and leaves the bottom of the trap when it accumulates enough to open the condensate discharge port.

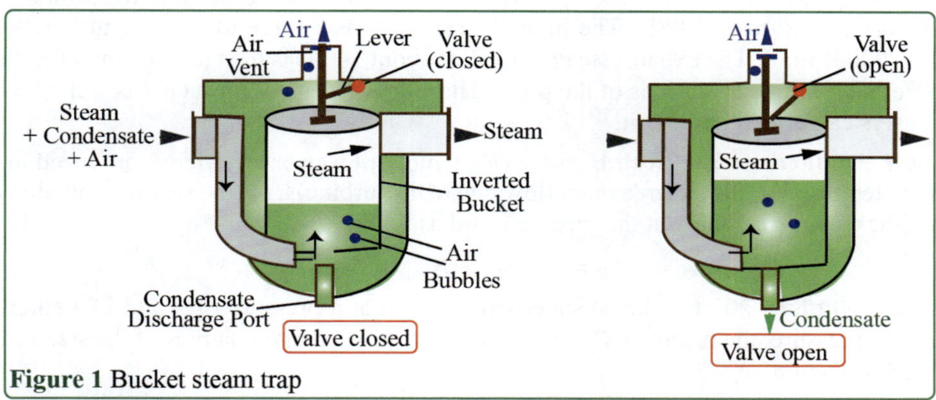

Figure 1 Bucket steam trap

S-119

STEAM TURBINES

A steam turbine (simply **turbine**) is a heat engine that converts the heat energy (E_Q, the enthalpy) in steam into kinetic energy (E_K) to perform shaft work (W_S), which then rotates the wire coil with many loops of an electric generator (simply **generator**). Based on Faraday's Induction Law, a turbine's W_S can rotate the generator's magnetic field (M-field), created by its electromagnet (stator), to generate alternating current (AC) electricity. The value of a turbine's W_S is *negative* because the steam (system) does work (W) on the turbine's shaft. In this way, W_S done by the steam *decreases* the E_Q of the steam as it turns the turbine's shaft. Figure 1 shows a typical steam turbine, consisting of the next main parts.

- A set of moving blades connected to the shaft,
- A set of stationary blades connected to the casing,
- Hydraulic governor for controlling shaft's movement at high RPM,
- Narrow nozzles for increasing the steam's pressure (P) to rotate the blades,
- Process control system for controlling process values in desired setpoint values,
- Lubricating system for preventing the rotating parts from friction, damage, and breakage.

A steam turbine's E_K depends on the following:

- Enthalpy (H, heat-energy) of the steam used,
- Mass flow rate ($\dot{M}$) of the steam used,

- Temperature (T) of the steam,
- Pressure (P) of the steam,
- friction losses.

Large steam turbines use supersaturated steam (simply **super steam** or **live steam**) produced in a steam boiler, typically at P of about 8 000 kPa (= 80 Bar = 1 180 PSI) and T of about 500°C (= 932°F). [Super-steam P of around 8 500 kPa (with T of around 525°C) is the maximum P that can be allowed to be used in a turbine (because high P causes high steam expansion, lowering its efficiency and creating corrosion problems.] The high-pressure steam, which enters the turbine through many narrow nozzles, forces the turbine's shaft to turn at a high RPM of up to 10 000. Several (in thousands) **moving blades** (rotors) are attached to the turbine's shaft. Several **stationary blades** are also there to direct the steam across the moving blades. The **hydraulic governor** of the turbine maintains a constant speed of the moving blades, which drive the generator. After turning the turbine's shaft, the steam leaves the turbine as the exhaust steam, which has lower energy than the super (live) steam entering the turbine.

Figure 2 shows a steam-and-power-production station in a chemical process plant. The station uses super steam with T of 200 to 255°C (= 390 to 490°F), produced in a high-pressure steam boiler with P of 1500 to 3500 kPa (= 15 to 35 bar or 220 to 510 PSI). The high-P steam acts as a force to turn the turbine's shaft at a high rotation (up to 10 000 R/min). The exhaust steam with T of about 140°C is then directed into the steam distributor to be sent to different steam-user stations of the plant. The exhaust steam with such T is well above the saturated state, so steam users can effectively use it.

Turbine Power Production: The electric power (P_E, simply **power** or electricity) produced in a steam generator can be calculated from $\dot{M}$ (the steam's mass flow rate to the turbine), H_{In} (the steam's enthalpy at the turbine's inlet), and H_{Out} (the steam's enthalpy at the turbine's outlet).

$$P_E = \dot{M}(H_{In} - H_{Out}) \qquad (1)$$

If, for example, 200 t/h (= 200 000 kg/h) super (live) steam at a pressure of 2 548 kPa enters a turbine and leaves it at 232 kPa pressure, the turbine's P_E can be calculated by using enthalpies of the steams, given in Table 1 in the book's table section.

$$P_E = 200000(2803 - 2713) = 8.9 \times 10^6 \text{ kJ/h} = 17.8{\times}10^6{\times}0.36{\times}10^{-6} = 6.4 \text{ MW/h}$$

Today's smaller turbines produce up to 30 MW/h of electricity, and larger ones from 30 to 100 MW/h.

Turbine Efficiency: Turbines are *not* 100% efficient in converting E_Q to E_K (mainly because of friction). Their efficiencies typically run between 45% for small turbines and 85% for larger turbo-generating turbines. A turbine's **efficiency** (e), which is the percentage ratio of the output E_Q to the input E_Q, can be determined by an enthalpy-entropy diagram (*H-S* or Mollier diagram) that its graph is given under the same topic. Part of the *H-S* diagram is given in Figure 3 to determine turbine efficiency. Assume that the efficiency expectancy from a turbine is 65%, then the enthalpy (heat) drop would be 65% of the full theoretical value (100%). From the input steam (live-steam) condition, a distance of 65% is drawn toward the vertical (entropy) line, and then a horizontal line is drawn to intersect the same pressure line (shown in **red**). The connection of the points gives the turbine's operation line (shown in **blue**). If a turbine were 100% efficient in converting E_Q to E_K, no E_Q loss would occur, and the steam's entropy (S) would remain constant.

The following two brief points are important to know about steam turbines:

- Horsepower (HP) is used to rate a steam turbine or steam boiler, where 1 HP = 735.5 W/h.
- Steam turbines produce most of the electricity used worldwide. In the USA, about 90% of the electricity is produced in ordinary power plants, and the rest is produced in nuclear power plants.

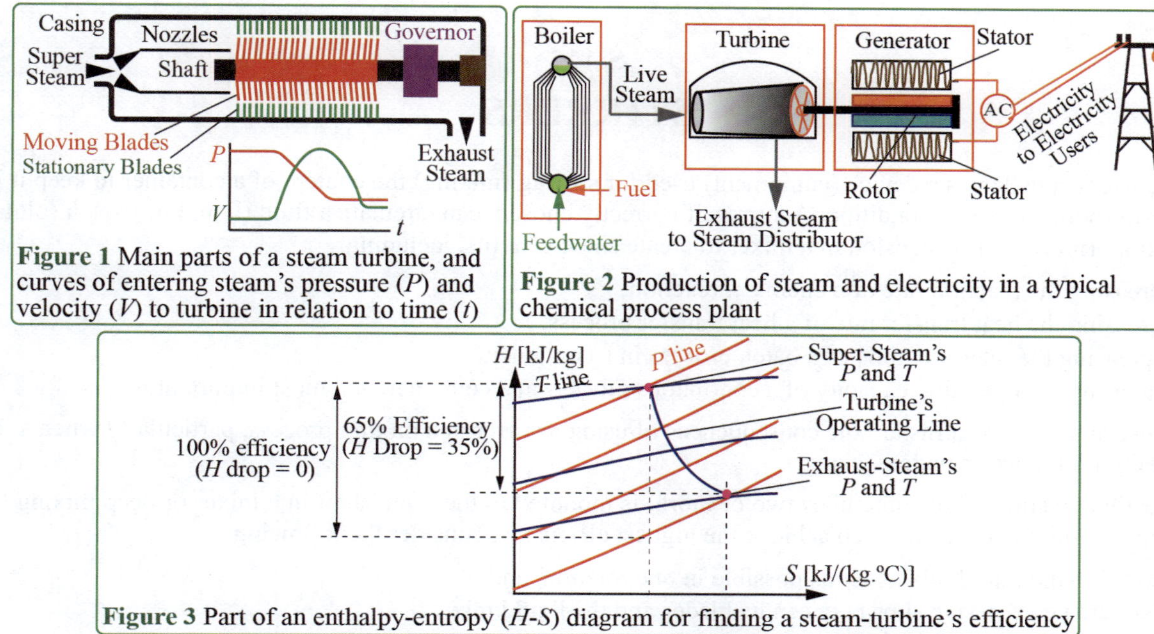

Figure 1 Main parts of a steam turbine, and curves of entering steam's pressure (*P*) and velocity (*V*) to turbine in relation to time (*t*)

Figure 2 Production of steam and electricity in a typical chemical process plant

Figure 3 Part of an enthalpy-entropy (*H-S*) diagram for finding a steam-turbine's efficiency

S-120

STEEL

See ALLOYANTS, ALLOYS, AND ALLOY STEELS.

S-121

STEFAN-BOLTZMANN'S CONSTANT

Study BOLTZMANN AND STEFAN-BOLTZMANN CONSTANTS.

S-122

STEREOISOMERS

Study ISOMERS AND STEREOISOMERS.

S-123

STIRRERS

A stirrer (impeller) is a device (equipment) used for stirring (mixing) the content of a container to keep it in a uniform (homogeneous) condition. A stirrer, if correctly chosen, can circulate a fluid (liquid or gas), a solution, a mixture (mix), or a suspension in a mixer to create some benefits, including:

- Increasing the reaction rate of a chemical reaction,
- Increasing the heat transfer rate of a heat transfer process,
- Decreasing the retention time of a batch process in a container,
- Increasing the operating capacity of a continuous process in a container, and most importantly

These and more benefits are the consequences of using a stirrer in a mixing process, particularly when a low-viscosity liquid mix is under stirring.

Mostly one stirrer (but sometimes two or more) is mounted to the same shaft in a mixer or deep mixing tank to improve mixing efficiency. To achieve the highest efficiency, consider the following:

- Moving the liquid mix as far as possible in one rotation, and
- Not create excessive slips between its blades and the liquid mix.

Stirrers come in different sizes but rarely exceed 0.5 m (= 20 In) in diameter, regardless of the mixing tank size. Depending on the duty, they usually have 3 to 6 blades and typically turn 20 to 150 R/min (revolution per minute, RPM). In a broad range, stirrers can be divided into the following four (4) types:

- **Marine Stirrers:** A marine stirrer, as shown in Figure 1A, has three pitched blades, like propellers used in boats for moving in the water. Marine stirrers are effective for low-viscosity (less than 5 Pa.s) liquid mixes and are used in large tanks when good vertical circulation is desired to keep solid particles in suspension. As shown in Figure 2 A, a marine stirrer mainly pushes the liquid mix in the vertical (axial) direction parallel to the axis of rotation (the stirrer's shaft).
- **Turbine Stirrers:** A turbine stirrer (see Figure 1B) has 4 to 6 short blades. The length of the blades is usually less than half the diameter of the mixer. Turbine stirrers are generally used for low-viscosity liquid mixes, such as dispersing a gas in a liquid. As shown in Figure 2 B, a turbine stirrer with flat blades and curved blades mainly moves the liquid mix in a circular direction so that the flow moves outward toward the tank's wall and then downward toward the bottom of the mixer.
- **Heavy-Duty Stirrers:** These are special stirrers used for high viscous duties (with viscosity up to 20 000 Pa.s). **Helical** (ribbon) stirrers (shown in Figure 1C) form a spiral (helical) flow, which moves axially (up to bottom). The ratio of the helix to the diameter of the mixing tank is about 0.9. Strong helical stirrers are used for extremely viscous mixes, which are active near the tank's wall, where the flow pattern is more effective. **Anchor stirrers** (shown in Figure 1D) form a circular flow, which moves the mix in the direction of rotation of the anchor. They are mainly used when a high-viscous liquid mix must be moved all over the tank, particularly near the bottom. They are also used to obtain good heat transferability in heated mixing tanks when a high-viscous liquid mix is under mixing.

The electric power (P_E, simply **power**) used by a stirrer can be calculated as

$$P_E = N_{PE}.D.N^3.d^5 \quad (1)$$

N_{PE} is the stirrer's power number (Newton's number), D is the density of the mix under mixing, N is the stirrer's rotational velocity (rotation per minute), and d is the stirrer's diameter. N_{PE} is dimensionless, so if D is given in kg/m^3, N in 1/s. and d in m, P_E becomes in kg.m^2/s^3, where 1 kg.m^2/s^3 = 1 W/h.

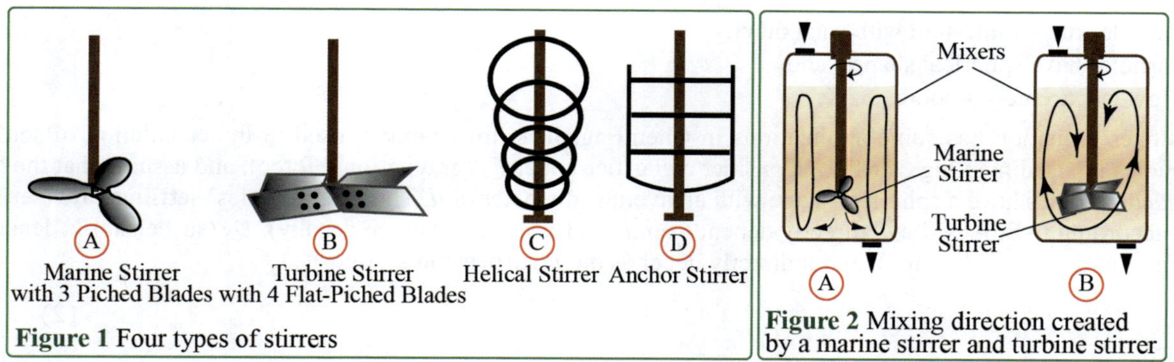

Figure 1 Four types of stirrers

Figure 2 Mixing direction created by a marine stirrer and turbine stirrer

S-124

STIRRING PROCESS

Discussed under MIXING PROCESS.

S-125

STOICHIOMETRY

Stoichiometry (pronounced **sto-keo-metry**) is a theoretical calculation for finding the amounts of the reactants and products of a chemical reaction (simply **reaction**). For example, the following reaction is stoichiometrically balanced:

$$H_2SO_4 + CaO \rightarrow CaSO_4 + H_2O$$

$$98\text{ g} + 56\text{ g} \rightarrow 136\text{ g} + 18\text{ g}$$

$$154\text{ g} \rightarrow 154\text{ g}$$

Thus, a balanced equation has the same number and type of atoms on both sides of the equation, and the mass of the reactants theoretically equates to the mass of the products. This means that the sum of the molecular masses of the reactants equates to that of the products.

S-126

STOKES' LAW

Stokes' Law is a principle in physics, named after George G. Stokes (1819–1903, a physicist from Ireland). It talks about suspended solid particles (simply **suspended particles** or **particles**) in a liquid. Mathematically, it determines the force (F) applied to a suspended particle in a suspension.

$$F = 6\pi.\eta.R.V \qquad (1)$$

In this form of Stocks' equation, η is the suspension's viscosity, R is the particle's radius, and V is the particle's velocity. This equation is valid only when the Reynolds number (N_R) is too small (smaller than 1). This means that the flow treated in this law is extremely smooth, called **creeping flow**. Such an extremely-smooth flow exists in a particle, settling in a suspension.

Stokes' Law considers the next simplifying assumptions.

- Particles do *not* interfere with each other,
- Particles have spherical shapes, and
- Flow is extremely smooth.

Stokes' equation has some applications in ChemEng. It is, for example, used in the calculation of settling particles in a sedimenting clarifier. Consider a clarifier under F_g (gravitational force), and assume that the suspended particles have a spherical shape with an average diameter of d. Then the particles' **settling rate** (settling V), according to Stokes' Law, directly depends on d, D_P (particles' average density), D_S (suspension's density), a_g (gravitational acceleration), and indirectly depends on η (suspension's viscosity).

$$V = \frac{d^2(D_P - D_S)a_g}{18\eta} \tag{2}$$

This equation tells us that the smaller particles (with smaller d) have lower settling rates. The equation works when the suspension flow is extremely smooth (when the flow's N_R is too small). Such a flow is called **creeping** (extremely smooth) **flow**.

Equation 2 is also valid for the calculation of settling V for settling of particles in a **sedimenting centrifuge** (see CENTRIFUGES) if a_g is replaced by a_C (centrifugal acceleration), where $a_C = R.\omega^2$ and R is the radius of the centrifuge's basket, and ω (omega) is the basket's rotational velocity.

$$V = \frac{d^2(D_P - D_L)a_c}{18\eta} = \frac{d^2(D_P - D_L)R.\omega^2}{18\mu} \tag{3}$$

S-127

STP

See STANDARD TEMPERATURE AND PRESSURE.

S-128

STREAM LAYERS AND STREAM LINES IN FLUID FLOW

Study BOUNDARY AND STREAM LAYERS IN FLUID FLOW.

S-129

STRENGTH AND HARDNESS OF MATERIAL

Strength and hardness of material are quantities used in material engineering in relation to the deformation of plastics due to a load (stress). Both strength and hardness depend on a material's molecular binding forces, so they are recoverable (get to their original shape if the load is removed). According to Hook's Law (when the force is doubled, the extension is also doubled), many elastics change directly to the applied force.

Strength

Strength is the maximum ability to hold a **stress** (a load in the form of force) without a **breakage** (fracture). In material engineering, a strength test with a strength tester determines the strength of a material by applying a force (F) on it to see if the material is the right one for a particular use. In the tester, a load in the form of a compressive force (as shown in Figure 1) is applied to the material under the test to deform it. The amount of the force applied by the tester is then recorded as **stress** (usually in the pressure unit), and the amount of the material's deformation is recorded as **strain** (usually in the length unit).

In material engineering, three different forces are usually used to test the materials (see Figures 1 and 2):

- **Tensile Force:** A tensile (elastic) force is a force that is applied on a material's surface in opposite directions at opposite places on opposite sides to **pull** the material.
- **Compressive Force:** A compressive force is a force that is applied on a material's surface in opposite directions at opposite places on opposite sides to **push** the material.
- **Shear Force:** A shear force is a force that is applied on a material's surface to push (or pull) the material.

Often, a **stress-strain diagram** is used to summarize the results of a strength test. Figure 3 shows a typical stress-strain diagram obtained from a strength test performed on plastic material. Under the test, the plastic first gets to its **elastic deformation point** (simply **elastic point**, point A), a temporary deformation (because it will get to its original shape if the force is removed). As the applied force continues, the material gets to its **plastic deformation point** (simply **plastic point**, point B), permanent deformation (it will *not* get to its original shape if the force is removed). More force gets the material to its **maximum strength point** (simply **strength point**, Point C), close to its **breaking point** (point D).

The portion of a stress-strain diagram until the material under the test reaches its elastic point is called the **elastic region**, which shows its stiffness (modulus). In this region, the material obeys Hook's Law. The portion until the material gets to its breaking point is called the **plastic region** (see Figure 3)

Strength is expressed in N/m^2. Materials are mainly characterized by their *ES*. Say, the *ES* of stainless steel is 207×10^6 N/m^2 =30×10^6 Lb/In^2), that of both iron and copper is 103×10^6 N/m^2 =15×10^6 Lb/In^2), and that of polyethylene is 4×10^5 N/m^2 = 0.6×10^5 Lb/In^2), where Lb is for pound-force and In is for inch.

Hardness

Hardness in material engineering is the resistance of a material's surface to penetration by a hard object (like a knife). [The term **hardening** is also used in material engineering to describe the increase in elastic strength (stretchable strength), as a metal is cold-worked (hardened by cooling).]

It is hard to express hardness in quantity (because most hardness scales are relative and, thus, qualitative). There are, however, different reliable hardness testers whose descriptions are beyond the scope of this book.

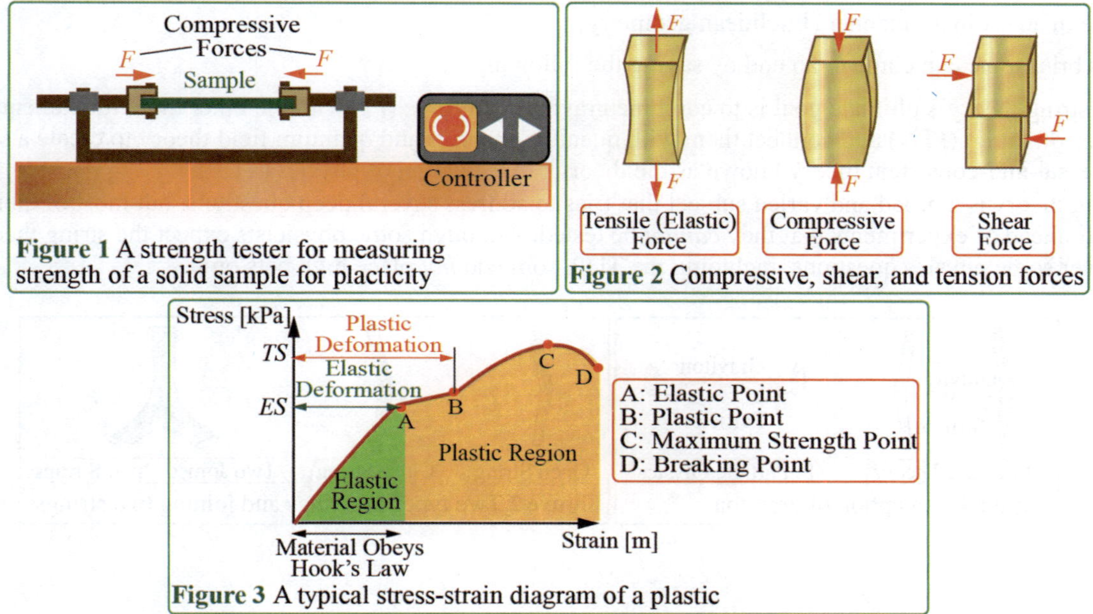

Figure 1 A strength tester for measuring strength of a solid sample for placticity

Figure 2 Compressive, shear, and tension forces

Figure 3 A typical stress-strain diagram of a plastic

S-130

STRESS, MODULUS, AND STRAIN OF MATERIAL

Study ELASTIC FORCE, MODULUS, AND STRAIN OF MATERIAL.

S-131

STRING THEORY

The string theory is a theoretical concept in particle physics starting in the late 1960s to describe the quantum elementary particles (simply **particles**) as 1-D (one-dimensional) vibrating strings, how the particles propagate in space, and how they interact with each other. Study the following:

- In string theory, a particle connects two strings, while a string connects two particles in particle physics. For example, in string theory, a graviton (the particle of the gravitational force, F_g) connects two strings, while in particle physics, a graviton connects two particles (see Figure 1).
- The strings are open and closed (see Figure 2), where both behave like particles with mass. In this way, a string's vibrational movement determines its type.
- String theory's earliest version considered the Bosons (photon, gluon, graviton, Z-Boson, W-Boson, Higgs Boson, and gauge Boson) as the strings. It also considers the Fermions (like quarks) as strings.

From its start, string theory has improved by offering new theories, including:

- **Bosonic String Theory:** This theory, developed in 1978, suggests that subatomic particles are spin-2 vibrating particles, called gravitons, which act as the carriers of the F_g.
- **M-Theory:** The M-theory (M for membrane) suggests that gravitons (the F_g carriers) are multi-layer membranes that act in a 4-D Universe, and the gravitons' shape is the reason for being so weak.
- **AdS/CFT:** The AdS/CFT (anti-de Sitter/conformal field theory), developed in 1997, considers the Universe as an anti-de Sitter space, in which the notion of distance between points is different from the notion of distance in an ordinary manner (Euclidean geometry).

This brief topic can come to an end by saying the following:

- The string theory's ultimate goal is to combine gravitational force (F_g) with the other three fundamental forces of nature (FFN) and connect them with quantum theories and quantum field theory to create a single universal-and-consistent theory known as the theory of unification of physics (TUP).
- String theory is a broad and varied subject that tries to address several deep questions, but most of them are so far ahead of experiments that they *cannot* be tested. Although some physicists expect the string theory to answer some physics questions, including the TUP, some do *not* place high bets on it.

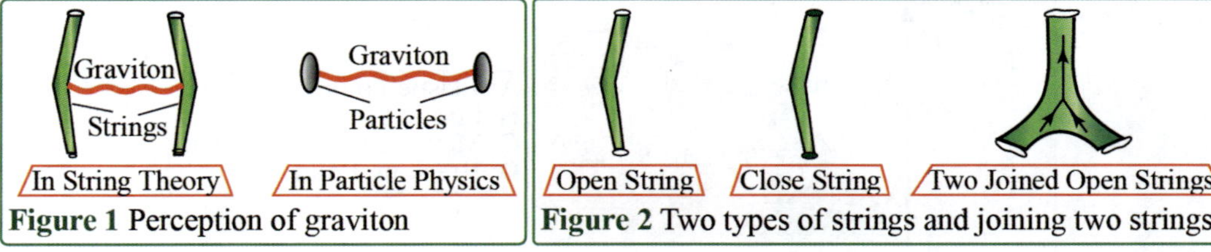

Figure 1 Perception of graviton

Figure 2 Two types of strings and joining two strings

S-132

STRONG NUCLEAR FORCE

Discussed under FUNDAMENTAL FORCES OF NATURE.

S-133

SUBATOMIC PARTICLES

Discussed under PARTICLES AND ITS TYPES.

S-134

SUBCOOLING

The term **subcooling** (also called **undercooling**) is often used in the evaporation process because *no* cooling occurs when condensate leaves an evaporator. Thus, at the exit, the condensate's temperature is *not* below its condensation temperature (T_C), and its enthalpy of condensation (H_{Con}) corresponds to the enthalpy (H) of water at the boiling point temperature (T_{BP}).

Always some subcooling occurs, but it is *not* significant in normal situations. However, if it occurs in a high quantity, a pool of stagnant condensate at the bottom of an evaporator accumulates that submerges some of the heating tubes, stopping their contact with the heating medium (say, vapor), as shown in Figure 1.

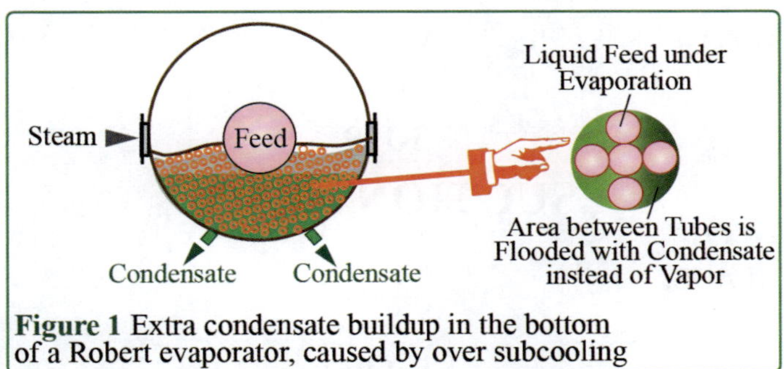

Figure 1 Extra condensate buildup in the bottom of a Robert evaporator, caused by over subcooling

S-135

SUBLIMATION POINT TEMPERATURE

The sublimation point temperature (T_{SP}, also called **sublimation point**) of a solid is the temperature (T) at which the sublimation process starts at the pressure (P) surrounding that solid. The T_S closely depends on the P (*at the same P, different solids sublimate at different temperatures*). Differences in the strength of molecular attractions explain why different solids have different T_S at the same P. For this reason, sublimation temperatures are usually specified at atmospheric pressure (P_{Atm} = 1 Atm = 760 mm Hg = 101 kPa), which is standard. T_S given for P_{Atm} is sometimes called **normal sublimation temperature**. At P_{Atm}, T_S is different for different substances. For example, solid CO_2 (dry ice) sublimes at 78.5°C (–109.3°F), and water ice sublimes below 0°C.

S-136

SUBLIMATION PROCESS

Sublimation is the change of a substance from a solid phase to a gaseous phase without going through the intermediate phase (the liquid phase). Some substances sublimize, meaning they do *not* melt from solid to liquid but go directly from solid to gaseous form. Sublimation requires additional heat energy (E_Q), so it is an endothermic process (an energy-absorbing process). It occurs at a substance's sublimation temperature (T_S), below its critical temperature (T_C). For example, at P_{Atm}, solid CO_2 (dry ice) sublimes at –78.5°C (–109.3°F). The T_C of CO_2 is 31°C (88°F). The value of –78.5°C is called **sublimation temperature** for CO_2. The triple point of CO_2 occurs at a much lower temperature (–57°C) and much higher pressure (5×10^5 Pa = 5 Atm) than water. Because CO_2 does *not* melt, solid CO_2 (dry ice) is used as a coolant. Dry ice looks like solid water (the ice). [Study Phase Diagram for sublimation graph of CO_2.] Ice (the solid water) sublimes slowly below its freezing temperature. This allows a wet cloth to be hung outdoors in freezing winter weather and later in a dry state.

S-137

SUBSTANCE

Study CHEMICAL SUBSTANCE.

S-138

SUCROSE

Study SUGARS AND SUGAR.

S-139

SUCTION HEAD

Study PUMP LIQUID HEADS.

S-140

SUGAR AND SUGARS

Sugar (sucrose) is discussed here under the subtopic of sugars (saccharides), as it is a family of sugars (saccharides).

Sugars

The word **sugars** is used as a general name for all kinds of sugars (scientifically **saccharides**, from the Latin *Saccharum*, meaning *sugar*). Sugars are a class of organic compounds consisting of C, O, and H and a functional group of –OH (hydroxyl group).

The quantity of OH groups in sugars contributes to their sweetness. Sucrose (sugar) with eight hydroxyl groups is sweeter than glucose (with five OH groups). In general, compounds with at least two OH groups are sweet. Glycerol (glycerin, $C_3H_8O_3$) with three OH groups, xylitol ($C_5H_{12}O_5$) with five, and glucitol (sorbitol, $C_6H_{14}O_6$) with six OH groups are less sweet than sucrose (sugar), the **standard reference** in sensory tests for comparing the sweeteners' sweetening power. In this standardization, sucrose is assigned a value of one. For example, sucralose sweetness is 600.

Sucrose, glucose, fructose, lactose, and many more are in the class of sugars, and sugars are in a larger class, known as carbohydrates. The ***ose*** suffix in sucrose (*soo'kros/Sue-k-Rose*), glucose (*gloo'kos*), fructose (*froo'ktos*), lactose (*la'ktos*), and so on identifies the sugars. In this way, we say that the sugar in sugarbeet and sugarcane is sucrose, the sugar in the blood is glucose, the sugar in honey is fructose, and the sugar in milk is lactose. The photosynthetic process makes sugars (saccharides) in plants.

Sugars are a large family with complicated chemistry. Here, we talk briefly about the three most common ones, **sugar** (sucrose), **glucose** (dextrose), and **fructose** (levulose), without going deep into their chemistry.

Sugar: Sugar ($C_{12}H_{22}O_{11}$, with the chemical name of **sucrose** and common name of **table sugar**), which is in the class of sugars (saccharides), is a disaccharide composed of two monosaccharides, glucose and fructose. Lactose (the milk sugar) and maltose (the malt sugar) are also disaccharides, with the same formulas of $C_{12}H_{22}O_{11}$ but different molecular structures.

As shown in Figure 1, a sugar molecule ($C_{12}H_{22}O_{11}$) consists of 12 atoms of carbon (C), 22 atoms of hydrogen (H), and 11 atoms of oxygen (O), so each mole of sugar consists of 12 moles of C, 22 moles of H_2, and 5½ moles of O_2. Expressing the composition in mass percentage, a sucrose molecule consists of 42% by mass carbon atoms [(12×12)/342 = 42%], 6.5% hydrogen atoms [(22×1)/342 = 6.5%], and 51.5% oxygen atoms [(11×16)/342 = 51.5%], where 12, 1, and 16 are the molecular mass (M_M) of C, H, and O, respectively.

Table-sugar crystals in a market-quality form that we use in our tea are among the world's most purified organic compounds, with a purity (P) of 99.95%. The difference, which is 0.05%, is mainly water (normally at 0.03%) and some minerals (in trace amounts) that remain in the crystal occlusions (small pockets on the faces of a crystal during crystallization).

The following bullets outline some of the chemical and physical properties of sucrose (sugar):

- It is a covalent compound,
- It is a nonionic compound,
- Its molar mass (M_n) is 342 g/mole,
- Its distribution coefficient (K_D) is 0.04 cm^2/h,
- Its enthalpy of formation (H_F) is about 6 494 kJ/kg,
- Its molar enthalpy of formation ($H_{n.F}$) is 2 221 kJ/mole,
- Its melting point temperature (T_{MP}) is about 185ºC (= 356ºF),
- Its bulk density (D_B) is approximately 873 kg/m^3 (= 55 Lb/Ft^3),
- Its particle density (D_P) is 1.588 g/cm^3 or 1588 kg/m^3 (= 99.2 Lb/Ft^3).

[Note 1: Because of generality in name, sugar (the table sugar) is the only one that gets the blame for all sugars about daily caloric intake and diabesity (the high level of glucose as the product of all carbohydrates in the body.)]

[Note 2: Although both **table sugar** and **table salt** are crystals and have some similarities, they are chemically dissimilar in some instances. Different properties of sugar and salt have helpful theoretical applications in using them as examples to simplify some complicated topics in chemistry. This author also followed this trend and used them as typical examples in some topics of this book. For instance, sugar (a nonionic compound) and salt (an ionic compound) are used in this book to compare their opposite behavior when they are dissolved in water.]

[Note 3: Interesting to know that a 0.5 kg (= 1.1 Lb) bag of medium-size sugar holds about 0.5 million crystals, and the total surface area covered with that amount of crystals is 3 950 m^2 (= 32 660 Ft^2).]

[Note 4: Because glucose and fructose promote the growth of microorganisms in the fermentation process, they are called **fermentable carbohydrates**.]

Glucose: Glucose ($C_6H_{12}O_6$, also called **dextrose** or **blood sugar**) is a monosaccharide and the isomer of fructose. It has an aldehyde group (H–C=O) bonded to carbon 1 (C–1), and fructose has a ketone group (–C=O) bonded to C–2, so glucose is an aldohexose and fructose is a ketohexose (see Figure 1).

Glucose exists in some fruits, such as grapes, figs, and dates. It is the building block of two important polysaccharides: starch and cellulose.

Fructose: Fructose ($C_6H_{12}O_6$, also called **levulose** or **fruit sugar**) is found in many fruits (apples, grapes, and more). Fructose is produced from sucrose (sugar) or **inulin** (a polysaccharide).

Polysaccharides: Polysaccharides are polymeric carbohydrates. They have long-chain molecules of monosaccharide units connected (bound) by glycosidic bonds (oxygen bonds) covalently. Starch, glycogen, and cellulose are polysaccharides composed of many glucose units with different molecular structures.

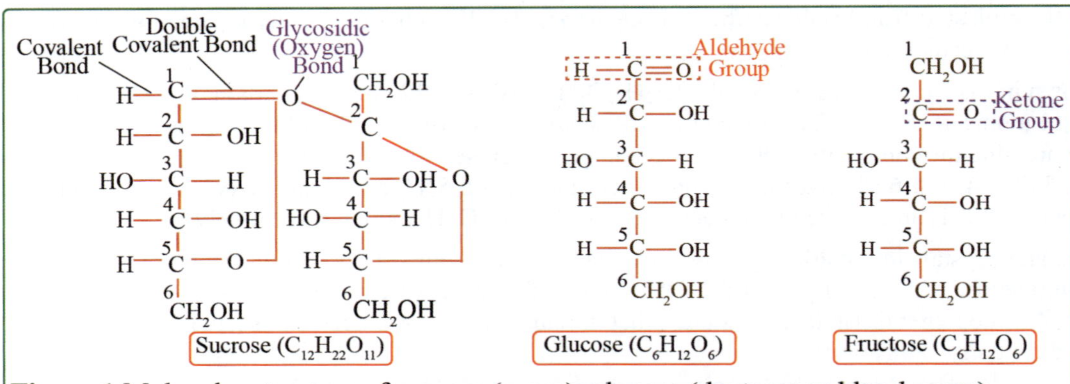

Figure 1 Molecular structure of sucrose (sugar), glucose (dextrose or blood sugar), and fructose (levulose or fruit sugar), shown in straight (Fischer) method

S-141

SULFUR AND SULFUR DIOXIDE

Sulfur: Sulfur (S) is a chemical element in group 16 and period 3 of the periodic table of elements. Its atomic mass number (N_A or A; the total number of protons and neutrons of an atom) is 16, its atomic mass (M_A, the actual mass of one atom of an element) is 32 AMU (simply 32 g), and its molar mass (M_n) is 32 g/mole.

Sulfur is a nonmetal and bright yellow crystalline solid at room temperature. It is insoluble in water, but almost soluble in nonpolar organic solvents, like benzene (C_6H_6) and toluene (C_7H_8). It burns in oxygen (O_2) with a **blue** flame to form sulfur dioxide (SO_2), an irritating odor. Sulfur has 23 isotopes, 19 of which are *not* stable. Some other properties of sulfur are:

- Its density (D) is 2017 kg/m^3(= 126 Lb/Ft^3),
- Its molar heat capacity ($C_{Q.n}$) is 22.8 J/mole.°C,
- Its melting point temperature is 115°C (= 239°F),
- Its boiling point temperature (T_{BP}) is 444°C (= 832°F).

Sulfur Dioxide: Sulfur dioxide (SO_2) is a colorless, odorous, toxic gas that can kill people at 500 PPM. SO_2 reacts with water in the air to form sulfurous acid (H_2SO_3), a component of acid rain.

In chemical process plants, SO_2 is produced by the combustion reaction of a fuel with oxygen from the air in a furnace. The SO_2 then moves with the furnace flue gas to the atmosphere. When the amount of SO_2 is high, a wet scrubber removes it from the flue gas. In SO_2 wet scrubbing (removal), calcium hydroxide [$Ca(OH)_2$] is added to the scrubbing water. Part of SO_2 reacts with water to form sulfurous acid (H_2SO_3), which reacts with the hydroxide to precipitate sodium sulfite (Na_2SO_3). The rest of SO_2 reacts directly with the hydroxide to precipitate Na_2SO_3.

$$SO_2 + H_2O \rightarrow H_2SO_3 \quad H_2SO_3 + 2\ NaOH \rightarrow Na_2SO_3 + 2\ H_2O \qquad SO_2 + 2\ NaOH \rightarrow Na_2SO_3 + H_2O$$

S-142

SULFURIC ACID

Sulfuric acid (H_2SO_4, also called **mineral acid**) is a water-soluble-colorless-odorless-and-viscous acid with a molar mass (M_n) of 98 g/mole. It is one of the four strongest inorganic acids; the other ones are nitric acid (HNO_3), hydrochloric acid (Cl, and perchloric acid ($HClO_4$). It usually comes in a concentration of 98.3%, known as **concentrated sulfuric acid**, with a density (D) of 1830 kg/m^3 (= 114 Lb/Ft^3).

In its pure anhydrous form, H_2SO_4 is highly corrosive (an oxidant) and dehydrating (removing water from a substance). It becomes, however, dehydrated by contacting with phosphorus dioxide (P_4O_{10}), which is a strong desiccant.

H_2SO_4 is used in various chemical productions, including plastics, batteries, iron, steel, detergent, fertilizer, paint, and pharmaceutical productions. [Today, about 50 million tons of H_2SO_4 are produced in the US of America, making it the most produced chemical.]

S-143

SUPERCRITICAL FLUIDS

A supercritical fluid is a chemical substance (simply **substance**) at a temperature (T) and pressure (P) above its critical point (C-point). In addition, at close to the C-point, small changes in P or T of a supercritical fluid result in large changes in its density (D). The C-point in water occurs at a critical temperature (T_C) of 374°C and critical pressure (P_C) of 218 Atm, as shown in Figure 2 under PHASE DIAGRAMS. [The water at its T_C and P_C has a D of 356 kg/m^3.]

S-144

SUPERFICIAL VELOCITY

The term superficial velocity (V_S) is usually used in engineering to express the velocity (V) of a fluid per area through which that fluid goes through. In ChemEng, the V_S is used in the fluidization process to express the velocity of a gas going through the area of a fluidized bed in a fluidized vessel. The terms critical velocity (V_C), superficial velocity (V_S), and minimum superficial velocity (V_{MS}) are also used.

S-145

SUPERFLUIDS

A superfluid is a system of electrically neutral atoms that flows without friction. Instead, an **insulating fluid** is a fluid that flows with friction. Superfluids are produced by pouring a lot of cold atoms into the lattice (structure) of some lasers. These atoms initially behave as a superfluid, but as the intensity of lasers is increased, the atoms gradually become less mobile, and the fluid suddenly changes to an insulating fluid. The decrease in the flow of the atoms depends on the temperature (T) and Planck's constant of the atoms.

S-146

SUPERSATURATED SOLUTIONS

Study SATURATED, UNSATURATED, AND SUPERSATURATED SOLUTIONS.

S-147

SUPERSATURATED STEAM

Discussed under the topic of VAPOR AND STEAM.

S-148

SUPERSATURATION

Study SATURATION, UNDERSATURATION, AND SUPERSATURATION.

S-149

SUPERSATURATION COEFFICIENT

Discussed under the topic of CRYSTALLIZATION COEFFICIENTS.

S-150

SURFACE ENERGY

Discussed under the topic of ENERGY AND ITS FORMS.

S-151

SURFACE FORCE

A surface force (F_S) is a force (F) that is applied by a fluid on the wall surface area (A) of that fluid's container. F_S also exists in the bulk (under-the-surface) of a fluid whose quantity is the same in all directions.

Like F, the F_S is given in Newton (N). Because pressure (P) is F/A and $A = L.W$ (where L is for length and W is for width), a P of 2 N/m^2 = 2 Pa (Pascal) per area of 20 m^2 produces an F_S of (2 Pa)(20 m^2) = 40 N.

S-152

SURFACE MOISTURE

Discussed under the topic of MOISTURE AND ITS TYPES.

S-153

SURFACE TENSION AND SURFACTANTS

Surface Tension: A surface tension (γ, gamma) in a liquid exists because that liquid's surface molecules contain more adhesive force (F_A) than its bulk (under-the-surface) molecules. So defined, the excess F_A in the surface molecules is called the **surface tension**. As illustrated in Figure 1, in a glass cup of water, a surface molecule is pulled by F_A only sideways and downward, while in bulk, the molecule is pulled in all directions. Because there is *no* F_A upward, the surface F_A pulls the surface molecule toward the bulk of water, and, thus, a surface tension occurs. Water, for example, has a high γ, which allows the insects to walk on water. This occurs because water's surface behaves like a thin elastic film, preventing the insects to become wet.

Surface tension (γ) affects some properties of liquids, including the following:

- It causes the surface of a liquid to be attracted to a substance, although the substance is denser than the liquid. For example, if we gently lay a small paper clip on the water's surface, it stays on its surface (because the water molecules' tension at the surface is strong).
- It causes a liquid drop to have a spherical shape. An oil drop or a rain drop is spherical because a drop's surface tends to contract, and this contraction forces the drop into a spherical shape, which has the least surface area for a given volume.
- It is affected by a compound's chemical polarity (simply **polarity**) because the surface tension of a polar compound is reduced when a nonpolar compound is mixed with it. When water (a polar compound) is added to a detergent (a nonpolar **surfactant**), the γ of water molecules is reduced (Figure 2). The reason follows. At the water's surface, the nonpolar end of the detergent molecules escapes the polarity of the water molecules, so the γ between the water and detergent molecules is reduced.
- It prevents a polar liquid (like water) from separating from a nonpolar solid's wet surface. This action occurs because water's surface behaves like an elastic film, preventing the surface of the nonpolar solid from being wet. We see this when a car's surface (a nonpolar solid surface) is polished with a polisher (a polar liquid).

The following are two important generalities of surface tension:

- Surface energy (E_S) and surface tension (γ) are identical quantities, except that the E_S applies to liquids and solids, while γ applies only to liquids. Thus, when talking about a liquid, its E_S and γ have the same meaning, value, and SI unit (or US unit).
- The SI unit of both E_S and γ is J/m^2 (= N/m), where N (Newton) is the SI unit of force (F) and m^2 (square meter) is the SI unit of area. Both E_S and γ of water at 25°C is 0.07 J/m^2 (= 0.07 N/m). The E_S of a sugar crystal (a solid) is 0.22 J/m^2.

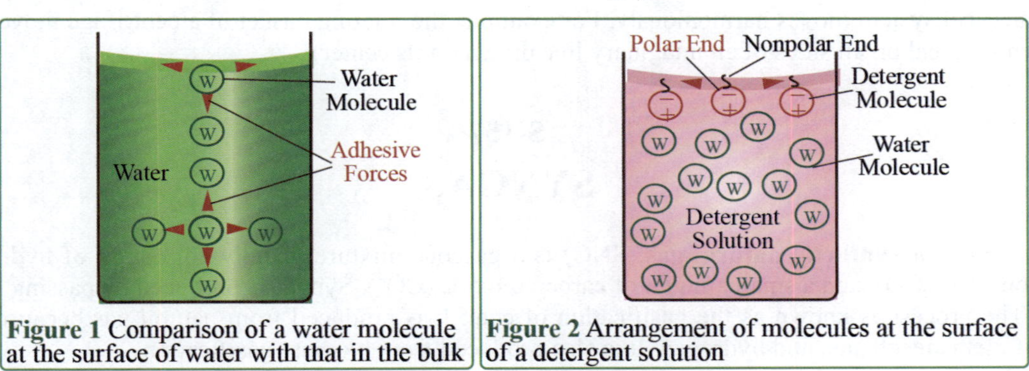

Figure 1 Comparison of a water molecule at the surface of water with that in the bulk

Figure 2 Arrangement of molecules at the surface of a detergent solution

Surfactants: A surfactant is a surface-active compound that lowers the surface tension (γ) between two liquids, between a liquid and a gas, or between a liquid and a solid. Soaps and detergents are good examples of surfactants. Because a polar compound's γ is reduced when a nonpolar compound is mixed with it, when water (a polar compound) is added to a detergent (a nonpolar compound), the water molecules γ is reduced.

Among other uses, a surfactant is used to position its molecules between the molecules of two phases in an emulsion to stabilize it by reducing the surface tension of its liquid phase.

S-154

SUSPENDED SOLID PARTICLES

Suspended solid particles (simply **suspended solids**, **suspended particles**, or **dust**) are all **filterable solid particles** (undissolved particles) left on a filtering medium after filtration of a suspension solution (simply **suspension** or slurry). Suspended particles present in a suspension are expressed in % by mass (see PERCENTAGES) or in PPM. In the chemical process industry, suspended solids existing in a suspension are removed by sedimentation, filtration, or both.

Suspended solids are invisible to the naked eye. They are important as pollutants and pathogens (disease creators). In the same unit mass, the smaller the size of particles, the greater is their total surface area and, therefore, the higher is the pollutant load in the air.

In the laboratories, total **suspended solids** (TSS) in wastewater are measured by filtration of a certain sample volume through a pre-weighed filter paper with a specified pore size. Then the filter paper is dried and weighed to determine the TSS content of the sample. [As related subjects, study DUST and TURBIDITY, also.]

S-155

SUSPENSIONS

Suspensions are in the large group of dispersions, so it is discussed under DISPERSIONS.

S-156

SYMMETRICAL SYSTEM

A symmetrical system moves harmoniously. For example, the rotating basket of a centrifuge moves symmetrically (symmetrical on all sides of an imaginary line drawn on its center).

S-157

SYNGAS

Syngas (short for **synthetic natural gas**, SNG) is a gaseous mixture, mainly consisting of hydrogen (H_2), carbon monoxide (CO), and a small amount of carbon dioxide (CO_2). Syngas is produced by passing steam over hot coal. The process is known as the gasification of coal. It is produced from natural gas because it mainly consists of methane, ethane, and hydrogen. It is also produced from biomass gasification.

Syngas is combustible and can be converted into synthetic gasoline and diesel to be used as a fuel. It is also used as an intermediate in methanol (CH_3OH) production or ammonia (NH_3).

S-158
SYNTHETIC ELEMENTS

A synthetic element is an element that is created in a laboratory and is not found in nature. Bohrium (Bh, in honor of Bohr), einsteinium (Es, in honor of Einstein), and rutherfordium (Rf, in honor of Rutherford) are examples of synthetic elements.

S-159
SYNTHETIC NATURAL GAS

Study SYNGAS.

S-160
SYSTEMS

Study CHEMICAL SYSTEMS.

T Section

LIST OF TOPICS

1. Tanks, Vessels, and Drums
2. Temperature Measurement
3. Temperature Pressure Phase Diagram
4. Temperature, Temperature Difference, and Temperature Gradient
5. Tensile Modulus and Tensile Strain
6. Ternary Mixtures and Triangular Diagrams
7. Tesla
8. Theoretical Air Requirement
9. Theoretical Plates
10. Theories of Relativity
11. Theory and Law (Physics)
12. Theory of Everything
13. Theory of General Relativity
14. Theory of Photoelectric Effect
15. Theory of Spacetime
16. Theory of Special Relativity
17. Theory of Unification of Physics
18. Thermal Conductance
19. Thermal Conductivity
20. Thermal Conductors and Thermal Insulators
21. Thermal Diffusivity
22. Thermal Equilibrium
23. Thermal Expansion
24. Thermal Insulators
25. Thermal Reactions
26. Thermal Reservoir
27. Thermal Resistance
28. Thermodynamic Equilibrium
29. Thermodynamic First Law
30. Thermodynamic Free Energy
31. Thermodynamic Laws
32. Thermodynamic Potential
33. Thermodynamic Second Law
34. Thermodynamic Stability
35. Thermodynamic System
36. Thermodynamic Temperature
37. Thermodynamic Third Law
38. Thermodynamic Zeroth Law
39. Thermodynamics and Thermodynamic Laws
40. Thermometers
41. Thickeners
42. Thin Film
43. Three- and Four-Dimensional Systems
44. Time
45. Time Dilation Theory
46. Titration
47. Titrimetric Analysis
48. TNT
49. Torque
50. Torricelli Equation
51. Total Dynamic Head
52. Total Energy
53. Total Head
54. Toxicity and Toxicology
55. Transformers
56. Transitional Flow
57. Transitional Metals
58. Transmittance
59. Triangular Diagrams
60. Triple Point and Critical Point
61. Tubes
62. Turbidity
63. Turbines
64. Turbulent Flow

T-1
TANKS, VESSELS, AND DRUMS

Tanks, vessels, and drums are containers used in all chemical process plants for different purposes. Tanks, vessels, and drums have their specifications, as you will study here. Before getting to these specifications, the differences between them are discussed. The main difference between **tanks** and **vessels** is that the tanks usually have *no* internal devices, while vessels have one (or more) devices. According to this statement, a container used, for example, to mix a solution is a vessel (but *not* a tank).

The major difference between **tanks** and **drums** is in their sizes. Tanks have several hours of retention (holdup) time, while drums have up to an hour. Some other differences between tanks and drums are:

- Tanks are usually installed vertically, while drums are installed vertically and horizontally.
- Tanks are usually cylindrical with a mildly curved bottom, while drums are cylindrical with a flat bottom.
- Tanks are used for major storing purposes, while drums are installed between devices to absorb fluctuations in a fluid flow process or disturbances in process control.

Tanks

A chemical process tank (simply **tank**) is a freely-ventilated container with a cylindrical shape, used mainly for storing a liquid or a solution (see Figure 1). Tanks are mostly made of alloy steel and, in some cases, stainless steel. They are equipped with maintenance holes for inspection, charge-and-discharge flange ports, holes for different sensors (like level and temperature sensors), a vent with a pressure-relief system, and some other attached parts. Thanks are of different types, like storage tank, pressure tank, flashing tank, water tank, supply tank, and special tank for storing reactive (corrosive) solutions. [Pressure and flashing tanks are discussed here.]

Tanks Design: To correctly design a tank, some factors must be considered, such as:

- The operating conditions of the tank, like pressure (*P*) and temperature (*T*).
- The size and material that must be used to build the tank.
- The properties of the liquid to be stored in the tank.

In relation to the size of **tanks** and **drums**, the following must be carefully considered (see Figure 1):

- **Size Ratio:** A tank's *h*-to-*d* (height-to-diameter) ratio must be 2 to 4.
- **Vapor Space:** Whether a drum is installed vertically or horizontally, the minimum vapor space must be 20% of the drum's volume or less than 0.3 m (= 13 In) from the top.

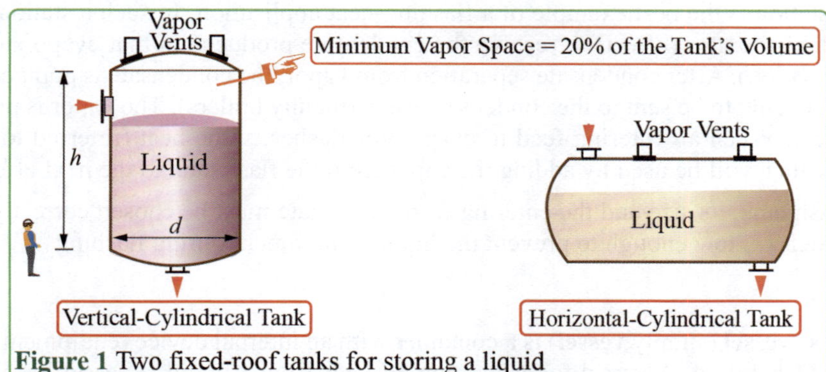

Figure 1 Two fixed-roof tanks for storing a liquid

Tanks Containment Basins: Some **safety rules** exist for the allowable distance between the storing tanks, the distance between a tank and the next building (like the delivery platform station), and the size of the **safety containment basin** (for ensuring safe retention in case of a leakage in a tank). Environmental concerns related to accidental liquid leakage require a storing system having a containment basin around a tank, or a set of tanks, in a tank yard, as shown in Figure 2 for three tanks and a **containment basin** in a **tank yard** (a location with tanks with or without a delivery platform).

[The safety rules are stricter for those chemical plants that produce liquid products with low flashing point temperatures (T_{FP}), like oil refineries and ethanol distilleries. In addition, an appropriate vapor space (a space that must be kept unfilled above a stored liquid) in a tank must be considered.]

Tanks Management: A tank can be a shift tank (supplying a process station for an 8-h operation) or a day tank. For example, three tanks can be used; one filled, one with the product tested in the lab before discharge to the final storage tank, and a third tank reserved for product out-of-specification (out-of-spec).

Large holding tanks in such a facility are interconnected by a ring of piping that allows the pumping of a tank content to another tank or a delivery platform.

Tanks Classification: In one classification, the storing tanks are classified into:

- **Fixed-Roof Tanks:** A typical fixed-roof tank has a conical-shaped roof permanently connected to its cylindrical body. It is freely vented or has a **breather valve**, allowing vapor release when high atmospheric P and T changes occur.
- **Floating-Roof Tanks**. A floating-roof tank (Figure 3) has an open-topped-cylindrical body and a roof that floats above the surface of the stored liquid. The roof can rise and fall by supporting legs with the liquid level in the tank, so *no* vapor space is needed in floating-roof tanks, except for when the liquid level in the tank is too low. The supporting legs are usually retractable to increase the operating volume of the tank. Floating tanks are usually used for environmental reasons to reduce the likelihood of volatile organic compound emissions (contaminations).

Pressure Tanks: A pressure tank (also called a **pressure vessel**) is a tank designed to hold a fluid (liquid or gas) at pressures above the atmospheric pressure (P_{Atm}). For safety reasons, the design of pressure tanks is important to perform according to the specific norms. The type and strength of the constructing material and maximum safe operating P and T are the two main factors in designing a pressure tank. The construction material becomes more important when the fluid kept under high pressure indicates **corrosion potential**. After construction, a new pressure tank must be tested using **non-destructive testing**, such as pressure testing and **ultrasound** (ultrasonic) **testing** for leak and strength. [Pressure tanks must be tested regularly.]

Flashing Tanks: A flashing tank (Figure 4) is used for flashing evaporation (simply **flashing**) on a liquid feed and separating condensate from vapor in the feed by lowering the P, T, or both. Using flashing tanks in a multiple-effect evaporation station is the best example of a flashing-heat application. In such a station, a flashing tank is installed under each evaporator (effect) to receive the condensate produced in that evaporator to flash (sudden cooling with condensation). After condensate separation from vapor, the condensate is pumped from the flashing tank to the condensate tank to be sent to the condensate users (mainly boilers). The vapor is pumped to the vapor line of the next effect. When an entering feed to evaporator flashes, some heat (referred to as heat energy) is suddenly released, which will be used by adding the vapor from the flash tank to the next effect's vapor line.

In designing a flash tank, its size and the entering feed's flow rate must be chosen correctly to ensure that the upward vapor's velocity is low enough to prevent the liquid entrainment during flashing.

Vessels

A chemical process vessel (simply **vessel**) is a container with an internal device (equipment) used for performing a process unit of ChemEng. A vessel for separation of a gas from a liquid, a vessel for mixing a solution, a vessel for sedimentation of a slurry, a vessel for evaporation of a solution, and a vessel for performing a chemical reaction (in this case, a chemical reactor) are examples of vessels.

In designing a vessel, its most appropriate shape (cylindrical-vertical, cylindrical-horizontal, or cubical) must be considered. In addition, the next factors must be studied:

- Constructing material that must be used in building the vessel.
- Operating conditions of the vessel, like pressure (*P*) and temperature (*T*).
- Properties of the chemical substance (or substances) to be processed in the vessel.
- Internal devices that must be used in the vessel, like a mixer for mixing a liquid, a baffle plate (weir) for separating light-and-heavy liquid streams, a vortex breaker for preventing vapor be drawn into the liquid's outlet or an outlet for exiting noncondensing gases from the vessel (like an evaporator).

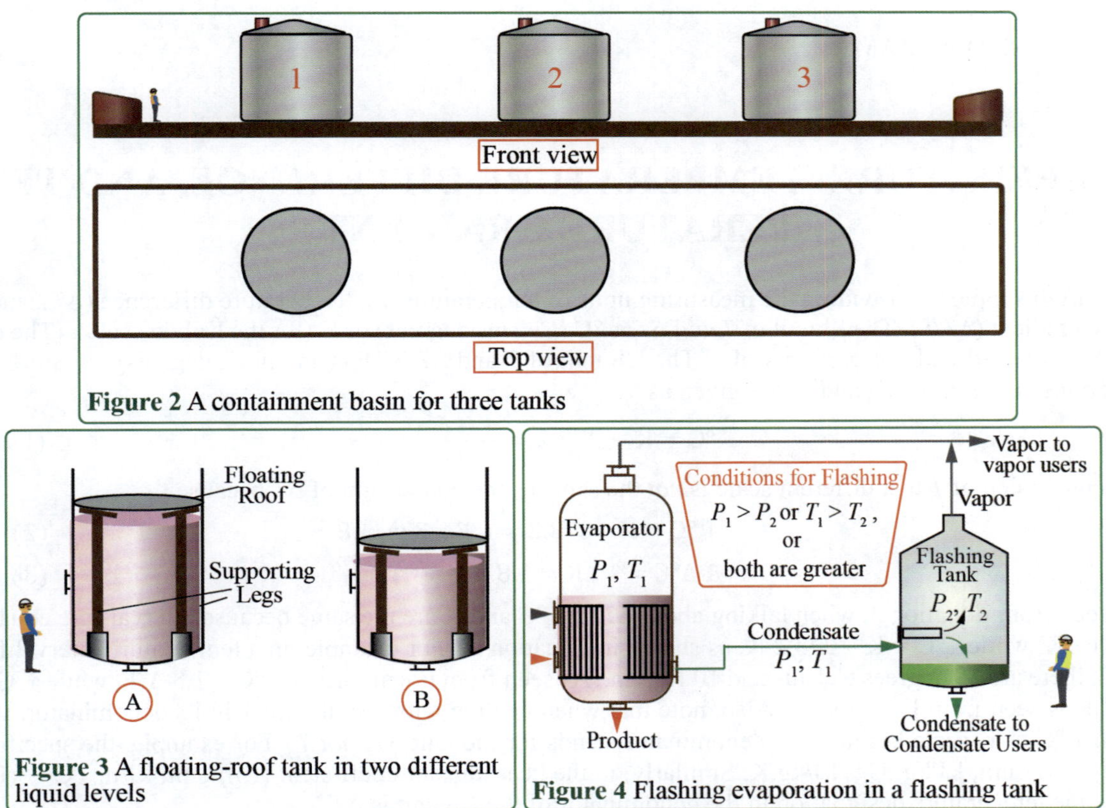

Figure 2 A containment basin for three tanks

Figure 3 A floating-roof tank in two different liquid levels

Figure 4 Flashing evaporation in a flashing tank

Drums

A chemical process drum (simply **drum**) is a small container used mainly to absorb fluctuations in a fluid flow process. For example, a **reflux drum** is installed in a distillation station between a condenser and a distillation column to adjust the operation of these two devices. In contrast, a **feed tank** (with a much bigger capacity) is installed in the same station to feed a distillation column for a few days.

An Example on Tanks

Calculate the diameter (*d*) of a cylindrical tank used to process 10^5 m^3 of wastewater. The height (*h*) of the tank is 9 m, and the retention time of the wastewater in the tank is 8 hours.

The volume (*V*) of the tank is $10^5/8 = 12\,500$ m^3, and its radius (*R*) and diameter (*d*) will be

$V = \pi.R^2.h \qquad R^2 = \frac{V}{\pi.h} = \frac{12500}{3.14\times9} = 442 \qquad R = 21 \text{ m} \qquad d = 21 \times 2 = 42 \text{ m } (= 70 \text{ Ft})$

T-2

TEMPERATURE MEASUREMENT

Discussed under the topic of PROCESS CONTROL OF CHEMICAL ENGINEERING.

T-3

TEMPERATURE PRESSURE PHASE DIAGRAM

Study PHASE DIAGRAM.

T-4

TEMPERATURE, TEMPERATURE DIFFERENCE, AND TEMPERATURE GRADIENT

We start this topic by providing the measuring units of temperature (T), temperature difference (ΔT), and temperature gradient ($\Delta T/L$). The SI unit of T and ΔT is °C (Celsius degrees) or K (for the Kelvin scale). [The degree sign (°) is *not* used with the Kelvin scale.] The US unit of T and ΔT is °F (Fahrenheit degrees). Figure 1 shows the relations between °C, K, and °F are given as

$$°\text{C} = \text{K} - 273.2 = \frac{°\text{F} - 32}{1.8} \quad (1)$$

The conversion of T to a different scale is *not* the same as the conversion of ΔT because

$$1\ °\text{C} = \text{K} - 273.2 = (°\text{F} - 32)/1.8 \quad (2)$$

$$1\ \Delta°\text{C} = 1\ \Delta\text{K} = 1.8\ \Delta°\text{F} \quad (3)$$

[As seen from Equation 3, when talking about ΔT, the °C and K are the same because intervals are equal, so 1 Δ°C = 1 ΔK, while 1°C = K – 273.2 K, as shown in Equation 2. For example, in a temperature interval from 0 to 10°C, there are 10 degrees Celsius and 10 Kelvin. As seen from Equation 3, 1 Δ°C = 1.8 Δ°F, while 1°C = (°F – 32)/1.8 as seen from Equation 2. Also, note that when dealing with a unit with T in its denominator, we can use either °C or K scale because the denominator stands for the unit ΔT, *not* T. For example, the specific heat capacity (C_Q) unit, kJ/kg.°C = kJ/kg.K. Similarly, in the heat transfer coefficient (U_Q) unit, kJ/m^2.°C = kJ/m^2.K because the temperature designation in the denominator of the U_Q unit is ΔT.]

The SI unit of $\Delta T/L$ (temperature gradient) is °C/m or K/m, and its US unit is °F/Ft, where m is for meter, Ft is for foot, and K is for Kelvin scale. [When talking about **temperature gradient** or **temperature difference**, °C and K are the same because two intervals are equal, so 1 Δ°C = 1 ΔK, while 1°C = K – 273.2 K.]

Temperature

Temperature (T) is the measurement of the **hotness** or **coldness** of a system (or a substance), which are molecular properties of that system. Specifically, the T affects every system in the Universe. At the molecular level, the T results from the average kinetic energy (E_K) of a system's molecules. When a system is heated, the E_K of its molecules increases, so the molecules begin moving faster, increasing the system's T. Thus, measuring a system's T tells us the molecular motion of that system. As heat (the simple term for heat energy, E_Q) is removed, the molecular movement slows down, the system gets colder, and its T decreases. In liquids and gases, molecules can move around in all directions (the *greater* the T, the *faster* their average speed). In solids, molecules are kept in fixed positions but can vibrate (the *greater* the T, the *faster* their vibration).

The T indicates the intensity of the E_Q, *not* its quantity, so they are related but *not* the same quantities. Two systems can be at the same T but with a different amount of E_Q. This can be viewed in two different-size heat exchangers at the same T but with different E_Q contents.

If two systems are in contact, heat moves from the higher-T system to the lower-T system until they become at the same T. When, thus, heat transfer occurs between two systems, T can determine the direction of heat transfer between them (heat flows toward the lower-T system). When two systems are at the same T, *no* heat transfer occurs. Thus, they are at **thermal stability** (stable system).

[Note 1: The centi- prefix in centigrade refers to the 100 equal degrees covering the range between the freezing point temperature of water (0ºC) and the boiling point temperature of water at sea level (100ºC).] [Note 2: Dry-bulb temperature and wet-bulb temperature are two ways of expressing the T of an air-vapor mixture or a gas-vapor mixture.] [Note 3: Some instruments used to measure T are discussed under TEMPERATURE MEASUREMENT.]

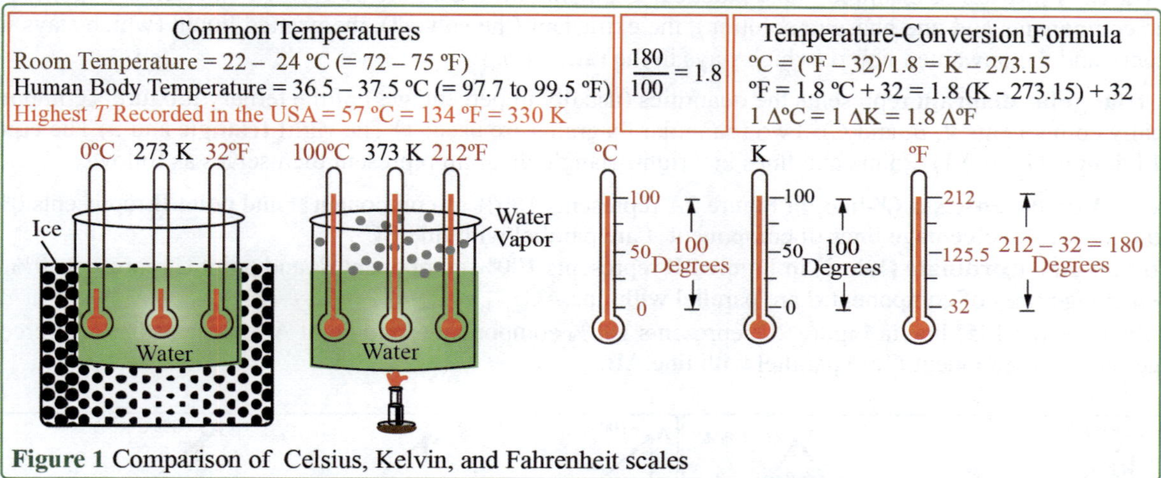

Figure 1 Comparison of Celsius, Kelvin, and Fahrenheit scales

Temperature Difference

Temperature difference (ΔT) is the difference in temperature (T) between two points in a system, two systems, two processes, two phases, or between two fluids that undergo the heat transfer process.

$$\Delta T = T_{\text{System2}} - T_{\text{System1}} = T_2 - T_1 \tag{4}$$

The ΔT is the cause (driving force) for most heat transfer processes. For example, in the evaporation process, ΔT between the steam at the entrance to an evaporator and the liquid at the exit ($\Delta T = T_S - T_L$) is the cause of the process, where subscript S is for steam and L is for liquid. In heating, the ΔT between the hot fluid (T_2) and cold fluid (T_1) is the cause of the process. The ΔT, similarly, between the vapor at the entrance to a heat exchanger and the liquid under heating is the cause of heating. [Instead of **temperature difference,** scientists consider **temperature gradient** ($\Delta T/L$) as the **cause** of heat transfers, where L is for length.]

Sign Assignment: When discussing the quantity of heat transfer, the sign rules for $\Delta T = T_2 - T_1$ are:

- **Positive Sign:** If $T_2 > T_1$, temperature increases, the ΔT is positive, and the E_Q will also be positive (+).
- **Negative Sign:** If $T_2 < T_1$, temperature decreases, the ΔT is negative, and the E_Q will also be negative (−).

Temperature Gradient

Temperature gradient ($\Delta T/L$) is the temperature difference (ΔT) per unit length (L) or per differential (final-minus-initial) length, shown as dL or dX. When using dX, we mean that the T changes only along the X-axis direction, so it is only a function of X. $\Delta T/L$, instead, describes how fast and in which direction a substance T changes along a given length. [A **gradient** is a change in the value of a quantity per change in L, such as $\Delta T/L$.]

T-5

TENSILE MODULUS AND TENSILE STRAIN

Other names for ELASTIC MODULUS AND ELASTIC STRAIN.

T-6

TERNARY MIXTURES AND TRIANGLE DIAGRAMS

A **ternary mixture** is a mixture (mix) with three (or more) chemical components (simply **components**) and one (or two) phase. For example, most practical extraction processes are performed on a ternary mixture with three components and one phase (a solution), the extractant (the solvent), the wanted liquid (which stays in the extract), and the unwanted liquid (which stays in the raffinate).

A **triangular diagram** represents the quantities (usually in percentages) of the ternary mixture's components (usually components *A*, *B*, and *C*). Two triangular diagrams are used: 1) The **right triangle** and 2) The **equilateral triangle** (Figure 1). Points and lines in a right-triangle diagram represent themselves as follows:

- Point A on the **abscissa** (*X*-line) in Figure 2A represents 100% of component *A* and point B represents 0% of component *A*. Percentage lines of component *A* are parallel with line BC.
- Point B on the **ordinate** (*Y*-line) in Figure 2B represents 100% component *B*, and point C represents 0% *B*. Percentage lines of component *B* are parallel with line AC.
- Point C on the 135° line in Figure 2C represents 100% component *C* and point A represents 0% *C*. Percentage lines of component *C* are parallel with line AB.

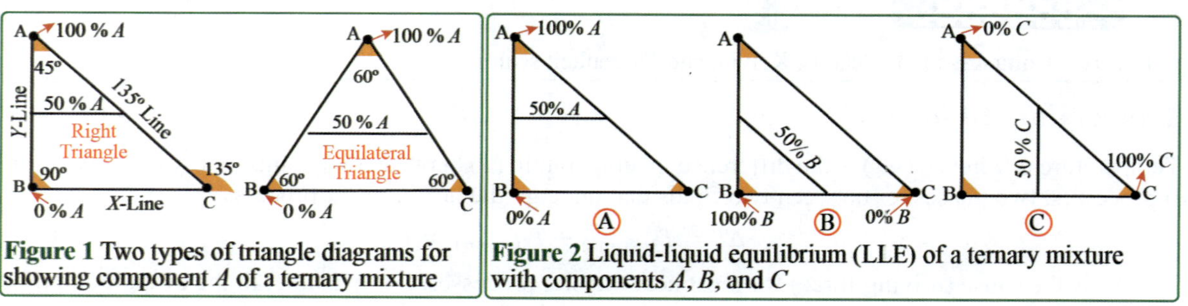

Figure 1 Two types of triangle diagrams for showing component *A* of a ternary mixture

Figure 2 Liquid-liquid equilibrium (LLE) of a ternary mixture with components *A*, *B*, and *C*

T-7

TESLA

Nicola Tesla (1856–1943) was a Serbian-American electrical inventor. He was born and raised in Serbia, moved to Hungary when he was 25 years old, and immigrated to the US of America three years later in 1884. In the USA, Tesla invented and developed many electrical devices and instruments, including alternating current (AC) electricity (1886), induction motor (1887), Tesla coil (1891), steam-powered generator (1893), radio-remote control (1898), bladeless turbine (1906), and more.

In honor of Tesla's scientific contributions, the SI unit of **magnetic flux density** (simply magnetic flux or **magnetic strength**) is named after him. 1 Tesla (T) = 1 N.s/C.m = Weber per m^2 = 10 000 gauss. [A magnet holding a small picture on a refrigerator door produces a magnetic flux of 0.01 T.]

T-8
THEORETICAL AIR REQUIREMENT

Discussed under COMBUSTION AIR REQUIREMENT.

T-9
THEORETICAL PLATES

See NUMBER OF THEORETICAL PLATES.

T-10
THEORIES OF RELATIVITY

Study EINSTEIN'S THEORIES OF RELATIVITY.

T-11
THEORY AND LAW (Physics)

Theory: A theory, in physics, is a scientific statement about a physical phenomenon (or phenomena) that is predicted, so it has *not* yet been tested and verified by observations and (or) experiments. A scientific theory survives if its predictions are mathematically verifiable on paper or testable in the laboratory. If *not*, it must be modified or rejected. Einstein's theory of general relativity is the most important in physics; based on its concept, many other theories (like blackhole theory) have been verified.

Law: A law in physics is a scientific statement about a physical phenomenon (or phenomena) that is verified repeatedly in a lab, on paper, or both. As a rule, the accuracy of a scientific law does *not* change when a new related theory is offered. [A law, however, does *not* have absolute certainty, so it *cannot* be taken as an **absolute-and-complete fact** (because it is possible to be contradicted or extended by future theories).] Laws of Conservation (Energy Conservation Law, Mass Conservation Law, Law of Linear Momentum Conservation, and Law of Rotational-Momentum Conservation) are examples of laws.

This topic can come to an end by saying the following:

- A theory can become a law when proved experimentally in a lab or theoretically on paper.
- A law differs from a **theory**, a **hypothesis** (a proposed explanation for a phenomenon), a **postulate** (a proposed explanation for a phenomenon that is taken to be true as a starting point), and a **paradigm** (a general idea) because those have *not* been verified to the same extent as a law has. [Several practical relationships that were first discovered with *no* theoretical explanation are often called laws, although they were later explained in the context of a broader theory.]

T-12

THEORY OF EVERYTHING

Another name for THEORY OF UNIFICATION OF PHYSICS.

T-13

THEORY OF GENERAL RELATIVITY

Discussed under the topic of EINSTEIN'S THEORIES OF RELATIVITY.

T-14

THEORY OF PHOTOELECTRIC EFFECT

Study EINSTEIN'S THEORY OF PHOTOELECTRIC EFFECT.

T-15

THEORY OF SPACETIME

Discussed under the topic of EINSTEIN'S THEORIES OF RELATIVITY.

T-16

THEORY OF SPECIAL RELATIVITY

Study EINSTEIN'S THEORIES OF RELATIVITY.

T-17

THEORY OF UNIFICATION OF PHYSICS

As one of the major yet-unsolved problems of physics, the theory of unification of physics (TUP, also called the **quantum unified theory** or **theory of everything**) is a concept about the connection of all four (4) fundamental forces of nature (FFN) to describe them in the context of their force-carrying quantum particles (particles with *no* subparticle). Physicists have *not* been successful in this difficult effort, mainly because

- The F_g (gravitational force) acts on a universal scale, so it *cannot* be quantized, unlike the other 3 FFN.
- The F_{EM} (electromagnetic force) acts at both atomic and universal (infinite) scales, and
- The F_{SN} (strong nuclear force) and F_{WN} (weak nuclear force) act only at the atomic scale with a tiny influence range of 10^{-15} m.

The successful inclusion of all FFN, mainly the F_g and F_{EM}, into the quantum field theories and Einstein's principle of spacetime-gravity can express all FFN and their elementary particles by unified equations.

Physics has been unable to quantize the F_g (the weakest of FFN); in other words, to provide a consistent quantum description and formulation of F_g, mainly because the general relativity is a non-quantum theory in a way that it talks about the F_g in large scales (from a few km to the size of the Universe), but *not* on the atomic (quantized) scale.

Hawking thought that string theory and particle physics, which are based on quantum physics, can solve the TUP to describe the Universe fully. He suggested that a necessary first step for achieving a unified theory is to consider space filled with the pairs (particles and antiparticles) because together, these pairs have an infinite amount of energy (E) and, thus, by Einstein's equation ($E = M.c^2$), they would have an infinite amount of mass (M). Thus, the F_g of pairs would be strong enough to curve (distort) the Universe (see CURVATURE OF SPACETIME) to an infinitely small size.

Several physicists, including Einstein in his last 20 years and a few other physicists, have already tried to have answers to the TUP's unsolved problems. But, this important work has *not* been completed yet (see the next Note). Let us hope that physics can soon solve this unified theory that can govern the entire Universe.

[Note: For those interested in details of TUP (theory of unification of physics), a good source is *Einstein's Theory of Unified Field*, authored by the French physicist M. A. Tonnelat, published in 1966.]

T-18

THERMAL CONDUCTANCE

Another name for **conductive heat transfer**. It is discussed under CONVECTIVE AND CONDUCTIVE HEAT TRANSFER COEFFICIENTS.

T-19

THERMAL CONDUCTIVITY

Another name for **conductive heat transfer coefficient**. It is discussed under CONVECTIVE AND CONDUCTIVE HEAT TRANSFER COEFFICIENTS.

T-20

THERMAL CONDUCTORS AND THERMAL INSULATORS

Thermal Conductors

A thermal (heat) conductor is a chemical compound (simply **compound**) that molecules can easily conduct the heat energy (E_Q), so its thermal conductance (K_T) is high. And its thermal resistance (R_Q) is low. Metals are good thermal conductors.

Thermal Insulators

A thermal (heat) insulator is a compound whose molecules *cannot* conduct the E_Q, so its K_T is low and its R_Q is high. A perfect thermal insulator does *not* exist, but some materials, like air, glass, plastic, fiberglass, and wood, are thermal insulators.

T-21

THERMAL DIFFUSIVITY

Thermal diffusivity (D_T or α) is the property of a chemical substance in relation to its thermal conductivity (K_T), density (D), and specific heat capacity (C_Q, simply **heat capacity**).

$$D_T = \frac{K_T}{D.C_Q} \tag{1}$$

The SI unit of D_T is m^2/s, usually measured at 20ºC and constant pressure ($\Delta P = 0$). For example, the D_T of moist air at 20ºC and 1 Atm is 0.14×10^{-6} m^2/s.

T-22

THERMAL EQUILIBRIUM

Discussed under the topic of EQUILIBRIUM.

T-23

THERMAL EXPANSION

Thermal expansion (X) is a measure of the expansion or contraction of a solid material when the material goes under a considerable temperature (T) change at constant pressure (P). Although the thermal expansion of solids has more applications, liquids and gases also expand (or contract) when heated (or cooled). [When discussing expansion in a material's length, the word **linear thermal expansion** is used, and when a material's volume goes under expansion, the word **volumetric thermal expansion** is used.]

Usually, the term **thermal expansion** is the **coefficient of thermal expansion**, which is the quantity of expansion divided by the change in T (the temperature difference, ΔT). The linear thermal expansion (X_L) of a material is given in relation to L (original length) and ΔT as

$$X_L = \frac{dL}{L.\Delta T} \tag{1}$$

In this equation, d is the symbol for differential, dL is the differential length, and $dL/\Delta T$ is the rate of differential length per unit ΔT. Usually, dL is given in μm (micrometer), L in m, and ΔT in °C, so the X_L becomes in μm/(m.°C). For example, the X_L of stainless steel is about 15 μm/(m.°C), meaning that for each °C increase in T, 1 m linear length of stainless steel goes through an expansion of 15 μm. The X_L of iron is 12 μm/(m.°C).

Most materials expand when they undergo an increase in T. Instead, several materials, like water, contract with increasing T. The term **thermal contraction** or equally **negative thermal expansion** is used for materials that behave like water. Water's thermal expansion decreases to zero as it is cooled to 4°C and decreases more (to below zero) when it is cooled to below 4°C. This means that water has a maximum density (D) at 4°C, so the D of warmer water is less than that of colder water. This trend continues until it reaches 4°C. At below 4°C, water becomes less dense as it freezes. This is why ice cubes always float to the top of a glass of water.

T-24

THERMAL INSULATORS

Study THERMAL CONDUCTORS AND THERMAL INSULATORS.

T-25

THERMAL REACTIONS

Another name for HEAT REACTIONS.

T-26

THERMAL RESERVOIR

Another name for HEAT RESERVOIR.

T-27

THERMAL RESISTANCE

Thermal resistance (R_T or R_Q, also called **heat resistance**) is a quantity that expresses how a material resists the flow of heat energy (E_Q, simply heat). A thermal resistor has a high R_T and a low K_T (thermal conductance). And a thermal conductor has a low R_T and a high K_T. The R_T is the reciprocal (inverse) of the K_T. A material's R_T can be calculated from the temperature change (ΔT) when an E_Q flows through that material.

$$R_T = \frac{1}{K_T} = \frac{\Delta T}{E_Q} \quad (1)$$

If T is in °C and E_Q is in W/h, the SI unit of R_T becomes in (h.°C)/W or equally in (s.°C)/J, where °C is for degrees centigrade, W is for Watt, the h is for an hour, the s is for second, and J is four Joule.

The R_Q can also be expressed in (h.°C.m)/W, the common unit of **specific thermal resistance**.

[Note: For simplicity, sometimes the term **specific thermal resistance** ($R_{T.Sp}$) is abbreviated to just **thermal resistance**. In such cases, the given unit of the quantity can determine the purpose of the writer because $R_{T.Sp}$ is expressed in (h.°C.m)/W, while R_T is given in (h.°C)/W.]

T-28

THERMODYNAMIC EQUILIBRIUM

Thermodynamic equilibrium (also known as **thermodynamic stability**; often abbreviated to **equilibrium**) is the condition of stability in a thermodynamic system (a heat-involving system) when *no* heat transfer occurs over the time between the system and its surrounding (outside). Because *no* heat flows through a stable thermodynamic system, *no* phase change occurs in the system. At such conditions, some thermodynamic potentials, like Gibbs free energy (E_{GF}) or Helmholtz free energy (E_{HF}), become minimized.

T-29

THERMODYNAMIC FIRST LAW

Discussed under THERMODYNAMICS AND THERMODYNAMIC LAWS.

T-30

THERMODYNAMIC FREE ENERGY

See GIBBS FREE ENERGY.

T-31

THERMODYNAMIC LAWS

Study THERMODYNAMICS AND THERMODYNAMIC LAWS.

T-32

THERMODYNAMIC POTENTIALS

The four (4) main thermodynamic potentials are internal energy (E_I), entropy (S), Gibbs free energy (E_{GF}), and Helmholtz free energy (E_{HF}). All of these are energy-related quantities. When a system is at thermodynamic equilibrium, *no* net mass flow, energy flow, and phase change occur in that system. At such conditions, some thermodynamic potential, like E_{GF} or E_{HF}, becomes minimized.

T-33

THERMODYNAMIC SECOND LAW

Study THERMODYNAMICS AND THERMODYNAMIC LAWS.

T-34

THERMODYNAMIC STABILITY

Another name for THERMODYNAMIC EQUILIBRIUM.

T-35

THERMODYNAMIC SYSTEM

A thermodynamic system is an energy-involving (heat-involving) system used to study the principles of Thermodynamic Laws. A thermodynamic system can be separated from its surrounding environment (outsides) by a boundary. Thus, the exchange of mass (M), energy (E), work (W), or all of the above between a thermodynamic system and its outside occur across the system's boundary.

As an example of a laboratory heat-involving system, consider a calorimeter. The solution under the test in the calorimeter is the system, and the calorimeter's wall and its immediate environment are the surroundings.

As an example of an industrial heat-involving system, consider an evaporator. The solution under evaporation is the system, and the evaporator's wall and its immediate environment are the surroundings. The evaporator uses the steam's heat energy (E_Q) to evaporate the solution to the desired concentration (C).

A steam-and-power production station in a chemical-process plant is also a large heat-involving system. The supersaturated steam (simply **super steam** or **live steam**) produced in the steam boiler runs the steam turbine, producing electricity (electric power) for the power users (like pumps). And the exhaust steam from the turbine is used by the heat users (like heat exchangers). Such a large thermodynamic system converts the E in fuel into E_Q in steam, vapor, and condensate for delivery to the process heat users.

T-36

THERMODYNAMIC TEMPERATURE

See ABSOLUTE TEMPERATURE.

T-37

THERMODYNAMIC THIRD LAW

Discussed under THERMODYNAMICS AND THERMODYNAMIC LAWS.

T-38

THERMODYNAMIC ZEROTH LAW

Discussed under THERMODYNAMIC AND THERMODYNAMIC LAWS.

T-39

THERMODYNAMICS AND THERMODYNAMIC LAWS

Thermodynamics

Thermodynamics is the foundation of most engineering courses, including ChemEng. In short, it studies the properties and functionalities of heat energy (E_Q, traditionally heat, and scientifically enthalpy). In more detail, it studies interactions of E_Q, T (temperature), M (mass), W (work), H (enthalpy), and S (entropy). In addition, thermodynamics is used in ChemEng to study heat transfer, mass transfer, and more.

Thermodynamic Laws

Thermodynamic laws are four (4) principles that define the temperature (T), energy (E), enthalpy (H), and entropy (S) of a thermodynamic system (a heat-involving system) and the conversion of E into its different forms. These laws apply to every thermodynamic system, like steam engines. A refrigerator is an example of a thermodynamic system. It does *not* add cold to our refrigerated foods. But, it takes the E_Q by compressing an expanding liquid through a condenser to become a cooling gas and returning to the refrigerator (see Figure 1).

Before talking about individual thermodynamic laws, it is helpful to mention the following:

- Thermodynamic Laws were developed by different scientists during the Industrial Revolution, starting in Europe around the 1760s when steam engines and machine-made mass products started.
- The principle involved with the definition of T (temperature) was formulized after the other principles, so it was named the **Thermodynamic Zeroth Law**. [We follow this trend in this book.]

Thermodynamic Zeroth Law: The zeroth law (some number it as the **first law** as reasoned a moment ago) defines the T of a thermodynamic system. It states that "if two closed systems (energy can enter or leave a closed system, but mass *cannot*) of A and B are each in thermal equilibrium with a third closed system of C, then A and B are also in thermal (heat) equilibrium with each other." The thermal equilibrium means a **temperature equilibrium**, which occurs in a closed system when it experiences *no* net change of its T with time. If, for example, we bring two (2) closed systems with different temperatures together to be in heat contact. Eventually, a situation occurs in which *no* further heat transfer occurs. This situation is called the **thermal equilibrium** in a heat-involved system. Thus, both systems have the same T.

Thermodynamic First Law: The first law (some number it as the **second law** as reasoned earlier) talks about the relation between the H (enthalpy) and W (work) of a thermodynamic system and the amount of heat energy (E_Q, simply heat) that is transferred (absorbed or released) in that system during a chemical process or a chemical reaction. The first law can be formulized as

$$H = E_Q + W \tag{1}$$

This equation shows that a closed system's H (or energy) is conserved (unchanged). For an open system (mass and energy can enter or leave the system), the first law can be written as the heat transfer rate (heat transfer per time).

$$\dot{H} = \dot{E}_Q + \dot{W} \tag{2}$$

The first law also has other expressions, including the next ones:

- The sum of E or M of a closed system remains constant (unchanged).
- For increasing a system's internal energy (E_I), two ways exist: to give the system some E_Q or do W on it. E_I, similarly, decreases if the system releases some E_Q or does some W.
- A system's total energy (E_T) can be considered as the sum of E_I, E_K (kinetic energy), and E_P (potential energy) if other energies are negligibly small, relatively.

The last expression can be written mathematically for a closed system, as

$$E_T = \Delta E_I + \Delta E_K + \Delta E_P \tag{3}$$

When heat energy (E_Q) and work (W) are added to a closed system, the system's E_I is

$$E_I = E_Q + W \tag{4}$$

This equation is like Equation 1. Two ways exist for increasing a system's E_I: give it some E_Q or do W (work) on it. Similarly, E_I decreases when the system releases some E_Q or does some W. Thus, the sign of E_T is + (positive) if heat enters a system from the surroundings (outsides) and – (negative) if heat leaves the system to the surroundings. This rule applies to W also.

In a condensed (liquid or solid), closed, and heat-involving system, the work term can be ignored because it is pressure-volume (PV) work, where P is for pressure and V is for volume. Similarly, E_K and E_P are *not* of importance, so the practical form of the first law is

$$E_T = E_I \tag{5}$$

This says that a system's E_T has the same meaning as its E_I if its E_K and E_P are negligibly small. The previous equation can be written in the differential form (d form) when the system goes through small state changes.

$$dE_T = dE_I \tag{6}$$

When a system is at **constant pressure** ($\Delta P = 0$), the PV work is negligibly small, thus

$$E_T = E_I = E_Q \tag{7}$$

We add another form of E, the H (enthalpy), to our discussion. We know that H is the heat-energy content of a substance (like fuel, vapor, or steam) at constant P. Enthalpy equation for a closed system is

$$H = E_I + P.V \tag{8}$$

In a chemical process, the **changes** (shown by Δ sign) between the initial enthalpy (H_1) and final enthalpy (H_2) are measured, but *not* the value of H. Thus,

$$\Delta H = H_2 - H_1 = E_I + P.V \tag{9}$$

Considering $E_I = E_Q$ and knowing that the product of PV is negligibly small when ΔP or ΔV is so small leads to the practical form of the First Thermodynamic Law.

$$\Delta H = E_Q \tag{10}$$

[This equation expresses the thermodynamic first law and, therefore, it is an important equation in ChemEng. It tells us that the **change in enthalpy** (ΔH) in a system equates to the amount of heat energy (E_Q) transferred (absorbed or released) by that system. Knowing that the ΔH and E_Q have the same meaning makes the heat transfer calculations easier because the ΔH values of many substances (such as vapor and steam) are determined and given in tables (such as Tables 1 and 2 in this book's table section.)]

Thermodynamic Second Law: The second law (some number it as the **third law** as reasoned earlier) started by saying that E_Q flows from a hot reservoir to a cold reservoir, but *not* in the other direction. The second law defines absolute temperature (T_{Abs}) as the lowest T that a system can be cooled (T_{Abs} = 0 K = – 273°C = –460°F), entropy (S) as a system's energy that *cannot* be used for doing work (W), and absolute entropy as the S at T_{Abs}. Mathematically, the second law defines a closed system's S in relation to its E_Q and T.

$$S = \frac{E_Q}{T} \tag{11}$$

The practical definition of the first law ($\Delta H = E_Q$) from one state to another can be combined with the practical definition of the second law ($\Delta S = \Delta E_Q/T$) to rewrite the entropy equation in a useful form.

$$\Delta S = \frac{\Delta H}{T} \tag{12}$$

This equation indicates the relation between the changes in entropy (ΔS, commonly entropy change), changes in enthalpy (ΔH, commonly enthalpy change), and T of a system from one state to another.

[Note: The second law predicts that as stars cool and die (for losing E), a gradual increase in S occurs in the Universe (a closed system) after billions of years. Thus, *not* enough E will remain to sustain any life (an effect so-called the **heat death of the Universe**). This can be prevented only by giving a huge E to the Universe in time.]

Thermodynamic Third Law: The third law (some call it the **fourth law** as reasoned earlier) states that S (entropy) in a system only approaches a constant value if the system's T (temperature) approaches T_{Abs} (absolute temperature = 0 K). This is the definition of T_{Abs}. Experimentally, the T_{Abs} may be approached but *cannot* be reached. At the T_{Abs}, the S of a pure system (like crystal molecules) is zero, so it is in the ground energy state.

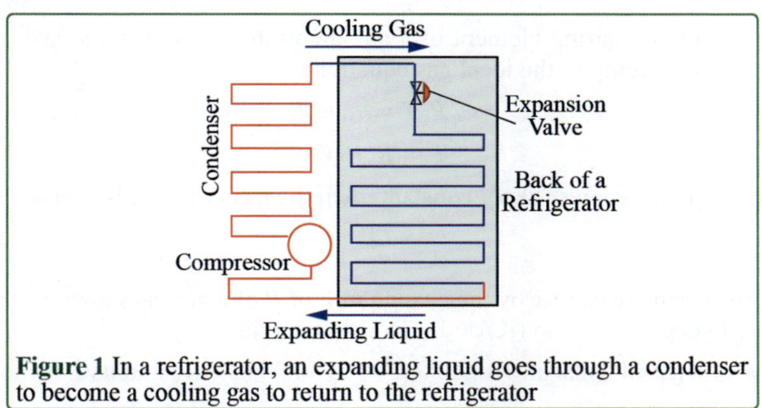

Figure 1 In a refrigerator, an expanding liquid goes through a condenser to become a cooling gas to return to the refrigerator

T-40

THERMOMETERS

A thermometer is an instrument for measuring the temperature (T) of a fluid (liquid or gases). [The first thermometer was developed by **Galileo** (1564–1642, Italian scientist). Its original form was a long narrow tube filled with colored alcohol that expands with increasing T and contracts with decreasing T.]

[Internationally, **mercury** is considered hazardous, so many countries recommend that **mercury thermometers** *not* be used in homes.]

Thermometers can be calibrated to three temperature scales, Celsius degrees (ºC), Fahrenheit degrees (ºF), and Kelvin scale (K). Temperature scales are based on absolute temperature (T_{Abs}). All four thermometers discussed here are portable (handy) and do *not* need a **power supply**.

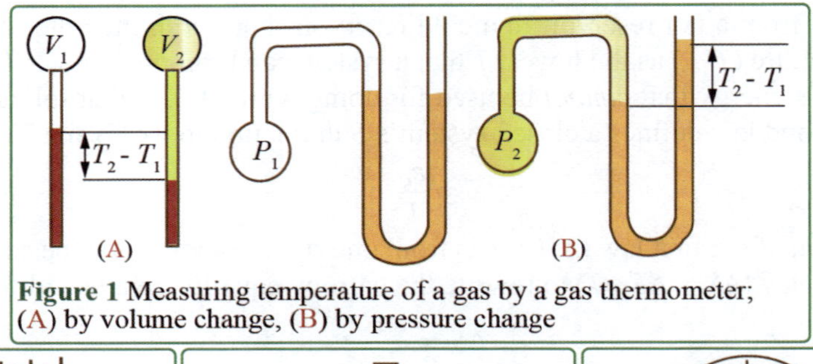

Figure 1 Measuring temperature of a gas by a gas thermometer; (A) by volume change, (B) by pressure change

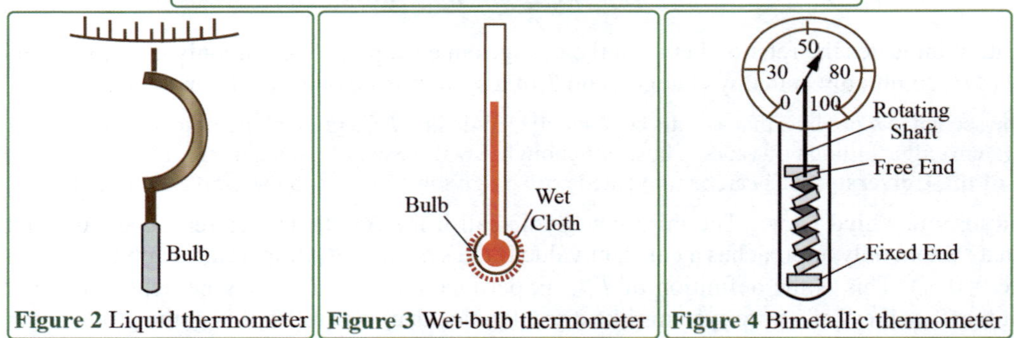

Figure 2 Liquid thermometer **Figure 3** Wet-bulb thermometer **Figure 4** Bimetallic thermometer

Gas Thermometers: The measuring element of a gas thermometer contains a gas whose V (volume) or P (pressure) changes with T (according to the ideal gas equation).

$$P.V = n.R.T \tag{1}$$

$$T = K.P.V \tag{2}$$

If the V of the gas in the thermometer is kept constant, then the ratio of the gas P and T is constant, so

$$\frac{P_1}{T_1} = \frac{P_2}{T_2} \tag{3}$$

A gas thermometer, thus, can measure T by the change in V or P of a gas, as shown in Figure 1. [Note that the T in Equation 3 must be in degrees Kelvin (K) and P in absolute units.]

If, for example, the P of a gas at constant V and 20ºC (= 293 K) is 3 Atm and its P is increased to 3.5 Atm, the T of the gas will be

$$T_2 = \frac{P_2}{P_1} T_1 = \frac{3.5}{3} \times 293 = 342 \text{ K} \quad \text{or} \qquad 342 - 273 = 69^{\circ}\text{C}$$

Liquid Thermometers: A liquid thermometer's measuring element contains a liquid whose V changes with T according to the following equation:

$$V_T = V_0(1 + \beta T) \quad (4)$$

V_T is the V of the liquid at T, V_0 is that at 0ºC, and β is the **volumetric thermal expansion coefficient** (it is in the range of 1×10^{-4} to 16×10^{-4} 1/K, where K is for degrees Kelvin).

As shown in Figure 2, a liquid thermometer contains a metal (or glass) tube, partly filled with a filling liquid and sealed on both sides. The filling liquid is often mercury, measuring temperatures between −40 to 500ºC. Methanol (−40 to 150ºC) or xylene (−40 to 400ºC) is also used. As the T around the thermometer's bulb increases, the liquid expands and rises in the tube, and the gauge moves.

Wet-Bulb Thermometers: A wet-bulb thermometer is a glass thermometer whose bulb is covered with a wet cloth (usually muslin), as shown in Figure 3, to measure air wet-bulb temperature. The air around a wet thermometer is saturated air, so the evaporation of a small portion of water in a wet cloth causes some water vapor to be produced. Part of the vapor condenses, which cools the remaining water in cloth, so the T_W, measured by the wet thermometer, is lower than T_D, measured by a dry-bulb (ordinary) thermometer. When a steady state is reached, the liquid T is the wet-bulb temperature (T_W).

Bimetallic Thermometers: A bimetallic thermometer uses the difference in thermal expansion between two different metals to measure the T of a substance. Thermal expansion (X) is the tendency of a solid, a liquid, or a gas to change in size in response to a change in T when undergoing a temperature change (ΔT). [When talking about expansion in a material's length (L), the term **linear thermal expansion** is used. And when a material's volume (V) goes under expansion, the term **volumetric thermal expansion** is used.] Assume that the change in linear dimension is L. The change in length that arises from a small change in T is ΔL. The ΔL (the small change in L) is proportional to the ΔT (the small change in T) and original L through a proportionality coefficient, the **linear thermal expansion coefficient** (K).

$$\Delta L = K.L.\Delta T \quad (5)$$

The value K for aluminum is 25×10^{-6} ºC, for copper is 17×10^{-6} ºC, and for stainless steel is 17×10^{-6} ºC. If, for example, we want to find the linear expansion of a 2 m long aluminum rod at 20ºC when its T changes from 0 to 100ºC, we have to calculate ΔL at 0 and 100.

$$\Delta L_0 = KL\Delta T = KL(T_0 - T_{20}) + L = 25 \times 10^{-6} \times 2(0 - 20) + 2 = 2.001 \text{ m}$$

$$\Delta L_{100} = KL(T_{100} - T_{20}) + L = 25 \times 10^{-6} \times 2(100 - 20) + 2 = 2.004 \text{ m}$$

$$L_{100} - L_0 = 2.004 - 2.001 = 0.003 \text{ m}$$

A bimetallic thermometer consists of spiral strips of two metals, which are connected (Figure 4). When, thus, one metal expands more than the other (as the result of a higher T), the resulting bend of the strip is translated into a T by a pointer.

T-41

THICKENERS

Study DECANTERS.

T-42

THIN FILM

The word **thin film** is used in ChemEng to refer to a **thin layer**, like the wall of a soup's bubble, with a thickness in the millimeter (mm) or nanometer (nm) range, depending on the origin of the thin film. For example, in the evaporation process in a thin-film (TF) tube evaporator, the thin films of a liquid feed created on the inside surface of the evaporator's heating tubes are in the mm range. While in the diffusion process in a diffuser, the diffusants diffuse through a thin film in the range of a few nm.

To become familiar with creating a thin film on the heating tubes, consider a TF tube evaporator, in which feed moves inside the tubes and steam moves outside the tubes. Because of heat transfer, the feed starts to boil, so it forms some vapor, whose pressure (P) presses the remaining liquid against the tubes' wall to form a thin film.

T-43

THREE- AND FOUR-DIMENSIONAL SYSTEMS

Three-Dimensional System: A three-dimensional (3D) system is a three-directional geometric model used to express space (with 3 dimensions). In the 3D system, which we are used to it, the directions are height (up/down), width (left/right), and depth (back/front), each at right angles to the other. Figure 1 shows a 3D system with three dimensions, each by a coordinate, where the Z-axis points toward the observer. In a 3D system,

- Dimensions are symmetrical, so *no* direction is different from any other direction,
- Each axis is perpendicular to the other two at the point of origin O (at which all axes cross), and
- A point (say, point P) in the system can be given by 3 coordinates (X, Y, and Z), as seen in the same figure.

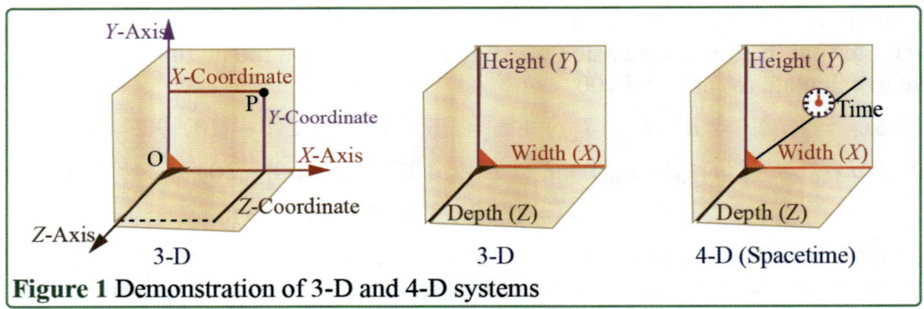

Figure 1 Demonstration of 3-D and 4-D systems

Four-Dimensional System: A four-dimensional (4D) system combines space (with 3 dimensions) and time (with 1 dimension) to a single concept, known as spacetime (with 4 dimensions). [Even though the **observable Universe** (the spherical space that can be observed from Earth with today's modern telescopes) is well described by a 4-D spacetime, some physicists prefer to work with a spacetime with more dimensions (because it is easier to perform the related calculations). For example, in string theory, spacetime is 10-dimensional. Similarly, in quantum gravity theory, spacetime is 11-dimensional, and in bosonic string theory, spacetime is even 26-dimensional. However, it is easier to describe some systems, like a condensed system, in 2-D or 3-D. In such a system, known as a **system with a compaction number of dimensions**, some of the extra dimensions are assumed to be overlaid to form a circle. When the overlaid dimensions become very small, we obtain a spacetime with fewer dimensions. Consider a garden hose. If viewing the hose from a distance, it appears to be 1-D (its **length**). If viewing the hose from a close distance, it appears to be 2-D (its length and depth or circumference). Thus, an ant moving on a hose surface would move in 2-D, while a person next to the hose would move in 3-D. In this way, some physicists think that the observable Universe is a 4-D subspace of higher space.]

T-44

TIME

Study SPACE, TIME, AND SPACETIME.

T-45

TIME DILATION THEORY

Discussed under EINSTEIN'S THEORIES OF RELATIVITY.

T-46

TITRATION

See TITRIMETRIC ANALYSIS.

T-47

TITRIMETRIC ANALYSIS

Titrimetric analysis (also called **volumetric titration** or simply **titration**) is a laboratory technique for determining a solution sample's concentration (*C*). It is based on adding a **titrant** (a solution with known *C*) and an indicator to a sample of unknown *C* until the sample's color changes at a certain pH. The point at which the color of the sample changes is called the **neutralization point** or **endpoint**. Then the unknown *C* is related to the titrant *C* and used *V* (volume) to determine the sample's *C*.

The general steps in performing a titration are outlined below.

- A certain volume (usually 20 or 25 mL) of a solution sample with unknown *C* is measured,
- A few (2 to 3) drops of an indicator are added to the sample to change its color at a certain pH, and
- The sample is titrated with a titrant with known *C* by a burette until an endpoint (neutralization point) is reached, and the concentration of the sample is calculated.

If, for example, sodium hydroxide solution (NaOH) of unknown *C* is under titration with 1.8 *N* nitric acid (HNO_3) solution, where *N* is for normality, you can proceed as follow (see Figure 1):

- Measure 20 mL of NaOH solution with a pipette and add it to an Erlenmeyer flask,
- Add a few drops of phenolphthalein indicator to the flask, and
- Titrate NaOH solution with HNO_3 solution until the pink color disappears entirely (endpoint of the phenolphthalein indicator is at the PH of 8).

The process of the neutralization reaction can be represented by a titration curve, like the one shown in Figure 2. Assume that the titration needed 18 mL of HNO_3. You can calculate the *N* of the NaOH (N_2).

$$V_1.N_1 = V_2.N_2 \qquad 20 \times 1.8 = 18 \times N_2 \qquad N_2 = \frac{36}{18} = 2$$

[In general, using a strong acid as **titrant** to determine the amount of a base gives a better result than a weak acid, as a strong acid creates a wider distinct endpoint.]

Similarly, the alkalinity of a solution sample is measured by the sample titration with a standardized acid solution, such as 0.036 N sulfuric acid solution, in the presence of phenolphthalein to the endpoint (PH of 8).

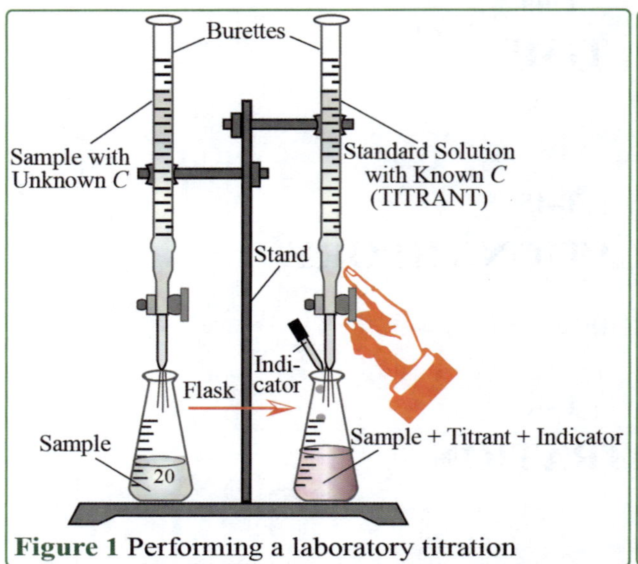

Figure 1 Performing a laboratory titration

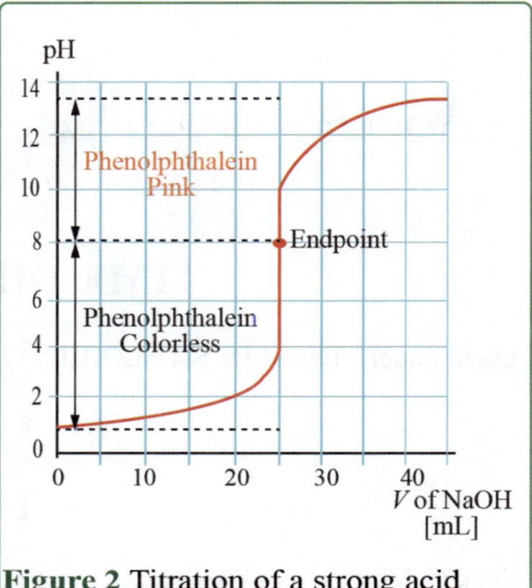

Figure 2 Titration of a strong acid with a strong base

T-48

TNT

TNT [trinitrotoluene, $C_6H_2(NO_2)_3CH_3$] is a yellow solid chemical compound. It melts at 80ºC (= 176ºF), far below the temperature (*T*) at which it explodes, allowing it to be safely combined with other compounds. As an explosive, some other properties of TNT are outlined below:

- It is easily handled.
- It is *not* soluble in water.
- It does *not* absorb the air's moisture, allowing it to be used effectively in a wet environment.
- It explodes when pressure is exerted on a starter explosive, known as the explosive booster.

As an explosive, TNT is used in the military, mining, and other industries. [The explosive effect of the TNT is used as a standard for the explosion of atomic weapons.]

T-49

TORQUE

Torque (T_R or τ, also called the **moment of force** or simply **moment**) is a twisting effect of a force (*F*) applied to a system, which is rotating (turning) in the distance from the axis of rotation of *R*. The concept originated with the studies by Archimedes (287 BC−212 BC, Greek scientist) for the use of lever by saying that a force applied to a lever multiplied by its distance from the lever's arm is its **torque**.

Not considering the gravitational force and friction, T_R is given as the product of *F* multiplied by *R* (perpendicular distance from the axis of rotation). Only the perpendicular component (F_1) produces a torque, so $F = F_1$, as shown in Figure 1.

$$T_R = F \times R \tag{1}$$

For example, a force of 2 N (Newton), applied 2 m from a lever's arm, exerts the same T_R as a force of 1N, applied 4 m from the arm. Figure 2 shows the top view of an ordinary door. The greatest T_R occurs (meaning the largest opening or closing occurs) when the force is applied,

- Perpendicular to the face of the door,
- Toward the hinges (the axes of rotation), and
- Farthest from the hinges (this is why the doorknobs are put there).

When the angle a exists between the applied force and the lever's arm vector, the torque equation becomes

$$T_R = F \times R \times \text{ Sin } a \tag{2}$$

The direction of torque can be determined by using the right-hand rule. When the fingers of the right hand are around the lever's arm, the thumb shows the direction of the torque.

The T_R is a vector quantity. It is expressed in N.m, where N is for Newton (the SI unit of force) and m is for the meter (the SI unit of length).

In shaft work (W_S) calculations, the W_S is the product of T_R multiplied by N (number of rotations per time, known as RPM, rotation per minute, or R/min).

$$W_S = 2T_R \times \pi \times N \tag{3}$$

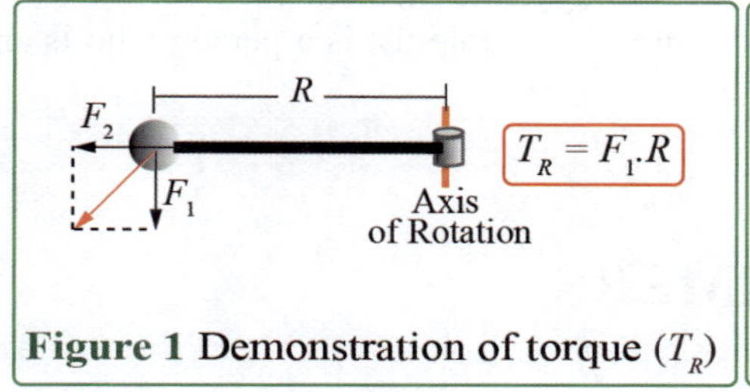

Figure 1 Demonstration of torque (T_R)

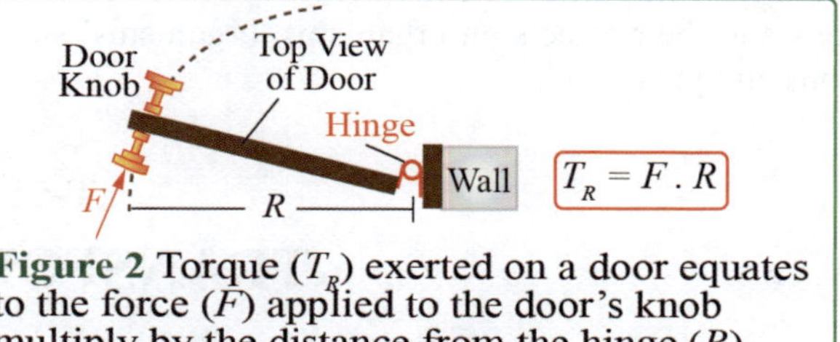

Figure 2 Torque (T_R) exerted on a door equates to the force (F) applied to the door's knob multiply by the distance from the hinge (R)

T-50

TORRICELLI EQUATION

Torricelli equation (named after Evangelista Torricelli, 1608–1647, Italian scientist) and Bernoulli equation (also called **mechanical-energy equation**), in their different forms, are used to calculating the energy balance involved in a liquid flow process in a pipe. [For a complete discussion about Bernoulli and Torricelli equations, refer to the topic of LIQUID FLOW PROCESS.]

T-51

TOTAL DYNAMIC HEAD

Another name for TOTAL PUMP HEAD.

T-52

TOTAL ENERGY

Discussed under the topic of ENERGY AND ITS FORMS.

T-53

TOTAL HEAD

Study PUMP LIQUID HEADS.

T-54

TOXICITY AND TOXICOLOGY

Toxicity: The term **toxicity** is used to express how bad a **toxicant** (see the Note below) can hurt an **organism** (any individual that embodies life, like a human or an animal) or on an organism's substructure (such as a human's eye) when it is exposed to that toxicant.

[Note: The terms **toxicant** and **toxin** should *not* be used equally, although both are **poisons** (poisonous chemical substances or mixtures of poisonous substances). This is because the word **toxicant** refers to a naturally-produced or artificial poison, while the word **toxin** is used to refer to a naturally-produced poison. A toxin, however, can be produced synthetically. For example, **biocides** (oxidizing disinfectants) are produced artificially.]

Toxicology: Toxicology is a subject study rooted in chemistry, biology, and medicine. It studies the properties of poisons and their effects on organisms, organisms' substructure. A toxicologist is a person who is an expert on poisons and poisoning.

T-55

TRANSFORMERS

Study ELECTRIC TRANSFORMERS.

T-56

TRANSITIONAL FLOW

Discussed under the topic of REYNOLD NUMBER.

T-57

TRANSITIONAL METALS

A transitional metal (also called **transition metal**) is a chemical element (simply **element**) with a partially filled *d* sub-shell. Transitional metals are in groups 3 through 11 of the periodic table of elements, shown in **blue** color in the periodic table given on the inside front cover of this book.

T-58

TRANSMITTANCE

Study LIGHT ABSORBANCE, INTENSITY, AND TRANSMITTANCE.

T-59

TRIANGULAR DIAGRAMS

Study TERNARY MIXTURES AND TRIANGULAR DIAGRAMS.

T-60

TRIPLE POINT AND CRITICAL POINT TEMPERATURES

Triple Point Temperature: The triple point temperature (simply T-point) of a pure chemical substance is the only temperature (*T*) and pressure (*P*) under which all three phases (solid, liquid, and gas) of that substance exist in equilibrium (see Figure 1). The T-point of, say, water is the *T* and *P*, at which liquid water, solid water (the ice), and water vapor are in equilibrium. The T-point of water occurs at *T* = 0°C (= 32°F = 273 K) and *P* = 0.006 Atm (= 0.6 kPa, a small *P*), as shown in Figure 2. At the conditions of the T-point, the system consists of water, ice, and vapor. Any variation in *T* and *P* causes these phases to deviate from equilibrium. The T-point of carbon dioxide gas (CO_2) occurs at a much lower *T* of –57°C and a much higher *P* of 5 Atm = 500 kPa than water (see Figure 3). [In Figures 2 and 3, the axes are *not* drawn to scale.]

[Note: The T-point of water is used to define the kelvin (K) degree, the SI unit for *T* (temperature).]

Critical Point Temperature: The critical point temperature (simply C-point) of a pure substance is the only *T* and *P*, at which the liquid phase and vapor phase of that substance approach each other, resulting in only one phase. The C-point in a substance occurs at the end of a liquid-vapor coexistence situation. The substance's liquid phase and vapor phase properties become so alike that they can *no* longer be distinguished as separate phases, resulting in only one phase with *no* phase boundary. Therefore, at a C-point, the following occur:

- No phase boundary exists between liquid and vapor phases.
- Liquid and vapor phases are at equilibrium (stable) conditions.
- The liquid phase and gaseous phase become undistinguishable (nonseparable).

The C-point in water occurs at a high critical temperature (T_C) of 374°C (= 705°F = 647 K) and high critical pressure (P_C) of 218 Atm [= 22 MPa = 3200 PSIA (Lb/In^2 absolute)], as shown in Figure 2. Considering these statements, we can say that the C-point represents the T_C and P_C. The T_C and P_C are the highest *T* and *P*, at which water can boil when heated or water vapor can condense when cooled. In CO_2, C-point occurs at about 31°C (= 87.8°F) and 73 Atm (= 1073 PSI), as shown in Figure 3.

The critical point is determined by heating a liquid-vapor mixture and visually observing when the boundary between the liquid and gas disappears. [A phase created above T_C and P_C is a supercritical fluid.]

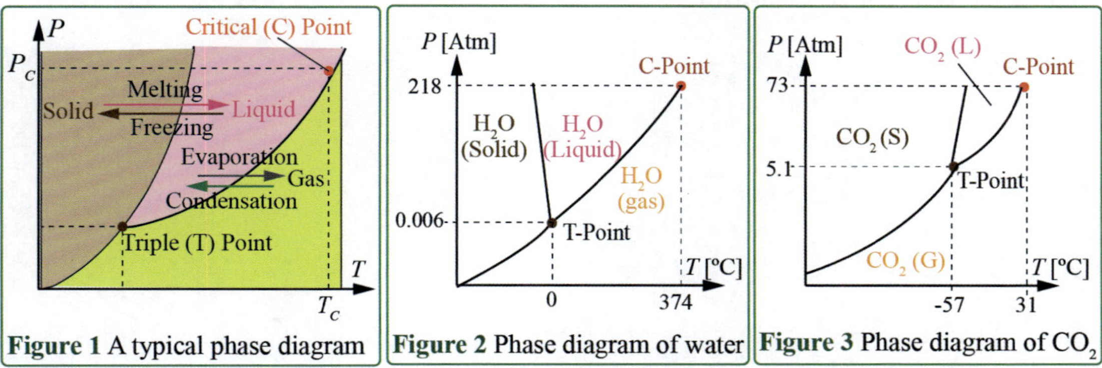

Figure 1 A typical phase diagram | **Figure 2** Phase diagram of water | **Figure 3** Phase diagram of CO_2

T-61

TUBES

A tube is a cylindrical or rectangular hollow shape device (equipment), mainly used to transport fluids (liquids and gases) or protect electrical wires or optical cables. [The term hose is usually used when the tube or pipe is flexible.]

The main differences between a tube and a pipe are outlined below.

- Tubes are usually specified by their inside diameter (ID, also called **nominal size**), while pipes are specified by their outside diameter (OD, also called **schedule size**).
- A tube may be formed or bent into the desired shape: while a pipe is shaped by pipe fittings, like tees and elbows. Some specifications call for using fittings to shape the tubes.

T-62

TURBIDITY

Turbidity is cloudiness (haziness) in a fluid (liquid or gas) caused by too many suspended solid particles invisible to the naked eye. Cloudy water, cloudy liquid sugar, and smoky air are examples of turbidity. Remember the following:

- Turbidity is one of the quality measures of water,
- Turbidity is measured in NTU (nephelometric turbidity units), and
- Water containing 1 mg of powdered silica per liter has a turbidity of 1 NTU.

T-63

TURBINES

Study STEAM TURBINES.

T-64

TURBULENT FLOW

Discussed under REYNOLDS NUMBER.

U Section

LIST OF TOPICS

1. Ultrafiltration Process
2. Ultrasonic Flowmeter
3. Ultraviolet Ray
4. Unit Operation of Chemical Engineering
5. Units of Measurement
6. Unsaturated, Saturated, and Supersaturated Solutions
7. Unstable Systems
8. Unsteady Flow
9. Uranium and its Isotopes
10. Uranium 235
11. Uranium 238
12. Uranium Enrichment Process
13. Uranium Yellowcake
14. US Unit System

U-1

ULTRAFILTRATION PROCESS

Discussed under MEMBRANE SEPARATION PROCESS.

U-2

ULTRASONIC FLOWMETER

Discussed under the topic of PROCESS CONTROL OF CHEMICAL ENGINEERING.

U-3

ULTRAVIOLET WAVE

Ultraviolet wave (UV wave, ultraviolet ray, or ultraviolet radiation) is an invisible wave to the human eye and one of the seven (7) types of electromagnetic waves (EM waves or EM radiations) with a wavelength (λ) shorter than that of visible light. The λ of the UV waves is between 10 to 400 nm, and their f (frequency) is 30 PHz to 750 THz, where P is for Pita (= 10^{15}), T is for Tera (= 10^{12}), and Hz is for Hertz (the SI unit of f).

[Note: The **EM waves** include radio wave, micro wave, infrared wave, visible light, ultraviolet wave, X-ray, and gamma ray, given in the longest to the shortest wavelengths. The *longer* the λ of a wave, the *smaller* is its f.]

U-4

UNIT OPERATIONS OF CHEMICAL ENGINEERING

Study PROCESS UNITS OF CHEMICAL ENGINEERING.

U-5

UNITS OF MEASUREMENT

Study SYSTEMS OF UNITS.

U-6

UNSATURATED SOLUTIONS

Study SATURATED, UNSATURATED, AND SUPERSATURATED SOLUTIONS.

U-7

UNSTABLE SYSTEMS

Study STABLE AND UNSTABLE SYSTEMS.

U-8

UNSTEADY FLOW

Study STEADY AND UNSTEADY FLOWS.

U-9

URANIUM AND ITS ISOTOPES

Uranium: Uranium (U, also called **uranium-238**, **U-238**, **natural uranium**, or **raw uranium**) is element 92 of the periodic table of elements. Its isotopes are uranium-235 (U-235) and uranium-234 (U-234).

U-238 is a silvery-gray radioactive element (radionuclide) when comes from a mine. Some properties of U-238 are outlined next.

- Its standard atomic mass (M_A) is 238.028 913.
- Its atomic mass number (N_A, the total number of protons and neutrons) is 238.
- Its atomic number (N_Z, the total number of protons) is 92, with 146 neutrons (n^0).

The three important nuclear properties of uranium are the following:

- Its nucleus is **unstable** and easily goes under nuclear decay (a radioactive element).
- Its nucleus contains 92 protons, the first natural element with the most protons. Neptunium (Np, with 93 protons) and a few more synthetically-produced elements have more protons than uranium.
- Its nucleus contains 146 neutrons, the seventh element with the greatest number of neutrons, after neptunium, plutonium, americium, curium, berkelium, and californium.

Listed next are three more properties of U-238.

- It is one of the heaviest elements.
- Its boiling point temperature (T_{MP}) is 4131°C (= 7468 °F).
- Its melting point temperature (T_{MP}) is 1132°C (= 2070 °F).

Furthermore, we can outline the following two other properties of U-238:

- It contains over 99% natural uranium (simply uranium) when it comes from a mine,
- It has a huge half lifetime (4.46 billion years), close to the age of the Earth (approximately 4.54 billion years). Because of its long halflife, U-238 has low radioactivity (it emits radiation at a low rate), so its total amount on the Earth stayed the same. [The uranium's slow nuclear decay creates the main heat energy (E_Q) resource inside the Earth.]

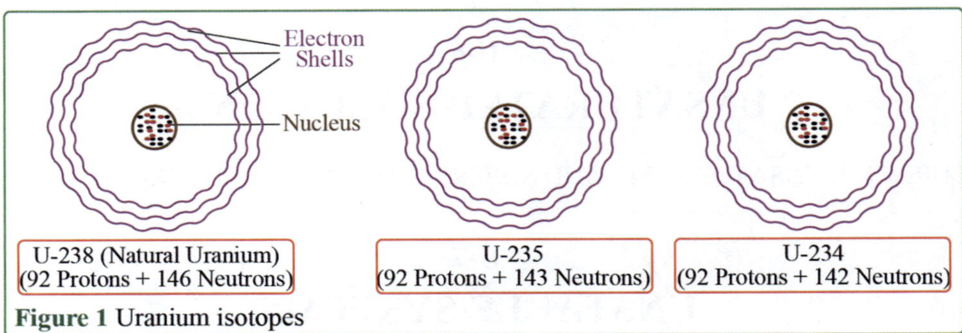

Figure 1 Uranium isotopes

Before **natural** (raw) **uranium** comes from a mine and becomes ready for use as nuclear fuel, it must go under the following processing steps:

- It is processed in crushers to produce **crushed uranium**,
- Crushed uranium is then mixed with a solvent (mostly concentrated acid) in an extractor to extract a uranium mixture containing different forms of uranium oxides, like UO_2 (uranium dioxide) and UO_3 (uranium trioxide), $UO_2(OH)_2$ (uranyl hydroxide), UO_2SO_4 (uranyl sulfate), and more.
- The uranium mixture is further filtered and dried to produce a coarse powder, known as the uranium yellowcake (simply **yellowcake**), which has a dark-brown color (unlike its name).

Uranium Isotopes: Natural uranium has the following three isotopes:

- **Uranium 238** (U-238): Its content in natural uranium is approximately 99.3%. It has 92 protons, 146 neutrons, and an N_A of 238. It is *not* fissile, so it *cannot* be used as a nuclear fuel in nuclear fission. However, it can absorb a neutron in a breeder reactor and, after two beta decays, become isotope platinum-239 (Pt-239, with N_A of 239), which is **fissile** so that it can be used in both nuclear power and nuclear weapons. If, however, it is enriched to contain 3% uranium 235 (U-235), it can be used as a fuel in nuclear power plants. And if it is enriched further to contain 90% U-235, it can be used for nuclear weapons.
- **Uranium 235** (U-235): Its content in natural U is about 0.7% (about 1 part in 140 parts). It has 92 protons, 143 neutrons, and an N_A of 235. Its half lifetime is 700 million years. It is fissile (can be used as a fuel to produce nuclear energy and nuclear weapons). Its radioactivity is more than U-238 but less than U-234.
- **Uranium 234** (U-234): Its content in natural uranium is in trace amounts. It has 92 protons, 142 neutrons, and thus, an N_A of 234. Its half-life time is 246 000 years. Its radioactivity is more than the other two isotopes. Its density is only 1.26% less than U-238. This makes uranium enrichment a difficult process.

[All three uranium isotopes are radioactive elements (radioactive isotopes or radionuclides) with an **unstable** nucleus. U-235 has the most unstable nucleus of all three, so it is the most important of three; therefore, it is used in nuclear fission and nuclear weapons.]

U-10
URANIUM 235

Discussed under URANIUM AND ITS ISOTOPES.

U-11
URANIUM 238

Discussed under URANIUM AND ITS ISOTOPES.

U-12

URANIUM ENRICHMENT PROCESS

Uranium enrichment is the process of increasing the content of uranium-235 (U-235) of the uranium yellow-cake (simply **yellowcake**), which consists of uranium-238 (at about 99.3%), uranium-235 (at about 0.7%), and uranium-234 (in trace amount). The enriched uranium is used in nuclear medicine, nuclear power plants, nuclear weapons, and other technologies. The enrichment process is important because each listed technology requires uranium with a certain purity. In more detail, the enrichment process is performed for the next reasons:

- The content of U-235 in the yellowcake is low (usually 0.7%). Thus, the yellowcake must be undergone the enrichment process to increase the purity of U-235. Most power-plant reactors are **light water reactors** (LWR) and require uranium to be enriched from 0.7% to 3 to 5% U-235 in their fuel. [Uranium used for nuclear weapons needs to be enriched in advanced enrichment plants to produce above 90% U-235.]
- The nucleus of U-235 is more unstable than that of U-238, so U-235 (a fissile) can be fissioned (see NUCLEAR FISSION) by absorption of a high-energy neutron. U-238, on the contrary, *cannot* be easily fissioned (because it needs neutron with much more energy).

Before the enrichment process, the yellowcake must be pretreated with hydrogen in a kiln to convert its main component, the U_3O_8, into uranium dioxide (UO_2).

$$U_3O_8 + 2H_2 \rightarrow 3\ UO_2 + 2H_2O$$

UO_2 is then treated with ClF_3 (chlorine trifluoride) to form UF_6 (uranium hexafluoride).

$$UO_2 + 2\ ClF_3 \rightarrow UF_6 + Cl_2 + O_2$$

UF_6 is solid at room temperatures. Because of its corrosiveness and extreme poisonousness, UF_6 is transported in internationally standardized containers.

Uranium enrichment is a difficult process because the isotopes U-235 and U-238 are chemically identical and have similar molecular mass (U-235 is only 1.26% lighter than U-238) and density. In addition, detailed information is unavailable in reference publications about this process (because of the nuclear secrecy of its technology). Based on the availability of information, the enrichment process is performed by the gas centrifugal process or diffusion process.

Enrichment by Gas Centrifugation: As the most common method for enriching uranium (U-235), the gas centrifugal process is a complicated centrifugal process. In this process, the container holding UF_6 is heated in an **autoclave** (a heated pressurized vessel) to become a gas (the boiling point temperature of liquid UF_6 is 56.5ºC). The gaseous UF_6 is adjusted for pressure before sending it to the centrifugal station. [Hazard Note: Gaseous UF_6 is colorless, soluble, corrosive, and extremely hazardous! When it reacts with moisture in the air, it forms hydrogen fluoride (HF, also called **hydrofluoric acid**), which is extremely dangerous if inhaled. Inhalation of UF_6 is the main hazard in the enrichment plants.]

In the centrifugal station, the gaseous UF_6 is processed in several gas centrifuges (known as a **cascade**), each operating at high speeds (about 90 000 R/min) and in connection with other centrifuges to separate U-235 (the wanted component) from its isotope U-238 (the less-wanted component). Figure 1 shows a typical enrichment process and front view of a gas centrifuge. The high speed of the centrifuge's rotor (the basket) creates a strong centrifugal force (F_C), which pushes the heavier U-238 closer to the wall of the rotor while the slightly lighter gas molecules (the U-235) move toward the center of the rotor. As a result, the gas closer to the rotor's wall becomes depleted (reduced) in U-235, whereas the gas near the center of rotation becomes slightly enriched in U-235. Then the slightly-enriched stream goes into the next stage of the cascade, while the slightly-depleted stream goes into the previous stage of the cascade. This process is repeated many times in the cascade until the desired level of enrichment is achieved. The enriched stream from the cascade is cooled to solidify the gaseous UF_6. Samples are taken from the cascade at certain intervals to test the content of U-235.

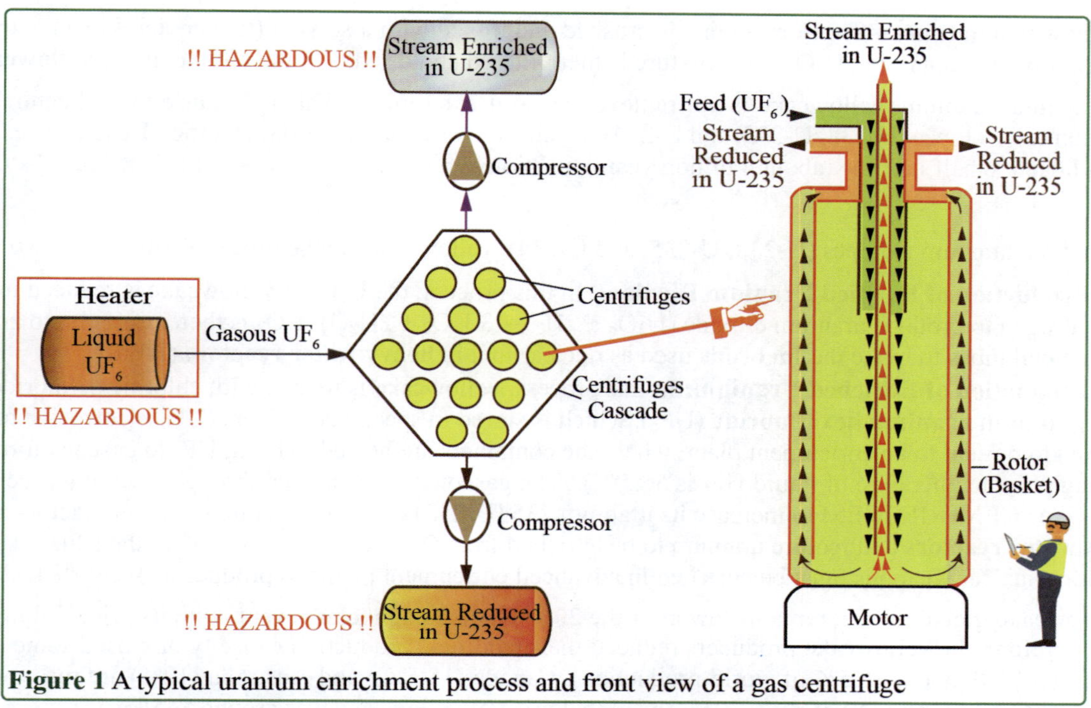

Figure 1 A typical uranium enrichment process and front view of a gas centrifuge

Enrichment by Gas Diffusion: The gas diffusion process is complicated. Gas centrifugation on UF_6 is *no* longer a common method for enriching uranium. The only enrichment facility in the United States that uses this process is Paducah in Kentucky. UF_6 is passed through many diffusional stages in the gas-diffusion process, separating uranium isotopes.

Based on the content of U-235, the enrichment process can be divided into three (3) steps:

- **Slightly-Enriched Uranium** (SEU): In this stage, the yellowcake is enriched to 1 to nearly 3% U-235. The SEU (U-235 with 1 to 3% purity) can be used in nuclear medicine.
- **Low-Enriched Uranium** (LEU): The SEU is enriched to produce U-235 with 3 to nearly 20% purity, depending on the usage of the product. The LEU with 3 to 5% U-235 is used as nuclear fuel.
- **High-Enriched Uranium** (HEU): The LEU is enriched to about 90% U-235 to be used in nuclear weapons.

[In addition to the listed uranium products, the enrichment process produces depleted uranium with about 0.3% U-235. The demand for the depleted uranium is much less than its production, so the countries with enrichment technology must store the rest of the depleted uranium in special disposal sites.]

U-13

URANIUM YELLOWCAKE

The uranium yellowcake (simply **yellowcake** or **urania**) is the product of a multiple-step process on the raw uranium (U) when it comes from a mine and before it goes under the uranium enrichment process. Urania is a yellowish-brown, coarse powder. It melts at approximately 2 880ºC. And it is *not* soluble in water. It mainly consists of U_3O_8 (a stable oxide). And to a less content, uranium dioxide (UO_2), uranium trioxide (UO_3), uranyl hydroxide [$UO_2(OH)_2$], uranyl sulfate (UO_2SO_4), and more. Of the total uranium content in yellowcake, 0.7% is uranium 235 (U-235). The yellowcake is then enriched to increase its content of U-235.

The **raw** (natural) **uranium** from a mine is crushed and mixed with a solvent (like an acid) in an extractor to extract a mixture containing U_3O_8. The mixture is then filtered and dried, and the product is the **yellowcake**.

Like natural uranium, yellowcake is *not* radioactive, so it is harmless. This is because the concentrations of three uranium isotopes (U-238, U-235, and U-234) in yellowcake are at their original ratio. Despite its extremely long radioactive half lifetime (about 4 billion years), its biological half lifetime is short (15 days).

With three uranium isotopes (U-238, U-235, and U-234), yellowcake can be processed further in two ways:

- **For Production of Purified Uranium Dioxide:** In this process, the U_3O_8 in yellowcake is reduced in a kiln by hydrogen to produce uranium dioxide ($U_3O_8 + 2H_2 \rightarrow 3\ UO_2 + 2H_2O$). UO_2 is then inserted into zirconium metal tubes to make the **fuel rods** used as nuclear fuel in **heavy water reactors** (HWR).
- **For Production of Enriched Uranium:** In this process, yellowcake is treated with chlorine trifluoride (ClF_3) to form **uranium hexafluoride** (UF_6), which is stored in special containers (UF_6 is corrosive to most metals) to be sent to an enrichment plant, where the containers are heated to bring UF_6 to gaseous form (the boiling point temperature of liquid UF_6 is 56.5°C). The gaseous UF_6 is passed through a set of gas centrifuges (see CENTRIFUGES) to increase its uranium 235 (U-235) content. Most power-plant reactors are **light water reactors** and require uranium to be enriched from 0.7% to 3 to 5% U-235 in their fuel. Uranium used for nuclear weapons must be enriched in advanced enrichment plants to produce above 90% U-235.

[Yellowcake global market remains low after the 2011 Fukushima nuclear event, with its price falling around 50%. Therefore, the yellowcake producers reduced their facilities' production capacity or closed some of them. Kazakhstan (with about 36.5% of world production), Canada (15.5%), and Australia (12%) are the world's top producers of yellowcake. As of early 2017, the global price of yellowcake was around $45/kg.]

U-14
US UNIT SYSTEM

Study SI AND US UNIT SYSTEMS.

V Section

LIST OF TOPICS

1. Vacuum
2. Vacuum Energy
3. Vacuum Filters
4. Vacuum Pressure
5. Vacuum Pressure Gauge
6. Vacuum Pumps
7. Vacuum State
8. Vacuum Test
9. Valence Electrons
10. Valence Number
11. Valves
12. Van der Waals Bond and Equation
13. Vapor and Steam
14. Vapor Bleeding Process
15. Vapor Cavitation
16. Vapor Compression
17. Vapor Density
18. Vapor Liquid Equilibrium
19. Vapor Liquid Equilibrium Diagrams
20. Vapor Liquid Equilibrium Mixtures
21. Vapor Pressure
22. Vapor Recompression Process
23. Vapor Shifting Process
24. Vapor Space
25. Vector and Scalar Quantities
26. Velocity
27. Velocity Gradient
28. Venturi Effect
29. Venturi Flowmeter
30. Venturi Scrubbers
31. Vessels
32. Viscoelasticity
33. Viscosity
34. Viscosity Equation
35. Viscosity Law
36. VLE Diagram
37. VLE Mixture
38. Void Fraction
39. Volatile Organic Compound
40. Volatility and Relative Volatility
41. Volt
42. Voltage
43. Volume
44. Volume Concentration
45. Volume Fraction
46. Volumetric Flow Rate
47. Volumetric Flux
48. Volumetric Mass Density
49. Vortex

V-1

VACUUM

The term **vacuum** (see upcoming Notes) is used in the following three (3) ways:

- When referring to a space with *no* mass (*M*), it designates that light travels in a vacuum with *no* interruption, refraction, and delay at 300 000 km/s.
- When referring to a system with *M* and a *P* (pressure) lower than P_{Atm} (atmospheric pressure) or equal to zero, it designates a system that its *P* is at vacuum pressure (P_{Vac}) or zero *P*. Such a vacuum can be created by pumping the air out of a vessel.

[Note 1: In this book, the word **vacuum** is used only when talking about the speed of light in a vacuum, and the word **vacuum pressure** is used when talking about a fluid (liquid or gas) whose *P* is below P_{Atm} or equal to zero. We (chemical engineers) say, for example, this evaporator operates under negative vacuum pressure of 0.8 Atm.]

[Note 2: The words **absolute vacuum**, **absolute vacuum pressure**, **perfect vacuum**, or **complete vacuum** refer to – 1 Atm (= – 14.7 PSIG). To remove confusion, these words are *not* used in this book.]

[Note 3: Absolute pressure (P_{Abs}) is always specified in vacuum-related subjects. Therefore, the "Abs" subscript can be omitted in these situations.]

V-2

VACUUM ENERGY

Discussed under the topic of ENERGY AND ITS FORMS.

V-3

VACUUM FILTERS

Discussed under FILTERS.

V-4

VACUUM PRESSURE

Discussed under ABSOLUTE, ATMOSPHERIC, GAUGE, AND VACUUM PRESSURES.

V-5

VACUUM PRESSURE GAUGE

A vacuum pressure gauge (simply **vacuum gauge**) is an instrument for measuring the pressure (*P*) of a system that is *below* vacuum pressure (P_{Vac}), the *P* below 1 Atm (= 101 kPa = 14.7 PSI). Some evaporators or condensers operate at *negative* P_{Vac}, so vacuum readings of a vacuum pressure gauge reading for the same source of *P* are less than atmospheric pressure (P_{Atm} = 1 Atm = 101 kPa = 14.7 PSI) and gauge pressure (P_G).

V-6

VACUUM PUMPS

A vacuum pump is a pump installed in a piping system (pipes, pumps, and valves) to move a gas (such as steam, vapor, or air) from a vessel (container), which operates under negative vacuum pressure (P_{Vac}). In other definition, a vacuum pump is a compressor that takes suction at a negative P_{Vac} and discharges it against atmospheric pressure (P_{Atm}). Thus, a vacuum pump works as a detached part for a device, such as a condenser, crystallizer, or evaporator, which operates under P_{Vac}.

Vacuum pumps use electric energy or steam as a source of energy to perform shaft work on a gas to

- Increase the mechanical energy (E_{Me}), pressure (P), and velocity (V) of the gas,
- Overcome the frictions (resistances to motion) that oppose the flow, and
- Compress the volume (V) of the gas under the process.

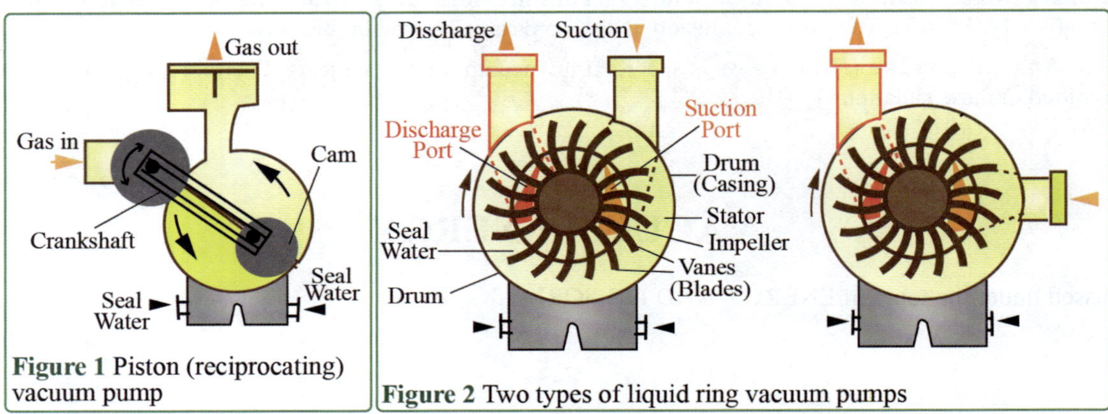

Figure 1 Piston (reciprocating) vacuum pump

Figure 2 Two types of liquid ring vacuum pumps

The following are two (2) typical types of vacuum pumps:

- **Piston** (Reciprocating) **Vacuum Pumps:** These pumps are energy efficient. A typical piston vacuum pump (see Figure 1) can create a vacuum pressure (P_{Vac}) up to 0.1 kPa. Or move 1 kg air at 10 kPa vacuum pressure using 24 kW/h, while a liquid-ring vacuum pump uses about 1/10th of this energy.
- **Liquid-Ring Vacuum Pumps:** These pumps are compact, easy to install and maintain, and energy-efficient. A typical liquid-ring pump (Figure 2) mainly consists of a cylindrical drum (casing), a shaft, and an impeller (wheel or propeller). The impeller has several radial vanes (blades), which rotate in the drum. The diameter of the vanes is less than the drum diameter, and the center of the shaft is located eccentrically in the drum. The liquid ring is formed by centrifugal force created by the rotating vanes. The liquid ring is arranged so that the space between vanes and liquid ring increases when it passes the inlet to suck the gas into the suction port. And then reduces, compressing the gas and discharging it at the outlet. Liquid-ring vacuum pumps are compact, reliable, and easy to operate. They operate well when quality seal water is used. Single-stage ring pumps are usually used for smaller devices (like condensers and vacuum filters), while double-stage pumps are usually used for larger devices (such as evaporators and crystallizers). [In some special cases, a jet ejector is used instead of the liquid-ring vacuum pump to move a gas or liquid as the motive fluid. For advantages and disadvantages of a jet ejector over a vacuum pump, refer to the topic of JET EJECTORS.]

A correction factor (K_C) is usually applied to the quoted capacity for the correct sizing of a liquid ring vacuum pump. The capacity of such a pump is determined by the following:

- Amount of incondensable gases that must be removed from a device that is under a vacuum.

- Temperature (T) of the **seal water**. Engineers use 15°C as the base T to calculate the correction factor (K_C) to be used in the pump-capacity equation. At this T, the water-vapor's partial pressure is 1.7 kPa and $K_C = 1$. K_C at different vapor pressures of seal water is calculated as

$$K_C = \frac{P - P_V}{P - 1.7} \quad (1)$$

In this equation, P is the pump's suction pressure, and P_V is vapor pressure at the seal-water temperature. [K_C, given by the pump manufacturer, usually varies slightly from the one obtained from Equation 1.]

V-7

VACCUM STATE

Study QUANTUM VACUUM.

V-8

VACCUM TEST

The vacuum test is used in chemical plants for indication of a leak (losing pressure, P) in a process vessel (such as a tank, a condenser, or a crystallizer). Consider a vessel containing a liquid that operates under a slight vacuum (vacuum pressure or a zero or negative pressure) of 80 kPa (0.8 Atm). The vessel is tested for leak by closing the vacuum and measuring P over a given time (30 or 60 minutes). In that period, the increase in P should *not* be more than a certain value, typically 10 kPa (0.1 Atm) for a medium-size vessel in 30 minutes. If a big leak exists in the vessel, the atmospheric pressure (P_{Atm} = 1 Atm = 101 kPa) increases the P of the vessel considerably, so the increase in P is more than usual (more than 0.1 Atm or 10 kPa).

V-9

VALENCE ELECTRONS

Discussed under the topic of FREE ELECTRONS AND VALENCE ELECTRONS.

V-10

VALENCE NUMBER

Study CHARGE AND CHARGE NUMBER.

V-11

VALVES

A valve is a device (equipment) that is installed in a piping system (pipes, pumps, valves, and more) to keep the flow of a fluid (liquid or gas) fully open, partially open, or fully closed.

In relation to pressure (P), all valves can control the P of a flow and keep it running in a certain direction and at a certain rate. A fluid flows from higher P to lower P in an open valve. A closed valve remains closed until a P is applied to open it.

Under the topic of LIQUID FLOW, we said that the existence of a valve in a pipe that carries a liquid creates some frictions (obstructions) in that pipe, and the energy (E) spent to overcome those frictions is generally known as friction energy loss (rather friction energy use). There, we also said that valves (or any other fittings) create pressure drop (generally known as the pressure difference, ΔP), which is usually specified with the volumetric flow rate of a flowing liquid ($\dot{V}$), the liquid specific density (D_{Sp}), and a coefficient known as **fitting friction factor** (f_{Fit}; also called **fitting friction coefficient**). The value of f_{Fit} is specific to a particular fitting, meaning that the factor, for example, used for a valve is different from that used for an elbow.

$$f_{Fit} = \dot{V}\sqrt{\frac{D_{Sp}}{\Delta P}} \quad (1)$$

A typical chemical process plant uses many (in thousands) valves of different sizes installed in different pipes. A flow can be controlled **manually** or **automatically**. In today's chemical plants, most valves are controlled automatically. In such a controlled valve, a flow is kept at the desired rate by using a **control loop** (see PROCESS CONTROL for definition) to adjust a valve's opening to a specific setpoint. And the valve prevents fluid from flowing if the process control system fails to operate. Many automatically-controlled valves operate with signals between 100 and 240 kPa (= 15 to 35 PSI).

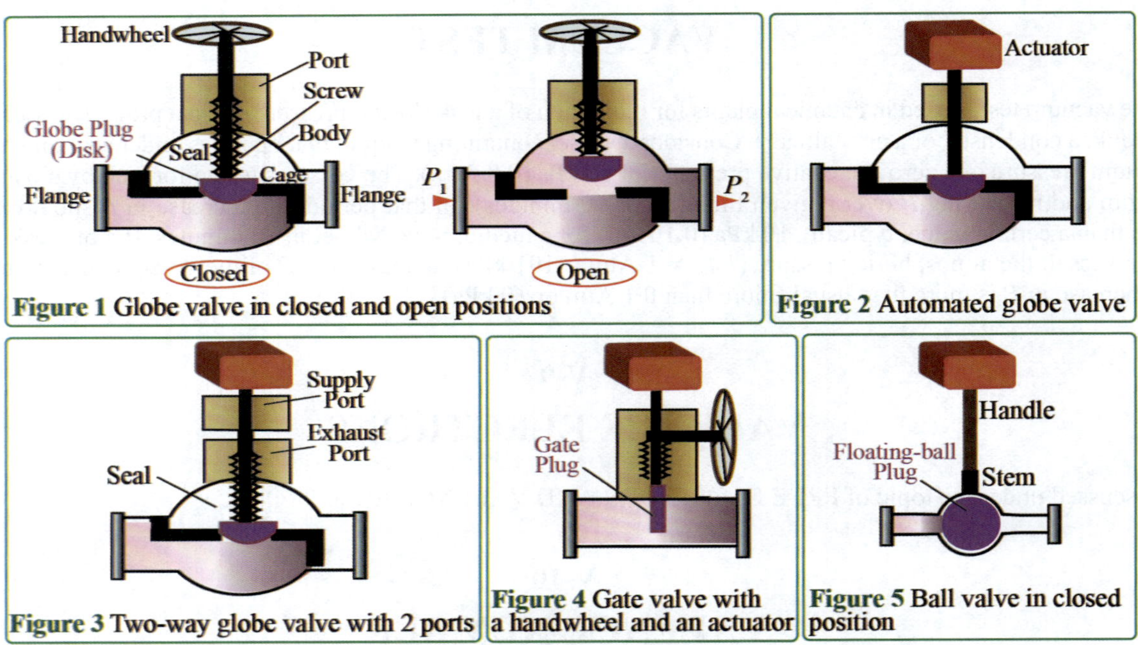

Figure 1 Globe valve in closed and open positions

Figure 2 Automated globe valve

Figure 3 Two-way globe valve with 2 ports

Figure 4 Gate valve with a handwheel and an actuator

Figure 5 Ball valve in closed position

VALVE TYPES

Valves come in many different types and sizes. Some special valves used in chemical plants have a diameter of up to 5 m. Next, a few typical types of valves are briefly described.

- **Globe Valves:** A globe valve opens by moving a **plug** (disk) up and closes by moving the plug down. A typical glove valve consists of an opening that forms a space (called a **seal**) in which a movable plug can open or close a fluid's flow. The plug is connected to a **stem** (handle), which screws up and down with a handwheel in hand-operated globe valves (as shown in Figure 1), or slides up and down with an **actuator** in electronically-operated valves (as shown in Figure 2). Globe valves are usually two-port valves (see Figure 3), although three-port designs are also used. The two-port valves with angled ports (usually 90º) are called **angle globe valves**. A 3-way globe valve can be used in a small-diameter pipe (up to 10-cm = 4-In) to split a flow between two lines. Usually, two open-close valves (one on each line) are used for pipes larger than the listed sizes. [Globe valves are named for the spherical body shape of old globe valves. The newer globe valves do *not* have much of a spherical shape.]

- **Gate Valves:** A gate valve opens by lifting a gate-type plug up and closes by moving it down (Figure 4). A typical gate valve needs a small space for installation in a pipeline. Gate valves are used to shut off liquids rather than for flow regulation. They are used in small-diameter pipes (since friction can cause a problem).
- **Ball Valve:** A ball valve (Figure 5) uses a hollow-perforated ball as a plug to control a flow. A ball valve is open when its handle is flat in line with a flow and closed when it is turned 90 degrees from the open position. [A ball valve is different from a globe valve.]
- **Solenoid Valves:** A solenoid valve operates electronically. Multiple solenoid valves can act together on a **manifold** (a regulator that can act as a switch to turn a flow on and off). Solenoid valves have many applications, including in the feed pipe of a centrifuge.

[Some special devices also function as valves for particular purposes. For example, a steam trap installed in a pipe is used as a valve to remove the condensate from the system. The trap automatically opens when condensate needs to be removed and closes when all the condensate is removed.]

V-12
VAN DER WAALS BOND AND EQUATION

These subjects are discussed under the topic of CHEMICAL BONDS and GAS LAWS.

V-13
VAPOR AND STEAM

Vapor

Vapor (in British-English **vapour**) is a substance in its gas phase, which is at a temperature (T) lower than its critical temperature (T_C). A vapor, like water vapor (generally **vapor**), can be condensed to a liquid by reducing its temperature (T) or by increasing its pressure (P). At ordinary temperatures, water vapor condenses to liquid water if its partial pressure (P_P) is increased to above P_{Atm} of 1 Atm. [Water vapor, which is the gas phase of water, is generally called **vapor** if *not* mentioned differently.]

Steam

Steam is the high-pressure vapor phase of water produced in a steam boiler (simply **boiler**). It is the most cost-effective source of heat energy (E_Q, traditionally heat) used industrially. The **heat value** (heat-energy value or enthalpy value) of steam is expressed by either its P or T, dependent on each other. When P in a boiler increases, the next dependent quantities increase:

- Boiling point temperature (T_{BP}) of the boiler's water,
- Temperature (T) of the steam produced in that boiler, and
- Heat energy (scientifically enthalpy, H) of the produced steam.

If thus, P or T of the produced steam is known, its H can be found from a steam table (Table 1, given in the Table Section of this book). Then H can calculate the amount of steam needed for a particular process, such as evaporating a liquid feed in an evaporator.

To practice the **steam efficiency** (steam economy, E_S) and familiarity with the mass balancing of steam, let us consider an evaporation station with only one evaporator. To mass-balance this evaporator, we must consider the feed's mass flow rate ($\dot{M}_F$) and the product's mass flow rate ($\dot{M}_P$) in relation to the feed's concentration ($C_{DS.F}$) and product's concentration ($C_{DS.F}$).

$$\dot{M}_F.C_{DS.F} = \dot{M}_P.C_{DS.P} \quad \text{or} \quad \dot{M}_P = \dot{M}_F \frac{C_{DS.F}}{C_{DS.P}} \tag{1}$$

Here the subscript *DS* is for dissolved solids, usually given in mass percentages, while mass flow rates are industrially given in t/h. Study the next Example for better clarity.

Example 1

Given: A single-effect evaporation station for concentrating a solution. The next data are available.

Feed's mass flow rate to the evaporator ($\dot{M}_F$)	21 t/h (5.8 kg/s)
Steam's mass flow rate, $\dot{M}_S$	15 t/h
Feed's dissolved solids concentration ($C_{DS.F}$)	15%
Product's dissolved solids concentration ($C_{DS.P}$)	45%

Wanted: 1) Product's mass ($\dot{M}_P$), 2) Evaporated-water mass ($\dot{M}_W$), and 3) Steam economy (E_S)

$$\dot{M}_P = \dot{M}_F \times \frac{C_{DS.F}}{C_{DS.P}} = 21 \times \frac{15}{45} = 7 \text{ t/h} \qquad \dot{M}_W = \dot{M}_F - \dot{M}_P = 21 - 7 = 14 \text{ t/h} (= 3.9 \text{ kg/s})$$

$$E_S = \frac{M_W}{M_S} = \frac{14}{15} = 0.9 \text{ t water/t steam}$$

In relation to the properties of steam, the following four (4) terms are used:

- Saturated steam,
- Exhaust (tail) steam,
- Saturated dry steam, and
- Supersaturated (super or live) steam.

The order above indicates the steam with the lowest **enthalpy** (*H*, heat value or **heat energy**, E_Q) to the highest and from the highest water content to the lowest. [Note that the first two listed steams' properties are close to each other and the last two properties.]

Saturated Steam: Saturated steam (commonly referred to as **saturated water steam**) is steam, which its *T* is above water's T_{BP} (boiling point temperature) at a certain *P*. If saturated steam is heated more in a boiler, steam's *T* and *P* increase and, therefore, **saturated dry steam** will be produced. More E_Q (heat energy) will produce supersaturated steam (simply **super steam** or **live steam**).

At the molecular level, steam is **saturated** when its molecules are maximally evaporated from its liquid form. Then the molecules exert a vapor pressure (P_V) on the surroundings.

The saturated steam has the following three (3) main advantages over the supers steam:

- It can coexist with liquid water at equilibrium (because it has some liquid water).
- It can be used in heating and evaporation processes (because of higher heat transfer).
- It can be used in sterilization process (because water can create a sufficient efficiency).

The supers steam, however, has the following advantages over-saturated:

- Acts as pure steam (because it has almost no traces of water),
- Has higher *T* and *P*, so it is the only steam that can be used in steam turbines,
- Needs less water in a boiler to be evaporated to produce the same volume of steam,
- Contains *no* water, so the boiler has *not* to be periodically drained (purged) for water, and
- Does *not* condense at high pressure (*P*), so does *not* damage the pipes and steam-user equipment.

Exhaust Steam: Exhaust steam is steam released from the exhaust (tail) of a steam turbine. Consider a typical chemical plant with a medium-size boiler with 15 Bar (= 220 PSI or 1500 kPa) pressure and a turbine. The boiler can produce a **supers steam** with a typical *T* of 200ºC (= 390ºF), which can be used in the turbine to discharge exhaust steam of about 140ºC, which is well below the *T* of a typical supers steam and well above typical **saturated steam**. [Exhaust steam and saturated steam *cannot* be used in a boiler but can be effectively used in the heat-user stations of a chemical plant, such as heating and evaporating stations.]

Saturated Dry Steam: Saturated dry steam (commonly refers to **saturated dry steam of water**; simply **dry steam**) is steam, which has been slightly supersaturated, so it has *no* water, and its *T* is slightly above the water's T_{BP}. The increase in *T* is insufficient to change the steam's E_Q greatly. However, it is a sufficient rise in *T* to avoid condensation, preventing damage to the steam supply systems and steam-user equipment in a chemical plant. Dry steam is produced in chemical plants by heating saturated steam in a boiler. Continued heat-energy input will then produce super steam. Saturated dry steam has slightly higher *T* and *P* than saturated steam but less than super steam.

Supersaturated Steam: Supersaturated steam (supersaturated water steam; also called **superheated steam** or simply **super steam** or **live steam**) is a steam with a high *P* and *T*. A supersaturated (live) steam produced in a high-pressure steam boiler, thus, has the next two properties.

- Its temperature is well above water's boiling point temperature (T_{BP}).
- It acts as pure steam (because its water's traces have been evaporated).

If saturated steam is heated in a boiler, steam's *T* and *P* will increase, so saturated dry steam will be produced. Applying more heat energy (E_Q) will then produce super steam.

The *P* of super steam is different in different chemical process plants, depending on the capacity of the steam boiler. Some modern chemical plants use high-pressure boilers with a typical *P* of 3500 kPa (= 35 bar = 510 Lb/In^2) to produce live steam with a typical *T* of 255ºC (= 490ºF). The live steam is then used to run the steam turbine to produce electricity. The exhaust steam discharged from the turbine, which has a lower *P* than live steam, is used in the heat-user stations, such as evaporation or distillation stations. In chemical plants with *no* turbine, the *P* of the live steam is typically reduced to around 230 kPa (33 Lb/In^2) by the steam pressure reduction process, and then it is used in the heat-user stations.

Steam Tables: Steam tables provide quick access to thermodynamic data of saturated steam and water, particularly their enthalpy (*H*) and entropy (*S*) at various *T* and *P*. At a given *T*, for example, *H* of a **saturated steam** (H_S) can be obtained from a steam table (such as Table 1 at the Table Section at the end of this book). H_C (enthalpy of the condensate) can also be obtained from the same table as enthalpy of saturated liquid at that *T* (so-known as saturated temperature). Then the enthalpy of evaporation of the saturated steam is the difference between the steam's enthalpy (H_S) and the condensate's enthalpy (H_C).

[Note 1: The properties of steam and water can also be obtained from software that applies IAPWS (International Association for the Properties of Water and Steam) standards.]

[Note 2: In almost all cases, as well as in the steam tables, the term **enthalpy** (*H*) is simply used to refer to specific enthalpy, which is enthalpy per mass, given in kJ/kg or BTU/Lb. Specific enthalpies, given in steam tables, are taken at 0°C and 1 Atm (called standard temperature and pressure, STP) and are based on a close-to-reality assumption that at 0ºC, the *H* of water is zero.]

V-14
VAPOR BLEEDING PROCESS

In a vapor-bleeding process (also called **additional-vapor-use**), the vapor is taken from different effects of a multiple-effect evaporation station to be used outside that station, as discussed and shown in Figures 3 and 5 under EVAPORATION PROCESS. For example, **vapor bleed 1** (the vapor leaving the first effect) can be used in a heat exchanger. The vapor-bleeding process and shifting process can improve the steam economy (E_S) of the heat-user stations. [The saving in heat energy (E_Q) is even better if the vapor is taken **from later effects**.]

V-15
VAPOR CAVITATION

Study PUMP CAVITATION.

V-16
VAPOR COMPRESSION

Study STEAM RECOMPRESSION AND VAPOR COMPRESSION.

V-17
VAPOR DENSITY

Discussed under the topic of DENSITY.

V-18
VAPOR LIQUID EQUILIBRIUM

Vapor-liquid equilibrium (VLE) is a condition under which equilibrium (stability) occurs between a mixture's vapor and liquid phases. Such a mixture is called a vapor-liquid equilibrium mixture (VLE mixture). At either constant temperature (T) or pressure (P), the VLE occurs when the liquid and vapor contact each other for enough time until the transfer of molecules between them stops, and the system reaches phase equilibrium. At VLE, *no* exchange of the molecules between the phases occurs. Or, if the exchange occurs slowly, the rates on the evaporation and condensation sides are the same. Because the system *cannot* hold its stability (equilibrium) forever, it constantly switches from the liquid to the vapor phase and vice versa.

If the liquid phase of a VLE mixture behaves as an ideal solution, the mixture is an ideal vapor-liquid-equilibrium mixture (ideal VLE mixture). If such a mixture is under the distillation process at moderate P (around P_{Atm}), the VLE for component A of the mixture in the vapor phase can be expressed as

$$Y_A = X_A(P_V)_A \quad (1)$$

In this equation, which is one form of Raoult's Law equations, Y_A is the molar fraction (a unitless quantity) of component A in the vapor phase, X_A is that in the liquid phase, and $(P_V)_A$ is the vapor pressure of pure component A above its liquid phase.

If the liquid phase of a VLE mixture behaves non-ideally (mostly the case), the mixture is called a **non-ideal VLE mixture**. For such a mixture, an activity coefficient (γ, sigma) for component A is used, so Equation 1 becomes

$$Y_A = X_A (P_V)_A \cdot \gamma_A \quad (2)$$

Equation 1, in which γ equates to one (as it represents an ideal mixture), is the basic equation for an ideal VLE mixture. Equation 2 is for a non-ideal VLE mixture, often used in distillation calculations. [Under ACTIVITY COEFFICIENT, we explained why a component in the liquid phase of a VLE mixture behaves non-ideally.]

V-19

VAPOR LIQUID EQUILIBRIUM DIAGRAM

A vapor-liquid equilibrium diagram (VLE diagram or XY diagram) illustrates the conditions of one mole of a binary (two-component) mixture, which is in vapor-liquid equilibrium (VLE). In a VLE diagram, the molar fraction (X, a unitless quantity) of the **lower-boiling component** (LBC, or component A) is usually plotted on X-axis. The VLE diagrams (VLE phase diagrams) are of three (3) kinds:

- ***TXY*** **(*T*-versus-*XY*) Diagrams:** When the liquid mixture's T is plotted on the Y-axis at constant pressure (P), the VLE diagram is called the TXY diagram (see Figure 1). A TXY diagram shows X (molar fraction of LBC in the liquid phase) and Y (molar fraction of LBC in the vapor phase) as functions of T at a constant P. In the figure, the **red** line represents the **liquid bubble-point curve** (simply **bubble-point curve** or ***X*** **curve**). The **silver** line represents the **vapor dew-point curve** (simply **dew-point curve** or ***Y*** **curve**). [Mostly, the phase diagrams are made for constant P, shown in Figure 1. The TXY diagrams are often used in the distillation process.]
- ***PXY*** **(*P*-versus-*XY*) Diagrams:** When the liquid mixture's P is plotted on the Y-axis at constant temperature (T), the VLE diagram is called the PXY diagram (see Figure 2). A PXY diagram shows X and Y as P functions at constant T.
- ***XY*** **(*X*** **versus** ***Y*****) Diagrams:** When the liquid mixture's composition (concentration, usually in molar fraction) is plotted on the X-axis and vapor molar fractions on the Y-axis, the VLE diagram is called the XY diagram (see Figure 3). [Usually, the XY diagrams are plotted at constant P.]

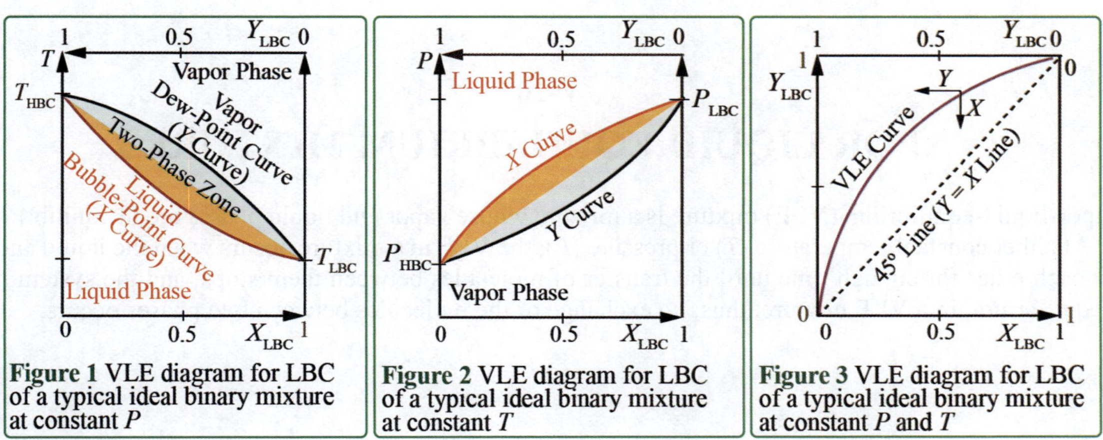

Figure 1 VLE diagram for LBC of a typical ideal binary mixture at constant P

Figure 2 VLE diagram for LBC of a typical ideal binary mixture at constant T

Figure 3 VLE diagram for LBC of a typical ideal binary mixture at constant P and T

A VLE diagram is determined experimentally by placing a binary liquid mixture in a closed vessel, held at constant T or P. Consider an experiment performed at constant P of 1 Atm. As phase equilibrium at P_{Atm} between the vapor and liquid occurs (it takes time to happen), T of the mixture is measured, and samples are taken to determine the vapor and liquid compositions (usually in molar fraction). After the T changes, more samples are taken to determine their compositions. These steps are repeated a few times until enough data are collected. Then the resulted data are plotted in the *TXY* diagram.

The two curves in a *TXY* diagram are in the following pattern (see Figure 1):

- **Lower Curve**: The lower curve, in this case, the bubble point temperature (T_{BBP}) curve (**saturated-liquid curve**), gives the molar fraction of the LBC in the liquid phase (X_{LBC} or just X) as a function of T. [The word **saturated** used here tells us that both the liquid and vapor phases have been reached their maximum limit and are in equilibrium.]
- **Upper Curve:** The upper curve, in this case, the dew point temperature (T_{DP}) curve (**saturated vapor curve**), gives the molar fraction of the LBC in the vapor phase (Y_{LBC} or just Y) as a function of T.

In Figure 1, which shows the *TXY* phase diagram of a binary liquid mixture, the lower curve is the **liquid bubble-point curve** (X curve), and the upper one is the **vapor dew-point curve** (Y curve). Both curves go through points $X = 1$, which represents pure LBC, and $X = 0$, which represents pure HBC (higher-boiling component). The point T_{LBC} at $X = 1$ represents the T_{BP} (boiling point temperature) of the pure LBC, and the point T_{HBC} at $X = 0$ is the T_{BP} of the pure HBC. The area below the X curve represents the liquid phase, and the Y curve represents the vapor phase. The area between the X and Y curves represents the two-phase (coexistent) area, where both phases are in equilibrium.

In Figure 2, which shows a *PXY* phase diagram, the lower curve is the Y curve, and the upper one is the X curve. The point P_{LBC} at $X = 1$ represents the vapor pressure (P_V) of LBC at the T, at which the data were collected, and the point P_{HBC} at $X = 0$ represents the P_V of the pure HBC at the same T. The area above the X curve represents the liquid phase, and below the Y curve represents the vapor phase. The P_V of LBC at a specified X and constant T can be read from a *PXY* diagram. Say, the liquid composition of LBC (that is, X_{LBC}) can be read from the intersection of X_1 with P_1 (the constant pressure line). Similarly, Y_A (vapor composition of A) can be determined from the intersection of Y_1 with P_1.

Figure 3, which shows the *XY* phase diagram of a binary liquid mixture, relates the compositions of the liquid phase and vapor phase of a pure substance when the phases are at equilibrium. Here, the equilibrium curve passes through the diagram's (0,0) and point (1,1). Usually, the **reference line** (also called the 45° line or $Y = X$ line) is also plotted on the diagram for reference purposes.

V-20

VAPOR LIQUID EQUILIBRIUM MIXTURES

A vapor-liquid-equilibrium (VLE) mixture is a mixture whose vapor and liquid phases are in equilibrium (stability). At either constant temperature (T) or pressure (P), the VLE in a mixture occurs when the liquid and vapor contact each other for enough time until the transfer of molecules between them stops, and the system reaches phase equilibrium. In a VLE mixture, thus, *no* exchange of the molecules between two phases occurs.

V-21

VAPOR PRESSURE AND RAOULT'S LAW OF VAPOR PRESSURE

Vapor Pressure

The vapor pressure (P_V, also called **saturated vapor pressure** or **equilibrium vapor pressure**) of a liquid in a closed container is the pressure (P) exerted by the vapor of that liquid on its surface at a certain temperature (T). Different liquids have different P_V. For example, the P_V of soda water in a closed bottle is much higher than the P_V of water in a similarly closed bottle, both at the same T. [The word **vapor pressure** is usually used when the P_V of water vapor (simply **vapor**) is under study unless it is mentioned.]

A liquid's P_V depends on the attractive forces between its molecules (the *higher* the attraction between a liquid's molecules, the *smaller* is its P_V). Say, water molecules (H_2O) have a strong attraction for each other, so it has a low P_V, while ethanol molecules (C_2H_5OH) have a weaker attraction, so it has a high P_V. And methanol molecules (CH_3OH) have the weakest, compared with ethanol and water. Because of the higher P_V, the methanol molecules escape from the liquid state more readily than ethanol and water molecules. Thus, at the same T, the P_V of these liquids is in the order of methanol > ethanol > water (see Figure 1).

If a non-volatile solute (a solute that does *not* evaporate, so its $P_V = 0$) is dissolved in a pure solvent (like water), the P_V of the final solution will be lower than that of the pure solvent. Thus, the P_V of water is greater than that of a solution containing water and sugar, as shown in Figure 2.

Tables 8 and 9 in the book's table section give the P_V of **water** and **ethanol** at various temperatures. When a binary solution (like ethanol-water mixture) is partially evaporated during distillation, the lower-boiling component (LBC, ethanol), which has higher volatility and the P_V concentrates in the vapor phase, resulting in a difference in composition between the liquid and vapor phases. The LBC's vapor can be cooled to produce condensate (distillate in distillation). The successive evaporation and condensation of the condensate are performed to increase the amount of LBC in the distillate (overhead) product.

At temperatures below 100°C, water does *not* boil because its P_V is lower than atmospheric pressure (P_{Atm} = 1 Atm). At 100°C, the water's boiling point temperature (T_{BP}), the P_V of water vapor is greater than P_{Atm}. Therefore, a liquid in a pot under boiling starts to boil when its P_V equates to the P_{Atm} acting on the liquid's surface. This tells us that a liquid's T_{BP} depends on its P (T_{BP} *decreases* with *decreasing* P). Water does *not* boil at room temperature (because its P_V is lower than the surrounding P_{Atm}), but if we raise its T to its T_{BP}, the vapor starts to be released (at that T, the P_V of water is greater than P_{Atm}).

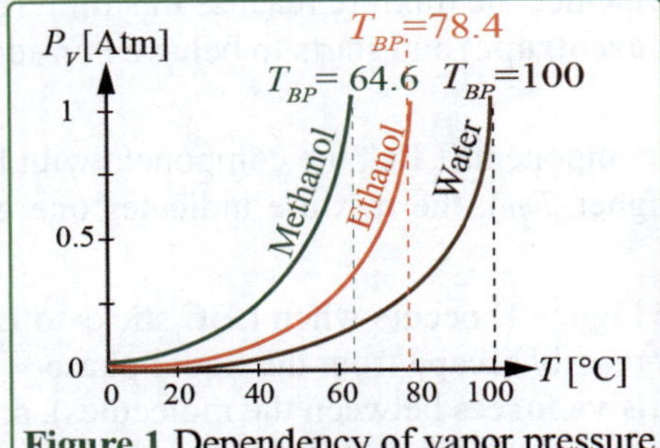

Figure 1 Dependency of vapor pressure (P_V) on temperature (T) for pure methanol, ethanol, and water

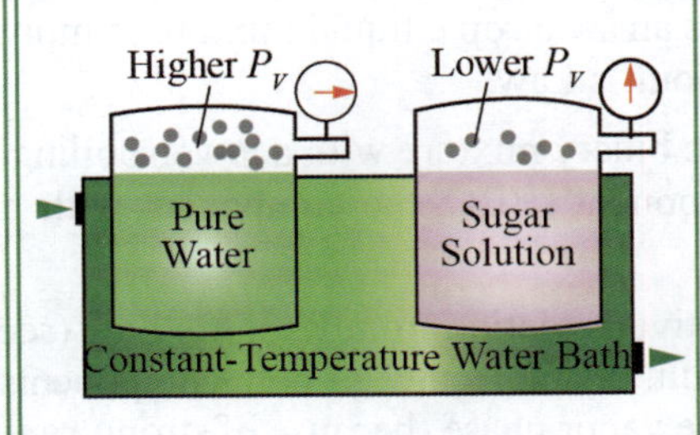

Figure 2 P_V of water (a pure liquid) is greater than that of a solution containing water and sugar

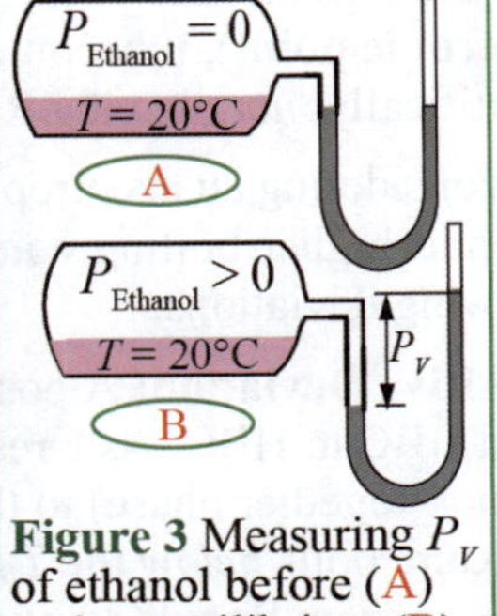

Figure 3 Measuring P_V of ethanol before (A) and at equilibrium (B)

From what has been discussed so far, we can say the following about P_V (vapor pressure):

- Every liquid has a P_V that acts on its surface.
- P_V has a direct relationship with T (the *greater* the T of a liquid, the *higher* is its P_V), as shown in Figure 1. In this way, a warm bottle of soda has a higher P_V than a cold bottle. This can be simply noticed by opening a warm bottle of soda. [Antoine equation is usually used to correlate (relate) a liquid's P_V with its T by using the Antoine coefficients (A, B, and C) of a component and its P_V at various T.]
- P_V has an indirect relationship with T_{BP} (the *lower* the T_{BP} of a liquid, the *higher* is its P_V); see Figure 1.

The P_V of a liquid is usually measured in a closed container when the equilibrium between its liquid phase and vapor phase (known as the vapor liquid equilibrium, simply VLE) is reached at a certain T, as shown in Figure 3 for measuring the P_V of ethanol. Then the T is changed, and another P_V is measured at the new T.

Like P, the P_V is usually expressed in absolute pressure (P_{Abs}) in Atm, kPa, mm Hg, or PSIA, and the T unit can be in °C, °F, or K.

Raoult's Law of Vapor Pressure

Raoult's Law of Vapor Pressure (simply **Raoult's Law**), which was offered in 1887 by Francois M. Raoult (French chemist), states that P_V of an ideal solution (diluted solution) at equilibrium equates to the molar fraction (X, a unitless quantity) of the solute in that solution multiplied by the solute's partial pressure (P_V) in the vapor phase above the solution. Formulizing this statement for component A results in the next equation.

$$P_{V.A} = X_{n.A} \cdot P_{P.A} \quad (1)$$

This equation can be written for a **binary ideal solution** that consists of components A and B when they reach a stable (equilibrium) condition, at which the total P_V of A and B above the solution (shown as $P_{V.AB}$) can be determined by combining general equation of Raoult's Law of vapor pressure with general equation of Dalton's Law of Partial Pressure.

$$P_{V.AB} = X_{n.A} \cdot P_{P.A} + X_{n.B} \cdot P_{P.B} \quad (2)$$

This equation tells us that the total P_V of a gaseous mixture equates to the total P_P of the components in that mixture. The Raoult-Dalton equation for a multicomponent solution is similar.

$$P_V = X_{n.A} \cdot P_{P.A} + X_{n.B} \cdot P_{P.B} + \cdots X_{n.I} \cdot P_{P.I} \quad (3)$$

Or

$$P_V = \sum_{I=A}^{N} X_{n.I} \cdot P_{P.I} \quad (4)$$

Raoult's Law is used in physical chemistry and ChemEng to study the differences between the behaviors of ideal and non-ideal binary (two-component) mixtures. For example, the ethanol-water mixture obeys Raoult's Law when its ethanol concentration (C) is below 96.5% (by volume). Once the mixture reaches this limit (called **azeotropic point**), it becomes an azeotropic liquid mixture (simply **azeotrope**) and starts to behave non-ideally; scientifically, *not* obeying Raoult's Law.

If considering an azeotropic binary mixture with a lower-boiling component (LBC, the component with lower T_{BP}) and higher-boiling component (HBC, the component with higher T_{BP}), the mixture indicates one of the following deviations:

- **Positive Deviation:** A positive deviation from Raoult's Law (see Figure 4) occurs when LBC sticks to LBC and HBC to HBC. As a result, the molecules of both components readily escape from the liquid phase (stuck-together phase) to the vapor phase (because of strong **repulsive forces** between the molecules), so the mixture boils *below* the T_{BP} of its pure LBC. For example, the ethanol-water mixture indicates a positive deviation from Raoult's Law when it reaches its azeotropic point. Ethanol boils at 78.4°C, water boils at 100°C, but their azeotropic mixture boils at 78.2°C (*lower* than the ethanol's T_{BP}).

- **Negative Deviation:** A negative deviation from Raoult's Law occurs when LBC sticks to HBC more strongly than LBC does to LBC and HBC does to HBC. As a result, the molecules of both components do *not* readily escape to the liquid phase (because of strong **repulsive forces** between the molecules), so the mixture boils *above* the T_{BP} of its pure HBC. For example, an HCl-water solution consisting of 20.2% (by mass) HCL (hydrochloric acid) and 79.8% H_2O indicates a negative deviation. HCl boils at −84ºC, and water boils at 100ºC, but their azeotropic mixture boils at 110ºC (*higher* than the water's T_{BP}).

Figure 5 shows the P_V of ethanol (as component A) and that of water (as component B) in relation to their molar fractions ($X_{n.A}$ and X_{nB}). The **purple line** in the figure is the $P_{P.T}$ (total P_P) as a function of $X_{n\text{-}A}$, the **red line** is the P_P of component A as a function of $X_{n\text{-}A}$, and the **green line** is the P_P of B as a function of $X_{n,B}$.

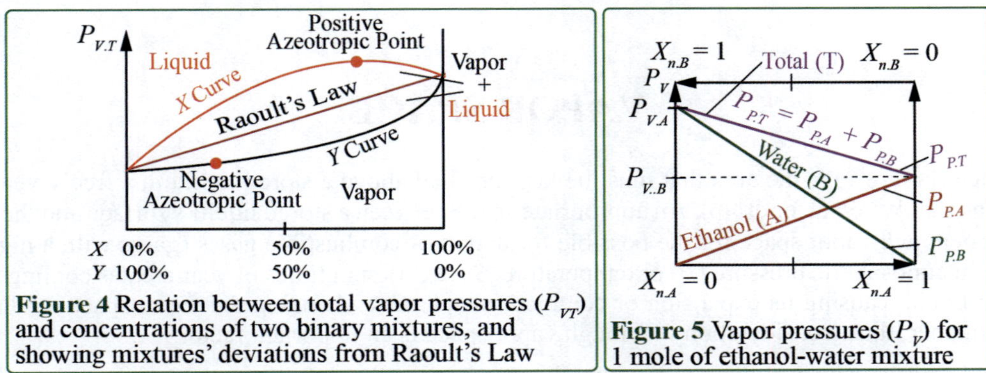

Figure 4 Relation between total vapor pressures (P_{VT}) and concentrations of two binary mixtures, and showing mixtures' deviations from Raoult's Law

Figure 5 Vapor pressures (P_V) for 1 mole of ethanol-water mixture

V-22

VAPOR RECOMPRESSION PROCESS

Study STEAM RECOMPRESSION AND VAPOR COMPRESSION.

V-23

VAPOR SHIFTING PROCESS

The vapor shifting process uses a vapor with lower heat energy (E_Q) in a vapor-user station instead of vapor with higher E_Q. This process can be performed in chemical plants with a multiple-effect evaporating station. [Multiple-effect evaporation is discussed under EVAPORATION PROCESS).] The process of taking vapor from different effects and used outside the evaporating station is called the vapor-bleeding process**.** The main purpose of the vapor shifting process and the vapor bleeding process is to save the E_Q of the evaporating station.

In chemical plants with a multi-effect evaporating station, vapor 1 (the vapor with higher E_Q from effect 1) and vapor 2 are used to heat the heat exchangers. Low-heat-demanding heaters are, instead, heated with vapor 3 or hot condensate. For example, the vapor can be taken from the first effect and used in a heater. In this case, the vapor is called **vapor bleed 1**. Heaters are the most users of the vapor bleeds. The vapor-shifting process saves E_Q, particularly when the vapor is taken from later effects (study the upcoming Example).

Vapor saving (V_S) can be calculated with the **vapor-shift formula**, which uses $\dot{M}$ (the mass rate of vapor used in a heater), V_1 (the effect from which the vapor was drawn before the change), V_2 (the effect from which the vapor was drawn after the change), and N_E (the number of effects in the evaporating station).

$$V_S = \dot{M}\,\frac{V_2 - V_1}{N_E} \qquad (1)$$

AN EXAMPLE OF A HEATING PROCESS

GIVEN: A four-effect evaporation station, from which a vapor must heat a heat exchanger that needs 100 kg vapor/hour ($\dot{M}$ = 100 kg/h).

WANTED: The vapor saving (V_S) and the amount of vapor saved; 1) If 1st vapor (vapor 1 bleed) is used in the exchanger instead of steam, 2) If 3rd vapor is used in the heat exchanger instead of 1st vapor.

$$V_{S1} = \dot{M} \times \frac{V_2 - V_1}{N_E} = 100 \times \frac{1-0}{4} = 25 \text{ kg/h} \qquad V_{S2} = 100 \times \frac{3-1}{4} = 50 \text{ kg/h}$$

Note that the difference between these two shifts confirms the next statement, "*it is more economical to take more vapor from later effects*."

V-24

VAPOR SPACE

Vapor space (Figure 1) is the area that must be kept unfilled above a stored liquid in a freely-ventilated container (such as a tank, vessel, or drum). An appropriate space between a stored liquid's surface and the container's roof provides enough vapor space for the possible formation of combustible gases (gases with a high fire risk). [The change in atmospheric pressure (*P*) or temperature (*T*) at different times of year creates cooling and heating of the stored liquid, causing its expansion or contraction and, thus, changing the vapor space's volume. In designing a container, thus, consideration of enough vapor space is an important factor.]

During cool days, some surrounding air enters the vapor space through the container's ventilators, increasing the vapor volume in the vapor space. Instead, some vapor escapes during hot days, causing emissions.

When a liquid containing volatile organic compounds is stored in a fixed-roof container, the vapor volume in the vapor space increases notably. This, as a result, increases the fire risk more. [To prevent fire risk and environmental emission, always a certain space (minimum 20%) of the container's volume must be kept unfilled above a stored liquid for, so known, **tank breathing**.]

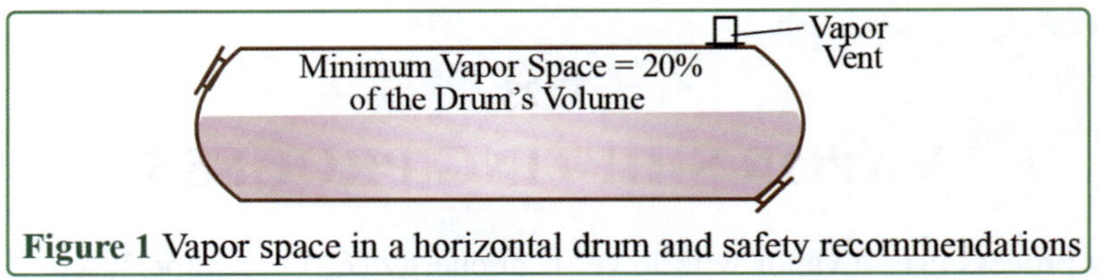

Figure 1 Vapor space in a horizontal drum and safety recommendations

V-25

VECTOR AND SCALAR QUANTITIES

Vector Quantities: A vector quantity (simply a **vector**) has both **magnitude** (size) and **direction**, indicating its direction at each point in space. Usually, 2 perpendicular components (*X*, *Y*) or 3 (*X*, *Y*, *Z*) are used to numerically describe the direction and quantity of a vector in space. Acceleration (*a*), force (*F*), momentum (*p*), position, velocity (*V*), and work (*W*) are vector quantities. When, for example, saying the *V* of a car is 100 km/h south, the number 100 indicates the car's speed (a scalar quantity), and the word **south** indicates its direction.

Scalar Quantities: A scalar quantity has only **magnitude**, so it *cannot* indicate its direction in space. Area (*A*), density (*D*), energy (*E*), length (*L*), mass (*M*), mole (*n*), pressure (*P*), speed (*U*), and temperature (*T*) are some examples of scalar quantities. For example, we say the speed of a car is 100 km/h. The car's speed tells us its quickness but *not* its direction in space. And the *T* at a given point is a quantity (say, 22°C) with *no* direction.

The following are the generalities of Vector and Scalar Quantities:

- Two vector quantities must be added with consideration of their directions. Two scalar quantities can be added without their directions (5 kg of water plus 3 kg of water makes 8 kg of water).
- A vector is graphically shown by an arrow (→) to show its direction in space. A vector that goes, for example, from point A (the start point or head point) to B (the endpoint or tail point) is shown as AB with an arrow sign above AB; that is $\overline{AB}$. Figure 1 shows vector A that lies in a vertical plane, with 2 components (A_X and A_Y) to describe the vector.
- A vector, like a vector F in Figure 2, is shown in the X, Y, and Z axes, and its components are accordingly shown as F_X, F_Y, and F_Z. In practice, a vector is simply described by two components: horizontal component (F_X, also called **parallel component**) and vertical component (F_Y, also called **perpendicular component**). Components, such as F_X and F_Y, are produced by drawing two lines at 90° to each other from the beginning of the vector. Usually, the vector and X-axis angles are shown by the symbol α (alpha). [If a component locates in the negative part of an axis, its magnitude is considered **negative**. If, for example, F_Y were downward in Figure 2 instead of upward and its length were equivalent to; say, a force (F) of 10 N, the F_Y axis should be written as $F_Y = -10$ N, where N is for Newton, the SI unit of force.]

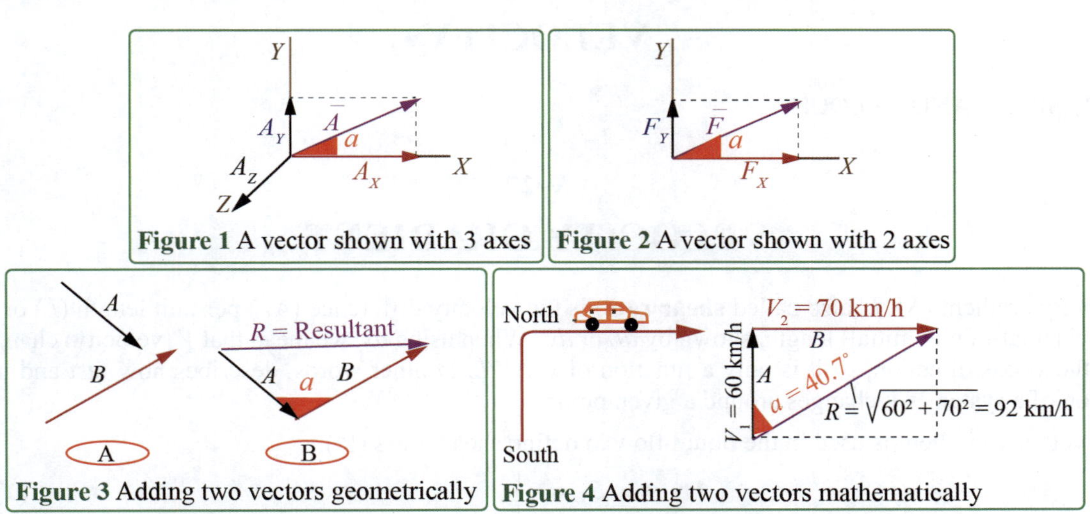

Figure 1 A vector shown with 3 axes
Figure 2 A vector shown with 2 axes
Figure 3 Adding two vectors geometrically
Figure 4 Adding two vectors mathematically

Vector Rules

Sum Rule: When two vectors (say, A and B) of the same kind are perpendicular to each other, they can be added geometrically by placing the tail of the second vector (vector B) at the head of the first vector (vector A), and the sum is the vector drawn from the tail of A to the head of B, as shown in Figure 3. Thus, the sum of vectors A and B is given as

$$\overline{AB} = \bar{A} + \bar{B}$$

The resultant (R) can be found with the Pythagorean Theorem.

$$R = \sqrt{A^2 + B^2}$$

[The same procedure is followed when more than two vectors of the same kind are added.]

Deduction Rule: The difference between two vectors is given as

$$\Delta\overline{AB} = \bar{A} - \bar{B}$$

Here the resultant (R) can also be found with the Pythagorean Theorem.

As a numerical example, we want to calculate the resultant velocity (V) of a car that, at $t_1 = 0$, is starting to move northward with a velocity of 60 km/h on a straight road and at $t_2 = 1$ min, is traveling eastward at the V of 70 km/h (Figure 4). Since V is a vector quantity, the difference between two velocities can be found.

$$\Delta\bar{v} = \bar{B} - \bar{A} = \bar{V}_2 - \bar{V}_1 = 70 - 60 = 10 \text{ km/h}$$

To find the quantity of the resultant velocity ($R = \Delta V$), the Pythagorean Theorem is used.

$$R = \Delta V = \sqrt{V_1^2 + V_2^2} = \sqrt{60^2 + 70^2} = 92 \text{ km/h}$$

And the tangent (tan) of the angle a between A and B can be found as

$$tan\ (a) = \frac{A}{B} = \frac{60}{70} = 0.86$$

By using a calculator, the $\tan^{-1}$ of 0.86 is 40.7°. This means that the car's movement resultant is in the northeast direction at an angle of 40.7°.

V-26

VELOCITY

Study SPEED AND VELOCITY.

V-27

VELOCITY GRADIENT

Velocity gradient ($\Delta V/L$, also called **shear rate**) is the velocity difference (ΔV) per unit length (L) or per differential (final-minus-initial) length, shown by dL or dx. When using dx, we mean that V (velocity) changes only along the x-axis direction, so it is only a function of x. $\Delta V/L$, in other words, describes how fast and in which direction of a system's V changes around a given point.

The velocity gradient is used in the liquid flow to define shear stress (S_S).

$$S_S = \eta \frac{V}{L} \tag{1}$$

Consider a liquid with viscosity η; the velocity gradient shows the liquid's V, at which it travels (in the direction of the flow) between two points that are apart by distance L. The distance (L, for length) is measured perpendicular to the direction of the flow.

V-28

VENTURI EFFECT

The Venturi effect, a principle in physics named after its inventor Giovanni Venturi (1746–1822, Italian physicist), can be expressed as follows. The pressure (P) of a flowing fluid (liquid or gas) decreases, and its velocity (V) increases as the fluid goes from the wider section of a **Venturi tube** to its narrower section. [A **Venturi tube** is a tube whose diameter decreases at one point and increases back to its original size. The narrow section between the sections is known as the **throat**.]

The Venturi effect occurs because of the fluid's contraction in a tube's narrower section. Bernoulli equation can calculate the fluid's pressure drop (pressure difference, ΔP) between the tube's sections.

$$\Delta P = P_1 - P_2 = \frac{D}{2}(V_2^2 - V_1^2) \qquad (1)$$

In this equation, D is the fluid's density, P_1 is the fluid's P in the wider section (the section with higher P and lower v), and P_2 is its P in the narrower section (the section with lower P and higher v).

Like an orifice flowmeter, a **Venturi flowmeter** (discussed under FLOW MEASUREMENT) works based on Bernoulli's principle (as a flowing fluid's V increases, its P and E_P (potential energy) decrease, and vice versa). A Venturi tube can measure the ΔP and, consequently, a fluid's flow rate when it goes through a contraction (as it goes through the throat of the tube).

The left side of Figure 1 shows the measurement of ΔP (pressure difference) when water goes through a Venturi flowmeter, and the right side of the same figure shows when air goes through a similar meter. In both figures, the tube's wider section and narrower section are connected to a manometer (a U-shaped tube) partially filled with water. Both figures show that the P in the first measuring tube (tube 1) is higher than in the second tube (tube 2). For the V of the fluid, the trend is the opposite (the V in tube 1 is lower than in tube 2). So, any decrease in P is associated with an increase in V. Considering the pressures in tubes 1 and 2, the ΔP in the manometer determines the fluid's liquid head (h, in cm or In).

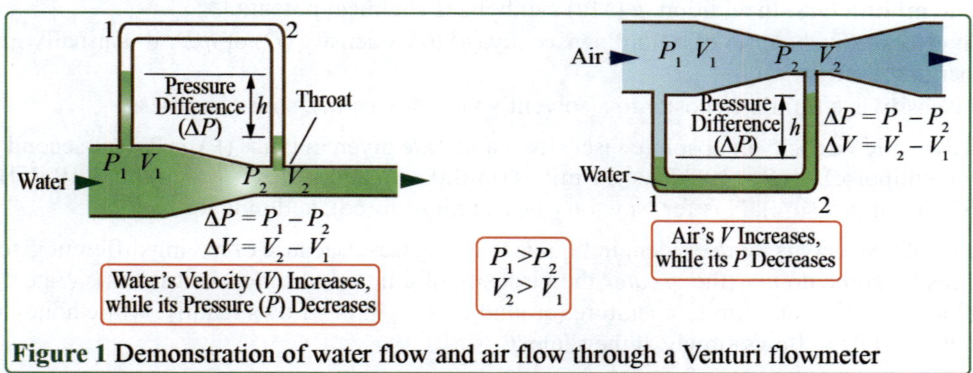

Figure 1 Demonstration of water flow and air flow through a Venturi flowmeter

V-29
VENTURI FLOWMETER

Discussed under the topic of PROCESS CONTROL OF CHEMICAL ENGINEERING.

V-30
VENTURI SCRUBBERS

Discussed under WET SCRUBBERS.

V-31
VESSELS

Study TANKS, VESSELS, AND DRUMS.

V-32

VISCOELASTICITY

Viscoelasticity is the response of a material, which has both viscous and elastic properties, to applied stress. This term is mostly used in polymer technology. Polymers can undergo permanent deformation at a high strain (deformation). The deformation can resemble viscous liquid flow.

V-33

VISCOSITY

Viscosity (η, eta, also called **dynamic viscosity** or **absolute viscosity**) is the resistance to the flow of a fluid (liquid or gas), so it can be viewed as a force (F) that acts against the flow of a fluid (the *greater* the η of a fluid, the *slower* it flows).

Knowing the following points about the terminology of viscosity is helpful:

- Instead of η (eta), some use μ (mu) to symbolize viscosity. This creates confusion because μ is usually used to abbreviate **millimeters**. In addition, μ (Mu) symbolizes chemical potential.
- **Kinematic viscosity** is the ratio of a fluid's viscosity (η) to its density (D) or η/D. It is usually given in surface area per unit time (m^2/s).
- **Relative viscosity** is a fluid's viscosity to a solvent's viscosity (η/η_1), so it is **unitless**.

Viscosity (dynamic viscosity or absolute viscosity) values are given in Poise (P) or Pascal-second (Pa.s), where 1 P = 100 cP (centipoise), 1 cP = 10^{-3} Pa.s = 1 mPa.s (milli Pa,s), and 1 Pa.s = 1 (N.s)/m^2 = 10 P. Here, Pa is for Pascal (the SI unit of pressure), N is for Newton (the SI unit of force), and m is for meter.

The presence of viscosity is more evident in liquids than in gases. Because of having different viscosities, some liquids flow easily; some do *not* (the *greater* the viscosity of a liquid, the *slower* it flows). Water (with a low η of about 1 cP (= 10^{-3} Pa.s) at room temperature (around 25°C = 77 °F) flows readily, while honey with a high η of about 100 P (= 10 Pa.s) flows slowly at the same T.

Viscosity can also be viewed as a resistance to the shear stress ($S_S = F_S/A$, where F_S is for shear force) when a liquid flows, say, in a pipe. A liquid flows in a direction when an S_S acts on it parallel to the liquid's surface. In a flowing liquid, therefore, η acts in the opposite direction of the flow, so η and S_S act against each other (η acts as the opposing force and S_S as the driving force of the flow). Thus, a liquid can move a distance (L, for length) when the S_S acting on it is greater than its η.

Viscosity plays an important role in many ChemEng process units, including filtration, evaporation, and crystallization. And in designing piping systems, pumps, mixers, stirrers, and more. For example, the viscosity reduces the heat-transfer rate in the evaporation process.

Viscosity (η) is expressed by the viscosity equation, which expresses the ratio of shear stress ($S_S = F_S/A$) to velocity gradient (V/L).

$$\eta = \frac{\frac{F_S}{A}}{\frac{V}{L}} = \frac{S_S}{\frac{V}{L}} = \frac{S_S.L}{V} \qquad (1)$$

In liquids, viscosity depends on the following:

- Pressure, P (the *greater* the P of a liquid, the *greater* is its η).
- Temperature, T (the *greater* the T of a liquid, the *smaller* is its η).
- Intermolecular forces, F_{Int} (the *greater* the F_{Int} of a liquid, the *greater* is its η).
- Molecular mass, M_M (the *greater* the M_M of a liquid, the *greater* is the liquid's η).

- Number of vacancies (N_H, also called **holes**). Therefore. the *greater* the N_H in a liquid, the *smaller* is its η. [According to the **hole theory**, there are holes (vacancies) in any liquid, and liquid molecules are continually moving into those holes so that the holes move around in a liquid. When the N_H in a liquid is comparatively great, the molecules move around easier, so the η is reduced.]

A few methods can measure a liquid's viscosity. In one method, it is determined by measuring the flow rate of a sphere through a capillary tube using the next equation.

$$\eta = \frac{P.\pi.R^4.t}{V.L} \qquad (2)$$

In this equation, P is for pressure, R is the sphere's radius, t is the time the sphere moves through the capillary tube, V is the liquid's volume, and L is the tube's length.

In another method, a liquid's viscosity is determined by measuring the settling rate of a sphere of known D (density) in a liquid. The force (F) causing the sphere to settle in the liquid equates to its mass (M) times the gravitational acceleration ($a_g = 9.8\ \text{m/s}^2$).

For rough estimation, chemical engineers use the next simple equation for practical purposes.

$$\eta = \frac{0.045}{T} \qquad (3)$$

The T is in °C, and η is in Pa.s. This equation does *not* create an error greater than 3%.

V-34
VISCOSITY EQUATION

Study LIQUID FLOW EQUATION.

V-35
VISCOSITY LAW

Study NEWTON'S VISCOSITY LAW.

V-36
VLE DIAGRAM

Study VAPOR LIQUID EQUILIBRIUM DIAGRAM.

V-37
VLE MIXTURE

Study VAPOR LIQUID EQUILIBRIUM MIXTURE.

V-38

VOID FRACTION

Void fraction ($\mathcal{E}_F$) is the empty spaces between the particles of a solid substance. [Instead of void fraction, some use the terms **void fraction of packing**, **voidage**, or **interparticle porosity**.]

$\mathcal{E}_F$ is related to D_B (bulk density) and D_P (particle density) in the following way:

$$D_B = D_P(1 - \mathcal{E}_F) \quad (1)$$

$$\mathcal{E}_F = 1 - \frac{D_B}{D_P} \quad (2)$$

Typically, $\mathcal{E}_F$ of solid particles is 0.4. If, for example, we use the D_B of medium-size sugar crystals as 860 kg/m^3 (= 54 Lb/Ft^3) and its D_P as 1588 kg/m^3 (99.2 Lb/Ft^3) in Equation 2, $\mathcal{E}_F$ becomes 0.46. This means that empty spaces occupy 46% of the medium-size bulk sugar. The $\mathcal{E}_F$ is highest with a bed of uniformly sized particles. In filtration and centrifugal processes, high void (empty) spaces between molecules of bulk material are advantageous. Instead, in the packing and storing processes, high porosity is disadvantageous.

V-39

VOLATILE ORGANIC COMPOUNDS

A volatile organic compound (VOC or simply **VO compound**) is an organic compound that has a low boiling point temperature (T_{BP}), so its molecules evaporate easily from liquid to gas or sublimate (see SUBLIMATION PROCESS) from solid to gas and enter the surrounding air. In addition to carbon (C) and hydrogen (H), Volatile organic compounds (VOCs) often contain oxygen, sulfur, nitrogen, fluorine, and chlorine also. [Air pollutants caused by VOCs are harmful to human health and the environment.]

Because of low T_{BP}, VOCs have a high vapor pressure (P_V) at room temperature (around 25°C or 77 °F). Formaldehyde (HCHO) with T_{BP} of – 19°C (= – 2°F) and ethanol with T_{BP} of 78.3°C (= 173°F) are examples of VOCs. Gasoline (C_8H_{18}, a fuel), butane, propane, smog, odor, and hot oil are VOCs.

VO compounds are produced by:

- Plants, animals, and microorganisms.
- Some human activities, such as combustion engines.

V-40

VOLATILITY AND RELATIVE VOLATILITY

Volatility

The volatility of a liquid is its evaporating ability into its gas phase (the easier a liquid evaporates, the higher its volatility is). When a solution evaporates, its volatile compound (or compounds) mixes with surrounding gases, so the vapor pressure (P_V) of the produced gas affects the total pressure (P) of the surrounding gases. Ammonia and water are examples of volatile inorganic compounds. Gasoline (C_8H_{18}, a fuel), butane, and propane are examples of volatile organic compounds (VOCs) with high volatility.

The volatility of liquids depends on the following:

- The temperature (T) of the surrounding air (volatility *increases* with *increasing* the air's T), and
- A liquid's volatility *increases* with *increasing* its vapor pressure (P_V).

The vapor-pressure test measures the volatility of a compound (like gasoline). Other methods are also used, depending on the compound under the test.

Relative Volatility

The relative volatility (α, alpha) of two components in a two-phase mixture is used to compare those components' volatility in that mixture when the phases are at equilibrium. It is usually used in a separation process (like distillation) to express its separation efficiency (S_E). Both α and S_E indicate the difficulty of separating two components from each other (the *greater* the α, the *greater* the S_E and, therefore, the *easier* is the separation of components from each other). When, therefore, α = 1, *no* separation can occur between the components (because both are equally volatile).

When a binary (two-component) mixture containing components *A* and *B* is under a separation process, α of *A* relative to *B*, shown as α_{AB}, is expressed as

$$\alpha_{AB} = \frac{\alpha_A}{\alpha_B} = \frac{\frac{Y_A}{X_A}}{\frac{Y_B}{X_B}} = \frac{Y_A.X_B}{X_A.Y_B} \quad (1)$$

Here Y_A is the molar fraction of *A* (the component with higher volatility and lower boiling point temperature, T_{BP}) in the vapor phase, and X_A is in the liquid phase. Y_B is the molar fraction of *B* (the component with lower volatility and higher T_{BP}) in the vapor phase, and X_B is that in the liquid phase. The term Y_A/X_A in Equation 1 is called the *K*-value (distribution coefficient) of component *A* in two phases when the phases are at equilibrium. For ideal components at equilibrium,

$$K_A = \frac{Y_A}{X_A} \quad (2)$$

When a binary system is under study, subscripts are usually *not* used in Equation 1. This is because if *X* and *Y* are the molar fractions of the LBC (lower boiling component, or component *A*), then (1 – *X*) and (1 – *Y*) are the molar fractions of the HBC (higher-boiling component, or component *B*). So, Equation 1 becomes

$$\alpha = \frac{\frac{Y}{X}}{\frac{(1-Y)}{(1-X)}} = \frac{Y(1-X)}{X(1-y)} \quad (3)$$

Solving this equation for *Y* gives a frequently used equation in distillation calculations.

$$Y = \frac{\alpha.X}{1+(\alpha-1)X} \quad (4)$$

Sometimes, α is expressed by each component's P_V (vapor pressure) in an ideal solution (a diluted solution that behaves like a pure solution and follows Raoult's Law of Vapor Pressure). For ideal components *A* and *B*, α_{AB} is given by the components' vapor pressure ratio (P_A/P_B).

$$\alpha_{AB} = \frac{\alpha_A}{\alpha_B} = \frac{P_A}{P_B} \quad (5)$$

In calculations, α is assumed to be the same as the vapor pressure of *A,* shown as $(P_V)_A$, which is the component with greater volatility.

$$\alpha_{AB} = (P_V)_A \quad (6)$$

α depends on the T_{BP} of the components (the *greater* is the difference between the T_{BP} of the components, the *smaller* is their α).

[More information on **relative volatility** under the topic of DISTILLATION PROCESS.]

V-41

VOLT AND VOLTMETERS

Volt: As the SI unit of electric voltage (V_E, simply **voltage**), the Volt (V), which is named after Italian physicist Alessandro Volta (1745–1827), is defined as the difference in V_E between two points on an electric conductor, which carries an electric current (I, simply current) of one Ampere (A), when the electric power (P_E) between the points is 1 W/h, where W is for Watt and h is for an hour.

A typical voltage for a flashlight AAA battery is 1.5 volts (DC). The voltage is 12 volts for a car battery (AC), where AC is for alternating current. Electricity for household usage in the US of America is 110 to 220 kV (AC). [If the voltage is too large (say, nuclear energy), it is expressed in MV (megavolts), where 1 MV = 10^6 V.]

Voltmeters: A voltmeter is an instrument that measures the V_E between two points in an **electric circuit** (a closed electric loop). The parallel arrangement does *not* increase the V produced in the resistor. Figure 1 shows a simple voltmeter with a fine wire coil in a strong magnetic field.

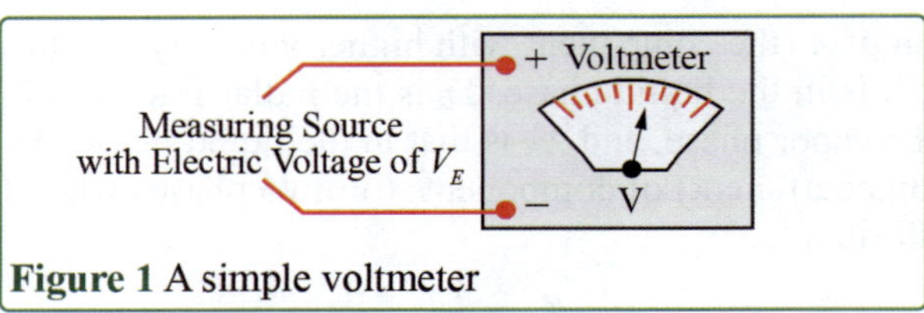

Figure 1 A simple voltmeter

V-42

VOLTAGE

Simplified name for ELECTRIC VOLTAGE.

V-43

VOLUME

The term volume (V) is used to designate a quantity that takes space, and its SI unit is m^3 (cubic meter). Volume is usually shown by a three-dimensional space enclosed by a boundary. V of a solid sample can be calculated in the following ways:

- **Geometric Formula Method:** It calculates the V of a sample with a geometric shape.
- **Liquid Displacement Method:** It determines the V of a sample with a non-geometric shape by immersing the sample in a liquid. In this method, V of an immersed sample equates to V of the displaced liquid, based on Archimedes' principle.

For example, the V of a tank with a diameter (d) of 4m and a height (h) of 5 m is

$$V = \pi \left(\frac{d}{2}\right)^2 h = 3.14\frac{4^2}{4} \times 5 = 62.8 \text{ m}^3 \ (= 2217 \text{ Ft}^3)$$

Using the liquid-displacement method, we can determine the V of a non-geometric shape solid sample with the help of a graduated cylinder. [The V of a non-geometric shape can also be determined by integration.]

V-44

VOLUME CONCENTRATION

The volume concentration of component A (shown as C_A) in a mixture is the volume of that component divided by the mixture's volume. As a ratio, volume concentration is a **unitless** number. For example, in the case of sugar solutions, the volume concentration of sugar is the greatest for a 56% sugar solution with a value of 0.03 or 3%.

Volume concentration, molar concentration (molarity), mass concentration, and number concentration are the four (4) types of expressing the concentration of a solution.

V-45

VOLUME FRACTION

Discussed under MASS FRACTION, MOLAR FRACTION, AND VOLUME FRACTION.

V-46

VOLUMETRIC FLOW RATE

The volumetric flow rate ($\dot{V}$, the rate of V) of a fluid (a liquid or gas) is its volume (V) when it flows to a reference system in unit time (t).

$$\dot{V} = \frac{V}{t} \tag{1}$$

Consider a liquid that flows into a tank. If its $\dot{V}$ is 1 m^3/min (= 266 Ga/min), the tank collects 4 m^3 of liquid in 4 minutes. Conversion between the $\dot{V}$ and $\dot{M}$ (mass flow rate) requires the D (density) of the fluid.

$$\dot{V} = \frac{\dot{M}}{D} \tag{2}$$

Differentially (infinitesimally), the $\dot{V}$ is the time differential of the V.

$$\dot{V} = \lim_{\Delta t \to 0} \frac{\Delta V}{\Delta t} = \frac{dV}{dt} \tag{3}$$

$\dot{V}$ of a liquid in a pipe is the product of the liquid's average velocity ($\bar{V}$) multiply by the pipe's cross-sectional area ($A = \pi R^2 = \pi d^2/4$, where d is the pipe's inside diameter).

$$\dot{V} = \bar{V}.A = \bar{V}.\pi.R^2 = \bar{V}.\pi\frac{d^2}{4} \tag{4}$$

This is known as the continuity equation, according to which $\dot{V}$ in a pipe with a different inside cross-sectional area (A) remains constant when the flow in the pipe is steady.

A liquid's $\dot{V}$ in a pipe can also be defined as the liquid's $\dot{M}$ per its D.

$$\dot{V} = \frac{\dot{M}}{D} = \frac{D.\bar{V}.A}{D} = \bar{V}.A \tag{5}$$

When $\dot{M}$ is in kg/s and D in kg/m^3, $\dot{V}$ becomes in m^3/s, and when $\bar{V}$ is in m/s and A in m^2, $\dot{V}$ also becomes in m^3/s.

The $\dot{V}$ of gas A in a mixture of gases can be calculated as

$$\dot{V} = \frac{\dot{M}_A}{D_A} \times \frac{P_{Atm}}{P_A} \times \frac{T}{273.2} \tag{6}$$

When the $\dot{M}$ of component A (shown as $\dot{M}_A$) is given in kg/min, the D of component A (shown as D_A) in kg/m^3, the atmospheric pressure (P_{Atm}) in kPa, the partial pressure of component A (P_A) in kPa, the gas mixture's temperature (T) in °C, then the $\dot{V}$ at that T and P_{Atm} becomes in m^3/min. [The value 273.2 in the last equation is the conversion factor from °C to Kelvin.]

We know from the topic of PARTIAL PRESSURE that in a mixture of two gases of A and B, the partial pressure of A (the $P_{P.A}$) can be calculated from its vapor pressure ($P_{V.A}$) and the mixture's total pressure (P_T).

$$P_{P.A} = \frac{P_{V.A}}{P_T} \quad (7)$$

Using this equation, we can calculate the $\dot{V}$ of gas A (volumetric flow rate of A) from the system's total $\dot{V}$.

$$\dot{V}_A = \dot{V}\frac{P_{V.A}}{P_T} \quad (8)$$

Obviously, $\dot{V}$ remains constant if the liquid flows under steady-state (uniform) velocity. In practice, $\dot{V}$ of a device (say, an evaporator) is considered its **volumetric capacity** (simply **capacity**). [A volume measuring instrument (like a Venturi meter) can be used to measure $\dot{V}$.]

If we have V (volume) of a tank and the $\dot{V}$ to it, we can calculate the **retention time** (t_R) of the fluid pumping to the tank.

$$t_R = \frac{V}{\dot{V}} \quad (9)$$

The SI unit of $\dot{V}$ is m^3/h, m^3/min, or m^3/s, and its US unit is Ga/h, Ga/min, or Ga/s. In US units, $\dot{V}$ is also expressed in Ft^3/min (cubic feet per minute), where 1 m^3/h = 0.59 Ft^3/min.

An Example on Volumetric Flow Rate

Given: A condenser uses air as a cooling medium for condensing a water vapor. The related data are:

Mass flow rate of the air in the condenser ($\dot{M}_A$)	100 kg/h
Vacuum pressure in the condenser (P_{Vac})	13.6 kPa
Temperature of the water vapor (T)	35°C (35 + 273.2 = 308 K)
Density of the air (D_A)	1.2 kg/m^3
Volume of the condenser (V)	50 m^3

Wanted: 1) Total volumetric flow rate of air ($\dot{V}$); 2) Volumetric flow rate of dry air ($\dot{V}_A$); 3) Volumetric flow rate of water vapor ($\dot{V}_V$), and 4) Retention time (t_R) of vapor in the condenser

From Table 8, the vapor pressure (P_V) of water vapor at 35°C is 5.6 kPa, so the partial pressure of air (P_{Air}) at 35°C is the difference between P_{Vac} (which is the condenser's total pressure, P_T) and P_V.

$$P_{Air} = P_{Vac} - P_V = 13.6 - 5.6 = 8 \text{ kPa}$$

Total $\dot{V}$ of air can be calculated from Equation 6, and that of dry air ($\dot{V}_A$) from Equation 8.

$$\dot{V} = \frac{\dot{M}_A}{D_A} \times \frac{P_{Atm}}{P_{Air}} \times \frac{T}{273.2} = \frac{100}{1.2} \times \frac{101}{8} \times \frac{308}{273.2} = 1186 \text{ m}^3\text{/h } (313\times10^3 \text{ Ga/h})$$

$$\dot{V}_A = \dot{V}\frac{P_{V.A}}{P_T} = 1186 \times \frac{8}{13.6} = 698 \text{ m}^3\text{/h } (184\times10^3 \text{ Ga/h})$$

From here, $\dot{V}$ of vapor ($\dot{V}_V$) will be

$$\dot{V}_V = 1186 - 698 = 488 \text{ m}^3\text{/h } (= 129\times10^3 \text{ Ga/h})$$

$$t_R = \frac{50}{1186} = 0.042 \text{ h} \times 60 = 2.5 \text{ min}$$

V-47
VOLUMETRIC FLUX

Volumetric flux (Q) is the quantity of volumetric flow per unit area (A). It is given in $m^3/m^2 = m$. In the same way, **volumetric flux rate** is the rate of volumetric flux or volumetric flux per unit time (t). Volumetric flux rate is given in m^3/m^2 per second (s) or hour (h); that is m/s or m/h. In the filtration process, for example, the filtrate's volumetric flux rate (with a unit of m/s) is used to represent the filtrate volume (V_F), which is produced during filtration time (t_F) per filter's surface area (A_F).

V-48
VOLUMETRIC MASS DENSITY

The complete name for DENSITY.

V-49
VORTEX

Study EDDY CURRENT.

W Section

LIST OF TOPICS

1. Waste and Waste Management
2. Wastewater and Wastewater Treatment
3. Water Activity
4. Water and Water Vapor
5. Water Cluster
6. Water Hammering
7. Water Softening Process
8. Watt and Watt Hour
9. Wave and Wavelength
10. Wave Particle Duality
11. Wavefunction
12. Weak Nuclear Force
13. Weight
14. Weighted Average
15. Wet Bulb Temperature
16. Wet Bulb Thermometer
17. Wet Gas Scrubbers
18. Wet Surface Air Coolers
19. Work and its Types

W-1

WASTES AND WASTE MANAGEMENT

Wastes

Waste in the chemical process industry is the unusable substance of a chemical process plant. Wastes are divided into solid wastes, liquid wastes, and gas wastes. The solid wastes are in either solid or semi-solid form and can be divided into two major groups, invaluable wastes, and valuable wastes. [An invaluable waste of a chemical facility may be processed further to become a valuable byproduct of that facility.]

Waste Management

To manage a chemical facility's environmental activities, the facility's environmental manager creates an **environmental management system** (EMS). In addition to the capital expenses, the following fall under the EMS programs:

- Environmental audits;
- Environmental permits;
- Environmental compliance program, and
- Environmental reports to the corresponding agencies.

Staying in compliance with all environmental regulations requires a good effort by the responsible individuals. Some of the responsibilities are step-outlined next.

- Upper management must make sure the resources are available to the environmental manager.
- The environmental manager must prepare an appropriate comprehensive departmental EMS.
- Front-line supervisors must follow the orders required by the environmental manager.
- Line operators must properly operate the devices according to their supervisor's orders.

W-2

WASTEWATER AND WASTEWATER TREATMENT

Wastewater

Wastewater is any water that has been processed, and some impurities (such as organic compounds) were added to it during the household, agricultural, or industrial activities. Sewer water from flush toilets, runoff water from a farm, and process water from a chemical plant are examples of wastewater. The quality of particular wastewater depends on the source of wastewater, which determines both the amount and type of impurities that exist in that wastewater. Some impurities of wastewater may be pollutants, and some *not*. Without treatment, however, discharging wastewater to a natural water source (like a river) is prohibited by environmental agencies (because it greatly damages the quality of the source and its marine life).

Wastewater Treatment

Wastewater treatment is the process of separating impurities (such as organic compounds) from wastewater of a chemical process plant to the extent that it can be used again in the water cycle of that plant or discharged to a natural water source (like a river) with *no* impact on the source quality. In a chemical plant, wastewater is treated in wastewater ponds or large tanks, aerobically or anaerobically.

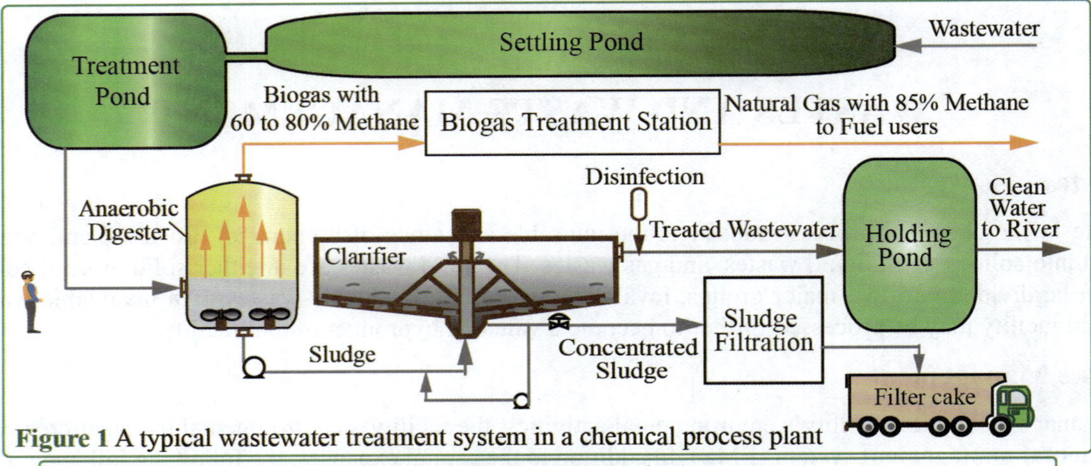

Figure 1 A typical wastewater treatment system in a chemical process plant

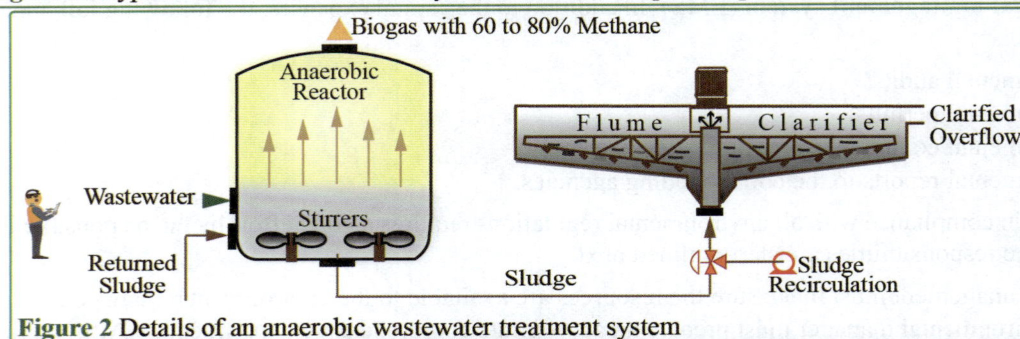

Figure 2 Details of an anaerobic wastewater treatment system

Figure 3 Typical wastewater treatment ponds of a chemical process plant

Wastewater Ponds

A wastewater pond (simply **pond**) is a concrete or earthen structure basin used to treat wastewater to improve its quality. A pond (Figure 1) used in a chemical process plant can perform from one to more functions. Based on the functionality, ponds can be divided into three (3) types (see Figure 3):

- **Settling** (primary) **Ponds:** In a settling pond, settleable solids of wastewater, such as large insoluble solids (such as dirt) and suspended solid particles (SS particles), are settled.
- **Treatment** (secondary) **Ponds:** In a treatment pond, nutrients (such as nitrogen and phosphorous), toxins (like pesticides), and heavy metals are removed from wastewater. Wastewater is treated **aerobically** (with aeration) or **anaerobically** (without aeration). Wastewater treatment uses microbes in a treatment pond to convert the organic compounds to carbon dioxide (CO_2), methane (CH_4), and sludge. The capacity of a typical treatment pond, usually several days, depends on the organic-compound load it must process and the required time for the microorganism population to grow. [In some chemical plants, the anaerobic treatment is performed in a **digester** (also called Anamet) instead of a pond. In a digester (see Figure 2), the operation

- and operating parameters (such as temperature and PH) are more controllable, so the treatment efficiency is greater than in a pond-anaerobic operation.]
- **Holding** (tertiary) **Ponds:** In a holding pond, which is usually built close to the discharge source (like a river), clean treated wastewater is temporarily stored to protect against flooding. After minor treatments, such as PH adjustment and chlorination, a certain amount of water is discharged into the river according to the permit criteria determined by an environmental agency.

Usually, ponds are connected so that wastewater enters the settling pond, gets some treatments, and leaves the holding pond as clean treated water. [Settling and treatment ponds need periodic cleaning.]

The aerobic reactions occur naturally in each pond. Sometimes, useful microorganisms are added to the treatment pond. Usually, the aeration process is done in the settling pond to increase the dissolved oxygen (DO) content for the **aerobic reactions** of microorganisms.

As outlined next, it is helpful to briefly compare a typical aerobic treatment system with an anaerobic one.

- An aerobic treatment system uses oxygen (O_2) for the reactions of useful microorganisms and bacteria, while an anaerobic system uses organic compounds as food for their reactions.
- An aerobic system produces mainly carbon dioxide (CO_2), nitrate (NO_3), and sulfate (SO_4), while an anaerobic system produces mainly biogas and ammonia (NH_3). [Because of biogas production, the facility with an anaerobic treatment system must burn the biogas or invest some money to install piping and filtering systems to use the biogas as a fuel in, say, steam boilers or dryers.]
- An aerobic system can release gases that are *not* odorous, toxic, and flammable, while an anaerobic system releases gases that are. [Existing hydrogen sulfide (H_2S) with a strong odor of rotten egg in biogas is the main problem of an anaerobic system. For toxicity purposes of biogas, operators must be trained.]
- An aerobic system produces more sludge for a given amount of organic load than an anaerobic system (aerobic bacteria fully utilize the energy in their food).
- An aerobic system requires more electric power (because it needs aerators).
- An aerobic system is larger than an anaerobic system.

W-3

WATER ACTIVITY

Water activity (A_W) is the ratio of a substance's vapor pressure (P_V) to the water's vapor pressure (P_W), both at the same temperature (T).

$$A_W = \frac{P_V}{P_W} \tag{1}$$

Because the P_V of a substance equates to the P_V of water present in that substance, a substance's A_W can be expressed in relation to its equilibrium relative humidity (W_{ER}) divided by 100.

$$A_W = \frac{W_{ER}}{100} \tag{2}$$

The A_W increases with increasing moisture content (W). Some properties of A_W are outlined next.

- It is a unitless quantity (because it is a ratio).
- Pure water (water with *no* dissolved solids) has an A_W of one.
- It increases with increasing T, except in some crystalline products (like sugar and salt).
- It is used in food products to measure the capability of water to support the growth of microorganisms. Bacteria usually require a medium with at least 0.9 and fungi with a medium with at least 0.7 A_W to grow.
- Water moves from areas of high A_W to areas of low A_W. If, for example, honey ($A_W \approx 0.6$) is exposed to air ($A_W \approx 0.7$), it absorbs water from the air.

W-4

WATER AND WATER VAPOR

Water

Water (H_2O), in addition to its liquid state, can also be in solid and gas states under different temperatures (T) and pressures (P). **Liquid water** (simply **water**), in its pure form, is a **standard reference** for liquids. It is widely used in chemical process plants in its pure or nearly pure form, both as process water and cooling water. It is also used to move heat energy (E_Q) in a heat transfer process. [Some properties of water and steam can be obtained from steam tables, such as Tables 1 and 2, given in the Table Section of this book.]

Water is an unusual (in a positive way) substance because

- It has the smallest molar mass (M_n) of all liquids (its M_n is 18 g/mole). The boiling point temperature (T_{BP}) increases with increasing M_n. Water with a T_{BP} of 100ºC (= 212ºF = 373 K) at atmospheric pressure (P_{Atm}) is an exception to this behavior because its T_{BP} is greater than we would expect in relation to its small M_n. [Because at higher altitudes, P_{Atm} is lower, water has lower T_{BP} at higher altitudes.]
- It is also an exception in the thermal expansion (its volume contracts as its T increases). Water's thermal expansion decreases to zero as it is cooled to 4°C. This trend also continues at below 4°C.
- It is among the very few substances whose liquid form is more compact than its solid form (the ice), so water has a greater density (D) than ice (because of the open molecular structure of ice). This property of water positively affects life on the Earth. Because ice floats, it covers the top of the water. Lakes and rivers freeze on the top, allowing life to continue under the ice. As shown in Figure 1, the D of water varies with T, but *not* linearly (as T increases, D increases to a peak at 4ºC). At 4ºC (= 39ºF), the D of water is 1000 kg/m^3 (= 62.4 Lb/Ft^3), which is its maximum D. The D of ice (water at 0ºC) is 916.7 kg/m^3. [The D of warmer water is less than colder water. This continues until it reaches 4°C (= 39ºF). At below 4°C, water becomes less dense as it freezes. This is why ice cubes float to the top of a glass of water.]
- It behaves, in one instance, as a base, and in another, as an acid. When mixed with an acid, water accepts a hydrogen ion (H+) from the acid molecule, behaving as a base. Instead, when water is mixed with a base, it donates an H^+ to the base molecule, behaving as an acid.
- It has a relatively high specific heat capacity (C_Q, simply **heat capacity**). Water's C_Q is 4.187 kJ/kg.ºC (= 1 BTU/Lb.ºF), meaning that for each ºC that 1 kg of water is heated, 4.187 kJ of E_Q is needed.

In many places, water boils at or near 100ºC. The P_{Atm} (= 1 Atm $\approx$ 100 kPa) is lower at higher altitudes, so water boils at lower temperatures. Therefore, food must be cooked longer to achieve the same result in a high-altitude area than at sea level.

The bonding properties between a water molecule' elements (H and O) and between a water molecule and its neighboring molecules can be summarized in the following ways:

- Covalent bonds bind a water molecule's hydrogen and oxygen (O) atoms (see Figure 2).
- Hydrogen bonds bind a water molecule to its neighboring molecules (Figure 3). [A water molecule in the liquid or solid state can form up to 4 hydrogen bonds with its neighboring molecules.]
- The bond angle between two hydrogen atoms in a water molecule is 104.5º, as shown in Figure 2.
- A water molecule, magnified one billion times, is shown on the right side of Figure 3.

Water is a weak electric conductor (because only one molecule in about 500 million forms ions). Water is a polar compound. Its approximate molecular size is about 0.28 nm, comparatively small (its small molecular mass of 18 AMU). Some other properties of water are outlined next.

- Its specific weight (w_{Sp}) at 4°C (= 39º) is 9.81 kN/m^3 (= 62.4 Lb$_F$/Ft^3),
- Its critical pressure (P_C) is 218 Atm (= 22 MPa = 3200 PSIA),
- Its critical temperature (T_C) is 374°C (= 705°F = 647 K),

- Its enthalpy of evaporation (H_E, λ_E, or λ_Q) is 2257 kJ/kg,
- Its enthalpy of condensation (H_{Con}) is 2257 kJ/kg,
- Its freezing point temperature (T_{FP}) is 0°C (32°F),
- Its surface tension at 25°C is 72 × 10–3 N/m,
- Its viscosity (η) at 25°C is about 10^{-3} Pa.s,
- Its refractive index is 1.333, and
- Its absorbance is 0.

Although water boils at 100ºC (= 212 ºF) to form water vapor, it can evaporate into its vapor at all temperatures above 0 (above 32ºF) in an **open container**. This process, called evaporative cooling, happens because all temperatures above zero have a non-zero vapor pressure (P_V) at that T. Thus, water evaporates for a while. Then it becomes in equilibrium with its liquid state. But the water vapor escapes, creating a non-equilibrium situation that causes the water to continue evaporation. When, however, water is in a **closed container**, it would evaporate until its P_V reaches the surrounding P at that T. The opposite process, the condensation process, also happens because water vapor starts to condensate when the surrounding P is greater than its P_V at that T. Figure 4 demonstrates the heating graph of water.

According to the type of hydrogen existing in the water's molecules, water is classed into

- **Light water** (ordinary water or hydrogen hydroxide, H_2O) with an M_n of 18 g/mole), and
- **Heavy water** (deuterium oxide, D_2O) with an M_n of 20 g/mole.

Heavy water was first produced in 1932, shortly after discovering **deuterium** (D, also called heavy hydrogen, with one proton and one neutron). A heavy-water molecule (D_2O) contains two deuterium atoms instead of two H atoms of ordinary water (H_2O). Pure heavy water consists of 99.75% deuterium oxide (D_2O) and a small amount of ordinary hydrogen oxide (H_2O). [The additional neutron changes some of deuterium's chemical and physical properties. For example, the hydrogen-oxygen bonds in deuterium are stronger than in ordinary water. This and other differences make deuterium used in other applications.]

Because **heavy water**, unlike light water, does *not* readily absorb neutrons, it is used in nuclear reactors.

Most properties of **heavy water**, including its taste, are the same as water. The density of pure heavy water is 1107 kg/m^3 (about 11% heavier than water), and its T_{BP} is 101.4 (= 214.5ºF = 374.5 K). It is much more expensive than light water and is *not* radioactive.

At high temperatures and pressures, such as in the interior of some planets, water exists as **ionic water**, so its molecules break down into hydrogen and oxygen ions. And at even higher temperatures, water exists as **superionic water**, in which the released O_2 ions crystallize, and the H ions float freely around them. Under such conditions, water is in plasma form.

Water Vapor

Water vapor is the gas phase of liquid water (simply water). [Water vapor is generally known as vapor if it is *not* mentioned differently. The term saturated vapor is also used to refer to **saturated water vapor**. In nature, water vapor is continuously produced by evaporation and removed by condensation. In industry, it is produced from the boiling or evaporation of water.]

Water vapor is a greenhouse gas. Some other properties of water vapor are outlined next.

- It is lighter than air,
- Its molar mass (M_n) is 22.4 L/mole at STP,
- Its density (D) is 804 kg/m^3 (0.804 kg/L or 0.047 Lb/Ft^3),
- Its specific enthalpy (H_{Sp}) at −71 to 124ºC is 1.88 kJ/(kg.ºC),
- Its specific heat capacity (C_Q) at 25ºC is 4.186 kJ/kg.ºC or 75.4 kJ/(kmole.°C), and
- It condenses to water if its partial pressure (P_P) increases above the atmospheric pressure.

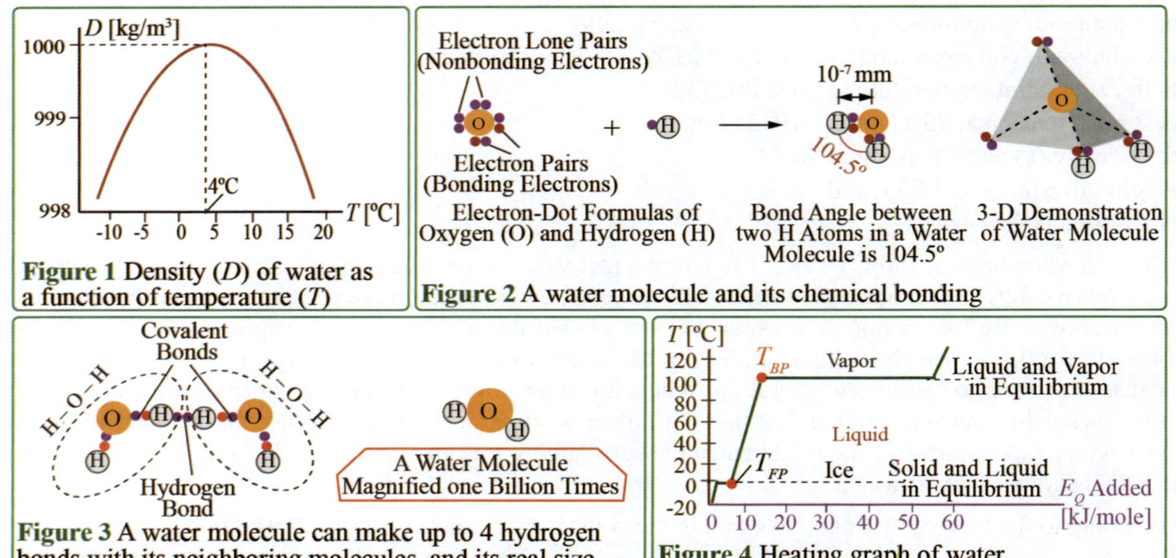

Figure 1 Density (D) of water as a function of temperature (T)

Figure 2 A water molecule and its chemical bonding

Figure 3 A water molecule can make up to 4 hydrogen bonds with its neighboring molecules, and its real size

Figure 4 Heating graph of water

The water vapor's specific gas constant (R_{Sp}) is determined using gas constant [R = 8314 kJ/(kg-mole.ºC)] and its molar mass (M_n = 18 kg/kg-mole).

$$R_{Sp} = \frac{R}{M_{Mol}} = \frac{8314}{18} = 461.5 \text{ J/(kg.ºC)}$$

The water vapor's specific volume (V_{Sp}) is expressed in m³/kg and calculated using its R_{Sp}, its P_P, and T (temperature) when it behaves like an ideal gas (this usually occurs below 66ºC).

$$V_{Sp} = \frac{R_{Sp}.T}{P_P} \quad (1)$$

When R_{SP} is in J/(kg.ºC), T is in ºC, and P_P is in Pa, the V_{Sp} becomes in m³/kg. When an ideal condition does *not* exist, the V_{Sp} is calculated as

$$V_{Sp} = (0.082T + 22.4)\left(\frac{1}{29} + \frac{W_{Sp}}{18}\right) \quad (2)$$

For example, if a water-vapor sample's W_{Sp} (specific humidity) at 95ºC is 0.015 kg water/kg dry air, the sample's V_{SP} will be

$$V_{Sp} = (0.082 \times 90 + 22.4)\left(\frac{1}{29} + \frac{0.015}{18}\right) = 1.066 \text{ m}^3\text{/kg dry air}$$

The water vapor's specific enthalpy (H_{Sp}) at a given T can be calculated using a reference temperature (T_R, usually 0C)

$$H_{Sp} = 2501.4 + 1.88(T - T_R) \quad (3)$$

W-5

WATER CLUSTER

A water cluster (also called a **hydrated cluster**, **hydrated cage**, **solvent cage**, or **salvation shell**) is formed when several water molecules surround a molecule of a nonionic compound.

Consider adding a few fine sugar crystals to a glass of water and stirring it to make a diluted sugar solution. In the solution, the water molecules move (scientifically diffuse) through the molecules of sugar (C_{12}, $H_{22}O_{11}$, a typical nonionic compound), and several water molecules surround a sugar molecule to form a **water-sugar cluster** (hydrated sugar cluster, H_2O-$C_{12}H_{22}O_{11}$-H_2O), as shown in Figure 1. As a result, each sugar molecule keeps its molecular structure the same as its solid form. A sugar molecule does *not* react with a water molecule, but it weakly bonds with several water molecules by hydrogen bonds to form a water-sugar cluster.

The number of molecules of solvent (in our example, water) surrounding each molecule of solute (in our example, sugar) in a hydrated solution is called the **hydration number** (N_H) of the solute. Some analytical methods can determine the N_H in a cluster, like NMR (nuclear magnetic resonance). The N_H can be calculated from the solute's activity coefficient, solute's molar volume (V_n), and solvent's V_n.

We now go to how water and sugar molecules get together to form a hydrated sugar solution. In a sugar molecule ($C_{12}H_{22}O_{11}$, with two rings of glucose and fructose), the bonds between two rings (–O–) and intermolecular bonds in each ring (C–H and C–O–H) are strong covalent bonds. Instead, the neighboring sucrose molecules are connected by weak hydrogen bonds. Thus, the neighboring molecules behave like the charged molecules, so they are only stable if each molecule is in contact with its nearest neighbor.

When sucrose crystals (each crystal contains many molecules) are mixed with water, water molecules (nonionic molecules) *cannot* penetrate between the sucrose molecules (nonionic molecules), although water is a good solvent. In addition, the **molecular distance** between the neighboring sucrose molecules depends on the amount of sucrose dissolved in a certain amount of water (the *less* concentrated a solution, the *greater* is the molecular distance). For example, in a 1% sucrose solution, the molecular distance is about 4 nm, while in a 40% solution, the distance is 1 nm. Instead, the molecular distance between the neighboring sucrose molecules is small (say, about 0.3 nm for 1 to 40% sucrose solutions). As a result, it is relatively easier for water molecules to move in between the sucrose molecules than sucrose molecules.

When the water and sucrose molecules are in touch, water molecules break the hydrogen bonds between the neighboring sucrose molecules (because of the weakness of hydrogen bonds) and form some new hydrogen bonds with the sucrose molecules. In this way, a few water molecules build a water cluster around each sucrose molecule. As a result, a solution with many **hydrated sucrose clusters** is formed. Note that water molecules *cannot* break the glycoside bond (–O–) between two rings of a sucrose molecule and intermolecular bonds in each ring (C–H and C–O–H) because they have covalent bond characteristics with a strong bonding ability. Thus far, we can say that the sucrose molecules in water do *not* decompose to individual components and stay intact. That is the reason that sucrose is a nonionic compound.

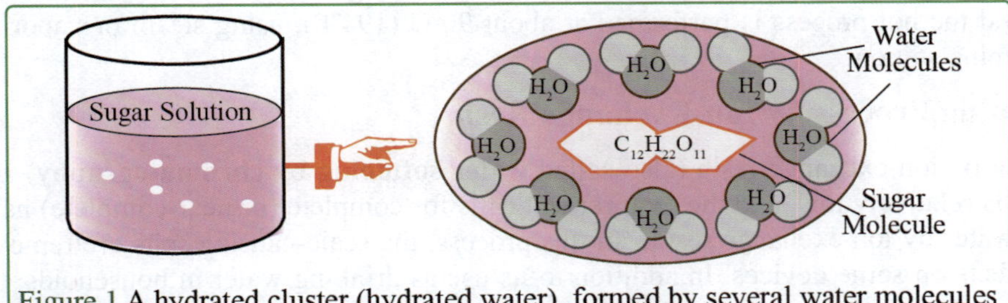

Figure 1 A hydrated cluster (hydrated water), formed by several water molecules around a sugar (sucrose) molecule in a pure sugar solution

W-6

WATER HAMMERING

Water hammering (cracking) is a symbolic term used in engineering to describe an action accompanied by discontinuous loud noises, like when a hammer hits a heavy object. In pumping operations, water hammering refers to the hitting of the bubbles formed by pump cavitation to the pump's blades, creating a loud noise.

In the condensation process, water hammering is an action in a condenser when the condensate accumulates in the condenser's vapor-receiving section, causing a loud noise. In the chemical process industry, water hammering is a serious operational problem (because it decreases the efficiency of the process).

W-7

WATER SOFTENING PROCESS

As a process unit (unit operation) of ChemEng, water softening is the process of removing scale-causing salts (also called **limesalt hardness** or simply **limesalts** or **hardness**) from hard water (like city water or well water) to produce soft water (water with minimum or *no* hardness).

Typically, hard water is classified into four (4) classes:

- **Slightly Hard Water:** It contains 17 to 60 PPM of limesalts hardness.
- **Moderately Hard Water:** It contains 60 to 120 PPM of hardness.
- **Hard Water:** It contains 120 to 180 PPM of hardness.
- **Extremely Hard Water:** It contains more than 180 PPM of hardness.

A quality soft water has a low specific conductance in the range of 0 to 4 μS/cm, corresponding to 0 to 2 PPM of scale causing salts (soluble salts of Ca and Mg, such as $CaCO_3$, $CaSO_4$, $MgSO_4$, and CaC_2O_4,)

Some chemical plants have a water-softening station to produce soft water used in different ways, including in the steam boilers to produce supersaturated steam (simply **super steam** or **live steam**). Hard water is usually softened in a chemical process plant by one of the following two methods: 1) Water softening process by chemicals. 2) Water softening process by an ion-exchange resin.

Water Softening Process by Chemicals

Water softening by chemicals is used when the hardness (scale-causing salts) content in water is relatively high, and the requirement does *not* call for complete hardness removal. It produces soft water from hard water (like city water or well water) using chemical compounds. In this process, caustic soda (NaOH), soda ash (Na_2CO_3), or a combination of both is used to precipitate (↓) scale-causing salts. In the **combination method**, liquid caustic and powdered soda ash are mixed with water to precipitate scale-causing salts. The precipitate is then removed from the water by filtration. Cold chemical softening is performed at room temperature (around 25°C or 77°F), and the hot process is performed at about 90°C (194°F), using steam or vapor to heat the feed water to the softening station.

Water Softening Process by Ion-Exchange Resin

Water softening by ion-exchange resin (also called **water softening by chromatography**) is used when the hardness content is relatively low, and the requirement calls for complete (or near-complete) hardness removal. It produces soft water by ion exchange resin. In this process, the scale-causing salts are removed to eliminate their negative effects on some devices. In addition to its use as drinking water in households, the soft water is produced in chemical plants to be mainly used as

- Feedwater in steam boilers and cooling towers, and

- Deionized water for making reagents in chemical laboratories.

The softening process is performed in two (or more) softening columns, usually filled with cationic ion-exchange resin to a certain level. As hard water enters the column, it passes through the resin bed. During the process, cations that cause water hardness are exchanged for sodium cations in the resin's functional group. At the same time, sodium cations leave the resin and dissolve in the water. As a result, undesirable hard-water cations (Ca^{2+} and Mg^{2+}) are exchanged for sodium cations (Na^+), *not* scale-causing cations.

Generally, the cationic resin (catex) in the Na^+ form is shown as $R\text{-}SO_3Na$ (or simply as R-Na), and scale-causing salts are shown as Ca^{2+} and Mg^{2+}. Considering these symbolizations, when hard water passes through the resin bed, the following exchanges take place:

$$2R\text{-}Na + Ca^{2+} \leftrightarrow R_2\text{-}Ca + 2Na^+ \qquad 2\ R\text{-}Na + Mg^{2+} \leftrightarrow R_2\text{-}Mg + 2\ Na^+$$

In these equations, R indicates the resin's structure (**matrix** in resin technology), R-Na is the resin's functional group, and Na is the resin's exchanging ion. The above-exchanging reactions are based on the resin's higher attractive energy (chemical affinity) for divalent cations in the solution than monovalent cations in the resin. Thus, sodium ions (Na^+) from the resin are replaced by Ca^{2+} and Mg^{2+} in the solution.

These reactions occur until the resin particles get exhausted (lose exchanging capacity). At this point, the resin is **regenerated**. For regeneration, saltwater containing Na ions is pumped through the resin to replace Ca and Mg ions for Na ions and bring the resin to its original Na^+ form with enough exchanging capacity. The following equations occur during regeneration:

$$R_2\text{-}Ca + 2\ Na^+ \leftrightarrow R\text{-}Na + Ca^{2+} \qquad 2\ R_2\text{-}Mg + 2Na^+ \leftrightarrow R\text{-}Na + Mg^{2+}$$

[Note 1: The mixed-bed softening is used to prepare better quality soft water. In this process, strong cationic and anionic resins are used separately in two different columns to take care of the hard water's cations and anions.]

[Note 2: If the raw-water source has too much suspended solid particles, a coagulant is first used to settle these particles. The process is followed by filtration before being fed to the softening column.]

Pressure Drop

Pressure drop (generally known as pressure difference, ΔP) across the resin bed is one of the most important factors in designing a water softening station. It is recommended that the softening columns be designed so that the pressure drop across the control valves does *not* exceed 7 kPa (about 1 PSI). The two most important factors that usually affect the pressure drop are the following:

- **Depth of Resin Bed:** The deeper the bed height, the more pressure drop the system has.
- **Feed Velocity to Softening Column:** The feed velocity should be kept at about 0.04 m^3/min per m^2 of resin bed (about 10 Ga/min per Ft^2 of resin area) to prevent high ΔP.

The surface area of the resin bed, column design, and type and size of control valves also affect the ΔP.

Determination of Operating Capacity of an Ion-Exchange Softening Station

The daily operating capacity of a softening station refers to the size of the softening columns, which dictates the size of pipes, valves, and other attached and detached devices. In calculations of a softening station's capacity, the softening-equipment suppliers usually use the following three practical rules:

- Pressure drop (ΔP) across each column should *not* be high.
- Each softening column should *not* be regenerated more than once a day.
- Feed velocity to each column should *not* be more than 0.5 m^3 per minute per m^2 of resin-bed surface area ($\approx$ 12 Ga/min/Ft^2 resin-bed area), ideally about 0.4 m^3/min per m^2 of resin bed (about 10 Ga/min per Ft^2).

To determine the capacity of a column, we need to know the amount of scale-causing salts in the hard water to be processed as feed in the columns. We base our calculations here on the assumption that hardness is 550 g in 1 m^3 of hard water (about 1.1 g hardness in 1 Ga of water). Further, we use the following data that softening columns manufacturers usually use:

- The amount of salt needed to regenerate is 160 kg per m^3 of resin (10 Lb per Ft^3 of resin),
- 1 kg of salt can remove 0.4 kg hardness from the hard water, and
- The amount of resin in each column is 3 m^3 (106 Ft^3).

The salt dosage of 160 kg per m^3 of resin means that 160 kg salt can remove 160 × 0.4 × 1000 = 64 000 g of hardness. Because we assumed that 3 m^3 resin is in each column, the total hardness removal in one column will be 64000 × 3 = 192 000 g. Thus, this amount divided by the amount of hardness in g/m^3 gives us the processing capacity of each column.

$$\frac{192000}{550} = 350 \text{ m}^3 \ (= 92400 \text{ Ga})$$

This value tells us that the column needs to be regenerated at a hardness content of 550 g/m^3 after processing 350 m^3 of hard water.

Salt Requirement for Regeneration: At 160 kg salt per m^3 of resin, the column would use 160 × 3 = 480 kg of salt per 350 m^3 of softened water. This equates to 1056 Lb salt per 92 400 Ga of water processed.

Station Capacity: The station's number of required columns (the station's capacity) is determined based on the amount of hard water softened a day. If the plant needs to soften 1 000 m^3/day, the softening station needs three (3) columns, each at 350 m^3 capacity. [Usually, one or two extra columns cover other columns under the regeneration process.]

W-8

WATT AND WATT HOUR

The word **Watt** (W) is used to refer to **Watt-hour** (more correctly Watt per hour or Watt/hour), which is the SI unit of electric energy (E_E = energy per time). Watt is named after Scottish scientist James Watt (1736 – 1819) and is defined as joule (J) per second (J/s), where 1 J/s = 1 W/h.

Watt hour (W.h or W/h) is defined as kJ (kilo joule) per hour (kJ/h), where 1 kJ/s = 1 kW/h (the amount of energy equivalent to a power of 1 kW running for 1 h). 1 kW/h = 1 000 W/h × 3600 = 3 600 000 W/s = 3 600 000 J = 3.6 MJ (mega joule), where 1 W/h = 1 J/s.

[Note: The term W/h is often written in reference books as Wh, W.h, or just W. Similarly, instead of kW/h, some write kWh or just kW. And instead of W/s (Watt per second), some write W.s and read watt-second.]

Watt per hour (W/h) is used to measure the following:

- The rate of electricity (electric energy) usage (also called **power consumption** or **energy consumption**). When, say, a light bulb with a rating of 100 W is on for 1 h, its electricity usage is 100 W/h (= 0.1 kW/h).
- The rate of energy transfer or heat transfer. For example, about 1 kW/h (1 kW per hour) of heat energy (E_Q) is transferred from Sun to 1 m^2 of the Earth's surface area on a clear day at midday.

To have a sense of the amount of W/h and kW/h, study the following:

- Household light bulbs are usually rated 60, 75, or 100 W/h.
- A small electric heater with one heating element can use 1 kW of electricity per hour (1 kW/h).
- A typical house with an electric range and an electric washer-and-dryer uses about 1000 kW per month.

W-9

WAVE AND WAVELENGTH

Wave

Wave is the periodic (repeating) movement of energy (E) through a **medium** (like air) from one point to another by vibration (oscillation). A wave can be viewed as an oscillation of particles that transfer E from one location of a medium to another. Thus, a wave moves the particles of its **medium** (an area consisting of particles of a solid, a liquid, or a gas). As a form of energy in a periodic motion, ocean waves vibrate the water molecules, and sound waves vibrate the air molecules.

The following are three (3) general properties of waves:

- Waves travel periodically but in different shapes and at different speeds.
- Waves are everywhere, in space and even in a vacuum that contains almost *no* particles.
- Waves move the particles of their media in different ways. For example, the light's waves move the photons (the light's particles) forward as fast as the waves move. And water's waves move its molecules forward, but *not* as fast as the waves move.

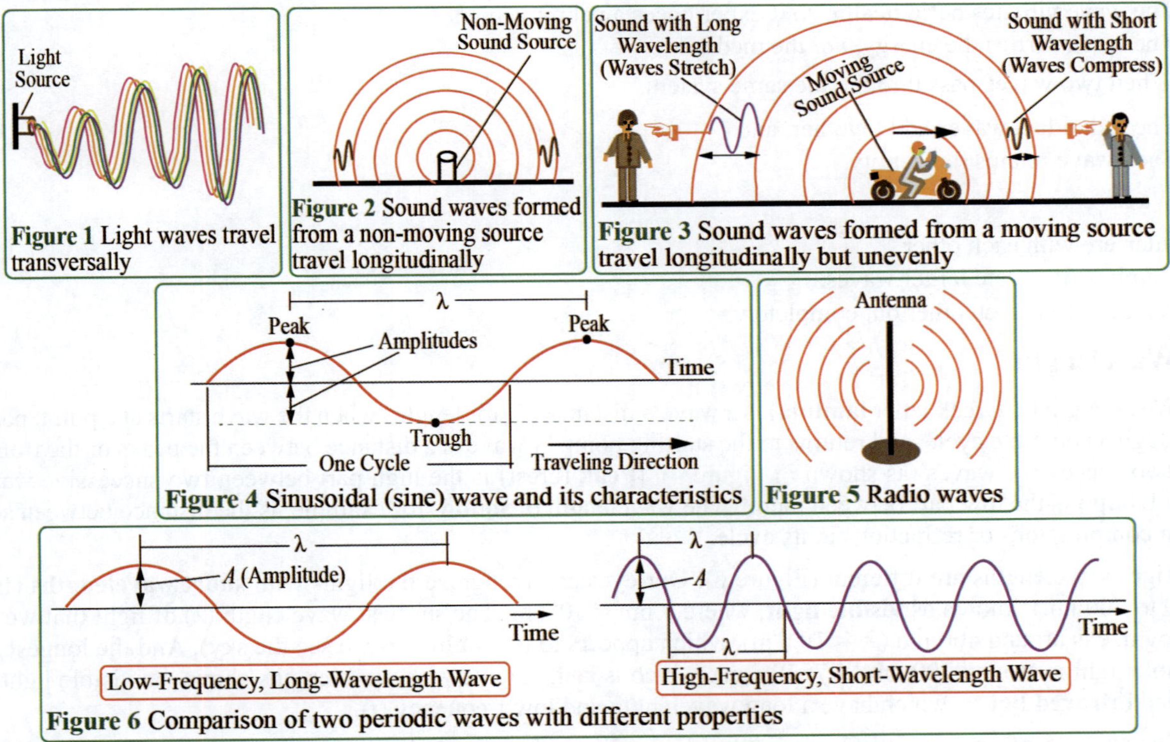

Figure 1 Light waves travel transversally

Figure 2 Sound waves formed from a non-moving source travel longitudinally

Figure 3 Sound waves formed from a moving source travel longitudinally but unevenly

Figure 4 Sinusoidal (sine) wave and its characteristics

Figure 5 Radio waves

Figure 6 Comparison of two periodic waves with different properties

The following are a few types of waves:

- **Transverse Waves:** In transverse waves, like light waves (Figure 1), the particles move at a right angle to the direction the waves are moving.
- **Longitudinal Waves:** In longitudinal waves, like sound waves (Figures 2 and 3), the particles move back and forth in the same direction the waves are moving.
- **Sinusoidal Wave:** In sinusoidal (sine) waves (Figure 4), all the pulses have the same size and shape as they move through a medium.

- **Electromagnetic Waves:** Electromagnetic waves (EM waves), like radio waves (Figure 5), do *not* need a medium to move through, so the E (energy) can be transferred by the waves even in a vacuum (because EM waves do *not* need a particle-containing medium to move through).

Aside from being an energy carrier, a wave has three (3) general characteristics:

- **Wavelength:** Wavelength (λ) is the distance between one peak (or one trough) and the next; in other words, it is the distance from the start of one wave cycle to the start of the next. As shown in Figure 5, the wavelength can be measured between any two corresponding points.
- **Amplitude:** Amplitude (A) is half the height of a wave from its peak or trough, as shown in Figure 5. It describes the maximum displacement at a peak (or trough).
- **Velocity:** Because velocity (V) is a vector quantity, a wave also has a vector that acts in the wave's direction. The V of a wave can be calculated from its λ as $2\pi/\lambda$.

[In the subjects of light and other EM waves, λ and f (frequency) are usually considered two sides of the same coin by specifying one instead of the other. If a wave travels one λ in a second, it has a 1 Hertz (Hz) frequency. An ocean wave might have an f of 0.2 Hz, but a light wave has an f of about 500 trillion Hz.]

When a wave moves through a medium,

- The medium vibrates in place; therefore, it experiences *no* net movement.
- The wave vibrates periodically, so it experiences a net movement.
- The wave carries the energy, *not* the medium.

When two waves pass through the same system,

- The individual waves add together, and
- Each wave retains its identity.

Waves can

- Interfere with each other.
- Combine to create larger waves.
- Cancel (stop) each other out completely.

Wavelength

Wavelength (λ, Greek letter **lambda**) is a wave's distance (L, for length) when the wave starts at a point, passes through a complete cycle, and returns to the starting point. A wave is a distance between the peaks or the troughs of two successive waves (as shown in Figure 4). [**Peak** (crest) is the high part between two successive waves, and **trough** is the low part between them.] The wavelength of **sound**, for example, is the distance between adjacent compressions or refractions in its cycle.

Light wavelengths are different (Figure 6). Our eyes can recognize the lights with **short wavelengths** (from 400 to 700 nm), known as **visible light**, where 1 nm = 10^{-9} m. The shortest wavelength (λ) of light that we can recognize is around 400 nm (= 4×10^{-7} m), which appears to us as **blue** (as we see the sky). And the longest λ of visible light is around 700 nm (= 7×10^{-7} m), which is **red**. Lights with wavelengths above the visible light are called **infrared lights**, which have a long wavelength and low frequency (f).

The strength of light is given by its λ (the *shorter* the λ, the *greater* is its E). Comparing the color of a fresh torch with a dying torch can make the subject clearer. The flame of the fresh torch appears blue because it comparatively has shorter λ and greater E (because it is hotter). When the torch is dying, it cools and thus appears red because it has longer λ and lowers E (because it is colder). Thus, the hotter the source, the more short-wavelength wave it releases. This is familiar to us from the glow of an electric heater as it warms. This rule *applies* to light and other electromagnetic waves (EM waves). An EM wave with shorter λ (or greater f) carries more E than an

EM wave with longer λ (or smaller *f*). Thus, if more *E* is in an EM wave, the wave's λ is shorter. Similarly, if a photon (the light's particle) has longer λ, it is less energetic.

The relation between a wave's *U* (speed), λ (wavelength), and its *f* (frequency) is

$$U = \lambda . f \qquad \text{or} \qquad \lambda = \frac{U}{f} \tag{1}$$

Because EM waves, including light, always travel through a vacuum at the speed of light constant (*c*), their λ is related to their *f* as

$$\lambda = \frac{c}{f} \tag{2}$$

Thus, the *longer* the λ (wavelength) of a wave, the *smaller* is its *f* (frequency).

The λ of a moving quantum particle (a particle with *no* subparticle, like an electron), which is called the **Broglie's wavelength**, is given as

$$\lambda = \frac{h}{M.V} \tag{3}$$

In this equation (called **Broglie's equation**), *h* is Planck's constant (= 6.625×10^{-34} J.s), *M* is the particle's rest mass, *V* is the particle's velocity, and the *M.V* is the particle's momentum. [Because EM waves can be treated as particles (called photons), particles may behave like waves under some conditions.]

Physics measures the speed of a wave by following the moving peaks (or troughs). Ocean waves, for instance, move at around 10 m/s, and sound travels at about 343 m/s through the air and 1500 m/s through the water. Physics uses the space between the peaks of the light's waves to measure its λ. If, for example, one light wave peaks 4 times in one second and the other peaks 8 times per second, then the second wave has shorter λ (because the waves' speed is the same).

[Note 1: In the subjects of EM waves, λ and *f* are usually considered as two sides of the same coin by specifying one instead of the other.]

[Note 1: The difference between the wavelength (λ) of electron and light is used in an electronic microscope, which gives far greater magnification (because λ of an electron beam is up to 100 000 times shorter than a light beam λ.]

W-10

WAVE PARTICLE DUALITY

The wave-particle duality is a theory that states an elementary particle (simply **particle**) can be described as a wave. First, this theory was explained by Einstein in his 1905's paper, in which he said that the light particles (the photons) *cannot* be described as particles or as waves but as a combination of both. In another context, the photons, and other electromagnetic radiations, have double (wave-and-particle) properties, but never both at the same time. Depending on the situation, they behave like waves at one time and like particles at another time, but they *cannot* behave as both at the same time. Later in 1926, Broglie published a paper proving that the particles of all matters, including electrons, atoms, and even molecules, demonstrate wavelike and particlelike properties.

The next important points can be made about Broglie's theory of duality of matter.

It is easier to detect an electron's wave property (because of its large wavelength and extremely tiny mass), so it is better to describe electrons with their wave property.

- It is not easy to detect a molecule's wave property (because of its extremely short wavelength), so it is better to describe molecules with their particle property.

[Study also EINSTEIN'S THEORY OF LIGHT DUALITY.]

W-11

WAVEFUNCTION

Study QUANTUM WAVEFUNCTION.

W-12

WEAK NUCLEAR FORCE

Discussed under FUNDAMENTAL FORCES OF NATURE.

W-13

WEIGHT

Study MASS AND WEIGHT.

W-14

WEIGHTED AVERAGE

Discussed under AVERAGES OF DATA.

W-15

WET BULB TEMPERATURE

Study AIR WET BULB TEMPERATURE.

W-16

WET BULB THERMOMETER

Discussed under THERMOMETERS.

W-17

WET GAS SCRUBBERS

Another name for **gas scrubbers**. It is discussed under GAS SCRUBBERS AND GAS CYCLONES.

W-18

WET SURFACE AIR COOLERS

Discussed under EVAPORATIVE COOLING DEVICES.

W-19

WORK AND ITS TYPES

Work

Work (W, refers to **mechanical work**) is the effect of force (F) applied on a system through a distance (L, for length). It can be viewed as the energy (E) transferred (because E can perform useful W), so sometimes it is called **work energy**. In equation form, W is the product of two vector quantities: force (F) in the direction of motion and distance (L).

$$W = F.L \tag{1}$$

The work, for example, done on a box, shown in Figure 1, to slide it along a flat surface is the product of a horizontal F applied to the box to overcome the friction between the floor and the bottom of the box multiplied by the displacement distance (L) of the box. Because W is a vector quantity, the angle (β) between the force that acts on the box and the displacement vector plays a role in the result of the W done on the box. As shown in the same figure, three cases may occur in relation to β:

- When F is parallel to L, where $\cos\beta = \cos 0° = 1$, the equation for work is $W = F.L$.
- When F is perpendicular to L, where $\cos\beta = \cos 90° = 0$, *no* work is done, so $W = 0$.
- When F is *not* parallel to L but separated by angle β, Equation 1 becomes,

$$W = F.L.\cos\beta \tag{2}$$

W can be positive or negative. W is **positive** when it is done **on** the system of interest by the system's surroundings. W is **negative** when it is done on the surrounding **by** a system. Figure 2 shows a system under a vacuum when a mass of M is applied to it. As shown on the left side of the figure, the mass M compresses the system to a new position when the stops are pulled out. Here the performed W is **positive** (because W is done **on** the system by its surroundings). The system is compressed on the right side of the figure, so when the stops are pulled out, the system expands to a new position. Here the performed W is **negative** (because W is done on the outside **by** the system).

Both work and heat energy (E_Q) are energies, but with the following two differences:

- W is caused by a force (F), while E_Q is caused by a temperature difference (ΔT),
- W is a higher-quality E (energy), while E_Q is a lower-quality E.

Based on the work-energy principle, the change in the kinetic energy (E_K) of a system equates to the net work done on the system; this is (final – initial) or (2 – 1).

$$W = \frac{1}{2}M.V_2^2 - \frac{1}{2}M.V_1^2 \tag{3}$$

This principle, which generally indicates the relation between W and E, is one of the Law of Energy Conservation applications.

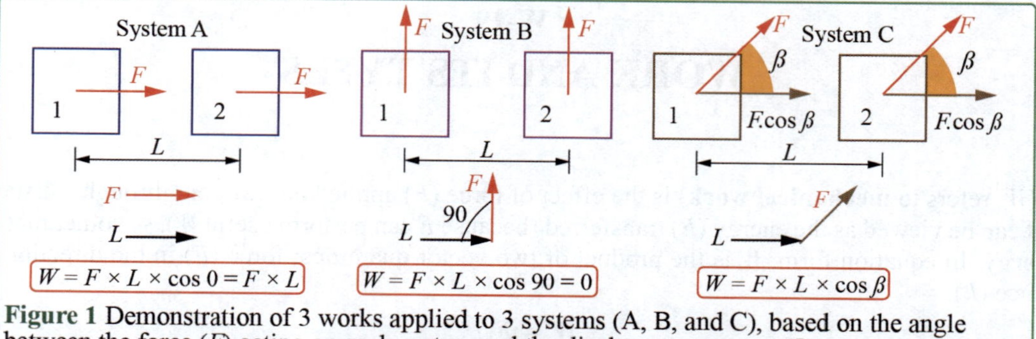

Figure 1 Demonstration of 3 works applied to 3 systems (A, B, and C), based on the angle between the force (*F*) acting on each system and the displacement vector (*L*)

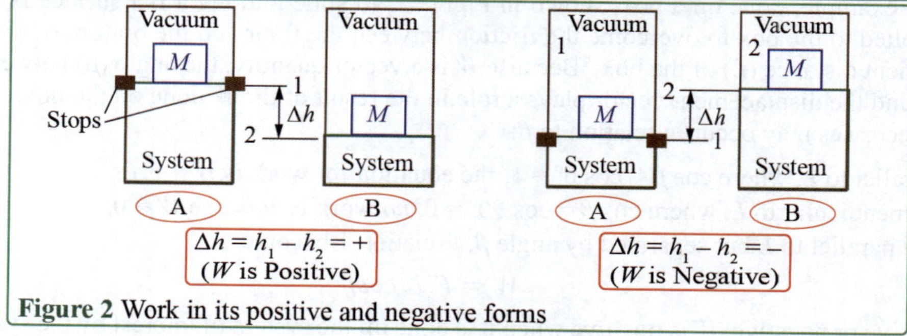

Figure 2 Work in its positive and negative forms

Work is

- A vector quantity (such vector has both magnitude and direction),
- A path quantity (it depends on the path taken to act), and
- A fixed quantity (it does *not* depend on time, *t*).

[Work, energy (*E*), and enthalpy (*H*) have the same unit, Joule (J).]

Work can be expressed in the differential form to calculate the rate of change infinitesimally (in an extremely small change). The dW done by a system when force (F) is parallel to L is given by

$$dW = F.dL \tag{4}$$

Work can also be expressed in the integral form to calculate it when the distance L changes in a tiny (infinitesimal) amount from point 1 to point 2. So, integrating Equation 4 over a limited (finite) distance of point 1 to point 2 will result

$$W = \int_1^2 F.dL = F(L_2 - L_1) \tag{5}$$

Work is usually measured by lifting a mass (M) to a height (h). In the Earth's gravitational field (which has a gravitational acceleration of a_g), the work needed to lift an M is given by the h, through which the mass is lifted.

$$W = M.a_g.h \tag{6}$$

This is known as the gravitational work (W_g). If, for example, work is done **by a system** to lift a mass of 1 kg in 2 m, the W_g will be

$$W_g = M.a_g.h = -1 \times 9.81 \times 2 = -19.62\ (\text{kg.m}^2)/\text{s}^2 = -19.62\ \text{J}$$

Work Types

Work has other kinds, including the following:

- Flow work ($W_F = P.V$), where P is for pressure and V is for volume, and
- Shaft work ($W_S = 2T_R\pi.N$), where T_R is for torque and N is for rotations per time (RPM, rotation per minute).

[Work (W) and electric power (P_E, simply **power**) are often confused. Work is the product of force (F) multiplied by the distance (L for length), while power is the product of W divided by t (time); in other words, power is a rate at which work is done. Study the upcoming example.]

When an adiabatic process (a process with *no* heat transfer) occurs in a closed system (energy can enter or leave the system, but mass *cannot*), a system's E_I (internal energy) can be calculated from W done on that system to change it from one state to another.

$$\Delta E_I = W \quad (7)$$

The symbol Δ indicates the value of E_I in the initial state (that is E_{I1}) minus that in the final state (that is E_{I2}), so $\Delta E_I = E_{I2} - E_{I1}$. Equation 7 tells us the following:

- W is done on the system by its surroundings,
- W and E_I are positive when W is done on the system by its surroundings, and
- E_I (internal energy) of the system increases when W is done on it by its surroundings.

The other form of Equation 7 is

$$\Delta E_I = -W \quad (8)$$

This equation, on the contrary, tells us that,

- W is done by the system on its surroundings,
- W and E_I are **negative** when W is done by the system on its surroundings, and
- The system's E_I (internal energy) decreases when it does some W (work) on its surroundings.

An Example on Work

Calculate a man's work (W) output and his power (P_E) output if he weighs 700 N walkups a ladder 4 m high in 4 s.

The work done by the man is against gravity through a distance (L) of 4 m

$$W = F.L = 700 \times 4 = 2800 \text{ N.m (or J)}$$

Then, power output will be

$$P_E = \frac{W}{t} = \frac{2800}{4} = 700 \text{ J/s (or w/h)}$$

It is worth mentioning that man would have done just as much work against gravity if he had climbed 4 m high if the ladder, supposedly, was in an exact vertical position.

X, Y, and Z Sections

LIST OF X-TOPICS

1. X-Rays

X- 1

X-RAYS

As an invisible wave to the human eye, an X-ray (X-wave) is one of the seven types of electromagnetic waves (EM waves or EM radiations), with a wavelength (λ) shorter than that of visible light. The λ of X-waves is between 0.01 nm and 10 nm, and its f (frequency) is between 30 EHz and 30 PHz, where E is for eta (10^{18}), P is for pita (10^{15}), and Hz is for Hertz (the SI unit of f).

The X-rays exhibit similar properties as EM waves, including the following:

- After gamma rays, the X-rays have the second shortest wavelengths of all seven.
- After gamma rays, the X-rays have the second-highest photon energy of all seven.
- Like gamma rays, the X-rays have an extreme penetrating ability on the human body.
- The X-ray photons carry hundreds to thousands of times more energy than the light photons.
- The X-rays are produced by systems that can create extremely high temperatures (in millions of °C).
- The X-rays produced by sunlight are absorbed by the atmosphere (despite their high penetrating ability).

Because of their extreme penetrating ability, the X-rays are used in medical and industrial uses. **Radiotherapy** (oncology for cancer treatment) is one of their medical uses. In industry, it is used in crystallography, by which a crystal structure can be studied.

LIST OF Y-TOPICS

1. Yeast
2. Yellowcake

Y-1

YEAST

See MOLD AND YEAST.

Y-2

YELLOWCAKE

Study URANIUM YELLOWCAKE.

LIST OF Z-TOPICS

1. Zero Point Energy
2. Zero Pressure
3. Zero Vacuum

Z-1

ZERO POINT ENERGY

Discussed under the topic of ENERGY AND ITS FORMS.

Z-2

ZERO PRESSURE

Study VACUUM PRESSURE.

Z-3

ZERO VACUUM

Study VACUUM PRESSURE.

Table Section

LIST OF TABLES

[Note 1: **Periodic Table of Elements** is given inside this book's front cover.]

[Note 2: **Table of Unit Conversion Factors** is given inside the back cover.]

Table 1 Saturated Steam Table for Steam and Water at Equilibrium (in SI and US units)

Temperature [ºC]	Vapor Pressure [kPa]	Enthalpy [kJ/kg]			Temperature [ºF]	Vapor Pressure [Lb/In²]	Enthalpy [BTU/Lb]		
		Vapor (H_V)	Liquid (H_L)	Enthalpy of Evaporation			Vapor (H_V)	Liquid (H_L)	Enthalpy of Evaporation
0	0.6	2501.6	0.0	2501.6	32	0.1	1075.4	0.0	1075.4
5	0.9	2510.7	21.0	2489.7	35	0.1	1076.7	3.0	1073.7
10	1.2	2519.9	42.0	2477.9	40	0.1	1078.9	8.0	1070.9
15	1.7	2528.9	62.9	2466.0	45	0.2	1081.1	13.0	1068.1
20	2.2	2538.2	83.9	2454.3	50	0.2	1083.3	18.1	1065.2
25	3.2	2547.3	104.8	2442.5	55	0.2	1085.5	23.1	1062.4
30	4.3	2556.3	125.8	2430.5	60	0.3	1087.7	28.1	1059.6
35	5.6	2565.4	146.6	2418.8	65	0.3	1089.9	33.1	1056.8
40	7.4	2574.3	167.6	2406.7	70	0.4	1092.0	38.1	1053.9
45	9.6	2583.2	188.5	2394.7	75	0.4	1094.2	43.1	1051.1
50	12.4	2592.1	209.3	2382.8	80	0.5	1096.4	48.1	1048.3
55	15.8	2600.9	230.2	2370.7	85	0.6	1098.6	53.1	1045.5
60	19.9	2609.6	251.1	2358.5	90	0.7	1100.7	58.1	1042.6
65	25.0	2618.3	272.1	2346.2	95	0.8	1102.9	63.1	1039.8
70	31.2	2626.8	293.0	2333.8	100	1.0	1105.0	68.1	1037.0
75	38.6	2635.3	313.0	2321.4	110	1.3	1109.3	78.0	1031.3
80	47.4	2643.7	314.9	2308.8	120	1.7	1113.5	88.0	1025.5
85	57.8	2651.9	355.9	2296.0	130	2.2	1117.8	98.0	1019.8
90	70.1	2660.1	376.9	2283.2	140	2.9	1121.9	108.0	1013.9
95	84.6	2668.1	398.0	2270.1	150	3.7	1126.1	118.0	1008.1
100	101.3	2676.1	419.0	2257.1	160	4.8	1130.1	128.0	1002.1
105	120.8	2683.8	440.2	2243.7	170	6.0	1134.2	138.0	996.2
110	143.3	2691.5	461.3	2230.2	180	7.5	1138.2	148.0	990.2
115	169.1	2699.0	482.5	2216.5	190	9.3	1142.1	158.0	984.1
120	198.5	2706.3	503.7	2202.6	200	11.5	1145.9	168.1	977.8
125	232.1	2713.5	525.0	2188.5	210	14.1	1149.7	178.1	971.6
130	270.1	2720.5	546.3	2174.2	220	17.2	1153.5	188.2	965.3
135	313.0	2727.3	567.7	2159.6	230	20.8	1157.1	198.3	958.8
140	361.3	2733.9	589.1	2144.8	240	25.0	1160.7	208.4	952.3
145	415.4	2740.3	610.6	2129.7	250	29.8	1164.2	218.6	945.6
150	475.8	2746.5	632.2	2114.3	260	35.4	1167.6	228.8	938.8
155	543.1	2752.4	653.8	2098.6	270	41.9	1170.9	239.0	932.0
160	617.8	2758.1	675.6	2082.6	280	49.2	1174.1	249.2	924.9
165	700.5	2763.5	697.3	2066.2	290	57.5	1177.2	259.4	917.8
170	791.7	2768.7	719.2	2049.5	300	67.0	1180.2	269.7	910.5
175	892.0	2773.6	741.2	2032.4	310	77.6	1183.0	280.1	902.9
180	1002	2778.2	763.2	2015.0	320	89.6	1185.8	290.4	895.4
190	1254	2786.4	807.6	1978.8	340	117.9	1190.8	313.3	879.5
200	1554	2793.2	852.5	1940.8	350	134.5	1193.1	321.8	871.3
225	2548	2803.3	966.8	1836.5	360	152.9	1195.2	332.4	862.9
250	3973	2801.5	1085.4	1716.1	370	173.2	1197.2	343.0	854.2
275	5942	2785.0	1210.1	1574.9	380	195.6	1199.0	353.6	845.4
300	8581	2749.0	1344.0	1405.0	390	220.2	1200.6	364.3	836.3

Abstracted from Steam Tables by Keenan (1969)

Table 2 Supersaturated (Superheated) Steam Table for Steam Specific Enthalpies (H_{Sp}, in kJ/kg)

Steam P_{Abs} [kPa]	Temperature [°C]							
	100	150	200	250	300	360	420	500
10	2687.5	2783.0	2879.5	2977.3	3076.5	3197.6	3320.9	3489.1
50	2682.5	2780.1	2877.7	2976.0	3075.5	3196.8	3320.4	3488.7
75	2679.4	2778.2	2876.5	2975.2	3074.9	3196.4	3320.0	3488.4
100	2676.2	2776.4	2875.3	2974.3	3074.3	3195.9	3319.6	3488.1
150		2772.6	2872.9	2972.7	3073.1	3195.0	3318.9	3487.6
400		2752.8	2860.5	2964.2	3066.8	3190.3	3315.3	3484.9
700			2844.8	2953.6	3059.1	3184.7	3310.9	3481.7
1000			2827.9	2942.6	3051.2	3178.9	3306.5	3478.5
1500			2796.8	2923.3	3037.6	3169.2	3299.1	3473.1
2000				2902.5	3023.5	3159.3	3291.6	3467.6
2500				2880.1	3008.8	3149.1	3284.0	3462.1
3000				2855.8	2993.5	3138.7	3276.3	3456.5

Abstracted from Steam Tables by Keenan (1969)

Table 3 Physical Properties of Saturated Water at Different Temperatures (T)

T [ºC]	Density D [kg/m³]	Specific Heat Capacity C_Q [kJ/(kg.ºC)]	Thermal Conductivity K_T [W/(m.ºC)]	Thermal Diffusivity D_T [$\times 10^{-6}$ m²/s]	Viscosity η [$\times 10^{-6}$ Pa.s]
0	999.9	4.226	0.558	0.131	1793.64
5	1000.0	4.206	0.568	0.135	1534.74
10	999.7	4.195	0.557	0.137	1296.44
15	999.1	4.187	0.587	0.141	1135.61
20	998.2	4.182	0.597	0.143	993.41
25	997.1	4.178	0.606	0.146	880.64
30	995.7	4.176	0.615	0.149	792.38
35	994.1	4.175	0.624	0.150	719.81
40	992.2	4.175	0.633	0.151	658.03
45	990.2	4.176	0.640	0.155	605.07
50	988.1	4.178	0.647	0.157	555.06
55	985.7	4.179	0.652	0.158	509.95
60	983.2	4.181	0.658	0.159	471.65
65	980.6	4.184	0.663	0.161	435.42
70	977.8	4.187	0.668	0.163	404.03
75	974.9	4.190	0.671	0.164	376.58
80	971.8	4.194	0.673	0.165	352.06
85	968.7	4.198	0.676	0.166	328.52
90	965.3	4.202	0.678	0.167	308.91
95	961.9	4.206	0.680	0.168	292.24
100	958.4	4.211	0.682	0.169	277.53
120	943.5	4.232	0.684	0.171	235.36
140	926.3	4.257	0.686	0.172	201.04
160	907.6	4.285	0.680	0.173	171.62
180	886.6	4.396	0.673	0.172	152.00
200	862.8	4.501	0.665	0.170	139.25
220	837.0	4.605	0.652	0.164	124.54
240	809.0	4.731	0.634	0.162	113.76

Table 4 Properties of Dry Air at Atmospheric Pressure and Different Temperatures

Temperature T [°C]	Density D [kg/m³]	Specific Heat Capacity C_Q [kJ/(kg.°C)]	Thermal Conductivity K_T [W/(m.°C)]	Thermal Diffusivity D_T [×10⁻⁶ m²/s]	Viscosity η [×10⁻⁶ Pa.s]
- 20	1.37	1.005	0.023	18.8	16.28
0	1.25	1.011	0.024	19.2	17.46
10	1.20	1.010	0.024	20.7	17.85
20	1.16	1.012	0.025	22.0	18.24
30	1.27	1.013	0.026	23.4	18.68
40	1.09	1.014	0.027	24.8	19.12
50	1.06	1.016	0.027	24.2	19.52
60	1.03	1.017	0.028	27.6	19.91
70	1.00	1.018	0.029	29.2	20.40
80	0.97	1.019	0.029	30.6	20.79
90	0.94	1.021	0.030	32.2	21.23
100	0.92	1.022	0.031	33.6	21.67
120	0.87	1.025	0.032	37.0	22.56
140	0.83	1.027	0.033	40.0	23.34
160	0.79	1.013	0.034	43.3	24.12
180	0.77	1.032	0.036	47.0	24.91
200	0.72	1.035	0.037	49.7	25.69
250	0.65	1.043	0.040	60.0	27.56

Table 5 Enthalpy of Formation of some Substances

Substances	Molar Enthalpy [kJ/mole]
Oxygen (G), O_2	0.0
Carbon Dioxide (G), CO_2	– 393.5
Nitrogen (G), N_2	0.0
Nitrogen Dioxide (G), NO_2	33.2
Ethanol (L), C_2H_5OH	– 277.0
Ethanol (G)	– 235.3
Methanol (L), CH_3OH	– 238.4
Water (L), H_2O	– 285.8
Water (G)	– 241.8

Table 6 Enthalpy of Combustion of some Fuels

Fuels	Specific Enthalpy [kJ/kg]	Specific Enthalpy [BTU/Lb]
Natural Gas	49000	21030
Gasoline	50000	21460
Coal	33000	14160
Coke	28000	12020
Wood	15000	6440

Table 7 Density (D), Specific Heat Capacity (C_Q), and Specific Thermal Conductivity ($K_{T.Sp}$) of some Materials

Materials	D [kg/m³]	C_Q [kJ/kg.°C]	$K_{T.Sp}$ [W/h.m.°C]
Aluminum (Al)	2707	0.90	204
Copper (Cu)	8954	0.38	386
Iron (Fe)	7874	0.45	80
Lead (Pb)	11373	0.13	35
Carbon Steel (Fe with 1% C)	7801	0.47	43
Chrome Steel (Fe with 5% Cr)	7689	0.46	40

Table 8 Vapor Pressure (P_V) of Water at Different Temperatures (T)

T [ºC]	P_V [kPa]	T [ºC]	P_V [kPa]	T [ºC]	P_V [kPa]	T [ºC]	P_V [kPa]	T [ºC]	P_V [kPa]	T [ºC]	P_V [kPa]
– 10	0.3	16	1.8	36	5.9	56	16.5	76	40.1	96	87.5
– 5	0.4	17	1.9	37	6.3	57	17.3	77	41.8	97	90.7
– 2	0.5	18	2.1	38	6.6	58	18.1	78	43.5	98	94.1
– 1	0.6	19	2.2	39	7.0	59	19.0	79	45.4	99	97.5
0	0.6	20	2.3	40	7.4	60	19.9	80	47.2	100	101.3
1	0.7	21	2.5	41	7.8	61	20.8	81	49.1	101	104.5
2	0.7	22	2.6	42	8.2	62	21.8	82	51.2	102	108.5
3	0.8	23	2.8	43	8.6	63	22.8	83	53.3	103	112.4
4	0.8	24	3.0	44	9.1	64	23.8	84	55.4	104	116.4
5	0.9	25	3.2	45	9.6	65	24.9	85	57.7	105	120.5
6	0.9	26	3.4	46	10.1	66	26.1	86	60.0	106	124.7
7	1.0	27	3.6	47	10.6	67	27.3	87	62.3	107	129.1
8	1.1	28	3.8	48	11.1	68	28.5	88	64.8	108	133.6
9	1.1	29	4.0	49	11.7	69	29.8	89	67.3	109	138.2
10	1.2	30	4.2	50	12.3	70	31.1	90	69.9	110	142.9
11	1.3	31	4.5	51	12.9	71	32.4	91	72.6		
12	1.4	32	4.7	52	13.6	72	33.9	92	75.4		
13	1.5	33	5.0	53	14.3	73	35.3	93	78.3		
14	1.6	34	5.4	54	15.0	74	36.9	94	81.2		
15	1.7	35	5.6	55	15.7	75	38.5	95	84.3		

Table 9 Vapor Pressure (P_V) of Ethanol at Different Temperatures (T)

Temperature	Vapor pressure of ethanol (C_2H_5OH)		
[ºC]	[kPa]	[Atm]	[mm Hg]
1	1.7	0.017	12.6
10	3.1	0.031	23.3
15	4.3	0.042	32.1
20	5.8	0.058	43.7
25	7.8	0.077	58.8
30	10.4	0.103	78.1
35	13.7	0.135	102.7
40	17.8	0.176	133.7
50	29.4	0.290	220.3
60	46.8	0.461	350.7
70	72.2	0.712	541.2
78.3	101.3	1.000	760.0
79	104.1	1.030	780.8
80	108.3	1.069	812.2

Table 10 Useful Formula from Geometry

Square

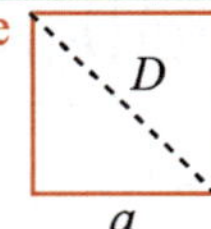

Area = $A = a^2$
Perimeter = $P = 4a$
Diagonal = $D = a\sqrt{2}$

Rectangle

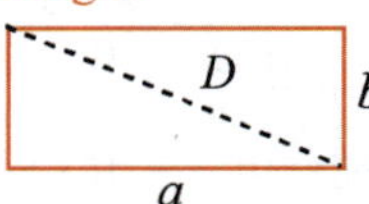

$A = a.b$
$P = 2a.b$
$D = \sqrt{a^2 + b^2}$

Parallelogram

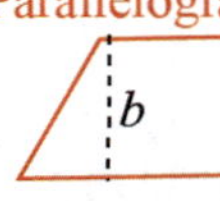

$A = a.b$
$P = 2a.b$

Triangle

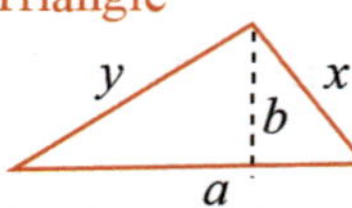

$A = \frac{a.b}{2}$
$P = a + x + y$

Cube

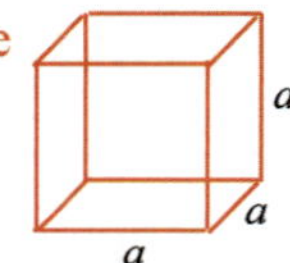

$A = 4a^2$
Volume = $V = 4a^3$

Cuboid (brick)

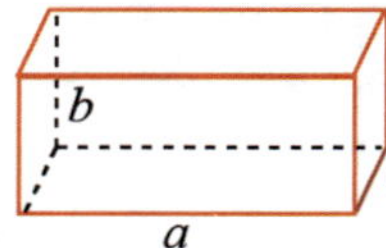

$A = 2\,(a.b + a.c + b.c)$
$V = 2\,(a.b + a.c + b.c)^2$

Circle

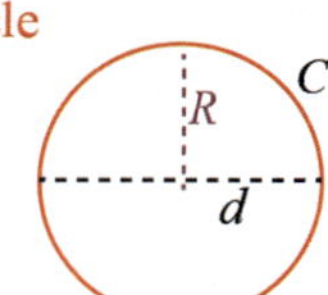

R : Radius
d : Diameter
C : Circumference
$\pi = C/d = 3.14$
$A = \pi.R^2 = \pi.d^2/4$
$C = 2\pi.R = \pi.d$

Sphere

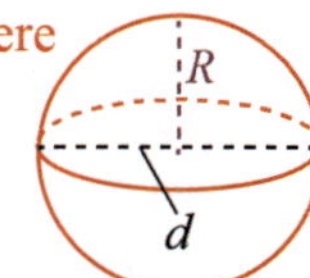

$A = 4\pi.R^2 = \pi.d^2$
$V = A.R = \frac{4\pi.R^3}{3} = \frac{\pi.d^3}{6}$

Solid in rotation

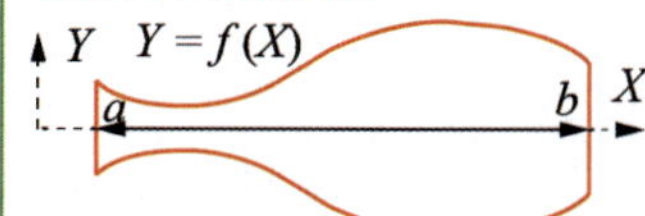

$V = \pi.\int_a^b f(x)^2\,dx$

Circular cylinder

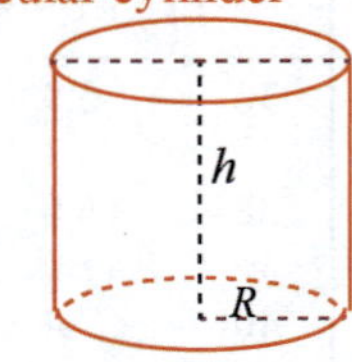

$A = \pi.R^2 = \frac{\pi.d^2}{4}$
$V = A.h = \pi R^2.h = \frac{\pi.d^2.h}{4}$

Hollow circular cylinder

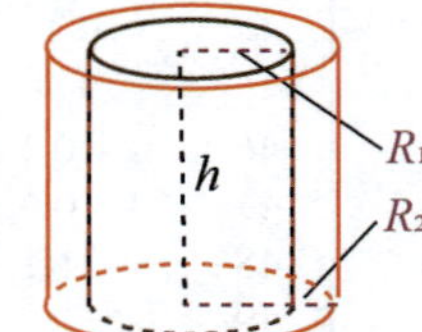

$A = \pi(R_2^2 - R_1^2)$
$V = \pi(R_2^2 - R_1^2)h$

Cone

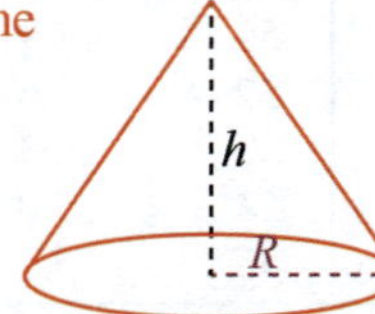

$A = \frac{\pi.R^2}{3}$
$V = \frac{\pi.R^2.h}{3}$

Truncated cone

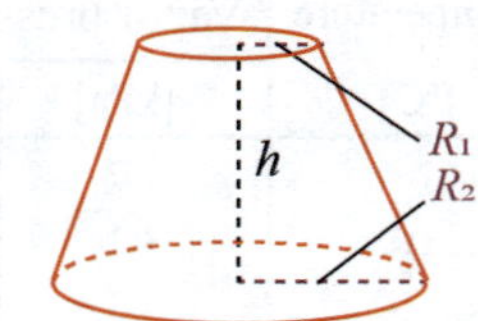

$A = \frac{\pi}{3}(R_1^2 + R_2^2 + R_1.R_2)$
$V = \frac{\pi.h}{3}(R_1^2 + R_2^2 + R_1.R_2)$

Pyramid

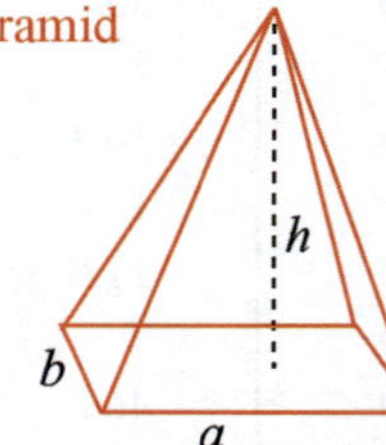

$A = \frac{a.b}{3}$
$V = \frac{a.b.h}{3}$

Truncated pyramid

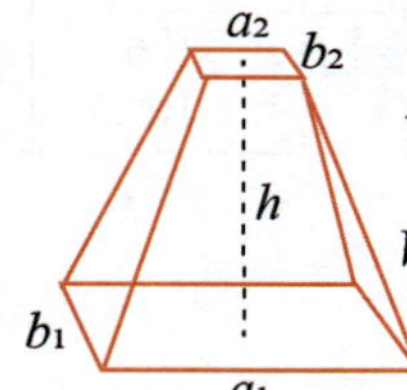

$A = \frac{a_1.b_1 + a_2.b_2 + \sqrt{(a_1.b_1)(a_2.b_2)}}{3}$
$V = \frac{h[a_1.b_1 + a_2.b_2 + \sqrt{(a_1.b_1)(a_2.b_2)}]}{3}$

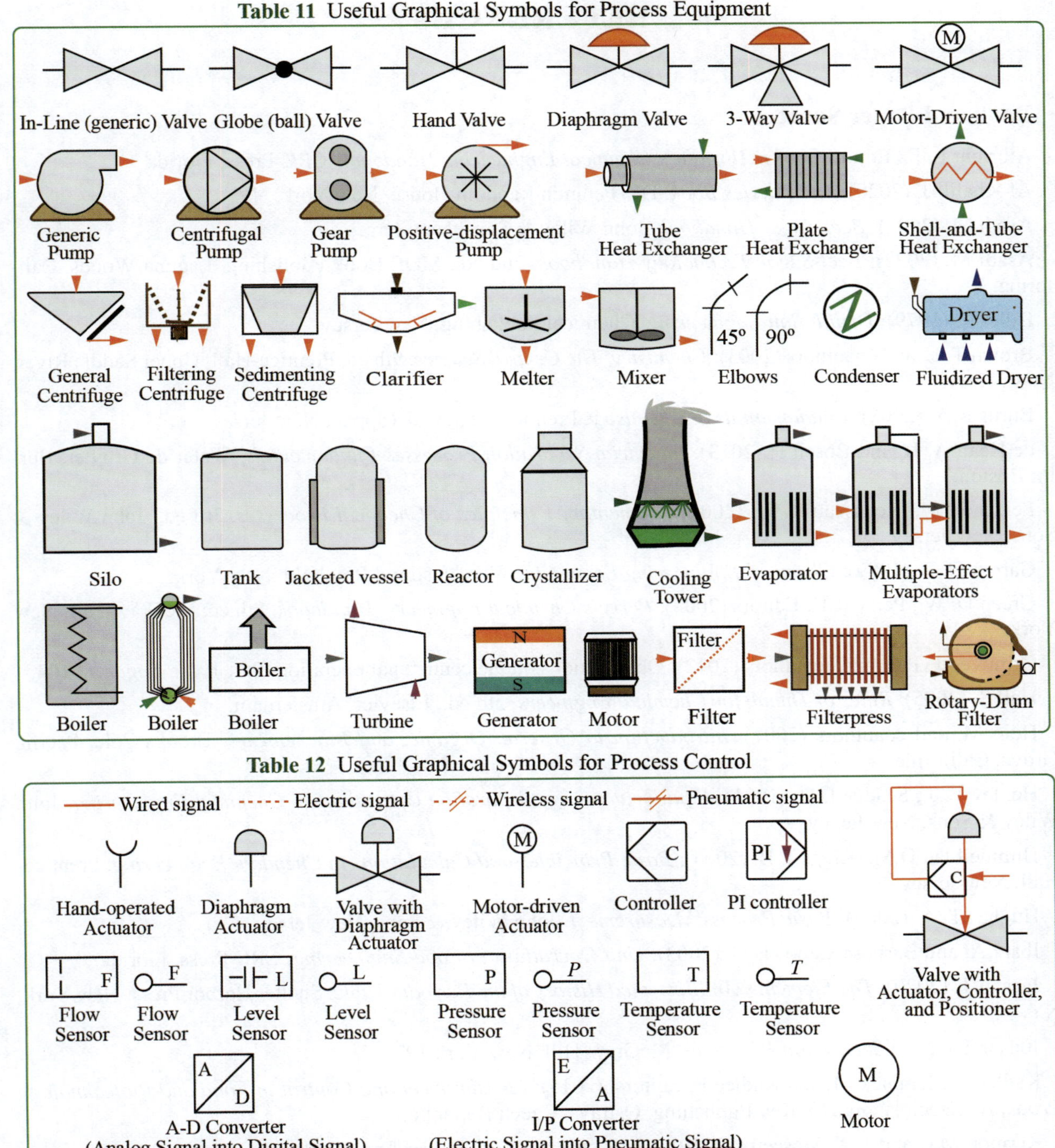

Table 11 Useful Graphical Symbols for Process Equipment

Table 12 Useful Graphical Symbols for Process Control

REFERENCES

Book and Paper Sources

Albright L. F., Editor (2009): *Albright's Chemical Engineering Handbook*. CRC Press, Florida.

Al-Khalili J. (2020): *The Physics Book*. DK-Penguin Random House, New York, NY.

Asadi M. (2007): *Beet-Sugar Handbook*. John Wiley & Sons, New Jersey.

Asadi M. (2022): *Beet-Sugar Technology Handbook*. 2nd ed., MOE Book Publishing, Laguna Woods, California.

Billet R. (1979): *Distillation Engineering*. Chemical Publishing, New Jersey.

Brown T. L. and coauthors (2003): *Chemistry, The Central Science*. 9th ed. Prentice-Hall, Upper Saddle River, New Jersey.

Burns R.A. (2003): *Fundamentals of Chemistry*. Prentice-Hall, Old Tappan, New Jersey.

de Haan A. B. and Bosch H (2013): *Industrial Separation Processes Fundamentals*. Water de Gruyter, Berlin/Boston.

Felder R. M., Rousseau R. W. (2005): *Elementary Principles of Chemical Processes*. 3rd ed., John Wiley & Sons, New Jersey.

Garrett D. E. (1989): *Chemical Engineering Economics*. Van Nostrand Reinhold, New York.

Green D. W., Perry R.H. Editors (2008): *Perry's Chemical Engineers' Handbook*. 8th ed. McGraw-Hill, New York.

Grimwood G. C. and coauthors (2012): Observations on the centrifugal operation. Part 1, *Int. Sugar J.*, **104**.

Hall S. (2005): *Rules of Thumb for Chemical Engineers*. 5th ed., Elsevier, Amsterdam.

Hein M. and coauthors (2001): *Introduction to General, Organic, and Biochemistry*. Brooks/Cole, Pacific Grove, California.

Henley E. J., Seader J. D. (1981): *Equilibrium-Stage Separation Operations in Chemical Engineering*. John Wiley & Sons, New Jersey.

Himmelblau D.M., Riggs J. B. (2004): *Basic Principles and Calculations in Chemical Engineering*. Prentice-Hall, New Jersey.

Hughes T. A. (2009): *Basic Process Measurement*. John Wiley & Sons, New Jersey.

Ibarz A. and Barbosa-Canovas G. (2003): *Unit Operations in Food Engineering*. CRC Press, Florida.

Jacson T. (2020): *The Elements. An Illustrated History of the Periodic Table*. Shelter Harbor Press, New York, NY.

Judson King C.: *Separation Processes*, McGraw-Hill, New York 1971

Kadlec. K, Kminek M, and Kadlec P. Editors. (2015): *Measurement and Control in Food and Biotechnology Products* (Czech language), Key Publishing, Ostrava, Czech Republic.

Kernion M.C and J. A. Mascetta (2019): *Chemistry, the Easy Way*. 6th ed. Kaplan Inc., New York, NY.

Kotz J. and Treichel P. (2003): *Chemistry & Chemical Reactivity*. 5th ed. Thomson Brooks/Cole, Toronto, Ontario.

Lange N. A. (1979): *Handbook of Chemistry*. 12th ed., McGraw-Hill, New York, NY.

Long R. B. (1995): *Separation Processes in Waste Minimization*, Macel Dekker, Inc. New York, NY.

Luyben W. L., Wenzel L.A. (1998): *Chemical Process Analysis Mass and Energy Balances*, Prentice-Hall, Englewood Cliffs, New Jersey.

McCabe W. L., Smith J. C., Herriott P. (2005): *Unit Operations of Chemical Engineering*, 7th Ed., McGraw-Hill, New York.

Mitchell B. S. (2004): *Material Engineering and Science for Chemical and Material Engineers*, McGraw-Hill, New York.

Nunes S.P., Peinemann K.V. (2006): *Membrane Technology in the Chemical Industry*, John Wiley & Sons, New Jersey.

Pickover C. A. (2015): The Physics Devotional, Sterling, New York, NY.

Pickover C.A. (2011): The Physics Book, Sterling, New York, NY.

Raju K. S. N. (2011): *Fluid Mechanics, Heat Transfer, and Mass Transfer*. John Wiley & Sons, New Jersey.

Rose L. M. (1985): *Distillation Design In Practice*. Elsevier, Amsterdam, Netherland.

Rousseau R.W. (1987): *Handbook of Separation Process Technology*, John Wiley & Sons, New Jersey.

Sattler K., Feindt H.J (1995): *Thermal Separation Processes, Principle and Design*, Weinheim, Germany.

Serway R. A., Faughn J. S. (2017): *Physics*, HMH Publishing, Illinois.

Silbey R.J. and coauthors (2005): *Physical Chemistry*, 4th ed. John Wiley & Sons, New Jersey.

Singh R.P., Helman D. R. (2009): *Introduction to Food Engineering*, 4th ed., Academic Press (Elsevier), San Diego, California.

Smith B. D. (1963): *Design of Equilibrium Stage Processes*, McGraw-Hill, New York, NY.

Smith J. M. and coauthors (2010): *Introduction to Chemical Engineering Thermodynamics*, 7th ed. McGraw-Hill Education, New York.

Smuts J. F. (2011): *Process Control for Practitioners*, OptiControls Inc., opticontrols.com.

Snyder C. H. (2002): *The Extraordinary Chemistry of Ordinary Things*. John Wiley & Sons, New Jersey.

Solen K. A., Harb J.N. (2011): *Introduction to Chemical Engineering*. John Wiley & Sons, New Jersey.

Sparks T., Chase G. (2015): *Filters and Filtration Handbook*, 6th ed., Elsevier, Amsterdam.

Still B. (2020): *Physics, How to Navigate the World of Science*. UniPress Books.

Stimus J. T. (2013): *The Beginner's Guide to Engineering: Chemical Engineering*, Quantum Scientific Publishing.

Sutherland K. (2008): *Filters and Filtration Handbook*, 5th ed, Elsevier, Amsterdam.

Tien C. (2012): *Principle of Filtration*, Elsevier, Amsterdam.

Van Winkle M. (1967): *Distillation*, McGraw-Hill, New York, NY.

Weast R. C. (1979): *Handbook of Chemistry and Physics*, CRC Press, Boca Raton, Florida.

Woodford C., Consultant (2019): Scientists Who Changed History, Dorling Kindersley, New York, NY.

Yu F. (2012): *Process Design for Chemical Engineers*. Ten Books, Inc., South Carolina.

Website Sources

Wikipedia.com

Britannica.com

Livescience.com

Mathtutor.com

References

[illegible]

[illegible] New York.

[illegible] New York.

[illegible] John Wiley & Sons [illegible]

[illegible]

Pickover, [illegible] The Physics Book. Sterling, New York, NY.

[illegible] John Wiley & Sons [illegible]

[illegible]

[illegible] John Wiley & Sons, New York.

[illegible]

[illegible]

[illegible] McGraw-Hill [illegible]

[illegible]

[illegible] McGraw-Hill [illegible]

Smith, J.M., Van Ness, H.C. [illegible] Introduction to Chemical Engineering Thermodynamics [illegible] McGraw-Hill Education, New York.

[illegible]

[illegible] The Extraordinary Chemistry of Ordinary Things. John Wiley & Sons [illegible]

[illegible] John Wiley & Sons [illegible]

[illegible]

[illegible]

[illegible]

[illegible]

[illegible]

[illegible]

[illegible] New York [illegible]

[illegible] South Carolina.

Website Sources

Wikipedia.com

Britannica.com

Livescience.com

[illegible].com